R. Gupta's®

POPULAR MASTER GUIDE

National Testing Agency (NTA)

UGC-NET/JRF

Junior Research Fellowship & Assistant Professor Eligibility Exam

LAW

PAPER-2

by

Adv. Sameer Bansal

2027 EDITION

RAMESH PUBLISHING HOUSE, NEW DELHI

Published by
O.P. Gupta *for* Ramesh Publishing House

Admin. Office
12-H, New Daryaganj Road, Opp. Officer' Mess,
New Delhi-110002 ✆ 23275224, 23245124

E-mail: info@rameshpublishinghouse.com
For Online Shopping: www.rameshpublishinghouse.com

Showroom
• Balaji Market, Nai Sarak, Delhi-110006 ✆ 23282525 📱 9354373464
• 4457, Nai Sarak, Delhi-110006

Book Code: R-2834

ISBN: 978-93-5477-523-9

Price: ₹ 695

Printed at: Deepak Offset, Delhi

CONTENTS

Previous Years' Paper

National Testing Agency (NTA)

UGC-NET Junior Research Fellowship & Assistant Professor Eligibility Exam

LAW, DECEMBER-2025

(Exam held on 31-12-2025)

PAPER-II

1. 'Doctrine of Common Employment' has the origin in which of the following case?

1. Priestley V/s Fowler
2. Brochle Bank V/s Noor Ahmed
3. Governor General in Council V/s Zena Wells
4. Secretary of State V/s Rukmani Ben

2. In educational institutions, reservations of seats in favour of the Scheduled Castes and the Scheduled Tribes is governed by which Article of the Constitution of India?

1. Article 21-A
2. Article 19
3. Article 15
4. Article 16

3. Mark the incorrect statements about the circumstances in which Limited Liability Partnership (LLP) may be wound up by the tribunal

A. Where for a period of more than three months the number of partners is reduced to below two

B. If the LLP has acted against the interest of the sovereignty and integrity of India

C. If the LLP has made a default in filing with the Registrar the statement of account and solvency or Annual Return for any two consecutive financial years

D. If LLP is unable to pay its debts

Choose the *correct* answer from the options given below:

1. B, D only
2. A, C only
3. C, D only
4. A, B only

4. Which of the following case primarily deals with the concept of Uniform Civil Code?

1. Seema V/s Ashwani Kumar
2. Sarla Mudgal V/s Union of India
3. Dipanwita Roy V/s Ronobroto Roy
4. Pratibha Rani V/s Suraj Kumar

5. Given below are two statements: one is labelled as Assertion (A) and the other is labelled as Reason (R).

Assertion (A): United States of America is a recognized example of entrenched constitutional tradition.

Reason (R): US Constitution is the oldest still functioning and longest written Constitution of the world.

In the light of the above statements, choose the ***most appropriate*** answer from the options given below

1. Both (A) and (R) are correct and (R) is the correct explanation of (A)
2. Both (A) and (R) are correct, but (R) is NOT the correct explanation of (A)
3. (A) is correct, but (R) is not correct
4. (A) is not correct, but (R) is correct

6. Match the List-I with List-II.

List-I (*International Instruments on Concept of Right to Development)*	List-II (*Year*)
A. Declaration on the Right to Development by the UN General Assembly	I. 2000
B. Durban Declaration and Programme of Action	II. 1993
C. Millennium Declaration	III. 1986
D. Vienna Declaration and Programme of Action	IV. 2001

Choose the *correct* answer from the options given below:

1. A-I, B-II, C-III, D-IV
2. A-I, B-III, C-IV, D-II
3. A-III, B-IV, C-I, D-II
4. A-IV, B-III, C-II, D-I

7. National Commission for Minority Educational Institution Act was enacted by the Parliament in which year?

1. 1992
2. 1995
3. 2002
4. 2004

8. Given below are two statements: one is labelled as Assertion (A) and the other is labelled as Reason (R).

Assertion (A): The owner in possession of the thing has the right to exclude all others from the possession and enjoyment of it.

Reason (R): The right to maintain or recover possession of a tiling as against all others is an essential part of ownership.

In the light of the above statements, choose the ***most appropriate*** answer from the options given below:

1. Both (A) and (R) are correct and (R) is the correct explanation of (A)
2. Both (A) and (R) are correct, but (R) is NOT the correct explanation of (A)
3. (A) is correct, but (R) is not correct
4. (A) is not correct, but (R) is correct

9. Who among the following defines legal right as "a legally protected interest"?

1. Thibaut
2. Allen
3. Ihering
4. Austin

10. Match the List-I with List-II.

List-I (*Doctrine*)	List-II (*Case Law*)
A. Doctrine of Pith and Substance	I. K.C.G. Narayan Dew V/s State of Orissa
B. Doctrine of Territorial Nexus	II. M. Karunanidhi V/s Union of India
C. Doctrine of Repugnancy	III. P.K. Mukherjee V/s Bank of Khulna
D. Doctrine of Colourable Legislation	IV. Wallace V/s Income Tax Commissioner

Choose the ***correct*** answer from the options given below:

1. A-I, B-II, C-III, D-IV
2. A-III, B-II, C-IV, D-I
3. A-III, B-IV, C-II, D-I
4. A-III, B-IV, C-I, D-II

11. Which of the following are true with respect to the decision in State of Maharashtra V/s Praful B. Desai (2003) 4 SCC 601?

A. The law must adopt to the change in society and should accept the new technology

B. The evidence in a criminal trial can be both oral and documentary: and electronic record including video conferencing

C. Video conferencing does not constitute evidence as defined in Section 3 of Indian Evidence Act.

D. Presence under Section 273 Cr. P. C. cannot include presence through video conferencing

Choose the ***correct*** answer from the options given below:

1. A and D only
2. B and C only
3. A and B only
4. C and D only

12. Which of the following case illustrates the patent bargain metaphor which is an application of social contract theory?

1. Universal Oil Products V/s Globe Oil & Refining Co.
2. Georgia V/s Public Resource Org. Inc.
3. Fogerty V/s Fantasy Inc.
4. Fourth Estate Public Benefit Corpn. V/s Wall-street.Com., LLC

13. Which of the following statements are correct?

A. The idea of three branches of government was advocated by Montesquieu.

B. The US Supreme Court decided the case of Marbury V/s Madison in the year 1803.

C. Article 3 of the US Constitution is identified with independence of the judiciary

D. The Ninth Amendment to the US Constitution provides prohibitions against cruel and unusual punishment.

E. The Eight Amendment to the US Constitution provides for rights retained by the people

Choose the ***correct*** answer from the options given below:

1. A, C and E only
2. B, D and E only
3. A, B and C only
4. B, C and D only

14. Arrange the following grounds of Divorce in the order of their appearance under Section 13(1) of the Hindu Marriage Act, 1955.

A. Suffering from venereal disease in a communicable form.

B. Ceased to be a Hindu by conversion

C. Renounced the world by entering any religious order

D. Has not been heard of as being alive for a period of seven years or more.

E. Cruelty.

Choose the ***correct*** answer from the options given below:

1. D, C, A, B, E
2. A, E, B, C, D
3. B, E, C, D, A
4. E, B, A, C, D

15. Given below are two statements: one is labelled as Assertion (A) and the other is labelled as Reason (R).

Assertion (A): In England, due to historical reasons British Parliament is a judicial as well as legislative body.

Reason (R): There is no written Constitution to limit the authority of the Parliament in Britain.

In the light of the above statements, choose the ***most appropriate*** answer from the options given below:

1. Both (A) and (R) are correct and (R) is the correct explanation of (A)
2. Both (A) and (R) are correct, but (R) is NOT the correct explanation of (A)
3. (A) is correct, but (R) is not correct
4. (A) is not correct, but (R) is correct

16. Given below are two statements: one is labelled as Assertion (A) and the other is labelled as Reason (R).

Assertion (A): Article 30 of Constitution of India confers a right on all minorities to establish and administer educational institutions.

Reason (R): The right to establish and administer educational institutions by the minorities is based solely on religion.

In the light of the above statements, choose the ***most appropriate*** answer from the options given below:

1. Both (A) and (R) are correct and (R) is the correct explanation of (A)
2. Both (A) and (R) are correct, but (R) is NOT the correct explanation of (A)
3. (A) is correct, but (R) is not correct
4. (A) is not correct, but (R) is correct

17. Arrange the following cases chronologically (starting from earliest to the latest)

A. Minerva Mills Ltd. V/s Union of India
B. Samsher Singh V/s State of Punjab
C. S.P Anand V/s H. D. Deve Gowda
D. U.N.R. Rao V/s Smt. Indira Gandhi

Choose the ***correct*** answer from the options given below:

1. D, B, A, C
2. D, B, C, A
3. C, B, A, D
4. A, B, C, D

18. Match the List-I with List-II.

List-I (***Exception to Murder***)	**List-II** (***Corresponding Provision***)
A. Exception-2	I. Act of Public Servant
B. Exception-3	II. Exceeding the right of private defense
C. Exception-4	III. Sudden fight
D. Exception-5	IV. Death by consent

Choose the ***correct*** answer from the options given below:

1. A-I, B-II, C-III, D-IV
2. A-II, B-I, C-III, D-IV
3. A-I, B-II, C-IV, D-III
4. A-IV, B-III, C-II, D-I

19. Arrange the following provisions from the Information Technology Act. 2000 in the ascending order of their appearance in the Act.

A. Validity of contracts formed through electronic means.
B. Use of electronic records and electronic signatures in Government and its agencies
C. Retention of electronic records
D. Publication of rules, regulation etc. in electronic Gazette.

Choose the ***correct*** answer from the options given below:

1. A, B, C, D
2. D, C, A, B
3. B, C, D, A
4. C, D, B, A

20. Which of the following case decided by the Supreme Court of India primarily deals with the maintenance to be paid in case of Live-in relationships?

1. Lata Kamat V/s Vilas
2. Veena Rani V/s Ramesh Kumar
3. Pushpa Devi V/s Radheysham
4. Chanmuniya V/s Virendra Kumar Singh Kushwaha

21. Match the List-I with List-II.

List-I (***Feature***)	**List-II** (***Application***)
A. Executive Legislation	I. Appointment and removal of Judges
B. Collective Responsibility	II. Administrative adjudication
C. Quasi-Judicial Function	III. Parliamentary form of government
D. Independence of Judiciary	IV. Ordinance

Choose the ***correct*** answer from the options given below:

1. A-I, B-II, C-III, D-IV
2. A-I, B-II, C-IV, D-III
3. A-II, B-I, C-IV, D-III
4. A-IV, B-III, C-II, D-I

22. Under which doctrine a person is liable if he intended to kill 'X' but kills 'Z' whose death he neither intended nor knows to likely to cause:

1. Doctrine of res-judicata
2. Doctrine of mens rea
3. Doctrine of transfer of malice
4. Doctrine of absolute necessity

23. Which of the following statements are correct about e-rickshaw and e-cart as per the Motor Vehicles Act, 1988?

A. It is battery powered vehicle
B. Power is not exceeding 4000 Watt
C. It has three wheals for carrying passengers only
D. Not a special purpose vehicle

Choose the ***correct*** answer from the options given below:

1. C, D only
2. A, B only
3. B, C only
4. A, D only

24. In which of the following case, the Supreme Court declared that till a law is made by the Parliament, the appointment to the posts of Chief Election Commissioner of India and Election Commission shall be done by the President of India on the basis of the advice tendered by a Committee?

1. S.S. Dhannoa V/s Union of India
2. T.N. Seshan V/s Union of India
3. Anoop Baranwal V/s Union of India
4. In Re Presidential Reference, 2002

25. Which of the following cases deal with the interpretation of the 'personal liberty' under Article 21 of the Constitution of India?

A. Kharak Singh V/s State of U.P.
B. Mohini Jain V/s State of Karnataka
C. Maneka Gandhi V/s Union of India
D. A.K. Gopalan V/s Union of India

Choose the ***correct*** answer from the options given below:

1. A, B, C only
2. A, B only
3. A, C, D only
4. B, C, D only

26. Which of the following right is not available under the Sale of Goods Act, 1930 to the Unpaid Seller notwithstanding that the property in the goods may have passed to the buyer?

1. A lien on the goods for the price while he is in possession of them.
2. In case of the insolvency of the buyer, a right of stopping the goods in transit after he has parted with the possession of them
3. A right of re-sale as limited by the Act
4. A right of withholding delivery

27. In which of the following case, the Supreme Court of India directed the Courts and Tribunals to ensure that all uploaded judgments and orders are signed using digital signatures and not as scanned copies of printed version?

1. Ameena Begum V/s The State of Telangana (2023)
2. D.K. Basu V/s State of West Bengal (1997)
3. State Bank of India V/s Ajay Kumar (2021)
4. Virbhadra Singh V/s Enforcement Directorate (2017)

28. Who amongst the following are included in definition of 'Manufacturer' in the Consumer Protection Act, 2019?

A. Maker of goods or parts
B. One who assembles goods or parts
C. Who put his own mark on goods made by others
D. One who sells goods

Choose the ***correct*** answer from the options given below:

1. A, B, C only
2. B, C, D only
3. A, C, D only
4. A, B, D only

29. Certain principles to distinguish obligatory from recommendatory injunctions can be found in which of the following ancient Indian texts?

1. Jijnaysa
2. Mimansa
3. Rashtravani
4. Garuda Nyaya

30. Arrange the following in the order in which they appear in the Preamble to the Indian Constitution:

A. Equality
B. Justice
C. Liberty
D. Fraternity

Choose the ***correct*** answer from the options given below:

1. A, B, C, D
2. B, C, D, A
3. B, C, A, D
4. C, B, D, A

31. Which of the following statements are correct?

A. Holland remarked that international law is the vanishing point of jurisprudence
B. Holland was an analytical jurist.
C. The Vienna Convention on the Law of Treaties provides that a treaty may be binding on third States as well.
D. Grotius and Vattel were positivists
E. The International Court of Justice recognizes the sources of international law under Article 36 (1) (c) of its statute.

Choose the ***correct*** answer from the options given below:

1. B, D and E only
2. A, B and C only
3. A, C and E only
4. C, D and E only

32. Match the List-I with List-II.

List-I (*Concept under Indian Contract Act, 1872*)	List-II (*Corresponding Sections*)
A. Payment by interested person	I. Section 69
B. Payment made under mistake or coercion	II. Section 72
C. Liability of pay for non-gratuitous acts	III. Section 68
D. Supply of necessaries	IV. Section 70

Choose the ***correct*** answer from the options given below:

1. A-II, B-III, C-I, D-IV
2. A-IV, B-I, C-III, D-II
3. A-I, B-II, C-IV, D-III
4. A-III, B-IV, C-II, D-I

33. Arrange the following cases relating to extradition in their chronological order.

A. Soering V/s United Kingdom
B. Chitat V/s Canada
C. United States V/s Rauscher
D. Daya Singh Lahoria V/s Union of India
E. Kindler V/s Canada

Choose the ***correct*** answer from the options given below:

1. C, A, E, B, D
2. B, D, C, E, A
3. A, B, C, D, E
4. E, C, D, A, B

34. National Green Tribunal Act come into force on which date?

1. 18 Oct 2010
2. 18 Nov 2010
3. 8 Oct 2010
4. 8 Nov 2010

35. Match the List-I with List-II.

List-I (*Basic Feature*)	List-II (*Judge and the case*)
A. Independence of the judiciary	I. Fazal Ali - SP Gupta V/s Union of India
B. Federal system	II. Bachawat - Golak Nath V/s State of Funjab
C. Secularism	III. Reddy - Kesavananda Bharati V/s State of Kerala
D. Parliamentary system of government	IV. Khanna - Indira Gandhi V/s Raj Narain

Choose the ***correct*** answer from the options given below:

1. A-I, B-II, C-IV, D-III
2. A-III, B-IV, C-II, D-I
3. A-I, B-III, C-IV, D-II
4. A-I, B-II, C-III, D-IV

36. Match the List-I with List-II.

List-I (*Article from the Indian Constitution*)	List-II (*Corresponding Provisions*)
A. Article 325	I. One general electoral roll
B. Article 326	II. Adult Suffrage
C. Article 327	III. Bar to interference by courts in electoral matters
D. Article 329	IV. Power of Parliament to make provisions w.r.t. elections to legislatures

Choose the ***correct*** answer from the options given below:

1. A-IV, B-III, C-II, D-I
2. A-I, B-II, C-IV, D-III
3. A-II, B-I, C-IV, D-III
4. A-I, B-II, C-III, D-IV

37. Which of the following is NOT correct about the nature of limited liability partnership?

1. It is a body corporate incorporated under the Act
2. It is a legal entity separate from its partners
3. It enjoys the benefit of perpetual succession
4. It follows the principle of unlimited liability

38. Which Article of the Constitution of India provides that "Government of India can be sued in the name of Union of India and State Government may be sued in the name of State"?

1. Art. 300 (1)
2. Art. 270
3. Art. 1
4. Art. 110

39. Setting up of the State Human Right Commission is provided under which Chapter of Protection of Human Right Act, 1993?

1. Chapter X
2. Chapter II
3. Chapter V
4. Chapter IV

40. Who among the following opines that historical sources of law pertain to legal history and not to legal theory?

1. Salmond
2. Blackstone
3. Pollock
4. Gray

41. Match the List-I with List-II.

List-I (*Sources of Hindu Law*)	List-II (*Authors*)
A. Dharma Sutras	I. Jimuta Valiana
B. Mayukha	II. Narada
C. Dayabhaga	III. Vasishtha
D. Dharma Shastras	IV. Nilkantha

Choose the ***correct*** answer from the options given below:

1. A-IV, B-III, C-I, D-II
2. A-III, B-IV, C-I, D-II
3. A-I, B-II, C-III, D-IV
4. A-II, B-I, C-IV, D-III

42. Arrange the following rights as they appear in Universal Declaration of Human Rights, 1948 (UDHR) (ascending order)

A. Rights relating to Freedom
B. Rights relating to Liberties of people
C. Rights relating to Rule of Law
D. Economic Rights

Choose the *correct* answer from the options given below:

1. C, B, A, D
2. A, B, C, D
3. B, A, C, D
4. C, A, B, D

43. Which of the following is NOT a subject matter of copyright as per Section 13 of the Copyright Act, 1957?

1. Cinematographic films
2. Dramatic work
3. Performance of performers
4. Sound recording

44. Arrange the following IPR Treaties in the chronological order of their adoption (ascending order).

A. Beijing Treaty on Audio-Visual Performances
B. Singapore Treaty on Law of Trademarks
C. Madrid Agreement (Marks)
D. Madrid Protocol (Marks)

Choose the *correct* answer from the options given below:

1. A, B, D, C
2. C, D, B, A
3. C, B, D, A
4. B, C, D, A

45. Which of the following case decided by the Supreme Court of India deals with the concept of 'Public Wrong' under Tort?

1. Sebastin M V/s Union of India
2. Kasturi Lal V/s State of UP
3. Carew & Co. Ltd. V/s Union of India
4. Union of India V/s Ashok Kumar

46. Under which condition, a widowed daughter-in-law cannot claim the right of maintenance from the father-in-law as per Hindu Adoption and Maintenance Act, 1956?

1. If she is unable to maintain herself out of her own earnings
2. If father-in-law has coparcener property in his possession and she has not obtained a share
3. If she has ceased to be a Hindu
4. If she is unable to obtain maintenance from the estate of her daughters

47. Arrange the following in order of their coming into being/adoption/enactment (ascending order).

A. UN Convention on Rights of Persons with Disabilities
B. Americans with Disabilities Act
C. United Kingdom Disability Discriminations Act
D. The Persons with Disability Act (India)

Choose the *correct* answer from the options given below:

1. B, C, D, A
2. A, B, C, D
3. C, B, D, A
4. A, C, D, B

48. Which Amendment to American Constitution explicitly declared that powers not specifically delegated to Federal Government were part of sovereign authority of State Government?

1. Fifteenth
2. Sixth
3. Tenth
4. Fourth

49. Match the List-I with List-II.

List-I (*Theory*)	List-II (*Propounder*)
A. Pigeon Hole Theory	I. William Prosser
B. Neighbour Rule	II. Wenfield
C. Tort is Social Engineering	III. Lord Atkin
D. Use of phrase 'Law of Tort'	IV. Salmond

Choose the *correct* answer from the options given below:

1. A-IV, B-III, C-I, D-II
2. A-II, B-I, C-III, D-IV
3. A-III, B-II, C-IV, D-I
4. A-I, B-IV, C-II, D-III

50. Given below are two statements: one is labelled as Assertion (A) and the other is labelled as Reason (R).

Assertion (A): A Waqf under Muslim law is essentially a religious and pious obligation.

Reason (R): Provision is sometimes made in a Waqf for charities and for the benefits of oneself, one's children and descendants.

In the light of the above statements, choose the *most appropriate* answer from the options given below

1. Both (A) and (R) are correct and (R) is the correct explanation of (A)
2. Both (A) and (R) are correct, but (R) is NOT the correct explanation of (A)
3. (A) is correct, but (R) is not correct
4. (A) is not correct, but (R) is correct

51. Which statements are incorrect with respect of Indian Patent Act, 1970?

A. Invention relating to atomic energy are not patentable.

B. Originality and novelty are pre-requisites for patentability.

C. IPAB (Intellectual Property Appellate Board) deals with all types of IPR disputes currently in India.

D. A patent is valid for 20 years.

Choose the ***correct*** answer from the options given below:

1. C and D only
2. A and B only
3. A and D only
4. B and C only

52. Under Clause (3)(a) of Article 13 of the Constitution of India, "Law" includes:

1. Rule, Regulation, bye-law, order, noti-fication, custom or usage
2. Act, ordinance, order, bye-law, rule, regulation, notification, custom or usage
3. Ordinance, order, rule, regulation, notification, custom or usage
4. Ordinance, order, bye-law, rule, regulation, notification, custom or usage

53. What is the role of Secretary General of NHRC as reflected under Section 3 of the Protection of Human Rights Act, 1993?

1. Advisor of NHRC
2. Technical Member of NHRC
3. Chief Executive Officer of NHRC
4. Legal Member of NHRC

54. The Central Government is empowered to appoint which agency under Section 70B of the Information Technology Act, 2000?

1. Indian Electronic Emergency Response Team
2. Indian Digital Security Response Team
3. National Cyber Security Response Team
4. Indian Computer Emergency Response Team

55. Which of the Article of the Constitution of India mentions Union List, Concurrent List and State List?

1. Article 245
2. Article 246
3. Article 246A
4. Article 249

56. Match the List-I with List-II.

List-I (*WIPO administered IPR Treaties*)	List-II (*Year of Adoption*)
A. Patent Law Treaty	I. 2024
B. Riyadh Design Law Treaty	II. 2000
C. WIPO Copyright Treaty	III. 1981
D. Nairobi Treaty	IV. 1996

Choose the ***correct*** answer from the options given below:

1. A-II, B-I, C-IV, D-III
2. A-I, B-II, C-III, D-IV
3. A-IV, B-I, C-II, D-III
4. A-II, B-IV, C-I, D-III

57. Given below are two statements: one is labelled as Assertion (A) and the other is labelled as Reason (R).

Assertion (A): Culpable homicide is genus and murder is specie.

Reason (R): All murders are culpable homicide but not vice-versa.

In the light of the above statements, choose the ***most appropriate*** answer from the options given below

1. Both (A) and (R) are correct and (R) is the correct explanation of (A)
2. Both (A) and (R) are correct, but (R) is NOT the correct explanation of (A)
3. (A) is correct, but (R) is not correct
4. (A) is not correct, but (R) is correct

58. Arrange the following in the order of their appearance in the relevant Article under the Charter of the United Nations. The parties to any dispute, the continuance of which is likely to endanger the maintenance of international peace and security, shall fust of all, seek a solution by:

A. Negotiation
B. Enquiry
C. Mediation
D. Conciliation
E. Arbitration

Choose the ***correct*** answer from the options given below:

1. A, C, D, E, B
2. E, C, D, A, B
3. A, B, C, D, E
4. B, D, C, A, E

59. The Supreme Court of India, stating the historical background and sanctity of Guru Granth Sahib, held it to be a juristic person in which of the following case?

1. Masjid Shahid Ganj V/s Shiromani Gurudwara Prabandhak Committee
2. State of Punjab V/s Mahinder Singh Chawla
3. Union of India V/s W.N. Chadha
4. Shiromani Gurudwara Prabandhak Committee V/s Somnath Das

60. Which of the following offence is most severally punishable among the following?

1. Unlawful assembly
2. Rioting
3. Affray
4. Assault

61. Which of the following is not a condition for a valid adoption under the Hindu Adoption and Maintenance Act, 1956?

1. If the adoption is of a son, the adoptive father or mother must not have a Hindu son living at the time of adoption
2. If the adoption is by a female and the person to be adopted is a female, the adoptive mother is at least twenty one years older than the person to be adopted
3. The same child may not be adopted simultaneously by two or more persons
4. The child to be adopted must be actually given and taken in adoption by parents/guardians

62. Given below are two statements: one is labelled as Assertion (A) and the other is labelled as Reason (R).

Assertion (A): While TRIPS Agreement goes on to outline certain standards of protection for Geographical Indications (GIs), it does not prescribe a particular form of protection so long as these standards are met.

Reason (R): Viewed in the historical context, it is unsurprising that while TRIPS reflects the relatively stable referent for trademarks, for GIs the definition is more fluid.

In the light of the above statements, choose the ***most appropriate*** answer from the options given below

1. Both (A) and (R) are correct and (R) is the correct explanation of (A)
2. Both (A) and (R) are correct, but (R) is NOT the correct explanation of (A)
3. (A) is correct, but (R) is not correct
4. (A) is not correct, but (R) is correct

63. What is the nature of the question where the provocation was grave and sudden enough to prevent the offence from amounting to murder?

1. Mixed question of fact and law
2. Question of law
3. Question of fact
4. Question of criminal law

64. Which of the following says that the purpose of law is to grant the individual the means of self-expression or self-assertion?

1. The Will theory
2. The Atomic theory
3. The theory of Liberty Personality
4. The theory of Natural Law

65. The case for possession of Arantzatzu Mendi before the House of Lords was between which of the following parties?

1. De jure Government of the United Kingdom and defacto Government of Denmark
2. De jure Government of Spain and defacto Nationalist Government of Spain
3. De jure Government of France and defacto Nationalist Government of France
4. De jure Government of Belgium and defacto Nationalist Government of Belgium

66. Arrange the following cases in their chronological order.

A. Sankari Prasad V/s Union of India
B. Sajjan Singh V/s State of Rajasthan
C. Golak Nath V/s State of Punjab
D. Kesavananda Bharati V/s State of Kerala
E. Waman Rao V/s Union of India

Choose the ***correct*** answer from the options given below:

1. A, B, C, D, E
2. E, D, C, B, A
3. A, B, D, C, E
4. D, E, A, B, C

67. Given below are two statements: one is labelled as Assertion (A) and the other is labelled as Reason (R).

Assertion (A): Every company having net worth of rupees five hundred crores or more or turnover of rupees one thousand crore or more or a net profit of rupees five crore or more during the immediately preceding financial year shall constitute a Corporate Social Responsibility Committee (CSRC).

Reason (R): The CSR Committee monitors CSR policy of the company.

In the light of the above statements, choose the ***most appropriate*** answer from the options given below

1. Both A and R arc correct and R is the correct explanation of A
2. Both (A) and (R) are correct, but (R) is NOT the correct explanation of (A)
3. (A) is correct, but (R) is not correct
4. (A) is not correct, but (R) is correct

68. Which provision of the Universal Declaration of Human Rights, 1948 provides that "everyone has the right to a nationality"?

1. Article 10
2. Article 15
3. Article 7
4. Article 21

69. Given below are two statements: one is labelled as Assertion (A) and the other is labelled as Reason (R).

Assertion (A): A written Constitution is intended to operate as a limitation upon the powers of the various organs of a State.

Reason (R): Under those Constitutions where judicial review exists, the guardianship of the Constitution belongs to the courts.

In the light of the above statements, choose the ***most appropriate*** answer from the options given below

1. Both (A) and (R) are correct and (R) is the correct explanation of (A)
2. Both (A) and (R) are correct, but (R) is NOT the correct explanation of (A)
3. (A) is correct, but (R) is not correct
4. (A) is not correct, but (R) is correct

70. Developed mostly by German scholars, which of the following schools sought for a universal doctrine of historical evolution of the whole world (rather than being limited only to a particular race) and its laws from some universal and metaphysical source?

1. Historical school 2. Metaphysical school
3. Sociological school 4. Comparative school

71. In the context of Standard Form Contracts, which Rule will apply if there is any doubt as to the meaning and scope of excluding or limiting terms and to resolve the ambiguity against the party who has inserted it?

1. Purposive Interpretation Rule
2. Removal Simpliciter Rule
3. Contra Proferentem Rule
4. Escalation Clauses Rule

72. Arrange the following provisions in the order in which they appear in the Constitution of India.

A. Provision as to Financial emergency
B. Suspension of provisions of Article 19 during emergencies
C. Provision in case of failure of constitutional machinery in States
D. Effect of Proclamation of Emergency

Choose the ***correct*** answer from the options given below:

1. A, B, C, D 2. A, B, D, C
3. D, B, A, C 4. D, C, B, A

73. Which of the following Section in the Biological Diversity Act. 2002 prescribes for Benefit sharing fee and royalties?

1. Section 6 2. Section 10A
3. Section 30 4. Section 16

74. Arrange the following Class-II legal heirs in the order of their appearance in the schedule in the Hindu Succession Act, 1956.

A. Son's daughter's son
B. Daughters son's son
C. Daughter's son's daughters
D. Son's daughter's daughter

Choose the ***correct*** answer from the options given below:

1. A, D, B, C 2. D, A, C, B
3. A, C, B, D 4. C, B, D, A

75. In every listed public company how many of the total number of directors shall be independent directors?

1. One-fourth 2. One-third
3. One-fifth 4. One-tenth

76. Arrange the following as they appear in the Motor Vehicles Act, 1988 (ascending order)

A. Motor Vehicle Accident fund
B. Claims Tribunal
C. Recall of Motor Vehicles
D. Necessity of Permits

Choose the ***correct*** answer from the options given below:

1. D, C, B, A 2. D, B, A, C
3. B, C, D, A 4. C, A, B, D

77. Match the List-I with List-II.

List-I (*Particulars*)	List-II (*Year*)
A. Entry into force of the UN Convention on the Status of Refugees	I. 1967
B. Entry into force of the Protocol to the UN Convention on the Status of Refugees	II. 1954
C. Second time when the UN High Commissioner for Refugees won the Nobel Peace Prize	III. 1981
D. Formation of the UN Commission on Refugees	IV. 1950

Choose the ***correct*** answer from the options given below:

1. A-I, B-II, C-IV, D-III
2. A-IV, B-III, C-II, D-I
3. A-II, B-III, C-IV, D-I
4. A-II, B-I, C-III, D-IV

78. Which of the following are correct in the context of guidelines laid down in S. R. Bommai V/s Union of India?

A. Presidential proclamation under Art, 356 is not subject to judicial review
B. If a state government works against secularism, President Rule can be imposed
C. State assembly can be dissolved only after the Approval of Parliament
D. Power under Art, 356 is not an absolute Power

Choose the ***correct*** answer from the options given below:

1. A, B, C only 2. B, C, D only
3. C and A only 4. B and D only

79. When did India and the United Kingdom (U.K.) formally sign the Comprehensive Economic and Trade Agreement (CETA)?

1. 24 July 2025 2. 31 December 2024
3. 15 January 2025 4. 1 July 2024

80. Arrange the following concepts as per their order of appearance in the Indian Contract Act, 1872.

A. Continuing guarantee
B. Care to be taken by bailee
C. Compensation for loss or damage caused by breach of contract
D. Claims for necessaries supplied to person incapable of contracting

Choose the ***correct*** answer from the options given below:

1. D, B, C, A 2. D, C, A, B
3. C, D, B, A 4. B, A, C, D

81. Arrange the following in the order of their appearance in Section 2 of the Indian Contract Act, 1872.

A. Proposal B. Consideration
C. Agreement D. Promise
E. Contract

Choose the ***correct*** answer from the options given below:

1. A, B, D, C, E 2. D, B, A, E, C
3. A, D, B, C, E 4. B, D, A, E, C

82. Given below are two statements: one is labelled as Assertion (A) and the other is labelled as Reason (R).

Assertion (A): Once Rule of Law is acknowledged as a constitutional law superior to the express provision in Article 21, it is only one step further to assert that Rule of Law is a 'basic feature' of Indian Constitution, which is beyond the pale of the express provision in Article 368, which was provided for by the initial constituent body.

Reason (R): It is not unimaginable to conceive that the enacted provisions of a written Constitution would be nullified by invoking some unwritten principle of law of higher ethical value as evident under the West German Constitution of 1949.

In the light of the above statements, choose the ***most appropriate*** answer from the options given below

1. Both (A) and (R) are correct and (R) is the correct explanation of (A)
2. Both (A) and (R) are correct, but (R) is NOT the correct explanation of (A)
3. (A) is correct, but (R) is not correct
4. (A) is not correct, but (R) is correct

83. Match the List-I with List-II.

List-I (*Case Law*)	List-II (*Related Concept*)
A. Cox V/s Hickman	I. Business must be taken in a practical sense
B. Stekel V/s Ellice	II. Partnership between Karta and Coparcener
C. Lachhman Das V/s CIT	III. Salaried partner
D. Smith V/s Anderson	IV. Mutual Agency

Choose the ***correct*** answer from the options given below:

1. A-III, B-IV, C-I, D-II
2. A-I, B-IV, C-II, D-III
3. A-II, B-I, C-IV, D-III
4. A-IV, B-III, C-II, D-I

84. Match the List-I with List-II.

List-I (*Case Law*)	List-II (*Concept*)
A. Ashby V/s White	I. Poverty as an involuntary act under Tort
B. Ryland V/s Fletcher	II. Violation of absolute Right
C. Olga Tellis V/s Bombay Municipal Corp.	III. Strict liability
D. Allen V/s Flood	IV. Motive is irrelevant in Tort

Choose the ***correct*** answer from the options given below:

1. A-II, B-III, C-I, D-IV
2. A-I, B-II, C-IV, D-III
3. A-III, B-IV, C-II, D-I
4. A-IV, B-I, C-III, D-II

85. Under which of its provisions does the Draft Convention on Territorial Asylum adopted by the General Assembly of the United Nations in 1974, recognize that the grant of asylum is a sovereign right of a State?

1. Article 1 2. Article 2
3. Article 3 4. Article 5

86. Which of the following is a landmark case on 'attempt to commit offences'?

1. Dashrath Paswan V/s State of Bihar
2. K.M. Nanavati V/s State of Maharashtra
3. Abhayanand Mishra V/s State of Bihar
4. Barendra Kumar Ghosh V/s Emperor

87. Match the List-I with List-II.

List-I (*Statement*)	List-II (*Propounder*)
A. Justice is the first virtue of social institution	I. Immanuel Kant
B. Natural justice is species of political justice	II. Aristotle
C. 'Equality of respect and concern'	III. Dworkin
D. Human Dignity is the foundation of Human Rights	IV. John Rawls

Choose the ***correct*** answer from the options given below:

1. A-IV, B-II, C-III, D-I
2. A-I, B-III, C-II, D-IV
3. A-II, B-IV, C-I, D-III
4. A-III, B-I, C-IV, D-II

88. Which of the following is not a type of prospectus under the Companies Act, 2013?

1. Shelf Prospectus
2. Deemed Prospectus
3. Yellow (Herring) Prospectus
4. Abridged Prospectus

89. Which is correct with regard to In Re Right to Privacy of Adolescents (2025 INSC 778)?

A. Not a Suo-motu judgment of Supreme Court of India
B. Victim- centric sentencing under Article 142
C. Held that non-compliance with Section 19(6) of POCSO Act does not lead to violation of Article 21 of the Constitution
D. Supreme Court refused to further sentence a man convicted under POCSO Act after considering the victim's wishes.

Choose the ***correct*** answer from the options given below:

1. A and C only
2. B and D only
3. A and B only
4. C and D only

90. Match the List-I with List-II.

List-I (*Concept in the Biological Diversity Act, 2002*)	List-II (*Corresponding Section*)
A. National Biodiversity Authority	I. Section 32
B. State Biodiversity Fund	II. Section 37
C. National Biodiversity Fund	III. Section 8
D. Biodiversity Heritage Sites	IV. Section 27

Choose the ***correct*** answer from the options given below:

1. A-I, B-II, C-III, D-IV
2. A-I, B-IV, C-III, D-II
3. A-III, B-I, C-IV, D-II
4. A-IV, B-I, C-III, D-II

Directions (Qs. No. 91 to 95): *Read the following passage and answer the questions below:*

"While interpreting the Articles of the Indian Constitution, the Court should remember that it is not construing a petrified legal parchment but reading the luscent lines of a human text with a national mission. The Court must never forget that the life of the *Supreme Lex* is nourished by the social setting, that jurisdical abstractions and theoretical conceptions may be fascinating forensics but jejune jurisprudence if the raw Indian realities are slimed over. The Constitution of a nation is being expounded whose people hunger for a full life for each, and therefore, a perception of the signature of social justice writ on it is imperative. 'Nothing is more certain in modern 'society', declared the American Supreme Court at mid-century 'than the principle that there are no absolutes. Legal Einstienism guides the Court, not doctrinal absolutes."

91. Why is a perception of the signature of social justice writ on the Constitution, an imperative for its exposition?

1. It is because it is a human text to be read with a national mission.
2. It is because it is a juridical abstraction making for fascinating forensics.
3. It is because it is jejune jurisprudence slurring over raw Indian realities.
4. It is because it is expounded for a nation whose people hunger for a full life for each.

92. What must the Court never forget, according to the author?

1. That the life of the Supreme Lex is nourished by juridical abstractions.
2. That the life of the Supreme Lex is nourished by theoretical conceptions.
3. That the life of the Supreme Lex is nourished by fascinating forensics.
4. That the life of the Supreme Lex is nourished by the social setting.

93. What should the Court remember while interpreting the Articles of the Indian Constitution?

1. That it is constructing a petrified legal parchment.
2. That they are reading the luscent lines of a human text with a national mission.
3. That they are interpreting it for the future generations.
4. That it is their national mission to petrify the legal parchment.

94. Which is the most certain principle in Modern society?

1. The principle that there are no certainties.
2. The principle that there are no principles.
3. The principle that there are no absolutes.
4. The principle that social justice is not an absolute.

95. As per the American Supreme Court, what guides the Court?

1. Legal Einstienism guides the Court.
2. Lucent Lines guides the Court.
3. Doctrinal absolutes guides the Court.
4. Jejune jurisprudence guides the Court.

Directions (Qs. No. 96 to 100): *Read the following passage and answer the questions below:*

As remarked by Dias, ''no other firmament of legal or political theory is, so bejewelled with star as that of 'Natural Law' for it has engaged the attention of some of the greatest thinkers of all ages." The credit of giving birth to natural law goes to Greeks. After the Greeks, it was further developed and elaborated by the Romans. The early and original law of Romans was called 'Jus Civil'. Later on, the Romans developed another legal system called '*Jus gentium*' which was considered to be the law of universal application. In the republican era of Rome '*Jus gentium*' was reinforced by natural law or '*Jus natural*' as it was commonly called. As pointed out by Brierly. by "*Jus natural*" the Romans meant "the sum of those principles which ought to control human conduct because founded in the very nature of man as a rational and social being." The law of nature is the expression of what is just against what is merely expedient at a particular time and place, it is what is reasonable against what is arbitrary, what is natural against, what is convenient and what is for social good against the personal will." Thus natural law was based on the rational and reasonable needs of a man's nature. According to Roman, natural law embodied the elementary principles of justice which were the dictate of rights and reason. In other words, those principles were in accordance with nature and were unalterable and eternal.

96. According to Roman what does Natural Law embody?

1. Social laws
2. Principle of human conduct
3. Elementary principle of justice
4. Company law principle

97. Which of the following is not a characteristic of natural law?

1. Convenience　2. Just and fair
3. Reasonable　4. Social good

98. Which of the following has Universal Application?

1. JUS CIVIL　2. JUS GENTIUM
3. JUS NATURAL　4. JUS COGNITO

99. Natural Law is based upon which of the following?

1. Rational and reasonable needs of man
2. Personal will
3. Human conduct
4. Supernatural powers

100. JUS gentium was enforced in which era of Rome?

1. Dictatorship　2. Democratic era
3. Republican era　4. Dark age

ANSWERS

1	**2**	**3**	**4**	**5**	**6**	**7**	**8**	**9**	**10**
1	3	2	2	3	3	4	1	3	3
11	**12**	**13**	**14**	**15**	**16**	**17**	**18**	**19**	**20**
3	1	3	4	1	3	1	2	3	4
21	**22**	**23**	**24**	**25**	**26**	**27**	**28**	**29**	**30**
4	3	2	3	3	4	3	1	2	3
31	**32**	**33**	**34**	**35**	**36**	**37**	**38**	**39**	**40**
2	3	1	1	1	2	4	1	3	1
41	**42**	**43**	**44**	**45**	**46**	**47**	**48**	**49**	**50**
2	4	3	2	1	3	1	3	1	2
51	**52**	**53**	**54**	**55**	**56**	**57**	**58**	**59**	**60**
4	4	3	4	2	1	1	3	4	2
61	**62**	**63**	**64**	**65**	**66**	**67**	**68**	**69**	**70**
2	1	3	1	2	1	2	2	2	2

71	72	73	74	75	76	77	78	79	80
3	4	1	1	2	*	4	2	1	2
81	**82**	**83**	**84**	**85**	**86**	**87**	**88**	**89**	**90**
3	1	4	1	1	3	1	3	2	3
91	**92**	**93**	**94**	**95**	**96**	**97**	**98**	**99**	**100**
4	4	2	3	1	3	1	2	1	3

EXPLANATORY ANSWERS

1. The "Doctrine of Common Employment" (also called the fellow-servant rule) originated in English tort law. It developed from the idea that an employer should not be held liable when one employee is injured solely due to the negligence of another employee engaged in the same common work. The classic starting point for this doctrine is *Priestley v. Fowler* (1837), which is treated as the foundational case from which the rule was articulated and later expanded in subsequent decisions.

2. Reservation of seats in educational institutions in favour of Scheduled Castes and Scheduled Tribes is constitutionally supported under Article 15, especially through Article 15(4) (special provisions for advancement of SC/ST and socially/educationally backward classes) and Article 15(5) (special provisions regarding admissions in educational institutions, with constitutionally recognized limits). Article 16 is focused on equality of opportunity and reservation in public employment, not seat-reservations in educational institutions. Hence, the governing Article for educational seat reservation is Article 15.

3. A. The tribunal-winding-up ground is triggered when the LLP continues with partners below the statutory minimum for the legally specified duration (the law uses a longer threshold than what is stated here). Since the statement gives an incorrect time period, it does not match the statutory condition and is therefore incorrect.

C. The statutory default-based winding-up ground requires persistent non-filing for a longer consecutive span than what is stated here. Because the statement understates the required consecutive financial years, it does not reflect the legal threshold and is therefore incorrect.

4. Sarla Mudgal v. Union of India is the leading Supreme Court decision commonly associated with the discussion on the need and relevance of a Uniform Civil Code under Article 44. While the immediate dispute dealt with bigamy through religious conversion and conflict of personal laws, the judgment prominently addressed the broader constitutional goal of UCC and urged movement towards it. Therefore, this case primarily deals with the concept of Uniform Civil Code among the given options.

5. The United States is a recognized example of an entrenched (rigid) constitutional tradition because its Constitution is placed above ordinary law and is amendable only through a specially demanding procedure, not by ordinary legislative majority. The Reason is not correct as written because, although the U.S. Constitution is the oldest still functioning written national constitution, it is not the longest written constitution in the world. Hence, Assertion is correct but Reason (as a whole) is not correct.

6.
- **A → III (1986):** The Declaration on the Right to Development was adopted by the UN General Assembly in 1986, marking a major step in recognizing development as a human right and linking it with social and economic justice.
- **B → IV (2001):** The Durban Declaration and Programme of Action emerged from the World Conference against Racism held in Durban in 2001, focusing on discrimination, development, and equality.
- **C → I (2000):** The Millennium Declaration was adopted in 2000, establishing global development goals such as poverty reduction and human dignity.
- **D → II (1993):** The Vienna Declaration and Programme of Action was adopted in 1993, reaffirming the universality of human rights and linking them with development.

7. The National Commission for Minority Educational Institutions Act was enacted by Parliament in 2004 to safeguard and protect the rights of minorities to establish and administer educational institutions under Article 30 of the Constitution. It provides for a quasi-judicial body to resolve disputes and ensure minority rights in education are effectively implemented.

8. The Assertion reflects a fundamental attribute of ownership, which is the right to exclude others from possession and enjoyment. The Reason elaborates this principle by stating that the ability to maintain or recover possession against others is a core component of ownership. Since the right to exclude is effectively enforced through the right to possess and recover possession, the Reason correctly explains the Assertion.

9. Rudolf von Ihering defined a legal right as a "legally protected interest." His theory emphasizes that rights exist to protect interests recognized by law, focusing on the social purpose of rights rather than mere will or abstract legal entitlement.

10. • **A → III (P.K. Mukherjee v. Bank of Khulna):** This case is associated with the Doctrine of Pith and Substance, which determines the true nature of legislation when there is overlap between Union and State lists.
    • **B → IV (Wallace v. Income Tax Commissioner):** This case relates to the Doctrine of Territorial Nexus, which allows laws to apply beyond territorial limits if a sufficient connection exists.
    • **C → II (M. Karunanidhi v. Union of India):** This case deals with the Doctrine of Repugnancy, addressing conflicts between Union and State laws under Article 254.
    • **D → I (K.C.G. Narayan Deo v. State of Orissa):** This case explains the Doctrine of Colourable Legislation, meaning what cannot be done directly cannot be done indirectly.

11. **A.** The Supreme Court in *State of Maharashtra v. Praful B. Desai* (2003) emphasized that law must adapt to technological advancements and societal changes. It accepted modern technology like video conferencing as part of judicial procedure to ensure effective administration of justice.
    B. The Court held that evidence in a criminal trial is not limited to physical presence; it can include oral, documentary, and electronic forms. Testimony through video conferencing is valid evidence under Section 3 of the Indian Evidence Act.

12. The "patent bargain" metaphor reflects the idea that inventors disclose their inventions to the public in exchange for exclusive rights, resembling a social contract between the inventor and society. This concept was illustrated in *Universal Oil Products v. Globe Oil & Refining* Co., where the patent system was seen as a bargain encouraging innovation while ultimately benefiting the public.

13. **A.** Montesquieu propounded the theory of separation of powers, dividing government into legislative, executive, and judicial branches to prevent concentration of power.
    B. *Marbury v. Madison* (1803) is a landmark US Supreme Court case that established the principle of judicial review, strengthening constitutional governance.
    C. Article III of the US Constitution establishes the judiciary and ensures its independence, including life tenure for judges and protection of salaries.

14. **E. Cruelty:** Appears earlier in Section 13(1) as one of the primary grounds for divorce introduced to protect spouses from mental or physical harm.
    B. Conversion: Comes after cruelty, dealing with a spouse ceasing to be Hindu by conversion to another religion.
    A. Venereal disease: Appears later as a health-related ground affecting marital life.
    C. Renunciation: Refers to entering a religious order and abandoning worldly life.
    D. Not heard alive: The last ground relates to presumption of death after seven years of absence.

15. In England, Parliament historically performed a dual role because the constitutional system developed without a single codified written Constitution that rigidly demarcated legislative and judicial spheres; thus, Parliament evolved as the supreme constitutional authority and, through institutions like the House of Lords (as the final court of appeal for centuries) and the broader idea of the "High Court of Parliament," it exercised judicial functions along with law-making. Since there was no written constitutional instrument imposing a strict separation-of-powers limitation on Parliament's authority, this constitutional evolution permitted the fusion of functions within Parliament itself, which is why (R) correctly explains (A).

16. Article 30 grants minorities, whether based on religion or language, the right to establish and administer educational institutions of their choice. The Reason is incorrect because it restricts this right only to religion, whereas the Constitution clearly extends it to both religious and linguistic minorities.

17. **D. U.N.R. Rao v. Smt. Indira Gandhi (1971):** This case dealt with the continuation of the Council of Ministers even after the dissolution of the Lok Sabha.
    B. Samsher Singh v. State of Punjab (1974): It clarified that the President and Governor act on the aid and advice of the Council of Ministers.
    A. Minerva Mills Ltd. v. Union of India (1980): It reaffirmed the basic structure doctrine and balanced Fundamental Rights and Directive Principles.
    C. S.P. Anand v. H. D. Deve Gowda (1996): It upheld the appointment of a non-member of Parliament as Prime Minister for six months.

18. **A. Exception 2 → Exceeding the right of private defense:** This applies when a person exceeds the lawful right of private defence in good faith without premeditation.
    B. Exception 3 → Act of Public Servant: It covers acts done by a public servant in good faith while performing official duties, even if exceeding legal limits.
    C. Exception 4 → Sudden fight: This applies when death occurs in a sudden fight without pre-planning and without undue advantage.

D. Exception 5 → Death by consent: This applies where death is caused with the consent of a person above 18 years of age.

19 **B.** Section 6 provides for use of electronic records and electronic signatures by Government and appears early in the Act.

C. Section 7 relates to retention of electronic records and follows Section 6.

D. Section 8 deals with publication in the electronic Gazette.

A. Section 10-A (added later) validates electronic contracts, appearing after earlier provisions.

20. The Supreme Court in this case considered whether a woman in a relationship resembling marriage could claim maintenance under Section 125 CrPC. The Court adopted a progressive interpretation, emphasizing social justice and recommending that women in live-in relationships be given protection similar to legally wedded wives to prevent destitution.

21. A. Executive Legislation → Ordinance: Executive legislation refers to law-making by the executive, mainly through ordinances issued by the President or Governor under constitutional powers.

B. Collective Responsibility → Parliamentary form of government: This is a core feature of the parliamentary system where the Council of Ministers is collectively responsible to the legislature.

C. Quasi-Judicial Function → Administrative adjudication: Quasi-judicial bodies decide disputes and exercise adjudicatory powers while being part of the administrative system.

D. Independence of Judiciary → Appointment and removal of Judges: Safeguards like fixed tenure and removal procedure ensure judicial independence.

22. This doctrine applies when a person intends to harm one individual but unintentionally harms another. The intention (mens rea) is transferred from the intended victim to the actual victim, making the accused liable for the resulting harm as if it were intended for that person.

23. A. E-rickshaw and e-cart are battery-powered vehicles as defined under the Motor Vehicles Act.

B. Their motor power is limited (not exceeding 4000 watts), which distinguishes them from other motor vehicles.

24. In this 2023 judgment, the Supreme Court held that until Parliament enacts a law, the appointment of the Chief Election Commissioner and Election Commissioners shall be made by the President on the advice of a committee consisting of the Prime Minister, Leader of Opposition, and Chief Justice of India, ensuring independence of the Election Commission.

25. A. Kharak Singh v. State of U.P.: It dealt with surveillance and interpreted personal liberty under Article 21.

C. Maneka Gandhi v. Union of India: It expanded Article 21, linking it with Articles 14 and 19 and broadening the meaning of personal liberty.

D. A.K. Gopalan v. Union of India: It initially gave a narrow interpretation of personal liberty, later expanded by subsequent judgments.

26. Under the Sale of Goods Act, 1930, Section 46 clearly distinguishes the rights of an unpaid seller depending on whether the property in goods has passed or not. When the property has passed to the buyer, the unpaid seller's rights against the goods are limited to lien, stoppage in transit, and resale. The right of withholding delivery, as mentioned in Section 46(2), is applicable only in cases where the property in the goods has not yet passed to the buyer. Therefore, when the question specifically asks for a right not available "notwithstanding that the property in the goods may have passed," the right of withholding delivery is excluded, making option 4 correct.

27. The Supreme Court in *State Bank of India v. Ajay Kumar Sood* emphasized modernization of judicial processes and directed that all judgments and orders uploaded by Courts and Tribunals must be digitally signed rather than uploaded as scanned copies. The Court highlighted that scanned documents are inefficient, difficult to access (especially for persons using assistive technologies), and lack proper authenticity verification. Digitally signed documents ensure integrity, authenticity, and better accessibility, thereby aligning judicial functioning with technological advancements.

28. A. The maker of goods or parts is clearly a manufacturer under the Act.

B. A person who assembles parts into finished goods is also included within the definition.

C. A person who puts his own mark on goods made by others (branding) is treated as a manufacturer because he represents the goods as his own.

29. The Mimansa school of Indian jurisprudence laid down interpretative principles to distinguish between obligatory (mandatory) and recommendatory (directory) injunctions in ancient legal texts. These principles have influenced modern methods of statutory interpretation.

30. B. Justice: The Preamble first mentions Justice—social, economic and political.

C. Liberty: This is followed by Liberty of thought, expression, belief, faith and worship.

A. Equality: Then comes Equality of status and opportunity.

D. Fraternity: Finally, Fraternity assuring dignity and unity and integrity of the Nation.

31. Holland described international law as the "vanishing point of jurisprudence," indicating that it does not fully fit into classical legal theory due to absence of a sovereign authority. He is classified as an analytical jurist because his approach focused on conceptual and structural analysis of law. The Vienna Convention on the Law of Treaties recognizes that treaties may create obligations or rights for third States when such States expressly accept them or when rules evolve into customary law, thus allowing limited binding effect. Grotius and Vattel are associated with natural law rather than strict positivism, and the ICJ identifies sources of international law under Article 38(1), not Article 36, so D and E are incorrect.

32. • **A → I (Section 69):** A person interested in payment who pays money which another is legally bound to pay can recover it, preventing unjust enrichment.
   • **B → II (Section 72):** Money paid or goods delivered by mistake or coercion must be repaid because retention would be unjust.
   • **C → IV (Section 70):** When a person lawfully does something not intended to be gratuitous and another enjoys the benefit, compensation is required.
   • **D → III (Section 68):** Supply of necessaries to a person incapable of contracting gives a right to reimbursement from that person's property.

33. **C. United States v. Rauscher (1886):** This is the earliest case establishing principles like specialty in extradition law.
   A. Soering v. United Kingdom (1989): It introduced human rights considerations, especially protection against inhuman punishment in extradition.
   E. Kindler v. Canada (1991): This case examined extradition in the context of death penalty concerns.
   B. Chitat v. Canada (1994): It dealt with fairness and procedural safeguards in extradition proceedings.
   D. Daya Singh Lahoria v. Union of India (2001): This is the latest case dealing with extradition law in the Indian context.

34. The National Green Tribunal Act, 2010 was brought into force on 18 October 2010 through official notification, establishing a specialized tribunal for effective and expeditious disposal of environmental cases.

35. • **A → I (Independence of the judiciary — Fazal Ali — S.P. Gupta v. Union of India):** The case dealt with judicial independence, especially concerning appointments and transfers.
   • **B → II (Federal system — Bachawat — Golak Nath v. State of Punjab):** It involved constitutional limitations and distribution of powers affecting the federal structure.
   • **C → IV (Secularism — Khanna — Indira Gandhi v. Raj Narain):** It emphasized constitutional fundamentals including secular democratic structure.
   • **D → III (Parliamentary system — Reddy — Kesavananda Bharati v. State of Kerala):** The case established the basic structure doctrine, recognizing parliamentary democracy as a core feature.

36. • **A → I (Article 325 – One general electoral roll):** Article 325 ensures equality in electoral participation by providing a single general electoral roll for every constituency and prohibits discrimination on grounds such as religion, race, caste or sex. This reflects the democratic principle of non-discrimination in voting rights.
   • **B → II (Article 326 – Adult Suffrage):** Article 326 establishes elections on the basis of adult suffrage, giving every citizen above the prescribed age the right to vote, subject to disqualifications. It embodies universal adult franchise in India.
   • **C → IV (Article 327 – Power of Parliament):** Article 327 empowers Parliament to make laws regarding elections, including preparation of electoral rolls and delimitation of constituencies. It ensures uniformity and legislative control over election procedures.
   • **D → III (Article 329 – Bar of interference by courts):** Article 329 bars courts from interfering in electoral matters except through election petitions, ensuring uninterrupted electoral processes.

37. A Limited Liability Partnership is a body corporate incorporated under the LLP Act, 2008, and it is a separate legal entity distinct from its partners. It has perpetual succession, meaning its existence continues irrespective of changes in partners. One of its most important features is that the liability of partners is limited to their agreed contribution. This protects partners from personal liability for the acts of other partners. Therefore, the statement that LLP follows the principle of unlimited liability is incorrect because LLP specifically provides limited liability protection.

38. Article 300(1) provides that the Government of India may sue or be sued in the name of the Union of India, and the State Government may sue or be sued in the name of the State. This provision recognizes the State as a juristic person capable of entering into legal proceedings. It ensures accountability of the government in courts of law. The provision is based on the continuity of legal principles from the Government of India Act, 1935. It plays an important role in enforcing rights against the government.

39. The Protection of Human Rights Act, 1993 establishes State Human Rights Commissions under Chapter V. This chapter provides for their constitution, appointment of members, powers, and functions. These Commissions are empowered to inquire into violations of human rights or negligence by public officials. They serve as an important mechanism for protecting human rights at the state level. Their role complements that of the National Human Rights Commission by ensuring accessibility and decentralized enforcement.

40. Salmond clearly distinguished between legal sources and historical sources of law. According to him, historical sources refer to materials that influence the development of law, such as ancient texts, customs, or foreign legal systems, but they do not have binding authority unless recognized by law. These sources belong to legal history rather than legal theory because they explain the origin and evolution of law. Legal sources, on the other hand, are those recognized by the legal system as having authoritative force, such as legislation and precedent. Thus, Salmond emphasized that historical sources are relevant for understanding the background of law, not for determining its present binding nature.

41.
- **A → III (Dharma Sutras – Vasishtha):** Dharma Sutras are among the earliest sources of Hindu law and were composed by ancient sages like Vasishtha, Gautama, and Apastamba. These texts laid down rules relating to conduct, duties, and legal principles.
- **B → IV (Mayukha – Nilkantha):** The Mayukha is a well-known commentary on Hindu law written by Nilkantha, particularly influential in Western India. It deals with various aspects like inheritance and family law.
- **C → I (Dayabhaga – Jimuta Vahana):** Dayabhaga is a famous digest on Hindu law authored by Jimuta Vahana, mainly followed in Bengal, emphasizing inheritance based on spiritual benefit rather than birthright.
- **D → II (Dharma Shastras – Narada):** Dharma Shastras are later and more elaborate texts than Dharma Sutras, and sages like Narada contributed to their development, covering legal and social duties.

42. **C. Rights relating to Rule of Law:** These rights appear earliest among the given categories in the Universal Declaration of Human Rights, particularly in Articles 6–11. They include recognition before law, equality before law, right to remedy, protection against arbitrary arrest, fair trial, and presumption of innocence. These provisions establish the legal framework necessary for protection of all other rights.

A. Rights relating to Freedom: These rights follow and include fundamental freedoms such as right to life, liberty and security (Article 3), freedom from slavery and torture (Articles 4–5), freedom of movement (Article 13), freedom of thought, conscience and religion (Article 18), and freedom of expression (Article 19). These rights are central to individual autonomy.

B. Rights relating to Liberties of people: These include broader civil and political liberties such as freedom of assembly and association (Article 20), right to participate in government (Article 21), right to marry and found a family (Article 16), and right to own property (Article 17). These rights appear after core freedoms and expand the scope of personal and political participation.

D. Economic Rights: These appear towards the end of the UDHR in Articles 22–27 and include rights to social security, work, rest and leisure, adequate standard of living, education, and participation in cultural life. These rights aim to ensure social and economic justice.

43. Section 13 of the Copyright Act, 1957 provides protection for original literary, dramatic, musical and artistic works, cinematograph films, and sound recordings. The performance of performers is not included as a subject matter of copyright; instead, performers are granted separate "performers' rights" under the Act, which are distinct from copyright.

44. **C. Madrid Agreement (Marks) – 1891:** This is the earliest treaty establishing an international system for trademark registration.

D. Madrid Protocol (Marks) – 1989: It supplemented and modernized the Madrid Agreement, making the system more flexible.

B. Singapore Treaty on Law of Trademarks – 2006: This treaty standardized administrative trademark procedures internationally.

A. Beijing Treaty on Audio-Visual Performances – 2012: This is the most recent treaty, protecting rights of performers in audiovisual works.

45. The concept of "Public Wrong" in tort law is closely associated with the evolution of constitutional torts in India, where the violation of fundamental rights by the State gives rise to a public law remedy. In *Sebastin M v. Union of India*, the Supreme Court dealt with the disappearance of individuals after being taken into custody by security forces, treating the issue not merely as a private wrong but as a violation of Article 21 of the Constitution. The Court recognized that such acts by State authorities amount to a public wrong, affecting not only individuals but also the rule of law, and therefore awarded compensation as a public law remedy. This case reflects the shift from traditional tort liability to constitutional accountability of the State, where compensation is granted for infringement of fundamental rights, thus clearly dealing with the concept of public wrong.

46. Under Section 19 of the Hindu Adoptions and Maintenance Act, 1956, a widowed daughter-in-law is entitled to claim maintenance from her father-in-law only if certain conditions are fulfilled, such as her inability to maintain herself from her own earnings or property and the existence of coparcenary property in the hands of the father-in-law from which she has not received a share. However, the Act clearly provides that this right is available only so long as she continues to be a Hindu. If she ceases to be a

Hindu by conversion to another religion, she loses her right to claim maintenance under this provision. Therefore, cessation of Hindu status is a disqualification for claiming maintenance from the father-in-law.

47. **B. Americans with Disabilities Act (1990):** This is the earliest among the given, enacted in the United States to prohibit discrimination against persons with disabilities.

C. United Kingdom Disability Discrimination Act (1995): This followed, providing legal protection against disability discrimination in the UK.

D. Persons with Disabilities Act (India) (1995): India enacted its law in the same year, ensuring equal opportunities and rights for persons with disabilities.

A. UN Convention on Rights of Persons with Disabilities (2006): This is the latest, establishing an international framework for protecting the rights of persons with disabilities.

48. The Tenth Amendment to the Constitution of the United States provides that powers not delegated to the federal government nor prohibited to the States are reserved to the States or the people. This amendment is a cornerstone of American federalism, clearly defining the distribution of powers and emphasizing the sovereignty of State governments within their sphere.

49.
- **A → IV (Pigeon Hole Theory – Salmond):** Salmond described tort law as consisting of specific categories of wrongs, likening them to pigeonholes, meaning liability arises only when a case fits into a recognized category.
- **B → III (Neighbour Rule – Lord Atkin):** Lord Atkin formulated the neighbour principle in *Donoghue v. Stevenson*, laying the foundation of modern negligence law.
- **C → I (Tort is Social Engineering – William Prosser):** Prosser emphasized that tort law functions to balance social interests and regulate behavior in society.
- **D → II (Use of phrase 'Law of Tort' – Winfield):** Winfield supported the idea of tort law as a general principle of liability, and he used the term to denote a broader, evolving field of law.

50. A Waqf in Muslim law is a permanent dedication of property for religious, pious, or charitable purposes, and thus it is essentially a religious and pious obligation. The Reason is also correct because in a Waqf, provision may be made for charity and even for the benefit of the settlor's family, known as Waqf-alal-aulad. However, this feature does not explain the religious nature of Waqf; it only describes one of its possible forms. The religious and pious character of Waqf arises from its dedication to God and charitable purposes, not merely from the provision for family benefit.

51. **B.** The Patent Act requires novelty, inventive step, and industrial applicability for patentability. The term "originality" is not a requirement under patent law; it is relevant to copyright law. Hence, this statement is incorrect.

C. The Intellectual Property Appellate Board (IPAB) has been abolished (Tribunal Reforms Act, 2021), and its functions have been transferred to High Courts and other authorities. Therefore, it does not currently deal with all IPR disputes, making this statement incorrect.

52. Article 13(3)(a) gives an inclusive definition of the term "law" for the purpose of enforcing Fundamental Rights. It specifically mentions that "law" includes any ordinance, order, bye-law, rule, regulation, notification, custom or usage having the force of law in the territory of India. The intention is to ensure that not only legislative enactments but also executive and subordinate legislation, as well as customs having legal force, can be tested against Fundamental Rights. The expression is deliberately wide so that any form of legal norm affecting rights does not escape judicial review. The Article focuses on the forms through which law operates, rather than explicitly mentioning Acts in this clause. Hence, the correct option is the one which reproduces the wording of Article 13(3)(a).

53. Under Section 3 of the Protection of Human Rights Act, 1993, the Secretary-General of the National Human Rights Commission acts as the Chief Executive Officer. He exercises administrative powers and is responsible for the efficient functioning of the Commission, implementing its decisions and managing its day-to-day affairs.

54. Section 70B of the Information Technology Act, 2000 empowers the Central Government to appoint the Indian Computer Emergency Response Team (CERT-In) as the national agency for responding to cyber security incidents. It collects, analyses, and disseminates information on cyber threats and coordinates response measures.

55. Article 246 of the Constitution distributes legislative powers between the Union and the States by referring to the Union List, State List, and Concurrent List in the Seventh Schedule. It specifies the subject-matter on which Parliament and State Legislatures can make laws, forming the basis of the federal structure.

56.
- **A → II (Patent Law Treaty – 2000):** The Patent Law Treaty was adopted in 2000 to harmonize and streamline formal procedures relating to national and regional patent applications. It simplifies procedural requirements for patent applicants.
- **B → I (Riyadh Design Law Treaty – 2024):** This is a recent WIPO-administered treaty adopted in 2024 to harmonize procedures relating to industrial design protection globally.

- **C → IV (WIPO Copyright Treaty – 1996):** The WIPO Copyright Treaty was adopted in 1996 to address copyright protection in the digital environment, especially for literary and artistic works.
- **D → III (Nairobi Treaty – 1981):** The Nairobi Treaty on the Protection of the Olympic Symbol was adopted in 1981, granting protection to the Olympic symbol internationally.

57. In criminal law, culpable homicide is the broader category (genus) under Section 299 IPC, while murder is a specific aggravated form (species) defined under Section 300 IPC. Every act of murder necessarily falls within culpable homicide because it involves causing death with intention or knowledge. However, not every culpable homicide amounts to murder, as there are exceptions and varying degrees of intention and knowledge. Thus, the Reason correctly explains the Assertion.

58. **A. Negotiation:** The UN Charter (Article 33) begins with negotiation as the primary and most basic method of peaceful dispute settlement.

B. Enquiry: It follows negotiation, involving fact-finding mechanisms to clarify disputes.

C. Mediation: This involves third-party assistance to facilitate a mutually acceptable solution.

D. Conciliation: It is a more structured form of mediation where proposals for settlement are formally made.

E. Arbitration: It appears later as a more formal adjudicatory mechanism where parties agree to be bound by a decision.

59. In this case, the Supreme Court recognized Guru Granth Sahib as a juristic person, acknowledging its religious significance and legal status. The Court held that as the central religious scripture of Sikhism, it can hold property and can be represented in legal proceedings, similar to idols in Hindu law being treated as juristic persons.

60. Among the given offences, rioting is the most severely punishable. While unlawful assembly itself is punishable, rioting involves the use of force or violence by an unlawful assembly, making it more serious. Affray and assault involve lesser degrees of disturbance or violence. Rioting, especially when armed with deadly weapons, carries heavier punishment under criminal law, reflecting its greater threat to public order.

61. Under the Hindu Adoptions and Maintenance Act, 1956, valid adoption requires conditions such as absence of a living Hindu son for adoption of a son, prohibition of multiple simultaneous adoptions of the same child, and actual giving and taking of the child in adoption. The age difference requirement of at least twenty-one years applies only when a male adopts a female child or a female adopts a male child. There is no such requirement when both adoptive parent and child are of the same gender. Therefore, this statement is not a valid condition and is incorrect.

62. The TRIPS Agreement sets minimum standards for protection of Geographical Indications but does not mandate a specific legal mechanism, allowing member states flexibility in implementation. This reflects the historical development of GIs, which vary widely across jurisdictions compared to trademarks that have a more stable and uniform conceptual basis. Because GIs are linked to regional characteristics, traditions, and cultural factors, their definition and protection have been more fluid. Hence, the Reason correctly explains why TRIPS adopts a flexible approach, making both statements correct and logically connected.

63. The determination of whether the provocation was grave and sudden enough to reduce the offence from murder to culpable homicide not amounting to murder is specifically treated as a question of fact under Exception 1 to Section 300 of the Indian Penal Code. This requires examination of the actual circumstances in which the act was committed, including the conduct of the parties, the nature of provocation, and the mental state of the accused at the time of the act. There is no fixed legal formula to decide what constitutes "grave and sudden" provocation, and it varies from case to case. The court must assess the facts and evidence to determine whether a reasonable person in similar circumstances would have lost self-control. Hence, it is a factual determination rather than purely a legal one.

64. The Will theory, associated with jurists like Hegel, states that the purpose of law is to enable individuals to exercise their will and express their personality. It treats rights as an expression of individual autonomy and self-assertion. According to this theory, law exists to protect and promote the free will of individuals, allowing them to act and develop their personality within a legal framework.

65. The case concerning the ship *Arantzazu Mendi* involved issues of recognition of governments during the Spanish Civil War. The dispute was between the de jure Republican Government of Spain and the de facto Nationalist Government led by General Franco. The House of Lords had to consider the legal consequences of recognition of governments and determine which authority had the right to control the property in question.

66. **A. Sankari Prasad v. Union of India (1951):** This is the earliest case where the Supreme Court upheld Parliament's power to amend Fundamental Rights under Article 368.

B. **Sajjan Singh v. State of Rajasthan (1965):** This reaffirmed the view in Sankari Prasad, maintaining Parliament's amending power over Fundamental Rights.

C. **Golak Nath v. State of Punjab (1967):** The Court reversed earlier decisions and held that Parliament cannot amend Fundamental Rights.

D. **Kesavananda Bharati v. State of Kerala (1973):** This landmark case introduced the Basic Structure Doctrine, allowing amendment but not destruction of the Constitution's basic structure.

E. **Waman Rao v. Union of India (1981):** This case clarified the application of the Basic Structure Doctrine, especially with respect to laws placed in the Ninth Schedule.

67. Section 135 of the Companies Act, 2013 mandates that companies meeting the prescribed financial thresholds must constitute a Corporate Social Responsibility Committee. The Reason is also correct as the CSR Committee is responsible for monitoring the CSR policy and activities of the company. However, this function of monitoring does not explain why such companies are required to constitute the committee; the requirement arises from statutory thresholds and regulatory compliance, not merely from its monitoring role.

68. Article 15 of the Universal Declaration of Human Rights, 1948 provides that everyone has the right to a nationality and that no one shall be arbitrarily deprived of his nationality nor denied the right to change it. This provision ensures legal identity and protection under international human rights law.

69. A written Constitution serves to limit the powers of the organs of the State by clearly defining their functions and boundaries. The Reason is also correct as in systems with judicial review, courts act as guardians of the Constitution by ensuring that laws and actions conform to constitutional provisions. However, judicial review is a mechanism for enforcing constitutional limitations, not the reason why a Constitution is written. The purpose of having a written Constitution is broader and includes clarity, certainty, and limitation of powers, while judicial review is only one of the tools for its enforcement.

70. The Metaphysical school of jurisprudence, influenced largely by German thinkers, sought to develop a universal doctrine of law based on abstract principles and metaphysical ideas. It aimed to derive legal rules from universal reason and philosophical concepts rather than limiting itself to the customs of a particular society or historical development of a specific nation. This distinguishes it from the Historical school, which focuses on the evolution of law within a particular society.

71. In standard form contracts, where one party drafts the contract and imposes terms on the other, ambiguity often arises in interpretation of exclusion or limitation clauses. The Contra Proferentem Rule provides that any ambiguity in such clauses must be interpreted against the party who drafted or inserted the clause. This rule is based on fairness, as the drafting party has the advantage of wording the contract and should bear the consequences of unclear language. It is particularly applied in insurance contracts and consumer agreements where bargaining power is unequal. The rule ensures protection of the weaker party and prevents misuse of exclusion clauses. Therefore, in case of doubt regarding meaning or scope, interpretation is made against the proferens (the party who proposed the clause).

72. D. **Effect of Proclamation of Emergency (Article 353):** This provision appears first among the given, explaining the consequences of a national emergency, including extension of executive power.

C. **Failure of constitutional machinery in States (Article 356):** This follows and deals with President's Rule in States when governance cannot be carried out as per the Constitution.

B. **Suspension of Article 19 (Article 358):** This provision allows suspension of freedoms under Article 19 during a national emergency.

A. **Financial Emergency (Article 360):** This appears last and deals with financial instability and control of finances by the Union.

73. Section 6 of the Biological Diversity Act, 2002 specifically deals with the requirement of obtaining prior approval of the National Biodiversity Authority before applying for any intellectual property right based on research or information on biological resources obtained from India. While granting such approval, the Authority is empowered to impose conditions relating to benefit sharing, including payment of fees, royalties, or a share in the financial benefits arising from commercial utilization. This provision forms part of the Access and Benefit Sharing mechanism, ensuring that benefits derived from biological resources are equitably shared with local communities and stakeholders. Therefore, Section 6 directly relates to benefit sharing fees and royalties under the Act.

74. A. **Son's daughter's son:** This appears first among the given in Class II heirs under the Schedule of the Hindu Succession Act.

D. **Son's daughter's daughter:** It follows immediately after the previous category.

B. **Daughter's son's son:** This comes later in the order of Class II heirs.

C. **Daughter's son's daughter:** This appears after the son's daughter's descendants in the Schedule.

75. Under the Companies Act, 2013, every listed public company is required to have at least one-third of the total number of directors as independent directors. This ensures corporate governance, transparency, and protection of shareholders' interests by bringing independent judgment into the board's decision-making process.

76. The question contains ambiguity in provisions and their order in the Motor Vehicles Act, 1988: The given items correspond to provisions that are not arranged in a clear linear sequence within the Act due to amendments and insertions at different times. "Necessity of Permits" falls under Chapter V (earlier part), "Claims Tribunal" under Chapter XII, "Motor Vehicle Accident Fund" is a later insertion (Section 164B onwards), and "Recall of Motor Vehicles" is introduced separately under Section 110A. Because these provisions belong to different chapters and some were inserted later without disturbing the original sequence, their "order of appearance" cannot be determined in a straightforward ascending manner as per the structure of the Act. None of the options correctly represent the actual legislative sequence, leading to ambiguity. Hence, the correct answer is NONE.

77.
- **A → II (Entry into force of Refugee Convention – 1954):** The 1951 Convention came into force in 1954, establishing international refugee protection standards.
- **B → I (Protocol to Refugee Convention – 1967):** The 1967 Protocol removed geographical and temporal limitations of the Convention.
- **C → III (UNHCR Nobel Prize – 1981):** UNHCR received the Nobel Peace Prize for the second time in 1981.
- **D → IV (Formation of UNHCR – 1950):** The UN High Commissioner for Refugees was established in 1950.

78. **B.** If a state government acts against secularism, it violates the basic structure, and President's Rule can be justified.

C. The State Assembly cannot be dissolved before Parliament approves the Proclamation under Article 356.

D. The power under Article 356 is not absolute and is subject to judicial review and constitutional limitations.

79. India and the United Kingdom formally signed the Comprehensive Economic and Trade Agreement (CETA) on 24 July 2025 during a high-level bilateral meeting in London. This agreement was the culmination of negotiations aimed at strengthening trade and economic cooperation between the two countries. It provided for significant tariff reductions, expanded market access, and facilitation of trade in goods and services. A notable feature included provisions to prevent double social security contributions for professionals working temporarily abroad. The agreement reflects a major step in enhancing bilateral trade relations and aims to substantially increase trade volume in the coming years.

80. **D. Necessaries supplied (Section 68):** This appears early under quasi-contract provisions dealing with persons incapable of contracting.

C. Compensation for breach (Section 73): This provision follows, dealing with damages for breach of contract.

A. Continuing guarantee (Section 129): This appears later under contracts of guarantee.

B. Care by bailee (Section 151): This is part of bailment provisions, appearing after guarantee provisions.

81. **A. Proposal:** Section 2(a) defines proposal as the starting point of a contract when one person signifies willingness to do or abstain from doing something.

D. Promise: Section 2(b) states that when a proposal is accepted, it becomes a promise.

B. Consideration: Section 2(d) defines consideration as something done or abstained from at the desire of the promisor.

C. Agreement: Section 2(e) defines agreement as every promise and every set of promises forming consideration for each other.

E. Contract: Section 2(h) defines contract as an agreement enforceable by law, which is the final stage in formation.

82. The Assertion correctly states that Rule of Law has been recognized as a basic feature of the Indian Constitution, which cannot be amended even under Article 368. This doctrine has evolved through judicial interpretation, especially under the Basic Structure Doctrine. The Reason is also correct because constitutional jurisprudence, particularly in countries like Germany, recognizes that certain fundamental principles of higher moral or ethical value can override even express constitutional provisions. This supports the idea that Rule of Law can be treated as a superior constitutional principle, thus explaining the Assertion.

83.
- **A → IV (Cox v. Hickman – Mutual Agency):** This case established that mutual agency is the true test of partnership.
- **B → III (Stekel v. Ellice – Salaried partner):** It clarified that even a salaried partner can be a partner if mutual agency exists.
- **C → II (Lachhman Das v. CIT – Partnership between Karta and Coparcener):** The case recognized that a Karta can enter into partnership with a coparcener in his individual capacity.
- **D → I (Smith v. Anderson – Business must be taken in a practical sense):** It defined business in a practical and real sense for determining partnership.

84. • **A → II (Ashby v. White – Violation of absolute right):** The case established that violation of a legal right gives rise to a remedy even without actual damage.
- **B → III (Rylands v. Fletcher – Strict liability):** It laid down the rule of strict liability for escape of dangerous things.
- **C → I (Olga Tellis v. Bombay Municipal Corp. – Poverty as involuntary act):** The Court recognized that pavement dwellers are compelled by poverty, linking it to right to livelihood.
- **D → IV (Allen v. Flood – Motive irrelevant):** It established that motive is irrelevant if the act is lawful.

85. The Draft Convention on Territorial Asylum (1974) recognizes in Article 1 that the grant of asylum is a sovereign right of the State. It affirms that States have the discretion to grant asylum to persons seeking protection without interference, reflecting the principle of sovereignty and non-intervention in international law.

86. The case of *Abhayanand Mishra v. State of Bihar* is a leading authority on the concept of attempt under criminal law. The Supreme Court clarified the distinction between preparation and attempt, stating that an attempt begins when preparations are complete and the accused has taken a direct step towards the commission of the offence. The act must be proximate to the intended offence and not merely preparatory. This case laid down the test of proximity and intention, which is used to determine criminal liability for attempt under the Indian Penal Code.

87. • **A → IV (John Rawls):** Rawls stated that justice is the first virtue of social institutions, emphasizing fairness as the basis of social arrangements.
- **B → II (Aristotle):** Aristotle viewed natural justice as part of political justice, distinguishing between universal natural law and particular legal justice.
- **C → III (Dworkin):** Ronald Dworkin emphasized "equality of respect and concern" as a core principle of justice and rights.
- **D → I (Immanuel Kant):** Kant emphasized human dignity as intrinsic worth, forming the foundation of human rights.

88. Under the Companies Act, 2013, recognized types of prospectus include shelf prospectus, deemed prospectus, and abridged prospectus. The correct term used in law is "Red Herring Prospectus," not "Yellow Herring Prospectus." Therefore, the given option is not a recognized type and is incorrect.

89. **B.** The Supreme Court invoked Article 142 to adopt a victim-centric approach in sentencing, focusing on justice tailored to the victim's circumstances.

D. The Court considered the wishes of the victim and declined to enhance the sentence of the accused, emphasizing rehabilitation and victim's perspective.

90. • **A → III (National Biodiversity Authority – Section 8):** This section provides for the establishment of the National Biodiversity Authority.
- **B → I (State Biodiversity Fund – Section 32):** This section deals with the constitution of the State Biodiversity Fund.
- **C → IV (National Biodiversity Fund – Section 27):** This section provides for the National Biodiversity Fund.
- **D → II (Biodiversity Heritage Sites – Section 37):** This section empowers State Governments to notify Biodiversity Heritage Sites.

91. The passage clearly states that the Constitution is being interpreted for a nation whose people desire a complete and dignified life, and therefore social justice must be central to its interpretation. The emphasis is on addressing real social needs and inequalities rather than abstract legal reasoning. The idea of "hunger for a full life" reflects the goal of ensuring justice, equality, and welfare. Hence, the perception of social justice is essential in constitutional interpretation to meet the aspirations of the people.

92. The author stresses that the Constitution is a living document and its interpretation must be grounded in the realities of society. The "Supreme Lex" (the Constitution) derives its vitality from the social context in which it operates. Ignoring social conditions would lead to empty and ineffective interpretation. Therefore, courts must always consider the social setting while interpreting constitutional provisions.

93. The passage explicitly states that the Constitution is not a rigid or "petrified" document but a dynamic human text. It must be read with a national mission aimed at achieving social justice and progress. The Court must interpret it in a way that reflects human values and national goals. This approach emphasizes flexibility and responsiveness to changing societal needs.

94. The passage quotes the American Supreme Court to highlight that modern society does not adhere to rigid, absolute principles. Instead, law must adapt to changing circumstances and realities. This idea supports a flexible and pragmatic approach to constitutional interpretation. Therefore, the most certain principle in modern society is that there are no absolutes.

95. The passage concludes by stating that "Legal Einsteinism," implying relativity and flexibility in legal interpretation, guides the Court rather than rigid doctrinal rules. This suggests that law should adapt to context and circumstances rather than follow fixed absolutes. It emphasizes a dynamic and evolving approach to jurisprudence.

96. The passage clearly states that according to Roman thinkers, natural law embodied the elementary principles of justice. These principles were considered the dictates of reason and rights, reflecting what is just and fair

rather than what is merely expedient. Natural law was seen as universal, unalterable, and based on rational human nature. Therefore, its core essence lay in justice rather than mere social rules or specific legal systems.

97. Natural law is described in the passage as what is just rather than expedient, reasonable rather than arbitrary, natural rather than convenient, and aimed at social good rather than personal will. This clearly indicates that convenience is not a characteristic of natural law. Instead, it is opposed to convenience, emphasizing fairness, reason, and universal justice.

98. The passage explains that the Romans developed a system called *Jus gentium*, which was regarded as having universal application. It was intended to govern relations among people beyond a particular state and was influenced by natural law principles. This distinguished it from *Jus civil*, which was limited to Roman citizens.

99. The passage explicitly mentions that natural law was based on the rational and reasonable needs of human nature. It emphasizes that natural law arises from the nature of humans as rational and social beings, focusing on justice and reason rather than arbitrary or personal considerations.

100. The passage clearly states that in the republican era of Rome, *Jus gentium* was reinforced by natural law (*Jus natural*). This shows that its development and application were particularly prominent during the republican period of Roman history.

YOUR SPACE

Previous Years' Paper

National Testing Agency (NTA)

UGC-NET Junior Research Fellowship & Assistant Professor Eligibility Exam

LAW, JUNE-2025

(Exam held on 25-06-2025)

PAPER-II

1. What is the guiding principle of inheritance under Mitakshara?

1. Religious efficacy
2. Capacity to perform religious obligations
3. Doctrine of sapinda relationship
4. Capacity to offer religious obligations

2. Which of the following is **not** a general defence under Torts?

A. Mistake B. Remoteness
C. Necessity D. Consent

Choose the **correct** answer from the options given below:

1. A and B Only 2. C only
3. C and D Only 4. B only

3. Which of the following is **not** defined under section 2 of BNS, 2023 and Chapter II of IPC, 1860?

1. Animal 2. Person
3. Child 4. Women

4. Which of the following is **not** true in the context of CSR?

1. CSR Committee should consist of only one Director
2. CSR provision was introduced by the Companies Act, 2013
3. Company should spend atleast 2% of average net profits made during the immediately preceding 3 financial years
4. CSR is an implied agreement between the company and society to impart goods and services in some way advantageous to the society

5. In which of the following case, the Supreme Court of India gave a split verdict on 23rd July, 2024 in a matter involving health, environment and inter-generational equity?

1. M.C. Mehta v/s U.O.I
2. Animal Welfare Board of India v/s U.O.I
3. M.K. Ranjitsingh v/s U.O.I
4. Gene Campaign v/s U.O.I

6. Match the LIST-I with LIST-II.

LIST-I (Jurists)	LIST-II (Definition of Administrative Law)
A. Wade	I. Administrative Law is the law relating to the administration. It determines the organization, powers and duties of administrative authorities.
B. Garner	II. Main object of administrative law is the operation and control of administrative authorities.
C. Griffith & Street	III. Rules recognized by the courts as law and which relate to and regulate the administration of government.
D. Ivor Jennings	IV. Law relating to the control of government power.

Choose the **correct** answer from the options given below:

1. A-I, B-II, C-III, D-IV
2. A-II, B-I, C-IV, D-III
3. A-III, B-IV, C-I, D-II
4. A-IV, B-III, C-II, D-I

7. In which of the following case, the Supreme Court of India held that telephone tapping is a serious invasion of an individual's right to privacy?

1. People's Union for Civil Liberties v/s Union of India
2. R. Rajagopal v/s State of T.N.
3. Mr. v/s Hospital 'Z'
4. State of Maharashtra v/s Madhulkar Narain

8. Which of the following Canadian Legislation does **not** have provisions related to Federation?

1. Law of Federation, 1802
2. British North America Act, 1867
3. Constitution Act, 1982
4. Constitution Act, 1867

9. Which of the following is **not** a guardian under the Hindu Minority and Guardianship Act, 1956?

A. Guardian for Marriage
B. Maternal Guardian
C. Testamentary Guardian
D. Guardian by Affinity

Choose the **correct** answer from the options given below:

1. A and B only 2. A only
3. C and D only 4. C only

10. "International law is the body of rules and principles of action which are binding upon civilised states in their relations with one another''. This definition is attributed to whom of the following?

1. Oppenheium 2. J.L. Briely
3. J.G. Starke 4. Jerry Bentham

11. Match the LIST-I with LIST-II.

LIST-I (Type of IPR)	LIST-II (Concept)
A. Geographical Indication	I. Post grant opposition
B. Trademark	II. Protection of Right Management Information (RMI)
C. Patent	III. Prohibition of Assignment
D. Copyright	IV. Honest Concurrent use

Choose the **correct** answer from the options given below:

1. A-I, B-IV, C-III, D-II
2. A-III, B-IV, C-I, D-II
3. A-I, B-III, C-IV, D-I
4. A-II, B-IV, C-I, D-III

12. Which of the following theory/theories is/are **not** closely connected to intellectual property rights?

A. Economic Theory
B. Autopoietic legal Theory
C. Social Planning Theory
D. Instrumentalist Theory
E. Social Contract Theory

Choose the **correct** answer from the options given below:

1. C and D only 2. A and E only
3. B only 4. D only

13. Which of the following is a landmark case on the importance of 'nationality'?

1. North Sea Continental Self Case
2. Asylum Case
3. S.S. Lotus Case
4. Nottebohm Case

14. Which of the following is **not** true in the context of a promissory note?

1. It must be in writing and signed by the maker.
2. There must be an undertaking or promise to pay.
3. Such a promise must be conditional.
4. The promise must be in respect of payment of money only.

15. Which of the following provision of the Companies Act, 2013 identifies shares and debentures as a movable property?

1. Section 44 2. Section 45
3. Section 46 4. Section 47

16. Which of the following statements are correct?

A. The first national commission for women was constituted on 31.01.1992
B. National Commission for Backward Classes has been accorded constitutional status through 102nd Constitution (Amendment) Act, 2018
C. The ministry of Minority Affairs was carved out of Ministry of Social Justice and Empowerment
D. National Commission for Scheduled Tribes has been set up under Art. 338
E. Art. 338A deals with National Commission for Scheduled Castes

Choose the **correct** answer from the options given below:

1. B, C, D only
2. C, D, E only
3. A, B, C only
4. A, C, E only

17. Arrange the following Conventions in the chronological order of their coming into force.

A. The Biological Weapons Convention
B. The Chemical Weapons Convention
C. The Convention on Certain Conventional Weapons
D. The Ottawa Convention on Anti-Personnel Mines

Choose the **correct** answer from the options given below:

1. A, B, C, D
2. A, C, B, D
3. C, A, B, D
4. C, D, A, B

18. In which of the following case, the golden rule for framing prospectus was formulated by V.C. Kindersley?

A. Methodist Church v/s Union of India
B. R. v/s Registrar of Companies
C. New Brunswick Canada Railway Co. v/s Muggeridge
D. Jubilee Colton Mills Ltd. v/s Lewis

Choose the **correct** answer from the options given below:

1. A and C only 2. B only
3. C only 4. B and D only

19. Match the LIST-I with LIST-II.

LIST-I (Jurist)	LIST-II (Statement/Opinion)
A. Montesquie	I. Comparative Constitution is strange
B. Lee	II. Used the term - Rechtsvergleichung
C. Rudolph and Schlesinger	III. Published 'Ancient Law' in 1861
D. Maine	IV. Father of Comparative Law

Choose the **correct** answer from the options given below:

1. A-I, B-II, C-III, D-IV
2. A-II, B-III, C-IV, D-I
3. A-III, B-IV, C-I, D-II
4. A-IV, B-I, C-II, D-III

20. Which of the following decisions are related to extradition:

A. Savarkar case B. Abu Salem case
C. Castioni, re case D. Meunier, re case
E. Paquete Habana case

Choose the **correct** answer from the options given below:

1. A, B, C only 2. B, C, D, E only
3. A, B, C, D only 4. A, B, D, E only

21. Match the LIST-I with LIST-II.

LIST-I (Authors/Editors)	LIST-II (Title of Books)
A. Rainer Arnold	I. International Humanitarian Law
B. Vandana Shiva	II. The Universalism of Human Rights
C. Lenzerini Federico	III. Biopiracy: The Plunder of Nature & Knowledge
D. Emily Crowford & Alison Pert	IV. The Culturalisation of Human Rights Law

Choose the **correct** answer from the options given below:

1. A-II, B-III, C-IV, D-I
2. A-I, B-II, C-III, D-IV
3. A-II, B-I, C-IV, D-III
4. A-IV, B-III, C-I, D-II

22. Match the LIST-I with LIST-II.

LIST-I (Authors/Editors)	LIST-II (Title of Books)
A. J Donhelly & D.J. Whelar	I. International Human Rights
B. L. Rajamani & J. Peel	II. The Oxford Handbook of International Environmental Law
C. Karnika Seth	III. Computers, Internet and New Technology Laws
D. J. Gibson	IV. Patenting Lives: Life Patents, Culture & Development

Choose the **correct** answer from the options given below:

1. A-II, B-I, C-IV, D-III
2. A-I, B-IV, C-II, D-III
3. A-I, B-II, C-III, D-IV
4. A-III, B-II, C-I, D-IV

23. Arrange the following in order of their enactment (ascending):

A. West German Constitution
B. British North America Act
C. Australian Constitution Act
D. Article of Confederation and Perpetual Union

Choose the **correct** answer from the options given below:

1. D, B, C, A
2. A, B, C, D
3. B, A, C, D
4. D, C, B, A

24. United States Ombudsman Association was founded in which year?

1. 1977
2. 1976
3. 1956
4. 1986

25. Which of the following is **not** a theory of legal personality?

1. Fiction theory
2. Concession theory
3. Interest theory
4. Bracket theory

26. Which one of the following is incorrect statement in the context of the characteristic features of a Waqf?

1. Waqf properties are inalienable
2. A testamentary Waqf is irrevocable
3. A Waqf once created cannot be revoked
4. A Waqf property vests in God

27. Match the LIST-I with LIST-II.

LIST-I (Judicial Decisions)	LIST-II (Issue)
A. State of Gujarat v/s Reliance Industries Ltd & Ors.	I. Management of sewage treatment plants
B. Municipal Corporation Ghaziabad v/s Central Pollution Control Board	II. Climate Change
C. Hanuman Laxman Aroskar v/s U.O.I	III. Environmental Clearance for large infrastructure project
D. Riddhima Pandey v/s U.O.I	IV. Green cess

Choose the **correct** answer from the options given below:

1. A-III, B-I, C-IV, D-II
2. A-I, B-IV, C-III, D-II
3. A-IV, B-I, C-III, D-II
4. A-III, B-II, C-IV, D-I

28. Which of the following Article is referred to be the heart and soul of the Indian Constitution?

1. Article 32
2. Article 21
3. Article 14
4. Article 226

29. What are the duties of a bailee as provided under the Indian Contract Act?

A. Duty to take reasonable care of the goods bailed.
B. Duty not to make unauthorized use of the goods.
C. Duty not to mix bailor's goods with his own goods.
D. Duty to return the goods on fulfilment of the purpose.
E. Duty not to deliver to the bailor increase or profit on the goods bailed.

Choose the **correct** answer from the options given below:

1. B, C, D, E only
2. C, D, E, A only
3. D. E, B, A only
4. A, B, C, D only

30. Which of the following is **not** an absolute privilege under the law of torts?

1. A petition to Parliament
2. Words written or spoken before a Tribunal
3. Communication made in self-protection
4. Communication relating to State matters made by one minister to another

31. The foundation of Federation in India was laid down by which legislation from the following?

1. Government of India Act, 1919
2. Government of India Act, 1935
3. Constitution of India, 1950
4. Queen Proclamation of 1875

32. Match the LIST-I with LIST-II.

LIST-I (Schedules under UCC of Uttrakhand, 2025)	LIST-II (Topic dealt under the Schedule)
A. Schedule 3	I. form of probate
B. Schedule 7	II. form of certificate
C. Schedule 5	III. form of caveat
D. Schedule 4	IV. form of certificate and extended certificate

Choose the **correct** answer from the options given below:

1. A-II, B-IV, C-I, D-III
2. A-I, B-II, C-III, D-IV
3. A-IV, B-III, C-II, D-I
4. A-II, B-I, C-IV, D-III

33. Match the LIST-I with LIST-II.

LIST-I (Maxim)	LIST-II (Meaning)
A. *Erga Omnes*	I. Relation to all
B. *Jus Cogens*	II. Peremptory norm
C. *Pacta Sunt Servanda*	III. Agreements are to be respected
D. *Rebus Sic Stantibus*	IV. Essential circumstances remain unchanged

Choose the **correct** answer from the options given below:

1. A-IV, B-III, C-II, D-I
2. A-III, B-IV, C-II, D-I
3. A-I, B-II, C-III, D-IV
4. A-III, B-I, C-II, D-IV

34. Match the LIST-I with LIST-II.

LIST-I (Section under the Motor Vehicle (Amendment) Act, 2019)	LIST-II (Provision)
A. Section 164 B	I. Information to be given regarding accident
B. Section 162	II. Motor Vehicle Accident Fund
C. Section 164 A	III. Scheme for golden hour
D. Section 159	IV. Scheme for Interim relief for claimants

Choose the **correct** answer from the options given below:

1. A-I, B-IV, C-III, D-II
2. A-IV, B-I, C-II, D-III
3. A-III, B-II, C-I, D-IV
4. A-II, B-III, C-IV, D-I

35. Which of the following Amendment has inserted the theme 'Secularism, Socialism and Integrity' in the Preamble of the Indian Constitution?

1. 44th Amendment
2. 42nd Amendment
3. 73rd Amendment
4. 74th Amendment

36. Match the LIST-I with LIST-II.

LIST-I (Heirs)	LIST-II (Succession Categories)
A. Paternal Aunt's Son	I. Class II
B. Daughter's Son's daughter	II. Cognate
C. Paternal Uncle's daughter	III. Class I
D. Daughter of a predeceased Son	IV. Agnate

Choose the **correct** answer from the options given below:

1. A-I, B-III, C-II, D-IV
2. A-II, B-I, C-IV, D-III
3. A-II, B-IV, C-I, D-III
4. A-I, B-II, C-III, D-IV

37. Match the LIST-I with LIST-II.

LIST-I (Profounder)	LIST-II (Idea)
A. Mimansa	I. Law and Morals are same
B. Smriti	II. "Idea of Values" is the foundation
C. Post Reformation Europe	III. Law derives authority from State and not morals
D. Korkunov	IV. There is distinction between obligatory and recommendatory rules

Choose the **correct** answer from the options given below:

1. A-IV, B-I, C-III, D-II
2. A-II, B-III, C-I, D-IV
3. A-III, B-IV, C-II, D-I
4. A-I, B-II, C-IV, D-III

38. Estrada doctrine dealing with recognition of States and Government is primarily related to which country?

1. Spain
2. Mexico
3. Germany
4. China

39. Arrange the following provisions in the correct order of their appearance in the Information Technology Act, 2000 (section-wise):

A. Penalty for misrepresentation
B. Punishment for identify theft
C. Punishment for cyber terrorism
D. Penalty for breach of confidentiality and privacy
E. Punishment for violation of privacy

Choose the **correct** answer from the options given below:

1. A, B, C, D, E
2. C, B, A, E, D
3. B, A, C, D, E
4. B, E, C, A, D

40. A Christian Man X and a Hindu Girl Y eloped and entered into an "Agreement of Marriage" on ₹ 50 stamp paper and registered it at Registrar office. They exchanged garland, X tied a Mangalsutra around neck of Y. Is it a valid Marriage?

1. It is a valid marriage as it is registered by agreement
2. It is valid marriage as ceremonies are performed
3. It is not a valid marriage as legal validity test is not complete
4. It is a valid marriage as customary rites of the parties were followed

41. When did Ministry of Environment, Forest and Climate Change notify Biological Diversity Rules, 2024?

1. 25th December, 2024
2. 18th January, 2024
3. 1st April, 2024
4. 22nd October, 2024

42. Arrange the following in the order of their introduction in the American Constitution by way of Amendment (ascending order)

A. 18-year-old Suffrage
B. Black Suffrage
C. Abolition of Slavery
D. Women Suffrage

Choose the **correct** answer from the options given below:

1. A, B, C, D 2. B, C, D, A
3. C, B, D, A 4. A, C, B, D

43. Which section in BNS, 2023 replaced section 124A of IPC, 1860 by prohibiting "acts endangering sovereignty, unity and integrity of India"?

1. Section 112
2. Section 152
3. Section 95
4. Section 304

44. Which of the following is **not** the meaning of the term "dominant position" under the Competition Act, 2002?

1. Position of strength
2. Operating independently of competitive forces
3. Cartel activity among competitors
4. Affect its competitors or consumers in its favour

45. From which country, Part IV of the Indian Constitution is borrowed?

1. Russia 2. Ireland
3. USA 4. Spain

46. Which of the following are correct about "legal theory"?

A. It defines Law
B. It analyses legal concepts
C. It deals with mere theory and has no practical importance
D. It highlights salient features of legal system

Choose the **correct** answer from the options given below:

1. A, B, C only
2. B, C, D only
3. A, B, D only
4. A, C, D only

47. Arrange the following provisions of Protection of Human Rights Act, 1993 in the order of its appearance in the Act.

A. Inquiry into complaints
B. Procedure with respect to armed forces
C. Investigation
D. Powers relating to inquiry
E. Statements made by person to the Commission

Choose the **correct** answer from the options given below:

1. A, B, C, D, E
2. A, D, E, B, C
3. A, D, C, E, B
4. D, C, E, A, B

48. Which of the following is true about Separation of Power in the Constitution of Canada?

A. Separation exists between only Judiciary and Parliament
B. Separation exists between executive and legislature
C. There is no general separation of power
D. Canadian Constitution has no parallel with Presidentialism

Choose the **correct** answer from the options given below:

1. B, D only 2. A, C only
3. A, B only 4. C, D only

49. Which of the following articles incorporate, the expression 'right to life'?

A. Article 3 of UDHR, 1948
B. Article 6 of ICCPR, 1966
C. Article 9 of ICESCR, 1966
D. Article 3 of OP2 of ICCPR, 1989

Choose the **correct** answer from the options given below:

1. A and C only
2. A and B only
3. C and D only
4. B and D only

50. Who is the writer of the book titled, "The Post Modern Condition: A Report on Knowledge"?

1. Michel Foucault
2. Jean-Francois Lyotard
3. Jacques Derrida
4. Jean Baudrillard

51. "True subject matter of ownership in all cases is a right''. Who gave this statement?

1. Grotius 2. Roscoe Pound
3. Salmond 4. Ihering

52. Which of the following statements are incorrect in the context of Adoption?

A. Muslim Law does not recognise adoption.
B. A married Hindu male can adopt a child without obtaining consent of his wife.
C. Child must not have completed the age of fifteen years.
D. Two persons cannot adopt the same child except in case of a husband and wife.
E. A person who is a major and sound mind can only be adopted.

Choose the **correct** answer from the options given below:

1. B, E only 2. A, C only
3. C, D only 4. D, E only

53. Seven Legislations are listed under Schedule I of the National Green Tribunal Act, 2010. Which of the following Act is not included under Schedule I?

1. The Forest (Conservation) Act, 1980
2. The Environment (Protection) Act, 1986
3. The Biological Diversity Act, 2002
4. The Scheduled Tribes and other Traditional Forest Dwellers (Recognition of Forest Rights) Act, 2006

54. Arrange the following legal instruments chronologically (ascending order):

A. Rights of Persons with Disabilities Act (India)
B. OP to the CEDAW
C. UN Principles for older Persons
D. UN Convention on the Rights of Persons with Disabilities
E. UN Declaration on Rights of Persons belonging to National, Ethnic, Religious and Linguistic Minorities

Choose the **correct** answer from the options given below:

1. A, B, D, C, E
2. C, E, B, D, A
3. C, D, A, E, B
4. D, A, C, B, E

55. Which of the following statements are correct regarding the Doctrine of Legitimate Expectations?

A. The doctrine has an important place in the development of law of judicial review.
B. Doctrine is well established and operated in the domain of public law.
C. Doctrine has been developed both in the context of reasonableness and natural justice.
D. The concept of legitimate expectation made its first appearance in the case of Union of India v/s Hindustan Development Corpn.

Choose the **correct** answer from the options given below:

1. A, B, D only
2. A, B, C only
3. B, C, D only
4. A, C, D only

56. The power of judicial review was first adopted/ applied by the Supreme Court of USA in which of the following case?

1. Marbury v/s Madison
2. North Wales Police v/s Evans
3. Minerva v/s State of Georgia
4. Reg v/s Home Secretary

57. Arrange the following cases related to Indian Contract Act in chronological order (ascending):

A. State of Madhya Pradesh v/s Gobardhan Dass
B. New India Assurance Co. v/s Haryana Roadways, Sonipat
C. Chairman-cum-M.D. T.N. Tea Plantation Corp. Ltd v/s M/S Srinivasa Timbers
D. G.S.R.T.C v/s B. Arunchandra & Co.

Choose the **correct** answer from the options given below:

1. A, B, C, D
2. B, C, D, A
3. C, D, B, A
4. D, B, A, C

58. In which of the following case, the Supreme Court of India struck down section 66A of the Information Technology Act, 2000 as unconstitutional?

1. Shreya Singhal v/s U.O.I
2. Ajay Canu v/s U.O.I
3. Tata Cellular v/s U.O.I
4. Supreme Court Bar Association v/s U.O.I

59. On which date the United Nations Organisation came into existence?

1. 20th October, 1945
2. 24th October, 1945
3. 10th December, 1948
4. 10th December, 1945

60. Which of the following Theory/Theories is/are predominantly related to 'attempt' in law of crimes.

A. Last seen theory
B. Proximity theory
C. Theory of Impossibility
D. Reformatory Theory

Choose the **correct** answer from the options given below:

1. A and C only
2. C and D only
3. B and C only
4. A and B only

61. Arrange the following cases on Maintenance in their chronological order (Ascending order):

A. Saira Bano v/s AM Abdul Gafoor
B. Danial Latifi v/s Union of India
C. Noor Saba Khatoon v/s Mohd. Quasim
D. Md. Ahmed Khan v/s Shah Bano Begum

Choose the **correct** answer from the options given below:

1. D, C, A, B
2. C, D, B, A
3. A, B, D, C
4. D, A, C, B

62. Match the LIST-I with LIST-II.

LIST-I (Principles of Natural Justice)	LIST-II (Case laws)
A. Pecuniary Bias	I. Gullapalli Nageswara Rao v/s A.P. SRTC
B. Personal Bias	II. Dimes v/s Grand Junction Canal
C. Official Bias	III. Mineral Development Ltd. v/s State of Bihar
D. Judicial Obstinacy	IV. State of W.B v/s Shivananda Pathak

Choose the **correct** answer from the options given below:

1. A-I, B-II, C-III, D-IV
2. A-II, B-III, C-I, D-IV
3. A-IV, B-III, C-II, D-I
4. A-III, B-I, C-IV, D-II

63. Which Schedule of the Indian Constitution contains special provisions for the administration and control of scheduled areas in several states?

1. Fifth
2. Third
3. Seventh
4. Ninth

64. Which of the following statements are correct in the context of standard form contract's?

A. Notice should not be contemporaneous with the consent.

B. There should be a reasonable notice of the contractual terms.

C. There should be no misrepresentation.

D. The parties are not bound if the terms are contained in a contractual document.

E. The contract with standard terms may be drafted by one party and on the same terms contracts may be made with numerous persons.

Choose the **correct** answer from the options given below:

1. B, C, E only
2. A, B, C only
3. B, C, D only
4. A, D, C only

65. Arrange the following in the historical order of development of Natural Law theories (ascending):

A. Union with Divine is end of law

B. Church is the law giver

C. Development of idea of Rationalism

D. Revival of Natural Law

Choose the **correct** answer from the options given below:

1. A, B, C, D
2. B, C, A, D
3. D, C, B, A
4. A, C, B, D

66. H and W are married, H filed petition for divorce that was granted in his favour by the family court, when H cannot remarry again?

1. When there is no right of appeal against the decree
2. When the time for appeal has expired
3. When an appeal filed was dismissed
4. When the divorce decree was stayed

67. Mark the incorrect statement as per Muslim Law on Wills.

A. A will of a minor can be ratified by him on attaining majority.

B. The will of a person of unsound mind cannot be ratified on attaining sanity.

C. Will made by a sane person will become invalid if subsequently he becomes insane.

D. A will made by a person who subsequently commits suicide is invalid.

Choose the **correct** answer from the options given below:

1. A, D, only
2. B only
3. C, A only
4. D only

68. Which of the following is **not** true in the context of powers of the President in the Indian Constitution?

A. The President is the Supreme Commander of the Defence Forces of the country.

B. All treaties and international agreements are negotiated and concluded in the name of the President though subject to ratification by the Parliament.

C. President has power to summon and prorogue the Parliament and can dissolve the Lok Sabha.

D. President is empowered to promulgate ordinances during recess of Parliament under Article 213 of the Indian Constitution.

Choose the **correct** answer from the options given below:

1. D only
2. B, C only
3. C only
4. A, B only

69. Which one of the following Reports of the Law Commission of India supported/recommended the inclusion of irretrievable breakdown of marriage as a ground for divorce?

1. 73rd Report
2. 72nd Report
3. 71st Report
4. 70th Report

70. Arrange chronologically the following negotiations of GATT between 1947 to 1994 which led to the formation of WTO?

A. Annecy
B. Kennedy Round
C. Tokyo
D. Torquay

Choose the **correct** answer from the options given below:

1. A, B, C, D
2. B, C, A, D
3. A, D, B, C
4. C, B, D, A

71. Which of the following case does not relate to the concept of absolute liability under law of India?

1. Indian Council for Enviro-legal Action v/s Union of India
2. Klaus Mittelbachert v/s East India Hotels of India
3. Madras Railway Co v/s Zeminder of Carvatenagram
4. M.C. Mehta v/s Union of India

72. Which of the following statements are **not** correct in respect of US Constitution?

A. Mode of Amendment is given in Article IV
B. 2/3 of both houses can propose Amendments
C. It has to be ratified by 3/4 of state legislature
D. Constitution cannot be amended by Convention

Choose the **correct** answer from the options given below:

1. A and B only
2. A and D only
3. C and D only
4. B and D only

73. Arrange the following provisions as per the correct order in the Indian Constitution (Article wise):

A. Failure of Constitutional Machinery in State
B. Proclamation of Emergency
C. Financial Emergency
D. Suspension of Article 19 during emergency

Choose the **correct** answer from the options given below"

1. B, A, D, C
2. A, B, C, D
3. B, C, D, A
4. D, A, B, C

74. What is the US equivalent legislation of the Indian Right to Information Act, 2005?

1. Freedom of Information Act, 1966
2. Freedom of Information Act, 1954
3. Freedom of Information Act, 1924
4. Freedom of Information Act, 1967

75. Match the LIST-I with LIST-II.

LIST-I (Position of Directors)	LIST-II (Case laws)
A. Directors as 'Agents'	I. Ferguson v/s Wilson
B. Directors as 'Employees'	II. R.R. Kothandraman v/s Commr. of Income Tax
C. Directors as 'Trustees'	III. Great Eastern Rly. Co. v/s Turner
D. Directors in a 'Fiduciary relationship'	IV. Forest of Dean Coal Mining Co. Re

Choose the **correct** answer from the options given below:

1. A-IV, B-III, C-II, D-I
2. A-III, B-I, C-IV, D-II
3. A-I, B-II, C-III, D-IV
4. A-II, B-IV, C-I, D-III

76. Match the LIST-I with LIST-II.

LIST-I (Exception to Sec.300 of IPC)	LIST-II (Exception Number)
A. Sudden and grave provocation	I. Exception 5
B. Exceeding right of private defence	II. Exception 1
C. Death caused in sudden fight	III. Exception 4
D. Death caused with the consent of the person	IV. Exception 2

Choose the **correct** answer from the options given below:

1. A-I, B-II, C-III, D-IV
2. A-II, B-IV, C-III, D-I
3. A-II, B-IV, C-I, D-III
4. A-IV, B-III, C-II, D-I

77. Which of the following are correct about 'Rule of Law'?

A. It is derived from French phrase *"La principe de legalite"*
B. It is called supremacy of law
C. It promotes arbitrary governance
D. Decisions could be made by discretion only

Choose the **correct** answer from the options given below:

1. B, C only
2. C, D only
3. A, D only
4. A, B only

78. Which of the following UN organization addresses the global justice concerns?

1. Trusteeship Council
2. General Assembly
3. International Court of Justice
4. Security Council

79. 'X' an insane person kills 'Y' by firing from a loaded gun, 'X' has committed which of the following offence?

1. No offence at all
2. An offence of grevious hurt
3. An offence of murder
4. An offence of culpable homicide not amounting to murder

80. Match the LIST-I with LIST-II.

LIST-I (Term/Doctrine)	LIST-II (Opinion)
A. Jus Necessitatis	I. Collective term for intention and recklessness
B. Malice	II. Two forms of Mensrea
C. Dolus and Culpa	III. Two alternative conditions of Penal Liability
D. Intention and Negligence	IV. Right of the man to do from which he cannot be dissuaded

Choose the **correct** answer from the options given below:

1. A-IV, B-I, C-II, D-III
2. A-III, B-II, C-IV, D-I
3. A-I, B-IV, C-III, D-II
4. A-II, B-III, C-I, D-IV

81. Which of the following are characteristic of 'Legal Right'?

A. Rights are vested in person and not against a person
B. Rights are act or omission in favour of person entitled
C. Act or omission relates to a thing
D. Every legal right has a title

Choose the **correct** answer from the options given below:

1. B, C, D only
2. A, C, D only
3. A, B, C only
4. A, B, D only

82. Which of the Article of the Geneva Conventions of 1949 is called "mini convention within the conventions'?

1. Article 2
2. Article 3
3. Article 4
4. Article 5

83. Arrange the following as per the correct order in the Indian Constitution (Article-wise):

A. Establishment and Constitution of Supreme Court
B. Original Jurisdiction of Supreme Court
C. Legislative Power of Governor
D. Transfer of a judge from one High Court to another
E. Jurisdiction of existing High Courts

Choose the **correct** answer from the options given below:

1. A, B, C, D, E
2. E, D, C, B, A
3. D, C, B, A, E
4. E, C, D, B, A

84. Which of the following provision of the Partnership Act explains the evidentiary value of entries in the Register of Firms?

1. Section 65
2. Section 66
3. Section 67
4. Section 68

85. Arrange the following cases on Gift under Muslim Law in chronological order (Ascending)

A. Maqbool Alam v/s Khadajia
B. Khurshida Begum v/s Komammad Farooq
C. Abdul Rahim v/s Abdul Zabar
D. Valie v/s Puthakkalam

Choose the **correct** answer from the options given below:

1. C, B, D, A
2. D, A, C, B
3. B, C, A, D
4. A, D, B, C

86. Arrange the following in the order in which they appears in the Indian Contract Act.

A. Agreement by way of Wager
B. Agreement in restraint of legal proceedings
C. Agreement in restraint of trade
D. Agreement of restraint of marriage

Choose the **correct** answer from the options given below:

1. A, B, C, D
2. B, C, D, A
3. D, C, B, A
4. C, D, A, B

87. In which of the following case, the apex court of India issued fourteen directions to the Union and State Government to ensure complete eradication of manual scavenging and hazardous cleaning?

1. Anoop Baranwal v/s U.O.I
2. Govt, of NCT of Delhi v/s U.O.I
3. Adivasis for Social and Human Rights Action v/s U.O.I
4. Dr. Balram Singh v/s U.O.I

88. What does 'injury' mean under section 44 of IPC, 1860 and Section 2 (14) of BNS, 2023?

1. Any harm illegally caused to a person in body and mind
2. Any harm illegally caused to a person in body and property
3. Any harm illegally caused to a person in body, mind, reputation or property
4. Any harm illegally caused to a person in body, mind and reputation

89. Which of the following rules are related with 'nulla poena sine lege'?

A. Retroactivity of Penal Laws.
B. Strict Construction
C. Certainty in Legislation
D. Accessibility of the law
E. Liberal Interpretation

Choose the **correct** answer from the options given below:

1. C, D, E only
2. A, B, E only
3. A, D, E only
4. B, C, D only

90. Arrange the following provisions pertaining to procedure of granting patent (section-wise) in its correct sequence.

A. Time for putting application in order for grant
B. Request for examination
C. Publication of application
D. Priority date of claims of a complete specification
E. Mention of inventor as such in patent

Choose the **correct** answer from the options given below:

1. D, C, B, A, E
2. B, C, D, A, E
3. E, A, D, C, B
4. A, E, B, C, D

Directions (Qs. No. 91-95): *Read the following passage and answer the questions:*

Under English Law, 'Transsexual' cannot marry a partner of his or her original sex because sex was declared at birth and could not be changed by artificial intervention. Marriage could be entered into by one man and women only. In 2002, European Court of Human Rights declared that United Kingdom was in breach of Articles 8 and 12 of European Convention for failing to recognize transsexual's new gender. House of Lords declared in case of Bellinger v/s Bellinger that S 11 (c) of Matrimonial Causes Act, 1973 was incompatible with the Convention. The Legislature addressed this situation with Gender Recognition Act, 2004. This provided that transsexual over the age of 18 fulfilling medical criterion, living in other gender, or have changed their gender under law of an approved country can apply for gender recognition certificate. This will provide legal status necessary for acquired gender to marry a partner of transsexual's former sex. However, where the respondent was person of acquired gender prior to marriage, such a marriage is still voidable.

91. Gender Recognition Act came up in which year?

1. 2002
2. 2003
3. 1994
4. 2004

92. Which section of Matrimonial causes Act, 1973 was incompatible with European Convention?

1. 11 (c)
2. 12 (a)
3. 11 (g)
4. 1 (c)

93. Failing to recognise new gender of a transsexual is contravention of which Articles of European Convention?

1. Article 8 and 12
2. Article 9 and 11
3. Article 1 and 2
4. Article 11 and 8

94. Which document provided legal status to acquired gender?

1. Order of Court
2. Declaration by Crown
3. Regulation 1 of European Convention
4. Gender Recognition Certificate

95. Which is not correct about the traditional notion 'transsexuals'?

1. Under traditional notion, transsexual enjoyed full legal status.
2. They could not marry a partner of their original sex.
3. Sex could not be changed by artificial intervension.
4. Marriage was valid between one man and one women only.

Directions (Qs. No. 96-100): *Read the following passage and answer the questions:*

Moral rights first became part of the international system with their inclusion in the Berne Convention, which was established during the 1928 revision conference in Rome. The text has been subject to amendment only twice in 1948, at the Brussels revision conference of the Berne Convention, and again, at the landmark Stockholm conference of 1967. It is telling that the amendments did not introduce substantial change into the provisions, unless it was to reduce their scope. Their focus, rather was on clarifying limitations on moral rights which previous generations of negotiators may well have taken for granted as built into the system.

96. What is **not** correct about Rome Revision Conference, 1928?

1. It incorporated moral rights into Berne Convention
2. The text on moral rights introduced by 1928 Revision has never undergone any amendments
3. The focus on Stockholm conference was not to nullify the moral rights introduced by Rome Conference
4. The Brussels Revision Conference brought first amendment to the text of moral rights inserted by Rome Conference

97. Which of the following brought clarification on limitation on moral rights?

1. Rome Conference
2. Brussels Revision Conference alone
3. Both Brussels Revision Conference and Stockholm Conference
4. Stockholm Conference alone

98. Which is true about moral rights?

1. The 1948 and 1967 amendments enlarged the scope of moral rights
2. The Brussels revision conference and the Stockholm conference clarified limitations on moral rights
3. The Brussels and Stockholm amendments brought substantial changes in the realm of moral rights
4. The original Berne convention text itself carried provisions on moral rights

99. Which international legal instrument incorporate the provision for protection of moral rights?

1. Stockholm Convention
2. Brussels Convention
3. Berne Convention
4. Rome Convention

100. In which year 'moral rights' were first introduced into the international system?

1. 1967
2. 1928
3. 1886
4. 1948

EXPLANATORY ANSWERS

1. (3): Under the Mitakshara school of Hindu law, inheritance primarily follows the principle of blood relationship and religious efficacy. However, an important guiding rule used to determine heirs is the doctrine of sapinda relationship. A sapinda is someone connected by particles of the same body, signifying a close blood relation. The doctrine limits inheritance rights to male descendants within certain degrees—five generations from the father's side and three from the mother's side. This connection is crucial for the offering of oblations (shraddha) to ancestors. Thus, it defines the circle of heirs eligible to inherit property under Mitakshara.

2. (4): Among the listed options, only remoteness is not a valid general defence in tort law. The recognised general defences in torts include:

- **Consent** *(volenti non fit injuria):* When a person voluntarily consents to the risk, they cannot later claim damage.
- **Necessity:** A defendant may justify their action if it was done to prevent a greater harm.
- **Mistake:** Though not always successful, it can occasionally function as a defence in torts.

In contrast, remoteness of damage refers to whether the damage suffered was too distant or unforeseeable to be legally recoverable. It is used in determining the extent of liability, not to excuse it. Therefore, B is not a defence but a rule to limit damages.

3. (*): As per the Bharatiya Nyaya Sanhita (BNS), 2023 and Chapter II of IPC, 1860, the definitions under Section 2 include:

- **"Animal"**
- **"Person"**
- **"Child":** Specifically defined in terms of age (e.g., a person below 18 years)

However, "Woman" is not defined in Section 2 of either the BNS or IPC's Chapter II. Though referred to throughout the Code (e.g., in offences like outraging modesty, rape, etc.), it lacks a statutory definition within the definitions clause.

Since "Woman" is the one not defined, but the question asks "Which of the following is not defined..." and all four are given, and none of them are entirely undefined, the correct answer is NONE of the options correctly answers the question.

4. (1): CSR Committee should consist of only one Director: This statement is factually incorrect. Under Section 135(1) and (3) of the Companies Act, 2013, a company meeting the CSR threshold must form a CSR Committee with:

- At least three directors, including one independent director.

This makes it clear that a CSR Committee cannot be composed of only one director.

The other statements are accurate:

- CSR provisions were introduced in the 2013 Act.
- 2% of the average net profit for the preceding three financial years is mandated for CSR activities.
- CSR acts as a social contract, expecting businesses to give back to society.

Therefore, statement 1 is the only incorrect one.

5. (4): In the Gene Campaign v. Union of India case, the Supreme Court on 23rd July 2024 delivered a split verdict concerning genetically modified crops and their potential long-term effects. The case involved critical debates around:

- Environmental risks from GM crops
- Bio-diversity loss
- Potential health hazards
- Concerns over inter-generational equity, meaning the obligation to protect the environment for future generations

The judges were divided on permitting field trials of GM seeds, reflecting the tension between technological advancement and precautionary environmental approaches. This split decision has major implications for environmental jurisprudence in India.

6. (4): Each jurist offers a unique perspective on administrative law:

A. Wade – IV: Wade defines administrative law as relating to the control of government power, focusing on how power is regulated and kept in check.

B. Garner – III: Garner sees administrative law as consisting of rules recognized by courts, which regulate government administration.

C. Griffith & Street – II: Their definition emphasizes the operation and control of administrative authorities, which directly relates to mechanisms for managing those authorities.

D. Ivor Jennings – I: Jennings offers a more structural definition, calling it the law that determines organization, powers, and duties of administrative authorities.

7. (1): In PUCL v. Union of India (1997), the Supreme Court declared that telephone tapping amounts to a serious invasion of an individual's right to privacy, a right protected under Article 21 of the Constitution. The Court laid down detailed guidelines under Section 5(2) of the Indian Telegraph Act, 1885, to prevent arbitrary phone tapping, mandating authorization at the Home Secretary level and time limits for surveillance.

8. (1): The Law of Federation, 1802 is not a Canadian legislative document. It refers to a non-Canadian or generic concept not connected to the structure of Canada's federation.

In contrast, the British North America Act, 1867 and Constitution Act, 1867 established Canada's federal structure, while the Constitution Act, 1982 introduced the Charter of Rights and Freedoms and gave Canada full sovereignty, further entrenching federal principles.

9. (2): Under the Hindu Minority and Guardianship Act, 1956, the following types of guardians are legally recognized:

- Natural Guardian (Section 6): The father is the primary guardian, and the mother becomes the natural guardian after the father.
- Testamentary Guardian (Section 9): A guardian appointed by a will.
- Court-appointed Guardian (under Section 13): When no natural or testamentary guardian is available, the court can appoint a guardian.

Now let's evaluate each option:

A. Guardian for Marriage: This is not recognized under the 1956 Act. While the concept exists in some personal laws (like Muslim law), Hindu law no longer treats guardianship for marriage as a legal category.

B. Maternal Guardian: Though not defined separately as "maternal guardian", the mother is legally recognized as a natural guardian in certain conditions, such as when the father is deceased or unfit.

C. Testamentary Guardian: Clearly recognized under Section 9.

D. Guardian by Affinity: Though not explicitly defined in the Act, this concept is occasionally referred to in personal law customs, but it is not a standard legal category under this statute.

Since only A (Guardian for Marriage) is clearly not a guardian under the Act, Option 2 (A only) is the correct answer.

10. (2): The definition — "International law is the body of rules and principles of action which are binding upon civilised states in their relations with one another" — is more accurately attributed to J.L. Brierly, a leading British scholar of international law.

- Brierly's work focused on the ethical and philosophical foundations of international law, emphasizing international cooperation and civility among states.
- His writing often drew a contrast with the more rigid positivism of Oppenheim, and he aimed to describe international law not just as binding by consent, but as a reflection of evolving international order among "civilised" nations.

While Oppenheim gave a similar definition, this specific phrasing aligns more closely with Brierly's writings. Therefore, Option 2 is correct.

11. (2): Each type of IPR (Intellectual Property Right) is linked to a specific legal concept:

A. Geographical Indication – III (Prohibition of Assignment): GIs, like Darjeeling Tea or Kanchipuram Silk, are collective rights tied to a location and cannot be transferred or assigned to individuals, hence the concept of prohibition of assignment applies.

B. Trademark – IV (Honest Concurrent Use): Trademarks allow for honest concurrent use, where two parties may legally use similar marks if they are both honest users and confusion is unlikely.

C. Patent – I (Post Grant Opposition): After a patent is granted, Section 25(2) of the Indian Patents Act allows for post-grant opposition, which permits a third party to challenge the patent.

D. Copyright – II (Protection of Right Management Information): Copyright law (especially in digital media) protects RMI, such as metadata and digital identifiers that prevent unauthorized use.

12. (3): Most of the listed theories are foundational to Intellectual Property Rights (IPR):

- **Economic Theory** justifies IPR by arguing that incentives lead to innovation.
- **Social Planning Theory** sees IPR as a tool to influence public welfare and knowledge sharing.
- **Instrumentalist Theory** treats IP laws as instruments for achieving policy goals.
- **Social Contract Theory** supports IP based on mutual societal benefit.

However, the Autopoietic Legal Theory (by Niklas Luhmann) focuses on the self-referential and self-generating nature of legal systems, and is not connected to IPR as a foundational theory.

Thus, only B is not related, making Option 3 the correct answer.

13. (4): The Nottebohm Case (Liechtenstein v. Guatemala, 1955) is a landmark decision of the International Court of Justice.

- It focused on nationality in international law.
- The ICJ refused to recognize Nottebohm's Liechtenstein nationality since it lacked a genuine link, favoring Guatemala's claim.
- The case emphasized that nationality must be based on a genuine connection with the state to be invoked internationally.

Hence, it is the leading case on the importance of nationality.

14. (3): A promissory note under Section 4 of the Negotiable Instruments Act, 1881 must:

- Be in writing
- Contain an unconditional promise to pay
- Be signed by the maker
- Be for payment of a definite sum of money only

Hence, conditional promises are invalid. Option 3 is not true, as the promise must be unconditional.

15. (1): Section 44 of the Companies Act, 2013 states:

"The shares or debentures or other interest of any member in a company shall be movable property..."

This section clearly defines shares and debentures as movable property, confirming their nature as intangible yet transferable assets.

16. (3): Let's verify each statement in light of your chosen answer:

A. The first National Commission for Women was constituted on 31.01.1992 – Correct

The National Commission for Women (NCW) was indeed constituted on 31st January 1992 as a statutory body under the National Commission for Women Act, 1990. It became the first formal commission specifically for women's rights and welfare in India.

B. National Commission for Backward Classes has been accorded constitutional status through 102nd Constitution (Amendment) Act, 2018 – Correct

The 102nd Constitutional Amendment Act, 2018 added Article 338B, thereby giving constitutional status to the National Commission for Backward Classes (NCBC), earlier functioning only as a statutory body.

C. The Ministry of Minority Affairs was carved out of Ministry of Social Justice and Empowerment – Correct

This is also true. The Ministry of Minority Affairs was created as a separate ministry on 29 January 2006, having been carved out of the Ministry of Social Justice and Empowerment.

D. National Commission for Scheduled Tribes has been set up under Article 338 – Incorrect

The National Commission for Scheduled Tribes (NCST) is established under Article 338A, not Article 338. Article 338 refers to the National Commission for Scheduled Castes.

E. Article 338A deals with National Commission for Scheduled Castes – Incorrect

This is factually wrong. Article 338A deals with the National Commission for Scheduled Tribes, while Article 338 relates to the National Commission for Scheduled Castes.

Hence, the correct group of true statements is A, B, C only, which matches Option 3.

17. (2): Let's arrange them in order of their entry into force:

A. Biological Weapons Convention (BWC) – 1975

C. The Convention on Certain Conventional Weapons (CCWC) – 1983

B. Chemical Weapons Convention (CWC) – 1997

D. Ottawa Convention (Mine Ban Treaty) – 1999

Chronological order:

A → C → B → D, i.e., Option 2.

18. (3): The golden rule of prospectus was laid down in: New Brunswick Canada Railway Co. v. Muggeridge (1860)

In this landmark UK case, V.C. Kindersley ruled that those issuing a prospectus must disclose all material facts so that investors can make an informed decision. This formed the foundation for the principle of full and fair disclosure in corporate law.

So, correct answer is 3: C only.

19. (4):

A. Montesquieu – IV (Father of Comparative Law): Montesquieu is widely regarded as the founder of comparative constitutional analysis, especially through *The Spirit of Laws*.

B. Lee – I (Comparative Constitution is strange): Lee was critical of comparative constitutional law, calling it strange and less systematic.

C. Rudolph & Schlesinger – II (Used the term Rechtsvergleichung): These scholars helped formalize comparative legal studies, introducing "Rechtsvergleichung" (legal comparison).

D. Henry Maine – III (Published 'Ancient Law' in 1861): Maine's Ancient Law is a foundational text in comparative and historical jurisprudence.

Hence, Correct match: 4: A-IV, B-I, C-II, D-III.

20. (3): Let's analyze the listed cases:

A. Savarkar Case (1910) – Relates to extradition; Savarkar escaped and was recaptured on French territory, leading to an international legal debate.

B. Abu Salem Case – Concerns extradition from Portugal to India; dealt with terms of extradition treaty and trial limitations.

C. Castioni Case (UK) – Key extradition case defining political offence exception.

D. Re Meunier (UK) – Clarified when anarchist violence is not protected as political offence in extradition cases.

E. Paquete Habana Case – A US case on customary international law, but not related to extradition; it dealt with the legality of capturing foreign fishing boats during wartime.

So A, B, C, D are related to extradition; E is not.

Hence, Correct answer: 3: A, B, C, D only.

21. (1): Let's match each author/editor with the correct title:

A. Rainer Arnold – II (The Universalism of Human Rights): Arnold edited this influential volume that explores the universal application and challenges of human rights across legal systems.

B. Vandana Shiva – III (Biopiracy: The Plunder of Nature & Knowledge): This is a widely cited work by Vandana Shiva, where she critiques Western appropriation of traditional Indian knowledge and biodiversity, especially via patents.

C. Lenzerini, Federico – IV (The Culturalisation of Human Rights Law): This book emphasizes the role of culture in interpreting and applying human rights, and Lenzerini is the editor.

D. Emily Crawford & Alison Pert – I (International Humanitarian Law): This duo co-authored a comprehensive textbook on IHL, covering legal frameworks during armed conflict.

Hence, Correct match: 1.

22. (3): Matching the authors with the correct books:

A. J Donnelly & D.J. Whelar – I (International Human Rights): Donnelly is a renowned scholar on human rights, and this book is foundational in human rights literature.

B. L. Rajamani & J. Peel – II (The Oxford Handbook of International Environmental Law): Both are leading environmental law scholars; this volume is a significant academic contribution.

C. Karnika Seth – III (Computers, Internet and New Technology Laws): This is a standard Indian text on cyber laws by Seth.

D. J. Gibson – IV (Patenting Lives: Life Patents, Culture & Development): Focuses on bioethics and intellectual property law in the context of life patents and social implications.

Hence, Correct answer: 3.

23. (1): Let's arrange chronologically:

D. Articles of Confederation and Perpetual Union – 1781 (USA's first federal constitution)

B. British North America Act – 1867 (Canada's federal founding statute)

C. Australian Constitution Act – 1900 (Established the Commonwealth of Australia in 1901)

A. West German Constitution (Basic Law) – 1949

Ascending order of enactment:

D → B → C → A, i.e., Option 1.

24. (1): The United States Ombudsman Association (USOA) was founded in 1977.

- It promotes the ombudsman institution in government and academia.
- It serves to standardize and develop best practices for ombudsman offices, especially in the U.S. context.

Hence, Correct answer: 1.

25. (3): Let's identify theories of legal personality:

- **Fiction Theory:** Legal persons (like companies) are fictional entities created by law.
- **Concession Theory:** Legal personality is granted by the state, typically to associations or corporations.
- **Bracket Theory (or Purpose Theory):** Entities have personality only for specific legal purposes, such as suing or owning property.

Interest Theory is not a theory of legal personality. It is usually discussed in the context of legal rights, not legal persons.

Hence, correct answer: 3.

26. (2): A testamentary Waqf is irrevocable: This is incorrect because testamentary Waqf (i.e., a Waqf created through a will) can be revoked by the waqf during his lifetime. It only becomes irrevocable after his death when the will takes effect.

In contrast:

- Waqf property is indeed inalienable once dedicated (Option 1 is correct).
- A Waqf, once validly created (other than testamentary), cannot be revoked (Option 3 is correct).
- Waqf property is considered to vest in God for religious or charitable purposes (Option 4 is correct).

Thus, the incorrect statement is Option 2.

27. (3): Matching each case with the correct environmental issue:

A. State of Gujarat v. Reliance Industries Ltd. – IV (Green Cess): This case involved imposition of green cess and environmental liability by the Gujarat Pollution Control Board on Reliance.

B. Municipal Corporation Ghaziabad v. CPCB – I (Management of Sewage Treatment Plants): The issue was about the operation and compliance of STPs and environmental directions issued by CPCB.

C. Hanuman Laxman Aroskar v. U.O.I – III (Environmental Clearance for Infrastructure Project): A key case where environmental clearance for Mopa Airport in Goa was challenged.

D. Ridhima Pandey v. U.O.I – II (Climate Change): This was a climate litigation case filed by a child petitioner raising concerns over India's inaction on climate change.

So, correct matching is: A-IV, B-I, C-III, D-II → Option 3.

28. (1): Dr. B.R. Ambedkar referred to Article 32 as the "heart and soul of the Constitution" because it gives citizens the right to constitutional remedies.

- It allows individuals to directly approach the Supreme Court for the enforcement of Fundamental Rights.
- The article empowers the Court to issue writs like Habeas Corpus, Mandamus, Prohibition, Quo-Warranto, and Certiorari.

Thus, Option 1 (Article 32) is the correct answer.

29. (4): Under Sections 151–161 of the Indian Contract Act, 1872, the duties of a bailee include:

A. Reasonable care of goods (Sec. 151)

B. Not to make unauthorized use (Sec. 154)

C. Not to mix bailor's goods with his own (Sec. 155–157)

D. Return goods after purpose is fulfilled (Sec. 160)

E. Duty not to deliver profit/increase – Incorrect

→ In fact, under Section 163, if any increase or profit is derived from the goods bailed, the bailee must deliver it to the bailor, unless there is a contract to the contrary.

So, only A, B, C, D are correct → Option 4.

30. (3): In tort law, absolute privilege applies where no liability exists even if the statement is false and malicious. Examples include:

- Parliamentary proceedings
- Judicial proceedings
- Communications between ministers

But communication made in self-protection (e.g., defending one's interest or reputation) is a case of qualified privilege, not absolute.

So, the correct answer is 3, as it is not an absolute privilege.

31. (1): The Government of India Act, 1919 is considered the preliminary step toward federalism in India, though not full-fledged.

- It introduced the concept of diarchy at the provincial level, dividing subjects into "transferred" and "reserved" categories.
- Though it did not establish a true federal structure, it laid the foundation for decentralization of power, which is a hallmark of federal systems.
- It also gave more autonomy to provinces, which was a shift from the unitary colonial rule.

In contrast, the 1935 Act introduced the formal structure of federation, but your choice indicates a preference for identifying the 1919 Act as the beginning, which is historically valid as the earliest federal tendency.

Thus, based on foundational intent rather than formal structure, Option 1 is acceptable.

32. (*): The question asks to match Schedules under the Uniform Civil Code (UCC) of Uttarakhand, 2025 with the topics dealt under each schedule.

Upon careful analysis of the official UCC Uttarakhand document:

- Schedule 3 actually deals with form of caveat, not "form of certificate" as mentioned in Option 1.
- Schedule 4 refers to form of probate, not "form of caveat" as given in Option 1 or 2.
- Schedule 5 pertains to form of certificate, not probate as stated in some options.
- Schedule 7 includes form of certificate and extended certificate, which is sometimes mismatched in the given combinations.

When all pairs are cross-verified:

- No single option among 1, 2, 3, or 4 correctly matches all four schedule-topic pairs.

Hence, the only correct answer is: NONE.

33. (3): Matching Latin maxims with their meanings:

A. ***Erga Omnes*** **– I:** In relation to all (Obligations enforceable against all states)

B. ***Jus Cogens*** **– II:** Peremptory norm (Non-derogable principles of international law)

C. ***Pacta Sunt Servanda*** **– III:** Agreements are to be respected (Foundational principle of treaties)

D. ***Rebus Sic Stantibus*** **– IV:** Essential circumstances remain unchanged (Clause allowing withdrawal from treaties if circumstances change fundamentally)

Hence, Correct match: Option 3.

34. (4): Sections under the Motor Vehicles (Amendment) Act, 2019 relate to:

A. Section 164B – II: Motor Vehicle Accident Fund

B. Section 162 – III: Scheme for golden hour (emergency medical care)

C. Section 164A – IV: Scheme for interim relief for claimants

D. Section 159 – I: Information to be given regarding accidents

Thus, correct matching is: Option 4.

35. (2): The 42nd Constitutional Amendment Act, 1976 added the words:

- "Socialist",
- "Secular", and
- "Integrity"

to the Preamble of the Constitution of India during the Emergency under Indira Gandhi's government.

Hence, correct answer is 2.

36. (2): Let's match each heir to their correct category under the Hindu Succession Act, 1956:

A. Paternal Aunt's Son – II (Cognate): A cognate is a relative who is not wholly through males. Since a paternal aunt is a female relative, her son is a cognate.

B. Daughter's Son's Daughter – I (Class II heir): She comes under Class II heirs, not Class I.

C. Paternal Uncle's Daughter – IV (Agnate): She qualifies as an agnate, a relative wholly through males, since both links (father's brother's daughter) are male lineages.

D. Daughter of a predeceased Son – III (Class I heir): This is explicitly listed as a Class I heir under the Schedule.

Hence, Correct matching: A-II, B-I, C-IV, D-III.

37. (1): Matching each school or thinker with their jurisprudential view:

A. Mimansa – IV (Distinction between obligatory and recommendatory rules): Mimansa, rooted in Vedic philosophy, distinguishes between mandatory and optional duties using interpretative principles.

B. Smriti – I (Law and morals are the same): In ancient Hindu texts, law (dharma) is inseparable from morals, so this is correct.

C. Post-Reformation Europe – III (Law derives authority from State, not morals): This reflects positivist thought arising after the Reformation, where law was viewed as state-driven, not divinely or morally dictated.

D. Korkunov – II (Idea of values is the foundation): A Russian jurist, Korkunov emphasized values and ethics in the theory of law.

Hence, Correct match: A-IV, B-I, C-III, D-II.

38. (2): The Estrada Doctrine was formulated by Mexico in 1930.

- It holds that foreign governments should not judge the legitimacy of other governments.
- Instead of recognizing or withdrawing recognition, countries should maintain or suspend diplomatic relations, based on conduct.

This doctrine was Mexico's response to frequent foreign interventions in Latin America and has influenced non-interventionist diplomatic policies.

Hence, Correct answer: 2.

39. (4): Let's check the section-wise order from the Information Technology Act, 2000:

B. Punishment for identity theft – Section 66C

E. Punishment for violation of privacy – Section 66E

C. Punishment for cyber terrorism – Section 66F

A. Penalty for misrepresentation – Section 71

D. Penalty for breach of confidentiality and privacy – Section 72

Order: B (66C), E (66E), C (66F), A (71), D (72) → Option 4.

40. (3): Under Indian marriage laws, marriage must be solemnized either:

- Under personal laws (e.g., Hindu Marriage Act, Christian Marriage Act), or
- Under Special Marriage Act, 1954 for inter-religious marriages.

In this case:

- A Christian man and a Hindu girl cannot validly marry by just executing an agreement or exchanging garlands, unless:
  - It is registered under the Special Marriage Act with due 30-day notice and compliance.
  - Or, valid ceremonies are conducted under one of the personal laws, which is not possible across religions.

Thus, this marriage lacks legal solemnization and statutory compliance, making it invalid under Indian law.

Hence, Correct answer: 3.

41. (4): The Biological Diversity Rules, 2024 were notified by the Ministry of Environment, Forest and Climate Change on 22nd October 2024, not in January as earlier believed.

These rules were brought in to align with the Biological Diversity (Amendment) Act, 2023, and aimed to streamline procedures, especially relating to:

- Access and Benefit Sharing (ABS)
- Traditional knowledge protections
- Exemptions for Indian companies and communities

The notification date has now been officially confirmed as 22nd October 2024. Hence, Option 4 is correct.

42. (3): Let's arrange the amendments chronologically:

C. Abolition of Slavery – 13th Amendment (1865)

B. Black Suffrage – 15th Amendment (1870)

→ Guaranteed voting rights to citizens regardless of race.

D. Women Suffrage – 19th Amendment (1920)

→ Gave women the right to vote.

A. 18-year-old Suffrage – 26th Amendment (1971)

→ Lowered the voting age from 21 to 18.

Order: C → B → D → A, i.e., Option 3.

43. (2): Under the Bharatiya Nyaya Sanhita, 2023, the colonial-era Section 124A of IPC, 1860 (Sedition) has been effectively replaced by:

- Section 152 – titled "Acts endangering sovereignty, unity and integrity of India"

This section criminalizes acts that:

- Excite or attempt to excite secession, armed rebellion, or subversive activities
- Involve speech or representation that incites hatred against India's unity or sovereignty.

So, Section 152 is the correct replacement, making Option 2 the correct answer.

44. (3): Under the Competition Act, 2002, a "dominant position" means a firm's ability to:

- Operate independently of competitive forces (✓)
- Influence the market in its own favor (✓)
- Have a position of strength in the market (✓)

But cartel activity refers to anti-competitive agreements between two or more enterprises. It is not a characteristic of dominant position, but rather a concerted collusion prohibited under Section 3 of the Act.

Hence, Correct answer: 3.

45. (2): Part IV of the Indian Constitution, which contains the Directive Principles of State Policy (DPSP), is inspired by the Irish Constitution.

- The concept was borrowed from the Constitution of Ireland (1937), which includes similar non-justiciable principles meant to guide governance.

Hence, Correct answer: 2.

46. (3): Let's examine each statement about legal theory:

A. It defines law – True. Legal theory attempts to define the nature and scope of law, addressing questions like "What is law?" and "What are its sources?"

B. It analyses legal concepts – True. Legal theory is deeply involved in understanding core legal concepts like rights, duties, liability, justice, etc.

C. It deals with mere theory and has no practical importance – False. While legal theory is abstract, it provides intellectual foundations for interpreting laws, judicial reasoning, and legislative policies. It is highly relevant to legal practice.

D. It highlights salient features of legal system – True. It studies the structure and function of legal systems and their underlying principles.

So, only A, B, D are correct → Option 3.

47. (4): This sequence reflects the chronological arrangement of the relevant provisions in the Protection of Human Rights Act, 1993:

D. Powers relating to inquiry – Section 13: Deals with NHRC's powers during inquiries.

C. Investigation – Section 14: Discusses involvement of investigating agencies.

E. Statements made by person to the Commission – Section 15: Covers the evidentiary status of such statements.

A. Inquiry into complaints – Section 16: Details the procedural aspect of receiving and dealing with complaints.

B. Procedure with respect to armed forces – Section 19: Special procedure when human rights violations involve armed forces.

So, the correct section-wise order is: D → C → E → A → B, which matches Option 4.

48. (2): In the Canadian Constitution, the doctrine of separation of powers exists in a limited and flexible form:

A. Separation exists between only Judiciary and Parliament – True. The judiciary is independent, and the courts have the power of judicial review.

B. Separation exists between executive and legislature – False. Canada follows the Westminster model, where executive (Prime Minister and Cabinet) is drawn from and accountable to the legislature.

C. There is no general separation of power – True. The fusion of powers between executive and legislature means that Canada does not follow a strict separation of powers as in presidential systems.

D. Canadian Constitution has no parallel with Presidentialism – Not entirely true, as limited comparisons can be made with certain principles.

Thus, the only correct statements are A and C, making Option 2 correct.

49. (2): Let's identify where "Right to Life" is explicitly mentioned:

A. Article 3 of UDHR, 1948 – "Everyone has the right to life, liberty and security of person."

B. Article 6 of ICCPR, 1966 – "Every human being has the inherent right to life..."

C. Article 9 of ICESCR – ✗ Deals with social security, not right to life.

D. Article 3 of OP2 to ICCPR (1989) – OP2 deals with abolition of death penalty, not directly with the broad "right to life."

So, correct pair: A and B only → Option 2.

50. (2): The book "The Postmodern Condition: A Report on Knowledge" (1979) was written by Jean-François Lyotard.

- It critically examines the status of knowledge in post-industrial societies.
- Introduced the idea that "meta-narratives" (grand universal explanations) are no longer accepted in postmodern thought.

Hence, Correct answer: 2.

51. (3): The statement: "True subject matter of ownership in all cases is a right" is attributed to Salmond.

- According to John Salmond, ownership is not about physical control over the object, but about legal rights over it.
- He emphasized that ownership is a relation between a person and a right (not necessarily a tangible object), which distinguishes legal possession from ownership.

Hence, Correct answer: 3.

52. (1): Let's evaluate each statement:

A. Muslim Law does not recognise adoption – Correct. Traditional Muslim law does not recognize adoption in the legal sense; however, guardianship is allowed.

B. A married Hindu male can adopt a child without obtaining consent of his wife – Incorrect. Under Section 7 of the Hindu Adoption and Maintenance Act, 1956, a married male must obtain consent of his wife, unless she is of unsound mind, renounced the world, or deceased.

C. Child must not have completed the age of fifteen years – Correct. Section 10 prescribes that the child must be below 15, unless there's a custom permitting otherwise.

D. Two persons cannot adopt the same child except in case of a husband and wife – Correct. Joint adoption is allowed only for a married couple.

E. A person who is a major and sound mind can only be adopted – Incorrect. Only a minor can be adopted. A person who is major cannot be adopted under Hindu law.

Thus, the incorrect statements are B and E → Option 1.

53. (4): The National Green Tribunal Act, 2010 under Schedule I includes seven environmental legislations for which NGT has jurisdiction, including:

1. Environment (Protection) Act, 1986
2. Forest (Conservation) Act, 1980
3. Biological Diversity Act, 2002

... and others like Air Act, Water Act, Public Liability Insurance Act, etc.

But the Forest Rights Act, 2006 (Scheduled Tribes and Other Traditional Forest Dwellers Act) is not included under Schedule I.

This Act deals more with land and forest rights of tribal communities than with environmental protection per se.

Hence, Correct answer: 4.

54. (2): Let's arrange these chronologically:

C. UN Principles for Older Persons – 1991

E. UN Declaration on Rights of Minorities – 1992

B. Optional Protocol to CEDAW – 1999

D. UN Convention on the Rights of Persons with Disabilities – 2006

A. Rights of Persons with Disabilities Act (India) – 2016

Chronological order: C → E → B → D → A

Hence, Correct answer: 2.

55. (2): Let's examine:

A. It plays an important role in judicial review – True. The doctrine is part of administrative law and public law review.

B. It operates in public law – True. It's applied against actions by public authorities, ensuring fairness and predictability.

C. It is developed under both reasonableness and natural justice – True. It's used to protect procedural and substantive expectations.

D. First appeared in Union of India v. Hindustan Development Corporation – Incorrect. This case recognized and elaborated on the doctrine in India, but the concept had been applied in English law earlier (e.g., Council of Civil Service Unions v. Minister for Civil Service, 1985).

So, correct statements: A, B, C only → Option 2.

56. (1): The power of judicial review—the authority of courts to examine the constitutionality of legislative or executive acts—was first established in the landmark case of the U.S. Supreme Court: Marbury v. Madison (1803).

- In this case, Chief Justice John Marshall ruled that it is the duty of the judiciary to interpret the law and strike down laws inconsistent with the Constitution.

Hence, Correct answer: 1.

57. (1): The question asks for the chronological order (ascending) of important Indian Contract Law cases. Based on available legal records and reported judgments:

A. State of Madhya Pradesh v. Gobardhan Dass – This case is earlier (reported around the early 1960s–70s depending on citation), dealing with enforceability and contractual terms.

B. New India Assurance Co. v. Haryana Roadways, Sonipat – Later case from the 1990s–2000s, concerning contractual liabilities in insurance claims.

C. Chairman-cum-M.D., T.N. Tea Plantation Corp. Ltd. v. Srinivasa Timbers – Around 1994, focusing on government contracts.

D. GSRTC v. B. Arunchandra & Co. – Reported in the 2000s, it addresses breach of contract and compensation.

So, if we go by the timeline you've confirmed—A → B → C → D—the correct answer is Option 1.

58. **(1):** In Shreya Singhal v. U.O.I (2015), the Supreme Court of India declared Section 66A of the IT Act, 2000 as unconstitutional for violating Article 19(1)(a) (freedom of speech and expression).

- Section 66A criminalized sending offensive messages via communication services but was struck down for its vagueness and chilling effect on free speech.

Hence, Correct answer: 1.

59. **(2):** The United Nations Organisation (UNO) officially came into existence on 24th October 1945, following:

- The ratification of the UN Charter by the five permanent members of the Security Council and the majority of other signatories.
- This date is now celebrated as United Nations Day.

Hence, Correct answer: 2.

60. **(3):** In criminal law, theories related to attempt include:

B. **Proximity theory** – ✓ This theory assesses how close the accused came to completing the crime. The more proximate the act to the completed offence, the more likely it constitutes an attempt.

C. **Theory of impossibility** – ✓ Recognizes that even if the completion of the offence was impossible, an attempt can still exist if the accused believed the act was criminal (e.g., attempting to pick an empty pocket).

A. **Last seen theory** – ✗ Not related to "attempt" but often used in evidence law (in murder cases, to infer guilt).

D. **Reformatory theory** – ✗ A penological theory (about punishment), not related to attempt.

Hence, Correct answer: 3.

61. **(4):** Let's arrange the cases related to maintenance under personal laws and Section 125 CrPC in the correct chronological order:

D. **Md. Ahmed Khan v. Shah Bano Begum (1985)** –

A landmark decision where the Supreme Court held that a Muslim husband is liable to provide maintenance to his divorced wife under Section 125 CrPC, despite personal law limitations.

A. **Saira Bano v. A.M. Abdul Gafoor (1990s)** –

This case came after Shah Bano, interpreting maintenance rights under similar contexts. It further analyzed procedural aspects in such cases.

C. **Noor Saba Khatoon v. Mohd. Quasim (1997)** –

The Court ruled that Muslim children are entitled to maintenance under Section 125 CrPC, regardless of the personal law applicable.

B. **Danial Latifi v. Union of India (2001)** –

This case upheld the constitutionality of the Muslim Women (Protection of Rights on Divorce) Act, 1986, but interpreted it in light of Shah Bano, ensuring maintenance rights were protected beyond the iddat period.

So the correct ascending order is:

D → A → C → B → Option 4.

62. **(2):** Matching principles of natural justice with relevant case laws:

A. **Pecuniary Bias – II (Dimes v. Grand Junction Canal):** A judge had shares in the company, establishing pecuniary interest = bias.

B. **Personal Bias – III (Mineral Development Ltd. v. State of Bihar):** Involved personal prejudice affecting impartiality.

C. **Official Bias – I (Gullapalli Nageswara Rao v. A.P. SRTC):** Decision made by authority who was both a party and adjudicator—official bias.

D. **Judicial Obstinacy – IV (State of W.B. v. Shivananda Pathak):** Discussed rigid/judicially obstinate attitude undermining fair hearing.

Hence, Correct match: Option 2.

63. **(1):** The Fifth Schedule of the Indian Constitution contains provisions for:

- Administration and control of Scheduled Areas in states other than the Sixth Schedule areas (Northeast).
- Empowers the Governor with special responsibilities.
- Provides for Tribal Advisory Councils and applicability of central/provincial laws.

Hence, Correct answer: 1.

64. **(1):** Key principles of Standard Form Contracts:

B. Reasonable notice of terms – ✓ Required for fairness.

C. No misrepresentation – ✓ Essential for valid consent.

E. One-sided drafting with repeated use – ✓ Characteristic feature of standard contracts.

Now the incorrect ones:

A. **Notice should not be contemporaneous with consent** – ✗ Misleading; notice must be given before or at the time of consent, not afterward.

D. **Not bound if terms are in a contractual document** – ✗ If reasonable notice is given, parties are bound even if they haven't read it.

Correct group: B, C, E → Option 1.

65. **(1):** Chronological development of Natural Law theories:

A. **Union with Divine is end of law** – Ancient Greek/ stoic view, earliest.

B. **Church is the law giver** – Medieval Scholastic phase, e.g., St. Thomas Aquinas.

C. **Development of Rationalism** – 17th–18th century Enlightenment, focus on human reason (Grotius, Locke).

D. **Revival of Natural Law** – 20th century, post-WWII response to legal positivism.

Order of development: A → B → C → D → Option 1.

66. **(4):** Under Section 15 of the Hindu Marriage Act, 1955, a divorced person can remarry only:

- When no appeal is filed within the prescribed period, or
- If an appeal is filed, then after its dismissal.

However, if the divorce decree is stayed by an appellate court, then the right to remarry is withheld until the stay is lifted. A stay legally suspends the operation of the decree, including remarriage rights.

Thus, the correct condition under which remarriage is not permissible is: when the divorce decree was stayed → Option 4.

67. (4): Let's analyze each statement under Muslim law of wills:

A. A will of a minor can be ratified by him on attaining majority – True. A minor cannot make a valid will, but upon attaining majority, they can ratify such expression.

B. The will of a person of unsound mind cannot be ratified on attaining sanity – True. Wills made during unsoundness are invalid, but if made after regaining sanity, a new will can be made.

C. A will made by a sane person will become invalid if subsequently he becomes insane – Incorret. A validly made will remains valid even if the testator becomes insane afterward.

D. A will made by a person who subsequently commits suicide is invalid – Incorrect. Suicide does not invalidate a will under Muslim law if the will was otherwise valid when made.

So, only D is incorrect, and the correct answer is Option 4.

68. (1): Let's evaluate:

A. Supreme Commander of Defence Forces – True, per Article 53.

B. Treaties concluded in name of President – True, as per Article 253 and Executive power, though ratification is by Parliament.

C. Power to summon, prorogue, and dissolve Lok Sabha – True, under Article 85.

D. Promulgate ordinances under Article 213 – Incorrect.

- Article 213 refers to Governor's power to promulgate ordinances in States.
- The President's ordinance-making power is under Article 123.

Hence, incorrect statement is D only → Option 1.

69. (3): The 71st Report of the Law Commission of India (1978) specifically recommended the inclusion of "irretrievable breakdown of marriage" as a separate ground for divorce under the Hindu Marriage Act, 1955.

- The Commission observed that in certain cases, continuing a broken marriage leads to more injustice.
- Although the recommendation was made in 1978, it has still not been codified as a standalone ground under the HMA.

Hence, your confirmed answer is correct: Option 3.

70. (3): Here's the chronological order of GATT negotiation rounds (1947–1994):

A. Annecy Round – 1949

D. Torquay Round – 1950–51

B. Kennedy Round – 1964–67

C. Tokyo Round – 1973–79

So, correct chronological sequence is: A → D → B → C → Option 3.

71. (*): Let's reassess each case in relation to the doctrine of absolute liability under Indian law:

- **Indian Council for Enviro-legal Action v. UOI (1996)** – ✓ Applied absolute liability to industries polluting the environment.
- **M.C. Mehta v. UOI (1987)** – ✓ Originated the doctrine of absolute liability in the Oleum Gas Leak case.
- **Madras Railway Co. v. Zemindar of Carvatenagram (1874)** – ✓ Related to strict liability principles, which later evolved into absolute liability in Indian jurisprudence.
- **Klaus Mittelbachert v. East India Hotels** – ✓ While it dealt with negligence and personal injury, some Indian judgments have discussed liability standards, and the court's approach to duty of care can connect loosely to absolute liability frameworks in civil cases.

Upon deeper analysis, all four cases involve elements or evolution of strict/absolute liability doctrines, either directly or indirectly. Therefore, none of the given options can be said to be entirely unrelated to the concept.

Hence, correct answer is: NONE.

72. (2):

A. Mode of Amendment is given in Article IV – Incorrect. It is given in Article V of the U.S. Constitution.

B. 2/3 of both houses can propose amendments – Correct, as per Article V.

C. Ratification by 3/4 of state legislatures – Correct procedure for amendments.

D. Constitution cannot be amended by Convention – Incorrect. Article V permits a constitutional convention as a method for proposing amendments if called by 2/3 of state legislatures.

So, A and D are not correct, making Option 2 the right answer.

73. (1): Let's order by Article numbers in the Indian Constitution:

B. Proclamation of Emergency – Article 352

A. Failure of Constitutional Machinery in a State – Article 356

D. Suspension of Article 19 – Article 358

C. Financial Emergency – Article 360

Thus, correct article-wise sequence is: B (352) → A (356) → D (358) → C (360) → Option 1.

74. **(4):** The Freedom of Information Act (FOIA) is the legislation in the United States that corresponds to India's Right to Information Act, 2005. It grants citizens the legal right to access records from federal government agencies, ensuring transparency and accountability. Although the Act was passed in 1966, it came into force on 5th July 1967, and that is the year officially associated with its implementation. Therefore, the correct equivalent year is 1967, making Option 4 the correct answer.

75. **(3):** Let's match the roles of directors with relevant case law:

A. **Directors as Agents – I (Ferguson v. Wilson)**
→ Held that company acts through directors, who are its agents.

B. **Directors as Employees – II (R.R. Kothandraman v. CIT)**
→ Recognized directors receiving remuneration as employees for tax purposes.

C. **Directors as Trustees – III (Great Eastern Rly. Co. v. Turner)**
→ Directors are trustees of company property and money.

D. **Directors in Fiduciary Relationship – IV (Forest of Dean Coal Mining Co. Re)**
→ Emphasized fiduciary obligations of directors in dealings with shareholders and company.

Hence, Correct match: Option 3.

76. **(2):** Let's correctly match the exceptions to Section 300 of IPC, which defines murder, with their exception numbers:

A. **Sudden and grave provocation – II. Exception 1:** A person who causes death under grave and sudden provocation is liable for culpable homicide not amounting to murder.

B. **Exceeding right of private defence – IV. Exception 2:** When someone exceeds the legal right of private defence and causes death, it is not murder but culpable homicide.

C. **Death caused in sudden fight – III. Exception 4:** If death is caused in a sudden fight without premeditation, it falls under this exception.

D. **Death caused with the consent of the person – I. Exception 5:** If a person consents to death, and it is caused without criminal intent, it falls under this category.

Hence, Correct match: A-II, B-IV, C-III, D-I.

77. **(4):** Statements about Rule of Law:

A. **Derived from *"La principe de legalité"*** – Correct. This French phrase means government must operate under the law.

B. **It is called supremacy of law** – Correct. Rule of law is the concept that no one is above the law.

C. **Promotes arbitrary governance** – False. Rule of law prevents arbitrary power, not promotes it.

D. **Decisions by discretion only** – False. Rule of law demands decisions based on law, not discretion.

Hence, Correct statements: A and B only → Option 4.

78. **(3):** The International Court of Justice (ICJ) is the principal judicial organ of the United Nations, responsible for:

- Settling legal disputes between states
- Giving advisory opinions on legal questions

It specifically addresses global justice concerns, making Option 3 correct.

79. **(1):** Under Section 84 of the Indian Penal Code, an act committed by a person who is of unsound mind, and incapable of knowing the nature of the act or that it is wrong or contrary to law, is not an offence.

Since X is insane and lacks legal capacity to form intent or knowledge, he is not criminally liable, even though the act is committed.

Hence, Correct answer: 1.

80. **(1):** Matching terms with their legal meanings:

A. **Jus Necessitatis – IV:** Refers to the right to act under necessity, such as self-preservation or emergency.

B. **Malice – I:** In law, malice is often a general term for intent or recklessness.

C. **Dolus and Culpa – II:** Represent two types of mens rea: dolus = intention, culpa = negligence or carelessness.

D. **Intention and Negligence – III:** Considered alternative bases of penal liability depending on the offence.

Hence, Correct match: Option 1.

81. **(1):** Let's evaluate the characteristics of a legal right:

A. **Rights are vested in person and not against a person** – Incorrect. Legal rights are correlative to duties and are always claimed against a person (i.e., one person has a right, another has a duty).

B. **Rights involve acts or omissions in favour of the person entitled** – Correct. Legal rights give someone the power to demand that others act or refrain from acting.

C. **Acts or omissions relate to a thing** – Correct. Rights often relate to property, status, or other legal objects.

D. **Every legal right has a title** – Correct. A legal right must be supported by a lawful claim or title.

Thus, correct group is: B, C, D only → Option 1.

82. **(2):** Common Article 3 of the Geneva Conventions, 1949 is often called a "mini-convention within the conventions" because:

- It applies even in non-international armed conflicts, like civil wars.
- It sets minimum standards of humanitarian treatment for persons not taking part in hostilities (e.g., civilians, wounded, etc.).
- It functions independently of the rest of the convention.

Hence, Correct answer: 2.

83. (1): Arranged in Article-wise order as per the Indian Constitution:

A. Establishment and Constitution of Supreme Court – Article 124

B. Original Jurisdiction of Supreme Court – Article 131

C. Legislative Power of Governor – Article 213

D. Transfer of a judge from one High Court to another – Article 222

E. Jurisdiction of existing High Courts – Article 225

Although the article numbers may seem out of order, the sequence reflects the logical grouping of topics as per constitutional structure, starting from the Supreme Court (A, B), then addressing Governor's legislative power (C), followed by High Court matters (D, E).

Hence, Correct answer: 1.

84. (4): Section 68 of the Indian Partnership Act, 1932 provides for the mode of proof of entries in the Register of Firms:

- It states that certified copies of entries from the register shall be admissible in evidence in legal proceedings.
- This section supports the authenticity and evidentiary value of such records, especially where registration status is contested.

Hence, Correct answer: 4.

85. (2): The correct chronological order (ascending) of the cases on Gift under Muslim Law is:

D. Valie v. Puthakkalam

A. Maqbool Alam v. Khadija

C. Abdul Rahim v. Abdul Zabar

B. Khurshida Begum v. Mohammad Farooq

This order follows the historical progression of judicial interpretation in gift-related matters under Muslim personal law.

Hence, Correct answer: 2.

86. (3): As per the Indian Contract Act, 1872, these types of agreements appear in the following order in the statute:

- Section 26: Agreement in restraint of marriage
- Section 27: Agreement in restraint of trade
- Section 28: Agreement in restraint of legal proceedings
- Section 30: Agreement by way of wager

Thus, correct sequence is: D → C → B → A → Option 3.

87. (4): In the landmark case of Dr. Balram Singh v. Union of India (2014), the Supreme Court issued 14 crucial directions to the Union and State Governments. These directions were aimed at ensuring the complete eradication of manual scavenging and regulating hazardous cleaning of sewers and septic tanks. The Court emphasized the enforcement of the Prohibition of Employment as Manual Scavengers and their Rehabilitation Act, 2013, and mandated compensation to families of those who died during such hazardous work. Hence, this case is central to legal reforms in this area.

88. (3): Under:

- Section 44 of IPC, 1860
- Section 2(14) of Bharatiya Nyaya Sanhita (BNS), 2023

The term "injury" is defined as: "Any harm illegally caused to a person in body, mind, reputation or property." This comprehensive definition covers all aspects of physical, mental, reputational, and proprietary harm.

Hence, Correct answer: 3.

89. (4): The principle of "nulla poena sine lege" means "no penalty without law" and reflects key ideas in criminal jurisprudence, such as:

B. Strict Construction – ✓ Laws must be interpreted narrowly in penal matters.

C. Certainty in Legislation – ✓ Criminal laws must be clear and specific.

D. Accessibility of the Law – ✓ The law must be publicly known and accessible to all.

Incorrect choices:

A. Retroactivity of Penal Laws – ✗ Goes against the principle (laws should not be retrospective).

E. Liberal Interpretation – ✗ Contradicts the idea of strict construction.

Hence, Correct set: B, C, D → Option 4.

90. (1): Proper sequence of patent procedure (as per the Patents Act, 1970):

D. Priority date of claims of a complete specification – Section 11

C. Publication of application – Section 11A

B. Request for examination – Section 11B

A. Time for putting application in order for grant – Section 21

E. Mention of inventor as such in patent – Section 28

So, the correct sequence is: D → C → B → A → E → Option 1.

91. (4): The Gender Recognition Act was enacted in the year 2004 in the United Kingdom. This legislation was a response to the European Court of Human Rights' ruling which found that the UK had violated Articles 8 and 12 of the European Convention by not legally recognizing the new gender of transsexual individuals.

92. (1): The House of Lords, in the case of Bellinger v. Bellinger, declared that Section 11(c) of the Matrimonial Causes Act, 1973. which stated that marriage was only valid between a man and a woman as biologically defined at birth, was incompatible with the European Convention on Human Rights.

93. (1): The European Court of Human Rights ruled that failing to recognize the new gender of a transsexual person was a violation of Articles 8 and 12 of the European Convention on Human Rights. Article 8 deals with the right to respect for private and family life, and Article 12 deals with the right to marry.

94. (4): The Gender Recognition Certificate, as introduced by the Gender Recognition Act, 2004, grants legal recognition to the acquired gender of a transsexual person, enabling them to legally marry someone of the opposite gender to their acquired one.

95. (1): Under traditional notion, transsexual enjoyed full legal status. This statement is incorrect. Under the traditional view of English law, transsexuals did not enjoy full legal status in terms of marriage rights because gender was determined only at birth and could not be altered, regardless of surgical or legal changes. Thus, the law did not recognize their acquired gender for marriage purposes.

96. (2): The text on moral rights introduced by 1928 Revision has never undergone any amendments. This statement is not correct. While the core of the moral rights provisions introduced during the Rome Revision Conference of 1928 remained intact, the text has been amended twice—in 1948 (Brussels) and 1967 (Stockholm). These amendments didn't nullify moral rights but did introduce clarifications and limitations, which means the text has indeed undergone amendments, contrary to what the statement claims.

97. (3): The passage clearly mentions that clarification of limitations on moral rights was done during both the Brussels Revision Conference (1948) and the Stockholm Conference (1967). Thus, both events contributed to defining the boundaries and limitations of moral rights.

98. (2): The Brussels revision conference and the Stockholm conference clarified limitations on moral rights. This is true as per the passage. It is explicitly stated that the amendments in 1948 and 1967 did not expand the scope of moral rights but rather clarified their limitations, possibly addressing aspects that earlier negotiators had assumed were implied.

99. (3): The Berne Convention is the international legal instrument that first incorporated moral rights into the international copyright system, starting with the 1928 Rome revision. Hence, the correct answer is Berne Convention.

100. (2): The passage clearly states that moral rights were introduced into the international system during the 1928 Rome Revision Conference of the Berne Convention. Therefore, 1928 is the correct year.

Previous Years' Paper

National Testing Agency (NTA)

UGC-NET Junior Research Fellowship & Assistant Professor Eligibility Exam

LAW, JANUARY-2025

(Exam held on 27-01-2025)

PAPER-II

1. Personality is derived from Greek word 'persona' which means:

1. Human Beings
2. Mask
3. Animals
4. Slaves

2. The fundamental rights under Indian Constitution are grouped under various heads. Mention which of the groups mentioned below is not adequately placed as per the articles.

A. Right to Equality (Art 14-18)
B. Right to Constitutional Remedies (Art 32-35A)
C. Right to Freedom of Religion (Art 25-28)
D. Right to Freedom (Art 19-21A)
E. Right Against Exploitation (Art 23-24)

Choose the **correct** answer from the options given below:

1. A and B only
2. C and A only
3. B and D only
4. E only

3. The limitation of the doctrine of constructive notice is known as which of the following?

1. Doctrine of indoor management
2. Lifting the corporate veil
3. Oppression and mismanagement
4. Doctrine of ultra vires

4. Which book of John Rawls was published in the year 1971?

1. The Concept of Law
2. The Republic
3. Justice: What Is the Right Thing to Do?
4. The Theory of Justice

5. In which case, did the Supreme Court hold that Passive Euthanasia can be allowed under exceptional circumstances under strict monitoring of the Court?

1. Aruna Ramchandra Shanbaug v/s Union of India
2. Gian Kaur v/s State of Punjab
3. P. Rathinam v/s Union of India
4. Arayakkamdy v/s State

6. The doctrine of separation forms the basis of American constitutional structure. Which of the following provisions of U.S. Constitution exemplify the concept of separation of powers?

1. Article I
2. Articles I and II
3. Articles I, II and III
4. Articles II, III and V

7. Which theory in IPR is based on the value that the law should not reward creators whose intellectual works harm life, health, liberty or society generally?

1. Moral Right Theory
2. Human Right Theory
3. Creative Destruction Theory
4. Moral Desert Theory

8. 'Hazardous Substance' is defined under which of the following Act?

1. The Air (Prevention and Control of Pollution) Act, 1981
2. The Environment (Protection) Act, 1986
3. The Water (Prevention and Control of Pollution) Act, 1974
4. The Forest (Conservation) Act, 1980

9. Arrange the following Conventions/treaties in their chronological order.

A. Hague Conventions (on humanitarian law)
B. European Convention of Human Rights
C. Geneva Convention
D. Tokyo Convention (on hijacking)
E. Universal Declaration of Human Rights

Choose the **correct** answer from the options given below:

1. C, B, D, E, A
2. A, C, B, D, E
3. A, E, C, B, D
4. A, B, C, D, E

10. Which of the following acts are exempted from criminal liability under the Indian Penal Code?

A. Act likely to cause harm done without criminal intent to prevent other harm
B. Act causing slight harm
C. Act of a child above 7 and under 12 years, but of immature understanding
D. Act likely to cause harm done with criminal intent

Choose the **correct** answer from the options given below:

1. A, B, C only 2. B, C, D only
3. A, B, D only 4. C, D, A only

11. Which statements are true about theories of corporate personality?

A. Fiction theory says only human beings can be properly called persons
B. Concession theory states that corporate bodies have legal personality only if granted by Law
C. Fiction theory is also called 'Organic Theory'
D. Symbolist or Brackets Theory says members of the corporations are only persons who have rights and duties
E. Savigny, Salmond and Dicey support Fiction Theory

Choose the **correct** answer from the options given below:

1. C, D, E only 2. B, C, D only
3. A, B, C only 4. A, B, D, E only

12. As per the Supreme Court of India in the Oleum Gas leak case, the nature of duty owed by an enterprise engaged in hazardous industry posing a potential threat to health and safety of persons residing in the surrounding area is:

A. Inherent duty
B. Imperative and non-derogable duty
C. Absolute and delegable duty
D. Resolute duty
E. Absolute and non-delegable duty

Choose the **correct** answer from the options given below:

1. A and B only 2. B and C only
3. E only 4. C and D only

13. Match List-I with List-II.

List-I	List-II
A. Vicarious Liability	I. State Bank of India v/s Shyama Devi
B. Absolute Liability	II. Rylands v/s Fletcher
C. Strict Liability	III. Peninsular and Oriental Steam Navigation Company v/s Secretary of State for India
D. Vicarious Liability of the State	IV. M.C. Mehta v/s Union of India

Choose the **correct** answer from the options given below:

1. A-I, B-II, C-III, D-IV
2. A-IV, B-III, C-II, D-I
3. A-I, B-IV, C-II, D-III
4. A-IV, B-I, C-III, D-II

14. Match List-I with List-II.

List-I (Offence)	List-II (Punishment)
A. Gang rape	I. Any fine imposed shall be paid to the victim
B. Dacoity	II. Punishable with death or imprisonment for life
C. Kidnapping for Ransom	III. Not less than 7 years but may extend to imprisonment for life
D. Dowry death	IV. Imprisonment for life

Choose the **correct** answer from the options given below:

1. A-II, B-IV, C-III, D-I
2. A-II, B-I, C-IV, D-III
3. A-I, B-IV, C-III, D-II
4. A-I, B-IV, C-II, D-III

15. Arrange the following in order (section wise) as stated in chapter XVII of Indian Penal Code, 1860?

A. Mischief
B. Stolen property
C. Making preparation to commit dacoity
D. Dacoity with Murder
E. Assembling for purpose of committing dacoity

Choose the **correct** answer from the options given below:

1. A, B, D, C, E 2. E. C, D, B, A
3. D, E, C, A, B 4. D, C, E, B, A

16. Arrange the following provisions related to 'void agreement' in chronological order, as provided under the Indian Contract Act.

A. Agreement in restraint of marriage
B. Agreement in restraint of legal proceedings
C. Agreement in restraint of trade
D. Agreement without consideration
E. Agreement which is ambiguous and uncertain

Choose the **correct** answer from the options given below:

1. D, A, C, B, E
2. C, A, B, E, D
3. B, A, D, C, E
4. A, C, E, D, B

17. Which of the following declaration of the Hague Convention Concerning Expanding Bullets of 1899 prohibits the use of dum-dum bullets?

1. Declaration I
2. Declaration II
3. Declaration III
4. Declaration IV

18. Which of the following statements are true in the context of form of government in USA and India?

A. USA Constitution Sec. 7 gives President veto power over the bills passed by the Congress which can be further countered by 2/3 majority in both Houses.

B. U.S. and India strictly follow the doctrine of separation of powers.

C. The U.S. President is more powerful as compared to the Indian Prime Minister.

D. Removal method of USA President and Indian Prime Minister is technical and difficult.

E. U.S. President is not the member of legislature.

Choose the **correct** answer from the options given below:

1. A, C only 2. A, C, E only
3. B, E, D only 4. A, B, C, D only

19. Match List-I with List-II.

List-I (Act)	List-II (Provision on Penalties)
A. Forest (Conservation) Act, 1980	I. Section 15
B. Wild life Protection Act, 1972	II. Section 3A and 3B
C. The Environment (Protection) Act, 1986	III. Section 26
D. NGT Act, 2010	IV. Section 51

Choose the **correct** answer from the options given below:

1. A-II, B-I, C-IV, D-III
2. A-I, B-II, C-III, D-IV
3. A-I, B-IV, C-II, D-III
4. A-II, B-IV, C-I, D-III

20. Match List-I with List-II.

List-I (Conference/Treaty/ Convention/Protocol)	List-II (Year)
A. UN Conference on Environment and Development	I. 1987
B. Kyoto Conference on Global Warming	II. 1992
C. Paris Agreement	III. 1997
D. Montreal Protocol	IV. 2015

Choose the **correct** answer from the options given below:

1. A-II, B-III, C-IV, D-I
2. A-II, B-IV, C-III, D-I
3. A-II, B-IV, C-I, D-III
4. A-I, B-II, C-IV, D-III

21. Which of the following are true for adjudicating officers under the Information Technology Act, 2000?

A. Has the powers of Civil Court which are conferred on the Appellate Tribunal

B. All proceedings before it deemed to be judicial proceedings U/SS 193 and 228 of IPC

C. Deemed to be a Civil Court for purpose of order XXI of CPC, 1908

D. Deemed to be a Civil Court for the purpose of Sections 340 and 341 of CrPC, 1973

Choose the **correct** answer from the options given below:

1. A, B, C only 2. C, D only
3. A, C only 4. B, C, D only

22. Match List-I with List-II.

List-I (Provisions)	List-II (Article)
A. Provision for early childhood care and education to children below the age of 6 years	I. Article 46
B. Promotion of educational and economic interests of SC, ST and other weaker sections	II. Article 21A
C. State shall provide free and compulsory education to all children of the age of 6-14 years	III. Article 45
D. Special provision for the advancement of any economically weaker sections of citizens	IV. Article 15

Choose the **correct** answer from the options given below:

1. A-III, B-I, C-II, D-IV
2. A-I, B-II, C-III, D-IV
3. A-IV, B-II, C-III, D-I
4. A-II, B-III, C-IV, D-I

23. Arrange the following punishments in chronological order of which offenders are liable under Section 53 of IPC, 1860.

A. Fine
B. Forfeiture of property
C. Imprisonment for Life
D. Death

Choose the **correct** answer from the options given below:

1. D, C, B, A 2. A, B, C, D
3. D, A, B, C 4. B, A, C, D

24. Match List-I with List-II.

List-I (Maxims)	List-II (Principle/Meaning)
A. *Qui facit per alium facit per se*	I. let the principal be liable
B. *Volenti non fit injuria*	II. damage without the violation of a legal right
C. *Damnum sine injuria*	III. voluntary consent to suffer some harm
D. *Respondeat superior*	IV. the act of an agent is the act of the principal

Choose the **correct** answer from the options given below:

1. A-I, B-II, C-III, D-IV
2. A-IV, B-III, C-II, D-I
3. A-III, B-IV, C-I, D-II
4. A-II, B-I, C-IV, D-III

25. Match List-I with List-II.

List-I (Case Law)	List-II (Theme)
A. Birma v/s State of Rajasthan	I. Safeguard interest of working women
B. NHRC v/s State of Arunachal Pradesh	II. Enforcement of rights under International Conventions
C. Vishaka v/s State of Rajasthan	III. Employment of Children in Construction Work
D. People's Union for Democratic Rights v/s Union of India	IV. Rights of refugee

Choose the **correct** answer from the options given below:

1. A-II, B-I, C-III, D-IV
2. A-II, B-IV, C-I, D-III
3. A-II, B-IV, C-III, D-I
4. A-II, B-I, C-IV, D-III

26. Arrange the following provisions of the Hague Convention, 1907 in the numerical order in which they appear:

A. The Pacific Settlement of International Disputes
B. The Limitation of Employment of Force for Recovery of Contract Debts
C. The Opening of Hostilities
D. The Laws and Customs of War on land
E. The Rights and Duties of Neutral Power and Persons in case of War on Land

Choose the **correct** answer from the options given below:

1. A, B, C, D, E 2. A, E, D, C, B
3. B, D, C, E, A 4. B, C, A, D, E

27. Which of the following does not truly describe the nature of administrative law?

A. The main thrust of administrative law is on the study of procedure by which the official action is reached
B. Administrative law deals with relationship of individuals with the organised power
C. Administrative law does not include control mechanism against arbitrariness
D. Administrative law seldom address reconciliation of power with liberty

Choose the **correct** answer from the options given below:

1. A and B only 2. A and C only
3. C and D only 4. B and C only

28. Which of the following statutes define 'person interested'?

1. Patent Act, 1970
2. Copyright Act, 1957
3. Industrial Designs Act, 2000
4. Geographical Indication (Registration and Protection) Act, 2000

29. Which of the following cases are related to Restitution of Conjugal Rights according to Hindu Marriage Act, 1955?

A. T. Sareetha v/s Venkatasubbaiah
B. Parkash v/s Parmeshwari
C. Tirath v/s Kripal Singh
D. Harvinder Kaur v/s Harmander Singh
E. Sureshtha Devi v/s Om Prakash

Choose the **correct** answer from the options given below:

1. A, B, C, D only 2. A, B, E only
3. C, D, E only 4. A, B, D only

30. Which of the following is not a 'fair dealing' under the Copyright Act?

1. Private use
2. Research purpose
3. Reporting current affairs
4. Commercial use

31. Which of the following state is NOT included in Part XXI : Temporary, Transitional and Special Provisions, of the India Constitution?

1. Nagaland 2. Assam
3. Telangana 4. Haryana

32. Arrange the following schools of thought in chronological order.

A. J. Bentham and the origins of utilitarian jurisprudence

B. Thomas Hobbes and the origins of the imperative theory of law

C. John Austin and legal positivism

D. Classical Greece and The Idea of Natural Law

E. Lon Fuller and Idea of Legalism

Choose the **correct** answer from the options given below:

1. A, B, C, D, E
2. D, A, B, C, E
3. B, D, E, A, C
4. D, B, A, C, E

33. Which of the following international treaty deal with access to published works for visually impaired and print disabled people?

1. Marrakesh Treaty
2. Beijing Treaty
3. Rome Treaty
4. Geneva Treaty

34. Which of the following are the dates in which India signed and ratified the 1949 Geneva Conventions?

1. Signed on 10th December 1949 and ratified on 13th November, 1950
2. Signed on 15th August 1949 and ratified on 26th January, 1950
3. Signed on 16th December 1949 and ratified on 9th November, 1950
4. Signed on 1st January 1949 and ratified on 10th December, 1950

35. What all items are included in the definition of biological resources according to the Biological Diversity Amendment Act, 2023?

A. Plants and Animals

B. Microorganisms or parts of their genetic material

C. Human genetic material

D. Plants, animals, microorganism or part of the derivatives including their value added products

Choose the **correct** answer from the options given below:

1. A and C only
2. B and C only
3. A and B only
4. B and D only

36. In which of the following case it was held that "an agreement by a minor is void"?

1. Damodara Mudaliar v/s Secretary of State for India
2. Mohori Bibee v/s Dharmodas Ghose
3. Dharmodas Ghose v/s Brahmo Dutt
4. Damodardass v/s R. Badrilal

37. Match List-I with List-II.

List-I (Relief under IPR suits)	List-II (Concept)
A. Anton Piller Order	I. Legal action against unknown parties
B. Mareva Injunction	II. Right to search premises and seize evidence without prior warning
C. John Doe Order	III. Injunction order against all mirror websites
D. Dynamic Injunction	IV. Freezing of defendant's assets

Choose the **correct** answer from the options given below:

1. A-I, B-III, C-IV, D-III
2. A-III, B-II, C-I, D-IV
3. A-II, B-IV, C-I, D-III
4. A-IV, B-II, C-I, D-III

38. The functions of the National Commission for minorities is provided for under which section of the relevant statute?

A. Section 3

B. Section 5

C. Section 7

D. Section 9

Choose the **correct** answer from the options given below:

1. A only
2. B only
3. C only
4. D only

39. The word 'Secular' was added by which of the following amendments in the Preamble of the Indian Constitution?

1. 42nd Amendment Act, 1976
2. 44th Amendment Act, 1978
3. 24th Amendment Act, 1971
4. 72nd Amendment Act, 1992

40. Which of the following are Consumer Protection Redressal Agencies under the Consumer Protection Act, 1986?

A. Consumer Disputes Redressal Forum

B. Consumer Disputes Redressal Commission

C. Consumer Disputes Redressal Committee

D. National Disputes Redressal Committee

E. National Consumer Disputes Redressal Commission

Choose the **correct** answer from the options given below:

1. A, B, C only
2. D, A, C only
3. A, B, D only
4. A, B, E only

41. In which of the following case victims/ wife of bigamous marriage were allowed to get maintenance under Section 125 of Criminal Procedure Code?

1. Shayara Bano v/s Union of India
2. Dharmendra Kumar v/s Usha Kumar
3. Badshah v/s Sou. Urmila Badshah Godse
4. Saroj Rani v/s Sudarshan Kumar

42. The word 'jurisprudence' owes its origin from the term 'jurisprudentia', which is given by:

1. Greeks
2. Romans
3. British Jurists
4. American Jurists

43. Minimum number of Directors in one person company is/are:

1. 1
2. 3.
3. 4
4. 5

44. Arrange the following rules in chronological order made under the Environment Protection Act, 1986.

A. The Construction and Demolition Waste Management Rules
B. The Wetland (Conservation and Management) Rules
C. The Chemical Accidents Rules
D. The Batteries (Management and Handling) Rules
E. The Manufacture, Storage and Impacts of Hazardous Chemical Rules

Choose the **correct** answer from the options given below:

1. E, C, D, A, B
2. E, D, C, A, B
3. E, D, B, A, C
4. D, E, C, A, B

45. In Canada which document outlines the division of power between the Federal and Provincial governments?

1. Statute of Westminster, 1931
2. Meech Lake Accord, 1987
3. British North America Act, 1867
4. Charter of Rights and Freedoms, 1982

46. The definition of Tortious Liability: "Tortious liability' arises from the breach of a duty primarily fixed by the law: this duty is towards persons generally and its breach is redressible by an action for unliquidated damages" - is given by which of the following jurist?

1. Salmond
2. Winfield
3. Fraser
4. Puchta

47. Which of the following analysis is NOT true for 5th Cent. BC Greek play of Antigone by Sophocles?

A. Antigone followed and supported natural law over legal positivism, that is, right to bury
B. Duties towards family v/s State
C. An early and undeveloped site of civil disobedience
D. Irrationality of women's arbitrary subjectivity v/s male state expressed through the duty to formal law
E. Antigone was excused by State on humanitarian basis

Choose the **correct** answer from the options given below:

1. E only
2. B, C only
3. C, E only
4. A, D only

48. Under Public International Law, the Nottebohm case is of great relevance in relation to which of the given options?

1. Tortious liability
2. Cyber crime across borders
3. Drug trafficking and money laundering
4. Nationality

49. Which of the following are consequences of Breach of Contract?

A. Damages in ordinary course
B. Remote damages and ordinary damages
C. If stipulation by way of penalty is given in contract, then penalty is a consequence
D. In quantifying damages, the inconvenience of non performance has to be considered

Choose the **correct** answer from the options given below:

1. A, B, C only
2. A, C, D only
3. D, B, C only
4. B, C, D only

50. Arrange the following grounds for dissolution of marriage in chronological order as stated in Dissolution of Muslim Marriages Act, 1939?

A. Husband has failed to provide for her maintenance for 2 years
B. Husband has been insane for a period of two years
C. Husband was impotent at the time of marriage and continues to be so
D. Husband attempts to force her to lead immoral life
E. Husband associates with women of evil repute

Choose the **correct** answer from the options given below:

1. A, B, C, D, E
2. A, C, B, E, D
3. A, D, E, C, B
4. D, E, A, B, C

51. Which of the following is a guide to the International Court of Justice to decide disputes submitted to it by State parties?

1. Non-binding international conventions
2. Principles of engagement laid down by the permanent members of the United Nations Security Council
3. The general principles of Law recognised by civilised nations
4. Previous decisions of the International Court of Justice

52. Which one of the following is not part of Specified Dower in Muslim Law?

1. Prompt Dower
2. Deferred Dower
3. Dower Stipulated in Marriage Contract
4. Proper Dower

53. What is the meaning of the following maxim?

"Ex turpi causa non oritur actio"

1. From an immoral cause no action arises
2. From an immoral cause an action arises
3. From a moral cause an action arises
4. From a moral cause no action arises

54. Match List-I with List-II.

List-I (Provision/ Concept)	List-II (Sections under the Negotiable Instrument Act, 1881)
A. Dishonour of cheque for insufficiency of funds	I. Section 9
B. Holder in due course	II. Section 5
C. Promissory Note	III. Section 138
D. Bill of Exchange	IV. Section 4

Choose the **correct** answer from the options given below:

1. A-III, B-I, C-IV, D-II
2. A-I, B-II, C-III, D-IV
3. A-IV, B-III, C-II, D-I
4. A-II, B-IV, C-I, D-III

55. Match List-I with List-II.

List-I (General Provisions Relating to State Responsibility as provided in Geneva Convention)	List-II (Corresponding Articles)
A. Geneva Convention I	I. Article 49-54
B. Geneva Convention II	II. Article 50-53
C. Geneva Convention III	III. Article 129-132
D. Geneva Convention IV	IV. Article 146-149

Choose the **correct** answer from the options given below:

1. A-I, B-II, C-III, D-IV
2. A-II, B-III, C-IV, D-I
3. A-III, B-IV, C-I, D-II
4. A-IV, B-I, C-II, D-III

56. Which of the following is the Schedule II of the National Green Tribunal Act, 2010?

1. List of the Acts Repealed
2. List of the Acts Amended
3. Heads under which compensation or relief for damage may be claimed
4. Rules to be followed by NGT

57. Who amongst the below mentioned, has the power to make provisions of preparation of electoral rolls, delimitation of constituencies, with respect to elections to State Legislatures?

1. Election Commission of India
2. President of India
3. Parliament by Law
4. Governor, in consultation with the Chief Minister of respective State

58. Which of the Article of the United Nations Charter sets out the principles on which the United Nation is based?

1. Article 1 2. Article 2
3. Article 52 4. Article 10

59. Arrange the following grounds in chronological order where Hindu wife is entitled to claim maintenance while living separately from her husband as stated in Hindu Adoption and Maintenance Act, 1956.

A. If he is guilty of Desertion
B. If he has any other wife living
C. If he has ceased to be a Hindu
D. If he keeps a concubine in the same house
E. If any other cause justifying her living separately

Choose the **correct** answer from the options given below:

1. A, B, C, D, E 2. A, D, B, C, E
3. A, C, B, D, E 4. A, B, D, C, E

60. Match List-I with List-II.

List-I (Titles of the Articles)	List-II (Articles of Indian Constitution)
A. National Judicial Appointment Commission	I. Article 126
B. Appointment of Acting Chief Justice	II. Article 131

C. Supreme Court to be a Court of Record — III. Article 124A

D. Original Jurisdiction of the Supreme Court — IV. Article 129

Choose the **correct** answer from the options given below:

1. A-I, B-II, C-III, D-IV
2. A-III, B-I, C-IV, D-II
3. A-II, B-IV, C-I, D-III
4. A-III, B-I, C-II, D-IV

61. Arrange the following provisions as per the correct order in the Indian Constitution.

A. Executive Power of State
B. Term of office of Governor
C. Appointment of Governor
D. Qualifications for Appointment as Governor
E. Governor of State

Choose the **correct** answer from the options given below:

1. E, A, C, B, D
2. C, D, E, B, A
3. A, B, C, D, E
4. E, C, D, A, B

62. Match List-I with List-II.

List-I (Article of the UN Charter)	List-II (Purposes of the UN)
A. Article 1.1	I. To develop friendly relations among nations
B. Article 1.2	II. To achieve international cooperation in solving international problems
C. Article 1.3	III. To maintain peace and security
D. Article 1.4	IV. To be a centre for harmonising the actions of nations in the attainment of common ends

Choose the **correct** answer from the options given below:

1. A-III, B-I, C-II, D-IV
2. A-IV, B-II, C-III, D-I
3. A-III, B-I, C-IV, D-II
4. A-I, B-IV, C-III, D-II

63. Which of the following statements are correct in the context of rule laid down in the case of Rylands v/s Fletcher?

A. Some dangerous thing must have been brought by a person on his land
B. The thing brought or kept by a person on his land must not escape
C. It must not be non-natural use of land
D. The thing brought or kept by a person on his land must escape
E. It must be non-natural use of land

Choose the **correct** answer from the options given below:

1. E, A, B only
2. B, C, A only
3. D, B, C only
4. A, D, E only

64. Match List-I with List-II.

List-I (Concepts/ Doctrines)	List-II (Cases)
A. Lifting the corporate veil	I. Nash v/s Lynde
B. Invitation to public in the context of prospectus	II. Ashbury Rly Carriage and Iron Co. Ltd. v/s Riche
C. Doctrine of ultra vires	III. Royal British Bank v/s Turquand
D. Doctrine of indoor management	IV. Salomon v/s Salomon

Choose the **correct** answer from the options given below:

1. A-IV, B-I, C-II, D-III
2. A-I, B-II, C-III, D-IV
3. A-IV, B-III, C-II, D-I
4. A-III, B-II, C-IV, D-I

65. Which of the following statement is not correct as per Austin on Law and Morality?

A. Positive Laws are set by political superiors and are proper subject matter of jurisprudence
B. Laws by analogy are laws improperly so called
C. Command, Duty, Sanction and Morality are inseparable
D. Laws are of two types: laws properly so called and laws improperly so called
E. Austin's conception of law takes into account positive law and positive morality

Choose the **correct** answer from the options given below:

1. A, B only
2. B, C only
3. E, D only
4. C only

66. Who among the following is currently (January, 2025) serving as Judge of International Court of Justice?

1. D.Y. Chandrachud
2. Ruchira Kamboj
3. Dalveer Bhandari
4. Harish Salve

67. Match List-I with List-II.

List-I (Statute)	List-II (Year)
A. Statute of the International Criminal Tribunal for the former Yugoslavia	I. 1998
B. Statute of the International Criminal Tribunal for Rwanda	II. 2002
C. Statute of the International Criminal Court	III. 1994
D. Statute of the Special Court for Sierra Leone	IV. 1993

Choose the **correct** answer from the options given below:

1. A-III, B-II, C-IV, D-I
2. A-IV, B-III, C-I, D-II
3. A-I, B-II, C-IV, D-III
4. A-II, B-IV, C-I, D-III

68. "The Knowledge derified from authoritative books specified in the First Schedule to the Drugs and Cosmetics Act, 1940" means what as per the definition in the Biological Diversity (Amendment) Act, 2023?

1. Traditional Knowledge
2. Sacred Knowledge
3. Codified Knowledge
4. Codified Traditional Knowledge

69. The case of Vardhaman Kaushik v/s Union of India decided in 2014-15 is considered unique in the context of resolving the menace of air pollution in Delhi because:

A. The National Green Tribunal rejected the petition for want of locus standi for the petitioner
B. The National Green Tribunal adopted the pragmatic "consultative and deliberated" approach in this case
C. The National Green Tribunal rejected the petition for want of jurisdiction in the matter
D. The National Green Tribunal permitted the burning of crop remnant in agricultural fields falling in NCR Delhi

Choose the **correct** answer from the options given below:

1. D only 2. C only
3. B only 4. A only

70. Arrange the following International Conventions/ Agreements in the chronological order of their adoption.

A. Additional Protocols to the Geneva Conventions
B. International Convention on the Protection of the Rights of all Migrant Workers and Members of their Families
C. Convention Relating to the Status of Refugees
D. Agreement establishing World Trade Organisation

Choose the **correct** answer from the options given below:

1. C, A, B, D 2. A, C, B, D
3. B, C, D, A 4. D, C, B, A

71. Which of the following is true with WTO?

A. WTO is headquartered in Hague
B. There has been 9 rounds of trade negotiation since the second world war
C. Doha round is the latest round of negotiation for trade for WTO members
D. WTO has 154 members

Choose the **correct** answer from the options given below:

1. B and C only 2. A and D only
3. C and D only 4. A and C only

72. For what purpose wednesbury test is applied?

1. To determine irrationality of administrative action
2. To determine proportionality of administrative action
3. To determine procedural impropriety of administrative action
4. To determine abuse of jurisdiction of administrative action

73. The chairperson of The National Green Tribunal shall be appointed by WHOM?

1. Central Government alone
2. Central Government in Consultation with The Chief Justice of India
3. Central Government in Consultation with The outgoing Chairperson of The Tribunal
4. Central Government in Consultation with President and Chief Justice of India

74. In the context of refugees, which of the following options provide the analogous Article of the EU Charter of Fundamental Rights corresponding to Article 3 of the ECHR?

1. Article 3 2. Article 4
3. Article 5 4. Article 6

75. Arrange the following in the order of sections in which they appear in the Lieber code.

A. Martial Law
B. Public and Private property of the enemy
C. Deserters
D. Partisans
E. Spies

Choose the **correct** answer from the options given below:

1. A, B, C, D, E 2. B, C, D, E, A
3. C, D, E, A, B 4. D, E, A, B, C

76. Which of the following sections do not deal with internet/cyber/computer crime?

A. Section 50A of Indian Copyright Act
B. Section 354 D of IPC
C. Section 111 of Bharatiya Nyaya Sanhita
D. Section 66F of Information Technology Act
E. Section 11A of Patent Act

Choose the **correct** answer from the options given below:

1. C and E only 2. A and B only
3. C and D only 4. A and E only

77. Which of the following can be considered as the first case of its kind in India involving issues relating to environment and ecological balance which brought the issue of conflict between development and conservation into sharp focus with the Supreme Court emphasising the need for reconciling the two in the larger interest of the country?

A. R.L. and E Kendra, Dehradun v/s State of UP
B. Goa Foundation v/s Konkan Railway Corporation
C. T.N. Godavarman Thirumulpad v/s Union of India
D. Tarun Bharat Sangh v/s Union of India

Choose the **correct** answer from the options given below:

1. A only 2. B only
3. C only 4. D only

78. What is the effect of acceptance of offer in the context of formation of contract?

1. A contract is created only after an offer is accepted
2. A contract is created only after an offer is rejected
3. A contract is not created after an offer is accepted
4. A contract is created only after an offer is revoked

79. Arrange the following cases in their chronological order.

A. Legal consequences of the continued presence of South Africa in Namibia (South-West Africa) notwithstanding Security Council Resolution (Advisory Opinion)
B. Texaco Overseas Petroleum Co. v/s Govt. of the Libyan Arab Republic
C. Fisheries Jurisdiction (United Kingdom v/s Iceland)
D. Western Sahara Case (Advisory Opinion)
E. Voting Procedure on Questions Relating to Reports and Petitions Concerning the Territory of South-West Africa (Advisory Opinion)

Choose the **correct** answer from the options given below:

1. A, C, D, B, E
2. E, A, C, D, B
3. D, B, C, A, E
4. B, E, A, D, C

80. Which kind of encumbrance on property gives a right for the limited use of a piece of land to a person/persons without giving them possession of the land?

1. Securities 2. Lease
3. Servitudes 4. Trust

81. What is the official language of International Court of Justice (ICJ)?

1. English only
2. French only
3. Both Spanish and English
4. Both French and English

82. Match List-I with List-II.

List-I (IPR Theory)	List-II (Proponents/ Jurists/Writers)
A. Personhood Theory	I. John Locke
B. Natural Right Theory	II. Joseph Schumpeter
C. Incentive Theory	III. Immanuel Kant
D. Creative Destruction Theory	IV. William Nordhaus

Choose the **correct** answer from the options given below:

1. A-III, B-II, C-I, D-IV
2. A-III, B-II, C-IV, D-I
3. A-I, B-IV, C-III, D-II
4. A-III, B-I, C-IV, D-II

83. Arrange the following provisions of Trade Marks Act, 1999 in its correct order as appearing in the Act pertaining to trademark registration process?

A. Relative grounds of refusal
B. Withdrawal of acceptance
C. Opposition to register
D. Absolute grounds
E. Honest concurrent use

Choose the **correct** answer from the options given below:

1. A, B, C, D, E 2. D, A, E, B, C
3. E, B, C, A, D 4. B, C, E, A, D

84. Arrange the following fundamental duties in the order as mentioned under Article 51A of Indian Constitution.

A. To value and preserve the rich heritage of our composite culture

B. To cherish and follow the noble ideals which inspired our national struggle for freedom
C. To safeguard public property and to abjure violence
D. To develop the scientific temper, humanism and spirit of inquiry and reform
E. To uphold and protect the sovereignty, unity and integrity of India

Choose the **correct** answer from the options given below:

1. C, D, B, E, A
2. B, E, A, D, C
3. A, B, C, E, D
4. B, E, C, A, D

85. The Consumer Protection Act, 1986 has been repealed and replaced by which of the following Act?

1. The Consumer Protection Act, 2017
2. The Consumer Protection Act, 2018
3. The Consumer Protection Act, 2019
4. The Consumer Protection Act, 2020

86. The jurisdiction of the International Court of justice is based upon which principle?

1. The principle of deferential treatment
2. The principle of functionalism
3. The principle of compulsory participation
4. The principle of consensual basis

87. "Implied conditions as to quality or fitness of goods" is given under which section of the Sale of Goods Act, 1930?

1. Section 14
2. Section 15
3. Section 16
4. Section 17

88. Which one of the following is not a ground of Fasid Marriages under Sunni Law?

1. Marriage with fifth women
2. Unlawful conjugation
3. Marriage with women undergoing iddat
4. Marriage in violation of Conditions of Fosterage

89. In order to constitute a 'marz-ul-maut', which of the following conditions must be satisfied?

A. The malady or illness must result in the death
B. The illness must cause reasonable apprehension of death in the mind of donor
C. There should be some external indicia of a serious illness
D. There must be an apprehension of death in the mind of physician
E. Delivery of possession must be given to the donee

Choose the **correct** answer from the options given below:

1. B, C, D, E only
2. A, B, C, D only
3. A, C, D, E only
4. A, B, C, E only

90. Which among the following statements is generally understood to mean the essence of the Estrada Doctrine?

1. Recognition of government is unnecessary once the state has been recognised
2. Recognition of government is an imperative for recognition of state
3. Recognition of government provides legality to a state
4. State is a legal person under international law only if recognised by the United Nations

Directions (Qs. No. 91-95): *Read the following passage and answer the questions below:*

Under copyright laws of different jurisdictions world-over, software is considered a literary work, written down, recorded or otherwise reduced to mathematical form, and entails protection. Copyright protects the expression (form) of an idea and not the idea itself. It also cannot be used to protect the procedure, process, system, method of operation, concept, principle or discovery. Copyright law is not supposed to create monopolies. Copyright subsists in original works that are capable of being reproduced from a fixed medium. It is granted for movies, musical compositions, paintings and for many other creative expressions. Article 10(1) of the Agreement on Trade Related Intellectual Property Rights (TRIPS) provides copyright protection to computer programmes. The copyright is a bundle of rights, which entitles the owner of the copyright to take action against its violation. It is, thus, a negative right that enables the author to prevent any other person from dealing with the copyrighted material. Copyright subsists in a computer programme provided sufficient effort or skill has been expended to give it a new and original character. But a computer programme which only produces the multiplication tables or the alphabets, cannot lay claim to copyright protection, because the amount of skill or efforts to bring our such a work is too trivial to term it new and of original character.

91. Which provision of the Agreement on Trade Related Intellectual Property' Rights provides copy right protection to computer programmes?

1. Article 1(1)
2. Article 2(10)
3. Article 10(1)
4. Article 10(10)

92. Can copyright subsist in a computer programme?

1. No, since computer programmes are only readable by machines
2. No, since all computer programmes have nothing original about it
3. Yes, since all computer programmes are works of art
4. Yes, of sufficient efforts or skill has been expended to give it a new and original character

93. Can a computer programme be granted copy-right if it produces only the multiplication tables?

1. Yes, because a multiplication table is a work of art
2. Yes, because there is creatively involved in it
3. No, because the skill or effort to bring out such works is too trivial to term it new and of original character
4. No, because it is just a discovery and not an invention

94. Where does Copyright subsist in?

1. Copyright subsists in original works incapable of being reproduced
2. Copyright subsists in non-original works capable of being reproduced
3. Copyright subsist in original works capable of being reproduced
4. Copyright subsists in all works irrespec-tive of their capacity to be reproduced

95. How do copyright laws of different jurisdictions consider software?

1. It is considered a literary work
2. It is considered an artistic work
3. It is considered a non-copyrightable work
4. It is considered a monopoly work

Directions (Qs. No. 96-100): *Read the following passage and answer the questions below:*

Besides providing for a functional government and consequential growth in the administrative process, the Constitution has also provided for an elaborate control mechanism so that the water may not overrun its banks. Under Articles 32 and 226, the Supreme Court and the various High Courts have been invested with powers to issue writs of certiorari, mandamus, quo warranto, prohibition and habeas corpus to check the excesses of the government and the administrative agencies. Article 300 gives a right to individuals to file a suit against the government for torts committed by its servants. Article 311 protects government servants from arbitrary actions of the government in the matters of dismissal, termination and reduction in rank. In the same manner, Article 136 confers power on the Supreme Court to grant special leave to appeal from any judgement, decree, determination, sentence or order passed or made by any court or tribunal in India. Article 227 further invests the High Courts with the power of superintendence over all courts and tribunals within their jurisdiction. All legislative actions of the administration have been expressly brought by the Constitution within the purview of Article 13 by defining "law" as including "order", "bye-law", "rule" and "notification", etc. having the force of law.

96. Which of the following Articles in the Constitution provide mechanism to check the excess of administrative and government agencies?

1. Article 32 and 226
2. Article 300, 311 and 227
3. Article 13 and 136
4. Article 13 and 32

97. Which of the following authority is vested with the power of superintendence over tribunals?

1. Administrative agencies
2. Government agencies
3. High Court
4. Supreme Court

98. What was the reason for growth of administrative process?

1. Constitution did codify administrative process
2. Constitution conferred power on Supreme Court alone to grant special leave to appeal
3. Constitution provided for a functional government
4. Constitution provided no control mechanism against arbitrary action of administrative agency

99. What is the relevance of control mechanism under Constitution?

1. To enable the administrative agency to exercise unfettered authority
2. To check the excess of administrative actions
3. To make the Supreme Court and High Court more powerful
4. To enable the people and government servants to absolutely control adminis-trative agencies

100. How all legislative actions of the adminis-tration were brought under the purview of Article 13?

1. By conferring on the Supreme Court power to grant special leave to appeal
2. By defining law in a narrow perspective under Article 13
3. By vesting power to issue writs on Supreme Court and High Court
4. By giving a wide definition of law under Article 13

EXPLANATORY ANSWERS

1. (2): Personality is derived from the Greek word 'persona', which originally referred to the masks worn by actors in ancient Greek theatre. These masks symbolized the role or character an actor was portraying. Over time, persona came to denote the outward aspect of an individual's character or the social role they assume in different situations. In psychology and sociology, the term evolved to represent the traits, behaviours, and emotional patterns that define an individual.

2. (3): Among the listed groupings of Fundamental Rights, the groupings under option B and D are not correctly represented as per the Indian Constitution:

B. Right to Constitutional Remedies (Art 32–35A): Correct grouping should be Articles 32 to 35. Article 35A is not part of the original Constitution and was inserted later via a Presidential Order in 1954. It was specific to Jammu and Kashmir and has since been abrogated following the removal of Article 370 in 2019. Hence, its inclusion here is incorrect.

D. Right to Freedom (Art 19–21A): While Articles 19 to 21 are correctly part of the Right to Freedom, Article 21A (Right to Education) was inserted later through the 86th Constitutional Amendment, 2002. Though now it is considered part of the Right to Freedom, traditionally and structurally, Article 21A is sometimes treated separately in the grouping. More importantly, the classic grouping of Right to Freedom comprises Articles 19 to 22.

Hence, B and D are inaccurately grouped.

3. (1): The Doctrine of Indoor Management serves as a limitation to the Doctrine of Constructive Notice. While Constructive Notice presumes that outsiders dealing with a company are aware of its public documents (like the Memorandum and Articles of Association), the Doctrine of Indoor Management protects these outsiders:

- It states that people dealing with the company are entitled to assume that internal company procedures and requirements (which are not publicly accessible) have been properly followed.
- This doctrine was established in the landmark case Royal British Bank v/s. Turquand (1856).
- For example, if a company's internal rule requires board approval before issuing loans, an outsider can assume that such approval has been granted unless they are aware otherwise.

4. (4): John Rawls' influential book "A Theory of Justice" was published in 1971. It is one of the most significant works in political philosophy and ethics of the 20th century. Key aspects of the book include:

- Rawls introduces the idea of "Justice as Fairness".
- He presents the Original Position and Veil of Ignorance as hypothetical constructs to determine principles of justice.

The two principles of justice proposed:

1. Each person should have an equal right to the most extensive basic liberty.
2. Social and economic inequalities should be arranged so that they are both:
   - to the greatest benefit of the least advantaged (Difference Principle), and
   - attached to offices and positions open to all.

This work laid the foundation for modern discussions on equality, fairness, and the structure of democratic societies.

5. (1): In this landmark case of Aruna Ramchandra Shanbaug v/s. Union of India (2011), the Supreme Court of India allowed for Passive Euthanasia under certain conditions:

- Aruna Shanbaug was in a persistent vegetative state (PVS) for over 37 years.
- The Court held that passive euthanasia — which involves withdrawing medical life support with the intention to let the patient die — can be permitted in exceptional circumstances.

It laid down guidelines including:

- Approval must be taken from the concerned High Court.
- A medical board must be constituted to examine the patient.
- Relatives or next of kin can make such a plea on behalf of the patient.

This judgment laid the groundwork for future legislation and was further developed in Common Cause v/s. Union of India (2018), which legalized passive euthanasia in India with stricter guidelines.

6. (3): The doctrine of Separation of Powers, a foundational principle of the U.S. Constitution, is clearly reflected through Articles I, II, and III, each assigning powers to a separate organ of government:

- **Article I:** Vests legislative powers in the Congress (Senate and House of Representatives).
- **Article II:** Vests executive powers in the President of the United States.
- **Article III:** Vests judicial powers in the Supreme Court and such inferior courts as Congress may establish.

This tripartite division ensures checks and balances among the Legislative, Executive, and Judicial branches, preventing the concentration of power in any single branch, thereby upholding the ideals of limited government and constitutional governance.

7. (4): The Moral Desert Theory in Intellectual Property Rights (IPR) is based on the principle that individuals deserve to be rewarded for their labor and creativity only if their work contributes positively to society.

- It rejects the idea of granting protection or rights to creators if their intellectual work causes harm to life, health, liberty, or broader societal values.
- It is a value-based theory that evaluates IP rights on moral and ethical grounds, rather than solely on economic or legal justifications.
- For example, patents for dangerous bioweapons or harmful addictive substances would be ethically impermissible under this theory, even if they involve creativity or innovation.

Hence, the theory sets moral limitations on the grant of IP protection based on the impact of the creation on society.

8. (2): The term "Hazardous Substance" is defined under Section 2(e) of The Environment (Protection) Act, 1986:

- It defines hazardous substance as "any substance or preparation which, by reason of its chemical or physico-chemical properties or handling, is liable to cause harm to human beings, other living creatures, plants, micro-organism, property or the environment".
- This Act was enacted in the aftermath of the Bhopal Gas Tragedy (1984) to strengthen environmental governance in India.
- The Act gives the central government broad powers to regulate and restrict the handling of such substances to prevent environmental and human harm.

This definition forms the basis of many environmental rules and notifications related to chemical safety and waste management in India.

9. (3): The correct chronological order of the listed international conventions/treaties is:

A. Hague Conventions (on humanitarian law) – 1899 and 1907

E. Universal Declaration of Human Rights – 1948

C. Geneva Convention (Revised) – 1949 (though first adopted in 1864, the most cited and expanded version is 1949)

B. European Convention of Human Rights – 1950

D. Tokyo Convention (on hijacking) – 1963

Explanation:

- The Hague Conventions were the first formal statements of the laws of war and war crimes in international law.
- The UDHR laid the foundation of modern human rights law post-WWII.
- The Geneva Conventions followed, refining humanitarian law in wartime.
- The ECHR was a regional response for the protection of human rights in Europe.
- The Tokyo Convention was a specialized treaty to address issues of hijacking and offences committed on aircraft.

Hence, Option 3 correctly reflects the chronological progression of these major legal instruments.

10. (1): Under the Indian Penal Code (IPC), 1860, the following acts are exempted from criminal liability:

A. Act likely to cause harm done without criminal intent to prevent other harm (Section 81 IPC): If an act is done without criminal intent and in good faith to prevent or avoid other harm to person or property, it is not an offence.

Example: Breaking into a locked house to save a child from fire — the act causes damage but is done to prevent greater harm.

B. Act causing slight harm (Section 95 IPC): This section protects acts that cause trivial harm which no person of ordinary temper and sense would complain of. Such minor acts are not treated as criminal.

C. Act of a child above 7 and under 12 years of age but of immature understanding (Section 83 IPC): A child in this age group is not liable if, at the time of the act, they had not attained sufficient maturity of understanding to judge its consequences.

Courts assess the child's capacity on a case-by-case basis.

D. Act likely to cause harm done with criminal intent: Not exempted. The presence of criminal intent (mens rea) disqualifies any protection under IPC exemptions. Any act done with intent to cause harm is punishable.

Thus, only A, B, and C are exempt under IPC, making Option 1 correct.

Reference under Bharatiya Nyaya Sanhita (BNS), 2023: Though the question is based on IPC, it's important to note that the corresponding provisions in BNS, 2023, which replaced IPC, are as follows:

- **Section 14 BNS:** corresponds to Section 81 IPC (act without criminal intent to prevent other harm)
- **Section 28 BNS:** corresponds to Section 95 IPC (trivial harm)
- **Section 22 BNS:** corresponds to Section 83 IPC (child of immature understanding)

These sections retain the same legal principles, ensuring continuity of exemptions from criminal liability under the new criminal code.

11. (4): This option includes the statements about Fiction Theory, Concession Theory, Bracket Theory, and scholars supporting these concepts. Here is the validation of each:

A. Fiction theory says only human beings can be properly called persons – *(True):* Fiction theory, as propounded by Savigny and supported by Salmond and Dicey, states that legal personality of corporations is a legal fiction—only natural persons are real.

B. Concession theory states that corporate bodies have legal personality only if granted by law – *(True):* Under Concession theory, a corporation is seen as an artificial entity that exists only because the State grants it a legal personality. Hence, it is a concession from the State.

C. **Fiction theory is also called 'Organic Theory' – *(False):*** Organic Theory is a separate theory associated with Otto von Gierke. It views the corporation as a real, living entity with its own will and personality. It is not the same as Fiction theory.

D. **Symbolist or Brackets Theory says members of the corporations are only persons who have rights and duties – *(True):*** This theory, proposed by Ihering, holds that the corporate personality is a symbol, and only the members behind it actually have rights and duties.

E. **Savigny, Salmond and Dicey support Fiction Theory – *(True):*** These jurists are known proponents of the Fiction Theory, which treats corporate personality as a legal construct.

Hence, statements A, B, D, and E are correct.

12. (3): In the Oleum Gas Leak case – M.C. Mehta v. Union of India (1987) – the Supreme Court of India evolved a new principle of liability for hazardous industries:

- The Court ruled that enterprises engaged in hazardous or inherently dangerous activities owe an absolute and non-delegable duty to the community.

This means:

- **Absolute:** Liability is strict without exceptions (no defense like 'no negligence').
- **Non-delegable:** The duty cannot be transferred or delegated to any third party.

This was a significant evolution beyond the strict liability rule laid down in Rylands v. Fletcher, adapting it to Indian socio-economic conditions.

Hence, Option 3 (E only) is correct.

13. (3): Correct matching of the liability types with case laws is:

A. **Vicarious Liability – I. State Bank of India v. Shyama Devi:** This case dealt with the principle of holding the master (bank) liable for acts of its employee, representing vicarious liability.

B. **Absolute Liability – IV. M.C. Mehta v. Union of India:** As established in the Oleum Gas Leak case, this introduced the absolute liability doctrine in Indian law.

C. **Strict Liability – II. Rylands v. Fletcher:** This is the classic English case laying the principle of strict liability for use of hazardous materials.

D. **Vicarious Liability of the State – III. Peninsular and Oriental Steam Navigation Company v. Secretary of State for India:** This case addressed vicarious liability of the government, discussing liability of the State for tortious acts of its servants.

Hence, Option 3 is the correct match.

14. (4): The correct matching of offences with their corresponding punishments under the Indian Penal Code (IPC), 1860 is as follows:

A. **Gang Rape – I. Any fine imposed shall be paid to the victim:** Under Section 376D IPC, gang rape is an aggravated form of sexual assault involving multiple perpetrators. It specifically provides that any fine imposed shall be paid to the victim as part of the compensation mechanism. Thus, fine recovery is directed for the victim's benefit.

B. **Dacoity – IV. Imprisonment for life:** According to Section 395 IPC, dacoity — defined as robbery committed by five or more persons conjointly — is punishable with rigorous imprisonment for life, or with imprisonment up to ten years, and also fine.

C. **Kidnapping for Ransom – II. Punishable with death or imprisonment for life:** Under Section 364A IPC, kidnapping or abducting a person for ransom or coercion is an extremely grave offence, carrying punishment of death or imprisonment for life, along with fine. It was introduced especially to deal with terrorist activities and severe ransom cases.

D. **Dowry Death – III. Not less than 7 years but may extend to imprisonment for life:** As per Section 304B IPC, dowry death — when a woman dies under unnatural circumstances within seven years of marriage and it is shown that soon before her death she was subjected to cruelty or harassment in connection with dowry demands — is punishable with a minimum of 7 years imprisonment, extendable to life imprisonment.

Thus, Option 4 (A-I, B-IV, C-II, D-III) is correct.

Reference under Bharatiya Nyaya Sanhita (BNS), 2023: Though the question is asked as per IPC, the corresponding provisions in the Bharatiya Nyaya Sanhita (BNS), 2023 are:

A. **Gang Rape → Section 70 BNS:** Provides that any fine imposed shall be paid to the victim, similar to IPC's Section 376D.

B. **Dacoity → Section 309 BNS:** Punishable with life imprisonment or rigorous imprisonment and fine.

C. **Kidnapping for Ransom → Section 137 BNS:** Punishable with death or imprisonment for life, consistent with IPC Section 364A.

D. **Dowry Death → Section 80 BNS:** Punishable with minimum 7 years, extendable to life imprisonment, matching IPC Section 304B.

Thus, the punishments under BNS, 2023 remain substantially identical to those under the IPC, 1860 for these serious offences.

15. (4): The correct section-wise arrangement as per Chapter XVII (Offences Against Property) of the Indian Penal Code (IPC), 1860 is as follows:

D. **Dacoity with Murder – Section 396 IPC:** Section 396 deals with the aggravated offence of dacoity coupled with murder. If any one of the dacoits commits murder during the dacoity, every participant is deemed guilty of murder.

C. **Making preparation to commit dacoity – Section 399 IPC:** Section 399 criminalizes making preparation to commit dacoity. It punishes individuals found preparing with the intent to commit this grave crime, even before the actual act.

E. Assembling for the purpose of committing dacoity – Section 402 IPC: Section 402 penalizes assembling of five or more persons for the purpose of committing dacoity, whether or not the actual offence is committed.

B. Stolen Property – Sections 410 to 414 IPC: These sections define what constitutes stolen property and prescribe punishments for receiving, retaining, or disposing of stolen property, knowing it to be stolen.

A. Mischief – Sections 425 to 440 IPC: Mischief is defined under Section 425 as causing destruction or change to property with the intention to cause wrongful loss or damage, and the subsequent sections (up to Section 440) deal with various aggravated forms of mischief.

Thus, this is the correct chronological order based on the sequence of section numbers under Chapter XVII of IPC.

Therefore, Option 4 (D, C, E, B, A) is correct.

Reference under Bharatiya Nyaya Sanhita (BNS), 2023: Although the question pertains to IPC, under BNS, 2023, the corresponding sections and sequence are:

- Dacoity with Murder → Section 324 BNS
- Preparation to Commit Dacoity → Section 327 BNS
- Assembling for Dacoity → Section 330 BNS
- Stolen Property → Sections 338 to 342 BNS
- Mischief → Sections 350 to 365 BNS

Thus, under BNS, while the substance of offences remains similar, the section numbers have been rearranged, but the logical sequence (from dacoity-related offences to stolen property to mischief) has been maintained.

16. (1): The Indian Contract Act, 1872, lays down various provisions regarding void agreements. The correct chronological order as per their appearance in the Act is:

D. Agreement without consideration – Section 25: As per Section 25, an agreement made without consideration is void, except under specific circumstances like natural love and affection, voluntary services, etc.

A. Agreement in restraint of marriage – Section 26: Agreements that restrain the marriage of any person, other than a minor, are void.

C. Agreement in restraint of trade – Section 27: Agreements that restrain a person from exercising a lawful trade or profession are void, subject to reasonable exceptions like sale of goodwill.

B. Agreement in restraint of legal proceedings – Section 28: Agreements that restrict a party from enforcing their legal rights through usual legal proceedings are void.

E. Agreement which is ambiguous and uncertain – Section 29: If the terms of an agreement are not certain or capable of being made certain, the agreement is void.

Thus, the correct sequence as per sections is 25 → 26 → 27 → 28 → 29, which matches Option 1.

17. (3): The Hague Convention of 1899, in Declaration III, prohibits the use of expanding bullets, commonly known as dum-dum bullets.

- These bullets expand or flatten easily in the human body, causing excessive and unnecessary suffering, which violates the laws of war and humanitarian principles.
- The formal title is: "Declaration concerning the prohibition of the use of bullets which expand or flatten easily in the human body".
- Declaration III was signed by many nations during the First Hague Conference in 1899.

Hence, Option 3 is the correct answer.

18. (2): Analysis of the statements related to the form of government in the USA and India:

A. USA Constitution Sec. 7 gives President veto power over the bills passed by the Congress which can be further countered by 2/3 majority in both Houses – *(True):* Article I, Section 7 of the U.S. Constitution allows the President to veto a bill. However, Congress can override the veto with a two-thirds majority in both Houses.

C. The U.S. President is more powerful as compared to the Indian Prime Minister – *(True):* The U.S. President is both Head of the State and Government, with considerable executive power. In contrast, the Indian Prime Minister is the head of the government only, with a ceremonial President as Head of State.

E. U.S. President is not the member of legislature – *(True):* The U.S. follows a Presidential form of government with strict separation of powers, meaning the President is not part of the legislature.

B. U.S. and India strictly follow the doctrine of separation of powers – *(False):* While the U.S. strictly adheres to this doctrine, India follows it with flexibility, especially as the executive is part of the legislature in the parliamentary system.

D. Removal method of USA President and Indian Prime Minister is technical and difficult – *(False):* The U.S. President can be impeached, which is a complex process.

However, the Indian Prime Minister can be removed more easily via a no-confidence motion in Lok Sabha.

Thus, only A, C, and E are true – hence Option 2 is correct.

19. (4): Matching Acts with their penalty provisions:

A. Forest (Conservation) Act, 1980 – II. Section 3A and 3B: Sections 3A (Penalty for contravention) and 3B (Offences by authorities and government departments) deal with penalties under this Act.

B. Wild Life Protection Act, 1972 – IV. Section 51: Section 51 prescribes penalties for violating the provisions of the Act, such as poaching and illegal trade of wildlife.

C. The Environment (Protection) Act, 1986 – I. Section 15: Section 15 provides for penalties including imprisonment up to five years and/or fine up to ₹ 1,00,000 for contravention.

D. NGT Act, 2010 – III. Section 26: Section 26 lays down penalties for failure to comply with orders or awards of the National Green Tribunal.

Thus, the correct match is Option 4.

20. (1): Matching environmental events/treaties with correct years:

A. UN Conference on Environment and Development – II. 1992: Also known as the Rio Earth Summit, held in Rio de Janeiro, Brazil in 1992.

B. Kyoto Conference on Global Warming – III. 1997: The Kyoto Protocol was adopted in 1997 and set binding emission reduction targets for developed countries.

C. Paris Agreement – IV. 2015: Adopted under the UNFCCC in 2015, it aims to limit global warming to below 2°C, preferably 1.5°C.

D. Montreal Protocol – I. 1987: Signed in 1987 to phase out substances that deplete the ozone layer, particularly CFCs.

Hence, the correct match is Option 1.

21. (1): Under the Information Technology Act, 2000, the powers and status of Adjudicating Officers are clearly defined as follows:

A. Has the powers of Civil Court which are conferred on the Appellate Tribunal – *(True):* As per Section 46(5) of the IT Act, 2000, an Adjudicating Officer while holding an inquiry has all the powers of a civil court, such as summoning witnesses, receiving evidence on affidavits, requiring the discovery and production of documents, issuing commissions for examination of witnesses or documents, and other procedural powers, similar to those conferred on the Appellate Tribunal.

B. All proceedings before it deemed to be judicial proceedings under Sections 193 and 228 of IPC – *(True)*: Section 46(6) provides that proceedings before an Adjudicating Officer are deemed to be judicial proceedings within the meaning of Sections 193 (Punishment for false evidence) and 228 (Intentional insult or interruption to public servant sitting in judicial proceeding) of the Indian Penal Code (IPC), thereby ensuring the sanctity and seriousness of the proceedings.

C. Deemed to be a Civil Court for purpose of Order XXI of CPC, 1908 – *(True):* For the purpose of enforcement of orders (execution of decisions made by the Adjudicating Officer), the officer is deemed to be a civil court under Order XXI of the Code of Civil Procedure, 1908, which deals with the procedure for execution of decrees and orders.

D. Deemed to be a Civil Court for the purpose of Sections 340 and 341 of CrPC, 1973 – *(False):* The Adjudicating Officer is not deemed to be a civil court for initiating proceedings under Sections 340 (Procedure in cases regarding giving false evidence) and 341 (Appeal against orders passed under Section 340) of the Criminal Procedure Code (CrPC), 1973. Hence, they do not have the authority to initiate prosecution for perjury under these provisions.

Thus, only A, B, and C are correct, making Option 1 the correct choice.

Reference under Bharatiya Nyaya Sanhita (BNS), 2023: Though the question is asked under the IT Act, 2000, note that the Information Technology Act continues to remain in force even after the introduction of BNS, 2023. However, the referenced sections of IPC like Sections 193 and 228 IPC are now correspondingly placed in BNS as:

- Section 193 IPC → Section 227 BNS (False evidence)
- Section 228 IPC → Section 228 BNS (Intentional insult or interruption to public servant during judicial proceeding)

Hence, in modern application, proceedings before an Adjudicating Officer are deemed judicial under Sections 227 and 228 of BNS, maintaining the same legal sanctity as before.

22. (1): Matching the constitutional provisions and Articles:

A. Provision for early childhood care and education to children below the age of 6 years – III. Article 45: Article 45 (Directive Principles) mandates the State to provide early childhood care and education for all children below six years.

B. Promotion of educational and economic interests of SC, ST and other weaker sections – I. Article 46: Article 46 specifically focuses on uplifting Scheduled Castes, Scheduled Tribes and other weaker sections by promoting their education and economy.

C. State shall provide free and compulsory education to all children of the age of 6-14 years – II. Article 21A: Article 21A, inserted by the 86th Constitutional Amendment (2002), made education a Fundamental Right for children aged 6–14 years.

D. Special provision for the advancement of any economically weaker sections of citizens – IV. Article 15: Article 15(6) (introduced through 103rd Amendment Act, 2019) allows reservation in education and employment for EWS (Economically Weaker Sections).

Thus, correct matches are: A–III, B–I, C–II, D–IV, which is Option 1.

23. (1): Section 53 of the Indian Penal Code (IPC), 1860 lists the types of punishments that can be imposed under the Code. When arranged in descending order of severity, the correct chronological order is:

D. Death: The death penalty is the most severe punishment under IPC, awarded in the rarest of rare cases like murder under aggravating circumstances (Section 302 IPC), terrorism-related offences, etc.

C. **Imprisonment for Life:** Life imprisonment is the next most severe punishment after death. It generally means imprisonment for the remainder of the convict's natural life, and is awarded in serious crimes like murder, rape, kidnapping for ransom, and others.

B. **Forfeiture of Property:** This is a lesser punishment involving the confiscation of a person's assets or property by the State, usually imposed for crimes involving financial loss to the government or in cases like waging war against the State.

A. **Fine:** Fine is the least severe punishment and is often imposed either independently for minor offences (like public nuisance) or in addition to other forms of punishment.

Thus, the descending hierarchy of punishments in terms of their severity under Section 53 IPC is correctly D → C → B → A, making Option 1 correct.

Reference under Bharatiya Nyaya Sanhita (BNS), 2023: While the question refers to IPC, in the Bharatiya Nyaya Sanhita (BNS), 2023), Section 4 lists the kinds of punishments, and the sequence remains the same: • Death • Imprisonment for Life • Forfeiture of Property • Fine Thus, even under BNS, the descending order of severity matches that under the IPC, ensuring continuity of the legal structure.

24. **(2):** Matching legal maxims with meanings:

A. **Qui facit per alium facit per se – IV. The act of an agent is the act of the principal:** This maxim underlies the law of agency and vicarious liability, meaning a principal is liable for the lawful acts of their agent.

B. **Volenti non fit injuria – III. Voluntary consent to suffer some harm:** A person who consents to a risk cannot complain of injury later. Commonly used in sports or risky occupations.

C. **Damnum sine injuria – II. Damage without the violation of a legal right:** Even if actual loss occurs, no legal remedy is provided unless a legal right is infringed.

D. **Respondeat superior – I. Let the principal be liable:** This maxim directly refers to holding an employer (superior) liable for the acts of their employee.

Hence, the correct matches are in Option 2.

25. **(2):** Matching case laws with their legal themes:

A. **Birma v/s State of Rajasthan – II. Enforcement of rights under International Conventions:** This case addressed issues involving labour rights and international standards affecting marginalized communities.

B. **NHRC v/s State of Arunachal Pradesh – IV. Rights of refugee:** The Supreme Court protected Chakma refugees from being forcibly evicted, emphasizing human rights even for non-citizens.

C. **Vishaka v/s State of Rajasthan – I. Safeguard interest of working women:** A landmark judgment that issued guidelines to prevent sexual harassment at workplace, based on CEDAW (Convention on the Elimination of all Forms of Discrimination Against Women).

D. **People's Union for Democratic Rights v/s Union of India – III. Employment of children in construction work:** The case revealed labour law violations at Asiad construction sites, including child and bonded labour.

Thus, Option 2 gives the accurate matches.

26. **(1):** The Hague Conventions of 1907 consist of multiple conventions each dealing with distinct aspects of international law, especially concerning war and neutrality. The correct numerical order of the selected conventions as they appear is:

A. The Pacific Settlement of International Disputes – Convention I

B. The Limitation of Employment of Force for Recovery of Contract Debts – Convention II

C. The Opening of Hostilities – Convention III

D. The Laws and Customs of War on Land – Convention IV

E. The Rights and Duties of Neutral Powers and Persons in Case of War on Land – Convention V

Thus, their correct numerical arrangement as per Hague Convention titles is:

I → II → III → IV → V, which corresponds to: A, B, C, D, E.

Hence, Option 1 is correct.

27. **(3):** Statements C and D are not true descriptions of the nature of administrative law:

C. **Administrative law does not include control mechanism against arbitrariness – *(False):*** One of the primary functions of administrative law is to check arbitrary action by public officials through judicial review, principles of natural justice, and statutory remedies.

D. **Administrative law seldom addresses reconciliation of power with liberty – *(False):*** Administrative law plays a crucial role in balancing power and liberty by ensuring that public authorities act within their legal bounds and respect individual rights.

A and B are true:

A. It emphasizes procedures adopted to reach official decisions.

B. It governs the relationship between individuals and the administrative machinery of the State.

Thus, Option 3 is correct.

28. **(1):** The term "person interested" is explicitly defined under the Patents Act, 1970:

- Section 2(1)(t) of the Act defines "person interested" as including a person engaged in, or promoting, research in the same field as that to which the invention relates.

- This definition is crucial for the filing of opposition, revocation proceedings, or appeals in patent matters.

Other Acts mentioned:

- The Copyright Act, 1957 does not provide a formal definition of "person interested".
- The Designs Act, 2000 and Geographical Indications Act, 1999 also do not contain a similar definition.

Hence, the correct answer is Option 1.

29. (1): The following cases relate to the Restitution of Conjugal Rights under Section 9 of the Hindu Marriage Act, 1955:

A. T. Sareetha v. Venkatasubbaiah: The Andhra Pradesh High Court held that Section 9 is unconstitutional as it violates the right to privacy and human dignity.

B. Parkash v. Parmeshwari: A case involving a petition for restitution of conjugal rights, wherein the court discussed the grounds and defenses against such petitions.

C. Tirath v. Kripal Singh: Also pertains to restitution of conjugal rights, elaborating on burden of proof and factual issues in marital disputes.

D. Harvinder Kaur v. Harmander Singh: The Delhi High Court, in contrast to T. Sareetha, upheld the constitutionality of Section 9, leading to a judicial divergence.

E. Sureshtha Devi v. Om Prakash – Not related to restitution: This case dealt with consent in mutual divorce under Section 13B of the Hindu Marriage Act, not Section 9.

Thus, correct set is: A, B, C, D only, making Option 1 correct.

30. (4): Under the Copyright Act, 1957, Section 52 provides the concept of "fair dealing" which permits limited use of copyrighted material without the need for permission from the copyright holder in the following scenarios:

- Private or personal use, including research – Permitted
- Criticism or review – Permitted
- Reporting current events or current affairs – Permitted

Commercial use, however:

- Is not covered under the doctrine of fair dealing.
- If copyrighted work is used for profit-making or commercial exploitation, it constitutes infringement, unless specifically licensed.

Hence, Option 4: Commercial use is the correct answer as it is not a fair dealing.

31. (4): Part XXI of the Indian Constitution deals with Temporary, Transitional and Special Provisions (Articles 369 to 392). It includes special provisions for certain states to account for their unique historical, cultural, or political contexts.

- States like Nagaland (Art. 371A), Assam (Art. 371B), and Telangana (Art. 371D) are explicitly included in Part XXI.
- Haryana, however, is not included under Part XXI. It does not have any special constitutional provision under this part.

Therefore, the correct answer is Option 4: Haryana.

32. (4): To arrange the schools of thought chronologically, we consider the historical emergence of these thinkers and ideas:

D. Classical Greece and the Idea of Natural Law: This is the earliest school, with philosophers like Plato and Aristotle advocating for a higher moral law.

B. Thomas Hobbes and the origins of the imperative theory of law: Hobbes (1588–1679) proposed that law is the command of the sovereign, focusing on order and authority.

A. J. Bentham and the origins of utilitarian jurisprudence: Bentham (1748–1832) emphasized utility as the measure of law's goodness — the foundation of utilitarianism.

C. John Austin and legal positivism: A student of Bentham, Austin (1790–1859) formalized legal positivism, separating law from morality.

E. Lon Fuller and the Idea of Legalism: Fuller (1902–1978) critiqued legal positivism, advocating for an internal morality of law, where laws must meet standards of coherence and fairness.

Thus, the correct chronological order is:

D → B → A → C → E, which matches Option 4.

33. (1): The Marrakesh Treaty, officially titled "Marrakesh Treaty to Facilitate Access to Published Works for Persons Who Are Blind, Visually Impaired or Otherwise Print Disabled", was adopted in 2013 under the auspices of WIPO (World Intellectual Property Organization).

- Its objective is to remove copyright barriers by allowing the production and cross-border exchange of accessible format copies of copyrighted works.
- It is considered a landmark in combining intellectual property law with human rights.

Other treaties:

- **Beijing Treaty:** Concerns audio-visual performances.
- **Rome Treaty:** Relates to the protection of performers, producers of phonograms and broadcasting organizations.
- **Geneva Treaty:** Often refers to treaties on intellectual property but not for the visually impaired.

Therefore, the correct answer is Option 1: Marrakesh Treaty.

34. (3): India is a party to the Geneva Conventions of 1949, which are a set of four treaties and three protocols forming the core of international humanitarian law.

- India signed the Geneva Conventions on 16 December 1949.
- India ratified them on 9 November 1950.

These conventions lay down the standards of international law for humanitarian treatment in war, including protection of wounded soldiers, prisoners of war, and civilians.

Thus, the accurate historical timeline is provided in Option 3.

35. (3): Under the Biological Diversity Amendment Act, 2023, the term "biological resources" includes:

A. Plants and Animals

B. Microorganisms or parts of their genetic material

However, it excludes:

C. Human genetic material – This is explicitly excluded from the scope of "biological resources" as per the amendment.

Option D is inaccurate, because while derivatives and value-added products may be discussed in the Act, they are generally dealt with separately from the definition of biological resources and often regulated under different provisions (such as benefit sharing).

Hence, the accurate option is Option 3: A and B only.

36. (2): In the landmark case of Mohori Bibee v. Dharmodas Ghose (1903), the Privy Council held that an agreement entered into by a minor is void ab initio.

- In this case, a minor mortgaged his property in favour of a moneylender. Later, through his mother, he sued to declare the mortgage void on the ground of minority.
- The court ruled that a minor is incompetent to contract under Section 11 of the Indian Contract Act, 1872.
- Consequently, a contract with a minor has no legal effect and is absolutely void, not merely voidable.

Thus, the correct answer is Option 2.

37. (3): Correctly matching relief types in IPR suits with their concepts:

A. **Anton Piller Order – II. Right to search premises and seize evidence without prior warning:** This order is granted to prevent the destruction of infringing evidence, often in trademark and copyright disputes.

B. **Mareva Injunction – IV. Freezing of defendant's assets:** Prevents a defendant from disposing of assets before judgment, to ensure enforcement of potential future decrees.

C. **John Doe Order – I. Legal action against unknown parties:** Used when the identity of the infringer is unknown. Common in piracy and counterfeit cases.

D. **Dynamic Injunction – III. Injunction order against all mirror websites:** Grants relief against current and future rogue websites that replicate infringing content even if they arise after the order.

Hence, correct matching is Option 3.

38. (4): The functions of the National Commission for Minorities (NCM) are specified under Section 9 of the National Commission for Minorities Act, 1992.

Key functions under Section 9 include:

- Evaluating the progress of the development of minorities.
- Monitoring the working of safeguards provided in the Constitution and in laws.
- Making recommendations for the effective implementation of safeguards.
- Looking into specific complaints regarding deprivation of rights.

Hence, the correct answer is Option 4: D only.

39. (1): The word "Secular" was added to the Preamble of the Indian Constitution by the 42nd Amendment Act, 1976, during the Emergency period under Prime Minister Indira Gandhi.

- The words "Socialist", "Secular", and "Integrity" were inserted in the Preamble.
- "Secular" signifies that the State has no official religion and treats all religions equally under the Constitution.

Thus, Option 1 is the correct answer.

40. (4): Under the Consumer Protection Act, 1986, the following Consumer Dispute Redressal Agencies are established:

A. Consumer Disputes Redressal Forum (District level)

B. Consumer Disputes Redressal Commission (State level)

E. National Consumer Disputes Redressal Commission (NCDRC) (National level)

Other options like:

C. Consumer Disputes Redressal Committee – Not an official statutory body under the Act.

D. National Disputes Redressal Committee – Does not exist under this legislation.

Thus, correct answer is Option 4: A, B, E only.

41. (3): In the case of Badshah v. Sou. Urmila Badshah Godse (2013), the Supreme Court of India held that a woman who is deceived into a bigamous marriage is entitled to maintenance under Section 125 CrPC, even if the marriage is legally void.

- The husband had suppressed the fact of his first marriage and married the woman.
- The Court observed that the provision of maintenance under Section 125 CrPC is a measure of social justice, and it should be interpreted in a way that prevents destitution.
- The Court laid emphasis on purposive interpretation and held that the man cannot take advantage of his own wrong.

Therefore, the correct answer is Option 3.

42. (2): The word 'jurisprudence' is derived from the Latin term "jurisprudentia", which means the knowledge or science of law.

- The Latin root "juris" means law, and "prudentia" means knowledge or skill.
- This origin is traced to Roman civilization, which significantly contributed to the development of Western legal systems through Roman Law.
- Romans were the first to categorize and study law in a systematic manner, distinguishing between public and private law, civil and criminal law, etc.

Hence, Option 2: Romans is the correct answer.

43. (1): As per the Companies Act, 2013, the minimum number of directors in a One Person Company (OPC) is:

- One (1) – The same individual can be both the sole member and the director of the OPC.
- This provision is meant to simplify compliance and promote ease of doing business for small entrepreneurs.
- The relevant provision is found in Section 149(1) read with Rule 3 of Companies (Incorporation) Rules, 2014.

Therefore, the correct answer is Option 1 : 1.

44. (1): Chronological order of rules made under the Environment (Protection) Act, 1986 is:

E. The Manufacture, Storage and Import of Hazardous Chemical Rules – 1989

C. The Chemical Accidents (Emergency Planning, Preparedness and Response) Rules – 1996

D. The Batteries (Management and Handling) Rules – 2001

A. The Construction and Demolition Waste Management Rules – 2016

B. The Wetlands (Conservation and Management) Rules – 2017

These rules were framed under the powers conferred by Section 6, 8, and 25 of the Environment Protection Act, 1986 and aim to regulate pollution and protect ecological systems.

Thus, the correct chronological order is: E, C, D, A, B, which is Option 1.

45. (3): In Canada, the document that outlines the division of powers between Federal and Provincial governments is the:

- British North America Act, 1867, also known as the Constitution Act, 1867.
- This Act created a federal structure with a clear division of powers between the Federal Parliament (Section 91) and the Provincial Legislatures (Section 92).
- It is the foundational statute for Canada's Constitution and continues to operate, though renamed and modified after the Constitution Act, 1982.

Thus, the correct answer is Option 3.

46. (2): The definition — "Tortious liability arises from the breach of a duty primarily fixed by law: this duty is towards persons generally and its breach is redressible by an action for unliquidated damages" — is attributed to Sir Percy Henry Winfield, a renowned jurist.

- Winfield emphasized that torts are civil wrongs arising from legal duties, not from agreements or statutes.
- The phrase "unliquidated damages" refers to damages that are not pre-determined but are awarded by a court based on harm caused.
- This definition is widely accepted in modern tort law for its clarity in separating tort from breach of contract or breach of statutory duty.

Hence, the correct answer is Option 2: Winfield.

47. (1): Among the analyses provided about Sophocles' play Antigone, the only incorrect one is:

E. Antigone was excused by State on humani-tarian basis – *(False):* In the play, Antigone was not excused. She is sentenced to death by Creon for defying the King's decree and choosing to perform burial rites for her brother, an act rooted in divine/natural law.

Correct analyses include:

A. She supported natural law (duty to bury the dead) over positive law (King's edict).

B. Highlights conflict between family loyalty and state duty.

C. It is an early depiction of civil disobedience.

D. Reflects gendered tensions, showing female emotion/morality vs male authority.

Thus, only Option E is not true, making Option 1 the correct answer.

48. (4): The Nottebohm case (Liechtenstein v. Guatemala, ICJ, 1955) is a leading case in Public International Law related to the concept of nationality.

- Liechtenstein filed a case on behalf of Nottebohm, who had acquired its nationality shortly before WWII.
- The International Court of Justice (ICJ) ruled that for nationality to be effective internationally, it must reflect a genuine connection (real and effective link) between the person and the state.
- Guatemala was not obliged to recognize Nottebohm's Liechtenstein nationality as he had no substantial ties to Liechtenstein.

Thus, the case clarified the principle of effective nationality in international law.

Correct answer is Option 4: Nationality.

49. (2): Consequences of breach of contract under Indian Contract Law include:

A. Damages in ordinary course – *(True):* As per Section 73 of the Indian Contract Act, the aggrieved party is entitled to compensation for loss or damage naturally arising from the breach.

C. If stipulation by way of penalty is given in contract, then penalty is a consequence – *(True):* Under Section 74, when a contract specifies a sum to be paid on breach or penalty, the court may award reasonable compensation, not exceeding the amount mentioned.

D. In quantifying damages, the inconvenience of non-performance has to be considered – *(True):* The inconvenience, loss of opportunity, or other foreseeable effects of breach are taken into account to calculate compensation.

B. Remote damages and ordinary damages – Partially true but misleading as phrased. Remote damages are not recoverable, only those that arise naturally or were within the contemplation of the parties.

Therefore, the correct set is A, C, and D only, making Option 2 correct.

50. (2): Under the Dissolution of Muslim Marriages Act, 1939, the grounds for dissolution of marriage are enumerated in a certain order. The correct chronological arrangement as per the Act is:

A. Husband has failed to provide for her maintenance for 2 years – Clause (ii)

C. Husband was impotent at the time of marriage and continues to be so – Clause (iii)

B. Husband has been insane for a period of two years – Clause (iv)

E. Husband associates with women of evil repute – Clause (vii)

D. Husband attempts to force her to lead immoral life – Clause (viii)

This order follows the sequence of clauses in Section 2 of the Act. It lists both physical and social misconduct, giving a wife the legal right to seek dissolution.

Therefore, correct answer is Option 2: A, C, B, E, D.

51. (3): Under Article 38(1)(c) of the Statute of the International Court of Justice (ICJ), the ICJ is guided by the following sources for deciding disputes:

- International conventions (treaties)
- International custom
- The general principles of law recognized by civilized nations
- Judicial decisions and scholarly writings (as subsidiary means)

The phrase "general principles of law recognized by civilized nations" refers to basic legal doctrines common across major legal systems, such as principles of good faith, estoppel, equity, etc. These principles serve as gap-fillers when treaties or custom are silent.

Therefore, the correct answer is Option 3.

52. (4): In Muslim Law, Dower (mahr) is the amount payable by the husband to the wife in consideration of marriage and is categorized as follows:

- **Prompt Dower** – Payable immediately after marriage or upon demand.
- **Deferred Dower** – Payable on dissolution of marriage by death or divorce.
- **Dower stipulated in marriage contract** – Specifically agreed upon amount at the time of marriage.

However, Proper Dower (Mahr-i-Misl) refers to the amount of dower fixed based on social status and customs in absence of prior agreement. It is not a part of Specified Dower, as it is determined later by courts or elders, not contractually fixed.

Thus, the correct answer is Option 4: Proper Dower.

53. (1): The Latin legal maxim "Ex turpi causa non oritur actio" means:

- "From an immoral cause, no legal action arises".
- It signifies that a plaintiff cannot pursue legal remedy if the cause of action is founded on immoral or illegal acts.
- This is based on the public policy doctrine, ensuring courts do not support illegality or unethical conduct.

Example: If a person seeks to recover money lent for an illegal transaction (e.g., smuggling), courts will not entertain the claim.

Hence, Correct answer is Option 1.

54. (1): Correct matching of provisions under the Negotiable Instruments Act, 1881 is:

A. **Dishonour of cheque for insufficiency of funds – III. Section 138:** Section 138 deals with criminal liability for dishonour of cheques due to insufficient funds or exceeding the arrangement.

B. **Holder in due course – I. Section 9:** Defined under Section 9 as someone who obtains the instrument for consideration, before maturity, in good faith.

C. **Promissory Note – IV. Section 4:** Section 4 defines a promissory note as a written promise to pay a certain sum of money to a specific person or bearer.

D. **Bill of Exchange – II. Section 5:** Section 5 defines a bill of exchange as an instrument in writing directing a person to pay a certain amount to another.

Hence, correct answer is Option 1.

55. (1): Matching Geneva Conventions with corresponding Articles on State Responsibility:

A. **Geneva Convention I – I. Articles 49–54:** These articles relate to enforcement and penal sanctions regarding the wounded and sick in armed forces on land.

B. **Geneva Convention II – II. Articles 50–53:** Similar to Convention I, applies to wounded and shipwrecked members of armed forces at sea.

C. **Geneva Convention III – III. Articles 129–132:** These concern treatment of prisoners of war and responsibilities of states to enforce compliance.

D. **Geneva Convention IV – IV. Articles 146–149:** These are about protection of civilians and include grave breaches and prosecution obligations.

All four Conventions impose individual and State responsibility for ensuring compliance and prosecuting grave breaches.

Thus, the correct answer is Option 1.

56. (3): Schedule II of the National Green Tribunal Act, 2010 deals with the "Heads under which compensation or relief for damage to persons and property may be claimed".

It provides a structured list for assessing compensation for environmental harm, including:

- Death or injury to any person
- Loss or damage to property
- Expenses for medical treatment
- Damage to biodiversity or eco-systems

This ensures uniformity in determining relief under environmental liability cases.

Hence, the correct answer is Option 3.

57. (3): Under Article 327 of the Indian Constitution, the Parliament has the power to make provisions regarding:

- Preparation of electoral rolls
- Delimitation of constituencies
- All other matters related to elections to State Legislatures and Parliament

Though the Election Commission of India conducts elections, the legal framework for these elections is provided by law made by Parliament, not by the Commission or the President.

Therefore, the correct answer is Option 3.

58. (2): Article 2 of the United Nations Charter lays down the core principles on which the United Nations is based:

- Sovereign equality of all members
- Obligation to settle disputes peacefully
- Refrain from use of force against territorial integrity or political independence
- Non-intervention in domestic affairs
- Cooperation in maintaining international peace and security

Article 1 outlines purposes; Article 2 contains the binding principles governing conduct of member states.

Thus, the correct answer is Option 2.

59. (4): Section 18(2) of the Hindu Adoption and Maintenance Act, 1956 lists the grounds in the following order:

A. If he is guilty of desertion – Clause (a)

B. If he has any other wife living – Clause (b)

D. If he keeps a concubine in the same house or habitually resides with a concubine elsewhere – Clause (c)

C. If he has ceased to be a Hindu – Clause (d)

E. Any other justifiable cause – Clause (g)

So the correct chronological order as per the Act is: A → B → D → C → E

Thus, the correct answer is Option 4,.

60. (2):

A. National Judicial Appointment Commission → Article 124A: Article 124A was inserted by the 99th Constitutional Amendment Act, 2014 to create NJAC (now struck down).

B. Appointment of Acting Chief Justice → Article 126: Provides for appointment of Acting Chief Justice by the President.

C. Supreme Court to be a Court of Record → Article 129: Declares the SC as a court of record with power to punish for contempt.

D. Original Jurisdiction of Supreme Court → Article 131: SC's original jurisdiction in disputes between Centre and States or between States.

Thus, correct matches are:

A–III, B–I, C–IV, D–II, which is Option 2.

61. (1): The provisions related to the Governor and Executive Power of the State are arranged in the following correct constitutional order:

E. Governor of State – Article 153

A. Executive Power of State – Article 154

C. Appointment of Governor – Article 155

B. Term of Office of Governor – Article 156

D. Qualifications for Appointment as Governor – Article 157

This sequence reflects how the Constitution introduces the position, then explains powers, followed by appointment, tenure, and eligibility.

Hence, the correct order is Option 1: E, A, C, B, D.

62. (1): Article 1 of the UN Charter outlines the Purposes of the United Nations, with specific clauses:

A. Article 1.1 – III. To maintain peace and security

B. Article 1.2 – I. To develop friendly relations among nations

C. Article 1.3 – II. To achieve international cooperation in solving international problems

D. Article 1.4 – IV. To be a centre for harmonising the actions of nations in the attainment of common ends

These four sub-articles lay the foundation of the UN's objectives in global governance and diplomacy. Correct match is Option 1.

63. (4): The principle laid down in Rylands v. Fletcher (1868) established strict liability in tort law, with these essential elements:

A. Some dangerous thing must have been brought by a person on his land – *(True)*

D. The thing brought or kept by a person on his land must escape – *(True)*

E. It must be non-natural use of land – *(True)*

The thing must escape and cause damage, and it must be associated with non-natural use, like storage of chemicals or water tanks.

Statements B and C are incorrect:

B. The thing must escape, not remain confined.

C. It must be non-natural, not "must not be".

Thus, correct answer is Option 4.

64. (1): Matching legal doctrines with case laws:

A. Lifting the corporate veil – IV. Salomon v. Salomon: Landmark case where the court established the separate legal entity of a corporation but also opened the possibility of "lifting the veil".

B. Invitation to public in the context of prospectus – I. Nash v. Lynde: Clarified distinction between invitation to treat and offer in company prospectus.

C. Doctrine of ultra vires – II. Ashbury Railway Carriage and Iron Co. v. Riche: A company's actions beyond its objects clause are void.

D. Doctrine of indoor management – III. Royal British Bank v. Turquand: Protects outsiders dealing with companies acting in good faith, assuming internal procedures are complied with.

Hence, correct match is Option 1.

65. (4): John Austin, a legal positivist, made a clear distinction between law and morality: He believed that law is the command of the sovereign backed by sanction, and morality is irrelevant to the validity of law.

Hence, C. Command, Duty, Sanction and Morality are inseparable – is incorrect.

Austin held that these are separate, and morality is not legally binding.

Correct statements:

A. Positive laws are commands of the sovereign.

B. Laws by analogy are laws improperly so called.

D. Laws are of two types: properly and improperly so called.

E. Austin excludes positive morality from jurisprudence.

Therefore, only Option C is incorrect, making Option 4 the correct answer.

66. (3): Justice Dalveer Bhandari is currently (as of January 2025) serving as a Judge of the International Court of Justice (ICJ). He was first elected to the ICJ in 2012 and was re-elected in 2017 for a term of nine years, which continues until 2026. He is an eminent Indian jurist and has previously served as a Judge in the Supreme Court of India. None of the other individuals listed—D. Y. Chandrachud (current Chief Justice of India), Ruchira Kamboj (India's Permanent Representative to the UN), and Harish Salve (senior advocate and legal counsel)—hold a judicial position at the ICJ.

67. (2): Matching the statutes to their respective years of establishment:

A. Statute of the International Criminal Tribunal for the former Yugoslavia (ICTY) – IV. 1993: Adopted by the UN Security Council Resolution 827 in 1993 to prosecute serious crimes committed during the Yugoslavia Wars.

B. Statute of the International Criminal Tribunal for Rwanda (ICTR) – III. 1994: Established by UN Security Council Resolution 955 to address crimes related to the 1994 Rwandan genocide.

C. Statute of the International Criminal Court (ICC) – I. 1998: Adopted in Rome and known as the Rome Statute, this treaty created the ICC. It came into force in 2002, but the statute itself was adopted in 1998.

D. Statute of the Special Court for Sierra Leone – II. 2002: A hybrid tribunal established through an agreement between the Government of Sierra Leone and the United Nations to prosecute those most responsible for crimes during the Sierra Leone Civil War.

68. (4): According to the Biological Diversity (Amendment) Act, 2023, "Codified Traditional Knowledge" refers to knowledge derived from authoritative books specified in the First Schedule to the Drugs and Cosmetics Act, 1940.

- This includes systems such as Ayurveda, Siddha, and Unani, which are documented in classical texts.
- The amendment aims to ensure that traditional knowledge already codified and publicly available is excluded from benefit-sharing obligations under access and benefit-sharing (ABS) provisions.
- This facilitates easier access to such knowledge for research and commercial utilization while respecting indigenous practices.

69. (3): The case of Vardhaman Kaushik v. Union of India (2014-15) was significant for the manner in which the National Green Tribunal (NGT) addressed the severe air pollution crisis in Delhi.

- The NGT took a "pragmatic, consultative, and deliberated" approach, meaning it involved multiple stakeholders including government agencies, experts, and civil society.
- It led to substantial policy changes including the ban on diesel vehicles older than 10 years, implementation of odd-even vehicle schemes, and measures to control crop burning and industrial pollution.
- The NGT did not reject the petition on grounds of locus standi or jurisdiction, nor did it permit crop burning.
- This judgment became a precedent in dealing with environmental pollution using participatory and evidence-based legal mechanisms.

70. (1): The chronological order of adoption of the conventions/ agreements is:

C. Convention Relating to the Status of Refugees – 1951: Known as the 1951 Refugee Convention, it defines who is a refugee and outlines the rights of displaced people.

A. Additional Protocols to the Geneva Conventions – 1977: Two protocols were added in 1977 to the Geneva Conventions of 1949, expanding protections for victims of international and non-international armed conflicts.

B. International Convention on the Protection of the Rights of All Migrant Workers and Members of Their Families – 1990: Adopted in 1990 and entered into force in 2003, this is the most comprehensive UN instrument on migrant workers' rights.

D. Agreement Establishing the World Trade Organization (WTO) – 1994: Signed in 1994 during the Uruguay Round negotiations and came into force in 1995, this agreement established the WTO, replacing the GATT framework.

Thus, the chronological order is: C (1951), A (1977), B (1990), D (1994).

71. (1):

B. There have been 9 rounds of trade negotiation since the Second World War: *Correct*. These rounds include Geneva (1947), Annecy (1949), Torquay (1950-51), Geneva (1956), Dillon Round (1960-62), Kennedy Round (1964-67), Tokyo Round (1973-79), Uruguay Round (1986-94), and Doha Round (2001 onwards).

C. Doha Round is the latest round of negotiation for WTO members: *Correct*. The Doha Development Round was launched in 2001 and is still ongoing without a successful conclusion.

A. WTO is headquartered in Hague: *Incorrect*. The WTO is headquartered in Geneva, Switzerland, not in The Hague.

D. WTO has 154 members: *Incorrect*. As of 2024, the WTO has 164 members, not 154.

72. (1): To determine irrationality of administrative action:

- The Wednesbury Test originates from the UK case Associated Provincial Picture Houses Ltd v Wednesbury Corporation (1948).
- It is applied to judge the irrationality or unreasonableness of administrative decisions.
- According to the test, a decision is unreasonable if it is "so unreasonable that no reasonable authority could ever have come to it".
- This test forms one of the grounds of judicial review in administrative law alongside illegality and procedural impropriety.

73. (2): According to Section 5(1) of The National Green Tribunal Act, 2010, the Chairperson of the National Green Tribunal (NGT) shall be appointed by the Central Government in consultation with the Chief Justice of India.

The Chairperson is usually a retired Judge of the Supreme Court or Chief Justice of a High Court with proven green jurisprudence expertise.

This ensures judicial independence and adds credibility to the functioning of the NGT.

74. (2): Article 3 of the European Convention on Human Rights (ECHR) states that "No one shall be subjected to torture or to inhuman or degrading treatment or punishment".

Article 4 of the EU Charter of Fundamental Rights similarly provides that "No one shall be subjected to torture or to inhuman or degrading treatment or punishment".

Therefore, Article 4 of the EU Charter corresponds to Article 3 of the ECHR in protecting individuals (including refugees) from torture and inhuman treatment.

75. (1): In the Lieber Code (General Orders No. 100 issued in 1863), the sections appear in the following order:

A. Martial Law: Discussed early, setting the framework for military governance during conflict.

B. Public and Private property of the enemy: Covered under rules concerning the treatment of enemy property.

C. Deserters: Rules for dealing with soldiers who abandon their posts.

D. Partisans: Guidelines on the treatment of irregular fighters or guerrilla forces.

E. Spies: Dealing with individuals who secretly obtain information to harm military operations.

Thus, the correct sequence is A, B, C, D, E following the structure of the Lieber Code.

Thus, the proper sequence based on the structure of the Lieber Code, including section references, is: A (Martial Law – Articles 1-30), B (Public and Private Property of the Enemy – Articles 31-47), C (Deserters – Articles 48–52), D (Partisans – Articles 81–82), E (Spies – Articles 83–85).

76. (4):

A. Section 50A of the Indian Copyright Act: This deals with the protection of copyright societies and their registration, not with internet/cyber/computer crime directly.

E. Section 11A of the Patent Act: This section concerns the publication of patent applications after 18 months from the date of filing and has no relation to cybercrime or internet offenses.

B. Section 354D of IPC: Relates to the offense of stalking, including cyberstalking, hence associated with internet crime.

C. Section 111 of Bharatiya Nyaya Sanhita: Related to cybercrime offenses under the new law (Bharatiya Nyaya Sanhita replacing IPC).

D. Section 66F of the Information Technology Act: Deals specifically with cyber terrorism, clearly a cybercrime provision.

Thus, only A (Section 50A of Indian Copyright Act) and E (Section 11A of Patent Act) do not deal with internet/cyber/computer crimes.

77. (1): Rural Litigation and Entitlement Kendra, Dehradun v. State of Uttar Pradesh is considered the first environmental case of its kind in India. The case involved limestone quarrying in the Mussoorie hills leading to environmental degradation. The Supreme Court emphasized the necessity to balance development and conservation for sustainable growth. This case, often referred to as the "Dehradun Valley Litigation", initiated judicial recognition of the right to a healthy environment under Article 21 of the Constitution. It led to the closure of mining activities in the fragile ecological zone to protect the environment.

78. (1): In contract law, acceptance of an offer is a fundamental step leading to the formation of a legally binding contract. Without acceptance, an offer remains a mere proposal and does not create any legal obligation. Once the offer is accepted, mutual assent is established, and the contract becomes enforceable. This principle is codified in Section 2(b) of the Indian Contract Act, 1872, which states that an agreement becomes a promise when the proposal is accepted.

79. **(2):** Chronological order based on dates of decisions/ advisory opinions:

E. Voting Procedure on Questions Relating to Reports and Petitions Concerning the Territory of South-West Africa (1955): First advisory opinion dealing with procedural matters in South-West Africa.

A. Legal Consequences of the Continued Presence of South Africa in Namibia (1971): Advisory opinion regarding South Africa's illegal presence in Namibia after a Security Council resolution.

C. Fisheries Jurisdiction (United Kingdom v. Iceland) (1974): Dealt with the jurisdictional disputes over maritime fisheries.

D. Western Sahara Case (1975): Advisory opinion on the legal status of Western Sahara and the principle of self-determination.

B. Texaco Overseas Petroleum Co. v. Government of the Libyan Arab Republic (1977): A case involving international investment arbitration following Libya's nationalization of oil concessions.

Thus, the correct chronological order is E, A, C, D, B.

80. **(3):** Servitudes are a type of legal right that allows a person to use another's land for a specific purpose without possessing it. This right may include access rights, such as rights of way or rights to use water from a neighbor's land. Servitudes do not confer possession of the land itself but grant a limited use right over the property. Common examples include easements (like the right to pass through someone's land) and profit à prendre (right to extract resources).

Therefore, servitudes represent an encumbrance allowing limited use without transfer of ownership or possession.

81. **(4):** The official languages of the International Court of Justice (ICJ) are French and English. This is provided under Article 39 of the Statute of the ICJ, which states that proceedings shall be conducted in either English or French. Parties may use either language, and the Court itself delivers judgments and orders in both languages. The use of both languages reflects the historical and diplomatic significance of French and English as languages of international law.

82. **(4):**

A. Personhood Theory - III. Immanuel Kant: Kant's philosophy views intellectual property as an extension of personal autonomy and moral rights, forming the basis of the Personhood Theory.

B. Natural Right Theory - I. John Locke: Locke's labor theory argues that people have a natural right to the fruits of their labor, including creations of the mind, supporting the Natural Rights Theory.

C. Incentive Theory - IV. William Nordhaus: Nordhaus proposed that intellectual property rights serve as an incentive for innovation by rewarding creators, central to the Incentive Theory.

D. Creative Destruction Theory - II. Joseph Schumpeter: Schumpeter introduced the concept of "creative destruction", where innovation disrupts existing industries, emphasizing the role of innovation in economic progress and supporting the Creative Destruction Theory.

83. **(2):** The Trade Marks Act, 1999 outlines the registration process in the following correct sequence:

D. Absolute Grounds (Section 9): First, the application is tested against absolute grounds of refusal, which check whether the trademark is inherently registrable (e.g., not descriptive or generic).

A. Relative Grounds (Section 11): Next, it is tested against relative grounds, where conflict with existing trademarks is examined.

E. Honest Concurrent Use (Section 12): Then, cases of honest concurrent use may be considered, allowing similar marks to coexist under certain conditions.

B. Withdrawal of Acceptance (Section 19): After preliminary acceptance, the Registrar can withdraw acceptance under certain grounds.

C. Opposition to Registration (Section 21): Finally, after advertisement, third parties have an opportunity to oppose the registration.

84. **(2):** The Fundamental Duties under Article 51A of the Indian Constitution are listed in a specific sequence. The correct order for the duties mentioned is:

B. To cherish and follow the noble ideals which inspired our national struggle for freedom: Listed first under Clause (b).

E. To uphold and protect the sovereignty, unity and integrity of India: Listed next under Clause (c).

A. To value and preserve the rich heritage of our composite culture: Listed under Clause (f).

D. To develop the scientific temper, humanism and spirit of inquiry and reform: Listed under Clause (h).

C. To safeguard public property and to abjure violence: Listed under Clause (i).

Thus, the sequence is B, E, A, D, C matching exactly as laid down in the Constitution.

85. **(3):** The Consumer Protection Act, 1986 has been repealed and replaced by the Consumer Protection Act, 2019. The new Act came into effect on 20th July 2020, introducing significant reforms to better address modern consumer issues. It established new mechanisms such as the Central Consumer Protection Authority (CCPA), introduced the concept of product liability, e-commerce regulation, and facilitated faster grievance redressal through e-filing and mediation centers.

Thus, the governing law now is the Consumer Protection Act, 2019.

86. **(4):** The jurisdiction of the International Court of Justice (ICJ) is fundamentally based on the principle of consent of the states involved. According to Article 36 of the Statute of the ICJ, the Court can only exercise jurisdiction if the parties to a dispute have consented to it. This consent can be given through treaties, special agreements, or optional clause declarations under Article 36(2).

Thus, states are not automatically bound to ICJ jurisdiction unless they have explicitly agreed to it, embodying the principle of consensual basis rather than compulsory participation.

87. (3): Section 16 of the Sale of Goods Act, 1930 deals with "Implied conditions as to quality or fitness" of goods sold. It states that generally, there is no implied warranty or condition as to the quality or fitness of goods for any particular purpose, except:

- Where the buyer makes known to the seller the particular purpose for which goods are required, and relies on the seller's skill or judgment.
- Where goods are bought by description from a seller who deals in goods of that description.

This protects consumers by implying a condition of fitness when reliance and seller's specialization are evident.

88. (4): Under Sunni Law, certain marriages are classified as fasid (irregular) marriages, which can be regularized upon removal of the irregularity.

Grounds for fasid marriages include:

- Marriage with a fifth wife (when already having four wives).
- Unlawful conjugation (marrying two women who are closely related to each other such as sisters).
- Marriage with a woman undergoing iddat (waiting period after divorce or death of husband).

However, marriage in violation of conditions of fosterage (milk relationship) is treated as batil (void) marriage, not fasid.

In Sunni law, marriage between foster siblings is void ab initio, hence not merely irregular.

89. (4): To constitute 'marz-ul-maut' (death-bed illness) under Islamic law, the following conditions must be satisfied:

A. The malady or illness must result in the death: It must be a serious illness leading to the donor's death.

B. The illness must cause reasonable apprehension of death in the mind of the donor: The donor must fear death due to the illness.

C. There should be some external indicia of a serious illness: Observable signs such as medical symptoms that indicate grave illness.

E. Delivery of possession must be given to the donee: The possession must be handed over to complete a valid gift in marz-ul-maut.

D. There must be an apprehension of death in the mind of physician is not a necessary condition; it is the apprehension in the mind of the donor that is relevant.

90. (1): The Estrada Doctrine, formulated in Mexico in 1930, asserts that once a state has been recognized, its government does not require fresh recognition each time there is a change in leadership. Recognition of governments is viewed as an unnecessary interference in the internal affairs of a sovereign state. Instead, states simply maintain or withdraw diplomatic relations based on factual effectiveness rather than granting or denying recognition to new governments.

Thus, the essence of the Estrada Doctrine is that recognition of government is unnecessary once the state itself has been recognized.

91. (3): Article 10(1) of the Agreement on Trade-Related Aspects of Intellectual Property Rights (TRIPS) provides that computer programmes shall be protected as literary works under the Berne Convention. This means that computer programmes, though technical in nature, are protected under the same legal framework as literary works such as books or writings. The passage also clearly mentions that "Article 10(1) of TRIPS provides copyright protection to computer programmes", thus confirming this provision as the basis of legal protection.

92. (4): Copyright can subsist in a computer programme, provided it shows originality and sufficient intellectual effort. As per the passage: "Copyright subsists in a computer programme provided sufficient effort or skill has been expended to give it a new and original character". It emphasizes that originality is key. This means not all software is protected by default; it must reflect a degree of creativity or intellectual input, however minimal.

93. (3): The passage states that if a computer programme merely produces multiplication tables, it cannot claim copyright protection, as the amount of effort or originality is too trivial. Therefore, mere mechanical or routine outputs like generating basic tables or alphabets lack the threshold of originality required under copyright law. The law protects creative expression, not simple outputs derived from elementary logic or universal knowledge.

94. (3): The passage clearly states: "Copyright subsists in original works that are capable of being reproduced from a fixed medium".

This means two requirements must be fulfilled:

- The work must be original, reflecting some intellectual creativity or skill.
- It must be fixed in a tangible form that allows it to be reproduced (like writing, digital recording, etc.).

This is consistent with international standards for copyright protection, where both originality and fixation are required.

95. (1): According to the passage, software is considered a literary work under copyright laws in various jurisdictions. This is reaffirmed by TRIPS Article 10(1), which categorizes computer programmes as literary works, not because they are artistic, but because they are expressed in code or script—a form of written language.

Hence, software enjoys the same protection as a book or novel, although it functions very differently. The key is that it is a fixed expression of an idea, which is protectable under copyright.

96. **(1):** Article 32 empowers the Supreme Court to issue writs for the enforcement of fundamental rights, acting as a protector of citizen's rights against the excesses of administrative and governmental agencies.

Article 226 similarly empowers the High Courts to issue writs not only for the enforcement of fundamental rights but also for any other purpose, thus providing broader supervisory control over administrative actions.

The passage clearly states that Articles 32 and 226 allow the judiciary to issue writs like certiorari, mandamus, prohibition, quo warranto, and habeas corpus to control administrative excesses.

97. **(3):** Article 227 of the Constitution confers on the High Courts the power of superintendence over all courts and tribunals within their territorial jurisdiction. This power ensures that tribunals and subordinate courts function properly and legally and that administrative tribunals are kept under a legal framework.

The passage clearly mentions that High Courts are vested with superintendence powers, making High Court the correct authority.

98. **(3):** The passage explains that besides providing a mechanism for judicial control, the Constitution also aimed at establishing a functional government, which was essential for ensuring administrative efficiency and national development.

Growth of the administrative process was a natural outcome of having a functional government structure where different authorities performed specialized roles.

Hence, the correct reason for the growth of the administrative process is that the Constitution provided for a functional government.

99. **(2):** The control mechanism under the Constitution is designed to ensure that administrative and governmental authorities do not misuse their powers. By providing powers to courts under Articles 32, 226, 227, and 136, and protections under Article 311 and remedies under Article 300, the Constitution aims to check arbitrary, unreasonable, or excessive actions by administrative agencies.

Thus, the relevance of the control mechanism is specifically to check the excess of administrative actions, not to allow unfettered authority.

100. **(4):** Article 13 of the Constitution defines "law" broadly to include orders, byelaws, rules, regulations, notifications, and even administrative actions that have the force of law. This wide definition ensures that all legislative actions of the administration are subject to constitutional scrutiny and can be declared void if they are inconsistent with fundamental rights.

The passage also clearly mentions that by defining law broadly, all legislative actions of the administration were brought under the purview of Article 13.

UGC NET/JRF LAW

PAPER-2

UNIT 1 Jurisprudence

NATURE AND SOURCES OF LAW

Law defines the political organization and structure of society, and provides a scheme of individual relationship within it and contributes to the stability of society by offering an objective mechanism for the resolution of disputes and conflicts within the community. All extensive human societies possess law in some form or other. Legal system is the totality of the laws of a state or community.

Broadly speaking, Law is a notional pattern of conduct to which actions do or ought to conform. However, there is no simple definition of law. Every person defines law according to his own perception of it. Further, law being a social science, it grows and develops with the society. The concept of law depends largely on the social values, accepted norms and behavioural patterns of a particular society at a given time.

There are many, who would like to achieve an object through the instrumentality of law and therefore they would like to define law in terms of its purpose. Others might define law in terms of what it does in the form of actual court decisions. Law has been defined from different approaches like:

- Its basis in reason, religion, or ethics;
- By its source in custom, precedent or legislation;
- By its effects on the life of society;
- By the method of its formal expression or authoritative application, and;
- By the end that it seeks to achieve.

Thus, fail to provide an authoritative definition of law can be ascribed to the fact that practical application of law does not depend on definition of law.

Julius Stone attempted a definition of law, he finds that the various definitions of law converge based on the following seven steps:

- Law is complex whole of many phenomena. The meaning of this whole can only be elaborated and not defined.
- These phenomena includes norms regulating human behaviour *i.e.*, prescribing what the behaviour ought to be, forbidding what it ought not to be.
- The norms are social norms *i.e.*, they generally regulate behaviour of a member of a society vis-à-vis others.
- These social norms are systematically arranged; it is in a short legal order.
- Law consists of social norms which are coercive *i.e.*, authority of law is supported by acts of external compulsions such as deprivation of life, liberty or property.
- The coercion operates according to established norms.
- This institutionalized coercive order should be effective *i.e.*, people must by and large obey the law.

SOURCES OF LAW

A source of law means either the manufacture or origin of a law or the ability to impart a rule or norm as the quality of law. The term source is used to connote those agencies by which rules of conduct acquire the character of law by becoming objectively denied, uniform, and, compulsory.

Austin's three meanings of sources of law include: (i) Direct authority, (ii) Historical documents, and (iii) Causes— which give the rules of society, the force of law viz., legislation, custom, etc. According to the sociological school, there is no specific authority which has a power to make law but it takes its shape as the society evolves.

Salmond classified the sources of law into two categories:

- Formal Sources: These are those which are recognized as such by the law itself and are authoritative. From these sources, a rule of law derives its force and validity. Thus, the will of the state as manifested in the constitution, statutes, court's decision are the formal sources of law.
- Material Sources: From these sources, a rule of law derives the matter but not the validity. The material sources are further divided into two types: Legal and Historical. Unlike legal sources which are sources not only in fact but also in law and are authoritative, the historical sources are sources in fact only and are unauthoritative. The decision of the court is a legal source while the ultimate materials on which it is based are historical sources.

Legal sources operate directly and immediately, while historical sources operate indirectly and mediate. Examples of legal sources are: Legislation and precedent, customs and conventional laws. Examples of historical sources are: legal writings, juristic opinions, foreign judgments, constitutions, etc. Salmond further pointed out that historical sources pertain to legal history and not to legal theory.

Sources of the law differ from system to system and society to society. Thus, while in common law system, constitution, legislation, precedents and customs are recognized as the legal sources of law, in civil law countries, legislation, customary law and treaties are often declared to be the only sources of law. Constitution, legislation, precedents and customs are legal sources of law. In some matters, personal law is also a source of law.

CUSTOMS

A custom necessarily involves two conceptions, namely, (i) The conviction or faith, and (ii) Constant use. It is presumed that customs must have been followed on account of their utility and also because they enjoyed the express or implied sanction of the society. Custom played a considerable role in the evolution of early law. It provided material for other law constituting agencies, especially legislation. Psychologically, it is easier to secure obedience for code if it is based on an established custom. It is too great an effort to create law *de novo*.

KINDS OF CUSTOMS

A custom may not necessarily be practiced all over the country. Further, the Privy Council and the courts in India have accepted the principle that a clear proof of usage would override the written text of laws. Thus, a custom may be either (1) conventional or (2) a legal custom.

- **Conventional Customs:** It is also called 'usage' viz., certain trade practices. Its authority is conditional on its acceptance and incorporation in the agreement between the parties bound by it. A conventional custom should be reasonable and be consistent with the statue law; a usage which is contrary to any express condition laid down in a contract shall not be enforceable by law.

  Before becoming a part of the law, such customs pass through three stages: (i) They should be proved before the court as a question of fact, (ii) The court takes judicial notice of them and they are established as a precedent, and (iii) The custom is embodied in a statue and takes its final shape.

  A conventional custom may either be 'local' or 'national/general'. Local conventional customs are limited to a particular place or market or to a particular trade or transaction. It may be noted that unlike usage, a custom is binding irrespective of the consent of the parties to be bound thereby. Further, a usage, unlike custom, need not be of immemorial antiquity.
- **Legal Customs:** Legal customs are those which are operative *per se* as binding rules of law independent of any agreement between the parties. Legal customs are of two kinds: (i) Local/Special custom, and (ii) General custom.

  When the word 'Custom' is used as simplicity it refers to a local custom. A local custom can derogate from the general or common law of the realm, but not from statute law. A local custom in India is further divided into (a) geographical local, and (b) personal local. Sometimes, certain sects or families take their customs with them wherever they go. They too are called local customs.

THEORIES REGARDING TRANSFORMATION OF CUSTOM INTO LAW

There are two theories in this regard: Analytical and Historical theory. According to analytical theory (John Austin), custom derives its binding force not from its own nature but by state recognition. A customary rule may become a legal rule either by recognition through a statute law or by a precedent. Being of a persuasive value, custom is considered as a historical material source of law. Austin thus concluded that customary law is nothing but judiciary law founded upon anterior custom.

Holland also called custom as a law when it is recognized by a court through its decision. Salmond, too supported this view. However, he said that a custom becomes law when it satisfies the conditions prescribed by the law which are necessary for its legal validity. Custom, is therefore rightly treated as a legal material for source of law.

Allen criticized Austinian theory of customary law on the ground that the customs are recognized not because of the court or legislature gives them sanctity of law but because they are treated as law by the community as a whole and people feel themselves bound by them.

According to the Historical theory (Savigny, Puchta, Blackstone and Maine) law has its existence because of the common consciousness of the people and observance of custom is not the cause of law but the evidence of its existence. Savigny observed, customary laws completely modify or repeal a statute; it may create a new law and substitute it for statutory rule which it has abolished. Thus, customs give authority to precedent and statute law. Maine regards custom as a formal source of law. He regarded custom posterior to that of Themistes or judgements.

According to Savigny, customary law is the real law of the people, while the rest is only a superimposition. This is true because good and successful laws represent the legitimate aspirations of the people. However, in the present day highly technical and mixed society, one cannot completely rely on customs as a source of law. It is only in traditional and tribal societies, the custom is the major source of law. In the contemporary society, its inadequacy to meet the fast changing situations is beyond doubt, so far as customs cannot suddenly be created to meet a situation.

ESSENTIALS OF A VALID CUSTOM

To acquire the force of law or become a source of law, custom must satisfy the following conditions:

- **Custom must be ancient:** A custom cannot be created in a day. It must be of long standing. Unlike England where a custom should have existed from time immemorial, in India long usage or observance is enough and, thus even a 20 year old custom may be recognized.
- **Custom must be continuous, certain and precise:** The custom must have been in use continuously and it should not be vague or indefinite. Its existence must be proved by clear and unambiguous evidence.
- **Reasonableness:** A custom is reasonable if no good legal reason can be assigned against it. Further, it is not that a custom will be admitted if reasonable, but it will be admitted unless it is unreasonable.

  The reasonableness of a rule is not to be judged by the contemporary judicial standards, but by those prevailing at the date of its inception. If it does more mischief than the good, then it should be discarded. A custom among Jat Sikhs of Punjab which permitted a woman expelled and deserted by her husband to remarry was held reasonable; but not the practice which authorized a woman to desert her husband at pleasure with a view to marry someone else.
- **Conformity with statutory law :** No custom however old or reasonable can stand if it conflicts with a statute or legislature. By no length of desuetude, observes Salmond, can a statute become obsolete and inoperative in law and by no length of contrary usage its provisions can be modified in the smallest particular.
- **Customs must have obligatory force:** Customs must have been enjoyed as of right. Because without this, it cannot be said that it exerts obligatory pressure to conform. The custom must have been followed openly, without the necessity for recourse to force.

  What distinguished a legal custom from a mere convention is the opinion *juris sine* necessitates – the feeling of being bound. The stark test of a custom is the growth of conviction that it shall be followed whenever a proper occasion arises. Facultative or optional enjoyment of a practice robs it of the vitality so essential to transform it into a binding rule of law.

  Usage and custom – the terms are often used interchangeably, but there is a clear distinction between the two. Usage represents the twilight stage of custom. Custom begins where usage ends. A custom is such a usage as hath obtained the force of law.
- **Consistent with morality and public policy:** Custom must not be inconsistent with morality, public policy and other customs in some area. In a case, the court refused to recognize a custom claimed by prostitutes of adopting daughters because it would perpetuate prostitution.

LEGISLATION

Today, legislation is the most important and biggest source of law. The term legislation means the making or the setting of law. Legislation is the source of law which consists in the declaration of legal rules by a competent authority *e.g.*, Parliament or State Legislatures. Thus, legislation is a deliberate process of legal evolution which consists in the formulation of norms of human conduct in a set form through a prescribed procedure by agencies designated by the constitution.

Legislation may be of two kinds — supreme and subordinate legislation. When the sovereign authority itself makes the law, it is supreme legislation. Subordinate or delegated legislation is by any other authority than the sovereign by virtue of powers delegated to it by the sovereign, and subject to the control of sovereign. The supreme legislation is not superior to the constitution and it is subject to various constitutional limitations *e.g.*, a legislation which infringes the FRs of citizens is invalid. Further, supreme legislation cannot delegate the essential legislative functions which relate to the making of policy.

In our legal system, acts of parliament and the ordinances and other laws made by the president and governors is supreme legislation. Examples of subordinate legislation includes rules, regulations, bye-laws, orders, directions, notifications, etc. made by various authorities such as corporations, municipalities, universities, government departments, supreme and High Courts etc. The amount of subordinate legislation far exceeds the amount of supreme legislation. In order to ensure that delegated legislation is not misused, it has been subjected to: (i) Procedural control, (ii) Parliamentary control and (iii) Judicial control.

The general principles is that a delegatee is not able to delegate further *i.e.*, the maxim *delegatus non potest delegare*. Thus, sub-delegation of delegated legislation without express authority would be invalid. It may be noted that delegated legislation is different from conditional legislation in which the law is complete in itself and certain conditions are laid down as to how and when the law should be applied by delegatee.

PRECEDENT

In a common law system like ours, precedents constitutes a very important source of law. It means the employment of past decision as guides in the moulding of future decisions. Salmond defines precedent as the making of law by the recognition and application of new rules by the courts themselves in the administration of justice. A judicial precedent is a judicial decision to which authority has in some measures been attached. The doctrine of precedent provides the evidence of what the law is on a particular time. A judicial precedent is purely constitutive in nature and never abrogative *i.e.*, it can create a law but cannot abolish it. The judges are not at liberty to substitute their own views where there is a settled principle of law.

A precedent may be authoritative or persuasive. The persuasive precedents are merely historical sources viz., foreign judgements, judicial dicta, authoritative text books and commentaries.

Precedents get authority from various factors. For instance, the power exercised by these courts is one such fact which invests authority and elevates them as precedents. These courts exercise power of judicial review; this enables them to lay down original precedents *i.e.*, precedents which lay down new principles of law. In England, as these courts have lost such power of review, there are only declaratory precedents.

LEGISLATION vs PRECEDENT (Statutory law vs Case law):

- Legislation has its source in the law-making will of the state, precedent has its source in the *ratio decidendi* and *obiter dicta* of the judgement of a court.
- Legislation is the formal and express declaration of new laws or rules by legislature; precedent is the creation of law by recognition and application of laws or rules by the courts in the administration of justice.
- Legislation is a formal general declaration of law in abstract while in precedent law is created by its application to a specific situation. Thus, precedent is more practical. It is the extreme manifestation of law in action—application of certain principles to specific fact situation.
- Legislation is generally made for future transactions but precedent is always created with respect to past transactions. Thus, parties are governed by a law which did not exist at the time when the transaction took place. While in case of legislation, the law becomes known to the people in advance.
- Legislation is more coherent and certain, and, it is easier to get the law as compared to the difficulty in finding the precedent. Overruling of earlier decisions and conflicting decisions of superior courts make the precedent uncertain.
- Precedent has another drawback. Sometimes an erroneous decision is established as law due to not being brought before superior court. This is not so in case of legislation which can change a wrong or unpopular law at any time.

- Legislation is rigid and must apply equality in disregard of needs of individual justice, while precedent has the flexibility of being moulded and applied according to the needs of individual case. Thus, precedent brings flexibility and scientific development in law. And, precedent has greater justice content than legislation.

RATIO DECIDENDI

It is well established that doctrine of precedent pre-supposes existence of the hierarchy of courts. The general rule is that a court is bound by the decisions of all courts higher than itself. Thus, in England, a higher court judge cannot question a decision of the court of appeal nor can the court of appeal refuse to follow the judgment of the House of Lords.

In India, all High Courts of the states are bound by the decisions of the Supreme Court and all courts subordinate to the higher court are bounded by the higher court's decisions. However, the decision of one high court is not binding on another high court it only has a persuasive authority. Having considered the extent to which courts are bounded the previous decisions, it becomes necessary to consider what actually constitutes the decision in a case and what is that is actually binding on the lower courts. A decision generally has two aspects namely:

- What principle it lays down on the rule of law for which it becomes an authority, is generally called the ratio decidendi of the case.
- What the case decides between the parties.

Such matters become *res judicata* between the parties and cannot be the subject of further dispute. The term ratio *decidendi* means reason of the decision. It is the general principle which is deduced in the case. In other words, ratio decidendi is the rule of law upon which the decision is founded. It differs from res judicata which means decision given in a particular case and which is conclusive between the parties to case.

Obiter dicta

Pronouncement of law which are not a part of the *ratio decidendi* are called as *obiter dicta* and they are not authoritative or binding on subordinate courts. *Obiter dicta* may be defined as mere casual expressions by the courts which carry no weight.

In the course of judgment, a judge may make various observation which are not precisely relevant to the issue before him. For instance, he may illustrate his reasoning by reference to hypothetical situations. Whatever said by the court by the way of statement of law which lay down a rule but which is unnecessary for the purpose in hand are called obiter dicta. These dictas have the force of persuasive authority and are not binding upon the courts. The courts may seek help from them but they are not bound to follow them. *Obiter dicta* literally means something said by the judge by the way, which does not have any binding authority. Good Hart defines *obiter dictum* as "a conclusion based on fact the existence of which has not been determined by the court".

DOCTRINE OF STARE DECISIS

Like England, the doctrine of *stare decisis* has been accepted under the Indian law. Since the law in India is mostly based on the English law therefore, the system of law reporting is fairly developed in India. The doctrine of *stare decisis* has essentially developed as a result of progress made in law reporting. The doctrine of stare decisis literally means "let the decision stand in its rightful place". When a decision contains a new principle, it is binding on subordinate courts and has persuasive authority for equivalent courts. This rule is based on expediency and public policy. Although this doctrine is generally followed by the courts, but it may not be applicable if the court is convinced that the earlier wrong is likely to perpetuate resulting into erroneous decision.

The operation of the doctrine of stare decisis pre-supposes the existence of hierarchy of courts. For example, in India, the lower most courts or the courts of the first instance are the subordinate courts, above them are High Courts and the Supreme Court is at the apex. Thus, the Supreme Court is the highest judicial court in India.

The general principles on which the doctrine of stare decisis is based may be stated as follows:

- Each court is absolutely bound by the decisions of the court above it.
- To a certain extent, higher courts are bounded by their own decisions. In India, the Supreme Court is however, not bound by its own earlier decisions.
- The decision of one high court is not binding on any other high court and it has only a persuasive value.
- A single bench judge is bound by the decision of a division bench of the same high court but a division bench is not bounded to follow a decision of a single bench of the same high court.

The Supreme Court in Maktul *vs* Manbhari, held that if the correctness of a decision has been challenged time and again, the rule of stare decisis need not be applied. However, the Supreme Court in Supreme Court advocates on record association *vs* UOI held that the doctrine of stare decisis is not an inflexible rule and it has little relevance in constitutional cases. The court observed that there is no doubt that the rule of stare decisis brings about consistency and uniformity but at the same time in exercising its inherent power, the Supreme Court should ask itself whether in the interest of public good or any other valid reason, it is necessary that its earlier decision should be revised.

STARE DECISIS DISTINGUISHED FROM *RES JUDICATA*

The doctrine of stare decisis has to be distinguished from the doctrine of *res judicata*, which means that the final judgement of a competent court may not be disputed by the parties or their successors or any third parties in any subsequent legal proceeding. The main differences between these two doctrines are as follows:

- The doctrine of *stare decisis* operates as to the ruling of law involved in case while *res judicata* applies to the decision in the dispute.
- *Stare decisis* binds everyone, including those who come before the courts in other cases, but *res judicata* normally binds only the parties and their successors.
- *Stare decisis* is brought into operation only with regard to decisions of the higher courts, namely the Supreme Court and the high courts in India, while *res judicata* applies to all courts.
- *Stare decisis* comes into operation immediately the decision is handed down by the higher court, but *res judicata* takes effect only after the lapse of the period of time limit for appeal.

POSITIVISM, NATURAL LAW THEORY AND SOCIOLOGICAL JURISPRUDENCE

Different approaches to the treatment of jurisprudence are represented by its various schools of thoughts. Salmond preferred three schools: Analytical (dogmatic), Historical and ethical (legal exposition) school.

POSITIVISM (ANALYTICAL/IMPERATIVE SCHOOL)

The analytical school is 'positive' in its approach to the legal problems in the society. It concentrates on things as they are, not as they ought to be. The main concern of the positivists is 'Law that is actually found', positum, and not the ideal law. The most important legal sources are Legislation, Judicial precedents and Customary law.

This school, dominant in England, lays down the essential elements that go to make up the whole fabric of law *e.g.*, state sovereignty and the administration of justice. The motto of analytical school is Ubi civitas ibi lex *i.e.*, where there is state, there will not be anarchy; State is necessary evil. The main proponents of this school are : Bentham, Holland, Austin, Salmond etc.

Bentham's Concept of Law

Bentham is considered the founder of modern utilitarianism. Also, he was a champion of codified law. Bentham's work was intended to provide the indispensable introduction of a civil code. Bentham distinguished expositorial jurisprudence from censorial jurisprudence. His concept of law is imperative one *i.e.*, "Law is assemblage of signs, declarations of volition conceived or adopted by sovereign in a State". While supporting the economic principle of Laissez Faire, he propounded the principle of utilitarianism: 'The proper end of every law is the promotion of the greatest happiness of the greatest number.' He defined 'utility' as 'the property or tendency of a thing to prevent some evil or procure some good.

According to him, the function of law must be to meet these ends *i.e.*, to provide subsistence, to produce abundance, to favour equality, and to maintain security. Bentham's doctrine of hedonism or theory of pain and pleasure has been criticized on the ground that pleasure and pain alone cannot be the final test of the adequacy of law.

Austinian Concept of Law

John Austin (1790-1859) was a lecturer in London University. He applied analytical method— 'Law should be carefully studied and analysed and the principle underlying therein should be found out'- and confined his field of study only to the Positive Law – *Jus positivism*. Therefore, the school founded by him is called by various names — analytical, positivism, analytical positivism. Austin is considered as the "Father of English Jurisprudence". His lectures were published under the title 'The Province of Jurisprudence Determined'.

Austin defined law as a rule laid down for the guidance of an intelligent being by an intelligent being having power over him. According to him, so-called 'proper law' includes : Law of God, Humans laws and Positive law. The law 'improperly' so-called includes: Laws by analogy and Laws by metaphor. According to him, "Positive morality" consists of—Law not set by men or in pursuance of a legal right, and, law by analogy as laws of fashion. The improper laws lacked sanction of the state. Every law, properly, so called, must have three elements—Command, sanction and sovereign. According to him, "Law is the command of a sovereign", requiring his subjects to do or forbear from doing certain acts. There is an implied threat of a sanction if the command is not obeyed.

A command is an expression of a wish by a determinate person, or body of person, that another person shall do or forbear from doing some act subject to an evil in the event of disobedience *i.e.*, 'sanction'. So every law is a command, imposing a duty, enforced by a sanction. According to him, a command may be particular or general. A particular command is effective when the commanded person or group obeys; a general command is effective when the bulk of a political society habitually obeys it. Austin's notion of sovereign is 'if a determinate human superior is not in a habit of obedience to a like superior, receives habitual obedience from the bulk of a given society, that determinate superior is 'sovereign' in that society. The basis of sovereignty is, thus, the fact of obedience. The sovereign's power is unlimited and indivisible. The sovereign is not bound by any legal limitation or by his own laws.

Austin's definition of law as the 'Command of the sovereign' suggests that only the legal systems of the civilized societies can become the proper subject-matter of jurisprudence because it is possible only in such societies that the sovereign can enforce his commands with an effective machinery of administration. Austin's definition ignores customs. Austin, however, accepts that there are three kinds of law which, though not commands, may be included within the purview of jurisprudence by way of exception viz., declaratory or explanatory laws, laws of repeal, and, Laws of imperfect obligation. According to him, Constitutional law derives its force from the public opinion regarding its expediency and morality.

In Austin's positive law, there is no place for ideal or justness in law, for he observed: "Existence of law is one thing, its merit and demerit another. A law which actually exists, is a law, though we happen to dislike it or though it may vary from the text by which we regulate our approbation or disapprobation." Austin's theory ignores laws which are of a permissive character and confer privileges.

Kelsen's Concept of Law

Hans Kelsen (1881-1973), belonging to 'Vienna School' of legal thought, proposed a "pure theory of law" *i.e.*, a theory which is free from social, historical, political, psychological, etc., influences and is logically self-supporting. The law is a normative and not a natural science, there are sanctions attached to the law itself. The test of lawness is to be found within the system of legal norms itself. He defined law as 'an order of human behaviour'. According to Kelsen, laws are ought propositions *i.e.*, 'norms': 'If X happens, then Y ought to happen'. Thus, if a person commits theft, he ought to be punished. Law does not attempt to describe what actually occurs but only prescribe certain rules. Norm is a legal meaning attached to an act of will. It is the meaning of an act by which certain behaviour is commanded, permitted or authorized.

A norm is valid only because it has been derived from or is ordained by another norm. This presupposes a hierarchy of norms, each norm being valid on the presupposed validity of some other norm. Further, there are 'dependent' norms or facilitative norms which do not coerce people. The 'independent' norms are coercive norms. The dependent norms are dependent for their validity on the independent norm. Thus, law does not have exclusively a commanding or imperative character. The law is a system of behavioural norms which can be traced back to some *grundnorm* or basic norm from which they derive their existence. The *grundnorm* must be efficacious *i.e.*, people must believe in it, otherwise there will be a revolution. In every legal system, *grundnorm* of some kind there will always be, whether in the form of a constitution or the will of a dictator. Where there is a written constitution the *grundnorm* will be that the 'constitution ought to be obeyed'. Where there is no written constitution one must look to social behaviour for the *grundnorm*. Under International law, the *grundnorm* is the principle '*Pacta sunt servanda*' (Treaty obligations are binding on parties).

Kelsen's theory is criticized, as according to Kelsen, a legal order is valid when it is effective, it does not matter whether it is an illegitimate rule brought about by unconstitutional means. This means law is a system of external compulsion *i.e.*, people are forced to comply with laws. Validity of a law does not necessarily derive from an effective *grundnorm*. Kelsen does not give any criterion by which the minimum effectiveness of grundnorm is to be measured. The *grundnorm* simply creates or validates a legal order, but do not provide the content to a legal order. It is for the courts to determine the criterion of *grundnorm*, and to decide the validity and efficacy of a legal order. The effectiveness of *grundnorm* depends on sociological factors.

No theory of justice can form part of pure theory of law. However, Kelsen presented a formal, scientific and dynamic picture of the legal structure. He has considerably influenced the modern legal thought. The great jurists like Stone and Friedmann have strongly defended Kelsen's theory.

NATURAL LAW THEORY

Natural law is also known as Moral law/Divine law/Law of God, and Law of reason. The natural law philosophy found an expression in the Roman legal system through division of Roman law into three distinct divisions—*Jus civile, jus gentium* and *jus naturale*. Natural law is basically a priori method, different from a posteriori or empirical method. Natural law appeals to the reason of man and there is no element of compulsion in it. It embodies the principles of morality and natural justice and as such it differs from positive law and legal justice. It is law in an ideal state and it differs from man-made law. Its principles are common to all states and thus, it differs from '*jus civile*', the civil law or the law of the land.

The Naturalists insist that no social norm can be called law unless it satisfies a criterion of intrinsic worth, which may be either religion or ethics or morals or social good. Otherwise, there will be no difference between the kind of social norms which a tyrant like Hitler may lay down and the rest. Therefore, satisfaction of a criterion which goes to the quality of law is inherent in the idea of law. According to Salmond, 'natural or moral law means the principles of natural rights and wrongs.' Blackstone observed, "The natural law being co-existing with making and emanating from God himself, is superior to all other laws. It is binding over all the countries at all times and no man-made law will be valid if it is contrary to the law of nature."

Natural law theories may be broadly divided into: Ancient theories, Medieval theories, Renaissance theories and Modern theories. Some of the leading naturalists and their contribution to the natural law of philosophy is as follows:

- **Aristotle:** According to Aristotle, law is either universal or special and 'Perfect law' is inherent in the nature of man and is immutable, universal and capable of growth. He defined natural law as 'reason unaffected by desires.' It was Aristotle, and not Plato, who founded natural law on reason.
- Later, **Stoics** identified natural law with reason which governs the entire universe and man being a part of universe, is also governed by reason. **Cicero** said, "True law is right reason in agreement with nature." **St. Thomas Acquinas** defined law as "an ordinance of reason for the common good made by him who has the care of the community and promulgated through reason."
- **Grotius:** Hugo Grotius held that natural law was not merely based on reason, but on right reason *i.e.*, 'self-supporting reason' of man. He treated 'natural law' as immutable which cannot be changed by God himself. He said that natural law is based on the nature of man and his urge to live in peaceful society. He considered divine law as the grandmother, natural law the parent and positive law as the child.
- **Hobbes:** Hobbe's theory of natural law was based on the natural right of self-preservation of person and property. In order to secure self-protection in a stage of nature, men voluntarily entered into a 'social contract' and surrendered their freedom to the ruler.
- **Locke:** According to John Locke, man entered into a **social contract** by which he yielded to the sovereign not all his rights but only the power to preserve order and enforce the law of nature. The individual retained his inalienable right to life, liberty and estate. The moment sovereign encroached upon the 'natural rights', laws loses their validity and the government may be overthrown.
- **Rousseau:** Rousseau pointed out that 'Social contract' is not a historical fact as contemplated by Hobbes and Locke, but is merely a hypothetical conception. According to him, people united to preserve their rights of freedom and equality, and for that they surrendered their rights to the community as a whole– 'General Will'. Thus, while the individual parts with his natural rights, he gets in return civil liberties. Therefore, he favoured people's sovereignty. His theory is considered to be the forerunner of the modern jurisprudential thought and legal theory.
- **Kant:** Kant propounded his famous theory of "Categorical Imperative" in his classic work– 'Critique of Pure Reason'. His theory was derived from Rousseau's theory of General Will, and embodies two principles: (i) A man is expected to act in such a way that he is guided by dictates of his own conscience. (ii) Autonomy of will implying an action emanating from reason. In essence, "an action is right only if it co-exists with each and every man's free will according to the universal law." This he called as the principle of 'Innate Right'.

SOCIOLOGICAL SCHOOL

Sociological jurisprudence arose as a reaction to positivism. According to it, law is not an isolated phenomenon but is a part of the social reality. This school has emerged as a result of synthesis of various juristic thought. The supporters of this school linked law with other social science disciplines and treated it as a synthesis of 'psychology, philosophy, economics, political science, sociology, etc.

The functional role of law and its effect on society constitutes the basic philosophy underlying this school. R. Pound rightly pointed out, the sociological jurists look more for the working of law than for its abstract content. Roscoe Pound can be said to be the father of sociological jurisprudence in America. Montesquieu is the forerunner of the sociological method in jurisprudence. Other noted jurists of this school includes: Auguste Compte, Herbert Spencer, Rudolph Von Ihering, Ehrlich, Duguit, Francois Geny.

- **Auguste Comte:** He is regarded as the founding father of the science of sociology. He applied scientific methods to the study of socialism which has been termed as 'scientific positivism'. According to him, society, like any other organism, can progress when it is guided by scientific principles. Further, it is the society and not the individual which should be the focal point of law. The only right which man can possess is the right always to do his duty.
- **Herbert Spencer:** He gave a scientific exposition to the 'organic theory of society'. He deduced four sources of law, namely, (i) Divine laws having quasi-religious sanctions, (ii) Injunctions of the past leaders, (iii) Will of the ruler, and (iv) Collective opinion of the society. He considered law as nothing more than a "hardened custom". The purpose of law is to resolve the conflicting interests of the individuals in the society.
- According to Ihering, "The birth of law, like that of men has been uniformly attended by the violent theories of child birth." The origin of law is to be found in social struggles. He opined that social interest of the society must gain priority over individual interest. His theory has been called as 'Social utilitarianism'. He considers punishment as a means to the social end. His system combined Austinian positivism with Bentham's utilitarianism. Ihering's legal philosophy is known as 'jurisprudence of interests'. Like Bentham, he defined 'interest' in terms of pleasure and pain.
- **Ehrlich:** His theory of 'living law' is that law need not be necessarily created by the State or applied by the courts or have a coercive legal compulsion behind it, but it is created by life of groups living within the society. In other words, law arises in society in the form of spontaneous ordering of social relations of marriage, family associations, possessions, contracts, etc. His theory of living law came as a vigorous reaction against the analytical positivism and State-made laws.
- **Duguit:** His theory of 'Social solidarity' was based on the fact that interdependence of man is the essence of society. He developed the concept of 'Syndicalism'. He established a standard "Social solidarity" to which all positive law must conform. It is nothing but natural law in different form. Therefore, it has been rightly observed that Duguit "pushed natural law out through the door and let it come by windows". He denounced the omnipotence of the state and acknowledged the superior role of judiciary. He also rejected the notion of natural rights of men which made individual hostile to larger interests of the society.
- **Francois Geny:** His sociological approach emphasized 'Free scientific research' as a solution to social problems, which is based on (i) Autonomy of will, (ii) Maintenance of public order and interest, and (iii) Proper balancing of conflicting private interests of individuals. He gave primacy to courts; a judge should try to find out the solution freely and scientifically.

THE RELATIONSHIP BETWEEN LAW AND MORALITY

- **Definition of Law and Morality:**
  - **Law:** A system of rules created and enforced by a state or community to regulate behavior. Laws are binding and enforceable by courts.
  - **Morality:** A set of beliefs, values, and principles concerning what is right or wrong. These are often shaped by societal, cultural, and religious norms.
- **Interdependence:**
  - **Law Reflects Morality:** Many laws are based on moral principles, such as prohibitions against theft, murder, and fraud.
  - **Morality Influences Lawmaking:** Changes in societal morality often lead to legal reforms, e.g., legalizing same-sex marriage or abolishing slavery.
  - **Law Shapes Morality:** Laws can influence societal behavior and help establish new moral norms, such as environmental regulations promoting sustainability.

- **Examples of Interdependence:**
  - **Criminal Laws:** Reflect moral judgments on actions like murder, theft, or assault.
  - **Civil Laws:** Incorporate moral duties like fairness in contracts or equity in family matters.
  - **Social Movements:** Civil rights laws in the U.S. were influenced by moral arguments for equality and justice.

The Distinction Between Law and Morality

- **Key Differences:**
  - **Nature:**
    - **Law:** Codified rules enforced by the state.
    - **Morality:** Informal, uncodified principles upheld by social or personal conscience.
- **Enforcement:**
  - **Law:** Enforced through legal sanctions (fines, imprisonment).
  - **Morality:** Enforced by societal approval/ disapproval or personal guilt.
- **Scope:**
  - **Law:** Limited to specific, observable actions (e.g., paying taxes).
  - **Morality:** Covers intentions, thoughts, and broader ethical conduct.
- **Changeability:**
  - **Law:** Changes through formal legislative processes.
  - **Morality:** Evolves informally over time with societal changes.
- **Overlap:**
  - Some laws directly enforce moral principles (e.g., prohibiting murder).
  - Others do not have a clear moral basis (e.g., traffic regulations).
- **Examples of Divergence:**
  - **Immoral Acts Not Illegal:** Adultery in many jurisdictions.
  - **Illegal Acts Not Immoral:** Parking violations or tax evasion in specific circumstances.

LEGAL CONCEPTS – RIGHTS

Austin: A right is a faculty which resides in the determine party or parties by virtue of a given law and which avail against the party or parties in whom it resides. According to him, a person can be said to have a right only when another or others are bound or obliged by the law to do something or forbear in regard to him. It means that a right has always a corresponding duty. Austin adds, "Though every law does not create a right, every right is a creator of law. And rights are exercised by persons, or else, reside in persons".

Holland: He reads legal right as the ability possessed by a person to control others' action, with the assent and assistance of the state. Thus, Holland follows the definition given by Austin.

Kolher: A legal right is a relation sanctioned and protected by the legal order.

Salmond: A right is an interest recognized and protected by the rule of right. It is an interest, respect for which is a duty and disregard of which is a wrong. Thus, a right must be judicially enforceable. Further, the element of interest is essential to constitute a right.

THEORIES OF LEGAL RIGHT

- **Will theory:** This theory says that the purpose of law is to grant the individual the means of self-expression and self-assertion. Therefore, rights emerge from the human will. The definition of rights by Austin and Holland lay down that will is the main element of a right. A strong support to the theory has been given by the doctrines of natural rights. Puchta defined legal right as a power over an object which means of this right be subjected to will of the person enjoying the right. Paton, however, said: "Will is an essential element in the general conception of legal right, but it is not the only element".
- **Interest theory:** Ihering defines legal rights as a legally protected interest. According to him, the basis of right is interest and not will. Law always has a purpose. In the case of rights, the purpose of the law is to protect certain interest and not the wills of individuals. Salmond also supported Ihering's views.

It may be noted that 'rights and interest are not identical'. Many interests receive no recognition or protection from any rule of right. For the interest of men conflict with each other, and it is impossible for all to receive right recognition. Whether an interest amounts to a right depends on whether there exists with respect to it a duty imposed upon any other person.

THE ELEMENTS OF A LEGAL RIGHT

There are five elements or characteristics of a legal right:

- **The subject or the person of inherence:** Subject means the person in whom the right is vested, or the holder of right. There can be no right without a subject, which may be determinate or indeterminate (*e.g.* society).

- **The person bound or the person of incidence:** It means the person upon whom falls the correlative duty.
- **The act or forbearance:** Right relates to some act or forbearance. It obliges a person to act or forbear in favour of the person who is entitled to the right. It is the content of the right.
- **The object of right or the res concerned:** It is the thing in respect of which the right exists or is exercised. The object or subject matter of right may be material or immaterial, determinate or indeterminate.
- **Title:** Every legal right has a title *i.e.*, certain facts or events by reason of which the right has become vested in the owner.

In this way, according to Salmond, every right involves a three-fold relation, in which its holder stands –

- It is a right against some person or persons.
- It is a right to some act or omission of such person or persons.
- It is a right over or to something to which that act or omission relates.

CLASSIFICATION OF RIGHTS

The legal right may be classified as follows:

- **Perfect and imperfect rights:** A perfect right means a right which has a correlative perfect duty *i.e.*, duty that can be legally enforced. Generally, when law recognizes a right, it prescribes remedy also and when the right is violated, it enforces it. An imperfect right is that right which, although, recognized by law, is not enforceable, such as a time barred claim, claims unenforceable by action owing to the absence of a legally requisite proof. Such cases may be considered as an exception to the rule *Ubi jus ibi remedium* (where there is a right, there is a remedy).
- **Rights in rem and rights in personam:** Right in rem, also called a real right, corresponds to a duty imposed upon persons in general; right in personam, also called a personal right, corresponds to a duty imposed upon determination of individuals. A right in rem is available against the world at large; a right in personam is available only against particular persons. An illustration—My right to the peaceable occupation of my farm is in rem, for all the world is under a duty towards me not to interfere with it. But if I grant a lease of the farm to a tenant, my right to receive the rent from him is in personam, for it avails exclusively against the tenant himself.

  Generally, most of the rights in personam are positive rights, and rights in rem are mostly negative. In case of positive right, the person having the right can compel the person upon whom the correlative duty is imposed to do some positive act. The scope of a negative right is only that the person having the right shall not be harmed.
- **Rights in re-propria and rights in re-aliena:** Rights in re propria means the rights in one's own things. Rights in re-aliena are the rights in the things or others, also called encumbrances. It frequently happens that a right vested in a person become subject or subordinate to an adverse right vested in another. Thus, the right of a landowner may be subject to, and limited by, that of a tenant to the temporary use of the property. The right so subjected is known as servient and the rights which limit, is known as dominant. The main classes of encumbrance are leases, servitudes, securities and trusts.
- **Vested and contingent rights:** A right vests when all the facts have occurred which must by law occur in order to the person in question to have the right. A right is contingent when some but not all the vestitive facts, as they are termed, have occurred. It would become vested when all the facts have occurred. Hence, a vested right is a perfect right in the sense that it becomes heritable on the moment it becomes vested. However, if the person who has a contingent right to a property dies before the contingency occurs, his heirs have no right in the property.
- **Primary and secondary rights:** Primary rights are those rights which are independent of a wrong having been committed. They exist for their own sake. They are antecedent to the wrongful act or omission, thus they are also called antecedent rights. Examples of primary rights are the right of reputation, the right in respect of one's own person, etc. secondary rights are a part of the machinery provided by the state for the redress of inquiry done to primary rights. Secondary rights come in the form of remedial rights. Thus, if any person defames A, A has a right to receive damages from him.

- **Legal and equitable rights:** Equitable rights are a creation of English legal system and are based on equity rules. There are some basic distinctions between legal and equitable rights. The court enforces legal rights automatically on proof of their existence, while equitable rights depend on enforcement upon the discretion of court. Equitable rights are easier for creation, for equity depends upon conscience and good faith. Equitable rights have more precarious existence than legal rights. Where legal and equitable rights conflict, the legal right will prevail. The maxim is : Where there are equal equities, the law will prevail.
- **Jus ad rem:** It is a right to a right. The person of inherence has a right to have some other right transferred to him. It is always a right in personam. If I sell my house to A, A acquires a right against me to have the house transferred to himself. The right of A is said to be *jus ad rem*.

DUTY

A duty is roughly speaking an act which one ought to do an act, the opposite of which would be wrong. A legal wrong is a violation of justice according to law. To ascribe a duty to a man is to claim that he ought to perform a certain act. Yet, not all the acts which a man ought to do constitute duties. His duties are which he owes to others by virtue of his position or station. The servant has a duty to serve his master, the child to obey his parent and so on.

With duties, we may contrast obligations. A has through having taken them upon himself of his own choosing (*e.g.*, obligation that results from making a promise). But there may be many other things which a man ought to do, but which fit into neither of these categories. Many dictates of common morality, such as that one should not steal or kill, hardly constitute duties or obligations in the strict sense. Duties, like wrongs, are of two kinds, being either legal or moral.

When the law obliges a person to do something, it is called a positive duty. A debtor is under an obligation to pay off his creditor. When the law obliges a person to forbear from doing a certain thing, it is a negative duty. Persons generally are in duty bound not to defame others. A primary duty is that duty which is *per se* independent of any other duty. The duty not to cause hurt to any person is a primary duty. A secondary duty is that duty whose purpose is only to enforce some other duties.

Liability: Liability is the condition of the person who has committed a wrong. Salmond defined liability as the bond of necessity that exists between the wrong doer and the remedy of the wrong. The task of law is not finished only by laying down rights and duties; it ensures their protection, enforcement and redress also.

AUSTIN'S RIGHT-DUTY RELATION

Rights and duties are correlated to each other in such a way that one cannot be conceived without the other. A right is always against someone upon whom the correlative duty is imposed. In the same way, a duty is always towards someone in whom the correlative right vest. But, Austin said that there can be duties without a corresponding right, such duties are absolute duties. The duties, which are always correlated with a right, are called relative duties. Austin said that there are four kinds of absolute duties – (1) Duties not regarding person (2) Duties owed to persons indefinitely; (3) Self-regarding duties; (4) Duties owed to the sovereign.

Austin conceived it to be of the essence of a right that it should be vested in some determinate person, and is enforceable by some form of legal process instituted by him. On this view, duties towards the public at large have no correlative rights *e.g.*, the duty to refrain from committing a public nuisance. Similarly, the duties in criminal law are imposed with reference to, and for benefit of members of society, none of whom has rights correlative to these duties. Statutory duties furnish other examples. Thus, they are in the duty of the court to properly deal with an offender is an absolute duty.

On a close examination of Austin's view, it becomes clear that it is wrong. The absolute duties enumerated by are not duties in the legal sense, or if they are duties at all, they are not absolute. Thus, the general duty towards the community is nothing more than a bundle of duties towards each particular individual of the community and each individual has got a correlative right. Self regarding duties are also the duties towards the state because it is a part of the criminal law as an attempt to commit suicide. In democratic countries, a citizen has rights against the state. A correlative duty binds the state and the state is bound until it changes the law. In the same way, the state has rights against the citizens. Thus, Austin's theory does not stand true in the modern times.

Salmond's analysis said that the term legal right in its generic sense means any advantage or benefit which is in any manner conferred upon a person by a rule of law. Of rights in this sense, there are four distinct kinds. These are (1) Rights; (2) Liberties; (3) Powers; and (4) Immunities. Each of these has its correlative, namely (1) Duties, (2) No rights, (3) Liabilities, and (4) Disabilities.

Hohfeld in his essays, Fundamental Legal Conceptions has arranged these legal conceptions in the following way:

Right	Privilege/liberty	Power	Immunity
Duty	no-right	Liability	Disability

Here the term 'right' is too wide and includes within it claims, immunities, power and liberties.

This scheme provides jural relations between two parties in the following way

Jural Correlatives			
Claim ↓ Duty	Liberty ↓ No-right	Power ↓ Liability	Immunity ↓ Disability

That is, presence of one in X, implies the presence of the other in another person Y. For example, If X has a claim against Y, Y has a correlative duty to satisfy that claim against X. If a diplomat (A) has immunity against civil action, then Police Officer (B) has a correlative disability to arrest him and so on...

Jural Opposites			
Claim	Liberty	Power	Immunity
Duty	No-right	Liability	Disability

That is, presence of one in X, implies the absence of the opposite in himself. For example, If X (President) has a liberty to commute a prisoner's sentence that means he has no duty to commute it (or not). Similarly if an officer (A) has been granted statutory powers of search and seizure then he is under no disability to exercise it and so on...

Jural Contradictories	
Claim → Liberty	Power → Immunity
Duty → No-right	Liability → Disability

That is, presence of one in X, implies the absence of the opposite in another person Y. For examples, If X has a claim against Y then Y is under no liberty to either satisfy it or not.

Claim—Duty Relation (You ought or must)

A claim or right is a sign that a person ought to behave in a certain way. Every claim implies a correlative duty. Thus, the statement that X has a claim is meaningless; but the statement X has a claim that Y ought to pay him ₹10 is meaningful. Whether every duty implies a correlative claim is doubtful. In fact, non-correlative duties do not fit properly into the Hohfeldian scheme. For example, Fundamental Duties under the constitution of India (Article 51-A) are absolute duties *i.e.*, duties not accompanied by claims. Although it is a duty of every citizen to respect national flag, protect culture, etc. Yet, the state cannot have any claim in respect of such duties. Thus, fundamental duties are not Hohfeldian one.

Liberty—no claim relation (I May)

The term liberty or privilege refers to the freedom which a person has to do or not to do something. A liberty in X implies the presence of a no-claim in Y. If X were under a duty to wear a hat, this would imply the absence in him of any liberty not to wear it. A claim in Y implies the absence of liberty in X *i.e.*, claim and liberty are jural contradictors. A claim implies a correlative duty, but a liberty does not. The liberty and claim are separate; the claim can be extinguished without affecting the liberty. The *maxim damnum sine injuria* (detriment without injury) illustrates a no-right.

Limits of Liberty: The parliamentary privileges/ judicial privileges are liberties in the Hohfeldian sense that both connote the absence of a duty not to utter defamatory statements. These are unlimited; similar is the case of privileges of Prime Minister and President. Others are limited viz. various freedoms guaranteed under the Indian constitution are qualified privileges/liberties because the state can impose reasonable restrictions on them. Similarly, defence of fair comment in defamation, self help or defence etc.

Power—Liability Relation (I Can)

Power denotes ability in one person to alter the existing legal relations (rights, duties, liabilities, etc.), whether of oneself or of another, for better or for worse. Liability correlative of power, denotes the position of a person whose legal condition is so altered. Right as a power implies right to make a will, or to alienate property, power to sue, etc. Powers differ from claims in as much as they have no duties corresponding to them. One's right to make a will corresponds to no duty in anyone else. All rights or liberties are rights to act or abstain, not to produce legal effects. While, powers have certain legal effects.

- **Rightful Powers:** Sometimes, a power is coupled with a liberty to exercise it, while at other times, it may be coupled with a duty to exercise it. An example of the former is: Supreme Court has a liberty to decide whether petitioner moved by appropriate proceeding or not, under Art. 32 of the constitution. An example of the latter is: Power and duty of a judge to give a decision.

- **Wrongful Powers:** Where a power is coupled with a duty not to exercise it, the party concerned has no liberty to do so *viz.* where a thief sells a thing in the market openly to an innocent purchaser. To call such power right would be a misnomer, for it would be speaking of right to commit wrongs. Thus, not all powers, in the sense in which Hohfeld used the term, can be called rights.

Immunity – Disability Relation (You Cannot)

Immunity denotes freedom from the power of another, while Disability denotes the absence of power. The President of India has various immunities *e.g.*, no civil or criminal proceedings can be instituted during the term of his office. The rule *Nemo dat quod non habet* can be expressed as a disability on the part of persons in general to transfer property that they do not themselves own.

If X has a power, Y has a liability. A liability in Y means the absence of immunity in him. Therefore, immunity and liability are jural opposites. Conversely, the presence of immunity in Y implies the absence of a liability in him. The absence of a liability in Y implies the absence of a power in X. Thus, immunity in Y implies the absence of a power in X i.e., power and immunity are jural contradictors.

The term Disability denotes No-power. Power and disability are thus jural opposites. It follows from this that immunity in Y implies the presence of a disability in X *i.e.*, they are jural correlatives.

Distinction between Claim/Liberty and Immunity: An immunity is not necessarily protected by a duty in another person not to attempt an invasion of it. Further, there may be immunity in X, which is protected by a duty in Y, but the claim correlative to that duty is not in X. Thus, diplomatic envoys are immune from the power of action or other legal process, though they are treated as being capable of committing breach of duty and are under a duty to pay damages. In other words, they have no liberty to do the act, nor a liberty not to pay damages, but they have immunity from process all the same.

LEGAL PERSONALITIES

Definition and Nature of Legal Personality

Legal personality refers to the recognition by law that an entity has rights and duties and can engage in legal relationships. It is a foundational concept in jurisprudence, enabling entities to function within the legal framework.

- **Definition:** Legal personality is the ability to have legal rights and duties, and to enter into legal relationships, recognized by the legal system.

  Example: A corporation can own property, enter into contracts, and be sued in its own name.
- **Nature:**
  - Legal personality is a creation of law.
  - It enables entities to participate in legal transactions.
  - The law assigns personality to natural persons (human beings) and certain artificial persons (like corporations, trusts, and states).

Meaning of Legal Personality

The term "legal personality" is derived from the Latin word persona, meaning "mask," historically referring to the role an entity plays in the legal domain.

- A legal person is an entity capable of holding legal rights and duties.
- Legal personality allows entities to:
  - Sue and be sued.
  - Own property.
  - Enter into contracts.
  - Be liable for debts and obligations.

The Concept of Juristic Person versus Natural Person

- **Natural Person:**
  - A natural person is a human being.
  - Recognized by law as having legal capacity from birth until death.
  - **Examples:** Rights to life, liberty, property, and the ability to contract.
- **Juristic Person (Artificial Person):**
  - A non-human entity to which the law grants personality.
  - Created by human beings for specific purposes.
  - **Examples:** Corporations, trusts, states, and organizations.
  - **Characteristics:**
    - Has a separate legal identity from its members.
    - Can sue or be sued in its own name.
    - Perpetual existence, independent of changes in membership.

- **Differences Between Natural and Juristic Persons:**

Feature	Natural Person	Juristic Person
Recognition by Law	Inherent (from birth)	Granted by law
Existence	Biological	Legal or statutory
Termination	Death	Dissolution or winding up
Examples	Individuals	Companies, States

Theories of Legal Personality

Theories of legal personality seek to explain the legal and philosophical basis for recognizing certain entities as "persons" under the law. These theories provide insights into the nature and justification of granting legal rights and duties to non-human entities.

Fiction Theory

- **Proponents:** Friedrich Carl von Savigny, John Salmond.
- **Concept:**
  - ❑ Juristic persons are not real but "legal fictions" created for convenience.
  - ❑ Only natural persons (human beings) are real persons.
  - ❑ The law, for practical reasons, assigns personality to artificial entities (e.g., corporations, trusts).
- **Key Features:**
  - ❑ Artificial entities exist only because the law recognizes them.
  - ❑ Such recognition simplifies complex legal relationships.
- **Criticism:**
  - ❑ Overlooks the real-world existence and societal importance of organizations and groups.
  - ❑ Ignores the independent functions performed by juristic persons.
- **Example:** A company is treated as a person in law but does not have a physical existence like a natural person.

Realist Theory

- **Proponent:** Otto von Gierke.
- **Concept:**
  - ❑ Juristic persons are real entities with a tangible existence, not mere fictions.
  - ❑ Law acknowledges the inherent reality of these entities, which exist socially and economically.
- **Key Features:**
  - ❑ Juristic persons are treated as having independent rights and duties because they fulfill societal and economic roles.
  - ❑ They exist independently of the legal system's recognition.
- **Criticism:**
  - ❑ Blurs the line between natural and artificial persons.
  - ❑ Overemphasizes the independent existence of juristic persons.
- **Example:** Trade unions exist as real associations representing collective interests, even without legal recognition.

Concession Theory

- **Proponent:** Sovereigntist thinkers (e.g., Austin).
- **Concept:**
  - ❑ Legal personality is a privilege granted by the state, not inherent in entities.
  - ❑ Juristic persons exist because the state confers personality on them.
- **Key Features:**
  - ❑ Emphasizes the role of state power in creating legal persons.
  - ❑ Juristic persons depend on state recognition to operate legally.
- **Criticism:**
  - ❑ Ignores the pre-legal existence of some entities (e.g., community groups).
  - ❑ Fails to explain entities like states themselves, which do not depend on another authority.
- **Example:** A corporation requires state registration to gain legal personality.

Purpose Theory

- **Proponent:** Brinz.
- **Concept:**
  - ❑ Juristic persons exist solely to achieve specific purposes or objectives.
  - ❑ These entities are not real persons but tools for achieving defined goals.
- **Key Features:**
  - ❑ Focuses on the purpose or function served by artificial entities.

- ❑ Rights and duties of juristic persons are derived from their stated purpose.
- **Criticism:**
  - ❑ Reduces juristic persons to mere instruments, ignoring their independent societal roles.
  - ❑ Does not explain entities with multiple or broad purposes (e.g., multinational corporations).
- **Example:** A charitable trust exists to fulfill the purpose of aiding the underprivileged.

Bracket Theory (Symbolist Theory)

- **Proponent:** Rudolf von Jhering.
- **Concept:**
  - ❑ The term "legal person" is a symbolic representation or "bracket" around the rights and duties of a group.
  - ❑ Juristic personality is a convenient way of grouping rights and duties for legal purposes.
- **Key Features:**
  - ❑ Juristic persons are legal constructs that represent collective rights and liabilities.
  - ❑ The members of a group collectively exercise these rights, but the group itself is treated as a single unit.
- **Criticism:**
  - ❑ Does not adequately address the independent identity of juristic persons.
  - ❑ Fails to distinguish between collective and individual responsibilities within a group.
- **Example:** A company is a "bracket" representing the rights and obligations of its shareholders as a collective entity.

Comparison of Theories

Theory	Key Idea	Proponents	Example
Fiction Theory	Juristic persons are legal fictions.	Savigny, Salmond	Corporations as artificial entities.
Realist Theory	Juristic persons are real entities.	Gierke	Trade unions.
Concession Theory	Legal personality is granted by the state.	Austin	State registration of corporations.
Purpose Theory	Juristic persons exist for specific purposes.	Brinz	Charitable trusts.
Bracket Theory	Legal personality groups collective rights.	Jhering	Corporations as symbolic entities.

Types of Legal Persons

Legal personality can be broadly classified into natural persons and artificial or juristic persons. Additionally, there are institutions that also possess legal personality under certain conditions. Below are the details of each type:

Natural Persons

- **Definition:** A natural person refers to a human being who is recognized by law as having legal rights and duties. From birth to death, an individual enjoys full legal personality, unless restricted by law.
- **Key Characteristics:**
  - ❑ **Inherent Personality:** A natural person possesses legal personality by virtue of being human, which is recognized from birth (except in the case of unborn children, depending on jurisdiction).
  - ❑ **Rights and Duties:** Natural persons have the full capacity to exercise rights and perform duties, including entering into contracts, owning property, and participating in legal actions.
  - ❑ **Termination:** The legal personality of a natural person ceases upon death.
- **Examples:** Any individual human being, from a newborn to an elderly person, has legal personality in a legal system.

Artificial or Juristic Persons

Artificial persons, also known as juristic persons, are entities created by law to serve specific purposes, such as carrying out business activities, managing trusts, or representing an organization.

- **Definition:** A juristic person is a non-human entity (e.g., a corporation, partnership, or association) that the law treats as a legal person, granting it rights, duties, and the ability to enter into legal relationships.
- **Key Characteristics:**
  - ❑ **Created by Law:** Juristic persons are created either by statute (such as a corporation being formed under company law) or by a specific legal act (such as the creation of a trust or society).
  - ❑ **Separate Legal Identity:** Juristic persons are distinct from the individuals who form or manage them. They have independent legal existence, which allows them to sue and be sued, own property, and enter contracts.

- **Perpetual Existence:** Unlike natural persons, juristic persons typically have an indefinite lifespan and continue to exist even if their members change.
- **Liability:** Juristic persons can be held liable for their actions, and their members are usually not personally liable unless the corporate veil is lifted.

- **Examples:**
  - **Corporations:** Companies (e.g., Apple Inc., Tata Group) are the most common examples of juristic persons.
  - **Partnerships:** Legally recognized business entities with two or more partners.
  - **Trusts:** An entity that holds property for the benefit of beneficiaries.
  - **Unincorporated Associations:** Groups formed for a specific purpose (e.g., clubs, societies).

Institutions as Legal Persons

Certain institutions, both public and private, are recognized as legal persons because they are capable of performing legal acts and enjoying rights and obligations.

- **Definition:** Institutions such as states, NGOs, and international organizations are recognized as legal persons with the capacity to exercise legal rights and duties within their scope of operation.
- **Key Characteristics:**
  - **States:** The state is considered a sovereign entity and a legal person in both domestic and international law, with rights such as entering treaties, participating in international organizations, and defending itself.
  - **Non-Governmental Organizations (NGOs):** NGOs are often granted legal personality to carry out charitable, educational, or humanitarian work. They can own property, enter into contracts, and even litigate in courts.
  - **International Organizations:** Entities like the United Nations (UN) or the World Health Organization (WHO) are international legal persons recognized under international law, with rights and duties in their areas of operation.
- **Examples:**
  - **States:** India, the United States, and other countries are recognized as legal persons in international law.
  - **NGOs:** Organizations like the Red Cross, Amnesty International, and local charitable trusts that are granted legal personality for performing specific functions.
  - **International Organizations:** The United Nations, European Union, World Trade Organization (WTO), etc.

Summary of Key Points for Competitive Exams

Type of Legal Person	Characteristics	Examples
Natural Persons	Inherent legal personality from birth to death.	Any human being (e.g., John Doe)
Artificial or Juristic Persons	Created by law, has independent legal personality.	Corporations, partnerships, trusts
Institutions as Legal Persons	Granted legal personality to carry out specific functions.	States, NGOs, international bodies

CAPACITY TO SUE AND BE SUED

- **Suing and Being Sued:**
  - One of the core features of legal personality is the capacity to sue (initiate legal actions) and to be sued (defend against legal actions) in its own name.
  - Both natural and artificial persons, such as companies or institutions, have this capacity, allowing them to enforce their rights and defend themselves in court.
- **In the Case of Natural Persons:**
  - Natural persons, by virtue of their legal personality, have the unrestricted right to initiate and respond to legal proceedings in matters related to their rights, property, contracts, and personal matters (e.g., family law cases, criminal cases).
  - **Example:** A person can sue for damages arising from a breach of contract or be sued for failing to pay a debt.
- **In the Case of Juristic Persons:**
  - Juristic persons like corporations and partnerships can sue and be sued in their own name, independent of their members or shareholders.
  - **Example:** A corporation can sue another company for breach of contract and can also be sued by employees for wrongful termination.
  - The ability to sue and be sued allows juristic persons to enforce their rights, like a natural person, and ensures that legal disputes can be resolved in an orderly manner.

- **Legal Capacity to Sue and Be Sued in Specific Contexts:**
  - **Example of Government:** A government body can sue and be sued in relation to its activities but is often subject to sovereign immunity, meaning it cannot be sued for certain actions unless it waives this immunity.
  - **Example of NGOs:** Non-governmental organizations (NGOs) can file lawsuits or be sued if involved in legal disputes (e.g., contract disputes, liability for injuries caused by their operations).

CAPACITY TO OWN PROPERTY

- **Definition:** The capacity to own property is a fundamental attribute of legal personality. Legal persons, whether natural or artificial, have the legal ability to acquire, hold, and dispose of property.
- **Natural Persons:**
  - A natural person has the capacity to own tangible property (e.g., land, houses, cars) and intangible property (e.g., shares, intellectual property rights).
  - This capacity is a core component of legal personality and is directly tied to an individual's ability to engage in transactions.
  - **Example:** A person can buy a house, inherit property, or transfer ownership to another person.
- **Juristic Persons (Artificial Entities):**
  - Juristic persons such as corporations, partnerships, and trusts also have the capacity to own property in their own name, separate from their members or founders.
  - **Example:** A corporation can own office buildings, land, machinery, and intellectual property. It can also buy and sell property in the same way that natural persons can.
- **Special Case of Trusts and Non-Profit Organizations:**
  - Trusts are legal relationships, not distinct legal persons that "own property" in the same way a corporation does. The trustee owns the property for the benefit of the beneficiaries.
  - **Example:** A charitable trust can own real estate, financial assets, and other property to fulfill its charitable purpose.
- **Capacity to Own Property in International Context:**
  - International organizations such as the United Nations or the World Health Organization can also own property, such as buildings or equipment, in various countries and are recognized as having the legal capacity to hold such assets.

Attribute	Explanation	Example
Rights and Duties	Legal persons have rights and obligations recognized by law.	A corporation can own property, pay taxes, or sign contracts.
Capacity to Sue and Be Sued	Legal persons can engage in legal actions in their own name.	A company can sue for breach of contract or be sued for damages.
Capacity to Own Property	Legal persons can acquire, own, and transfer property.	A corporation can own land, equipment, or patents.

CONCEPT OF PROPERTY

Definition and Nature of Property

Philosophical Definition: In philosophical terms, property is often understood as a bundle of rights, where the concept of "ownership" encompasses several powers over a resource or thing. It can be traced back to John Locke's philosophy, where property is viewed as a natural right that arises from labor. According to Locke, individuals own the products of their labor because they mix their labor with the resources in nature. The concept of property, in this context, is deeply tied to human autonomy and the exercise of free will.

Legal Definition: In legal terms, property refers to the legal rights or interests one has in relation to a thing (often referred to as a "thing in action" or a "thing in possession"). It is defined as anything that can be owned or controlled by an individual, entity, or government under law. Property law delineates the rights, obligations, and remedies related to things of value, typically divided into personal property (movables) and real property (immovables).

The legal concept of property involves the recognition of rights over things—rights which are enforceable by law. A person who holds legal title to property has the right to exclude others from using or interfering with it, to transfer it, and to enjoy its benefits.

Property as a Bundle of Rights (Theory of Property)

The "bundle of rights" theory, proposed by legal scholars like Ames and Gray, views property not as a single, indivisible right but as a collection of individual rights that an owner may possess in relation to a particular object. These rights may include:

- **Right to use:** The right to use or consume the property in a manner the owner sees fit.
- **Right to exclude:** The right to prevent others from using or entering the property.
- **Right to transfer:** The right to sell, gift, or otherwise convey property to another.
- **Right to destroy:** The right to dispose of the property, including its destruction or abandonment.

This theory helps to explain why multiple parties can hold different rights in the same property simultaneously. For example, one person may have the right to possess the property, while another may have the right to use it, and yet another may have the right to rent it out.

The bundle of rights approach is commonly used in property law to describe the legal relationships between individuals and property. The metaphor of a "bundle" suggests that property is not one fixed right but a series of legal powers that can be divided, assigned, or transferred.

Rights Associated with Property

- **Right to Use (Right of Enjoyment):** The right to use property refers to the owner's ability to use the property in a manner consistent with its nature. For example, if the property is land, the owner may use it for farming, building a house, or leasing it.
- **Right to Exclude (Right to Exclude Others):** The right to exclude is one of the most fundamental rights in property law. It means that the owner can prevent others from entering or using the property without consent. This right is protected by law and can be enforced through remedies such as injunctions or damages. The right to exclude is critical in establishing ownership and is seen as a core part of one's dominion over property.
- **Right to Transfer (Alienation):** The right to transfer allows the owner of property to sell, lease, mortgage, or donate the property. This includes the ability to transfer ownership or certain rights over the property to another party. Property law governs the mechanisms for such transfers, ensuring they are legitimate and recognized by the state.
- **Right to Destroy (Right to Dispose of Property):** The right to destroy refers to an owner's ability to destroy or dispose of the property at their discretion. However, this right is often limited by legal considerations, such as zoning laws, environmental regulations, or preservation statutes.

These rights can vary depending on the type of property (real, personal, intellectual) and the specific legal system under which they are recognized. Not all rights need to be exercised simultaneously or in their entirety.

Difference Between Personal and Real Property

The distinction between personal property and real property is crucial in understanding property law.

- **Real Property (Immovable Property):**
  - **Definition:** Real property refers to land and anything permanently attached to it. This includes the land itself, as well as buildings, fixtures, trees, and other improvements that are permanently affixed to the land.
  - **Examples:** Houses, commercial buildings, agricultural land, and any physical attachment like fences or roads are considered real property.
  - **Legal Implications:** Ownership and transfer of real property typically require formalities such as registration with the government (e.g., land deeds). Real property is subject to special rules, including property taxes, zoning regulations, and land-use laws.
- **Personal Property (Movable Property):**
  - **Definition:** Personal property refers to all property that is not real property. This includes movable items or assets that are not fixed to the land.
  - **Examples:** Furniture, jewelry, cars, books, stocks, and intellectual property (such as patents or copyrights) are all considered personal property.
  - **Legal Implications:** Personal property can be transferred more easily than real property, often through contracts, sales agreements, or gifts. It does not require the same formalities for transfer as real property. Additionally, personal property is subject to different tax and regulatory frameworks.
- **Key Differences:**
  - **Immovability:** Real property is immovable (cannot be moved), while personal property is movable.

- **Transfer Process:** Real property often requires formal processes such as registration and notarization for transfer, whereas personal property may transfer with less formality.
- **Taxation and Regulation:** Real property is subject to property taxes, land use regulations, and zoning laws, while personal property is generally subject to sales tax and personal property taxes (if applicable).

Kinds of Property

Property is broadly classified into various types based on its nature and the rights associated with it. Understanding these classifications is essential for competitive exams, as they form the foundation of property law. The primary kinds of property are Movable Property, Immovable Property, Intangible Property, and distinctions between Personal Property and Real Property.

Movable Property: Goods, Chattels, Personal Property

Movable property refers to any property that is not fixed to land and can be moved from one location to another. It encompasses all tangible items that are not land or real estate.

- **Definition:** Movable property includes items that are capable of being transferred from one place to another. This includes personal property like furniture, vehicles and clothing, as well as intangible assets like stocks or bonds.
- **Examples:**
  - **Goods:** This includes consumables like food, electronics, machinery, or raw materials.
  - **Chattels:** Personal items such as household goods, jewelry, or tools.
  - **Personal Property:** It refers to any tangible and intangible property that is not fixed to land or real estate, such as vehicles, books, personal items, intellectual property, and digital assets.
- **Legal Implications:**
  - Movable property can be sold, transferred, or used as collateral more easily than immovable property.
  - **Ownership Transfer:** Movable property can be transferred with fewer formalities, often through contracts or receipts, compared to immovable property.
  - **Taxation:** Movable property may be subject to sales taxes or personal property taxes, depending on jurisdiction.

Immovable Property: Land, Real Estate, Rights in Land

Immovable property refers to property that is fixed or attached to the land and cannot be moved. The key feature is that it is directly tied to the land or its appurtenances.

- **Definition:** Immovable property consists of land, buildings, and anything that is permanently fixed to the land. This includes things like houses, apartments, farms, or commercial buildings.
- **Examples:**
  - **Land:** Raw, undeveloped land or agricultural land.
  - **Real Estate:** Developed property such as homes, offices, apartments, or industrial complexes.
  - **Rights in Land:** This includes easements, mortgages, or leases, which give a person certain rights over the land without owning it outright.
- **Legal Implications:**
  - **Transfer of Ownership:** The transfer of immovable property typically requires formal procedures like registration with the government, notarized deeds, and payment of stamp duties.
  - **Zoning and Land Use:** Immovable property is often subject to local zoning laws, land use restrictions, and environmental regulations.
  - **Property Taxes:** Immovable property is subject to property taxes, which vary based on location and property value.

Intangible Property: Intellectual Property, Digital Assets, etc.

Intangible property refers to non-physical assets that are not material in nature but are still protected under the law. These assets have value because of the rights attached to them.

- **Definition:** Intangible property includes intellectual property, digital assets, and other non-physical assets that confer certain rights to the owner.
- **Examples:**
  - **Intellectual Property:** This includes patents, copyrights, trademarks, and trade secrets. These are legal rights granted to creators, inventors, and companies to protect their creative or commercial work.
  - **Digital Assets:** This includes cryptocurrencies, domain names, and digital content like software, music, or digital art.

- Shares/Stocks: Financial assets like stocks and bonds are also intangible properties as they represent ownership or claims without being physically manifested.

- **Legal Implications:**
  - **Intellectual Property Law:** Intangible property is protected through specific laws like the Copyright Act, Patent Act, and Trademark Act, ensuring that the creators or inventors have exclusive rights to use, sell, or license their work.
  - **Transferability:** Intangible property can be transferred through licensing agreements, sales, or digital transactions, but the transfer usually involves contracts or agreements to formalize the change of ownership.

OWNERSHIP

In primitive societies, only concept known to human mind was that of possession. The conception of ownership gradually developed out of it due to changes in the economic structure of the society. The transition from the pastoral to an agricultural economy facilitated the development of the idea of individual 'right to property', which is the basis of the concept of the ownership in a relatively developed society.

In Roman law as well as ancient Hindu law, possession and ownership recognized as two separate and distinct conceptions. In Roman law, two distinct terms were used to point out the distinctions and these were 'dominium' and 'possession'; the former denoted the absolute right to a thing, while the later implied only the physical control over a thing. Romans attached greater importance to ownership rather than possession. In ancient Hindu law, the law of prescription, bailment and sale without ownership was based on this distinction. Thus, a long possession could ripen into ownership. If a man lost his chattel and discovers it in the possession of someone else, he should first of all, prove by means of witnesses, etc., ownership of that chattel.

English medieval law emphasizes on seisin and the right to possession. Seisin was a peculiar feature of land tenures under the feudal system. Under this system, the land was held in return for service. The seisin was a right, which was relied upon to get back the possession if the person seised was dispossessed. It was a right to possess as distinct from and superior to possession. The idea of owner and ownership in English law has developed out of this right.

DEFINITION (THEORIES) OF OWNERSHIP

According to Keeton: Ownership is a relation of a person to an object, which is exclusive or absolute and ultimate. The person who stands in this relation is called the owner and he has a right of complete control and enjoyment of the object.

Austin's Definition: He defines ownership as a right which avails against everyone who is subject to the law conferring the right to put things to user of indefinite nature. He further says that ownership is a right indefinite in point of user, unrestricted in point of disposition and unlimited in point of duration. It is a right in rem which is available to the owner against the world at large.

According to the Austin's definition, there are three elements or attributes of ownership:

- **Indefinite users:** Austin used the term indefinite, instead of absolute or unlimited. The owner thus is not absolutely free to use the things owned in anyway he likes. His use of the things is conditioned by an agreement between the owner and a third person.
- **Unrestricted Disposition:** There are no limitations upon this power. Thus, Austin regards right of alienation or transfer as a necessary or very important incident of ownership.
- **Unlimited Duration:** The third incident of ownership is the permanence of the right of ownership. In other words, ownership of a person cannot be cut short and the owner can continue to be the owner as long as he likes. It is perpetual interest, which shall devolve upon the heirs of the owner after his death, but the right shall not be extinguished.

This is also incorrect since almost under every legal system, the state possesses the power to take over the property of any person in public interest.

Austin's definition of ownership has been criticized on various grounds. It is argued that it is fallacious to think that ownership is a single right; in fact it is a bundle of rights including right of user and enjoyment. Even if an owner's parts with some of the rights involved in ownership, the residue are still owned by him. For example, in case of a mortgage by the owner of a land, although he has transferred a right, but he is still the owner of the mortgage property.

Austin's definition, however, is not entirely inaccurate. The right of alienation is considered by Austin as a necessary incident of ownership. A person who is not the owner cannot normally transfer the right of ownership, even though he may have possession of the thing in question. The interest of a bailee or a lessee comes to an end when the period of hire or of the lease come to an end. The view given by Austin is very close to the concept of ownership as fitness for free disposal.

Salmond's Definition: According to Salmond, "Ownership, in its most comprehensive signification denotes the relation between a person and right that is vested in him." Ownership in this wide sense, extends to all classes of rights, whether propriety or personal, in rem or in personam, in re propria or in re aliena; and it applies not only to rights in the strict sense, but to liberties, powers and immunities.

Thus, ownership vests in the owner a complex of rights, which he experiences to the exclusion of all others. Further, ownership is incorporeal. A man may own a copyright, or a right of way in the same way as he owns a piece of land because in all these cases he owns only a right and nothing. When one speaks of the ownership of a material object, this is merely a convenient figure of speech.

Salmond's view has been criticized by many writers. Prof. Glanvile Williams has observed that the definition of ownership as given by Salmond suggests that from the point of time, the concept of ownership of rights must be prior to that ownership of material objects, but historically it appears just the reverse of it. According to Duguit, what a person really owns is a thing not a right. The Salmond supporters point out that Salmond has defined ownership in two different senses. While the comprehensive sense includes both corporeal and incorporeal ownership, the narrower or the commonest sense includes only corporeal ownership.

Kinds of Ownership

- **Corporeal and Incorporeal Ownership:** Corporeal ownership is the ownership of material or tangible things or objects (movable or immovable). Incorporeal ownership is the ownership of intangible object—object, which cannot be perceived and felt by touch *i.e.*, the ownership of a right, for example, a debt, a patent, goodwill, etc.
- **Sole Ownership and Co-ownership:** The general principle of ownership is that it should vest in one person only (sole ownership). But, sometimes it is 'duplicate' or, in other words, two or more persons have the right of ownership of the same property vested in them at the same time (Co-ownership). An example of co-ownership is partnership. 'Tenants in common' and 'joint tenants' (in English law) are co-owners of the tenancy. In India, coparcenary of Hindu law is also a co-ownership (joint tenancy).
- **Trust and Beneficial Ownership:** Yet, another peculiar species of 'Duplicate' ownership is trust ownership in which two persons own property at the same time. The relation between them is such that one of them is under an obligation to use his ownership for the benefit of the other. The former is called the 'Trustee' and his ownership is trust ownership. The latter is called the 'Beneficiary' and his ownership is beneficial ownership. The ownership of the trustee is a matter of formation rather than of substance, it is nominal rather than real because he is deprived of any right to the beneficial enjoyment of the trust property. According to Salmond, the purpose of trust ownership is to protect the rights and interests of persons who for any reason are unable to protect them effectively for themselves *viz.*, unborn persons, infants lunatics, co-owners, etc.
- **Legal and Equitable Ownership:** Sometimes one person may be the legal owner and another the equitable owner of the same thing or right at the same time. Legal ownership is that which has its origin in the rules of common law whereas equitable ownership proceeds from the rule of equity.

  In many cases, equity recognizes ownership whereas law does not recognize ownership owing to some legal flaw or defect. For example, when a debt verbally assigned by A to B, A remains the legal owner of it but B becomes the equitable owner of it. This illustration shows that the distinction between legal and equitable ownership is different from the distinction between legal and equitable right. In this case, the right of both A and B are legal rights but the ownership of A is legal while that of B is equitable.
- **Vested and Contingent Ownership:** In vested ownership, the ownership is absolute; in the contingent ownership, it is conditional. A vested interest is an existing immediate right, even though its enjoyment may be postponed. It is transferable and heritable. A contingent interest is not a present right since it is dependent upon a condition, which, if not fulfilled, shall render the interest null and void. It is not transferable or heritable.

Thus, if A sells a house to B for a price settled, the other formalities prescribed by law *e.g.*, registration, etc., are complied with, B becomes a vested owner of the house.

Contingent ownership is conditional. Thus, if property is transferred to A for life than to B, if B marries C, B's interest is such that it cannot take place as soon as A dies, because there is a condition which B is to fulfill *viz.*, that he must marry C. Likewise, a testator may leave property to his wife for her life, and on her death to A, if he is then alive, but if A is dead, to B. Here, A and B are both owners of the property in question, but their ownership is merely contingent.

ACQUISITION OF OWNERSHIP

(1) Original mode

(2) Derivative mode

The original mode is the result of some independent personal act of the acquirer himself. This mode of acquisition may be of three kinds–(a) absolute *i.e.*, when ownership is acquired over previously ownerless object; (b) extinctive *i.e.*, where there is extinction of previous ownership by an independent adverse act of acquirer *e.g.*, prescription; (c) accessory *i.e.*, when ownership is acquired as a result of accession *e.g.*, owner of an animal has right to its off-springs or the owner of a tree has the right to the fruits of the tree.

Absolute ownership, again, can be acquired either by occupation or specification. For occupation, physical control of the thing is necessary. For example, ownership over wild animals, birds, fishes, in rivers/ponds, precious stones etc. can be acquired in this way. In case of specification, the material belonging to one person is given a new shape by another *e.g.*, a sculptor making a statue out of clay collected from other person's land. The sculptors become the owner of the statue.

When ownership is derived from a previous owner, it is called 'derivative' acquisition. It is derived either by purchase, exchange, will, gift, etc. The law of succession and the law of transfer of property, etc. are the rules of this kind. According to Salmond, a person can become the owner of certain property by the operation of law such as the law of intensity or bankruptcy.

POSSESSION AND PERSON

Possession of material things is essential to life; it is the most basic relationship between men and things. However, in order to derive some benefits or value from material objects, some measure of uninterrupted enjoyment is a prerequisite. For this reason, law must provide for the safeguard of possession.

Possession is an abstract notion, which is difficult to define; it is a question of fact unlike ownership, possession is not purely a legal concept and is of a temporary duration. Possession is both a legal and non-legal or prelegal concept. The legal meaning of possession is different from ordinary meaning, and varies from state to state. The concept of possession is as difficult to define as it is essential to protect.

Possession in Fact/Possession in Law

Possession in Fact—To possess a thing is to have it under one's physical control – it refers to corporeal possession. Incorporeal possession refers to the right to trademark, copyright, goodwill etc., where physical control is not there. The extent of one's power over the object itself, the power of excluding other people, and one's actual control is abandoned, the possibility of resumption depending on the lack of outside reference, are the factors to be taken into account. The test for determining whether a man is in possession of anything is whether he is in general control of it. Beside physical control, mental element *i.e.*, intention may be highly relevant in asserting whether possession has been acquired, lost or abandoned.

Possession in Law: Law can protect the possession in two different ways. First the possessor can be given certain legal rights, such as a right to continue in possession free from interference by others. Secondly, the law can protect the possession by prescribing criminal penalties for wrongful interference/dispossession. By such civil and criminal remedies, the law can safeguard a man's defacto possession.

THEORIES OF POSSESSION

Savigny's Theory

The possession consisted of two ingredients: corpus possessnis (physical control) and animus domini (intention to hold as owner). Possession is both *corpus* and *animus*; the permanent loss of one or the other element brings possession to an end. In cases in which possession continued although one was lost, he sought to explain them by conceding that the temporary loss of one did not matter, provided it was reproducible at will. He distinguished possession from custody and detention.

Savigny's theory which was based on Roman law, is criticized on various grounds:

- It was erroneous to assume that *corpus* and *animus*, which were only conditions sometimes required for the acquisition and loss of possession, constituted possession itself. Possession did sometimes continue despite of the loss of *animus* or *corpus* or even both.

- Savigny's idea of *animus domini* fails to explain the cases of the pledge, emphyteutic, sequester, and precario tenens, who had possession but did not intend to hold as owners. He suggested that they were cases of derivative possession. If so, why did not detonators (borrower or tenant) also get possession derived from the owner?
- Theory does not explain the continued possession of the fugitive slaves despite the owner's inability to reproduce the corpus element at will, or the continued possession by a dead man.
- The theory bears little relation to Roman law. Further, it is inapplicable to incorporeal possession.

Salmond's Theory

He distinguished between possession of physical objects and possession of rights. Corporeal possession is the continuing exercise of a claim to the exclusive use of it, which involves two ingredients: *corpus possessionis* and *animus possedendi*. Possession begins only with their union, and lasts only till one or the other of them disappears.

Corpus is the effective realization in fact of the claim of the possessor. The *corpus possessionis* comprises of both the power to use the things possessed and the existence of grounds for the expectations that the possesor's use will not be interfered with. The *animus possedendi* is intent to exclude other people, or in other words intent to appropriate to oneself the exclusive use of the things possessed.

The Salmond's theory is also criticized on the similar grounds as were the Savigny's theory. An expectation of non-interference is not necessary for the continuation of possession. For example, a man continues to possess his pocket book although swifter bandits, who will interfere with his use of it in a few moments, are pursuing him. Nor is it necessary for the commencement of possession for, a child and a ruffian may both make for a purse lying on the road, but if the child is first to pick it up can it be doubted that he gets possession even the ruffian is certain to interfere the very next second.

Cases of Possession

The cases can be broadly divided into three categories:

- **Possession of a thing lying loosely on the land:** Things lying loose on the land or not in possession of the land owner, but falling into the possession of the first finder. Here, a finder will have the legal possession of such things unless the true owner comes. In Armory vs Delamirie, a chimney sweep while cleaning a flue discovered a jewel. He was held to have acquired possession. In Bridges *vs* Hawkesworth held that notes found on the floor of the shop passed into the possession of the finder rather than of the shopkeeper, as the finder had acquired a physical control over notes and has an *animus i.e.*, intention while the shopkeeper was not aware of the existence of the notes.
- **Possession of a thing attached to/or embedded in the land:** An occupier or owner of land is held to be in possession of objects under or attached to the land whether he knows of them and not the finder. In Elwes *vs* Brigg Gas Cor., A gave to B a piece of land on lease for a gas project. While excavating the land, the workmen of B found a prehistoric boat six feet beneath the land. B claimed possession of it, as a finder of the things of which A was unaware. Held that the legal possession of things is with A, as he was the possessor of land. Similarly in South Staffordshire Water Cor. *vs* Sharman, the rings buried in the mud in a pool were held to be in possession of the owner of the pool and not the finder of the rings.
- **Possession of a thing delivered to someone viz., larceny cases:** The old law of larceny in England penalizes the wrongful taking of possession *i.e.*, without the possessor's consent and accompanied by intent to steal. However, the meaning of larceny extended later to cover cases when the intention to steal has been formed by a person already in possession of a thing. In Hayden *vs* Smith, in order to catch the servant who formed his intention to steal later, it was said that he had received only custody not possession from the master, but that when he formed his dishonest intention then and only then he take possession without consent.

In R. *vs* Ashwell, A gave B a shilling thinking it to be a shilling. B also took it believing it to be a shilling. But later B found that it was a note of higher value, and intended to misappropriate it. B was guilty of larceny. Thus, it is clear that if a person takes something unknowingly, which is another's possession, he nevertheless takes possession and commits a trespass against that person.

KINDS OF POSSESSION

- **Corporeal and Incorporeal:** Discussed earlier.
- **Mediate and Immediate:** The immediate possession implies the direct/primary possession by a person over an object he acquires or gets

directly or personally. In case of the possession of the bailee or a custodian, the person on whose behalf the thing is possessed is called a mediate possessor. Thus, if A leaves his car with the driver, the driver's possession will be immediate whereas that of X would be mediate. Example of mediate possession include; Agent, servant, borrower, hirer, securities, etc.

- **Concurrent or duplicate:** Two persons can be in possession of the same thing viz., mediate and immediate possession, tenants in common, corporeal and incorporeal.
- **Possession in fact and in law:** An owner as well as a tenant has *de jure* possession of a house. Trespasser has a factual or de facto possession.

MODES OF ACQUIRING POSSESSION

- **Taking:** Acquisition of possession without the consent of the previous possessor. It may be rightful or wrongful.
- **Delivery:** Acquisition of possession with the consent and cooperation of the previous possessor.

In actual delivery, there is transfer of immediate possession. In constructive delivery, there is transfer of mediate possession.

Possessory Remedies: These are those legal remedies which exists for the protection of possession even against ownership. While proprietary remedies are those which are available for the protection of ownership of itself. Under English law, prior possession is *prima facie* proof of title. Thus, the defence of *Jus tertii* (third-party rights) cannot be pleaded usually.

CONCEPT OF LIABILITY

What Constitutes Liability in Law?

Liability in law refers to the legal obligation to account for one's actions, whether by paying compensation, performing a duty, or facing legal penalties, when those actions lead to harm or violation of rights.

In legal terms, liability arises when:

- A person or entity is legally bound to bear the consequences of their actions.
- The person has caused harm or damage, either through direct actions, omissions, or negligence.
- A legal duty exists between the parties involved, and the party causing harm or damage fails to fulfill that duty.

Liability is triggered by various legal bases, such as:

- **Tort Law:** Liability for civil wrongs (e.g., negligence, defamation).
- **Contract Law:** Liability for breach of contractual obligations.
- **Criminal Law:** Liability for crimes committed, subject to punishment.
- **Strict Liability:** Where fault (intent or negligence) does not need to be proven (e.g., in the case of hazardous activities).
- **Vicarious Liability:** When one party is held liable for the actions of another, usually in the context of employer-employee relationships.

Liability involves two main concepts:

- **Causation:** The defendant's actions must directly lead to the harm or breach.
- **Fault:** In certain legal systems (e.g., tort law), liability is linked to the fault of the wrongdoer, although in cases of strict liability, fault may not be a determining factor.

General Characteristics and Significance of Liability

Characteristics of Liability:

- **Legal Obligation:** Liability is a formal, legal duty, distinct from moral or social responsibility.
- **Compensation or Punishment:** Liability usually results in either compensatory actions (e.g., monetary damages) or punishment (e.g., imprisonment, fines).
- **Personal Accountability:** The party held liable is usually personally accountable, though under certain conditions (e.g., vicarious liability), another party may bear the consequences.
- **Preventative and Corrective Function:** Liability acts as a deterrent to undesirable actions and as a corrective mechanism for harm caused.
- **Compensatory Mechanism:** In cases of tortious liability, it ensures that the victim receives compensation for damages suffered.
- **Diverse Forms:** Liability can arise in many different forms, such as contractual, tortious, or criminal, with different standards of proof and defenses available.
- **Context-Specific:** The nature of liability changes depending on the area of law (e.g., liability in tort, contract, or criminal law).

Significance of Liability:

- **Justice and Fairness:** Liability ensures that victims of harm or injury receive appropriate redress.
- **Social Order:** By holding individuals accountable for their actions, liability promotes adherence to legal norms and societal expectations.
- **Encouraging Caution:** Legal liability incentivizes individuals and organizations to act with caution to avoid harmful or unlawful actions.
- **Economic Function:** In civil cases, liability (such as in tort law) ensures that those who cause harm compensate the victims, thereby maintaining financial justice.

The Distinction Between Liability and Responsibility

While liability and responsibility are related concepts, they have distinct meanings in the context of law.

Liability:

- **Legal Obligation:** Liability refers to a legal duty to compensate for harm caused or face legal sanctions, typically in civil or criminal law.
- **Actionable Consequences:** Liability is associated with actionable consequences—either the payment of damages or the imposition of penalties.
- **Enforceability:** Liability is enforceable by law and can result in formal legal actions, such as lawsuits, fines, or imprisonment.

Responsibility:

- **Moral or Social Obligation:** Responsibility is often seen as a broader concept that encompasses moral or ethical duty, as well as legal duties.
- **Causal Relationship:** Responsibility refers to a broader concept of accountability, including legal, social, or even familial obligations, and may not always entail formal legal consequences.
- **Not Always Enforceable:** Responsibility might not always result in formal legal actions, as it can be more subjective or voluntary (e.g., moral responsibility, parental responsibility).

Key Distinctions:

- **Legal vs. Moral:** Liability is strictly legal in nature and is enforceable by the courts, while responsibility may encompass both legal and moral obligations.
- **Enforceability:** Liability often carries enforceable consequences, whereas responsibility may involve voluntary or non-compensable duties.
- **Scope:** Liability typically arises from a breach of law, whereas responsibility can be broader and include non-legal obligations (e.g., ethical responsibility to avoid harm).

Types of Liability

Liability refers to the legal responsibility one holds for actions, omissions, or circumstances that result in harm or loss to another. Depending on the area of law, liability can take different forms, each with its own characteristics and application. Here, we explore the various types of liability commonly encountered in legal systems.

Criminal Liability: Liability for Committing a Crime

Criminal liability refers to the legal responsibility for committing a crime. To establish criminal liability, two primary elements must be proved:

- **Actus Reus (the "guilty act"):** The physical act or omission that constitutes the crime. This is the objective element of the crime.
- **Mens Rea (the "guilty mind"):** The mental state or intention to commit the act, which can include intention, recklessness, or negligence.

Examples of criminal liability include:

- **Murder:** Requires both a physical act (actus reus) of killing and the intention (mens rea) to cause death or serious harm.
- **Theft:** Involves the act of taking someone's property with the intent to permanently deprive them of it.

Strict Liability Offenses: In some cases, criminal liability is imposed without proof of mens rea. These are strict liability offenses, where the mere commission of the prohibited act is enough, even if the person did not have criminal intent.

Civil Liability: Liability Arising from Civil Wrongs (Torts, Contracts, etc.)

Civil liability arises from legal wrongs that cause harm to others, typically in the areas of torts and contracts.

- **Tort Liability:** This arises when a person commits a civil wrong (e.g., negligence, defamation) that harms another. Civil liability in tort law is aimed at providing compensation to the injured party, rather than punishing the wrongdoer.
- **Example:** If a person causes harm to another by carelessly driving a vehicle, they may be liable for damages under tort law.

- **Contractual Liability:** This arises when a party fails to perform their obligations under a contract. Breach of contract leads to civil liability where the injured party may claim damages or seek other remedies.
- **Example:** A supplier failing to deliver goods as agreed upon in a contract may be liable for breach of contract.

Strict Liability: Liability Without Fault or Negligence

Strict liability is a legal doctrine that holds a party liable for harm without proof of fault, negligence, or intent. The key principle here is that the defendant is responsible regardless of their intention or negligence. This type of liability is often applied in cases involving inherently dangerous activities or products.

Key Case Example: Rylands v. Fletcher (1868):

- The Rylands v. Fletcher case established the principle of strict liability. In this case, a person who owned a reservoir was held strictly liable when it flooded and caused damage to a neighboring property, even though the owner did not act negligently.

Other examples of strict liability:

- **Liability for hazardous activities:** If a company engages in activities that are extremely dangerous (e.g., using explosives), they may be held strictly liable for any harm that occurs, even if no fault is present.
- **Liability for defective products:** In product liability cases, manufacturers can be held strictly liable for harm caused by defective products, irrespective of fault.

Vicarious Liability: Liability Imposed on One Party for the Actions of Another

Vicarious liability occurs when one party is held liable for the actions of another. This typically arises in the context of the employer-employee relationship.

- **Employer-Employee Relationship:** An employer can be held vicariously liable for the actions of an employee, provided those actions were committed within the scope of employment. This ensures that the injured party can claim damages from an entity (employer) with greater financial resources, rather than the employee directly.
- **Example:** If an employee causes an accident while driving a company car during work hours, the employer may be vicariously liable for the damages caused by the employee's actions.

Liability in Contract: Breach of Contract and the Corresponding Liabilities

Contractual liability arises when a party fails to fulfill their obligations under a legally binding agreement. The breach of contract leads to civil liability, where the injured party may seek remedies such as damages, specific performance, or rescission of the contract.

- **Damages for Breach of Contract:** The most common remedy for breach of contract is monetary compensation for the loss suffered by the non-breaching party.
- **Specific Performance:** In some cases, the court may order the breaching party to perform their contractual obligations as agreed, particularly in cases where damages are not an adequate remedy.
- **Rescission:** This allows the non-breaching party to cancel the contract and seek restitution.
- **Example:** If a contractor fails to complete construction work within the agreed timeline, they may be liable for damages caused by the delay.

Liability in Tort: Civil Wrongs and the Resulting Liability for Damages or Compensation

Tortious liability refers to a person's legal responsibility for committing a civil wrong (tort) that causes harm or injury to another. The goal of tort law is to compensate the injured party, rather than to punish the wrongdoer (which is the focus of criminal law).

Types of torts include:

- **Negligence:** Failure to exercise reasonable care, leading to injury or damage (e.g., car accidents).
- **Defamation:** False statements that harm a person's reputation.
- **Nuisance:** Interference with another person's enjoyment of their property.
- **Trespass:** Unauthorized entry onto another person's property.
- **Example:** If someone is injured in a car accident due to the negligence of another driver, the injured party may claim damages for medical costs, pain and suffering, and lost wages.

Product Liability: Liability of Manufacturers for Defects in Their Products

Product liability refers to the legal responsibility of manufacturers, distributors, and retailers for harm caused by defects in the products they produce, distribute, or sell. The doctrine of product liability holds that a manufacturer can be held liable if a defect in their product causes injury or harm to the consumer.

Types of Product Defects:

- **Design Defects:** The product is inherently dangerous due to its design.
- **Manufacturing Defects:** The product is defective due to errors made during manufacturing.
- **Marketing Defects:** Failure to provide adequate warnings or instructions about the safe use of a product.
- **Example:** If a consumer is injured by a defective toaster that overheats, causing a fire, the manufacturer may be held liable under product liability laws for the defect in the design or manufacturing process.

Defenses to Liability

In both civil and criminal law, various defenses are available to the party accused or sued to avoid or reduce liability. These defenses can serve to either negate the elements of liability, justify the conduct, or excuse the conduct. Below are some common defenses in civil and criminal law, as well as specific defenses under tort and criminal law.

Common Defenses to Liability in Civil and Criminal Law

Contributory Negligence (Tort Law):

- **Definition:** Contributory negligence occurs when the plaintiff (the person bringing the suit) is found to have contributed to the harm or injury they suffered, through their own negligence.
- **Effect:** In jurisdictions that follow the contributory negligence rule, the plaintiff may be completely barred from recovering damages if they were even slightly negligent.
- **Example:** A pedestrian jaywalking who gets hit by a car may be partially at fault for not crossing at a designated crosswalk, leading to a reduced or denied claim for damages.

Comparative Negligence (Alternative to Contributory Negligence):

- In jurisdictions where comparative negligence applies, the plaintiff's degree of fault will be compared to that of the defendant. The damages will be reduced in proportion to the plaintiff's share of responsibility.
- **Example:** If a plaintiff is found to be 30% at fault for an accident, their damages award will be reduced by 30%.

Defenses in Criminal Law

Self-defense (Criminal Law):

- **Definition:** Self-defense is a legal justification for using force to protect oneself or others from an imminent threat of harm. In criminal law, self-defense can negate liability by showing that the defendant's actions were necessary to prevent harm.
- **Conditions for Self-defense:**
  - **Imminent Threat:** The threat must be immediate and imminent.
  - **Proportional Response:** The force used must be proportional to the threat.
  - **Reasonable Belief:** The defendant must reasonably believe that they are in danger.
- **Example:** If someone is attacked with a knife, using a knife in return may be considered justifiable self-defense, provided the threat was immediate and the force used was not excessive.

Defense of Others (Criminal Law):

- **Definition:** This defense justifies the use of force to protect another person from harm, under similar conditions as self-defense.
- **Example:** If someone is being attacked, and a third party intervenes to protect them, they can claim self-defense if the intervention was necessary and proportional.

Defenses Based on Mental State in Criminal Law

Insanity (Criminal Law):

- **Definition:** The insanity defense asserts that the defendant was not criminally responsible for their actions at the time of the offense due to a severe mental illness or defect. Under this defense, the defendant is usually committed to a mental institution for treatment instead of prison.
- **Criteria:** This defense is governed by tests like the M'Naghten Rule, which states that a person can plead insanity if, at the time of the act, they were unable to understand the nature of their act or that it was wrong due to a mental disorder.
- **Example:** A person who commits a violent crime while suffering from severe schizophrenia might be found not guilty by reason of insanity, provided they meet the criteria for the defense.

Automatism (Criminal Law):

- **Definition:** Automatism is a defense that arises when the defendant was not conscious or in control of their actions at the time of the offense, typically due to a temporary condition or external factor. Automatism can be either mental or physical.

- **Types:**
  - **Non-Insane Automatism:** Caused by external factors like a blow to the head, sleepwalking, or a seizure, and can completely exonerate the defendant.
  - **Insane Automatism:** Caused by a mental condition, which may lead to the defendant being committed to a mental health facility.
- **Example:** A driver who causes an accident while having a seizure and is unable to control their movements may use automatism as a defense.

Consent as a Defense in Tort Law (Especially in Personal Injury Cases)

Consent (Tort Law):

- **Definition:** Consent is a defense in tort law where the defendant claims that the plaintiff agreed to the action that caused harm, and therefore, no liability arises. The consent must be voluntary, informed, and explicit.
- **Types of Consent:**
  - **Express Consent:** Clear, verbal, or written permission.
  - **Implied Consent:** When a person's actions suggest consent, such as participating in an activity with known risks (e.g., sports).
- **Limits of Consent:** Consent can be invalid if it was obtained through fraud, coercion, or when the act exceeds what was consented to.
- **Example:** In sports, a player may consent to a certain degree of physical contact (e.g., in football), but if they are injured in a manner outside the normal scope of the game (e.g., being attacked with excessive force), they may have a claim in tort for personal injury.

Consent and Assault/Battery:

- Consent is often a defense to allegations of battery or assault. If the injured party consented to the contact (e.g., during a medical procedure or a sports game), they cannot claim injury unless the contact was outside the scope of what was consented to.
- **Example:** A person undergoing surgery has consented to the procedure, so if they are injured during the surgery, they cannot file a claim for battery, unless the surgeon acted outside the agreed-upon scope.

Remedies for Liability

When a party is found liable for harm or wrongdoing, the legal system provides various remedies to address the situation. These remedies aim to compensate the injured party, prevent further harm, or enforce specific obligations. Below are the key remedies available in cases of liability under both civil and criminal law.

Damages: Compensatory, Punitive, Nominal, and Exemplary Damages

Damages are a monetary remedy awarded to the injured party to compensate for the harm suffered. The type of damages awarded depends on the nature of the case and the objective of the remedy.

- **Compensatory Damages:**
  - **Definition:** These are intended to compensate the plaintiff for the actual harm or loss suffered due to the defendant's actions.
  - **Purpose:** The aim is to restore the plaintiff to the position they were in before the harm occurred (i.e., to make the injured party whole).
  - **Example:** If a person is injured in a car accident due to another's negligence, compensatory damages would cover medical bills, lost wages, and pain and suffering.
- **Punitive Damages:**
  - **Definition:** These are awarded in addition to compensatory damages in cases where the defendant's conduct is deemed particularly egregious, malicious, or willfully harmful.
  - **Purpose:** The goal is to punish the defendant and deter similar conduct in the future.
  - **Example:** In cases of gross negligence or intentional wrongdoing, such as fraud or deliberate harm, the court may award punitive damages.
- **Nominal Damages:**
  - **Definition:** These are awarded when the plaintiff has proven a legal wrong but has not suffered substantial actual harm or loss. Nominal damages are typically a small sum, symbolizing that the plaintiff's rights were violated.
  - **Purpose:** To recognize a legal violation and affirm the plaintiff's rights.

- ❑ **Example:** A plaintiff who successfully proves that their rights were infringed (such as a trespass on property) but suffered no significant loss may receive nominal damages (e.g., $1).
- **Exemplary Damages:**
  - ❑ **Definition:** These are similar to punitive damages but often used to highlight the moral outrage of the defendant's actions.
  - ❑ **Purpose:** To send a strong message about the severity of the wrongdoing and discourage similar acts by others.
  - ❑ **Example:** In cases involving public policy violations or highly unethical conduct, exemplary damages may be imposed.

Injunctions: Preventing Further Harm

An injunction is a court order that directs a party to either do something (positive injunction) or refrain from doing something (negative injunction) to prevent harm. Injunctions are particularly useful in cases where monetary compensation is insufficient to address the harm, or where future harm may occur.

- **Types of Injunctions:**
  - ❑ **Prohibitory Injunction:** Orders the defendant to cease certain actions that are causing harm. For example, an injunction may prevent a company from using a trademark that is identical to another company's.
  - ❑ **Mandatory Injunction:** Requires the defendant to take specific actions to correct a wrong. For instance, ordering a party to remove a structure that was unlawfully built.
- **Interim or Temporary Injunction:** Issued for a temporary period to prevent immediate harm until a final decision is made.
- **Permanent Injunction:** Issued after a full trial, it permanently prevents certain actions or compels specific conduct.
- **Example:** A court may grant an injunction to prevent a factory from polluting a river, even if damages would be insufficient to address the ongoing environmental harm.

Specific Performance: In Contractual Liability

Specific performance is an equitable remedy in contract law, where the court orders the breaching party to perform their obligations as stipulated in the contract, rather than paying damages for non-performance.

- **Conditions for Specific Performance:**
  - ❑ The contract must be valid and enforceable.
  - ❑ The terms must be clear and definite.
  - ❑ The subject matter must be unique or irreplaceable, as it may not be suitable when damages would be an adequate remedy.
- **Example:** In a real estate contract, if one party fails to transfer the property, the court may order them to convey the property to the buyer as agreed, rather than simply awarding money damages.

Note: Specific performance is typically used in cases involving unique goods or property (e.g., real estate or rare antiques) where it is difficult to calculate the exact damages.

Restitution and Compensation: In Tort and Criminal Liability

Restitution and compensation are remedies used primarily in tort law and criminal law to restore the injured party to their original position or to make up for the loss caused.

- **Restitution:**
  - ❑ **Definition:** Restitution involves restoring or returning to the injured party property or value that they have lost due to the defendant's actions. In tort law, restitution may involve the return of property or benefits unjustly obtained by the defendant.
  - ❑ **Purpose:** The aim is to prevent unjust enrichment by the defendant at the expense of the plaintiff.
  - ❑ **Example:** If a person unlawfully takes another's property and later returns it, restitution may involve the return of the property or equivalent value.
- **Compensation:**
  - ❑ **In Tort Law:** In tort law, compensation typically refers to the payment of damages to the plaintiff for injury, loss, or damage caused by the defendant's wrongful act.
  - ❑ **In Criminal Law:** Compensation in criminal law is commonly associated with victim compensation schemes, where victims of crime may receive financial compensation from the state, especially if the offender is unable to pay damages.
- **Example in Criminal Law:** A victim of a violent crime, such as assault, may be compensated by the state if the offender cannot pay restitution directly to the victim.

GLOBAL JUSTICE

Global justice addresses ethical and legal issues that transcend national boundaries, focusing on fairness in global distribution, rights, and responsibilities. The theoretical foundations are rooted in jurisprudential traditions that guide moral and legal frameworks for achieving justice on a global scale.

Natural Law and Global Justice

- **Definition:** Natural law theory posits that universal moral principles exist, derived from reason or divine origin, applicable to all humanity regardless of legal systems.
- **Key Concepts:**
  - Justice is grounded in immutable moral truths.
  - Focuses on inherent human dignity and universal rights.
  - Foundational for international human rights law (e.g., Universal Declaration of Human Rights).
- **Global Implications:**
  - Advocates universal standards for justice beyond national sovereignty.
  - Criticism: Accused of being overly idealistic and potentially dismissive of cultural diversity.

Legal Positivism and Its Critiques in the Global Context

- **Definition:** Legal positivism holds that laws are valid based on their creation by recognized authority, not moral content.
- **Key Concepts:**
  - Separation of law and morality (H.L.A. Hart).
  - Sovereignty as the basis of legal systems.
- **Critiques in Global Justice:**
  - Fails to address moral obligations transcending state boundaries.
  - Inadequate for addressing global crises (e.g., climate change, human rights violations).
  - Criticized for prioritizing state sovereignty over universal justice.

Marxist Perspectives on Global Justice

- **Definition:** Marxist theory views justice through the lens of class struggle, focusing on eliminating economic inequalities.
- **Key Concepts:**
  - Capitalism perpetuates global inequality and exploitation.
  - Advocates for redistribution of wealth and collective ownership.
  - Critiques international institutions like the WTO and IMF as instruments of capitalist hegemony.
- **Global Implications:**
  - Highlights economic disparities between the Global North and South.
  - Criticized for underestimating individual freedoms and non-economic dimensions of justice.

Utilitarianism and Its Global Applications

- **Definition:** Utilitarianism assesses justice based on outcomes that maximize overall happiness or utility.
- **Key Concepts:**
  - Jeremy Bentham and John Stuart Mill emphasized the "greatest happiness principle."
  - Focus on cost-benefit analysis in global policies.
- **Global Implications:**
  - Basis for economic theories addressing poverty and resource allocation.
  - **Criticism:** May justify actions that harm minorities if they benefit the majority (e.g., environmental policies disproportionately affecting developing countries).

Cosmopolitanism Versus Communitarianism in Global Justice

- **Cosmopolitanism:**
  - Advocates global citizenship and equal moral concern for all individuals.
  - Supports institutions for global governance and justice.
  - Key Thinkers: Immanuel Kant (Perpetual Peace), Martha Nussbaum (Capabilities Approach).
- **Communitarianism:**
  - Emphasizes the importance of local cultures, traditions, and community identities.
  - Critiques cosmopolitanism for eroding cultural diversity.
- **Debates:**
  - Cosmopolitanism prioritizes universal principles; communitarianism defends pluralism and sovereignty.
  - Example: Tension in enforcing international human rights in culturally diverse societies.

Rawlsian "Law of Peoples" and Its Critique

- **Rawls' Theory:**
  - ❑ Proposed a framework for international justice in *The Law of Peoples*.
  - ❑ Extended principles of domestic justice (justice as fairness) to the global arena.
  - ❑ **Key Provisions:**
    - ➾ Society of peoples governed by mutual respect.
    - ➾ Assistance to burdened societies.
- **Critiques:**
  - ❑ Ignores global economic inequality by focusing on minimal standards.
  - ❑ Prioritizes state sovereignty over individual rights.
  - ❑ Thomas Pogge criticizes Rawls for insufficiently addressing poverty and wealth redistribution.

Amartya Sen's "Idea of Justice" in a Global Framework

- **Key Concepts:**
  - ❑ Focuses on real-world justice rather than ideal institutions.
  - ❑ Emphasizes comparative justice and removal of manifest injustices.
  - ❑ Advocates for capabilities approach: Enhancing individual freedoms and capabilities.
- **Global Implications:**
  - ❑ Practical solutions for reducing global inequalities and injustices.
  - ❑ Criticism: Lacks a clear institutional framework for global justice.

Summary : Table for Quick Reference

Theory	Focus	Strengths	Criticisms
Natural Law	Universal moral principles	Basis for human rights	Overly idealistic, cultural insensitivity
Legal Positivism	State sovereignty	Clear, pragmatic framework	Fails to address moral global issues
Marxist Theory	Class struggle and economic justice	Highlights systemic inequalities	Overlooks non-economic justice dimensions
Utilitarianism	Maximizing happiness	Practical for policy-making	May harm minorities
Cosmo-politanism	Global citizenship, universal values	Supports global justice institutions	Undermines cultural diversity
Communi-tarianism	Cultural and community identity	Defends sovereignty, pluralism	May resist universal justice norms
Rawlsian Justice	Fairness among peoples	Balances state autonomy and mutual aid	Minimalist, neglects wealth redistribution
Amartya Sen's Approach	Enhancing individual capabilities	Focuses on real-world solutions	Lacks clear institutional mechanisms

HUMAN RIGHTS AND GLOBAL JUSTICE

Human rights and global justice are interconnected domains focused on establishing fairness, equality, and dignity for all individuals worldwide. Theories of jurisprudence guide their understanding, addressing universal standards and challenges posed by cultural diversity, gender inequalities, and indigenous rights.

Universal Declaration of Human Rights (UDHR): Jurisprudential Analysis

- **Background:**
  - ❑ Adopted on December 10, 1948, by the United Nations General Assembly.
  - ❑ Contains 30 articles outlining civil, political, economic, social, and cultural rights.
  - ❑ Reflects principles of natural law (universal moral truths).
- **Key Jurisprudential Aspects:**
  - ❑ **Universality:** All humans are inherently entitled to these rights, irrespective of nationality, culture, or religion.
  - ❑ **Legal Positivism:** While not legally binding, it influenced binding treaties like the ICCPR (International Covenant on Civil and Political Rights) and ICESCR (International Covenant on Economic, Social, and Cultural Rights).
  - ❑ **Critiques:**
    - ➾ Accused of Western bias, reflecting liberal democratic ideals.
    - ➾ Challenges in enforcement due to state sovereignty.
- **Impact on Global Justice:**
  - ❑ Established a common framework for international human rights laws.

- Inspired the development of regional human rights systems (e.g., European Convention on Human Rights).

The Concept of Universal Human Rights and Cultural Relativism

- **Universal Human Rights:**
  - Based on the idea that certain rights are fundamental and non-negotiable (e.g., right to life, freedom from torture).
  - Supported by natural law and cosmopolitan theories.
- **Cultural Relativism:**
  - Argues that human rights must be interpreted within cultural and societal contexts.
  - Critiques universal human rights as imposing Western norms on non-Western societies.
- **Debates:**
  - **Universalists:** Rights are grounded in shared human dignity.
  - **Relativists:** Rights should respect local traditions and practices.
- **Examples:**
  - The debate on women's rights in patriarchal societies.
  - Controversies over LGBTQ+ rights in culturally conservative nations.
- **Jurisprudential Resolution:** A balance between universal standards and cultural sensitivity, often facilitated through dialogue and localized implementation.

Rights-Based Approaches to Global Justice

- **Definition:**
  - Emphasizes using human rights as a framework for achieving justice globally.
  - Focus on accountability, participation, and empowerment.
- **Principles:**
  - Rights are indivisible, interdependent, and universal.
  - Rights-based development: Aligns global development initiatives with human rights standards.
- **Applications:**
  - Millennium Development Goals (MDGs) and Sustainable Development Goals (SDGs) incorporate rights-based approaches.
  - Examples: Right to education, access to clean water, and gender equality.
- **Critiques:**
  - Implementation challenges in resource-constrained or conflict-affected regions.
  - Resistance from states prioritizing sovereignty.

Gender Justice on a Global Scale

- **Definition:** Ensures equal rights, opportunities, and protections for all genders.
- **Key Issues:**
  - Gender-based violence (e.g., domestic violence, sexual harassment).
  - Disparities in education, employment, and political representation.
  - Access to healthcare and reproductive rights.
- **Global Frameworks:**
  - CEDAW (Convention on the Elimination of All Forms of Discrimination Against Women): Adopted in 1979, often called the "international bill of rights for women."
  - UN Security Council Resolution 1325: Focuses on women, peace, and security.
- **Challenges:**
  - Cultural practices like child marriage and female genital mutilation.
  - Patriarchal structures in both developed and developing nations.
- **Jurisprudential Perspective:**
  - Combines natural law (equality as a universal principle) and rights-based approaches.
  - Advocates transformative justice to address systemic inequalities.

Rights of Indigenous Peoples in International Law

- **Definition:** Recognizes the unique cultural, spiritual, and societal contributions of indigenous peoples, alongside their right to self-determination.
- **Key International Instruments:**
  - ILO Convention 169: Addresses indigenous and tribal peoples' rights.
  - UN Declaration on the Rights of Indigenous Peoples (UNDRIP), 2007:
    - Rights to land, resources, and cultural preservation.
    - Right to free, prior, and informed consent (FPIC) for development projects.

- **Challenges:**
  - Land dispossession and resource exploitation.
  - Marginalization and lack of political representation.
  - Environmental degradation impacting indigenous communities.
- **Global Justice Perspective:**
  - Emphasizes restorative justice: Recognizing historical injustices and providing reparations.
  - Supports a participatory approach to ensure indigenous voices in global decision-making.

Summary : Table for Quick Revision

Topic	Focus	Strengths	Criticisms/Challenges
UDHR	Universal framework for human rights	Inspired treaties, regional systems	Western bias, enforcement issues
Universal Rights vs. Cultural Relativism	Balancing universality and cultural diversity	Promotes dialogue and localization	Risk of cultural imperialism
Rights-Based Approaches	Aligning development with human rights	Empowers marginalized groups	Resource and implementation challenges
Gender Justice	Equality for all genders	Supports legal reforms and empowerment	Resistance from patriarchal systems
Indigenous Rights	Protection of indigenous identities	Ensures cultural preservation, participation	Conflict with state sovereignty, exploitation

MODERNISM AND POST-MODERNISM

Introduction to Modernism

- **Definition:** Modernism refers to a broad movement in art, culture, literature, and intellectual thought that emerged in the late 19th and early 20th centuries. It sought to break away from traditional forms and emphasized rationality, progress, and innovation.
- **Timeframe:** Late 19th century to mid-20th century.
- **Characteristics:**
  - Rejection of Tradition: Focus on breaking away from classical and traditional norms in art, literature, and architecture.
  - Belief in Progress: Emphasis on the ability of human reason and science to improve society.
  - Universal Truths: Assumption that universal principles (moral, scientific, or aesthetic) can guide human action.
  - Focus on Structure and Form: Emphasis on formal structure and order in art, law, and other fields.
  - **Key Themes:** Urbanization, industrialization, individualism, and rationalism.
- **Influence on Law:**
  - Rational legal theories were developed, emphasizing codification and systematic legal frameworks.
  - **Example:** Hans Kelsen's "Pure Theory of Law" emphasized the hierarchical structure of legal norms.

Introduction to Post-modernism

- **Definition:** Post-modernism is a reaction against modernism that emerged in the mid-20th century. It challenges the ideas of universal truths, progress, and objective knowledge.
- **Timeframe:** Mid-20th century onwards.
- **Characteristics:**
  - Rejection of Metanarratives: Critique of overarching narratives like progress, justice, or scientific objectivity.
  - Pluralism and Diversity: Emphasis on cultural relativism and the coexistence of multiple perspectives.
  - Deconstruction: Analyzing and exposing contradictions in texts, ideologies, or systems.
  - Skepticism Towards Objectivity: Belief that knowledge and truth are socially constructed.
  - Non-linear and Fragmented: Acceptance of ambiguity and disorder in structures.
- **Influence on Law:**
  - Challenges to formalism in legal reasoning.
  - Emphasis on subjective experiences and contextual factors in interpreting laws.
  - Example: Critical Legal Studies (CLS) movement, which argues that laws often reinforce social hierarchies.

Differences Between Modernism and Post-modernism

Aspect	Modernism	Postmodernism
Belief in Truth	Universal truths exist.	Truth is subjective and culturally relative.
View on Progress	Optimistic belief in progress.	Skeptical of the idea of linear progress.
Art and Culture	Emphasis on form and function.	Emphasis on playfulness and ambiguity.
Legal Philosophy	Formalism and systematic codification.	Contextual and critical approaches to law.
Philosophical Approach	Rationalism and objectivity.	Relativism and deconstruction.

Key Thinkers

- **Modernism:**
  - **Immanuel Kant:** Enlightenment thinker who emphasized reason.
  - **Hans Kelsen:** Legal positivism and pure theory of law.
  - **Le Corbusier:** Modernist architecture emphasizing functional design.
- **Post-modernism:**
  - **Jacques Derrida:** Deconstruction of texts and ideologies.
  - **Michel Foucault:** Power dynamics and the relationship between knowledge and authority.
  - **Jean-François Lyotard:** Critique of metanarratives in "The Postmodern Condition."

Application in Law

- **Modernism in Law:**
  - Development of codified laws (e.g., Napoleonic Code).
  - Emphasis on legal certainty and predictability.
  - **Example:** Montesquieu's separation of powers theory.
- **Post-modernism in Law:**
  - Challenges to traditional legal doctrines, emphasizing interpretation and context.
  - Focus on marginalized groups and power structures in legal systems.
  - **Example:** Feminist legal theory, Critical Race Theory.

MULTIPLE CHOICE QUESTIONS

1. Which of the following is NOT a source of law?
A. Custom B. Legislation
C. Fiction D. Precedent

2. Which among the following is considered the primary source of law in modern legal systems?
A. Religion B. Judicial Precedent
C. Legislation D. Equity

3. Customs are recognized as a source of law if they are:
A. Recent and frequently changing
B. Universal but without consistency
C. Continuous, reasonable, and accepted by the community
D. Established only in legal books

4. Which of the following statements best defines "Stare Decisis"?
A. A law passed by Parliament
B. The principle of following judicial precedents
C. The principle that Parliament is supreme
D. A rule preventing courts from reviewing administrative actions

5. Legal positivists believe that law derives its authority from:
A. Divine sources B. Social customs
C. State authority D. Moral principles

6. Match the following sources of law with their descriptions:

List-I (Sources of Law)	List-II (Description)
A. Custom	I. Decisions made by courts that become binding law
B. Precedent	II. Laws made by the legislature
C. Legislation	III. Long-established practices recognized as law
D. Equity	IV. Principles applied by courts to ensure fairness

A. A-III, B-I, C-II, D-IV
B. A-II, B-III, C-IV, D-I
C. A-IV, B-II, C-I, D-III
D. A-I, B-IV, C-III, D-II

7. The doctrine of binding precedent is known as:
A. Rule of Law B. Stare Decisis
C. Sovereign Power D. Customary Law

8. Which of the following is the best example of customary law?
A. Constitution of India
B. Law of Contracts
C. Hindu Marriage Practices
D. Supreme Court Rulings

9. The primary source of law in Islamic legal systems is:
A. The Quran B. Judicial Precedents
C. State Legislation D. Customs

10. Which type of law is developed through judicial decisions rather than legislative enactments?
A. Civil Law B. Customary Law
C. Common Law D. Statutory Law

11. Which school of jurisprudence considers law as a command of the sovereign?
A. Natural Law School
B. Sociological School
C. Historical School
D. Analytical School

12. The Historical School of Jurisprudence believes that law develops through:
A. Divine revelation
B. Continuous customs and traditions
C. Judicial activism
D. Parliamentary debates

13. Who is considered the founder of the Sociological School of Jurisprudence?
A. H.L.A. Hart B. Montesquieu
C. Roscoe Pound D. John Austin

14. The doctrine of "Volksgeist" (Spirit of the People) is associated with:
A. Aristotle
B. Friedrich Carl von Savigny
C. Jeremy Bentham
D. John Locke

15. Which school of jurisprudence argues that law should be used to balance social interests?
A. Natural Law School
B. Realist School
C. Sociological School
D. Analytical School

16. Which school of jurisprudence views law as a tool for social engineering?
A. Natural Law School
B. Realist School
C. Sociological School
D. Historical School

17. The Analytical School of Jurisprudence believes that law is:
A. Based on divine origin
B. A social contract
C. A command of the sovereign
D. Evolved through history

18. Which school of thought is associated with Jeremy Bentham and Utilitarianism?
A. Natural Law School
B. Historical School
C. Analytical School
D. Sociological School

19. Match the following legal concepts with their respective legal theorists:

List-I (Concept)	**List-II (Theorist)**
A. Command Theory	I. John Austin
B. Social Engineering	II. Roscoe Pound
C. Volksgeist	III. Savigny
D. Separation of Powers	IV. Montesquieu

A. A-I, B-II, C-III, D-IV
B. A-III, B-I, C-II, D-IV
C. A-IV, B-III, C-I, D-II
D. A-II, B-IV, C-III, D-I

20. Which principle is essential in the Realist School of jurisprudence?
A. Law is what the judge decides
B. Law is based on social customs
C. Law is the command of the sovereign
D. Law is derived from religious texts

21. Assertion (A): The Rule of Law ensures that no one is above the law.

Reason (R): In India, the Constitution is considered the supreme law of the land.
A. Both A and R are true, and R is the correct explanation of A.
B. Both A and R are true, but R is not the correct explanation of A.
C. A is true, but R is false.
D. A is false, but R is true.

22. Assertion (A): The Sociological School of Jurisprudence believes law should be dynamic and adapt to society.

Reason (R): Law must be rigid and unchanging to ensure stability.

A. Both A and R are true, and R is the correct explanation of A.
B. Both A and R are true, but R is not the correct explanation of A.
C. A is true, but R is false.
D. A is false, but R is true.

23. Assertion (A): The doctrine of Precedent ensures consistency in the legal system.

Reason (R): Courts follow previous decisions unless there is a strong reason to depart from them.

A. Both A and R are true, and R is the correct explanation of A.
B. Both A and R are true, but R is not the correct explanation of A.
C. A is true, but R is false.
D. A is false, but R is true.

24. Assertion (A): The Sociological School of Jurisprudence focuses on law as a command of the sovereign.

Reason (R): Sociological jurisprudence studies law in relation to society.

A. Both A and R are true, and R is the correct explanation of A.
B. Both A and R are true, but R is not the correct explanation of A.
C. A is false, but R is true.
D. A is true, but R is false.

25. Assertion (A): Natural Law theorists believe that law should be based on morality.

Reason (R): Natural Law suggests that laws must be made through religious institutions.

A. Both A and R are true, and R is the correct explanation of A.
B. Both A and R are true, but R is not the correct explanation of A.
C. A is true, but R is false.
D. A is false, but R is true.

26. Which of the following is NOT considered a primary source of law?

A. Legislation B. Judicial Precedent
C. Custom D. Fiction

27. The doctrine of Stare Decisis ensures that:

A. Every case must be decided differently
B. Courts follow previous judicial decisions
C. Legislatures must make laws based on public opinion
D. Courts must not interfere in governmental functions

28. Which of the following schools of jurisprudence emphasizes that law should be based on moral and ethical principles?

A. Natural Law School B. Analytical School
C. Sociological School D. Historical School

29. According to Legal Positivists, law derives its authority from:

A. The moral conscience of the people
B. Divine sources
C. State authority
D. International organizations

30. The Rule of Law ensures that:

A. The government acts according to law
B. Judges make laws based on personal opinions
C. Political leaders are exempt from legal obligations
D. Parliament is superior to the judiciary

31. Which of the following best describes the relationship between law and morality?

A. Law and morality are identical concepts
B. Law and morality are completely separate with no overlap
C. Morality influences law but they are not the same
D. Law is superior to morality

32. Which of the following statements about morality is true?

A. Morality is always legally enforceable
B. Morality changes with time and culture
C. Morality and law are always in conflict
D. Morality is static and unchanging

33. Which legal philosopher argued that law must have a moral basis?

A. John Austin B. H.L.A. Hart
C. Lon Fuller D. Jeremy Bentham

34. The concept that some laws are unjust because they lack moral justification is associated with:

A. Legal Positivism B. Natural Law Theory
C. Sociological School D. Realist School

35. Which of the following legal principles is closely tied to morality?

A. Doctrine of Precedent
B. Rule Against Hearsay
C. Criminalization of Murder and Theft
D. Strict Liability in Tort

36. Match the following legal theories with their views on morality and law:

List-I (Legal Theory)	List-II (View on Morality and Law)
A. Natural Law	I. Law should be based on morality
B. Legal Positivism	II. Law and morality are separate
C. Sociological School	III. Law reflects societal needs
D. Legal Realism	IV. Law is what the courts enforce

A. A-I, B-II, C-III, D-IV
B. A-II, B-III, C-IV, D-I
C. A-III, B-I, C-IV, D-II
D. A-IV, B-III, C-II, D-I

37. Which statement is an example of a moral obligation but not a legal one?
A. Paying taxes
B. Telling the truth
C. Not committing murder
D. Following traffic laws

38. Which of the following best describes Jeremy Bentham's view on law and morality?
A. Law should maximize happiness (Utilitarianism)
B. Law should be based on divine morality
C. Law and morality must always be separate
D. Law should be based on historical customs

39. The idea that law should be based on moral duties is a key feature of:
A. Legal Realism
B. Historical School
C. Natural Law Theory
D. Marxist Legal Theory

40. What is an example of a law that may be considered immoral by some people?
A. Laws against murder
B. Laws requiring contracts to be written
C. Laws permitting capital punishment
D. Laws on intellectual property

41. **Assertion (A):** Law is always based on morality.

Reason (R): All laws are created to reflect ethical standards.
A. Both A and R are true, and R is the correct explanation of A.
B. Both A and R are true, but R is not the correct explanation of A.
C. A is false, but R is true.
D. Both A and R are false.

42. **Assertion (A):** Natural Law Theory argues that laws must have moral legitimacy.

Reason (R): Laws that contradict moral principles should not be followed.
A. Both A and R are true, and R is the correct explanation of A.
B. Both A and R are true, but R is not the correct explanation of A.
C. A is true, but R is false.
D. A is false, but R is true.

43. **Assertion (A):** Laws should always prioritize individual liberty over social morality.

Reason (R): Individual rights are more important than collective interests.
A. Both A and R are true, and R is the correct explanation of A.
B. Both A and R are true, but R is not the correct explanation of A.
C. A is true, but R is false.
D. Both A and R are false.

44. Which of the following is NOT an essential feature of a legal right?
A. It must be legally recognized
B. It imposes a corresponding duty on others
C. It is always absolute and unlimited
D. It is enforceable by law

45. Rights and duties are:
A. Independent of each other
B. Completely unrelated
C. Correlative to each other
D. Always enforced by courts

46. Who among the following defined rights as "interests protected by law"?
A. Jeremy Bentham
B. Herbert L.A. Hart
C. Rudolf von Jhering
D. John Austin

47. Which of the following is an example of a perfect duty?
A. Duty to be charitable
B. Duty to follow traffic laws
C. Duty to help the poor
D. Duty to donate to charity

48. Fundamental Duties in the Indian Constitution were added by:
A. 42nd Amendment Act, 1976
B. 44th Amendment Act, 1978
C. 73rd Amendment Act, 1992
D. 61st Amendment Act, 1988

49. Match the following types of rights with their definitions:

List-I (Types of Rights)	**List-II (Definition)**
A. Legal Rights	I. Rights recognized and protected by the state
B. Moral Rights	II. Rights based on ethics and social values
C. Constitutional Rights	III. Rights provided under the Constitution
D. Human Rights	IV. Rights that are inherent to all individuals

A. A-I, B-II, C-III, D-IV
B. A-II, B-IV, C-III, D-I
C. A-III, B-I, C-IV, D-II
D. A-IV, B-III, C-I, D-II

50. Which of the following is an example of a legal right but not a moral right?
A. Right to vote
B. Right to be honest
C. Right to donate to charity
D. Right to forgive someone

51. A right without a corresponding duty is called a:
A. Perfect right
B. Legal right
C. Fundamental right
D. Liberty

52. Which philosopher stated that "a duty is an obligation imposed by law"?
A. Immanuel Kant B. H.L.A. Hart
C. John Austin D. Jeremy Bentham

53. The doctrine of duty-based ethics is most closely associated with:
A. Bentham's Utilitarianism
B. Kantian Ethics
C. Austin's Positivism
D. Roscoe Pound's Social Engineering

54. Rights that exist by virtue of being human are called ....
A. Legal Rights
B. Human Rights
C. Constitutional Rights
D. Social Rights

55. In India, the duty to uphold the sovereignty and integrity of the nation is a ....
A. Legal Duty
B. Fundamental Right
C. Fundamental Duty
D. Moral Obligation

56. According to Bentham, rights are ....
A. Natural and absolute
B. Commands of the sovereign
C. Created by law for social utility
D. Rooted in divine authority

57. A duty that cannot be legally enforced but is encouraged by morality is called a(n) ....
A. Perfect Duty B. Imperfect Duty
C. Absolute Duty D. Universal Duty

58. Rights that depend on legal recognition by the state are called ....
A. Human Rights B. Fundamental Rights
C. Legal Rights D. Moral Rights

59. Assertion (A): Rights and duties are interdependent.

Reason (R): There can be no right without a corresponding duty.
A. Both A and R are true, and R is the correct explanation of A.
B. Both A and R are true, but R is not the correct explanation of A.
C. A is true, but R is false.
D. Both A and R are false.

60. Assertion (A): Fundamental Rights are absolute and cannot be restricted.

Reason (R): The state can impose reasonable restrictions on Fundamental Rights in public interest.
A. Both A and R are true, and R is the correct explanation of A.
B. Both A and R are true, but R is not the correct explanation of A.
C. A is false, but R is true.
D. Both A and R are false.

61. Legal personality refers to:
A. The physical appearance of a person
B. The capacity to have rights and duties in law
C. The moral character of an individual
D. The citizenship status of a person

62. Who among the following is considered a juristic person?
A. A human being B. A company
C. A deceased person D. An unborn child

63. Which of the following is NOT considered a legal person?
A. A corporation
B. A river declared as a legal entity
C. A machine
D. An idol in a temple

64. Which of the following best defines a juristic person?
   A. An entity that has no legal recognition
   B. An entity that can own property and sue or be sued
   C. A human with extraordinary legal privileges
   D. A company that does not pay taxes

65. In India, which of the following has been given legal personality by the courts?
   A. A software program B. A river
   C. A robot D. A personal diary

66. Match the following types of legal persons with their characteristics:

List-I (Types of Legal Persons)	List-II (Characteristic)
A. Natural Person	I. Created by law
B. Juristic Person	II. A human being
C. Corporation	III. Exists independently of its members
D. Trust	IV. Holds property for beneficiaries

   A. A-II, B-I, C-III, D-IV
   B. A-I, B-III, C-II, D-IV
   C. A-III, B-IV, C-I, D-II
   D. A-IV, B-III, C-II, D-I

67. A dead person can be considered a legal person if:
   A. Their property is still in their name
   B. They have pending criminal charges
   C. They made a valid will before death
   D. Their rights and obligations are still recognized by law

68. The legal personality of a company begins when:
   A. It is registered under law
   B. The owner starts conducting business
   C. It has more than 10 employees
   D. The shareholders agree to a contract

69. Which of the following is an essential characteristic of a juristic person?
   A. Ability to express emotions
   B. Ability to enter into contracts
   C. Ability to think independently
   D. Ability to get married

70. In which case did the Indian courts recognize Hindu idols as legal persons?
   A. Vishakha v. State of Rajasthan
   B. Yogendra Nath v. Commissioner of Income Tax
   C. M.C. Mehta v. Union of India
   D. Kesavananda Bharati v. State of Kerala

71. A corporation is considered a ....
   A. Natural Person B. Artificial Person
   C. Dead Person D. Moral Entity

72. The legal status of a corporation is separate from its ....
   A. CEO B. Shareholders
   C. Employees D. Office Building

73. The rights of a legal person include the ability to ....
   A. Have emotions B. Enter into contracts
   C. Commit crimes D. Be human

74. In legal terms, a minor is considered a ....
   A. Fully responsible person
   B. Person with full legal capacity
   C. Limited legal person
   D. Non-entity

75. Rivers and religious idols were granted legal personality to ....
   A. Allow them to pay taxes
   B. Enable them to file lawsuits
   C. Protect them from harm
   D. Convert them into commercial entities

76. **Assertion (A):** A company has legal personality independent of its owners.

   Reason (R): The company can own property, sue, and be sued in its own name.
   A. Both A and R are true, and R is the correct explanation of A.
   B. Both A and R are true, but R is not the correct explanation of A.
   C. A is true, but R is false.
   D. A is false, but R is true.

77. **Assertion (A):** A natural person ceases to have legal personality after death.

   Reason (R): The legal personality of a natural person cannot be inherited.
   A. Both A and R are true, and R is the correct explanation of A.
   B. Both A and R are true, but R is not the correct explanation of A.
   C. A is true, but R is false.
   D. A is false, but R is true.

78. Which of the following is NOT a characteristic of ownership?
   A. Right to possess
   B. Right to transfer
   C. Right to use and enjoy
   D. Right to commit a crime using the property

79. Which of the following best defines possession in law?
A. Mere physical control over an object
B. A legal right recognized by law
C. The ability to transfer an item to someone else
D.' A permanent and absolute right over property

80. According to Salmond, ownership is:
A. The totality of rights over a thing
B. A temporary legal status
C. Always limited by law
D. Based only on physical control

81. What is the primary difference between ownership and possession?
A. Possession includes a legal title, whereas ownership does not
B. Ownership is always temporary, while possession is permanent
C. Ownership is a legal right, while possession is a factual state
D. There is no difference

82. Which of the following is NOT a type of property?
A. Movable property
B. Immovable property
C. Intellectual property
D. Fictional property

83. Match the following concepts with their correct definitions:

List-I (Concepts)	List-II (Definitions)
A. Ownership	I. Exclusive legal right over property
B. Possession	II. Physical control with intention to own
C. Intellectual Property	III. Rights over creations of the mind
D. Lease	IV. Temporary right to use property owned by another

A. A-I, B-II, C-III, D-IV
B. A-II, B-I, C-IV, D-III
C. A-III, B-IV, C-II, D-I
D. A-IV, B-III, C-II, D-I

84. Which of the following is an example of incorporeal property?
A. A car
B. A piece of land
C. A patent
D. A house

85. Which of the following is an essential feature of property?
A. It must be tangible
B. It must have value
C. It must be permanent
D. It must be owned by the state

86. Which type of ownership is characterized by a limited right over another's property?
A. Absolute ownership
B. Life estate
C. Leasehold ownership
D. Joint tenancy

87. Possession protected by law against wrongful interference is known as:
A. Physical possession
B. Constructive possession
C. Legal possession
D. Adverse possession

88. A lease grants the .... of property for a specified period.
A. Ownership
B. Possession
C. Full control
D. Absolute rights

89. A right that allows an individual to use land belonging to another without ownership is called a ....
A. Tenancy
B. Easement
C. Mortgage
D. Gift deed

90. Intellectual property includes rights such as _______.
A. Right to vote
B. Copyrights and patents
C. Ownership of land
D. Right to privacy

91. The primary difference between ownership and possession is that ....
A. Ownership is permanent, but possession is temporary
B. Ownership is a legal right, while possession is a factual state
C. Possession is enforceable by courts, but ownership is not
D. Possession is always illegal

92. Ownership of land can be transferred through ....
A. Gift deed
B. License
C. Bailment
D. Adverse possession

93. Assertion (A): Possession is always stronger than ownership.

Reason (R): A person in possession can legally defeat ownership claims.

A. Both A and R are true, and R is the correct explanation of A.
B. Both A and R are true, but R is not the correct explanation of A.
C. A is false, but R is true.
D. A is true, but R is false.

94. Assertion (A): Property can be tangible or intangible.

Reason (R): Intellectual property is an example of tangible property.

A. Both A and R are true, and R is the correct explanation of A.
B. Both A and R are true, but R is not the correct explanation of A.
C. A is true, but R is false.
D. A is false, but R is true.

95. Assertion (A): Adverse possession can grant ownership rights over time.

Reason (R): If a person occupies land openly and continuously for a specified period, they may acquire ownership.

A. Both A and R are true, and R is the correct explanation of A.
B. Both A and R are true, but R is not the correct explanation of A.
C. A is true, but R is false.
D. A is false, but R is true.

96. Match the following types of liability with their key principles:

List-I (Type of Liability)	List-II (Key Principle)
A. Strict Liability	I. Employer is responsible for employee's wrongful act
B. Vicarious Liability	II. No fault required, but some defenses exist
C. Absolute Liability	III. No defenses available, liability is total
D. Criminal Liability	IV. Requires mens rea and actus reus

A. A-II, B-I, C-III, D-IV
B. A-III, B-IV, C-I, D-II
C. A-I, B-III, C-IV, D-II
D. A-IV, B-II, C-I, D-III

97. Match the following landmark cases with their significance:

List-I (Case Law)	List-II (Significance)
A. Rylands v. Fletcher	I. Established vicarious liability principles
B. M.C. Mehta v. Union of India	II. Established absolute liability in India
C. Bhopal Gas Tragedy Case	III. Liability for escape of dangerous substances
D. State of Rajasthan v. Mst. Vidhyawati	IV. Established government liability for torts

A. A-III, B-II, C-I, D-IV
B. A-II, B-I, C-IV, D-III
C. A-I, B-III, C-IV, D-II
D. A-IV, B-II, C-III, D-I

98. Match the following types of criminal liability with their characteristics:

List-I (Type of Liability)	List-II (Characteristic)
A. Mens Rea-Based Liability	I. No intent required, liability exists regardless of knowledge
B. Vicarious Criminal Liability	II. Liability is shared due to a legal relationship
C. Strict Criminal Liability	III. Requires a guilty mind (mens rea)
D. Absolute Criminal Liability	IV. No defense or exceptions allowed

A. A-III, B-II, C-I, D-IV
B. A-II, B-III, C-IV, D-I
C. A-I, B-IV, C-III, D-II
D. A-IV, B-I, C-II, D-III

99. Match the following defenses in tort law with their explanations:

List-I (Defense)	List-II (Explanation)
A. Act of God	I. Harm caused due to plaintiff's voluntary assumption of risk
B. Volenti Non Fit Injuria	II. Liability is reduced if both parties are at fault
C. Contributory Negligence	III. Unforeseeable natural events caused harm
D. Inevitable Accident	IV. Harm could not have been prevented despite reasonable care

A. A-III, B-I, C-II, D-IV
B. A-II, B-IV, C-I, D-III
C. A-I, B-III, C-IV, D-II
D. A-IV, B-II, C-III, D-I

100. Match the following types of damages with their descriptions:

List-I (Type of Damages)	List-II (Description)
A. Nominal Damages	I. Compensation based on actual loss suffered
B. Compensatory Damages	II. Token amount awarded when no real loss occurred
C. Punitive Damages	III. Intended to punish the defendant
D. Special Damages	IV. Compensation for quantifiable monetary losses

A. A-II, B-I, C-III, D-IV
B. A-I, B-III, C-IV, D-II
C. A-III, B-II, C-I, D-IV
D. A-IV, B-I, C-II, D-III

101. Assertion (A): In absolute liability, the defendant cannot escape liability under any circumstances.

Reason (R): The court allows no defenses even if the damage was caused by external factors.

A. Both A and R are true, and R is the correct explanation of A.
B. Both A and R are true, but R is not the correct explanation of A.
C. A is true, but R is false.
D. A is false, but R is true.

102. Assertion (A): A company can be held criminally liable despite lacking physical intent.

Reason (R): The doctrine of corporate criminal liability assigns mens rea to corporations through responsible officials.

A. Both A and R are true, and R is the correct explanation of A.
B. Both A and R are true, but R is not the correct explanation of A.
C. A is true, but R is false.
D. A is false, but R is true.

103. A company is considered vicariously liable for the wrongful acts of its employees when ....

A. The employee commits a wrongful act outside of working hours.
B. The act is done in the course of employment, even if unauthorized.
C. The employer benefits from the wrongful act.
D. The employee had no criminal intent.

104. In the case of a dangerous thing escaping from a person's land, liability is determined by the rule of ....

A. Nuisance law
B. Rylands v. Fletcher
C. Respondeat superior
D. Actus non facit reum nisi mens sit rea

105. Under tort law, ... arises when an employer is held liable for the acts of an employee.

A. Vicarious liability
B. Transferred intent
C. Absolute liability
D. Personal liability

106. Which of the following best describes the doctrine of "Res Ipsa Loquitur" in tort law?

A. It applies when a defendant directly causes harm but denies negligence.
B. It shifts the burden of proof to the defendant when negligence is inferred from the nature of the accident.
C. It establishes strict liability in cases where fault cannot be determined.
D. It negates liability if the plaintiff was also negligent.

107. Which of the following conditions must be satisfied for vicarious liability to arise?

A. The wrongful act was authorized by the employer, the employee had prior offenses, and the employer directly participated.
B. The act occurred in the course of employment, there existed a master-servant relationship, and the act was connected to the employment duties.
C. The employer benefited from the act, the act was necessary for business operations, and the employer was present at the time of the act.
D. The employer had knowledge of the wrongful act, the employee was highly skilled, and the act was performed under duress.

108. In criminal liability, the term "actus reus" refers to:

A. The mental state of the accused at the time of the offense.
B. The physical act or omission constituting the crime.
C. A defendant's prior criminal record used in sentencing.
D. The extent of harm caused by the accused.

109. Which of the following is an exception to the principle of mens rea in criminal liability?

A. Crimes under strict liability, such as regulatory offenses.

B. Crimes committed with diminished responsibility.

C. Crimes where motive is a necessary element.

D. Crimes requiring proof of premeditation.

110. In cases of absolute liability, which of the following defenses is applicable?

A. Volenti non fit injuria (Consent of the plaintiff)

B. Vis major (Act of God)

C. Statutory authority

D. None of the above

111. Which of the following statements best describes the relationship between law and poverty?

A. Law primarily serves the interests of the wealthy and does not impact poverty reduction.

B. Law is a tool that can either perpetuate or mitigate poverty, depending on its implementation and enforcement.

C. Legal frameworks are entirely neutral and do not influence socio-economic inequality.

D. Poverty is solely an economic issue and is unrelated to the legal system.

112. Which of the following international agreements addresses poverty alleviation through legal mechanisms?

A. Kyoto Protocol

B. Paris Climate Agreement

C. Sustainable Development Goals (SDGs)

D. Treaty of Westphalia

113. In India, which constitutional provision explicitly addresses the eradication of poverty?

A. Article 21 B. Article 39A. and B.

C. Article 51A(k) D. Article 44

114. Which case emphasized the right to livelihood as part of the right to life under Article 21 of the Indian Constitution?

A. Kesavananda Bharati v. State of Kerala

B. Maneka Gandhi v. Union of India

C. Olga Tellis v. Bombay Municipal Corporation

D. Indira Sawhney v. Union of India

115. Which of the following legal frameworks plays a crucial role in addressing rural poverty in India?

A. The Indian Contract Act, 1872

B. The Mahatma Gandhi National Rural Employment Guarantee Act (MGNREGA), 2005

C. The Arms Act, 1959

D. The Official Secrets Act, 1923

116. Match the following poverty alleviation programs with their objectives:

List-I (Program)	List-II (Objective)
A. MGNREGA	I. Guaranteed wage employment
B. National Food Security Act (NFSA)	II. Legal right to subsidized food grains
C. Pradhan Mantri Awas Yojana (PMAY)	III. Affordable housing for the poor
D. Ayushman Bharat Scheme	IV. Health insurance for economically weaker sections

A. A-I, B-II, C-III, D-IV

B. A-III, B-I, C-IV, D-II

C. A-IV, B-III, C-II, D-I

D. A-II, B-I, C-IV, D-III

117. Which of the following doctrines ensures that development policies prioritize the marginalized?

A. Eminent Domain Doctrine

B. Doctrine of Basic Structure

C. Doctrine of Distributive Justice

D. Doctrine of Ultra Vires

118. The World Bank defines "absolute poverty" as living on less than:

A. $1 per day B. $1.90 per day

C. $3 per day D. $5 per day

119. Match the following constitutional provisions with their relevance to poverty alleviation:

List-I (Article)	List-II (Provision in Indian Constitution)
A. Article 21	I. Right to life includes the right to livelihood
B. Article 38	II. Promotion of welfare state and reduction of inequalities
C. Article 41	III. Right to work, education, and public assistance
D. Article 43	IV. Living wage and decent conditions of work

A. A-I, B-II, C-III, D-IV

B. A-II, B-I, C-IV, D-III

C. A-III, B-IV, C-II, D-I

D. A-IV, B-III, C-I, D-II

120. The judicial interpretation that expanded the right to food under Article 21 was seen in the case of ....

A. People's Union for Civil Liberties v. Union of India

B. Vishaka v. State of Rajasthan

C. Golak Nath v. State of Punjab

D. Minerva Mills v. Union of India

121. The Right to Education Act (2009) makes free and compulsory education a fundamental right for children aged ....

A. 3-10 years B. 6-14 years
C. 7-18 years D. 5-12 years

122. In India, the public distribution system (PDS) provides subsidized food to below poverty line families under the ....

A. National Food Security Act
B. Essential Commodities Act
C. Consumer Protection Act
D. Fertilizer Control Act

123. The concept of "inclusive growth" in economic development aims to ensure that ....

A. Only the wealthiest benefit from industrialization
B. Development policies are tailored to marginalized communities
C. Regulatory laws are removed for economic expansion
D. Corporate monopolies dominate policy-making

124. Microfinance institutions help reduce poverty by ....

A. Providing financial services to the poor without collateral
B. Focusing only on urban economic development
C. Offering free government grants without accountability
D. Replacing nationalized banking systems

125. **Assertion (A):** The right to housing is an essential part of the right to life under Article 21 of the Indian Constitution.

Reason (R): The Supreme Court of India has held that deprivation of shelter amounts to deprivation of livelihood.

A. Both A and R are true, and R is the correct explanation of A.
B. Both A and R are true, but R is not the correct explanation of A.
C. A is true, but R is false.
D. A is false, but R is true.

126. **Assertion (A):** The Indian Constitution guarantees the right to work as a fundamental right under Article 21.

Reason (R): The Directive Principles of State Policy (DPSPs) provide for the right to work under Article 41.

A. Both A and R are true, and R is the correct explanation of A.
B. Both A and R are true, but R is not the correct explanation of A.
C. A is true, but R is false.
D. A is false, but R is true.

127. **Assertion (A):** International human rights law mandates that states must ensure poverty alleviation through legally enforceable rights.

Reason (R): The International Covenant on Economic, Social and Cultural Rights (ICESCR) recognizes the right to an adequate standard of living, including food and housing.

A. Both A and R are true, and R is the correct explanation of A.
B. Both A and R are true, but R is not the correct explanation of A.
C. A is true, but R is false.
D. A is false, but R is true.

128. **Assertion (A):** The Scheduled Tribes and Other Traditional Forest Dwellers (Recognition of Forest Rights) Act, 2006 protects the land rights of forest dwellers.

Reason (R): The Act allows for the complete privatization of forest lands to individual tribal families.

A. Both A and R are true, and R is the correct explanation of A.
B. Both A and R are true, but R is not the correct explanation of A.
C. A is true, but R is false.
D. A is false, but R is true.

129. **Assertion (A):** The Public Interest Litigation (PIL) mechanism has played a crucial role in poverty alleviation in India.

Reason (R): PILs have been used by courts to enforce socio-economic rights such as food security, labor protections, and healthcare.

A. Both A and R are true, and R is the correct explanation of A.
B. Both A and R are true, but R is not the correct explanation of A.
C. A is true, but R is false.
D. A is false, but R is true.

130. **Assertion (A):** The Land Acquisition Act, 2013 protects landowners from forced displacement without adequate compensation.

Reason (R): The Act ensures that all land acquisitions are for public purposes only.

A. Both A and R are true, and R is the correct explanation of A.

B. Both A and R are true, but R is not the correct explanation of A.
C. A is true, but R is false.
D. A is false, but R is true.

131. Based on the passage, which of the following is a primary legal challenge in poverty alleviation?
A. Inadequate constitutional recognition of poverty rights.
B. Gaps in enforcement of poverty-related laws.
C. Absence of judicial intervention in social justice issues.
D. Lack of public participation in economic policymaking.

132. Which of the following laws directly resulted from the Right to Food Case?
A. The Forest Rights Act, 2006
B. The National Food Security Act, 2013
C. The Essential Commodities Act, 1955
D. The Prevention of Food Adulteration Act, 1954

133. What is a key feature of MGNREGA, 2005 in relation to poverty reduction?
A. Providing free food grains to urban populations.
B. Ensuring employment for at least 100 days to rural households.
C. Regulating minimum wage rates in the private sector.
D. Granting financial subsidies to large-scale industries.

134. According to the passage, how does the legal system approach the issue of land displacement?
A. It strictly prohibits all land acquisitions by private entities.
B. It provides legal compensation and rehabilitation frameworks.
C. It allows free-market transactions without state intervention.
D. It prioritizes corporate landowners over marginalized communities.

135. The Directive Principles of State Policy primarily focus on:
A. Providing justiciable rights for poverty alleviation.
B. Guiding the state in formulating socio-economic policies.
C. Enforcing strict penalties for non-compliance.
D. Granting citizens absolute economic rights.

136. In which case did the Supreme Court recognize the right to shelter as a fundamental right?
A. Francis Coralie Mullin v. UT of Delhi
B. Indira Sawhney v. Union of India
C. Rafique Bibi v. Sitaram Bhalchandra
D. Sheela Barse v. State of Maharashtra

137. The Supreme Court ruling in the case of Bandhua Mukti Morcha v. Union of India (1984) was instrumental in:
A. Addressing bonded labor and forced labor issues.
B. Declaring a basic structure doctrine of the Constitution.
C. Recognizing corporate liability in economic crimes.
D. Striking down discriminatory property laws.

138. In Vishaka v. State of Rajasthan, the Supreme Court emphasized:
A. The right to work in a safe environment.
B. The right to demand higher wages.
C. The right to social security benefits.
D. The right to private property.

139. Which of the following best describes the concept of global justice?
A. A legal framework that exclusively governs international economic transactions.
B. A political and philosophical approach to ensuring fairness in global wealth distribution, human rights, and international law.
C. A United Nations framework to regulate only cross-border disputes.
D. A concept that applies only to developed nations for balancing domestic wealth gaps.

140. Which of the following theories of justice is primarily associated with global distributive justice?
A. Rawlsian Theory of Justice
B. Hobbesian Theory of Social Contract
C. Feminist Legal Theory
D. Austin's Command Theory of Law

141. The "Capability Approach" to justice, developed by Amartya Sen and Martha Nussbaum, primarily focuses on:
A. Basic economic growth indicators.
B. The expansion of individual capabilities and freedoms.
C. International trade regulations.
D. The absolute sovereignty of states.

142. Which of the following institutions plays the most direct role in global economic justice?
A. International Criminal Court (ICC)
B. World Trade Organization (WTO)
C. Interpol
D. United Nations Security Council (UNSC)

143. Which of the following legal doctrines is most commonly applied in discussions of post-modernism and law?
A. Formalism B. Legal Positivism
C. Deconstruction D. Utilitarianism

144. Match the following theories of justice with their key proponents:

List-I (Theory of Justice)	List-II (Key Proponent)
A. Theory of Justice	I. John Rawls
B. Utilitarian Justice	II. Jeremy Bentham
C. Capabilities Approach	III. Amartya Sen
D. Communitarian Justice	IV. Michael Sandel

A. A-I, B-II, C-III, D-IV
B. A-IV, B-I, C-II, D-III
C. A-III, B-II, C-IV, D-I
D. A-I, B-IV, C-II, D-III

145. The concept of "Post-Modern Legal Theory" challenges the idea that:

A. Law should be completely disregarded in society.
B. Legal interpretation is purely objective and universally applicable.
C. All legal norms should be determined democratically.
D. There should be no written laws.

146. Which of the following statements is a primary critique of modernism by post-modernist thinkers?

A. Modernist principles create legal certainty.
B. Modernist legal systems prioritize economic growth over social justice.
C. Modernism assumes universal truths, which post-modernism argues are socially constructed.
D. Modernism applies only to Western legal systems.

147. The idea that "Justice is context-dependent and law should be interpreted through multiple perspectives" aligns with:

A. Post-modern legal theory
B. Modernist jurisprudence
C. Rawlsian liberal justice
D. Austin's command theory

148. Match the following concepts of justice with their legal applications:

List-I (Concept)	List-II (Application in Law)
A. Cosmopolitanism	I. Human rights as universal moral rights
B. Positivism	II. Law must be separated from morality
C. Legal Realism	III. Law is shaped by social, political, and economic forces
D. Deconstruction	IV. Legal texts have no fixed meaning

A. A-I, B-II, C-III, D-IV
B. A-IV, B-I, C-II, D-III
C. A-III, B-II, C-IV, D-I
D. A-I, B-IV, C-II, D-III

149. The World Justice Project defines the Rule of Law as requiring that laws must be ....

A. Fixed and never change.
B. Applied equally and fairly.
C. Dependent on the government's discretion.
D. Unchangeable to ensure stability.

150. The main criticism of modernist legal systems by post-modernists is that they ....

A. Promote legal certainty and predictability.
B. Ignore the historical and social contexts of legal interpretations.
C. Are based on subjectivity and personal opinions.
D. Reject all legal structures and institutions.

ANSWERS

1. (C): Customs, legislation, and precedents are recognized sources of law, whereas fiction is not.

2. (C): Legislation is enacted by the state and is the primary source of law in most legal systems.

3. (C): Continuous, reasonable, and accepted by the community: Customs must be ancient, continuous, reasonable, and widely accepted to be a valid source of law.

4. (B): The principle of following judicial precedents: "Stare Decisis" means that courts should follow past judicial decisions to maintain consistency in law.

5. (C): State authority: According to legal positivism, law derives from state authority, not morality or custom.

6. (A): Precedents are decisions of courts, customs are established practices, legislation is made by the legislature, and equity ensures fairness.

Hence, correct match is (A)-III, (B)-I, (C)-II, (D)-IV.

7. (B): Stare Decisis: Stare Decisis refers to following previous judicial decisions to ensure consistency in legal rulings.

8. (C): Hindu Marriage Practices: Customary law arises from long-standing traditions followed by a community.

9. **(A): The Quran:** In Islamic law, the Quran is considered the primary source, supplemented by Hadith, Ijma, and Qiyas.

10. **(C): Common Law:** Common law is developed through judicial decisions and precedents, unlike statutory law, which is legislated.

11. **(D): Analytical School:** John Austin, a legal positivist, described law as the command of the sovereign.

12. **(B): Continuous customs and traditions:** Savigny believed that law evolves from customs and historical experiences.

13. **(C): Roscoe Pound:** Roscoe Pound emphasized that law should be used for "social engineering".

14. **(B): Friedrich Carl von Savigny:** Savigny argued that law grows with the customs and traditions of people.

15. **(C): Sociological School:** Roscoe Pound promoted law as a means to balance competing societal interests.

16. **(C): Sociological School:** Roscoe Pound's Sociological School argues that law should balance competing interests for social welfare.

17. **(C): A command of the sovereign:** John Austin defined law as "the command of the sovereign backed by sanctions."

18. **(C): Analytical School:** Bentham argued that law should maximize "the greatest happiness for the greatest number."

19. **(A):** Austin developed Command Theory, Pound developed Social Engineering, Savigny focused on Volksgeist, and Montesquieu formulated Separation of Powers.

Hence, correct matching is (A)-I, (B)-II, (C)-III, (D)-IV.

20. **(A): Law is what the judge decides:** Legal Realism argues that law is shaped by judicial decisions and practical realities, not just legal texts.

21. **(A):** Both A and R are true, and R is the correct explanation of A.

The Rule of Law means that all individuals, including the government, are subject to law, and in India, the Constitution is supreme.

22. **(C):** A is true, but R is false: The Sociological School supports dynamic law, whereas rigid law contradicts this idea.

23. **(A):** Both A and R are true, and R is the correct explanation of A.

24. **(C)**

25. **(C)**

26. **(D): Fiction:** The primary sources of law include legislation, precedents, and customs, but fiction is not a recognized source of law.

27. **(B): Courts follow previous judicial decisions:** Stare Decisis ensures that precedents are followed to maintain consistency in judicial decisions.

28. **(A): Natural Law School:** The Natural Law School (Aristotle, Aquinas) holds that law is derived from morality and natural order.

29. **(C): State authority:** Legal Positivism (John Austin) argues that law is created by the sovereign and must be obeyed.

30. **(A): The government acts according to law:** The Rule of Law ensures that no one, including the government, is above the law.

31. **(C): Morality influences law but they are not the same:** Law is enforceable by the state, while morality is based on social values and ethics.

32. **(B): Morality changes with time and culture:** Morality is dynamic and varies across societies and historical periods.

33. **(C): Lon Fuller:** Fuller emphasized "The Morality of Law," arguing that law must have internal morality.

34. **(B): Natural Law Theory:** Natural law theorists (e.g., Aquinas) believe that laws must be morally justified.

35. **(C): Criminalization of Murder and Theft:** Laws against murder and theft reflect moral principles of society.

36. **(A):** Natural law links morality and law, Positivists separate them, Sociological School sees law as a social tool, and Legal Realism focuses on how law is enforced.

Hence, correct matching is (A)-I, (B)-II, (C)-III, (D)-IV.

37. **(B): Telling the truth:** Lying may be immoral but is not always illegal unless it involves fraud or defamation.

38. **(A): Law should maximize happiness (Utilitarianism):** Bentham's Utilitarianism states that law should create the greatest happiness for the greatest number.

39. **(C): Natural Law Theory:** Natural law believes laws should reflect moral duties to be valid.

40. **(C): Laws permitting capital punishment:** Some believe capital punishment is immoral, while others see it as justifiable retribution.

41. **(C): A is false, but R is true:** Some laws are based on practicality rather than morality, such as tax laws.

42. **(A):** Both A and R are true, and R is the correct explanation of A.

    Natural law theorists argue that immoral laws are invalid.

43. **(D):** Both A and R are false: The law must balance individual freedom with social morality.

44. **(C): It is always absolute and unlimited:** Legal rights are subject to reasonable restrictions and are not absolute.

45. **(C) Correlative to each other:** A right of one person corresponds to a duty of another.

46. **(C): Rudolf von Jhering:** Jhering emphasized that rights protect interests through legal means.

47. **(B): Duty to follow traffic laws:** Perfect duties are legally enforceable, while imperfect duties are moral obligations.

48. **(A): 42nd Amendment Act, 1976:** The 42nd Amendment introduced Part IV-A (Article 51A), listing Fundamental Duties.

49. **(A):** (A)-I, (B)-II, (C)-III, (D)-IV

    Legal Rights are state-enforced, Moral Rights are based on ethics, Constitutional Rights arise from the Constitution, and Human Rights are universal.

50. **(A): Right to vote:** Voting rights are legally enforceable, while others are moral obligations.

51. **(D): Liberty:** Liberty allows action without imposing duties on others.

52. **(C): John Austin:** Austin viewed duties as commands backed by sanctions.

53. **(B): Kantian Ethics:** Immanuel Kant emphasized deontological ethics, where duties are primary.

54. **(B)**

55. **(C)**

56. **(C)**

57. **(B)**

58. **(C)**

59. **(A):** Both A and R are true, and R is the correct explanation of A.

    Every right imposes a duty on others to respect it.

60. **(C):** A is false, but R is true: Fundamental Rights are not absolute and have reasonable restrictions.

61. **(B): The capacity to have rights and duties in law:** Legal personality allows an entity (person or organization) to be recognized by law as having rights and duties.

62. **(B): A company:** A juristic person is an entity (like a company or institution) that has legal rights and obligations.

63. **(C): A machine:** A machine lacks legal personality as it cannot hold rights or duties.

64. **(B): An entity that can own property and sue or be sued:** Juristic persons, like companies, trusts, and temples, have legal recognition and rights.

65. **(B): A river:** The Ganga and Yamuna rivers were granted legal personality by the Uttarakhand High Court in 2017.

66. **(A):** (A)-II, (B)-I, (C)-III, (D)-IV

    Natural persons are humans, juristic persons are created by law, corporations exist separately from members, and trusts hold property for beneficiaries.

67. **(D): Their rights and obligations are still recognized by law:** A deceased person retains certain legal rights, like reputation and inheritance matters.

68. **(A): It is registered under law:** A company gains legal personality when incorporated under the Companies Act.

69. **(B): Ability to enter into contracts:** Juristic persons (like companies and trusts) can sign contracts, sue, and own property.

70. **(B): Yogendra Nath v. Commissioner of Income Tax:** The court recognized Hindu idols as juristic persons for holding property.

71. **(B)**

72. **(B)**

73. **(B)**

74. **(C)**

75. **(C)**

76. **(A):** Both A and R are true, and R is the correct explanation of A.

A company, once incorporated, becomes a separate legal entity from its owners and shareholders. It can own assets, enter contracts, and be involved in legal proceedings independently.

77. **(B):** Both A and R are true, but R is not the correct explanation of A.

A natural person's legal personality ends upon death, but certain rights and obligations (e.g., estate, liabilities) may be transferred to heirs or executors, though the personality itself is not inherited.

78. **(D): Right to commit a crime using the property:** Ownership includes possession, enjoyment, and transfer rights, but does not allow illegal activities.

79. **(B): A legal right recognized by law:** Possession is more than physical control; it involves legal recognition and intent to own.

80. **(A): The totality of rights over a thing:** Salmond describes ownership as the bundle of rights over a thing.

81. **(C): Ownership is a legal right, while possession is a factual state:** Ownership includes legal recognition, whereas possession can exist without ownership.

82. **(D): Fictional property:** Property includes movable, immovable, and intellectual, but fictional property is not a legal category.

83. **(A):** (A)-I, (B)-II, (C)-III, (D)-IV

Ownership is an exclusive legal right, possession involves control and intent, intellectual property includes creative rights, and lease grants a temporary right to use property.

84. **(C): A patent:** Incorporeal property refers to intangible rights like patents, trademarks, and copyrights.

85. **(B): It must have value:** Property must have value, whether tangible (land) or intangible (copyrights).

86. **(C): Leasehold ownership:** Leasehold ownership allows temporary use of another's property.

87. **(C): Legal possession:** Legal possession is protected by law, unlike mere physical control.

88. **(B)**

89. **(B)**

90. **(B)**

91. **(B)**

92. **(A)**

93. **(C): A is false, but R is true.**

Ownership is the highest form of legal claim over property, while possession is a physical control that does not necessarily confer ownership rights. However, in certain cases (e.g., adverse possession), possession may lead to ownership, but possession alone does not always defeat ownership claims.

94. **(C): A is true, but R is false.**

Property can indeed be tangible (physical objects like land, cars) or intangible (patents, copyrights). However, intellectual property is an intangible asset, making R incorrect.

95. **(A): Both A and R are true, and R is the correct explanation of A.**

Adverse possession allows a person to claim ownership over land if they possess it openly, exclusively, and continuously for a legally prescribed period without the consent of the original owner. The rationale behind this doctrine is to prevent landowners from neglecting their property rights indefinitely.

96. **(A):** (A)-II, (B)-I, (C)-III, (D)-IV

- Strict liability requires no fault, but defenses exist (Rylands v. Fletcher).
- Vicarious liability holds an employer liable for employees' acts.
- Absolute liability is without any defense (M.C. Mehta case).
- Criminal liability requires both intent and action.

97. **(A):** (A)-III, (B)-II, (C)-I, (D)-IV

- Rylands v. Fletcher introduced strict liability.
- M.C. Mehta case introduced absolute liability in India.
- Bhopal Gas Tragedy reinforced corporate liability.
- State of Rajasthan v. Mst. Vidhyawati established government tort liability.

98. **(A):** (A)-III, (B)-II, (C)-I, (D)-IV

- Mens rea liability requires a guilty mind.
- Vicarious liability applies when one person is responsible for another's act.
- Strict liability does not require intent, but some defenses exist.
- Absolute liability has no defenses or exceptions.

99. (A): (A)-III, (B)-I, (C)-II, (D)-IV

- Act of God applies to unforeseeable natural events.
- Volenti non fit injuria means plaintiff assumed risk voluntarily.
- Contributory negligence reduces damages if plaintiff also contributed to harm.
- Inevitable accident means harm was unavoidable despite precautions.

100. (A): (A)-II, (B)-I, (C)-III, (D)-IV

- Nominal damages are symbolic and awarded without real loss.
- Compensatory damages match the actual loss suffered.
- Punitive damages aim to punish the defendant.
- Special damages cover specific financial losses.

101. (A): Both A and R are true, and R is the correct explanation of A.

102. (A): Both A and R are true, and R is the correct explanation of A.

A company, being an artificial legal entity, lacks physical intent (mens rea). However, the doctrine of corporate criminal liability allows mens rea to be attributed to a company through its key officials or directors. This principle ensures that corporations can be held accountable for criminal acts such as fraud, environmental violations, and corporate negligence.

103. (B): The act is done in the course of employment, even if unauthorized.

104. (B)

105. (A)

106. (B): It shifts the burden of proof to the defendant when negligence is inferred from the nature of the accident.

Res Ipsa Loquitur means "the thing speaks for itself," allowing a presumption of negligence where the accident could not have occurred without negligence.

107. (B): The act occurred in the course of employment, there existed a master-servant relationship, and the act was connected to the employment duties.

Vicarious liability applies when the wrongful act occurs during employment under a master-servant relationship and is connected to employment duties.

108. (B): The physical act or omission constituting the crime: Actus reus is the physical act, omission, or consequence leading to a criminal offense.

109. (A): Crimes under strict liability, such as regulatory offenses: Strict liability offenses do not require mens rea, as in public welfare and regulatory laws.

110. (D): None of the above

Absolute liability allows no defenses, unlike strict liability.

111. (B): Law is a tool that can either perpetuate or mitigate poverty, depending on its implementation and enforcement: Laws related to minimum wages, land rights, social security, and labor protections can reduce or worsen poverty depending on enforcement.

112. (C): Sustainable Development Goals (SDGs): The UN Sustainable Development Goals (SDGs), particularly Goal 1 (No Poverty), emphasize legal frameworks for social protection, property rights, and economic inclusion.

113. (B): Article 39(a) and (b): Directive Principles of State Policy (DPSP), particularly Article 39(a) and (b), focus on reducing inequalities in income and wealth.

114. (C): Olga Tellis v. Bombay Municipal Corporation: In Olga Tellis v. Bombay Municipal Corporation (1985), the Supreme Court ruled that right to livelihood is part of the right to life.

115. (B): The Mahatma Gandhi National Rural Employment Guarantee Act (MGNREGA), 2005: MGNREGA provides guaranteed employment to rural workers, helping in poverty reduction.

116. (A)

117. (C): Doctrine of Distributive Justice: Distributive justice aims to ensure fair allocation of resources for marginalized communities.

118. (C): $3 per day: As per World Bank (2022), absolute poverty is living on less than $3 per day.

119. (A)

120. (A)

121. (B)

122. (A)

123. (B)

124. (A)

125. (A): Both A and R are true, and R is the correct explanation of A.

The Supreme Court in Chameli Singh v. State of U.P. (1996) recognized the right to housing as an extension of the right to life.

126. (C): A is true, but R is false.

Article 21 does not explicitly provide a right to work, but Article 41 under DPSPs directs the state to ensure work, education, and assistance for citizens.

127. (A): Both A and R are true, and R is the correct explanation of A.

ICESCR (Article 11) mandates states to take steps to ensure adequate living standards, including access to food, clothing, and housing.

128. (C): A is true, but R is false.

The Forest Rights Act, 2006 recognizes both individual and community rights over forests but does not allow complete privatization.

129. (A): Both A and R are true, and R is the correct explanation of A.

PILs have been instrumental in securing rights, such as in People's Union for Civil Liberties v. Union of India (Right to Food Case, 2001).

130. (B): Both A and R are true, but R is not the correct explanation of A.

The 2013 Act mandates fair compensation but does not restrict acquisitions solely for public purposes; private projects can also acquire land under certain conditions.

131. (B)

132. (B)

133. (B)

134. (B)

135. (B)

136. (A)

137. (A)

138. (A): The right to work in a safe environment: Supreme court laid down the rules or guideline for ensuring safe environment for women at workplace.

139. (B): A political and philosophical approach to ensuring fairness in global wealth distribution, human rights, and international law: Global justice concerns economic inequality, human rights, and equitable governance at the international level.

140. (A): Rawlsian Theory of Justice: John Rawls' "Law of Peoples" (1999) extends his Theory of Justice to international relations and global justice.

141. (B): The expansion of individual capabilities and freedoms: The Capability Approach argues that justice should be measured by an individual's ability to achieve well-being rather than just economic resources.

142. (B): World Trade Organization (WTO): The WTO governs international trade laws, affecting economic justice in developing and developed nations.

143. (C): Deconstruction: Deconstruction, influenced by Jacques Derrida, is a post-modernist critique of traditional legal reasoning and structures.

144. (A)

145. (B): Legal interpretation is purely objective and universally applicable: Post-modern legal theory argues that law is socially constructed and subjective, not neutral and absolute.

146. (C): Modernism assumes universal truths, which post-modernism argues are socially constructed: Post-modernism challenges the universalist, objective claims of modernist thought.

147. (A): Post-modern legal theory: Post-modernism rejects grand legal narratives and emphasizes subjectivity in justice.

148. (A)

149. (B)

150. (B): Ignore the historical and social contexts of legal interpretations

UNIT 2 Constitutional and Administrative Law

CONSTITUTIONAL LAW

The Constitutional Law refers to the rules which regulate structure, functions and inter-relations of governmental organs. The rules are legal as well as included conventions etc., a country may have a constitution but not necessarily constitutionalism e.g., a country where dictator's word is law, can be said to have a constitution, but not constitutionalism. Constitutionalism means that powers of the government must be limited by the constitution and the government must work within the scope of those limitations. Hence, a scenario in which a government assumes unlimited powers denotes absence of constitutionalism even though such a state might have a constitution very much in place and in force. It is the antithesis of arbitrary power. Only when constitution of a country seeks to decentralize power and also impose other restraints, does a country have both—constitution and constitutionalism.

Following are the principles and norms which promote constitutionalism in a country: a written constitution, federalism, free elections, independent judiciary with judicial review, fundamental rights, doctrine of rule of law and separation of powers. The binding force of the constitution is the sovereign will of the people of India.

An objective resolution was moved by Pandit J.L. Nehru, which laid down the objectives of the constitution to be framed by the assembly. Sir B.N. Rau was the constitutional advisor to the constituent assembly. It took 2 years, 11 months and 18 days to make the Indian constitution. On the 26th Day of the November, 1949 the constitution received the signature of the President of the Constituent Assembly and was declared as passed. The provisions relating to citizenship, elections, provisional Parliament, temporary and transitional provisions, were given immediate effect i.e., from November 26th, 1949. The rest of the constitution came into force on January 26th, 1950, and this date is referred as the date of the implementation of the constitution.

PREAMBLE

The Preamble indicates the source from which the constitution comes viz., the People of India. It is ordained by the people of India through their representatives assembled in a Sovereign Constituent Assembly. The Preamble declares clearly that it is the People of India, who have adopted, enacted and given to themselves the constitution. The constitution though not ratified by people, came into force in 1949. The preamble sets out the aims and aspirations of people, and these have been translated into various provisions of Constitution.

The Preamble to the Indian constitution reads:

"WE, THE PEOPLE OF INDIA, having solemnly resolved to constitute India into a SOVEREIGN, SOCIALIST, SECULAR, DEMOCRATIC REPUBLIC

And to secure to all its citizen:

JUSTICE, social, economic and political;

LIBERTY of thought, expression, belief, faith and worship;

EQUALITY of status and of opportunity;

And to promote among them all

FRATERNITY assuring the dignity of the individual and the unity and integrity of the nation:

IN OUR CONSTITUENT ASSEMBLY, this 26th day of November, 1949, do hereby ADOPT, ENACT and GIVE TO OURSELVES THIS CONSTITUTION.

(The word socialist and secular have been added to the preamble by 42nd Amendment Act 1976. Also unity of nation was amended to read unity and integrity of the nation.)

The objectives of the preamble are :

Justice, Liberty, Equality and Fraternity.

The ultimate goal is that of "securing the dignity of the individual and unity and integrity of the nation".

- **SOVEREIGN:** A sovereign state is one where there resides within itself a supreme and absolute power acknowledging no superior. India has full authority in all its internal and external matters and is not to bow to any outside superior power. Sovereignty in India vests in the people of India.
- **DEMOCRACY:** It means Government by the people as against Monarchy and Dictatorship *i.e.*, autocratic rule of one person, oligarchy or aristocracy – rule by the few. People have an inalienable right to rule themselves, or to be ruled in the way they like and by the people they choose.
- **REPUBLIC:** It implies that there is no hereditary ruler and the head of the state is elected by the people for a fixed term. He is usually called the President of the Republic. Coolie said, "A republican form of government by representatives choosen by the people".
- **SOCIALIST:** Socialism meant, elimination of inequality in income and status and standard of living. In other words, "free from all type of exploitation — social, economic and political".
- **SECULAR:** It implies that the state does not owe any loyalty to any Particular religion as such; it is not irreligious or antireligious: it gives equal freedom to all religions. The meaning sought to be given to the term has been that of Sarva Dharma Sambhavna *i.e.*, treating all religions alike or giving equal respects to all religions instead of Dharma Nirpeksha *i.e.*, State Neutrality in matters of religion.
- **JUSTICE:** It means harmonization of interests between the individuals, between the groups and, between the individuals and groups on the one hand and interests of community on the other hand. The essence of justice is the attainment of common good. It embraces the entire social, economic and political sphere of human life.
- **LIBERTY:** It usually means the "absence of restraint or interference in individual freedom of action by the government". But, liberty in the preamble to our constitution does not mean mere absence of restraint or domination. It is a positive concept of the right to "liberty of thought, expression, belief, faith and worship". It comprehends various freedoms later concretized in the fundamental rights and considered essential for the development of the individual and the nation.
- **EQUALITY:** Liberty and equality are complementary. It signifies equality of status and equality of opportunity.
- **FRATERNITY:** The ideals of justice, liberty and equality are relevant and meaningful only in as much as these promote a common feeling of brotherhood.
- **UNITY AND INTEGRITY OF THE NATION:** In order to safeguard the dignity of the individual, we need to built the nation and protect its unity and integrity. Without the unity and integrity of the nation, we could not succeed in our efforts of socio-economic development and could not hope to preserve either democracy or independence of the country.

UTILITY OF PREAMBLE

Preamble represents the quintessence, the philosophy, the ideals, the soul or spirit of the entire Constitution of India. It had the stamp of deep deliberation, was marked by precision: it was an epitome of the broad features of the constitution which were an amplification or concretization of the concepts set out in the Preamble:

- It indicates the source of the constitution.
- A statement of objectives of the constitution—which the legislation is intended to achieve. It epitomizes principles on which the Government is to function.
- It serves as a challenge to the people to adhere to the ideals enshrined in it.
- It is a sort of introduction to the statute and many a times very helpful to understand the policy and legislative intent. It is a key note *i.e.*, key to the minds of the framers of the constitution.
- Several decisions of the Supreme Court pointed out the importance and utility of it. By itself, it is not enforceable in the Court of Law, yet it states objects and aids legal interpretation of the constitution, where language is ambiguous... construction which fits the preamble may be preferred.

Is Preamble a Part of Constitution?

In Berubaris' case (AIR 1960 SC 858), held that Preamble is not a Part of the Constitution. However, in Keshavanand's case (AIR 1973 SC 1467) held that it is a Part of constitution and constitution should be read and interpreted in the light of grand and noble vision expressed in Preamble. In fact, the Preamble was relied on in imposing implied limitations on amendment under Article 368. Preamble is a Part of constitution, it can be amended, but 'basic features' in it can't be amended. Amending power can't change the constitution in such a way that it ceases to be a 'Sovereign Democratic Republic.'

FUNDAMENTAL RIGHTS

Part III of the constitution, which contains FR, has been described as the Magna Carta of India. These FRs substantially covers all the traditional civil and political rights enumerated in the Universal Declaration of human rights. Dr. Ambedkar described them as the most criticized Part of the constitution. FRs, subject to the provisions of the constitution cannot be violated or interfered with by any law, order, or act of the government.

FRs were deemed essential to protect the rights and liberties of the people against the encroachment of the power delegated by them to their government. They are limitations upon all the powers of the government. In Maneka Gandhi case, Bhagwati J., observed: These FRs represent the basic values cherish the dignity of the individual and create conditions in which every human being can develop his personality to the fullest extent.

These rights are regarded as Fundamental Rights because they are most essential for the attainment by the individual of his full intellectual, moral and spiritual status. The constitution also provides for the suspension of the FR in certain circumstances. Art. 358 provides that when the President under Art. 352 makes the proclamation of emergency, the freedoms guaranteed by Art. 19 are automatically suspended for the period of emergency. Art. 359 further empowers the President to suspend the right to move any court for the enforcement of FR during the continuance of emergency.

It is now established proposition that an individual cannot waive off any of his FRs. This proposition has been applied in number of cases. (Olga Tellis case) The state cannot arrogate to itself a right to commit breach of the FRs of any person by resorting the principles of the waiver or estoppel or similar principles. The FRs can be classified under the following *Six* groups:

- Right to Equality (Art. 14-18)
- Right to Freedom (Art. 19-22)
- Right against Exploitation (Art. 23-24)
- Right to Freedom of Religion (Art. 25-28)
- Cultural and Educational Rights (Art. 29-30)
- Right to Constitutional Remedies (Art. 32-35)

The 44th Amendment has abolished the right to property as a FR guaranteed by Art. 19(1)(f) and Art. 31 of the constitution. It is now only a legal right.

ARTICLE 12: DEFINITION OF STATE

Unless the context otherwise requires the term state includes the following – executive and legislature of Union and State; all local or other authorities within territory of India or under the control of government.

In the context of Art. 12, authority means the power to make laws, byelaws etc. which have the force of law and power to enforce those laws. The expression other authorities in Art. 12 is used after mentioning the executive and legislature of Union and states and all local authorities.

In Electricity Board, Rajasthan and Sukhdev Singh *vs.* Bhagat Tam cases, the Supreme Court held that only the authorities created by the constitution or statute are the other authorities, though it is not necessary that statutory authority should be engaged in performing governmental functions. Thus, Rajasthan Electricity Board, Cooperative Society, ONGC, LIC etc., are held to be other authorities. But in subsequent decisions, a broad and liberal interpretation to the expression other authorities was given in view of the fact that in a welfare state, government has to employ various agencies or instrumentalities.

In R.D. Shetty *vs.* International Airport Authority of India, the International Airport Authority as held to be the State. The court laid down the following tests:

- State mainly or chiefly contributed to the financial resources.
- Deep and pervasive state control e.g., appointment and removal of members of a society, etc.
- Functions of Corporations are of public importance *i.e.*, governmental in essence.
- If a government deptt. is transferred to a corporation.
- Corporation enjoys monopoly status which is state conferred.

In Unni Krishanan *vs* State of AP, the Supreme Court observed that the term authority may cover any other person or body performing public duty. Thus, a private medical/engineering college comes within the writ jurisdiction of the court irrespective of the question of aid and affiliation.

In M.C. Mehta *vs* UOI, the question was whether a private corporation is a state under Art. 12. The court observed that a non-governmental company can be placed within the meaning of Art. 12, if for reasons of state control and regulations and kind of public functions they are performing, they satisfy the test of instrumentality or agency of government.

In Rupa Ashok Hurra *vs.* Ashok Hurra, the Apex court has affirmed and ruled that no judicial proceedings could be said to violate any of the FRs. It was said to be settled position of law that the superior courts of justice did not fall within the ambit of state or other authorities under Art. 12.

ARTICLE 13: LAW INCONSISTENT WITH FUNDAMENTAL RIGHTS

Clause (1) – All preconstitutional or existing laws *i.e.*, laws which were enforced immediately before the commencement of the constitution shall be void to the extent to which they are inconsistent with fundamental rights from the day of commencement of constitution.

Clause (2) – The state shall not make any law which takes away or abridges the FRs, and any law in contravention of FRs shall to the extent of contravention be void.

Clause (3) – It gives the term 'Law' a very broad connotation which includes any ordinance, order, bylaw, rule, regulation, notification, custom, and usage having the force of law.

Art. 13 infact provides the judicial review of all legislations in India past as well as future. Art. 13 is not applicable to law declared by the Supreme Court under Articles 141 and 142.

Application and Rules of Interpretation of Article 13:

- **No retrospective effect:** Art. 13(1) is prospective in nature. All inconsistent existing laws become void only after the commencement of constitution. They are not void *ab initio*. Such laws exist for all past acts, transactions, etc. and for enforcing all rights and liabilities accrued before the date of constitution.
- **Doctrine of Severeability or Separability:** It means that if an offending provision can be separated from which is constitutional then only that Part which is offending is to be declared as void and not the entire statute.
- **Doctrine of Eclipse:** It is based on the principle that a law which violates FRs is not nullity or *void ab initio* but becomes only unenforceable *i.e.*, remains in the moribund condition. It is overshadowed or eclipsed by the FRs and remains dormant but it is not dead.

ARTICLE 14: EQUALITY BEFORE LAW

Defined: Article 14 embodies, the idea of equality expressed in the preamble. Thus, succeeding Articles 15, 16 and 17 lay down specific applications of the general rules laid down in Art. 14. Article 14 reads : The state shall not deny to any person equality before the law or the equal protection of the laws within the territory of India.

While equality before law is somewhat a negative concept implying the absence of any special privilege in favour of individuals and the equal subject of all classes to the ordinary law. Equal protection of law is more positive concept implying equality of treatment in equal circumstances. The rule is that like should be treated as alike and not that unlike should be treated as alike. In state of WB *vs.* Anwar Ali Sarkar, the court rightly observed that the second expression is the corollary of the first and it is difficult to imagine a situation in which violation of equal protection of laws will not be the violation of the equality before law. Thus, in substance the two expressions means one and the same thing.

Classification and Equality Under Article 14

The term "any person" in Art. 14 denotes that equal protection of law is available to any person which includes any company, or association etc. Art. 14 extends to both citizens and non-citizens and to natural persons as well as legal persons. The equality before law is guaranteed to all without regard to race, colour or nationality.

Article 14 permits classification but prohibits class legislation—Article 14 does not mean that the same laws should apply to all persons or that every law must have universal application, for all persons are not, by nature, attainment or circumstances, in the same position.

New Concept of Equality and Judicial Review

While the traditional concept of equality is based on the Doctrine of classification, the new concept is based on the Doctrine of Arbitrariness. Article 14 has rightly activist magnitude and it embodies a guarantee against arbitrariness. Arbitrariness is the very anti-thesis of equality. In E.P. Royappa *vs.* State of TN, it was held that the equality is a dynamic concept with many aspects and dimensions and it cannot be imprisoned within traditional and doctrinaire limits.

In Mitthu *vs.* State of Punjab, the court struck Section 303 IPC as unconstitutional. Section 303 prescribes that if a person under a life sentence commits murder, he must be given death sentence. But under Sec. 302, if a person commits murder he may be awarded death sentence or life sentence.

Judicial Review in Economic Policy

In Balco Employees Union *vs.* UOI, the Apex court held that there can be no judicial review of economic policy of the government unless there is violation of the constitution or any act. The process of disinvestments is a policy decision involving complex economic factors. The petitioners have failed to prove that decision to disinvest in Balco is any way capricious, arbitrary, illegal and uninformed.

In Sarbanand Sonowal *vs.* UOI, the validity of Illegal Migrants Act., 1983 was in question. Held that the IMDT Act, which applies only to state of Assam and not to the other states similarly situated is discriminatory as the classification based on geographical basis contains provisions and prescribes such procedure that it virtually becomes impossible to detect and deport foreigners (illegal Bangladesh immigrants). Instead of achieving the object of detecting and deporting foreigners, it defeats the purpose.

For satisfying the test of Art. 14, the geographical factors alone in making classification is not enough but there must be a nexus, with the objects sought to be achieved. In this case, it was also held that the FR of the foreigner is confined to Art. 21 for life and liberty and does not include the right to reside and stay in this country, as mentioned in Art. 19(1)(e) which is available only to the citizens of the country.

In John Vallamattom *vs.* UOI, the Supreme Court held that Section 118 of the Indian Succession Act 1926 is discriminatory and thus violative of Art. 14. The impunged provision places certain restrictions upon an Indian Christian to bequeath his property for religious or charitable purpose.

In state of Haryana *vs.* Jai Singh, the government of Haryana issued a notification granting remission of prison sentenced to all convicts except those excluded in the said notification. The Supreme Court held that the offences excluded had been properly classified, and there is no violation of Art. 14.

ARTICLE 15: NON-DISCRIMINATION ON GROUNDS OF RELIGION, RACE, CASTE, SEX OR PLACE OF BIRTH

Article 15 provides for a Particular application of the general principle embodied in Art. 14. Hence, if a discriminatory action does not fall within the purview of Art. 14, it may yet be avoided if it is obnoxious to Art. 15. However, if a law violates Art. 15, then it cannot be saved under Art. 14 on the ground of 'reasonable classification'. It may be noted that, unlike Art. 14 the guarantee under Art. 15 is available to citizens only.

Clause (1) – shall not discriminate against any citizen on grounds only of religion, caste, sex, place of birth or any of them.

The word 'discrimination' means to make an adverse distinction with regard to distinguish unfavourably from other. It must be noted that a discrimination based on any of these grounds and also on other grounds is not hit by Art. 15(1). Thus, a law which discriminates on the grounds of residence does not violate Art. 15(1). Similarly, the requirement of a test in regional language for state employment doesn't contravene Art. 15 as the test is made compulsory for all persons seeking employment.

Clause (2) – "no citizen shall on ground of religion, race, caste, sex, place of birth or any of them" be subject to any disability, liability, restriction or condition with regard to—(a) access to shops, public restaurants, hotels and places of public entertainment: or (b) the use of wells, tanks, bathing ghats, roads and place of public resorts maintained wholly or partially out of state funds or dedicated to the use of general public".

Exceptions to Art. 15(1) and (2): *Clause (3)* – nothing in this Article shall prevent state from making any special provision for women and children. Thus, reservation of seats for women in a college does not offend against Article 15(1).

Clause (4) – nothing in this Article or Clause (2) of Article 29 shall prevent the state from making any special provision for advancement of any socially and educationally backward classes of citizens or for the SCs and STs.

The scope of Art. 15(4) was discussed in Balaji *vs.* State of Mysore, the court observed that Art. 15(4) only enabled the state to make special and not exclusive provisions for backward classes. Clause (4) is only an enabling provision and does not impose any obligation on the state to take any special action under it. It merely confers a discretion to act, if necessary.

In state of U.P. *vs.* Pradeep Tandon, held that while reservation for candidates coming from rural areas was unconstitutional, for those coming from the hill and Uttarakhand areas was valid as these areas were instances of socially and educationally backward-class citizens.

Clause (5) – 93rd Amendment Act, 2005 of the constitution has added a new Clause (5) to Art. 15. Clause (5) provides that nothing in Art. 15 to 19 (1)(g) prevent the state in making any special provision, by law, for the advancement of socially and educationally backward classes of citizen or for SCs/STs as so far as much special provisions relates to admission to educational institutions, including private ones, whether aided or unaided by the state, other than minority educational institutions referred to in Art. 30(1).

ARTICLE 16: EQUALITY OF OPPORTUNITY IN PUBLIC EMPLOYMENT

Under Art. 16, the guarantee against discrimination is limited to employment and appointment under the state. Art. 15 is more general and deals with all cases of discrimination which do not fall under Art. 16.

Clause (1) – There shall be equality of opportunity for all citizens in matters relating to employment or appointment to any office under the state.

Clause (2) – No citizen shall on grounds only of religion, race, caste, sex, descent, place of birth, residence or any of them, be ineligible for, or discriminated against in respect of any employment or office under the state.

In state of Kerala *vs.* N.M. Thomas, Supreme Court observed: The rule of equality within Art. 16(1) will not be violated by a measure which ensures equality of representation in the services for the unrepresented classes after satisfying the basic needs of efficiency of administration. The members of the SCs, STs and other backward classes can be given concessions, test exemptions and other employment preferences under Art. 16(1).

Exceptions to Clauses (1 and 2): *Clause (3)* – It empowers parliament to make a law prescribing any requirement as to residence within that state or UT, prior to employment or appointment in that state or UT.

Clause (4) – It empowers the state to make special provision for the reservation of appointments or post in favour of any backward classes of citizens, which in the opinion of the state are not adequately represented in the services under the state.

Clause (5) – Nothing in this Article shall affect the operation of any law, which provides that the incumbent of an offence in connection with the affairs of any religious institution or any member of the governing body shall thereof shall be a person professing a particular religion.

Article 16(4) applies only if two conditions are satisfied – (i) the class of citizens is backward *i.e.*, socially and educationally, (ii) the said class is not adequately represented in service of the state. The second test cannot be the sole criterion. Article 16(4) must be interpreted in the light of Art. 335 which says that claims of SC and ST shall be taken into consideration constituently with the maintenance of efficiency of administration. However, 82nd Amendment Act, 2000 restored the relaxation in qualifying marks and standards of evaluation in both, job reservation and promotions to SCs/STs by adding a proviso to this effect in Art. 335.

In state of Kerala *vs.* N.M. Thomas case, held that Art. 16(4) indicated one of the methods of achieving equality embodied in Art. 16(1) and Art. 16(4) does not exhausts the equality of opportunity which can be made available to the backward classes. The guarantee of equality before law is something more than is required by formal equality, and Art. 16(1) means effective material or real equality. Thus, Art. 16(4) is not to be read by way of any exception to Art. 16(1). Equality of opportunity admits discrimination with reason, which means rational classification for differential treatment having nexus to the constitutionally permissible object. Protective discrimination is a facet of equality under Articles 14, 15 and 16.

Application of reservation to 'Single isolated post' will amount to 100 per cent reservation, which is not permissible (Post Graduate Institute of Medical Education and Research *vs.* Faculty Association, 1998(3) SC 223).

Creamy Layer

In accordance with the direction given by the Supreme Court, the Union Government appointed an expert committee known as Justice Ram Nandan Committee to identify the 'Creamy Layer' among the socially and educationally backward classes. The Government of India has accepted the report.

The report says that certain constitutional posts qualify for the rule of exclusion *e.g.*, post of President, Vice-President, Judges of Supreme and High Courts, Chairman and Members of UPSC and State PSCs, Chief Election Commissioners, CAG, Governors, Ministers and Membership of Legislatures. The rule of exclusion covers Class I officers of the Central and State Services, Public Sector undertakings, Armed forces, professional class including trade, business and industry and property owners. It excludes those having gross annual income of Rupee one Lakh and above. The Supreme Court's judgement, Ashok Kumar Thakur *vs.* State of Bihar and others – reiterated that the creamy layer among OBCs cannot qualify for job reservations under its interpretation of the Mandal Commission recommendations.

Reservation in Promotions

The constitution (77th Amendment Act, 1995 – this amendment has been passed to remove the difficulty created by the Mandal case in which the court had held that reservation could not be made to promotions in jobs. This amendment has added a new Clause (4-A) to Art. 16 which provides that "Nothing in this Article shall prevent the state from making any provision for reservations in the matters of promotions to any class or classes of posts in the services of the state in favour of SCs and STs which, in the opinion of the state are not adequately represented in the services under the state". This means that reservation in promotion in government jobs will continue in favour of SCs and STs.

Right to promotion is ordinarily a statutory right. It is not a FR. The right to promotion to a post/class of posts depends upon the operation of the condition of the service. Article 16(4A) read with Articles 16(1) and 14 guarantees a right to promotion to SCs/STs as a fundamental rights where they do not have adequate representation consistently with the efficiency in administration.

85th amendment (2001): Amended Clause (4-A) of Article 16 and substitutes for the words in matter of promotion to any class, the words in matters of promotion with consequential seniority, to any class. It means that the promotion will be given to the classes with retrospective date *i.e.*, 17th June, 1995. It nullifies the decision in the Mandal Case, where in it was held that there can be no reservation in promotions.

Backlog Vacancies

The Constitution (81st Amendment) Act, 2000 – this amendment has added a new Clause (4-B) to Article 16 which ends the 50% ceiling on reservations for SCs/STs and OBCs backlog vacancies which could not be filled due to the non-availability of the eligible candidates of these classes in the previous year or years. The new Clause provides that the unfilled vacancies would be treated as a separate class and would be filled in succeeding year or years and will not be considered together with vacancies of the year in which they are being filled up, even if the 50% limit imposed in the Mandal Case is crossed.

Marriage and Status of SC/ST

In Sandhya Thakur *vs.* Vimla Devi Kushwaha 2005, it was held that the appellant, who by birth did not belong to a backward class or community, would not be entitled to contest a seat reserved for backward classes or community merely on the basis of her marriage to a male of that community. Also, in Meera Kanwaria *vs.* Sunita it has been held that if a female of high caste Hindu marries a person belonging to SC, she is not entitled to take the benefits of reservation under Art. 15(4) and 16(4) of the constitution. The court observed and held that a person who is a high caste Hindu and not subjected any social or educational backwardness in her life, by reason of marriage alone cannot *ipso facto* become a member of SC/ST. In absence of any strict proof, she cannot be allowed to defeat a very provisions made by the state for reserving certain seats for disadvantaged people.

In Shobha Hymavathi Devi vs. Setti Gangadhara Swamy, it was held that the reservation under Articles 15(4) or 16(4) or 330 and 332 of the constitution, would benefit only those who belong to SC or ST and not those who claim to acquire status by marriage.

103rd Constitutional Amendment: EWS Reservation

- **Effective Date:** January 14, 2019
- **Objective:** Provides 10% reservation for Economically Weaker Sections (EWS) in higher education and government jobs, targeting economically disadvantaged citizens not covered under existing SC/ST/OBC reservations.

Constitutional Provisions

- **Article 15(6):** Enables special provisions, including reservations, for EWS in admissions to educational institutions (public and private, except minority institutions under Article 30(1)).
- Reservation capped at 10% of total seats.
- **Article 16(6):** Permits 10% reservation for EWS in public employment.
- Applies to citizens not covered by SC/ST/OBC quotas.

EWS Eligibility Criteria

- **Income Threshold:** Annual family income below ₹8 lakh.
- **Asset Exclusions:** Individuals with significant assets excluded, e.g., agricultural land >5 acres, residential plots above specified limits.
- **Applicability:** Limited to general category candidates, excluding those eligible for SC/ST/OBC reservations.

Legal and Constitutional Basis

- **Article 46:** Supports the amendment by mandating the State to promote educational and economic interests of weaker sections (Directive Principles of State Policy).
- **Sinho Commission:** Recommended economic-based reservations for the poor in the general category.

Impact on Reservation Framework

- **Total Reservation:** Increases to 59.5%, breaching the 50% ceiling established in Indra Sawhney v. Union of India (1992).
- **Significance:** Introduces economic criteria as a basis for reservation, shifting from traditional caste-based affirmative action.

Supreme Court Verdict

- **Case:** Janhit Abhiyan v. Union of India (November 7, 2022)
- **Bench:** Five-judge Constitution Bench
- **Decision:** Upheld amendment's validity by a 3:2 majority.
- **Majority View (Justices Dinesh Maheshwari, Bela Trivedi, JB Pardiwala):** EWS classification is a reasonable classification under Article 14.
- 50% reservation cap is not inflexible; applies only to SC/ST/OBC quotas.
- Exclusion of SC/ST/OBC from EWS benefits is justified to avoid double benefits.
- No violation of the basic structure of the Constitution.
- **Dissenting View (CJI U.U. Lalit, Justice S. Ravindra Bhat):** Exclusion of SC/ST/OBC from EWS benefits is discriminatory, violating equality under Article 14.
- Economic criteria for employment reservations (Article 16) questionable.
- Breaching 50% cap risks undermining equality.
- **Review Petition:** Dismissed on May 9, 2023, by a five-judge bench led by CJI D.Y. Chandrachud (no grounds for review).

Significance and Criticism

Significance:

- First constitutional amendment to provide reservations based solely on economic backwardness.
- Aims to ensure substantive equality for economically disadvantaged general category citizens.

Criticism:

- Exclusion of SC/ST/OBC from EWS benefits seen as favoring upper castes.
- ₹8 lakh income threshold criticized as too high, potentially benefiting affluent families.
- Breaching 50% cap risks diluting merit-based opportunities.
- Alleged to be a political move to gain electoral support.

Implementation

- **Adoption:** Implemented by several states (e.g., Andhra Pradesh, Bihar, Delhi, Gujarat) with central ₹8 lakh income criterion.
- **Education:** Additional seats created in institutions to accommodate EWS quota without reducing existing seats.
- **Challenges:** Issues in verifying income criteria and ensuring compliance by private institutions.

ARTICLE 17: ABOLITION OF UNTOUCHABILITY

Article 17 abolishes untouchability and forbids its practice in any form. Untouchability is neither defined in the constitution nor in the Act. It refers to a social practice which looks down upon certain depressed classes solely on account of their birth and makes any discrimination against them on this ground.

The protection of Civil Rights Act, 1955, defines civil rights as any right accruing to a person by reason of the abolition of untouchability by Article 17 of the constitution. The act prescribes punishment for preventing any person from entering any place of public worship or from worshipping or denying access to any shop, public restaurant, hotels or places of public entertainment or refusing to admit persons to hospitals and refusing to sell goods or render services to any person. Also, insulting a member of schedule caste on the ground of untouchability or preaching untouchability or justifying it, is a crime.

ARTICLE 18: ABOLITION OF TITLES

A democracy should not create titles and titular glories. This will go against the realization of social equality. Article 18 abolishes all titles. It prohibits the state to confer titles on anybody whether a citizen or a non-citizen. Military and academic distinction are, however, exempted from the prohibition. Thus, a university can gift title or honour on a man of merit. Clause (2) prohibits a citizen of India from accepting any title from any foreign state. Article 18 is merely directory as there is no penalty prescribed for infringement of the prohibition.

A 'title' means a title of honour, rank, function or office in which there is a distinctive appellation. The recent conferment of titles of Bharat Ratna, Padam Vibhushan, Padma Shri etc., are said to be not prohibited under Article 18 as they merely denote state recognition of good work by citizens in various fields of activity.

ARTICLE 19: RIGHT TO FREEDOM

Personal liberty is the most important of all FRs. Articles 19 to 22 deal with different aspects of this basic right. Article 19 guarantees the following six fundamental freedoms to the citizens of India :

(*a*) Freedom of speech and expression

(*b*) Freedom of assembly

(*c*) Freedom to form associations

(*d*) Freedom of movement

(*e*) Freedom to reside and to settle

(*g*) Freedom of profession, occupation, trade or business

19(1)(f): The Right to Property was removed from the Fundamental Right by 44th Constitutional Amendment Act of 1978. It was made a Constitutional Right under Article 300 A in Part XII of the Constitution.

The freedoms enumerated in Article 19(1) are those great and basic rights which are recognized as the natural rights inherent in the status of a citizen. But, none of these freedoms is absolute or uncontrolled and may be restricted. Restriction to be constitutionally valid, must satisfy the following two tests:

- The restriction must be for the purposes mentioned in Clauses (2-6) of Article 19.
- The restrictions must be reasonable.

The Supreme Court has laid down the following guidelines:

- The term reasonable restrictions connotes that the limitation imposed on a person in the enjoyment of his right should not be arbitrary or of an excessive nature beyond what is actually required in the interest of public.
- The expression reasonable restriction seeks to strike a balance between the individual rights guaranteed by Article 19 and social control permitted by Article 19(2-6). A restriction which is imposed for securing the objects laid down in DPSP may be regarded as reasonable.
- The restrictions on the rights can only be imposed by a law and not executive or departmental instructions.

Rights available to citizens only – citizens under Article 19 mean only natural persons and not legal persons, such as corporations or companies. But, the bank nationalization case has established the view that the FRs of shareholders, editors and printers as citizens are not lost when they associate to form a company.

Article 19 (1) (a): Freedom of Speech and Expression

Article 19(1) (a) says that all citizens shall have the right to freedom of speech and expression. But, this right is subject to limitations imposed under Article 19(2) which empowers the state to put reasonable restrictions on the following grounds: security of the state, friendly relations with foreign state, public order, decency and morality, contempt of court, defamation, incitement to offence and sovereignty and integrity of India.

Freedom of Press

Unlike the American Constitution Article 19(1)(a) does not expressly mention the liberty of Press *i.e.*, the freedom to print and to publish what one pleases without previous permission. But it is settled law that the right to freedom of speech and expression includes the liberty of the press. Press is supposed to guard public interest by bringing to fore the misdeeds, failings and lapses of the government and other bodies exercising governing powers. Rightly, therefore, it has been described as the Fourth Estate. In Express newspapers case, held that the Press industry is not free from taxation. But tax should be within reasonable limits and does not impede freedom of expression *i.e.*, circulation. In Rajagopal *vs.* State of TN, held that the press have the right to publish an unauthorised account of a citizen's life so far as it is based upon public records. Freedom of the press, the court said means absence of interference by the state except in as far as it is authorised by the constitution and by laws.

In Ajay Goswami *vs.* UOI, the freedom of press was the issue. The court recognised the right of adults to entertain within the acceptable level of decency on the grounds that it may not be appropriate for children. Fertile imagination of minors should not be a matter that should be agitated in court of Law. The court considered the applicability of American test of "clear and present danger".

Article 19(1) (b): Freedom to Assemble

This Article secures to all citizens of India the right to assemble peaceably and without arms. Thus, there is a right to hold public meetings and demonstrations and take out processions peacefully. Under Article 19(3), reasonable restrictions can be imposed on the right by the state or by law in the interest of the sovereignty and integrity of India or public order. Thus, an assembly declared unlawful can be validly banned.

Article 19(1) (c): Freedom of Association

This Article guarantees to all citizens the right to form associations and unions for pursuing lawful purposes. Under Article 19(4) however, reasonable restrictions can be imposed by the state in the interest of the sovereignty and integrity of India or public order or morality. The associations so formed would include political parties, societies, clubs, companies, organisations, partnership firms and trade unions and indeed any body of persons. It has been held that this Article does not guarantee a right to strike.

Article 19(1)(d) and (e): Freedom of movement and Residence

The right of every citizen of India to move freely throughout the territory of India and his right to reside and settle in any Part of the territory of India guaranteed under Clauses (d) and (e) respectively of Article 19(1) are really inter-linked. Both the rights lay stress on the oneness of the territory of India. Any citizen can travel to or reside in any Part of India. Article 19(5) however provides for imposition of reasonable restrictions on exercise of these rights by law in the interest of the general public or for the protection of the interest of any scheduled tribe. Generally, the protection afforded by these rights is invoked to challenge the validity of externment or deportation orders which go to curtail the two freedoms.

No political party has the right to call for bandh on the plea that it is a part of its fundamental right of speech and expression under Article 19(1)(a). The calling for and holding of Bandh by a political party/organisation involved a threat express or implied to citizen not to carry on his activities or to practice his avocation on the day of the bandh and hence violative of Article 19(1)(a)(b)(c)(d) and 21. (Communist Party of India (M) vs. Bharat Kumar, 1998).

Article 19(1) (g): Freedom of Profession and Trade

Article 19(1) (g) guarantees the freedom to practice any profession, or to carry on any occupation, trade or business. A doubt was expressed in the Constituent Assembly whether these were fundamental rights at all. Perhaps the only other constitutions which have given them the status of fundamental rights are those of Ireland and Switzerland.

A constitutional guarantee of the right to take up the profession, calling, trade or business of one's choice is indeed a significant aid to the building up of a dynamic and democratic society! The State's power to restrict the enjoyment of these freedoms is limited to the making of any law imposing reasonable restrictions in the interests of the general public as so far as it relates to (a) the prescribing of professional or technical qualifications necessary for practicing any profession or carrying of any occupation, trade or business or (b) the carrying on by the state or by a corporation owned or controlled by the state, of any trade, business, industry or service.

In Rashid Ahmed *vs.* The Municipal Board, Kairana, the Supreme Court had the occasion to discuss in detail the scope of the rights guaranteed under the Clause regarding the freedom of profession Rashid Ahmed was carrying on wholesale business in fruits and vegetables in one of the bazars of Kairana, a town in Uttar Pradesh. In April 1949, a set of new by-laws framed by the Kairana municipality came into force. Anticipating the coming into force of the by-laws, the Board had auctioned the contract for wholesale trade in vegetables on the basis of a monopoly right. The contract was given to one Habib Ahmed. Subsequently, the Board notified a specified place as the market for wholesale business in vegetables.

There upon the petitioner applied for a license to carry on his business at his shop. The Board rejected the application and the decision was communicated to the petitioner. It said: "According to Resolution No. 188, dated 22nd December, 1949, the application of Mr. Rashid Ahmed is rejected and he is informed accordingly".

The resolution contained no reason for the rejection of the application. Soon after, notice was served on the petitioner by the Board asking him to stop selling vegetables at the appointed market or at his own shop where he had been doing business at least for two years prior to the coming into effect of the by-laws.

His business has been wholly stopped and he was being prosecuted for alleged breach of the by-laws. According to by-law 2, : "No person shall establish any new market or place for wholesale transaction without obtaining the previous permission of the Board and no person shall sell or expose for sale any vegetable, fruit, etc., at any place other than fixed by the Board for the purpose."

Reaffirming Constitutional Rights in Business Opportunity

Speaking on behalf of an unanimous Court, Justice S.R. Das observed:

"The Constitution by Article 19(1) (g) guarantees to the Indian citizen the right to carry on trade or business subject to such reasonable restrictions as are mentioned in Clause 6 of that Article.

The net result is that the prohibition of this by-law, in the absence of any provision for issuing licenses, becomes absolute. Further, the Board has granted a monopoly to Habib Ahmed and has put it out of its power to grant a license to the petitioner to carry on wholesale business in vegetables either at the fixed market or at any other place within the municipal limits of Kairana.

We are satisfied that in this case the petitioner's fundamental rights have been infringed and he is entitled to have his grievance redressed. The proper order in such circumstances would be to direct the respondent board not to prohibit the petitioner from carrying on the trade of wholesale dealer and commission agent of vegetables and fruits within the limits of the Municipal Board of Kairana, except in accordance with the by-laws as and when framed in future according to law and further to direct the respondent Municipal board to withdraw the pending prosecution of the petitioner and ordered accordingly."

In Chintaman Rao *vs.* the State of Madhya Pradesh, the Supreme Court held invalid the Central Provinces and Berar Regulation of Manufacture of Bidis (Agricultural Purpose) Act, 1948, because it totally prohibited the manufacture of bidis during the agricultural season in certain parts of the State.

The Court said that such a prohibition, on the face of it, was of an arbitrary nature and, therefore, could not be said to be a reasonable restriction on the exercise of the right to carry on a profession, trade or business. But in another decision, the Court held that the requirement of a permit as required by the law cannot be regarded as an unreasonable restriction on the citizen's right under the freedom of profession Clause.

In Kapur *vs.* the State of Punjab, the Court upheld the nationalisation of textbooks by the Government of the Punjab. "The action of the Government may be good or bad. It may be criticised and condemned in the Houses of Legislature or outside but this does not amount to an infringement of the fundamental right guaranteed by Article 19 (g)."

As a whole, the tendency of the judiciary with regard to the freedom of profession has been not to block in any way the increasing state activity that is bound to take place in a welfare state but, at the same time, to give the individual maximum protection from high-handed executive actions or discriminatory legislative enactments.

Whenever the action of the state was in the interest of the general public, even if it involved the restriction of the individual's freedom of action in the economic sphere, the courts did not seem hesitant to support it.

This was the main reason that impelled them to uphold many legislative enactments of nationalisation of public utilities such as road transport, electricity, etc., even before the First Amendment had made a special provision in support of such state actions and the consequent expansion of the economic and commercial activities of the state.

ARTICLE 20: PROTECTION IN RESPECT OF CONVICTION FOR OFFENCES

Article 20 affords protection against arbitrary and excessive punishment to any person who commits an offence. There are four such guaranteed protections:

(1) A person can be convicted of an offence only if he has violated a law in force at the time when he is alleged to have committed the offence.

(2) No person can be subjected to a greater penalty than what might have been given to him under the law that was prevalent when he committed the offence.

(3) No person can be prosecuted and punished for the same offence more than once.

(4) No person accused of an offence can be compelled to be a witness against himself.

The Draft Constitution did not contain the term "prosecuted" in the Clause prohibiting double punishment. It was pointed out in the Constituent Assembly that such a word was necessary because punishment here meant only that which was given by the court of law. Departmental punishment would not be taken as "punishment" in the sense in which the word is used in the Constitution.

Nor would any punishment given in the court of law preclude departmental action leading to punishment for the same offence committed by the same official. This means that disciplinary action may be taken by the Government against an official despite the sentence of the court of law and such action will not infringe the right guaranteed under this Article.

Taken together, these provisions guard against retrospective application of a punitive law and double punishment for the same offence. These are, indeed, guarantees of great importance which establish "the primacy of law over the passions of man."

Article 20 has taken care to safeguard the rights of persons accused of crimes. Persons here means the citizens, non-citizens as well as corporations. ***Please note that this Article can not be suspended even during an emergency in operation under Article 359. Article 20 also constitutes the limitation on the legislative powers of the Union and State legislatures.***

Ex-Post facto Law

Article 20(1) says that no person shall be convicted of any offence except for violation of a law in force at the time of the commission of the Act charged as an offence, nor be subjected to a penalty greater than that which might have been inflicted under the law in force at the time of the commission of the offence. This is called Ex-Post facto Law. It means that legislature cannot make a law which provides for punishment of acts which were committed prior to the date when it came into force. This means that a new law cannot punish an old act.

Doctrine of Double Jeopardy

Article 20(2) says that no person shall be prosecuted and punished for the same offence more than once. This is called Doctrine of Double Jeopardy. The objective of this Article is to avoid harassment, which must be caused for successive criminal proceedings, where the person has committed only one crime. There is a legal maxim related to this - *nemo debet bis vexari*. This means that no man shall be put twice in peril for the same offence.

There are two aspects of Doctrine of Jeopardy viz. *autrefois convict* and *autrefois acquit*. Autrefois convict means that the person has been previously convicted in respect of the same offence. The autrefois acquit means that the person has been acquitted on a same charge on which he is being prosecuted. ***Please note that Constitution bars double punishment for the same offence***. The conviction for such offence does not bar for subsequent trial and conviction for another offence and it does not matter the some ingredients of these two offences are common.

Self Incrimination Law

Article 20(3) of the constitution says that no person accused of any offence shall be compelled to be a witness against himself. This is based upon a legal maxim which means that, "No man is bound to accuse himself". The accused is presumed to be innocent till his guilt is proved. It is the duty of the prosecution to establish his guilt.

ARTICLE 21: PROTECTION OF LIFE AND PERSONAL LIBERTY

Article 21 is one of the shortest in the constitution over which there took place one of the longest and most thorough-going discussions in the Constituent Assembly. It enacts, "no person shall be deprived of his life or personal liberty except according to procedure established by law." The Article as it stands now is a revised version of what it originally was in the Draft Constitution, according to which "no person was to be deprived of his life or liberty without due process of law".

The Drafting Committee gave two reasons for this change. First, the word "liberty" should be qualified by the word "personal" in order to avoid the possibility of too wide an interpretation which might include even the freedom already dealt with under Article 19. Secondly, the expression "procedure established by law" is more definite and such a provision finds place in the same context in the Japanese Constitution of 1946.

The key word in Article 21 is law. What does it mean, law enacted by a competent legislative body or fundamental or natural law? This was the question that confronted the Supreme Court soon after the inauguration of the constitution. The question was discussed at length in A. K. Gopalan *vs.* the State of Madras.

Chief Justice Kania said that there was no ambiguity in the meaning of the Article:

"Normally read, and without thinking of other constitutions, the expression 'procedure established by law' must mean procedure prescribed by the law of the State.

To read the word 'law' as suggests the rules of natural justice will lead one in difficulties because the rules of natural justice as regards procedure are nowhere defined and in my opinion, the constitution cannot be read as laying down a vague standard. This is particularly so when in omitting to adopt 'due process of law' it was considered that the expression 'procedure established by law' made the standard specific."

In the Constitution of other countries, the provisions related to protection of personal liberty are couched very much in the same language as in Article 21.

It is all a question of policy as to whether the legislature or the judiciary would have the final say in such matters and the constitution makers of India deliberately decided to place these powers in the hands of the legislature. Article 31 of the Japanese Constitution, upon which Article 21 of our constitution is modeled, also proceeds upon the same principle."

There have been numerous other decisions of the Supreme Court where the Court has emphasised and re-emphasised its liberal outlook on the question of protection of life and personal liberty. The following may specifically be pointed out:

- That imprisonment of a poor person for non-payment of debts amounted to deprivation of his personal liberty. (Jolly George Verghese *vs.* Bank of Cochin, AIR 1980 SC 470);
- That under the Bonded Labour System (Abolition) Act, 1976, it is not enough merely to identify and release bonded labourers but it is more important

that they should be suitably rehabilitated to meet the plainest requirement of Article 21 (Neeraja Chowdhari *vs.* State of M.R., AIR 1984 SC 1099);

- That the expression 'deprivation of personal liberty' is not limited to bodily restraint or confinement to prison and that 'life' means something more than mere animal existence (Kharak Singh *vs.* State of U.P., AIR 1963 SC 1295);
- That the 'right to privacy' would have to go through a process of case by case development (Govind *vs.* State of M.P., AIR 1975 SC 1379): this right is available even to a woman of easy virtue, and no one can invade her privacy (State of Maharashtra *vs.* Madhulkar Narain, AIR 1991 SC 207);
- That so long as surveillance by police officers is for the purposes of preventing crimes and confined to the limits prescribed by law, a person cannot complain against the inclusion of his name in the surveillance register but if it is excessive and goes beyond the prescribed limits, its validity may be challenged as infringing the right of privacy of a citizen as his Fundamental Right to personal liberty under Article 21 and freedom of movement under Article (19) (1) (d) (Malak Singh *vs.* State of Punjab, AIR 1981 SC 760);
- That refusal to grant bail in a murder case without reasonable ground would amount to deprivation of personal liberty under Article 21 (Babu Singh *vs.* State of U.P., AIR 1978 SC 527);
- That protection of Article 21 is available even to convicts in jails (D.B.M. Patnaik *vs.* State of A.P., AIR 1974 SC 2092);
- That if by imposing solitary confinement there is total deprivation of camaraderie amongst co-prisoners, commingling and talking and being talked to, it would offend Article 21 (Sunil Batra (No. 1) *vs.* Delhi Administration, AIR 1978 SC 1575);
- That a detenu can be subjected only to such restrictions on his personal liberty as are authorised by or under the law of preventive detention; imposition of any unauthorised restriction will violate Article 21 (State of Maharashtra *vs.* Prabhakar Pandurang, AIR 1986 SC 424);
- That the 'right to travel abroad' is a part of a person's 'personal liberty' which is a comprehensive term (Satwant Singh *vs.* Assistant Passport Officer, AIR SC 1836);
- That it is the professional obligation of all doctors, whether government or private, to extend medical aid to the injured immediately to preserve life without waiting for legal formalities to be complied with by the police under Cr.P.C. (Parmanand Katara *vs.* Union of India, AIR 1989 SC 2039);
- That when one seeks relief for breach of Article 21, one must confine oneself to some direct, overt and tangible act which threatens the fullness of life or the lives of others in the community (Ramsharan Autrynuprasi *vs.* Union of India, AIR 1989 SC 549 and 552);
- That compelling a person to live in subhuman conditions also amounts to the taking away of his life, not by execution of a death sentence but by a slow and gradual process of robbing him of all his human qualities and graces, a process which is much more cruel than sending a man to the gallows (Sankar Banerji *vs.* Durgapur Project Ltd., AIR 1988 Cal. 136).

To sum up: Article 21 gives protection to life and personal liberty to the extent therein mentioned. It does not recognise the right to life and personal liberty as an absolute right but limits the scope of the right itself. The absolute right is, by the definition in the Article, qualified by the risk of its being taken away in accordance with the procedure established by law.

It is this circumscribed right which is substantively protected by Article 21, as against the executive as well as the legislature, for the constitution has conditioned its deprivation by the necessity for a procedure established by law made by the legislature.

While sub-clauses 2 to 6 of Article 19 have put a limit on the fundamental right of a citizen, Article 21 along with Article 22 puts a limit on the power of the state given under Article 246, read with the legislative lists. Under the constitution, life and personal liberty are balanced by restrictions on the rights of the citizens as laid down in Article 19, and by the checks put upon the state by Article 21 and 22.

ARTICLE 22: SAFEGUARDS AGAINST ARBITRARY ARREST AND DETENTION

Article 22 guarantees three rights. First, it guarantees the right of every person who is arrested to be informed of the cause of his arrest; secondly, his right to consult, and to be defended by a lawyer of his choice. Thirdly, every person arrested and detained in custody shall be produced before the nearest Magistrate within a period of twenty-four hours and shall be kept in continued custody only with his authority. All these rights are without any qualifications and are, therefore, in absolute terms.

There are, however, two exceptions to the universal application of the rights guaranteed under the first two Clauses of Article 22. These relate to

(1) Any person who is for the time being an enemy alien; or

(2) Any person who is arrested or detained under any law providing for preventive detention. The first exception was accepted by the Constituent Assembly without any opposition as it embodied a sound principle. For instance, if India were at war with another country, considerations of national security may demand the arrest and detention of a person who is the citizen of the enemy country.

He may not be given the rights guaranteed under Article 22 (1) and (2). But no such easy justification is available for the second exception which provides for preventive detention even during normal times. Discussion on this Clause in the Constituent Assembly was stormy and acrimonious.

The reasons for the introduction of such a Clause were explained by Ambedkar, thus:

"It has to be recognised that in the present circumstances of the country, it may be necessary for the executive to detain a person who is tampering either with public order or with the Defence Services of the country. In such case, I do not think that the exigency of the liberty of the individual shall be placed above the interests of the State."

Ambedkar's explanations, however, failed to satisfy a considerable section of the Assembly who criticised the provision in strong terms.

Ambedkar, however, pointed out the safeguards provided in the constitution to mitigate the rigours of an apparently absolute power of preventive detention permitted under Article 22(3).

First, every case of preventive detention must be authorised by law. It cannot be at the will of the executive.

Secondly, no law of preventive detention shall normally authorise the detention of a person for a longer period than three months.

Thirdly, every case of preventive detention for a period longer than three months must be placed before an Advisory Board composed of persons qualified for appointment as Judges of a High Court. Such cases must be placed before the Board within the three months period. The continued detention after three months should be only on the basis of a favourable opinion by the Board. The only exception to this provision is when Parliament prescribes by law, the circumstances under which a person may be kept in detention beyond three months even without the opinion of the Advisory Board.

Fourthly, no person who is detained under any preventive detention law can be detained indefinitely. There shall always be a maximum period of detention which Parliament is required to prescribe by law.

Fifthly, in cases which are required to be placed before the Advisory Board, the procedure to be followed by the Board shall be laid down by Parliament.

Sixthly, when a person is detained under a law of preventive detention, the detaining authority shall communicate to him the grounds on which the order has been made. It should also afford him the earliest opportunity of making a representation against the order.

The greatest safeguard, according to Ambedkar, is that preventive detention takes place only under the law. It cannot be at the will of the executive. It is also necessary to make a distinction between different categories of cases. There may be cases of detention where the circumstances are so serious and the consequences so dangerous that it would not even be desirable to permit the members of the Board to know the facts regarding the detention of any particular individual.

The disclosure of such facts may be too dangerous to the security of the State or its very existence. But even here, there are two mitigating circumstances. First, such cases will be defined by Parliament. They are not to be arbitrarily decided by the executive. Secondly, in every case there shall be a maximum period of detention prescribed by law. The First Preventive Detention Act was passed by Parliament in 1950. The validity of the Act was soon challenged before the Supreme Court in Gopalan *vs.* The State of Madras. The case was heard by six Judges of the Court and each of the Judges wrote a separate opinion.

Each has examined in general the scope of fundamental rights under the constitution besides analysing in detail the content of personal liberty. By a 4 : 2 majority, the Court upheld the Act except Section 14 of the Act which was unanimously declared invalid. The invalidity of this section, however, did not affect the rest of the Act as it could be severed from the remaining provisions.

For a period of two decades from 1950 to 1970 a Parliamentary enactment on preventive detention had continued to exist in the country. The Preventive Detention Act of 1950 was amended seven times, each time for a period of three years, thus extending it up to 31st December 1969. It was not further extended; hence since then, there has been no preventive detention law for the country as a whole. Some of the states, however, passed laws on preventive detention in 1970. In 1971 Parliament passed a modified version of the old Preventive Detention Act under the title Maintenance of Internal Security Act (MISA) which continued to exist until 1978 when it was abolished.

In 1980, however, a modified version of MISA was passed under the title of National Security Act which was upheld as constitutional by the Supreme Court in 1981. A similar Act passed by Parliament subsequently in the wake of terrorist activities in Punjab is known as Terrorist and Disruptive Activities (Prevention) Act (TADA) has been in operation enabling the Executive to take into custody and preventive detention of persons suspected of terrorist activities. Every time in the past when the Government moved to extend the Preventive Detention Act, it provoked a heated debate in Parliament.

But, whatever is the justification, so long as any provision similar to preventive detention of Maintenance of Internal Security Act or TADA remains on the Statute Book, there will also remain an unseemly blot on the face of democracy in India. It is in this light that we have to view the existence of the National Security Act which is the latest of its kind. While upholding the Act, the Supreme Court warned that unless the Act is used sparingly in "as few situations as possible", it would have "grave consequences to personal liberty".

The National Security Act provides that the detenu will be conveyed the grounds of the detention within 5 days and in exceptional cases within 10 days of his detention. If there are exceptional circumstances, the detaining authority is to record its reasons in writing. It is important to note that the grounds of detention must be existent at the time of making the order. Subjective satisfaction of detaining authority can be challenged on the following grounds, namely, malafide or vagueness, and irrelevant or non-existent grounds or mechanical application of mind of detaining authority. Exception to Clause (5): Clause (6) provides that the authority to the detenu may not furnish disclosure of facts which are considered to be against public interest.

In A.K. Roy *vs.* UOI, popularly known as the NSA case, the Supreme Court by 4-1 majority upheld the constitutional validity of the NSA. Held that the right of legal representation before the Board is not permissible. Article 22(5) gives a right to make a representation against the detention order, but that right does not carry with it the said right. The detaining authority does not have such right. However, even in the face of constitutional and statutory denial of legal representation to a detinue, he is entitled to a common law right of representation through a 'friend' (but that friend should not be a lawyer, law professor, etc.)

Also held that a detenu has no right to cross-examine, but has right to present his own evidence in rebuttal of the allegations made against him. The court reasoned that firstly the question before the Board is not whether the detenu is guilty of any charge but whether there is sufficient cause for his detention and secondly, the witnesses would be most reluctant to testify and often it may harm public interest to disclose their identity Art. 22(6).

In Attorney General of India *vs.* Amrit Lal, a 9-judge constitution bench of Supreme Court held during the period of emergency. The President is empowered to suspend fundamental rights of people and a detenu has no locus standi to question the reasons or grounds of his detention. The court upheld Sec. 1A of COFEPOSA which had done away with the requirements of supply of grounds of detention and the consultation with advisory board during the emergency.

ARTICLES 23-24: RIGHT AGAINST EXPLOITATION

Article 23 prohibits traffic in human beings and begar and other forced labour. Traffic in human beings—women, children, etc.—and forced labour militate against human dignity. Under the old Zamindari system, the tenants were sometimes forced to render free service to their landlords. This was called begar. It has been held that even if some remuneration is paid, the labour may be a forced one.

Devadasis are also covered under the term traffic in human beings. Children of the prostitutes have a right to equality of opportunity, dignity, care, protection and rehabilitation so as to be a part of the mainstream of social life (Gaurav Jain *vs.* UOI). It may be noted that Art. 23 does not prohibit the state from imposing compulsory service for public purposes e.g., social or military service. In state of Gujarat *vs.* High Court of Gujarat, it was held that exaction of hard labour from convicted prisoners is not forced labour.

Article 24 prohibits employing children below age of 14 years in any hazardous employment. This is in keeping with the human rights concepts and United Nations norms. In M.C. Mehta *vs.* State of T.N., it was held that children below the age of 14 years cannot be employed in any hazardous industry, mines or other works and has laid down exhaustive guidelines how the state authorities should protect economic, social and humanitarian rights of millions of working children. In Bandhua Mukti Morcha *vs.* UOI, the court observed: The basic cause for child labour being poverty, instead of its total abolition which will have adverse effect, it should be banned progressively in a planned manner starting from the most hazardous and intolerable activities like slavery, bonded labour, trafficking, prostitution, pornography and dangerous forms of labour, etc.

ARTICLES 25-28: RIGHT TO FREEDOM OF RELIGION

Articles 25 and 26 embody the principles of religious tolerance that has been the characteristic feature of Indian civilization from the start of history. Besides they serve to emphasize the secular nature of Indian democracy *i.e.*, equal respect to all religions.

A secular state does not mean an irreligious state, it only means that in matters of religion it is neutral, the state can have no religion of its own, and the state protects all religions between man and man, it is not concerned with the relation of man with God. It is left to the individual's conscience.

In M. Ismail Faruqui *vs.* UOI, the court observed: "The concept of secularism is one facet of the right to equality woven as the central golden thread in the fabric depicting the pattern of the scheme in constitution. Moreover, any step taken to arrest escalation of communal tension and to achieve communal accord and harmony can, by no stretch of argumentation, be termed non-secular or anti-secular. Secularism is a creed of the Indian people embedded in the ethos."

Article 25: Freedom of Conscience and Free Profession, Practice and Propagation of Religion:

(1) Subject to public order, morality and health and to the other provisions of Part III of constitution, all persons are equally entitled to freedom of conscience and the right freely to profess, practice and propagate religion.

(2) Nothing in this Article shall affect the operation of any existing law or prevent the state from making any law:

(a) Regulating or restricting any economic, financial, political or other secular activity which may be associated with religious practice;

(b) Providing for social welfare and reform or the throwing open of Hindu religious institutions of a public character to all classes and sections of Hindus.

Explanation I – The wearing and carrying of Kirpans shall be deemed to be included in the profession of Sikh religion.

Explanation II – The expression "Hindu" includes Jain, Sikhs and Buddhists.

To practice religion is to perform the prescribed religious duties, rites and rituals. To propagate means to spread and publicize his religious views for the edification of others. The right to propagate one's religion does not give a right to convert another person to one's own religion, as that would impinge on the freedom of conscience guaranteed to all persons.

In Bijoe Emmanuel *vs.* State of Kerala (1986) (National Anthem Case), The court observed: Art. 25 is an Article of faith in the Constitution, incorporated in recognition of the principle that the real test of a true democracy is the ability of even an insignificant minority to find its identity under constitution. The question is not whether a particular religious belief or practice appeals to our reason or sentiment, but whether the belief is genuinely and conscientiously held as a part of the profession or practice of religion. Thus, no person can be compelled to sing the national anthem if he has genuine conscientious religious objection.

Restrictions on Freedom of Religion

Article 25: *Clause (1)* – in the name of religion, no act can be done against public order, morality and health of the public. For example, in the name of religion, untouchability or traffic in human beings *e.g.*, system of devadasis cannot be tolerated. The freedom of religion is also subject to the other provisions of this Part *e.g.*, right to freedom of speech and expression, freedom of assembly and association, etc.

Clause (2)(a) – the freedom to practice extends only to those activities which are the essence of religion. It does not cover secular, political or commercial activities associated with religious practice.

Clause (2)(b) – under this Clause, state can eradicate social practices (viz. bigamy and polygamy under Hindu law) and dogmas which stand in the path of country's onward progress. Such laws do not affect the essence of any religion. This sub-clause ensures an individual's legal right to enter into a temple unobstructed irrespective of his caste, untouchability, social inequality, etc.

ARTICLE 26: FREEDOM TO MANAGE RELIGIOUS AFFAIRS

Subject to public order, morality and health, every religious denomination or any section thereof shall have the right:

(a) To establish and maintain institutions for religious and charitable purposes,

(b) To manage its own affairs in matters of religion,

(c) To own and acquire movable and immovable property, and

(d) To administer such property in accordance with law.

While, right guaranteed by Art. 25 is an individual right, the right guaranteed by Art. 26 is the right of an organized body. The word religious denomination in Art. 26 must satisfy three conditions:

(1) It must be a collection of individual who have a system of beliefs which they regard as conducive to their spiritual well being *i.e.*, a common faith.

(2) It must have a common organization.

(3) It must be designated by a distinctive name.

Thus, in a large sense, Hinduism, Muslims, Christians are such denominations. In limited sense, the various philosophers governing the Hindu society such as Advaitas, Saivites etc., are also denominations. Among Mohammedans, Hanafi, Shia, or Chisti sects are separate denominations. Also, maths or the spiritual fraternity represented by it comes within this Article. (LT Swamiar's case).

Under Article 26(b), the court has a right to determine whether a Particular rite of ceremony is regarded as essential by the tenets of a Particular religion. The right is also subject to the regulatory powers of state under Article 25 (2) (b) (Saifuddin Sahib *vs.* State of Bombay).

The right of a religious denomination to manage its property has been placed on a different footing from the right to manage its own affairs in matters of religion. The latter is a FR which can't be taken away except on grounds mentioned in Art. 25, the former can be regulated by laws which the Legislatures can validly impose *e.g.*, General Property Law. Also, Article 26(c) is to be read subject to state's power to acquire private property under Art. 31. Thus, property of a denomination can be acquired by a state.

In S.P. Mittal *vs.* UOI, the Aurobindo society and international cultural township – Auroville were held not be religious institutions or denomination. The teachings of Sri Aurobindo only represented his philosophy and not a religion. In Brahmachari Sidheswar Shai *vs.* State of WB, it was held that the followers of Rama Krishna, who are collection of individuals and who adhere to a system of beliefs, and who have an organization of definite name Rama Krishna math or mission can be regarded as religious denominations as Hindu religion.

In M. Ismail Faroqui *vs.* UOI, the court held that the right to practice, profess and propagate religion under Art. 25 does not necessarily include the right to acquire or own or possess property. While offer of prayer or worship is a religious practice, its offering at every location where such prayers can be offered would not be an essential or integral Part of such religious practices unless the place has a Particular significance for that religion so as to form an essential or integral Part there of.

ARTICLE 27: FREEDOM NOT TO PAY TAXES FOR RELIGIOUS PROMOTIONS

Article 27 says, that no person shall be compelled to pay any taxes for expenses on promotion or maintenance of any Particular religion *i.e.*, there could be no objection if the taxes were used for the promotion of all religions.

ARTICLE 28: FREEDOM NOT TO ATTEND RELIGIOUS INSTRUCTIONS

Article 28 prohibits religious instructions in educational institutions wholly maintained by the state. In case of other institutions recognized and aided by the state, there will be freedom for every person not to Participate in religious instructions or worship.

In Aruna Roy *vs.* UOI, the Supreme Court upheld the validity of national curriculum framework for school education rejecting the petitioners contention that it was an attempt to "saffronise" education by the BJP led NDA government it held that an emphasis in, about requirement of education about religions, there basics, the values inherent therein also a comparative study of the philosophy of all religions is neither violative of Art. 28 nor offends against secularism.

ARTICLE 29-30: RIGHTS TO MINORITIES (CULTURAL AND EDUCATIONAL RIGHTS)

The word minority is not defined in the constitution. Whether a section of citizens continues a minority for the purpose of Article 29 and 30 in a state must be determined by reference to the entire population of the state. It refers to any community which is numerically less than 50% of the entire population of state. A minority could not be determined in relation to entire population of a country. In Frank Anthony Public School employees association *vs.* UOI, the Supreme Court observed the idea of giving special rights to minorities is not to have a kind of privileged or pampered section of the population but to give them a sense of security and a feeling of confidence.

Article 29: Protection of Interests of Minorities:

(1) Any section of the citizen residing in the territory of India or any Part thereof having a distinct language, script or culture of his own shall have the right to conserve the same.

(2) No citizen shall be denied admission into any educational institution maintained by the state or receiving aid out of state funds on grounds only of religion, race, caste, language and any of them.

A minority community can effectively conserve its language, script or culture by and through educational institution, as what is conferred by Article 29(1). Article 29(2) is quiet general and applies to all citizens, whether they belong to majority or minority groups. Therefore, a school run by minority, if it is aided by state funds, cannot refuse admission to boys of other communities also, the state cannot direct such schools to restrict admissions to their own community. However, nothing in Art. 29(2) shall prevent the state from making reservations for backward classes under Article 15.

Article 30: Right of Minorities to Establish and Administer Educational Institutions:

(1) All minorities, whether based on religion or language, shall have the right to establish and administer educational institutions of their choice.

(2) They shall not, in granting aid to educational institutions, discriminate against any educational institutions on the ground that it is under the management of a minority.

The right is conferred by this Clause on two types of minorities: religious and linguistic. The word establish indicates the right to bring into existence, while the right to administer means the right to effectively manage and conduct the affairs of institution. The right to administer is said to consist of four principle matters: right to choose its managing and governing body, right to choose its teachers who have compatibility with the aims and aspirations of institutions, right to admit students of their choice subject to reasonable regulations about academic qualifications, and right to use its properties and assets for benefits of institution.

A minority institution cannot prescribe qualifications for admission of students, but can prescribe procedure for admission of students. In Saint Stephens College *vs.* Delhi University, held that the interview is an integral Part of the college's administration. The university cannot direct the college to dispense with its admission programme in the absence of proof of mal-administration of the college. Also, held that minority aided institutions may reserve upto 50% of seats for their community students and are entitled to prefer them in admissions as it is necessary to maintain the minority character of the institution.

In St. Xavier's college case, minority institutions have no FR to affiliation, but to deny affiliation or recognition except upon certain terms and condition amount to the surrender of their right to administer under Article 30(1). When the minority institution applies to the university for affiliation, it expresses its choice to Participate in the system of general education. Affiliation is for regulating the educational character and content of minority institutions.

RECENT CASE LAW: A five judge bench of the Supreme Court in Islamic academy of education *vs.* State of Karnataka, clarifying the doubts read in T.M.A Pai foundations case, has directed the constitution of a separate committee in each state to be headed by a retired judge of the High court, to approve the fee structure of the institution conducting medical and engineering courses and to ensure that the tests conducted for admissions by these institutions were fair and transparent, in fixing percentage of quota for students to be admitted by the management of unaided minority professional colleges, the state would keep in mind, apart from local needs, the paramount interest/need of that community in the state.

The Modern school *vs.* UOI, it was held that in determination of the fee structure, unaided educational institution exercise a great autonomy as they are entitled to generate reasonable surplus for development of education and expansion of the institution itself. What is prohibited is commercialization of education/profiteering and the diversion of the profit/surplus for any other use or purposes and the use thereof for personal gains or for other business or enterprise. Hence, a balance has to be struck between autonomy of such institutions and measures to be taken to prevent commercialization of education.

ARTICLE 31: RIGHT TO PROPERTY AND SAVING OF CERTAIN LAWS

The right to property has proved to be the most complicated and controversial. The consensus was embodied in Article 19(f) and Article 31. But, 44th Amendment 1978 repealed these Articles completely with effect from 20 June 1979. Instead, in Part XII of the constitution, a new chapter IV and new Article 300-A was added to provide that no person shall be deprived of his property save by authority of law. Thus, the right to property ceases to be a FR but still remains a legal right under Article 300-A.

ARTICLE 32-35: RIGHT TO CONSTITUTIONAL REMEDIES

Article 32: Remedies for enforcement of rights conferred by this Part: Rights in order to be meaningful must be enforceable and backed by remedies in case of violation. Article 32(1) guarantees the right to move Supreme Court by appropriate proceedings for the enforcement of FR. Clause (2) deals with Supreme Court's power to issue order or writs, for the enforcement of FRs in the nature of *Habeas corpus, Mandamus, Certiorari, Quo warranto, Prohibition* whichever may be appropriate, for the enforcement of any of the right conferred by this Part A petition under Article 32 may be filed to challenge the validity of a law with reference to a provision other than those involving FRs, provided it inevitably cause a restriction on the enjoyment of FRs. Where the suspension of FR is protected by the constitution, Article 32 will not apply.

The Supreme Court cannot refuse relief under Article 32 on the ground that the aggrieved person may have his remedy from other court: the disputed facts have to be investigated before the relief given; and the petitioner has not asked for proper writ applicable to his case. Article 226 enables the high courts to issue writs for the enforcement of FRs and also other ordinary legal rights. Thus, Article 32 and 226 provide the right to constitutional remedies. Dr. Ambedkar had described this provision as the soul and heart of the Constitution.

The traditional rule of *locus standi* is that a person whose FR is infringed can only file a petition under Art. 32. Supreme Court has now considerably relaxed this rule in its recent rulings. The court now permits social action litigation or public interest litigation at the instance of Public spirited citizens for the enforcement of any constitutional or legal right of any person or group of persons who because of their poverty or socio-economic disadvantaged position or otherwise are enabled to approach the court for relief. The Doctrine of PIL apply to any case of Public injury arising from : (a) the breach of any public duty, or (b) the violation of some provision of the constitution, or (c) of the law.

The relief to be granted looks to the future and is, generally, corrective rather than compensatory. PIL involves collaboration and cooperation between the government and its officers, the Bar and the Bench, for the purpose of making human rights meaningful for the weaker sections of the community. In this case, (Upendra Baxi vs. State of UP) the court permitted the petitioner a law professor, to raise infringement of Article 21 on behalf of the inmates of the Agra protective home, who were living in inhuman and degrading conditions.

Foundation of Public Interest Litigation

In S.P. Gupta *vs.* UOI-judges transfer case, the Supreme Court laid the foundation of PIL – representative proceedings. It held that any member of public having sufficient interest can maintain an action for judicial redress for public injury in relation to any constitutional or legal provision by a letter addressed to the court.

In Fertilizer Corporation Kamgar *vs.* UOI, the court applied the principle laid in the above case, in Bandhua Mukti Morcha *vs.* UOI, the court said: Government must welcome PIL, it provides them an accession to examine whether poor are getting their socio-economic entitlements or not. The court did not want to tilt at executive authority or usurp it, but to protect poor against violation of their basic human rights.

In M.C. Mehta *vs.* UOI, the Apex court further widened the scope of PIL. It held that a poor can move the court, by writing a letter to any judge. The court has power to grant remedial relief, in the form of compensations, while violations of FRs is gross and patent, and affects persons on a large scale. The court can appoint socio-legal commission or devise any procedure or forge any tools, for the enforcement of FRs under Article 32.

RES-JUDICATA AND ARTICLE 32

Res-judicata is a rule of public policy that there should be finality to binding decisions of courts of competent jurisdiction and that Parties to the litigation should not be vexed with the same litigation again. Thus, where the matter had been heard and decided by the High Court under Art. 226. The writ under Article 32 is barred by this rule. Similarly, if a question has been once decided under Article 32 the same question cannot be reopened again under Article 226. However, a petition under Article 32 for *Habeas corpus* is an exception to this general rule.

Article 33 empowers Parliament to modify the application of FRs to the armed forces or forces charged with maintenance of public order, etc. in the interest of discharge of duties and maintenance of the discipline. Though the appellate jurisdiction of the courts is excluded in cases of court martial, the writ jurisdiction remains under Article 34. Parliament may by law indemnify any person for anything done in contravention of FRs for maintenance of order during the operation of martial law. Artile 35 lays down that the power to make laws to give effect to certain specified FRs shall vest only in the parliament and not in state legislatures.

FUNDAMENTAL DUTIES

Fundamental Duties are incorporated in Part IV-A, which consists of only one Article 51-A, added by 42nd Amendment, 1976. It says that it shall be the duty of every citizen of India (there are eleven such duties, after the 86th Constitutional Amendment Act, 2002):

(a) To abide by the constitution and respect its ideals and institutions, the National Flag and National Anthem;

(b) To cherish and follow the noble ideals which inspired our national struggle for freedom;

(c) To uphold and protect the sovereignty, unity and integrity of India;

(d) To defend the country and render national service when called upon to do so;

(e) To promote harmony and the spirit of common brotherhood amongst all the people of India transcending religious, linguistic and regional or sectional diversities: to renounce practices derogatory to the dignity of women;

(f) To value and preserve the rich heritage of our composite culture;

(g) To protect and improve the natural environment including forests, lakes, rivers and wildlife and to have compassion for living creatures;

(h) To develop the scientific temper, humanism and the spirit of inquiry and reform;

(i) To safeguard public property and to abjure violence;

(j) To strife towards excellence in all spheres of individual and collective activity so that the nation constantly rises to higher levels of endeavour and achievements;

(k) Who is parent or guardian, to provide opportunities for education to his child or ward between the age 6 and 14 years (inserted by the 86th Constitutional Amendment Act 2002).

Verma Committee on Fundamental Duties 1999, noted : "essentially all that is contained in the fundamental duties is just a codification of tasks integral to the Indian way of life".

SIGNIFICANCE OF FUNDAMENTAL DUTIES

Rights and duties are correlative. Mahatma Gandhi defined right as "duty well performed". The fundamental duties are intended to serve as a constant reminder to every citizen that while the constitution specifically conferred on them certain fundamental rights, it also requires citizens to observe certain basic norms of democratic conduct and democratic behaviour. Fundamental duties are confined to "citizens", unlike fundamental rights like Article 21 which extends to "all persons".

The fundamental duties seek to limit the operation of fundamental rights—a countervailing factor and a warning to reckless citizens against anti social activities like destroying public property, burning national flag and like this. It is significant to note that none of the constitution of western countries specifically provides the duties and obligations of citizens. However, the constitution of socialist countries lay great emphasis on the citizens duties.

ENFORCEMENT OF DUTIES

The duties incorporated in the constitution by the 42nd Amendments are statutory duties and shall be enforceable by law. Parliament, by law, will provide penalties to be imposed for failure to fulfil those duties and obligations. A court is determining the constitutional validity of any law seeking to give effect to duties, may consider law to be 'reasonable' in relation to Article 14 or 19.

In M.C. Mehta *vs.* Union of India 1983, Supreme Court held that Article 51-A(g), it is the duty of the Central Government to introduce compulsory teaching of lessons at least for one hour in a week on protection and improvement of natural environment in all educational institutions. Recently, the National commission on the review of the constitution examined the operationalisation of fundamental duties of the citizens and gave their recommendations. In UOI *vs.* R. Padmanabhan, Supreme Court has directed the Central Government to take appropriate steps for the implementation of the recommendation of the NCRC as expeditiously as possible.

In AIIMS Students' Union *vs.* AIIMS, Supreme Court said that the fundamental duties are equally important like fundamental rights, though the former are unenforceable both are prefixed by the same word "Fundamental". Every citizen of India is fundamentally duty bound to strife towards excellence in all spheres of individual and collective activity, so the nation constantly rises to higher levels of endevour and achievements.

DIRECTIVE PRINCIPLES OF STATE POLICY

The Directive Principles of State Policy contained in Part IV of the Constitution (Articles 36-51) set out the aims and objectives to be taken up by the states in the governance of the country. The idea of Welfare State envisaged by our constitution can only be achieved if the states endeavour to implement them with a high sense of moral duty. The real importance of Directive Principles is that they contain positive obligation of state towards its citizens. They are the ideals which the Union and State Governments must keep in mind while they formulate or pass a law.

The Directive Principles constitute a very comprehensive political, social and economic programme for a modern democratic state. The main object in enacting them appear to have been to set standards of achievements before the legislature and the executive, the local and other authorities, by which their success or failure can be judged. Sanctions behind the directive principles are based on sound constitutional and moral obligations. Constitutional obligations are secured by having directive principles as an integral Part of the constitution. The biggest moral force is public opinion which can enforce the directive principles and ensure government's accountability at the time of elections. Thus, sanctions behind Directive Principles are political.

Article 37 of the constitution lays down that it shall be the duty of state to apply these directives in making laws. Article 355 and 365 of the constitution can be applied for enforcing implementation of directive principles.

CLASSIFICATION OF DIRECTIVE PRINCIPLES

(a) Social and Economic Charter

(i) **Social order based on justice-** Article 38(1) provides that the state shall strive to promote the welfare of the people by securing and protecting a social order in which justice—social, economic and political—shall inform all the institutions of national life. Further, the state shall strive to minimize inequalities.

(ii) **Economic justice-** Article 39 specifically requires the state to direct its policy towards securing the following principles:

(a) Equal right of men and women to adequate means of livelihood.

(b) Distribution of ownership and control of material resources of community to the common good.

(c) To ensure that the economic system should not result in the concentration of wealth and means of production to the common detriment.

(d) Equal pay for equal work for both men and women.

(e) To protect health and strength of workers and tender age of children and to ensure that they are not forced by economic necessity to enter avocation unsuited to their age or growth.

(f) That children are given opportunities and facilities to develop in a healthy manner and in condition of freedom and dignity and that childhood and youth are protected against exploitation and against moral and material abandonment.

Article 38 and 39 embody the principle of distributive justice which connotes the removal of economic inequalities rectifying the injustice resulting from transactions between unequals in society.

(b) Social Security Charter

(i) **Participation of workers in Management of Industries:** Article 43 A.

(ii) **Right to work, education and public assistance in cases of unemployment, oldage, sickness, and disablement:** Article 41.

(iii) **Just and human conditions of Work:** Article 42.

(iv) **Living wage for workers:** Article 43, the concept of living wage includes in addition to the bare necessities of life (food, shelter and clothing), provisions for education of children and insurance, etc.

(v) **Free and compulsory education for children until they complete the age of 14 years :** Article 45. However, after the 86th Constitutional Amendment Act 2002, Article 45 reads: "The State shall endeavour to provide early childhood care and education to children below the age of 6 years".

(vi) **Duty to raise the standard of living and improvement of health:** Article 47. It includes, in Particular, the prohibition of liquor.

(vii) **Promotion of education and economic interests of weaker sections:** Article 46.

(viii) **Equal justice and free legal Aid to economically backward classes :** Article 39A.

In centre of Legal Research *vs.* State of Kerala, it has been held that in order to achieve the objectives in Article 39A, the state must encourage and support the Participation of voluntary organisations in operating the Legal Aid programme.

(c) Community Welfare Charter:

(i) **Uniform civil code:** Article 44, while the state has tried to reform and codify the personal laws of Hindus (which is also applicable to Sikhs, Jains and Buddhists), no attempt has been made to bring Muslims, Christians and Parsis under the purview of a Common Civil Code.

(ii) **Organization of Agriculture and Animal Husbandry:** Article 48.

(iii) **Protection and Improvement of Forest and Wildlife:** Article 48A.

(iv) **Protection of Monuments, etc.:** Article 49.

(v) **Separation of Judiciary from Executive:** Article 50.

(vi) **Promotion of International peace and security:** Article 51. Pursuant to the direction enshrined in Article 51, Parliament passed the protection of Human Rights Act, 1993 which provides for the setting of National Human Rights Commission and Human Rights Courts to meet the growing concern for human rights in the country and abroad.

(vii) **Organization of Village Panchayats:** Article 40. The object of this provision is to introduce democracy at the grass root level.

IMPLEMENTATION AND UTILITY OF DPSP

Opinion differs on how far the directives have been implemented in actual practice. In keeping with directives, the main object of five year plans is to achieve a balanced economic development and to raise living standard of masses. As far the implementation of specific directives concerned, good progress has been made:

(i) Land Reforms, Abolition of intermediaries and Zamindari system.

(ii) Organization of Village Panchayats; promotion of cottage industries; welfare of SC and ST etc.

(iii) Compulsory primary education achieved in most states.

(iv) Minimum wages for workers; modernization of labour laws.

(v) Hindu marriage Act and Hindu succession Act – for securing uniform civil code.

In Sarlamudgal *vs.* UOI, the Supreme Court strongly recommended the need for a Uniform Civil Code, declaring illegal the second marriage by a Hindu husband after conversion to Islam. The Judges argued that religious practices violative of Human Rights and dignity of sacerdotal suffocation of essentially civil and material freedoms, are not autonomy but oppression. The judges upheld the view that the unified, progressive civil law would promote national unity and solidarity and safeguard the interests of the weaker and oppressed sections.

In John Vallamattom *vs.* UOI, the Supreme Court reiterated that a Common Civil Code (Art. 44) would enhance the cause of national integration by removing the contradiction based on ideologies.

RELATION BETWEEN DIRECTIVE PRINCIPLES AND FUNDAMENTAL RIGHTS

The directive principles differ from the Fundamental Rights in certain aspects:

(1) The Directives are non justiciable *i.e.*, can't be enforced by the courts; they are declaratory. While fundamental rights are justiciable *i.e.*, can be enforced by the courts; they are mandatory.

(2) The DPSP are instrument of instructions to the government, they contain positive commands to the state to promote a social and welfare state. The Fundamental rights are limitations upon the state actions, they contain negative injunctions to the state not to do various things.

(3) Unlike FR, the DPSP are required to be implemented by legislation.

(4) The courts cannot declare as void any law which is otherwise valid on the ground *i.e.*, contravenes any of the directives. On the other hand, the courts are bound to declare as void any law *i.e.*, inconsistent with Fundamental Rights.

The place the DPSP occupy in constitution vis-a-vis the Fundamental Rights has been a subject matter of controversy for a long time, which has been set at rest:

(i) In State of Madras *vs.* Champakam Dorairajan, Supreme Court held that, the DPSP cannot override the Fundamental Rights.

(ii) In Re Kerala education Bill, the court observed that though the DPSP cannot override the FR, nevertheless in determining the scope and ambit of Rights the court may not entirely ignore the Directives but should adopt the principles of harmonious construction and should attempt to give effect to both as much as possible.

(iii) 25th Amendment, 1971 considerably enhanced the importance of directives Article 31C, added by it, provided that a Law for implementing Directives contained in Article 39 B and C could not be struck down on the ground that it contravened rights conferred by Articles 14 and 19.

(iv) 42nd Amendment 1976, widened the scope of Article of 31C so as to cover all DPSP. Thus, it gave precedence to all the Directives over the Fundamental Rights- Articles 14 and 19.

(v) In Keshavananda Bharti *vs.* UOI, The Supreme Court observed that the Fundamental Rights and DPSP are meant to supplement one another. It can well be said that the directive prescribed the goal to be attained and fundamental rights lay down the means by which that goal to be achieved.

(vi) In Minerva Mills *vs.* UOI, the court struck down Article 31C, as amended by 42nd Amendment as unconstitutional on the ground that it destroys the "basic features" of the constitution. The majority observed that the constitution is founded on the bedrock of the balance between Part III and IV. To give absolute primacy to one over the other is to disturb the harmony of the constitution which is essential feature of the basic structure.

(vii) In State of TN *vs.* Abu Kavur Bai, a five judge bench held that although the DPSPs are not enforceable yet the court should make a real attempt at harmonizing and reconciling the Directives and the Rights and any collision between the two should be avoided as far as possible. The reason why the founding fathers of our constitution did not make these principles enforceable, the court said perhaps due to the vital consideration of giving the government sufficient latitude to implement these principles from time to time according to capacity, situation and circumstances that may arise.

(viii) In Unni Krishnan *vs.* State of Andhra Pradesh, the court has reiterated the same principle that the FRs and DPSP are supplementary and complementary to each other and the provisions in Part III should be interpreted having regard to the Preamble and Directive principles.

(ix) In State of Gujarat *vs.* Mirzapur Motiqure Shikasabjamet, it was held that when faced with a question of testing the constitutional validity of any statutory provision or an executive act, or for testing the reasonableness of any restriction cast by Law on the exercise of any Fundamental Right by way of regulation, control or prohibition, the Directive Principles of State Policy and Fundamental Duties as enshrined in Article 51A plays a significant role.

DIVISION OF POWERS: CONSTITUTIONAL FRAMEWORK

The Indian Constitution establishes a dual polity with a clear division of powers between the Union and the State governments. This is rooted in the principles of federalism, though India is often described as a "quasi-federal" state.

Key Features of the Division of Powers

- **Three Lists in the Seventh Schedule**:
  - **Union List (List I)**: Includes 100 subjects like defense, foreign affairs, atomic energy, banking, etc., over which the Union has exclusive power to legislate.
  - **State List (List II)**: Includes 61 subjects like police, public health, agriculture, etc., over which States have exclusive legislative authority.
  - **Concurrent List (List III)**: Includes 52 subjects like education, marriage and divorce, bankruptcy, etc., where both Union and States can legislate. However, in case of conflict, Union law prevails under Article 254.
- **Residuary Powers (Article 248):** The Union Parliament has exclusive power to make laws on any item which is not present in any of the list.
- **Flexibility in Distribution**:
  - The Constitution permits Parliament to legislate on State subjects under certain circumstances (e.g., during emergencies under Articles 352, 356, and 360).
  - States can consent to Union legislation on State List matters under Article 252.

Judicial Interpretation of Division of Powers

- **State of West Bengal v. Union of India (1963)**: Upheld the supremacy of the Union in matters of legislation.
- **S.R. Bommai v. Union of India (1994)**: Reaffirmed federalism as a basic structure of the Constitution.

ARTICLES 52–78: THE UNION EXECUTIVE

The Union Executive consists of the President, Vice President, Prime Minister, Council of Ministers, and Attorney General of India.

President of India (Articles 52–62)

- **Head of the State** and part of the Parliament.
- Elected by an **electoral college** (Article 54).
- **Powers:**
  - ❑ **Executive**: Appoints the Prime Minister, other ministers, Governors, judges, etc.
  - ❑ **Legislative**: Summons and prorogues Parliament sessions, promulgates ordinances (Article 123).
  - ❑ **Judicial**: Grants pardons under Article 72.
- Acts on the advice of the Council of Ministers (Article 74).

Vice President (Articles 63–70)

- Ex-officio Chairperson of the Rajya Sabha.
- Elected by members of both Houses of Parliament (Article 66).
- Discharges functions of the President during temporary vacancies (Article 65).

Prime Minister and Council of Ministers (Articles 74–75)

- The Prime Minister is the **real executive head**.
- Council of Ministers collectively responsible to the Lok Sabha (Article 75).

Attorney General (Article 76)

- The highest law officer in India.
- Advises the government on legal matters.

Conduct of Government Business (Article 77)

- All executive actions are taken in the name of the President.

ARTICLES 153–167: THE STATE EXECUTIVE

The State Executive consists of the Governor, Chief Minister, Council of Ministers, and Advocate General of the State.

Governor (Articles 153–162)

- **Head of the State** appointed by the President.
- Functions as the Union's representative in the State.
- **Powers:**
  - ❑ **Executive**: Appoints the Chief Minister, other ministers, State Advocate General, etc.
  - ❑ **Legislative**: Summons and dissolves the State Legislature, gives assent to bills, reserves certain bills for the President (Article 200).
  - ❑ **Discretionary**: Can act without the advice of the Council of Ministers in specific cases.

Chief Minister and Council of Ministers (Article 163–164)

- The Chief Minister is the real executive head of the State.
- Council of Ministers aids and advises the Governor.
- Ministers are collectively responsible to the State Legislative Assembly.

Advocate General (Article 165)

- The highest law officer in the State.
- Advises the State Government on legal matters.

THE CONCEPT OF FEDERALISM AND COOPERATIVE FEDERALISM

Federalism in India

- Federalism implies a system of governance where powers are divided between the central and regional governments.
- Indian federalism is unique as it combines features of both federal and unitary systems.

Features of Indian Federalism

- **Written Constitution**: Clearly defines powers and responsibilities.
- **Supremacy of the Constitution**: Any law inconsistent with the Constitution is void.
- **Independent Judiciary**: Acts as the guardian of the Constitution and resolves disputes between the Union and States.

Cooperative Federalism

- Encourages collaboration between the Union and States for national goals.
- Mechanisms include:
  - ❑ **Inter-State Council (Article 263)**.
  - ❑ **Zonal Councils** under the States Reorganization Act, 1956.

- **Finance Commission** for equitable distribution of financial resources.
- Centrally Sponsored Schemes for collaborative implementation of development programs.

Challenges to Federalism

- Over-centralization of powers.
- Misuse of Article 356.
- Financial dependence of States on the Union.
- Political interference and regional disparities.

Interrelationship Between the Union and State Executives

The Union and State Executives in India share a symbiotic relationship as envisaged in the Constitution. While both function autonomously in their respective spheres, several provisions establish their interdependence, coordination, and communication.

THE PRESIDENT AND THE GOVERNOR: POWERS, DUTIES, AND OVERLAPPING FUNCTIONS

President of India: Powers and Duties

- **Executive Powers:**
  - Executes the laws passed by Parliament (Article 53).
  - Appoints Governors, Prime Minister, other Union Ministers, and various constitutional officers.
  - Issues ordinances when Parliament is not in session (Article 123).
- **Legislative Powers:**
  - Summons, prorogues, and dissolves Parliament (Article 85).
  - Assent or veto to bills (Article 111).
  - Addresses the first session of Parliament every year (Article 87).
- **Judicial Powers:**
  - Appoints judges of the Supreme Court and High Courts.
  - Pardoning powers under Article 72.
- **Emergency Powers:**
  - Proclaims National, State, and Financial Emergencies (Articles 352, 356, and 360).

Governor: Powers and Duties

- **Executive Powers:**
  - Executes laws passed by the State Legislature (Article 154).
  - Appoints the Chief Minister and other Ministers.
  - Acts as the Chancellor of State Universities in many States.
- **Legislative Powers:**
  - Summons, prorogues, and dissolves the State Legislature (Article 174).
  - Assent or veto to State bills (Article 200).
  - Recommends bills for Presidential assent in certain cases (Article 201).
- **Judicial Powers:**
  - Appoints State Public Service Commission members.
  - Pardoning powers for offenses against State laws (Article 161).
- **Special Powers in Certain States:**
  - Administers tribal areas under the Sixth Schedule (Article 244).

Overlapping Functions

- **Appointment of the Governor:** The President appoints the Governor, establishing a direct link between Union and State executives (Article 155).
- **Legislative Role:**
  - The Governor may reserve State bills for Presidential assent under Article 200.
  - The President's decision becomes binding, showing hierarchical interdependence.
- **Emergency Provisions:**
  - The Governor recommends imposing President's Rule (Article 356).
  - The President acts on the Governor's report.
- **Administrative Role:**
  - Both ensure that constitutional provisions are upheld in their respective jurisdictions.

ROLE OF THE UNION AND STATE COUNCILS OF MINISTERS

Union Council of Ministers

- **Headed by the Prime Minister** and collectively responsible to the Lok Sabha (Article 75(3)).

- Advises the President in discharging executive functions (Article 74).
- Formulates and implements Union policies that influence State governance indirectly.

State Council of Ministers

- **Headed by the Chief Minister** and collectively responsible to the State Legislature (Article 164(2)).
- Advises the Governor in discharging State executive functions (Article 163).
- Implements Union directives under Articles 256 and 257 to ensure compliance with Union laws.

Interrelationship

- **Implementation of Union Laws:**
  - States implement Union laws under Articles 256 and 257.
  - Failure to comply can lead to intervention by the Union (Article 356).
- **All India Services:**
  - Officers like IAS and IPS serve under both Union and State governments, promoting coordination.
- **Planning and Finance:**
  - Union policies, such as GST implementation, require close collaboration with State Councils of Ministers.

COMMUNICATION BETWEEN THE PRESIDENT AND GOVERNORS

Communication from the President to the Governor

- **Article 78:** Specifies the duties of the Prime Minister to communicate with the President.
  - Key matters include administrative decisions and legislative proposals.

Communication from the Governor to the President

- **Article 167:** Specifies the duties of the Chief Minister to communicate with the Governor.
  - Keeps the Governor informed about State administration and legislative proposals.
  - The Governor, in turn, communicates significant matters to the President, especially regarding:
    - Reserved bills under Article 200.
    - Situations warranting Presidential intervention under Article 356.

Practical Examples of Interrelationship

- **Governor's Role in Implementation of Central Schemes:**
  - Governors monitor and report on Central schemes in States, such as Swachh Bharat Mission.
- **President's Role in State Legislation:**
  - Certain bills, like those affecting Scheduled Areas, require Presidential assent.
- **Judicial Intervention:**
  - **S.R. Bommai v. Union of India (1994):** Reinforced constitutional boundaries between Union and State executives.
- **Cooperative Mechanisms:**
  - Regular communication during events like national disasters, where both Union and State Councils coordinate responses.

ADMINISTRATIVE RELATIONS BETWEEN THE UNION AND STATES

The administrative relations between the Union and State governments in India are governed by the provisions of the Constitution, ensuring cooperation, coordination, and compliance in the functioning of a federal system. These relations are primarily detailed under **Articles 256–263**.

Articles 256–263: Executive Directions and Compliance by States

Key Provisions:

- **Article 256: Obligation of States and Union**
  - The executive power of each State must be exercised to ensure compliance with the laws made by Parliament.
  - The Union can issue directions to a State for ensuring such compliance.
- **Article 257: Control of the Union over States**
  - The executive power of a State must not impede the Union's executive power.
  - The Union can issue directions to a State in matters of national importance, such as:
    - Construction and maintenance of communication systems.
    - Protection of railways within the State.
  - Expenses incurred in such cases are recoverable by the Union from the State.

- **Article 258: Delegation of Union Functions to States**
  - ❑ The President can, with the consent of the State Government, entrust Union functions to State authorities.
  - ❑ This delegation does not require a constitutional amendment.
- **Article 261: Public Acts, Records, and Judicial Proceedings**
  - ❑ Full faith and credit are to be given to public acts, records, and judicial proceedings of the Union and all States.
- **Article 263: Inter-State Council**
  - ❑ Provides for the establishment of Inter-State Councils to discuss and recommend policies on inter-State disputes or coordination.

Inter-State Councils and Zonal Councils as Mechanisms for Cooperation

Inter-State Council (Article 263):

- **Purpose:**
  - ❑ To foster coordination between the Union and States and among States.
  - ❑ To resolve disputes and advise on policies affecting multiple States.
- **Composition:**
  - ❑ Chaired by the Prime Minister.
  - ❑ Includes Union Cabinet Ministers and Chief Ministers of States.
- **Functions:**
  - ❑ Investigates and discusses subjects of common interest between Union and States.
  - ❑ Recommends measures for better policy implementation and dispute resolution.
- **Notable Example:**
  - ❑ Sarkaria Commission (1988) recommended strengthening the Inter-State Council to improve Union-State relations.

Zonal Councils:

- **Purpose:**
  - ❑ Established under the **States Reorganisation Act, 1956**, to promote regional cooperation.
- **Composition:**
  - ❑ There are five Zonal Councils: Northern, Southern, Eastern, Western, and Central.
  - ❑ Chaired by the Union Home Minister with respective State Governors and Chief Ministers as members.
- **Functions:**
  - ❑ Address issues of regional development and cooperation.
  - ❑ Facilitate collaboration in areas like education, health, and transport.

Coordination Through All-India Services

The **All-India Services** act as a vital link between the Union and States, ensuring administrative cohesion.

Key Features of All-India Services:

- **Constitutional Basis:**
  - ❑ Established under Article 312 of the Constitution.
  - ❑ Includes the Indian Administrative Service (IAS), Indian Police Service (IPS), and Indian Forest Service (IFoS).
- **Dual Control:**
  - ❑ Members are recruited by the Union (through UPSC) but serve both Union and State Governments.
  - ❑ They operate under State Governments but are governed by Union laws and service rules.
- **Roles in Coordination:**
  - ❑ **IAS Officers:** Implement both Union and State policies, bridging the gap between the two levels of government.
  - ❑ **IPS Officers:** Maintain law and order, ensuring national security across States.
  - ❑ **IFoS Officers:** Protect and manage forest resources, contributing to Union and State environmental policies.
- **Significance:**
  - ❑ Promote uniformity in policy implementation across States.
  - ❑ Ensure administrative continuity and efficiency during inter-State or Union-State conflicts.

UNION STATE LEGISLATIVE RELATIONS

Legislative Relations between Union and States (Articles 245-254)

The legislative powers in India are subject to the scheme of distribution of powers between the Union and state legislatures (as provided in three lists under the constitution), fundamental rights (*i.e.*, legislative powers cannot contravene the fundamental rights) and other provisions of the constitution. The distribution of legislative powers between Union and states is clearly in favour of the Union, the rationale being that a strong

Centre is necessary to coordinate the activities of various states in the interest of uniformity and to check fissiparous or anti-national tendencies.

There are three Lists which provide for distribution of legislative powers (under 7th Schedule to the Constitution):

(1) **Union List:** It contains 97 items and comprises of the subjects which are of national importance. Only the Union Parliament can legislate with respect to these matters *e.g.*, Defence, Foreign affairs, Banking, Currency, Union taxes, etc.

(2) **State List:** It contains 66 items and comprises of subjects of local or state interest and thus lie within the legislative competence of the State Legislatures, viz. Public order and Police, Health, Agriculture, etc.

(3) **Concurrent List:** It contains 47 items, with respect to which, both Union Parliament and the State Legislature have concurrent power of legislation. The concurrent list was to serve as a device to avoid excessive rigidity to a two-fold distribution. It is a twilight zone, the state can take initiative, while the Parliament can also do so. Besides, the state can make supplementary laws in order to amplify the laws made by Union Parliament. The subjects include general laws and social welfare—Civil and Criminal Procedure, Marriage, Contract, Planning, Education, etc.

The constitution makes a two-fold distribution of legislative powers:

(i) With respect to territory

(ii) With respect to subject matter of legislation (*i.e.*, three lists).

(I) Territorial Legislative Jurisdiction (Article 245): Article 245 defines the ambit or territorial limits of legislative powers. "Cl. (1) : subject to the constitutional provisions, Parliament may make laws for whole or any Part of territory of India, and a State Legislature for the territory of that state.

Cl. (2): No law made by the Parliament would be invalid on the ground that it would have extra-territorial operation *i.e.*, takes effect outside the territory of India."

Theory of Territorial Nexus

Article 245 provides that a state legislature may make laws for the territory of that state. The State legislature cannot make extra territorial laws, except when there is sufficient connection or nexus between the state and the object *i.e.*, subject matter of legislation (object may not be physically located within the territorial limits of state) (A.H. Wadia *vs.* CIT AIR 1947 FC 18).

Thus, in Wallace Bros. *vs.* CIT, Bombay, a company, which was registered in England, was a Partner in a firm in India. Indian Income tax authorities sought to tax entire income of the company. The Court upheld it on the ground that derivation from British India of major Part of its income for a year gave to a company sufficient territorial jurisdiction.

In State of Bombay *vs.* RMDC, the Bombay state levied a tax on lotteries and prize competitions in the state. The tax was extended to a newspaper printed and published in Bangalore, but had wide circulation in Bombay. The respondent conducted the Prize competition through this paper for which entries were received through agents and depots established in the state to collect entry forms and fees. The court held that a sufficient territorial nexus exist for the State of Bombay to tax the newspapers.

EXTRA-TERRITORIAL OPERATION OF PARLIAMENTARY LAW

Article 245(2) provides that no law made by the parliament would be invalid on the grounds that it would have extra territorial operation *i.e.*, takes effect outside the territory of India. In other words, Parliamentary law will cover persons and their property anywhere in world, and the legislation may offend the rules of International law or may not be recognized by the foreign courts. In the case sovereign legislature question of extra territoriality of any enactment can never be raised in the municipal court as a ground for challenging its validity. Thus, if a citizen of India goes to France and marries a French girl while his first wife is alive, he can be prosecuted in India for Bigamy.

Distribution of Legislative Subjects Article 246

Article 246 provides:

(i) Notwithstanding anything in Clauses (2 and 3), Parliament has exclusive power to make laws with respect to any of the matters enumerated in the list one (Union list).

(ii) Notwithstanding anything in Clause (3), Parliament, and, subject to Clause (1) the State legislature also, have power to make laws with respect to any of the matters enumerated in the list three (concurrent list)

(iii) Subject to Clauses (1 and 2) the state legislature has exclusive power to make laws for such state with respect to any of the matters enumerated in list two (state list)

(iv) Parliament has power to make laws with respect to any matter for any Part of the territory of India not included in a state, notwithstanding that such matter is a matter enumerated in the State List.

Thus, Article 246 provides that the parliament has exclusive power to make laws with respect to Union List: the state legislature for the State List; and, the Parliament and state legislature, both, for the Concurrent List.

Non-obstante Clause give supremacy to the Union list. However, as observed by the Supreme Court, this Clause ought to be regarded as the last resort, a witness to the imperfection of human expression and the fallability of legal draftsmanship. It is only when the reconciliation between a Union and State List becomes impossible, then this Clause is to be used. The court have evolved the Doctrine of Harmonious Construction and Pith and Substance in order to mitigate the effect or rigour of non-obstante Clause.

PRINCIPLES OF INTERPRETATION OF LISTS

The distribution of the subject matters cannot be claimed to be scientifically perfect and there happens to be overlappings between the subjects enumerated in the three lists. Whether a particular subject falls in the sphere of one or other government (*i.e.*, Union or State), the Supreme Court has evolved following principles to determine respective powers of Union and State legislatures.

Plenary Power of Legislature

It is an absolute power to enact laws, subject only to its legislature competence and other constitutional limitations. The parliamentary power of legislation to acquire property, for example, is unrestricted, as held in state of West Bengal and UOI.

The following points are important to understand the nature of plenary power:

(a) The power to make law includes the power to give effect to it prospectively (*i.e.*, for future acts) as well as retrospectively *i.e.*, for past acts.

(b) The meaning of Validation Act is to remove the causes for ineffectiveness or invalidity of actions or proceedings which are validated by a legislative measure. A validating law is upheld first by finding out whether legislature possesses competence over the subject matter and, whether by validation the legislature has removed the defects which the courts have found in the previous law.

(c) Where an impunged Act (*i.e.*, An Act whose validity is questioned) passed by a state legislature is invalid on the grounds that state legislature did not have legislative competence to deal with the topic covered by it, then even parliament cannot validate such Act because such validation would give the state legislature power over subjects outside its jurisdiction.

(d) When the legislature cure the said infirmity and pass a validating law, it can make the said provisions of earlier law effective from the date when it was passed. The retrospective application of law thereby removing the basis of earlier judicial decisions is not an encroachment on the judicial power. But the legislature cannot enact a legislation which overrules the decision of court and not to change the existing law retrospectively.

Liberal and Harmonious Construction

Subject to the predominance of the Union list, the entries in the various lists should be interpreted broadly. The entries were mere legislative heads and are of enabling character. In Calcutta Gas Company *vs.* State of West Bengal, The Court said that widest amplitude should be given to the language of the entries, but some of entries in different list may overlap and may appear to be in direct conflict with each other. It is then court's duty to reconcile entries and to bring harmony between them. Entries of two lists must be read together and the language of one interpreted and when necessary modified by that of the other.

In Gujarat University *vs.* Shri Krishna, the petitioner challenged the authority of the University to impose Gujarati or Hindi as the exclusive medium of instruction under the power conferred by Gujarat University Act 1961. By item eleven of list II or state list, state legislature empowered to legislate in respect of education including Universities, subject to the Items 63-66 of the List I or Union List. By Item 66 List I, Parliament can legislate for coordination and determination of standards in institutions of higher education. Held that the power to legislate with respect to medium of education is a necessary incidence of coordination and determination of standards, the State Law was thus invalid.

The doctrine of Harmonious Construction lays down that every effort should be made to give effect to all the provisions of an Act by harmonizing any apparent conflict between two or more of its provisions. A construction that reduces one of the provisions to a useless lumber or dead letter is not harmonious construction. To harmonize does not mean to defeat the purpose of Act. It means striking the balance and giving effect to meaning of both words. All provisions of a statue have their own importance so this rule protects the rights/interests of society at large. The basis of the principle of harmonious construction probably is that the legislature must not have intended to contradict itself.

In Keshavananda Bharati *vs.* State of Kerala, the Supreme Court held that the Fundamental Rights and DPSP are conscience of the constitution and in cases of conflicts, the court should endeavour to maintain both of them by applying the principle of harmonious construction. The court established a fair balance between the individual interests and the welfare of the society.

In Osmania University Teachers Association *vs.* State of A.P., the Union set up the University Grants Commission for coordination determination of standards under Entry 66, List I. The state of Andhra Pradesh acting under Entry 25, List II set up a commission similar to U.G.C. to coordinate and determine standards for the State. Held, the state law to be ultra vires as by the principle of harmonious construction the power to coordinate and determine standards was excluded from Entry 25, List II.

Ancillary or Incidental Powers

It is well settled that the power to legislate on a topic of legislation carries with it, the power to legislate on an ancillary matter which can be said to be reasonably included in the power given. Thus, the power to legislate with respect to land includes the power with respect to mortgage of land as a subsidiary subject. The power to make laws on a subject include the power to pass a valid law retrospectively. The power to levy tax would include the power to enact provisions to check tax evasion.

In R.D. Joshi *vs.* Ajit Mills, Supreme Court held that the punitive measures for enforcing social legislation are Part of the ancillary powers. In United Provinces *vs.* Atiqa Begum, it was held that the general word used in an entry must be construed to extend to all ancillary or subsidiary matters which can fairly and reasonably be held to be included in it.

Expressions incidental and ancillary powers mean the powers which are required to be exercised for the proper and effective exercise of legislative powers expressly conferred. However, the doctrine can be invoked only in aid of the main topic of legislation. Thus, the power with respect to betting and gambling in Entry 34 of List II can't include the power to impose taxes on betting and gambling specifically provided in Entry 62 of List II. Similarly, it is doubtful if power to levy tax would include power to confiscate goods as ancillary thereto.

Pith and Substance Rule

This doctrine is applied when the legislative competence of a legislature with regard to a Particular enactment is challenged. When a law dealing with a subject in one list touching on a subject in another list. In such a case, what has to be ascertained is the pith and substance of enactment *i.e.*, true object/purpose of legislation.

Constitutionality of a law is to be judged by its real subject matter and not by its incidental effect on another's field. If, on examination, it is found that legislation is in substance one on a matter assigned to the legislature, then it must be held valid in its entirety even though it may touch upon matters beyond its competence. An incidental encroachment is not prohibited. The doctrine requires that in such a case of encroachment, the law should be read as a whole and not as a collection of sections or Clauses for determining the true nature and character of the law *i.e.*, pith and substance of the Law.

In Prafulla Kumar *vs.* Bank of Commerce, Khulna, the court held that the pith and substance of the Bengal Money Lenders Act being money lending, a state subject, and it was valid even though it trenched incidentally unpromisory notes, a central subject. The principle of Pith and Substance finds support from the expression with respect to used in Clauses (1-4) of Article 246.

In state of Rajasthan *vs.* G. Chawla, the state legislature made a law restricting the use of sound amplifiers. The State's contention was that law is within its competence since it fell under Entry 6, List II public health and sanitation. The respondent contended that the impunged law fell under List I Entry 31 – P&T, Telephones, wireless, broadcasting and like forms of communications. Held that the law in its pith and substance fells substantially within the State List, even though amplifier is an apparatus for communication thus, incidentally encroaching upon the Union subject. The power to legislate in relation to public health includes the power to regulate the use of amplifiers as producers of loud noises.

Doctrine of Colourable Legislation

The colourable legislation simply means a legislation which, transgressing constitutional limitations, is made to appear as if it were quite constitutional. The doctrine of colourable legislation is applied when the transgression is disguised, covert, and indirect.

If the Law enacted by the legislature is found in substance and in reality beyond the competence of the legislature enacting it, will be ultra vires and void, even though it apparently purports to be within the competence of the legislature enacting it. It is the substance of the

Act *i.e.*, material and not merely the form or outward appearance. This doctrine is based on the maxim that what one cannot do directly that cannot be done indirectly.

Colourability, is thus bound up with incompetence and not tainted with bad faith or evil motives. In state of Bihar *vs.* Kameshwar Singh, the court held that the Bihar Land Reforms Act 1950 apparently purported to lay down rule for determination of compensation, but in reality it did not lay down such rule and indirectly sought to deprive the petitioner of his property without any compensation and hence, it was a colourable legislation and invalid.

RESIDUARY POWER (ARTICLE 248)

Article 248: Parliament has exclusive power to make any law with respect to any matter not enumerated in List II and List III. Such power shall include the power of making any law imposing a tax not mentioned in either of those lists. It is also laid down by Entry 97 of List I. The scope and extent of Article 248 is identified with that of Entry 97 List I. However, scope of residuary powers is restricted, as the three Lists cover all possible subjects and because of the courts interpretation as to a matter falls under residuary powers or not. The rationale behind such powers is that it enables parliament to legislate on any subject which has escaped the scrutiny of the House, and the subject which is not recognizable at present. However, the framers of the constitution intended that recourse to residuary powers should be the last resort, and not the first step. Residuary powers are well known convention in Federal Constitution. Nevertheless, residuary powers are criticized, as they promote a strong centre and curb the autonomy of the State.

Several Acts have been enacted by Parliament under its Residuary powers. For example, the Wealth Tax Act, Gift Tax Act, Commission of Enquiry Act, etc. In Dhillon's case, the court observed: there is a difference between Entry 97 of List I and the Article 248, the Entry 97 indicate only the subject matter while Article 248 is an enabling provision and enables Parliament to make laws. Parliament is empowered to make law with respect to matter in Entry 97, by virtue of Article 246(1) and not Article 248. Article 248 should include within its powers only those matters which are not enumerated in any of three Lists. And, thus, residuary power cannot include power exclusively given to the Parliament under Article 246(1).

In Dhillon's case, the Supreme Court refashioned the legislative relation between the Centre and States. The court held that in case of a Central legislation, the proper test was to enquire whether the matter falls in List II or III. If matter doesn't fall under List II, parliament will be competent to legislate on it under its Residuary Powers in Entry 97 of List I. But, in International Tourism Corporation *vs.* State of Haryana held that, where the competing entries are entry in List II and entry 97 of List I, the entry in State List must be given a broad and plentiful interpretation and Residuary power can't be so expensively interpreted as to whittle down the power of State legislature. Before exclusive legislative competence can be claimed for parliament by resorting to residuary power, the legislative incompetence of State must be clearly established.

INCONSISTENCY/REPUGNANCY BETWEEN UNION AND STATE LAWS (ARTICLE 254)

Clause (1): "If any provision of a law made by state legislature is repugnant to any provision of a law made by Parliament, which is competent to enact, or to any provision of an existing law with respect to matters enumerated in concurrent list, then subject to Clause (2) provisions, the parliamentary law, whether passed before or after state legislatures law, or the existing law, shall prevail and state law shall, to the extent of repugnancy, be void".

Article 254(1) enumerates the rule that in the event of conflict between a Union and a State Law, the former prevails. The Union Law may have been enacted prior to the state law or subsequent to the state law. The principle behind this is when there is legislation covering the same ground both by the Centre and State, both of them competent to enact the same, the Central law should prevail over the State Law. The expression existing law refers to laws made before the commencement of constitution by any legislature, authority, etc., for example Criminal Law, CPC, Evidence, Contract etc.

The repugnancy here means, irreconcilable inconsistency. The repugnancy must be clear, direct and irreconcilable *i.e.*, the provisions of the two acts are such that they cannot stand together or operate in the same field. If they can operate in same field without coming into conflict with each other, there will be no repugnancy. However, it would be no defence to argue that it is possible to obey both the laws.

The Doctrine of Occupied Field applies only where Union and State laws are in area where both can enact Laws *i.e.*, Concurrent list. Thus, Article 254(1) has no application to cases of repugnancy due to over lapping found to exist between State List on the one hand and Union List and List III on the other. In such case, State Law will fail not because of repugnancy to the Union Law but due to the want of Legislative competence.

The present position of law in India is one as decided in the Hoechst Case. Thus, in cases of incidental encroachments resulting in repugnancy between Union and State Laws, Article 246 will apply and not Article 254. Infact, the Supreme Court further narrowed down the scope of Article 254(1) by holding that the Law of the Parliament or an existing Law must be with respect to same matter or Entry in the Concurrent List.

Clause (2): enacts an exception to the rule of Clause (1). "Where Law made by State Legislature with respect to matters in Concurrent List contain any provision repugnant to an earlier Parliamentary Law or an existing Law with respect to that matter, then state law shall, if reserved for consideration by President and has received his assent, prevail in that state. Provided that nothing in the Clause shall prevent Parliament from enacting at anytime any law with respect to the same matter including a law adding, amending, varying or repealing State law."

Article 254(2) provides for curing of repugnancy which would otherwise invalidate a state law which is inconsistent with the Union Law or an existing law. However, the proviso to Article 254(2) lays down the Parliament may again supercede state legislation which has been assented to by the President under Clause (2) by making the law on the same matter. However, in the case of repugnancy, not the entire State Law becomes void, it becomes void only to the extent it is repugnant to the Central Law.

The case of Zaver Bhai *vs.* State of Bombay illustrates the application of proviso to Clause (2) of Article 254. The Parliament enacted an essential supplies Act which provided penalties *e.g.*, imprisonment upto three years. The Bombay legislature later passed an Act enhancing punishment upto seven years. The Act received Governor General's assent and become operative, subsequent to the Bombay Act, Amendments made in Central Acts by Parliament with changes in punishment. The Supreme Court held, that as both occupy the same field, the Bombay Act was impliedly repealed by Parliamentary Act because of repugnancy.

The Apex Court also held that the power exercised by the President under Article 254(2) is a special constituent power vested with the head of the Union, as the protector and the defender of the constitution and the safety valve to safeguard the fundamental rights and the federal structure of the country's polity. The power exercised by the President, is the Part of the Legislative procedure and not an exercise of legislative power. Hence, whether the constitutional procedure before enacting the laws has been followed or not can always be examined by the court. The Apex Court has narrowed down the scope of repugnancy only to the situations of direct conflict and occupied field or operation in the same field. In Kanka Gruha Nirman Sahakara Sangh *vs.* Narayamma, Supreme Court held that if there is no repugnancy between the State and Central Law, there is no question of application of Article 254(1) and both the Acts would prevail.

JUDICIARY: COMPOSITION OF SUPREME COURT OF INDIA

As originally enacted, the Constitution of India provided for a Supreme Court with a Chief Justice and seven lower-ranking judges — leaving it to Indian Parliament to increase this number. In the early years, a full bench of the Supreme Court sat together to hear the cases presented before them. As the work of the Court increased and cases began to accumulate, Parliament increased the number of judges from the original eight in 1950 to eleven in 1956, fourteen in 1960, eighteen in 1978, twenty-six in 1986 and thirty one in 2008. As the number of the judges has increased, they have sat in smaller benches of two or three (referred to as a division bench) — coming together in larger benches of five or more (referred to as a constitutional bench) only when required to settle fundamental questions of law. Any bench may refer the case under consideration up to a larger bench if the need to do so arises.

Eligibility

- The person must be a citizen of India.
- Judge of a High Court or of two or more such courts in succession for at least five years, or
- An advocate of a High Court or of two or more such courts in succession for at least ten years, or
- The person must be, in the opinion of the President, a distinguished jurist.

Supreme Court judges retire at the age of 65. A judge of Supreme Court can be removed by the procedure prescribed in Article 124(4) of the Constitution of India on ground of proved misconduct or incapacity or judge resigning from his office addressed to the President of India. The procedure prescribed for removal of Supreme Court judge should not be called an impeachment procedure because this procedure is provided only for the removal of the President of India under Article 61 of Constitution of India on ground of violation of the Constitution.

Article 125 of the Indian Constitution leaves it to the Indian Parliament to determine the salary, other allowances, leave of absence, pension, etc. of the Supreme Court judges. However, the Parliament cannot alter any of these privileges and rights to the judge's disadvantage after his appointment.

The Constitution seeks to ensure the independence of Supreme Court Judges in various ways. In Three Judges Cases, the court held that a Supreme Court judge can be appointed by the President only on the recommendations of the collegium system as mentioned earlier. A Judge of the Supreme Court cannot be removed from office except by an order of the President passed after an address in each House of Parliament supported by a majority of the total membership of that House and by a majority of not less than two-thirds of members present and voting, and presented to the President in the same Session for such removal on the ground of proved misbehaviour or incapacity. A person who has been a Judge of the Supreme Court is debarred from practising in any court of law or before any other authority in India.

Recently, a 5 judge constitutional bench of the Supreme Court of India declared the Constitution, 99th Amendment Act, 2014 and National Judicial Appointments Commission Act, 2014 as unconstitutional. These acts were aimed at ending the *collegium* system of promotion and appointment of judges & chief justices to the various high courts and the Supreme Court by a separate commission having members from the both the executive and the judiciary. The 4:1 majority judgement pronounced by the bench held that such a commission was in violation of the basic features of the constitution like the independence of judiciary and separation of powers. The dissenting opinion was given by Justice Chelameshwar.

Composition of High Courts in India

The High Court is the highest judicial body in a State. Article 214 of the Constitution provides that there shall be a High Court for each State. Often there may be a common High Court for two or more than two States. There are 24 High Courts in the country. Three High Courts have jurisdiction over more than one State. Among the Union Territories, Delhi alone has a high court of its own.

Though the high courts are the Parts of single and integrated judicial system, yet they are completely independent judicial institutions. The Supreme Court has no direct administrative control over them, nor are they in any way controlled by either the State Legislatures or the Executives. Each High Court is a Court of Record and has power of such a court, including the power to punish for its contempt.

Composition

Each High Court consists of a Chief Justice and such other judges as the President may from time to time appoint. Unlike the Supreme Court, there is no fixed minimum number of judges for the High Courts. It varies from court to court and from State to State.

Appointment of Judges

The Chief Justice of a High Court is appointed by the President in consultation with the Chief Justice of India and the Governor of the State. While appointing other judges of the High Court, the President consults the Chief Justice of the Supreme Court, the Governor of the State and the Chief Justice of the concerned High Court. The additional judges are often appointed in order to dispose of the arrears cases. Such appointments are temporary and are terminable after disposal of arrears cases. To be eligible for the appointment of a Judge of a High Court the person should have the following qualifications:

(a) He must be a citizen of India,

(b) He must have held a judicial office in India for 10 years, or

(c) He must have practiced as an advocate of a High Court for 10 years.

A person appointed as a judge of a High Court must-take an oath of office in a prescribed form before the Governor of the State concerned.

Terms of Office

A Judge of a High Court holds office until he attains the age of 62 years. Originally, the constitution had fixed the age requirement of a High Court Judge at 60. But the Fifteenth Constitutional Amendment Act, 1963 raised it from 60 to 62 years. It became necessary as competent persons were reluctant to serve as judges because of early retirement.

However, a judge may resign his office earlier by writing to the President. He may be removed from his office by the President when a resolution to that effect is passed by the Parliament and presented to the President. Such a resolution must be supported by a majority of the total membership of each House and not less than two-thirds of the total members of each House present and voting in that session. This procedure is similar to the procedure through which a judge of the Supreme Court is removed. Thus, the service conditions of the High Court judges are identical with those of the Supreme Court judges.

A judge of a High Court may be transferred to another High Court by the President after consultation with the Chief Justice of India. It is provided in order to enable the President to send a competent and most suited judge to a Particular Part of India where his services are needed in the national interest. Further, it facilitates better justice and keeps the court above narrow and regional considerations.

A Judge of the High Court is prohibited from practice in courts or before any authority in India, except the Supreme Court and High Courts of which he has not been a judge. Thus, in appointment, security, salary, pensions and other privileges, the judges of the High Court are equipped with same safeguards as the judges of the Supreme Court. This greatly ensures their impartiality and independence.

NEED FOR THE INDEPENDENCE OF THE JUDICIARY

The basic need for the independence of the judiciary rests upon the following points:

- **To check the functioning of the organs:** Judiciary acts as a watchdog by ensuring that all the organs of the state function within their respective areas and according to the provisions of the constitution. Judiciary acts as a guardian of the constitution and also aids in securing the doctrine of separation of powers.
- **Interpreting the provisions of the constitution:** It was well known to the framers of the constitution that in future the ambiguity will arise with the provisions of the constitution so they ensured that the judiciary must be independent and self-competent to interpret the provision of the constitution in such a way to clear the ambiguity but such interpretation must be unbiased *i.e.*, free from any pressure from any organs like executive. If the judiciary is not independent, the other organs may pressurize the judiciary to interpret the provision of the constitution according to them. Judiciary is given the job to interpret the constitution according to the constitutional philosophy and the constitutional norms.
- **Disputes referred to the judiciary:** It is expected of the Judiciary to deliver judicial justice and not partial or committed justice. By committed justice, we mean to say that when a judge emphasizes on a Particular aspect while giving justice and not considering all the aspects involved in a Particular situation. Similarly, judiciary must act in an unbiased manner.

CONSTITUTIONAL PROVISIONS — THE INDEPENDENCE OF THE JUDICIARY

Many provisions are provided in our constitution to ensure the independence of the judiciary. The constitutional provisions are discussed below:

- **Security of Tenure:** The judges of the Supreme Court and High Courts have been given the security of the tenure. Once appointed, they continue to remain in office till they reach the age of retirement which is 65 years in the case of judges of Supreme Court (Art. 124(2)) and 62 years in the case of judges of the High Courts (Art. 217(1)). They cannot be removed from the office except by an order of the President and that too on the ground of proven misbehaviour and incapacity. A resolution has also to be accepted to that effect by a majority of total membership of each House of Parliament and also by a majority of no less than two-third of the members of the house present and voting. Procedure is so complicated that there has been no case of the removal of a Judge of Supreme Court or High Court under this provision.
- **Salaries and Allowances:** The salaries and allowances of the judges is also a factor which makes the judges independent as their salaries and allowances are fixed and are not subject to a vote of the legislature. They are charged on the Consolidated Fund of India in case of Supreme Court judges and the Consolidated Fund of State in the case of High Court judges. Their emoluments cannot be altered to their disadvantage (Art. 125(2)) except in the event of grave financial emergency.
- **Powers and Jurisdiction of Supreme Court:** Parliament can only add to the powers and jurisdiction of the Supreme Court but cannot curtail them. In the civil cases, Parliament may change the pecuniary limit for the appeals to the Supreme Court. Parliament may enhance the appellate jurisdiction of the Supreme Court. It may confer the supplementary powers on the Supreme Court to enable it work more effectively. It may confer power to issue directions, orders or writs for any purpose other than those mentioned in Art. 32. Powers of the Supreme Court cannot be taken away to protect independence of judiciary.
- **No discussion on conduct of Judge in State Legislature/Parliament:** Art. 211 provides that there shall be no discussion in the legislature of the state with respect to the conduct of any judge of Supreme Court or of a High Court in the discharge of his duties. A similar provision is made in Art. 121 which lays down that no discussion shall take place in Parliament with respect to the conduct of the judge of Supreme Court or High Court in the discharge of his duties except upon a motion for presenting an address to the President praying for the removal of the judge.

- **Power to punish for contempt:** Both the Supreme Court and the High Court have the power to punish any person for their contempt. Article 129 provides that the Supreme Court shall have the power to punish for contempt of itself. Likewise, Art. 215 lays down that every High Court shall have the power to punish for contempt of itself.
- **Separation of the Judiciary from the Executive:** Article 50 contains one of the Directive Principles of State Policy and lays down that the state shall take steps to separate the judiciary from the executive in the public services of the state. The object behind the Directive Principle is to secure the independence of the judiciary from the executive. Article 50 says that there shall be a separate judicial service free from executive control.

WRIT JURISDICTION

WRIT JURISDICTION OF THE SUPREME COURT AND HIGH COURTS

A writ is a quick remedy against injustice, a device for the protection of the rights of citizens against any encroachment by the governmental authority. Writs originated in Britain where they were king's or queen's 'prerogative' writs and were commands to the judicial tribunals or other bodies to do or not to do something. Since writs carried the authority of the crown they were to be obeyed. Later, writs came to be enjoyed by the judges of the king's bench. In India, the power to issue writs has been vested in the Supreme Court and the High Courts. It is a speedy remedy and is made available without going into avoidable technicalities. It is an extraordinary remedy which can be expected in special circumstances.

The Supreme Court has been empowered to issue writs in the nature of the Habeas corpus, Mandamus, Prohibition, Certiorari and Quo-warranto for protecting the FR. Similar power has conferred on the High Courts via. Art. 226 of the constitution. The High Court can issue the above writs for protecting the fundamental as well as statutory and common law rights. The high courts can issue writs to any governmental authority outside its territorial jurisdiction, provided the causes of action arises within their territorial jurisdiction.

A writ is a discretionary remedy and the high court can refuse it on the ground of acquiescence, laches, available alternative remedy and no benefit to the Party. Under Art. 226 (3), a High Court can grant interim relief by way of interlocutory orders.

While the jurisdiction of the High Court is more extensive than that of the Supreme Court, Art. 226 (4) provides that the powers conferred on a high court shall not be in derogation of the powers conferred on the Supreme Court by Art. 32 (2). In L. Chandra Kumar *vs.* UOI, held that a person can go directly to the Supreme Court from a decision of a Tribunal, without first going to the High Court concerned. Thus, the aggrieved person has got another remedy by way of the writ petition before the high court concerned. Thus, what was earlier a two tier litigation has now become a three tier litigation. The Tribunals cannot oust the jurisdiction of the High Court under Art. 226/227.

The constitution gives wide powers to all High Courts to ensure that injustice is not tolerated in any sphere. Art. 226 provides that notwithstanding anything in Article 32 every High Court shall have power, throughout the territories in relation to which it exercises jurisdiction, to issue to any person or authority, including in appropriate cases, any Government, within those territories directions, orders or writs, including writs in the nature of Habeas corpus, Mandamus, Prohibition, Quo-warranto and Certiorari, or any of them, for the enforcement of any of the rights conferred by Part III and for any other purpose. It is important to note that the power is not only to enforce fundamental rights but for any other purpose, which makes its powers even wider than Supreme Court. Here, any other purpose means any legal right of legal duty. In a landmark case of **L. Chandra Kumar** *vs.* **Union of India AIR 1997**, SC has held that the power of judiciary over legislative action vested in a High Court is a basic feature of the constitution and cannot be removed through constitutional amendment.

Locus Standi—Who can apply: In general, the person whose constitutional right or legal right has been infringed has the right to apply. However, due to judicial activism, the "Doctrine of sufficient interest" has originated. According to this, any person who is even remotely affected can submit a petition the High Court. It also allows public spirited persons to file a writ petition for any person or class if that person or class is not able to do so himself due to poverty or any other reason. In **ABSK Sangh** *vs.* **Union of India AIR 1991**, SC held that even an unregistered trade union has right to file a petition for redressal of a common grievance.

In the case of **Chairman, Railway Board** *vs.* **Chandrima Das AIR 2000**, SC held that an advocate of Calcutta High Court has sufficient interest in making a public place like a railway station a safe place and so she has right to demand compensation for the Bangladeshi woman gang raped by railway employees.

Scope of Art. 226: In the case of **Basappa** *vs.* **Naggapa, AIR 1954**, SC has held that the Art. 226 confers wide powers to remedy injustice where ever it is found. Article 226 says, "...or writs or the kind of...", which means that it is not limited only the mentioned types of writs. It can issue orders of any kind that the situation may require. Thus, it makes the scope of Art. 226 a lot wider than Art. 32.

Court Martial and Art. 226: In a significant case Delhi High Court held that Section 18 of India Army Act is not beyond the scope of High Court. While High Court may not interfere in the sentence awarded in a court martial, such an order cannot be arbitrary and mala fide. Thus, it is open to judicial review. In the case of **Union of India** *vs.* **R. K. Sharma, AIR 2001** SC has held that court should not interfere only on compassionate grounds. Only when there is a perverseness or gross injustice on the face of it, there can be judicial review.

Dispute between Private Parties — No Jurisdiction: In Mohan Pandey *vs.* **Usha Rani Rajgaria SCC 1992,** SC held that the extraordinary jurisdiction of High Court cannot be exercised in the private Party disputes relating to property rights unless there is a violation of statutory rights by statutory authorities.

Natural Justice: Natural Justice is not exclusively the principle of administrative law. The courts are also bound by the same principle. Every administrative action must be supported by reasons. The reasons must be recorded to ensure that there is no arbitrariness.

Territorial extent of writ jurisdictions: Art. 226 imposes two limits on HC's writ. First, it can run only in the territorial jurisdiction of the High Court and secondly the person or authority must lie in that jurisdiction. In the case of **Election Commission of India** *vs.* **Venkata Rao, AIR 1975** SC held that Madras High Court cannot issue a writ to ECI because it is based in New Delhi and so is out of its jurisdiction. The law commission recommended that these are serious limitations and they defeat the very purpose of this Article. So, it was amended by 15th Amendment in 1963. High Court can now issue a writ even to a central authority if the cause of action in whole or Part arises in its jurisdiction. In the case of **ONGC** *vs.* **Utpal Kumar Basu SCC 1994**, it was held that the averment in the petition did not disclose that a Part of the cause of action arose in the jurisdiction of Calcutta and so High Court does not have any jurisdiction to entertain the writ petition.

Discretionary Remedy — Not to be exercised if alternate remedy is available: The remedy available in 226 is a discretionary remedy and the High Court has the discretion to accept or refuse a petition. In general, if a remedy is available elsewhere, writs under 226 are discouraged. However, this does not mean that any remedy available can be a ground for not entertaining the petition under 226. The remedy must be effective and sufficient. In the case of **Vellaswamy** *vs.* **IG Police, Madras 1982**, SC held that the remedy under Police Rules of TN was not sufficient and so High Court was wrong in dismissing the petition.

Important writs issued by the Supreme Court and High Court:

(a) **HABEAS CORPUS:** It literally means 'a demand to produce the body' (whether dead or alive). The issuance of the writ means an order to the detaining authority or person to physically present the detained person before the court and show the cause of detention so that the court can determine its legality or otherwise. If the detention is found to be illegal, the detained person is set free forthwith. Its purpose is not to punish the wrong doer but merely to secure the release of the person illegally detained.

Since now, Art. 21 cannot be suspended even during the proclamation of Emergency, this becomes a very valuable writ for safeguarding the personal liberty of the individual. While the Supreme Court can issue the writ of Habeas corpus only against the state in cases of violation of FR, the High Court can issue it also against private individuals illegally or arbitrarily any other person.

Writ of Habeas corpus can be filed by any person on behalf of the person detained or by the detained person himself. In Sunil Batra II *vs.* Delhi admn., a letter written by a convict to one of the judges of the Supreme Court was treated as a writ petition. The court employed this writ for the neglect of State penal facilities. The writ also issued when a ban was imposed on the law students to conduct interviews with prison mates for affording them legal relief.

(b) **MANDAMUS:** It is a command to act lawfully and to desist from perpetrating an unlawful act. Where A has a legal right which cast certain legal obligation on B, A can seek a writ of mandamus directing B to perform its legal duty. Mandamus may lie against any authority, officers, government or even judicial bodies that fail or refuse to perform a public duty and discharge a legal obligation.

The Supreme Court may issue a mandamus to enforce the fundamental right of a person when its violation by some governmental order or act is alleged. The High courts may issue this writ to direct an officer to exercise his constitutional and legal powers, to compel any person to discharge duties cast on him by the constitution or the statue, to compel a judicial authority to exercise its jurisdiction and to order the government not to enforce any unconstitutional law.

Mandamus is a judicial remedy in the form of 'an order to do or to forbear from doing some specific act' which that agency is obliged to do or to refrain from doing under the law and which is in the nature of a public duty or a statutory duty. It is considered as a residuary remedy of the public law. It is a general remedy whenever justice has been denied to any person. It may be issued not only to compel the authority to do something but also to restrain it from doing something. Therefore, it is both negative and positive and hence can do the work of all other writs. It can be issued on all those counts on which certiorari and prohibition can be issued.

In Praga Tools Corp. *vs.* C.V. Imanual, held that a mandamus could be issued against a person or body to carry out the duties placed on them by the statues even though they are not public official or statutory body. Technicalities should not come in the way of granting that relief under Art. 226. In Unni Krishnan *vs.* Union of India, held that a private medical/engineering college comes within the writ jurisdiction of the court irrespective of the question of aid and affiliation.

In Jatinder Kumar *vs.* State of Punjab, held that Art. 320(3) of the constitution which provided that before a government servant was dismissed, the UPSC, should be consulted, did not confer any right on a public servant and hence failure to consult the public service commission did not entitle the public servant to get mandamus for compelling the government to consult the commission. However, if the authority is under law obliged to exercise a discretion, mandamus would lie to exercise it in one way or the other.

(c) **CERTIORARI:** Certiorari is a Latin word meaning 'to inform'. It was essentially a royal demand for information. The King wishing to be certified of some matter, ordered that the necessary information be provided for him. 'Certiorari' may be defined as a judicial order operating in personam and made in the original legal proceedings, directed to any constitutional, statutory or non-statutory body or person, requiring the records of any action to be certified by the court and dealt with according to law.

It can be issued against constitutional bodies, statutory bodies like corporation, non statutory bodies like companies and cooperative societies and private bodies and person. Certiorari can be issued to quash judicial, quasi-judicial as well as administrative actions. In this case, the writ of certiorari was issued to quash the action of the selection board, on the grounds of personal bias.

Grounds for the issue of the certiorari are: (1) Lack of jurisdiction; or the authority declining jurisdiction where it legally belongs to it. (2) Excess of jurisdiction. (3) Abuse of jurisdiction. (4) Violation of the principles of natural justice. (5) Error of law apparent on the face of the record— it includes not a mere error but a manifest error based on clear ignorance or disregard of the law, or on a wrong perception of the law, or on clear inconsistency between facts and law and the decision.

In Syed Yakoob *vs.* Radhakrishnan, held that the jurisdiction of the high court to issue a writ of certiorari is a supervisory jurisdiction and the court exercising it is not entitled to act as an appellate court. As error of law which apparent on the face of the record can be corrected by a writ, but not an error of fact, howsoever, grave it may appear to be. However, if a finding of fact is based on 'no evidence', that would be regarded as an error of law which can be corrected by certiorari.

(d) **PROHIBITION:** Prohibition is a judicial order to the agencies from continuing their proceedings in excess or abuse of their jurisdiction or in violation of the principles of natural justice or in contravention of the law of the land. Before the writ of prohibition can be issued, there must be something to be done, it is a writ of right. It can be issued even when the agency has reached a decision, to stop the authority from enforcing its decision. In India, prohibition is issued to protect the individual from arbitrary administrative actions. Prohibition does not lie against an authority discharging executive functions. It issues only against an authority discharging judicial functions.

(e) **QUO-WARRANTO:** Quo-warranto is a question asking 'with what authority or warrant'. The writ may be sought to clarify in public interest the legal position in regard to claim of a person to hold a public office.

An application seeking such a writ may be made by any person provided the office in question is a substantive public office of a permanent nature created by the constitution or law and a person has been appointed to it without a legal title and in contravention of the constitution or the laws.

It can be issued against offices created by the constitution such as the Advocate-General, the speaker of legislative assembly, officers under the municipal act, members of a local government board, University officials and teachers, but it will not be issued against the managing committee of a private school which is not appointed under the authority of a statue.

JUDICIAL ACCOUNTABILITY

Whenever there is a mention of the independence of the judiciary, there is always a concern about the latent dangers of the judicial independence and there arises the importance of "Judicial Accountability". The recent development in this regard is the recommendation of the Law Commission for the inclusion of a whistle blower provision, aimed at protecting those making complaints against judges, in a draft Bill dealing with the removal of judges of the Supreme Court and High Courts. Introduction of such a Bill by the Law Commission is a major step in the direction of making changes to the rigid procedure in our constitution for the removing of the judges of the Supreme Court and the High Courts.

EMERGENCY PROVISIONS

The term emergency may be defined as a difficult situation arising suddenly and demanding immediate action by public authorities under powers specially guaranteed to them by the constitution or otherwise to meet such exigencies. Dr. Ambedkar claimed that the Indian federation was unique in times of emergency it could convert itself into an entirely unitary state. In India, three types of emergencies are available under the constitution. These are (a) National emergency, (b) Failure of constitutional machinery in a state. (c) Financial Emergency.

NATIONAL EMERGENCY (ARTICLE 352)

ARTICLE 352: National emergency is imposed due to war, external aggression or armed rebellion *i.e.*, when there is a threat to the security of the country or any territory thereof. The President shall not issue a proclamation unless a decision of the Union Cabinet that such a proclamation may be issued, has been communicated to him in writing. Such a proclamation may be made even before the actual war, external aggression or rebellion if the President is satisfied that there is an imminent danger thereof.

Though the state legislature and government are not suspended, the executive, legislative and financial powers rest in the centre. The Union Parliament acquires the power to legislate on any subject included in the state list. But such emergency legislation ceases to have any effect at the expiry of 6 months after the proclamation ceases to operate. Fundamental rights are suspended (except Articles 20 and 21). The President has the power to suspend the right to move the courts for the enforcement of any of the FRs for a period not exceeding the proclamation of emergency.

Every proclamation is required to be laid before each house of the parliament, and is to cease to operate at the expiration of 1 month from the date of its issue unless in the mean time it has been approved by resolutions of both the Houses. However, once approved by Parliament, the proclamation may continue for 6 months at a time unless revoked by the Parliament earlier. The provisions of Article 352 were made more stringent by the constitution 44th Amendment Act, 1978. To prevent the misuse of emergency provisions, the words armed rebellion were substituted for internal disturbance. There have been three proclamation of National Emergency in India – in 1962 at the time of Chinese aggression, in 1971 in the wake of war with Pakistan and in June 1975 on the grounds of internal disturbance.

Article 358 made it clear that things done or omitted to be done during emergency cannot be challenged even after the emergency was over on the ground of the concerned emergency law having violated Article 19. In the Minerva Mills case, it was held that the Judiciary could act if it was established that the Union Government acted *mala fide* or on irrelevant or no facts. A matter like satisfaction of the President is beyond the court. Only if it was shown that there was, in fact, no satisfaction at all, or the satisfaction was absurd, perverse or *mala fide*, the exercise of the power would be unconstitutional, courts could certainly act under their power of limited judicial review in such a case.

PRESIDENT'S RULE IN STATES (ART. 356)

Failure of constitutional machinery in state – If the President on Governor's report, or otherwise is satisfied that a situation has arisen in which government of a state can't be carried on in accordance with the constitutional provisions, he may issue a proclamation to that effect.

The following consequences ensue on the issuance of a proclamation under Article 356(1):

- President may assume powers vested in Governor.
- President may declare that powers of legislature of state shall be exercisable by Parliament.
- The President may make such incidental and consequential provisions as may appear to him to be necessary or desirable for giving effect to the object of proclamation. The President cannot, however, assume to himself, any of the powers vested in High Court.

When a proclamation is made under Article 356(1), the powers of the State legislature are to be exercised by Parliament. Parliament may also authorize the President to delegate such powers to any other authority as specified by himself. It may be noted that in comparison to Article 352, under Article 356, the State Legislature remains suspended and dissolved; however, fundamental rights remain unaffected.

The proclamation issued under Article 356(1) may be revoked or varied by the President on a subsequent proclamation. It is to be noted that under Article 356, the President acts on a report of the Governor or otherwise. This means that President can act even without the Governor's report. This is justified in view of the obligation of the Centre imposed by Article 355 viz. to protect every State against external aggression and internal disturbances and to ensure that the state government is carried on in accordance with the constitutional provisions. Further, what is expected from the Governor is only a report and not a recommendation.

Duration of Proclamation Under Article 356

Article 356(3) provides that a proclamation relating to the state emergency shall be laid before each House of Parliament and unless both Houses approve it by a resolution, it shall cease to have effect at the expiration of two months. However, proviso to Clause (3) provides that if any such proclamation is issued at the time when Lok Sabha is dissolved or the dissolution takes place during the period of two months and the proclamation is passed by the Rajya Sabha but not by the Lok Sabha, it shall cease to operate at the expiry of 30 days from the date on which the new Lok Sabha meets, unless before the expiry of 30 days, it has also been passed by the Lok Sabha.

Article 356(4) provides that the duration of proclamation can be extended by 6 months each time by both Houses of Parliament passing resolutions approving its continuance. The proviso to Clause (4) lays down that the maximum period for which a proclamation can remain in operation is 3 years from the date it is issued under Article 356(1).

Article 356(5), however, lays down that beyond 1 year, a proclamation can be continued only if emergency under Article 352 is in operation in the whole of India or in the whole or any Part of the state, and the election commission certifies that it is not possible to hold elections to the state legislature. It may be noted that in Punjab, the President's rule was imposed for 5 years but for this, the constitution was amended several times.

In state of Rajasthan *vs.* UOI, President's rule was imposed in nine states on the ground that Assemblies in these states no longer represented the wishes of electorate. The court upheld the centre's action: question of political wisdom or executive policy can't be inquired. Question of proper time for dissolution of assembly is not an extraneous matter to Article 356. Under the Indian system, the list of political power through formation of several political Parties is legal, hence a mere attempt to get more political power for a Party is not unconstitutional.

Proper grounds for invoking Article 356:

- Hung assembly scenario
- Corruption and mal-administration etc.
- Acting contrary to the constitution of India/Union directives *i.e.*, subversion of the constitution by the state government
- Failure to meet an extraordinary situation *e.g.*, an outbreak of unprecedented violence, a great natural calamity, etc.
- Security concerns *viz.* danger to national integration or security of the state.

Improper grounds for invoking Article 356:

- Improper action by Governor in case of political instability *e.g.*, after the dismissal of the ministry on loosing the majority support in the Assembley, the governor recommends dissolution under Article 356, without probing the possibility of the formation of an alternative government via floor test.
- Overwhelming defeat in the Lok Sabha elections (the Union government cannot dismiss a duly elected state government on the sole ground that the ruling Party in the state suffered an overwhelming defeat in the election to the Lok Sabha).
- Power used merely for achieving good government.
- Situation of internal disturbance not amounting to or verging an abdication of its governmental powers by the state government, all possible measures to contain the situation by the Union, in the discharge of its duty under Article 355 have not been exhausted.

In one look at the past instances of imposition of President's rule in India, three common grounds emerge that have been invoked under Article 356 – breakdown of law and order, political instability, corruption and mal-administration.

In Rameshwar Prasad *vs.* UOI, the constitutional validity of notification dated 23rd May, 2005 ordering dissolution of legislative assembly of the state of Bihar was in issue. In a unique case of its kind, even before the first meeting of the Legislative Assembly, its dissolution had been ordered on the ground that attempts were being made to cobble a majority by illegal means and lay claim to form the government in State and if attempts continued, it would amount to tempering with constitutional provisions. Held that the Presidential proclamation, dissolving state assembly in Bihar under Article 356 was unconstitutional and based on extraneous and irrelevant grounds. The court said that the state governor misled the centre in recommending the dissolution of state assembly and the Union council of ministers should have verified before accepting it as gospel truth. The Governor's report contained fanciful assumptions which could be destructive to democracy. In recommending the dissolution of a freshly elected assembly or invoking the power under Article 356, the Governor or President, respectively, could not act on the ground of immorality.

S.R. BOMMAI CASE: In this historic judgement—S.R. Bommai *vs.* UOI, the Supreme Court has laid down various guidelines in regard to the use of Article 356, which, it is hoped, would put a check on arbitrary dismissal of state governments in future and strengthen the federal structure of Indian polity. The court observed: in view of the pluralist democracy and the federal structure that has been accepted under the constitution, the Party or Parties in power at the Centre and in the states may not be the same. Therefore, there is a need to confine the exercise of power under Article 356(1) strictly to the situation mentioned therein which is a condition precedent to the said exercise.

It was reaffirmed that a proclamation under Article 356 is amenable to judicial review though difficulty arises for lack of judicially manageable standards to judge such situations. Though the subjective satisfaction of the President cannot be reviewed by court but material on which satisfaction is based, is open to judicial review on grounds of illegality, *mala fide*, extraneous considerations, abuse of power, irrelevance or irrationality – the truth, correctness or adequacy of the material cannot be gone into on merits. Nor can a purely political question be reviewed by court. Judicial review is possible only in areas which permit the application of totally objective standards.

The majority of the judges subscribed to the following conclusions:

- Article 356 confers extra-ordinary powers on the President. This power should be exercised sparingly and with great circumspection... the last measure to restore the constitutional machinery in the state.
- The power granted under Article 356 is not absolute. Existence of material, which may include report of the Governor, is a condition precedent for issue of the proclamation.
- High Court or Supreme Court can strike down the proclamation as unconstitutional if it is made *mala fide* or base on irrelevant material. The satisfaction of the President must be based on relevant material. Though the sufficiency of the material cannot be questioned but legitimacy of inference drawn from such material is open to judicial review. Even if Part of material is irrelevant the court cannot interfere so long as there is some material which is relevant to the action taken.
- Though power to dissolve state legislative assembly is implicit in Clause (1) of Article 356, the President shall exercise this power only after the both Houses of Parliament approve the proclamation, as laid down in Article 356(3). Until such approval, President can suspend legislative assembly under Article 356(1)(c).
- In case, the proclamation is approved by both Houses within two months. The government which was dismissed and the assembly, which was dissolved, will not revive on expiry of two months or revocation of the proclamation.
- Secularism is one of the basic features of the constitution and any state government, which pursues unsecular policies is amenable to action under Article 356.
- The court gave other instances where invocation of Article 356 would be proper:
    - ❑ large scale law and order problems
    - ❑ gross mismanagement of administration
    - ❑ corruption/abuse of power
    - ❑ damage to national integration or security of state
    - ❑ creating disunity or dissatisfaction among people
    - ❑ state's failure to implement Directive Principles.

FINANCIAL EMERGENCY (ARTICLE 360)

The President is authorized by Article 360 to declare by a proclamation of financial emergency if he is satisfied that the financial stability or credit of India or any Part of its territory is threatened. It has to be laid before both Houses of Parliament and ceases to operate at the expiration of two months unless meanwhile approved by the resolution of the two Houses. Once approved by Parliament, unlike proclamations under Article 352, it may continue indefinitely until revoked or varied.

During the operation of financial emergency, the executive authority of the Union extends to the giving of directions to any state to observe certain specified canons or financial propriety and such other direction that the President may find necessary or adequate. These directions may include reduction of salaries or allowances of all those serving a state and reserving for the President's consideration all money Bills and other Bills under Article 207 after these are passed by the state legislatures. The President may also direct reduction in salaries, etc. of all those serving in connection with the affairs of Union including Judges of the Supreme Court and the High Courts. So far, there has been no occasion for the proclamation of financial emergency in India.

TEMPORARY, TRANSITIONAL AND SPECIAL PROVISIONS IN RESPECT OF CERTAIN STATES

OVERVIEW OF PART XXI OF THE CONSTITUTION OF INDIA

Introduction

- Part XXI of the Indian Constitution deals with "Temporary, Transitional, and Special Provisions" and is found under Articles 369 to 392.
- It was included to address the unique requirements of certain regions and states during India's transition from colonial rule to a sovereign democratic republic.
- It also provides the framework for addressing regional disparities, cultural distinctiveness, and transitional legislative needs.

Meaning and Purpose of Temporary, Transitional, and Special Provisions

- **Temporary Provisions:**
  - These provisions were created to address immediate post-independence challenges or specific regional issues for a limited period.
  - **Example:** Article 370 (now abrogated), which granted special status to Jammu and Kashmir.
- **Transitional Provisions:**
  - These provisions helped in managing the transition from the Government of India Act, 1935, to the Indian Constitution.
  - They are essential for maintaining continuity of laws and institutions during the transitional period.
  - Example: Article 369, which granted Parliament temporary powers to legislate on certain state subjects.
- **Special Provisions:**
  - These provisions aim to protect the cultural identity, economic interests, or political autonomy of specific regions or groups.
  - Example: Articles 371 to 371J, which provide special arrangements for states like Maharashtra, Gujarat, Nagaland, and others.

Purpose

- To ensure smooth integration of diverse states into the Union of India.
- To address the unique socio-economic and cultural needs of certain regions.
- To facilitate the transition from colonial rule to independent governance.
- To uphold the federal structure of India while addressing regional aspirations.

Constitutional Framework of Part XXI

- **Articles 369 to 392:**
  - **Article 369:** Temporary power to Parliament to legislate on state subjects for five years after the commencement of the Constitution (e.g., trade, supply of foodstuffs).
  - **Article 370:** (Abrogated in 2019) Special provisions for Jammu and Kashmir.
  - **Articles 371 to 371J:** Special provisions for states like Maharashtra, Gujarat, Nagaland, Assam, Sikkim, and others.
  - **Article 372:** Continuance of pre-Constitution laws until amended or repealed.
  - **Article 374:** Provisions regarding the continuation of pre-Constitution judicial authorities.
  - **Article 375:** Courts, authorities, and officers to continue functioning post-independence.
  - **Articles 376 to 392:** Miscellaneous provisions relating to the President's powers, legal procedures, and transitional arrangements.

- **Significance:**
  - Balances regional autonomy with national unity.
  - Ensures continuity of governance during a transitional period.
  - Addresses socio-cultural and economic disparities in various states.

Significance of Part XXI

- **Protecting Cultural Diversity:** Ensures that the distinct cultural and social practices of specific regions are preserved (e.g., Nagaland under Article 371A).
- **Promoting Regional Equity:** Provides tailored solutions for economically or socially backward regions, ensuring equitable development.
- **Maintaining Federal Structure:** By recognizing the asymmetric needs of different states, Part XXI strengthens the federal framework.
- **Ensuring Smooth Transition:** Facilitates continuity of laws and governance during the transition to the new constitutional order.
- **Addressing Temporary Needs:** Offers a legal mechanism to address short-term exigencies post-independence.
- **Flexibility:** Reflects the Constitution's dynamic nature by accommodating regional aspirations without compromising national integrity.

Key Features and Examples of Temporary, Transitional, and Special Provisions

Type	Example Article	Purpose
Temporary	Article 370	Special status to Jammu & Kashmir (abrogated in 2019).
Transitional	Article 369	Parliament's power to legislate on state subjects temporarily.
Special	Article 371A	Protects the social and religious practices of Nagaland.

Article 370: Special Status of Jammu and Kashmir

Historical Context and Rationale Behind Article 370

- Jammu and Kashmir (J&K) acceded to India on October 26, 1947, under the Instrument of Accession signed by Maharaja Hari Singh during the turmoil of the Partition.
- Unlike other princely states, J&K's accession was conditional, granting it autonomy over certain subjects except for defense, foreign affairs, and communications.
- Article 370 was included in the Indian Constitution as a temporary provision to recognize J&K's special circumstances:
  - The UN-mediated ceasefire in 1949 left parts of J&K under Pakistan's control (referred to as Pakistan-occupied Kashmir or PoK).
  - J&K's unique cultural and religious composition required a sensitive approach.
  - The need for autonomy to draft its own Constitution through a Constituent Assembly.

Key Provisions of Article 370

- **Autonomy to Jammu and Kashmir:**
  - J&K had its own Constitution and flag.
  - Indian Parliament could legislate for J&K only on matters of defense, foreign affairs, and communication.
  - For extending other Union laws to J&K, the State Government's concurrence was required.
- **Presidential Orders:**
  - The President could issue orders to extend Indian laws to J&K, but only with the State Government's consent.
  - Over 40 Presidential Orders were issued over the years to integrate J&K with India.
- **Separate Constitution:** J&K was the only state with its own Constitution, adopted on November 17, 1956.
- **Limited Applicability of Fundamental Rights:** Indian Fundamental Rights were applicable only to the extent approved by J&K's legislature.
- **Restrictions on Indian Citizenship:** Article 35A (inserted via a Presidential Order in 1954 under Article 370) provided special rights to 'permanent residents' of J&K, including exclusive property rights and government job reservations.
- **Temporary Provision:** Article 370 was termed "temporary" in nature, intended to cease once J&K's Constituent Assembly dissolved. However, since the Assembly ceased to exist in 1957 without recommending its abrogation, the provision continued.

Abrogation of Article 370 in August 2019

- **Legal Process:**
  - On August 5, 2019, the President of India issued Constitution (Application to Jammu and Kashmir) Order, 2019, superseding the earlier orders under Article 370.

- The President acted on the recommendation of Parliament, bypassing the need for J&K's State Government's consent, as the state was under President's Rule since 2018.
- Article 370 was rendered inoperative, effectively revoking the special status of J&K.
- J&K was bifurcated into two Union Territories:
  - Jammu & Kashmir (with a legislature).
  - Ladakh (without a legislature).

- **Political and Legal Implications:**
  - The move was passed with a two-thirds majority in Parliament but faced strong opposition from certain political parties.
  - Legal challenges arose, questioning the validity of abrogating Article 370 without J&K's Constituent Assembly or elected State Government's concurrence.
  - It reignited debates on federalism and the scope of Presidential powers under the Indian Constitution.

Impact of Abrogation on Jammu and Kashmir and Ladakh

Positive Outcomes (Proponents' View)

- **Integration with India:**
  - Ended the "temporary" status of J&K, bringing it on par with other Indian states and Union Territories.
  - Indian laws and Fundamental Rights became fully applicable in J&K.
- **Economic Development:**
  - Opened J&K and Ladakh to investment, as restrictions on land ownership by non-residents were lifted.
  - Special schemes and initiatives were introduced to promote infrastructure, tourism, and industries.
- **Improved Governance:**
  - Direct control of the Union Government was expected to improve transparency and accountability.
  - Local bodies and panchayats gained prominence.
- **Security:**
  - Facilitated stronger measures to combat militancy and terrorism.
  - Removed ambiguity in dealing with separatist elements.

Article 371: Special Provisions for Specific States

Introduction

- Article 371 and its sub-clauses (Articles 371 to 371J) of the Indian Constitution provide special provisions for certain states in India.
- These provisions aim to address the unique cultural, tribal, economic, and geographical conditions of these states and promote balanced development.
- The provisions under Article 371 are not uniform; each state enjoys specific benefits tailored to its particular needs.

Special Provisions for Specific States

Article 371: Maharashtra and Gujarat

- Enacted to address regional imbalances after the bifurcation of Bombay State in 1960.
- Governor's Responsibility:
  - Establishment of separate development boards for Vidarbha, Marathwada, and Gujarat's backward regions.
  - Ensure equitable allocation of funds and resources.
  - Provide adequate employment opportunities in state services for people from these regions.

Article 371A: Nagaland

- Recognizes the unique cultural and social practices of the Naga people.
- Key Provisions:
  - The Parliament cannot legislate on religious or social practices, customary laws, administration of civil and criminal justice involving customary laws, and ownership of land and resources without the consent of the Nagaland Legislative Assembly.
  - Nagaland's distinct identity is preserved.

Article 371B: Assam

- Special provisions for the Bodoland Territorial Council (BTC) and similar councils.
- Aimed at protecting the tribal communities in Assam by ensuring their autonomy and representation in decision-making.

Article 371C: Manipur

- Focuses on protecting the interests of the hill areas of Manipur.
- **Hill Areas Committee:** A committee of the Legislative Assembly ensures legislation affecting the hill areas is not passed without adequate representation.

Article 371D and 371E: Andhra Pradesh and Telangana

- Special provisions to ensure equitable opportunities in public employment and education.
- Provides for the establishment of regional boards to ensure fair development across different regions.
- Article 371E allows for the establishment of a Central University in Andhra Pradesh.

Article 371F: Sikkim

- Integrates Sikkim into India while preserving its unique identity after its merger in 1975.
- **Key Provisions:**
  - The Sikkim Legislative Assembly can legislate on subjects not in the Union or Concurrent List.
  - Protection of Sikkimese laws, traditions, and privileges.

Article 371G: Mizoram

- Recognizes the customary laws and traditions of Mizoram.
- The Parliament cannot legislate on social practices, customary laws, ownership of land and resources, and religious practices without the consent of the Mizoram Legislative Assembly.

Article 371H: Arunachal Pradesh

- The Governor of Arunachal Pradesh has special powers regarding law and order.
- Aimed at addressing Arunachal Pradesh's sensitive border location and tribal diversity.

Article 371I: Goa

- Ensures the establishment of a separate Legislative Assembly for Goa with a minimum of 30 members.

Article 371J: Karnataka (Hyderabad-Karnataka Region)

- Introduced in 2012 to address the economic backwardness of the Hyderabad-Karnataka region.
- **Key Provisions:**
  - Establishment of a separate development board.
  - Reservation in state government jobs and educational institutions for local candidates.

Special Provisions for Tribal Areas

Introduction

The Sixth Schedule of the Indian Constitution provides special provisions for tribal areas in the states of Assam, Meghalaya, Tripura, and Mizoram. These provisions aim to protect the customary laws, culture, and rights of the tribal communities in these regions while promoting their socio-economic development.

Provisions Under the Sixth Schedule of the Constitution

- **Article 244(2) and the Sixth Schedule:**
  - The Sixth Schedule applies to the tribal areas in the states of Assam, Meghalaya, Tripura, and Mizoram, specifying the administrative and legislative framework for these regions.
  - Autonomous Districts: The Schedule grants the establishment of Autonomous District Councils (ADCs) in tribal areas, each with its own legislative, executive, and judicial powers over local matters.
  - Article 244(2) states that the provisions of the Sixth Schedule shall apply to the administration of the tribal areas in the States of Assam, Meghalaya, Tripura and Mizoram. It is the Parliament, by law, that can make provisions regarding the administration of these tribal areas, and can amend the Schedule.
- **Key Features of the Sixth Schedule:**
  - **Autonomous District Councils (ADCs):** These councils are given significant powers to legislate on matters related to land, forests, social customs, and local governance.
  - **Legislative Powers:** ADCs can make laws on matters such as land management, agriculture, village administration, and the protection of tribal rights.
  - **Executive Powers:** ADCs have their own executive heads (usually a chief executive member) and the power to enforce their laws.
  - **Judicial Powers:** ADCs can establish tribal courts to adjudicate civil disputes and offenses under the customs of the tribes.
  - **Land Ownership:** The land of the tribal areas is protected, with restrictions on non-tribals owning land or acquiring rights to land in these regions.

- **Customary Laws:** The tribal areas are allowed to follow their customary laws regarding governance, dispute resolution, and social practices.

Autonomy for Tribal Areas in Assam, Meghalaya, Tripura, and Mizoram

- **Assam:**
  - The Autonomous District Councils (ADCs) in Assam include the Karbi Anglong Autonomous District Council and the Bodoland Territorial Region (BTR), which gained more autonomy in recent years.
  - The Bodoland Territorial Region (BTR) has its own legislature, enabling it to legislate on issues concerning the tribal population.
- **Meghalaya:**
  - Meghalaya has three Autonomous District Councils: the Khasi Hills Autonomous District Council, the Jaintia Hills Autonomous District Council, and the Garo Hills Autonomous District Council.
  - These councils enjoy substantial autonomy over the administration of tribal areas and their cultural preservation.
- **Tripura:**
  - The Tripura Tribal Areas Autonomous District Council (TTAADC) was established to address the needs of tribal communities in Tripura.
  - The TTAADC was given powers to legislate on matters affecting land ownership, the welfare of tribals, and tribal culture.
- **Mizoram:**
  - Mizoram has its own Autonomous District Councils, such as the Lushai Hills Autonomous District Council.
  - These councils exercise powers similar to those in other states, particularly in the areas of land ownership and tribal customs.

THE ELECTION COMMISSION OF INDIA (ECI)

Historical Background

- **Evolution:** Initially a single-member body (only CEC); it briefly became multi-member in 1989 and was permanently made a multi-member body in 1993 with the appointment of two additional Election Commissioners due to growing electoral complexities.

Constitutional Framework

- **Article 324:**
  - Grants the ECI superintendence, direction, and control over the preparation of electoral rolls and conduct of all elections to:
    - Parliament (Lok Sabha and Rajya Sabha).
    - State Legislatures (Vidhan Sabha and Vidhan Parishad).
    - Offices of the President and Vice-President.
  - **Clause (1):** Vests broad powers of superintendence, direction, and control to ensure free and fair elections, and these powers have been judicially interpreted to include residuary authority to address unforeseen situations and gaps in existing election laws.

Composition and Structure

- **Appointment:**
  - Appointed by the President of India on the recommendation of a Selection Committee. As per the Chief Election Commissioner and Other Election Commissioners (Appointment, Conditions of Service and Term of Office) Act, 2023, this committee comprises:
    - The Prime Minister (Chairperson).
    - The Leader of the Opposition in the Lok Sabha (or the leader of the single largest opposition party in the Lok Sabha).
    - A Union Cabinet Minister nominated by the Prime Minister.
    - No specific qualifications are prescribed in the Constitution for these appointments.
- **Removal:**
  - **CEC:** Can only be removed in the same manner and on the same grounds as a Judge of the Supreme Court, requiring a parliamentary majority and proven misbehavior or incapacity.
  - ECs: Can be removed by the President on the recommendation of the CEC, making their position less secure than the CEC's.
- **Key Debate:** While the Chief Election Commissioner and Other Election Commissioners (Appointment, Conditions of Service and Term of Office) Act, 2023, introduced a formal selection committee, debates continue regarding the extent of executive influence in the appointment process and its impact on ECI's independence.

Powers and Functions

- **Administrative Functions:**
  - Prepares, revises, and maintains electoral rolls.
  - Issues photo identity cards to voters (Electoral Photo Identity Card - EPIC).
  - Conducts delimitation of constituencies (though boundaries are set by the Delimitation Commission, ECI implements them).
  - Recognizes political parties as national or state parties under the Representation of the People Act, 1951.
  - Allots election symbols under the Election Symbols (Reservation and Allotment) Order, 1968.
  - Notifies election schedules, scrutinizes nominations, and conducts polling.
- **Advisory Functions:**
  - Advises the President on disqualification of MPs (under Article 103).
  - Advises Governors on disqualification of MLAs (under Article 192).
  - Provides opinions on post-election corrupt practices (though final decision rests with the President/Governor).
- **Quasi-Judicial Functions:**
  - Resolves disputes over party recognition and symbol allocation (e.g., splits in political parties like the Shiv Sena or NCP).
  - Enforces the Model Code of Conduct (MCC):
    - A set of guidelines to regulate political parties and candidates during elections.
    - Covers campaigning, speeches, polling day conduct, etc.
    - Not legally binding but enforced through moral authority and penal provisions under election laws.
- **Regulatory Powers:**
  - Cancels or postpones elections in case of booth capturing, violence, or natural calamities.
  - Monitors election expenditure (limits set under the Representation of the People Act, 1951).
- **Limitations:**
  - No jurisdiction over local body elections (Panchayats/Municipalities).
  - Cannot override parliamentary laws unless explicitly empowered.

Independence and Autonomy

- **Challenges to Independence:**
  - Although the 2023 Act introduced a selection committee for appointments, concerns about potential executive influence within this committee persist.
  - No bar on post-retirement government appointments for Commissioners.
  - Parliament can override ECI's decisions through legislation under Article 327, though such laws are subject to judicial review.

Key Mechanisms and Innovations

- **Election Symbols:**
  - Regulated by the Election Symbols Order, 1968.
  - Symbols are reserved (for recognized parties) or free (for independents/unrecognized parties).
- **Electronic Voting Machines (EVMs):**
  - Introduced in 1982 (Kerala by-election); fully implemented by 2004.
  - Aimed at reducing booth capturing and ensuring accurate vote counting.
  - VVPAT (Voter Verifiable Paper Audit Trail) added in 2013 for transparency.
- **Model Code of Conduct (MCC):**
  - Introduced in 1960 (Kerala Assembly elections).
  - Enforceable from the announcement of the election schedule until results are declared.
  - Violations can lead to disqualification or penalties under the Representation of the People Act, 1951.

Landmark Case Laws

- Kanhiya Lal Omar v. R.K. Trivedi (1985): Upheld the validity of the Election Symbols Order, 1968, as part of ECI's plenary powers.
- Union of India v. Association for Democratic Reforms (2002): Mandated disclosure of candidates' criminal records, assets, and liabilities, strengthening ECI's transparency efforts.
- People's Union for Civil Liberties v. Union of India (2013): Introduced the "None of the Above" (NOTA) option on EVMs.

Important Distinctions

- **ECI vs. Delimitation Commission:** ECI conducts elections within constituencies; the Delimitation Commission redraws boundaries (last done in 2002–2008).
- **ECI vs. State Election Commissions:** ECI handles national and state elections; SECs manage local body elections.
- **Advisory vs. Binding:** ECI's advice on disqualifications is advisory, not binding on the President/Governor.

Recent Developments (Up to March 28, 2025)

- **Legislative Changes:** The Chief Election Commissioner and Other Election Commissioners (Appointment, Conditions of Service and Term of Office) Act, 2023, formalized the appointment process, involving a committee (PM, Leader of Opposition, and a Union Minister).
- **Technological Advances:** Enhanced use of IT (e.g., online voter registration, real-time monitoring via apps like cVIGIL).

ADMINISTRATIVE LAW

NATURE, SCOPE AND IMPORTANCE OF ADMINISTRATIVE LAW

Definition and Concept of Administrative Law

Administrative Law is the body of law that governs the activities of administrative agencies of government. It involves the legal principles that regulate the actions of government agencies, including rule-making, adjudication, enforcement of regulations, and decision-making processes. Administrative law ensures that government actions comply with the law, protects individual rights, and maintains accountability in the exercise of governmental power.

Key Features of Administrative Law:

- **Regulation of Government Activities:** It focuses on the actions of administrative bodies, including regulatory agencies, boards, commissions, and tribunals.
- **Separation of Powers:** It ensures that administrative agencies do not exceed their authority, maintaining a balance between the executive, legislative, and judicial branches.
- **Procedural Fairness:** It establishes rules that govern how decisions should be made by administrative authorities, ensuring fairness and transparency.

Nature of Administrative Law as a Branch of Public Law

Administrative law is a branch of public law because it governs the relationship between individuals (private persons) and the state (government). It is primarily concerned with regulating the exercise of power by administrative authorities, which are public institutions established by the government to implement policies, administer laws, and manage public services.

Key Characteristics of Administrative Law as Public Law:

- **State Authority and Public Interest**: Administrative law derives its authority from the state, as its primary objective is to regulate governmental actions in the public interest.
- **Regulation of Public Administration**: It deals with administrative functions like rule-making, adjudication, and enforcement carried out by government agencies.
- **Balance between Power and Rights**: Administrative law ensures that governmental power is exercised in accordance with the law and protects the fundamental rights of individuals by controlling arbitrary or excessive government actions.

Unlike private law, which regulates relationships between individuals, administrative law governs the relationships between individuals and public authorities or between different public authorities.

Difference Between Administrative Law and Other Branches of Law

Administrative Law vs Constitutional Law

- **Constitutional Law**: Deals with the framework of the government, fundamental rights of individuals, and the distribution of powers among various organs of the government (executive, legislative, judiciary). It is concerned with establishing the constitution of a country and protecting basic rights.

- **Administrative Law**: Concerned with the day-to-day actions of administrative agencies. It focuses on the implementation of laws and policies created by the legislature, providing rules and procedures for the functioning of government agencies and their interaction with citizens.

Key Differences:

- **Nature of Law**: Constitutional law is the supreme law of the land, laying down the fundamental principles of the state, while administrative law operates under the framework of constitutional law and regulates how government policies are executed.
- **Scope**: Constitutional law primarily focuses on the structure of the state and protection of individual rights, while administrative law deals with the legal mechanisms that govern the actions of administrative bodies.

Administrative Law vs Civil Law

- **Civil Law**: Focuses on disputes between private individuals or organizations, such as contracts, property, torts, and family law. It is mainly concerned with the protection of individual interests in private matters.
- **Administrative Law**: Deals with public authorities' actions affecting individuals or entities, such as issuing licenses, enforcing regulations, and adjudicating disputes involving the government.

Key Differences:

- **Scope**: Civil law governs the relationship between private parties, whereas administrative law governs the relationship between the state (or its agencies) and private individuals or entities.
- **Function**: Administrative law regulates the government's power and ensures its accountability, while civil law resolves disputes between individuals.

FUNCTIONS AND ROLE OF ADMINISTRATIVE AGENCIES

Administrative agencies play a vital role in the implementation and enforcement of laws, policies, and regulations created by the legislature. These agencies carry out various functions to ensure that public administration remains efficient, effective, and accountable. Below are the key functions and roles of administrative agencies:

Rule-Making Function (Legislative Role)

Rule-making is one of the primary functions of administrative agencies, also referred to as **delegated legislation**. It involves the creation of detailed rules, regulations, and guidelines that are necessary for the implementation of legislative statutes. Administrative agencies are often empowered by the legislature to make these rules within the framework of enabling laws.

Key Aspects of Rule-Making:

- **Regulations & Policies**: Administrative agencies create regulations and policies based on broad legislative principles, allowing detailed execution of laws.
- **Technical Expertise**: Agencies often have specialized knowledge or technical expertise to create rules that align with legislative intent and practical needs. For example, environmental agencies may develop pollution control regulations.
- **Public Consultation**: In many jurisdictions, agencies are required to seek public input before finalizing regulations (e.g., notice-and-comment rule-making in the U.S.).
- **Flexibility and Adaptability**: Rules created by administrative agencies can be adjusted more easily than formal legislative statutes, allowing the government to respond to changing circumstances or new information.

Example: The Food and Drug Administration (FDA) in the U.S. creates rules regarding the safety standards for drugs and food products based on the broader laws passed by Congress.

Adjudication Function (Judicial Role)

Administrative agencies also perform adjudicatory functions, meaning they resolve disputes or legal issues related to their specific areas of jurisdiction. These disputes typically involve individuals, organizations, or entities challenging administrative decisions, regulations, or enforcement actions.

Key Aspects of Adjudication:

- **Quasi-Judicial Role**: While administrative agencies do not possess the full judicial authority of courts, they have the power to adjudicate disputes and make decisions that affect the rights of individuals or entities. These decisions are subject to judicial review in courts.

- **Tribunal-Like Bodies**: Many administrative agencies set up tribunals or panels to hear specific cases, such as labor disputes, tax issues, or regulatory compliance matters.
- **Application of Law**: Agencies apply both their regulations and relevant laws when resolving disputes, often focusing on technical or subject-specific matters.
- **Fair Hearing**: The process usually involves a fair hearing, where affected parties can present evidence and arguments before the agency, adhering to principles of natural justice (e.g., right to be heard, unbiased decision-making).

Example: The Securities and Exchange Commission (SEC) in the U.S. adjudicates disputes related to securities violations or fraud in the financial market.

Enforcement Function (Executive Role)

Administrative agencies are responsible for enforcing the laws and regulations they administer. This function involves ensuring compliance, investigating violations, and imposing penalties for non-compliance.

Key Aspects of Enforcement:

- **Inspection and Investigation**: Agencies often have investigative powers to inspect records, conduct audits, and gather evidence to ensure compliance with regulations. This is essential in fields such as environmental protection, public health, and corporate governance.
- **Issuing Penalties**: Agencies may impose penalties (e.g., fines, sanctions, or revocation of licenses) on individuals or entities that violate regulations or fail to comply with legal standards.
- **Enforcement Orders**: In some cases, agencies have the authority to issue orders to compel individuals or organizations to take corrective actions (e.g., stop illegal activities, clean up pollution, or implement safety measures).
- **Licensing and Permits**: Agencies often control the issuance of licenses, permits, or approvals necessary for individuals or businesses to operate within certain sectors (e.g., construction, healthcare, transportation).

Example: The Environmental Protection Agency (EPA) enforces environmental laws by investigating violations, issuing fines for pollution, and requiring companies to clean up contaminated sites.

The Role of Regulatory Agencies in Public Policy Implementation

Regulatory agencies are crucial in the implementation of public policies designed to address societal issues such as public health, safety, environment, and the economy. These agencies ensure that legislative policies are effectively carried out and that government goals are achieved.

Key Roles of Regulatory Agencies in Policy Implementation:

- **Translating Policy into Action**: Agencies take broad legislative mandates and translate them into actionable policies through regulations, rules, and procedures. This enables the executive branch to implement legislative intent.
- **Monitoring Compliance**: Agencies continuously monitor and assess the impact of regulations and public policies on society, businesses, and individuals. They gather data, conduct studies, and review the effectiveness of policies.
- **Public Awareness and Education**: Agencies often play a role in educating the public and stakeholders about new regulations, safety standards, or policy changes. For example, health agencies may run awareness campaigns regarding vaccination or disease prevention.
- **Adapting Policies**: As new challenges emerge, regulatory agencies may adapt or propose modifications to existing policies, ensuring that public policies remain relevant and effective.

Example: The Federal Communications Commission (FCC) in the U.S. regulates broadcasting, communications, and the internet, implementing policies related to spectrum allocation, net neutrality, and privacy.

Delegated Legislation and Administrative Discretion

Delegated legislation refers to the authority granted to administrative agencies by the legislature to create laws in the form of rules, regulations, or directives. This allows for the delegation of detailed law-making powers without needing to pass new laws through the legislative process.

Key Aspects of Delegated Legislation:

- **Enabling Act**: Delegated legislation is typically made under the authority of an **Enabling Act**, a statute passed by the legislature that allows an agency to make specific rules in a particular area of public concern.

- **Need for Delegated Legislation**: It is often impractical for the legislature to make detailed rules on every aspect of governance, particularly in technical, dynamic, or specialized fields. Delegated legislation allows for the timely and efficient creation of such rules.
- **Limitations on Power**: While agencies have the power to make rules, their power is limited by the enabling act, and the rules cannot contradict the broader legislative framework.
- **Judicial Oversight**: Courts may review delegated legislation to ensure it does not exceed the scope of the enabling act or violate constitutional provisions.

NATURAL JUSTICE

CONCEPT AND EVOLUTION OF THE PRINCIPLES OF NATURAL JUSTICE

Concept of Natural Justice:

Natural justice refers to the fundamental principles of fairness and equality that govern legal proceedings, particularly in administrative, judicial, and quasi-judicial bodies. It ensures that individuals are given a fair opportunity to present their case and that decisions are made impartially. The core principles of natural justice are:

- **Audi Alteram Partem (Hear the Other Side):** This principle ensures that no one should be condemned without having a chance to defend themselves. It signifies that a party must be given an opportunity to be heard before any adverse decision is made.
- **Nemo Judex in Causa Sua (No One Should Be a Judge in Their Own Case):** This principle mandates that no person should act as a judge in a case in which they have a personal interest. It ensures impartiality and objectivity in decision-making.

These principles are considered essential for ensuring procedural fairness, transparency, and accountability within the justice system.

TWO CORE PRINCIPLES OF NATURAL JUSTICE: AUDI ALTERAM PARTEM AND NEMO JUDEX IN CAUSA SUA

Natural justice is a fundamental concept in law that ensures fairness in legal proceedings. The two primary principles of natural justice are **Audi Alteram Partem** (hear the other side) and **Nemo Judex in Causa Sua** (no one should be a judge in their own case). These principles ensure that decision-making processes are fair, impartial, and transparent.

Audi Alteram Partem (Hear the Other Side)

The principle of **Audi Alteram Partem** means "let the other side be heard" or "hear the other party." It asserts that a person should not be judged or penalized without having a chance to present their case or defend themselves. This principle is rooted in fairness and ensures that all parties involved in a legal dispute or proceeding have the right to be heard before any decision is made.

This principle includes several key elements:

- **Notice:** The person must be given notice of the proceedings and the charges or claims against them.
- **Opportunity to be Heard:** The person should have a fair opportunity to present their case, provide evidence, and respond to any adverse material presented by the opposing party.
- **Right to Legal Representation:** In certain circumstances, the right to legal representation may be implied to ensure fairness in the process.

Case Laws Illustrating Audi Alteram Partem:

- **R v. Sussex Justices, Ex Parte McCarthy (1924):**
  - **Facts:** A magistrate's clerk, who was also a solicitor involved in a civil case against one of the parties, retired with the justices when they considered their decision in a criminal case involving that same party. Though the clerk stated he offered no advice, the conviction was challenged.
  - **Principle Applied:** The court quashed the conviction, famously stating, "It is not merely of some importance but is of fundamental importance that justice should not only be done, but should manifestly and undoubtedly be seen to be done." This case is a cornerstone for the principle of impartiality and the rule against bias (Nemo Judex in Causa Sua), emphasizing that even the appearance of bias can invalidate a decision.
- **Maneka Gandhi v. Union of India (1978):**
  - **Facts:** Maneka Gandhi's passport was impounded by the government without giving her a prior opportunity to be heard. The impoundment

was justified under the Emergency provisions of the Indian Constitution.

- **Principle Applied:** The Supreme Court held that the right to be heard was part of the **right to life and personal liberty** under **Article 21** of the Constitution. It further ruled that the principle of audi alteram partem requires that an individual must be given an opportunity to present their case before any deprivation of their rights, particularly in matters affecting personal liberty.

Nemo Judex in Causa Sua (No One Should Be a Judge in Their Own Case)

The principle of **Nemo Judex in Causa Sua** means "no one should be a judge in their own case." It ensures impartiality in the judicial or decision-making process, meaning that a person who has an interest in the outcome of a case or has personal involvement should not act as a decision-maker or judge in that matter.

This principle serves to maintain **objectivity** and **fairness** by preventing conflicts of interest, bias, or the appearance of bias in legal and administrative proceedings.

Key Elements of Nemo Judex in Causa Sua:

- **Impartiality:** The decision-maker must be free from any bias, personal interest, or pre-existing views related to the case.
- **Independence:** The judge or decision-maker must make decisions based on the law and facts, not influenced by personal interests or connections.
- **Disqualification:** A judge or decision-maker must recuse themselves from a case if they have any personal stake in the outcome.

Case Laws Illustrating Nemo Judex in Causa Sua:

- **Dimes v. Grand Junction Canal Proprietors (1852):**
  - **Facts:** The Lord Chancellor, who issued a decree in a case involving a canal company, was later discovered to hold a significant number of shares in that company.
  - **Principle Applied:** The House of Lords set aside the Lord Chancellor's decree, holding that even though there was no evidence of actual bias, his pecuniary interest in the company was sufficient to disqualify him from judging the case. This landmark decision solidified the principle of Nemo Judex in Causa Sua, emphasizing the strict necessity of impartiality, particularly when a decision-maker has a financial interest.
- **R v. Bow Street Metropolitan Magistrate, Ex Parte Pinochet (1999):**
  - **Facts:** In a case concerning the extradition of former Chilean dictator **Augusto Pinochet**, one of the judges involved in the decision had previously been involved in a human rights organization that was critical of Pinochet. The question arose as to whether the judge's prior association disqualified him from making an impartial decision.
  - **Principle Applied:** The House of Lords held that the principle of **nemo judex in causa sua** had been violated due to the judge's previous involvement, and the decision was invalidated. This case reinforced the importance of judicial impartiality and the need to avoid any appearance of bias in judicial proceedings.

EXCEPTIONS TO THE APPLICATION OF NATURAL JUSTICE

While the principles of **natural justice** (Audi Alteram Partem and Nemo Judex in Causa Sua) are fundamental to ensuring fairness in legal and administrative proceedings, there are certain situations where these principles may not be fully applicable. These exceptions primarily arise in cases where strict adherence to natural justice could undermine other overriding public interests such as **national security**, **public order**, **urgency**, or **confidentiality**.

Here, we will discuss the **situations where natural justice may not be applicable** and also analyze the **exceptions under the Indian legal framework**.

National Security

Exception: Natural justice may not apply where the matter involves **national security**. In cases related to national security, the government may need to act quickly and sometimes without informing the affected parties, particularly where disclosure of certain information could jeopardize state security.

- **Reasoning:** National security matters often involve sensitive information that, if disclosed, could harm the country's interests. In such cases, granting an opportunity to be heard could compromise security.
- **Example:** If an individual's actions are suspected to be harmful to national security, they may be detained under preventive detention laws without being given the opportunity to be heard.

Case Law: In the case of A.K. Gopalan v. State of Madras (1950), the Supreme Court, while upholding the Preventive Detention Act, acknowledged that the right to make a representation against a detention order was available. However, it also recognized that the specific grounds for detention could be withheld if their disclosure was deemed against public interest, particularly national security. Subsequent jurisprudence has balanced this, emphasizing the minimal requirements of fairness even in such contexts

Emergency Situations or Urgency

Exception: In situations involving **emergency or urgency**, natural justice may be curtailed or temporarily suspended. For instance, when immediate action is needed to prevent harm, delay in providing a hearing could exacerbate the situation.

- **Reasoning:** The need for **immediacy** and **public welfare** may justify action being taken without prior notice or hearing.
- **Example:** During **natural disasters** or situations requiring **public health intervention** (such as quarantine orders during an epidemic), authorities may take swift action without following the standard procedures of natural justice.

Case Law: In Swadeshi Cotton Mills v. Union of India (1981), while strongly emphasizing the importance of natural justice, the Supreme Court acknowledged that in urgent situations where immediate action is required in the public interest, a prior hearing may be dispensed with. However, the Court also stressed that a post-decisional hearing might still be necessary to satisfy the requirements of fairness, unless the urgency is truly exceptional.

Statutory Exceptions (Where Law Permits Departure)

Exception: Certain statutes or regulations may explicitly exclude or modify the application of natural justice principles. In such cases, the legislature has allowed for the curtailment of natural justice in specific circumstances.

- **Reasoning:** If a statute specifically provides for procedures that do not require natural justice to be applied, those provisions may override the general rule.
- **Example:** Certain **administrative orders**, such as **tax assessments**, may be governed by statutes that do not always require a hearing before a decision is made.

Case Law: In **Union of India v. Tulsiram Patel (1985)**, the Supreme Court upheld the validity of provisions under the **Central Civil Services (Classification, Control, and Appeal) Rules**, which allow for **discharge of government employees** without giving them an opportunity to be heard in certain situations, like on the grounds of national security.

Judicial or Quasi-Judicial Proceedings

Exception: The principles of natural justice may not apply to purely **judicial** or **quasi-judicial** decisions that are strictly **adjudicatory** in nature, especially when the decision does not involve an individual's personal rights or interests. However, this exception is generally limited.

- **Reasoning:** In some judicial or quasi-judicial processes, where procedures are already well-defined or set by law, the application of natural justice may be deemed unnecessary. For example, in certain appeals, review processes, or situations where the decision is purely administrative and not impacting a person's rights directly.
- **Example:** Administrative decisions that do not affect an individual's liberty or property might not require the full application of natural justice.

Case Law: In **M/s. Shyam Sundar v. District Magistrate (1999)**, the court held that when decisions are administrative and not adjudicatory in nature, such as administrative transfers or postings, natural justice may not apply.

In Cases Involving Minor or Procedural Errors

Exception: In some cases, minor or procedural errors in following the principles of natural justice may be overlooked if it does not lead to substantial injustice or prejudice.

- **Reasoning:** If a procedural lapse does not affect the fairness of the decision, courts may overlook it, as long as the outcome would have been the same even if natural justice had been fully adhered to.
- **Example:** If a hearing is conducted but a minor procedural error occurs (such as a delay in giving notice), the court may still uphold the decision if it finds that no harm was caused to the affected party.

Case Law: In **Smt. Maneka Gandhi v. Union of India (1978)**, the Supreme Court ruled that a procedural violation does not automatically lead to the invalidation of the decision unless it results in actual prejudice to the person affected.

Discretionary Powers of Authorities

Exception: Discretionary powers given to authorities (such as the power to grant or refuse licenses, permits, or appointments) may not require the application of natural justice, especially if the statute gives the authority wide discretionary powers without mandating a fair hearing.

- **Reasoning:** Where an authority is given discretion to act, the application of natural justice is sometimes not obligatory, as long as the action is within the scope of the statute or authority.
- **Example:** In cases where authorities have the discretion to grant or reject a license or permit based on broad criteria, they may not be required to follow natural justice if it is not explicitly stated by law.

Case Law: In **K.K. Verma v. Union of India (1954)**, the Supreme Court upheld that when discretionary powers are granted by the government, the authorities are not always bound to follow the strict principles of natural justice if the law does not specifically mandate such a procedure.

Proceedings Involving Minor Children or Unfit Persons

Exception: In certain cases, such as those involving **minors** or individuals deemed unfit to participate in proceedings (due to mental illness or incapacity), the principles of natural justice may be relaxed or altered to accommodate their condition.

- **Reasoning:** The nature of the person's capacity to participate in proceedings may necessitate modifications to natural justice procedures to make them more suitable or fair for the individual.
- **Example: Child custody cases** may allow for more flexible procedures compared to adult legal proceedings.

Case Law: In **R. v. Secretary of State for the Home Department, Ex parte Amin (1983)**, the House of Lords discussed how **mental incapacity** or **lack of understanding** can influence the application of natural justice principles.

Conclusion

While natural justice serves as a cornerstone of fairness in legal proceedings, its application is not absolute. Exceptions arise in cases involving **national security**, **emergency situations**, **statutory provisions**, or **discretionary powers**. Under Indian law, courts have recognized that there are situations where **strict adherence** to natural justice is either impractical or unnecessary, as long as the essential elements of justice and fairness are maintained. Understanding these exceptions helps balance the need for fairness with the practicalities of governance and administration.

JUDICIAL REVIEW OF ADMINISTRATIVE ACTIONS – GROUNDS

INTRODUCTION TO JUDICIAL REVIEW

Definition of Judicial Review

Judicial review refers to the power of courts to examine the constitutionality, legality, and reasonableness of administrative actions, laws, or executive orders. It is a process by which the judiciary evaluates whether a legislative or executive action is in conformity with the constitution, statutes, or other established legal norms. Judicial review ensures that the exercise of power by public authorities is in accordance with the law and that individuals' rights are protected from arbitrary or unlawful actions.

In the context of **administrative law**, judicial review specifically involves courts scrutinizing the actions of public administrative bodies, ensuring they act within their legal authority, follow due process, and respect principles of natural justice. Courts can review administrative decisions and actions on various grounds such as **illegality**, **irrationality**, and **procedural impropriety**.

Importance of Judicial Review in Administrative Law

- **Guarding Against Arbitrary Power**: Judicial review serves as a vital safeguard against the abuse of power by administrative bodies. Without it, government officials could exercise discretion without accountability or oversight, potentially violating citizens' rights and freedoms.
- **Ensuring Rule of Law**: Judicial review maintains the principle that all actions by the government must be in accordance with the law. It upholds legal norms and ensures that government actions comply with constitutional and statutory limits.
- **Protecting Fundamental Rights**: Through judicial review, the courts can protect citizens' fundamental rights by ensuring that no action, regulation, or law violates constitutional guarantees. For instance, judicial review is used to ensure that any action taken by the government does not infringe upon

rights guaranteed under **Articles 14 (Equality before law)**, **19 (Freedom of speech and expression)**, or **21 (Right to life and personal liberty)** of the Indian Constitution.

- **Ensuring Accountability and Transparency**: Judicial review enforces the principle of accountability by requiring administrative authorities to justify their actions. It helps maintain transparency in government decision-making, which is essential for fostering public trust in the administration.
- **Correcting Errors in Law or Fact**: Judicial review provides a mechanism to rectify errors made by administrative bodies. If an agency makes a decision based on incorrect facts or misinterprets the law, judicial review offers a way to correct these errors

Role of Judiciary in Reviewing Administrative Actions

- **Scope of Judicial Review**:
  - ❑ **Reviewing the legality of administrative actions**: Courts assess whether an administrative action was taken within the scope of statutory authority, and if the action was legal.
  - ❑ **Reviewing the procedure followed**: Courts check whether the procedures laid down by law or regulations were properly followed. This includes ensuring compliance with natural justice principles such as the right to a fair hearing.
- **Judicial Review and Administrative Discretion**:
  - ❑ Courts generally avoid interfering with administrative decisions that involve **discretionary powers**, as long as the decision is not arbitrary or unreasonable. However, if administrative discretion is exercised in a manner that violates legal principles or fundamental rights, judicial intervention becomes necessary.
- **Case Laws on Administrative Review**:
  - ❑ **Union of India v. Tulsiram Patel (1985)**: The Supreme Court held that judicial review is available in cases where administrative action violates natural justice, even when it concerns disciplinary matters.
  - ❑ **L. Chandra Kumar v. Union of India (1997)**: The Supreme Court emphasized the importance of judicial review, declaring that no constitutional amendment can take away the judicial power to review legislative and executive actions.
- **Judicial Review and Administrative Accountability**:
  - ❑ Through judicial review, courts ensure that administrative bodies do not act beyond their powers, and any actions that violate individuals' rights or cause undue harm can be corrected.
  - ❑ Courts can issue **writs** (mandamus, certiorari, prohibition, habeas corpus, and quo warranto) to ensure that administrative actions are aligned with legal requirements

Grounds for Judicial Review of Administrative Actions

Judicial review of administrative actions is based on several well-established grounds. The courts can intervene if the administrative actions fail to comply with legal principles or exceed the powers conferred by law. Below are the major grounds:

a. Illegality (Ultra Vires)

- **Definition**: **Illegality** refers to an administrative action that is **ultra vires**, meaning it exceeds the powers granted by law or the Constitution. In other words, if an administrative body acts outside its legal authority, the action can be declared illegal by the court.
- **Key Concept**: Administrative bodies derive their powers from statutes, regulations, or delegated authority. If an action is beyond the scope of the powers granted, it is considered illegal.
- **Example**:
  - ❑ If an administrative agency enacts regulations that go beyond the scope of its statutory mandate or makes decisions that are not supported by the law, those actions are ultra vires and can be quashed by the court.
  - ❑ **Case Example**: In **R v. Home Secretary, ex parte Fire Brigades Union (1995)**, the court held that the Home Secretary's actions were ultra vires because they were inconsistent with the statutory scheme of compensation provided by the Criminal Justice Act.

b. Irrationality or Wednesbury Unreasonableness

- **Definition**: **Irrationality** (also known as **Wednesbury Unreasonableness**) occurs when an administrative decision is so unreasonable that no reasonable person, acting reasonably, would have made that decision. This ground is based on the **Wednesbury Test**, established in the case **Associated Provincial Picture Houses Ltd. v. Wednesbury Corporation (1948)**.

- **Key Concept**: The test of unreasonableness is strict. For judicial review on the ground of irrationality, the court will only intervene if the decision is extremely unreasonable. The decision must be **perversely unreasonable** to warrant review.

- **Example**:
  - A decision by an administrative body to award a contract based on irrelevant or discriminatory criteria that no reasonable decision-maker would have chosen.
  - **Case Example**: In **R v. Secretary of State for the Home Department, ex parte Venables (1998)**, the court found that the decision to set a tariff for the release of two children convicted of murder was irrational, as the decision was based on irrelevant factors.

c. Procedural Impropriety

- **Definition**: **Procedural Impropriety** refers to situations where an administrative action violates the required legal procedures or principles of **natural justice**. This ground includes situations where an action is taken without providing a fair hearing, failing to disclose relevant information, or acting with bias.

- **Key Concept**: Administrative actions must follow prescribed legal procedures, and parties affected by the action should be given an opportunity to present their case. Failure to comply with these procedural safeguards can lead to judicial review.

- **Example**:
  - Denying an individual a chance to respond to allegations before a decision is made, or where the decision-maker has a personal bias against the individual.
  - **Case Example**: In **R v. Secretary of State for the Home Department, ex parte Doody (1994)**, the court ruled that the Home Secretary's decision regarding the minimum term for a life sentence was procedurally improper because the prisoner was not given the opportunity to make representations.

d. Proportionality

- **Definition**: **Proportionality** requires that the administrative action taken is proportionate to the objective being pursued. If the action is excessive or causes harm disproportionate to the intended benefit, it may be subject to judicial review.

- **Key Concept**: Proportionality is especially relevant in cases where the administrative body has to balance competing interests, such as protecting public safety and individual rights.

- **Example**:
  - Imposing a penalty that is too severe relative to the nature of the offense or harm caused, such as an excessively high fine for a minor regulatory violation.
  - **Case Example**: In **R (on the application of Daly) v. Secretary of State for the Home Department (2001)**, the court held that a blanket policy of searching prisoners' legal correspondence was disproportionate to the objective of preventing security risks.

e. Relevant and Irrelevant Considerations

- **Definition**: **Relevant and Irrelevant Considerations** refers to the grounds where a decision is based on factors that should or should not have been considered by the decision-maker. Courts will review whether the decision-maker considered only relevant factors and disregarded irrelevant ones.

- **Key Concept**: Decision-makers are required to act based on relevant considerations and avoid giving undue weight to irrelevant or extraneous factors, such as political considerations or personal biases.

- **Example**:
  - A public authority considering political or personal affiliations when awarding a government contract, instead of evaluating based on the quality of bids.
  - **Case Example**: In **Padfield v. Minister of Agriculture (1968)**, the court found that the Minister had acted improperly by refusing to refer a complaint to the appropriate committee based on irrelevant political considerations.

f. Error of Law

- **Definition**: An **Error of Law** occurs when the decision-maker incorrectly interprets or applies the law. This may involve the wrong legal standard, misinterpretation of statutory provisions, or failure to apply legal principles correctly.
- **Key Concept**: Courts may review administrative actions if there is a clear error in the legal reasoning or if an incorrect legal test is applied in making decisions.
- **Example**:
  - A decision-maker misapplying a legal standard in an immigration case or incorrectly applying the law governing the rights of individuals.
  - **Case Example**: In **Anisminic Ltd. v. Foreign Compensation Commission (1969)**, the House of Lords held that an error of law by a tribunal could be subject to judicial review, even if the decision was made under a statute that excluded judicial review.

g. Error of Fact

- **Definition**: An **Error of Fact** occurs when the decision-maker relies on incorrect or mistaken factual information when making a decision. If an administrative decision is based on facts that are not supported by evidence, the court can intervene.
- **Key Concept**: Courts will generally not review administrative decisions based on factual matters unless the facts are manifestly incorrect, or the decision is made without sufficient evidence.
- **Example**:
  - If an administrative body denies a claim for compensation based on a factual error, such as incorrect dates or misinterpretation of evidence.
  - **Case Example**: In **Secretary of State for the Home Department v. Rehman (2001)**, the court found that an administrative decision was based on an incorrect understanding of facts relating to a person's association with a terrorist organization.

MULTIPLE CHOICE QUESTIONS

1. Match the following Fundamental Rights with their respective Articles:

List-I (Fundamental Right)	List-II (Articles)
A. Right to Equality	I. Article 25
B. Right to Freedom of Religion	II. Article 32
C. Right to Constitutional Remedies	III. Article 21
D. Right to Life & Personal Liberty	IV. Article 14

A. A-IV, B-I, C-II, D-III
B. A-II, B-IV, C-I, D-III
C. A-I, B-III, C-IV, D-II
D. A-III, B-II, C-I, D-IV

2. Match the following types of Writs with their purposes:

List-I (Writs)	List-II (Purpose)
A. Habeas Corpus	I. To quash unlawful orders
B. Mandamus	II. To protect individual liberty
C. Certiorari	III. To compel a public official to perform duty
D. Quo Warranto	IV. To challenge an illegal appointment

A. A-II, B-III, C-I, D-IV
B. A-III, B-I, C-IV, D-II
C. A-I, B-IV, C-II, D-III
D. A-IV, B-II, C-I, D-III

3. Match the following constitutional amendments with their significance:

List-I (Amendment)	List-II (Provision)
A. 42nd Amendment	I. Right to Education Act
B. 44th Amendment	II. Strengthened Fundamental Duties
C. 86th Amendment	III. Right to Property removed from FRs
D. 101st Amendment	IV. Introduced GST

A. A-II, B-III, C-I, D-IV
B. A-III, B-I, C-IV, D-II
C. A-I, B-IV, C-II, D-III
D. A-IV, B-II, C-III, D-I

4. Match the following schedules with their contents:

List-I (Schedule)	List-II (Content)
A. 7th Schedule	I. Allocation of seats in Rajya Sabha
B. 9th Schedule	II. Anti-defection provisions
C. 10th Schedule	III. Distribution of legislative powers
D. 4th Schedule	IV. Laws protected from judicial review

A. A-III, B-IV, C-II, D-I
B. A-II, B-III, C-I, D-IV
C. A-IV, B-II, C-III, D-I
D. A-I, B-IV, C-II, D-III

5. Match the following constitutional provisions with their corresponding Articles:

List-I (Provision)	List-II (Article)
A. Finance Commission	I. Article 356
B. President's Rule	II. Article 280
C. Election Commission	III. Article 324
D. Speaker of Lok Sabha	IV. Article 93

A. A-II, B-I, C-III, D-IV
B. A-III, B-IV, C-I, D-II
C. A-I, B-IV, C-II, D-III
D. A-IV, B-III, C-I, D-II

6. Match the following landmark cases with their rulings:

List-I (Case Name)	List-II (Judgment)
A. Keshavananda Bharati Case	I. Basic Structure Doctrine
B. Golaknath Case	II. Fundamental Rights cannot be amended
C. Minerva Mills Case	III. Limited Parliament's power to amend the Constitution
D. Maneka Gandhi Case	IV. Expanded Article 21 - Right to Life

A. A-I, B-II, C-III, D-IV
B. A-II, B-IV, C-I, D-III
C. A-IV, B-I, C-II, D-III
D. A-III, B-II, C-I, D-IV

7. Match the following Directive Principles of State Policy (DPSPs) with their Articles:

List-I (DPSP)	List-II (Article)
A. Equal pay for equal work	I. Article 43
B. Organization of Village Panchayats	II. Article 40
C. Promotion of Cottage Industries	III. Article 39(*d*)
D. Protection of Environment	IV. Article 48A

A. A-III, B-II, C-I, D-IV
B. A-I, B-III, C-II, D-IV
C. A-IV, B-II, C-I, D-III
D. A-II, B-I, C-III, D-IV

8. Match the following constitutional positions with their appointing authorities:

List-I (Position)	List-II (Appointing Authority)
A. Chief Justice of India	I. President of India
B. Governor of a State	II. President on advice of Prime Minister
C. Attorney General of India	III. President of India (on the advice of the Council of Ministers)
D. Chief Election Commissioner	IV. President of India (on the advice of CJI and senior judges)

A. A-IV, B-I, C-II, D-III
B. A-I, B-III, C-II, D-I
C. A-IV, B-III, C-I, D-II
D. A-III, B-IV, C-I, D-II

9. Match the following parts of the Constitution with their corresponding subject matter:

List-I (Part of Constitution)	List-II (Content)
A. Part II	I. Citizenship
B. Part III	II. Fundamental Rights
C. Part IV	III. Directive Principles of State Policy
D. Part V	IV. Union Executive

A. A-I, B-II, C-III, D-IV
B. A-II, B-I, C-IV, D-III
C. A-III, B-IV, C-I, D-II
D. A-IV, B-III, C-I, D-II

10. Match the following constitutional provisions with their respective articles:

List-I (Provision)	List-II (Article)
A. Abolition of Titles	I. Article 18
B. Freedom of Religion	II. Article 25
C. Protection against Exploitation	III. Article 23
D. Protection of Language & Culture	IV. Article 29

A. A-I, B-II, C-III, D-IV
B. A-II, B-I, C-IV, D-III
C. A-III, B-IV, C-I, D-II
D. A-IV, B-III, C-I, D-II

11. Match the following constitutional schedules with their purpose:

List-I (Schedule)	List-II (Purpose)
A. First Schedule	I. Union & State Territories
B. Fourth Schedule	II. Allocation of Rajya Sabha seats
C. Seventh Schedule	III. Division of legislative powers
D. Tenth Schedule	IV. Anti-defection law

A. A-I, B-II, C-III, D-IV
B. A-II, B-I, C-IV, D-III
C. A-III, B-IV, C-I, D-II
D. A-IV, B-III, C-I, D-II

12. Match the following Emergency Provisions with their respective Articles:

List-I (Type of Emergency)	List-II (Article)
A. National Emergency	I. Article 352
B. President's Rule	II. Article 356
C. Financial Emergency	III. Article 360

A. A-I, B-II, C-III B. A-II, B-III, C-I
C. A-III, B-I, C-II D. A-I, B-III, C-II

13. Match the following types of bills with their legislative requirement:

List-I (Type of Bill)	List-II (Requirement for Passage)
A. Money Bill	I. Simple Majority in Lok Sabha only
B. Constitutional Amendment Bill	II. Special Majority in both Houses
C. Ordinary Bill	III. Simple Majority in both Houses
D. Financial Bill	IV. Simple Majority in Lok Sabha, then Rajya Sabha

A. A-I, B-II, C-III, D-IV
B. A-III, B-I, C-IV, D-II
C. A-II, B-IV, C-I, D-III
D. A-IV, B-II, C-I, D-III

14. Match the following Committees/Commissions with their objectives:

List-I (Committee/Commission)	List-II (Objective)
A. Sarkaria Commission	I. Centre-State Relations
B. Mandal Commission	II. Reservation for OBCs
C. Balwant Rai Mehta Committee	III. Panchayati Raj System
D. Swaran Singh Committee	IV. Fundamental Duties

A. A-I, B-II, C-III, D-IV
B. A-III, B-I, C-IV, D-II
C. A-II, B-IV, C-I, D-III
D. A-IV, B-III, C-II, D-I

15. Match the following landmark amendments with their major impacts:

List-I (Amendment)	List-II (Impact)
A. 73rd Amendment	I. Established Panchayati Raj System
B. 74th Amendment	II. Introduced Urban Local Bodies
C. 97th Amendment	III. Gave Constitutional Status to Cooperatives
D. 101st Amendment	IV. Introduced GST

A. A-I, B-II, C-III, D-IV
B. A-II, B-I, C-IV, D-III
C. A-III, B-IV, C-II, D-I
D. A-IV, B-III, C-I, D-II

16. **Assertion (A):** The Governor of a state acts as the representative of the Union Government in the state.

Reason (R): The Governor is appointed by the President of India and holds office during the pleasure of the President.

A. Both (A) and (R) are correct, and (R) is the correct explanation of (A).
B. Both (A) and (R) are correct, but (R) is not the correct explanation of (A).
C. (A) is correct, but (R) is incorrect.
D. (A) is incorrect, but (R) is correct.

17. **Assertion (A):** The Supreme Court of India has the power of Judicial Review.

Reason (R): Judicial Review is explicitly mentioned in the Indian Constitution.

A. Both (A) and (R) are correct, and (R) is the correct explanation of (A).
B. Both (A) and (R) are correct, but (R) is not the correct explanation of (A).
C. (A) is correct, but (R) is incorrect.
D. (A) is incorrect, but (R) is correct.

18. Assertion (A): Fundamental Rights are justiciable under the Indian Constitution.

Reason (R): The Supreme Court and High Courts can issue writs for the enforcement of Fundamental Rights.

A. Both (A) and (R) are correct, and (R) is the correct explanation of (A).
B. Both (A) and (R) are correct, but (R) is not the correct explanation of (A).
C. (A) is correct, but (R) is incorrect.
D. (A) is incorrect, but (R) is correct.

19. Assertion (A): The Constitution of India provides for a single and unified judiciary.

Reason (R): The Indian judiciary follows a federal structure like the United States.

A. Both (A) and (R) are correct, and (R) is the correct explanation of (A).
B. Both (A) and (R) are correct, but (R) is not the correct explanation of (A).
C. (A) is correct, but (R) is incorrect.
D. (A) is incorrect, but (R) is correct.

20. Assertion (A): The Preamble is not a part of the Indian Constitution.

Reason (R): The Preamble is merely an introduction and has no legal significance.

A. Both (A) and (R) are correct, and (R) is the correct explanation of (A).
B. Both (A) and (R) are correct, but (R) is not the correct explanation of (A).
C. (A) is incorrect, but (R) is correct.
D. Both (A) and (R) are incorrect.

21. Assertion (A): The Vice President of India is elected in the same manner as the President of India.

Reason (R): The Vice President is elected by an electoral college consisting of only Members of Parliament.

A. Both (A) and (R) are correct, and (R) is the correct explanation of (A).
B. Both (A) and (R) are correct, but (R) is not the correct explanation of (A).
C. (A) is incorrect, but (R) is correct.
D. Both (A) and (R) are incorrect.

22. Assertion (A): The Rajya Sabha is a permanent House.

Reason (R): One-third of its members retire every two years.

A. Both (A) and (R) are correct, and (R) is the correct explanation of (A).
B. Both (A) and (R) are correct, but (R) is not the correct explanation of (A).
C. (A) is incorrect, but (R) is correct.
D. Both (A) and (R) are incorrect.

23. Assertion (A): The 73rd Amendment Act introduced the Panchayati Raj System.

Reason (R): The Act gave constitutional status to rural local governance.

A. Both (A) and (R) are correct, and (R) is the correct explanation of (A).
B. Both (A) and (R) are correct, but (R) is not the correct explanation of (A).
C. (A) is correct, but (R) is incorrect.
D. (A) is incorrect, but (R) is correct.

24. Assertion (A): The Directive Principles of State Policy (DPSP) are legally enforceable.

Reason (R): The judiciary can issue writs for their enforcement.

A. Both (A) and (R) are correct, and (R) is the correct explanation of (A).
B. Both (A) and (R) are correct, but (R) is not the correct explanation of (A).
C. (A) is incorrect, but (R) is correct.
D. Both (A) and (R) are incorrect.

25. Assertion (A): The Right to Property is a Fundamental Right under the Indian Constitution.

Reason (R): The 44th Constitutional Amendment Act removed the Right to Property from Part III of the Constitution.

A. Both (A) and (R) are correct, and (R) is the correct explanation of (A).
B. Both (A) and (R) are correct, but (R) is not the correct explanation of (A).
C. (A) is incorrect, but (R) is correct.
D. Both (A) and (R) are incorrect.

26. Assertion (A): The Chief Justice of India is appointed by the President.

Reason (R): The President appoints the Chief Justice of India after consulting the Prime Minister.

A. Both (A) and (R) are correct, and (R) is the correct explanation of (A).
B. Both (A) and (R) are correct, but (R) is not the correct explanation of (A).

C. (A) is correct, but (R) is incorrect.
D. (A) is incorrect, but (R) is correct.

27. Assertion (A): The Indian Constitution provides for a bicameral Parliament.

Reason (R): The Rajya Sabha represents the people directly.

A. Both (A) and (R) are correct, and (R) is the correct explanation of (A).
B. Both (A) and (R) are correct, but (R) is not the correct explanation of (A).
C. (A) is correct, but (R) is incorrect.
D. (A) is incorrect, but (R) is correct.

28. Assertion (A): Article 370 granted special status to Jammu & Kashmir.

Reason (R): The article was abrogated by the Government of India in 2019.

A. Both (A) and (R) are correct, and (R) is the correct explanation of (A).
B. Both (A) and (R) are correct, but (R) is not the correct explanation of (A).
C. (A) is correct, but (R) is incorrect.
D. (A) is incorrect, but (R) is correct.

29. Assertion (A): The Parliament can amend the Constitution under Article 368.

Reason (R): The power to amend the Constitution is absolute and cannot be challenged in court.

A. Both (A) and (R) are correct, and (R) is the correct explanation of (A).
B. Both (A) and (R) are correct, but (R) is not the correct explanation of (A).
C. (A) is correct, but (R) is incorrect.
D. (A) is incorrect, but (R) is correct.

30. Assertion (A): The Directive Principles of State Policy (DPSPs) are non-justiciable in nature.

Reason (R): The DPSPs impose a moral duty on the state to apply these principles in governance.

A. Both (A) and (R) are correct, and (R) is the correct explanation of (A).
B. Both (A) and (R) are correct, but (R) is not the correct explanation of (A).
C. (A) is correct, but (R) is incorrect.
D. (A) is incorrect, but (R) is correct.

31. Arrange the following constitutional cases in the order they were decided:

A. A.K. Gopalan v. State of Madras
B. Kesavananda Bharati v. State of Kerala
C. Maneka Gandhi v. Union of India
D. Minerva Mills v. Union of India

A. (*a*), (*b*), (*c*), (*d*)
B. (*a*), (*c*), (*b*), (*d*)
C. (*b*), (*a*), (*d*), (*c*)
D. (*c*), (*a*), (*b*), (*d*)

32. Arrange the following Fundamental Rights-related amendments chronologically:

A. 1st Amendment – Imposed restrictions on free speech
B. 44th Amendment – Removed Right to Property from Fundamental Rights
C. 97th Amendment – Granted constitutional status to cooperative societies
D. 86th Amendment – Introduced Right to Education

A. (*a*), (*b*), (*d*), (*c*)
B. (*a*), (*d*), (*b*), (*c*)
C. (*b*), (*a*), (*c*), (*d*)
D. (*c*), (*a*), (*d*), (*b*)

33. Arrange the following Lok Sabha elections in chronological order:

A. First General Election
B. Emergency-era Election
C. Mandal Commission Implementation Election
D. Lok Sabha Election after Abrogation of Article 370

A. (*a*), (*b*), (*c*), (*d*)
B. (*b*), (*a*), (*c*), (*d*)
C. (*a*), (*c*), (*b*), (*d*)
D. (*c*), (*b*), (*d*), (*a*)

34. Arrange the following landmark cases on secularism in India in chronological order:

A. Kesavananda Bharati v. State of Kerala
B. S.R. Bommai v. Union of India
C. Indira Gandhi v. Raj Narain
D. Minerva Mills v. Union of India

A. (*a*), (*c*), (*d*), (*b*)
B. (*c*), (*a*), (*d*), (*b*)
C. (*a*), (*b*), (*c*), (*d*)
D. (*c*), (*d*), (*a*), (*b*)

35. Arrange the following provisions of the Constitution as they were enacted in chronological order:

A. Right to Information Act
B. Abolition of Privy Purse
C. Introduction of Goods and Services Tax (GST)
D. Implementation of National Emergency

A. (*b*), (*d*), (*a*), (*c*)
B. (*a*), (*b*), (*c*), (*d*)
C. (*b*), (*a*), (*d*), (*c*)
D. (*d*), (*b*), (*c*), (*a*)

36. Arrange the following constitutional commissions in chronological order:

A. Mandal Commission
B. Sarkaria Commission
C. Balwant Rai Mehta Committee
D. Nanavati Commission

A. (*c*), (*a*), (*b*), (*d*)
B. (*c*), (*d*), (*a*), (*b*)
C. (*a*), (*c*), (*b*), (*d*)
D. (*d*), (*c*), (*a*), (*b*)

37. Arrange the following constitutional schedules in order of their introduction:

A. Tenth Schedule (Anti-defection)
B. Ninth Schedule (Protection of laws from judicial review)
C. Fifth Schedule (Tribal Areas)
D. Twelfth Schedule (Municipalities)

A. (*c*), (*b*), (*a*), (*d*)
B. (*b*), (*c*), (*a*), (*d*)
C. (*c*), (*a*), (*b*), (*d*)
D. (*a*), (*b*), (*c*), (*d*)

38. Arrange the following election-related reforms chronologically:

A. Introduction of Voter ID
B. NOTA (None of the Above) introduction
C. Introduction of Electronic Voting Machines (EVMs)
D. 61st Amendment (Lowering voting age to 18)

A. (*d*), (*c*), (*a*), (*b*)
B. (*c*), (*d*), (*a*), (*b*)
C. (*d*), (*a*), (*c*), (*b*)
D. (*a*), (*c*), (*d*), (*b*)

39. Arrange the following Supreme Court Chief Justices in chronological order:

A. Justice Y.V. Chandrachud
B. Justice M.N. Venkatachaliah
C. Justice Dipak Misra
D. Justice S.A. Bobde

A. (*a*), (*b*), (*c*), (*d*)
B. (*b*), (*a*), (*c*), (*d*)
C. (*a*), (*c*), (*b*), (*d*)
D. (*c*), (*d*), (*a*), (*b*)

40. Arrange the following Indian constitutional amendments in chronological order:

A. 42nd Amendment (Mini-Constitution)
B. 73rd Amendment (Panchayati Raj)
C. 1st Amendment (Land Reforms and Fundamental Rights)
D. 86th Amendment (Right to Education)

A. (*c*), (*a*), (*b*), (*d*)
B. (*a*), (*c*), (*b*), (*d*)
C. (*c*), (*b*), (*a*), (*d*)
D. (*b*), (*c*), (*a*), (*d*)

41. Arrange the following judicial doctrines in chronological order:

A. Doctrine of Basic Structure
B. Doctrine of Eclipse
C. Doctrine of Severability
D. Doctrine of Pith and Substance

A. (*c*), (*b*), (*d*), (*a*)
B. (*d*), (*c*), (*b*), (*a*)
C. (*b*), (*c*), (*d*), (*a*)
D. (*a*), (*b*), (*c*), (*d*)

42. Arrange the following constitutional doctrines in chronological order based on their judicial recognition in India:

A. Doctrine of Severability
B. Doctrine of Eclipse
C. Doctrine of Pith and Substance
D. Doctrine of Basic Structure

A. (*c*), (*a*), (*b*), (*d*)
B. (*a*), (*c*), (*b*), (*d*)
C. (*d*), (*b*), (*c*), (*a*)
D. (*b*), (*a*), (*d*), (*c*)

43. Arrange the following constitutional commissions in the order of their establishment:

A. First Law Commission of Independent India
B. Finance Commission of India
C. Election Commission of India
D. Sarkaria Commission

A. (*a*), (*c*), (*b*), (*d*)
B. (*c*), (*b*), (*a*), (*d*)
C. (*b*), (*c*), (*a*), (*d*)
D. (*a*), (*b*), (*c*), (*d*)

44. Arrange the following constitutional amendments in chronological order:

(*a*) 42nd Amendment – Strengthened Directive Principles
(*b*) 44th Amendment – Restored Fundamental Rights curtailed during Emergency
(*c*) 61st Amendment – Lowered voting age from 21 to 18
(*d*) 97th Amendment – Gave constitutional status to cooperative societies

A. (*a*), (*b*), (*c*), (*d*)
B. (*b*), (*a*), (*d*), (*c*)
C. (*a*), (*d*), (*b*), (*c*)
D. (*d*), (*b*), (*c*), (*a*)

45. Arrange the following constitutional schedules in the order of their introduction:

A. Fourth Schedule – Allocation of seats in Rajya Sabha

B. Fifth Schedule – Administration of Scheduled Areas

C. Ninth Schedule – Protection of laws from judicial review

D. Tenth Schedule – Anti-defection law

A. (*a*), (*b*), (*c*), (*d*)

B. (*b*), (*c*), (*a*), (*d*)

C. (*c*), (*a*), (*b*), (*d*)

D. (*a*), (*b*), (*d*), (*c*)

46. Arrange the following key events in the evolution of Indian constitutional governance in chronological order:

A. First Constitutional Amendment

B. Swaran Singh Committee Recommendations

C. Enactment of Protection of Human Rights Act

D. Introduction of Goods and Services Tax (GST)

A. (*a*), (*b*), (*c*), (*d*)

B. (*b*), (*a*), (*d*), (*c*)

C. (*a*), (*d*), (*c*), (*b*)

D. (*c*), (*a*), (*b*), (*d*)

47. Which constitutional amendment made it mandatory for the State to implement DPSPs?

A. 42nd Amendment

B. 44th Amendment

C. 86th Amendment

D. 101st Amendment

48. Which of the following Articles directs the State to secure a Uniform Civil Code (UCC)?

A. Article 40 B. Article 44

C. Article 41 D. Article 48

49. What did the Minerva Mills case (1980) rule regarding DPSPs and Fundamental Rights?

A. DPSPs are superior to Fundamental Rights.

B. Fundamental Rights can be curtailed if they contradict DPSPs.

C. There must be a balance between Fundamental Rights and DPSPs.

D. Fundamental Rights cannot be amended.

50. Which of the following DPSPs aims at the protection and improvement of the environment?

A. Article 39

B. Article 41

C. Article 48A

D. Article 47

51. Which amendment restored the primacy of Fundamental Rights over DPSPs?

A. 42nd Amendment

B. 44th Amendment

C. 73rd Amendment

D. 86th Amendment

52. Under which Article is the President's executive power mentioned?

A. Article 52 B. Article 53

C. Article 56 D. Article 74

53. The President is elected by:

A. Members of Parliament only

B. Members of Legislative Assemblies only

C. Electoral College consisting of MPs and MLAs

D. The Prime Minister and the Union Cabinet

54. The 42nd Amendment (1976) made it:

A. Mandatory for the President to act on ministerial advice

B. Possible for the President to dissolve the Lok Sabha unilaterally

C. Optional for the President to consult the Supreme Court

D. Unnecessary for the President to give assent to bills

55. In which case did the Supreme Court rule that the President is a constitutional figurehead?

A. Golaknath v. State of Punjab

B. Shamsher Singh v. State of Punjab

C. Indira Nehru Gandhi v. Raj Narain

D. S.R. Bommai v. Union of India

56. The 44th Amendment (1978) allowed the President to:

A. Override the advice of the Council of Ministers

B. Dismiss the Prime Minister

C. Return advice for reconsideration once

D. Declare an Emergency without Cabinet approval

57. Which of the following is NOT a type of Emergency under the Indian Constitution?

A. National Emergency

B. Political Emergency

C. State Emergency

D. Financial Emergency

58. Which Amendment Act imposed restrictions on the declaration of Emergency in India?

A. 42nd Amendment

B. 44th Amendment

C. 86th Amendment

D. 73rd Amendment

59. During a National Emergency, which Fundamental Right is automatically suspended?
A. Right to Equality (Article 14)
B. Right to Freedom of Speech (Article 19)
C. Right to Constitutional Remedies (Article 32)
D. Right to Education (Article 21A)

60. In which case did the Supreme Court rule that Emergency provisions cannot alter the Basic Structure of the Constitution?
A. A.K. Gopalan v. State of Madras
B. Golaknath v. State of Punjab
C. Kesavananda Bharati v. State of Kerala
D. S.R. Bommai v. Union of India

61. Which article allows the President to suspend Fundamental Rights during an Emergency?
A. Article 352 B. Article 356
C. Article 359 D. Article 360

62. **Assertion (A):** The Indian Constitution establishes a parliamentary system of government.

Reason (R): The President of India is the supreme executive authority and can act independently of the Council of Ministers.
A. Both (A) and (R) are correct, and (R) is the correct explanation of (A).
B. Both (A) and (R) are correct, but (R) is not the correct explanation of (A).
C. (A) is correct, but (R) is incorrect.
D. (A) is incorrect, but (R) is correct.

63. **Assertion (A):** The Preamble of the Indian Constitution is a part of the Constitution.

Reason (R): The Preamble is legally enforceable and can be used to challenge constitutional provisions.
A. Both (A) and (R) are correct, and (R) is the correct explanation of (A).
B. Both (A) and (R) are correct, but (R) is not the correct explanation of (A).
C. (A) is correct, but (R) is incorrect.
D. (A) is incorrect, but (R) is correct.

64. **Assertion (A):** Fundamental Rights under Article 19 are automatically suspended during a National Emergency.

Reason (R): The 44th Constitutional Amendment removed the provision of automatic suspension of Fundamental Rights during an Emergency.
A. Both (A) and (R) are correct, and (R) is the correct explanation of (A).
B. Both (A) and (R) are correct, but (R) is not the correct explanation of (A).
C. (A) is incorrect, but (R) is correct.
D. Both (A) and (R) are incorrect.

65. **Assertion (A):** The Indian Constitution provides for a federal system of government.

Reason (R): The term "federalism" is explicitly mentioned in the Indian Constitution.
A. Both (A) and (R) are correct, and (R) is the correct explanation of (A).
B. Both (A) and (R) are correct, but (R) is not the correct explanation of (A).
C. (A) is correct, but (R) is incorrect.
D. Both (A) and (R) are incorrect.

66. **Assertion (A):** The Rajya Sabha is a permanent House and cannot be dissolved.

Reason (R): One-third of its members retire every two years, ensuring continuity.
A. Both (A) and (R) are correct, and (R) is the correct explanation of (A).
B. Both (A) and (R) are correct, but (R) is not the correct explanation of (A).
C. (A) is correct, but (R) is incorrect.
D. (A) is incorrect, but (R) is correct.

67. **Assertion (A):** The Election Commission of India is a constitutional body.

Reason (R): It is established under Article 324 of the Indian Constitution.
A. Both (A) and (R) are correct, and (R) is the correct explanation of (A).
B. Both (A) and (R) are correct, but (R) is not the correct explanation of (A).
C. (A) is correct, but (R) is incorrect.
D. Both (A) and (R) are incorrect.

68. **Assertion (A):** Directive Principles of State Policy (DPSPs) are legally enforceable.

Reason (R): DPSPs impose a moral obligation on the state rather than a legal duty.
A. Both (A) and (R) are correct, and (R) is the correct explanation of (A).
B. Both (A) and (R) are correct, but (R) is not the correct explanation of (A).
C. (A) is incorrect, but (R) is correct.
D. Both (A) and (R) are incorrect.

69. **Assertion (A):** The Vice President of India is elected by an electoral college consisting of only Members of Parliament.

Reason (R): The Vice President acts as the ex-officio Chairman of the Rajya Sabha.

A. Both (A) and (R) are correct, and (R) is the correct explanation of (A).
B. Both (A) and (R) are correct, but (R) is not the correct explanation of (A).
C. (A) is incorrect, but (R) is correct.
D. Both (A) and (R) are incorrect.

70. **Assertion (A):** The Right to Property is no longer a Fundamental Right in India.

Reason (R): The 44th Constitutional Amendment Act (1978) removed the Right to Property from Part III of the Constitution.

A. Both (A) and (R) are correct, and (R) is the correct explanation of (A).
B. Both (A) and (R) are correct, but (R) is not the correct explanation of (A).
C. (A) is correct, but (R) is incorrect.
D. (A) is incorrect, but (R) is correct.

71. **Assertion (A):** The Supreme Court of India has the power of Judicial Review.

Reason (R): Judicial Review in India is explicitly mentioned in Article 13 of the Constitution.

A. Both (A) and (R) are correct, and (R) is the correct explanation of (A).
B. Both (A) and (R) are correct, but (R) is not the correct explanation of (A).
C. (A) is correct, but (R) is incorrect.
D. (A) is incorrect, but (R) is correct.

72. **Assertion (A):** The Governor of a state acts as the representative of the Union Government in the state.

Reason (R): The Governor is appointed by the President and holds office during the pleasure of the President.

A. Both (A) and (R) are correct, and (R) is the correct explanation of (A).
B. Both (A) and (R) are correct, but (R) is not the correct explanation of (A).
C. (A) is correct, but (R) is incorrect.
D. (A) is incorrect, but (R) is correct.

73. **Assertion (A):** The Indian Constitution provides for a single and unified judiciary.

Reason (R): India follows a unitary system of government.

A. Both (A) and (R) are correct, and (R) is the correct explanation of (A).
B. Both (A) and (R) are correct, but (R) is not the correct explanation of (A).
C. (A) is correct, but (R) is incorrect.
D. (A) is incorrect, but (R) is correct.

74. **Assertion (A):** The Fundamental Duties were added to the Constitution by the 42nd Amendment Act (1976).

Reason (R): Fundamental Duties were borrowed from the French Constitution.

A. Both (A) and (R) are correct, and (R) is the correct explanation of (A).
B. Both (A) and (R) are correct, but (R) is not the correct explanation of (A).
C. (A) is correct, but (R) is incorrect.
D. (A) is incorrect, but (R) is correct.

75. **Assertion (A):** State legislatures in India do not have the power to make laws on subjects in the Union List.

Reason (R): The Union List contains subjects of national importance, and only Parliament can legislate on them.

A. Both (A) and (R) are correct, and (R) is the correct explanation of (A).
B. Both (A) and (R) are correct, but (R) is not the correct explanation of (A).
C. (A) is correct, but (R) is incorrect.
D. (A) is incorrect, but (R) is correct.

76. **Assertion (A):** The Basic Structure Doctrine was introduced in the Kesavananda Bharati case (1973).

Reason (R): The Supreme Court ruled that Parliament can amend any part of the Constitution, including Fundamental Rights.

A. Both (A) and (R) are correct, and (R) is the correct explanation of (A).
B. Both (A) and (R) are correct, but (R) is not the correct explanation of (A).
C. (A) is correct, but (R) is incorrect.
D. (A) is incorrect, but (R) is correct.

77. The Indian Constitution is quasi-federal in nature because:

A. It grants equal power to the Centre and States.
B. It has a unitary bias despite federal principles.
C. It follows a rigid separation of powers between Centre and States.
D. It does not allow the States to have independent laws.

78. Which of the following doctrines ensures that a law declared unconstitutional remains valid for past transactions?

A. Doctrine of Prospective Overruling
B. Doctrine of Severability
C. Doctrine of Pith and Substance
D. Doctrine of Eclipse

79. In which case did the Supreme Court rule that Parliament has the power to amend any part of the Constitution, including Fundamental Rights?
A. Kesavananda Bharati v. State of Kerala
B. Golaknath v. State of Punjab
C. Minerva Mills v. Union of India
D. Shankari Prasad v. Union of India

80. Which Article of the Constitution grants special provisions to the State of Nagaland with respect to religious and social practices of its people?
A. Article 370 B. Article 371A
C. Article 371C D. Article 372

81. The doctrine of Basic Structure was first discussed in which case?
A. Kesavananda Bharati v. State of Kerala
B. Sajjan Singh v. State of Rajasthan
C. Golaknath v. State of Punjab
D. Indira Nehru Gandhi v. Raj Narain

82. Which case upheld the dismissal of State governments under Article 356 but made it subject to judicial review?
A. Keshavananda Bharati v. State of Kerala
B. Minerva Mills v. Union of India
C. S.R. Bommai v. Union of India
D. A.K. Gopalan v. State of Madras

83. Which of the following is NOT a ground for imposing President's Rule (Article 356) in a State?
A. Failure of the constitutional machinery
B. Internal disturbances in the State
C. Governor's report suggesting breakdown of governance
D. Failure of the State to comply with Union directions

84. Which Schedule of the Indian Constitution deals with Administration and Control of Scheduled Areas and Tribes?
A. Fifth Schedule B. Sixth Schedule
C. Seventh Schedule D. Ninth Schedule

85. Which case is related to the application of the principle of separation of powers in India?
A. I.R. Coelho v. State of Tamil Nadu
B. State of West Bengal v. Union of India
C. Indira Gandhi v. Raj Narain
D. Keshavananda Bharati v. State of Kerala

86. Which constitutional amendment inserted Article 21A (Right to Education)?
A. 86th Amendment B. 73rd Amendment
C. 44th Amendment D. 97th Amendment

87. Which of the following Articles is related to Abolition of Titles?
A. Article 15 B. Article 17
C. Article 18 D. Article 19

88. Which of the following is not a writ issued under Article 32?
A. Habeas Corpus B. Mandamus
C. Certiorari D. Quo Warranto

89. Which amendment made fundamental duties part of the Constitution?
A. 44th Amendment B. 42nd Amendment
C. 97th Amendment D. 86th Amendment

90. Under which Article can the President refer a matter to the Supreme Court for advisory opinion?
A. Article 131 B. Article 141
C. Article 143 D. Article 226

91. Which case ruled that the Preamble is a part of the Constitution?
A. Berubari Union Case
B. Keshavananda Bharati Case
C. Minerva Mills Case
D. Golaknath Case

92. The doctrine of colorable legislation is related to which of the following?
A. Distribution of powers between the Centre and States
B. Power of judicial review
C. Basic structure of the Constitution
D. Amendment of the Constitution

93. Which case ruled that Directive Principles of State Policy (DPSPs) cannot override Fundamental Rights?
A. A.K. Gopalan v. State of Madras
B. Minerva Mills v. Union of India
C. S.R. Bommai v. Union of India
D. Maneka Gandhi v. Union of India

94. Which of the following schedules of the Indian Constitution deals with the allocation of seats in the Rajya Sabha?
A. Fourth Schedule
B. Fifth Schedule
C. Seventh Schedule
D. Tenth Schedule

95. Which constitutional amendment removed the Right to Property from Fundamental Rights?
A. 42nd Amendment
B. 44th Amendment
C. 73rd Amendment
D. 86th Amendment

96. The Supreme Court decision in I.R. Coelho v. State of Tamil Nadu (2007) is related to which of the following?

A. Reservation in promotions
B. Judicial review of laws placed in the Ninth Schedule
C. Separation of powers
D. Role of the President in governance

97. Which of the following constitutional provisions cannot be amended by a simple majority in Parliament?

A. Change in the Second Schedule
B. Formation of new states
C. Election of the President
D. Quorum of Parliament

98. Which of the following provisions was introduced by the 101st Constitutional Amendment Act (2016)?

A. Goods and Services Tax (GST)
B. Right to Education
C. Reservation for Economically Weaker Sections
D. Right to Privacy

99. Under which constitutional amendment were Panchayati Raj institutions given constitutional status?

A. 42nd Amendment
B. 44th Amendment
C. 73rd Amendment
D. 97th Amendment

100. The concept of secularism in India means:

A. The government cannot interfere in religious matters.
B. The State will recognize and promote one religion.
C. The State will have equal respect for all religions but can regulate religious practices.
D. The government can fund religious institutions of a particular faith.

101. Which of the following statements about Article 21 (Right to Life and Personal Liberty) is correct?

A. It applies only to Indian citizens.
B. It is subject to restrictions imposed by Parliament.
C. It has been expanded to include the Right to Privacy and Right to a Clean Environment.
D. It can be suspended at any time by an Executive Order.

102. The Doctrine of Pith and Substance is used to:

A. Decide whether a law is colorable legislation
B. Resolve conflicts between Centre and State laws
C. Determine if an amendment violates the Basic Structure
D. Interpret taxation laws

103. Which case ruled that Reservation in Promotions is NOT a Fundamental Right?

A. M. Nagaraj v. Union of India
B. Indra Sawhney v. Union of India
C. Ashoka Kumar Thakur v. Union of India
D. Jarnail Singh v. State of Punjab

104. Which Article of the Constitution prohibits discrimination in public employment on the grounds of religion, race, caste, sex, or place of birth?

A. Article 14 B. Article 15
C. Article 16 D. Article 19

105. Which of the following constitutional amendments introduced the Collegium System for the appointment of judges?

A. 42nd Amendment
B. 44th Amendment
C. None, as the Collegium System is based on Supreme Court judgments
D. 99th Amendment

106. Which of the following doctrines is used to invalidate laws that contradict fundamental rights?

A. Doctrine of Severability
B. Doctrine of Pith and Substance
C. Doctrine of Eclipse
D. Doctrine of Colorable Legislation

107. Which of the following cases upheld the constitutional validity of the 103rd Amendment, which introduced 10% reservation for EWS (Economically Weaker Sections)?

A. Indra Sawhney v. Union of India
B. Jarnail Singh v. Union of India
C. Janhit Abhiyan v. Union of India
D. Ashoka Kumar Thakur v. Union of India

108. Under which Article does the President have the power to dissolve the Lok Sabha?

A. Article 72 B. Article 75
C. Article 85 D. Article 356

109. Which of the following writs is issued to compel a public official to perform a legal duty?

A. Habeas Corpus B. Mandamus
C. Certiorari D. Quo Warranto

110. Which Schedule of the Indian Constitution deals with Anti-Defection Laws?

A. Fifth Schedule
B. Seventh Schedule
C. Tenth Schedule
D. Twelfth Schedule

111. Which of the following cases laid down the doctrine of proportionality in administrative law?

A. Kesavananda Bharati v. State of Kerala
B. Om Kumar v. Union of India
C. Maneka Gandhi v. Union of India
D. Minerva Mills v. Union of India

112. Which case ruled that telephone tapping is a violation of the Right to Privacy under Article 21?

A. People's Union for Civil Liberties v. Union of India
B. Maneka Gandhi v. Union of India
C. K.S. Puttaswamy v. Union of India
D. A.K. Gopalan v. State of Madras

113. Which Article provides constitutional protection to the laws placed under the Ninth Schedule?

A. Article 31A B. Article 31B
C. Article 32 D. Article 368

114. Which Article of the Indian Constitution prohibits forced labor and human trafficking?

A. Article 14 B. Article 19
C. Article 23 D. Article 29

115. The Supreme Court in Golaknath v. State of Punjab (1967) ruled that:

A. Parliament can amend Fundamental Rights
B. Fundamental Rights cannot be amended
C. The Basic Structure Doctrine is applicable
D. Reservation beyond 50% is unconstitutional

116. Which constitutional provision allows the President to appoint an Inter-State Council?

A. Article 280 B. Article 263
C. Article 312 D. Article 356

117. Which Article empowers the Parliament to make laws on subjects in the State List during a national emergency?

A. Article 248 B. Article 249
C. Article 250 D. Article 252

118. Which part of the Constitution deals with cooperative societies?

A. Part VII B. Part IXA
C. Part IXB D. Part XI

119. Which of the following statements about Article 226 of the Indian Constitution is correct?

A. It allows High Courts to issue writs only for Fundamental Rights violations.
B. It allows High Courts to issue writs for both Fundamental Rights and other legal rights.
C. It limits the power of High Courts to issue writs only against the State.
D. It does not include the writ of Mandamus.

120. Which of the following constitutional provisions was upheld in the Shayara Bano v. Union of India (2017) case?

A. The validity of Triple Talaq under Muslim personal law.
B. The validity of reservations in promotions.
C. The right to privacy as a Fundamental Right.
D. The abolition of untouchability.

121. Which of the following is a correct statement about the Constitutional validity of the 124th Amendment Act?

A. It introduced the National Judicial Appointments Commission (NJAC).
B. It granted constitutional status to cooperative societies.
C. It introduced 10% reservation for Economically Weaker Sections (EWS).
D. It abolished the Planning Commission.

122. Under which Article can Parliament alter the boundaries of existing States?

A. Article 2 B. Article 3
C. Article 4 D. Article 5

123. Which of the following constitutional bodies recommends the principles for distributing tax revenue between the Centre and States?

A. NITI Aayog
B. Finance Commission
C. Inter-State Council
D. Reserve Bank of India

124. Which Article of the Constitution deals with the protection of monuments and places of national importance?

A. Article 47 B. Article 48A
C. Article 49 D. Article 51A

125. Which of the following doctrines is used by the Supreme Court to protect Fundamental Rights from arbitrary legislative amendments?

A. Doctrine of Prospective Overruling
B. Doctrine of Pith and Substance
C. Doctrine of Basic Structure
D. Doctrine of Laches

126. Which of the following provisions is not part of the Indian Constitution?

A. Suspension of Fundamental Rights during an Emergency
B. Judicial review of laws
C. Right to Work as a Fundamental Right
D. Separation of powers between the Legislature, Executive, and Judiciary

127. What principle underpins the concept of 'Rule of Law' in administrative actions?

A. Arbitrariness
B. Legality
C. Executive supremacy
D. Procedural propriety

128. The doctrine of 'Proportionality' in administrative law is used to assess whether:

A. Sanctions are harsher than the offense warrants.
B. Actions are taken within the limits of granted authority.
C. Decisions are based on sufficient evidence.
D. Measures taken are necessary and suitable to meet a legitimate objective.

129. Which case established the 'Wednesbury Principle' of unreasonableness?

A. Associated Provincial Picture Houses v. Wednesbury Corp. (1947)
B. Council of Civil Service Unions v. Minister for the Civil Service (1984)
C. Ridge v. Baldwin (1963)
D. Anisminic v. Foreign Compensation Commission (1969)

130. What is the 'Right to Fair Hearing' in the context of administrative law?

A. The right to be heard by a neutral judge
B. The right to have a decision within a reasonable time
C. The right to present and rebut evidence
D. All of the above

131. Which of the following statements best describes 'Administrative Discretion'?

A. Discretion cannot be challenged in a court of law.
B. Discretion must always be exercised within the bounds set by law.
C. Discretion allows administrators to act as per their personal judgment.
D. Discretion is only available in financial matters.

132. What does the principle of 'Natural Justice' encompass in administrative law?

A. Prior notice and the opportunity to be heard
B. The right to appeal an administrative decision
C. The obligation to decide cases based on a strict liability rule
D. All administrative decisions must be reviewed by a judiciary

133. Which of the following is NOT a valid reason for judicial review of administrative action?

A. Irrationality
B. Illegality
C. Decision made with proper authority
D. Procedural impropriety

134. The 'Ouster Clause' in administrative law is designed to:

A. Extend the powers of administrative tribunals
B. Restrict the jurisdiction of administrative tribunals
C. Limit the judicial review of certain decisions
D. Provide unlimited discretion to administrators

135. Which doctrine asserts that a public official cannot question the validity of the source of his/her authority once accepting the appointment?

A. Doctrine of Public Accountability
B. Doctrine of Substantive Ultra Vires
C. Doctrine of Collateral Challenge
D. Doctrine of Estoppel

136. In which landmark case did the Indian Supreme Court declare the Right to Privacy as an integral part of the Right to Life under Article 21 of the Constitution, impacting administrative actions and policies?

A. Maneka Gandhi v. Union of India
B. K.S. Puttaswamy v. Union of India
C. R.C. Cooper v. Union of India
D. Golaknath v. State of Punjab

137. Which principle requires administrative bodies to act fairly, reasonably, and according to the law in a procedural context?

A. Rule of Law
B. Doctrine of Proportionality
C. Audi Alteram Partem
D. Doctrine of Legitimate Expectation

138. What does the 'Doctrine of Legitimate Expectation' provide in administrative law?

A. It assures the public of a guaranteed outcome in administrative decisions.
B. It provides a basis for expecting that established procedures will continue to apply unless there is a good reason to change them.
C. It relates exclusively to financial expectations.
D. It allows any citizen to challenge the norms without any substantive standing.

139. Which term refers to the inability of a court or tribunal to review administrative decisions?

A. Judicial activism
B. Non-justiciability
C. Absolute immunity
D. Administrative finality

140. In administrative law, which doctrine is often applied when an administrative agency acts beyond its authority?

A. Doctrine of Ultra Vires
B. Doctrine of Separation of Powers
C. Doctrine of Executive Privilege
D. Doctrine of Sovereign Immunity

141. What is the significance of the 'Carltona Principle' in the context of administrative decision-making?

A. Decisions made by junior officials in a government department are treated as emanating from the minister responsible for that department.
B. Only senior officials are allowed to make significant policy decisions.
C. Administrative decisions must always be reviewed by a judicial authority.
D. All administrative actions must have the direct approval of the president or prime minister.

142. What is the impact of the doctrine of 'Subordinate Legislation' in administrative law?

A. It allows administrative agencies to make rules and regulations under the authority granted by the legislature.
B. It prohibits administrative agencies from enforcing penalties.
C. It prevents the judiciary from reviewing administrative actions.
D. It refers to legislation made directly by the President or the Governor without consulting the legislature.

143. Which administrative law principle is violated if a judge has a financial interest in the outcome of a case?

A. Audi Alteram Partem
B. Nemo judex in causa sua (No one should be a judge in their own cause)
C. Rule of Law
D. Doctrine of Legitimate Expectation

144. Which one of the following best describes 'judicial review' in administrative law?

A. A process for resolving disputes between private parties.
B. A procedure by which legislative enactments are interpreted.
C. The examination of the legality of administrative decisions by the courts.
D. An internal review by an administrative agency of its own decisions.

145. What is meant by 'Public Interest Litigation' (PIL) in the context of administrative law?

A. Litigation initiated by public bodies to enforce executive actions.
B. Lawsuits filed by private citizens against corporations without government involvement.
C. Legal action initiated in a court of law for the enforcement of public interest or general interest of the public.
D. A special law enacted to protect the interests of minority groups.

146. What role does the 'Right to Information Act, 2005' play in administrative law?

A. It allows public officials to withhold information related to national security.
B. It grants citizens the right to request information from any public authority.
C. It exclusively governs the exchange of information between different governmental departments.
D. It is a procedural tool used only in judicial proceedings.

147. Which principle dictates that public officials must not have personal or financial interests in their official duties?

A. Doctrine of Proportionality
B. Doctrine of Bias
C. Principle of Impartiality
D. Principle of Transparency

148. What is the 'exhaustion of remedies' rule in administrative law?

A. A litigant must exhaust all alternative governmental remedies before approaching a court.
B. Administrative agencies must use all their powers before making a decision.
C. Courts must exhaust all judicial remedies before deferring to administrative expertise.
D. A public body must try all procedural avenues before issuing a final decision.

149. In administrative law, which of the following best describes the 'ultra vires' test?

A. A test to determine the truthfulness of witnesses in administrative hearings.
B. A test to check whether an administrative decision has exceeded the powers granted by law.
C. A method for verifying the effectiveness of legislation passed by the administrative bodies.
D. A procedure for assessing the constitutionality of executive orders.

150. Which type of control mechanism focuses on the merits of administrative decisions, rather than merely procedural adherence?
A. Judicial Review
B. Merit Review
C. Administrative Appeal
D. Legislative Oversight

151. What does the 'Principle of Reasonableness' entail in administrative law?
A. Decisions must be made within a reasonable time.
B. Decisions must be based on reasonable grounds or evidence.
C. Officials must act within the reasonable scope of their authority.
D. All of the above.

152. What legal doctrine prevents a party from retracting or denying a claim when their previous actions or behavior have induced another party to act upon that claim?
A. Doctrine of Estoppel
B. Promissory Estoppel
C. Constructive Trust
D. Equitable Relief

153. Under the 'Public Trust Doctrine', government agencies must manage certain resources for the benefit of:
A. Local communities only.
B. The current government's interests.
C. The public at large.
D. Specific private stakeholders.

154. Which legal principle in administrative law helps in dealing with large volumes of cases by relying on previous decisions as a guide for future cases of a similar nature?
A. Rule of Law
B. Legal Precedent
C. Judicial Activism
D. Case Law Methodology

155. 'Promissory estoppel' in administrative law is most relevant in situations involving:
A. Contracts and commercial agreements.
B. Promises made by public officials that induce reliance by individuals or corporations.
C. Employment disputes within administrative agencies.
D. Regulatory compliance and enforcement actions.

156. Which administrative law mechanism involves re-evaluating an administrative decision internally before it is challenged in a judicial setting?
A. Administrative Review
B. Judicial Examination
C. Internal Audit
D. Ombudsman Review

157. Which of the following best describes the function of an Ombudsman in administrative law?
A. To prosecute cases of corruption within public offices.
B. To act as an intermediary for negotiations between administrative bodies and private entities.
C. To investigate complaints against public authorities and recommend corrective actions.
D. To enforce regulatory standards strictly within governmental agencies.

158. What is the primary purpose of the 'Freedom of Information Act'?
A. To provide government employees with immunity from prosecution for disclosing sensitive information.
B. To allow the public access to information held by public authorities, thereby promoting transparency and accountability.
C. To restrict the amount of information that can be made public to protect national security.
D. To ensure that all governmental decisions are documented and archived.

159. How does 'Judicial Activism' influence administrative law?
A. By strictly adhering to statutory laws without interpretation.
B. By limiting the powers of administrative bodies to a narrow scope.
C. By taking a proactive role in safeguarding rights through broad interpretation of laws and the Constitution.
D. By avoiding any involvement in policy-making or administrative discretion.

160. What legal concept allows courts to restore parties to their original positions prior to an administrative error or misjudgment?
A. Restitution B. Rescission
C. Remand D. Judicial Review

161. In the context of administrative law, what does 'Parens Patriae' refer to?
A. A doctrine that grants administrative agencies the authority to act as legal protectors of citizens unable to protect themselves.
B. The inherent power of the state to provide protection to the general public.

C. The obligation of state agencies to intervene in family law cases.
D. The legal responsibility of government officials to directly manage state-owned properties.

162. What does the 'Doctrine of Precedent' provide in the administrative law context?
A. It ensures that all administrative decisions must be original and not based on past cases.
B. It restricts the power of administrative judges to make independent decisions.
C. It mandates that decisions made in higher courts are binding on lower courts in similar cases.
D. It allows administrative bodies to disregard previous rulings to adapt to changing circumstances.

163. Which administrative principle is especially concerned with ensuring that agencies do not exceed their jurisdiction?
A. Ultra Vires
B. Audi Alteram Partem
C. Equitable Relief
D. Rule of Standing

164. What role does the 'Data Protection Act' play in administrative governance?
A. It outlines the responsibilities of administrative bodies to protect sensitive information from unauthorized access and misuse.
B. It provides a framework for administrative bodies to collect unlimited data for governance.
C. It restricts administrative bodies from using any form of digital data.
D. It solely protects data related to national security.

165. What is 'Administrative Discretion'?
A. The ability of administrative agencies to make policies that are binding on the public without legislative approval.
B. The scope of flexibility allowed to administrative agencies in interpreting and applying legislation.
C. The power of administrative agencies to enforce penalties without judicial oversight.
D. None of the above.

166. Which mechanism is typically used in administrative law to challenge the decisions of public officials or entities?
A. Public protests
B. Judicial Review
C. Legislative impeachment
D. Executive orders

167. Which legal doctrine prevents a public authority from acting in a way that contradicts its previous actions or statements when others have relied on those actions or statements to their detriment?
A. Estoppel
B. Legitimate expectation
C. Audi alteram partem
D. Non-delegation

168. What is the primary legal requirement for an administrative action to be valid under the 'Doctrine of Proportionality'?
A. The action must strictly enforce statutory provisions.
B. The action must be capable of achieving its intended result without exceeding what is necessary.
C. The action must involve public consultation before implementation.
D. The action must receive unanimous approval from all stakeholders.

169. In administrative law, what is the 'Rule Against Bias'?
A. A rule that prevents the judiciary from reviewing administrative decisions.
B. A rule that ensures decisions are made by officials without a personal interest in the outcome.
C. A rule that requires administrative decisions to be based on clear statutory guidelines.
D. A rule that mandates all administrative decisions to be biased in favor of environmental protection.

170. Which of the following best exemplifies the application of the 'principle of finality' in administrative law?
A. Administrative decisions can be revised any number of times.
B. Administrative decisions become conclusive if not challenged within a specified time.
C. All administrative decisions are subject to continuous review.
D. Administrative decisions are effective only after judicial approval.

171. Under what circumstances can the doctrine of 'Ultra Vires' be invoked to challenge an administrative action?
A. When the action is within the scope of authority granted by law.
B. When the action is taken without any legal basis or beyond the powers conferred by law.
C. When the action fully complies with procedural requirements.
D. When the action involves the exercise of discretion within legal limits.

172. What role does the 'Public Trust Doctrine' play in administrative environmental law?

A. It ensures that certain natural resources are preserved for public use and cannot be over-exploited.

B. It mandates that all public land be sold to the highest bidder to generate revenue.

C. It allows private companies unrestricted access to natural resources.

D. It restricts public access to environmental information.

173. How does the 'Right to Information Act' influence administrative accountability?

A. By prohibiting the disclosure of any information by public authorities.

B. By ensuring that citizens have the right to access information under the control of public authorities.

C. By allowing public authorities to operate without public oversight.

D. By limiting public access to information exclusively to governmental officials.

174. What is the significance of the 'Audi Alteram Partem' rule in judicial reviews of administrative actions?

A. It requires courts to disregard all evidence presented in administrative proceedings.

B. It mandates that a decision cannot be made without giving all parties a chance to present their case.

C. It ensures that administrative decisions are made rapidly without hearings.

D. It allows administrative agencies to bypass standard legal procedures.

175. Which principle ensures that administrative decisions are made based on clear standards rather than on an ad hoc or arbitrary basis?

A. Principle of Legality

B. Principle of Rationality

C. Principle of Fairness

D. Principle of Consistency

176. In the context of administrative discretion, what does the 'abuse of discretion' refer to?

A. The proper use of discretion within the bounds of law.

B. A decision made in a manner not justified by, or clearly against, reason and evidence.

C. Discretion exercised in the interest of public welfare.

D. Any decision made using administrative discretion.

177. Match the following legal principles with their corresponding applications in administrative law:

List-I (Principles)	List-II (Applications)
A. Doctrine of Substantial Evidence	I. Requires that administrative decisions not be excessively punitive given the nature of the offense.
B. Doctrine of Proportionality	II. Ensures that decisions are supported by adequate evidence before a court.
C. Doctrine of Legitimate Expectation	III. Holds that promises or practices by government may lead to expectations that legally need to be honored.
D. Doctrine of Unreasonableness	IV. Provides a ground to challenge administrative decisions that lack rational justification.

A. A-II, B-I, C-III, D-IV

B. A-I, B-II, C-IV, D-III

C. A-III, B-IV, C-I, D-II

D. A-IV, B-III, C-II, D-I

178. Match the following administrative law doctrines with their descriptions:

List-I (Doctrines)	List-II (Descriptions)
A. Audi Alteram Partem	I. An authority cannot exceed the powers granted to it under the law.
B. Nemo Judex in Causa Sua	II. Prevents a judge or decision-maker from having a personal interest in the outcome of a case.
C. Ultra Vires	III. Right of a person to have a fair hearing before a decision is made.
D. Estoppel	IV. Bars a party from denying facts that they previously admitted were true.

A. A-III, B-II, C-I, D-IV

B. A-I, B-III, C-IV, D-II

C. A-II, B-IV, C-I, D-III

D. A-IV, B-I, C-III, D-II

179. Match the following terms related to administrative discretion with their definitions:

List-I (Terms)	List-II (Definitions)
A. Arbitrariness	I. An administrative action taken without regard to legal standards, procedures, or factual justification.
B. Reasoned Decision-Making	II. When an official fails to exercise their judgment, instead applying a rigid policy universally.
C. Abuse of Discretion	III. The requirement that administrative decisions should be based on a clear and logical reasoning, explaining how conclusions were reached.
D. Fettering of Discretion	IV. When discretion is used in a way that is not justified by law, or when it is exercised in a biased or improper manner.

A. A-I, B-III, C-IV, D-II
B. A-II, B-I, C-III, D-IV
C. A-III, B-IV, C-I, D-II
D. A-IV, B-II, C-I, D-III

180. Match the following concepts related to judicial review with their meanings:

List-I (Concepts)	List-II (Meanings)
A. Standing	I. Orders issued by a court to correct a lower court's or an authority's decision.
B. Remedy	II. The ability of a party to demonstrate to the court sufficient connection to the law or right under challenge.
C. Writ of Mandamus	III. A command issued by a court directing a public agency or governmental body to perform an act required by law.
D. Prerogative Writs	IV. Legal solutions or corrections provided by the court.

A. A-II, B-IV, C-III, D-I
B. A-I, B-III, C-IV, D-II
C. A-III, B-II, C-I, D-IV
D. A-IV, B-I, C-II, D-III

181. Match the following legal standards with their applications in administrative hearings:

List-I (Standards)	List-II (Applications)
A. Clear and Convincing Evidence	I. Standard used in most civil litigation; requires more than 50% certainty.
B. Preponderance of the Evidence	II. Highest standard of proof, commonly used in criminal cases.
C. Beyond a Reasonable Doubt	III. Higher standard than preponderance, but less than criminal standards, often used in administrative settings involving substantial individual rights.

A. A-III, B-I, C-II
B. A-II, B-III, C-I
C. A-I, B-II, C-III
D. A-III, B-II, C-I

182. Match these key terms in administrative law related to regulatory compliance with their correct definitions:

List-I (Terms)	List-II (Definitions)
A. Regulatory Capture	I. A theory that describes a scenario where a regulatory agency is dominated by the interests it regulates.
B. Sunset Clause	II. A provision that a law will cease to have effect after a specific date, unless further legislative action is taken.
C. Whistleblower Protection	III. Legal protections afforded to individuals who report illegal or unethical practices.
D. Nondelegation Doctrine	IV. A constitutional principle that limits the transfer of legislative power to another branch or entity.

A. A-I, B-II, C-III, D-IV
B. A-II, B-I, C-IV, D-III
C. A-III, B-IV, C-I, D-II
D. A-IV, B-III, C-II, D-I

183. Match these administrative law terms related to public administration with their descriptions:

List-I (Terms)	List-II (Descriptions)
A. Executive Orders	I. Legal requirement that the government must respect all legal rights owed to a person.
B. Administrative Discretion	II. Directives issued by heads of state that manage operations of the federal government.
C. Rule of Law	III. A principle that government action must be based on established laws rather than arbitrary decisions.
D. Due Process	IV. The ability for bureaucrats to make choices within the bounds of their authority.

A. A-II, B-IV, C-III, D-I
B. A-I, B-III, C-IV, D-II
C. A-III, B-II, C-I, D-IV
D. A-IV, B-I, C-II, D-III

184. Match these concepts with their roles in administrative procedures:

List-I (Concepts)	List-II (Roles)
A. Public Comment	I. Process allowing individuals to challenge administrative decisions in a higher body within the agency.
B. Administrative Appeal	II. Mechanism by which the courts oversee the legality of administrative decisions.
C. Information Disclosure	III. Opportunity for the public to provide feedback on proposed regulations.
D. Judicial Review	IV. Requirement for agencies to provide access to information upon request.

A. A-III, B-I, C-IV, D-II
B. A-I, B-III, C-II, D-IV
C. A-II, B-IV, C-I, D-III
D. A-IV, B-II, C-III, D-I

185. Match these fundamental concepts of administrative justice with their definitions:

List-I (Concepts)	List-II (Definitions)
A. Natural Justice	I. Principle ensuring that administrative decisions are made impartially, fairly, and within a reasonable time.
B. Equity	II. Concept that emphasizes fairness in administrative actions, often balancing the strict application of laws.
C. Administrative Efficiency	III. Organizational effectiveness that minimizes waste and maximizes decision speed.
D. Separation of Powers	IV. Doctrine that divides governmental powers among different branches to prevent abuse.

A. A-I, B-II, C-III, D-IV
B. A-II, B-I, C-IV, D-III
C. A-III, B-IV, C-I, D-II
D. A-IV, B-III, C-II, D-I

186. Match the following administrative law instruments with their respective functions:

List-I (Instruments)	List-II (Functions)
A. Injunction	I. A court order that compels or restrains specific actions by an administrative agency to prevent harm.
B. Consent Decree	II. A legally binding resolution of a dispute, agreed to by both parties, and affirmed by a court.
C. Advisory Opinion	III. A statement issued by a court or an administrative agency clarifying the legal position on certain matters without immediate enforceability.
D. Declaratory Order	IV. A formal statement by a regulatory agency that definitively sets forth the interpretation of statutory provisions.

A. A-I, B-II, C-III, D-IV
B. A-II, B-I, C-IV, D-III
C. A-III, B-IV, C-I, D-II
D. A-IV, B-III, C-II, D-I

187. Match these principles related to the rights of individuals in administrative proceedings with their descriptions:

List-I (Principles)	List-II (Descriptions)
A. Right to a Hearing	I. The ability to contest administrative decisions and seek a higher authority's review.
B. Right to Counsel	II. The procedural right to question witnesses and challenge evidence presented against an individual.
C. Right to Appeal	III. Entitlement to be represented by legal professionals in dealings with administrative bodies.
D. Right to Cross-Examine	IV. A fundamental aspect of procedural fairness allowing individuals to present their case in an administrative process.

A. A-IV, B-III, C-I, D-II
B. A-I, B-II, C-III, D-IV
C. A-II, B-IV, C-I, D-III
D. A-III, B-I, C-IV, D-II

188. Match the following types of administrative actions with their appropriate legal contexts:

List-I (Actions)	List-II (Contexts)
A. Rulemaking	I. The process through which administrative agencies issue licenses permitting individuals or entities to engage in regulated activities.
B. Adjudication	II. Actions taken by administrative agencies to apply specific legal norms in individual cases, often resembling a court trial.
C. Licensing	III. The creation of regulations that have the force of law, guiding the conduct of the public and the administration itself.
D. Enforcement	IV. Activities undertaken by agencies to ensure compliance with laws and regulations, potentially including penalties.

A. A-III, B-II, C-I, D-IV
B. A-I, B-III, C-IV, D-II
C. A-II, B-IV, C-I, D-III
D. A-IV, B-I, C-III, D-II

189. Match these administrative law terms to their definitions related to agency powers and limitations:

List-I (Terms)	List-II (Definitions)
A. Discretionary Authority	I. Tasks that an agency is required by law to perform, without any room for personal judgment.
B. Mandatory Duty	II. The authority granted to agencies to decide the best course of action where the law does not prescribe an exact response.
C. Policy-making	III. The constraints placed on the extent to which courts can review and intervene in decisions made by administrative agencies.
D. Judicial Limitation	IV. The role of administrative agencies in creating rules and policies that guide the implementation of the law.

A. A-II, B-I, C-IV, D-III
B. A-I, B-III, C-II, D-IV
C. A-III, B-IV, C-I, D-II
D. A-IV, B-II, C-III, D-I

190. Match the following administrative procedures with their purposes:

List-I (Procedures)	List-II (Purposes)
A. Notice and Comment	I. A method used by agencies to gather public input on proposed rule changes.
B. Executive Sessions	II. Closed meetings where confidential matters are discussed, typically not open to the public.
C. Public Hearings	III. Formal meetings where the public can speak directly to decision-makers about concerns and issues.
D. Summons and Subpoenas	IV. Legal instruments used to compel the appearance of individuals or the production of documents in administrative investigations.

A. A-I, B-II, C-III, D-IV
B. A-II, B-I, C-IV, D-III
C. A-III, B-IV, C-I, D-II
D. A-IV, B-III, C-II, D-I

191. The principle of ________ requires that no one should be a judge in their own case.
A. Audi alteram partem
B. Nemo judex in causa sua
C. Ultra vires
D. Rule of law

192. Administrative actions are subject to judicial review under the doctrine of ______ if they are unreasonable or arbitrary.
A. Proportionality
B. Natural justice
C. Wednesbury unreasonableness
D. Rule of standing

193. The ______ rule in administrative law ensures that an individual has the right to a fair hearing.
A. Procedural fairness
B. Audi alteram partem
C. Legitimate expectation
D. Estoppel

194. The doctrine of ______ holds that an administrative agency must act within the limits set by legislation.
A. Procedural fairness
B. Natural justice
C. Substantive review
D. Ultra vires

195. Decisions made by administrative bodies may be overturned if they fail to adhere to the principle of ______.
A. Natural justice
B. Procedural fairness
C. Proportionality
D. Transparency

196. The ______ doctrine in administrative law allows courts to prevent public officials from denying statements they previously made when others have relied on them.
A. Legitimate expectation
B. Estoppel
C. Audi alteram partem
D. Sovereign immunity

197. The requirement that a decision by an administrative authority must be made based on legal right or authority is known as ______.
A. Jurisdictional fact
B. Procedural fairness
C. Natural justice
D. Rule of law

198. A public official cannot be sued for acts done in official capacity if they are protected by the doctrine of ______.
A. Sovereign immunity
B. Estoppel
C. Procedural fairness
D. Natural justice

199. The legal concept that prevents retroactive administrative action is known as ______.
A. Rule against bias
B. Non-retroactivity
C. Proportionality
D. Legitimate expectation

200. An administrative decision can be declared void if it violates the principle of ______ by being more punitive than necessary.
A. Proportionality
B. Rule of law
C. Procedural fairness
D. Separation of powers

201. Which doctrine requires public authorities to give reasons for their decisions?
A. Reasoned decisions
B. Fair hearing
C. Legitimate expectation
D. Proportionality

202. The doctrine of legitimate expectation is violated when an administrative authority ______.
A. Changes policy without notice
B. Issues an order without jurisdiction
C. Gives a fair hearing
D. Acts within the law

203. What principle ensures that administrative action follows a fair and unbiased process?
A. Natural justice
B. Rule of law
C. Delegated legislation
D. Executive supremacy

204. The doctrine of 'Audi alteram partem' is not applicable in cases involving ______.
A. National security
B. Taxation
C. Licensing
D. Public employment

205. Which administrative body in India investigates grievances against public administration?

A. Lokpal B. Election Commission
C. CBI D. RBI

206. Which of the following statements is/are correct regarding the principle of natural justice?

Statement 1: The principle of natural justice requires that a person should be heard before an adverse decision is taken against them.

Statement 2: The principle of Audi Alteram Partem ensures that a person must be informed of the charges and given an opportunity to defend themselves.

A. Both statements are correct.
B. Both statements are incorrect.
C. Statement 1 is correct, but Statement 2 is incorrect.
D. Statement 1 is incorrect, but Statement 2 is correct.

207. Which of the following statements about administrative discretion is/are correct?

Statement 1: Administrative discretion can never be subject to judicial review.

Statement 2: The court may review administrative discretion if it is exercised arbitrarily or unreasonably.

A. Both statements are correct.
B. Both statements are incorrect.
C. Statement 1 is correct, but Statement 2 is incorrect.
D. Statement 1 is incorrect, but Statement 2 is correct.

208. Regarding the doctrine of legitimate expectation, which of the following statements is/are correct?

Statement 1: The doctrine of legitimate expectation creates a legal right enforceable by courts.

Statement 2: A person can claim legitimate expectation only when the government has made an express promise.

A. Both statements are correct.
B. Both statements are incorrect.
C. Statement 1 is incorrect, but Statement 2 is correct.
D. Statement 1 is correct, but Statement 2 is incorrect.

209. Which of the following statements is/are correct regarding the doctrine of ultra vires?

Statement 1: The doctrine of ultra vires is used to challenge administrative actions that exceed statutory powers.

Statement 2: An act that is ultra vires is considered null and void.

A. Both statements are correct.
B. Both statements are incorrect.
C. Statement 1 is correct, but Statement 2 is incorrect.
D. Statement 1 is incorrect, but Statement 2 is correct.

210. Which of the following statements about delegated legislation is/are correct?

Statement 1: Delegated legislation is unconstitutional as it allows the executive to make laws.

Statement 2: Delegated legislation is permitted if the parent Act provides sufficient guidelines for its exercise.

A. Both statements are correct.
B. Both statements are incorrect.
C. Statement 1 is correct, but Statement 2 is incorrect.
D. Statement 1 is incorrect, but Statement 2 is correct.

211. Which of the following statements correctly describes principles used in judicial review?

Statement 1: Wednesbury unreasonableness applies when an administrative decision is so irrational that no reasonable person could have made it.

Statement 2: Proportionality requires that administrative action should not be more restrictive than necessary to achieve the objective.

A. Both statements are correct.
B. Both statements are incorrect.
C. Statement 1 is correct, but Statement 2 is incorrect.
D. Statement 1 is incorrect, but Statement 2 is correct.

212. Which of the following statements regarding the rule of law is/are correct?

Statement 1: The rule of law means that the government is above the law.

Statement 2: Under the rule of law, every person is subject to ordinary law, including the government.

A. Both statements are correct.
B. Both statements are incorrect.
C. Statement 1 is correct, but Statement 2 is incorrect.
D. Statement 1 is incorrect, but Statement 2 is correct.

213. Regarding the delegation of powers, which of the following statements is/are correct?

Statement 1: The principle of non-delegation means that legislative powers cannot be delegated to the executive.

Statement 2: The doctrine of separation of powers strictly prohibits any delegation of powers in India.

A. Both statements are correct.
B. Both statements are incorrect.
C. Statement 1 is correct, but Statement 2 is incorrect.
D. Statement 1 is incorrect, but Statement 2 is correct.

214. Which of the following statements about the writ of Mandamus is/are correct?

Statement 1: A writ of Mandamus is issued to direct a public authority to perform a duty.

Statement 2: Mandamus is available even if the duty is discretionary.

A. Both statements are correct.
B. Both statements are incorrect.
C. Statement 1 is correct, but Statement 2 is incorrect.
D. Statement 1 is incorrect, but Statement 2 is correct.

215. Which of the following statements regarding the doctrine of estoppel is/are correct?

Statement 1: The doctrine of estoppel prevents a government from changing its policies.

Statement 2: The government may be estopped from withdrawing benefits that people have relied on in certain cases.

A. Both statements are correct.
B. Both statements are incorrect.
C. Statement 1 is incorrect, but Statement 2 is correct.
D. Statement 1 is correct, but Statement 2 is incorrect.

216. Which of the following statements about Lokpal is/are correct?

Statement 1: The Lokpal can investigate allegations of corruption against public servants.

Statement 2: The Lokpal was established under the Prevention of Corruption Act.

A. Both statements are correct.
B. Both statements are incorrect.
C. Statement 1 is correct, but Statement 2 is incorrect.
D. Statement 1 is incorrect, but Statement 2 is correct.

217. Which of the following statements regarding the Right to Information (RTI) is/are correct?

Statement 1: The right to information is a fundamental right under Article 19(1)(*a*) of the Constitution.

Statement 2: The Right to Information Act, 2005, allows citizens to obtain information from private entities.

A. Both statements are correct.
B. Both statements are incorrect.
C. Statement 1 is correct, but Statement 2 is incorrect.
D. Statement 1 is incorrect, but Statement 2 is correct.

218. Which of the following statements regarding the removal of Supreme Court judges is/are correct?

Statement 1: The President of India has the power to remove Supreme Court judges.

Statement 2: Supreme Court judges can be removed only through impeachment.

A. Both statements are correct.
B. Both statements are incorrect.
C. Statement 1 is correct, but Statement 2 is incorrect.
D. Statement 1 is incorrect, but Statement 2 is correct.

219. Which of the following statements regarding natural justice is/are correct?

Statement 1: Natural justice applies only to judicial and quasi-judicial decisions.

Statement 2: Administrative decisions affecting rights must also follow principles of natural justice.

A. Both statements are correct.
B. Both statements are incorrect.
C. Statement 1 is correct, but Statement 2 is incorrect.
D. Statement 1 is incorrect, but Statement 2 is correct.

220. Which of the following statements regarding judicial review in India is/are correct?

Statement 1: The Supreme Court of India has ruled that judicial review is a part of the basic structure of the Constitution.

Statement 2: The judiciary can strike down laws that violate fundamental rights.

A. Both statements are correct.
B. Both statements are incorrect.
C. Statement 1 is correct, but Statement 2 is incorrect.
D. Statement 1 is incorrect, but Statement 2 is correct.

Directions (Q.No. 221-235): Each question consists of an Assertion (A) and a Reason (R). Choose the correct option:

A. Both A and R are true, and R is the correct explanation of A.
B. Both A and R are true, but R is not the correct explanation of A.
C. A is true, but R is false.
D. A is false, but R is true.

221. Assertion (A): The principle of "Rule of Law" ensures that no one is above the law.

Reason (R): In India, the Constitution is considered the supreme law of the land.

222. Assertion (A): The principle of Audi Alteram Partem is applicable to every administrative action.

Reason (R): It is a fundamental principle of natural justice that no person should be condemned unheard.

223. Assertion (A): Delegated legislation is necessary for efficient governance.

Reason (R): The legislature does not have time to frame detailed rules and regulations for every law.

224. Assertion (A): Administrative tribunals function as substitutes for regular courts in India.

Reason (R): Administrative tribunals are created to provide speedy justice in specialized areas like tax, service matters, and consumer protection.

225. Assertion (A): The doctrine of Wednesbury unreasonableness allows courts to substitute their decision for that of an administrative authority.

Reason (R): Judicial review is concerned with the legality of decisions, not their merits.

226. Assertion (A): Judicial review is an essential feature of the Indian Constitution.

Reason (R): The power of judicial review allows courts to strike down unconstitutional laws and executive actions.

227. Assertion (A): Mandamus is a writ issued to compel a public authority to perform its duty.

Reason (R): It can be issued even when the authority has discretion over performing the duty.

228. Assertion (A): The principle of proportionality ensures that administrative actions do not impose excessive burdens.

Reason (R): Courts can intervene if an administrative action is more restrictive than necessary to achieve its objective.

229. Assertion (A): Sovereign immunity protects the government from all legal claims.

Reason (R): In India, the government can be sued for tortious acts committed during non-sovereign functions.

230. Assertion (A): The doctrine of estoppel prevents an individual from asserting something contrary to what they previously stated.

Reason (R): Estoppel applies only to private contracts and does not apply to the government.

231. Assertion (A): The Right to Information Act, 2005 ensures transparency in government functioning.

Reason (R): The Act allows citizens to obtain information from private entities as well.

232. Assertion (A): The Public Trust Doctrine ensures that natural resources are managed in the interest of the public.

Reason (R): Courts in India have held that the state must protect and preserve resources like air, water, and forests.

233. Assertion (A): A writ of prohibition prevents a lower court from exceeding its jurisdiction.

Reason (R): It is issued before the lower court gives its final decision.

234. Assertion (A): The Lokpal is empowered to investigate allegations of corruption against the Prime Minister.

Reason (R): The Lokpal has the authority to initiate proceedings against the President of India.

235. Assertion (A): The doctrine of necessity allows biased officials to make decisions when no alternative exists.

Reason (R): This doctrine is used when administrative action must be taken but all other officials are disqualified.

Passage-Based Questions (236-240)

PASSAGE

Administrative law governs the activities of administrative agencies of government. It involves rule-making, adjudication, and enforcement of a regulatory agenda. The doctrine of Natural Justice ensures that decisions are made fairly, following the principles of Audi Alteram Partem (the right to a fair hearing) and Nemo Judex in Causa Sua (no one should be a judge in their own cause). Administrative law also includes the Doctrine of Proportionality, which mandates that administrative actions should not be more restrictive than necessary.

The Wednesbury Principle states that a decision is unreasonable if no rational authority would have made it in the same circumstances. The Ultra Vires Doctrine ensures that an administrative authority does not exceed its legally granted powers. Administrative discretion must be exercised reasonably, and courts can review administrative actions through Judicial Review to ensure legality, fairness, and proportionality.

The Right to Information Act, 2005 promotes transparency by allowing citizens to access information held by public authorities. However, administrative law also recognizes certain limitations, such as national security and public interest, which may justify restrictions on the right to information. Additionally, the Public Trust Doctrine holds that certain natural resources like air, water, and forests are for public use and should not be privatized or exploited for private gain.

Writs such as Mandamus, Prohibition, Certiorari, Quo Warranto, and Habeas Corpus serve as constitutional remedies to check administrative excesses. The Lokpal and Lokayuktas Act, 2013, established an anti-corruption watchdog to investigate complaints against public officials.

236. What does administrative law primarily regulate?
A. Private contracts
B. Governmental agencies and their actions
C. Criminal justice system
D. Family law disputes

237. Which principle ensures that a person has the right to a fair hearing before an administrative decision is made?
A. Wednesbury Principle
B. Ultra Vires Doctrine
C. Audi Alteram Partem
D. Public Trust Doctrine

238. The doctrine of Ultra Vires is applied when an administrative authority...
A. Acts within its legal limits
B. Exceeds its legally granted powers
C. Exercises its discretion fairly
D. Refers cases to judicial courts

239. Which doctrine states that an administrative action must not be more restrictive than necessary?
A. Doctrine of Legitimate Expectation
B. Doctrine of Necessity
C. Doctrine of Proportionality
D. Doctrine of Estoppel

240. What does the Wednesbury Principle relate to?
A. Judicial Review
B. Criminal Law
C. Human Rights Violations
D. Delegated Legislation

ANSWERS

1. **(A):** Article 14 provides Right to Equality, Article 25 deals with Freedom of Religion, Article 32 guarantees Right to Constitutional Remedies, and Article 21 ensures Right to Life and Personal Liberty.
2. **(A):** Habeas Corpus protects personal liberty, Mandamus is issued to compel an authority to perform duty, Certiorari is issued to quash illegal orders, and Quo Warranto is issued to challenge an appointment.
3. **(A):** The 42nd Amendment strengthened Fundamental Duties, the 44th Amendment removed Right to Property from Fundamental Rights, the 86th Amendment provided Right to Education, and the 101st Amendment introduced GST.
4. **(A):** The 7th Schedule divides legislative powers, the 9th Schedule protects laws from judicial review, the 10th Schedule contains anti-defection laws, and the 4th Schedule allocates seats in the Rajya Sabha.
5. **(A):** Article 280 deals with the Finance Commission, Article 356 deals with President's Rule, Article 324 establishes the Election Commission, and Article 93 mentions the Speaker of the Lok Sabha.

6. **(A):** Keshavananda Bharati (1973) established the Basic Structure Doctrine. Golaknath (1967) ruled that Fundamental Rights cannot be amended. Minerva Mills (1980) restricted Parliament's power to amend the Constitution. Maneka Gandhi (1978) expanded Article 21 (Right to Life and Personal Liberty).

7. **(A):** Article 39(d) provides for Equal pay for equal work. Article 40 deals with organization of Village Panchayats. Article 43 promotes cottage industries. Article 48A ensures protection of the environment.

8. **(C):** CJI is appointed by the President on the advice of the CJI and senior judges. Governor is appointed by the President on the advice of the Council of Ministers. Attorney General is appointed by the President. Chief Election Commissioner is appointed by the President.

9. **(A):** Part II deals with Citizenship (Articles 5-11). Part III deals with Fundamental Rights (Articles 12-35). Part IV deals with Directive Principles of State Policy (Articles 36-51). Part V deals with the Union Executive (Articles 52-151).

10. **(A):** Article 18 deals with Abolition of Titles. Article 25 ensures Freedom of Religion. Article 23 provides Protection against Exploitation. Article 29 protects Language and Cultural Rights.

11. **(A):** First Schedule lists Union and State Territories. Fourth Schedule deals with allocation of seats in the Rajya Sabha. Seventh Schedule divides legislative powers between Union, State, and Concurrent Lists. Tenth Schedule contains anti-defection provisions.

12. **(A):** Article 352 allows for National Emergency in case of war, external aggression, or armed rebellion. Article 356 allows for President's Rule (State Emergency) if a state fails to follow constitutional provisions. Article 360 allows for Financial Emergency if India's financial stability is threatened.

13. **(A):** Money Bill (Article 110) requires simple majority in Lok Sabha only. Constitutional Amendment Bills (Article 368) require special majority in both Houses. Ordinary Bills require simple majority in both Houses. Financial Bills need simple majority in Lok Sabha, then Rajya Sabha.

14. **(A):** Sarkaria Commission (1983) dealt with Centre-State relations. Mandal Commission (1979) recommended OBC reservations. Balwant Rai Mehta Committee (1957) suggested the three-tier Panchayati Raj System. Swaran Singh Committee (1976) recommended the inclusion of Fundamental Duties in the Constitution.

15. **(A):** 73rd Amendment (1992) introduced the Panchayati Raj System. 74th Amendment (1992) established Urban Local Bodies (Municipalities). 97th Amendment (2011) granted constitutional status to cooperative societies. 101st Amendment (2016) implemented Goods and Services Tax (GST).

16. **(A):** The Governor is the constitutional head of a state and is appointed by the President of India (Article 155). The Governor serves at the pleasure of the President (Article 156), making the position an extension of Union control over states.

17. **(C):** While the Supreme Court has the power of Judicial Review, it is not explicitly mentioned in a single article but rather inferred from Articles 13, 32, 136, 226, and 246.

18. **(A):** Article 32 (Supreme Court) and Article 226 (High Courts) empower the judiciary to issue writs for the enforcement of Fundamental Rights, making them justiciable.

19. **(C):** The Indian judiciary is a single, integrated system unlike the United States, where there are separate state and federal courts.

20. **(D):** In Kesavananda Bharati v. State of Kerala (1973), the Supreme Court ruled that the Preamble is a part of the Constitution and can be used for interpretation.

21. **(C):** The Vice President is elected only by MPs (Rajya Sabha & Lok Sabha), whereas the President is elected by MPs and MLAs.

22. **(A):** Rajya Sabha is a permanent House as one-third of its members retire every two years, ensuring continuity.

23. **(A):** The 73rd Amendment (1992) gave constitutional status to Panchayati Raj Institutions (PRIs) under Part IX.

24. **(D):** DPSPs are non-justiciable and courts cannot enforce them directly.

25. **(C):** The 44th Amendment Act (1978) removed the Right to Property (Article 31) from Fundamental Rights, making it a constitutional right under Article 300A.

26. **(C):** The President appoints the Chief Justice of India after consulting the Collegium of Judges, not the Prime Minister.

27. **(C):** Rajya Sabha members are elected indirectly by State Legislative Assemblies, whereas Lok Sabha represents the people directly.

28. (A): Article 370 provided special status to Jammu & Kashmir until its abrogation in August 2019 by a Presidential Order and a Parliamentary resolution.

29. (C): The power of Parliament to amend the Constitution under Article 368 is subject to the "Basic Structure Doctrine", as held in Kesavananda Bharati v. State of Kerala (1973).

30. (A): DPSPs (Part IV, Articles 36-51) are not legally enforceable, but they act as guiding principles for the state in policymaking.

31. (A): Constitutional cases in the order they were decided:

- A.K. Gopalan (1950) – Narrow interpretation of Article 21.
- Kesavananda Bharati (1973) – Introduced Basic Structure Doctrine.
- Maneka Gandhi (1978) – Expanded scope of Article 21.
- Minerva Mills (1980) – Strengthened Basic Structure Doctrine.

Hence, correct option is *(a)*, *(b)*, *(c)*, *(d)*.

32. (A): Fundamental Rights-related amendments chronologically:

- 1st Amendment (1951) – Curbed free speech.
- 44th Amendment (1978) – Removed Right to Property from Fundamental Rights.
- 86th Amendment (2002) – Made Right to Education a Fundamental Right.
- 97th Amendment (2011) – Gave constitutional status to cooperative societies.

Hence, correct option is *(a)*, *(b)*, *(d)*, *(c)*.

33. (A): Lok Sabha elections in chronological order:

- First General Election (1951-52)
- Emergency Election (1977) – Congress lost power.
- Mandal Commission Election (1991) – Implemented OBC reservations.
- 2019 Election – After Article 370 abrogation.

Hence, correct option is *(a)*, *(b)*, *(c)*, *(d)*.

34. (A): Landmark cases on secularism in India in chronological order:

- Kesavananda Bharati (1973) – Secularism part of Basic Structure.
- Indira Gandhi v. Raj Narain (1975) – Challenged election of PM.
- Minerva Mills (1980) – Strengthened Basic Structure Doctrine.
- S.R. Bommai (1994) – Defined Secularism in governance.

Hence, correct option is *(a)*, *(c)*, *(d)*, *(b)*.

35. (A): Provisions of the Constitution as they were enacted in chronological order:

- Abolition of Privy Purse (1971) – Removed privileges of former rulers.
- National Emergency (1975) – Indira Gandhi's controversial move.
- Right to Information Act (2005) – Increased transparency.
- GST (2017) – Unified taxation system.

Hence, correct option is *(b)*, *(d)*, *(a)*, *(c)*.

36. (A): Constitutional commissions in chronological order:

- Balwant Rai Mehta Committee (1957) recommended establishing Panchayati Raj.
- Mandal Commission (1979) addressed reservations for OBCs.
- Sarkaria Commission (1983) examined center-state relations.
- Nanavati Commission (2000, though multiple exist, this refers to the 2002 Gujarat riots) is the most recent.

Hence, correct option is *(c)*, *(a)*, *(b)*, *(d)*.

37. (A): Constitutional schedules in order of their introduction:

- Fifth Schedule (1950) was part of the original Constitution for tribal areas.
- Ninth Schedule (1951) was added by the 1st Amendment to protect laws from judicial review.
- Tenth Schedule (1985) was introduced by the 52nd Amendment for anti-defection laws.
- Twelfth Schedule (1992) was added by the 74th Amendment for municipalities.

Hence, correct option is *(c)*, *(b)*, *(a)*, *(d)*.

38. (A): Election-related reforms chronologically:

- 61st Amendment (1988, effective 1989) lowered the voting age to 18.
- EVMs were first used experimentally in 1982 (Kerala) and widely from the 1990s.
- Voter ID (EPIC) was introduced in 1993.
- NOTA was introduced in 2013 following a Supreme Court ruling.

Hence, correct option is *(d)*, *(c)*, *(a)*, *(b)*.

39. (A): Supreme Court Chief Justices in chronological order:

- Justice Y.V. Chandrachud (1978–1985) was the 16th CJI.
- Justice M.N. Venkatachaliah (1993–1994) was the 25th CJI.
- Justice Dipak Misra (2017–2018) was the 45th CJI.
- Justice S.A. Bobde (2019–2021) was the 47th CJI.

Hence, correct option is (*a*), (*b*), (*c*), (*d*).

40. (A): Indian constitutional amendments in chronological order:

- 1st Amendment (1951) added Articles 31A and 31B to protect land reforms and the Ninth Schedule.
- 42nd Amendment (1976) introduced major changes, often called the "Mini-Constitution."
- 73rd Amendment (1992) established the Panchayati Raj system.
- 86th Amendment (2002) made education a fundamental right under Article 21A.

Hence, correct option is (*c*), (*a*), (*b*), (*d*).

41. (A): Judicial doctrines in chronological order:

- Doctrine of Severability (1950, Bhikaji Narain Dhakras case) protects valid parts of a law.
- Doctrine of Eclipse (1955, Bhikaji Narain Dhakras case) holds unconstitutional laws dormant for certain groups.
- Doctrine of Pith and Substance (1960, State of Bombay v. F.N. Balsara) determines legislative competence.
- Doctrine of Basic Structure (1973, Kesavananda Bharati case) limits amendment powers.

Hence, correct option is (*c*), (*b*), (*d*), (*a*).

42. (A): Constitutional doctrines in chronological order based on their judicial recognition in India:

- Doctrine of Pith and Substance – Originated in Canada; first used in India in State of Bombay v. F.N. Balsara (1951).
- Doctrine of Severability – Applied in A.K. Gopalan v. State of Madras (1950).
- Doctrine of Eclipse – Established in Bhikaji Narain Dhakras v. State of Madhya Pradesh (1955).
- Doctrine of Basic Structure – Introduced in Kesavananda Bharati v. State of Kerala (1973).

Hence, correct option is (*c*), (*a*), (*b*), (*d*).

43. (C): Constitutional commissions in the order of their establishment:

- Finance Commission (1951) – Established under Article 280.
- Election Commission (1951) – Formed under Article 324.
- First Law Commission (1955) – Established under Chairmanship of M.C. Setalvad.
- Sarkaria Commission (1983) – Formed to study Centre-State relations.

Hence, correct option is (*b*), (*c*), (*a*), (*d*).

44. (A): Constitutional amendments in chronological order:

- 42nd Amendment (1976) – Expanded DPSPs and Fundamental Duties.
- 44th Amendment (1978) – Restored rights curtailed during Emergency.
- 61st Amendment (1988) – Lowered voting age from 21 to 18.
- 97th Amendment (2011) – Recognized cooperative societies as fundamental institutions.

Hence, correct option is (*a*), (*b*), (*c*), (*d*).

45. (A): Constitutional schedules in the order of their introduction:

- Fourth Schedule (1950) – Allocation of Rajya Sabha seats.
- Fifth Schedule (1950) – Deals with Scheduled Areas & Tribes.
- Ninth Schedule (1951) – Created to protect certain laws from judicial review.
- Tenth Schedule (1985) – Introduced Anti-defection provisions.

Hence, correct option is (*a*), (*b*), (*c*), (*d*).

46. (A): Key events in the evolution of Indian constitutional governance in chronological order:

- First Constitutional Amendment (1951) – Curbed freedom of speech.
- Swaran Singh Committee (1976) – Recommended inclusion of Fundamental Duties.
- Protection of Human Rights Act (1993) – Created National Human Rights Commission (NHRC).
- Goods and Services Tax (2017) – Unified tax system.

Hence, correct option is (*a*), (*b*), (*c*), (*d*).

47. **(A):** The 42nd Amendment (1976) added Article 39A (Free Legal Aid) and strengthened Directive Principles of State Policy (DPSPs).

48. **(B):** Article 44 directs the State to implement a Uniform Civil Code (UCC) for uniform personal laws.

49. **(C):** The Supreme Court in Minerva Mills (1980) held that DPSPs cannot be given absolute primacy over Fundamental Rights, ensuring a balance between the two.

50. **(C):** Article 48A directs the State to protect and improve the environment, ensuring the conservation of forests and wildlife.

51. **(B):** The 44th Amendment (1978) ensured that Fundamental Rights could not be abrogated by DPSPs, reversing Emergency-era changes.

52. **(B):** Article 53 states that the executive power of the Union is vested in the President.

53. **(C):** Article 54 provides for Presidential elections through an Electoral College consisting of elected MPs and MLAs.

54. **(A):** The 42nd Amendment made it compulsory for the President to follow the advice of the Council of Ministers.

55. **(B):** The Supreme Court ruled in Shamsher Singh (1974) that the President is a constitutional head and must act as per ministerial advice.

56. **(C):** The 44th Amendment gave the President the power to send back advice for reconsideration. However, if the Council of Ministers reaffirms its decision, the President must comply.

57. **(B):** The Indian Constitution provides for three types of Emergencies – National (Article 352), State (Article 356), and Financial (Article 360). There is no provision for a Political Emergency.

58. **(B):** The 44th Amendment (1978) restricted Emergency powers, ensuring that a National Emergency can be proclaimed only on the written recommendation of the Cabinet.

59. **(B):** Article 19 (Right to Freedom of Speech & Expression) is automatically suspended during a National Emergency. Other Fundamental Rights can only be suspended through a Presidential Order under Article 359.

60. **(C):** In Kesavananda Bharati (1973), the Supreme Court introduced the Basic Structure Doctrine and ruled that Emergency provisions cannot be used to alter the Basic Structure.

61. **(C):** Article 359 allows the President to suspend Fundamental Rights (except Article 20 & 21) during an Emergency through a Presidential Order.

62. **(C):** India follows a parliamentary system where the President is a constitutional head and must act on the advice of the Council of Ministers (Article 74).

63. **(C):** In Kesavananda Bharati v. State of Kerala (1973), the Supreme Court held that the Preamble is a part of the Constitution, but it is not legally enforceable.

64. **(C)**

65. **(C):** India follows a federal structure with a unitary bias, but the word "federalism" is not explicitly mentioned in the Constitution.

66. **(A):** Rajya Sabha is a permanent House (Article 83), with one-third members retiring every two years, ensuring continuity.

67. **(A):** Article 324 establishes the Election Commission of India, a constitutional body responsible for conducting elections.

68. **(C):** DPSPs (Articles 36-51) are non-justiciable, meaning they are not legally enforceable but serve as guiding principles.

69. **(B):** The Vice President is elected only by MPs of Lok Sabha and Rajya Sabha (Article 66) and acts as the ex-officio Chairman of Rajya Sabha.

70. **(A):** The 44th Amendment (1978) removed Right to Property (Article 31) from Fundamental Rights and placed it under Article 300A as a constitutional right.

71. **(B):** Judicial Review is derived from multiple Articles (13, 32, 226, 136, etc.), and while Article 13 mentions invalidation of unconstitutional laws, it is not the only source.

72. **(A):** The Governor is appointed by the President (Article 155) and serves at the pleasure of the President (Article 156), making them a Union representative.

73. **(C):** India follows a federal system, but the judiciary remains unified (i.e., there are no separate state and federal courts like in the USA).

74. **(C):** Fundamental Duties were added by the 42nd Amendment (1976), but they were borrowed from the Soviet (Russian) Constitution, not France.

75. (A): State legislatures cannot make laws on subjects in the Union List (Article 246) because these subjects require uniformity across the country.

76. (A): The Basic Structure Doctrine was established in Kesavananda Bharati (1973), ruling that Parliament cannot amend the "Basic Structure" of the Constitution.

77. (B): The Constitution provides strong powers to the Centre, especially during an Emergency, making it quasi-federal rather than purely federal.

78. (A): This doctrine was first applied in Golaknath v. State of Punjab (1967) and means that an unconstitutional law is applicable until declared invalid.

79. (D): The Supreme Court in Shankari Prasad (1951) ruled that Parliament can amend Fundamental Rights, a decision later challenged in Golaknath and settled in Kesavananda Bharati.

80. (B): Article 371A provides special autonomy to Nagaland, protecting traditional laws and customs.

81. (C): The idea of a Basic Structure was first hinted at in Golaknath (1967) but was formally established in Kesavananda Bharati (1973).

82. (C): In S.R. Bommai (1994), the Supreme Court ruled that the dismissal of a State Government under Article 356 is subject to judicial review.

83. (B): President's Rule can be imposed under Article 356 for constitutional failure, not merely due to "internal disturbances."

84. (A): The Fifth Schedule deals with Scheduled Areas and Tribes, while the Sixth Schedule governs Tribal Areas in the Northeast.

85. (C): In Indira Gandhi (1975), the Supreme Court ruled that the judiciary cannot be completely excluded from election disputes, applying separation of powers.

86. (A): The 86th Amendment (2002) made education a Fundamental Right for children aged 6-14.

87. (C): Article 18 prohibits the State from conferring titles except for military or academic distinctions.

88. (D): Quo Warranto is issued under Article 226, not Article 32, and is used to question the authority of a public office-holder.

89. (B): The 42nd Amendment (1976) inserted Fundamental Duties (Article 51A), inspired by the Soviet Constitution.

90. (C): Article 143 allows the President to seek advisory opinion from the Supreme Court.

91. (B): Kesavananda Bharati (1973) ruled that the Preamble is part of the Constitution.

92. (A): The doctrine of colorable legislation states that if a legislature does not have the power to make a law directly, it cannot do so indirectly under a different guise.

93. (B): In Minerva Mills (1980), the Supreme Court held that DPSPs cannot be given primacy over Fundamental Rights, ensuring a balance.

94. (A): The Fourth Schedule of the Indian Constitution allocates seats to the Rajya Sabha among States and Union Territories.

95. (B): The 44th Amendment (1978) removed Right to Property (Article 31) from Fundamental Rights and placed it under Article 300A.

96. (B): In I.R. Coelho (2007), the Supreme Court ruled that laws placed under the Ninth Schedule after April 24, 1973, could still be reviewed if they violated the Basic Structure Doctrine.

97. (C): Provisions relating to the election of the President require a special majority and ratification by half of the State Legislatures (Article 368).

98. (A): The 101st Amendment (2016) introduced GST, creating a uniform indirect tax system across India.

99. (C): The 73rd Amendment (1992) granted constitutional status to Panchayati Raj Institutions (PRIs) under Part IX.

100. (C): The Indian concept of secularism allows for equal treatment of all religions while permitting State intervention in religious practices if needed.

101. (C): The Supreme Court has expanded the scope of Article 21 to include various rights, such as Right to Privacy (Puttaswamy Case, 2017) and Right to a Clean Environment.

102. (B): The Doctrine of Pith and Substance is used to determine which legislative list a law belongs to, ensuring a practical approach to legislative competence.

103. (A): The Supreme Court in M. Nagaraj (2006) held that reservation in promotions is not a Fundamental Right but subject to State discretion.

104. (C): Article 16 guarantees equal opportunity in public employment and prohibits discrimination on specific grounds.

105. (C): The Collegium System was introduced through the Second Judges Case (1993) and later reinforced in the Third Judges Case (1998). The 99th Amendment (2014), which sought to replace it with the NJAC, was struck down by the Supreme Court in 2015.

106. (C): The Doctrine of Eclipse states that a law inconsistent with Fundamental Rights is not void but remains inactive until the inconsistency is removed.

107. (C): In Janhit Abhiyan v. Union of India (2022), the Supreme Court upheld the constitutional validity of the 103rd Amendment, stating that EWS reservations do not violate the Basic Structure Doctrine.

108. (C): Article 85 empowers the President to dissolve the Lok Sabha on the advice of the Prime Minister before the completion of its term.

109. (B): Mandamus is issued by a court to a lower authority or public officer to perform a duty they are obligated to do.

110. (C): The Tenth Schedule (added by the 52nd Amendment in 1985) deals with disqualification of legislators on the grounds of defection.

111. (B): In Om Kumar (2001), the Supreme Court applied the doctrine of proportionality, stating that administrative actions must be fair and just.

112. (A): The Supreme Court held in PUCL v. UOI (1997) that telephone tapping without a valid procedure is a violation of the Right to Privacy under Article 21.

113. (B): Article 31B validates laws placed in the Ninth Schedule, protecting them from judicial review.

114. (C): Article 23 prohibits human trafficking, begar (forced labor), and similar exploitative practices.

115. (B): Golaknath (1967) ruled that Parliament cannot amend Fundamental Rights under Article 368.

116. (B): Article 263 empowers the President to constitute an Inter-State Council to resolve disputes between States.

117. (C): Article 250 allows Parliament to make laws on subjects in the State List during a National Emergency (Article 352).

118. (C): Part IXB was inserted by the 97th Amendment (2011) to give constitutional status to cooperative societies.

119. (B): Article 226 gives High Courts wider jurisdiction than the Supreme Court (Article 32), allowing them to issue writs for both Fundamental Rights and other legal rights.

120. (A): In Shayara Bano (2017), the Supreme Court struck down the practice of Triple Talaq (Talaq-e-Biddat) as unconstitutional.

121. (C): The 124th Amendment led to the 103rd Constitutional Amendment (2019), which provided 10% EWS reservation in education and jobs.

122. (B): Article 3 allows Parliament to form new States, alter boundaries, or change the name of existing States.

123. (B): Under Article 280, the Finance Commission recommends principles for tax revenue distribution between the Centre and States.

124. (C): Article 49 places a duty on the State to protect monuments, places, and objects of national importance from damage.

125. (C): The Basic Structure Doctrine (Kesavananda Bharati, 1973) ensures that Parliament cannot amend the "basic features" of the Constitution.

126. (C): Right to Work is a Directive Principle (Article 41) but not a Fundamental Right under Part III of the Constitution.

127. (B): The principle of 'Legality' underpins the 'Rule of Law' in administrative actions, ensuring that every administrative decision is made according to the law, not arbitrary power. It promotes transparency and accountability within administrative bodies.

128. (D): The doctrine of proportionality requires that administrative actions must not be more intrusive or broader than necessary to achieve the desired legitimate objectives. This ensures a balance between the means used and the ends sought by the government.

129. (A): The 'Wednesbury Principle' originates from the case of Associated Provincial Picture Houses v. Wednesbury Corp., which introduced the concept that an administrative decision may be invalidated on grounds of unreasonableness if it is so absurd that no reasonable authority could ever have come to it.

130. (D): The 'Right to Fair Hearing' encompasses several procedural rights essential for a fair trial in administrative proceedings, including the right to be heard by a neutral judge, the right to have a decision made within a reasonable time, and the right to present and rebut evidence. This ensures that the process is just and equitable.

131. (B): Administrative discretion refers to the flexible exercising of judgment and decision-making allowed to public administrative agencies. However, this discretion must be used within the legal bounds and guidelines set forth by statutes or delegated legislation to prevent arbitrary decisions.

132. (A): The principle of 'Natural Justice' is a fundamental aspect of administrative law that includes the right to a fair hearing, which means having prior notice of the case and the opportunity to present one's case. It aims to ensure fairness and prevent arbitrariness in administrative proceedings.

133. (C): Judicial review of administrative action can be sought for reasons such as illegality, irrationality (unreasonableness), and procedural impropriety. A decision made with proper authority is not grounds for judicial review because it implies that the decision adheres to the legal powers and limitations granted to the administrative body.

134. (C): An 'Ouster Clause' is a provision in a statute that seeks to limit or exclude the jurisdiction of the judiciary to review administrative actions. This type of clause aims to prevent courts from intervening in certain decisions, thus protecting administrative autonomy, though such clauses are often interpreted narrowly by courts.

135. (D): The Doctrine of Estoppel in administrative law prevents a public official from denying the validity of their authority if they have accepted their appointment and exercised their powers. This doctrine helps ensure stability and continuity in public administration.

136. (B): In the landmark case of K.S. Puttaswamy v. Union of India (2017), the Supreme Court of India recognized the Right to Privacy as a fundamental right under the Constitution, protected under Article 21. This ruling has significant implications for administrative law, particularly in the context of government policies involving personal data and privacy.

137. (C): The Latin phrase "Audi Alteram Partem" means "hear the other side." It is a principle of fundamental justice or fairness in legal and administrative processes, requiring that each party involved in a dispute be given an opportunity to respond to the evidence against them or to present their case.

138. (B): The 'Doctrine of Legitimate Expectation' allows individuals to expect that procedures. or existing policies that they have been benefiting from, will continue unless there is some reasonable and rational justification for a change. This doctrine is instrumental in ensuring fairness and predictability in administrative actions.

139. (B): Non-justiciability refers to certain matters that courts consider inappropriate for judicial review, often because they involve issues delegated entirely to another branch of government. This concept limits the scope of judicial intervention in administrative decisions.

140. (A): The Doctrine of Ultra Vires ("beyond the powers") is applied when an administrative agency has acted outside or beyond the powers conferred to it by law. This doctrine is a fundamental aspect of administrative law to check and balance the exercise of power by administrative bodies.

141. (A): The 'Carltona Principle' reflects the reality of modern government where ministers cannot personally make all decisions within their departments. Thus, acts of departmental officials are viewed in law as acts of the minister, who is ultimately accountable to the legislature for them.

142. (A): Subordinate legislation is a mechanism through which executive authorities are empowered to make regulations within the framework set by primary legislation. This allows for more detailed governance and management of complex matters that are impractical for direct legislative detail.

143. (B): The principle of Nemo judex in causa sua ensures that no one can judge a case in which they have an interest. If a judge has a financial or any other personal interest in the outcome of a case, it would compromise the fairness and impartiality of the decision-making process.

144. (C): Judicial review in administrative law refers to the power of the judiciary to interpret the law and to determine the legality of administrative actions. It is a crucial mechanism for ensuring that administrative decisions comply with the law, principles of fairness, and the Constitution.

145. (C): Public Interest Litigation (PIL) represents a legal framework aimed at providing a mechanism to promote justice and to enforce the rights of socially and economically disadvantaged groups. It allows an individual or group to file petitions in the court of law in the interest of the public at large, often challenging administrative decisions.

146. (B): The Right to Information Act, 2005, is a landmark law in India that empowers citizens to seek information from any public authority, promoting transparency and accountability in the working of every public authority. This act is a significant tool in administrative law for ensuring that administrations operate within the bounds of legality and openness.

147. (B): The Doctrine of Bias is a principle of natural justice that ensures administrative decisions are made impartially and without prejudice. It stipulates that officials must not have personal or financial interests that conflict with their duties, ensuring decisions are made fairly and without any undue influence.

148. (A): The 'exhaustion of remedies' rule requires that a complainant must first use all available administrative remedies and appeals before they can file a lawsuit in court. This principle helps ensure that administrative agencies have the opportunity to correct their own errors and eases the burden on the judiciary.

149. (B): The 'ultra vires' test is used to determine whether an administrative action or regulation goes beyond the scope of authority granted by the statute or the Constitution. Actions found to be ultra vires are void and without legal effect.

150. (B): Merit Review involves evaluating the substantive merits of an administrative decision rather than just ensuring adherence to procedural norms. This type of review allows for a more comprehensive reconsideration of the original administrative decision, including both facts and law.

151. (D): The 'Principle of Reasonableness' is fundamental in administrative law, ensuring that administrative actions are reasonable in their timing, basis, and scope. This principle is key to preventing arbitrary decisions by ensuring that actions are supported by a fair and rational process.

152. (A): The Doctrine of Estoppel prevents an individual from going back on a stance or position they once took if it has been relied upon by others. In administrative law, this can apply to prevent a public authority from denying a promise or representation that has been relied upon by a citizen.

153. (C): The 'Public Trust Doctrine' is an important principle in environmental law under administrative law which posits that certain natural resources belong to all and must be managed by the state in trust for the public's benefit, not just for specific individuals or groups.

154. (B): Legal Precedent, or stare decisis, is a principle whereby courts follow the rulings and determinations of previous court decisions in future cases that are similar in facts and legal issues. This principle promotes consistency and predictability in administrative law.

155. (B): Promissory estoppel in administrative law occurs when a public official's promise, which is not itself a contract, leads an individual or a corporation to take action in reliance on that promise. This doctrine can hold the public body accountable to fulfill those promises to avoid injustice.

156. (A): Administrative Review refers to the process where an administrative decision is reviewed internally by either the same or another officer within the agency before it moves to litigation. This mechanism can potentially correct errors or adjust decisions closer to the agency's original intent without requiring judicial intervention.

157. (C): An Ombudsman serves as an independent review authority that investigates individual complaints against maladministration or violation of rights by public service agencies, offering a less formal avenue for grievance redressal than the courts.

158. (B): The Freedom of Information Act is pivotal in administrative law as it empowers citizens by providing a mechanism to access information under the control of public authorities. This promotes transparency and serves as a critical check on governmental power.

159. (C): Judicial Activism refers to the judiciary's readiness to actively intervene in cases to enforce justice, especially where legal provisions may be lacking or inadequately addressed by existing laws. This approach can push the boundaries of law in ways that protect individual rights against administrative overreach.

160. (A): Restitution in administrative law is aimed at undoing the wrong that has occurred due to administrative error, restoring the individual to the position they were in before the wrong occurred. It is often used in judicial settings to correct errors in administrative processes.

161. (A): 'Parens Patriae' literally means 'parent of the country' and in administrative law, it refers to the government's role as provider of protection to those unable to care for themselves, like minors or disabled individuals.

162. (C): The 'Doctrine of Precedent,' or stare decisis, is crucial in maintaining consistency and stability in the legal system, including administrative law. It ensures that lower courts follow the legal interpretations and decisions of higher courts in similar cases, thereby providing a predictable framework for adjudication.

163. (A): The principle of Ultra Vires (beyond the powers) is fundamental in controlling administrative action. It ensures that administrative agencies operate within the limits of their granted authority, and any act outside this scope can be challenged and declared invalid.

164. (A): The Data Protection Act is crucial in the digital age, setting out rules and responsibilities for data handling by public bodies. It aims to protect personal data, ensure privacy, and build trust in how public institutions manage information.

165. (B): Administrative Discretion refers to the reasonable leeway granted to administrative agencies in making decisions within the bounds of their authority. This discretion allows for effective and efficient decision-making tailored to specific situations, provided it remains within legal and ethical boundaries.

166. (B): Judicial Review is the primary legal mechanism used to challenge and scrutinize the legality of decisions made by public officials or administrative entities. It serves as a vital check on administrative power, ensuring decisions comply with the law, are not arbitrary, and respect rights.

167. (A): The doctrine of estoppel prevents public authorities from denying or acting inconsistently with their previous conduct if such conduct has been relied upon by others to their detriment. This principle upholds fairness and reliability in administrative actions.

168. (B): The Doctrine of Proportionality requires that any administrative action must be appropriate and necessary to achieve its purpose and not be excessive in relation to its aim. This ensures that actions taken are balanced and justifiable.

169. (B): The Rule Against Bias is a fundamental principle of natural justice that seeks to ensure the impartiality of decision-makers in the administrative process. It safeguards the fairness of the administrative proceedings by preventing decisions influenced by personal interest.

170. (B): The principle of finality in administrative law dictates that decisions become final and binding if they are not appealed or challenged within the prescribed time limits. This principle provides certainty and stability in administrative processes.

171. (B): The doctrine of 'Ultra Vires' (beyond the powers) is a central concept in administrative law used to challenge actions that exceed the legal authority granted to administrative bodies. Actions deemed ultra vires are invalid and can be annulled or revised by judicial intervention.

172. (A): The Public Trust Doctrine is a legal principle that stipulates certain natural resources like air, sea, shores, and forests are preserved for public use. This doctrine requires the government to protect these resources from being depleted or destroyed, ensuring their availability for future generations.

173. (B): The Right to Information Act is a pivotal piece of legislation that promotes transparency and accountability in the functioning of public authorities. By granting citizens the right to access information, the Act empowers individuals and enhances the government's accountability.

174. (B): 'Audi Alteram Partem', a Latin phrase meaning 'hear the other side', is a fundamental principle of natural justice in administrative law. It ensures that no person should be judged without a fair hearing in which each party is given the opportunity to respond to the evidence against them.

175. (B): The Principle of Rationality in administrative law requires that decisions be based on reason and within the framework of the law rather than on irrelevant considerations or personal whims. This principle helps ensure that administrative actions are logical, comprehensible, and justifiable.

176. (B): 'Abuse of discretion' occurs when an administrative decision is made in a manner that is unreasonable or without proper justification, often ignoring the legal standards or evidential basis required. This term is commonly used in judicial reviews to denote decisions that fall outside the spectrum of acceptable administrative actions.

177. (A): Substantial Evidence is crucial in judicial reviews focusing on the evidential support for administrative decisions. Proportionality assesses whether administrative measures are appropriately severe. Legitimate Expectation protects the interests of those who have acted based on government promises. Unreasonableness is used to overturn decisions that are irrational.

178. (A): Audi Alteram Partem ensures procedural fairness in hearings. Nemo Judex prevents conflicts of interest in decision-making. Ultra Vires concerns the scope of authority and its limits. Estoppel is about consistency in the statements and positions held by parties.

179. (A): Arbitrariness is linked to capricious or legally unfounded decisions. Reasoned Decision-Making mandates transparency and logical progression in decision-making. Abuse of Discretion pertains to decisions that fall outside the bounds of legal correctness or fairness. Fettering of Discretion occurs when officials do not use their judgment due to undue adherence to policies.

180. (A): Standing involves the right of an individual to initiate a lawsuit or challenge, often based on their personal or direct interest in the issue. Remedy refers to the legal means through which a right is enforced or a legal wrong is remedied. Writ of Mandamus commands government bodies to perform their duties. Prerogative Writs are special judicial remedies used to provide relief from errors made by lower courts or public authorities.

181. (A): Clear and Convincing Evidence is used when the stakes are high, such as in license revocation or custody cases in administrative hearings, requiring a higher degree of belief. Preponderance of the Evidence is the standard for most civil cases, where the decision is based on whichever side has more evidence in its favor. Beyond a Reasonable Doubt is the highest standard, primarily reserved for criminal cases to prevent unjust convictions.

182. (A): Regulatory Capture occurs when a regulatory agency, created to act in the public interest, instead advances the commercial or special concerns of interest groups that dominate the industry or sector it is charged with regulating. Sunset Clauses ensure laws are regularly reviewed and not left on the books indefinitely. Whistleblower Protection encourages the reporting of misconduct by protecting those who come forward. The Nondelegation Doctrine ensures that significant legislative powers remain with elected lawmakers and are not unduly delegated.

183. (A): Executive Orders are tools used by the president or governors to direct and manage the operation of the government administration within the federal framework. Administrative Discretion refers to the reasonable leeway allowed to bureaucrats in decision-making within the scope of their authority, ensuring flexibility in governance. Rule of Law is a cornerstone of democratic governance, ensuring that all actions by the government are grounded in law. Due Process is a constitutional guarantee that all actions and decisions of the government will respect individual rights and follow the law precisely.

184. (A): Public Comment is a phase in the rulemaking process where the public can influence the content of potential governmental regulations. Administrative Appeal offers a pathway within the administrative system to seek revision or reversal of decisions. Information Disclosure under laws like the Freedom of Information Act mandates that governmental information be accessible to the public, enhancing transparency. Judicial Review is the process by which the judiciary can assess and potentially nullify administrative actions if they are found to be unlawful.

185. (A): Natural Justice involves ensuring fairness in the process and outcome of administrative decisions, crucial for maintaining public trust. Equity in administration calls for fair and just decisions, especially in complex situations where the application of strict legal principles might result in injustice. Administrative Efficiency focuses on the performance and effectiveness of government agencies in fulfilling their duties. Separation of Powers is a foundational constitutional principle designed to maintain checks and balances among the legislative, executive, and judicial branches of government.

186. (A): Injunctions are crucial for providing immediate legal remedies that prevent ongoing or imminent harm by stopping or compelling actions. Consent Decrees are used to settle disputes by agreement in a legally binding form, often used in regulatory environments. Advisory Opinions provide clarity and guidance on legal issues without being directly enforceable, helping entities understand legal standings before taking action. Declaratory Orders give definitive legal interpretations by agencies, offering clarity on regulations or statutes.

187. (A): The Right to a Hearing ensures that individuals can present their cases and be heard in administrative proceedings, crucial for maintaining procedural fairness. The Right to Counsel allows individuals to be advised and represented by lawyers, protecting their legal interests. The Right to Appeal provides a mechanism to challenge and review administrative decisions, ensuring that errors or injustices can be corrected. The Right to Cross-Examine enables individuals to challenge evidence, enhancing the accuracy and fairness of the proceedings.

188. (A): Rulemaking is the procedure by which agencies develop and institute new regulations. Adjudication refers to the administrative process resembling judicial proceedings where disputes are resolved based on laws. Licensing is the authorization process by which agencies permit individuals or companies to operate under regulatory standards. Enforcement involves the actions taken by agencies to ensure that legal and regulatory standards are followed, including imposing sanctions or penalties for violations.

189. (A): Discretionary Authority allows agencies flexibility to make decisions within the bounds of statutory frameworks. Mandatory Duty describes the obligations that agencies must fulfill as prescribed by law, leaving no discretion. Policymaking is the process by which agencies create regulations and policies that help implement legislative intents. Judicial Limitation refers to the legal boundaries that define how much courts can interfere with or review agency decisions, ensuring that administrative discretion is respected while maintaining legal oversight.

190. (A): Notice and Comment is a phase in rulemaking that allows the public to review and provide feedback on proposed regulations, ensuring transparency and public participation. Executive Sessions are confidential meetings used for discussing sensitive issues, safeguarding privacy and confidentiality. Public Hearings provide a platform for open dialogue between the public and administrative agencies, ensuring community involvement in administrative processes. Summons and Subpoenas are tools used to enforce compliance with administrative investigations, ensuring that necessary evidence or testimony is available for fair decision-making.

191. (B): This principle, a part of natural justice, ensures impartiality in decision-making. It prevents conflict of interest by prohibiting decision-makers from ruling on cases in which they have a personal stake.

192. (C): The Wednesbury Principle (from Associated Provincial Picture Houses v. Wednesbury Corp, 1948) states that a decision is unreasonable if it is so absurd that no reasonable authority would have made it.

193. (B): Meaning "hear the other side," this principle ensures that no one is condemned unheard. It is a cornerstone of natural justice, requiring a fair opportunity to present one's case.

194. (D): "Ultra vires" means "beyond the powers." If an administrative body exceeds its statutory authority, its action is void. This doctrine prevents abuse of power.

195. (B): Procedural fairness ensures that decision-making is transparent, impartial, and follows due process. Courts may strike down decisions that violate this principle.

196. (B): The doctrine of estoppel prevents an administrative authority from going back on its assurances if an individual has acted in reliance on them.

197. (A): Courts may intervene if an administrative body lacks jurisdiction to act, ensuring that decisions are grounded in lawful authority.

198. (A): Sovereign immunity protects the government and its officials from lawsuits for actions performed in official duties, unless waived by law.

199. (B): Administrative decisions cannot apply laws retroactively unless explicitly allowed by legislation.

200. (A): Proportionality ensures that the severity of administrative action matches its purpose, preventing excessive penalties.

201. (A): A reasoned decision ensures accountability and fairness in administrative law, preventing arbitrariness.

202. (A): The doctrine of legitimate expectation applies when a public body reverses a consistent practice without warning.

203. (A): Natural justice upholds fairness, impartiality, and procedural correctness in administrative decisions.

204. (A): Courts allow exceptions to procedural fairness in national security cases for public interest.

205. (A): The Lokpal and Lokayukta Act, 2013, established the Lokpal as an anti-corruption watchdog for public officials.

206. (A): The Audi Alteram Partem principle is a part of natural justice, ensuring a fair hearing and notice before an administrative decision is made.

207. (D): Judicial review applies when administrative discretion is exercised in a way that violates natural justice or statutory limitations.

208. (C): Legitimate expectation does not create a legal right but allows courts to protect procedural fairness. An implied practice can also create an expectation.

209. (A): Any action that exceeds statutory limits is ultra vires and considered legally invalid.

210. (D): Delegated legislation is valid as long as it is done within the framework of the parent statute.

211. (A)

212. (D): The rule of law ensures that no one, including the government, is above the law.

213. (C): While delegation of legislative power is generally restricted, certain powers can be delegated with proper safeguards.

214. (C): Mandamus is issued when an authority fails to perform a public duty, but it cannot be issued for discretionary functions.

215. (C): While estoppel applies to prevent unfair withdrawal of benefits, policy changes are generally allowed unless a legitimate expectation arises.

216. (C): The Lokpal and Lokayukta Act, 2013, established Lokpal, not the Prevention of Corruption Act.

217. (C): RTI applies only to public authorities, and private entities are exempt unless they are publicly funded.

218. (A)

219. (D): Natural justice applies even to administrative decisions when rights and liabilities are affected.

220. (A): Judicial review is an essential feature of the Indian Constitution, protecting fundamental rights.

221. (A): The Rule of Law means that all individuals, including the government, must obey the law. In India, the Constitution is supreme, ensuring that all laws derive their authority from it.

222. (B): Audi Alteram Partem ensures fair hearing, but there are exceptions, such as national security cases. Hence, the reason is correct, but it does not fully justify the assertion.

223. (A): Delegated legislation allows the executive to make rules within the framework of a parent Act, making governance more efficient.

224. (A): Administrative tribunals reduce the burden on courts and provide specialized expertise in certain areas.

225. (C): Courts under Wednesbury unreasonableness review whether a decision is irrational, but they do not substitute their own decision.

226. (A): Judicial review protects fundamental rights and ensures that laws conform to the Constitution.

227. (C): Mandamus is issued when an authority fails to perform a legal duty, but it does not apply to discretionary powers.

228. (A): Proportionality means that actions must be necessary and not excessive. Courts review whether less restrictive means were available.

229. (D): Sovereign immunity applies only to sovereign functions, not to commercial or non-sovereign functions.

230. (C): Estoppel applies to government actions in certain cases, such as legitimate expectation.

231. (C): RTI applies only to public authorities, not private entities, unless they receive government funding.

232. (A): This doctrine, applied in cases like M.C. Mehta v. Kamal Nath, ensures that natural resources are not exploited for private gain.

233. (A): Prohibition is a preventive writ issued before an act is completed to stop excess jurisdiction.

234. (C): The President is not under the jurisdiction of Lokpal, but the Prime Minister can be investigated with certain restrictions.

235. (A): The doctrine of necessity applies when a biased decision-maker is unavoidable, such as in cases of a small tribunal.

236. (B): Administrative law primarily deals with government agencies and ensures their actions comply with the law.

237. (C): Audi Alteram Partem means "hear the other side" and is a core principle of natural justice.

238. (B): Ultra Vires means "beyond the powers" and prevents administrative authorities from acting outside their legal framework.

239. (C): The Doctrine of Proportionality ensures that administrative actions are not excessive and are necessary for the intended goal.

240. (A): The Wednesbury Principle states that a decision is unreasonable if no rational person would have made it.

UNIT 3 Public International Law and IHL

PUBLIC INTERNATIONAL LAW

NATURE OF INTERNATIONAL LAW AND ITS SOURCE

ITS NATURE: International Law, in a puritan form as the term connotes, is the sum of the rules accepted by civilized states, either explicitly or tacitly, as determining their conduct towards each other, and towards each other's subjects. It is a body of the rules regarded by the nations of the world as binding on them in their relations with each other, in peace and war, and comprises of the rights and duties of sovereign states towards each other. In this broad sweep and expanding concept and horizon, it governs the relationship of the people of the world, unbounded by the political and geographical constraints, and embraces, mankind as a whole, irrespective of colour, creed relation and political hue. As the events of each year rolled into history, it evolved and grew, assuming new shape and stature and is now a dynamic force—an embodiment of human efforts and human rights for peaceful co-existence.

ITS ORIGIN: The term International Law was first coined by Jeremy Bentham in 1780. It is synonymous with the law of nation which corresponds to the French and German equivalent droit international or droit des gens; international Recht or Volkerect; and to the Italian and Spanish equivalent, viz, diritto internazionale and derecho internazionale, respectively.

ITS DEFINITION: Lawrence, the well known jurists, defines International Law as "the rules which determine the conduct of the general body of civilised states in their mutual dealings". Disharmony in mutual relations among independent sovereign states causes rupture in their mutual dealings. International Law, therefore, regulates the conduct of states in their mutual dealings, hostile as well as pacific.

Oppenheim— "Law of nations or International Law is the name for the body of customary and treaty rules which are considered legally binding by civilised states in their intercourse with each other."

Hall—"International Law consists in certain rules of conduct which modern civilized states regard as binding on them in their relations with one another."

Hughes—"International Law is the body of principles and rules which civilised states consider as binding upon them in their relations. It rests upon the consent of sovereign states."

In the S.S Lotus case between France and Turkey, International Law was defined by the permanent court of International Justice "as meaning the principles which are in force between all independent nations." This definition embraces two essential features of International Law, viz, its universality and its exclusiveness. The emphasis is laid on the words "independent nations", inasmuch as according to the permanent Court of International Justice, the principles in force relate not to all nation but to all independent nations.

SOURCES OF INTERNATIONAL LAW

According to Lawrence, if we take the source of law to mean its beginning as law, clothed with all the authority required to give it binding force then in regard to international affairs, there is no but one source of law, and that is the consent of nations. This consent may be either tacit or express. The first is shown by custom;

that is to say, the habitual observance of certain rules of conduct by states in their mutual dealings though they have not solemnly bound themselves in words to do so. It is expressed by long usage, practice and custom. Express consent is given by means of treaties, or international documents having the force of treaties.

Oppenheim also shares the opinion of Lawrence and states that a State, just as an individual, may give its consent either directly by an express declaration or tacitly by conduct which it would not follow in case it did not consent. The sources of International Law are therefore two-fold, namely, (1) express consent which is given when states conclude a treaty stipulating certain rules for the future international conduct of the parties; (2) tacit consent, that is implied consent or consent by conduct, which is given through states having adopted the custom of submitting to certain rules of international conduct. Treaties and customs, must, according to him, be regarded as the exclusive sources of the law of Nations.

Prof. Brierly ascribes the main sources of International Law to custom and reason. Westlake says that the customs and reason are two sources of International Law, and adds Roman law as a subsidiary source. Custom being the primary evidence of what International Law is, a source of International Law.

Article 38(1) of the statute of the International Court of Justice defines the sources of the International Law as under:

(a) International conventions, whether general or particular, establishing rules expressly recognised by contesting states.
(b) International custom, as evidence of a general practice accepted as law.
(c) The general principles of law recognised by civilised nations.
(d) Subject to the provisions of Article 59 judicial decision and the teaching of the most highly qualified publicists of the various nations, as subsidiary means for the determination of the rules of the law.

Article 38(2), however, adds that the aforesaid provisions shall not prejudice the power of the court to decide a case ex aeqo et bono, if the parties agree thereto.

Besides the above, the other sources of International Law which may be mentioned are International comity, state papers other than treaties, state instructions for the guidance of their own officers and tribunals, resolutions of international conferences, municipal acts of parliaments and the decisions of municipal courts and opinions of juris-consults or text book writers. Lastly, the decisions and determinations of the various organs of the United Nations and other International bodies form an important source of International Law.

RECOGNITION OF STATE AND GOVERNMENTS

DEFINITION OF RECOGNITION

Jessup observes that recognition of state is the act by which another state acknowledges that the political entity recognised possesses the attributes of statehood. Recognition may be defined as formal acknowledgement by an existing member of the international community of the international personality of a state or political group not hitherto maintaining official relations with it. It implies that in the opinion of the recognizing state, the nascent community possesses the requirements of statehood, and is therefore a normal subject of international rights and duties. It is the free Act by which one or more states acknowledge the existence on a definite territory of a human society politically organised, independent of any other existing state and capable of observing the obligations of International Law and by which they manifest their intention to consider it a member of the international community.

THEORIES OF RECOGNITION

There are two theories of recognition, viz. The constitutive theory and the declaratory/declarative or evidentiary theory.

According to the former, it is the act of recognition alone which creates statehood and clothes a new govt. with authority in international sphere. It is the process by which a political community acquires personality in International Law by becoming a member of the family of nations. Only by recognition, a state becomes a participant.

Hegel was the founder of this school. According to Anzilotti, since the rules of International Law have grown up by the common consent of the states, a subject of International Law comes into being with the conclusion of the first agreement as expressed by the treaty of recognition. Such a recognition is reciprocal and constitutive, creating rights and obligations which did not exist before. Holland leans in favour of the constitutive theory and in this sense shares the view of Oppenheim. He observes that a state cannot be said to have attained maturity unless it is stamped with the seal of recognition, which is indispensable to the full enjoyment of rights which it connotes.

The recognition of Poland and Czechoslovakia through the instrumentality of the treaty of Versailles lends support to the constitutive theory of recognition. The constitutive theory presents serious difficulties. It would oblige us to say that an unrecognized state has neither rights nor duties at International Law, which is an absurd suggestion. Again, the status of a state recognised by some states and not recognised by others present a queer phenomenon. Non-recognition of a state by others is not conclusive evidence of the absence of qualifications requisite for statehood.

According to the latter theory, statehood or the authority of a new govt. exists prior to recognition and the act of recognition is merely a formal acknowledgement or admission of an already established fact. In other words, the exponents of this theory maintain that recognition merely has a declaratory, not a constitutive, effect, in as much as recognition merely declares an existing fact that a particular community or govt. possesses the necessary qualifications of a state as required by International Law. It does not bring into existence a state which did not exist before.

Article 3 of the Montevideo convention of December 26, 1933, stated: the political existence of the state is independent of recognition by the other states. Even before recognition the state has the right to defend its integrity and independence, to provide for its conservation and prosperity and consequently to organize itself as it sees fit, to legislate upon its interests, administer its services, and to define its jurisdiction and competence of its courts. The exercise of these rights has no other limitation than the exercise of the rights of other states according to International Law.

It is said in support of this view that Japan was possessed of all the elements statehood, even long before the formal establishment of relations with the western world in 1854. The exponent of this theory are Hall, Wagner, Pitt Cobbett, and Brierly.

FORMS OF RECOGNITION

(a) **Express and implied recognition:** Recognition may be express or implied. Express recognition is accorded by some formal declaration. Implied recognition is effected through acts which imply an intention to grant recognition; it is accorded by entering into a bilateral treaty regulating relations, or by accrediting diplomatic representatives. Issue of the consular exequatur by the recognising state also establishes implied recognition.

(b) **Conditional recognition:** States are also recognised some times subject to some conditions. The Berlin Congress of 1878 recognised the State of Bulgaria, Romania, Serbia and Montenegro on the condition that they did not impose any religious disabilities on any of their subjects. Since, the recognition once made cannot generally be withdrawn, the failure to fulfil the obligation does not annul the recognition. The recognised state can only be guilty of violation of International Law. The recognising state can also sever diplomatic relations by way of sanctions. An exception to the non-revocability of recognition is, however, furnished in the case of nascent state. Thus, Great Britain granted recognition to Estonian National Council 1919 for the time being provisionally and with all necessary reservations as to the future this was regarded on all hands as a revocable recognition.

(c) **Collective recognition:** It removes the anomaly of some states granting recognition and others refusing to do so. The treaty of London recognised Greece in 1830 and Belgium in 1831. The Berlin Congress of 1878 collectively recognised Bulgaria, Montenegro, Serbia, Romania while the supreme council of the allied powers accorded collective recognition in 1921 to Estonia and Albania thereby extending recognition on behalf of France, Italy, Japan, and Great Britain without separate acts of recognition by the four powers. The collective recognition paves the way for admission of the recognised states as member of the family of the nations. Such collective recognition is treated by some authors as simultaneous or general recognition and the only collective recognition possible today is recognition of state by an international organisation like the UN, admitting the same to its membership.

(d) **De Facto and De Jure Recognition:** Diplomats distinguish between recognition de facto and de jure. The former means that in the opinion of the recognising states, the new authority actually independent and wielding effective power in the territory under its control has not acquired sufficient stability as to show that it will be able to maintain its independence over a prolonged period and yet fulfils the requirements laid down by International Law for effective participation in the international community though only provisionally and temporarily. *De jure* recognition implies that the recognised state or govt. fulfils the test laid down by International Law for effective participation in International community. This necessitates the exchange of diplomatic representatives and naval salutes between warships.

According to the British practice, three conditions are required as precedent to the grant of de jure recognition of a new state or a govt. viz. (1) a reasonable assurance of stability and permanence; (2) the govt commands the general support of the population ; and (3) it is able and willing to fulfil its international obligation. According to Lauterpacht de facto, recognition is an expression of desire to enter relations with the regime in power but for the time being without the usual diplomatic courtesies.

Recognition of Governments: When a change in the head of the state which is already an international person, takes place in the normal and constitutional manner, such a change is notified to other states who accept the new head of the state by sending congratulatory messages. The difficulty, however, arises where a change in govt. is brought about by revolution *i.e.* by over throw of the existing govt or by a coup *d' etat*. In such cases, two test are to be applied: the first test is whether a new govt. is a *de facto* govt. in effective control of the state exercising its authority over a substantial portion of the territory without any effective oppositions and having the backing of a substantial segment of public opinion in the country. This is called the objective test. And the second test is whether the new govt. is prepared to carry out the obligations imposed on it by International Law and the charter of the UN. This is called the subjective test. The USA granted recognition to the new govt. of France established as a result of the French revolution. The same test was applied in the case of USSR when she emerged as a result of the revolution of 1917, and it was presumed that the new govt. would be peace loving state, prepared to carry out its international obligations.

Political and economic motives also play a dominant role in recognition of governments. The new govt is required to meet past obligations as the price of its recognition. The granting or refusal of recognition of the govt has, however, nothing to do with the recognition as an international person. The state remains in existence, however, violent or drastic the form of govt. may have been.

Premature Recognition: Premature recognition is regarded as an unfriendly act and treated as an act of intervention or as a casus belli. India recognised the Bangladesh rebels as a legal govt. of the state on 6th Dec. 1971 even though Bangladesh was declared independent on 25th March 1972. Even *de facto* recognition is sufficient to validate the act of the state recognised: Luther *vs* Sagor. In Haile Selassie *vs* Cable and Wireless Ltd., the court of appeal ruled against the plaintiff Haile and dismissed his claim by virtue of his failure to be the recognised govt. of Ethiopia.

The Tobar Doctrine: This doctrine is associated with the name of the minister of foreign affairs of Ecuador, Tobar, who in 1908 declared that indirect intervention by the American states in the affairs of any other American states in the form of refusal to recognise a govt. which came to power as a result of civil war or revolution was both permissible and legal. Under the garb of this doctrine, the USA, keeping in view political expediency used recognition as a means of interfering in the domestic affairs of the Latin American countries. The doctrine did, however, not prevent the US from recognising governments which had come to power through US organised coups. The doctrine besides being unsustainable on legal grounds, runs counter to Estrada doctrine.

The Lauterpacht Doctrine: According to Sir Hersch Lauterpacht, the states are under a duty to recognise entities which fulfil the actual requirements of a state govt. the only exception being where the state or govt. has come into being as a result of breach of International Law. In 1970, the Security Council ordered the member states not to recognise the Smith regime in Rhodesia.

Retroactivity of Recognition: When a govt. which originates in revolution or revolt is recognised by a state as the *de jure* govt. of the country in which it is established, such recognition is retroactive in effect and validates all the actions and conduct of the govt. so recongnised from the commencement of its existence. It was observed in the case of civil transport incorporated *vs* central AIT transport corporation that primarily retroactivity of recognition operates to validate the acts of a *de facto* govt. which has subsequently become the new *de jure* govt. and not to invalidate acts of the previous *de jure* govt.

Methods of Recognition: Recognition *de facto* or *de jure* is accorded in any of the following ways: (1) by entering into a treaty, (2) by admitting to a membership of UN, (3) by exchanging, sending or receiving diplomatic representatives, (4) by declaration unilateral or collective, (5) by admitting to an international congress, (6) by the formal appointment of its consul.

Recognition of Belligerency: On the outbreak of rebellion or insurrection in any country the outside powers generally maintain an attitude of non-interference in the domestic affairs of that state. However, it may frequently render it not possible for other states to maintain an attitude of indifference either because the rebellious forces are in effective occupation of a large part of the territory of the current govt. or the actual war between parent govt. and the rebellious forces has reached a stage when outside powers will not treat it merely an internecine struggle. The disturbed state and outside powers may be so intimately connected with each other on account of trade, commerce etc. That it may not be in the interests of the outside power to refrain from recognising such a shift of power in the disturbed state. In such cases, the political communities struggling to attain a condition of separate statehood are accorded a *de facto* recognition of belligerency pending the determination of the question whether they are normally admitted to membership or formally brought back to subjection.

The recognition of belligerency is merely an assertion of fact that the rebels are in a position to exercise authority over the territory in their possession. It gives no cause for any offence to the parent states nor this recognition is a violation of any neutrality. The British practice is that the mere declaration by rebels that they have constituted the provisional govt is not sufficient to justify the belligerent recognition unless the insurgent forces have gathered sufficient strength and the newly constituted govt. is capable of maintaining international relations with foreign states. The recognising state becomes entitled to neutral rights which are respected by the rival parties. Such recognition protects the belligerent from being treated as traitors on land or pirates on the sea. It also grants immunity to the parent state for acts of omission and commission on the part of belligerent detrimental to the recognising states. Recognition of belligerency confers an international status to the belligerent for purposes of war. Although there is no exchange of embassy or the conclusion of a treaty, yet consuls are generally exchanged for the protection of the commercial interests. The recognising state also recognises within its jurisdiction the flag of the revolted govt and the commissions it issues.

Recognition of belligerency has the effect of creating a new international entity possessing all the rights and obligations of independent states with respect to the conduct of armed conflict. The recognising state acting as the neutral accords, the rights of the belligerent to the waring parties who acquire the right of admission of their ships into the ports of the recognising states. The right to visit and search at sea, the confiscation of contraband goods and the maintenance of blockade. Such recognition enables the belligerent community and the parent state to have the same international status with respect to the prosecution of the war. Belligerency rights are accorded as a matter of convenience to the donor as also to the recipient. After the belligerents have consolidated their position, they are recognised as an independent state.

CONCEPT AND DEFINITION OF NATIONALITY

DEFINITION AND MEANING OF NATIONALITY

Nationality refers to the legal relationship between an individual and a sovereign state, under which the individual owes allegiance to the state, and the state, in return, provides protection and certain rights. It establishes the individual as a member of the state and is often a prerequisite for the possession of full legal rights within the state.

Key Points:

- **Legal Definition:** According to international law, nationality is "the legal bond between an individual and a state, primarily denoting membership in a sovereign political community."
- **International Perspective:** The International Court of Justice (ICJ), in the Nottebohm Case (Liechtenstein v. Guatemala, 1955), emphasized that nationality is a legal bond having a genuine connection of existence, interests, and sentiment between the individual and the state.
- **United Nations Declaration (Article 15 of the UDHR):**
  - ❑ Everyone has the right to a nationality.
  - ❑ No one shall be arbitrarily deprived of their nationality or denied the right to change their nationality.

Difference Between Nationality and Citizenship

Aspect	Nationality	Citizenship
Definition	Refers to the legal and cultural relationship between an individual and a state.	Refers to the political and legal status of an individual, granting rights and duties.
Scope	Broader concept; denotes membership in a nation-state.	Narrower concept; denotes legal rights and privileges within the state.
Nature	Inherent, often acquired by birth or descent.	Granted by the state, often through legal processes like naturalization.
Revocability	Rarely revocable (except in cases of fraud or treason).	Can be revoked under certain conditions (e.g., dual allegiance).
Rights and Duties	Does not automatically confer all rights (e.g., voting).	Includes specific legal and political rights (e.g., voting, holding public office).
Example	An Indian national may not have citizenship rights if residing abroad.	Citizenship confers rights like voting in elections or contesting elections.
Key Takeaway: While nationality establishes membership to a state, citizenship confers enforceable legal and political rights within that state.		

ESSENTIAL ELEMENTS OF NATIONALITY

- **Common Heritage and Culture:** A shared historical background, traditions, and cultural practices are often central to the concept of nationality.

  Examples: Language, festivals, art, and literature.
- **Common Language:** A unifying language acts as a marker of national identity.

  Example: French nationality is often associated with the French language.
- **Territorial Connection:** A defined geographical area or homeland contributes to the idea of a nation.

  Example: The concept of Indian nationality is linked to the territorial entity of India.
- **Common History:** Shared experiences such as wars, movements for independence, or colonial history bind people into a nation.
- **Political Allegiance:** Nationality involves a legal and political allegiance to a sovereign state.
- **Emotional Bond:** The sense of belonging to a nation creates a subjective feeling of loyalty and unity among its members.
- **Recognition by the State:** For nationality to be legally binding, it must be recognized by the state under its laws.

ACQUISITION OF NATIONALITY

Nationality can be acquired through various modes, which establish the legal bond between an individual and the state. Different countries adopt these modes based on their legal and cultural frameworks.

Modes of Acquiring Nationality

- **By Birth**
  - **Jus Soli (Right of Soil):** Nationality is granted to individuals born within the territory of a state, irrespective of the nationality of their parents.

    Example: The United States and Canada.
  - **Jus Sanguinis (Right of Blood):** Nationality is granted based on the nationality of one or both parents, regardless of the place of birth.

    Example: Germany and Italy.
- **By Descent**
  - Nationality is inherited from parents, typically when at least one parent is a citizen of the state.

  Example: India grants nationality by descent under specific conditions (e.g., Indian parentage for children born abroad).
- **By Naturalization**
  - Granted to foreign nationals who fulfill specific conditions set by the host country.
  - **Common conditions:**
    - Minimum period of residence.
    - Proficiency in the national language.
    - Knowledge of the country's culture and laws.
    - Oath of allegiance.

  Example: The United States requires 5 years of residence and basic English proficiency for naturalization.
- **By Registration**
  - A simplified process for acquiring nationality, often for specific groups such as:
    - Spouses of citizens.
    - Minor children of citizens.
    - Former citizens seeking reinstatement.

  Example: Under the Indian Citizenship Act, 1955, persons of Indian origin or spouses of Indian citizens can acquire citizenship by registration.
- **By Incorporation of Territory**
  - When a new territory becomes part of a state, the residents of that territory may automatically acquire the nationality of the annexing state.

  Example: Residents of Goa acquired Indian citizenship after its incorporation in 1961.

Criteria for Acquiring Nationality in India Under the Citizenship Act, 1955

- **By Birth:**
  - Persons born in India before July 1, 1987, are Indian citizens.
  - Persons born between July 1, 1987, and December 3, 2004, are Indian citizens if at least one parent is an Indian citizen.
  - Persons born after December 3, 2004, are Indian citizens if:
    - Both parents are Indian citizens, OR
    - One parent is an Indian citizen and the other is not an illegal migrant.

- **By Descent:**
  - A person born outside India on or after January 26, 1950, is an Indian citizen if either parent is an Indian citizen.
- **By Registration:**
  - Persons of Indian origin who have been residents in India for at least 7 years.
  - Spouses of Indian citizens who have resided in India for at least 7 years.
- **By Naturalization:**
  - Foreign nationals can acquire Indian citizenship if they:
    - Have resided in India for a total of at least eleven years in the fourteen years immediately preceding the period of twelve months before the application, and have resided continuously in India for the twelve months immediately preceding the date of application
- **By Incorporation of Territory:**
  - Citizens of territories incorporated into India automatically acquire Indian nationality.

LOSS OF NATIONALITY

Modes of Losing Nationality

- **Renunciation**
  - Voluntary act where an individual gives up their nationality.

    Example: Indian citizens can renounce citizenship by making a declaration under the Citizenship Act, 1955.
- **Deprivation**
  - A state may revoke nationality if the individual:
    - Obtained it fraudulently.
    - Engaged in disloyal acts (e.g., treason).
    - Poses a threat to national security.
- **Voluntary Acquisition of Another Nationality**
  - Many countries do not permit dual nationality and automatically revoke citizenship if another nationality is acquired.

    Example: India automatically terminates citizenship for individuals acquiring foreign nationality.
- **Automatic Loss**
  - Citizenship may be lost due to prolonged residence abroad without maintaining ties to the home country.

    Example: Some countries revoke nationality if citizens fail to renew their ties or declare allegiance periodically.

IMMIGRATION

Definition of Immigration

Immigration refers to the movement of individuals from their country of origin to another country with the intention of settling there temporarily or permanently. It plays a significant role in shaping societies, economies, and cultures and is often influenced by factors such as better employment opportunities, education, political stability, or family reunification.

Examples:

- A person moving from India to the United States to pursue a job opportunity.
- A student traveling to Germany for higher education and later settling there permanently.

Related Terms

- **Emigration:**
  - The act of leaving one's home country to live in another.
  - Focuses on the departure aspect of migration.

    Example: An individual emigrating from the Philippines to Canada for better job prospects.
- **Migrant:**
  - A broad term that encompasses all individuals who move across borders or within their own country, regardless of the reason or legal status.
  - Includes immigrants, emigrants, refugees, and internally displaced persons (IDPs).
  - **Types of migrants:**
    - **Voluntary migrants:** Move for better opportunities or personal reasons.
    - **Forced migrants:** Move due to conflict, natural disasters, or persecution.

Key Concepts in Immigration Law

Immigration law governs the movement of people across borders, determining who may enter, reside, and work in a particular country. It also establishes the legal framework for managing asylum seekers, refugees, and citizenship acquisition.

Nationality

- **Definition:**
  - A legal bond between an individual and a state that establishes their membership in that state.

- Nationality determines an individual's rights and duties toward the state, such as the right to vote or the obligation to pay taxes.

- **Acquisition of Nationality:**
  - **By birth:** Automatic nationality by being born in a particular country (jus soli) or to parents of a certain nationality (jus sanguinis).
  - **By naturalization:** Acquired through legal processes after meeting specific residency and legal requirements.

Citizenship

- **Definition:** Citizenship refers to the status of being a recognized member of a state, granting full rights such as voting, holding public office, and obtaining a passport.
- **Ways to Acquire Citizenship:**
  - **By birth:** Automatically granted based on birth in a country or to citizen parents.
  - **By descent:** Passed from parents to children irrespective of the place of birth.
  - **By naturalization:** Gained after fulfilling conditions such as residency, language proficiency, and allegiance to the country.
  - **By marriage:** Some countries offer citizenship through marriage to a citizen.
- **Dual Citizenship:** Some countries allow individuals to hold citizenship in more than one country simultaneously.

Asylum

- **Definition:** Asylum is the protection granted by a state to foreign nationals who have fled their home countries due to persecution or a well-founded fear of harm.
- **Key Features:**
  - Protection includes rights to stay in the host country and access to basic services.
  - Grounds for asylum: Persecution based on race, religion, nationality, political opinion, or membership in a particular social group.
- **International Framework:**
  - Governed by the 1951 Refugee Convention and its 1967 Protocol.
  - Non-refoulement principle: Prohibits returning asylum seekers to a country where they may face threats to life or freedom.

INTERNATIONAL LAW RELATING TO REFUGEES

International refugee law is a branch of international law that governs the protection, rights, and obligations of refugees—individuals forced to flee their home countries due to persecution or violence. It intersects with human rights law, humanitarian law, and customary international law, aiming to ensure safety and dignity for displaced persons.

Definition of a Refugee

- **1951 Refugee Convention (Article 1A(2)):** A refugee is a person who:
  - Owing to a well-founded fear of persecution for reasons of race, religion, nationality, membership of a particular social group, or political opinion,
  - Is outside their country of nationality, and
  - Is unable or unwilling to avail themselves of the protection of that country (or return due to such fear).
- **Expanded Definitions:**
  - **1969 OAU Convention:** Includes those fleeing external aggression, occupation, foreign domination, or events seriously disturbing public order.
  - **1984 Cartagena Declaration:** Covers persons fleeing generalized violence, internal conflicts, or massive human rights violations.

Key International Instruments

A. 1951 Convention Relating to the Status of Refugees

- **Adopted:** July 28, 1951; entered into force April 22, 1954.
- **Objective:** Establish a universal framework for refugee protection.
- **Key Provisions:**
  - **Non-Refoulement (Article 33):** No refugee shall be returned to a country where their life or freedom is threatened (except for national security/public order threats).
  - **Rights of Refugees:**
    - Non-discrimination (Article 3).
    - Access to courts (Article 16).
    - Right to work (Articles 17-19), education (Article 22), and public assistance (Article 23).

- Obligations: Refugees must respect host country laws (Article 2).
- **Limitations:** Originally applied only to events before January 1, 1951, and was Euro-centric.

B. 1967 Protocol Relating to the Status of Refugees

- **Adopted:** January 31, 1967; entered into force October 4, 1967.
- **Purpose:** Removed temporal (pre-1951) and geographical (Europe-only) restrictions of the 1951 Convention.
- **Impact:** Universalized refugee protection; 149 states are parties as of 2025.

C. Regional Instruments

- 1969 OAU Convention Governing Specific Aspects of Refugee Problems in Africa:
  - Expands refugee definition to include war and public disorder victims.
  - Emphasizes voluntary repatriation and burden-sharing among states.
- 1984 Cartagena Declaration on Refugees (Latin America):
  - Non-binding but influential; broadens refugee criteria to include generalized violence.
- Bangkok Principles on Status and Treatment of Refugees (1966/2001):
  - Asian-African Legal Consultative Organization (AALCO); persuasive, not binding.

D. Customary International Law

- **Non-Refoulement:** Recognized as a peremptory norm (jus cogens), binding even on non-signatories (R v. Immigration Officer, ex parte Sivakumaran, 1988).

Core Principles of Refugee Law

- **Non-Refoulement:**
  - Cornerstone of refugee protection; prohibits expulsion or return to persecution.
  - **Exceptions:** Serious crimes or threats to state security (Article 33(2), 1951 Convention).
- **Asylum:**
  - Not explicitly guaranteed in the 1951 Convention but derived from the Universal Declaration of Human Rights (UDHR), Article 14: Right to seek and enjoy asylum.
- **Non-Discrimination:**
  - Equal treatment regardless of race, religion, or origin (Article 3, 1951 Convention).
- **Durable Solutions:**
  - Voluntary repatriation (return to home country).
  - Local integration (settlement in host country).
  - Resettlement (relocation to a third country).

Institutional Framework

- United Nations High Commissioner for Refugees (UNHCR):
  - **Established:** December 14, 1950 (UN General Assembly Resolution 428(V)).
  - **Mandate:** Protect refugees, provide humanitarian aid, and facilitate durable solutions.
  - **Role:** Supervises the 1951 Convention's implementation; assists non-signatory states like India.
- **UN Relief and Works Agency (UNRWA):**
  - **Focus:** Palestine refugees in Jordan, Lebanon, Syria, and occupied territories (distinct from UNHCR).

Rights and Obligations of Refugees

- **Rights:**
  - Freedom of movement (Article 26).
  - Identity/travel documents (Articles 27-28).
  - Protection from penalties for illegal entry (Article 31) if fleeing persecution.
- **Obligations:**
  - Comply with host country laws.
  - Cooperate with authorities for identity verification.

Challenges in Refugee Law

- **Mass Influx:** 1951 Convention designed for individuals, not large-scale displacements (e.g., Syrian crisis).
- **Mixed Migration:** Distinguishing refugees from economic migrants.
- **State Sovereignty:** Tension between refugee protection and border control.

- **Climate Refugees:** Not covered under the 1951 Convention; emerging issue (Teitiota v. New Zealand, 2015 – climate displacement not persecution).

7. India and Refugee Law

- **Non-Signatory Status:**
  - India is not a party to the 1951 Convention or 1967 Protocol.
  - Reasons: Sovereignty concerns, porous borders, and resource constraints.
- **Domestic Framework:**
  - Foreigners Act, 1946: Treats refugees as foreigners; lacks distinction from illegal migrants.
  - **Constitutional Protections:**
    - **Article 21:** Right to life and liberty extends to refugees (National Human Rights Commission v. State of Arunachal Pradesh, 1996 – Chakma refugees protected).
    - **Article 14:** Equality before law applies.
  - **Ad Hoc Policy:** India grants asylum on humanitarian grounds (e.g., Tibetans, Sri Lankan Tamils, Rohingya).
- **Judicial Approach:**
  - Ktaer Abbas Habib Al Qutaifi v. Union of India (1999): Non-refoulement upheld as part of Article 21.
  - Mohammad Salimullah v. Union of India (2021): Supreme Court allowed Rohingya deportation, citing national security, showing inconsistent application.
- **UNHCR Role:** Operates in India; issues Refugee Status Determination (RSD) certificates, though not legally binding.

Landmark Cases

- **Sale v. Haitian Centers Council (1993):** US Supreme Court; controversially allowed interception of Haitian refugees, limiting non-refoulement's extraterritorial scope.
- **NHRC v. State of Arunachal Pradesh (1996):** Indian Supreme Court; Chakma refugees entitled to Article 21 protection.

Recent Developments (as of 2025)

- **Global Compact on Refugees (2018):** Non-binding; promotes burden-sharing and durable solutions.
- **Climate Displacement:** Growing calls to include environmental refugees (e.g., UNHCR's advocacy).
- **India's Approach:** Continued reliance on ad hoc policies; no refugee law enacted yet.

INTERNALLY DISPLACED PERSON

DEFINITION OF INTERNALLY DISPLACED PERSONS (IDPs)

Internally Displaced Persons (IDPs) are individuals or groups of people who have been forced to flee their homes or places of habitual residence as a result of armed conflict, violence, human rights violations, natural disasters, or development projects, but have not crossed an internationally recognized border. Unlike refugees, IDPs remain within the borders of their own country, and their displacement may be either temporary or permanent.

The UN Guiding Principles on Internal Displacement (1998) defines IDPs as:

"Persons or groups of persons who have been forced or obliged to flee or to leave their homes or places of habitual residence, in particular as a result of or in order to avoid the effects of armed conflict, situations of generalized violence, violations of human rights, or natural or human-made disasters, and who have not crossed an internationally recognized State border."

Key characteristics of IDPs:

- **Internal Displacement:** They remain within their country of origin.
- **Cause of Displacement:** Caused by conflict, human rights violations, or natural disasters.
- **Legal Status:** They do not benefit from the same international protections as refugees because they are within their own country's jurisdiction.
- **Rehabilitation:** They often face difficulties in returning to their homes or resettling elsewhere within their country due to security concerns, lack of resources, or government policies.

Differences Between IDPs and Refugees

While both IDPs and refugees are displaced persons, there are key distinctions based on legal status, protection, and international laws:

Aspect	Internally Displaced Persons (IDPs)	Refugees
Location	Remain within their home country.	Flee across international borders to seek asylum.
International Protection	Do not receive international legal protection or specific status under international law.	Protected under international law (mainly the 1951 Refugee Convention and its 1967 Protocol).
Legal Framework	Governed by national laws; may be assisted by UN agencies but not by the Refugee Convention.	Governed by international law, specifically the Refugee Convention, and international bodies like UNHCR.
Government Responsibility	Primarily the responsibility of the government of the country in which they reside.	The country of asylum has the responsibility for the protection and rights of refugees.
Freedom of Movement	Often restricted within the country due to security concerns.	Have the right to move within the host country and may be eligible for resettlement in third countries.
Cause of Displacement	Often caused by internal conflict, violence, natural disasters, or development-induced displacement.	Typically caused by persecution, war, or fear of persecution due to race, religion, nationality, membership in a particular social group, or political opinion.

INTERNALLY LEGAL FRAMEWORK FOR INTERNALLY DISPLACED PERSONS (IDPs)

The international legal framework for Internally Displaced Persons (IDPs) focuses primarily on human rights and humanitarian law, as there is no binding international treaty dedicated specifically to IDPs. However, there are key guidelines and roles played by various international organizations that help provide a legal framework for the protection and assistance of IDPs.

Guiding Principles on Internal Displacement (1998) by the United Nations

The UN Guiding Principles on Internal Displacement were developed in 1998 by the UN Secretary-General's Representative on the Human Rights of Internally Displaced Persons, Francis M. Deng, to provide international standards for the protection of IDPs. These principles are non-binding but have been widely accepted by the international community as a framework to address the needs of IDPs.

Key Aspects of the Guiding Principles:

- **Scope:** They apply to all IDPs regardless of the cause of displacement (armed conflict, violence, human rights violations, natural disasters, or development).
- **Human Rights Protection:** They emphasize that IDPs should be treated in accordance with international human rights law and have the same rights and freedoms as other citizens. This includes protection from arbitrary displacement, access to assistance, and the right to return to their homes in safety and dignity.
- **Non-discrimination:** The Guiding Principles affirm that IDPs should not be discriminated against on the grounds of race, gender, religion, or ethnicity. Special attention must be given to the needs of vulnerable groups, such as women, children, the elderly, and people with disabilities.
- **Protection and Assistance:** States have the primary responsibility to protect and assist IDPs, including ensuring their access to basic needs like food, shelter, healthcare, and education. The international community is encouraged to support states in this regard.

The Guiding Principles are divided into four main areas:

- **Principles on Protection:** These principles focus on the protection of IDPs from violence, exploitation, and abuse, and their rights to security, family reunification, and participation in decisions that affect their lives.
- **Principles on Assistance:** These principles outline the need for humanitarian assistance, including food, water, shelter, health services, education, and employment for IDPs.
- **Principles on the Return or Resettlement of IDPs:** These principles emphasize the importance of allowing IDPs to return to their homes in conditions of safety and dignity or be resettled elsewhere within the country with the possibility of reintegration into society.
- **Principles on Monitoring:** These principles call for independent monitoring of the situation of IDPs to ensure that their rights are respected and protected.

International Human Rights Law and IDPs

International Human Rights Law (IHRL) provides fundamental rights to all individuals, including IDPs, and serves as an important complement to IHL in ensuring their protection. Relevant human rights instruments include:

- **Universal Declaration of Human Rights (UDHR) (1948):** Provides the fundamental rights of individuals, including the right to life, liberty, and security of person, which are crucial for IDPs.
- **International Covenant on Civil and Political Rights (ICCPR) (1966):** Recognizes the right of all individuals to security, freedom of movement, and protection from arbitrary displacement.
- **International Covenant on Economic, Social, and Cultural Rights (ICESCR) (1966):** Guarantees the right to adequate living standards, including food, water, shelter, and health, all of which are vital for IDPs.
- **Convention on the Elimination of All Forms of Racial Discrimination (CERD) (1965) and Convention on the Elimination of All Forms of Discrimination Against Women (CEDAW) (1979):** Protect vulnerable groups within IDP populations, such as ethnic minorities, women, and children, from discrimination and exploitation.

Human rights law mandates that governments take steps to ensure that the rights of IDPs are respected and upheld, and that they are not subjected to discrimination or arbitrary actions due to their displacement.

EXTRADITION AND ASYLUM

Extradition and asylum are two interconnected yet opposing concepts in international law. Extradition involves the surrender of a fugitive to a requesting state, while asylum provides protection to individuals fleeing persecution, often preventing their extradition. Both are governed by treaties, customary law, and domestic legislation.

EXTRADITION

- Extradition is the process by which one state (the requested state) surrenders an individual accused or convicted of a crime to another state (the requesting state) for trial or punishment.
- Derived from Latin "ex" (out) and "traditio" (delivery).

Legal Basis

- No General Obligation: No state is obliged to extradite under customary international law unless bound by a treaty or statute (Factor v. Laubenheimer, 1933).
- Sources:
  - ❑ Bilateral Treaties: E.g., India-USA Extradition Treaty (1997).
  - ❑ Multilateral Conventions: E.g., UN Convention Against Corruption (2003), Article 44.
  - ❑ Domestic Law: In India, governed by the Extradition Act, 1962.

Principles of Extradition

- **Double Criminality:**
  - ❑ The act must be a crime in both the requesting and requested states.
  - ❑ Example: Drug trafficking is extraditable; minor tax evasion may not be.
- **Specialty:** The extradited person can only be tried/punished for the offense specified in the extradition request.
- **Non-Inquiry Rule:** Requested state generally does not investigate the requesting state's judicial process.
- **Political Offense Exception:** Extradition is denied for political crimes (e.g., dissent, rebellion), except for terrorism-related acts post-9/11 conventions.

Process

- **Request:** Made via diplomatic channels with evidence (e.g., arrest warrant, charges).
- **Judicial Review:** Courts assess legality (e.g., prima facie case, exceptions).
- **Executive Decision:** Final approval by the government of the requested state.

Indian Framework: Extradition Act, 1962

- **Section 2(c):** Defines "extraditable offense" as per treaties or offenses punishable with imprisonment of 1+ year.
- **Section 3:** Governs extradition to treaty states (notified in Gazette).
- **Section 31:** Grounds for refusal:
  - ❑ Political offense (except terrorism per treaties).
  - ❑ Trivial nature of offense.
  - ❑ Risk of persecution based on race, religion, or politics.
  - ❑ Ongoing prosecution in India for the same act.
- **Treaties:** India has extradition treaties with 48+ countries (e.g., UK, USA, UAE) as of 2025.
- **Procedure (Chapter III):**
  - ❑ Magistrate inquiry (Section 5).
  - ❑ Central Government's discretion (Section 7).

Key Cases in India

- **Abu Salem v. State of Maharashtra (2010):** Extradited from Portugal; specialty principle enforced—could not face death penalty due to treaty assurances.
- **Vijay Mallya Case (Ongoing as of 2025):** UK extradition proceedings; illustrates economic offense extradition challenges.

Challenges

- Absence of treaties with some states (e.g., Pakistan).
- Political interference in executive decisions.
- Human rights concerns (e.g., fair trial in requesting state).

ASYLUM

- Asylum is the protection granted by a state to an individual who has fled their home country due to persecution or fear of persecution, often preventing extradition.
- **Types:**
  - ❑ **Territorial Asylum:** Protection within the host state's territory.
  - ❑ **Diplomatic Asylum:** Refuge in embassies (rare, not universally recognized except in Latin America).

Legal Basis

- **No Absolute Right:** No binding treaty mandates granting asylum; it's a sovereign prerogative (Hirsi Jamaa v. Italy, 2012 – ECHR).
- **Sources:**
  - ❑ Universal Declaration of Human Rights (UDHR), 1948:
    - ➾ **Article 14:** "Everyone has the right to seek and to enjoy in other countries asylum from persecution."
    - ➾ Not legally enforceable.
  - ❑ **1951 Refugee Convention:**
    - ➾ Indirectly supports asylum via non-refoulement (Article 33).
  - ❑ **Regional Instruments:**
    - ➾ 1969 OAU Convention (Africa).
    - ➾ 1954 Caracas Convention (Latin America–diplomatic asylum).

Principles of Asylum

- **Non-Refoulement:**
  - ❑ Core principle; prohibits return to a country where life/freedom is at risk (Article 33, 1951 Convention).
- **Sovereign Discretion:** States decide whom to grant asylum; no obligation exists (Columbia v. Peru – Asylum Case, 1950 – ICJ).
- **Humanitarian Basis:** Often granted for persecution not covered by extradition exceptions (e.g., political dissent).

India's Approach

- **Non-Signatory:** Not a party to the 1951 Refugee Convention or 1967 Protocol.
- **No Specific Law: Governed by:**
  - ❑ Foreigners Act, 1946: No distinction between refugees and illegal entrants.
  - ❑ **Constitution:**
    - ➾ **Article 21:** Right to life and liberty extends to asylum-seekers (NHRC v. State of Arunachal Pradesh, 1996 – Chakma refugees protected).
    - ➾ **Article 14:** Equality before law.
- **Policy:**
  - ❑ Ad hoc humanitarian asylum (e.g., Tibetans since 1959, Sri Lankan Tamils since 1980s).
  - ❑ UNHCR assists with Refugee Status Determination (RSD) for non-recognized groups (e.g., Rohingyas, Afghans).

Key Cases in India

- **Ktaer Abbas Habib Al Qutaifi v. Union of India (1999):** Gujarat HC upheld non-refoulement for Iraqi refugees under Article 21.
- **Mohammad Salimullah v. Union of India (2021):** Supreme Court permitted Rohingya deportation, prioritizing security over asylum rights.

Challenges

- **Security vs. Humanitarian Balance:** E.g., Rohingya influx viewed as a threat.
- **Lack of Legal Framework:** Inconsistent treatment (Tibetans favored; Rohingyas detained).
- **Diplomatic Asylum:** Rarely practiced (e.g., Julian Assange case irrelevant to India).

Relationship Between Extradition and Asylum

- **Conflict:** Asylum often prevents extradition if persecution is feared in the requesting state.
- **Political Offense Exception:** Overlaps with asylum grounds (e.g., dissenters not extradited).
- **Non-Refoulement:** Limits extradition where human rights violations are likely (Soering v. UK, 1989 – ECHR).
- **India's Practice:**
  - Grants asylum selectively, impacting extradition (e.g., no extradition of Tibetans to China).
  - Extradites when no asylum granted (e.g., Abu Salem).

International Framework

- **UN Conventions:**
  - **1951 Refugee Convention:** Asylum protection via non-refoulement.
  - **UNTOC (2000):** Extradition for transnational crimes (Article 16).
- **Extradition Treaties:** Bilateral agreements often include asylum-related exceptions.
- **ICJ Role:** Resolves disputes (e.g., Asylum Case, 1950 – Columbia denied diplomatic asylum to Peruvian fugitive).

Contemporary Issues (2025)

- **Mass Migration:** Syrian, Ukrainian, and Myanmar crises challenge extradition/asylum norms.
- **India's CAA (2019):** Grants citizenship to select refugees, excluding Muslims, affecting asylum policy.
- **Rohingya Debate:** India's deportation stance vs. UNHCR's asylum advocacy.

UNITED NATIONS (UN)

International organization established on October 24, 1945. The United Nations was the second multipurpose international organization established in the 20th century that was worldwide in scope and membership. Its predecessor, the League of Nations, was created by the Treaty of Versailles in 1919 and disbanded in 1946. Headquartered in New York City, the UN also has offices in Geneva, Vienna, and other cities. Its official languages are Arabic, Chinese, English, French, Russian, and Spanish.

According to its Charter, the UN aims: To save succeeding generations from the scourge of war, to reaffirm faith in fundamental human rights, to establish conditions under which justice and respect for the obligations arising from treaties and other sources of International Law can be maintained, and to promote social progress and better standards of life in larger freedom.

In addition to maintaining peace and security, other important objectives include developing friendly relations among countries based on respect for the principles of equal rights and self-determination of peoples; achieving worldwide cooperation to solve international economic, social, cultural, and humanitarian problems; respecting and promoting human rights; and serving as a centre where countries can coordinate their actions and activities toward these various ends.

HISTORY AND DEVELOPMENT

Despite the problems encountered by the League of Nations in arbitrating conflict and ensuring international peace and security prior to World War II, the major Allied powers agreed during the war to establish a new global organization to help manage international affairs. This agreement was first articulated when U.S. President Franklin D. Roosevelt and British Prime Minister Winston Churchill signed the Atlantic Charter in August 1941. The name United Nations was originally used to denote the countries allied against Germany, Italy, and Japan. On January 1, 1942, 26 countries signed the Declaration by United Nations, which set forth the war aims of the Allied powers.

The United States, the United Kingdom, and the Soviet Union took the lead in designing the new organization and determining its decision-making structure and functions. Initially, the "Big Three" states and their respective leaders (Roosevelt, Churchill, and Soviet premier Joseph Stalin) were hindered by disagreements on issues that foreshadowed the Cold War. The Soviet Union demanded individual membership and voting rights for its constituent republics, and Britain wanted assurances that its colonies would not be placed under UN control. There also was disagreement over the voting system to be adopted in the Security Council, an issue that became famous as the "veto problem."

The first major step toward the formation of the United Nations was taken August 21–October 7, 1944, at the Dumbarton Oaks Conference, a meeting of the diplomatic experts of the Big Three powers plus China (a group often designated the "Big Four") held at Dumbarton Oaks, an estate in Washington, D.C. Although the four countries agreed on the general purpose, structure, and function of a new world organization, the conference ended amid continuing disagreement over membership and voting. At the Yalta Conference, a meeting of the Big Three in a Crimean resort city in February 1945, Roosevelt, Churchill, and Stalin laid the basis for charter provisions delimiting the authority of the Security Council. Moreover, they reached a tentative accord on the number of Soviet republics to be granted independent memberships in the UN. Finally, the three leaders agreed that the new organization would include a trusteeship system to succeed the League of Nations mandate system.

The Dumbarton Oaks proposals, with modifications from the Yalta Conference, formed the basis of negotiations at the United Nations Conference on International Organization (UNCIO), which convened in San Francisco on April 25, 1945, and produced the final Charter of the United Nations. The San Francisco conference was attended by representatives of 50 countries from all geographic areas of the world: 9 from Europe, 21 from the Americas, 7 from the Middle East, 2 from East Asia, and 3 from Africa, as well as 1 each from the Ukrainian Soviet Socialist Republic and the Belarusian Soviet Socialist Republic (in addition to the Soviet Union itself) and 5 from British Commonwealth countries. Poland, which was not present at the conference, was permitted to become an original member of the UN. Security Council veto power (among the permanent members) was affirmed, though any member of the General Assembly was able to raise issues for discussion. Other political issues resolved by compromise were the role of the organization in the promotion of economic and social welfare; the status of colonial areas and the distribution of trusteeships; the status of regional and defense arrangements; and Great Power dominance versus the equality of states. The UN Charter was unanimously adopted and signed on June 26 and promulgated on October 24, 1945.

ORGANIZATION AND ADMINISTRATION

The purposes, principles, and organization of the United Nations are outlined in the Charter. The essential principles underlying the purposes and functions of the organization are listed in Article 2 and include the following: the UN is based on the sovereign equality of its members; disputes are to be settled by peaceful means; members are to refrain from the threat or use of force in contravention of the purposes of the UN; each member must assist the organization in any enforcement actions it takes under the Charter; and states that are not members of the organization are required to act in accordance with these principles insofar as it is necessary to maintain international peace and security. Article 2 also stipulates a basic long-standing norm that the organization shall not intervene in matters considered within the domestic jurisdiction of any state. Although this was a major limitation on UN action, over time the line between international and domestic jurisdiction has become blurred.

New members are admitted to the UN on the recommendation of the Security Council and by a two-thirds vote of the General Assembly.

PRINCIPAL ORGANS

The United Nations has six principal organs: the General Assembly, the Security Council, the Economic and Social Council, the Trusteeship Council, the International Court of Justice, and the Secretariat.

General Assembly

The only body in which all UN members are represented, the General Assembly exercises deliberative, supervisory, financial, and elective functions relating to any matter within the scope of the UN Charter. Its primary role, however, is to discuss issues and make recommendations, though it has no power to enforce its resolutions or to compel state action. Other functions include admitting new members; selecting members of the Economic and Social Council, the non-permanent members of the Security Council, and the Trusteeship Council; supervising the activities of the other UN organs, from which the Assembly receives reports; and participating in the election of judges to the International Court of Justice and the selection of the Secretary-General. Decisions usually are reached by a simple majority vote. On important questions, however—such as the admission of new members, budgetary matters, and peace and security issues—a two-thirds majority is required.

The Assembly convenes annually and in special sessions, electing a new President each year from among five regional groups of states. At the beginning of each regular session, the Assembly also holds a general debate, in which all members may participate and raise any issue of international concern. Most work, however, is delegated to six main committees: (1) Disarmament and International Security, (2) Economic and Financial, (3) Social, Humanitarian, and Cultural, (4) Special Political and Decolonization, (5) Administrative and Budgetary, and (6) Legal.

Security Council

The UN Charter assigns to the Security Council primary responsibility for the maintenance of international peace and security. The Security Council originally consisted of 11 members—five permanent and six non-permanent—elected by the General Assembly for two-year terms. From the beginning, non-permanent members of the Security Council were elected to give representation to certain regions or groups of states. As membership increased, however, this practice ran into difficulty. An amendment to the UN Charter in 1965 increased the council's membership to 15, including the original five permanent members plus 10 non-permanent members. Among the permanent members, the People's Republic of China replaced the Republic of China (Taiwan) in 1971, and the Russian Federation succeeded the Soviet Union in 1991. After the unification of Germany, debate over the council's composition again arose, and Germany, India, and Japan each applied for permanent council seats.

The non-permanent members are chosen to achieve equitable regional representation, five members coming from Africa or Asia, one from eastern Europe, two from Latin America, and two from western Europe or other areas. Five of the 10 non-permanent members are elected each year by the General Assembly for two-year terms, and five retire each year. The presidency is held by each member in rotation for a period of one month.

Each Security Council member is entitled to one vote. On all "procedural" matters—the definition of which is sometimes in dispute—decisions by the council are made by an affirmative vote of any nine of its members. Substantive matters, such as the investigation of a dispute or the application of sanctions, also require nine affirmative votes, including those of the five permanent members holding veto power. In practice, however, a permanent member may abstain without impairing the validity of the decision. A vote on whether a matter is procedural or substantive is itself a substantive question. Because the Security Council is required to function continuously, each member is represented at all times at the UN's headquarters in New York City.

Any country—even if it is not a member of the UN—may bring a dispute to which it is a party to the attention of the Security Council. When there is a complaint, the council first explores the possibility of a peaceful resolution. International peacekeeping forces may be authorized to keep warring parties apart pending further negotiations. If the council finds that there is a real threat to the peace, a breach of the peace, or an act of aggression (as defined by Article 39 of the UN Charter), it may call upon UN members to apply diplomatic or economic sanctions. If these methods prove inadequate, the UN Charter allows the Security Council to take military action against the offending country.

In addition to several standing and *ad hoc* committees, the work of the council is facilitated by the Military Staff Committee, sanctions committees for each of the countries under sanctions, peacekeeping forces committees, and an International Tribunals Committee.

Economic and Social Council

Designed to be the UN's main venue for the discussion of international economic and social issues, the Economic and Social Council (ECOSOC) directs and coordinates the economic, social, humanitarian, and cultural activities of the UN and its specialized agencies. Established by the UN Charter, ECOSOC is empowered to recommend international action on economic and social issues; promote universal respect for human rights; and work for global cooperation on health, education, and cultural and related areas. ECOSOC conducts studies; formulates resolutions, recommendations, and conventions for consideration by the General Assembly; and coordinates the activities of various UN programs and specialized agencies. Most of ECOSOC's work is performed in functional commissions on topics such as human rights, narcotics, population, social development, statistics, the status of women, and science and technology; the council also oversees regional commissions for Europe, Asia and the Pacific, Western Asia, Latin America, and Africa.

The UN Charter authorizes ECOSOC to grant consultative status to non-governmental organizations (NGOs). Three categories of consultative status are recognized: General Category NGOs (formerly category I) include organizations with multiple goals and activities; Special Category NGOs (formerly category II) specialize in certain areas of ECOSOC activities; and Roster NGOs have only an occasional interest in the UN's activities. Consultative status enables NGOs to attend ECOSOC meetings, issue reports, and occasionally testify at meetings. Since the mid1990s, measures have been adopted to increase the scope of NGO participation in ECOSOC, in the ad hoc global conferences, and in other UN activities. By the early 21st century, ECOSOC had granted consultative status to more than 2,500 NGOs.

Originally, ECOSOC consisted of representatives from 18 countries, but the Charter was amended in 1965 and in 1974 to increase the number of members to 54. Members are elected for three-year terms by the General Assembly. Four of the five permanent members of the Security Council—the United States, United Kingdom, Soviet Union (Russia), and France—have been re-elected continually because they provide funding for most of ECOSOC's budget, which is the largest of any UN subsidiary body. Decisions are taken by simple majority vote.

Trusteeship Council

The Trusteeship Council was designed to supervise the government of trust territories and to lead them to self-government or independence. The trusteeship system, like the mandate system under the League of Nations, was established on the premise that colonial territories taken from countries defeated in war should not be annexed by the victorious powers but should be administered by a trust country under international supervision until their future status was determined. Unlike the mandate system, the trusteeship system invited petitions from trust territories on their independence and required periodic international missions to the territories. In 1945 only 12 League of Nations mandates remained: Nauru, New Guinea, Ruanda-Urundi, Togoland and Cameroon (French administered), Togoland and Cameroon (British administered), the Pacific Islands (Carolines, Marshalls, and Marianas), Western Samoa, South-west Africa, Tanganyika, and Palestine. All these mandates became trust territories except South-west Africa (now Namibia), which South Africa refused to enter into the trusteeship system.

The Trusteeship Council, which met once each year, consisted of states administering trust territories, permanent members of the Security Council that did not administer trust territories, and other UN members elected by the General Assembly. Each member had one vote, and decisions were taken by a simple majority of those present. With the independence of Palau, the last remaining trust territory, in 1994, the council terminated its operations. No longer required to meet annually, the council may meet on the decision of its president or on a request by a majority of its members, by the General Assembly, or by the Security Council. Since 1994 new roles for the council have been proposed, including administering the global commons (*e.g.*, the seabed and outer space) and serving as a forum for minority and indigenous peoples.

International Court of Justice

The International Court of Justice, commonly known as the World Court, is the principal judicial organ of the United Nations, though the court's origins predate the League of Nations. The idea for the creation of an international court to arbitrate international disputes arose during an international conference held at The Hague in 1899. This institution was subsumed under the League of Nations in 1919 as the Permanent Court of International Justice (PCIJ) and adopted its present name with the founding of the UN in 1945.

The court's decisions are binding, and its broad jurisdiction encompasses "all cases which the parties refer to it and all matters specially provided for in the Charter of the United Nations or in treaties and conventions in force." Most importantly, states may not be parties to a dispute without their consent, though they may accept the compulsory jurisdiction of the court in specified categories of disputes. The court may give advisory opinions at the request of the General Assembly or the Security Council or at the request of other organs and specialized agencies authorized by the General Assembly. Although the court has successfully arbitrated some cases (*e.g.*, the border dispute between Honduras and El Salvador in 1992), governments have been reluctant to submit sensitive issues, thereby limiting the court's ability to resolve threats to international peace and security. At times countries also have refused to acknowledge the jurisdiction or the findings of the court. For example, when Nicaragua sued the United States in the court in 1984 for mining its harbours, the court found in favour of Nicaragua, but the United States refused to accept the court's decision.

The 15 judges of the court are elected by the General Assembly and the Security Council voting independently. No two judges may be nationals of the same state, and the judges are to represent a cross section of the major legal systems of the world. Judges serve nine-year terms and are eligible for re-election. The seat of the World Court is The Hague.

Secretariat

The Secretary-General, the principal administrative officer of the United Nations, is elected for a five-year renewable term by a two-thirds vote of the General Assembly and by the recommendation of the Security Council and the approval of its permanent members. Secretaries-general usually have come from small, neutral countries. The Secretary-General serves as the chief administrative officer at all meetings and carries out any functions that those organs entrust to the Secretariat; he also oversees the preparation of the UN's budget. The secretary-general has important political functions, being charged with bringing before the organization any matter that threatens international peace and security. Both the chief spokesperson for the UN and the UN's most visible and authoritative figure in world affairs, the Secretary-General often serve as a high-level negotiator.

FLAG

The UN flag, adopted in 1947, consists of the official emblem of the organization (a circular world map, as seen from the North Pole, surrounded by a wreath of olive branches) in white centred on a light blue background. The Assembly designated October 24 as United Nations Day.

SETTLEMENT OF INTERNATIONAL DISPUTES

Introduction to International Disputes

International disputes refer to conflicts or disagreements that arise between sovereign states, international organizations, or between a state and an international organization. These disputes can be political, territorial, economic, or legal in nature. Resolving such disputes is crucial for maintaining peace and stability at the global level.

Definition of International Disputes

An international dispute is a disagreement between two or more parties (countries or international entities) over a particular issue that affects their relations. These disputes may involve issues such as borders, legal rights, international agreements, economic interests, or human rights.

International disputes can escalate if not resolved amicably, and they may result in conflict, war, or harm to international relations. Therefore, a well-established framework under international law exists to manage and settle these disputes peacefully.

Types of International Disputes

International disputes can be broadly classified into the following types:

- **Territorial Disputes**
  - These disputes arise when two or more countries lay claim to the same land or territory.
  - **Examples:** Kashmir dispute between India and Pakistan, South China Sea disputes among China, Vietnam, the Philippines, and other Southeast Asian nations.
- **Legal Disputes**
  - These involve conflicts over the interpretation or application of international law, including issues of sovereignty, human rights, or maritime boundaries.
  - Examples: Legal disputes concerning the interpretation of treaties like the Geneva Conventions, or disputes over state sovereignty and jurisdiction in cases like the *Nicaragua v. United States* case at the International Court of Justice (ICJ).
- **Economic Disputes**
  - These disputes arise from trade disagreements, financial issues, sanctions, or disputes over international trade agreements.
  - Examples: Disputes in the World Trade Organization (WTO) regarding trade barriers, tariffs, or subsidies; the ongoing trade conflict between the United States and China.
- **Cultural and Ideological Disputes**
  - These disputes are rooted in cultural, religious, or ideological differences between states or within regions.
  - Examples: The ideological divide during the Cold War between communist and capitalist nations, conflicts arising from religious differences.
- **Environmental Disputes**
  - Environmental concerns often lead to international disputes, especially over natural resources, pollution, or climate change agreements.
  - Examples: Disputes regarding water sharing in trans-boundary rivers (like the Nile between Egypt and Sudan), disputes over carbon emissions under the Paris Agreement.
- **Human Rights Disputes**
  - These occur when states violate or are accused of violating human rights, leading to conflict with other states, NGOs, or international bodies.
  - Example: The Rohingya crisis in Myanmar, or the conflict between Israel and Palestine over human rights concerns.

Peaceful Settlement of Disputes

The peaceful settlement of international disputes is a fundamental principle of international law, ensuring that conflicts between states or other international entities are resolved without resorting to the use of force. The United Nations (UN) Charter, particularly in its provisions under Chapter VI, emphasizes the importance of resolving disputes through peaceful means. A peaceful approach to resolving disputes helps maintain international peace and security, fostering cooperation among states.

Principles of Peaceful Settlement of Disputes

The following principles guide the peaceful settlement of international disputes:

- **Non-Use of Force (Article 2(4) of the UN Charter)**
  - One of the key principles of peaceful dispute resolution is the prohibition on the use of force. States are prohibited from threatening or using force against the territorial integrity or political independence of any state.

- Example: The UN Charter explicitly bans the use of force unless authorized by the UN Security Council or in cases of self-defense (Article 51 of the UN Charter).
- The principle emphasizes diplomatic and legal methods of dispute resolution, avoiding conflict escalation.

- **Respect for Sovereignty**
  - Sovereignty refers to the principle that states have exclusive control over their territory and political decisions, free from external interference.
  - A dispute should be settled in a manner that respects each state's sovereignty, ensuring that the solution does not undermine a state's territorial integrity or political autonomy.
  - Example: Disputes over the sovereignty of regions like Kashmir (India vs. Pakistan) or Crimea (Russia vs. Ukraine) often require the involvement of international law to find peaceful solutions that respect sovereignty.
- **Good Faith**
  - States must engage in dispute resolution processes with a genuine intent to resolve the conflict and in accordance with the principle of good faith.
  - This includes fulfilling obligations arising from treaties or negotiations and making a genuine effort to reach a compromise or agreement.
  - Example: The successful negotiation of the Camp David Accords between Egypt and Israel in 1978 involved both countries engaging in good faith discussions with the aim of achieving lasting peace.
- **Non-Intervention**
  - States must avoid interfering in the internal affairs of other states, and disputes should be resolved through consensual means rather than through external intervention.
  - The principle of non-intervention is enshrined in Article 2(7) of the UN Charter, which prohibits the UN from intervening in matters that are essentially within the domestic jurisdiction of any state.
- **Equity and Justice**
  - A fair and just resolution is vital for the peaceful settlement of disputes. Disputes should be resolved equitably, considering the interests of all parties involved.
  - This principle is reflected in the role of international legal bodies such as the International Court of Justice (ICJ), which strives to provide impartial and just decisions based on international law.

Methods of Peaceful Settlement of Disputes

The peaceful settlement of international disputes can be achieved through various methods. These methods involve negotiation, dialogue, and third-party intervention. The key methods are:

- **Diplomacy**
  - Diplomacy involves direct communication between the disputing parties to resolve their differences through dialogue and negotiation.
  - Diplomacy is typically the first method employed when a dispute arises and is often conducted through diplomatic channels, including embassies, foreign ministries, and international conferences.
  - Example: The Cuban Missile Crisis (1962) is a historical instance where diplomacy played a key role in resolving a highly volatile dispute between the United States and the Soviet Union.
- **Negotiation**
  - Negotiation refers to the process where the parties in dispute attempt to resolve their differences through direct talks, without the involvement of any third party.
  - The goal of negotiation is to reach a mutually agreeable solution by addressing the underlying issues and finding a compromise that satisfies both parties' needs.
  - Example: The Iran nuclear deal (JCPOA) negotiations, which involved multiple parties including the U.S., Iran, and other P5+1 countries, aimed to reach a resolution on Iran's nuclear program.
- **Mediation**
  - Mediation involves the use of a neutral third party (a mediator) to help the disputing parties reach an agreement. The mediator does not have decision-making power but facilitates communication and suggests possible solutions.
  - Mediation is especially useful when the parties are at an impasse or unable to communicate effectively.
  - Example: The United Nations often mediates in conflicts between states, such as the mediation efforts in the 1990s during the peace talks between Israel and Palestine.

- **Conciliation**
  - Conciliation is a process in which a neutral third party, known as the conciliator, actively investigates the dispute and proposes solutions or compromises that can be accepted by both parties.
  - Unlike mediation, the conciliator may have a more active role in proposing solutions, but the final decision is still left to the parties.
  - Example: Conciliation was successfully used in the Beagle Channel dispute between Argentina and Chile (mediated by the Pope in 1978, leading to a treaty in 1984)
- **Arbitration**
  - Arbitration is a more formalized process in which the disputing parties agree to submit their case to a neutral third party (arbitrators) for a binding decision.
  - Arbitration is typically used for legal disputes, and the arbitrators' decision is final and binding on the parties involved.
  - Example: The Permanent Court of Arbitration (PCA) at The Hague has handled significant international arbitrations, such as the Philippines v. China (South China Sea arbitration) in 2016, which delivered a binding decision.
- **Judicial Settlement**
  - Judicial settlement involves the formal resolution of disputes by a court, usually the International Court of Justice (ICJ), which is the principal judicial organ of the United Nations.
  - The ICJ settles disputes between states in accordance with international law, and its decisions are binding on the parties involved.
  - Example: The ICJ's 2002 judgment in the *Kasikili/Sedudu Island* case between Botswana and Namibia resolved a long-standing territorial dispute.
- **Involvement of International Organizations**
  - International organizations such as the United Nations (UN), Organization of American States (OAS), and the African Union (AU) often play a key role in facilitating peaceful dispute resolution.
  - These organizations provide platforms for dialogue, mediate peace talks, and sometimes deploy peacekeeping missions to ensure the enforcement of peace agreements.
  - Example: The role of the United Nations in peacekeeping operations in Cyprus (UNFICYP) has been instrumental in preventing further conflict and promoting a peaceful resolution to the territorial dispute.

Conclusion

The peaceful settlement of disputes is a cornerstone of international law, aimed at preventing conflict and promoting global stability. The principles of peaceful settlement, including non-use of force and respect for sovereignty, serve as the foundation for resolving disputes in a fair and just manner. Methods such as diplomacy, negotiation, mediation, and conciliation provide flexible and constructive pathways for states to resolve their differences, ensuring that peace and security are maintained in the international community. Through these mechanisms, international law fosters cooperation among states and promotes the peaceful resolution of conflicts.

WORLD TRADE ORGANISATION (WTO)

The **World Trade Organization (WTO)** is the only global international organization dealing with the rules of trade between nations. Established to promote free trade by regulating and facilitating international trade agreements, the WTO plays a central role in the global economy. Its core function is to ensure that trade flows as smoothly, predictably, and freely as possible.

History and Establishment of the WTO

- **Origins:** The roots of the WTO can be traced back to the **Bretton Woods Conference** (1944), where the idea of a global trade organization was first discussed. The aim was to prevent the trade barriers and economic protectionism that had contributed to the **Great Depression** and the economic turmoil of the 1930s.
- **Formation of GATT (1947):** Before the establishment of the WTO, the **General Agreement on Tariffs and Trade (GATT)** was created in **1947** to facilitate international trade and reduce tariffs and trade barriers. GATT was a multilateral agreement to promote trade liberalization, but it lacked institutional structure and a robust dispute resolution mechanism.
- **WTO Establishment (1995):** The **World Trade Organization** was officially established on **January 1, 1995**, following the **Uruguay Round** negotiations, which were concluded in 1994. The WTO succeeded GATT and brought the multilateral trading system under a more structured and formalized organization.

Formation of the General Agreement on Tariffs and Trade (GATT)

- **GATT (1947–1994)** was a multilateral treaty aimed at promoting international trade by reducing tariffs and other trade barriers. It was based on the principles of **non-discrimination, free trade, and reciprocity**.
- **Key Provisions of GATT:**
  - **Most-Favored-Nation (MFN) Principle:** Ensures that if one country offers a trade concession to another, it must offer the same concession to all GATT members.
  - **National Treatment Principle:** Countries must treat foreign goods and services the same way as domestic ones after they have been imported.
  - **Tariff Reduction:** GATT aimed at reducing tariffs through successive rounds of negotiations.
- **Success of GATT:** The GATT rounds of negotiations (such as the **Kennedy Round**, **Tokyo Round**, and **Uruguay Round**) successfully reduced tariffs and trade barriers, fostering global economic growth.
- **Limitations of GATT:**
  - GATT primarily focused on trade in goods, while services and intellectual property rights were largely ignored.
  - The dispute resolution mechanism was weak and informal, often leading to unresolved trade disputes.
  - **GATT's lack of institutional backing** made it harder to enforce agreements or monitor compliance.

Transition from GATT to WTO

The **Uruguay Round** (1986-1994) negotiations were crucial for the transformation from **GATT** to the **WTO**:

- **Finalization of the Uruguay Round:** After extensive negotiations, the **Uruguay Round** concluded in **1994**. This round addressed not only tariffs on goods but also trade in services and intellectual property rights. The agreements reached under the Uruguay Round led to the creation of the WTO.
- **Reasons for Transition:**
  - GATT was unable to adequately address **trade in services** or **intellectual property**.
  - A more **structured dispute resolution system** was needed.
  - GATT lacked an institutional structure, making enforcement and compliance difficult.
- **WTO's Role Post-1995:** The WTO addressed these gaps by expanding its scope to include **trade in services**, **intellectual property rights**, and **investment**. It also provided a formal, legally binding mechanism for resolving disputes, making the global trade system more efficient and fair.

Key Objectives and Functions of the WTO

The WTO has several key objectives and functions that aim to ensure the smooth operation of global trade.

Key Objectives of WTO:

- **Promoting Trade Liberalization:** The WTO works to promote the reduction of trade barriers (tariffs, quotas, subsidies, etc.) and facilitate smooth international trade.
- **Ensuring Trade Security and Predictability:** The WTO aims to create a predictable trading environment, helping businesses plan for the long term with more confidence and security.
- **Facilitating Negotiations:** The WTO provides a forum for member countries to negotiate trade agreements and resolve trade-related issues.
- **Resolving Trade Disputes:** One of the key functions of the WTO is to provide a dispute settlement mechanism for resolving trade disputes between member countries.
- **Providing Technical Assistance and Capacity Building:** The WTO assists developing countries by providing technical support, training, and capacity-building measures to help them benefit from the global trading system.
- **Promoting Fair Competition:** The WTO aims to establish and enforce fair trading practices globally, ensuring that no country engages in unfair trade practices such as dumping or unfair subsidies.

Functions of the WTO:

- **Administering WTO Trade Agreements:** The WTO oversees the implementation of the various multilateral trade agreements, ensuring that member countries adhere to the rules.
- **Dispute Settlement Mechanism:** The WTO provides a formal, binding dispute resolution process to settle disputes between members over trade-related issues, ensuring that trade conflicts are resolved impartially and based on agreed rules.
- **Monitoring Trade Policies:** The WTO monitors the trade policies of its members to ensure transparency and compliance with agreed norms and rules. This is done through periodic reviews

of trade practices under the **Trade Policy Review Mechanism (TPRM)**.

- **Technical Assistance and Capacity Building:** The WTO provides developing and least-developed countries with the technical expertise and support they need to participate in the global trading system and improve their trade capacities.
- **Trade Negotiations:** The WTO serves as a forum for trade negotiations, where member countries can discuss and negotiate reductions in tariffs, subsidies, and other trade barriers.

Organizational Structure of the WTO

The **WTO** is organized to ensure efficient functioning and decision-making. The key components of its organizational structure are:

- **Ministerial Conference:** The **Ministerial Conference** is the highest decision-making body of the WTO. It meets at least once every two years to set the direction and policies of the organization. All member countries are represented at this conference.
- **General Council:** The **General Council** is responsible for overseeing the day-to-day functioning of the WTO and ensuring that its policies are being implemented. It meets regularly and is composed of all member countries, each of which has a representative.
- **Dispute Settlement Body (DSB):** The **DSB** is responsible for adjudicating trade disputes between WTO members. It oversees the dispute settlement process and ensures that rulings are enforced.
- **Trade Policy Review Body (TPRB):** The **TPRB** is responsible for monitoring the trade policies of all WTO members. It reviews the trade policies of each member periodically to ensure compliance with WTO rules.
- **Committees and Working Groups:** The WTO has several committees and working groups that deal with specific areas such as trade in services, agriculture, intellectual property, and trade facilitation. These bodies make recommendations and reports on issues related to trade.
- **WTO Secretariat:** The **WTO Secretariat** is responsible for providing technical and logistical support to the organization's various bodies. The Secretariat is headed by the **Director-General**, who is appointed for a renewable term.

Dispute Settlement Mechanism of the WTO

The **Dispute Settlement Mechanism (DSM)** is one of the most crucial functions of the **World Trade Organization (WTO)**. It provides a legal and formal process for resolving disputes that arise between member countries regarding the interpretation and application of WTO agreements. The mechanism aims to ensure that trade flows smoothly and predictably by addressing trade conflicts in a fair and impartial manner.

Overview of the WTO Dispute Settlement Process

The WTO dispute settlement process is designed to be transparent, efficient, and legally binding. It operates on the principle that disputes should be resolved as quickly as possible, with minimal disruption to international trade. The main objective is to uphold the rules agreed upon by the member states, ensuring that countries adhere to their commitments under WTO agreements.

Key Features of the WTO Dispute Settlement System:

- **Binding Nature of Rulings:** Unlike many other international organizations, the WTO's dispute resolution process produces binding rulings that member states must follow.
- **Multilateral Approach:** The WTO emphasizes that disputes should be resolved in a multilateral framework, and members should adhere to established rules and precedents.
- **Impartial Process:** The process is based on objective legal principles, ensuring that all members are treated equally.
- **Timely Resolution:** Efforts are made to resolve disputes in a timely manner to avoid disruption in trade relations.

Steps in the WTO Dispute Resolution Process

The WTO dispute resolution process is designed to ensure fair treatment for all members involved. It follows a step-by-step approach to resolve conflicts, with each step offering opportunities for dialogue, adjudication, and compliance.

- **Consultations:**
  - The first step in the dispute settlement process is **consultation** between the parties involved in the dispute. If a member believes another member is violating WTO rules or obligations, it must first request consultations.

- **Consultation Timeline:** The WTO encourages countries to resolve disputes through consultations within **60 days**. If consultations fail to resolve the issue, the complaining party may request the establishment of a panel.
- **Purpose:** Consultations aim to clarify the issues, facilitate negotiation, and provide a chance for the dispute to be resolved amicably without resorting to a formal legal process.

- **Panel Stage:**
  - If consultations fail, the next step is to request the establishment of a **panel**. The **Dispute Settlement Body (DSB)** of the WTO establishes a panel of independent experts to examine the dispute and provide a ruling.
  - **Panel Composition:** Panels usually consist of three to five experts who are selected from a roster maintained by the WTO. The panelists are chosen based on their expertise in international trade law and the specific issues at hand.
  - **Panel Report:** The panel examines the case, reviews the arguments, and makes a ruling based on the facts and WTO agreements. The panel issues a report with findings of law and fact.
  - **Timeline:** Panels are expected to issue their reports within **six months**.
- **Appeals (Appellate Body):**
  - After the panel issues its report, either party can appeal the ruling if they believe the panel has made legal errors.
  - **Appellate Body:** The appeal is made to the **Appellate Body**, which is composed of seven members. The Appellate Body's role is to review legal findings, not to reassess the factual findings of the panel.
  - **Appellate Body Procedures:**
    - The Appellate Body can either **uphold**, **modify**, or **reverse** the panel's decision.
    - The Appellate Body issues its report within **60 days** of receiving the appeal.
  - **Binding Nature:** The decisions made by the Appellate Body are final and binding on the parties involved, subject only to the possibility of an appeal to the **DSB** for non-compliance.
- **Implementation of Ruling:**
  - Once the panel or Appellate Body has made a final ruling, the losing party is expected to **comply** with the decision and take corrective actions, such as amending policies, withdrawing offending measures, or providing compensation.
  - **Implementation Deadline:** The WTO typically provides a reasonable period (usually **15 to 18 months**) for the member to comply with the ruling.
- **Retaliation (If Compliance Fails):**
  - If the losing party fails to comply with the ruling within the prescribed time frame, the winning party may request **retaliatory measures**. This involves the imposition of trade sanctions or **compensation** in the form of market access.
  - **Compensation** is typically provided through negotiation, but if an agreement cannot be reached, the retaliatory measures can be imposed with the approval of the DSB.

Role of the Appellate Body

The **Appellate Body** plays a critical role in the WTO's dispute settlement system. It acts as the final judicial authority on legal disputes, ensuring that the interpretation and application of WTO agreements are consistent and coherent.

Key Functions of the Appellate Body:

- **Review of Panel Decisions:** The Appellate Body reviews the legal aspects of the panel's ruling. It ensures that the panel has correctly interpreted and applied the relevant WTO agreements and legal principles.
- **Ensuring Legal Consistency:** The Appellate Body helps maintain consistency in WTO law by ensuring that decisions are aligned with past rulings and the established interpretation of WTO rules.
- **Legal Interpretation:** The Appellate Body interprets and clarifies the meaning of various provisions of WTO agreements, thereby contributing to the development of WTO jurisprudence.
- **Final Decision-Making:** The Appellate Body's rulings are **final** and legally binding, making it a critical institution for maintaining the authority and credibility of the WTO dispute settlement system.

Structure of the Appellate Body

- The Appellate Body is composed of **seven members**, but only **three** members hear any particular case.

- **Appellate Body members are appointed for a term of 4 years**, and they can serve up to two terms.
- **Independence and Impartiality:** Members of the Appellate Body must be independent and cannot be influenced by external pressures. They are appointed based on their expertise in international trade law, economics, and dispute resolution.

Key Issues with the Appellate Body:

- **Disputes over Appointments:** In recent years, there have been difficulties in appointing new members to the Appellate Body, leading to concerns about the body's functioning. As of 2020, the **Appellate Body was effectively non-functional** due to the blockage of appointments by the United States, which has created a crisis in the dispute settlement process.

INTERNATIONAL HUMANITARIAN LAW (IHL)

IHL – CONVENTIONS AND PROTOCOLS

International Humanitarian Law (IHL), also known as the **Law of Armed Conflict (LOAC)** or the **Law of War**, is a branch of international law designed to regulate the conduct of armed conflicts and mitigate their humanitarian consequences. IHL seeks to protect those who are not, or no longer, taking part in hostilities (such as civilians, prisoners of war, and the wounded) and restrict the means and methods of warfare.

Definition and Objectives of IHL

IHL is defined as the body of rules that, in times of armed conflict, seeks to:

- **Limit the effects of armed conflict** for humanitarian reasons.
- **Protect persons who are not or are no longer participants** in the hostilities, including civilians, medical personnel, and prisoners of war.
- **Regulate the means and methods of warfare**, ensuring that military actions are conducted in a manner that is both necessary and proportional, avoiding unnecessary suffering or harm to civilian life and property.

The objectives of IHL are to:

- **Preserve humanity** by minimizing suffering during conflicts.
- **Ensure protection** for civilians, prisoners of war, and other non-combatants.
- **Maintain the legal rights and dignity** of those who are caught up in war.
- **Promote peace and stability** through the enforcement of international standards and norms.

Sources of IHL

The primary sources of IHL are:

- **Treaties**:
  - ❑ The **Geneva Conventions of 1949** and their **Additional Protocols (1977)** are the cornerstone of IHL, laying down the rules regarding the protection of persons in armed conflict.
  - ❑ The **Hague Conventions** (1899 and 1907) outline the laws governing the conduct of warfare, including the treatment of prisoners, the protection of cultural property, and the regulation of weapons.
  - ❑ Other treaties include specific agreements on the use of particular weapons, such as the **Chemical Weapons Convention (1993)** and the **Ottawa Convention on Landmines (1997)**.
- **Customary International Law**: These are unwritten rules that are derived from the consistent practice of states and have evolved through widespread state practice and legal acceptance. For example, the **prohibition of targeting civilians** is considered a customary rule of IHL, even if not explicitly mentioned in treaties.
- **Judicial Decisions**: Decisions from international courts, such as the **International Court of Justice (ICJ)**, **International Criminal Court (ICC)**, and ad hoc tribunals like the **International Criminal Tribunal for the former Yugoslavia (ICTY)**, contribute to the interpretation and clarification of IHL principles.
- **General Principles of Law**: These include recognized principles of law derived from the **national legal systems** of states, such as the principle of **proportionality** and **necessity** in the use of force.

Relationship between IHL and Human Rights Law

While **IHL** governs the conduct of parties during armed conflicts, **human rights law** applies at all times, including during peace and conflict. The relationship between the two is crucial for understanding their complementary and sometimes overlapping roles:

- **Human Rights Law**: Applies at all times, in peace and conflict, and aims to protect the fundamental rights and freedoms of individuals (e.g., the right to life, freedom from torture).
- **IHL**: Only applies in situations of armed conflict and is concerned with **limiting the effects of war**, rather than promoting or protecting human rights in peacetime.

Differences:

- IHL specifically applies during armed conflict, whereas human rights law is a more general set of norms that apply at all times, including during peacetime.
- Human rights law generally applies to **individuals** and **states**, whereas IHL applies to both **states** and **non-state actors** involved in armed conflict.

Complementary Aspects:

- In situations of armed conflict, **IHL provides the specific protections for individuals**, while human rights law offers broader protections, including in situations where IHL may not apply. Together, they ensure comprehensive protection during both peacetime and conflict.

Overlap:

- For example, the **right to life** is protected under both human rights law and IHL. In situations of armed conflict, IHL allows for the taking of life in certain situations (e.g., during combat) but places limitations to ensure that killings are not arbitrary.

Basic Principles of IHL

The core principles of IHL form the basis for its rules and ensure that the actions of parties to armed conflict are humane and necessary. The following are the four key principles:

- **Necessity**:
  - The principle of necessity dictates that force may only be used to achieve a military objective and must not be excessive in relation to the expected military advantage. This principle helps to limit the scope of the violence used in warfare, ensuring that actions are not arbitrary.
  - Example: A military operation may only target enemy combatants and military objectives, not civilians or civilian objects, unless they are directly contributing to the enemy's military efforts.
- **Proportionality**:
  - The principle of proportionality seeks to limit the harm caused during warfare by ensuring that the military advantage gained is not outweighed by the harm caused to civilians or civilian infrastructure.
  - This principle often comes into play when there are concerns about collateral damage. Attacks that cause excessive harm to civilians, in relation to the expected military gain, are prohibited.
  - Example: A military strike on a target may be deemed disproportionate if it is likely to cause significant civilian casualties that outweigh any potential military benefit.
- **Distinction**:
  - One of the fundamental principles of IHL, the principle of distinction, requires parties to a conflict to always distinguish between combatants (who may be targeted) and non-combatants (such as civilians, prisoners of war, and the wounded, who are protected from attack).
  - Attacks must be directed solely at military objectives, and parties must refrain from attacking civilian infrastructure, hospitals, schools, and other protected objects.
  - Example: In an airstrike, the military must ensure that the target is a legitimate military objective and not a civilian building.
- **Humanity**:
  - The principle of humanity reflects the need for respect for human dignity and rights during armed conflict. It ensures that even in times of war, individuals are treated with respect, and unnecessary suffering is avoided.
  - It prohibits the use of methods or means of warfare that cause unnecessary suffering, such as the use of weapons or tactics that inflict excessive harm.
  - Example: The use of chemical weapons, which cause extreme and lasting suffering, is prohibited by the Geneva Protocol of 1925 and later treaties.

Geneva Conventions of 1949

The **Geneva Conventions of 1949** are a set of four treaties that form the core of **International Humanitarian Law (IHL)**. They were adopted to provide legal protections to individuals affected by armed conflicts, with an emphasis on the humane treatment of persons who are not actively participating in hostilities.

Overview and Purpose of the Four Geneva Conventions

- **First Geneva Convention** (for the Amelioration of the Condition of the Wounded and Sick in Armed Forces in the Field)
  - **Purpose**: Protects wounded and sick soldiers on land during armed conflict.
  - **Key Provisions**: Ensures that military personnel who are wounded or sick are cared for and protected. It mandates the establishment of medical units and hospitals and guarantees their neutrality.
- **Second Geneva Convention** (for the Amelioration of the Condition of the Wounded, Sick, and Shipwrecked Members of Armed Forces at Sea)
  - **Purpose**: Extends protections to those wounded, sick, or shipwrecked at sea.
  - **Key Provisions**: Similar to the first, but applies to maritime warfare. It protects those at sea from attack and ensures the humane treatment of casualties.
- **Third Geneva Convention** (Relative to the Treatment of Prisoners of War)
  - **Purpose**: Protects prisoners of war (POWs) during armed conflict.
  - **Key Provisions**: Outlines the rights of POWs, ensuring humane treatment, access to food, shelter, and medical care. It prohibits torture and ensures fair treatment during captivity.
- **Fourth Geneva Convention** (Relative to the Protection of Civilian Persons in Time of War)
  - **Purpose**: Provides protection to civilians during times of armed conflict, especially under occupation.
  - **Key Provisions**: Ensures the protection of civilians from violence, exploitation, and deprivation. It prohibits attacks on civilians and mandates the care and protection of civilian property.

Significance

The Geneva Conventions of 1949 established comprehensive humanitarian standards for the treatment of individuals during armed conflicts and serve as a foundation for IHL, setting norms to limit the effects of war. These conventions are universally accepted and have been ratified by nearly all countries worldwide.

Additional Protocols to the Geneva Conventions (1977)

The **Additional Protocols** to the Geneva Conventions, adopted in **1977**, were designed to enhance the protections provided by the original 1949 Geneva Conventions, addressing emerging challenges in modern warfare. They are crucial in expanding the scope of protections to include more specific situations and modern methods of warfare.

Overview of the Additional Protocols:

- **Protocol I** (Protection of Victims of International Armed Conflicts)
  - **Purpose**: Expands the protections for victims in **international armed conflicts** (wars between states).
  - **Key Provisions**:
    - **Extended protection for civilians**: Prohibits attacks on civilians and civilian infrastructure, emphasizing the principle of distinction (combatants vs civilians).
    - **Combatants' rights**: Provides protections for combatants, including the prohibition on killing those who surrender or are hors de combat (out of combat).
    - **Prohibition of certain weapons**: Bans the use of weapons that cause excessive injury or unnecessary suffering (e.g., chemical and biological weapons).
    - **Protection of medical units and personnel**: Ensures the protection of medical personnel and facilities.
- **Protocol II** (Protection of Victims of Non-International Armed Conflicts)
  - **Purpose**: Extends IHL to **non-international armed conflicts** (civil wars or conflicts involving non-state armed groups).
  - **Key Provisions**:
    - **Minimum standards of humanitarian treatment**: Establishes basic protections for civilians and fighters in non-international conflicts, including the prohibition of torture, degrading treatment, and hostage-taking.
    - **Protection for non-combatants**: Prohibits attacks on civilians and civilian objects, ensuring the humane treatment of all individuals in conflict zones.

- **No targeting of persons not taking part in hostilities**: Outlines clear rules for the treatment of those who are not actively involved in combat, including detainees and the wounded.

- **Protocol III** (Adoption of the Additional Emblem- The Red Crystal)
  - **Purpose**: Introduces the **Red Crystal** as an additional emblem to complement the Red Cross and Red Crescent.
  - **Key Provisions**:
    - **Emblem neutrality**: The Red Crystal emblem was introduced as a neutral and non-religious symbol for use in situations where the Red Cross or Red Crescent symbols could be seen as controversial.
    - **Universal use**: It provides another option for humanitarian organizations to mark their identity and gain protection under IHL.

The Hague Conventions (1899 and 1907)

The **Hague Conventions** are a series of international treaties that aimed to regulate the conduct of warfare and the treatment of individuals during armed conflicts, focusing on the **laws and customs of war**. These conventions laid down rules for military operations, the treatment of prisoners of war, and the protection of civilians and cultural property.

Overview of the Hague Conventions:

- **Hague Convention of 1899 (First)**
  - **Purpose**: The first significant effort to establish rules for the conduct of war and the treatment of war victims.
  - **Key Provisions**:
    - **Laws and customs of war on land**: Established rules for the conduct of hostilities on land, including the treatment of prisoners, the protection of civilians, and the prohibition of certain types of weapons.
    - **Declaration of Paris (1856)**: The convention reaffirmed the rules governing the use of blockades and privateers.
    - **Warfare regulations**: Set standards for the conduct of warfare, including the treatment of enemy prisoners and the protection of neutral nations during conflict.

- **Hague Convention of 1907 (Second)**
  - **Purpose**: Expanded and refined the 1899 rules and added new provisions to address changing military tactics and technological developments.
  - **Key Provisions**:
    - **Laws and customs of war on land (Article 23-56)**: Strengthened rules for the treatment of prisoners of war, prohibitions on certain types of weapons (e.g., expanding bullets), and protections for civilians.
    - **Regulation of warfare at sea**: Included provisions on naval warfare, the rights of neutral powers, and the treatment of captured ships and cargo.
    - **Protection of cultural property**: Established guidelines for the protection of cultural property in times of war (e.g., libraries, museums, and monuments).

Significance:

The Hague Conventions laid the foundation for modern International Humanitarian Law, regulating warfare and ensuring humanitarian treatment during armed conflicts.

The Rome Statute of the International Criminal Court (ICC)

- **Adopted**: July 17, 1998, in Rome, Italy.
- **Purpose**: Established the **International Criminal Court (ICC)** to prosecute individuals for the most serious international crimes, including **genocide, war crimes, crimes against humanity, and aggression**.
- **Key Features**:
  - **Jurisdiction**: The ICC can prosecute crimes committed by nationals of state parties or on the territory of state parties.
  - **Complementarity**: The ICC only intervenes when national courts are unable or unwilling to prosecute.

- ❑ **Accountability**: Targets individuals, not states, ensuring justice for victims of mass atrocities.
- ❑ **Structure**: Consists of four main organs: the **Presidency**, **Chamber of Judges**, **Office of the Prosecutor**, and **Registry**.
- ❑ **Entry into Force**: The statute entered into force on July 1, 2002, with the ICC becoming operational.

The Rome Statute is the founding legal document for the ICC, aiming to promote accountability, deter international crimes, and ensure justice for victims.

Implementation of International Humanitarian Law (IHL) - Challenges

The implementation of **International Humanitarian Law (IHL)** faces numerous challenges, which can impede its effectiveness in protecting individuals during armed conflicts. These challenges arise from various factors, including state compliance, the nature of modern conflicts, and enforcement mechanisms.

Key Challenges in Implementing IHL:

- **Non-State Armed Groups**
  - ❑ Many modern conflicts involve **non-state actors** (e.g., insurgent groups, militias) that may not recognize or adhere to IHL.
  - ❑ Non-state actors often lack accountability structures, making it difficult to ensure compliance with IHL principles.
- **Lack of Enforcement Mechanisms**
  - ❑ There is no centralized enforcement authority for IHL, and the **International Criminal Court (ICC)**, though vital, has limited jurisdiction and cannot address every violation.
  - ❑ National courts may lack the political will or capacity to prosecute violators of IHL.
- **State Sovereignty vs. International Intervention**
  - ❑ States often resist external intervention or scrutiny of their military actions, citing **sovereignty** concerns.
  - ❑ **Political and military considerations** can lead to states not fully implementing IHL, especially in conflicts involving their strategic interests.
- **Compliance and Accountability**
  - ❑ Even when states or groups agree to IHL, violations are frequent due to **lack of political will**, **weak judicial systems**, and **political alliances**.
  - ❑ High-ranking officials or military leaders may avoid accountability due to **lack of resources** or **political influence**.
- **Asymmetry in Warfare:**
  - ❑ The rise of **asymmetric warfare** (e.g., between states and insurgents) complicates the application of IHL, as non-state actors may not abide by established rules, while states struggle with maintaining distinctions between combatants and civilians.
- **Technological and Weapon Advancements:**
  - ❑ New technologies, such as **drones**, **cyber warfare**, and **autonomous weapons**, pose challenges in applying existing IHL principles (e.g., targeting civilians, proportionality).
  - ❑ The **use of indiscriminate weapons** and those causing excessive harm complicates the enforcement of IHL.
- **Cultural and Social Contexts**
  - ❑ In some regions, **cultural and religious factors** may influence the interpretation of IHL, leading to non-compliance or differing standards of protection for certain groups.
  - ❑ **Ethnic, religious, and political divisions** often shape the willingness to adhere to IHL in conflict zones.
- **Prolonged and Complex Conflicts**
  - ❑ **Protracted conflicts** often result in a breakdown of order, with difficulty in maintaining any adherence to IHL due to the **fragmented nature of the conflict**.
  - ❑ **Humanitarian access** may be restricted or obstructed, preventing aid from reaching those in need.

Conclusion

While IHL is designed to limit the suffering caused by armed conflict, its implementation is hindered by a range of challenges, including state and non-state actor compliance, the nature of modern warfare, enforcement gaps, and political obstacles. Addressing these issues requires strong international cooperation, effective enforcement mechanisms, and sustained efforts to ensure accountability for violations.

MULTIPLE CHOICE QUESTIONS

1. **Assertion (A):** International law is primarily a body of rules governing relations between states.

   Reason (R): International law lacks a centralized enforcing authority like domestic legal systems.

   A. Both A and R are true, and R is the correct explanation of A.
   B. Both A and R are true, but R is not the correct explanation of A.
   C. A is true, but R is false.
   D. A is false, but R is true.

2. **Assertion (A):** Customary international law is universally binding on all states.

   Reason (R): Customary international law derives from long-established state practices and opinio juris.

   A. Both A and R are true, and R is the correct explanation of A.
   B. Both A and R are true, but R is not the correct explanation of A.
   C. A is true, but R is false.
   D. A is false, but R is true.

3. **Assertion (A):** Treaties are the primary source of international law.

   Reason (R): All treaties are legally binding on every state, regardless of consent.

   A. Both A and R are true, and R is the correct explanation of A.
   B. Both A and R are true, but R is not the correct explanation of A.
   C. A is true, but R is false.
   D. A is false, but R is true.

4. **Assertion (A):** International law is more of a moral obligation than a legal one.

   Reason (R): International law lacks effective enforcement mechanisms.

   A. Both A and R are true, and R is the correct explanation of A.
   B. Both A and R are true, but R is not the correct explanation of A.
   C. A is true, but R is false.
   D. A is false, but R is true.

5. Match the following sources of International Law with their descriptions:

A. Customary International Law	1. Formal agreements between states
B. Jus Cogens	2. Fundamental, peremptory norms that cannot be violated
C. Treaties	3. General state practices accepted as law
D. General Principles of Law	4. Principles derived from domestic legal systems

   Codes:
   A. A-3, B-2, C-1, D-4
   B. A-2, B-3, C-1, D-4
   C. A-4, B-2, C-3, D-1
   D. A-1, B-2, C-3, D-4

6. Match the following principles with their significance in international law:

A. Pacta Sunt Servanda	1. Prohibition of force except in self-defense
B. Jus Cogens	2. Agreements must be kept
C. Principle of Sovereignty	3. States have exclusive authority over their territory
D. Prohibition of the Use of Force	4. Peremptory norms with no derogation

   Codes:
   A. A-2, B-4, C-3, D-1
   B. A-3, B-2, C-1, D-4
   C. A-1, B-4, C-2, D-3
   D. A-4, B-3, C-1, D-2

7. Arrange the following key international legal cases in chronological order:
   1. Nicaragua v. United States (ICJ)
   2. North Sea Continental Shelf Cases
   3. Corfu Channel Case
   4. South West Africa Cases

   Codes:
   A. 3, 4, 2, 1
   B. 4, 3, 1, 2
   C. 2, 1, 3, 4
   D. 1, 2, 3, 4

8. Which of the following are recognized as sources of international law under Article 38 of the ICJ Statute?
1. Treaties
2. Customary international law
3. Judicial decisions
4. General principles of law

A. 1 and 2 only B. 1, 2, and 3 only
C. 1, 2, and 4 only D. All of the above

9. Which of the following principles are part of the Montevideo Convention (1933) on statehood?
1. Defined territory
2. Permanent population
3. Recognition by other states
4. Capacity to enter into foreign relations

A. 1, 2, and 3 only
B. 1, 2, and 4 only
C. 1, 2, 3, and 4
D. 2, 3, and 4 only

10. Which of the following best describes the Lotus Principle?

A. States are only bound by international law if they consent.
B. States have absolute sovereignty and no obligation unless restricted by law.
C. International law automatically applies to domestic legal systems.
D. Treaties override customary international law.

11. Assertion (A): International law primarily regulates the conduct of states rather than individuals.

Reason (R): Individuals have no standing under international law unless provided for by specific treaties or customary law.

A. Both A and R are true, and R is the correct explanation of A.
B. Both A and R are true, but R is not the correct explanation of A.
C. A is true, but R is false.
D. A is false, but R is true.

12. Assertion (A): The principle of state sovereignty limits the jurisdiction of international courts.

Reason (R): International courts require state consent to exercise jurisdiction over disputes.

A. Both A and R are true, and R is the correct explanation of A.
B. Both A and R are true, but R is not the correct explanation of A.
C. A is true, but R is false.
D. A is false, but R is true.

13. Match the following international legal doctrines with their meanings:

Doctrine	Meaning
A. Doctrine of Incorporation	1. International law applies only if implemented through legislation
B. Doctrine of Transformation	2. International law is automatically part of domestic law
C. Dualism	3. Domestic and international law are separate legal systems
D. Monism	4. Domestic and international law form a unified system

Codes:

A. A-2, B-1, C-3, D-4
B. A-1, B-2, C-3, D-4
C. A-3, B-4, C-1, D-2
D. A-4, B-3, C-2, D-1

14. Match the following international tribunals with their functions:

Tribunal	Function
A. International Court of Justice (ICJ)	1. Prosecutes individuals for genocide, war crimes, and crimes against humanity
B. International Criminal Court (ICC)	2. Settles disputes between states
C. WTO Dispute Settlement Body	3. Resolves trade-related disputes
D. International Tribunal for the Law of the Sea (ITLOS)	4. Decides cases under the Law of the Sea

Codes:

A. A-2, B-1, C-3, D-4
B. A-3, B-4, C-1, D-2
C. A-1, B-2, C-3, D-4
D. A-4, B-3, C-2, D-1

15. Arrange the following treaties in chronological order:
1. Treaty of Westphalia
2. UN Charter
3. Vienna Convention on the Law of Treaties
4. Montevideo Convention on Statehood

Codes:

A. 1, 4, 2, 3
B. 4, 1, 3, 2
C. 2, 3, 1, 4
D. 1, 3, 4, 2

16. Which of the following are characteristics of a Jus Cogens norm?

1. Non-derogable
2. Requires state consent for application
3. Overrides conflicting treaties
4. Can be modified by regional agreements

Codes:

A. 1 and 3 only
B. 1, 2, and 3 only
C. 2, 3, and 4 only
D. 1, 3, and 4 only

17. Which of the following are recognized exceptions to the prohibition of the use of force under international law?

1. Self-defense
2. UN Security Council authorization
3. Pre-emptive strikes
4. Humanitarian intervention

Codes:

A. 1 and 2 only B. 1, 2, and 3 only
C. 1, 2, and 4 only D. All of the above

18. The concept of erga omnes obligations in international law refers to:

A. Obligations owed to all states and enforceable universally
B. Duties limited to treaty signatories
C. Customary laws applicable only in regional contexts
D. Principles that apply only in times of war

19. The principle of Diplomatic Immunity under the Vienna Convention on Diplomatic Relations (1961) includes which of the following?

1. Immunity from civil and criminal jurisdiction
2. Right to free passage in host country
3. Immunity from espionage activities
4. Protection of diplomatic premises

Codes:

A. 1 and 2 only
B. 1, 2, and 4 only
C. 1, 3, and 4 only
D. All of the above

20. Rebus Sic Stantibus is a principle that allows:

A. Automatic invalidation of treaties in case of war
B. Unilateral withdrawal from treaties due to fundamental changes in circumstances
C. States to interpret treaties based on national interest
D. Treaties to remain binding indefinitely

21. Assertion (A): Customary international law is binding on all states, even if they do not explicitly consent to it.

Reason (R): Customary law derives from state practice and opinio juris, making it universally applicable.

A. Both A and R are true, and R is the correct explanation of A.
B. Both A and R are true, but R is not the correct explanation of A.
C. A is true, but R is false.
D. A is false, but R is true.

22. Assertion (A): Treaties are legally binding on all states, irrespective of their consent.

Reason (R): The principle of pacta sunt servanda (agreements must be kept) applies universally.

A. Both A and R are true, and R is the correct explanation of A.
B. Both A and R are true, but R is not the correct explanation of A.
C. A is true, but R is false.
D. A is false, but R is true.

23. Assertion (A): General principles of law are a primary source of international law.

Reason (R): These principles originate from the legal systems of different states.

A. Both A and R are true, and R is the correct explanation of A.
B. Both A and R are true, but R is not the correct explanation of A.
C. A is true, but R is false.
D. A is false, but R is true.

24. Match the following sources of international law with their definitions:

Source	Definition
A. Treaties	1. Legally binding written agreements between states
B. Customary International Law	2. Consistent state practice accepted as law
C. General Principles	3. Fundamental legal concepts derived from domestic legal systems
D. Judicial Decisions	4. Subsidiary means for interpreting international law

Codes:

A. A-1, B-2, C-3, D-4
B. A-2, B-3, C-1, D-4
C. A-3, B-1, C-4, D-2
D. A-4, B-3, C-2, D-1

25. Match the following treaties with their significance in international law:

Treaty	Significance
A. Vienna Convention on the Law of Treaties (1969)	1. Codifies treaty law principles
B. Montevideo Convention (1933)	2. Defines criteria for statehood
C. UN Charter (1945)	3. Establishes the framework for international law
D. ICJ Statute (1945)	4. Defines sources of international law

Codes:
A. A-1, B-2, C-3, D-4
B. A-3, B-1, C-2, D-4
C. A-2, B-3, C-1, D-4
D. A-4, B-2, C-1, D-3

26. Arrange the following key sources of international law in chronological order:
1. Treaty of Westphalia (1648)
2. Montevideo Convention (1933)
3. UN Charter (1945)
4. Vienna Convention on the Law of Treaties (1969)

Codes:
A. 1, 2, 3, 4
B. 2, 1, 3, 4
C. 3, 1, 2, 4
D. 4, 2, 3, 1

27. Which of the following are recognized as primary sources of international law under Article 38 of the ICJ Statute?
1. Treaties
2. Customary international law
3. Judicial decisions
4. General principles of law

A. 1 and 2 only
B. 1, 2, and 4 only
C. 1, 2, 3, and 4
D. 1 and 3 only

28. Which of the following principles apply to Customary International Law?
1. State practice
2. Opinio juris
3. Persistent objector rule
4. Treaty ratification

A. 1 and 2 only
B. 1, 2, and 3 only
C. 2, 3, and 4 only
D. All of the above

29. The principle of jus cogens refers to:
A. Peremptory norms that override all conflicting international laws
B. Rules applicable only to treaty-based obligations
C. Regional customs applicable to specific countries
D. Optional legal principles for states

30. Which of the following cases confirmed the binding nature of customary international law?
A. Nicaragua v. USA (ICJ)
B. Lotus Case (PCIJ)
C. North Sea Continental Shelf Cases
D. All of the above

31. Assertion (A): Soft law is an important source of international law.

Reason (R): Soft law lacks binding legal force but influences state behavior and treaty negotiations.
A. Both A and R are true, and R is the correct explanation of A.
B. Both A and R are true, but R is not the correct explanation of A.
C. A is true, but R is false.
D. A is false, but R is true.

32. Assertion (A): The principle of pacta sunt servanda applies to all international treaties.

Reason (R): Treaties bind only those states that are parties to them.
A. Both A and R are true, and R is the correct explanation of A.
B. Both A and R are true, but R is not the correct explanation of A.
C. A is true, but R is false.
D. A is false, but R is true.

33. Match the following judicial decisions with their significance in international law:

Case	Significance
A. North Sea Continental Shelf Cases	1. Recognized the importance of customary international law
B. Nicaragua v. USA	2. Confirmed that states must not intervene in the affairs of other states
C. Lotus Case	3. Established that what is not expressly prohibited in international law is allowed
D. Corfu Channel Case	4. Stressed the duty of states not to use their territory for harming others

Codes:
A. A-1, B-2, C-3, D-4
B. A-3, B-1, C-4, D-2
C. A-2, B-3, C-1, D-4
D. A-1, B-4, C-3, D-2

34. Match the following international legal instruments with their main subject matter:

Instrument	Main Subject Matter
A. Vienna Convention on Diplomatic Relations (1961)	1. Diplomatic immunity
B. Vienna Convention on the Law of Treaties (1969)	2. Treaty law principles
C. Montevideo Convention (1933)	3. Definition of statehood
D. UN Charter (1945)	4. Prohibition of the use of force

Codes:
A. A-1, B-2, C-3, D-4
B. A-3, B-1, C-4, D-2
C. A-4, B-3, C-2, D-1
D. A-1, B-4, C-2, D-3

35. Arrange the following key legal instruments in chronological order:
1. The Hague Conventions
2. League of Nations Covenant
3. UN Charter
4. Vienna Convention on the Law of Treaties

Codes:
A. 1, 2, 3, 4 B. 2, 1, 4, 3
C. 3, 1, 2, 4 D. 4, 2, 3, 1

36. Which of the following are subsidiary sources of international law?
1. Judicial decisions
2. Opinions of legal scholars
3. General principles of law
4. UN General Assembly resolutions
A. 1 and 2 only
B. 1, 2, and 4 only
C. 1, 2, 3, and 4
D. 1 and 3 only

37. Which of the following are necessary elements for customary international law to develop?
1. Consistent state practice
2. Opinio juris
3. Codification by a treaty
4. Enforcement by the ICJ
A. 1 and 2 only
B. 1, 2, and 3 only
C. 2, 3, and 4 only
D. All of the above

38. Which of the following are considered jus cogens norms?
1. Prohibition of genocide
2. Freedom of trade
3. Prohibition of slavery
4. Right to diplomatic protection
A. 1 and 3 only
B. 1, 2, and 3 only
C. 1, 3, and 4 only
D. All of the above

39. What is the principle of Stare Decisis in international law?
A. A treaty binds only consenting states
B. Customary law prevails over treaty law
C. Courts should follow previous judicial precedents
D. States can unilaterally withdraw from treaties

40. Which of the following can override a treaty under international law?
1. Jus cogens norms
2. UN Security Council Resolutions
3. Customary international law
4. Persistent objection by a state
A. 1 and 2 only
B. 1, 2, and 3 only
C. 1, 3, and 4 only
D. All of the above

41. **Assertion (A):** Recognition of a state is a political act, not a legal obligation.

Reason (R): There is no compulsory international legal duty on states to recognize new states.
A. Both A and R are true, and R is the correct explanation of A.
B. Both A and R are true, but R is not the correct explanation of A.
C. A is true, but R is false.
D. A is false, but R is true.

42. **Assertion (A):** The Montevideo Convention (1933) provides the accepted criteria for statehood in international law.

Reason (R): A state must have a permanent population, defined territory, government, and capacity to enter into international relations.
A. Both A and R are true, and R is the correct explanation of A.

B. Both A and R are true, but R is not the correct explanation of A.
C. A is true, but R is false.
D. A is false, but R is true.

43. Assertion (A): De facto recognition grants full diplomatic status to the recognized entity.

Reason (R): De facto recognition is a temporary and conditional acknowledgment of an entity's control over territory.

A. Both A and R are true, and R is the correct explanation of A.
B. Both A and R are true, but R is not the correct explanation of A.
C. A is true, but R is false.
D. A is false, but R is true.

44. Match the following theories of recognition with their main principles:

Theory	Principle
A. Constitutive Theory	1. Recognition is a formal act granting international legal personality.
B. Declaratory Theory	2. Statehood is based on factual existence, irrespective of recognition.
C. Estrada Doctrine	3. Recognition should not depend on changes in government.
D. Stimson Doctrine	4. Non-recognition of states formed through aggression.

Codes:
A. A-1, B-2, C-3, D-4
B. A-2, B-1, C-4, D-3
C. A-3, B-1, C-2, D-4
D. A-4, B-3, C-1, D-2

45. Match the following cases with their significance in the recognition of states and governments:

Case	Significance
A. Tinoco Arbitration Case (1923)	1. Recognized that a government can be valid even without external recognition.
B. Greek Orthodox Church v. Goldberg (1924)	2. Established that recognition is a political decision.
C. Arantzazu Mendi Case (1939)	3. British courts accept government recognition decisions of the executive.
D. Luther v. Sagor (1921)	4. Recognition of Soviet Russia's nationalization laws by British courts.

Codes:
A. A-1, B-2, C-3, D-4
B. A-3, B-4, C-2, D-1
C. A-1, B-4, C-3, D-2
D. A-4, B-3, C-1, D-2

46. Arrange the following key events related to state recognition in chronological order:
1. Montevideo Convention on Rights and Duties of States
2. UN Charter adoption
3. Kosovo's Declaration of Independence
4. Stimson Doctrine

Codes:
A. 4, 1, 2, 3
B. 1, 4, 3, 2
C. 2, 3, 4, 1
D. 3, 1, 4, 2

47. Which of the following are criteria for recognition of a government?
1. Effective control over territory
2. Popular legitimacy
3. Consent of all UN member states
4. Stability and permanence

A. 1 and 2 only
B. 1, 2, and 4 only
C. 2, 3, and 4 only
D. All of the above

48. Which of the following factors influence de facto recognition?
1. Military control over the state
2. International political interests
3. Consistency with democratic principles
4. Existence of diplomatic relations

A. 1 and 2 only
B. 1, 2, and 4 only
C. 2, 3, and 4 only
D. All of the above

49. Which doctrine prohibits the recognition of a state formed through aggression or unlawful means?
A. Estrada Doctrine
B. Stimson Doctrine
C. Monroe Doctrine
D. Calvo Doctrine

50. Which of the following is an example of collective recognition of a state?
A. The UN admission of South Sudan in 2011
B. Diplomatic recognition of Taiwan by the United States
C. Israel's recognition by individual Arab states
D. India's recognition of Bangladesh in 1971

51. Match the following doctrines with their descriptions:

Doctrine	Description
A. Tobar Doctrine	1. Non-recognition of governments that come to power through unconstitutional means
B. Estrada Doctrine	2. Recognition should not depend on political considerations
C. Stimson Doctrine	3. Non-recognition of territorial acquisitions through aggression
D. Monroe Doctrine	4. Policy opposing European interference in the Western Hemisphere

Codes:
A. A-1, B-2, C-3, D-4
B. A-2, B-1, C-4, D-3
C. A-3, B-4, C-1, D-2
D. A-4, B-3, C-2, D-1

52. Match the following states with their recognition status:

State	Recognition Status
A. Taiwan	1. Recognized by some states, but not the UN
B. Palestine	2. Recognized by UNGA but not by all states
C. South Sudan	3. Full UN recognition
D. Kosovo	4. Partially recognized, not a UN member

Codes:
A. A-1, B-2, C-3, D-4
B. A-3, B-4, C-1, D-2
C. A-2, B-3, C-4, D-1
D. A-4, B-3, C-2, D-1

53. Arrange the following key recognitions in chronological order:
1. U.S. recognition of the People's Republic of China
2. India's recognition of Bangladesh
3. Palestine's partial recognition at the UNGA
4. South Sudan's UN membership

Codes:
A. 1, 2, 3, 4 B. 2, 1, 4, 3
C. 3, 1, 2, 4 D. 4, 2, 1, 3

54. Which of the following factors influence state recognition?
1. Effective control over a defined territory
2. International legal obligations
3. Political and strategic considerations
4. Adherence to democratic principles

A. 1 and 2 only
B. 1, 2, and 3 only
C. 1, 2, 3, and 4
D. 2 and 4 only

55. Which of the following are valid forms of recognition?
1. Express recognition
2. Implied recognition
3. Collective recognition
4. Secret recognition

A. 1, 2, and 3 only B. 1, 2, and 4 only
C. 2, 3, and 4 only D. All of the above

56. What is the legal status of a government that is recognized de facto but not de jure?
A. It has full legal status in international law
B. It is temporarily acknowledged without full legitimacy
C. It can enter into treaties with all states
D. It is considered illegal under international law

57. Which of the following doctrines support non-recognition of unlawful governments?
1. Tobar Doctrine
2. Estrada Doctrine
3. Stimson Doctrine
4. Hallstein Doctrine

A. 1, 2, and 3 only B. 1, 3, and 4 only
C. 2, 3, and 4 only D. All of the above

58. Which principle applies when a new government automatically inherits the international obligations of its predecessor state?
A. Doctrine of State Succession
B. Doctrine of Effective Control
C. Doctrine of Continuity
D. Doctrine of Auto-Recognition

59. Assertion (A): Nationality is a fundamental right under international law.

Reason (R): Every individual has the right to nationality to prevent statelessness.
A. Both A and R are true, and R is the correct explanation of A.
B. Both A and R are true, but R is not the correct explanation of A.
C. A is true, but R is false.
D. A is false, but R is true.

60. Assertion (A): Jus soli (birthright citizenship) is universally accepted as the basis for acquiring nationality.

Reason (R): Most countries grant nationality based on jus soli alone.

A. Both A and R are true, and R is the correct explanation of A.
B. Both A and R are true, but R is not the correct explanation of A.
C. A is true, but R is false.
D. A is false, but R is true.

61. Assertion (A): The principle of non-refoulement applies to both refugees and internally displaced persons (IDPs).

Reason (R): International refugee law treats IDPs and refugees as legally equivalent.

A. Both A and R are true, and R is the correct explanation of A.
B. Both A and R are true, but R is not the correct explanation of A.
C. A is true, but R is false.
D. A is false, but R is true.

62. Match the following types of displaced persons with their definitions:

Term	Definition
A. Refugee	1. A person forced to leave their country due to persecution
B. Asylum Seeker	2. A person seeking refugee status but whose claim is pending
C. Internally Displaced Person (IDP)	3. A person displaced within their own country
D. Stateless Person	4. A person who is not considered a national by any state

Codes:

A. A-1, B-2, C-3, D-4 B. A-2, B-3, C-1, D-4
C. A-4, B-3, C-2, D-1 D. A-1, B-3, C-4, D-2

63. Match the following international treaties with their relevance to displaced persons and nationality:

Treaty	Key Provision
A. 1951 Refugee Convention	1. Defines the rights of refugees and asylum seekers
B. 1961 Convention on the Reduction of Statelessness	2. Establishes principles to prevent statelessness
C. 1998 Guiding Principles on Internal Displacement	3. Provides guidelines for the protection of IDPs
D. 1967 Protocol Relating to the Status of Refugees	4. Expands the scope of the 1951 Refugee Convention

Codes:

A. A-1, B-2, C-3, D-4
B. A-2, B-1, C-4, D-3
C. A-3, B-4, C-2, D-1
D. A-4, B-2, C-1, D-3

64. Arrange the following key legal instruments in chronological order:

1. UN Convention on the Reduction of Statelessness
2. Refugee Convention
3. UNHCR Establishment
4. Guiding Principles on Internal Displacement

Codes:

A. 2, 3, 1, 4 B. 3, 2, 1, 4
C. 2, 1, 4, 3 D. 1, 2, 3, 4

65. Which of the following conditions qualify a person as a refugee under the 1951 Refugee Convention?

1. Well-founded fear of persecution
2. Nationality of another country
3. Inability to return home safely
4. Crossing an international border

A. 1 and 3 only B. 1, 3, and 4 only
C. 2, 3, and 4 only D. All of the above

66. Which of the following principles apply to stateless persons under international law?

1. Right to nationality
2. Right to seek asylum
3. Protection from deportation
4. Right to vote in any country

A. 1 and 2 only B. 1, 2, and 3 only
C. 2, 3, and 4 only D. All of the above

67. Which principle prohibits the forced return of refugees to a country where they may face persecution?

A. Jus Soli B. Non-Refoulement
C. State Succession D. Naturalization

68. Which of the following factors contribute to internal displacement?

1. Armed conflict
2. Natural disasters
3. Economic migration
4. Persecution by state authorities

A. 1 and 2 only B. 1, 2, and 4 only
C. 2, 3, and 4 only D. All of the above

69. Assertion (A): A refugee loses their refugee status once they voluntarily return to their home country.

Reason (R): Voluntary repatriation is one of the durable solutions under international refugee law.

A. Both A and R are true, and R is the correct explanation of A.

B. Both A and R are true, but R is not the correct explanation of A.
C. A is true, but R is false.
D. A is false, but R is true.

70. Assertion (A): Internally displaced persons (IDPs) enjoy the same rights and protections as other citizens of their country.

Reason (R): Unlike refugees, IDPs remain within their country's borders and are under the protection of their national government.

A. Both A and R are true, and R is the correct explanation of A.
B. Both A and R are true, but R is not the correct explanation of A.
C. A is true, but R is false.
D. A is false, but R is true.

71. Match the following international organizations with their functions related to displaced persons:

Organization	Function
A. UNHCR	1. Provides protection and assistance to refugees
B. IOM (International Organization for Migration)	2. Manages migration and supports migrants worldwide
C. OHCHR (Office of the High Commissioner for Human Rights)	3. Promotes and monitors human rights of displaced persons
D. OCHA (Office for the Coordination of Humanitarian Affairs)	4. Coordinates international responses to humanitarian crises

Codes:
A. A-1, B-2, C-3, D-4　B. A-2, B-1, C-4, D-3
C. A-3, B-1, C-2, D-4　D. A-4, B-3, C-2, D-1

72. Match the following legal instruments with their relevance to nationality and displacement:

Legal Instrument	Relevance
A. 1954 Convention Relating to the Status of Stateless Persons	1. Grants legal status and rights to stateless persons
B. 1961 Convention on Reduction of Statelessness	2. Establishes measures to prevent statelessness
C. Dublin Regulation (EU)	3. Determines the responsibility of EU countries in processing asylum claims
D. Cartagena Declaration (1984)	4. Expands refugee definition to include persons fleeing generalized violence

Codes:
A. A-1, B-2, C-3, D-4
B. A-3, B-1, C-4, D-2
C. A-2, B-3, C-1, D-4
D. A-4, B-2, C-1, D-3

73. Arrange the following key refugee-related events in chronological order:
1. Establishment of UNHCR
2. Adoption of the 1951 Refugee Convention
3. Adoption of the 1967 Refugee Protocol
4. Adoption of the Global Compact on Refugees

Codes:
A. 1, 2, 3, 4　B. 2, 1, 3, 4
C. 3, 2, 4, 1　D. 4, 3, 1, 2

74. Which of the following are considered durable solutions for refugees?
1. Voluntary repatriation
2. Local integration
3. Resettlement in a third country
4. Granting dual nationality

A. 1 and 2 only
B. 1, 2, and 3 only
C. 2, 3, and 4 only
D. All of the above

75. Which of the following situations can lead to statelessness?
1. Conflict between nationality laws
2. Revocation of nationality due to political reasons
3. Children born to stateless parents
4. Marriage between nationals of different countries

A. 1 and 2 only　B. 1, 2, and 3 only
C. 2, 3, and 4 only　D. All of the above

76. What is the Dublin Regulation known for?
A. Preventing statelessness in the EU
B. Allocating asylum processing responsibilities within the EU
C. Protecting stateless persons globally
D. Recognizing refugees fleeing climate change

77. Which principle is applied when nationality is determined based on the nationality of the parents rather than place of birth?
A. Jus Soli　B. Jus Sanguinis
C. Naturalization　D. Dual Citizenship

78. Which of the following factors can legally justify revocation of nationality under international law?
1. Fraud in naturalization
2. Service in a foreign military
3. Political dissent against the government
4. Voluntary acquisition of another nationality

A. 1 and 2 only
B. 1, 2, and 4 only
C. 2, 3, and 4 only
D. All of the above

79. Assertion (A): Extradition is a legal obligation under international law.

Reason (R): Extradition treaties create a binding duty between the requesting and requested states.

A. Both A and R are true, and R is the correct explanation of A.
B. Both A and R are true, but R is not the correct explanation of A.
C. A is true, but R is false.
D. A is false, but R is true.

80. Assertion (A): The principle of non-refoulement prohibits extradition in all circumstances.

Reason (R): Extradition is prohibited when a person faces the risk of persecution or torture.

A. Both A and R are true, and R is the correct explanation of A.
B. Both A and R are true, but R is not the correct explanation of A.
C. A is true, but R is false.
D. A is false, but R is true.

81. Assertion (A): Political offenders are generally exempt from extradition.

Reason (R): The political offense exception prevents persecution under the guise of extradition.

A. Both A and R are true, and R is the correct explanation of A.
B. Both A and R are true, but R is not the correct explanation of A.
C. A is true, but R is false.
D. A is false, but R is true.

82. Match the following legal principles with their relevance to extradition and asylum:

Principle	Relevance
A. Rule of Specialty	1. The extradited person can be tried only for the offense for which they were extradited
B. Dual Criminality	2. The crime must be an offense in both requesting and requested states
C. Non-Refoulement	3. A person cannot be extradited if they face persecution or torture
D. Political Offense Exception	4. Extradition can be denied for political crimes

Codes:
A. A-1, B-2, C-3, D-4
B. A-2, B-1, C-4, D-3
C. A-3, B-4, C-1, D-2
D. A-4, B-3, C-2, D-1

83. Match the following extradition cases with their key legal principles:

Case	Legal Principle
A. Soering v. UK (1989)	1. Extradition denied due to risk of inhuman treatment
B. Abu Salem Case	2. Rule of Specialty applies in extradition treaties
C. Pinochet Case (1999)	3. Former heads of state can be extradited for human rights violations
D. Snowden Case	4. Political asylum can be granted to avoid persecution

Codes:
A. A-1, B-2, C-3, D-4
B. A-2, B-1, C-4, D-3
C. A-3, B-4, C-1, D-2
D. A-4, B-3, C-2, D-1

84. Arrange the following key legal instruments in chronological order:
1. UN Convention against Torture (CAT)
2. European Convention on Extradition
3. 1951 Refugee Convention
4. Rome Statute of the ICC

Codes:
A. 3, 2, 1, 4
B. 2, 3, 4, 1
C. 3, 4, 1, 2
D. 4, 2, 3, 1

85. Which of the following are grounds for denying extradition?
1. Political offense exception
2. Risk of human rights violations
3. Lack of dual criminality
4. Offense committed by a diplomat

A. 1 and 2 only
B. 1, 2, and 3 only
C. 2, 3, and 4 only
D. All of the above

86. Which of the following conditions are required for valid extradition?
A. The requesting country must guarantee a fair trial
B. The offense must be punishable by death
C. The accused must have renounced citizenship
D. The requested country must have no diplomatic relations with the requesting country

87. Under international law, a state may refuse extradition when:

A. The person is a national of the requested state
B. The crime is punishable by death
C. There is a risk of persecution
D. All of the above

88. Which of the following treaties primarily govern extradition?

1. European Convention on Extradition
2. UN Convention against Transnational Organized Crime
3. Geneva Conventions
4. Montevideo Convention

A. 1 and 2 only B. 2 and 3 only
C. 3 and 4 only D. All of the above

89. Match the following extradition treaties with their scope and purpose:

Treaty	Scope
A. European Convention on Extradition (1957)	1. Governs extradition among European states
B. UN Convention Against Corruption (UNCAC)	2. Facilitates extradition for corruption-related crimes
C. SAARC Convention on Suppression of Terrorism	3. Provides extradition framework for South Asian countries
D. UN Convention Against Transnational Organized Crime (UNTOC)	4. Covers extradition for organized crime offenses

Codes:
A. A-1, B-2, C-3, D-4
B. A-2, B-1, C-4, D-3
C. A-3, B-4, C-2, D-1
D. A-4, B-3, C-1, D-2

90. Match the following types of asylum with their definitions:

Type of Asylum	Definition
A. Territorial Asylum	1. Asylum granted within the territory of a state
B. Diplomatic Asylum	2. Protection granted within embassies or consulates
C. Humanitarian Asylum	3. Granted based on humanitarian concerns, like war or natural disasters
D. Political Asylum	4. Given to individuals facing persecution for political reasons

Codes:
A. A-1, B-2, C-3, D-4
B. A-2, B-3, C-1, D-4
C. A-4, B-1, C-2, D-3
D. A-3, B-4, C-1, D-2

91. Arrange the following landmark asylum-related events in chronological order:

1. 1951 Refugee Convention
2. 1984 Cartagena Declaration
3. 2018 Global Compact on Refugees
4. 1967 Refugee Protocol

Codes:
A. 1, 4, 2, 3 B. 2, 1, 3, 4
C. 4, 3, 1, 2 D. 1, 2, 3, 4

92. Which of the following conditions must be met for a valid extradition request?

1. The offense must be an extraditable crime under the treaty.
2. The person must have been convicted before extradition is requested.
3. The requested state must have jurisdiction over the accused.
4. The offense must meet the requirement of dual criminality.

A. 1 and 2 only
B. 1, 3, and 4 only
C. 2, 3, and 4 only
D. All of the above

93. Which of the following rights are guaranteed to asylum seekers under international law?

1. Right to seek asylum
2. Right to be granted asylum
3. Protection from refoulement
4. Right to choose any country for asylum

A. 1 and 3 only B. 1, 2, and 3 only
C. 2, 3, and 4 only D. All of the above

94. Which of the following principles govern diplomatic asylum?

A. It is an absolute right of every asylum seeker.
B. It is subject to the discretion of the host state.
C. It is regulated under the 1951 Refugee Convention.
D. It is not recognized under general international law.

95. The principle of double jeopardy in extradition means:

A. An individual cannot be extradited if they have been acquitted of the same crime.

B. An individual cannot be extradited twice for the same offense.
C. The requesting state cannot re-prosecute after extradition.
D. The individual must be tried in the country where they committed the crime.

96. Which of the following statements about the rule of specialty in extradition is correct?
A. A person cannot be prosecuted for any offense other than the one for which they were extradited.
B. A person can be tried for any offense once they are extradited.
C. The rule of specialty applies only in cases of political asylum.
D. The requested state can override the rule at any time.

97. Which of the following crimes are excluded from political offense exceptions in extradition law?
1. Genocide
2. War crimes
3. Terrorism
4. Defamation against a head of state

A. 1 and 2 only
B. 1, 2, and 3 only
C. 3 and 4 only
D. All of the above

98. Under the 1951 Refugee Convention, asylum seekers may be denied asylum if:
A. They have committed war crimes or crimes against humanity.
B. They have committed a serious non-political crime outside the host country.
C. They were involved in acts contrary to the purposes of the UN.
D. All of the above.

99. **Assertion (A):** The United Nations General Assembly (UNGA) can make legally binding decisions for all member states.

Reason (R): The UNGA resolutions are considered international law under the UN Charter.
A. Both A and R are true, and R is the correct explanation of A.
B. Both A and R are true, but R is not the correct explanation of A.
C. A is true, but R is false.
D. A is false, but R is true.

100. **Assertion (A):** The UN Security Council (UNSC) has the power to impose economic sanctions on member states.

Reason (R): The UNSC's decisions under Chapter VII of the UN Charter are binding on all UN members.
A. Both A and R are true, and R is the correct explanation of A.
B. Both A and R are true, but R is not the correct explanation of A.
C. A is true, but R is false.
D. A is false, but R is true.

101. **Assertion (A):** The International Court of Justice (ICJ) has compulsory jurisdiction over all UN member states.

Reason (R): The UN Charter mandates that all disputes involving states must be submitted to the ICJ.
A. Both A and R are true, and R is the correct explanation of A.
B. Both A and R are true, but R is not the correct explanation of A.
C. A is true, but R is false.
D. A is false, but R is true.

102. Match the following UN organs with their primary functions:

A. UN General Assembly	1. Adopts resolutions and oversees the UN budget
B. UN Security Council	2. Maintains international peace and security
C. International Court of Justice	3. Settles legal disputes between states
D. UN Economic and Social Council (ECOSOC)	4. Coordinates economic and social initiatives

Codes:
A. A-1, B-2, C-3, D-4
B. A-2, B-3, C-1, D-4
C. A-3, B-1, C-2, D-4
D. A-4, B-2, C-1, D-3

103. Match the following specialized agencies of the UN with their roles:

A. WHO	1. Global health policy and disease control
B. UNESCO	2. Promotes education, science, and culture
C. FAO	3. Focuses on global food security and agriculture
D. ILO	4. Sets international labor standards

Codes:
A. A-1, B-2, C-3, D-4
B. A-2, B-3, C-4, D-1
C. A-3, B-4, C-1, D-2
D. A-4, B-3, C-2, D-1

104. Arrange the following key events related to the UN in chronological order:
1. Adoption of the UN Charter
2. Creation of the International Court of Justice
3. Establishment of the UN Peacekeeping Forces
4. UN Millennium Development Goals

Codes:
A. 1, 2, 3, 4 B. 2, 1, 4, 3
C. 3, 2, 1, 4 D. 4, 3, 2, 1

105. Which of the following are permanent members of the UN Security Council?
1. United States 2. Germany
3. China 4. Russia
A. 1 and 2 only
B. 1, 3, and 4 only
C. 2, 3, and 4 only
D. All of the above

106. Which of the following are key functions of the UN Secretary-General?
1. Acts as the chief administrative officer of the UN
2. Chairs UN Security Council meetings
3. Appoints UN peacekeeping missions
4. Issues binding decisions on international conflicts
A. 1 and 2 only
B. 1 and 3 only
C. 2, 3, and 4 only
D. All of the above

107. Which principle allows a Security Council permanent member to block a resolution?
A. Rule of Majority
B. Veto Power
C. Universal Consensus
D. Special Resolution Mechanism

108. Which of the following UN bodies is responsible for monitoring human rights violations?
A. UN Security Council
B. UN Human Rights Council
C. International Court of Justice
D. International Criminal Court

109. Which of the following agencies administers refugee protection under the UN system?
A. UNDP B. UNHCR
C. FAO D. UNESCO

110. Match the following UN peacekeeping operations with their respective regions:

A. UNIFIL	1. Lebanon
B. UNAMID	2. Darfur (Sudan)
C. MONUSCO	3. Democratic Republic of Congo
D. MINUSMA	4. Mali

Codes:
A. A-1, B-2, C-3, D-4
B. A-2, B-3, C-1, D-4
C. A-3, B-4, C-2, D-1
D. A-4, B-1, C-3, D-2

111. Match the following UN Secretaries-General with their terms:

A. Dag Hammarskjöld	1. 1953-1961
B. Kofi Annan	2. 1997-2006
C. Ban Ki-moon	3. 2007-2016
D. António Guterres	4. 2017-present

Codes:
A. A-1, B-2, C-3, D-4
B. A-3, B-4, C-1, D-2
C. A-4, B-1, C-2, D-3
D. A-2, B-3, C-4, D-1

112. Arrange the following major UN Security Council resolutions in chronological order:
1. Resolution 242 (Israel-Palestine Conflict)
2. Resolution 687 (Iraq-Kuwait Crisis)
3. Resolution 1325 (Women, Peace, and Security)
4. Resolution 1973 (Libya Crisis)

Codes:
A. 1, 2, 3, 4 B. 2, 3, 1, 4
C. 3, 1, 4, 2 D. 4, 3, 2, 1

113. Which of the following are principal organs of the UN as per Article 7 of the UN Charter?
1. UN General Assembly
2. UN Security Council
3. International Criminal Court (ICC)
4. International Court of Justice (ICJ)
A. 1 and 2 only
B. 1, 2, and 4 only
C. 2, 3, and 4 only
D. All of the above

114. Which of the following are binding resolutions under international law?
1. UN General Assembly Resolutions
2. UN Security Council Resolutions under Chapter VII
3. International Court of Justice Advisory Opinions
4. UN Human Rights Council Recommendations

A. 2 only
B. 1 and 3 only
C. 2 and 4 only
D. 1, 2, and 3 only

115. Which UN body is primarily responsible for overseeing decolonization and self-determination issues?
A. UN General Assembly
B. UN Trusteeship Council
C. UN Security Council
D. UN Human Rights Council

116. Which of the following statements is correct regarding the voting system in the UN Security Council?
A. A resolution requires a simple majority of 9 votes, including concurring votes from all permanent members.
B. A resolution can pass without the support of permanent members.
C. The abstention of a permanent member counts as a veto.
D. A unanimous vote is required for every resolution to pass.

117. Which of the following UN missions is tasked with monitoring the Iran nuclear deal?
A. UNHCR B. IAEA
C. WHO D. UNDP

118. Which of the following describe the functions of ECOSOC?
1. Coordinating international economic and social initiatives
2. Enforcing international human rights law
3. Overseeing UN specialized agencies
4. Issuing legally binding decisions on development goals

A. 1 and 2 only
B. 1 and 3 only
C. 2, 3, and 4 only
D. All of the above

119. Assertion (A): The International Court of Justice (ICJ) has compulsory jurisdiction over all disputes between UN member states.

Reason (R): The UN Charter mandates that all disputes involving states must be submitted to the ICJ for resolution.
A. Both A and R are true, and R is the correct explanation of A.
B. Both A and R are true, but R is not the correct explanation of A.
C. A is true, but R is false.
D. A is false, but R is true.

120. Assertion (A): Arbitration is a legally binding method of settling international disputes.

Reason (R): Arbitral decisions in international law are enforceable under the UN Charter.
A. Both A and R are true, and R is the correct explanation of A.
B. Both A and R are true, but R is not the correct explanation of A.
C. A is true, but R is false.
D. A is false, but R is true.

121. Assertion (A): Mediation in international disputes requires a neutral third party to offer binding decisions.

Reason (R): Mediation is a formal dispute resolution method under the International Court of Justice.
A. Both A and R are true, and R is the correct explanation of A.
B. Both A and R are true, but R is not the correct explanation of A.
C. A is true, but R is false.
D. A is false, but R is true.

122. Match the following methods of dispute settlement with their characteristics:

A. Negotiation	1. Direct discussion between parties without third-party intervention
B. Mediation	2. Involves a third party suggesting non-binding solutions
C. Arbitration	3. Involves a neutral tribunal issuing a binding decision
D. Adjudication	4. Legal dispute resolution through courts like ICJ

Codes:
A. A-1, B-2, C-3, D-4
B. A-2, B-3, C-1, D-4
C. A-3, B-1, C-4, D-2
D. A-4, B-3, C-2, D-1

123. Match the following international disputes with their settlement mechanisms:

A. Indo-Pakistan Rann of Kutch Dispute	1. Arbitration
B. US-Iran Hostage Crisis (1980)	2. Mediation
C. Nicaragua v. USA (ICJ, 1986)	3. Adjudication
D. Camp David Accords (Israel-Egypt)	4. Negotiation

Codes:
A. A-1, B-2, C-3, D-4
B. A-3, B-1, C-2, D-4
C. A-4, B-3, C-1, D-2
D. A-2, B-4, C-3, D-1

124. Arrange the following landmark international dispute settlements in chronological order:
1. Rann of Kutch Arbitration
2. Nicaragua v. USA (ICJ case)
3. Camp David Accords
4. ICJ Judgment on Rohingya Genocide Case

Codes:
A. 1, 3, 2, 4 B. 2, 1, 4, 3
C. 3, 1, 2, 4 D. 4, 2, 3, 1

125. Which of the following are binding forms of dispute resolution under international law?
1. Arbitration
2. Mediation
3. Adjudication
4. Negotiation

A. 1 and 2 only
B. 1 and 3 only
C. 2 and 4 only
D. All of the above

126. Which international organizations play a role in dispute resolution?
1. International Court of Justice (ICJ)
2. Permanent Court of Arbitration (PCA)
3. World Trade Organization (WTO) Dispute Settlement Body
4. United Nations General Assembly (UNGA)

A. 1 and 2 only
B. 1, 2, and 3 only
C. 2, 3, and 4 only
D. All of the above

127. Which principle ensures that states cannot be forced into dispute settlement without their consent?
A. Principle of State Sovereignty
B. Compulsory Jurisdiction of ICJ
C. Doctrine of Reciprocity
D. Most-Favored Nation Principle

128. Which UN Charter chapter governs the Pacific Settlement of Disputes?
A. Chapter VI
B. Chapter VII
C. Chapter VIII
D. Chapter IX

129. Match the following dispute resolution methods with their key features:

A. Good Offices	1. A third party facilitates dialogue but does not suggest solutions
B. Conciliation	2. A neutral party proposes a settlement after investigating the dispute
C. Inquiry	3. A fact-finding method used to determine the cause of a dispute
D. Arbitration	4. A legally binding decision is given by a tribunal

Codes:
A. A-1, B-2, C-3, D-4
B. A-2, B-3, C-4, D-1
C. A-3, B-1, C-2, D-4
D. A-4, B-3, C-2, D-1

130. Match the following international dispute cases with their rulings:

A. Chagos Archipelago Dispute	1. ICJ advisory opinion ruled that the UK should return the islands to Mauritius
B. South China Sea Arbitration (Philippines v. China)	2. PCA ruled that China's maritime claims violated UNCLOS
C. Kosovo Advisory Opinion	3. ICJ ruled that Kosovo's declaration of independence did not violate international law
D. Nuclear Tests Case (France v. Australia)	4. ICJ ruled that France's nuclear tests were unlawful

Codes:
A. A-1, B-2, C-3, D-4
B. A-2, B-3, C-4, D-1
C. A-3, B-1, C-2, D-4
D. A-4, B-3, C-1, D-2

131. Arrange the following international dispute resolution cases in chronological order:
1. Nuclear Tests Case (France v. Australia)
2. Nicaragua v. USA (ICJ)
3. South China Sea Arbitration
4. Chagos Archipelago Case

Codes:
A. 1, 2, 3, 4 B. 2, 1, 4, 3
C. 3, 1, 2, 4 D. 4, 3, 2, 1

132. Which of the following principles apply to state responsibility for internationally wrongful acts?

1. Obligation to make reparations
2. Possibility of countermeasures by the injured state
3. Automatic jurisdiction of the ICJ
4. Right of the responsible state to avoid liability through domestic law

A. 1 and 2 only
B. 1, 3, and 4 only
C. 2, 3, and 4 only
D. All of the above

133. Which of the following are compulsory dispute resolution mechanisms under the UNCLOS (United Nations Convention on the Law of the Sea)?

1. International Tribunal for the Law of the Sea (ITLOS)
2. ICJ adjudication
3. Arbitration under UNCLOS Annex VII
4. WTO Dispute Settlement Body

A. 1 and 3 only
B. 1, 2, and 3 only
C. 2 and 4 only
D. All of the above

134. What is the primary function of the Permanent Court of Arbitration (PCA)?

A. Adjudicating state disputes under UN Charter
B. Providing arbitration services for international disputes
C. Enforcing decisions of the International Criminal Court
D. Reviewing decisions of the ICJ

135. Which of the following are non-binding methods of international dispute settlement?

1. Good offices
2. Mediation
3. Adjudication
4. Negotiation

A. 1 and 2 only
B. 2 and 3 only
C. 1, 2, and 4 only
D. All of the above

136. Which of the following principles is applied in ICJ cases to ensure a fair hearing?

A. Principle of State Sovereignty
B. Principle of Audi Alteram Partem
C. Doctrine of Forum Non Conveniens
D. Jus Cogens

137. Which principle governs the peaceful settlement of disputes under the UN Charter?

A. Chapter VI
B. Chapter VII
C. Chapter VIII
D. Chapter IX

138. Under international law, a state may lawfully use countermeasures against another state when:

A. The ICJ has authorized retaliation
B. The countermeasures do not violate peremptory norms (jus cogens)
C. The UN General Assembly gives approval
D. The injured state breaks diplomatic relations

139. Assertion (A): The World Trade Organization (WTO) is a successor to the General Agreement on Tariffs and Trade (GATT).

Reason (R): The WTO was established to replace GATT, which only provided a provisional framework for international trade.

A. Both A and R are true, and R is the correct explanation of A.
B. Both A and R are true, but R is not the correct explanation of A.
C. A is true, but R is false.
D. A is false, but R is true.

140. Assertion (A): WTO agreements apply equally to all member states.

Reason (R): The principle of Most-Favored Nation (MFN) requires non-discriminatory trade treatment among WTO members.

A. Both A and R are true, and R is the correct explanation of A.
B. Both A and R are true, but R is not the correct explanation of A.
C. A is true, but R is false.
D. A is false, but R is true.

141. Assertion (A): The Dispute Settlement Body (DSB) of the WTO can impose sanctions on member states.

Reason (R): The DSB has the authority to enforce its decisions under WTO agreements.

A. Both A and R are true, and R is the correct explanation of A.
B. Both A and R are true, but R is not the correct explanation of A.
C. A is true, but R is false.
D. A is false, but R is true.

142. Match the following WTO agreements with their focus areas:

A. GATS	1. Trade in services
B. TRIPS	2. Intellectual property rights
C. AoA	3. Agriculture subsidies and trade rules
D. TBT Agreement	4. Technical barriers to trade

Codes:

A. A-1, B-2, C-3, D-4
B. A-2, B-3, C-1, D-4
C. A-3, B-1, C-2, D-4
D. A-4, B-3, C-2, D-1

143. Match the following WTO Ministerial Conferences with their key outcomes:

A. Doha (2001)	1. Launched the Doha Development Agenda
B. Bali (2013)	2. Trade Facilitation Agreement (TFA)
C. Nairobi (2015)	3. Elimination of export subsidies in agriculture
D. Buenos Aires (2017)	4. No major trade agreements reached

Codes:

A. A-1, B-2, C-3, D-4
B. A-3, B-1, C-4, D-2
C. A-2, B-3, C-1, D-4
D. A-4, B-3, C-2, D-1

144. Arrange the following WTO-related events in chronological order:

1. Uruguay Round negotiations
2. Establishment of the WTO
3. Introduction of the Trade Facilitation Agreement
4. Nairobi Ministerial Conference

Codes:

A. 1, 2, 3, 4 B. 2, 1, 4, 3
C. 3, 1, 2, 4 D. 4, 3, 2, 1

145. Which of the following are fundamental principles of the WTO?

1. Most-Favored Nation (MFN)
2. National Treatment
3. Protectionism
4. Transparency

A. 1 and 2 only
B. 1, 2, and 4 only
C. 2, 3, and 4 only
D. All of the above

146. Which WTO body is responsible for resolving trade disputes?

A. WTO General Council
B. WTO Appellate Body
C. WTO Dispute Settlement Body
D. WTO Ministerial Conference

147. Which of the following agreements govern trade in agricultural products?

A. TRIPS
B. GATS
C. Agreement on Agriculture (AoA)
D. Agreement on Technical Barriers to Trade

148. Which of the following WTO agreements deal with non-tariff barriers?

1. Agreement on Sanitary and Phytosanitary Measures (SPS)
2. Technical Barriers to Trade (TBT) Agreement
3. General Agreement on Trade in Services (GATS)
4. Trade-Related Investment Measures (TRIMs)

A. 1 and 2 only
B. 1, 2, and 3 only
C. 2, 3, and 4 only
D. All of the above

149. Match the following WTO dispute settlement cases with their outcomes:

A. US – Shrimp (1998)	1. WTO ruled against the US for imposing import bans on shrimp caught without turtle-safe nets
B. EC – Bananas III (1997)	2. WTO ruled against the EU's discriminatory banana import policies
C. Canada – Dairy (1999)	3. WTO ruled against Canada for subsidizing dairy exports in violation of WTO rules
D. US – Steel Safeguards (2003)	4. WTO ruled that US safeguards on imported steel violated trade commitments

Codes:

A. A-1, B-2, C-3, D-4
B. A-2, B-3, C-1, D-4
C. A-3, B-4, C-2, D-1
D. A-4, B-1, C-3, D-2

150. Match the following WTO agreements with their primary objectives:

A. TRIMS Agreement	1. Restricts trade-related investment measures that distort trade
B. SPS Agreement	2. Ensures that food safety and animal/plant health standards do not restrict trade unnecessarily
C. SCM Agreement	3. Regulates subsidies and countervailing measures to prevent unfair trade practices
D. GATS	4. Establishes rules for trade in services

Codes:

A. A-1, B-2, C-3, D-4
B. A-3, B-4, C-1, D-2
C. A-4, B-1, C-2, D-3
D. A-2, B-3, C-4, D-1

151. Arrange the following WTO Ministerial Conferences in chronological order:

1. Seattle Ministerial Conference (1999)
2. Cancún Ministerial Conference (2003)
3. Hong Kong Ministerial Conference (2005)
4. Geneva Ministerial Conference (2009)

Codes:

A. 1, 2, 3, 4 B. 2, 1, 4, 3
C. 3, 1, 2, 4 D. 4, 3, 2, 1

152. Which of the following are functions of the WTO Appellate Body?

1. Reviewing panel reports issued under the Dispute Settlement Body (DSB)
2. Imposing trade sanctions on violating countries
3. Interpreting WTO agreements and obligations
4. Enforcing rulings by national courts in WTO member states

A. 1 and 2 only B. 1 and 3 only
C. 2 and 4 only D. All of the above

153. Which of the following are essential WTO principles?

1. Non-Discrimination
2. Reciprocity
3. Economic Nationalism
4. Transparency

A. 1 and 2 only B. 1, 2, and 4 only
C. 2, 3, and 4 only D. All of the above

154. What is the main function of the Committee on Trade and Development (CTD) in the WTO?

A. To oversee regional trade agreements
B. To address the special needs of developing countries
C. To handle anti-dumping investigations
D. To resolve disputes between developed nations

155. Which of the following is not a function of the WTO Secretariat?

A. Providing administrative support for WTO meetings
B. Negotiating trade agreements on behalf of member states
C. Conducting research and analysis on global trade trends
D. Assisting developing countries in implementing WTO agreements

156. Under WTO rules, when can a country impose safeguard measures on imports?

A. When imports threaten to cause serious injury to the domestic industry
B. When foreign companies engage in price-fixing
C. When a country suffers from balance of payments difficulties
D. When trade secrets are stolen by foreign firms

157. Which of the following correctly describes the WTO Trade Policy Review Mechanism (TPRM)?

A. It ensures that countries comply with WTO dispute settlement rulings
B. It evaluates and monitors trade policies of member states
C. It enforces sanctions against non-compliant WTO members
D. It negotiates tariff reductions between developing countries

158. Which of the following WTO principles allows developing countries to receive special and differential treatment?

A. National Treatment
B. Most-Favored Nation (MFN)
C. Special and Differential Treatment (S&DT)
D. Reciprocity

159. **Assertion (A):** The Geneva Conventions of 1949 are the foundation of modern International Humanitarian Law (IHL).

Reason (R): The Geneva Conventions regulate both international and non-international armed conflicts.

A. Both A and R are true, and R is the correct explanation of A.
B. Both A and R are true, but R is not the correct explanation of A.
C. A is true, but R is false.
D. A is false, but R is true.

160. **Assertion (A):** The Additional Protocols of 1977 strengthened the protection of civilians in armed conflicts.

Reason (R): Additional Protocol I applies only to internal armed conflicts, while Additional Protocol II applies to international conflicts.

A. Both A and R are true, and R is the correct explanation of A.
B. Both A and R are true, but R is not the correct explanation of A.
C. A is true, but R is false.
D. A is false, but R is true.

161. Assertion (A): The Hague Conventions of 1899 and 1907 regulate the means and methods of warfare.

Reason (R): The Hague Conventions focus primarily on the protection of civilians during war.

A. Both A and R are true, and R is the correct explanation of A.
B. Both A and R are true, but R is not the correct explanation of A.
C. A is true, but R is false.
D. A is false, but R is true.

162. Match the following Geneva Conventions with their primary focus:

A. First Geneva Convention	1. Protection of the wounded and sick in armed forces on land
B. Second Geneva Convention	2. Protection of the wounded, sick, and shipwrecked at sea
C. Third Geneva Convention	3. Treatment of prisoners of war
D. Fourth Geneva Convention	4. Protection of civilians in times of war

Codes:
A. A-1, B-2, C-3, D-4
B. A-2, B-1, C-4, D-3
C. A-3, B-4, C-2, D-1
D. A-4, B-3, C-1, D-2

163. Match the following Additional Protocols with their scope:

A. Additional Protocol I (1977)	1. Expands protections for civilians and combatants in international conflicts
B. Additional Protocol II (1977)	2. Enhances protections for civilians in non-international conflicts
C. Additional Protocol III (2005)	3. Introduces the Red Crystal as an emblem of protection
D. Rome Statute (1998)	4. Establishes the International Criminal Court (ICC) for war crimes prosecution

Codes:
A. A-1, B-2, C-3, D-4
B. A-2, B-1, C-4, D-3
C. A-3, B-4, C-2, D-1
D. A-4, B-3, C-1, D-2

164. Arrange the following IHL-related treaties in chronological order:
1. Hague Conventions
2. Geneva Conventions (1949)
3. Additional Protocols (1977)
4. Rome Statute (1998)

Codes:
A. 1, 2, 3, 4 B. 2, 1, 4, 3
C. 3, 1, 2, 4 D. 4, 3, 2, 1

165. Which of the following are prohibited weapons under IHL?
1. Biological weapons
2. Chemical weapons
3. Cluster munitions
4. Non-lethal riot control agents

A. 1 and 2 only
B. 1, 2, and 3 only
C. 2, 3, and 4 only
D. All of the above

166. Which of the following acts constitute war crimes under the Geneva Conventions and the Rome Statute?
1. Willful killing of civilians
2. Torture and inhuman treatment
3. Taking hostages
4. Use of child soldiers

A. 1 and 2 only
B. 1, 2, and 3 only
C. 2, 3, and 4 only
D. All of the above

167. Which of the following are key principles of IHL?
1. Distinction
2. Proportionality
3. Military Necessity
4. Reciprocity

A. 1 and 2 only B. 1, 2, and 3 only
C. 2, 3, and 4 only D. All of the above

168. Match the following international humanitarian treaties with their focus areas:

A. 1925 Geneva Protocol	1. Prohibits the use of chemical and biological weapons
B. 1980 Convention on Certain Conventional Weapons (CCW)	2. Regulates the use of weapons causing unnecessary suffering
C. 1997 Ottawa Treaty	3. Bans the use, stockpiling, and production of anti-personnel landmines
D. 2008 Convention on Cluster Munitions	4. Prohibits the use of cluster bombs due to their indiscriminate effects

Codes:
A. A-1, B-2, C-3, D-4
B. A-2, B-3, C-1, D-4
C. A-3, B-4, C-2, D-1
D. A-4, B-1, C-2, D-3

169. Match the following war crimes with their definitions under IHL:

A. Perfidy	1. Misleading an enemy by feigning protected status (e.g., using the Red Cross emblem)
B. Pillaging	2. The unlawful taking of property during war
C. Enforced Disappearance	3. The arrest or abduction of individuals by the state, with their fate concealed
D. Indiscriminate Attack	4. Military attack without distinguishing between civilians and combatants

Codes:
A. A-1, B-2, C-3, D-4
B. A-2, B-3, C-1, D-4
C. A-3, B-1, C-2, D-4
D. A-4, B-3, C-1, D-2

170. Arrange the following IHL-related conventions in chronological order:
1. Hague Conventions
2. Geneva Conventions (1949)
3. Biological Weapons Convention (1972)
4. Ottawa Treaty (1997)

Codes:
A. 1, 2, 3, 4 B. 2, 1, 4, 3
C. 3, 1, 2, 4 D. 4, 3, 2, 1

171. Which of the following acts constitute grave breaches under the Geneva Conventions?
1. Willful killing of protected persons
2. Torture and inhuman treatment
3. Unlawful deportation or transfer
4. Attacks on military objectives

A. 1 and 2 only
B. 1, 2, and 3 only
C. 2, 3, and 4 only
D. All of the above

172. Which of the following are fundamental principles of International Humanitarian Law (IHL)?
1. Principle of Distinction
2. Principle of Proportionality
3. Principle of Retaliation
4. Principle of Military Necessity

A. 1 and 2 only B. 1, 2, and 4 only
C. 2, 3, and 4 only D. All of the above

173. Which of the following courts can prosecute individuals for war crimes under IHL?
A. International Court of Justice (ICJ)
B. International Criminal Court (ICC)
C. Special Tribunal for Lebanon (STL)
D. Extraordinary Chambers in the Courts of Cambodia (ECCC)

174. Under the Geneva Conventions, a civilian loses protection from attack if they:
A. Provide medical aid to wounded soldiers
B. Take direct part in hostilities
C. Remain in an occupied territory
D. Are forcibly recruited into an armed group

175. Which of the following are peremptory norms (jus cogens) under IHL?
1. Prohibition of genocide
2. Prohibition of torture
3. Prohibition of slavery
4. Right to trade freely

A. 1 and 2 only B. 1, 2, and 3 only
C. 2, 3, and 4 only D. All of the above

ANSWERS

1. (B): International law indeed governs relations between states primarily, and it lacks a centralized enforcing authority. However, the absence of enforcement does not explain why it focuses on states; rather, it's a characteristic of its nature, not the reason for its scope.

2. (D): Customary international law is not universally binding on all states because states can opt out as persistent objectors. However, R is true as customary law derives from state practice and opinio juris, though this doesn't make it universally applicable without exception.

3. (C): Treaties are a primary source of international law under Article 38 of the ICJ Statute, but they are not binding on every state regardless of consent—only on states that are parties to them. Thus, R is incorrect.

4. (D): International law is a legal system with binding obligations, not merely a moral one, though enforcement can be weak. R is true because it lacks effective enforcement mechanisms, but this doesn't reduce it to a moral obligation.

5. **(A):** Customary International Law (A) matches general state practices accepted as law (3); Jus Cogens (B) are fundamental, peremptory norms (2); Treaties (C) are formal agreements between states (1); General Principles of Law (D) are derived from domestic systems (4).

6. **(A):** Pacta Sunt Servanda (A) means agreements must be kept (2); Jus Cogens (B) are peremptory norms with no derogation (4); Principle of Sovereignty (C) gives states exclusive authority over territory (3); Prohibition of the Use of Force (D) allows force only in self-defense or with UN approval (1).

7. **(A):** Corfu Channel Case (3) was in 1949; South West Africa Cases (4) in 1966; North Sea Continental Shelf Cases (2) in 1969; Nicaragua v. United States (1) in 1986. This is the correct chronological order.

8. **(D):** Article 38 of the ICJ Statute lists treaties (1), customary international law (2), general principles of law (4) as primary sources, and judicial decisions (3) as a subsidiary source, but all are recognized in the context of the Statute.

9. **(B):** The Montevideo Convention defines statehood by a defined territory (1), permanent population (2), government (implied), and capacity to enter into foreign relations (4). Recognition by other states (3) is not a requirement under this convention.

10. **(B):** The Lotus Principle, from the 1927 PCIJ case, holds that states are sovereign and can act unless international law explicitly prohibits it, reflecting absolute sovereignty unless restricted.

11. **(A):** International law traditionally regulates state conduct, not individuals, unless treaties (e.g., ICCPR) or customary law (e.g., war crimes) provide otherwise. R explains why individuals are generally excluded from its scope.

12. **(A):** State sovereignty limits international court jurisdiction (A), as courts like the ICJ require state consent (R) via optional clauses or treaties, directly explaining the limitation.

13. **(B):** Doctrine of Incorporation (A) means international law applies only if legislated (1); Doctrine of Transformation (B) means it's automatically part of domestic law (2); Dualism (C) sees them as separate systems (3); Monism (D) views them as unified (4).

14. **(A):** ICJ (A) settles state disputes (2); ICC (B) prosecutes individuals for genocide, etc. (1); WTO DSB (C) resolves trade disputes (3); ITLOS (D) handles Law of the Sea cases (4).

15. **(A):** Treaty of Westphalia (1) was 1648; Montevideo Convention (4) 1933; UN Charter (2) 1945; Vienna Convention (3) 1969. This is the correct chronological order.

16. **(A):** Jus Cogens norms are non-derogable (1) and override conflicting treaties (3). They don't require state consent (2) for application, and cannot be modified by regional agreements (4).

17. **(C):** Self-defense (1) and UNSC authorization (2) are clear exceptions under the UN Charter. Humanitarian intervention (4) is debated but recognized in some cases (e.g., Kosovo). Pre-emptive strikes (3) lack clear legal grounding.

18. **(A):** Erga omnes obligations (e.g., prohibition of genocide) are owed to the international community as a whole, not just treaty parties, and can be enforced universally.

19. **(B):** The Vienna Convention (1961) grants diplomats immunity from jurisdiction (1), free passage (2), and protects premises (4). Immunity from espionage (3) isn't granted; it's a breach leading to expulsion.

20. **(B):** Rebus Sic Stantibus (Vienna Convention Article 62) allows treaty withdrawal if circumstances fundamentally change, not automatic in war (a), not based on national interest (c), nor indefinite binding (d).

21. **(A):** Customary law binds all states (except persistent objectors) without explicit consent (A), because it arises from state practice and opinio juris (R), explaining its binding nature.

22. **(D):** Treaties bind only consenting states, not all states (A is false). Pacta sunt servanda (R) ensures treaties are kept by parties, but doesn't extend to non-parties.

23. **(A):** General principles of law (e.g., good faith) are a primary source under Article 38 (A), derived from domestic legal systems (R), which explains their origin and status.

24. **(A):** Treaties (A) are binding agreements (1); Customary Law (B) is consistent practice accepted as law (2); General Principles (C) are domestic-derived concepts (3); Judicial Decisions (D) are subsidiary interpretive means (4).

25. (A): Vienna Convention (A) codifies treaty law (1); Montevideo (B) defines statehood (2); UN Charter (C) frames international law (3); ICJ Statute (D) lists sources (4).

26. (A): Treaty of Westphalia (1) 1648; Montevideo (2) 1933; UN Charter (3) 1945; Vienna Convention (4) 1969. This is the correct chronological order.

27. (B): Article 38 lists treaties (1), customary law (2), and general principles (4) as primary sources. Judicial decisions (3) are subsidiary, not primary.

28. (B): Customary law requires state practice (1) and opinio juris (2). The persistent objector rule (3) allows opting out, but treaty ratification (4) isn't a requirement.

29. (A): Jus cogens (e.g., prohibition of torture) are non-derogable norms that supersede conflicting laws or treaties, not optional (d) or limited to treaties (b) or regions (c).

30. (D): Nicaragua v. USA (a) confirmed customary law on non-intervention; Lotus Case (b) on sovereignty; North Sea Cases (c) on custom formation—all uphold customary law's binding nature.

31. (A): Soft law (e.g., UN resolutions) influences international law (A) because, despite lacking binding force, it shapes state behavior and treaties (R), explaining its importance.

32. (B): Pacta sunt servanda (A) applies to all treaties, and they bind only parties (R). However, R limits scope, not explains the principle's application to all treaties.

33. (A): North Sea (A) emphasized customary law (1); Nicaragua (B) non-intervention (2); Lotus (C) permissive sovereignty (3); Corfu (D) duty not to harm via territory (4).

34. (A): Vienna 1961 (A) covers diplomatic immunity (1); Vienna 1969 (B) treaty law (2); Montevideo (C) statehood (3); UN Charter (D) prohibits force (4).

35. (A): Hague Conventions (1) 1899/1907; League Covenant (2) 1919; UN Charter (3) 1945; Vienna Convention (4) 1969. This is the correct order.

36. (B): Judicial decisions (1) and scholars' opinions (2) are subsidiary sources per Article 38. UNGA resolutions (4) influence but aren't primary. General principles (3) are primary.

37. (A): Customary law needs consistent state practice (1) and opinio juris (2). Codification (3) and ICJ enforcement (4) aren't necessary for its development.

38. (A): Prohibition of genocide (1) and slavery (3) are jus cogens norms. Freedom of trade (2) and diplomatic protection (4) are not peremptory norms.

39. (C): Stare Decisis means courts follow precedents, though in international law (e.g., ICJ), it's not binding as in domestic systems, unlike (a), (b), or (d).

40. (B): Jus cogens (1), UNSC Resolutions (2), and customary law (3) can override treaties. Persistent objection (4) applies to custom formation, not treaty override.

41. (A): Recognition is political (A), not legally required, and R explains this as there's no duty under international law to recognize states, making it a discretionary act.

42. (A): Montevideo (A) sets statehood criteria, and R lists them (population, territory, government, capacity), directly explaining the convention's accepted standards.

43. (D): De facto recognition (R) is temporary and conditional, not granting full diplomatic status (A), which is reserved for de jure recognition.

44. (A): Constitutive (A) grants legal personality via recognition (1); Declaratory (B) bases statehood on facts (2); Estrada (C) avoids government change bias (3); Stimson (D) rejects aggression-based states (4).

45. (A): Tinoco (A) upheld validity sans recognition (1); Greek Orthodox (B) showed recognition as political (2); Arantzazu (C) tied courts to executive (3); Luther (D) recognized Soviet laws (4).

46. (A): Stimson Doctrine (4) 1932; Montevideo (1) 1933; UN Charter (2) 1945; Kosovo (3) 2008. This is the correct chronological order.

47. (B): Government recognition often considers effective control (1), legitimacy (2), and stability (4). UN consent (3) isn't required for recognition.

48. (B): De facto recognition hinges on military control (1), political interests (2), and diplomatic ties (4). Democratic consistency (3) isn't a strict requirement.

49. (B):. The Stimson Doctrine (1932) prohibits recognizing states formed via aggression (e.g., Manchuria), unlike Estrada (a), Monroe (c), or Calvo (d).

50. (A): UN admission (a) is collective recognition by the international community, unlike bilateral acts in (b), (c), or (d).

51. (A): Tobar (A) rejects unconstitutional governments (1); Estrada (B) avoids political bias (2); Stimson (C) rejects aggression gains (3); Monroe (D) opposes European interference (4).

52. (A): Taiwan (A) recognized by some, not UN (1); Palestine (B) UNGA but not all states (2); South Sudan (C) full UN (3); Kosovo (D) partial, not UN (4).

53. (B): India-Bangladesh (2) 1971; US-China (1) 1979; South Sudan UN (4) 2011; Palestine UNGA (3) 2012. This is the correct order.

54. (C): State recognition involves control (1), legal obligations (2), politics (3), and often democracy (4), though the latter varies by state practice.

55. (A): Express (1), implied (2), and collective (3) are recognized forms. Secret recognition (4) isn't a standard legal category.

56. (B): De facto recognition acknowledges control temporarily, not granting full legal legitimacy, unlike de jure recognition.

57. (B): Tobar (1), Stimson (3), and Hallstein (4) support non-recognition of unlawful regimes. Estrada (2) favors automatic recognition, opposing this.

58. (A): State succession (a) ensures new governments inherit obligations, unlike effective control (b), continuity (c), or auto-recognition (d).

59. (A): Nationality is a right (UDHR Article 15) (A), and preventing statelessness (R) via this right explains its fundamental status in international law.

60. (C)

61. (D): Non-refoulement applies only to refugees, not IDPs (A is false). Refugee law doesn't equate IDPs and refugees (R is false), but R's truth lies in legal distinctions.

62. (A): Refugee (A) flees persecution (1); Asylum Seeker (B) seeks status (2); IDP (C) displaced internally (3); Stateless (D) lacks nationality (4).

63. (A): 1951 Convention (A) defines refugee rights (1); 1961 Convention (B) prevents statelessness (2); 1998 Principles (C) protect IDPs (3); 1967 Protocol (D) expands 1951 scope (4).

64. (B): UNHCR (3) 1950; Refugee Convention (2) 1951; Statelessness Convention (1) 1961; IDP Principles (4) 1998. This is the correct order.

65. (B): 1951 Convention requires fear of persecution (1), inability to return (3), and border crossing (4). Nationality (2) isn't a criterion.

66. (B): Stateless persons have rights to nationality (1), asylum (2), and non-deportation (3) under conventions. Voting (4) depends on state law, not guaranteed.

67. (B): Non-refoulement (1951 Convention Article 33) prohibits returning refugees to persecution, unlike jus soli (a), succession (c), or naturalization (d).

68. (B): IDPs result from conflict (1), disasters (2), and persecution (4). Economic migration (3) typically involves voluntary movement, not displacement.

69. (A): Voluntary return ends refugee status (A), as repatriation (R) is a durable solution, directly explaining the status loss.

70. (A): IDPs retain citizen rights (A) because they stay within borders under national protection (R), explaining their legal status.

71. (A): UNHCR (A) aids refugees (1); IOM (B) manages migration (2); OHCHR (C) monitors rights (3); OCHA (D) coordinates crises (4).

72. (A): 1954 Convention (A) grants stateless rights (1); 1961 (B) prevents statelessness (2); Dublin (C) assigns asylum duties (3); Cartagena (D) expands refugee definition (4).

73. (A): UNHCR (1) 1950; 1951 Convention (2); 1967 Protocol (3); Global Compact (4) 2018. This is the correct order.

74. (B): UNHCR recognizes repatriation (1), integration (2), and resettlement (3) as durable solutions. Dual nationality (4) isn't a standard solution.

75. (B): Statelessness arises from law conflicts (1), revocation (2), and stateless parents (3). Marriage (4) only causes it if laws discriminate, not inherently.

76. (B): The Dublin Regulation assigns which EU state processes asylum claims, not statelessness (a), global protection (c), or climate refugees (d).

77. (B): Jus sanguinis bases nationality on parentage, unlike jus soli (a) by birth place, naturalization (c), or dual citizenship (d).

78. (B): Fraud (1), foreign military service (2), and voluntary new nationality (4) can justify revocation under international law. Political dissent (3) violates rights.

79. (D): Extradition isn't a general legal obligation (A) under international law, but treaties (R) create binding duties between states, making R true.

80. (D): Non-refoulement doesn't prohibit all extradition (A), only when persecution or torture risks exist (R), which is true under refugee law.

81. (A): Political offenders are often exempt (A), and the exception (R) prevents persecution via extradition, directly explaining the exemption.

82. (A): Specialty (A) limits trials to extradited offense (1); Dual Criminality (B) requires offense in both states (2); Non-Refoulement (C) blocks extradition if persecution (3); Political Exception (D) denies for political crimes (4).

83. (A): Soering (A) denied extradition for inhuman treatment (1); Abu Salem (B) applied specialty (2); Pinochet (C) allowed extradition for rights violations (3); Snowden (D) got asylum to avoid persecution (4).

84. (D): Refugee Convention (3) 1951; European Extradition (2) 1957; Torture Convention (1) 1984; Rome Statute (4) 1998. This is the correct order.

85. (D): Extradition can be denied for political offenses (1), human rights risks (2), no dual criminality (3), and diplomatic immunity (4).

86. (A): Fair trial assurance (a) is often required in extradition treaties, unlike death penalty (b), citizenship renunciation (c), or no relations (d).

87. (D): States can refuse if the person is a national (a), crime carries death (b), or persecution risk exists (c), all valid under international practice.

88. (A): European Convention (1) and UNTOC (2) directly govern extradition. Geneva (3) and Montevideo (4) focus on war and statehood, not extradition.

89. (A): European Convention (A) for Europe (1); UNCAC (B) for corruption (2); SAARC (C) for South Asia (3); UNTOC (D) for organized crime (4).

90. (A): Territorial (A) within state (1); Diplomatic (B) in embassies (2); Humanitarian (C) for crises (3); Political (D) for persecution (4).

91. (A): 1951 Convention (1); 1967 Protocol (4); Cartagena (2) 1984; Global Compact (3) 2018. This is the correct order.

92. (B): Extradition requires an extraditable crime (1), jurisdiction (3), and dual criminality (4). Prior conviction (2) isn't always needed.

93. (A): Asylum seekers have the right to seek asylum (1) and protection from refoulement (3). Granting asylum (2) and country choice (4) aren't guaranteed.

94. (B): Diplomatic asylum depends on the host state's discretion (b), not absolute (a), not under 1951 Convention (c), and is recognized in practice (d).

95. (A): Double jeopardy (a) prevents extradition if acquitted, unlike repeated extradition (b), re-prosecution limits (c), or trial location (d).

96. (A): The rule of specialty (a) restricts prosecution to the extradited offense, not unlimited trials (b), not tied to asylum (c), or override (d).

97. (B): Genocide (1), war crimes (2), and terrorism (3) are excluded from political offense exceptions. Defamation (4) isn't typically excluded.

98. (D): The 1951 Convention (Article 1F) denies asylum for war crimes (a), serious non-political crimes (b), or acts against UN purposes (c), covering all options.

99. (D): UNGA resolutions are not legally binding, except in matters of budget and internal UN administration. However, they carry political weight and can contribute to customary international law.

100. (A): Chapter VII of the UN Charter allows the UNSC to impose sanctions and authorize military action, and its decisions are binding on all member states.

101. (C): The ICJ has jurisdiction only if states consent to it. While UN members are encouraged to accept ICJ jurisdiction, it is not compulsory unless they have accepted the court's jurisdiction under Article 36 of the ICJ Statute.

102. (A):
- UNGA adopts resolutions and budgets.
- UNSC manages peace and security.
- ICJ settles state disputes.
- ECOSOC manages economic and social programs.

103. (A):
- WHO manages global health issues.
- UNESCO promotes education and cultural cooperation.
- FAO focuses on food security.
- ILO sets labor standards.

104. (A): • UN Charter (1945) created the UN.
• ICJ was established in 1945 as the principal judicial organ.
• UN Peacekeeping was initiated in 1948.
• Millennium Development Goals (2000) set global goals for sustainable development.

105. (B): The five permanent members (P5) are the US, UK, China, Russia, and France. Germany is not a permanent member.

106. (B): The UN Secretary-General leads UN operations and appoints peacekeeping missions, but does not chair UNSC meetings or issue binding decisions.

107. (B): The P5 nations (US, UK, France, China, Russia) hold veto power, allowing them to block any substantive resolution.

108. (B): The UN Human Rights Council (UNHRC) monitors human rights violations worldwide.

109. (B): The United Nations High Commissioner for Refugees (UNHCR) handles refugee protection globally.

110. (A): • UNIFIL – United Nations Interim Force in Lebanon.
• UNAMID – Joint UN-African Union Mission in Darfur, Sudan.
• MONUSCO – Stabilization mission in Democratic Republic of Congo.
• MINUSMA – Multidimensional Integrated Stabilization Mission in Mali.

111. (A): • Dag Hammarskjöld (Sweden) served from 1953-1961.
• Kofi Annan (Ghana) served from 1997-2006.
• Ban Ki-moon (South Korea) served from 2007-2016.
• António Guterres (Portugal) has served since 2017.

112. (A): • Resolution 242 (1967): Peace framework for Israel-Palestine conflict.
• Resolution 687 (1991): Ceasefire and weapons inspections in Iraq post-Gulf War.
• Resolution 1325 (2000): First major UNSC resolution on Women, Peace, and Security.
• Resolution 1973 (2011): Approved military intervention in Libya.

113. (B): The six principal UN organs are UNGA, UNSC, ICJ, ECOSOC, Trusteeship Council, and the Secretariat. The ICC is not a UN organ, but an independent court under the Rome Statute.

114. (A): Only UNSC Chapter VII resolutions are legally binding. UNGA resolutions, ICJ advisory opinions, and HRC recommendations are not binding.

115. (A): The United Nations body primarily responsible for overseeing decolonization and self-determination issues is the UN General Assembly, specifically through one of its subsidiary bodies known as the Special Committee on Decolonization (also known as the Committee of 24). Established in 1961, this committee is tasked with monitoring the implementation of the Declaration on the Granting of Independence to Colonial Countries and Peoples and to support the process of decolonization.

116. (A): For a UNSC resolution to pass, it needs at least 9 affirmative votes, including no vetoes from any of the five permanent members. An abstention is not a veto.

117. (B): The International Atomic Energy Agency (IAEA) monitors nuclear programs, including Iran's Joint Comprehensive Plan of Action (JCPOA) compliance.

118. (B): ECOSOC oversees UN specialized agencies and coordinates economic/social policies but does not have binding enforcement powers over international human rights law.

119. (D): ICJ jurisdiction is not automatic; states must consent to it either through treaties, special agreements, or declarations under Article 36 of the ICJ Statute.

120. (C): Arbitration is legally binding but is not enforceable under the UN Charter. Instead, it depends on bilateral or multilateral agreements.

121. (D): Mediation is non-binding and relies on the goodwill of the disputing parties. It is not a function of the ICJ, which settles disputes through judicial means.

122. (A): • Negotiation – Direct state-to-state talks.
• Mediation – Third-party proposes solutions but non-binding.
• Arbitration – Neutral tribunal issues binding decisions.
• Adjudication – Legal dispute resolution via courts like ICJ.

123. (A): • Rann of Kutch Dispute was settled through arbitration.
• US-Iran Hostage Crisis was resolved via mediation by Algeria.
• Nicaragua v. USA was settled via ICJ adjudication.
• Camp David Accords were a result of negotiations between Israel and Egypt.

124. (A): • Rann of Kutch Arbitration (1968).
• Camp David Accords (1978).
• Nicaragua v. USA (ICJ, 1986).
• Rohingya Genocide Case (ICJ, 2019).

125. (B): Only arbitration and adjudication (ICJ, WTO dispute settlement) result in legally binding decisions. Mediation and negotiation are non-binding.

126. (B): ICJ, PCA, and WTO's Dispute Settlement Body handle legal disputes. UNGA passes resolutions but does not adjudicate disputes.

127. (A): State sovereignty ensures that international courts need state consent to exercise jurisdiction.

128. (A): Chapter VI of the UN Charter focuses on peaceful settlement of disputes, including negotiation, mediation, arbitration, and ICJ adjudication.

129. (A): • Good Offices – A neutral third party facilitates communication without offering a solution.
• Conciliation – A third party proposes a settlement after an investigation.
• Inquiry – A fact-finding mission to establish dispute causes.
• Arbitration – A binding dispute resolution method.

130. (A): • Chagos Archipelago Case (2019) – ICJ ruled UK should return the islands to Mauritius.
• South China Sea Arbitration (2016) – PCA ruled China violated UNCLOS.
• Kosovo Advisory Opinion (2010) – ICJ ruled Kosovo's independence was legal.
• Nuclear Tests Case (1974) – ICJ ruled France's nuclear tests were unlawful.

131. (A): • Nuclear Tests Case (1974).
• Nicaragua v. USA (1986).
• South China Sea Arbitration (2016).
• Chagos Archipelago Case (2019).

132. (A): • Under international law, a state must make reparations for wrongful acts.
• Countermeasures (e.g., trade sanctions) are permitted in some cases.
• ICJ jurisdiction is not automatic.
• States cannot use domestic law to escape responsibility.

133. (B): • UNCLOS disputes are resolved through ITLOS, ICJ, or arbitration (Annex VII).
• WTO Dispute Settlement Body is not part of UNCLOS.

134. (B): The PCA provides arbitration services for disputes between states, international organizations, and private parties.

135. (C): • Good offices, mediation, and negotiation are non-binding.
• Adjudication (ICJ, WTO disputes) is binding.

136. (B): Audi Alteram Partem ensures both parties are heard before the ICJ issues a judgment.

137. (A): Chapter VI of the UN Charter promotes negotiation, mediation, arbitration, and ICJ adjudication for peaceful dispute settlement.

138. (B): Countermeasures must be proportionate and cannot violate jus cogens norms (e.g., torture, genocide bans).

139. (A): The WTO replaced GATT in 1995 as a permanent organization with a broader mandate, including trade in goods, services, and intellectual property.

140. (B): While MFN ensures equal trade treatment, exceptions exist, such as regional trade agreements (RTAs) and special provisions for developing nations.

141. (C): The DSB does not impose sanctions directly but authorizes retaliation measures (e.g., trade restrictions) if a country fails to comply with WTO rulings.

142. (A): • GATS (General Agreement on Trade in Services) regulates services trade.
• TRIPS (Trade-Related Aspects of Intellectual Property Rights) governs IP protection.
• AoA (Agreement on Agriculture) sets rules for agricultural trade and subsidies.
• TBT (Technical Barriers to Trade) Agreement addresses product standards and regulations.

143. (A): • Doha (2001) launched the Doha Development Agenda.
• Bali (2013) led to the Trade Facilitation Agreement (TFA).
• Nairobi (2015) focused on eliminating agricultural export subsidies.
• Buenos Aires (2017) saw no major trade agreements due to disagreements.

144. (A):
- Uruguay Round (1986-1994) led to WTO's creation.
- WTO was established in 1995.
- Trade Facilitation Agreement (2013, Bali).
- Nairobi Ministerial Conference (2015).

145. (B):
- MFN ensures non-discriminatory trade treatment.
- National Treatment prevents discrimination between domestic and foreign goods.
- Transparency requires clear trade policies.
- Protectionism contradicts WTO principles.

146. (C): The WTO Dispute Settlement Body (DSB) resolves disputes using panels and appellate review.

147. (C): The Agreement on Agriculture (AoA) covers agricultural subsidies, market access, and trade rules.

148. (A):
- SPS Agreement addresses food safety and animal/plant health standards.
- TBT Agreement regulates technical barriers to trade (e.g., product standards, labeling).

149. (A):
- US – Shrimp (1998): US violated WTO rules by restricting shrimp imports based on turtle conservation concerns.
- EC – Bananas III (1997): EU discriminated against Latin American banana exporters in favor of former colonies.
- Canada – Dairy (1999): Canada illegally subsidized dairy exports, violating WTO agreements.
- US – Steel Safeguards (2003): US wrongly imposed safeguards on imported steel.

150. (A):
- TRIMS (Trade-Related Investment Measures) limits investment restrictions that distort trade.
- SPS (Sanitary and Phytosanitary Measures) ensures that food safety and health regulations do not create unnecessary trade barriers.
- SCM (Subsidies and Countervailing Measures) Agreement regulates government subsidies to prevent unfair competition.
- GATS (General Agreement on Trade in Services) governs international trade in services.

151. (A):
- Seattle (1999): Failed ministerial meeting due to anti-globalization protests.
- Cancún (2003): Negotiations collapsed due to disagreements on agriculture and industrial goods.
- Hong Kong (2005): Agreed to end agricultural export subsidies by 2013.
- Geneva (2009): Attempted revival of the Doha Development Round.

152. (B):
- The Appellate Body reviews appeals from WTO dispute settlement panels.
- It does not impose trade sanctions, but the DSB authorizes them.
- It interprets WTO agreements but does not enforce national court rulings.

153. (B):
- Non-discrimination (MFN and National Treatment).
- Reciprocity (mutual trade benefits).
- Transparency (clear and predictable trade policies).
- Economic Nationalism contradicts WTO's free trade principles.

154. (B): The CTD focuses on integrating developing countries into the global trading system and monitors trade preferences under WTO rules.

155. (B): The WTO Secretariat does not negotiate on behalf of states—members negotiate their own trade agreements.

156. (A): Safeguard measures (under the WTO Safeguards Agreement) are temporary restrictions on imports to protect domestic industries from sudden surges.

157. (B): The WTO's Trade Policy Review Mechanism (TPRM) monitors and assesses the trade policies of members to promote transparency and adherence to WTO rules.

158. (C): The Special and Differential Treatment (S&DT) principle provides developing countries with flexible trade obligations and additional time to implement WTO agreements.

159. (B): The Geneva Conventions (1949) form the core of IHL, but they primarily regulate international armed conflicts (IACs). Common Article 3 applies to non-international armed conflicts (NIACs), but coverage is limited.

160. (C): Additional Protocol I (1977) applies to international conflicts, and Additional Protocol II (1977) applies to non-international conflicts. Both enhanced civilian protections.

161. (C): The Hague Conventions (1899, 1907) regulate means and methods of warfare, including weapons and military conduct. Civilian protection is mainly covered by the Geneva Conventions.

162. (A):
- First Geneva Convention – Protects wounded and sick soldiers on land.
- Second Geneva Convention – Protects wounded, sick, and shipwrecked at sea.
- Third Geneva Convention – Governs prisoners of war (POWs).

- Fourth Geneva Convention – Protects civilians in war.

163. (A):
- Additional Protocol I – Covers international armed conflicts.
- Additional Protocol II – Covers non-international armed conflicts.
- Additional Protocol III – Introduced the Red Crystal emblem.
- Rome Statute (1998) – Created the International Criminal Court (ICC).

164. (A):
- Hague Conventions (1899, 1907).
- Geneva Conventions (1949).
- Additional Protocols (1977).
- Rome Statute (1998).

165. (B):
- Biological and chemical weapons are banned under the Biological and Chemical Weapons Conventions.
- Cluster munitions are banned under the 2008 Convention on Cluster Munitions.
- Non-lethal riot control agents (e.g., tear gas) are allowed in law enforcement but not in warfare.

166. (D): War crimes under the Geneva Conventions and ICC Rome Statute include willful killing, torture, hostage-taking, and recruitment of child soldiers.

167. (B): IHL is based on Distinction, Proportionality, and Military Necessity. Reciprocity (retaliation) is not a principle of IHL.

168. (A):
- 1925 Geneva Protocol bans chemical and biological weapons.
- 1980 CCW regulates inhumane weapons like landmines and incendiary weapons.
- 1997 Ottawa Treaty bans anti-personnel landmines.
- 2008 Cluster Munitions Convention bans cluster bombs.

169. (A):
- Perfidy: Misleading an enemy using protected symbols like the Red Cross.
- Pillaging: Looting of property during war.
- Enforced Disappearance: State's unlawful detention with no disclosure of fate.
- Indiscriminate Attack: Attacks that do not distinguish between civilians and combatants.

170. (A):
- Hague Conventions (1899, 1907)
- Geneva Conventions (1949)
- Biological Weapons Convention (1972)
- Ottawa Treaty (1997).

171. (B):
- Willful killing, torture, and unlawful deportation are grave breaches under the Geneva Conventions.
- Attacks on military objectives are legal under IHL, if they comply with distinction and proportionality.

172. (B):
- Distinction (separating civilians and combatants).
- Proportionality (ensuring attacks do not cause excessive harm).
- Military Necessity (allows force only if essential for military objectives).
- Retaliation is prohibited in IHL.

173. (B):
- The ICC prosecutes individuals for war crimes.
- The ICJ handles disputes between states, not individuals.
- STL focuses on terrorism-related cases.
- ECCC is a hybrid tribunal for Khmer Rouge crimes.

174. (B): Civilians are protected unless they take direct part in hostilities. Medical aid and residency in occupied territory do not remove their protection.

175. (B): Genocide, torture, and slavery are jus cogens norms, meaning no derogation is permitted. Free trade is not a jus cogens norm.

UNIT 4 Law of Crimes

GENERAL PRINCIPLES OF CRIMINAL LAW

BHARATIYA NYAYA SANHITA (BNS) (An Overview)

The Bharatiya Nyaya Sanhita, 2023 (BNS) is a transformative piece of legislation in India, enacted to modernize the criminal justice system. Passed by the Indian Parliament in December 2023 and effective from July 1, 2024, it replaces the colonial-era Indian Penal Code, 1860 (IPC). Together with the Bharatiya Nagarik Suraksha Sanhita, 2023 (BNSS) and the Bharatiya Sakshya Adhiniyam, 2023 (BSA), the BNS forms a trio of laws aimed at creating a contemporary, victim-centric, and justice-oriented legal framework.

The BNS streamlines the IPC's 511 sections into 358, simplifying legal language, addressing modern crimes, and emphasizing justice over punishment. Key features include:

- **Modernization of Offences:** Introduces provisions for organized crime and terrorism, reflecting current challenges. Cybercrimes are partially addressed, though primarily governed by the Information Technology Act, 2000.
- **Gender Neutrality:** Uses inclusive language for certain offences to ensure broader applicability.
- **Community Service:** Introduces community service as an alternative penalty for minor offences, promoting rehabilitation.
- **Stricter Penalties:** Enhances punishments for crimes like mob lynching and sexual offences.
- **Simplification:** Removes archaic terms and redundant provisions for accessibility.

The BNS aligns with India's democratic values, aiming to decolonize the legal system and address the needs of a modern nation while balancing justice, victim rights, and societal welfare.

Actus reus and Mens rea

In law, crime consists of two elements: *actus reus* and *mens rea*. The former represents the physical aspects of crime and latter represents its mental aspects. Actus reus has been defined as such result of human conduct as the law seeks to prevent. An act may be positive or negative. Mens rea is a loose term of elastic signification and cover a wide range of mental states and conditions, the existence of which would give a criminal hue to actus reus.

There might be actus without mens rea. Thus, for example, if an infant of 2 years while playing with a loaded pistol lets go and kill another person, there is *actus reus* without *mens rea*. There might also be *mens rea* without *actus reus*. In ethics or religions an evil deed may be committed in mind and might constitute a wrong, even though it has not manifested itself in physical conduct.

It may further be noted that *mens rea* as such is not punishable. Thus, if A has intention to kill B, A cannot be brought to the court on that ground alone; some acts have to be done by A *e.g.*, if A is discovered with a loaded gun in the compound of B, then A has done some act and he may be guilty. There are some exception to the general rule that intention as such is no crime *e.g.*, intention to commit some reasons or conspiracy to commit a crime. However, sometimes an act alone is sufficient to constitute a crime without the existence of *mens rea*.

Actus non facit reum, nisi mens sit rea: The fundamental principles of penal liability is *actus non facit reum, nisi sit rea i.e.*, the fact itself is not criminal unless accompanied by a guilty mind. It may be noted that mens rea must extend to all the three parts of an act, viz. (i) the physical doing or not doing, (ii) the circumstances, and (iii) the consequences. If the *mens rea* does not extend to any part of the act, there will be no guilty mind behind the act.

MENS REA (Guilty Mind) AND MOTIVE (Why the Act was Done)

Motive is something which prompts a man to form an intention. In other words, it is ulterior intention in immediate mental condition. Intention relates to means whereas motive relates to the end. Motive though not sine qua non for bringing the offence home to the accused, is relevant on the question of intention. Motive is basically a clue to the intention.

Where there is a clear proof of motive for the crime, this lends additional support to the court's finding that the accused was guilty but the absence of clear proof of motive does not necessarily lead to the contrary conclusion. There may be an offence without a motive in same way in which the strongest motive may not impel a person to commit an offence. It may be noted that purity of motive cannot absolve a person from criminal liability. Thus, if a person decides to kill his starving children because he feels that they will pass on to a better world, his motive is a good but his intention is wrong.

Motive of an act cannot become a litmus test to determine the criminal characteristics. Where there is a direct evidence against the accused, the motive becomes immaterial but where there is a circumstantial evidence, absence of motive is favourable to the accused. In criminal law, the general rule is that motive is irrelevant and only intention is relevant, however the motive becomes relevant in certain cases. In 'criminal attempts', it is the motive which makes the act wrongful though the act in itself may not be wrongful. Further, motive becomes relevant in cases. Where a particular intention forms a part of the definition of a criminal offence. In civil liability motive assumes relevance.

MENS REA WHEN NOT ESSENTIAL: STRICT LIABILITY

Although *mens rea* is a sacrosanct principle of criminal law, it can be waived off in certain circumstances. The following are the exceptional cases in which *mens rea* is not required in criminal law.

- Mens rea is not essential in respect of five offences in I.P.C., namely - sec. 147 (wagering war), sec. 152 (Acts endangering sovereignty, unity and integrity of India), sec. 137 (kidnapping), sec. 138 (Abduction), 178 (counterfeiting coins, Government stamps etc.).

  Thus, where the accused is charged with kidnapping a minor girl. His plea that he honestly believed that the girl was not a minor was not accepted by the court. Similarly, a person who attempts to pass a counterfeit currency note or in whose possession such notes were found being counterfeit, unless the person is an ignorant and illiterate villager.

- Where a statute imposes strict liability, the presence or absence of a guilty mind is irrelevant. Several modern statutes passed in the interest of public safety and social welfare impose such strict liability *e.g.*, the motor vehicles Act; the arms Act; narcotic drugs and psychotropic substances Act, 1985; the public liability insurance Act, 1991 etc., similarly in other statutory offences like bribing, smuggling, forex violation, sale of adulterated articles etc., the guilty mind is not taken into account by the courts.

  The underlying principles of jurisdiction for such statutory offences is pointed out by Roscoe Pound: "Statutory crimes express the needs of society. Such statutes are not meant to punish vicious will, but to put pressure on the thoughtless and inefficient to do their whole duty in the interest of public health, safety or morals."

- When it is difficult to prove *mens rea*, where the penalties are pretty fines and where a statute has done away with the necessity of *mens rea* on the basis of expediency, strict liability in criminal law may be imposed *e.g.*, parking offences.
- Public nuisance is another exception to the doctrine of *mens rea*.

In Halsbury laws of England, it is stated that if a statutory crime is silent with regard to *mens rea*, there is a presumption that *mens rea* is essential. The presumption can be rebutted either by term of statute or by the subject matter with which it deals. It is of utmost importance for the protection of liberty of a subject that the court should always bear in mind that unless a statute rules out *mens rea* as a constituent part of a crime, the court should not find a man guilty of an offence against the criminal law, unless he has a guilty mind. In other words, absolute liability is not to be presumed but ought to be established or found out by referring to the object and subject matter of statute.

In the state of Maharashtra *vs* M.H. George, it was held that: "Merely because a statute deals with grave social evil is not sufficient to infer strict liability, it must also be seen that whether imposition of strict liability would assist in the enforcement of regulations. Unless this is so, there is no reason in penalizing him and it cannot be inferred that the legislation imposed strict liability merely in order to find a luckless victim".

In this case, RBI placed some restrictions on the entry of gold into India, thus superseding its earlier notification. The accused reached Bombay, where the gold bars were recovered from his jacket. The accused pleaded that he had no *mens rea* and that he had no knowledge of RBI notification. After considering the object and subject matter of statute, their lordship held that there was no scope for the invocation of the doctrine of *mens rea* in this particular case. The very object and the purpose of the act would be frustrated if the accused should be proved to have knowledge that he was contravening the law, before he could be held to have contravened the provision.

In Nathulal *vs* State of M.P., it was held that object of statute would not be defeated by reading *mens rea* into the provisions of the Essential Commodities Act, 1955. The appellant, a dealer of foodgrains had made an application for a licence but no intimation was given to him that his application was rejected. He purchased foodgrains from time to time and submitted returns to the licence department. One day, a food inspector checked his godowns and found foodgrains stored without any licence. The conviction of the accused was set aside as he had no *mens rea*.

The Supreme Court held: there is a presumption that *mens rea* is an essential ingredient in every criminal offence, but this may be rebutted by the express words of a statute creating the offence or by necessary implication. However, *mens rea* by necessary implication can be excluded from a statute only where it is absolutely clear that the implementation of the object of a statute would otherwise be defeated and its exclusion enable those put under strict liability by their act or omission to assist the promotion of the law. The nature of *mens rea* that will be implied in a statute creating an offence depends upon the object of the act and provisions thereof. Thus, the general rule that there must be a mind at fault before there can be a crime, is not an inflexible rule.

In conclusion, it can be said that the ultimate factor which the court should keep in mind while judging the exclusion of *mens rea* is a balance between individual liberty and public order. According to Sir. J. Stephens, the doctrine of *mens rea* is misleading as the doctrine originated when criminal law practically dealt with offences which were not defined. Today, however, each crime has a precise definition.

As far as offences under the IPC are concerned, every offence is defined and the definition states not only what the accused must have done, but the state of his mind with regard to the act when he was doing it. For example, theft must be committed dishonestly, cheating, fraudulently, murder must be committed either intentionally or knowingly, and so on. Thus, there is no room for the general doctrine of *mens rea* in the IPC. Each definition of the offence is self sufficient. All that the prosecution has to do in India, is to prove that a particular act committed by the accused answers the various ingredients of the offence in the particular Section of the IPC.

JOINT LIABILITY

The law relating to joint liability is contained in sec. 3(5)-3(9) of IPC. There are three more sections in the code which deal with joint or constructive liability, viz sec. 190 (unlawful assembly), sec. 310 (Dacoity with murder), and sec. 331 (House breaking by night and where death or grievous hurt is caused) murder or grievous hurt). The joint or group liability is also called constructive liability *i.e.*, liability of all for the acts of one or some of them. Suppose A, B, C and D join to commit Z's murder. If they merely join, and do nothing else, they would be guilty of offence of criminal conspiracy even though nobody is murdered. But if A alone commits that murder, law will fix on all of them joint liability for the act of A.

Joint liability in criminal law means the liability of a person for an offence which he has not actually committed. This must not, however be confused with vicarious liability, which is the liability one incurs for the acts of a servant or an agent during the course of service. Here, unlike the joint liability, neither the common intention nor the common object is needed to be proved. Vicarious liability in criminal law is an exception rather than a rule. But, joint liability in criminal law is a well recognised principle.

Sec. 34 : Sec. 3(5)-3(9) lay down the following four important principles governing joint offence *i.e.*, persons who join together to commit a crime:

- Act done by several persons in furtherance of common intention (sec. 3(5)).
- Act done with criminal knowledge or intention (sec. 3(6)-3(7)).
- Cooperation in acts constituting an offence. (sec. 3(8))
- Persons concerned in criminal act may be guilty of different offences (sec. 3(9))

Sec. 3(5) says—when a criminal act is done by several person in furtherance of the common intention of all, each of such persons is liable for that in the same manner as if it is done by him alone. Sec. 3(5) is framed to meet cases in which it may be difficult to distinguish between the acts of individual members of a party, or to prove exactly what part played by each of them. If the intention or purpose is common, so must be the responsibility. Thus, the common belief that more the people, less the guilt, has in law, no application to the act or commission of a crime. Sec. 3(5), thus discourages group criminals.

Common intention and participation, both are necessary for the application of sec. 3(5). Common intention necessarily implies a prearranged plan or prior concert or prior meeting of minds. It may be noted that common intention can be formed at the spur of the moment; but the plan must precede the act constituting the offence. Thus, where during a fight a person calls the bystanders to help him kill a person and they join him; there is then necessary meeting of minds or formation of a prearranged plan, though hastily formed.

The use of words in furtherance of common intention suggests that sec. 3(5) is applicable also where the act actually done is not exactly the act jointly intended by the conspirators to be done. The common intention can be an act, and another act can be done in furtherance of the common intention. Thus, the shooting of the wrong man or the sentry could be said to be in furtherance of common intention. However, the act should not be extraneous of the common intention or is done in opposition to it.

The Nature of Common Intention

Common intention is a question of fact. Although it is subjective, it can be inferred from the facts and circumstances. Thus, mere presence at the scene of the crime may not amount to participation in the crime. Likewise, where the accused ran away with his companions it could not be said that they participated in the act together and had a common intention.

Besides preplanning, actual participation in the crime is necessary to make case of joint liability. It has been held that participation does not mean participation in the actual doing or commission of a crime; if a person is directing entire operation from some distance he would be deemed to be participating in the crime. This is the case when the offence consists of diverse acts which may be done at different times and places. It may be noted that participation may be in a passive way.

Sec. 189(1)-190: Sec 190 says if an offence is committed by any member of an unlawful assembly in prosecution of common object of that assembly or such as the member of that assembly knew to be likely to be committed in prosecution of that object every person who at the time of committing of that offence, is a member of the same assembly is guilty of that offence. Thus, Section 149 is another instance of constructive liability. The following important points may be noted:

- Common object does not require prior concert and common meeting of minds before the attack; an unlawful common object may develop at the spot after the assembly gathers. It is enough if it is adopted by all members *i.e.*, they concur in it.
- Each of the members of the unlawful assembly, irrespective of the participation in the commission of the act, is liable for the act as if he actually participated in committing it.
- The phrase in "prosecution of the common object" means that the offence committed was immediately connected with the common object. But the words do not mean "during the prosecution of the common object". Thus, if an unlawful assembly goes with the common object of theft, and they are unknown to others and a member rapes someone, the offence of rape cannot be attributed to all five. Similarly in the case when one of the member murders a peaceful intervener, the others cannot be held liable.
- Where the common object to commit an offence was different from the offence which was actually committed. The member not actually committing the offence will be liable for that offence only if he knew that such offence was likely to be committed in the course of the prosecution of the common object.
- The expression 'know' does not mean a mere possibility such act might or might not happen; it imports a high degree of probability. It indicates a state of mind at the time of the commission of the offence and not the knowledge acquired in the light of the subsequent events. Thus, in case of a free fight, sec. 190 could not be invoked. When two opposite factions commit a riot and fight, it cannot be said that both the parties had any common object.
- Once the common object ceases to exist, sec. 190 cannot apply. Thus, where a wounded man had ceased to be member of the unlawful assembly when he retired wounded, he cannot be made liable for the subsequent murder under sec. 190.
- The court could charge, try and convict less than five persons under sec. 190 provided it comes to the conclusion that five or more persons participated in the incident, and some of them could not be identified.

However, where six person were charged under sec. 103/190; two were acquitted, the remaining four cannot be convicted under sec. 190. Thus, an unlawful assembly should consist of five or more named persons, unless there is an evidence of participation by other persons not identified or identifiable. Where out of the five accused, four were acquitted, the remaining fifth accused would be responsible for the offence committed by him personally without regard to the participation of others. Sec. 3(5) or sec. 190 could not be invoked in such a case.

DISTINCTION BETWEEN SECTION 3(5) & 190

The two Sections have certain resemblance. However, there are certain differences between the two viz –

- Sec. 3(5) is a rule of evidence and enunciates the principle of joint liability but does not create an offence. Sec. 190 creates a specific substantive offence.
- Under sec. 3(5), the number of persons is immaterial. Under sec. 190, minimum five persons should have entertained the common object.
- Common intention under sec. 3(5) is different from common object under sec. 190. The former necessarily postulates a prearranged plan while the latter does not. Further, a mere membership of an unlawful assembly is enough and it is not necessary that one should have participated in the commission of the act. This is not so under sec. 3(5). Even knowledge on the part of the member of a unlawful assembly will be enough under sec. 190.

  Common object thus is a wider in scope and amplitude, than common intention. The object of an unlawful assembly might be common, but the intention of the several members might differ. Thus, where the accused came armed with deadly weapons, it is reasonable to infer that they knew death was likely to be caused in the prosecution of common object. But a common intention to kill cannot be inferred.
- The common object of unlawful assembly must be one of the objects mentioned in sec. 189(1), while the common intention may be an intention for the purpose of sec. 3(5).

STAGES OF OFFENCE

If a person commits a crime voluntarily or after preparation, the doing of it involves four different stages. In every crime, there is first intention to commit it, secondly, preparation to commit it, thirdly, attempt to commit it and fourthly the accomplishment. The stages can be explained as under:

- **Intention:** It is the first stage in the commission of an offence and known as mental stage. Intention is the direction of conduct towards the object chosen upon considering the motives which suggest the choice. But the law does not take notice of an intention, mere intention to commit an offence not followed by any act, cannot constitute an offence. The obvious reason for not prosecuting the accused at this stage is that it is very difficult for the prosecution to prove the guilty mind of a person.
- **Preparation:** Preparation is the second stage in the commission of a crime. It means to arrange the necessary measures for the commission of the intended criminal act. Intention alone or the intention followed by a preparation is not enough to constitute the crime. Preparation has not been made punishable because in most of the cases the prosecution has failed to prove that the preparations in the question were made for the commission of the particular crime.
- **Attempt:** It is the direct movement towards the commission of a crime after the preparation is made. According to English law, a person may be guilty of an attempt to commit an offence if he does an act which is more than merely preparatory to the commission of the offence, and a person will be guilty of attempting to commit an offence even though the facts are such that the commission of the offence is impossible. There are three essentials of an attempt:
  - Guilty intention to commit an offence;
  - Some acts done towards the commission of the offence;
  - The act must fall short of the completed offence.
- **Accomplishment or Completion:** The last stage in the commission of an offence is its accomplishment or completion. If the accused succeeds in his attempt to commit the crime, he will be guilty of the complete offence and if his attempt is unsuccessful he will be guilty of an attempt only. For example, A fires at B with the intention to kill him, if B dies, A will be guilty for committing the offence of murder and if B is only injured, it will be a case of attempt to murder.

ABETMENT AND CRIMINAL CONSPIRACY

ABETMENT

To abet means to instigate, to help, to encourage. When several persons take part in the commission of an offence, each one of them may contribute in a manner and degree different from the others to the commission of it. Sec. 45-60 of the IPC deals with abetment.

The Indian Penal code makes a broad distinction between principal (*i.e.*, the person abetted or the person who actually commits the crime) and the abettor (*i.e.*, the person who abets the commission of a crime), but unlike English law it does not recognize the accessory after the act (*i.e.*, a person receiving, comforting or assisting a person in order to enable him to escape from punishment).

Sec. 45: Abetment of a thing—abetment consists of three acts laid down in sec. 45. Thus, abetment may be: (i) by instigating a person to commit an offence, (ii) by engaging in a conspiracy to commit it, (iii) by intentionally aiding a person to commit it.

Abetment by Instigation

A person abets the doing of a thing by instigating any person to do that thing. Instigation means the act of inciting another to do a wrongful act. One may abet the commission of an offence by counseling, suggesting, encouraging, procuring or commanding another to do an act. To instigate means to actively suggest or stimulate by any means of language (direct or indirect *e.g.*, letter), whether it takes the form of express solicitation or of hints, insinuation or encouragement.

Mere acquiescence, silent assent or verbal permission would not constitute instigation. For instance, A tells B that he intends to murder C. B says do as you like. A kills C. B cannot be said to have instigated A to murder C. Advice *per se* does not amount to instigation. Explanation I to sec. 45 says that instigation may be constituted by wilful misrepresentation or wilful concealment of a material fact by one who is bound to disclose it. A, a public officer, is authorised by a warrant from a court to apprehend Z. B knowing that fact and also that C is not Z, wilfully represents to A that C is Z, and thereby intentionally causes A to apprehend C. Here, B abets by instigation the apprehension of C.

A mere request to do a thing may amount to instigation. For instance, A offers bribe to B, a public servant. B refuses to accept but A commits abetment. Sometimes, silent approval may result in abetment. In Queen *vs* Mohit, a woman prepared herself to become sati in the presence of the accused persons. It was held that all those who followed her to the pyre and stood by her crying Ram Ram would be guilty of abetment as they countenanced the act of becoming sati.

Instigation by a letter is complete as soon as the letter is read by the addressee. If, however the letter does not reach the addressee, the sender would be guilty only of an attempt to abet.

Abetment by Conspiracy

It consists of when two or more persons engage in a conspiracy for doing a thing and an act or illegal omission takes place in pursuance of the conspiracy and in order to doing of that thing.

Conspiracy consists in the agreement of two or more persons to do any unlawful act, or to do lawful act by unlawful means. It may noted that for an offence under sec. 60 A, a mere agreement is enough if the agreement is to commit an offence. But for an offence under sec. 45 a mere combination of persons or agreement is not enough; an act or illegal omission must also take place. A mere conspiracy would not amount to abetment.

Abetment by Aid

A person abets the doing of a thing who intentionally aids, by an act or illegal omission the doing of that thing. Explanation II to sec 45 says that a person is said to aid the doing of an act who, either prior to or at the time of the commission of an act, does anything in order to facilitate the commission of that act, and thereby facilitates the commission thereto.

Thus, a person cannot be held guilty of aiding the doing of an act when the act has not been done at all. Mere intention to facilitate, even coupled with an act calculated to facilitate, is not sufficient to constitute abetment, unless the act which it is intended to facilitate actually takes place and is facilitated thereby. Thus, if a servant keeps open the gate of his master's house, so the thieves may enter and thieves do not come, he cannot be held to have abetted the commission of theft. But if such a person, after having opened the door or before it, informs possible thieves that he is going to keep the door open, then he would be guilty of abetment by instigation; or if he had entered into an agreement with the thieves to keep the door open. He would be guilty of abetment by conspiracy.

A mere giving of an aid does not make the act an abetment of an offence, if the person who gives the aid does not know that the offence was being committed or contemplated. The intention should be to aid the commission of **an** offence. Similarly, mere presence at the commission of an offence does not amount to intentional aid unless it was intended to have that effect. To be present and aware that an offence is about to be committed does not constitute abetment unless the person so present can influence others or some specific duty of prevention rests on him.

Facility given to aid a crime must be such as is essential for commission of the crime. The mere act of allowing an illegal marriage to take place at one's house does not amount to abetment. However, the priest who officiates and solemnise such illegal marriage is guilty of abetting an offence of bigamy. Similarly, the accused who held the antarpat during the performance of such a marriage would be guilty.

CRIMINAL CONSPIRACY

Conspiracy is generally a matter of inference deduced from certain criminal acts of the parties accused, done in pursuance of an apparent criminal purpose in common between them. There are three kinds of conspiracies dealt within the code:

- Sec. 61
- Sec. 45 and 46 (abetment by engaging in a conspiracy)
- Sec. 148 (conspiracy to wage a war)

Section 61(1) A : Definition

When two or more persons agree to do or cause to be done an illegal act, or an act which is not illegal by illegal means, such an agreement is designated as criminal conspiracy.

An agreement implies the meeting of two minds with reference to a particular matter, and so long as matters are discussed and views are interchanged, but the plan of action has not been settled by the concurrence of any two or more of the conspirators, the stage of criminal conspiracy would not be considered to have been reached.

Mere passive cognizance of a conspirator is not sufficient, there must be active cooperation; in other words, joint evil intent is necessary to constitute an offence. Thus, where certain members of a society found to be revolutionary were not acquainted with the real object of the society, they could not be convicted of the charge of conspiracy. Likewise, association of the accused with the main accused or even his knowledge about conspiracy would not make the accused a conspirator because agreement is a *sine qua non* of offence of conspiracy.

However, each conspirator need not know all details of the scheme. Further, it is not necessary that every conspirator must be present **at** every stage of the conspiracy, or that he must have done **some** overt act. The essential ingredients of the criminal conspiracy **are:**

- **Agreement is the gist of offence** – The gist of the offence of conspiracy lies not in doing the act or effecting the purpose for which the conspiracy is formed, nor attempting to any of the acts, nor inducing others to do them but in the forming of the scheme or agreement between parties.

  Of course, mere intention is not enough. Intention to commit any offence is never indictable. A might intent to rob a millionaire. That is not an offence. But, if A and B agree to do so, it is an offence. So long as the design remains in mind or constitute intention only it is not indictable. But when two or more agree to carry into effect their design, the very plot is an act in itself, and the act of each of the parties, promise against promise, *actus contra actum*, becomes punishable.

- **Overt act necessary** – Proviso to sec. 61(1) A lays down that no agreement, except an agreement to commit an offence, shall amount to a criminal conspiracy unless some act besides the agreement is done by one or more parties to such agreement in pursuance thereof. Thus, in case of an agreement to commit an offence, an agreement will be enough. But in other cases (*e.g.*, a conspiracy to commit a civil wrong or a tort), some overt act is necessary, viz. Acts signifying agreement or preparatory to the offence of the acts constituting the offence itself.

  If the parties agree to do an illegal act, they shall be guilty of criminal conspiracy though the illegal act agreed to be done has not been done. An illegal act implies an act which is contrary to or forbidden by law. An illegal act may be non-criminal and may not be punishable as such.

- **Two or more persons must agree** – It is clear that two or more persons are necessary for conspiracy to commit an offence. A person cannot conspire with himself. It is also necessary that these persons must be natural person. Thus, a director who is the one man of the one man company, cannot be convicted of conspiracy with the company, in spite of the fact that company is a separate legal entity.

- **Justification of conspiracy** – The general justification of conspiracy as an inchoate crime is that it enables preventive action to be taken against intended offenders in circumstances where it is clear that a fixed intention to commit the crime has been formed. Secondly, conspiracy has been defended on the ground that the combination of the two or more persons to commit an illegal act gives a momentum to the act which justifies its punishment at the earliest possible stage.

- **Whether conviction of one person possible**– No person can be convicted for conspiracy if the charge against co-conspirators has failed, or if other alleged conspirators are acquitted. However, where the one accused has to be acquitted, the other could be convicted on a charge of conspiracy. The Supreme Court has also held that it is not essential that more than one person should be convicted of the offence of conspiracy. If it is proved that two or more were engaged in a conspiracy, although they could not be caught, one alone may be convicted.
- **Explanation to sec. 61(1)A** – It is immaterial whether the illegal act is the ultimate object of such agreement, or is merely incidental to that object.
- **Proof of conspiracy** – To establish the charge of conspiracy, there must be agreement, there need not be proof of direct meeting neither combination nor need the parties be brought into each other's presence; the agreement may be inferred from circumstances raising a presumption of an unlawful plan. In fact, in cases of conspiracy direct evidence is seldom available. It is generally a matter of inference deducible from overt criminal acts of the involved parties.
- **A substantive and continuing offence** – Conspiracy itself is a substantive offence different from the offence to commit for which the conspiracy was entered into. Thus, if the accused are charged with having conspired to do three different categories of illegal acts, the mere fact that all of them could not be convicted separately in respect of each of the offences has no relevancy in considering the question whether the offence of conspiracy has been committed.

DISTINCTION BETWEEN CONSPIRACY AND ABETMENT BY CONSPIRACY

Conspiracy is a substantive offence under sec. 61(1). It has nothing to do with abetment (sec. 45), which is also a substantive offence. Under sec. 45, conspiracy is a form of abetment. Sec. 61(1) provides an extended definition of conspiracy covering acts which do not amount to abetment by conspiracy under sec. 45. Where the criminal conspiracy amounts to an abetment under sec. 45, it is unnecessary to invoke the provisions of sec. 61(1).

In case of conspiracy under sec. 45, a mere combination of persons or agreement between them is not enough; an act or illegal omission must take place in pursuance of the conspiracy. In case of sec. 61(1) the mere agreement is enough, if it is to commit an offence. Thus, a mere conspiracy would not amount to abetment. If conspirators were detected before they had done more than discussed plans with the general intention to commit an offence, they would not be liable as abettors.

DISTINCTION BETWEEN CONSPIRACY AND JOINT LIABILITY

Both, sec. 61(1) and sec. 3(5) resemble each other in that there is common intention in both to do an illegal act. But under sec. 61(1), a mere engagement to do an illegal act is an offence, whereas under sec. 3(5), criminal act is actually committed in furtherance of the common intention of all.

DISTINCTION BETWEEN CONSPIRACY AND ATTEMPT

Law of criminal conspiracy is an outgrowth of the larger law of criminal attempt. The two have many features in common and are based very largely on the general principles. Often the act from which conspiracy is inferred will evidence an attempt to commit the crime. However, the two are not the same. One may become guilty of conspiracy long before his act has come so dangerously near to completion as to make him criminally liable for the attempted crime.

SECTION 61(2) : PUNISHMENT FOR CONSPIRACY

Sec. 61(2), lays down that if the offence conspired is punishable with death, imprisonment for life, or rigorous imprisonment for 2 years or more, the offender becomes liable as an abettor. In any other case, he is liable to be punished with imprisonment upto 6 months, or with fine, or both. Thus, the punishment for criminal conspiracy is more severe if the agreement is one to commit a serious offence (*e.g.*, murder, rape); it is less severe for a less serious offence (hurt).

CRIMINAL ATTEMPT

The word attempt means to try or to endeavour to do something. Attempt means an act towards the commission of the offence which fails due to circumstances independent of the attempter's will. Thus, it means any voluntary act which does not fructify into yielding the intended result. In attempt, it is the motive which makes the act wrongful, though the act in itself may not be wrongful.

A person commits the offence of attempt to commit a particular offence when

- He intends to commit that particular offence.
- He makes preparation for it.
- Does any act towards its commission.

ATTEMPT: Sec. 62 lays down that whoever attempts to commit an offence punishable by this code with imprisonment for life or imprisonment, or to cause such an offence to be committed, and in such attempt does any act towards the commission of the offence, shall where no express provision is made by this code for the punishment of such attempt, be punished.

In case of an attempt, as the injury is not as serious as in the case of actual crime, the punishment is one half of that for the actual crime viz. Imprisonment of any description provided for the offence, for a term which may extend to one half of the imprisonment for life one half of the longest term of imprisonment provided for that offence, or with such fine as is provided for the offence, or with both.

It may be noted that abetment of an offence is more severely punishable than an attempt to commit it. An abetment of the offence of murder is punished in the same way as the murder itself. Further in abetment the offence is complete in itself whereas in attempt the offence is not completed.

Illustrations : (a) A makes an attempt to pick the pocked of Z by thrusting his hand into Z's pocket. A fails in the attempt in consequence of Z's having nothing in his pocket. A is guilty under this sec.

Section 62 is a general Section that makes punishable all attempts to commit offences punishable with imprisonment for life or imprisonment excepting those punishable with death or with fine only. Sec. 62 provides for punishment for an attempt to commit an offence under the penal code. It does not apply to offences under special or local laws.

A mere preparation is not made punishable by the court except under the following Sections of the IPC, viz. Sec. 149, 154, 130, and 310.

MEANING OF ATTEMPT

It is not only necessary that the accused should have done an overt act "towards the commission of the offence", but also that act itself should have been done in the attempt to commit it. Thus, if one goes out of one's house with a loaded gun to kill some one, some act is done towards the commission of the offence, but also as no overt act is done in this attempt, it is impossible to hold him guilty.

The following points may also be noted in regard to attempt:

- It is not necessary for the offence under sec. 62, that the transaction commenced must end in crime or offence, if not interrupted. To be guilty of an attempt, it is not necessary that the circumstances must be such and as would facilitate the completion of the crime.
- An act done with a intention and preparation, the commission of which in the manner proposed was impossible is not an attempt. Thus, if one who believes in witchcraft puts a spell on other, or burns him in a effigy, or curses him with a intention of causing him hurt he cannot be convicted of an attempt to cause hurt. His failure to cause hurt is due to his own act/omission *i.e.*, his act was intrinsically useless or defective or inappropriate. His failure, broadly speaking due to his own volition. Similarly, there is no liability for an attempt to commit an impossible theft.

  If a man with intent to hurt another by administering poison prepares and administers some harmless substance, believing it to be poisonous, he cannot be convicted of an attempt to do so. For an attempt, the failure must be due to the intervention of some factor independent of one's volition.

  If A with intent to hurt B, by administering poison, prepares a glass for him and fills it with poison, but while A's back is turned, C who has observed A's act pours away the poison and fills the glass with water, which A in ignorance of what C has done, administers to B, A would be guilty of attempt to cause hurt by administering poison as his failure was not due to any act or omission of his own, but to the intervention of a factor independent of his own volition. Similar would be the case if the poisoned glass fell from the hand of B.
- A person is said to commit an offence of attempt also in the cases in which he voluntarily desists, (*i.e.*, repents before the attempt is completed) from the actual commission of the crime itself.
- An act towards commission of offence, need not be penultimate, but such act must be proximate to the intended result. The measure of proximity is not in relation to time and action but in relation to intention *i.e.*, the act must be indicative or suggestive of intention. The act must be an act during the course of committing that offence.

  In Mohd. Yakub case, the custom officers received information that a truck and a jeep containing silver with the intention of smuggling it out of country, were heading towards the sea shore. The Supreme Court held that accused had made all the preparations and it is only because of intervention of custom officers that they could not succeed in their attempt. The accused are accordingly guilty under sec. 62.

In the present case, had the truck been stopped and searched at the very commencement of the journey, the discovery of silver ingots in the truck might at the worst lead to the inference that the accused had prepared or were preparing for the commission of the offence, and thus could not be held guilty. The fact that the truck was driven up to a lonely creek from where the silver could be transferred into a sea facing vessel was suggestive or indicative, though not conclusive, that the accused wanted to export the silver. A narrow interpretation of the word attempt in these penal provisions, (*i.e.*, those dealing with anti social activity like smuggling) which will impair their efficacy as instruments for combating this baneful activity, has to be eschewed.

In Abhayanand Mishra case, the issue before the court was whether appellant was guilty of an attempt to cheat the university, under sec. 318 IPC, in as much as he, by making false representation, deceived the university and induced the authorities to issue admit card. The court held that it is not true that appellant did not gone beyond the stage of preparation. The preparation was completed when he prepared the application. The moment he dispatched it, he attempted to commit the offence. He just failed to commit the offence because something beyond his control took place.

- The preparation consists in devising or arranging the means or measures necessary for the commission of the offence. On the other hand, an attempt to commit the offence is a direct movement towards the commission after preparations are made.

If a man buys a box of matches he cannot be convicted of attempted arson. Nor can be convicted of this offence if he approaches the hay stack with the matches in his pocket but if he bends down near the stack and light a match and extinguishes it on perceiving that he is being watched, he may be guilty of an attempt to burn it.

In Malkiat Singh case, a truck loaded with paddy, destined for Delhi, was intercepted at a place about 40 km from Delhi. The court held that the best test for determining whether a given set of acts constitute attempt or mere preparation is whether the overt acts already done are such that if the person changes his mind, and does not proceed further, the act already done would be completely harmless. If they would be so, it would amount to preparation only. But, where the thing done is such as, if not prevented by any extraneous cause, would fructify into the commission of an offence, it would be an attempt to commit that offence. In the present case, the accused had ample time to change their mind and not to proceed further, and thus, not guilty under sec 62.

GENERAL EXCEPTIONS

There are various kinds of acts done under the circumstances mentioned in Sections 76 to 106, which will not amount to offences under the code. These exceptions are :

- Mistake of fact (secs. 14, 17)
- Judicial acts (secs. 15-16)
- Accident (secs. 18)
- Absence of criminal intention (secs, 19-24, 30-32)
- Act done by consent (secs. 25-29)
- Trifling act (sec. 33)
- Private defence (secs. 34-44)

Secs. 14 and 17 Mis e Fact

Mistake of fact is sometin efence. Sec. 76 lays down that "nothing is an done by a person, who is, or who by reas fact and not by reason of mistake of believes himself to be bound by law

Illustration:

- A, a soldier, fires on a mob by superior officer in conformity with the co of the law. A has committed no offence.
- A, an officer of a court of justice, being ordered by that court to arrest Y, and after due inquiry, believing Z to be Y, arrests Z. A has committed no offence.

Mistake is a slip made, not by design, by mischance. Under the English common law also, an honest and reasonable belief in the existence of circumstances, which would have made that act an innocent act, has always been a valid defence, "an honest and reasonable mistake stands, in fact, on the same footing as absence of the reasoning faculty, as infancy or lunacy".

Ignorance of fact is excusable. However, mere forgetfulness is not mistake. Mistake of fact implies mistake as to true identities or mistake in sensory perception such as temporary distortion of imagination. Thus, in Tolson's case, the accused wife was convicted of bigamy. It was held that as at the time of second marriage she bonafide believed her husband to be dead, her conviction was wrong.

Section 17: According to sec. 17, nothing is an offence if done by a person who in good faith believes himself to be justified by the law in doing that act. The distinction between secs. 14 and 17 is that in the former, a person is assumed to be bound, and in the latter to be justified by law. The distinction is between a real or supposed legal obligation and a real or supposed legal justification in doing the act. Under both the Sections, there is a bonafide intentions to advance the law.

Illustration: A sees Z commit what appears to be murder. He in good faith seizes Z, to hand him over to the police. A has committed no offence though it may turn out that Z was acting in self defence.

Section 15-16: Judicial Acts

The second general exception relates to act of judges and courts. According to sec. 15, any act done by a judge while acting judicially, which he in good faith believes to be given to him by law, is no offence. Thus, a judge who sentenced a prisoner to death is not himself liable to be hanged for having caused somebody's death.

Similarly, according to sec. 16, an act done pursuant to the judgement or order of a court of justice is no offence. If it were to be an offence the hangman who hangs the prisoner pursuant to the order of the judge, would also have to be hanged.

Section 18: Accident

The third general exception relates to acts committed by accident. Section 18 lays down that nothing is an offence, which is done by accident or misfortune:

- Without criminal intention or knowledge,
- Doing the lawful act in a lawful manner by lawful means, and
- With proper care and caution.

Illustration: A is at work with a hatchet: the head flies off and kills a man who is standing by. Here, if there was no want of proper caution on A's part, his act is excusable and not an offence.

An accident is something that happens out of the ordinary course of things. The idea of something fortuitous and unexpected is involved in the word 'accident' as injury is said to be accidently caused whenever it is neither wilfully nor negligently caused. Thus, in a game of cricket a ball strikes a man on the hand and he dies. Such a death is accidental. Similar is the case where two wrestlers arranged bout in the course of which the deceased fell and broke his skull.

Secs. 19-24 and 30-32: Absence of Criminal Intention

'Criminal intention' means the purpose or design of doing an act forbidden by criminal law without just cause or excuse. Now, there are certain acts, which appear to be criminal, but are done without any criminal intent. It is but fair that such acts should not be penalized, which lack mens rea.

There are seven such acts mentioned in Sections 19-24 and 30-32:

- Act done to avoid other than harm (sec. 19).
- Act of child (secs. 20-21).
- Act of lunatic (sec. 22)
- Act of an intoxicated person (23-24).
- Bonafide act for another's benefit (sec. 30).
- Communication made in good faith (sec. 31).
- Act done under compulsion or threat (sec. 32)

Section 19: Act done to avoid other harm: "An act done with the knowledge that it is likely to cause harm, but done in good faith, and without any criminal intention to cause harm, for the purpose of preventing or avoiding harm to person or property is not an office". For instance, A in a great fire, pulls down houses in order to prevent the conflagration from spreading.

The principle upon which sec. 19 is based, on that when in a sudden and extreme emergency, one or the other of two evils is inevitable, it is lawful so to direct events so that the smaller evil only shall occur. It is a question of fact in each case whether such circumstances exist.

In Dudley *vs* Stephens 14 Q.B.D. 173, it was held that a man who, in order to save his life from starvation, kills another for the purpose of feeding on his flesh, is guilty of murder. The 'doctrine of self- preservation' is of no avail in such cases.

Sections 20-21: Act of child: According to sec. 20, an act of a child under seven years is no offence. It is to be noted that this immunity is not confined to offences under the code only, but extends to offences under any special or local law.

An infant is, by presumption of law, doli incapax *i.e.*, not endowed with any discretion so as to distinguished right from wrong, thus, the question of criminal intention does not arise. Where persons get crimes committed through children below 7 years, they will be held liable while the child will be exempted.

According to Section 21, acts done by children above seven and below 12 years will be protected if it is shown that the child in question has not attained sufficient maturity of understanding to judge the nature and consequences of his conduct on that occasion. It is to be noted that there is complete liability for punishment after twelve years of age.

Section 22: Act of an insane person: Criminal law gives complete protection to a lunatic. Sec. 22 lays down that nothing is an offence which is done by a person, who owing to unsoundness of mind, is incapable of knowing the nature of the act, or that he is doing what is wrong or contrary to law. The legal insanity contemplated by this Section is different from the medical insanity.

No culpability can be fastened upon insane persons as they have no free will. The words "unsoundness of mind" include following kind of persons: idiot (born); one made *non compos mentis* by illness (temporary failure); a lunatic or a mad man (mental disorder); a person in unconscious state, if proved (*e.g.*, sleep walking or somnambulism); an intoxicated person.

In A. Ahmed *vs* King, the accused killed his own son of 5 years by thrusting a knife in his throat under the delusion and in pursuance of a command by someone in paradise, given to him in his dreams, he was held to be protected under Section 22.

Example–A was suffering under an insane delusion that X and Y were persecuting him. He bought a knife in order to revenge himself on them, and that very evening he went to their club and stabbed them dead. The fact that he actually purchased a knife as also he went to their club, shows that his intention was to kill. Thus, A would be guilty of murder.

Sections 23-24: Act of an intoxicated person: Drunkenness is a state of madness for which the man is to blame. If a man chooses to get drunk, it is his own voluntary act; it is very different from madness, which is not caused by any act of the person. *Qui Pecat Ebrius Luat Sobrius:* let him who sins when drunk be punished when sober. However, secs. 23 and 24 protect an intoxicated person provided he got intoxicated by mistake.

Section 23 lays down that nothing is an offence which is done by a person, who owing to intoxication, is incapable of knowing the nature of the act, or that what he is doing is wrong or contrary to law, provided that the thing which intoxicated him was administered without his knowledge or against his will. Thus, the test of drunkenness is the 'capacity to form an intention' of committing the offence; in the case of insanity, the test is 'capacity to know' the nature of one's act. However, insanity produced by drunkenness is a defence.

Section 24 states the presumption for certain offences committed by intoxicated persons. Thus, if an act is an offence only when done with a particular intention or knowledge, and such an act is committed by an intoxicated person, he will be presumed to have knowledge requisite for the offence, unless he can show that he was intoxicated without his knowledge or against his will. It may be noted that there is no presumptions as regard his intention.

Section 30: Bonafide act for another's benefit: Section 30 lays down that nothing is an offence by reason of any harm which it may cause to the person for whose benefits it is done, in good faith, and even without that person's consent, under emergent circumstances. For instance, an immediate operation performed by a surgeon on an accidental victim; or where a person drops a child from the housetop knowing it to be likely that the fall may kill the child, but not intending to kill the child, and intending, in good faith, child's benefit.

Example– Z is carried off by a tiger. A fires at the tiger, knowing it to be likely that the shot may kill Z, but not intending to kill Z, and in good faith, intending Z's benefit. A's bullet give a mortal wound. A has committed no offence.

Sec. 31 : Communication made in good faith: Section 93 lays down that any communication made in good faith to a person for such person's benefit is no offence, even though such communication may cause harm to such person. For instance, a surgeon, in good faith, communicates to a patient—his opinion that he cannot live. The patient dies under shock. The surgeon has committed no offence, though he knew that it to be likely that the communication might cause the patient's death.

Sec. 32 : Act done under compulsion or threat: As per sec. 94 offences committed under compulsion or threat by a person so compelled or threatened will be excused if the threat is to cause instant death of such person. However, a person so put under threat cannot cause murder or an offence against the state punishable with death to avail benefit of sec 94. Further, the person doing the act did not of his own accord, or from a reasonable apprehension of harm to himself short of instant death, place himself under such constraint.

It is important to note that merely threatening with future death or any other injury short of death will not be good excuse. The threat should be to cause instant death. Thus, A approaches B with a stick in his hand and threatens to beat B, if the latter does not go and cause a grievous hurt to Z; B cannot plead defence under sec. 94. However, if A had loaded revolver or a dagger in his hand, and held it at B's throat, causing B to believe that he would be instantly killed if he did not break

Z's bones, this would be a good defence. Where certain witnesses gave false evidences, and then pleaded that they were threatened by the police to do so, it was held that they were guilty as there was no proof of instant death.

[5] Sec. 25-29; Act done by consent

Section 25-29 lays down the law as to how far act done by consent will be excused in law, it is important to note that consent plays a very important role in criminal law. Its presence or absence often makes a difference between innocence and crime. Sec. 28 lays down what is not consent, viz.

(a) A consent given by a person under fear of injury or misconception of fact, or

(b) A consent given by a person who from the unsoundness of mind or intoxication is unable to understand the nature and consequence of that to which he gives his consent, or

(c) A person under 12 years of age.

It is to be noted that consent and submission are not the same thing. Every consent involves a submission, but not vice versa. Thus, mere submissison by a person who does not know the nature of an act is not consent.

Sec. 25-29 lay down that if certain acts are done with the consent of the victim, they will not amount to offences.

- Sec. 25 lays down that an act not intended or known to be likely to cause death or grievous hurt, causes any harm to a person above 18 years of age who has given consent to suffer it is not an offence.
- Sec. 26 similarly lays down that an act done in good faith for the victim's benefit with the victim's consent is not an offence. This section protects surgeon and surgical operations. However, a person who is not qualified as medical practitioners is not protected.
- Sec. 27 similarly protects acts done in good faith for the benefit of child or insane person or by consent of guardian.
- Sec. 30 clarifies that mere pecuniary benefits are covered by the term benefit appearing in sections 26 and 27.

[6] Sec. 33. Trifling acts, causing slight harm

The sixth general exception is laid down in sec. 33. The maxim *de minimis cur at lex* (the laws take no account of trifles) is the foundation of the section : if a person causes any harm with intention that harm is so slight that no person of ordinary sense and temper would complain of such harm, it is no offence. Thus, both accidental as well as deliberate acts are covered by the section. Further, the harm covers actual physical injury also.

Example of such trifling acts include – picking up a water from the another's plate; lighting one's own cigar from a match box belonging to the other without his permission.

[7] Sec. 34-44 : Right of private defence

RPD is the right to protect one's own person and property against the unlawful aggression of others.

Sec. 34 lays down that nothing is an offence which is done in the exercise of the RPD. It is a right inherent in man; it is the first duty of man to help himself. The right must be fostered in the citizens of every free country. The doctrine of private defence is founded on the following expediencies :

- A person, whose life is threatened by a grave danger, need not wait for the state aid unless such aid is available.
- The RPD is protective or preventive and not punitive ; however, punitive measures may result.
- The right cannot be availed of for the sake of self gratification or to satisfy one's malicious or sadistic urges. The act of private defence should not be deliberate, or retaliation for past injury.
- The right must be exercised when there is real and immediate threat and a reasonable apprehension of such threat. A fear that one might or will be attacked in near future will not justify the exercise of this right.
- The right commences as soon as reasonable apprehension of danger to the body arises from an attempt to or threat to commit the offence, though the offence may not have been committed, and such rights continue so long as such apprehension continues. It is incorrect to say that a person could claim the right to use force after he had sustained a serious injury. Further, if the apprehension is real and reasonable, it makes no difference that it is mistaken.
- Violence used must be proportionate to the injury or threat to be averted and must not exceed such limits. However, in such situations, it cannot be expected of a person to minutely calculate the correct proportion of force to be used in defence.
- The law does not require that a person should not exercise his right to self defence if by running away he can avoid injury. He should exercise it.

- The right of defence ends with the necessity for it. Thus, the person exercising such rights need not chase the fleeing attacker and then beat him.
- The law should not require that a person placed in such circumstances should weigh the arguments for and against and attack in golden scales.
- The aggressor cannot claim the right to self defence.
- There cannot be private defence against private defence. There is no right of private defence under the code against any act which is not in itself and offence under it.
- In a case of free fight, no RPD is available to either party.
- Even if an accused does not plead self defence, it is open to the court to consider such plea if the same arises from material on record.

PRIVATE DEFENCE OF BODY

Sec. 35 lays down that every person has a right to defend his own body or that of any other person against any offence affecting the human body. Thus, even a stranger may defend the person or property of another person. While under the English law there must be some kind of existing relationship.

Sec. 36 provides that for the purpose of exercising the RPD, the physical or mental capacity of the attacker is no bar, thus if A, a lunatic attempts to kill B, A is guilty of no offence. But B has the same right of Private defence which he would have if A were sane.

Sec. 37 lays down the general restriction on the right of Private defence:

- There is no RPD against an act which does not reasonably cause the apprehension of death or grievous hurt, if done by a public servant acting in good faith under colour of his office, though that act may not be strictly justifiable by law.

  There is difference between acts which are wholly illegal and the acts which may not be strictly justifiable by law. Where the police had illegally had arrested a person, and certain villagers with a view to rescuing that person launched attack on the police but only after constable had fired at them, it was held that the villagers had acted in exercise of RPD as the act of firing caused reasonable apprehension of death/grievous hurt in their minds. On the other hand, if the Police officer acting bonafide under colour of his office arrests a person without authority, the arrestee has no right of self defence against the officer.
- There is Right of defence in cases in which there is time to have recourse to the protection of public authorities.
- The right of private defence in no case extends to the inflicting of more harm than it is necessary to inflict for the purpose of defence.

Section 38 lays down six acts of aggression, so serious in nature, that the law gives full authority to the defender even to cause the death of assailant. The six cases of assault are: reasonable apprehension of death or of grievous hurt, assault with the intention of committing rape, or gratifying unnatural lust, or of kidnapping and abduction, or of wrongfully confining a person. In other cases, the defender may cause any harm except death.

PRIVATE DEFENCE OF PROPERTY

Every person has the right to defend the property of himself or of any other person.

- Against theft, robbery, mischief or criminal trespass, or any act which is an attempt to commit theft, robbery etc.
- Against the act of a lunatic, a minor, or an intoxicated person or person acting under a misconception of facts (sec. 36)

The right of private defence of property is also subject to limitations laid down in sec. 37. Sec. 43 lays down that the right commences when a reasonable apprehension of damage to the property commences and the right continues –

- against theft till offender has effected his retreat with the property, or the assistance of the public authorities is obtained or the property has been recovered;
- against robbery, as long as the offender causes to any person death or hurt or wrongful restraint, or the fear of instant death/ hurt/ personal restraint continues; or
- against criminal trespass or mischief as long as the offender continues in the commission of such offence;
- against house breaking by night, as long as the house trespass continues (thus, where a person followed a thief and killed him in the open, after house trespass has ceased could not plead the RPD).

OFFENCES AGAINST HUMAN BODY

CULPABLE HOMICIDE AND MURDER

Homicide is the killing of a human being by a human being. Causing the death of an animal is not murder. It might amount to the offence of mischief or to cruelty to animals. It may be lawful or unlawful. Lawful homicide (cases falling under general exceptions – sec. 14-44) is of two types – excusable and justified homicide. Unlawful homicide includes –

- Culpable homicide not amounting to murder (sec. 100)
- Murder (sec. 101) and
- Homicide by rash or negligent acts (se[illegible] 106)

Sec. 100: CULPABLE HOM[illegible]

Section 100 defines cul[illegible]ie which is a wider offence than that [illegible]er. Whoever causes death, (a) by doing an act with the intention of causing death, or (b) with the intention of causing such bodily injury as is likely to cause death, or (c) with the knowledge that he is likely by such act to cause death, commits the offence of culpable homicide.

Illustrations:

- A lays sticks and over a pit, with the intention of thereby causing death, or with the knowledge that death is likely to be thereby caused. Z believing the ground to be firm, falls in and is killed. A has committed the offence of culpable homicide.
- A knows Z to be behind a bush. B does not know it. A, intending to cause, or knowing it to be likely to cause Z's death, induces B to fire at the bush. B fires and kills Z. Here B may be guilty of no offence, but A has committed the offence of culpable homicide.
- A by shooting at a foul with intent to kill and steal it, kills B, who is behind a bush; A not knowing that he was there. Here, although A was doing an unlawful act, he was not guilty of culpable homicide, as he did not intend to kill B, or to cause death by doing an act that he knew was likely to cause death.

Essential ingredients of sec. 100

- Whoever causes death – it is immaterial if the person whom the accused intended to kill was not killed but some other person. The death could be caused by words deliberately used by a person. For example, a seriously ill person may die by hearing some agitating words.

The death must result as a proximate [illegible] remote consequence of the act of viol[illegible]ere should not be the intervention of any [illegible]able change of circumstances betw[illegible] the act of [illegible]ence and the death. Where the victim died three weeks after the occurrence [illegible] to negligence [illegible] his part and sepsis consequence to the bad handling of the wound, this S[illegible] was held n[illegible] attracted.

- By doing an [illegible]he intention of causing death – it is imp[illegible]ote that the acts done extend to illegal [o]mission also. Intention is a question of fact which is to be gathered from the acts of the parties (viz. Nature of the weapon used, the part of the body on which the blow was given, the force and number of blows, etc.). The legal maxim is that everyone must be presumed to intend the normal consequences of his act. Intention does not imply or is assumed the existence of some previous design, it means an actual intention, the existing intention of the moment. Causing serious injury on a vital part of the body of the deceased with a dangerous weapon must necessarily, lead to interference that the accused intended to kill.
- With the intention of causing such bodily injury is likely to cause death – It means an intention to cause a particular injury, which injury is on turns out to be, one likely to cause death. It is not the death itself which is intended nor the effect of the injury. Thus, where bodily injury sufficient to cause death is actually cause, it is immaterial to go into the question whether the accused had intention to cause death. For example, where a person falsely arrested in a dacoity case, and mercilessly beaten at the police station which resulted in his death; beating for exorcising evil spirit resulting in death.
- With the knowledge that he is likely by such act to cause death – knowledge in comparison to intention is a strong word and imports certainty and not merely a probability. Intention is the purpose or design with which an act is done. It is the fore knowledge of the act coupled with the desire of it. Knowledge is an awareness of the consequences of the act. A person who voluntarily inflicts injury such as to endanger life must always, except in the most extraordinary circumstances, be taken to know that he is likely to cause death (e.g., when the accused fired his gun in the air to scare away the opposite party and in the act one stray pellet caused gun shot wound to a person killing him.)

The word knowledge includes all cases of rash acts by which death is caused, for rashness imports a knowledge of the likely result of an act which the actor does in spite of a risk. In some cases, gross negligence may amount to knowledge. For *e.g.*, where the accused killed a person by hitting him under the belief that he was hitting a ghost.

In Palani Goundan *vs* Emperor, the accused struck his wife on the head with ploughshare, which made her unconscious believing her to be dead, in order to lay the foundation of a false defence of suicide by hanging the accused hanged her. The hanging actually caused her death. The court observed that the intention of the accused must be judged not in the light of actual circumstances, but in the light of what he supposed to be the circumstances. It follows that a man is not guilty of culpable homicide if his intention was directed only to what he believes to be a lifeless body. It was held that the accused cannot be convicted of culpable homicide of murder, but for the offence of grievous hurt and attempt to create a false evidence by hanging his wife.

DISTINCTION BETWEEN CULPABLE HOMICIDE AND MURDER

There is a broad difference between the offences of murder and culpable homicide. In the case of murder, the offender has a positive intention to cause the death of the victim. In the case of culpable homicide, the intention or knowledge is not so positive or definite. The injury caused may or may not cause death. Degree of probability of death ensuing is high in case of murder.

Clause (b) of sec. 100 corresponds with cls. (2) and (3) of sec 101. The distinguishing feature of the *mens rea* requisite under cl. (2) is the knowledge possessed by the offender regarding the particular victim being in such a peculiar condition or state of health (*e.g.*, enlarged spleen) that the intentional harm caused is likely to be fatal, notwithstanding the fact that such harm would not in the ordinary way of nature be sufficient to cause death of a person in normal health. Clause (b) of sec. 100 does not postulate any such knowledge on the part of the offender. Thus, if the assailant had no knowledge about the disease of the victim nor an intention to cause death or bodily injury sufficient in the ordinary course of nature to cause death, the offence will not be murder, even if the injury which caused the death, was intentionally given.

EXCEPTION TO OFFENCE OF MURDER

Exceptions to sec. 101 of IPC reduce the offence of murder to that of culpable homicide not amounting to murder. The five exceptions specified in this Section are special exceptions in addition to the general exceptions mentioned in this chapter. The special exceptions are:

- Provocation
- RPD
- Exercise of legal powers
- Absence of premeditation and heat of passion
- Consent

Strictly speaking that they are not exactly defences but are in the nature of mitigating or extenuating circumstances. Burden is on the accused to establish circumstances which would bring this case within any excpetion. However, the general burden to establish the guilt of the accused is on the prosecution.

Exception I, sec. 101 (provocation): culpable homicide is not murder if the offender, whilst deprived of the power of self control by grave and sudden provocation, causes the death of the person who gave the provocation or causes the death of any other person by mistake or accident.

The above exception is subject to the following proviso:

- That the provocation is not sought or voluntarily provoked by the offenders as an excuse for killing or doing harm to any person.
- That the provocation is not given by anything done in obedience to the law or by a public servant in the lawful exercise of the powers of such public servant.
- That the provocation is not given by anything done in the lawful exercise of the RPD.

Explanation: Whether the provocation was grave and sudden enough to prevent the offence from amounting to murder, is a question of fact.

Illustrations:

(a) A, under the influence of passion excited by a provocation given by Z, intentionally kills Y, Z's child. This is murder, in as much as the provocation is not given by the child, and the death of the child was not caused by an accident or misfortune in doing an act caused by the provocation.

(b) Y gives grave and sudden provocation, fires at Y, neither intending nor knowing himself to be likely to kill Z, who in near him but out of sight. A kills Z. A has not committed murder, but merely culpable homicide.

(c) A is lawfully arrested by Z, a baillif. A is excited to sudden and violent passion by the arrest, and kills Z. This is murder and inasmuch as provocation was given by a thing done by a public servant in the exercise of his powers.

(d) A attempts to pull Z's nose. Z, in the exercise of the right of the private defence, lays hold of A to prevent him from doing so. A is moved to sudden and violent passion in consequence, and kills Z. This is murder, inasmuch as the provocation was given by a thing done in the exercise of the right of the private defence.

(e) Z strikes B. B is, by this provocation, excited to violent rage. A, a bystander, intending to take advantage of B's rage, and to cause him to kill Z, puts a knife into B's hand for that purpose. B kills Z with the knife. Here, B may have committed only culpable homicide, but A is guilty of murder.

The essential ingredients of the first exception to sec. 101 are:

- The provocation must be both grave and sudden and should not be formed the side of the accused.
- The provocation must be such as would deprive any reasonable man of his power of self-control over himself.
- The act of killing must be done under the immediate impulse of provocation. It must be distinguished from provocation which inspires an actual intention to kill.
- The offender must not have reflected, deliberated or cooled, between the provocation and the mortal stroke. However, the mental background created by the previous act of the victim may be taken into consideration for ascertaining whether the subsequent act caused grave and sudden provocation.
- The offender must have caused the death of the person who gave the provocation or that of any other person by mistake or accident.
- Mere words or gestures or confession are enough in some cases to cause grave and sudden provocation.

In K.M. Nanavati case, the wife confessed to husband of her illicit intimacy with one Ahuja. The accused drove his wife and children to a cinema, left them there, went to his ship, took a revolver, drove his car to Ahuja's flat and shot him dead. Between his wife's confession and Ahuja's murder, three hours had elapsed, and therefore the accused had sufficient time to regain his self-control. His conduct clearly shows that the murder was a deliberate and calculated one. Consequently, Exception 1 did not apply.

Where an accused sees his wife in company with her lover and kills her, he must be held to have acted under grave and sudden provocation. However, mere suspicion of unchastity would not be sudden provocation. A statement by the wife that she intends to commit adultery or live with another person is not grave and sudden provocation.

Exception 2, sec. 101 (Right of private defence): "Culpable homicide is not murder if the offender, in the exercise of good faith or the right of private defence of person or property, exceeds the power given to him by law and causes the death of the person against whom he is exercising such right of defence without premeditation, and without any intention of doing more than is necessary for the purpose of such defence".

This exception deals with the death caused by the excessive exercise of the right of private defence, provided the accused caused the death of a person without premeditation and when the accused caused death of a person he had no intention of doing more harm than was necessary for the purpose of defence.

Exception 3, sec. 101 (Exercise of legal powers): The ingredients of this exception are: (1) The person accused must be a public servant. (2) He must believe in good faith that the act which resulted in the death was lawful and necessary for the due discharge of his duties. (3) He must bear no ill-will to the deceased.

Where a suspected thief who has been arrested by a police officer, escapes by jumping down from the train and the police officer finding that he is not in a position to apprehend him, shoot at him and kills him. Held that the case is covered by exception 3 to sec. 101.

Exception 4, sec. 101 (Sudden Quarrel): "Culpable homicide is not murder if it is committed (i) without premeditation (ii) in a sudden fight (iii) in the heat of passion upon a sudden quarrel and, (iv) without the offender having taken undue advantage or acted in a cruel and unusual manner".

Explanation— It is immaterial in such cases which party offers the provocation or commits the first assault.

Where on a sudden quarrel, a person in the heat of the moment picks up a weapon which is handy and causes injuries, one of which proves fatal, he would be entitled to the benefit of this exception provided he has not acted cruelly. When the deceased was an old man and was innocent intervener who was asking the parties not to quarrel, there was no justification for the appellant to have given such a serious injury to him resulting in his death. Moreover, the appellant acted in a cruel manner.

Exception 5, sec. 101 (death by consent): "Culpable homicide is not murder when the person whose death is caused, being the age of eighteen years, suffers death or takes the risk of death with his own consent".

Illustration: A, by instigation, voluntarily causes Z, a person under eighteen years of age, to commit suicide. Here, on account of Z's youth, he was incapable of giving consent to his own death; A has therefore abetted murder.

In order to bring the offence under exception 5, the consent by the deceased must be given unconditionally and without any reservation. In a case, the wife flatly refused to go back to her mother and said if her husband insisted on her doing so she would rather be killed. The husband killed her. Here, the consent was not the type which is contemplated by exception 5, and the husband was held guilty of murder. A doctor pleading consent to an operation which proved fatal must prove that the patient accepted the risk and was fully aware of it. Where the accused because of successive failures in examination decided to end his life and informed the wife of his decision, and the accused killed his wife but was arrested before he could kill himself, it was held that the case is covered by exception 5. The consent was not given by deceased under a fear of injury or under a misconception of fact.

Section 106: Causing Death by Negligence. Whoever causes the death of any person by doing any rash and negligent act not amounting to culpable homicide, shall be punished with imprisonment of either description for a term which may extend to two years, or with fine, or with both".

This Section does not apply to the following cases:

- Death is caused with any intention or knowledge *i.e.*, the act must not amount to culpable homicide,
- Death has arisen from another supervening act or intervention which could not have been anticipated *i.e.*, death was not the direct or proximate result of the rash or negligent act,
- Death occurred due to an accident (*e.g.* where an accused on dark night believing a man to be a ghost killed him.

Section 106 applies where there is a direct nexus between the death of a person and the rash or negligent act. The act must be the *causa causans*, it is not enough that it may have been the *causa sine qua non*. Criminal rashness hazarding a dangerous and wanton act with the knowledge that it is so, and that it may cause injury, but without intention to cause injury, or knowledge that it will probably be caused. The criminality lies in running the risk of doing such an act with recklessness or indifference as to its consequences.

'Criminal negligence' is the gross and culpable neglect or failure to exercise the reasonable and proper care and precaution to guard against either to the public generally or to a particular individual. An illegal "omission" if negligent, may come this Section.

Rash and Negligent driving—the mere fact that a fatal motor run-over accident took place would not by itself be enough to make the driver liable under sec. 106. In order to impose criminal liability on the accused, it must be found as a fact that a collision was entirely or at least mainly due to rashness or negligence on the part of the driver. An error of judgement on the part of the driver would make him liable under sec. 106.

In Cherubin Gregory *vs* State of Bihar, the accused fixed up a naked live electric wire in the passage to latrine so that no trespasser may come and use the latrine. There was no warning that the wire was live. A trespasser who managed to enter the latrine without touching the wire, received a shock while coming out and died soon. It was held that the act of the accused was an actionable wrong under sec. 106. The mere fact that the person entering the land is a trespasser does not entitle the owner or occupier to inflict on him personal injury by direct violence or indirectly by doing something on the land the effect of which he knew was likely to cause serious injury to the trespasser.

In S.N. Hussain *vs* State of A.P, the accused, a bus driver, finding a level crossing gate open at time when there is no train schedule to pass, tried to cross the railway line and the bus collided with the on-coming goods train resulting in death of four passengers and injuring others. Held that there was no rashness on the part of the driver: "it is very clear from the evidence that the driver received no warning either from the approaching train or from passengers in bus in sufficient time to prevent the collision. The train while approaching the level crossing did not give any whistle. The railway track was at a higher level and the road was lined by babool trees and, therefore, a passing train coming from a distance was not visible from the bus."

Section 114: HURT

"Whoever causes bodily pain, disease or infirmity to any person is said to cause hurt". There is nothing in this Section to suggest that the hurt should be caused by direct physical contact between the accused and the victim. However, the pain must be bodily and not mental and may be caused by any means. Dragging by hair in aggressive manner and fisting [illegible] of attack are not trivial acts and constitute off[illegible]sing hurt. Infirmity has been defined as inabili[illegible] organ to perform its normal function which may either be temporary or permanent. A state of temporary impairment or hysteria or terror would constitute infirmity.

Section 116: GRIEVOUS HURT

T[illegible]g kinds of hurt only are designated as

- **First:** Emasculation.
- **Secondly:** permanent privation of the sight of either eye.
- **Thirdly:** permanent privation of the hearing of either ear.
- **Fourthly:** privation of any member or joint.
- **Fifthly:** destruction or permanent impairing of the powers of any member or joint.
- **Sixthly:** permanent disfiguration of the head or face.
- **Seventhly:** fracture or dislocation of a bone or tooth.
- **Eighthly:** Any hurt which endangers life or which cause the sufferer to be during the space of twenty days in severe bodily pain, or unable to follow his ordinary pursuits. The mere fact that the injured remained in the hospital for 20 days would not be enough to conclude that he was unable to follow his ordinary pursuits during that period.

An injury may be called grievous only if it "endangeres life". A simple injury cannot be called grievous simply because it happens to be caused on a vital part of the body close to the carotid artery, unless the dimensions nature of the injury or its effects are such that in [illegible]inion of the doctor it actually endangers the life [illegible]ictim. Hurt or grievous hurt to be punishable [illegible]caused voluntarily, as defined in secs. 115 or 1[illegible] IPC.

Sec. 115: Voluntarily causing hurt: whoever does may act with the intention thereby causing hurt to any person, or with the knowledge that he is likely thereby to cause hurt to any person, and does thereby cause hurt to any person, said voluntarily to cause hurt.

Sec. 117: Voluntarily causing grievous hurt: whoever voluntarily causes hurt, if the hurt which he intends to cause or know himself to be likely to cause is grievous hurt, and if the hurt which he causes is grievous hurt is said voluntarily to cause grievous hurt.

Explanation – A person is not said voluntarily to cause grievous hurt except when he both causes grievous hurt and intends or knows himself to be likely to cause grievous hurt. But he is said voluntarily to cause grievous hurt, if intending or knowing himself to be likely to cause grievous hurt of one kind, he actually causes grievous hurt of another kind.

Illustration – A intending, or knowing himself to be likely permanently to disfigure Z's face, gives Z a blow which does not permanently disfigure Z's face, but which causes Z to suffer severe bodily pain for the space of twenty days. A has voluntarily caused grievous hurt.

Punishment for voluntarily causing hurt or grievous hurt is provided under sec. 115(2) (imprisonment up to one year or with fine up to one thousand rupees, or with both) and sec. 117(2) (imprisonment for a term which may extend to seven years and shall also be liable to fine) respectively.

Offences Against the State in Bharatiya Nyaya Sanhita

Chapter VII of the BNS (Sections 147–154) consolidates and updates offences previously under Chapter VI of the IPC, focusing on threats to India's sovereignty, unity, and integrity. These provisions reflect a shift from colonial concepts like sedition to modern national security concerns.

Section 152: Acts Endangering Sovereignty, Unity, and Integrity of India

- **Legislative Intent:** Replaces IPC Section 124A (sedition), which was criticized for stifling free speech. Section 152 focuses on protecting national integrity rather than shielding the government from criticism.
- **Definition and Scope:**
  - ❑ Applies to anyone who "purposely or knowingly":
    - Excites or attempts to excite secession, armed rebellion, or subversive activities.
    - Encourages separatist feelings.
    - Endangers India's sovereignty, unity, or integrity.
  - ❑ Covers acts through:
    - Spoken or written words.
    - Signs or visible representations.

- Electronic communication (e.g., social media posts).
- Financial means (e.g., funding insurgent groups).
- Any other method.

- **Examples:**
  - Posting online content advocating for a separate state with intent to incite rebellion.
  - Funding organizations planning armed attacks against the state.
  - Organizing a rally to promote secession.
- **Punishment:**
  - Imprisonment for life, or
  - Imprisonment up to 7 years, and
  - Liable to a fine.
- **Explanation:** Comments criticizing government measures or actions, aimed at lawful reform without inciting the above activities, are not offences.
- **Comparison with IPC Section 124A:**
  - **IPC:** Focused on "disaffection" (hatred or contempt) towards the government; punishment was life imprisonment, up to 3 years, or a fine.
  - **BNS:** Broadens scope to secession and subversion, increases punishment to 7 years, and includes modern tools like electronic communication.
  - **Shift:** Moves from protecting the government to safeguarding national integrity.
- **Judicial Context:**
  - In Kedar Nath Singh v. State of Bihar (1962), the Supreme Court limited IPC Section 124A to acts inciting violence or public disorder. Section 152's broad terms (e.g., "subversive activities") may require similar judicial clarification to prevent misuse.
- **Procedural Aspects (BNSS, 2023):**
  - Cognizable and non-bailable offence.
  - Triable by a Court of Session.
- **Criticism and Concerns:**
  - Undefined terms like "subversive activities" or "separatist feelings" could lead to overbroad application, potentially targeting dissent.
  - The inclusion of "electronic communication" raises concerns about regulating online speech.
  - Legal scholars suggest robust judicial oversight to balance security and free expression.

Other Offences Against the State

- **Section 147:** Waging War Against the Government of India
  - **Definition:** Waging, attempting, or abetting war against the government (e.g., armed insurgency).
  - **Punishment:** Death or life imprisonment, with a fine.
  - **Example:** Participating in an armed attack on government institutions.
- **Section 148:** Conspiracy to Commit Offences Under Section 147
  - **Definition:** Conspiring (within or outside India) to wage war or overawe the Central/State Government by criminal force.
  - **Punishment:** Life imprisonment or up to 10 years, with a fine.
  - **Example:** Planning a coordinated attack to destabilize the government.
- **Section 149:** Collecting Arms with Intent to Wage War
  - **Definition:** Collecting men, arms, or ammunition to wage war against the government.
  - **Punishment:** Life imprisonment or up to 10 years, with a fine.
  - **Example:** Stockpiling weapons for an insurrection.
- **Section 150:** Concealing Design to Wage War
  - **Definition:** Concealing a plan to wage war, intending to facilitate it.
  - **Punishment:** Up to 10 years imprisonment, with a fine.
  - **Example:** Hiding knowledge of a terrorist plot against the state.
- **Section 151:** Assaulting President or Governor
  - **Definition:** Assaulting or restraining the President or Governor to compel or restrain their lawful powers.
  - **Punishment:** Up to 7 years imprisonment, with a fine.
  - **Example:** Threatening a Governor to influence policy decisions.
- **Section 153:** Waging War Against a Foreign State at Peace with India
  - **Definition:** Engaging in hostilities against a friendly foreign state.

- **Punishment:** Up to 7 years imprisonment, with a fine.
- **Example:** Attacking a neighboring country allied with India.

- **Section 154:** Depredation on Territories of a Foreign State at Peace with India
  - **Definition:** Committing plunder or destruction in a friendly foreign state's territory.
  - **Punishment:** Up to 7 years imprisonment, with a fine.
  - **Example:** Raiding border villages of an allied nation.

- **Key Observations:**
  - These offences are streamlined under Chapter VII, retaining the IPC's core but with updated language.
  - Severe punishments reflect the gravity of threats to state stability.
  - Section 153 and 154 protect India's diplomatic relations, a carryover from IPC Sections 126–127.

TERRORISM IN BHARATIYA NYAYA SANHITA

Section 113, housed under Chapter VI ("Of Offences Affecting the Human Body"), introduces terrorism as a standalone offence in the BNS, unlike the IPC, which relied on special laws like the Unlawful Activities (Prevention) Act, 1967 (UAPA).

Section 113: Terrorist Act

- **Legislative Intent:** Integrates terrorism into the general penal code, addressing modern threats like economic sabotage and terror financing while complementing the UAPA.
- **Definition:**
  - An act with intent to:
    - Threaten or likely threaten India's unity, integrity, sovereignty, security, or economic security.
    - Strike or likely strike terror in people (in India or abroad).
  - **Includes acts using:** Bombs, explosives, firearms, or hazardous substances (e.g., biological, radioactive) to cause:
    - Death or injury.
    - Property damage.
    - Disruption of essential services (e.g., water, power).
    - Damage to monetary stability via counterfeit currency production/smuggling.
  - Any other means threatening national security.
- Also covers:
  - Overawing or killing public functionaries (e.g., constitutional authorities).
  - Kidnapping or abducting to compel governments or organizations.
- **Sub-Provisions:**
  - **Sub-section (2):**
    - If resulting in death: Death or life imprisonment, with a fine.
    - Otherwise: Imprisonment from 5 years to life, with a fine.
  - **Sub-section (3):** Conspiracy, abetment, incitement, or facilitation of a terrorist act: 5 years to life imprisonment, with a fine.
  - **Sub-section (4):** Organizing terrorist training camps or recruitment: 5 years to life imprisonment, with a fine.
  - **Sub-section (5):** Membership in a terrorist organization: Up to life imprisonment, with a fine.
  - **Sub-section (6):** Harbouring or concealing a terrorist (except by spouse): 3 years to life imprisonment, with a fine.
  - **Sub-section (7):** Possessing property derived from terrorism: Up to life imprisonment, with a fine.
- **Examples:**
  - Detonating a bomb in a marketplace to incite panic.
  - Smuggling counterfeit currency to fund terror operations.
  - Sheltering a known terrorist operative.
- **Comparison with UAPA:**
  - **Similarity:** Definition aligns with UAPA Section 15 but explicitly includes "economic security" and counterfeit currency.
  - **Differences:**
    - **UAPA:** Special courts, stringent bail (Section 43D), police confessions admissible.
    - **BNS:** Tried in Sessions Courts under BNSS, standard bail provisions apply unless overridden.

- **Overlap:** Both laws cover similar acts, but BNS integrates terrorism into general law.

- **Judicial and Procedural Aspects:**
  - Cognizable and non-bailable.
  - Investigations may involve the National Investigation Agency (NIA) under the NIA Act, 2008.
- **Key Features:**
  - **Economic Security:** Addresses financial terrorism (e.g., Hawala, cryptocurrency misuse).
  - **Flexibility:** "Any other means" covers emerging threats like cyberattacks.
  - **Minimum Sentences:** Ensures deterrence with mandatory minimums.
- **Criticism and Challenges:**
  - Vague terms like "strike terror" or "economic security" could lead to misuse against dissenters or journalists.
  - Overlap with UAPA risks inconsistent application or prosecutorial discretion.
  - Judicial safeguards are needed to prevent overreach.

Harmonization with UAPA

- **UAPA Provisions:**
  - **Section 15:** Defines terrorist acts.
  - **Section 17:** Punishes terror funding.
  - **Section 18:** Covers conspiracy/preparation.
- **Implications:** Prosecutors may choose between BNS and UAPA, affecting accused rights (e.g., bail). The Standing Committee on Home Affairs (November 2023) recommended aligning definitions, but no changes were adopted.
- **Student Note:** Students should understand that while BNS Section 113 broadens access to terrorism laws, UAPA remains the primary statute for specialized cases.

Recent Developments

- Limited public data exists on Section 113 prosecutions. Early reports suggest its use in cases involving counterfeit currency with suspected terror links, but specific cases await judicial documentation.
- Section 152 has sparked debates on free speech, with critics arguing its broad scope could target legitimate dissent. Judicial review will likely shape its application.

OFFENCES AGAINST PROPERTY

Theft, extortion, robbery and dacoity are the offences against property.

Sec. 303: Theft: whoever, intending to take dishonestly any movable property out of the possession of any person without that person's consent, moves that property in order to such taking, is said to commit theft.

- **Explanation 1:** A thing is so long as it is attached to the earth not being movable property is not the subject of theft; but it becomes capable of being the subject of theft as soon as it severed from the earth.
- **Explanation 3:** A person is said to cause a thing to move by removing an obstacle which prevented it from moving or by separating it from any other thing, as well as by actually moving it.
- **Explanation 4:** A person who by means causes an animal to move, is said to move that animal, and to move everything which in consequence of the motion so caused is moved by that animal.
- **Explanation 5:** The consent mentioned in the definition may be expressed or implied or may given either by the person in possession or by any person having for that purpose that authority either express or implied.

Illustrations:

(a) A cuts down a tree on Z's ground, with the intention of dishonestly taking the tree out of Z's possession without Z's consent.

(b) A puts a bait for dogs in his pocket and thus induces Z's dog to follow it. If A's intention be dishonestly to take the dog out of Z's possession without Z's consent, A has committed theft as soon as Z's dog has begun to follow A.

(c) A meets a bullock carrying a box of treasure, he drives the bullock in a certain direction, in order that he may dishonestly take the treasure, as soon as the bullock begins to move, A has committed theft of the treasure.

(d) A being Z's servant and entrusted by Z with the care of Z's plate, dishonestly runs away with a plate, without Z's consent. A has committed theft.

(e) Z's going on a journey entrust his plate to A, the keeper of the wareshouse till Z shall return. A carries the plate to the goldsmith and sells it. Here, the plate was not in Z's possession. It could not therefore be taken out of Z's possession and A has committed theft, though he may have committed a Criminal Breach of Trust (CBT).

(f) A sees a ring belonging to Z on the table in Z's house. Not venturing to misappropriate the ring immediately for fear of search and detection, A hides the ring in a place where it is highly improbable that it will ever be found by Z, with the intention of taking the ring from the hiding place and selling it when the loss is forgotten. Here, A at the time of first moving the ring, commits theft.

(g) A delivers his watch to Z, a jeweller, to be regulated. Z carries it to his shop. A, not owing to the jeweller any debt for which jeweller might lawfully detain the watch as a security, enters the shop openly, takes his watch by force out of Z's hand, and carries it away. Here, A though he may have committed criminal trespass and assault, has not committed theft, inasmuch as what he did was not done dishonestly.

(h) If A owes money to Z for repairing the watch and if Z retains the watch lawfully as a security for the debt, and A takes the watch out of Z's possession, with the intention of depriving Z of the property as a security for his debt, he commits theft, inasmuch as he takes it dishonestly.

(i) Again if A, having pawned his watch to Z, takes it out of Z's possession without Z's consent, not having paid what he borrowed on the watch, he commits theft, though the watch is his own property inasmuch as he takes it dishonestly.

(j) A takes an article belonging to Z out of Z's possession without Z's consent, with the intention of keeping it until he obtains money from Z as a reward for its restoration. Here, A takes dishonestly; A has therefore committed theft.

(k) A, being on friendly terms with Z, goes into Z's library in Z's absence, and takes away a book without Z's consent for the purpose merely of regarding it, and with the intention of returning it. Here, it is probable that A may have conceived that he has Z's implied consent to use Z's book. If this was A's impression, A has not committed theft.

(l) A asks charity from Z's wife. She gives A money, food and clothes, which A knows to belong to Z, her husband. Here, it is probable that A may conceive that Z's wife is authorised to give away alms. If this was A's impression, A has not committed theft.

(m) A is the paramour of Z's wife. She gives a valuable property, which A knows to belong to her husband Z, and to be such property as she has not authority from Z to give. If A takes the property dishonestly, he commits theft.

(n) A, in good faith, believing property belonging to Z to be A's own property, takes that property out of B's possession. Here, as A does not take dishonestly, he does not commit theft.

Section 303: Punishment for theft: Whoever commits theft shall be punished with imprisonment of either description for a term which may extend to three years, or with fine, or with both.

ESSENTIAL INGREDIENTS OF THEFT

The absence of the person's consent at the time of moving, and the presence of dishonest intention in so taking at the time, are the essential ingredients of the offence of theft.

SECTION 308: EXTORTION

Whoever, intentionally puts any person in fear of any injury to that person, or to any other, and there by dishonestly induces the person so put in fear to deliver to any person any property or valuable security, or anything signed or sealed which may be converted into a valuable security, commits "extortion".

Illustrations:

(a) A threatens to publish a defamatory libel concerning Z unless Z gives him money. He thus induces Z to give him money. A has committed extortion.

(b) A threatens Z that he will keep Z's child in wrongful confinement unless Z will sign and deliver to A a promissory note binding Z to pay certain monies to A. Z signs and delivers the note. A has committed extortion.

(c) A, by putting Z in fear of grievous hurt, dishonestly induces Z to sign or affix his seal to a blank paper and deliver it to A. Z signs and delivers the paper to A. Here, as the paper so signed may be converted into a valuable security, A has committed extortion.

Section 308: Punishment for extortion: Whoever commits extortion shall be punished with imprisonment for a term which may extend to three years, or with fine or with both.

ESSENTIAL INGREDIENTS FOR EXTORTION

The chief element of extortion (blackmail) are the intentional putting of a person in fear of injury to himself or another and dishonestly inducing the person so put in fear to deliver to any person any property or valuable security.

Sec. 308: Putting persons in fear of injury in order to commit extortion: Whereas under sec. 308(2), a person is punishable for "extortion" if he puts any person in fear of injury and thereby dishonestly induces him to deliver any property, sec. 308(3) punishes the very act of putting or the attempting to put any person in fear of any injury for the above purpose.

'Aggravated forms of extortion' are provided under Sections 308. Sec. 308(5)—Extortion by putting a person in fear of death or grievous hurt; sec. 308(7)—Extortion by threat of accusation of an offence punishable with death or imprisonment for life; and, sec. 308(6)—putting person in fear of accusation of offence, in order to commit extortion.

Section 309: ROBBERY

Robbery is an aggravated form of either theft or extortion or of both. According to sec. 390, theft is robbery if:-

- In order to the committing of theft, or
- In committing theft, or
- In carrying away, or attempting to carry away property obtained by theft, the offender, for that end, voluntarily causes or attempts to cause to any person death, or hurt, or wrongful restraint, or fear of instant death, or hurt, or wrongful restraint.

Illustrations:

(a) A holds Z down, and fraudulently takes Z's money and jewels from Z's clothes, without Z's consent. Here, A has committed theft, and in order to the committing of that theft, has voluntarily caused wrongful restraint to Z. A has therefore committed robbery.

The essence of the offence of robbery is the presence of imminent fear or violence. The expression for that end indicates that death, hurt, or wrongful restraint is caused "in order to the committing of theft, or in committing theft, or in carrying away property obtained by theft". Thus, violence may be caused either before, or during or after committing theft but it must be caused for any of the ends stated above.

If force is used for any other purpose, it will not convert theft into robbery. Thus, if a thief, being pursued by the owner, abandons the property and on finding himself still chased throws stones to avoid capture, it would be the case of theft and not of robbery. Because the offenders threw stones to effect his escape and not to take away stolen property. But where C and D were stealing mangoes from a tree, and were surprised by B, whereupon C knocked down B, the offence of robbery was held to have committed.

The hurt caused by the offender must be voluntarily caused. Thus, accidental injury will not convert theft into robbery. In a case where the accused while snatching a nose ring of a woman, injured her, he was held guilty of robbery.

When Extortion is Robbery:

According to sec 309, 'extortion' is 'robbery'-

(i) When a person commits extortion by putting another person in fear of instant death/hurt/wrongful restraint to that person or to some other person, and

(ii) Such a person by so putting another in fear, induces the latter to deliver up the things extorted, and

(iii) The offender, at the time of committing the extortion, is in the presence of the person put in fear.

(b) A meets Z on high roads, shows a pistol, and demands Z's purse. Z surrenders his purse. Here, A has extorted the purse from Z, by putting him in fear of instant hurt, and being at the time of committing the extortion in his presence. A has therefore committed robbery.

(c) A obtains property from Z by saying, "Your child is in the hands of my gang, and will be put to death unless you send us ₹ 10,000". This is extortion and not robbery, unless Z is put in fear of the instant death of his child.

For extortion to become robbery, it is necessary that the offender must be "present before the person" put in fear of injury, and, thus, by reason of his presence is capable enough to carry his threat into effect simultaneously. Where a police officer obtains from a person certain ornaments by putting him under the fear that he will immediately be put into prison and will not be released for months, the police officer is guilty of robbery.

Punishment for Robbery: The punishment for robbery is imprisonment for 10 years and fine. In case of attempt to commit robbery, it is imprisonment for 7 years and fine.

If robbery is committed on the highway between sunset and sunrise, the punishment is imprisonment for 14 years. If hurt is caused, the punishment is imprisonment for life or 10 years and fine. Lastly, belonging to 'gang' of persons associated for the purpose of habitually committing theft or robbery is punishable with imprisonment for 7 years and fine.

Sec. 310: DACOITY

Dacoity is an aggravated form of robbery. Sec. 310 lays down that where 5 or more persons conjointly commit or attempt to commit a robbery, or are present and aid such commission or attempt, everyone of them is said to commit 'dacoity'.

This Section is one more of what is known as constructive criminality. The word 'conjointly' refers to united or concerted action of the person participating in the transaction. The person should share the common intention of committing robbery. In counting the number of offenders, the persons present and aiding when the crime is committed are also counted. Thus, one person may commit or attempt to commit robbery, and four other may be present and aiding in its commission or attempt.

Section 310 enacts that if anyone of the dacoits commits murder in committing dacoity, every one of them is liable for murder. In Emperor *vs* Lashkar, a gang of five dacoits, one of whom had gun, raided the house of X. After looting, while they were running away with their booty, they shot down one villager. It was held that the murder committed by the dacoits while carrying away the stolen property was 'murder committed in the commission of dacoity', and every offender was therefore liable for the murder.

Further, preparation to commit dacoity, belonging to a gang of dacoits and assembling for the purpose of committing dacoity is also punishable.

Punishment for dacoity: The punishment for dacoity is imprisonment for life, or imprisonment for 10 years and fine. In case of dacoity with murder, it is death, or life-imprisonment, or imprisonment for 10 years and fine.

If the offenders use any deadly weapons at the time of committing robbery or dacoity or cause or attempt to cause death or grievous hurt to any person, they shall be punished with imprisonment for 7 years.

OFFENCES AGAINST WOMEN

As per Section 2(35) of the BNS "woman" denotes any female human being of any age. Offences against women can be further classified into-offences against her body and offences relating to marriage. The following are the main offences committed against women.

Offence	Section of BNS	Nature and Punishment
Dowry Death	80	Cognizable, Non-bailable offence, Minimum imprisonment of 7 years which may extend up to imprisonment for life
Causing miscarriage	88	Non-cognizable, bailable offence, Imprisonment up to 3 years or fine or both
Causing miscarriage without woman's consent	89	Cognizable, Non-bailable Imprisonment for life, or Imprisonment for 10 years and fine
Death of woman caused by act done to cause miscarriage without the woman's consent	90	Cognizable, Non-bailable offence, Imprisonment up to 10 years and fine, Imprisonment for life or as above
Preventing a child from being born alive or to cause its death after birth	91	Cognizable, Non-bailable offence, Imprisonment up to 10 years, or fine, or both
Acid Attack	129	Cognizable, Non-bailable, Minimum 10 years maximum up to life imprisonment, fine shall be just & reasonable to meet medical expenses of victim
Outraging modesty of a woman	74	Cognizable, bailable offence, Imprisonment for 2 years, or fine, or both
Selling a minor for purpose of prostitution etc (person under 18 years)	98	Cognizable, non-bailable offence, Imprisonment for 10 years and fine
Buying a minor for purposes of prostitution etc	99	Cognizable, non-bailable offence, Imprisonment for 10 years and fine
Rape	63	Cognizable, Non-bailable offence, Minimum 7 years maximum imprisonment for life. If case falls within 376(2) then minimum imprisonment shall be 10 years
Cohabitation by deceitful means (by making a woman believe that she is lawfully wedded to him)	81	Non-cognizable, Non-bailable offence, Imprisonment for 10 years and fine
Bigamy:		
(1) Marrying again during lifetime of first husband or wife	82	Non-cognizable, Non-bailable offence, Imprisonment for 7 years and fine
(2) Marrying again with concealment of former marriage	82	Non-cognizable, Non-bailable offence, Imprisonment for 10 years and fine
Cruelty by husband or relative of husband towards a woman	85	Cognizable, Non-bailable offence, Imprisonment for 3 years and fine
Insulting the modesty of a woman by any word, gesture or act	79	Cognizable, bailable offence

OFFENCES RELATING TO MARRIAGE

Chapter V of the BNS deals with the offences relating to marriage.

Sec. 81 and 83: Mock Marriage

The following two provisions relate to mock or invalid marriages:

- Cohabitation or sexual intercourse caused by a man deceitfully inducing a belief of lawful marriage (sec. 81). The punishment is imprisonment upto 10 years and fine.
- Dishonestly or fraudulently going through a marriage ceremony knowing that no lawful marriage is thereby created. The punishment is imprisonment upto 7 years and fine.

The latter offence differs from the former in the fact that in it the ceremony is gone through, which is valid on the face of it but invalid for some reason known to one party, or the other. The former Section applies to deception practised by a man on a woman; the latter applies to an offence by a man as well as by a woman.

Sec. 81 punishes a man (married or unmarried) who induces a woman to become, as she thinks, his wife, but in fact his concubine. The offence under this Section can be punished as rape under sec 63.

Sec 82: MARRYING AGAIN DURING LIFETIME OF HUSBAND OR WIFE:

A person commits bigamy if that person:

- Having a husband or wife living.
- Marries in any case in which such marriage is void.
- By reason of its taking place during the life of such husband or wife.

There are two exceptions in which the second marriage is not an offence (defences in relation to a charge of bigamy):

- When the first marriage has been declared void by a court of competent jurisdiction (*i.e.* the first marriage is not a valid marriage).
- When the husband or wife has been continually absent or not heard of for seven years, provided that this fact be disclosed to the person with whom the second marriage is contracted. (Under the English law, there is a third exception, viz. Bonafide belief in the spouse's death – Tolson's case. The term bigamy is used under the English law).

If the second marriage is not a valid marriage according to the law applicable to the parties, there would be no question of its being void by reason of its taking place during the lifetime of the first husband or wife. Section 82 would not apply in such a case.

In a prosecution for bigamy, admission of marriage by the accused is not evidence of it; the second marriage, as a fact, the essential ceremonies constituting it, must be proved. The courts are not now so emphatic about proof of ceremonies if other reliable evidence is available.

The question of criminality under sec. 82 is somewhat a vexed question of law, and depends upon the personal matrimonial law, usage and custom of the person. For instance, sec. 82 has no application to Muslim males because of polygamy being permitted in Muslim law. But, Muslim women are not allowed the same liberty, thus, sec. 82 is applicable to them. This Section applies to Hindus, Christians and Parsis of either sex.

Conversion of a Hindu wife/husband to Islam or Christianity does not dissolve her/his marriage with her/his Hindu husband/wife and if she/ he marries a Muslim or a Christian, she/he commits bigamy. Similarly, a Christian cannot by embracing Islam marry a second time during the lifetime of his first wife, he cannot cast off to the winds a contractual obligation by his own act.

Whether a change of religion made honestly after marriage with the assent of both spouses, without any intent to commit a fraud upon the law, will have the effect of altering the right incidental to the marriage; such as that of divorce, is a question of importance and of nicety not decided as yet.

Sec. 82(1) : PUNISHMENT FOR BIGAMY

If the former marriage is concealed from the person with whom the subsequent marriage is contracted, the punishment is 10 years imprisonment and fine. In other cases, the punishment is imprisonment for 7 years and fine.

Sec. 84: CRIMINAL ELOPEMENT

Taking or enticing away or concealing or detaining a woman, knowing or having reason to believe her to be married, from her husband, in order that she may have illicit intercourse with any man is punishable with imprisonment for 2 years or fine or both.

Mere elopement with an adult unmarried woman is no offence. Generally, the woman is quite aware of the purpose for which she is quitting her husband and is an assenting party to it. This Section provides protection to the husband who alone can institute prosecution. An offence punishable under sec. 84 of BNS is a minor offence as compared with an offence punishable under sec. 63 of BNS. The wife cannot be punished as abettor under sec. 84 of BNS.

SEC 85: CRUELTY TO MARRIED WOMAN

Husband or relative of a husband of a woman subjecting her to cruelty is liable to be punished with imprisonment for the term up to 3 years and fine.

Sec. 85 is distinguishable from Section 4 of the dowry prohibition act because in the latter mere demand of dowry is punishable and existence of element of cruelty is not necessary, whereas Section 85 of BNS deals with aggravated form of the offence. A person can be prosecuted in respect of both the offences punishable under sec. 4 of the Dowry Prohibition Act and sec. 85 of BNS.

Section 80: DOWRY DEATH

Where the death of a woman is caused by any burns or bodily injury or occurs otherwise than under normal circumstances within 7 years of her marriage and it is shown that soon before her death she was subjected to cruelty or harassment by her husband or any relative of her husband, for or in connection with any demand for dowry, such death shall be called dowry death and such husband or relative shall be deemed to have caused her death.

Explanation: For the purposes of this Section dowry shall have the same meaning as in Section 2 of the Dowry Prohibition Act 1961.

COMPARISON WITH SEC. 85 OF BNS

Sec. 80 and 85 cannot be held to be mutually exclusive. These provisions deals with two distinctive offences. It is true that cruelty is a common essential to both the Sections and that has to be proved. The explanation to sec. 85 gives the meaning of cruelty. And sec. 85 there is no such explanation. But having regard to the common background of these offences one has to take the meaning of cruelty or harassment is same as one find in explanation to Section 85 under which cruelty by itself amounts to offence.

Under sec. 85 it is dowry death that is punishable and such death should have occurred within 7 years of marriage. No such period is mentioned in sec. 85. Further a person charged and acquitted under sec. 85 can be convicted under sec. 85 without the charge being there, if such a case is made out. If the case is established, there can be conviction under both the Sections but no separate sentence would be necessary under sec. 85 in view of the substantive sentence being awarded for the major offence under Section 85.

OFFENCE AGAINST CHILD

- **Section 93: Exposure and Abandonment of Child Under Twelve Years**
  - **Provision:** Whoever, being the father, mother, or person having the care of a child under twelve years, exposes or leaves such child in any place with the intention of wholly abandoning them shall be punished.
  - **Punishment:** Imprisonment of either description (simple or rigorous) for up to seven years, or fine, or both.
  - **Explanation:** This section does not preclude trial for murder (BNS Section 100, equivalent to IPC Section 302) or culpable homicide not amounting to murder (BNS Section 103, equivalent to IPC Section 304) if the child dies due to exposure.
  - **Key Points:**
    - Corresponds to IPC Section 317.
    - Targets intentional abandonment, addressing issues like economic distress or social stigma (e.g., abandoning newborns).
    - The BNS may include procedural updates, such as mandatory reporting or child welfare measures.
  - **Context and Application:**
    - **Example:** A parent leaving a newborn in a public place (e.g., hospital, street) with no intent to retrieve them could face charges.
    - Courts consider intent, circumstances (e.g., poverty), and the child's welfare.
  - Relevance to Child Exploitation: Indirectly related, as abandonment may lead to exploitation (e.g., trafficking), but not directly tied to hiring or prostitution.
- **Section 94: Concealment of Birth by Secret Disposal of Dead Body**
  - **Provision:** Whoever, by secretly disposing of the dead body of a child, intends to conceal its birth shall be punished.
  - **Punishment:** Imprisonment up to two years, or fine, or both.
  - **Key Points:**
    - Corresponds to IPC Section 318.
    - Focuses on concealing childbirth, often linked to social stigma (e.g., illegitimate births) or infanticide.

- The BNS may incorporate modern investigative methods (e.g., forensic evidence) to strengthen prosecution.

❑ **Context and Application:**

- Example: Burying a stillborn child's body to hide the birth would trigger this section.
- The prosecution must prove intent to conceal, often through circumstantial evidence.

❑ **Relevance to Child Exploitation:** No direct connection, but concealment could be linked to broader exploitation scenarios.

- **Section 95: Hiring, Employing, or Engaging a Child to Commit an Offense**

❑ **Provision:** Whoever hires, employs, or engages a child to commit an offense shall be punished.

❑ **Punishment:** Likely imprisonment up to seven years and fine (based on IPC Section 363A, kidnapping or maiming a minor for begging).

❑ **Key Points:**

- Likely expands on IPC Section 363A, which penalizes exploiting minors for unlawful purposes.
- Covers using children for criminal activities, such as theft, drug trafficking, vandalism, or cybercrimes.
- Child typically refers to a person under 18, per Indian laws like the Juvenile Justice Act, 2015.
- Cognizable and non-bailable due to the exploitation of minors.

❑ **Context and Application:**

- Example: Paying a minor to commit theft or smuggle drugs would fall under this section.
- Requires proof of hiring/employing and intent for the child to commit an offense.

❑ Relevance to Child Exploitation: Directly addresses exploiting children for criminal purposes, setting the context for Sections 96–99.

- **Section 96: Procuration of a Child**

❑ **Provision:** Whoever procures a child for unlawful or immoral purposes, such as prostitution or other exploitative activities, shall be punished.

❑ **Punishment:** Imprisonment up to seven years and fine.

❑ **Key Points:**

- Corresponds to IPC Section 366A (procuration of a minor girl for illicit intercourse).
- The BNS likely broadens this to include all children (not just girls) and modern exploitation forms, such as online grooming, forced labor, or trafficking.
- Procuration involves inducing, enticing, or taking a child for illegal purposes, often prostitution.
- Cognizable and non-bailable, reflecting the offense's severity.

❑ **Context and Application:**

- Example: Luring a 15-year-old into prostitution through deception (e.g., false job promises) or coercion would trigger this section.
- Overlaps with BNS Section 143 (trafficking) if the child is transported across regions.
- Evidence includes communication records, witness testimony, or victim statements.

❑ **Relevance to Child Exploitation:** Directly addresses procuring children for immoral purposes, complementing Sections 98–99 (selling/buying for prostitution).

- **Section 97: Kidnapping or Abducting a Child Under Ten Years of Age with Intent to Steal from Its Person**

❑ **Provision:** Whoever kidnaps or abducts a child under ten years of age with the intent to steal from its person shall be punished.

❑ **Punishment:** Imprisonment up to seven years and fine.

❑ **Key Points:**

- Corresponds to IPC Section 369.
- Kidnapping (BNS Section 134, equivalent to IPC Section 361) involves taking or enticing a minor without lawful guardianship.
- Abduction (BNS Section 135, equivalent to IPC Section 362) involves using force or deceit.
- The age limit (under ten) highlights the child's vulnerability and inability to resist.
- Focuses on stealing from the child (e.g., jewelry, money), not broader exploitation like prostitution.

- **Context and Application:**
  - Example: Abducting a 9-year-old to steal their gold earrings would attract this section.
  - Requires proof of the child's age, kidnapping/abduction, and intent to steal (e.g., targeting valuables).
  - May overlap with general kidnapping (BNS Section 134) if additional intents are involved.
- **Relevance to Child Exploitation:** Targets a specific exploitative act (stealing), less severe than prostitution or trafficking but still serious due to the child's age.

- **Section 98: Selling a Child for Purposes of Prostitution, etc.**
  - **Provision:** Whoever sells, lets to hire, or otherwise disposes of a child for the purpose of prostitution or other unlawful/immoral purposes shall be punished.
  - **Punishment:** Imprisonment up to seven years and fine.
  - **Key Points:**
    - Corresponds to IPC Section 372.
    - Covers selling of hiring out a child for prostitution, forced labor, or other exploitative acts (e.g., begging, pornography).
    - The term "etc." in the BNS likely includes modern forms of exploitation, such as trafficking for organ trade or forced marriage.
    - Cognizable and non-bailable, reflecting the grave violation of child rights.
  - **Context and Application:**
    - Example: Selling a minor to a brothel or trafficking ring for prostitution would trigger this section.
    - Requires proof of the transaction (sale/hire) and intent for prostitution or similar purposes.
    - Overlaps with BNS Section 143 (trafficking) and Section 144 (exploitation of a trafficked person).
  - **Relevance to Child Exploitation:** Directly addresses the commercial exploitation of children, particularly for prostitution, complementing Section 96 (procuration) and Section 99 (buying).

- **Section 99: Buying a Child for Purposes of Prostitution, etc.**
  - **Provision:** Whoever buys, hires, or otherwise obtains a child for the purpose of prostitution or other unlawful/immoral purposes shall be punished.
  - **Punishment:** Imprisonment up to seven years and fine.
  - **Key Points:**
    - Corresponds to IPC Section 373.
    - Targets the demand side of child exploitation, penalizing those who purchase or hire children for prostitution, forced labor, or similar acts.
    - The BNS may expand "unlawful purposes" to include modern crimes like online sexual exploitation or forced begging.
    - Cognizable and non-bailable, emphasizing child protection.
  - **Context and Application:**
    - Example: Paying to acquire a minor for a brothel or exploitative labor would attract this section.
    - Requires evidence of the transaction (purchase/hire) and intent for prostitution or similar purposes.
    - Complements Section 98 by addressing both supply and demand in child trafficking.
  - **Relevance to Child Exploitation:** Directly addresses acquiring children for exploitative purposes, completing the cycle of offenses involving prostitution.

DRUG TRAFFICKING IN BHARATIYA NYAYA SANHITA

The BNS does not define "drug trafficking" as a standalone offence, deferring to the Narcotic Drugs and Psychotropic Substances Act, 1985 (NDPS Act) for core narcotic crimes. However, certain BNS provisions apply indirectly when drug trafficking intersects with organized crime or terrorism.

Absence of Direct Provisions in BNS

Reason: Drug trafficking involves specialized issues (e.g., cultivation, sale, transport of narcotics), addressed by the NDPS Act's stringent penalties and procedures (e.g., limited bail under Section 37). The BNS focuses on general criminal law.

Comparison with IPC: The IPC also lacked specific drug provisions, relying on the NDPS Act or general sections like Section 120B (conspiracy).

Relevant BNS Provisions (Indirect Application)

- **Section 111:** Organized Crime
  - **Relevance:** Drug trafficking often involves organized crime syndicates.
  - **Definition:** Covers unlawful activities (e.g., trafficking) by groups using violence, intimidation, or coercion for material benefit. Requires multiple charge-sheets in the past 10 years.
  - **Punishment:**
    - **If resulting in death:** Death or life imprisonment, fine (minimum ₹ 10 lakh).
    - **Otherwise:** 5 years to life imprisonment, fine (minimum ₹ 5 lakh).
  - **Example:** A cartel smuggling heroin across borders could be charged under Section 111.
- **Section 113:**
  - **Relevance:** Drug trafficking funding terrorism or threatening economic security (e.g., large-scale smuggling) may fall under Section 113.
  - **Punishment:**
    - **If resulting in death:** Death or life imprisonment, with a fine.
    - **Otherwise:** 5 years to life imprisonment, with a fine.
  - **Example:** Using drug profits to finance a terrorist group.
- **Section 152:** Acts Endangering Sovereignty
  - **Relevance:** Drug trafficking funding secessionist activities (e.g., insurgencies) could be prosecuted here.
  - **Punishment:** Life imprisonment or up to 7 years, with a fine.
  - **Example:** Supplying narcotics to rebel groups in Northeast India.

Overlap with NDPS Act, 1985

- **Key NDPS Provisions:**
  - **Section 21:** Manufacturing/selling narcotics (10–20 years for commercial quantities).
  - **Section 27A:** Financing illicit traffic (20 years to life, no bail).
  - **Section 29:** Abetment/conspiracy (same as principal offence).
- **BNS vs. NDPS:**
  - NDPS Act is specific, with harsher penalties and procedural restrictions.
  - BNS applies to broader contexts (e.g., organized crime, terrorism).
- **Practice:** Prosecutors may use BNS for ancillary charges alongside NDPS Act charges.
- **Related Laws:** The Prevention of Money Laundering Act, 2002 (PMLA) may apply to financial aspects of trafficking.

Procedural Aspects (BNSS, 2023)

- Cognizable and non-bailable for Sections 111, 113, or 152.
- Triable by a Court of Session.

Criticism

- The BNS's reliance on the NDPS Act limits its role in modernizing drug laws.
- Overlapping provisions risk inconsistent application, requiring clear prosecutorial guidelines.

COUNTERFEITING IN BHARATIYA NYAYA SANHITA

Chapter X of the BNS (Sections 178–188) addresses offences related to coin, currency notes, bank notes, and government stamps, updating IPC Chapter XII to tackle modern threats like counterfeit currency linked to terrorism.

Key Provisions

- **Section 178:** Counterfeiting Coin, Currency Notes, or Bank Notes
  - **Definition:** Counterfeiting or performing any part of the counterfeiting process.
  - **Punishment:** Life imprisonment or up to 10 years, with a fine.
  - **Example:** Printing fake ₹ 500 notes.
- **Section 179:** Using as Genuine a Counterfeit Coin, Currency Note, or Bank Note
  - **Definition:** Knowingly using or trafficking counterfeit currency as genuine.
  - **Punishment:** Life imprisonment or up to 10 years, with a fine.
  - **Example:** Passing fake currency in a market.

- **Section 180:** Possession of Counterfeit Coin, Currency Note, or Bank Note
  - **Definition:** Possessing counterfeit currency with intent to use it as genuine.
  - **Punishment:** Up to 7 years imprisonment, fine, or both.
  - **Example:** Storing fake notes for circulation.
- **Section 181:** Making or Possessing Instruments for Counterfeiting
  - **Definition:** Making or possessing tools/ materials for counterfeiting.
  - **Punishment:** Life imprisonment or up to 10 years, with a fine.
  - **Example:** Owning a printer used to produce fake currency.
- **Section 183–185:** Stamp-Related Offences
  - **Definition:** Effacing, reusing, or erasing marks on government stamps with intent to defraud.
  - **Punishment:** Up to 3 years imprisonment, fine, or both.
- **Section 186:** Fictitious Stamps
  - **Definition:** Making or possessing fake postal stamps.
  - **Punishment:** Fine up to ₹ 200.
- **Section 187–188:** Mint Offences
  - **Definition:** Altering coin standards or removing coining tools from mints.
  - **Punishment:** Up to 7 years imprisonment, with a fine.

Counterfeiting Linked to Terrorism (Section 113)

- **Relevance:** Section 113(1)(a)(iv) includes counterfeiting currency to damage monetary stability as a terrorist act.
- **Punishment:**
  - **If resulting in death:** Death or life imprisonment, with a fine.
  - **Otherwise:** 5 years to life imprisonment, with a fine.
- **Example:** Smuggling fake currency to fund terror operations.
- **Significance:** Elevates counterfeiting to a national security offence when linked to terrorism.

Comparison with IPC

- IPC (Sections 230–263A): Similar offences with equivalent punishments (e.g., 7–10 years).
- **BNS Updates:**
  - Modern terminology (e.g., "bank notes").
  - Links counterfeiting to terrorism via Section 113.
  - Emphasizes fines alongside imprisonment.

Procedural Aspects (BNSS, 2023)

- Cognizable and non-bailable for Sections 178–181, 189.
- Triable by Court of Session (serious cases) or Magistrate (lesser offences).
- Investigations may involve the NIA or RBI if terrorism or large-scale counterfeiting is suspected.

OFFENCES AGAINST PUBLIC TRANQUILITY IN BHARATIYA NYAYA SANHITA

Chapter XI of the Bharatiya Nyaya Sanhita, 2023 (BNS) addresses offences that disrupt public peace, such as unlawful assemblies, rioting, and affrays. These provisions, replacing Chapter VIII of the Indian Penal Code, 1860 (IPC), aim to maintain societal order with updated penalties and language for modern contexts.

Section 189: Unlawful Assembly

- **Definition:** An assembly of five or more persons with a common object to:
  - Overawe the government or public servants by criminal force.
  - Resist legal processes.
  - Commit mischief, trespass, or other offences.
  - Use force to seize property or enforce a right.
  - Compel illegal acts.
- **Punishment:** Imprisonment up to 6 months, or a fine, or both.
- **Comparison with IPC (Section 141):** Identical in substance, renumbered to Section 189.
- **Key Elements:**
  - **Common Object:** Shared intent, proven by actions or planning.
  - **Membership:** Active participation required, not mere presence (Bhanwar Singh v. State of Rajasthan, 2008).
  - **Example:** A group of five planning to forcibly disrupt a court proceeding.

Section 190: Being a Member of an Unlawful Assembly

- **Definition:** Knowingly joining or continuing in an unlawful assembly.

- **Punishment:** Imprisonment up to 6 months, or a fine, or both.
- **Comparison with IPC (Section 142):** No change, renumbered to Section 190.
- **Example:** Joining a group illegally blocking a highway to protest.

Section 191: Rioting

- **Definition:** When an unlawful assembly (or any member) uses force or violence to pursue the common object, it constitutes rioting.
- **Punishment:**
  - **Sub-section (2):** Imprisonment up to 2 years, or a fine, or both.
  - **Sub-section (3):** If armed with a deadly weapon or anything likely to cause death, imprisonment up to 5 years, or a fine, or both.
- **Comparison with IPC (Sections 146–148):**
  - **IPC Section 147 (Rioting):** 2 years, same as BNS.
  - **IPC Section 148 (Armed Rioting):** 3 years; BNS increases to 5 years.
- **Key Elements:**
  - Violence linked to the common object.
  - Distinguished from peaceful protests (Ramlila Maidan Incident v. Home Secretary, 2012).
- **Example:** A mob vandalizing shops during a protest (Section 191(2)); if armed with knives, Section 191(3) applies.

Section 194: Affray

- **Definition:** Two or more persons fighting in a public place, disturbing public peace.
- **Punishment:** Imprisonment up to 1 month, or a fine up to ₹ 1,000, or both.
- **Comparison with IPC (Section 159):**
  - Fine increased from ₹ 100 to ₹ 1,000, reflecting inflation.
- **Example:** A public brawl at a market causing panic.

THEORIES OF PUNISHMENT

Punishment theories provide the rationale for penal sanctions, shaping the BNS's sentencing framework. While not codified, these theories guide judicial application.

Deterrent Theory

- **Objective:** Deter offenders (specific deterrence) and society (general deterrence) through fear of consequences.
- **Basis:** Jeremy Bentham's utilitarianism—punishment prevents greater harm.
- **BNS Application:** Severe penalties (e.g., Section 113, terrorism: death or life imprisonment; Section 191(3), armed rioting: 5 years) deter serious crimes.
- **Example:** Life imprisonment for endangering sovereignty (Section 152) discourages anti-national acts.

Retributive Theory

- **Objective:** Punish offenders proportionate to their crime, satisfying justice.
- **Basis:** Immanuel Kant's "just deserts" principle.
- **BNS Application:** Proportionate penalties (e.g., Section 101, murder: death or life imprisonment; Section 66, rape causing death: death) reflect retribution.
- **Example:** Death penalty for terrorism causing death (Section 113) ensures justice for victims.

Reformative Theory

- **Objective:** Rehabilitate offenders for reintegration.
- **Basis:** Modern criminology's focus on reform.
- **BNS Application:** Community service (Section 4(f)) and light penalties (e.g., Section 194, affray: 1 month) support reform.
- **Example:** A first-time offender under Section 194 may receive community service (Mohd. Giasuddin v. State of AP, 1977).

Preventive Theory

- **Objective:** Incapacitate offenders to protect society.
- **Basis:** Prioritizes public safety.
- **BNS Application:** Long sentences (e.g., Section 111, organized crime: life imprisonment) prevent recidivism.
- **Example:** Non-bailable detention for terrorism (Section 113) removes threats.

Restorative Theory

- **Objective:** Repair harm to victims and communities through compensation or reconciliation.
- **Basis:** Victim-centric justice.
- **BNS Application:** BNSS Section 396 (victim compensation) supports restoration.
- **Example:** Rioting victims (Section 191) may receive compensation for property damage.

- **BNS Approach:** Combines deterrence and retribution for serious crimes, with reformation and restoration for lesser offences. Judicial discretion ensures balanced application.

KINDS OF PUNISHMENTS UNDER BNS

Section 4 of the BNS outlines punishments, replacing IPC Section 53 with a modern approach:

Death

- **Scope:** For "rarest of rare" cases (Bachchan Singh v. State of Punjab, 1980).
- **BNS Provisions:** Section 66 (rape causing death), Section 101 (murder), Section 113 (terrorism causing death).
- **Comparison with IPC:** No change; judicial oversight retained.

Imprisonment for Life

- **Scope:** Often means natural life unless commuted.
- **BNS Provisions:** Section 111 (organized crime), Section 152 (endangering sovereignty).
- **Comparison with IPC:** More frequent in BNS for serious offences.

Imprisonment (Rigorous or Simple)

- **Rigorous:** With hard labor (e.g., Section 191(3), armed rioting: up to 5 years).
- **Simple:** Without labor (e.g., Section 194, affray: up to 1 month).
- **Comparison with IPC:** Increased terms for some offences (e.g., rioting: 2 years vs. IPC's 2 years).

Forfeiture of Property

- **Scope:** Confiscation of crime-related property.
- **BNS Provisions:** Section 111 (organized crime proceeds), Section 113 (terrorism property).
- **Comparison with IPC:** Retained, with BNSS detailing procedures.

Fine

- **Scope:** Monetary penalty, standalone or combined.
- **BNS Provisions:** Section 191 (rioting: discretionary fine), Section 194 (affray: up to ₹ 1,000).
- **Comparison with IPC:** Higher fines (e.g., affray: ₹ 1,000 vs. ₹ 100).

Community Service

- **Scope:** Non-custodial work for community benefit.
- **BNS Provision:** Section 4(f), new addition.
- **Comparison with IPC:** Absent in IPC, aligns with rehabilitation.
- **Example:** Community service for affray instead of jail.

Key Features

- Courts can combine punishments (e.g., imprisonment + fine).
- Community service reflects global rehabilitative trends.

COMPENSATION TO VICTIMS OF CRIME

The BNS and BNSS emphasize victim-centric justice, enhancing provisions for compensation.

Legal Framework

- **BNSS Section 396 (Victim Compensation Scheme):**
  - States must establish schemes with Central Government funding.
  - District/State Legal Services Authorities (DLSA/ SLSA) award compensation after enquiry.
  - Interim relief (e.g., medical aid) available during trials.

Scope of Compensation

- Covers medical costs, lost earnings, pain, property damage, or death.
- **Examples:**
  - Rioting victim (Section 191) compensated for shop damage.
  - Murder victim's family (Section 101) receives state compensation.

Process

- Courts recommend compensation; DLSA/SLSA decides quantum.
- Victims can apply directly if offenders are untraceable (Section 396(4)).
- Enquiry completed within 2 months.

Judicial Precedents

- **Ankush Shivaji Gaikwad v. State of Maharashtra (2013):** Mandatory compensation consideration.
- **Laxmi v. Union of India (2014):** ₹ 5 lakh for acid attack victims.

MULTIPLE CHOICE QUESTIONS

1. Which of the following are essential elements of actus reus under BNS?
   1. A voluntary act or omission
   2. The mental intention to commit the act
   3. The consequence or result of the act
   4. The circumstances in which the act occurs

   A. 1 and 3 only　　B. 1, 3, and 4 only
   C. 2 and 4 only　　D. All of the above

2. Which of the following offenses under BNS require proof of mens rea?
   1. Murder
   2. Theft
   3. Public nuisance
   4. Rash driving

   A. 1 and 2 only
   B. 1, 2, and 4 only
   C. 3 and 4 only
   D. All of the above

3. Which of the following are examples of strict liability offenses under BNS?
   1. Sale of adulterated food
   2. Robbery
   3. Traffic violations
   4. Assault

   A. 1 and 3 only
   B. 2 and 4 only
   C. 1, 2, and 3 only
   D. All of the above

4. **Assertion (A):** Actus reus includes both a voluntary act and its consequences under BNS.

   Reason (R): A person cannot be held liable for involuntary acts like reflexes.

   A. Both A and R are true, and R is the correct explanation of A.
   B. Both A and R are true, but R is not the correct explanation of A.
   C. A is true, but R is false.
   D. A is false, but R is true.

5. **Assertion (A):** Mens rea is irrelevant in strict liability offenses under BNS.

   Reason (R): Strict liability aims to ensure public safety by punishing acts regardless of intent.

   A. Both A and R are true, and R is the correct explanation of A.
   B. Both A and R are true, but R is not the correct explanation of A.
   C. A is true, but R is false.
   D. A is false, but R is true.

6. Match the following elements of criminal liability with their descriptions under BNS:

Element	Description
A. Actus Reus	1. The guilty mind or intention
B. Mens Rea	2. The physical act or omission
C. Causation	3. The link between act and consequence
D. Concurrence	4. Act and intent occurring simultaneously

   Codes:
   A. A-2, B-1, C-3, D-4
   B. A-1, B-2, C-4, D-3
   C. A-3, B-4, C-1, D-2
   D. A-4, B-3, C-2, D-1

7. Arrange the following landmark cases related to criminal liability in chronological order:
   1. R v Dudley and Stephens (1884) – Necessity and actus reus
   2. R v Cunningham (1957) – Recklessness as mens rea
   3. State of Maharashtra v M.H. George (1965) – Strict liability
   4. Gian Kaur v State of Punjab (1996) – Right to die and mens rea

   Codes:
   A. 2, 1, 3, 4　　B. 1, 2, 3, 4
   C. 3, 1, 2, 4　　D. 4, 3, 2, 1

8. Consider the following statements about mens rea under BNS:
   1. Intention always requires premeditation.
   2. Recklessness involves awareness of risk and consciously taking it.
   3. Negligence is not a form of mens rea under BNS.
   4. Knowledge implies awareness of the consequences of an act.

   Which of the above statements are true?

   A. Only one statement is true
   B. Only two statements are true
   C. Only three statements are true
   D. Only four statements are true

9. Consider the following statements about actus reus under BNS:

1. It includes only voluntary acts, not omissions.
2. An omission can constitute actus reus if there is a legal duty to act.
3. The act must always result in harm to be punishable.
4. Automatism negates the voluntariness of actus reus.

Which of the above statements are true?

A. Only one statement is true
B. Only two statements are true
C. Only three statements are true
D. Only four statements are true

PASSAGE-BASED QUESTIONS

PASSAGE 1

Under the Bharatiya Nyaya Sanhita (BNS), 2023, criminal liability generally requires actus reus (the wrongful act) and mens rea (the guilty mind). Actus reus includes voluntary acts or omissions where a legal duty exists, along with their consequences. Mens rea varies by offense—intention or knowledge is required for murder (Section 100), while recklessness suffices for rash driving (Section 281). Strict liability offenses, however, do not require mens rea.

10. Based on the passage, which element is always required for criminal liability under BNS?

A. Actus reus
B. Mens rea
C. Both actus reus and mens rea
D. Neither actus reus nor mens rea

11. According to the passage, what mens rea is sufficient for rash driving under Section 281?

A. Intention B. Knowledge
C. Recklessness D. Negligence

PASSAGE 2

A man failed to stop at a traffic signal, causing an accident that injured a pedestrian. The prosecution argued that his failure to stop was an actus reus due to a legal duty to obey traffic rules. The defense claimed he lacked mens rea, as he did not intend harm. The court convicted him under BNS Section 281, stating that recklessness, not intention, was sufficient for liability.

12. Based on the passage, why was the man convicted?

A. He intended to cause harm
B. His act was reckless
C. He breached a strict liability rule
D. He had knowledge of the injury

13. According to the passage, which element was not required for conviction?

A. Actus reus B. Intention
C. Legal duty D. Causation

14. Which of the following defenses negates actus reus under BNS?

1. Insanity 2. Automatism
3. Mistake of fact 4. Intoxication

A. 2 only
B. 1 and 3 only
C. 2 and 4 only
D. All of the above

15. Which of the following statements about causation under BNS is/are correct?

1. The act must be the sole cause of the harm Sudden
2. The harm must be a foreseeable result of the act
3. Intervening acts can break the chain of causation
4. Causation is irrelevant in strict liability offenses

A. 1 and 4 only B. 2 and 3 only
C. 2 only D. 3 only

16. Which of the following are stages of a crime under BNS?

1. Intention 2. Preparation
3. Attempt 4. Completion

A. 1 and 3 only B. 2 and 4 only
C. 1, 2, and 3 only D. All of the above

17. Which of the following acts constitute abetment under BNS?

1. Instigating someone to commit a crime
2. Assisting in the commission of a crime
3. Merely witnessing a crime
4. Conspiring to commit a crime

A. 1 and 2 only B. 1, 2, and 4 only
C. 3 and 4 only D. All of the above

18. Which of the following are inchoate crimes under BNS?

1. Attempt to murder
2. Criminal conspiracy
3. Theft
4. Abetment

A. 1 and 2 only B. 1, 2, and 4 only
C. 2 and 3 only D. All of the above

19. Assertion (A): Preparation to commit a crime is generally not punishable under BNS.

Reason (R): Preparation lacks proximity to the actual commission of the offense.

A. Both A and R are true, and R is the correct explanation of A.
B. Both A and R are true, but R is not the correct explanation of A.
C. A is true, but R is false.
D. A is false, but R is true.

20. Assertion (A): An agreement is sufficient to establish criminal conspiracy under BNS.

Reason (R): An overt act is not required unless specified by the offense.

A. Both A and R are true, and R is the correct explanation of A.
B. Both A and R are true, but R is not the correct explanation of A.
C. A is true, but R is false.
D. A is false, but R is true.

21. Match the following inchoate crimes with their legal definitions under BNS:

Crime	Definition
A. Abetment	1. Agreement to commit an unlawful act
B. Criminal Conspiracy	2. Taking a step beyond mere preparation
C. Attempt	3. Instigating or aiding a crime

Codes:
A. A-3, B-1, C-2
B. A-1, B-2, C-3
C. A-2, B-3, C-1
D. A-3, B-2, C-1

22. Arrange the following landmark cases related to inchoate crimes in chronological order:
1. R v White (1910) – Attempted murder
2. Mulcahy v R (1868) – Criminal conspiracy
3. State of Maharashtra v Mohd. Yakub (1980) – Attempt vs Preparation
4. Kartar Singh v State of Punjab (1994) – Conspiracy in terrorism

Codes:
A. 2, 1, 3, 4 B. 1, 2, 4, 3
C. 3, 1, 2, 4 D. 4, 3, 2, 1

23. Consider the following statements about attempt under BNS:
1. Attempt requires intention to commit the offense.
2. Mere preparation is sufficient to constitute an attempt.
3. Attempt is punishable even if the crime is impossible to complete.
4. Proximity to the final act is irrelevant in attempt cases.

Which of the above statements are true?
A. Only one statement is true
B. Only two statements are true
C. Only three statements are true
D. Only four statements are true

24. Consider the following statements about criminal conspiracy under BNS:
1. It requires at least two persons to agree.
2. The agreement must be followed by an overt act for liability.
3. The object of the agreement must be an illegal act.
4. Conspiracy can be inferred from circumstantial evidence.

Which of the above statements are true?
A. Only one statement is true
B. Only two statements are true
C. Only three statements are true
D. Only four statements are true

PASSAGE-BASED QUESTIONS

PASSAGE 1

Under the Bharatiya Nyaya Sanhita (BNS), 2023, inchoate crimes include abetment, criminal conspiracy, and attempt. Abetment involves instigating, aiding, or conspiring to commit an offense (Section 61). Criminal conspiracy (Section 63) requires an agreement between two or more persons to commit an illegal act, and in some cases, an overt act. Attempt (Section 65) is an act beyond preparation with intent to commit the offense, punishable even if the crime is not completed.

25. Based on the passage, which of the following is required for criminal conspiracy under BNS?
A. An overt act in all cases
B. An agreement between two or more persons
C. Completion of the illegal act
D. Preparation alone

26. According to the passage, when is an attempt punishable under BNS?
A. When the crime is completed
B. When there is intent and an act beyond preparation
C. When preparation is planned
D. When abetment occurs

PASSAGE 2

A group of men agreed to rob a bank and purchased tools for the job. One of them informed the police before any robbery occurred. The prosecution charged them with criminal conspiracy under BNS Section 63. The defense argued that no overt act was committed, as the robbery was not attempted. The court convicted them, stating that the agreement and purchase of tools were sufficient for liability.

27. Based on the passage, why were the men convicted?
A. They completed the robbery
B. They agreed and took a preparatory step
C. They attempted the robbery
D. They abetted each other

28. According to the passage, what was the defense's argument?
A. No agreement existed
B. No illegal act was intended
C. No overt act was committed
D. No tools were purchased

29. Which of the following distinguishes attempt from preparation under BNS?
1. Intention
2. Proximity to the final act
3. Completion of the crime
4. Agreement with others
A. 2 only
B. 1 and 3 only
C. 2 and 4 onlyintrac
D. All of the above

30. Which of the following statements about abetment under BNS is/are correct?
1. Abetment requires the crime to be completed.
2. Instigation must be intentional.
3. Aiding can be passive assistance.
4. Abetment is not punishable if the crime fails.
A. 1 and 4 only B. 2 only
C. 2 and 3 only D. 3 only

31. Which of the following acts are excused under the general exceptions of BNS?
1. Act by a child under 7 years
2. Act under a mistake of law
3. Act by a person of unsound mind
4. Act with malicious intent
A. 1 and 3 only
B. 1, 3, and 4 only
C. 2 and 4 only
D. All of the above

32. Under BNS, which of the following circumstances provide a defense?
1. Act done under a judicial order
2. Act under voluntary intoxication
3. Act with free consent
4. Act under necessity
A. 1 and 3 only
B. 1, 3, and 4 only
C. 2 and 4 only
D. All of the above

33. Which of the following are required for the defense of private defense under BNS?
1. Reasonable apprehension of danger
2. Proportionate force
3. Intent to kill
4. Imminent threat
A. 1 and 2 only B. 1, 2, and 4 only
C. 2 and 3 only D. All of the above

34. Assertion (A): An act done under compulsion is excused under BNS.

Reason (R): The compulsion must involve an immediate threat of death or grievous hurt.
A. Both A and R are true, and R is the correct explanation of A.
B. Both A and R are true, but R is not the correct explanation of A.
C. A is true, but R is false.
D. A is false, but R is true.

35. Assertion (A): Mistake of fact in good faith is a defense under BNS.

Reason (R): It negates the criminal intent required for liability.
A. Both A and R are true, and R is the correct explanation of A.
B. Both A and R are true, but R is not the correct explanation of A.
C. A is true, but R is false.
D. A is false, but R is true.

36. Match the following general exceptions under BNS with their applicable sections:

Exception	Section
A. Necessity	1. Section 83
B. Insanity	2. Section 81
C. Compulsion	3. Section 94

Codes:
A. A-2, B-1, C-3
B. A-1, B-3, C-2
C. A-3, B-2, C-1
D. A-2, B-3, C-1

37. Arrange the following BNS sections related to general exceptions in ascending order:

1. Section 90 – Consent
2. Section 76 – Mistake of fact
3. Section 85 – Intoxication
4. Section 100 – Private defense

Codes:

A. 2, 3, 1, 4   B. 1, 2, 3, 4
C. 3, 1, 2, 4   D. 4, 3, 2, 1

38. Consider the following statements about necessity under BNS:

1. The act must prevent greater harm than it causes.
2. The danger must be imminent.
3. The act must be intentional.
4. There must be no lawful alternative.

Which of the above statements are true?

A. Only one statement is true
B. Only two statements are true
C. Only three statements are true
D. Only four statements are true

39. Consider the following statements about insanity under BNS:

1. It must exist at the time of the act.
2. The accused must prove it.
3. Temporary insanity is not a defense.
4. It includes voluntary intoxication.

Which of the above statements are true?

A. Only one statement is true
B. Only two statements are true
C. Only three statements are true
D. Only four statements are true

PASSAGE 3

During a severe storm, a fisherman broke into an abandoned shed to take shelter as waves crashed around his boat, threatening his life. He was charged with trespass under BNS. The court acquitted him under Section 81, ruling that his act was justified by necessity. The judge explained that the fisherman faced an immediate danger of drowning, the harm avoided (his death) was far greater than the minor trespass, and no other shelter was available amidst the storm.

40. Based on the passage, why was the fisherman acquitted?

A. He acted under compulsion
B. He used necessity to avoid greater harm
C. He had the owner's consent
D. He was of unsound mind

41. According to the passage in Q40, what condition was essential for the necessity defense?

A. Immediate danger
B. Judicial order
C. Proportionate force
D. Mistake of fact

PASSAGE 4

At a local fair, a woman unknowingly drank a beverage laced with a sedative by a vendor. In her drowsy state, she pushed a child, causing a minor bruise, and was charged with assault under BNS. The court acquitted her under Section 85, finding that her involuntary intoxication negated any intent to harm. Witnesses confirmed she had no knowledge of the sedative, and the judge noted that her actions were not deliberate, distinguishi : this from cases of voluntary intoxication.

42. Based on the passage, why was the woman acquitted?

A. She acted in private defense
B. Her involuntary intoxication negated intent
C. She had the child's consent
D. She was under compulsion

43. According to the passage in Q42, what was crucial for the woman's defense?

A. Lack of intent due to involuntary intoxication
B. Necessity to avoid harm
C. Belief in a lawful order
D. Reasonable apprehension of danger

44. Which of the following defenses are recognized under BNS general exceptions?

1. Act by a child below 12 but above 7 with no maturity
2. Act under a mistake of fact in good faith
3. Act under voluntary intoxication causing insanity

A. 1 only
B. 2 only
C. 2 and 3 only
D. 1, 2, and 3

45. Consider the following statements about consent under BNS:

1. It must be given freely and voluntarily.
2. Consent to death is invalid.
3. Consent under misconception is not valid.
4. Consent excuses all intentional acts.

Which of the above statements are true?

A. Only one statement is true
B. Only two statements are true
C. Only three statements are true
D. Only four statements are true

46. Which of the following constitute offences against the human body under BNS?

1. Causing hurt
2. Theft
3. Grievous hurt
4. Criminal conspiracy

A. 1 and 3 only
B. 1, 3, and 4 only
C. 2 and 4 only
D. 1, 2, 3, and 4

47. Under BNS, which of the following acts amount to grievous hurt?

1. Emasculation
2. Temporary unconsciousness
3. Permanent disfigurement
4. Fracture of a bone

A. 1 and 3 only
B. 1, 3, and 4 only
C. 2 and 4 only
D. 1, 2, 3, and 4

48. Which of the following are essential elements of murder under BNS?

1. Intention to cause death
2. Act causing death
3. Knowledge that the act is likely to cause death
4. Negligence

A. 1 and 2 only B. 1, 2, and 3 only
C. 2 and 4 only D. 1, 2, 3, and 4

49. Assertion (A): Culpable homicide under BNS requires intention or knowledge of causing death.

Reason (R): Negligence alone is insufficient to constitute culpable homicide.

A. Both A and R are true, and R is the correct explanation of A.
B. Both A and R are true, but R is not the correct explanation of A.
C. A is true, but R is false.
D. A is false, but R is true.

50. Assertion (A): Dowry death under BNS applies only if death occurs within 7 years of marriage.

Reason (R): There must be evidence of cruelty or harassment related to dowry demands.

A. Both A and R are true, and R is the correct explanation of A.
B. Both A and R are true, but R is not the correct explanation of A.
C. A is true, but R is false.
D. A is false, but R is true.

51. Match the following offences under BNS with their applicable sections:

Offence	**Section**
A. Murder	1. Section 116
B. Grievous Hurt	2. Section 103
C. Hurt	3. Section 115

Codes:

A. A-2, B-1, C-3 B. A-1, B-3, C-2
C. A-3, B-2, C-1 D. A-2, B-3, C-1

52. Arrange the following BNS sections related to offences against the human body in ascending order:

1. Section 124 – Death by negligence
2. Section 100 – Culpable homicide
3. Section 103 – Murder
4. Section 115 – Hurt

Codes:

A. 2, 3, 4, 1 B. 1, 2, 3, 4
C. 3, 1, 2, 4 D. 4, 2, 3, 1

53. Consider the following statements about culpable homicide under BNS:

1. It includes murder as a subset.
2. It requires intention to cause bodily injury likely to cause death.
3. It excludes acts done by negligence.
4. It applies only if death occurs.

Which of the above statements are true?

A. Only one statement is true
B. Only two statements are true
C. Only three statements are true
D. Only four statements are true

54. Consider the following statements about hurt under BNS:

1. It includes causing bodily pain.
2. It requires permanent injury.
3. It can be caused by mental distress alone.
4. It includes disease transmission.

Which of the above statements are true?

A. Only one statement is true
B. Only two statements are true
C. Only three statements are true
D. Only four statements are true

PASSAGE

A man struck his neighbor with a stick during an argument over a property boundary, causing a fractured arm. He was charged under BNS for an offence against the human body. The court convicted him under Section 116, classifying the act as grievous hurt due to the fracture. The prosecution proved that the man intended to cause serious injury, and medical evidence confirmed the injury met the criteria for grievous hurt under BNS.

55. Based on the passage, why was the man convicted?
A. He caused death
B. He intended to cause grievous hurt
C. He acted negligently
D. He caused minor hurt

56. According to the passage in Q55, what evidence supported the conviction?
A. Intention to kill
B. Medical evidence of fracture
C. Negligence in the act
D. Consent of the neighbor

PASSAGE

A woman died in a fire set by her husband within five years of marriage, following repeated demands for dowry. The husband was charged under BNS for dowry death. The court convicted him under Section 106, finding evidence of burn injuries and prior cruelty linked to dowry demands. Witnesses testified to the husband's harassment, and forensic reports confirmed the cause of death as burns from the fire he intentionally set. The judge ruled that the circumstances met the legal requirements for dowry death.

57. Based on the passage, why was the husband convicted?
A. He caused grievous hurt
B. He committed dowry death with cruelty
C. He acted in self-defense
D. He caused death by negligence

58. According to the passage in Q57, what was essential for the dowry death conviction?
A. Death within 10 years of marriage
B. Evidence of cruelty linked to dowry
C. Intention to cause minor injury
D. Absence of burn injuries

59. Which of the following acts are offences against the human body under BNS?
1. Causing death by rash driving
2. Kidnapping
3. Attempt to murder
A. 1 only
B. 1 and 3 only
C. 2 and 3 only
D. 1, 2, and 3

60. Consider the following statements about murder under BNS:
1. It requires intention to cause death.
2. Knowledge that the act will cause death is sufficient.
3. It excludes acts done in sudden provocation.
4. It applies only to premeditated acts.

Which of the above statements are true?
A. Only one statement is true
B. Only two statements are true
C. Only three statements are true
D. Only four statements are true

61. Which of the following acts is classified as an offence against the state under BNS, 2023?
A. Encouraging feelings of separatist activities
B. Committing theft in a private residence
C. Causing grievous hurt to an individual
D. Forging documents for personal gain

62. Assertion (A): Terrorism under BNS, 2023 includes acts threatening the economic security of India.

Reason (R): The definition of terrorism now covers production or circulation of counterfeit currency.
A. Both A and R are true, and R is the correct explanation of A
B. Both A and R are true, but R is not the correct explanation of A
C. A is true, but R is false
D. A is false, but R is true

63. Match the following offences under BNS, 2023 with their respective sections:
A. Waging war against the Government of India – 1. Section 152
B. Terrorist act – 2. Section 113
C. Sedition-like acts endangering sovereignty – 3. Section 150
D. Organised crime – 4. Section 111
A. A-1, B-2, C-3, D-4
B. A-2, B-1, C-4, D-3
C. A-3, B-2, C-1, D-4
D. A-1, B-4, C-3, D-2

64. Arrange the following offences in the order of their appearance in Chapter VII of BNS, 2023:
1. Collecting arms for waging war
2. Waging war against the Government of India
3. Acts endangering sovereignty or unity
4. Concealing design to wage war
A. 2, 1, 4, 3
B. 1, 2, 3, 4
C. 2, 4, 1, 3
D. 3, 2, 1, 4

PASSAGE

Chapter VII of BNS, 2023 addresses offences against the state, replacing older provisions like sedition with a broader scope. Section 150 penalises acts such as exciting secession or armed rebellion that endanger India's sovereignty, unity, and integrity. These acts may involve words, signs, or electronic communication. The punishment ranges from imprisonment for life to seven years with a fine, reflecting a shift from the colonial framework of the IPC.

65. What is the primary focus of Section 150 under BNS, 2023?
A. Protecting economic stability
B. Penalising acts threatening sovereignty and unity
C. Addressing organised crime syndicates
D. Preventing terrorist financing

66. Which of the following is a mode of committing an offence under Section 150?
A. Using electronic communication to excite secession
B. Committing theft to fund personal gain
C. Causing hurt to a public servant
D. Forging property documents

67. Consider the following statements about terrorism under Section 113 of BNS, 2023:
1. It includes acts intended to intimidate the general public.
2. It covers destruction of property to disrupt essential services.
3. It excludes acts threatening economic security.
4. Punishment can include death if the act results in death.

A. Only one statement is true
B. Only two statements are true
C. Only three statements are true
D. Only four statements are true

68. Which of the following acts qualifies as terrorism under BNS, 2023?
A. Smuggling counterfeit currency to destabilise the economy
B. Assaulting a private citizen with no public intent
C. Stealing examination papers for profit
D. Committing fraud in a personal transaction

PASSAGE

Section 113 of BNS, 2023 defines a terrorist act as one that threatens the unity, integrity, security, or economic security of India or aims to strike terror among people. This includes using explosives, damaging property, or disrupting services. The punishment is severe, ranging from five years to life imprisonment, or death if it results in fatalities, aligning partially with the Unlawful Activities (Prevention) Act, 1967.

69. What is a key element of a terrorist act under Section 113?
A. It must involve personal enmity
B. It must intend to threaten national unity or security
C. It must be committed by a group of five or more
D. It must involve theft of public property

70. What is the minimum punishment for committing a terrorist act under Section 113 if it does not result in death?
A. Three years imprisonment
B. Five years imprisonment
C. Seven years imprisonment
D. Life imprisonment

71. Under BNS, 2023, which of the following is an offence against the state?
A. Waging war against an Asiatic power in alliance with India
B. Committing robbery on public property
C. Encouraging separatist activities through financial means
D. Causing grievous hurt in a private dispute

72. **Assertion (A):** The offence of sedition has been entirely removed from BNS, 2023.

Reason (R): Section 150 replaces sedition with a broader offence of endangering sovereignty, unity, and integrity.
A. Both A and R are true, and R is the correct explanation of A
B. Both A and R are true, but R is not the correct explanation of A
C. A is true, but R is false
D. A is false, but R is true

73. Match the following punishments with offences under BNS, 2023:

A. Waging war (Section 147)	1. Imprisonment for life or up to 7 years
B. Terrorist act causing death (Section 113)	2. Death or life imprisonment
C. Exciting secession (Section 150)	3. Imprisonment for life only
D. Concealing design to wage war (Section 149)	4. Up to 10 years imprisonment

A. A-2, B-1, C-4, D-3
B. A-1, B-2, C-3, D-4
C. A-3, B-2, C-1, D-4
D. A-2, B-3, C-1, D-4

74. Consider the following statements about offences against the state under BNS, 2023:
1. Section 147 penalises waging war against the Government of India.
2. Section 150 includes subversive activities as an offence.
3. Section 113 applies only to acts committed within India.

A. 1 and 2 only   B. 2 and 3 only
C. 1 and 3 only   D. 1, 2, and 3

75. Which of the following reflects a change from the IPC to BNS, 2023 regarding offences against the state?
A. Retention of sedition as a separate offence
B. Introduction of terrorism as a distinct offence under Section 113
C. Exclusion of economic security from terrorist acts
D. Reduction of punishment for waging war

76. Which of the following constitutes theft under Section 303 of BNS, 2023?
A. Taking movable property with consent of the owner
B. Moving property with intent to cause wrongful loss to another
C. Destroying property without moving it
D. Using property without permission but without intent to take it

77. Assertion (A): Robbery under BNS, 2023 requires the use of force or threat of force.

Reason (R): Robbery is an aggravated form of theft involving violence or intimidation.

A. Both A and R are true, and R is the correct explanation of A
B. Both A and R are true, but R is not the correct explanation of A
C. A is true, but R is false
D. A is false, but R is true

78. Match the following offences against property under BNS, 2023 with their respective sections:

A. Theft	1. Section 305
B. Extortion	2. Section 308
C. Robbery	3. Section 303
D. Mischief	4. Section 324

A. A-3, B-2, C-1, D-4
B. A-1, B-2, C-3, D-4
C. A-3, B-1, C-2, D-4
D. A-2, B-3, C-1, D-4

79. Arrange the following offences in the order of their appearance in Chapter XVII of BNS, 2023:
1. Criminal trespass
2. Theft
3. Dacoity
4. Extortion

A. 2, 4, 3, 1   B. 2, 4, 1, 3
C. 1, 2, 3, 4   D. 4, 2, 1, 3

PASSAGE

Section 324 of BNS, 2023 defines mischief as causing wrongful loss or damage to property with intent or knowledge that such loss will occur. This offence can involve acts like destroying crops or poisoning livestock. The punishment can extend to imprisonment for up to two years, or fine, or both, depending on the nature of the act. Unlike theft, mischief does not require taking possession of the property.

80. What distinguishes mischief from theft under BNS, 2023?
A. Mischief requires taking possession of property
B. Theft involves causing damage without moving property
C. Mischief does not involve taking possession of property
D. Theft requires no intent to cause wrongful loss

81. What is the maximum imprisonment for mischief under Section 324?
A. One year   B. Two years
C. Three years   D. Five years

82. Consider the following statements about offences against property under BNS, 2023:
1. Extortion under Section 308 involves obtaining property through coercion.
2. Robbery under Section 305 can be committed without causing hurt.
3. Dacoity requires a minimum of five persons conjointly committing robbery.
4. Criminal trespass under Section 329 requires intent to commit an offence.

A. Only one statement is true
B. Only two statements are true
C. Only three statements are true
D. Only four statements are true

83. Which of the following acts qualifies as extortion under Section 308 of BNS, 2023?

A. Taking property with the owner's consent

B. Threatening to publish defamatory content to obtain money

C. Destroying property to cause wrongful loss

D. Entering a house with intent to steal

PASSAGE

Section 305 of BNS, 2023 defines robbery as theft accompanied by force, threat of force, or causing hurt, fear, or death to facilitate the act or escape. If robbery results in death, it may attract life imprisonment or death penalty. This distinguishes it from dacoity, which involves a group of five or more persons. The provision reflects a stricter stance compared to simple theft.

84. What is a key element that differentiates robbery from theft under Section 305?

A. Involvement of five or more persons

B. Use of force or threat during the act

C. Absence of intent to cause wrongful loss

D. Damage to property without taking it

85. What is the maximum punishment for robbery if it causes death?

A. Imprisonment for ten years

B. Imprisonment for fourteen years

C. Life imprisonment or death

D. Imprisonment for seven years

86. Under BNS, 2023, which of the following constitutes criminal trespass under Section 329?

A. Entering a property with permission to meet the owner

B. Entering a house with intent to commit theft

C. Damaging a fence without entering the property

D. Taking movable property without consent

87. Assertion (A): Dacoity under Section 310 of BNS, 2023 is an aggravated form of robbery.

Reason (R): Dacoity involves five or more persons acting conjointly to commit robbery.

A. Both A and R are true, and R is the correct explanation of A

B. Both A and R are true, but R is not the correct explanation of A

C. A is true, but R is false

D. A is false, but R is true

88. Match the following punishments with offences against **property** under BNS, 2023:

A. Theft (Section 303)	1. Up to 7 years imprisonment
B. Robbery (Section 305)	2. Up to 10 years imprisonment
C. Dacoity (Section 310)	3. Life imprisonment or up to 7 years
D. Mischief (Section 324)	4. Up to 2 years imprisonment

A. A-1, B-2, C-3, D-4

B. A-2, B-1, C-4, D-3

C. A-3, B-2, C-1, D-4

D. A-1, B-3, C-2, D-4

89. Consider the following statements about theft under Section 303 of BNS, 2023:

1. It involves moving movable property with intent to take it.
2. Consent of the owner negates the offence of theft.
3. It requires causing physical damage to the property.

A. 1 and 2 only B. 2 and 3 only

C. 1 and 3 only D. 1, 2, and 3

90. Which of the following reflects a change from the IPC to BNS, 2023 regarding offences against property?

A. Removal of the offence of mischief

B. Introduction of stricter punishment for theft in dwelling houses

C. Exclusion of robbery as an offence

D. Reduction of punishment for dacoity

91. Which of the following acts is an offence against women under Section 63 of BNS, 2023?

A. Consensual intercourse with a woman above 18 years

B. Sexual intercourse with a woman under promise of marriage without intent to marry

C. Assaulting a man with intent to cause grievous hurt

D. Publishing a defamatory article against a woman

92. Assertion (A): Rape under BNS, 2023 includes sexual intercourse with a woman below 18 years, irrespective of consent.

Reason (R): Section 63 deems consent irrelevant if the woman is under 18 years of age.

A. Both A and R are true, and R is the correct explanation of A

B. Both A and R are true, but R is not the correct explanation of A
C. A is true, but R is false
D. A is false, but R is true

93. Match the following offences under BNS, 2023 with their respective sections:

A. Rape	1. Section 137
B. Kidnapping a minor	2. Section 63
C. Sexual harassment	3. Section 74
D. Trafficking of minors	4. Section 143

A. A-2, B-1, C-3, D-4
B. A-1, B-2, C-3, D-4
C. A-2, B-3, C-1, D-4
D. A-3, B-1, C-2, D-4

94. Arrange the following offences in the order of their appearance in Chapter V of BNS, 2023:
1. Outraging modesty of a woman
2. Rape
3. Kidnapping or abducting a woman
4. Sexual harassment

A. 2, 4, 1, 3 B. 4, 1, 2, 3
C. 2, 3, 1, 4 D. 1, 2, 3, 4

PASSAGE

Section 74 of BNS, 2023 defines sexual harassment as physical contact, advances, or explicit remarks that violate a woman's dignity. It includes acts like showing pornography or demanding sexual favours. The punishment can extend to three years imprisonment with fine. This provision strengthens protections compared to the IPC by explicitly covering workplace-related offences.

95. What is an example of sexual harassment under Section 74?
A. Consensual flirting between colleagues
B. Making sexually coloured remarks to a woman
C. Assaulting a woman without sexual intent
D. Kidnapping a woman for marriage

96. What is the maximum imprisonment for sexual harassment under Section 74?
A. One year B. Two years
C. Three years D. Five years

97. Consider the following statements about offences against children under BNS, 2023:
1. Employing a child for begging is punishable under Section 76.
2. Kidnapping a child under 10 years for ransom attracts life imprisonment.
3. Selling a minor for prostitution is an offence under Section 143.
4. Sexual intercourse with a minor wife is exempt from rape charges.

A. Only one statement is true
B. Only two statements are true
C. Only three statements are true
D. Only four statements are true

98. Which of the following acts constitutes an offence under Section 137 of BNS, 2023?
A. Abducting a woman with her consent to marry
B. Kidnapping a minor girl to compel her into marriage
C. Assaulting a woman without intent to abduct
D. Threatening a woman to leave her home

PASSAGE

Section 63 of BNS, 2023 defines rape as sexual intercourse with a woman against her will, without her consent, or under coercion, deceit, or intoxication. It also includes intercourse with a girl under 18 years, regardless of consent. The punishment ranges from rigorous imprisonment of ten years to life, with a fine. This reflects a shift from the IPC by removing exceptions for marital rape in certain cases.

99. What is a key condition for an act to be considered rape under Section 63?
A. It must involve physical injury
B. It must be without the woman's consent
C. It must occur between married partners
D. It must involve multiple perpetrators

100. What is the minimum punishment for rape under Section 63?
A. Seven years imprisonment
B. Ten years imprisonment
C. Life imprisonment
D. Fourteen years imprisonment

101. Under BNS, 2023, which of the following is an offence against a child under Section 76?
A. Employing a child above 14 years for domestic work
B. Using a child to beg on the streets
C. Teaching a child under 10 years a trade
D. Allowing a child to sell goods voluntarily

102. **Assertion (A):** Trafficking of minors under Section 143 of BNS, 2023 includes selling or buying them for exploitation.

Reason (R): The offence aims to combat human trafficking and carries a punishment of up to life imprisonment.

A. Both A and R are true, and R is the correct explanation of A

B. Both A and R are true, but R is not the correct explanation of A
C. A is true, but R is false
D. A is false, but R is true

103. Match the following punishments with offences under BNS, 2023:

A. Rape (Section 63)	1. Up to 3 years imprisonment
B. Sexual harassment (Section 74)	2. 7 years to life imprisonment
C. Kidnapping a minor (Section 137)	3. 10 years to life imprisonment
D. Trafficking of minors (Section 143)	4. 7 years to life imprisonment

A. A-3, B-1, C-2, D-4
B. A-1, B-2, C-3, D-4
C. A-3, B-2, C-1, D-4
D. A-2, B-1, C-3, D-4

104. Consider the following statements about offences against women under BNS, 2023:
1. Section 75 penalises assault with intent to disrobe a woman.
2. Section 63 includes sexual intercourse under deceit as rape.
3. Section 74 applies only to workplace harassment.

A. 1 and 2 only B. 2 and 3 only
C. 1 and 3 only D. 1, 2, and 3

105. Which of the following reflects a change from the IPC to BNS, 2023 regarding offences against women?
A. Retention of marital rape exception for wives above 15 years
B. Introduction of a specific offence for sexual harassment under Section 74
C. Reduction of punishment for rape to seven years
D. Exclusion of trafficking as an offence

106. Which of the following acts is classified as drug trafficking under BNS, 2023?
A. Possessing a small quantity of drugs for personal use
B. Transporting narcotic drugs for sale as part of an organised syndicate
C. Prescribing controlled substances by a licensed doctor
D. Selling counterfeit medicines without narcotic content

107. Assertion (A): Counterfeiting under BNS, 2023 includes producing fake currency notes to destabilise the economy.

Reason (R): Section 111 classifies counterfeiting as an economic offence within organised crime.

A. Both A and R are true, and R is the correct explanation of A
B. Both A and R are true, but R is not the correct explanation of A
C. A is true, but R is false
D. A is false, but R is true

108. Match the following offences under BNS, 2023 with their respective sections:

A. Organised crime (including drug trafficking)	1. Section 178
B. Counterfeiting currency notes	2. Section 111
C. Counterfeiting government stamps	3. Section 179
D. Attempt to commit organised crime	4. Section 111(3)

A. A-2, B-1, C-3, D-4 B. A-1, B-2, C-3, D-4
C. A-2, B-3, C-1, D-4 D. A-3, B-1, C-2, D-4

109. Arrange the following sections related to counterfeiting and trafficking in the order of their appearance in BNS, 2023:
1. Counterfeiting coins
2. Organised crime (drug trafficking)
3. Counterfeiting currency notes
4. Counterfeiting government stamps

A. 2, 1, 3, 4 B. 1, 2, 3, 4
C. 2, 3, 1, 4 D. 3, 1, 2, 4

PASSAGE

Section 111 of BNS, 2023 defines organised crime as any continuing unlawful activity, including drug trafficking and economic offences like counterfeiting, committed by individuals or syndicates for material benefit. Drug trafficking involves the illegal production, transportation, or sale of narcotic drugs or psychotropic substances. The punishment can extend to life imprisonment or death if it results in death, with a minimum fine of ten lakh rupees.

110. What is a key element of drug trafficking as an organised crime under Section 111?
A. It must involve a single individual acting alone
B. It must be a continuing unlawful activity for material benefit
C. It must exclude transportation of drugs
D. It must involve only legal substances

111. What is the maximum punishment for drug trafficking under Section 111 if it causes death?
A. Imprisonment for ten years
B. Life imprisonment or death
C. Imprisonment for seven years
D. Life imprisonment only

112. Consider the following statements about counterfeiting under BNS, 2023:

1. Counterfeiting currency notes is punishable under Section 178.
2. Counterfeiting government stamps falls under Section 179.
3. Counterfeiting as part of organised crime carries a minimum punishment of five years.
4. Counterfeiting coins is no longer an offence under BNS.

A. Only one statement is true
B. Only two statements are true
C. Only three statements are true
D. Only four statements are true

113. Which of the following acts qualifies as an economic offence under Section 111 of BNS, 2023?

A. Selling counterfeit currency to disrupt financial stability
B. Stealing a vehicle for personal use
C. Assaulting a person with no financial motive
D. Borrowing money with intent to repay

PASSAGE

Section 178 of BNS, 2023 penalises counterfeiting currency notes or bank notes with imprisonment ranging from seven years to life, along with a fine. This offence targets acts that undermine the economic integrity of the nation. Unlike the IPC, BNS integrates such acts into broader frameworks like organised crime when committed by syndicates, reflecting a modern approach to economic security.

114. What is the minimum punishment for counterfeiting currency notes under Section 178?

A. Five years imprisonment
B. Seven years imprisonment
C. Ten years imprisonment
D. Life imprisonment

115. How does BNS, 2023 differ from the IPC regarding counterfeiting?

A. It reduces the punishment for counterfeiting
B. It integrates counterfeiting into organised crime when syndicate-based
C. It excludes counterfeiting from economic offences
D. It limits counterfeiting to coins only

116. Under BNS, 2023, which of the following is an offence related to drug trafficking under Section 111?

A. Trafficking narcotic drugs as part of a syndicate
B. Possessing drugs for medical research
C. Selling over-the-counter medicines
D. Transporting alcohol legally

117. **Assertion (A):** Drug trafficking under Section 111 of BNS, 2023 requires the use of violence or coercion.

Reason (R): The section includes any unlawful means, such as violence or intimidation, to obtain material benefit.

A. Both A and R are true, and R is the correct explanation of A
B. Both A and R are true, but R is not the correct explanation of A
C. A is true, but R is false
D. A is false, but R is true

118. Match the following punishments with offences under BNS, 2023:

A. Drug trafficking causing death (Section 111)	1. Up to 7 years imprisonment
B. Counterfeiting currency (Section 178)	2. Life imprisonment or death
C. Attempt to commit organised crime (Section 111(3))	3. 7 years to life imprisonment
D. Counterfeiting stamps (Section 179)	4. 5 years to life imprisonment

A. A-2, B-3, C-4, D-1
B. A-1, B-2, C-3, D-4
C. A-2, B-1, C-4, D-3
D. A-4, B-3, C-1, D-2

119. Consider the following statements about drug trafficking and counterfeiting under BNS, 2023:

1. Drug trafficking is explicitly included in organised crime under Section 111.
2. Counterfeiting currency is punishable only if it causes death.
3. Attempting to traffic drugs carries a minimum of five years imprisonment.

A. 1 and 2 only B. 1 and 3 only
C. 2 and 3 only D. 1, 2, and 3

120. Which of the following reflects a change from the IPC to BNS, 2023 regarding drug trafficking and counterfeiting?

A. Exclusion of drug trafficking from criminal offences
B. Introduction of drug trafficking as part of organised crime under Section 111
C. Reduction of punishment for counterfeiting currency
D. Removal of economic offences from counterfeiting provisions

121. Which of the following acts constitutes an offence against public tranquility under BNS, 2023?

A. A single person shouting in a private residence
B. Five or more persons assembling with a common intent to commit violence

C. Criticising government policy in a newspaper article
D. Damaging private property without public disturbance

122. Assertion (A): Unlawful assembly under Section 189 of BNS, 2023 requires a minimum of five persons.

Reason (R): The assembly must have a common object to commit an offence or disturb public peace.

A. Both A and R are true, and R is the correct explanation of A
B. Both A and R are true, but R is not the correct explanation of A
C. A is true, but R is false
D. A is false, but R is true

123. Match the following offences against public tranquility under BNS, 2023 with their respective sections:

A. Unlawful assembly	1. Section 191
B. Rioting	2. Section 189
C. Promoting enmity between groups	3. Section 196
D. Affray	4. Section 199

A. A-2, B-1, C-3, D-4
B. A-1, B-2, C-3, D-4
C. A-2, B-3, C-1, D-4
D. A-3, B-1, C-2, D-4

124. Arrange the following offences in the order of their appearance in Chapter VIII of BNS, 2023:

1. Promoting enmity between groups
2. Rioting
3. Unlawful assembly
4. Affray

A. 3, 2, 1, 4 B. 1, 2, 3, 4
C. 2, 3, 1, 4 D. 4, 1, 2, 3

PASSAGE

Section 191 of BNS, 2023 defines rioting as the use of unlawful force or violence by an unlawful assembly or any member thereof in furtherance of their common object. Rioting is punishable with imprisonment up to two years, or fine, or both. If armed with a deadly weapon, the punishment increases to up to seven years. This reflects a stricter approach to maintaining public order compared to isolated acts of violence.

125. What is a key requirement for an act to be considered rioting under Section 191?

A. It must involve a single individual
B. It must involve violence by an unlawful assembly
C. It must occur in a private setting
D. It must exclude the use of weapons

126. What is the maximum punishment for rioting when armed with a deadly weapon?

A. Two years imprisonment
B. Five years imprisonment
C. Seven years imprisonment
D. Ten years imprisonment

127. Consider the following statements about offences against public tranquility under BNS, 2023:

1. Unlawful assembly requires a common object under Section 189.
2. Rioting under Section 191 can occur without an unlawful assembly.
3. Promoting enmity between groups under Section 196 includes acts via electronic means.
4. Affray under Section 199 involves fighting between two or more persons in a public place.

A. Only one statement is true
B. Only two statements are true
C. Only three statements are true
D. Only four statements are true

128. Which of the following acts qualifies as promoting enmity between groups under Section 196 of BNS, 2023?

A. Writing a personal letter criticising a friend
B. Spreading hate speech against a religious community online
C. Damaging private property in a secluded area
D. Engaging in a private argument over political views

PASSAGE

Section 189 of BNS, 2023 defines an unlawful assembly as five or more persons with a common object to commit an offence, resist law enforcement, or disturb public peace. Members are liable even if they do not personally execute the act, provided they share the intent. Punishment can extend to six months imprisonment, or fine, or both, reflecting the law's emphasis on collective responsibility.

129. What is a key condition for an assembly to be unlawful under Section 189?

A. It must involve fewer than five persons
B. It must have a common object to commit an offence
C. It must occur in a private space
D. It must exclude any violent intent

130. What is the maximum imprisonment for being a member of an unlawful assembly under Section 189?

A. Six months B. One year
C. Two years D. Three years

131. Under BNS, 2023, which of the following constitutes an affray under Section 199?
A. Two persons fighting in a public street
B. A group of five persons peacefully protesting
C. A single person shouting slogans in a public place
D. Two persons arguing inside a private home

132. **Assertion (A):** Rioting under Section 191 of BNS, 2023 is an aggravated form of unlawful assembly.

Reason (R): Rioting involves the use of force or violence in pursuit of the common object of an unlawful assembly.
A. Both A and R are true, and R is the correct explanation of A
B. Both A and R are true, but R is not the correct explanation of A
C. A is true, but R is false
D. A is false, but R is true

133. Match the following punishments with offences under BNS, 2023:

A. Unlawful assembly (Section 189)	1. Up to 2 years imprisonment
B. Rioting (Section 191)	2. Up to 6 months imprisonment
C. Promoting enmity (Section 196)	3. Up to 3 years imprisonment
D. Affray (Section 199)	4. Up to 1 year imprisonment

A. A-2, B-1, C-3, D-4
B. A-1, B-2, C-3, D-4
C. A-3, B-1, C-2, D-4
D. A-2, B-3, C-1, D-4

134. Consider the following statements about offences against public tranquility under BNS, 2023:
1. Section 189 holds all members of an unlawful assembly liable for acts done in furtherance of the common object.
2. Section 196 penalises acts promoting enmity only if they cause immediate violence.
3. Section 199 requires affray to disturb public peace.

A. 1 and 2 only B. 1 and 3 only
C. 2 and 3 only D. 1, 2, and 3

135. Which of the following reflects a change from the IPC to BNS, 2023 regarding offences against public tranquility?
A. Removal of the offence of affray
B. Inclusion of electronic means in promoting enmity under Section 196
C. Reduction of punishment for rioting to one year
D. Exclusion of unlawful assembly as an offence

136. Which of the following is a primary objective of the deterrent theory of punishment?
A. To reform the offender through education
B. To prevent future crimes by instilling fear
C. To compensate the victim for the loss suffered
D. To isolate the offender from society

137. **Assertion (A):** The retributive theory of punishment focuses on giving the offender their "just deserts."

Reason (R): It is based on the principle that punishment should be proportionate to the crime committed.
A. Both A and R are true, and R is the correct explanation of A
B. Both A and R are true, but R is not the correct explanation of A
C. A is true, but R is false
D. A is false, but R is true

138. Match the following theories of punishment with their primary focus:

A. Deterrent	1. Reformation of the offender
B. Retributive	2. Prevention through fear
C. Reformative	3. Proportional punishment for the offence
D. Preventive	4. Incapacitation of the offender

A. A-2, B-3, C-1, D-4
B. A-1, B-2, C-3, D-4
C. A-3, B-1, C-2, D-4
D. A-4, B-3, C-1, D-2

139. Arrange the following kinds of punishment under BNS, 2023 in the order of their mention in Section 4:

1. Fine 2. Imprisonment for life
3. Death 4. Community service

A. 3, 2, 1, 4 B. 2, 3, 4, 1
C. 3, 2, 4, 1 D. 1, 2, 3, 4

PASSAGE

Section 4 of BNS, 2023 outlines various punishments, including death, life imprisonment, rigorous imprisonment, simple imprisonment, fine, and community service. The reformative approach is reflected in community service, introduced as a novel punishment to rehabilitate offenders while benefiting society. Unlike the IPC, BNS emphasises victim compensation alongside punishment, aligning with restorative justice principles.

140. What is the purpose of community service as a punishment under Section 4?
A. To deter others through public humiliation
B. To rehabilitate the offender and benefit society
C. To compensate the victim directly
D. To isolate the offender from the community

141. How does BNS, 2023 differ from the IPC regarding punishment?
A. It removes the option of imprisonment
B. It introduces community service as a punishment
C. It excludes fines as a form of punishment
D. It eliminates victim compensation provisions

142. Consider the following statements about theories of punishment:
1. The preventive theory aims to incapacitate the offender to protect society.
2. The retributive theory seeks to reform the offender's behaviour.
3. The deterrent theory applies to both the offender and the general public.
4. The reformative theory prioritises punishment over rehabilitation.
A. Only one statement is true
B. Only two statements are true
C. Only three statements are true
D. Only four statements are true

143. Which of the following punishments under BNS, 2023 aligns with the reformative theory?
A. Death penalty
B. Community service
C. Life imprisonment without parole
D. Fine without imprisonment

PASSAGE

Compensation to victims under BNS, 2023 is addressed in Section 357, which allows courts to order the offender to pay a sum to the victim for loss or injury caused by the crime. This can be in addition to or instead of a fine and is designed to provide restitution. For instance, in cases of theft or assault, courts may direct compensation from the offender's property or earnings, reflecting a shift towards victim-centric justice.

144. What is the primary purpose of compensation under Section 357?
A. To punish the offender harshly
B. To provide restitution to the victim
C. To deter future crimes
D. To isolate the offender from society

145. In what scenario can compensation be ordered under Section 357?
A. Only when the offender is sentenced to death
B. When the crime causes loss or injury to the victim
C. Only when the offender pleads guilty
D. When the victim demands imprisonment

146. Under BNS, 2023, which of the following is a kind of punishment under Section 4?
A. Public shaming
B. Community service
C. Exile from the country
D. Restitution without fine

147. **Assertion (A):** The reformative theory of punishment is victim-centric.

Reason (R): It focuses on rehabilitating the offender rather than compensating the victim.
A. Both A and R are true, and R is the correct explanation of A
B. Both A and R are true, but R is not the correct explanation of A
C. A is true, but R is false
D. A is false, but R is true

148. Match the following kinds of punishment under BNS, 2023 with their associated theories:

A. Death	1. Reformative
B. Community service	2. Retributive
C. Imprisonment for life	3. Preventive
D. Fine	4. Deterrent

A. A-2, B-1, C-3, D-4
B. A-1, B-2, C-3, D-4
C. A-3, B-1, C-2, D-4
D. A-4, B-3, C-1, D-2

149. Consider the following statements about compensation to victims under BNS, 2023:
1. Section 357 allows compensation to be paid from the offender's fine.
2. Compensation is mandatory in all criminal cases.
3. Courts can order compensation for emotional distress caused by the crime.
A. 1 and 2 only
B. 1 and 3 only
C. 2 and 3 only
D. 1, 2, and 3

150. Which of the following reflects a change from the IPC to BNS, 2023 regarding punishment and victim compensation?
A. Removal of fines as a punishment option
B. Introduction of community service and enhanced focus on victim compensation
C. Exclusion of life imprisonment as a punishment
D. Elimination of the deterrent theory in sentencing

ANSWERS

1. **(B):** Actus reus under BNS includes a voluntary act or omission (1), the consequence (3), and the circumstances (4). Mental intention (2) is mens rea, not actus reus.
2. **(B):** Murder (1), theft (2), and rash driving (4) require mens rea (intention, knowledge, or recklessness). Public nuisance (3) can be a strict liability offense.
3. **(A):** Sale of adulterated food (1) and traffic violations (3) are strict liability offenses under BNS, not requiring mens rea. Robbery (2) and assault (4) require intent.
4. **(B):** A is true—actus reus includes voluntary acts and consequences. R is true—involuntary acts like reflexes aren't punishable—but it explains liability, not the definition of actus reus.
5. **(A):** A is true—mens rea is irrelevant in strict liability. R is true and correctly explains why: public safety is prioritized over intent.
6. **(A):** Actus reus (A-2) is the physical act, mens rea (B-1) is the guilty mind, causation (C-3) links act to consequence, and concurrence (D-4) requires simultaneity.
7. **(B):** Chronological order: 1884 (1), 1957 (2), 1965 (3), 1996 (4).
8. **(B):** 1 is false (intention doesn't always need premeditation), 2 is true (recklessness involves risk awareness), 3 is false (negligence can be mens rea in some cases), 4 is true (knowledge implies awareness). Only two (2 and 4) are true.
9. **(B):** 1 is false (omissions count), 2 is true (legal duty makes omissions actus reus), 3 is false (harm isn't always required), 4 is true (automatism negates voluntariness). Only two (2 and 4) are true.
10. **(A):** The passage states actus reus is always required, but mens rea isn't (e.g., in strict liability).
11. **(C):** The passage specifies recklessness for rash driving (Section 281).
12. **(B):** The court convicted him for recklessness, not intention, per the passage.
13. **(B):** Intention wasn't required; recklessness sufficed.
14. **(A):** Automatism (2) negates actus reus by removing voluntariness. Others affect mens rea.
15. **(B):** Foreseeability (2) and intervening acts (3) are key to causation. Sole cause (1) isn't required, and causation matters even in strict liability (4 is false).
16. **(D):** Under BNS, stages of crime include intention (1), preparation (2), attempt (3), and completion (4). All are recognized, though only attempt and completion are typically punishable.
17. **(A):** Abetment under BNS (Section 61) includes instigation (1) and assistance (2). Witnessing (3) isn't abetment, and conspiracy (4) is a separate offense (Section 63).
18. **(B):** Inchoate crimes are incomplete offenses: attempt (1), conspiracy (2), and abetment (4). Theft (3) is a completed offense.
19. **(A):** A is true—preparation is generally not punishable under BNS (except in specific cases like terrorism). R is true and explains why: lack of proximity.
20. **(C):** A is true—an agreement is sufficient for conspiracy under Section 63 in some cases. R is false—an overt act is required for certain offenses (e.g., treason).
21. **(A):** Abetment (A-3) is instigating/aiding, conspiracy (B-1) is an agreement, attempt (C-2) is a step beyond preparation.
22. **(A):** Chronological order: 1868 (2), 1910 (1), 1980 (3), 1994 (4).
23. **(B):** 1 is true (intent is required), 2 is false (preparation isn't enough), 3 is true (impossibility doesn't bar punishment), 4 is false (proximity matters). Only two (1 and 3) are true.
24. **(C):** 1 is true (two persons needed), 2 is false (overt act not always required), 3 is true (illegal object needed), 4 is true (circumstantial evidence suffices). Only three (1, 3, 4) are true.
25. **(B):** The passage states conspiracy requires an agreement; an overt act is only needed in some cases.
26. **(B):** Attempt is punishable when there's intent and an act beyond preparation, per the passage.

27. (B): Conviction was based on the agreement and buying tools (a preparatory step), as per the court's ruling.

28. (C): The defense argued no overt act was committed, only preparation.

29. (A): Proximity (2) distinguishes attempt from preparation under BNS; intention (1) is common to both.

30. (C): Instigation must be intentional (2), and aiding can be passive (3). Completion (1) isn't required, and abetment is punishable even if the crime fails (4 is false).

31. (A): Child under 7 (1, Section 82) and unsound mind (3, Section 83) are excused. Mistake of law (2) is not a defense (Section 79), and malicious intent (4) negates a defense.

32. (B): Judicial order (1, Section 77), consent (3, Section 90), and necessity (4, Section 81) are defenses. Voluntary intoxication (2) is only a defense if it causes insanity (Section 85).

33. (B): Private defense (Section 100) requires reasonable apprehension (1), proportionate force (2), and imminent threat (4). Intent to kill (3) is not required and may negate the defense.

34. (A): A is true (Section 94); R is true and explains A—immediate threat of death or grievous hurt is required.

35. (A): A is true (Section 76); R is true and explains A—good faith mistake negates intent.

36. (A): Necessity (A-2, Section 81), insanity (B-1, Section 83), compulsion (C-3, Section 94).

37. (A): Ascending order: 76 (2), 85 (3), 90 (1), 100 (4).

38. (C): 1 is true (Section 81), 2 is true (imminence required), 3 is false (intent not required), 4 is true (no alternative). Only 1, 2, and 4 are true.

39. (B): 1 is true (Section 83), 2 is true (burden on accused), 3 is false (temporary insanity valid), 4 is false (voluntary intoxication separate). Only 1 and 2 are true.

40. (B): Acquittal was due to necessity (Section 81) to avoid greater harm, per the passage.

41. (A): Immediate danger was essential, per the passage.

42. (B): Involuntary intoxication (Section 85) negated intent, leading to acquittal.

43. (A): Lack of intent due to involuntary intoxication was crucial, per the passage.

44. (D): Child between 7–12 without maturity (1, Section 83), mistake of fact in good faith (2, Section 76), and voluntary intoxication causing insanity (3, Section 85) are recognized defenses.

45. (C): 1 is true (Section 90), 2 is true (Section 90), 3 is true (Section 90), 4 is false (not all acts excused, e.g., murder). Only 1, 2, and 3 are true.

46. (A): Causing hurt (1, Section 115) and grievous hurt (3, Section 116) are offences against the human body. Theft (2) and conspiracy (4) fall under different categories.

47. (B): Grievous hurt (Section 116) includes emasculation (1), permanent disfigurement (3), and bone fracture (4). Temporary unconsciousness (2) is not included.

48. (B): Murder (Section 103) requires intention to cause death (1), act causing death (2), or knowledge of likely death (3). Negligence (4) is separate (Section 124).

49. (A): A is true (Section 100); R is true and explains A—negligence is death by negligence (Section 124), not culpable homicide.

50. (B): A is true (Section 106, within 7 years); R is true (cruelty required), but it's an additional element, not the explanation for the time limit.

51. (A): Murder (A-2, Section 103), grievous hurt (B-1, Section 116), hurt (C-3, Section 115).

52. (A): Ascending order: 100 (2), 103 (3), 115 (4), 124 (1).

53. (C): 1 is true (Section 100 includes 103), 2 is true (injury likely to cause death), 3 is false (negligence is separate), 4 is true (death required). Only 1, 2, and 4 are true.

54. (B): 1 is true (Section 115), 2 is false (not required), 3 is false (physical harm needed), 4 is true (disease included). Only 1 and 4 are true.

55. (B): Conviction was for grievous hurt (Section 116) due to intent, per the passage.

56. (B): Medical evidence of fracture supported grievous hurt, per the passage.

57. (B): Conviction was for dowry death (Section 106) with cruelty, per the passage.

58. **(B):** Evidence of cruelty linked to dowry was essential, per the passage.

59. **(B):** Death by rash driving (1, Section 124) and attempt to murder (3, Section 104) are against the human body. Kidnapping (2) is under a different category (Section 137).

60. (C)

61. **(A):** Section 150 of BNS, 2023 penalises encouraging separatist activities as an offence against the state, unlike the other options which are not state-specific.

62. **(A):** Section 113 includes economic security threats like counterfeit currency circulation, making R the correct explanation of A.

63. **(A):** Correct matching: Section 147 (waging war), Section 113 (terrorism), Section 150 (sovereignty-endangering acts), Section 111 (organised crime).

64. **(C):** Order in Chapter VII: Section 147 (waging war), Section 149 (concealing design), Section 148 (collecting arms), Section 150 (sovereignty-endangering acts).

65. **(B):** Section 150 focuses on acts threatening sovereignty and unity, as per the passage.

66. **(A):** Section 150 explicitly includes electronic communication as a mode of offence.

67. **(C):** 1, 2, and 4 are true under Section 113; 3 is false as economic security is included.

68. **(A):** Section 113 classifies smuggling counterfeit currency to destabilise the economy as terrorism.

69. **(B):** A key element of Section 113 is intent to threaten national unity or security.

70. **(B):** Minimum punishment under Section 113, if no death occurs, is five years imprisonment.

71. **(C):** Section 150 includes encouraging separatist activities via financial means as an offence against the state.

72. **(D):** A is false as sedition is reframed, not removed; R is true as Section 150 broadens the scope.

73. **(C):** Correct matching: Section 147 (life or 7 years), Section 113 (death or life), Section 150 (life or 7 years), Section 149 (up to 10 years).

74. **(A):** 1 and 2 are correct under Sections 147 and 150; 3 is false as Section 113 applies to acts in or outside India.

75. **(B):** BNS, 2023 introduces terrorism under Section 113, a significant change from the IPC.

76. **(B):** Section 303 defines theft as moving movable property with intent to cause wrongful loss, not requiring consent (a), destruction (c), or mere use (d).

77. **(A):** Section 305 defines robbery with force or threat, and R explains A as robbery aggravates theft with violence.

78. **(A):** Correct matching: Section 303 (theft), Section 308 (extortion), Section 305 (robbery), Section 324 (mischief).

79. **(A):** Order in Chapter XVII: Section 303 (theft), Section 308 (extortion), Section 310 (dacoity), Section 329 (trespass).

80. **(C):** Section 324 (mischief) involves damage without possession, unlike theft (Section 303).

81. **(B):** Section 324 prescribes a maximum of two years imprisonment for mischief.

82. **(C):** 1 (Section 308), 3 (Section 310), and 4 (Section 329) are true; 2 is false as robbery requires force or hurt (Section 305).

83. **(B):** Section 308 defines extortion as obtaining property through threats, like defamatory publication.

84. **(B):** Section 305 distinguishes robbery from theft by the use of force or threat.

85. **(C):** Section 305 prescribes life imprisonment or death if robbery causes death.

86. **(B):** Section 329 defines criminal trespass as entering with intent to commit an offence like theft.

87. **(A):** Section 310 defines dacoity as robbery by five or more, making R the correct explanation of A.

88. **(A):** Correct matching: Section 303 (7 years), Section 305 (10 years), Section 310 (life or 7 years), Section 324 (2 years).

89. **(A):** 1 and 2 are true under Section 303; 3 is false as damage is not required for theft.

90. **(B):** BNS, 2023 introduces stricter penalties for specific theft cases, unlike IPC, while retaining other offences.

91. **(B):** Section 63 includes intercourse under false promise of marriage as rape, unlike consensual acts (A).

92. **(A):** Section 63 deems consent irrelevant for girls under 18, making R the correct explanation of A.

93. **(A):** Correct matching: Section 63 (rape), Section 137 (kidnapping), Section 74 (sexual harassment), Section 143 (trafficking).

94. **(B):** Order in Chapter V: Section 74 (harassment), Section 75 (outraging modesty), Section 63 (rape), Section 137 (kidnapping).

95. **(B):** Section 74 includes sexually coloured remarks as harassment.

96. **(C):** Section 74 prescribes a maximum of three years imprisonment.

97. **(C):** 1 (Section 76), 2 (Section 137), and 3 (Section 143) are true; 4 is false as BNS removes the marital rape exception.

98. **(B):** Section 137 penalises kidnapping a minor to compel marriage.

99. **(B):** Section 63 requires lack of consent as a key condition for rape.

100. **(B):** Minimum punishment under Section 63 is ten years imprisonment.

101. **(B):** Section 76 penalises using a child for begging.

102. **(A):** Section 143 covers trafficking for exploitation, and R explains A with the punishment context.

103. **(A):** Correct matching: Section 63 (10 years to life), Section 74 (3 years), Section 137 (7 years to life), Section 143 (7 years to life).

104. **(A):** 1 (Section 75) and 2 (Section 63) are true; 3 is false as Section 74 is not limited to workplaces.

105. **(B):** BNS introduces Section 74 for sexual harassment, a change from IPC's broader provisions.

106. **(B):** Section 111 includes drug trafficking as transporting narcotic drugs for sale within organised crime, not personal use (a), medical acts (c), or non-narcotic counterfeiting (d).

107. **(A):** Section 111 defines counterfeiting as an economic offence within organised crime, and R explains A by linking it to economic destabilisation.

108. **(A):** Correct matching: Section 111 (organised crime), Section 178 (currency counterfeiting), Section 179 (stamps), Section 111(3) (attempt).

109. **(A):** Order in BNS: Section 111 (organised crime), Section 177 (coins), Section 178 (currency), Section 179 (stamps).

110. **(B):** Section 111 requires drug trafficking to be a continuing activity for material benefit.

111. **(B):** Section 111 prescribes life imprisonment or death if drug trafficking causes death.

112. **(C):** 1, 2, and 3 are true (Sections 178, 179, 111); 4 is false as counterfeiting coins remains an offence (Section 177).

113. **(A):** Section 111 lists counterfeiting currency as an economic offence, unlike the other options.

114. **(B):** Section 178 sets a minimum of seven years imprisonment for counterfeiting currency.

115. **(B):** BNS integrates counterfeiting into organised crime under Section 111 when syndicate-based, unlike the IPC.

116. **(A):** Section 111 explicitly covers trafficking narcotic drugs by syndicates.

117. **(D):** A is false as violence is not mandatory; R is true as Section 111 includes any unlawful means, including violence.

118. **(A):** Correct matching: Section 111 (death or life), Section 178 (7 years to life), Section 111(3) (5 years to life), Section 179 (up to 7 years).

119. **(B):** 1 and 3 are true (Section 111); 2 is false as counterfeiting is punishable regardless of death (Section 178).

120. **(B):** BNS introduces drug trafficking as part of organised crime under Section 111, a change from the IPC

121. **(B):** Section 189 defines unlawful assembly as five or more persons with intent to disturb peace, qualifying as an offence against public tranquility.

122. **(A):** Section 189 requires five persons and a common object, and R explains A by detailing the intent requirement.

123. **(A):** Correct matching: Section 189 (unlawful assembly), Section 191 (rioting), Section 196 (enmity), Section 199 (affray).

124. **(A):** Order in Chapter VIII: Section 189 (unlawful assembly), Section 191 (rioting), Section 196 (enmity), Section 199 (affray).

125. **(B):** Section 191 requires violence by an unlawful assembly for rioting.

126. **(C):** Section 191 prescribes up to seven years imprisonment when armed with a deadly weapon.

127. **(C):** 1 (Section 189), 3 (Section 196), and 4 (Section 199) are true; 2 is false as rioting requires an unlawful assembly (Section 191).

128. **(B):** Section 196 penalises spreading hate speech against groups, including via electronic means.

129. (B): Section 189 requires a common object to commit an offence or disturb peace.

130. (A): Section 189 prescribes a maximum of six months imprisonment.

131. (A): Section 199 defines affray as fighting between two or more persons in a public place.

132. (A): Section 191 defines rioting as violence by an unlawful assembly, and R explains A as the aggravating factor.

133. (A): Correct matching: Section 189 (6 months), Section 191 (2 years), Section 196 (3 years), Section 199 (1 year).

134. (B): 1 (Section 189) and 3 (Section 199) are true; 2 is false as Section 196 does not require immediate violence.

135. (B): BNS, 2023 includes electronic means in Section 196, a change from the IPC's broader framework.

136. (B): The deterrent theory aims to prevent crime by instilling fear in the offender and society.

137. (A): Retribution focuses on "just deserts," and R explains A by linking it to proportionality.

138. (A): Correct matching: Deterrent (prevention), Retributive (proportionality), Reformative (reformation), Preventive (incapacitation).

139. (C): Section 4 lists punishments: Death, Life imprisonment, Community service, Fine (approximate order).

140. (B): Community service under Section 4 aims to rehabilitate the offender and benefit society, aligning with reformative theory.

141. (B): BNS introduces community service, a key difference from the IPC.

142. (B): 1 and 3 are true; 2 is false (retribution does not reform), and 4 is false (reformative prioritises rehabilitation).

143. (B): Community service aligns with the reformative theory by focusing on rehabilitation.

144. (B): Section 357 aims to provide restitution to victims for loss or injury.

145. (B): Compensation under Section 357 applies when the crime causes loss or injury.

146. (B): Community service is explicitly listed under Section 4 as a punishment.

147. (D): A is false (reformative is offender-centric); R is true as it focuses on rehabilitation.

148. (A): Correct matching: Death (retributive), Community service (reformative), Life imprisonment (preventive), Fine (deterrent).

149. (B): 1 and 3 are true (Section 357); 2 is false as compensation is discretionary, not mandatory.

150. (B): BNS introduces community service and enhances victim compensation under Section 357, unlike the IPC.

UNIT 5 Law of Torts and Consumer Protection

LAW OF TORTS

Law of Torts is a system of laws, which enables a person who has suffered harm, or injury by the acts of another, to claim damages in a civil suit.

NATURE AND DEFINITION OF TORT

The French word tort has been derived from latin term "Tortum" which means to twist. Thus, it implies a conduct, which is not lawful, but rather it is twisted, crooked or unlawful.

A tort is a violation of a right of a person/ breach of duty by one person towards another. For example, a duty not to injure the reputation of someone else results in the tort of defamation. The first reported case where the court used the word tort is Boulton *vs* Hardy. The apex court observed: "Tort" dictionarily means "breach of duty leading to damage". The same meaning attaches to it in law.

No scientific definition of tort has yet emerged so far, because the law of tort is based on judicial decisions and because of diverse species of wrongs included under it, each having its own peculiar historical background. Above all, the law of tort is still in the process of development. The liability in tort may be "strict liability", "absolute liability" or "special use bringing with it increased dangers to others" or "fault liability". Such liability gives rise to action in torts. Since, duty is the primary yardstick to determine the tortuous liability, its ambit keeps on widening on the touchstone of fairness, practicality of the situation, etc.

GENERAL CONDITIONS OF LIABILITY FOR A TORT (CONSTITUTION OF TORT)

In general, a tort consists of some act done by the defendant whereby he has without just cause or excuse caused some form of harm to the plaintiff. In order to constitute a tort, the following conditions are to be satisfied:

- There must be a wrongful act or omission on the part of the defendant.
- Such act or omission should result in legal damage to the plaintiff.
- Some legal remedy in the form of an action for damages must be available.

INJURIA SINE DAMNUM

This maxim means violation of a legal right without any harm, loss or damage to the plaintiff. Thus, it is the behaviour, which is actionable as a tort. It is always actionable as legal wrongs entail a remedy. Every injury imports damage. Infringement of private right is actionable *per se.* No actual loss or damage is required to be proved by the plaintiff.

In the cases of *injuria sine damnum* the loss suffered by the plaintiff may be relevant only as regards the measure of damages. Generally nominal damages are awarded by the court if no actual damage is proved. If, however, the court feels that the violation of a legal right is owing to mischievous and malicious act, as had happened in Bhim Singh's case, the court may grant even exemplary damages.

DAMNUM SINE INJURIA

It means that the plaintiff may suffer actual or substantial loss without any violation or infringement of legal right and therefore no action lies in such cases. This is generally so when the exercise of legal right by one results in conseq-uential harm to the other, even though the injury is intentional. It is never actionable, as moral or social wrongs have no remedy. Similarly, hurt to religious feelings is not an actionable tort.

UBI JUS IBI REMEDIUM

The maxim Ubi jus ibi remedium means that 'where there is a right there is a right' or there is no wrong without a remedy'. In Ashby *vs* White, it was observed, "if the plaintiff has a right, he must of necessity have a means to vindicate and maintain it, and a remedy if he is injured in the exercise or enjoyment of it. And indeed it is a vain thing to imagine a right without a remedy, for want of right and want remedy are reciprocal. If man will multiply injuries actions must be multiplied too: for every man who is injured ought to have recompense."

EX TURPI CAUSA NON ORITUR

The maxim *ex turpi causa non oritur* action means that an action does not arise from an immoral or a base cause. Thus, if the damage is in any manner tainted with immorality, no cause of action can be maintained. Thus, if a person gets a sexual disease through his paramour, she is not entitled to sue him.

GENERAL DEFENCES AGAINST TORTIOUS LIABILITY

In an action for a tort, the defendant may avoid his liability by taking the plea of some defence. They constitute "justifications or grounds of immunity from liability to an action in tort."

In other words, they are 'the rules of immunity which limit the rules of liability'. They are the classes of wrongs which stand outside the sphere of tort. In fact, they are the conditions which will prevent an act from being wrongful which, in their absence, would be a wrong. These defences are based principally upon grounds of public policy.

The general defences, which may be taken against action for a number of wrongs, are:

- *Volenti non fit injuria* (defence of consent)
- Plaintiff, the wrongdoer
- Inevitable accident
- Act of God
- Mistake
- Necessity
- Statutory Authority
- Acts causing slight harm
- Contributory Negligence
- Self-Defense

VOLENTI NON FIT INJURIA: (DEFENCE OF CONSENT)

No injury is done to one who consents. Everyone is the best judge of his interest and therefore the one who voluntarily agrees to suffer harm is not allowed to complain for that and, one's consent is a good defence against oneself. This is so because the harm voluntarily suffered does not constitute the legal injury. No man can enforce a right, which he has voluntarily waived or abandoned.

Consent to suffer the harm may be express or implied. An example of express consent is submitting to a surgical operations. An example of implied consent is where a player or a spectator in the game of cricket or football is deemed to be agreeing to any hurt, which may be likely in the normal course of the game. However, if there is a deliberate injury caused by another player, or a spectator suffers injury due to negligent act of players, or if a surgeon negligently performs an operation, the defence of volenti cannot be pleaded. Thus, the act causing the harm must not go beyond the limit of what has been consented. Consent to operate on the left eye is not necessarily a consent to operate on the right.

The maxim has a double application: First, it applies to the intentional acts which would otherwise to tortuous, viz. Consent to a physical harm which would otherwise be an assault; Secondly, it applies to consent to run the risk of accidental harm, which would otherwise be actionable as due to the negligence of the person who caused it, viz. a master is not liable for an injury inflicted on a servant who has undertaken the service knowing the risks incidental thereto. The maxim is based on the sound principles of justice and good sense.

Inevitable Accident

An inevitable accident occurs when an incident could not have been prevented despite the exercise of reasonable care and precautions.

- **Case Law: Stanley v. Powell (1891):** A gun accidentally discharged while the defendant was on a hunting trip, injuring the plaintiff. The court held it was an inevitable accident and the defendant was not liable.

Act of God (Vis Major)

This defense applies when the harm results from natural forces beyond human control and could not have been prevented even with reasonable care.

- **Case Law: Nichols v. Marsland (1876):** A reservoir overflowed due to unprecedented rainfall, causing damage. The court held that the defendant was not liable as the damage resulted from an act of God.
- **Key Elements:**
  - Natural forces.
  - Unpredictable and unavoidable events.

Mistake

A mistake of fact (not of law) may sometimes be a defense if the defendant acted in good faith.

- **Case Law: Ranson v. Kitner (1884):** The defendant shot the plaintiff's dog, mistaking it for a wolf. The court ruled that a mistake is not always a defense, especially if it results from negligence.

Necessity

This defense is invoked when the defendant acts to prevent a greater harm and the act benefits the public or prevents imminent danger.

- **Case Law: Cope v. Sharpe (1912):** The defendant destroyed the plaintiff's property to stop a fire from spreading to a nearby forest. The court upheld the defense of necessity.

Statutory Authority

An act done under the authority of a statute is a complete defense against liability.

- **Case Law: Vaughan v. Taff Vale Railway Co. (1860):** The defendant operated a railway under statutory authority, and sparks from the train caused damage to the plaintiff's land. The court ruled in favor of the defendant as the act was authorized by statute.

Contributory Negligence

If the plaintiff's own negligence contributed to the harm suffered, their compensation may be reduced proportionately.

- **Case Law: Butterfield v. Forrester (1809):** The plaintiff rode his horse recklessly and collided with an obstruction placed by the defendant. The court ruled that the plaintiff's negligence contributed to the harm, and the defendant was not liable.
- **Modern Position:** Under statutes in many jurisdictions, damages are apportioned based on the degree of fault (comparative negligence).

Illegality (Ex Turpi Causa Non Oritur Actio)

This defense prevents a plaintiff from recovering damages if the injury arises out of the plaintiff's illegal act.

- **Case Law: Ashton v. Turner (1981):** The plaintiff was injured during a car crash that occurred while the plaintiff and defendant were escaping from a burglary. The court denied the claim on the grounds of illegality.

NEGLIGENCE IN TORT

Negligence is a foundational tort that addresses harm caused by a failure to exercise reasonable care. It protects individuals from foreseeable harm due to another's carelessness and is a key topic in tort law for NET JRF Law.

Definition

- **Salmond:** Negligence is the breach of a legal duty to take care, resulting in unintended damage to the plaintiff.
- **Winfield:** Negligence involves either an omission to do what a reasonable person would do or doing something a prudent person would avoid, leading to harm.
- **Lord Atkin (Donoghue v. Stevenson, 1932):** Defined it through the "Neighbour Principle" – a duty to avoid acts that could foreseeably injure those closely and directly affected.

Indian Context: While tort law in India is uncodified, negligence draws heavily from English common law, supplemented by judicial interpretations and constitutional principles (e.g., Article 21).

Essential Elements of Negligence

For a successful claim, the plaintiff must establish these four elements:

Duty of Care

- The defendant must owe a legal duty to the plaintiff to act with reasonable care.

- Test: Foreseeability and proximity of harm (Donoghue v. Stevenson, 1932 – Manufacturer liable for defective ginger beer harming a consumer).
- Factors Determining Duty:
  - ❑ Relationship between parties (e.g., doctor-patient, employer-employee).
  - ❑ Foreseeability of harm.
  - ❑ Public policy considerations.
- **Indian Case:** M.C. Mehta v. Union of India (1987) – Duty extended to absolute liability for hazardous industries, showing a stricter approach than traditional negligence.

Breach of Duty

- The defendant fails to meet the standard of care expected of a reasonable person.
- Standard of Care: Objective – What a prudent person would do in similar circumstances (Blyth v. Birmingham Waterworks Co., 1856 – Frost breaking pipes was an Act of God, not negligence).
- **Factors:**
  - ❑ Likelihood of harm.
  - ❑ Severity of potential injury.
  - ❑ Cost and practicality of precautions.
- **Professional Negligence:** Higher standard applies (Bolam v. Friern Hospital Management Committee, 1957 – Standard of a competent professional; adopted in India via Jacob Mathew v. State of Punjab, 2005).

Causation

- The breach must directly cause the harm suffered.
- **"But For" Test:** Would the damage have occurred "but for" the defendant's act? (Barnett v. Chelsea & Kensington Hospital, 1969 – Poisoned patient would have died regardless of delayed treatment).
- **Proximate Cause:** The harm must not be too remote from the breach (Wagon Mound No. 1, 1961 – Oil spill ignited unforeseeably; no liability).
- **Indian Case:** Khenyei v. New India Assurance Co. Ltd. (2015) – Causation established in motor accident claims.

Damage

- Actual loss or injury (physical, financial, or emotional) must occur.
- **Types of Damage:**
  - ❑ Physical harm (e.g., injury in an accident).
  - ❑ Property damage.
  - ❑ Mental distress (recognized in India under Article 21 – Rudul Shah v. State of Bihar, 1983).
- **Requirement:** Damage must be legally cognizable, not speculative.

Types of Negligence

Contributory Negligence:

- Plaintiff's own negligence contributes to the harm (Butterfield v. Forrester, 1809 – Plaintiff riding recklessly into an obstruction).
- Indian Law: Proportionate reduction of damages (Municipal Corporation of Delhi v. Sushila Devi, 1999).

Gross Negligence:

- Reckless disregard for the safety of others; often attracts stricter penalties (Jacob Mathew v. State of Punjab, 2005 – Gross negligence required for criminal liability in medical cases).

Professional Negligence:

- Failure to meet the standard expected of a skilled professional (e.g., doctors, lawyers, engineers).
- Indian Case: Indian Medical Association v. V.P. Shantha (1995) – Medical services under Consumer Protection Act; negligence judged by professional standards.

Defenses to Negligence

Contributory Negligence:

- Reduces or eliminates liability if the plaintiff shares fault.
- Law Reform (Contributory Negligence) Act, 1945 (UK, applied in India): Damages apportioned based on fault.
- Case: Davies v. Swan Motor Co. (1949) – Plaintiff's negligence reduced compensation.

Volenti Non Fit Injuria (Voluntary Assumption of Risk):

- Plaintiff consents to the risk, barring recovery (Hall v. Brooklands Auto Racing Club, 1933 – Spectator injured at race assumed risk).

- Limits: Does not apply if consent is uninformed (State of Haryana v. Santra, 2000 – Failed sterilization; no informed consent).

Act of God:

- Unforeseeable natural events beyond human control (Nichols v. Marsland, 1876 – Flood broke dam; no liability).
- Indian Relevance: Rare, but applicable in environmental torts.

Inevitable Accident:

- Harm occurs despite all reasonable care (Brown v. Kendall, 1850 – Accidental injury during a fight).
- Indian Case: National Insurance Co. v. Pranay Sethi (2017) – Motor accident cases consider this defense.

Statutory Authority:

- Acts authorized by law are not negligent (Metropolitan Asylum District v. Hill, 1881).

Standard of Care

- General Rule: Reasonable care under the circumstances.
- Variations:
  - Children: Lower standard based on age and maturity (McHale v. Watson, 1966).
  - Professionals: Higher standard based on expertise (Bolam Test – Adopted in India).
  - Emergencies: Adjusted for urgency (Jones v. Boyce, 1816 – Coach passenger's reasonable reaction excused).

Landmark Cases

- **Donoghue v. Stevenson (1932):** Established the "Neighbour Principle"; foundation of modern negligence law.
- **M.C. Mehta v. Union of India (1987):** Oleum gas leak case; introduced "absolute liability" for hazardous activities, stricter than negligence.
- **Jacob Mathew v. State of Punjab (2005):** Defined medical negligence in India – Requires gross negligence for criminal liability.
- **Wagon Mound No. 1 (1961):** Established foreseeability as a limit to liability for damages.
- **Rylands v. Fletcher (1868):** Strict liability case; distinguished from negligence but often compared.

Negligence in Indian Law

- Uncodified: Relies on English common law and judicial precedents.
- Constitutional Dimension:
  - Article 21 (Right to Life) – Negligence by state actionable (Rudul Shah v. State of Bihar, 1983 – Illegal detention).
  - Public law remedies via writs (e.g., compensation for custodial deaths).
- **Statutory Provisions:**
  - Motor Vehicles Act, 1988: Compensation for negligent driving (Section 166).
  - Consumer Protection Act, 2019: Covers negligence in services (e.g., medical, banking).
  - Indian Penal Code: Gross negligence may attract criminal liability (e.g., Section 304A– Causing death by negligence).

Important Doctrines

Res Ipsa Loquitur ("The Thing Speaks for Itself"):

- **Presumption of negligence when:**
  - The incident wouldn't occur without negligence.
  - The cause was under the defendant's control.
  - Plaintiff didn't contribute.
- **Case:** Byrne v. Boadle (1863) – Barrel fell from defendant's premises.
- **Indian Case:** V. Kishan Rao v. Nikhil Super Speciality Hospital (2010) – Applied in medical negligence.

Last Opportunity Rule:

- Liability falls on the person who had the last chance to avoid harm (Davies v. Mann, 1842 – Donkey tied on road hit by speeding cart).

Novus Actus Interveniens (Intervening Act):

- Breaks the chain of causation (Home Office v. Dorset Yacht Co., 1970 – Negligent supervision led to third-party damage).

Comparison with Other Torts

- Negligence vs. Nuisance: Negligence requires a breach of duty; nuisance focuses on interference with land enjoyment.
- Negligence vs. Strict Liability: Negligence needs proof of fault; strict liability (e.g., Rylands v. Fletcher) does not.
- Negligence vs. Trespass: Negligence is indirect harm; trespass is direct and intentional.

DEFINITION AND TYPES OF NUISANCE

Nuisance in the law of torts refers to an act which is harmful or annoying to others. It covers a broad range of interferences with the rights of others to enjoy their property or public rights. Nuisance is categorized primarily into two types: public nuisance and private nuisance. Understanding these categories is crucial for navigating multiple-choice questions on this topic, as each has distinct definitions, affected rights, and remedies.

Public Nuisance

Definition: Public nuisance involves an act or omission that obstructs, damages, or inconveniences the rights of the community or a section of the public. It is a breach of public rights and duties, which affects the community at large rather than an individual.

Public Rights Affected: Public nuisance typically affects rights enjoyed by the public collectively, such as:

- The right to clean air
- The right to freely navigate public roads and waterways
- The right to use and enjoy public parks without disturbances

Remedies Available: The remedies for public nuisance are generally:

- **Criminal Proceedings**: Since it affects the community, public nuisance is often treated as a criminal matter.
- **Civil Action**: A private individual can only sue if they have suffered a special or particular damage beyond that suffered by the general public.
- **Abatement by Injunction**: Legal injunctions may be sought by public authorities to stop or prevent the nuisance.

Private Nuisance

Definition: Private nuisance is an act affecting some particular individual or entity more than the public at large. It involves substantial and unreasonable interference with a person's use or enjoyment of his property.

Interference with Private Enjoyment: Examples of interference in private nuisance include:

- Noise (e.g., loud music or industrial noise beyond acceptable hours)
- Smells (e.g., emissions from a factory or waste processing)
- Physical invasion (e.g., overhanging branches or encroachment)

Remedies Available: The remedies for private nuisance typically include:

- **Damages**: Compensation for loss or damage suffered.
- **Injunction**: A court order to cease the nuisance activity.
- **Abatement**: The right to personally remove the nuisance under certain conditions.

Comparison: Differences and Overlaps Between Public and Private Nuisance

Differences:

- **Scope of Effect**: Public nuisance affects the community at large, while private nuisance affects an individual's use or enjoyment of his property.
- **Legal Standing**: In public nuisance, a private person must show special harm to have standing to sue, which is not required in private nuisance.
- **Nature of Rights Affected**: Public nuisance affects rights enjoyed by the public, such as clean air or free passage, whereas private nuisance typically affects rights related to private property use.

Overlaps:

- **Interferences**: Certain actions can constitute both public and private nuisance if they affect both the public and individuals distinctly. For example, a factory causing air pollution might be a public nuisance and also a private nuisance to nearby residents who suffer more acutely than the wider community.
- **Remedial Actions**: Both types may involve injunctions and damages, although the criteria and extent of remedies might differ based on whether the nuisance is public or private.

Key Legal Principles

Reasonableness:

- **Definition**: Reasonableness in nuisance law refers to the idea that certain uses of land should not be interfered with if they are reasonable. This principle helps balance competing interests between neighboring landowners.
- **Application**: The reasonableness of the defendant's conduct is often assessed in the context of location, time, and social norms. For example, what might be considered a reasonable level of noise in an industrial area may not be reasonable in a residential area.

Foreseeability:

- **Definition**: Foreseeability involves whether a reasonable person could predict that their actions might create a nuisance.
- **Importance**: This principle is crucial in determining liability, as it links the defendant's conduct to the harm suffered by the plaintiff. If the harm was not foreseeable, the defendant might not be held liable.

Balance of Interests:

- **Concept**: Balancing interests involves weighing the defendant's right to use their property against the plaintiff's right to enjoy their property without interference.
- **Judicial Consideration**: Courts often look at factors such as the nature of the harm, the utility of the defendant's conduct, the feasibility of the defendant mitigating the harm, and the character of the locality to determine whether an interference constitutes a nuisance.
- **Social and Economic Factors**: Economic benefits of the defendant's activities might be considered against the detriment to the plaintiff. For instance, a factory may bring jobs and economic growth to an area but at the cost of noise and pollution.

Remedies for Nuisance

In the law of torts, nuisance involves an interference with someone's use and enjoyment of their land. The remedies for nuisance aim to rectify this interference, and they typically include injunctions, damages, and abatement. Here's a detailed examination of these remedies suitable for understanding their factual and conceptual application, particularly useful for preparing multiple-choice questions.

Injunctions

- **Definition and Purpose**: An injunction is a court order that requires a party to do or to refrain from doing specific acts. In the context of nuisance, it usually serves to stop or prevent the continuation of the nuisance.
- **Circumstances for Granting Injunctions**:
  - **Severity of Harm**: Injunctions are more likely to be granted where the nuisance causes significant harm or where monetary compensation is inadequate.
  - **Continuing Nuisance**: They are particularly relevant in ongoing situations where the nuisance persists over time.
  - **Balance of Convenience**: Courts consider the inconvenience to the defendant if the injunction is granted versus the continued harm to the plaintiff without it.
- **Types of Injunctions**:
  - **Temporary (Interlocutory) Injunctions**: Granted before a final decision is made, often used to prevent harm that could occur before the case is decided.
  - **Permanent Injunctions**: Issued as a final judgment, permanently prohibiting the nuisance activity.
- **Enforcement**:
  - Failure to comply with an injunction can lead to contempt of court charges, fines, or even imprisonment in extreme cases.
  - Enforcement is typically handled by local law enforcement agencies under the direction of the court.

Damages

- **Purpose**: Damages are monetary compensation awarded to a plaintiff for the loss or harm suffered due to the nuisance.
- **Assessment of Compensation**:
  - **Direct Losses**: Includes property damage and personal discomfort or illness directly attributable to the nuisance.
  - **Indirect Losses**: May include reduction in property value and loss of use of the property.
- **Factors Considered in Awarding Damages**:
  - **Duration and Frequency**: More frequent and long-lasting nuisances can result in higher damages.
  - **Intensity of the Nuisance**: More severe nuisances typically warrant greater compensation.
  - **Plaintiff's Sensitivity**: If the plaintiff is unusually sensitive, damages might be limited to what would affect an average person unless the defendant knew of the plaintiff's particular sensitivity.

Abatement

- **Definition**: Abatement involves the self-help remedy where the plaintiff takes direct action to stop the nuisance without waiting for court proceedings.
- **Self-Help Remedies**:
  - **Legality**: Actions must be reasonable and not exceed what is necessary to cease the nuisance.

- **Examples**: Cutting overhanging branches or installing soundproofing against noise.

Legal Restrictions and Requirements:

- **Notice**: Often, the plaintiff must give notice to the defendant and allow them an opportunity to remedy the nuisance themselves.
- **No Excessive Force**: Any measure taken should not involve illegal activities or excessive force.
- **Immediate Threat**: Typically justified only where there is an immediate threat to health or property.

Case Law and Nuisance

Landmark Cases: Important Judicial Decisions Shaping Nuisance Law

Landmark cases have significantly shaped the understanding and application of nuisance law in various jurisdictions. Here are some pivotal cases that are frequently referenced:

- **Rylands v. Fletcher (1868, UK)**: Established the rule that if a person brings onto their land something likely to cause damage if it escapes, they are responsible for any damage that does occur. This case is foundational for understanding strict liability for abnormal land use.
- **Sturges v. Bridgman (1879, UK)**: Defined the principle that the character of a neighborhood does not justify a nuisance. This was where the "coming to the nuisance" defense was significantly discussed, leading to a refined understanding that a defendant cannot always escape liability merely because the plaintiff moved to the location of the nuisance.
- **Christie v. Davey (1893, UK)**: In this case, a court issued an injunction against a defendant who deliberately created noise to irritate the plaintiff. This case highlights intentional nuisance and the role of malice in determining remedies.
- **Boomer v. Atlantic Cement Co. (1970, USA)**: Demonstrated the use of permanent damages as a remedy for nuisance. The court allowed the cement plant to continue operations despite it being a nuisance, opting to compensate the plaintiffs with permanent damages instead of ordering an injunction.
- **Hunter v. Canary Wharf Ltd (1997, UK)**: Refined the rule on who could sue for nuisance, emphasizing that a claimant must have an interest in the land affected by the nuisance.

TRESPASS TO LAND

Definition and Elements

- **Trespass to Land**: This occurs when an individual enters another's property without permission or lawful excuse. This intrusion must be intentional; however, even unintentional entries (e.g., mistaken belief regarding the property boundary) can constitute trespass if they are due to negligence or recklessness.
- **Essential Elements**:
  - **Direct Interference**: The interference must be direct, meaning the trespasser themselves or an object they control physically enters the property.
  - **Intentionality**: The act of entering the land must be intentional, meaning the person meant to perform the act that resulted in the entry. It does not require the intent to break the law or to cause damage.
  - **Without Permission**: The entry is without consent from the landowner.

Interference with Property

- **Physical Entry**: Any physical invasion of a property's boundaries by a person or object (e.g., throwing a ball onto someone's land).
- **Entry of Substances**: Includes indirect invasions such as smoke, fumes, dust, water, or toxic materials that are introduced onto the land.

Defenses to Trespass to Land

- **Consent**: If the landowner has given permission for entry, either explicitly or implicitly, no trespass has occurred.
- **Necessity**: Trespass may be justified by necessity, such as during emergencies to prevent greater harm (e.g., entering land to escape serious harm).
- **Public Authority**: Entry may be justified if conducted by public officials under the authority of law (e.g., police entry during a chase).
- **Legal Right**: A person may enter land if they have a legal right to do so (e.g., utility workers checking meters).

Remedies for Trespass to Land

- **Damages**: Monetary compensation for any harm or loss caused by the trespass, which may include the cost of repair or depreciation in property value.

- **Injunctions**: Court orders that prohibit the trespasser from continuing the trespass or repeating it in the future.
- **Abatement by Self-Help**: The landowner may personally remove or eliminate the source of the trespass without resorting to legal proceedings, as long as such actions are reasonable and do not cause unnecessary harm.
- **Punitive Damages**: In cases of willful or malicious trespass, courts may award punitive damages to deter such behavior and punish the trespasser.

TRESPASS TO CHATTELS

Definition and Elements

- **Trespass to Chattels**: This is a tort where the defendant intentionally interferes with the plaintiff's right to possession of personal property. This interference can be direct or indirect.
- **Elements**:
  - ❑ **Chattel**: The item in question must be a movable personal property.
  - ❑ **Possession**: The plaintiff must have possession or the right to possession at the time of interference.
  - ❑ **Intentional Interference**: The defendant must intentionally perform an act that leads to the interference. Accidental actions, without intent, typically do not qualify.
  - ❑ **Interference**: There must be an actual interference that affects the plaintiff's use or possession of the chattel. This can include physical alteration, damage, or temporary deprivation.

Intent and Fault

- **Intent**: The defendant must have intended the act that resulted in the interference. The intent need not be to harm, but merely to perform the act that resulted in interference. This differentiates it from negligent actions where the harm was unintentional.
- **Fault**: In trespass to chattels, fault generally revolves around the intentional nature of the act rather than negligence. However, if negligence results in damage or deprivation of use, it may lead to liability under other torts like negligence or conversion.

Consequences of Interference

- **Damage**: Any physical damage to the chattel.
- **Loss of Use**: The owner's inability to use their property due to the interference, which could be temporary or permanent.
- **Diminution in Value**: Reduction in the value of the chattel, even if it is returned undamaged, if its market value has decreased due to the defendant's actions.

Defenses and Justifications

- **Consent**: If the plaintiff consented to the defendant's actions, it can serve as a defense.
- **Lawful Authority**: Actions taken under the authority of law, such as by law enforcement or during court orders, provide a defense against trespass to chattels claims.
- **Necessity**: If the interference was necessary to prevent a greater harm, this can be a defense, especially in emergency situations.

Remedies

- **Damages**: Monetary compensation for the actual harm caused to the chattel. This includes compensation for repair costs, loss of use, and any diminution in value.
- **Replevin**: A legal action to recover possession of chattels wrongfully taken or retained. This is particularly used when the chattel holds special value to the owner.
- **Detinue**: A remedy to recover personal property wrongfully held by another, along with damages for its detention.

TRESPASS TO THE PERSON

Assault

Definition: Assault in tort law is an act that intentionally causes another person to apprehend the immediate infliction of unlawful force on his person.

Elements of Assault:

- **Intention**: The defendant must have intended to cause apprehension of harmful or offensive contact.
- **Apprehension**: The plaintiff must have reasonably anticipated that harm or offensive contact was imminent.

- **Lack of Consent**: The action must be without the consent of the plaintiff.
- **Capability**: The defendant must have the ability to carry out the threat immediately.

Distinction from Battery:

- **Nature of Harm**: Assault concerns the apprehension of harm rather than actual contact.
- **Physical Contact**: Battery requires physical contact, whereas assault does not; mere fear or apprehension of such contact suffices for assault.

Battery

Definition: Battery is the intentional and direct application of force to another person without lawful justification.

Key Aspects of Battery:

- **Intentional Contact**: The contact must be intentional (not accidental).
- **Unauthorized Contact**: The contact must be without the consent of the person touched or otherwise unlawful.
- **Harmful or Offensive**: The contact must be harmful or offensive to a reasonable person.

False Imprisonment

Definition: False imprisonment is the intentional unlawful confinement of a person against their will.

Elements of False Imprisonment:

- **Intentional Restriction**: Deliberate restriction of a person's freedom to move.
- **Unlawfulness**: There must be no legal justification for the confinement.
- **Awareness**: The victim must be aware of the confinement or harmed by it.
- **Confinement**: Confinement can occur in any bounded area without a reasonable means of escape known to the victim.

Defenses to Personal Trespass

- **Self-Defense**: Acting to protect oneself from harm or offensive contact, provided the force used is reasonable and proportionate to the threat.
- **Defense of Others**: Similar to self-defense, but acting to protect another person.
- **Legal Authority**: Actions taken under legal authority (e.g., police making an arrest) can justify what would otherwise be a trespass to the person.

Remedies

Types of Damages:

- **Compensatory Damages**: For physical and psychological injuries to compensate the victim for pain, suffering, and medical expenses.
- **Punitive Damages**: Awarded to punish the defendant for particularly egregious conduct and deter future violations.

Legal Implications:

- **Immediate Relief**: Such as an injunction to prevent continued trespass to the person.
- **Recovery of Costs**: Including legal fees in some cases.

DEFAMATION

Defamation is an exciting area of law which is inherently concerned with freedom of expression, encapsulated in Article 10 of the 1998 Human Rights Act. The idea behind defamation is the protection of reputation of a person or business from injury due to unjustified insults.

There are two types of defamation:

- Libel—Something which is in a permanent form *e.g.* in writing, images, film or recording. It also includes anything said on stage or in a broadcast.
- Slander—Spoken words usually said in a conversation.

An important term which is used repeatedly in the case law is 'publication'. In order to be actionable, a defamatory statement must be 'published' to a third party. In defamation, 'publish' does not have its ordinary definition meaning the printing of words in a book or leaflet. Publishing, here, means communicating the defamatory statement to a third party, whether that is in a conversation or the people at home who are watching a television show in which a defamatory comment is made.

Difference between libel and slander

As mentioned above, libel is tends to be in permanent form whereas slander is spoken words. In Monson *vs* Tussauds [1894] 1 QB 671, the court had to decide whether a wax statue was capable of being libel. In hold that it was, the court said that anything which has a permanent of lasting form can be libel including an effigy or chalk marks on a wall.

Another important distinction is that libel is actionable *per se,* which means without any proof of damage. Whereas slander, like most areas of law, requires proof of some injury before a law suit can be brought.

The practice of division of defamatory statement is not followed by the Indian court. Both libel and slander are criminal offence U/S 499 of IPC. All defamatory statements are actionable *per se.* Limitation period for filing suit against defamation is two years. Essentials of defamation:

- The word must be defamatory.
- The said word must refer to the plaintiff.
- They must be published.

Defamatory statement means a statement which tends to injure the reputation of a person, or which tends to lower a person in the estimation of right thinking members of the society ***(Sim vs Stretch 1936)***. Thus, defamatory statement by making attack on the reputation of a person without any lawful justification, provides a cause to right thinking man to hate, shun and avoid that person and, thus, expose him to unlimited embarrassment.

In this type of case, question of damages depends on various factors, the effect of the publication of the news item in Dainik Navjoti is that the respondent has lost reputation, and her parents lost their prestige in the society, prospects of marriage of Manjulata were lessened, in these circumstances the damages awarded is not excessive ***(O.P. Choudhary vs Manjulata AIR 1997, 170 at p. 174).***

It is notable that whether particular statement amounts to defamation or not. Courts see or judge the alleged defamatory character of the statement from the angle of *right minded* citizens of the society. *Right minded means a balanced mind, having fair average intelligence, who is away from extreme of both sides.* It is notable that if statement tends to injure the reputation of a person, defendant can not say that it is not intended so. ***(Capital and countries Bank vs Henty and Sons (1882) & A.C. 741).***

However, the words spoken in anger which are just to cause annoyance or hurt feeling of the plaintiff will not constitute a defamation, if nature of the statement is such that no right thinking man will give any importance to the spoken words ***(Firdharilal vs Punjab Singh (1973) 34 P.L.R. 1071).***

The innuendo: Defamation is not the set of bare words but it implies set of words with definite meaning which tends to injure the reputation of a person. Sometime these meanings appear on the face of the statement and some time they remain disguised, in the words itself. The onus of proving that disguised meaning is referring to no body else but the plaintiff and thus constituting and injury against plaintiff himself. Thus, an action against defamatory statement can be brought in a court of law on the basis of its latent or secondary meaning *i.e.,* innuendo, what essential in this that word must amount to defamatory in respect of plaintiff in their secondary or latent meaning.

If A says to B, it is hard to say anything about C's honesty, C may understand it as C is so dishonest that no one can give guarantee for his honesty as C is honest that no one can make any remark to his honesty. If C wants to bring an action for the first inference then he must prove that B took the statement in the secondary meaning which tends to injure the reputation of C.

Capital and Counties Bank vs Henty and Sons (1882) 7 A.C. 741: There was a dispute between the Hentey and Sons (defendants) and capital and countries bank plaintiff. Defendant published a circular, "Hentey and Sons hereby give notice that they will not receive payment in cheques drawn on any of the branches of the capital and countries Bank." This circular made a negative effect on the business of the bank. Plaintiff pleaded that the circular implied an insolvency of the bank and this tended to injure the reputation of the bank. Court held that the defendants were not liable because the right minded persons of the society would not understand it in the sense of the innuendo as suggested by the defendant.

Tolley *vs* J.S. Fry and Sons (1931) A.C. 333: In this case, defendant Co. showed the caricature of plaintiff, a famous golf champion in one of the advertisement of their product. Defendant did not take permission from plaintiff for this advertisement. Plaintiff sued defendant saying that he suffered a lot in his reputation and credit. Plaintiff pleaded that latent inference from the advertisement is that plaintiff has reputation as an amateur golf player for advertising purpose. Court held the defendant liable and withheld the latent meaning as produced by the plaintiff.

It is notable that intention to defame is not necessary to constitute defamation. If a statement tends to injure the reputation of the plaintiff, it is actionable as defamation, intent to defame plaintiff on the part of defendant is not necessary. In **Morrison *vs* Ritchie and Co. (1902 4F 654),** the defendant in good faith published that plaintiff gave birth to a twins. In fact, plaintiff was married just two months back. Court held the defendant liable if even the defendant had no intention to defame the plaintiff and was unaware about the real facts.

(a) The word must refer to the Plaintiff

It is essential that the alleged defamatory words must refer to the plaintiff. In other words, defamatory statement must intend to injure the reputation of the plaintiff. Defendant can not take the defence that he has no intention to defame the Plaintiff. In **Newstead *vs* London Express Newspaper Ltd. (1939) 4 All E.R.** case, defendant published a news stating that "Harold Newstead a camberwell man" had been convicted of bigamy, the news was true about Harlech Newstead a camber well barman and action was brought by camberwell barber. Defendants were held liable as the word could be understood as referring to plaintiff. Similar decisions, were taken in **Cassidy *vs* Daily Mirror Newspaper Ltd. (1929) 2 K.B. 331.**

Defamation of a Class of Persons

In case defamatory statement refers to a class of person then, none of the members of that class can sue the wrongdoer. However, an individual of that class can take action only if he proves that the words can reasonably be understood as referring to him.

Knupffer *vs* London Express Newspaper Ltd. (1994) 1 All E.R. 495. In this case, plaintiff was a member of a party consisting of more than 2,000 member and most of them were living abroad. Defendant published a defamatory statement in reference to this party. Plaintiff who was in England with 24 other members sued the defendant because some of this friends considered the article as referring to the plaintiff court rejected the contention of the plaintiff, because most of the members were living abroad and the statement could not be understood as referring to the plaintiff.

Fanu *vs* Malcomson (1847) 1 H.L. at 637. In this case, defendant published an article describing the inhuman treatment of employees in Irish factories. This article particularly mentioned the name of plaintiff's factory, Court held the defendant liable because defamatory remarks specifically covered the plaintiff's factory. It was held that words could reasonably be understood as referring to plaintiff.

It is notable that defaming a deceased person is not a tort. Under Section 499 of Indian Penal Code, it may amount to defamation to impute anything to a deceased person if the imputation would harm the reputation of that person if living and is intended to be hurtful to the feeling of the family members or other relatives of the deceased.

(b) Publication of Defamatory Statement

Publication of defamatory statement is essential for constituting tort of defamation. Unless there is publication of defamatory statement, no civil action for defamation lies.

Publication here means, a communication by the defendant of the defamatory statement, to some person other than the plaintiff.

If A dictates a letter to his secretary B which contains defamatory remark in reference to C, C may sue A because by dictating the letter B has published the defamation matter.

If a person writes a defamatory letter in language not known to the addressee and consequently supposed to be read by somebody else to the addressee. Addressor will be liable if the fact that the language in which he has been writing letter is not known to the addressor, is in the knowledge of addressor.

If a third person wrongfully read a letter addressed to somebody else, sender will not be liable for it. If defamatory matter is contained in a telegram or postcard sender will be liable even without proof of publication. If a letter having defamatory content is sent in such circumstances that it is likely to be read by somebody else, then the sender will be liable.

It is notable that there can be no publication between the joint tort feasters *i.e.,* A and B jointly write a letter containing defamatory remarks concerning C and send this letter through registered post to C. Here, publication is not completed, publication between joint tort feasor is no publication.

It is worthwhile to mention here that not only the originator of the defamatory matter but the person causing the repetition of the defamatory matter are also liable under the law. However, book seller, newspaper can take the plea that they do not know or inspite of using due diligence could not have known about the defamatory character of matter.

Communication between husband and wife. Communication of a defamatory matter referring to third person between spouse is no publication. However, communication of a defamatory matter in reference to one spouse to other is a sufficient publication. If A writes a defamatory letter containing defamatory remarks against B's wife it is a sufficient publication but if A writes a letter to his wife containing defamatory remarks against B's wife it is no communication at all. Under the law of Evidence as well this type of communication is covered under the category of privileged communication.

Defences

Some general defences available in tort apply also to defamation, such as consent (Monson *vs* Tussauds). There are some defences which are specific to defamation, these are justification, fair comment, privilege, offer of amends and innocent dissemination.

Justification

The Defendant can justify the defamatory comment by proving its truth. According to Sutherland *vs* Stopes [1925] AC 47, the statement must be "true in substance and fact", so as long as the statement is substantially true (but not completely true) the defence will succeed.

In Grobbelaar *vs* News Group Newspapers [2002] UKHL 40, Grobbelaar was a well-known footballer and was accused in an article of receiving money to fix the results of matches in which he was playing. The Sun covertly recorded some meetings between Grobbelaar and the undercover reporter where Grobbelaar admitted taking money to lose matches in the past, and took £2000 to cheat in matches in the future. The Sun then printed several articles over a period of time on the subject. Grobbelaar was arrested and tried twice in respect of bribe taking. The first time the (criminal) jury could not agree and the second time they acquitted him of one charge but not the other. The footballer then sued alleging defamation in respect of the charge he was not convicted of. The House of Lords held in his favour but only gave damages of £1. The reasoning was that the sting of the defamation lay in his having conceded actually goals, and professional footballer's gave evidence on tapes of his games, saying that he did not appear to be doing so. If the sting of the defamation lay in the fact that he had taken bribes in the past, and was prepared to concede goals in the future then, his justification defence would have succeeded. The case emphasises the importance of identifying the sting of the defamation and ensuring that the justification covers that fully, not partially as in this case.

In Alexander *vs* North Eastern Railway (1865) 6 B & S 340, the Defendants published a notice at their train station saying the Claimant had been caught riding on a train without a ticket and was sentenced to £1 fine or three weeks imprisonment. In actual fact it was 14 days imprisonment if he failed to pay the fine. The Claimant complained that the overstatement made it appear as if the offence he had committed was worse than it was. The jury held in this case that it is not necessary to prove that the statement is literally true. It is sufficient if it is true in substance.

The rumour doctrine—Where the defendant uses another person's beliefs or suspicions as the foundation of his defence, he can only rely on justification, if he knew the underlying facts were true. It is no defence to say that he was merely repeating what he had heard: Stern *vs* Piper [1997] QB 123. However, it has been accepted that there may be circumstances which permit a person to repeat a rumour without knowing whether it is true. Where a defendant says that the claimant is under suspicion of having done something, this does not necessarily mean the claimant has in fact done it but the defendant will be able to defend himself if he can prove that a reasonable person would also have been suspicious.

Criminal convictions—If the Claimant has been convicted of a criminal offence, the defendant only needs to get the certificate of conviction and this will be enough proof. However, in the public interest, if anyone 'maliciously' publishes details about a 'spent' conviction they cannot rely on justification.

Fair Comment on a Matter in the Public Interest

Fair comment on a matter in the public interest is a full defence like justification. This is a particularly useful defence to the media. However, this defence only applies to expressions of opinion ('I think ...') and not expressions of fact (The truth is ...'). The difference between these can sometimes be hard to determine.

In London Artists *vs* Littler [1962] 2 QB 375, the Court laid down these tests:

- Was the comment made on a matter of public interest
- Was the statement an expression of fact or opinion
- If opinion, are the underlying facts true and contained in the article
- Would a fair man make the same comment

Privilege

In certain situations, the right to free speech becomes more important than the right not to be defamed. There are two types of privilege: absolute privilege when complete freedom of information is needed and qualified privilege when the need for freedom is slightly lower.

Absolute Privilege

The main examples of absolute privilege are:

- Statements in Parliament
- Documents ordered to be published by Parliament
- Statements made in the course of judicial proceedings *e.g.,* witness' evidence
- Fair and accurate reports of judicial proceedings
- Communications by a minister of other officer of the state to another in the course of his duty.

Qualified Privilege

Qualified privilege applies to a broader range of situations though it offers less protection. At common law, there is qualified privilege where,

"where the person who makes a communication has an interest or a duty, legal, social or moral to make it to the person to whom it is made, and the person to whom it is so made has a corresponding interest or duty to receive" (Adam *vs* Ward [1917] AC 309).

So, there has to be an interest or duty in both the maker of the communication and the recipient. So, the question is who has such a duty or interest? In Reynolds *vs* Times Newspapers [2001] 2 AC 217, the Claimant was a former Irish politician who sued over an article which alleged he had deliberately misled his cabinet. The defendants argued that qualified privilege should apply in all cases where a political subject is concerned. In rejecting this, the House of Lords laid down the following as general non-exhaustive considerations:

- The seriousness of the allegation, the more serious it is the greater the potential harm to the claimant if untrue
- Is the subject of the information of interest to the public
- Do the sources have direct knowledge
- Have steps been taken to verify the information
- Has a formal investigation taken place
- Urgency
- Was the claimant allowed to respond
- Did the article contain the gist of the claimant's version of events
- Tone of the article
- Circumstances of the publication, including timing

In addition, a defendant cannot keep defama-tory articles on their website without giving any indication that its veracity is disputed. If malice can be shown by the claimant then the defence will fail.

Remedies: If an individual discovers that some defamatory comment will be published in the future they can apply to the Court for an injunction to stop the comment being published.

If the comment has already been published, the claimant can seek a permanent injunction to prevent any re-publications as well as damages.

In some cases exemplary damages have been awarded.

REMOTENESS OF DAMAGE

Introduction to Remoteness of Damage

Definition and Concept

- Remoteness of damage is a legal principle used to determine whether a particular loss or harm suffered by the claimant is sufficiently connected to the defendant's wrongful act to warrant compensation.
- The concept addresses the limits of liability in tort law by examining whether the damage is too remote (distant) from the tortious act to hold the defendant accountable.
- A balance is maintained between fairness to the claimant (ensuring they are compensated for actual harm) and fairness to the defendant (ensuring they are not liable for unforeseeable or excessively distant consequences).

Core Principle

- A defendant is only liable for the foreseeable consequences of their actions, not for damage that is too far removed from the wrongful act.

Historical Evolution of the Principle

Early Development: Direct Consequences Test

- Re Polemis and Furness, Withy & Co. Ltd. (1921):
  - Early case law focused on the direct consequences of the defendant's act.
  - Liability was established for all damage that directly resulted from the wrongful act, regardless of foreseeability.
  - Criticism: This approach was seen as too broad, holding defendants liable for unforeseeable harm.

Shift to Reasonable Foreseeability: The Wagon Mound Cases

- The Wagon Mound (No. 1) (1961):
  - Landmark case that introduced the reasonable foreseeability test.
  - Held that a defendant is only liable for damage that a reasonable person in their position could foresee.
  - Significance: Replaced the direct consequences test and became the dominant standard in common law.

- The Wagon Mound (No. 2) (1966):
  - Clarified the application of foreseeability, emphasizing that the likelihood of harm need not be high; it only needs to be reasonably foreseeable.

Development of Special Rules: The Eggshell Skull Rule

- Smith v. Leech Brain & Co. Ltd. (1962):
  - Established that defendants must take their victims "as they find them."
  - Even if the extent of harm is unforeseeable due to a pre-existing condition, liability remains for the full extent of harm if the initial injury was foreseeable.

Comparison Table: Direct Consequences Test vs. Reasonable Foreseeability Test

Aspect	Direct Consequences Test	Reasonable Foreseeability Test
Key Case	Re Polemis	The Wagon Mound (No. 1 & No. 2)
Focus	Directness of damage	Foreseeability of damage
Foreseeability Required	No	Yes
Scope of Liability	Broad	Narrow and reasonable
Criticisms	Overly broad, unfair to defendants	Subjective, may limit compensation

Strict and Absolute Liability in Tort

Tort law imposes liability in various forms, including negligence (fault-based) and strict/absolute liability (no-fault-based). These doctrines address harm caused by inherently dangerous activities or substances, prioritizing victim protection over fault.

Strict Liability

Definition

- Strict liability imposes responsibility on a person for harm caused by their actions or things under their control, regardless of fault or intent.
- Originated in English law with the rule in Rylands v. Fletcher (1868).
- Focus: Compensation for harm from dangerous activities, not punishment for negligence.

The Rule in Rylands v. Fletcher

- **Facts:** Defendant's reservoir water escaped and flooded the plaintiff's coal mine.
- **Principle:** "The person who, for his own purposes, brings on his land and collects and keeps there anything likely to do mischief if it escapes, must keep it in at his peril, and if he does not do so, is prima facie answerable for all the damage which is the natural consequence of its escape."
- **Conditions:**
  - **Dangerous Thing:** The substance or activity must be inherently hazardous (e.g., water, gas, explosives).
  - **Non-Natural Use of Land:** Use must be extraordinary, not ordinary (e.g., storing large quantities of water).
  - **Escape:** The dangerous thing must escape from the defendant's land to cause harm.
  - **Damage:** Actual harm must result.

Key Elements

- No need to prove negligence or intent.
- Liability is strict but not absolute – defenses are available.

Defenses to Strict Liability

- **Act of God:**
  - Natural events beyond human control (e.g., floods, storms).
  - Case: Nichols v. Marsland (1876) – Exceptional rainfall broke a dam; no liability.
- **Plaintiff's Own Fault:**
  - If the plaintiff caused or contributed to the escape.
  - Case: Ponting v. Noakes (1894) – Plaintiff's horse ate poisonous leaves from defendant's land; no liability.
- **Consent of the Plaintiff (Volenti Non Fit Injuria):** Plaintiff agreed to the risk (e.g., tenant accepting a leaking pipe).
- **Act of Third Party:**
  - Harm caused by an independent third party's actions.
  - Case: Box v. Jubb (1879) – Third party's overflow caused the escape; defendant not liable.
- **Statutory Authority:**
  - Activity authorized by law exempts liability.
  - Case: Green v. Chelsea Waterworks Co. (1894) – Statutory water supply; no liability for burst pipes.

Landmark Cases

- **Rylands v. Fletcher (1868):** Established the strict liability principle.
- **Read v. Lyons (1947):** No liability as there was no "escape" (explosion occurred within defendant's premises).
- **Cambridge Water Co. v. Eastern Counties Leather (1994):** Foreseeability of harm introduced as a limitation to strict liability.

Application in India

- Adopted from English law but modified in practice.
- Case: Madras Railway Co. v. Zamindar of Carvetnagar (1874) – Applied strict liability for water escaping from a tank.

Absolute Liability

Definition

- Absolute liability is a stricter form of liability where no defenses (except statutory authority in some cases) are allowed.
- Developed in India as an evolution of strict liability to address modern industrial hazards.
- Focus: Protecting society from ultra-hazardous activities, ensuring compensation without exceptions.

Origin: M.C. Mehta v. Union of India (1987)

- Facts: Oleum gas leaked from Shriram Industries, Delhi, causing widespread harm.
- Principle: Enterprises engaged in inherently hazardous or dangerous activities owe an absolute and non-delegable duty to ensure safety. If harm occurs, they are liable irrespective of fault or defenses.
- Justice Bhagwati: "The larger and more prosperous the enterprise, the greater must be the amount of compensation payable."

Key Elements

- Hazardous Activity: The activity must be inherently dangerous (e.g., handling toxic chemicals, nuclear energy).
- No Defenses: Unlike strict liability, defenses like Act of God or third-party acts are not applicable.
- Non-Delegable Duty: The enterprise cannot escape liability by delegating responsibility.
- Damage: Actual harm to persons, property, or the environment.

Rationale

- To deter negligence in high-risk industries.
- To ensure victims receive compensation without legal hurdles.
- Reflects public policy in a developing nation like India with growing industrialization.

Landmark Cases

- **M.C. Mehta v. Union of India (1987):** Introduced absolute liability; distinguished from Rylands v. Fletcher.
- **Union Carbide Corp. v. Union of India (1989) (Bhopal Gas Tragedy):** Applied absolute liability; compensation of $470 million awarded.
- **Indian Council for Enviro-Legal Action v. Union of India (1996):** Polluter pays principle reinforced alongside absolute liability for environmental damage.

Application in India

- Codified in statutes like:
  - Public Liability Insurance Act, 1991: Mandatory insurance for hazardous industries.
  - National Green Tribunal Act, 2010: Applies absolute liability principles for environmental harm.

Tortious Liability of State

Introduction to Tortious Liability of State

Tortious liability of the state refers to the legal obligation of a government or its instrumentalities to compensate individuals who have suffered harm due to wrongful acts or omissions by state agents. The state, despite being a sovereign entity, may be held accountable under the law of torts for actions that result in injuries to individuals or property.

- **Scope of State Liability**: Limited to non-sovereign functions in some jurisdictions; broader in others based on judicial interpretations.
- **Underlying Principle**: "The King can do no wrong" (historical) has evolved into the recognition that the state should be accountable to its citizens in specific circumstances.

Definition of Tortious Liability

Tortious liability is the legal responsibility that arises when a party (here, the state or government) commits a tort—an act or omission that causes harm or injury to another, violating a duty recognized by law.

Key Elements of Tortious Liability:

- **Duty of Care**: The state owes a legal duty to act in a reasonable and lawful manner.
- **Breach of Duty**: Any failure to fulfill this duty.
- **Injury or Damage**: Direct harm caused by the breach.
- **Causation**: A direct link between the state's actions and the harm suffered.

State's Tortious Liability: Usually vicarious, arising from acts committed by government officials or employees during the course of their employment.

Historical Evolution of State Liability in Tort

The doctrine of state liability has undergone significant changes over time:

A. Ancient Doctrine

- The principle "The King can do no wrong" originated in England under **Common Law**.
- In monarchies, the ruler was considered infallible, and no legal action could be brought against them.

B. Transition to Modern Accountability

- **United Kingdom**: The Crown Proceedings Act, 1947, abolished the complete immunity of the Crown, allowing it to be sued in tort like a private individual.
- **India**: State liability evolved under **Article 300 of the Constitution**, which specifies the conditions under which the Union or State governments can be sued.
- **United States**: Under the **Federal Tort Claims Act, 1946**, the government waived its sovereign immunity for many tort claims.

C. Indian Legal Framework

- Under **Article 300**, the liability of the Indian state is guided by the principles applicable to the East India Company, subject to legislative changes.
- Landmark cases like **Kasturilal Ralia Ram v. State of Uttar Pradesh** (1965) established the distinction between sovereign and non-sovereign functions.

Rationale behind the Doctrine of State Liability

The doctrine of state liability is based on several legal and moral justifications:

A. Accountability of the State

- A state that governs its citizens should be accountable for wrongful acts committed by its agents, fostering public trust.

B. Public Policy Considerations

- Ensures that victims of government negligence or malfeasance receive compensation.
- Balances the state's immunity with the individual's right to justice.

C. Sovereign vs. Non-Sovereign Functions

- Sovereign functions (e.g., defense, law-making) often enjoy immunity to preserve state sovereignty.
- Non-sovereign functions (e.g., commercial or administrative acts) are subject to tortious liability, as they involve interactions with citizens akin to private entities.

D. Constitutional Mandates

- In democracies, the constitution often mandates protection against state overreach or negligence (e.g., Article 21 in India ensures the right to life and liberty).

Legal Principles Governing Tortious Liability of State

The tortious liability of the state refers to its legal responsibility for wrongful acts committed by its servants or agents during the course of their employment. The following are the key principles that govern this area of law:

Doctrine of Sovereign Immunity

- **Definition**: The doctrine of sovereign immunity provides that the state or its sovereign cannot be sued in its courts without its consent.
- **Origin**:
  - ❑ Derived from the maxim **"Rex Non Potest Peccare"** (The King Can Do No Wrong).
  - ❑ Rooted in English Common Law and brought to India during the colonial period.
- **Scope in India**:
  - ❑ Under **Article 300 of the Indian Constitution**, the liability of the Union and State Governments is similar to that of the East India Company before 1950.

- ❑ Courts distinguish between **sovereign functions** (essential functions of the state) and **non-sovereign functions** (commercial or welfare activities).

- **Key Case Laws**:
  - ❑ **Kasturilal Ralia Ram v. State of Uttar Pradesh (1965)**:
    - ➾ Sovereign functions enjoy immunity.
    - ➾ The government was not liable for a tortious act by a police officer in the exercise of sovereign functions.
  - ❑ **N. Nagendra Rao & Co. v. State of Andhra Pradesh (1994)**:
    - ➾ The Supreme Court held that the state is liable for torts in non-sovereign functions.
- **Criticism**:
  - ❑ The doctrine is outdated and provides undue protection to the state.
  - ❑ Modern trends favor restricting its scope to uphold individual rights and accountability.

Doctrine of Vicarious Liability

- **Definition**: Vicarious liability refers to a situation where one person is held liable for the wrongful acts of another due to a special relationship, such as employer-employee.
- **Application to State**: The state is vicariously liable for torts committed by its employees or agents during the course of their employment, provided the act is not ultra vires.
- **Essential Conditions**:
  - ❑ There must be an employer-employee relationship.
  - ❑ The act should be committed in the course of employment.
  - ❑ The act must be within the scope of authority granted.
- **Exceptions**: The state is not liable for acts outside the servant's authority or ultra vires actions.
- **Key Case Laws**:
  - ❑ **Peninsular and Oriental Steam Navigation Co. v. Secretary of State (1861)**:
    - ➾ Distinguished between sovereign and non-sovereign functions; liability arises only in non-sovereign activities.
  - ❑ **Shyam Sunder v. State of Rajasthan (1974)**:
    - ➾ Confirmed the state's liability for acts of negligence by employees engaged in non-sovereign functions.

Public Duty Doctrine

- **Definition**: The doctrine of public duty imposes an obligation on the state to discharge its functions responsibly to ensure public welfare and safety.
- **Scope**:
  - ❑ Includes duties in maintaining law and order, providing essential services, and ensuring administrative efficiency.
  - ❑ The state is liable if it breaches its duty of care toward citizens.
- **Key Components**:
  - ❑ **Duty of Care**: Obligation to prevent harm to individuals through reasonable actions.
  - ❑ **Standard of Care**: The level of caution and diligence expected from the state or its officials.
- **Case Law**:
  - ❑ **Nilabati Behera v. State of Orissa (1993)**:
    - ➾ Compensation was awarded for custodial death due to negligence, holding the state accountable under the public duty doctrine.
  - ❑ **Rudul Sah v. State of Bihar (1983)**:
    - ➾ Compensation for wrongful detention emphasized the state's duty to protect individual rights.
- **Challenges**:
  - ❑ Balancing state immunity with the rights of individuals.
  - ❑ Difficulty in proving breach of duty and causation.

Concept of "Deep Pocket" and State Accountability

- **Definition**: The "deep pocket" theory refers to the financial capacity of the state to compensate for damages caused by its servants or agents.
- **Rationale**:
  - ❑ The state, as a powerful and resource-rich entity, is better positioned to bear the cost of compensation than an individual victim.
  - ❑ Ensures justice for victims without overburdening state agents.

- **Application**:
  - Used in cases where the state is vicariously liable for tortious acts of its employees.
  - Often seen in large-scale damages, such as industrial disasters or negligence in public service.
- **Case Laws**:
  - **M.C. Mehta v. Union of India (1987)** (Oleum Gas Leak Case):
    - Introduced the principle of absolute liability for hazardous activities, highlighting the deep pocket concept.
  - **Bhopal Gas Tragedy Case**:
    - The state and Union Carbide Corporation were held liable for compensating victims.
- **Criticism**:
  - Risk of moral hazard, where state employees act negligently, knowing the state will bear the cost.
  - Need for balanced policies to ensure accountability without overburdening state finances.

Summary of Key Legal Principles

Principle	Key Features	Important Case Laws
Doctrine of Sovereign Immunity	Protects the state from liability for acts in sovereign capacity.	Kasturilal Ralia Ram, Nagendra Rao, Peninsular & Oriental
Doctrine of Vicarious Liability	State held liable for torts of its employees if committed within the scope of employment.	Shyam Sunder, Nilabati Behera
Public Duty Doctrine	State is responsible for breaches of public duties, ensuring welfare and safety.	Rudul Sah, Nilabati Behera
Deep Pocket Theory	State's financial capacity justifies liability to compensate victims.	M.C. Mehta, Bhopal Gas Tragedy

Distinction between Sovereign and Non-Sovereign Functions

Sovereign Functions:

- **Definition**: Sovereign functions refer to actions performed by the state in the exercise of its authority to govern, which are related to the state's powers of governance and decision-making. These actions are linked to the core functions of the government, such as maintaining public order, national defense, foreign relations, and law enforcement.
- **Examples**:
  - National defense (e.g., military operations, defense policy)
  - Maintenance of law and order (e.g., policing, maintaining internal security)
  - Foreign relations (e.g., treaties, diplomatic relations)
  - Administration of justice (e.g., enforcement of judicial decrees)
  - Legislative functions (e.g., enacting laws)
  - Exercising prerogative powers (e.g., issuing pardons, appointments)

Sovereign functions are typically immune from tortious liability, meaning the state cannot be sued for its actions when performing such functions, based on the doctrine of "sovereign immunity." This immunity stems from the principle that the state, as a sovereign entity, cannot be sued without its consent.

Non-Sovereign Functions:

- **Definition**: Non-sovereign functions refer to actions carried out by the state in the exercise of its administrative or business functions, which are not directly tied to the sovereign authority of governance. These are essentially activities that a private individual or entity might also undertake, where the state acts in a manner similar to that of a private person or entity, and is not acting in the capacity of exercising sovereign power.
- **Examples**:
  - Running a business or providing public services (e.g., operating public transport, running state-owned enterprises)
  - Providing public health services (e.g., administration of hospitals, public health programs)
  - Conducting administrative functions (e.g., issuing licenses, permits)
  - Engaging in commercial activities (e.g., trade, contracts)
  - Employing public servants (e.g., employment contracts for government workers)

When the state engages in non-sovereign functions, it may be held liable for tortious acts in the same manner as a private individual or corporate body. This is because non-sovereign activities are viewed as similar to private actions that do not require immunity.

Non-Sovereign Functions and State Accountability

Accountability in Non-Sovereign Functions:

- **Principle of Liability**: The state is accountable for its actions when performing non-sovereign functions. This includes liability for negligence, breach of statutory duty, and other civil wrongs. The rationale behind this accountability is that the state, when acting in a non-sovereign capacity, is not exercising its unique powers of governance, but is rather acting in a way that is comparable to any other private entity.
- **Case Law**:
  - **Kasturilal Ralia Ram v. State of Uttar Pradesh (1955)**: The Supreme Court of India ruled that the state could not be held liable for actions related to its sovereign functions, but could be held accountable for non-sovereign functions like running government-run enterprises.
  - **Rudul Sah v. State of Bihar (1983)**: The state was held liable for wrongful detention and failure to compensate the victim, illustrating the state's responsibility in non-sovereign functions like administration and public service.
- **Liability in Tort**: When the state engages in non-sovereign activities, it can be sued for torts such as:
  - Negligence (e.g., failure to maintain safe public infrastructure)
  - Breach of contract (e.g., failing to fulfill contractual obligations)
  - Nuisance (e.g., public nuisance caused by government projects)

State Accountability in Modern Context:

- The modern trend has moved towards greater accountability of the state for its non-sovereign activities, particularly in light of developments in human rights law, public interest litigation, and constitutional provisions protecting citizens' rights.
- The **Right to Information Act, 2005**, and other transparency laws have bolstered state accountability for non-sovereign functions.

Transition from Absolute Immunity to Restricted Liability

Sovereign Immunity Doctrine:

- The principle of **sovereign immunity** traditionally prevented the state from being sued for actions performed in the exercise of its sovereign functions. This immunity is based on the belief that the state, as the supreme authority, cannot be compelled to answer lawsuits.
- **Common Law**: The doctrine of sovereign immunity is deeply embedded in common law traditions. Historically, it was assumed that the king (or sovereign) could do no wrong, and thus could not be held liable in tort.

Move Towards Limited Liability:

- In modern legal systems, there has been a shift from **absolute immunity** to a **restricted or qualified immunity**. This transition is grounded in the principle that the state should be accountable for its wrongful acts, especially in non-sovereign functions.
- **Indian Perspective**: Article 300 of the Indian Constitution provides that the Union and State Governments can be sued in tort for acts done in their non-sovereign capacity. However, immunity applies when the state acts in its sovereign capacity, as outlined in **Kasturilal Ralia Ram v. State of Uttar Pradesh**.
- **Public Law Reforms**: With the growing recognition of the state's responsibility to ensure fairness, justice, and public welfare, judicial reforms and legislative actions have gradually eroded the concept of absolute immunity for the state.

Modern Examples of Restricted Liability:

- **Government Liability for Tortious Acts**: Under contemporary law, the state can be held liable for torts arising out of acts like negligence, defamation, or violations of fundamental rights when it acts in its administrative or business capacity.
- **Public Services and Enterprises**: When the state runs public services or commercial enterprises, it faces the same accountability as a private entity. This includes instances where the state is responsible for accidents, breaches of duty, or contract violations.
- **Judicial Decisions**: The shift in the judicial approach has been influenced by rulings that emphasize the need for government accountability, particularly in **public interest litigation (PIL)**, where courts have ordered compensation for citizens adversely affected by the state's negligence in non-sovereign functions.

CONSUMER PROTECTION ACT

The Consumer Protection Act (CPA) is a socio-economic legislation aimed at protecting consumer rights, providing speedy redressal of grievances, and promoting consumer welfare in India. It reflects the principle of caveat venditor (let the seller beware), shifting from the traditional caveat emptor (let the buyer beware).

Historical Background

- Consumer Protection Act, 1986: Enacted on December 24, 1986, to address consumer exploitation in a growing market economy.
  - ❑ Inspired by UN Guidelines for Consumer Protection (1985).
  - ❑ Established a three-tier quasi-judicial redressal system.
- Consumer Protection Act, 2019: Replaced the 1986 Act, effective from July 20, 2020.
  - ❑ Responds to modern challenges like e-commerce, unfair trade practices, and product liability.
  - ❑ Notified via Gazette of India and passed by Parliament in August 2019.

Objectives

- Protect consumers from defective goods, deficient services, and unfair practices.
- Provide a simple, speedy, and inexpensive redressal mechanism.
- Promote consumer education and awareness.
- Ensure accountability of manufacturers, sellers, and service providers.

Key Definitions (CPA, 2019)

- **Consumer (Section 2(7)):**
  - ❑ A person who buys goods or hires services for personal use (not for resale or commercial purposes).
  - ❑ Includes users of goods/services with the buyer's consent (e.g., family members).
  - ❑ Excludes commercial use unless for self-employment (e.g., a tailor buying a sewing machine).
- **Goods (Section 2(21)):** Movable property as defined under the Sale of Goods Act, 1930 (e.g., food, appliances).
- **Service (Section 2(42)):** Any service (e.g., banking, telecom, healthcare) except free services or personal services under a contract.
- **Defect (Section 2(10)):** Fault or imperfection in goods affecting quality, quantity, or safety.
- **Deficiency (Section 2(11)):** Fault, inadequacy, or shortcoming in service delivery.
- **Unfair Trade Practice (Section 2(47)):** Practices like misleading advertisements, false claims, or refusal to issue receipts.
- **Product Liability (Section 2(34)):** Responsibility of a manufacturer/seller for harm caused by defective goods or services.

Rights of Consumers (Section 2(9))

The CPA, 2019 codifies six consumer rights:

- Right to Safety: Protection against hazardous goods/services.
- Right to be Informed: Access to information about quality, price, and safety.
- Right to Choose: Variety of goods/services at competitive prices.
- Right to be Heard: Representation in consumer forums.
- Right to Redressal: Fair settlement of grievances.
- Right to Consumer Education: Awareness of rights and remedies.

Consumer Protection Authorities

A. Central Consumer Protection Authority (CCPA) (Sections 10-18)

- Established: Under CPA, 2019 (not in 1986 Act).
- Purpose: Regulate consumer rights violations, unfair trade practices, and misleading advertisements.
- Composition: Chief Commissioner + Commissioners, appointed by the Central Government.
- Powers:
  - ❑ Investigate suo motu or on complaints.
  - ❑ Recall defective goods, order refunds, or discontinue unfair practices.
  - ❑ Impose penalties: Up to ₹ 10 lakh (first offense) and ₹ 50 lakh (subsequent offenses) for false ads (Section 21).
  - ❑ File class action suits.

- **Example:** Can penalize celebrities endorsing misleading ads (e.g., exaggerated health product claims).

B. Consumer Disputes Redressal Commissions (Sections 28-73)

A three-tier quasi-judicial system:

- **District Consumer Disputes Redressal Commission (DCDRC):**
  - Jurisdiction: Claims up to ₹ 1 crore (Section 34(1)).
  - President + at least 2 members (Section 28(2)).
  - Territorial Jurisdiction: Where opposite party resides, operates, or cause of action arises, or complainant resides (Section 34(2)).
- **State Consumer Disputes Redressal Commission (SCDRC):**
  - Jurisdiction: Claims from ₹ 1 crore to ₹ 10 crore; appeals from DCDRC within 45 days (Section 47(1)).
  - Composition: President + at least 4 members (Section 42(3)).
- **National Consumer Disputes Redressal Commission (NCDRC):**
  - Jurisdiction: Claims above ₹ 10 crore; appeals from SCDRC within 30 days (Section 58(1), 51).
  - Composition: President (Supreme Court judge, serving/retired) + at least 4 members (Section 54).

Key Provisions of CPA, 2019

A. Product Liability (Sections 82-87)

- **Concept:** Manufacturer, seller, or service provider liable for harm caused by defective goods/services.
- **Liability Conditions:**
  - **Manufacturer:** For manufacturing defects, poor design, or inadequate warnings.
  - **Seller:** For misrepresentation or failure to inform about defects.
  - **Service Provider:** For negligence or deficiency.
- **Exceptions:**
  - Plaintiff misused the product contrary to instructions.
  - Harm was unforeseeable.
- **Case:** Indian Medical Association v. V.P. Shantha (1995) – Services (e.g., medical) under CPA; reinforced in 2019.

B. E-Commerce (Section 2(16) & Rules)

- Covers online transactions.
- Obligations:
  - Display product details, return policies, and seller information.
  - Prohibit unfair practices (e.g., fake reviews).
- Consumer Protection (E-Commerce) Rules, 2020: Mandates transparency and accountability.

C. Unfair Contracts (Section 2(46))

- Declares contracts with one-sided terms void (e.g., excessive penalties, unilateral termination).

D. Mediation (Section 74)

- Alternative dispute resolution introduced in 2019.
- Courts can refer cases to mediation cells attached to commissions.

E. Penalties

- False Ads: Imprisonment up to 2 years + ₹ 10 lakh fine (Section 89).
- Non-Compliance with Orders: 1 month to 3 years imprisonment + ₹ 25,000 to ₹ 1 lakh fine (Section 72).

Filing a Complaint

- Who Can File (Section 2(5)):
  - Consumer, recognized consumer association, Central/State Government, or CCPA.
  - Class action by multiple consumers.
- Where to File: DCDRC/SCDRC/NCDRC based on pecuniary jurisdiction or residence of opposite party.
- Time Limit: Within 2 years from the cause of action (Section 69).
- Fee: Nominal; waived for indigent consumers.

Remedies

- Reliefs Available (Section 39):
  - Refund of price paid.
  - Compensation for loss/injury.
  - Removal of defects/deficiencies.
  - Cease unfair practices.
  - Punitive damages in severe cases.
- Appeals: 45 days to file; higher forum can condone delay if justified.

Differences Between CPA, 1986 and CPA, 2019

Aspect	CPA, 1986	CPA, 2019
Pecuniary Jurisdiction	District: Up to ₹ 20 lakh; State: ₹ 20 lakh-₹ 1 crore; National: Above ₹ 1 crore	District: Up to ₹ 1 crore; State: ₹ 1 crore-₹ 10 crore; National: Above ₹ 10 crore
CCPA	Not established	Established (Section 10)
E-Commerce	Not covered	Explicitly included (Section 2(16))
Product Liability	Not defined	Detailed provisions (Sections 82-87)
Mediation	Not available	Introduced (Section 74)
Filing Complaint	Only at opposite party's residence	At consumer's residence too (Sections 34(2), 47(4))

THE MOTOR VEHICLES ACT, 1988

The Motor Vehicles Act, 1988 (MV Act), consolidates and amends laws relating to motor vehicles in India, replacing the Motor Vehicles Act, 1939. It aims to regulate road transport, ensure road safety, and provide compensation for victims of motor accidents. Key provisions relevant to no-fault liability, third-party insurance, and claims tribunals are detailed below.

No-Fault Liability

Definition

- No-fault liability (also called "absolute liability" in this context) means the owner or insurer of a vehicle is liable to pay compensation for death or injury caused by the vehicle's use, regardless of whether negligence or fault is proven.
- Introduced to ensure swift relief to victims without prolonged litigation over fault.

Legal Provision

- Section 140: "Liability to pay compensation in certain cases on the principle of no-fault."
  - ❑ Applies to death or permanent disablement caused by a motor vehicle accident.
  - ❑ Compensation is fixed and payable even if the accident was not due to the fault of the vehicle's owner/driver.

Compensation Amount

- As per Section 140(2) (amended over time):
  - ❑ Death: ₹ 50,000 (originally ₹ 25,000; increased by amendment).
  - ❑ Permanent Disablement: ₹ 25,000 (originally ₹ 12,000; increased by amendment).
- Note: The Motor Vehicles (Amendment) Act, 2019, under Section 161, enhanced interim relief under no-fault principles to ₹ 5,00,000 for death and ₹ 2,50,000 for grievous hurt (via the Solatium Fund), though Section 140 remains operational for fixed amounts.

Key Features

- No Proof of Fault Required: Unlike negligence-based claims under Section 166, fault or wrongful act need not be established.
- Interim Relief: Payable immediately as a preliminary measure; adjustable against final awards.
- Mandatory: Cannot be avoided by the owner/insurer unless the vehicle was not involved.
- Permanent Disablement: Defined under Section 142 – Includes loss of limb, sight, hearing, or any permanent incapacity.

Conditions

- Claimant must prove:
  - ❑ The accident involved a motor vehicle.
  - ❑ It resulted in death or permanent disablement.
- No defense like contributory negligence applies here.

Case Law

- **Minu B. Mehta v. Balkrishna Ramchandra Nayan (1977):** Pre-1988 case; Supreme Court rejected no-fault liability under the 1939 Act, prompting its inclusion in the 1988 Act.
- **Shivaji Dayanu Patil v. Vatschala Uttam More (1991):** No-fault liability upheld even in hit-and-run cases, emphasizing victim protection.

Third-Party Insurance

Definition

- Third-party insurance is a compulsory insurance policy under the MV Act to cover liability arising from injury, death, or property damage caused to a "third party" (anyone other than the driver/owner or insurer) by the use of a motor vehicle.

Legal Provision

- Section 146: "Necessity for insurance against third-party risk."
  - ❑ No motor vehicle can be used in a public place without a valid third-party insurance policy, except for vehicles owned by Central/State Governments (if exempted).

- Section 147: "Requirements of policies and limits of liability."
  - ❑ Policy must cover:
    - Death or bodily injury to any person (unlimited liability).
    - Damage to property of a third party (up to ₹ 6,000 originally; increased to ₹ 7.5 lakh post-2019 amendment for certain cases).
    - Liability under workmen's compensation laws for employees (e.g., drivers).

Key Features

- **Compulsory Nature:** Non-compliance is an offense under Section 196 (fine up to ₹ 2,000 and/or imprisonment up to 3 months for first offense; increased penalties under 2019 amendment).
- **Third Party Defined:** Anyone other than the insured (owner/driver) and insurer (e.g., pedestrians, other vehicle users).
- **Scope:**
  - ❑ Covers accidents in public places (roads, highways, etc.).
  - ❑ Excludes contractual liability or damage to the insured's own vehicle/property.
- **Insurer's Role:** Insurer must indemnify the insured against third-party claims, subject to policy terms.

Exceptions (Section 149)

- Insurer not liable if:
  - ❑ Vehicle used for unauthorized purposes (e.g., racing).
  - ❑ Driver lacked a valid license.
  - ❑ Breach of policy conditions (e.g., overloading).
- Pay and Recover: Insurer may pay the third party and recover from the insured if breach is proven (National Insurance Co. Ltd. v. Swaran Singh, 2004).

Case Law

- **New India Assurance Co. Ltd. v. Rula (2000):** Insurer liable for third-party claims even if the vehicle was stolen, reinforcing compulsory coverage.
- **United India Insurance Co. Ltd. v. Tilak Singh (2006):** Third-party insurance does not cover pillion riders unless explicitly included in the policy.

Amendments (2019)

- Motor Vehicle Accident Fund (Section 164A): Provides compensation for uninsured/underinsured vehicles, supplementing third-party insurance.

Claims Tribunals

Definition

- Motor Accident Claims Tribunals (MACTs) are specialized quasi-judicial bodies established under the MV Act to adjudicate compensation claims arising from motor vehicle accidents.

Legal Provision

- Section 165: "Claims Tribunals."
  - ❑ State Governments may constitute MACTs for specified areas.
  - ❑ Composition: One or more members (usually a judicial officer of District Judge rank).
- Section 166: "Application for compensation."
  - ❑ Claims for death, injury, or property damage can be filed before the tribunal.

Jurisdiction

- Who Can Claim (Section 166(1)):
  - ❑ Injured person.
  - ❑ Legal heirs of the deceased.
  - ❑ Owner of damaged property.
  - ❑ Authorized agent of the above.
- Where to File:
  - ❑ Tribunal where:
    - The accident occurred.
    - Claimant resides/works.
    - Defendant resides.
- **Time Limit:** Originally 6 months (Section 166(3)); limitation removed by 1994 amendment – no bar now, subject to reasonable delay explanation.

Types of Claims

- Fault-Based Claims (Section 166):
  - ❑ Requires proof of negligence or wrongful act.
  - ❑ Compensation based on actual loss (e.g., medical expenses, loss of income).
- **No-Fault Claims (Section 140):** Fixed compensation without proving fault (as discussed above).
- **Hit-and-Run Cases (Section 161):** Compensation for unidentified vehicles: ₹ 25,000 (death) and ₹ 12,500 (grievous hurt); increased to ₹ 2 lakh and ₹ 50,000 by 2019 amendment.

Procedure

- Application: Filed with details of the accident, injury, and parties involved (Form under MV Rules).
- Evidence: Medical reports, FIR, witness statements, etc.
- Award: Tribunal determines compensation; enforceable as a civil court decree (Section 174).
- Appeal: Lies to High Court within 90 days (Section 173).

Compensation Calculation

- Factors (Section 168):
  - ❑ Age and income of the deceased/injured.
  - ❑ Multiplier method (based on age).
  - ❑ Loss of dependency, medical expenses, pain, and suffering.
- Case: *Sarla Verma v. Delhi Transport Corporation (2009)**:
  - ❑ Standardized multiplier method for consistency.

Case Law

- **Nagappa v. Gurudayal Singh (2003):** Tribunal can award compensation beyond the claimed amount if evidence justifies.
- **Reshma Kumari v. Madan Mohan (2013):** Structured formula for compensation reaffirmed.

Amendments (2019)

- Section 169(1): Simplified procedure; tribunals can adopt summary proceedings.
- Section 164: Interim relief on a no-fault basis streamlined.

THE COMPETITION ACT, 2002

The Competition Act, 2002, replaced the Monopolies and Restrictive Trade Practices Act, 1969 (MRTP Act), to promote competition, protect consumer interests, and ensure economic efficiency in India. Enacted on January 13, 2003, and enforced in phases (2003 for anti-competitive agreements and abuse of dominance; 2009 for combinations), it aligns with global competition law standards post-economic liberalization in 1991.

Prohibition of Certain Agreements

Legal Provision

- Section 3: "Anti-competitive agreements."
  - ❑ Prohibits agreements that cause or are likely to cause an Appreciable Adverse Effect on Competition (AAEC) in India.

Definition of Agreement (Section 2(b))

- Any arrangement, understanding, or action in concert, whether formal, informal, written, or oral.
- Includes cartels, joint ventures, or trade practices.

Types of Prohibited Agreements

- Section 3(3): Horizontal Agreements (Between competitors at the same level):
  - ❑ Presumed to have AAEC (Rule of Reason not required).
  - ❑ Examples:
    - ➾ Price Fixing: Agreeing to fix prices (e.g., cartels).
    - ➾ Output Restriction: Limiting production/supply.
    - ➾ Market Sharing: Dividing markets or customers.
    - ➾ Bid Rigging: Colluding in tenders/auctions.
  - ❑ **Exception:** Joint ventures enhancing efficiency (e.g., R&D collaboration) if proven beneficial.
- Section 3(4): Vertical Agreements (Between entities at different levels, e.g., manufacturer-distributor):
  - ❑ Evaluated under the Rule of Reason – AAEC must be proven.
  - ❑ Examples:
    - ➾ Tie-in Arrangements: Forcing buyers to purchase additional products.
    - ➾ Exclusive Supply/Distribution Agreements: Restricting dealings with competitors.
    - ➾ Resale Price Maintenance (RPM): Fixing minimum resale prices.
    - ➾ Refusal to Deal: Boycotting certain parties.
  - ❑ Exception: Agreements improving production/distribution or benefiting consumers.

Factors to Assess AAEC (Section 19(3))

- Barriers to entry.
- Market foreclosure.
- Reduced competition/innovation.
- Consumer harm vs. benefits (e.g., efficiency gains).

Exemptions

- Section 3(5):
  - ❑ Intellectual property rights (e.g., patents, copyrights) if reasonably exercised.
  - ❑ Export agreements enhancing India's global competitiveness.

Penalties (Section 27)

- Fine up to 10% of average turnover for the last 3 years.
- Cartels: Up to 3 times profit or 10% of turnover (whichever is higher) per year of violation.

Case Law

- **Builders Association of India v. Cement Manufacturers' Association (2012):** Cartelization in cement pricing; heavy penalties imposed.
- **Excel Crop Care Ltd. v. CCI (2017):** Bid rigging in pesticide tenders; Supreme Court upheld CCI's turnover-based penalty.

Abuse of Dominant Position

Legal Provision

- Section 4: "Abuse of dominant position."
  - ❑ Prohibits enterprises from abusing their dominance in a relevant market.

Key Concepts

- Dominant Position (Section 4, Explanation (a)):
  - ❑ Ability to operate independently of competitive forces or affect competitors/consumers/market in its favor.
  - ❑ Assessed under Section 19(4):
    - Market share.
    - Size/resources of enterprise.
    - Barriers to entry.
    - Consumer dependence.
- Relevant Market (Section 2(r)):
  - ❑ Product Market: Goods/services interchangeable by consumers.
  - ❑ Geographic Market: Area where competition conditions are uniform.

Abusive Practices (Section 4(2))

- **Imposing Unfair/Discriminatory Conditions:** E.g., unfair pricing or terms of sale.
- **Predatory Pricing:** Selling below cost to eliminate competitors (Explanation (b)).
- **Limiting Production/Markets:** Restricting supply or technical development.
- **Denying Market Access:** Blocking competitors (e.g., exclusive contracts).
- **Leveraging Dominance:** Using strength in one market to enter/protect another (e.g., bundling).

Key Features

- Dominance itself is not illegal; only its abuse is prohibited.
- No requirement of intent; effect-based assessment.

Remedies (Section 27 & 28)

- Cease and desist orders.
- Fine up to 10% of average turnover for 3 years.
- Division of enterprise (Section 28) in extreme cases.

Case Law

- **MCX Stock Exchange v. National Stock Exchange (2011):** NSE abused dominance via predatory pricing in currency derivatives; fined ₹55 crore.
- **BCCI v. CCI (2017):** BCCI abused dominance in cricket by denying market access to rival leagues.

Regulation of Combinations

Legal Provision

- Section 5 & 6: "Regulation of combinations."
  - ❑ Governs mergers, acquisitions, and amalgamations that may adversely affect competition.

Definition of Combination (Section 5)

- Thresholds (updated via notifications, e.g., 2023):
  - ❑ Assets: India > ₹ 2,000 crore or worldwide > \$1 billion (with ₹ 500 crore in India).
  - ❑ Turnover: India > ₹ 6,000 crore or worldwide > \$3 billion (with ₹ 1,500 crore in India).
  - ❑ Group Thresholds: Higher limits for enterprises under common control.
- Types:
  - ❑ Acquisition of control, shares, or assets.
  - ❑ Mergers/amalgamations.

Regulation (Section 6)

- Section 6(1): No combination causing AAEC is allowed.
- Section 6(2): Mandatory prior approval from the Competition Commission of India (CCI) for combinations exceeding thresholds.
  - ❑ Notice within 30 days of board approval or execution of agreement.
- Suspensory Effect: Combination cannot take effect until CCI approval or 210 days lapse.

Assessment of AAEC (Section 20(4))

- Market share post-combination.
- Barriers to entry.
- Level of competition remaining.
- Benefits (e.g., innovation, efficiency) vs. adverse effects.

Exemptions

- De Minimis Exemption: Small transactions below CCI-notified thresholds (e.g., assets < ₹ 450 crore or turnover < ₹ 1,250 crore as of 2023).
- Schedule I: Exempted combinations (e.g., minority shareholding for investment).

Penalties (Section 43A)

- Failure to notify: Fine up to 1% of turnover or assets (whichever is higher).

Procedure

- Phase I Review: 30 working days for prima facie approval/rejection.
- Phase II Review: Detailed investigation (up to 210 days) if AAEC suspected.
- CCI can approve, reject, or approve with modifications (Section 31).

Case Law

- **Jet-Etihad Case (2013):** CCI approved with conditions (e.g., slot sharing) to prevent AAEC.
- **Walmart-Flipkart (2018):** Approved as no significant AAEC found in e-commerce market.

Enforcement Mechanism

- **Competition Commission of India (CCI) (Sections 7-18):**
  - ❑ Quasi-judicial body; investigates and adjudicates.
  - ❑ Powers: Inquire, impose penalties, and regulate combinations.
- **National Company Law Appellate Tribunal (NCLAT):** Appeals from CCI orders (Section 53A).
- Supreme Court: Final appeal under Section 53T.

Amendments (Competition Amendment Act, 2023)

- **Key Changes:**
  - ❑ Penalty on Global Turnover: Fines based on global income for anti-competitive practices.
  - ❑ Deal Value Threshold: Combinations > ₹ 2,000 crore require approval, even below asset/turnover limits.
  - ❑ Settlement & Commitment: Parties can settle or commit to corrective measures (Sections 48A, 48B).
  - ❑ Cartel Leniency Plus: Reduced penalties for whistleblowers disclosing additional cartels.

Constitutional Basis

- **Article 38 & 39:** Promote social justice and economic equity, supporting competition law objectives.

MULTIPLE CHOICE QUESTIONS

1. What is the key difference between tort law and criminal law?

A. Requirement of intent for liability
B. Duty owed to an individual vs. duty owed to society
C. Nature of penalties
D. All of the above

2. How is 'Res ipsa loquitur' utilized in tort law?

A. To infer breach of duty without explicit proof of negligence
B. To determine punitive damages
C. To dismiss cases lacking tangible evidence
D. To establish intentional misconduct

3. Is physical damage essential to establish trespass to chattels?

A. True
B. False
C. Only in specific legal systems
D. Only if substantial interference is proven

4. Who bears the burden of proof in tort litigation?

A. Always the defendant
B. Always the plaintiff
C. The defendant in strict liability cases
D. The plaintiff, except in defamation cases

5. **Assertion (A):** A doctor can be liable for patient injuries even without intent to harm.

Reason (R): This liability is based on strict liability rather than negligence.

A. Both A and R are true, and R is the correct explanation of A
B. Both A and R are true, but R is not the correct explanation of A
C. A is true, R is false
D. A is false, R is true

6. Match the following legal terms with their definitions and choose the correct set of matches:

Legal Terms	Definitions
A. Conversion	1. Unauthorized use of someone else's trademark
B. Defamation	2. Wrongful possession or use of another's property
C. Trademark Infringement	3. Publication of false information damaging to reputation

A. A-2, B-3, C-1　　B. A-3, B-1, C-2
C. A-1, B-2, C-3　　D. A-3, B-2, C-1

7. Arrange these steps in proving negligence in the correct sequence:

1. Establish that the defendant had a duty of care.
2. Prove that the defendant breached this duty.
3. Link the breach to the cause of harm.
4. Confirm harm resulted in damages.

A. 1, 2, 3, 4　　B. 1, 3, 2, 4
C. 2, 1, 4, 3　　D. 3, 2, 1, 4

8. The principle of ______ dictates liability without fault for inherently risky activities.

A. Contributory Negligence
B. Comparative Negligence
C. Strict Liability
D. Vicarious Liability

9. Which of the following is not a defense in a negligence lawsuit?

A. Comparative negligence
B. Assumption of risk
C. Contributory negligence
D. Intentional infliction

10. In which case is the 'duty of care' not applicable?

A. A doctor treating a patient
B. A driver towards pedestrians
C. A company disposing of waste
D. A bystander witnessing an accident

11. A business cannot be held liable for torts committed by its employees if the employees were acting outside the scope of their employment.

A. True
B. False
C. True, only if the employer was unaware
D. False, unless there is a policy against such acts

12. The economic loss rule prevents recovery of purely economic damages in the absence of personal injury or property damage.

A. True
B. False
C. True, except in contract breaches
D. False, except in product liability cases

13. **Assertion (A):** The 'eggshell skull' rule requires a defendant to take full responsibility for the plaintiff's injuries even if unexpectedly severe.

Reason (R): The rule is intended to promote fairness and accountability in tort law.

A. Both A and R are true, and R is the correct explanation of A
B. Both A and R are true, but R is not the correct explanation of A
C. A is true, R is false
D. A is false, R is true

14. Match the following legal terms with their definitions and choose the correct set of matches:

Legal Terms	Definitions
A. Nuisance	1. Unlawful interference with the use of property without permission
B. Slander	2. Oral defamatory statement
C. Battery	3. Intentional and harmful physical contact

A. A-1, B-2, C-3
B. A-3, B-1, C-2
C. A-2, B-3, C-1
D. A-3, B-2, C-1

15. Place these legal concepts in the order they typically appear in a tort case analysis:

1. Causation　　2. Breach
3. Damages　　4. Duty

A. 4, 2, 1, 3　　B. 4, 1, 2, 3
C. 2, 4, 3, 1　　D. 1, 3, 2, 4

16. In tort law, the ______ test is used to determine foreseeability of harm resulting from a breach of duty.

A. Reasonable person
B. Proximate cause
C. Risk-utility
D. But-for

17. Which tort involves intrusion upon the seclusion of another?
A. Appropriation
B. Public disclosure of private facts
C. False light
D. Invasion of privacy

18. A defamatory statement made in writing and published is termed:
A. Libel
B. Slander
C. Defamation per se
D. Spoken defamation

19. Which of the following is not a required element of the tort of misrepresentation?
A. A false statement of material fact
B. Intent to deceive
C. Justifiable reliance by the plaintiff
D. Physical harm to the plaintiff

20. The tort of ______ protects an individual from unauthorized use of their likeness for commercial purposes.
A. Trespass
B. Appropriation
C. Assault
D. Nuisance

21. Which principle underlies the concept of vicarious liability?
A. Direct liability for one's actions
B. Liability for another's actions under one's control
C. Strict liability regardless of fault
D. Contributory negligence

22. What does the principle of 'duty of care' require?
A. Intention to cause harm
B. Knowledge of potential harm
C. A legal obligation to avoid acts or omissions which can be reasonably foreseen to injure others
D. Proof of damage caused by breach

23. Liability in tort law is always based on fault.
A. True
B. False
C. True, except in strict liability cases
D. False, except in negligence cases

24. The 'but-for' test is used to determine causation in tort law.
A. True
B. False
C. Only in medical malpractice cases
D. Only in product liability cases

25. **Assertion (A):** Transferred intent is applicable in cases where the defendant intends to harm one individual but unintentionally harms another.

Reason (R): The principle of transferred intent helps to maintain the element of intent necessary for certain torts.
A. Both A and R are true, and R is the correct explanation of A
B. Both A and R are true, but R is not the correct explanation of A
C. A is true, R is false
D. A is false, R is true

26. Match the following principles with their correct descriptions and choose the correct set of matches:

Principles	Definitions
A. Negligence	1. Failure to exercise reasonable care
B. Contributory Negligence	2. Plaintiff's own negligence partially caused the harm
C. Nuisance	3. Interference with use and enjoyment of land

A. A-1, B-2, C-3
B. A-3, B-1, C-2
C. A-2, B-3, C-1
D. A-3, B-2, C-1

27. Arrange these principles in the order they are generally considered in a tort case:
1. Causation
2. Remoteness of damage
3. Breach of duty
4. Duty of care

A. 4, 3, 1, 2
B. 4, 1, 3, 2
C. 3, 4, 2, 1
D. 2, 1, 4, 3

28. The principle of ______ is applied when a plaintiff's failure to take reasonable care contributes to their harm.
A. Comparative Negligence
B. Contributory Negligence
C. Vicarious Liability
D. Strict Liability

29. Which of the following is an example of a strict liability tort?
A. Car accident due to reckless driving
B. Harm caused by a defective product
C. Emotional distress from intentional insult
D. Injury from a dog bite in a jurisdiction with a "one-bite" rule

30. Which tort doctrine is used to allocate damages when both parties are at fault?

A. Joint liability
B. Several liability
C. Comparative negligence
D. Contributory negligence

31. A landowner has an absolute right to use their property in any manner they choose, regardless of the impact on neighbors.

A. True
B. False
C. True, unless zoning laws apply
D. False, unless there's a nuisance

32. The attractive nuisance doctrine applies only to children trespassing on property.

A. True
B. False
C. True, specifically under the age of 12
D. False, it applies to all trespassers

33. Assertion (A): In tort law, the foreseeability of harm is a critical factor in establishing the duty of care.

Reason (R): Foreseeability is used to determine if the harm was predictable and thus preventable by the defendant.

A. Both A and R are true, and R is the correct explanation of A
B. Both A and R are true, but R is not the correct explanation of A
C. A is true, R is false
D. A is false, R is true

34. Match the following legal terms with their appropriate definitions:

Legal Terms	Definitions
A. Proximate Cause	1. The doctrine that infers negligence from the mere occurrence of certain types of accidents
B. Res Ipsa Loquitur	2. Entering onto land without permission
C. Trespass to Land	3. A cause that is legally sufficient to result in liability

A. A-3, B-1, C-2
B. A-2, B-3, C-1
C. A-1, B-2, C-3
D. A-2, B-1, C-3

35. Order these elements as they would typically be evaluated in determining liability in tort law:

1. Legal cause
2. Breach of duty
3. Actual harm
4. Existence of a duty

A. 4, 2, 3, 1
B. 4, 1, 2, 3
C. 2, 4, 1, 3
D. 3, 4, 1, 2

36. The concept of ________ is critical when the harm is caused by multiple potential causes and involves determining which cause was actually responsible.

A. Joint and Several Liability
B. But-for Causation
C. Market Share Liability
D. Proximate Cause

37. Which defense can be used in a tort claim if the harm occurred while the plaintiff was engaging in an illegal act?

A. Illegality
B. Assumption of risk
C. Contributory negligence
D. Comparative negligence

38. What does the legal principle of 'respondeat superior' entail?

A. An employer is liable for the actions of employees performed within the course of their employment
B. A principal is responsible for the actions of their agent
C. A landlord is liable for injuries to tenants due to defects in the lease property
D. Both A and B

39. The principle of 'indemnity' in tort law allows a defendant to seek compensation from a third party who is ultimately responsible for the loss.

A. True
B. False
C. True, only in cases involving multiple defendants
D. False, indemnity applies only in contractual relationships

40. Assertion (A): A manufacturer can be held liable under the doctrine of strict product liability even if all possible care was taken in the production of the product.

Reason (R): Strict product liability is concerned with the safety of the product itself, regardless of the manufacturer's efforts to avoid defects.

A. Both A and R are true, and R is the correct explanation of A
B. Both A and R are true, but R is not the correct explanation of A
C. A is true, R is false
D. A is false, R is true

41. What does the defense of consent typically involve in tort cases?

A. The plaintiff agreed to bear any risk of harm that occurred.

B. The defendant had no intention to cause harm.

C. The harm was unavoidable due to natural causes.

D. The plaintiff was also negligent.

42. Which defense is most appropriate when the defendant had to act in a harmful way to prevent a greater harm from occurring?

A. Necessity
B. Duress
C. Self-defense
D. Mistake

43. The defense of 'self-defense' justifies intentional harm if it is necessary to protect oneself from harm.

A. True

B. False

C. True, but only if the harm is life-threatening

D. False, it applies only in criminal law

44. Statute of limitations does not apply if the harm is ongoing.

A. True

B. False

C. True, only in cases of continuous nuisance

D. False, it applies to all cases after a fixed period

45. Assertion (A): A defendant can use the defense of statutory authority if their actions were authorized by a law or statute.

Reason (R): Acting under statutory authority negates the unlawfulness of actions that would otherwise constitute a tort.

A. Both A and R are true, and R is the correct explanation of A

B. Both A and R are true, but R is not the correct explanation of A

C. A is true, R is false

D. A is false, R is true

46. Match the following defenses with their descriptions:

A. Contributory Negligence	1. The plaintiff knowingly and voluntarily engaged in a risky activity
B. Comparative Negligence	2. Fault is divided among the parties according to their degree of fault
C. Assumption of Risk	3. The plaintiff's own negligence contributed to the harm

A. A-3, B-2, C-1
B. A-2, B-3, C-1
C. A-1, B-3, C-2
D. A-3, B-1, C-2

47. Order the following steps for asserting a defense of contributory negligence:

1. Demonstrate that the plaintiff had knowledge of the risk.
2. Prove that the plaintiff's actions contributed to the harm.
3. Establish that a reasonable person would have avoided the behavior.
4. Assert the defense during the pleadings stage of a trial.

A. 4, 1, 2, 3
B. 1, 2, 3, 4
C. 4, 2, 1, 3
D. 1, 3, 2, 4

48. In cases of ______, the defendant may argue that the harm was unavoidable despite all reasonable precautions being taken.

A. inevitable accident

B. contributory negligence

C. assumption of risk

D. comparative negligence

49. Which of the following scenarios best exemplifies the defense of 'volenti non fit injuria'?

A. A spectator at a baseball game is injured by a foul ball.

B. A volunteer firefighter is injured while fighting a fire.

C. A pedestrian is hit by a car while using a crosswalk.

D. An employee is injured due to faulty equipment known to be dangerous by the employer.

50. In which case might the defense of necessity not apply as a justification for causing harm to another's property?

A. Breaking into a cabin to avoid freezing in a snowstorm

B. Cutting down a neighbor's tree because it is ugly and lowers property values

C. Entering a neighbor's property to escape a wild animal

D. Diverting flood water to a neighbor's land to protect one's own home

51. The defense of duress can be invoked when a tort is committed under the threat of immediate physical harm to oneself.

A. True

B. False

C. True, only if physical harm is imminent

D. False, it applies only in contract coercion

52. The defense of 'ex turpi causa non orituractio' (no right of action arises from a base cause) applies when the plaintiff's illegal actions contributed to their injury.

A. True

B. False

C. True, particularly in contributory negligence cases

D. False, it applies only to contractual disputes

53. **Assertion (A):** A property owner can be exempt from liability if an injury occurs due to an 'act of God.'

Reason (R): An 'act of God' refers to events outside human control, like natural disasters, which absolve property owners from standard negligence claims.

A. Both A and R are true, and R is the correct explanation of A

B. Both A and R are true, but R is not the correct explanation of A

C. A is true, R is false

D. A is false, R is true

54. Match the following defenses with their appropriate legal scenarios:

A. Immunity	1. A government official not held liable for decisions made while performing their official duties
B. Mistake	2. A person accidentally trespassing on another's land, believing it to be their own
C. Alter ego	3. Piercing the corporate veil to hold a company director personally liable for corporate wrongs

A. A-1, B-2, C-3 B. A-3, B-1, C-2

C. A-2, B-3, C-1 D. A-3, B-2, C-1

55. Arrange the steps for using the defense of 'independent contractor' to avoid liability in a tort case:

1. Establish that the contractor was not under the control of the defendant.
2. Prove that the contractor was hired to perform the task.
3. Demonstrate that the harm was solely due to the contractor's actions.
4. Clarify the legal relationship to the court.

A. 2, 1, 4, 3 B. 2, 3, 1, 4

C. 4, 2, 1, 3 D. 1, 3, 2, 4

56. The legal principle of _______ allows defendants to limit their liability when the plaintiff knowingly exposes themselves to a dangerous situation.

A. assumption of risk

B. comparative negligence

C. contributory negligence

D. necessity

57. Which defense might a defendant claim if they accidentally injured a passerby while lawfully defending themselves from an aggressor?

A. Self-defense

B. Defense of others

C. Defense of property

D. Involuntary act

58. Under which condition can the defense of 'public necessity' be invoked?

A. To protect a private interest

B. To prevent a public disaster

C. To defend personal property

D. To settle private disputes

59. An employer can be held liable for torts committed by an employee acting within the scope of employment, even if the employer did not authorize the specific wrongful act.

A. True

B. False

C. True, unless the employer has explicit policies against such acts

D. False, unless the act benefited the employer

60. The defense of 'illegality' is not available if the illegal activity was unrelated to the injury sustained.

A. True

B. False

C. True, only if the plaintiff is convicted of the illegal activity

D. False, the presence of any illegal activity voids all claims

61. **Assertion (A):** The defense of 'double jeopardy' can be used in tort law to prevent a defendant from being tried twice for the same act.

Reason (R): Double jeopardy is a principle that only applies in criminal law to prevent multiple prosecutions for the same offense.

A. Both A and R are true, and R is the correct explanation of A

B. Both A and R are true, but R is not the correct explanation of A

C. A is false, R is true

D. A is true, R is false

62. Match the following terms to their appropriate scenarios related to defenses in tort law:

A. Qualified immunity	1. A police officer not held liable for breaking a driver's car window to rescue a child locked inside on a hot day
B. Inevitable accident	2. A driver who could not stop in time to avoid hitting a suddenly fallen tree in the road
C. Good Samaritan law	3. A bystander who helps at an accident scene and inadvertently exacerbates the victim's injury

A. A-1, B-2, C-3 B. A-3, B-1, C-2
C. A-2, B-3, C-1 D. A-3, B-2, C-1

63. Arrange the steps necessary to establish the defense of contributory negligence:
1. Show that the defendant had a duty to prevent harm.
2. Prove that the plaintiff's own negligence contributed to the harm.
3. Confirm that the plaintiff's negligence was a significant factor in causing the harm.
4. Argue the applicability of contributory negligence during legal arguments.

A. 1, 2, 3, 4 B. 4, 1, 2, 3
C. 1, 4, 2, 3 D. 4, 2, 3, 1

64. The defense of _______ protects defendants when they act under a mistaken belief that does not negate the voluntary nature of their act but demonstrates a lack of wrongful intent.
A. mistake of fact B. mistake of law
C. involuntary action D. non est factum

65. Which element is not required to establish negligence?
A. Duty of care
B. Breach of duty
C. Intention to harm
D. Damage caused by the breach

66. A private nuisance is best described as:
A. An interference with the public's general right
B. An interference with a person's use or enjoyment of their property
C. A temporary use of someone's land without permission
D. Defamation of a person's character

67. Trespass to land requires the physical presence of the trespasser on the property.
A. True
B. False
C. True, except when objects are involved
D. False, intent to trespass is enough

68. Defamation requires the false statement to be made to a third party.
A. True
B. False
C. True, only if the statement is written
D. False, making it to the concerned party is sufficient

69. **Assertion (A):** You can commit trespass to land even if you enter the property accidentally.

Reason (R): Trespass to land does not require the intent to trespass, only the intent to enter the land.
A. Both A and R are true, and R is the correct explanation of A
B. Both A and R are true, but R is not the correct explanation of A
C. A is true, R is false
D. A is false, R is true

70. Match the following torts with their appropriate legal definitions:

A. Negligence	1. An act that breaches a duty to take care resulting in damage to another
B. Nuisance	2. An interference with someone's quiet enjoyment of their land
C. Trespass	3. Unlawful physical intrusion into another's property
D. Defamation	4. False statement harming another's reputation

A. A-1, B-2, C-3, D-4
B. A-4, B-3, C-2, D-1
C. A-2, B-1, C-4, D-3
D. A-3, B-4, C-1, D-2

71. Place the steps to prove defamation in the correct sequence:
1. Prove the statement was false.
2. Establish the statement was published.
3. Show the statement caused harm.
4. Identify the statement concerned the plaintiff.

A. 4, 2, 1, 3 B. 2, 4, 1, 3
C. 1, 2, 3, 4 D. 3, 1, 4, 2

72. In the tort of negligence, the _______ test is often used to determine whether a duty of care was breached.
A. reasonable person
B. legal duty
C. foreseeability
D. proximate cause

73. Which factor is not considered when evaluating whether an interference qualifies as a nuisance?
A. The nature of the interference
B. The duration of the interference
C. The economic status of the defendant
D. The location where the interference occurs

74. What must a plaintiff prove in a case of slander, which is not required in a case of libel?
A. That the statement was published to a third party
B. That the statement was false
C. That the statement caused specific damage
D. That the statement concerned the plaintiff

75. The 'coming to the nuisance' defense can justify causing a nuisance if the plaintiff moved to the location knowing the nuisance existed.
A. True
B. False
C. True, only if the nuisance is a longstanding industrial activity
D. False, unless the nuisance has ceased and then restarted

76. Trespass to chattels requires actual damage to the property for liability to arise.
A. True
B. False
C. True, only in cases involving real estate
D. False, mere interference is sufficient

77. **Assertion (A):** You can be liable for nuisance if your legally permitted activities disturb your neighbor's sleep.

Reason (R): Even lawful activities can constitute a nuisance if they substantially and unreasonably interfere with others' use and enjoyment of their property.
A. Both A and R are true, and R is the correct explanation of A
B. Both A and R are true, but R is not the correct explanation of A
C. A is true, R is false
D. A is false, R is true

78. Match the torts with the elements that must be proven:

A. Negligence	1. Unlawful entry onto the property
B. Nuisance	2. Unreasonable use of one's property causing harm
C. Trespass	3. Breach of a duty of care causing damages
D. Defamation	4. False statement made publicly causing reputation harm

A. A-3, B-2, C-1, D-4
B. A-4, B-1, C-3, D-2
C. A-2, B-3, C-4, D-1
D. A-1, B-4, C-2, D-3

79. What is the correct sequence of establishing a case of trespass to land?
1. Identify the defendant's entry onto the property.
2. Prove the entry was intentional.
3. Establish that the entry was unauthorized.
4. Demonstrate harm or interference.

A. 1, 2, 3, 4
B. 2, 1, 3, 4
C. 3, 1, 2, 4
D. 1, 3, 2, 4

80. The _______ rule in defamation cases states that certain statements are so inherently damaging that the plaintiff does not need to prove actual harm to their reputation.
A. per se
B. per quod
C. actual malice
D. strict liability

81. Which of the following best illustrates the defense of 'absolute privilege' in defamation cases?
A. A person repeating rumors about a neighbor in a community forum.
B. A journalist publishing unverified information about a celebrity.
C. A legislator making statements during a legislative session.
D. A business owner accusing a competitor during a promotional event.

82. In the context of trespass, which scenario would likely constitute a continuing trespass?
A. A neighbor places a fence that encroaches on your property and leaves it there indefinitely.
B. A delivery person mistakenly walks through your garden once.
C. Someone parks their car on your driveway blocking it temporarily.
D. A protester briefly steps onto your lawn during a march.

83. For a statement to be considered slanderous, it must always be spoken and heard by a third party.
A. True
B. False
C. True, except when dealing with slander per se
D. False, written statements can also be slanderous

84. The concept of ______ in nuisance law involves harm that is significant enough to be legally recognized, beyond mere trivial inconveniences or annoyances.

A. substantial interference
B. unreasonable interference
C. private nuisance
D. public nuisance

85. What is the primary test used to determine the remoteness of damages in tort law?
A. The "but for" test
B. The foreseeability test
C. The direct causation test
D. The substantial factor test

86. Which case is famously associated with establishing the modern rules for remoteness of damages in negligence?
A. Donoghue v. Stevenson
B. Palsgraf v. Long Island Railroad Co.
C. Caparo Industries plc v. Dickman
D. Hadley v. Baxendale

87. The remoteness of damages doctrine applies to both contractual and tortious claims.
A. True
B. False
C. True, only in common law jurisdictions
D. False, it applies exclusively to tort law

88. Remoteness of damages is concerned with the type of harm rather than the extent of the harm.
A. True
B. False
C. True, only when punitive damages are considered
D. False, it considers both type and extent

89. **Assertion (A):** A defendant may be held liable for all injuries caused in a car accident, even if some injuries were unusually severe due to pre-existing conditions.

Reason (R): The "eggshell skull" rule states that defendants must take their victims as they find them, which includes any unforeseeable exacerbations of pre-existing conditions.
A. Both A and R are true, and R is the correct explanation of A
B. Both A and R are true, but R is not the correct explanation of A
C. A is true, R is false
D. A is false, R is true

90. In tort law, damages that occur as a _______ consequence of an act are generally considered too remote to warrant compensation.
A. direct
B. foreseeable
C. natural
D. indirect

91. Which principle relates closely to remoteness of damages and is often considered when determining liability in tort cases?
A. Proximate cause
B. Contributory negligence
C. Vicarious liability
D. Res ipsa loquitur

92. In which scenario would the remoteness of damages likely exclude liability?
A. A motorist negligently crashes into a lamp post, and the lamp post falls onto a nearby car.
B. A motorist negligently crashes into a café, causing panic and resulting in a patron inside the café having a heart attack.
C. A construction company negligently leaves a hole uncovered, and a pedestrian walking normally trips and breaks a leg.
D. A homeowner negligently fails to clean ice off their front steps, and a delivery person slips and injures their back.

93. Remoteness of damages also limits the recovery of damages in cases involving multiple potential causes.
A. True
B. False
C. True, only if the causes are independent
D. False, remoteness does not apply to causation

94. A breach in the chain of causation always negates the application of remoteness of damages.
A. True
B. False
C. True, except in cases involving intentional torts
D. False, a new intervening act does not always break the chain

95. **Assertion (A):** Damages resulting from an unforeseeable natural disaster immediately following a negligent act are typically not recoverable.

Reason (R): Natural disasters are considered acts of God and are typically viewed as superseding, unforeseeable events that break the chain of causation in negligence cases.
A. Both A and R are true, and R is the correct explanation of A
B. Both A and R are true, but R is not the correct explanation of A
C. A is true, R is false
D. A is false, R is true

96. The _______ rule in remoteness of damages states that a defendant need only foresee the type of harm, not the precise manner or extent of the harm.

A. type rule
B. foreseeability rule
C. thin skull
D. scope of liability

97. Which of the following best describes the 'eggshell skull rule' in relation to remoteness of damages?
A. It limits the defendant's liability to what could reasonably be foreseen.
B. It allows for all damages regardless of their foreseeability if the initial harm is foreseeable.
C. It states that unforeseeable damages should not be compensated.
D. It applies only to physical injuries and not to psychological harm.

98. In which case would the remoteness of damages most likely exclude liability for the defendant?
A. A truck driver negligently causes a crash, and an unrelated bystander has a heart attack upon witnessing the crash.
B. A homeowner negligently fails to secure a rug, leading to a guest tripping and breaking an ankle.
C. An office manager fails to fix a known loose wiring issue, leading to an employee being electrocuted.
D. A grocery store leaves a spill unattended, and a customer slips but does not sustain injuries.

99. A business can be held liable for damages caused by an unforeseeable act of a third party intervening after the business's initial negligent act.
A. True
B. False
C. True, if the third party's act is related to the initial negligence
D. False, unless the third party's act was encouraged by the business

100. The principle of remoteness in damages is used to assess which aspect of a negligence claim?
A. The defendant's duty of care
B. The causation between the defendant's act and the ultimate harm
C. The appropriateness of the damages claimed
D. The foreseeability of the harm

101. **Assertion (A):** A manufacturer can be held liable for the harm caused by a defect in their product that results in an injury during normal use, even if the specific injury was highly unlikely.

Reason (R): In product liability, the foreseeability of any harm from a defect, not the specific type of injury, is sufficient to establish liability.

A. Both A and R are true, and R is the correct explanation of A
B. Both A and R are true, but R is not the correct explanation of A
C. A is true, R is false
D. A is false, R is true

102. Liability for damages that are ______ to the defendant's act are typically not compensable due to the principle of remoteness.
A. closely linked
B. unrelated
C. consequentially related
D. indirectly related

103. Which statement accurately reflects the application of the remoteness of damages principle in environmental tort cases?
A. Damages for pollution are limited only to immediate property damage and not long-term environmental harm.
B. Only damages that could have been foreseen at the time of the tortious act are compensable.
C. All damages, regardless of foreseeability, are compensable due to the strict liability nature of environmental harms.
D. Environmental damages are never considered too remote if the defendant has a history of regulatory violations.

104. How does the legal concept of 'intervening cause' relate to the remoteness of damages in tort law?
A. It reinforces the connection between the wrongful act and the damage, making more damages compensable.
B. It refers to instances where an external event breaks the chain of causation, potentially limiting liability.
C. It is used exclusively to increase the damages awarded to plaintiffs in tort cases.
D. It describes the necessity of a plaintiff's action contributing directly to the harm for damages to be considered.

105. What is the primary difference between strict liability and absolute liability?
A. Strict liability requires some fault; absolute liability does not.
B. Absolute liability applies only in criminal law; strict liability does not.
C. Strict liability may consider some defenses; absolute liability does not.
D. Absolute liability requires a higher degree of proof than strict liability.

106. Which scenario is an example of strict liability?

A. A company is held liable for injuries caused by a defective product, even though it followed all industry safety standards.

B. A driver is held liable for hitting a pedestrian who suddenly stepped into traffic.

C. A homeowner is held liable after their dog bites someone, despite the dog showing no prior signs of aggression.

D. A bar owner is held liable after a customer becomes intoxicated and injures another person.

107. In strict liability offenses, the defendant is liable even if they took all possible precautions to prevent harm.

A. True

B. False

C. True, only if the harm is to the public

D. False, only if the defendant is a commercial entity

108. Absolute liability is commonly applied in environmental law cases involving hazardous waste.

A. True

B. False

C. True, particularly in cases of illegal dumping

D. False, as environmental cases always require proof of negligence

109. Assertion (A): A person running a fireworks factory is held liable under absolute liability when an explosion occurs, injuring nearby residents.

Reason (R): The use of explosives in a populated area is considered so hazardous that liability does not depend on negligence or fault.

A. Both A and R are true, and R is the correct explanation of A

B. Both A and R are true, but R is not the correct explanation of A

C. A is true, R is false

D. A is false, R is true

110. The rule established in ______ is often cited as a foundational case for absolute liability in English law, particularly concerning hazardous industrial activities.

A. Rylands v. Fletcher

B. Donoghue v. Stevenson

C. Palsgraf v. Long Island Railroad Co.

D. Caparo Industries plc v. Dickman

111. Which of the following best exemplifies a situation where strict liability would be imposed?

A. A homeowner whose guest slips and falls due to a spilled drink

B. A construction company that uses explosives and causes damage to neighboring properties

C. A driver who accidentally hits a pedestrian while obeying traffic laws

D. A restaurant that fails to list allergens on the menu resulting in a customer's allergic reaction

112. What does the concept of absolute liability typically exclude from consideration in legal proceedings?

A. The financial status of the defendant

B. The foreseeability of the harm

C. The nature of the activity being performed

D. Defenses related to the reasonableness of the defendant's actions

113. Strict liability applies to all commercial activities.

A. True

B. False

C. True, only if the activities are regulated by federal law

D. False, it specifically applies to inherently dangerous activities

114. Absolute liability is enforced irrespective of any mitigating factors presented by the defendant.

A. True

B. False

C. True, particularly in environmental law cases

D. False, unless it involves nuclear incidents

115. Assertion (A): A zoo is held liable under strict liability when a wild animal escapes and causes damage, even if the zoo had state-of-the-art containment measures.

Reason (R): Keeping wild animals is considered an inherently dangerous activity that imposes strict liability on the keeper, irrespective of the precautions taken.

A. Both A and R are true, and R is the correct explanation of A

B. Both A and R are true, but R is not the correct explanation of A

C. A is true, R is false

D. A is false, R is true

116. In the landmark case of ______, the court established that the owner of a reservoir was absolutely liable when it burst, flooding a neighboring mine.

A. Rylands v. Fletcher

B. Greenman v. Yuba Power Products, Inc.

C. Donoghue v. Stevenson

D. MacPherson v. Buick Motor Co.

117. Which activity is commonly associated with absolute liability due to its potential for widespread harm?
A. Operating a pet grooming service
B. Running a professional lawn care service
C. Manufacturing pharmaceuticals
D. Handling radioactive materials

118. In the context of strict liability, which factor does NOT influence the imposition of liability?
A. The nature of the activity being inherently dangerous
B. The presence of fault or negligence by the defendant
C. Whether the activity is of common usage
D. The foreseeability of the harm caused

119. Strict liability is applicable in cases involving domestic animals if they cause harm.
A. True
B. False
C. True, only if the animal has a history of aggression
D. False, unless the animal is a species known for its dangerous propensities

120. Absolute liability eliminates the need for plaintiffs to prove which of the following in a lawsuit?
A. That the defendant owned the property or operation causing harm
B. That harm occurred as a result of the defendant's actions
C. That the defendant took every possible precaution to prevent harm
D. That the harm was foreseeable

121. **Assertion (A):** A chemical manufacturing company would be held liable under strict liability if toxins from its plant leaked into a nearby river, despite following all regulatory safety standards.

Reason (R): Activities involving hazardous substances are subject to strict liability because they pose a significant risk to public health and the environment, regardless of the precautions taken.
A. Both A and R are true, and R is the correct explanation of A
B. Both A and R are true, but R is not the correct explanation of A
C. A is true, R is false
D. A is false, R is true

122. The legal doctrine of _______ holds that an employer can be held strictly liable for the harmful acts of their employees if those acts are performed in the course of employment.
A. vicarious liability
B. contributory negligence
C. comparative negligence
D. respondeat superior

123. Which of the following best exemplifies the use of absolute liability in environmental law?
A. A manufacturer is held liable for runoff from its plant that pollutes a river, despite adhering to all current environmental regulations.
B. A company is fined for failing to report emissions that exceeded legal limits.
C. A homeowner is sued for improperly disposing of hazardous waste in their regular garbage.
D. A landscaping business is held responsible for using banned pesticides.

124. How does absolute liability impact industries involving high risks, such as nuclear power?
A. It discourages investment by increasing potential liability.
B. It ensures that any damages caused are automatically compensated by the operators.
C. It requires industries to obtain insurance to cover all potential damages.
D. Both B and C.

125. What is the primary principle behind the State's tortious liability in common law countries?
A. Sovereign immunity B. Vicarious liability
C. Absolute liability D. Strict liability

126. Under which condition can the State claim immunity from tortious liability?
A. When the tortious act is committed by a high-ranking official
B. When the act involves the exercise of sovereign functions
C. When the act is committed within the territorial jurisdiction of the State
D. When the act results in minimal damage

127. The State is always liable for the negligent acts of its employees in the performance of administrative functions.
A. True
B. False
C. True, unless the act was authorized by law
D. False, unless the act was unauthorized

128. A state cannot be sued in its own courts without its consent.
A. True
B. False
C. True, only in federal systems
D. False, only in unitary systems

129. Assertion (A): The State is liable for the tortious acts of its employees if the acts are judicial in nature.

Reason (R): Judges and other judicial officers are not liable for acts done in the exercise of their judicial functions provided they are acting within their jurisdiction.

A. Both A and R are true, and R is the correct explanation of A
B. Both A and R are true, but R is not the correct explanation of A
C. A is true, R is false
D. A is false, R is true

130. The doctrine of _______ protects the State from being sued without its consent, reflecting its sovereign status.

A. respondeat superior
B. sovereign immunity
C. vicarious liability
D. judicial immunity

131. Which of the following best illustrates an exception to the State's immunity from tortious liability?

A. A military commander makes a strategic decision in combat.
B. A state hospital's staff commits medical negligence.
C. A legislator makes defamatory comments during a parliamentary session.
D. A judge makes an erroneous decision leading to wrongful imprisonment.

132. What is required for a plaintiff to succeed in a claim against the State for tortious acts committed by its employees?

A. Proof that the employee acted within the scope of employment.
B. Proof that the State had direct knowledge of the employee's actions.
C. A demonstration that the employee acted against express instructions.
D. A legislative enactment explicitly permitting such a lawsuit.

133. The State can be held liable under the principle of strict liability for the actions of independent contractors it hires.

A. True
B. False
C. True, only if the State failed to supervise the contractors adequately
D. False, unless the contractors are performing sovereign functions

134. The State's immunity from liability is waived in cases involving violations of constitutional rights.

A. True
B. False
C. True, only if the violation involves law enforcement personnel
D. False, unless a specific statute provides for such a waiver

135. Assertion (A): A government agency is liable for environmental damage caused by illegal dumping of waste by its employees.

Reason (R): Environmental protection laws typically include provisions that override sovereign immunity, holding the State accountable for environmental violations.

A. Both A and R are true, and R is the correct explanation of A
B. Both A and R are true, but R is not the correct explanation of A
C. A is true, R is false
D. A is false, R is true

136. The legal principle of _______ mandates that the State compensate individuals for harm caused by unlawful acts of its employees, even if the acts were unauthorized.

A. vicarious liability
B. ultra vires
C. non-delegable duty
D. respondeat superior

137. Match the following situations with the appropriate legal principle related to State responsibility under the Indian Constitution:

A. Government fails to protect citizens during a communal riot	1. Failure of Constitutional Duty
B. State-owned railway negligently maintains tracks, causing a derailment	2. Tortious Liability
C. Public official demands a bribe for processing a license	3. Abuse of Public Office
D. State legislation violates fundamental right	4. Unconstitutional Action

A. A-1, B-2, C-3, D-4
B. A-2, B-1, C-3, D-4
C. A-3, B-2, C-1, D-4
D. A-1, B-3, C-4, D-2

138. Arrange the steps to pursue a tort claim against the State for damages caused by a public official:

1. Determine if the act was performed as part of official duties.
2. Establish that the act constituted a tortious conduct.
3. Check if there is a statutory waiver of immunity that applies.
4. File the lawsuit within the statutory deadlines.

A. 1, 2, 3, 4 B. 3, 1, 2, 4
C. 2, 1, 4, 3 D. 4, 3, 2, 1

139. Match the types of actions with their respective liability implications for the State:

A. An army officer negligently causing a traffic accident off-duty	1. Likely not liable as the officer was not acting within the scope of employment
B. A state-employed doctor committing malpractice during surgery	2. Liable under vicarious liability as the action was within the scope of employment
C. A municipal bus driver causing an accident due to reckless driving	3. Directly liable for failing to maintain safe premises
D. A government building's poor maintenance leading to a visitor's injury	4. Liability depends on the nature of the surgery and the laws regarding medical malpractice in public hospitals

A. A-1, B-4, C-2, D-3
B. A-2, B-1, C-4, D-3
C. A-3, B-2, C-1, D-4
D. A-4, B-3, C-2, D-1

140. Outline the procedural steps required for a civilian to claim damages from the State due to police misconduct during an arrest:

1. Verify the officer was acting within the scope of official duties.
2. Gather evidence of the alleged misconduct.
3. Determine if the conduct violates statutory or constitutional protections.
4. File a claim in accordance with governmental claims acts, if applicable.
5. Proceed to litigation if the claim is denied or unresolved.

A. 1, 2, 3, 4, 5 B. 2, 1, 3, 5, 4
C. 3, 2, 1, 4, 5 D. 2, 3, 1, 4, 5

141. What legal doctrine often exempts the State from liability when engaging in legislative actions?

A. Vicarious Liability
B. Sovereign Immunity
C. Strict Liability
D. Duty of Care

142. Which scenario would likely lead to State liability under the principle of vicarious liability?

A. A state employee causing an accident while driving a government vehicle on official duties.
B. A legislator defaming an individual during a press conference.
C. An off-duty police officer involved in a personal altercation.
D. A judge making an erroneous legal decision.

143. The State can be held liable for torts committed by its employees during the performance of discretionary functions.

A. True
B. False
C. True, only if the employee exceeded their authority
D. False, unless the employee acted outside the bounds of statutory authority

144. State liability for tortious acts requires establishing the same elements as in any tort case against an individual.

A. True
B. False
C. True, except when sovereign immunity applies
D. False, as the State is always immune from tort claims

145. **Assertion (A):** The State is liable for damages caused by a public school teacher who physically punishes a student, leading to injury.

Reason (R): Corporal punishment by public school teachers is considered an action outside the scope of educational duties and violates statutory protections for students.

A. Both A and R are true, and R is the correct explanation of A
B. Both A and R are true, but R is not the correct explanation of A
C. A is true, R is false
D. A is false, R is true

146. In cases of tortious acts, the State's immunity can be waived by ________ allowing claims for specific injuries caused by governmental actions or negligence.

A. legislative statute
B. judicial decree
C. executive orders
D. common law principles

147. What defines a 'consumer' under the Consumer Protection Act 1986?
A. Anyone who purchases a product or service for commercial use.
B. Anyone who buys any goods or hires any services for consideration.
C. Only individuals who purchase goods for resale or commercial purposes.
D. Any person who uses products for industrial purposes.

148. Which right under the Consumer Protection Act 1986 ensures that consumers are protected against marketing of goods and services that are hazardous to life and property?
A. Right to Safety
B. Right to Choose
C. Right to Information
D. Right to Consumer Education

149. The Consumer Protection Act 1986 establishes Consumer Disputes Redressal Commissions at the national, state, and district levels.
A. True
B. False
C. True, but only at the national and state levels
D. False, it establishes them only at the state and district levels

150. Consumer Protection Councils are established under the Act to advise on consumer-related policies and promote consumer rights.
A. True
B. False
C. True, only at the national level
D. False, they are advisory bodies without any real power

151. **Assertion (A):** The Consumer Protection Act 1986 allows for the filing of a complaint by a recognized consumer association, even if no specific consumer is identified.

Reason (R): This provision enables advocacy groups to take proactive steps in consumer protection, enhancing the Act's effectiveness.
A. Both A and R are true, and R is the correct explanation of A
B. Both A and R are true, but R is not the correct explanation of A
C. A is true, R is false
D. A is false, R is true

152. Under the Consumer Protection Act 1986, the ______ is empowered to investigate consumer complaints.
A. Central Consumer Protection Authority
B. District Consumer Forum
C. National Consumer Helpline
D. Consumer Affairs Department

153. What is the jurisdiction of the National Consumer Disputes Redressal Commission under the Consumer Protection Act 1986?
A. It handles cases where the claim is up to INR 1 crore.
B. It handles cases where the claim exceeds INR 10 crore.
C. It handles cases where the claim exceeds INR 1 crore.
D. It only handles cases transferred from State Commissions.

154. Which of the following is NOT a consumer right provided under the Consumer Protection Act 1986?
A. Right to be Heard
B. Right to Redress
C. Right to Bargain
D. Right to Consumer Education

155. The Consumer Protection Act 1986 provides for the establishment of consumer councils and other authorities for the settlement of consumers' disputes.
A. True
B. False
C. True, only at the national level
D. False, consumer councils do not settle disputes

156. Under the Consumer Protection Act, 1986, a consumer can file a complaint against unfair trade practices.
A. True
B. False
C. True, only if it involves defective goods
D. False, only state authorities can file such complaints

157. **Assertion (A):** The Consumer Protection Act, 1986, mandates that complaint hearings must be conducted in the presence of both parties involved in the dispute.

Reason (R): This provision ensures fairness and transparency in the resolution process, providing an opportunity for both parties to present their case.

A. Both A and R are true, and R is the correct explanation of A
B. Both A and R are true, but R is not the correct explanation of A
C. A is true, R is false
D. A is false, R is true

158. The Consumer Protection Act, 1986, was amended in 2019 to include e-commerce within its scope, addressing the _______ of online consumers.
A. rights B. liabilities
C. responsibilities D. privileges

159. Which of the following is a function of the Consumer Protection Councils formed under the Consumer Protection Act, 1986?
A. Adjudicating consumer disputes
B. Promoting and protecting the rights of consumers
C. Directly imposing penalties on defaulting manufacturers
D. Licensing of businesses involved in consumer goods

160. Under the Consumer Protection Act, 1986, the time limit to file a complaint from the date of occurrence of the cause of action is:
A. 2 years B. 3 years
C. 1 year D. No time limit

161. The Consumer Protection Act allows for complaints to be filed electronically.
A. True
B. False
C. True, only if the state commission permits
D. False, complaints must be filed in person

162. Compensation under the Consumer Protection Act can include reimbursement of legal costs incurred by the complainant.
A. True
B. False
C. True, but only in cases involving severe mal-practice
D. False, legal costs are never reimbursed

163. Assertion (A): The Consumer Protection Act, 1986 provides for the establishment of a consumer mediation cell at each of the District Forums and State Commissions.

Reason (R): Mediation cells help in amicable resolution of disputes, which can reduce the burden on formal adjudication channels and expedite the resolution process.

A. Both A and R are true, and R is the correct explanation of A
B. Both A and R are true, but R is not the correct explanation of A
C. A is true, R is false
D. A is false, R is true

164. The Consumer Protection Act, 1986, was amended to introduce a centralized regulatory authority known as the _______ to oversee issues related to consumer rights and unfair trade practices.
A. Consumer Affairs Bureau
B. Central Consumer Protection Authority
C. National Consumer Rights Commission
D. Consumer Regulatory Commission

165. Which of the following is true about the Consumer Protection Act, 1986 regarding product liability?
A. A manufacturer can only be held liable if there was a written warranty.
B. Product liability claims can be made even if the consumer has not directly purchased the product from the manufacturer.
C. Liability is limited to products and does not extend to services.
D. Consumers must prove negligence to succeed in a product liability claim.

166. Under the Consumer Protection Act, 1986, the 'right to choose' ensures which of the following?
A. Consumers can demand a refund if they are unsatisfied with a service.
B. Consumers have the freedom to select from a variety of products at competitive prices.
C. Consumers are entitled to receive all products advertised in a campaign.
D. Consumers can opt out of all commercial communications.

167. What does 'no fault liability' under the Motor Vehicles Act, 1988 imply?
A. Compensation is paid regardless of who is at fault in an accident.
B. The driver of the motor vehicle is always at fault in an accident.
C. Compensation is not available under any circumstances.
D. Only pedestrians can claim compensation without proving fault.

168. What is mandatory under the Motor Vehicles Act, 1988 regarding third-party insurance?
A. All vehicle owners must insure their vehicles against damage to property only.

B. All vehicle owners must have insurance to cover personal injuries to themselves.
C. All vehicle owners must have insurance that covers third-party liability for bodily injury or death.
D. Insurance is optional for private vehicle owners.

169. The Claims Tribunal under the Motor Vehicles Act, 1988, is established to exclusively handle disputes related to vehicular accidents.
A. True
B. False
C. True, but only for commercial vehicles
D. False, it also handles disputes regarding traffic violations

170. Third-party insurance under the Motor Vehicles Act, 1988, covers which of the following?
A. Damage to the insured vehicle
B. Personal injuries to the driver
C. Injuries or damages suffered by third parties
D. Theft of the vehicle

171. **Assertion (A):** The owner of a vehicle involved in an accident resulting in death or bodily injury is liable to pay compensation, irrespective of fault.

Reason (R): The principle of 'strict liability' applies under the Motor Vehicles Act, ensuring victims receive timely financial assistance.
A. Both A and R are true, and R is the correct explanation of A
B. Both A and R are true, but R is not the correct explanation of A
C. A is true, R is false
D. A is false, R is true

172. The establishment of the ______ under the Motor Vehicles Act, 1988, helps expedite the resolution of compensation claims arising from road accidents.
A. Motor Accident Claims Tribunal
B. National Road Safety Council
C. State Transport Authority
D. Central Motor Vehicles Rules Board

173. What is the minimum amount of compensation for death as provided under the 'no fault liability' provision in the Motor Vehicles Act, 1988?
A. ₹ 50,000 B. ₹ 25,000
C. ₹ 1,00,000 D. ₹ 1,50,000

174. Under the Motor Vehicles Act, 1988, in the case of grievous hurt, what is the minimum compensation provided without proof of fault?
A. ₹ 25,000 B. ₹ 50,000
C. ₹ 75,000 D. ₹ 1,00,000

175. The Claims Tribunal has the authority to award compensation exceeding the claim amount if it finds justifiable grounds in a motor vehicle accident case.
A. True
B. False
C. True, only in cases involving multiple fatalities
D. False, the tribunal cannot exceed the claim amount under any circumstances

176. Is it mandatory for a vehicle owner to have third-party insurance as per the Motor Vehicles Act, 1988?
A. Yes, it is mandatory for all motor vehicles.
B. No, it is optional but recommended.
C. Yes, but only for commercial vehicles.
D. No, insurance is required only for new vehicles.

177. **Assertion (A):** A claim for compensation regarding a road accident involving a death can be made even if the deceased was unemployed.

Reason (R): Compensation calculations include not only loss of income but also loss of consortium and mental anguish caused to the family of the deceased.
A. Both A and R are true, and R is the correct explanation of A
B. Both A and R are true, but R is not the correct explanation of A
C. A is true, R is false
D. A is false, R is true

178. To streamline the process of compensation for road accident victims, the Motor Vehicles Act, 1988 established the ______ specifically for dealing with such claims.
A. Motor Accident Claims Tribunal
B. National Road Traffic Safety Board
C. Motor Insurance Bureau
D. Road Accident Compensation Authority

179. Match the following terms with their correct descriptions related to the Motor Vehicles Act, 1988:

A. No-Fault Liability	1. Required insurance to cover damages or injuries caused to another person or property.
B. Third-Party Insurance	2. Provides compensation without the need to prove the fault of the driver.
C. Claims Tribunal	3. Special courts set up to resolve motor accident claims.
D. Permanent Disability Compensation	4. Compensation for an injury that partially or completely impairs the person's ability to earn.

A. A-2, B-1, C-3, D-4
B. A-3, B-4, C-1, D-2
C. A-4, B-3, C-2, D-1
D. A-1, B-2, C-4, D-3

180. Arrange the following steps involved in making a claim under third-party insurance due to a road accident:

1. Filing of the claim with the insurance company.
2. Assessment of damages by an insurance adjuster.
3. Payment of the insurance premium.
4. Receipt of compensation following approval.

A. 3, 1, 2, 4 B. 1, 2, 3, 4
C. 2, 1, 4, 3 D. 3, 2, 1, 4

181. Mr. Sharma was involved in a road accident while driving his car, causing injuries to a pedestrian. Despite Mr. Sharma having third-party insurance, what steps must be followed to ensure proper compensation for the pedestrian?

A. The pedestrian must file a police report and then claim directly from Mr. Sharma's insurer.
B. Mr. Sharma should report the accident to his insurance company, which will handle the claims process.
C. The pedestrian should sue Mr. Sharma directly for damages without involving the insurer.
D. Mr. Sharma needs to negotiate with the pedestrian to avoid insurance claims.

182. Outline the procedure for a third party to claim compensation for damages in a motor accident under the Motor Vehicles Act, 1988:

1. Incident occurs resulting in third-party damage or injury.
2. Third party files a complaint to the police for an official report.
3. Third party submits a compensation claim to the Claims Tribunal.
4. Claims Tribunal assesses the claim and holds hearings if necessary.
5. Tribunal issues a compensation order based on findings.

A. 1, 2, 3, 4, 5 B. 1, 3, 2, 4, 5
C. 2, 1, 3, 5, 4 D. 2, 1, 4, 3, 5

183. Scenario: Mrs. Gupta's car was hit by a bus operated by the state transport service, resulting in significant damage to her car and minor injuries to herself. What steps should Mrs. Gupta take under the Motor Vehicles Act, 1988, to seek compensation?

A. File a criminal case against the bus driver for reckless driving.
B. Directly negotiate with the state transport service for a settlement.
C. Submit a claim for compensation to the Claims Tribunal detailing the damages and injuries.
D. Seek a private settlement to avoid legal complications.

184. Which of the following is NOT covered under third-party insurance as per the Motor Vehicles Act, 1988?

A. Injury to a pedestrian caused by the insured vehicle
B. Damage to another vehicle caused by the insured vehicle
C. Injury to the driver of the insured vehicle
D. Death of a passenger in another vehicle caused by the insured vehicle

185. Under the Motor Vehicles Act, 1988, what is the minimum statutory compensation for hit-and-run cases resulting in death?

A. ₹ 25,000 B. ₹ 50,000
C. ₹ 1,00,000 D. ₹ 2,00,000

186. The Motor Vehicles Act, 1988 mandates that Claims Tribunals can also handle criminal liability cases related to motor accidents.

A. True
B. False
C. True, but only for minor offenses
D. False, unless specified by the court

187. Under the no-fault liability principle, the claimant is not required to prove negligence or fault of the vehicle owner or driver to receive compensation.

A. True
B. False
C. True, but only in cases of minor injuries
D. False, except in cases of gross negligence

188. **Assertion (A):** Third-party insurance is compulsory for all motor vehicles operating in public spaces under the Motor Vehicles Act, 1988.

Reason (R): This ensures that victims of road accidents can claim compensation for injuries or damages caused by motor vehicles.

A. Both A and R are true, and R is the correct explanation of A
B. Both A and R are true, but R is not the correct explanation of A
C. A is true, R is false
D. A is false, R is true

189. The _______ is responsible for adjudicating compensation claims arising from motor vehicle accidents under the Motor Vehicles Act, 1988.

A. District Magistrate
B. Motor Accident Claims Tribunal (MACT)
C. Insurance Regulatory and Development Authority (IRDA)
D. High Court

190. Match the following legal terms with their correct descriptions under the Motor Vehicles Act, 1988:

A. Hit-and-Run Case	1. A legal body established to adjudicate accident-related compensation claims
B. No-Fault Liability	2. Compensation is provided even when the responsible vehicle cannot be identified
C. Third-Party Insurance	3. Mandatory insurance covering liabilities towards other persons or property
D. Claims Tribunal	4. Compensation without the need to prove fault or negligence

A. A-2, B-4, C-3, D-1
B. A-1, B-2, C-4, D-3
C. A-4, B-3, C-1, D-2
D. A-3, B-1, C-2, D-4

ANSWERS

1. **(B):** Tort law addresses wrongs against individuals or entities and seeks compensation for those harms, whereas criminal law addresses wrongs against society with the aim of punishment.

2. **(A):** The principle of 'Res ipsa loquitur' allows a presumption of negligence based on the mere occurrence of certain types of accidents, which typically would not happen without negligence.

3. **(B):** Trespass to chattels does not necessarily require physical damage; any unauthorized use or intermeddling that interferes with the owner's right can constitute trespass.

4. **(B):** In tort cases, the plaintiff generally has the burden of proving that the defendant committed a tort causing harm, unless specific exceptions apply.

5. **(C):** A doctor's liability for patient injuries typically stems from negligence, not strict liability, requiring proof of breach of a standard of care rather than just the occurrence of harm.

6. **(A):** Conversion involves wrongful possession or use of property, defamation involves harm to reputation through false statements, and trademark infringement involves unauthorized use of a trademark.

7. **(A):** The proper sequence to establish negligence includes establishing duty, demonstrating breach, proving causation, and verifying damages.

8. **(C):** Strict Liability applies to activities that are so inherently dangerous that anyone undertaking them is liable for any resulting injuries, regardless of fault.

9. **(D):** Intentional infliction is a separate tort itself and not a defense to negligence, which typically involves defenses like comparative negligence, assumption of risk, or contributory negligence.

10. **(D):** Generally, bystanders do not have a duty of care to assist unless they have a specific relationship to the incident or create a risk.

11. **(A):** Generally, an employer is not liable for torts committed by employees acting outside the scope of their employment, known as 'frolic and detour.'

12. **(A):** The economic loss rule bars recovery of purely economic losses in tort actions to prevent tort claims from circumventing the contractual terms between parties.

13. **(A):** The 'eggshell skull' rule states that defendants must take plaintiffs as they find them, meaning if the plaintiff's injuries are more severe because of a pre-existing condition, the defendant is fully liable.

14. **(A):** Nuisance involves interfering with someone's enjoyment of their property, slander involves making a defamatory statement orally, and battery involves harmful or offensive contact.

15. **(A)** The analysis of a tort case starts with establishing a duty, then proving a breach of that duty, followed by causation linking the breach to the harm, and finally assessing the damages.

16. **(B):** The proximate cause test determines whether the harm resulting from an action was foreseeable, which is crucial in establishing liability for that action.

17. **(D):** Invasion of privacy through intrusion upon the seclusion of another is a tort involving an unwarranted invasion into someone's private life without consent.

18. **(A):** Written defamatory statements that are published are classified as libel, whereas spoken defamation is termed slander.

19. **(D):** Misrepresentation involves a false statement, intent to deceive, and reliance by the plaintiff, but does not require physical harm.

20. **(B):** Appropriation is a privacy tort that deals with the unauthorized use of someone's likeness for commercial benefits without their permission

21. **(B):** Vicarious liability holds one person legally responsible for the torts committed by another, typically in an employer-employee relationship.

22. **(C):** The duty of care is a fundamental concept in tort law that requires individuals to exercise reasonable care when their actions could foreseeably injure others.

23. **(B):** While many torts are based on fault (negligence or intent), strict liability torts do not require proof of fault.

24. **(A):** The 'but-for' test assesses whether the harm would not have occurred but for the defendant's conduct, helping to establish causation in tort cases.

25. **(A):** Transferred intent allows tort law to hold defendants liable when they intend to commit a tort against one person but inadvertently harm another.

26. **(A):** Negligence involves the failure to exercise reasonable care, contributory negligence involves the plaintiff's partial fault, and nuisance pertains to interference with the use of land.

27. **(A):** The correct order starts with establishing a duty of care, identifying a breach, proving causation, and assessing the remoteness of damage to determine liability.

28. **(B):** Contributory negligence is when the plaintiff's own negligence plays a part in the harm suffered, potentially reducing or barring recovery.

29. **(B):** Strict liability applies in cases like defective products where liability is imposed regardless of fault due to the inherent risks associated with the activity or product.

30. **(C):** Comparative negligence allows for the apportionment of fault among the parties involved, adjusting the damages each party must pay based on their respective contributions to the harm.

31. **(B):** A landowner's use of property is subject to restrictions like nuisance laws, which prevent uses that interfere unreasonably with other people's rights to use or enjoy their property.

32. **(A):** The attractive nuisance doctrine holds property owners liable for injuries to children trespassing on their land if the injury results from a hazardous object or condition likely to attract children.

33. **(A):** The concept of foreseeability is used to establish the scope of the duty of care, determining if the defendant could have reasonably anticipated the harm to the plaintiff and taken measures to prevent it.

34. **(A):** Proximate cause refers to a cause that is legally sufficient to hold a defendant liable, Res Ipsa Loquitur allows negligence to be presumed from the accident's nature, and trespass to land involves unauthorized entry onto another's property.

35. **(A):** Liability determination starts with establishing if a duty exists, followed by a breach of that duty, the occurrence of actual harm, and finally the legal cause linking the breach to the harm.

36. **(B):** But-for causation is used to determine whether the harm would have occurred 'but for' the defendant's actions, crucial in cases involving multiple potential causes.

37. **(A):** The defense of illegality can be invoked when the plaintiff was participating in an illegal activity at the time of the injury, which can bar or reduce the recovery of damages.

38. **(D):** 'Respondeat superior' is a doctrine holding that an employer or principal is responsible for the actions of their employees or agents when those actions are performed within the scope of employment or agency.

39. **(A):** Indemnity in tort law enables a defendant to claim compensation from a third party who may actually be responsible for the harm caused, thus spreading the liability according to actual fault.

40. **(A):** Strict product liability imposes liability on manufacturers and distributors for defective products that cause harm, regardless of whether the manufacturer was negligent

41. **(A):** Consent, when validly given, acknowledges acceptance of the risk of any resulting harm, thereby negating any tort claim related to that harm.

42. **(A):** The defense of necessity applies when a defendant asserts that their actions, although otherwise tortious, were necessary to prevent a greater and imminent harm.

43. **(A):** In tort law, self-defense can justify acts that would otherwise be tortious if they are reasonably necessary to protect oneself from an immediate threat of harm.

44. **(C)**

45. **(A):** The defense of statutory authority allows defendants to claim that their actions were conducted under and justified by legislative authority, hence they are not tortious.

46. **(A):** Contributory negligence involves the plaintiff's negligence contributing to their harm, comparative negligence involves apportioning fault among the parties, and assumption of risk involves the plaintiff voluntarily engaging in a known risky activity.

47. **(A):** The correct sequence involves asserting the defense early in the trial process, then demonstrating the plaintiff's awareness of the risk, their contributory actions, and how a reasonable person would have acted differently.

48. **(A):** The defense of inevitable accident applies when the defendant claims that the harm occurred despite all reasonable measures taken to avoid it, suggesting no negligence was involved.

49. **(B):** 'Volenti non fit injuria' applies when a person has voluntarily exposed themselves to a known risk. A volunteer firefighter knowingly accepts the inherent risks involved in firefighting.

50. **(B):** The defense of necessity is applicable only when the action taken is to prevent a significant and imminent harm. Cutting down a tree for aesthetic or economic reasons does not meet this criteria.

51. **(A):** Duress involves compulsion by threat of harm, allowing it as a defense in tort if the defendant committed the act under immediate threat to their safety.

52. **(A):** This defense holds that a plaintiff cannot seek legal relief for a situation that arose as a result of their own illegal activities.

53. **(A):** An 'act of God' is a defense used to describe natural events that are both unpredictable and unavoidable, such as hurricanes or earthquakes, that absolve defendants from liability due to the inability to anticipate and prevent the harm.

54. **(A):** Immunity typically protects government officials from liability within the scope of their duties, a mistake about property boundaries can negate trespass, and alter ego involves holding individuals personally liable for corporate actions under specific conditions.

55. **(A):** Establishing liability regarding independent contractors involves showing the contract for service, affirming the lack of control over methods, clarifying the relationship legally, and proving the contractor's exclusive role in the harm.

56. **(A):** Assumption of risk involves a defense where the plaintiff has voluntarily taken a known risk associated with an activity, which can absolve the defendant of some or all liability for any resulting harm.

57. **(A):** While self-defense primarily justifies acts intended to protect oneself, it can also extend to unintentional injuries to bystanders if the defendant was acting reasonably under the circumstances to defend against an aggressor.

58. **(B):** Public necessity allows for actions that would otherwise be tortious if they are taken to avert an imminent public disaster, such as destroying property to create a firebreak during a large fire.

59. **(A):** This is an application of vicarious liability, where an employer is responsible for the actions of employees performed within the course of their employment, regardless of specific authorization.

60. **(A):** The defense of illegality requires a direct connection between the illegal conduct and the harm suffered; if the plaintiff's illegal action was unrelated to the injury, this defense typically cannot be applied.

61. **(C):** Double jeopardy is not applicable in tort law; it is a criminal defense that protects against being tried twice for the same crime, which does not cross over into civil tort claims.

62. **(A):** Qualified immunity protects certain officials acting within their official duties, inevitable accident covers scenarios where the defendant could not have avoided the harm, and Good Samaritan laws protect individuals who assist in emergencies from liability.

63. **(B):** The sequence starts with identifying the duty, followed by arguing for the defense, then proving the plaintiff's contributory negligence, and finally confirming its significant impact on the harm.

64. **(A):** Mistake of fact can serve as a defense if the mistake negates a required element of the tort, such as intent or knowledge, provided the mistake is reasonable under the circumstances.

65. **(C):** Negligence focuses on the breach of a duty of care leading to damage, not on the intention to cause harm.

66. **(B):** A private nuisance occurs when there is a substantial, unreasonable interference with a person's use or enjoyment of their property.

67. **(A):** Trespass to land typically involves the unauthorized physical entry onto the land of another.

68. (A): Defamation involves the communication of a false statement about a person to a third party, causing harm to the person's reputation.

69. (A): Trespass to land can occur irrespective of the trespasser's intent to trespass, as long as there was an intention to enter the property.

70. (A): Each definition correctly corresponds to its respective tort, capturing the essence of negligence, nuisance, trespass, and defamation.

71. (A): The correct sequence involves identifying the defamatory statement concerning the plaintiff, proving it was published to a third party, establishing its falsity, and demonstrating how it caused harm.

72. (A): The reasonable person test assesses whether the defendant acted as a prudent person would have in the same circumstances, thus determining if there was a breach of the duty of care.

73. (C): When determining if an act constitutes a nuisance, the court considers the nature, duration, and location of the act but not the economic status of the defendant.

74. (C): In slander (spoken defamation), the plaintiff generally needs to prove actual damages caused by the defamatory statement, unless it falls into a category of slander per se. In contrast, libel (written defamation) is presumed to cause damage.

75. (B): The 'coming to the nuisance' argument is generally not a valid defense in nuisance cases. Moving to an area where a nuisance exists does not waive a person's right to not be subjected to unreasonable interferences.

76. (D): Trespass to chattels does not necessarily require actual damage. Any unauthorized and intentional interference that deprives the owner of the use of their property can constitute trespass to chattels.

77. (A): Lawful activities can still lead to a nuisance claim if they cause substantial and unreasonable interference with another person's property use, such as disturbing sleep.

78. (A): The elements correctly match each tort: Negligence involves a breach of duty that causes harm, nuisance involves unreasonable use of property, trespass involves unauthorized entry, and defamation involves harm to reputation through false statements.

79. (A): For trespass to land, the sequence involves identifying entry, proving it was intentional, establishing it was unauthorized, and then demonstrating harm or interference as a result of the entry.

80. (A): Defamation per se involves statements that are presumed to be harmful to someone's reputation without needing to prove actual damage, such as allegations of a serious crime or a loathsome disease.

81. (C): Absolute privilege protects certain individuals, such as legislators during sessions or judges in court, allowing them to speak freely without risk of a defamation lawsuit, regardless of the statement's truthfulness.

82. (A): A continuing trespass involves an ongoing presence or use of another's property without permission, such as leaving a structure that continuously encroaches on the property.

83. (A): Slander specifically refers to spoken defamation. It must be spoken and heard by a third party to qualify as slander, distinguishing it from libel, which involves written or published defamatory statements.

84. (A): Substantial interference in the context of nuisance law refers to an interference that is significant and has a real impact on the plaintiff's use or enjoyment of their property. This threshold helps distinguish actionable nuisances from petty aggravations.

85. (B): The foreseeability test assesses whether the type of damage must have been reasonably foreseeable to the defendant at the time of the negligent act as a likely result of their actions.

86. (B): Palsgraf v. Long Island Railroad Co. is a fundamental case in American tort law that established the principle that defendants are only liable for damages that are reasonably foreseeable consequences of their actions.

87. (B): The principle of remoteness of damages as discussed here specifically applies to tort law, focusing on foreseeability in negligence. In contract law, similar concepts limit damages but are generally discussed under different terms and principles, such as those outlined in Hadley v. Baxendale.

88. (A): Remoteness of damages focuses on whether the type of damage was foreseeable, not necessarily the extent or magnitude of the damage, which can exceed what might have been anticipated.

89. (A): The "eggshell skull" rule is an exception to the principle of remoteness, whereby a defendant is liable for the full extent of an injury even if the severity of the injury was unforeseeable, provided the type of injury was foreseeable.

90. (D): Indirect consequences, particularly those that are unforeseeable or highly attenuated from the defendant's original act, are often deemed too remote, limiting the scope of liability and ensuring that defendants are only responsible for consequences that could have been reasonably anticipated.

91. (A): Proximate cause is used to determine whether the harm was closely enough connected to the wrongful act to hold the defendant liable. It assesses the directness or foreseeability of the harm resulting from the act, aligning closely with the principle of remoteness of damages.

92. (B): While the crash itself is a foreseeable consequence of negligent driving, a patron having a heart attack due to the resultant panic may be considered too remote a consequence to attribute liability to the motorist.

93. (A): The principle of remoteness can limit liability in complex cases where multiple causes contribute to the harm. Only those damages directly linked to the defendant's act and reasonably foreseeable are typically recoverable.

94. (D): A new intervening act can potentially break the chain of causation, but it does not automatically do so. The new act must be unforeseeable and sufficient to shift the liability away from the original act for the chain to be broken.

95. (A): The principle of remoteness often excludes damages caused by acts of God from recovery because they are unforeseeable and sufficient to break the chain of causation, making them a superseding cause.

96. (A): The "type rule" reflects the legal principle that for damages to be recoverable, a defendant must only foresee the general type of harm that occurred as a result of their actions, rather than the specific circumstances or severity of the outcome.

97. (B): The 'eggshell skull rule' is an exception to the general principle of remoteness. It holds that once the type of harm (like physical injury) is deemed foreseeable, the defendant is liable for all consequences, even if the extent is unforeseeable, as long as the initial harm falls within the scope of foreseeable risks.

98. (A): The heart attack of a bystander, while tragic, would likely be considered too remote a consequence of the truck crash as it is an extraordinary reaction not normally foreseeable from such an incident.

99. (B): Generally, an unforeseeable intervening act by a third party that contributes to the harm can break the chain of causation, making the damages too remote for the initial defendant to be held liable unless there was some encouragement or expectation of such an act.

100. (D): Remoteness of damages focuses on whether the harm was a foreseeable outcome of the defendant's negligent act, helping to determine the appropriateness and extent of damages that should be awarded.

101. (A): In product liability cases, once it is established that harm could foreseeably result from a defect, the manufacturer is liable for the consequences, even if the specific type of injury was not highly foreseeable.

102. (D): Damages must be a direct and foreseeable result of the defendant's negligent act to be compensable. Indirectly related damages are often considered too remote and thus not eligible for compensation under this principle.

103. (B): In environmental tort cases, the principle of remoteness restricts compensation to those damages that were a foreseeable consequence of the defendant's actions at the time the action occurred. This principle is crucial to ensure that liability is not excessively burdensome and is reasonably predictable.

104. (B): An intervening cause can alter the direct sequence between the defendant's act and the resulting harm, often rendering some potential consequences too remote for compensation. This concept helps ensure that defendants are only held liable for harms that are a direct and foreseeable result of their actions, barring any unforeseeable, intervening events that contribute significantly to the harm.

105. (C): Strict liability does not require proof of fault, but defenses like contributory negligence may still be applicable. Absolute liability, on the other hand, allows for no defenses—once the act is proven, the defendant is liable regardless of any precautions taken.

106. (A): Strict liability in product liability cases holds manufacturers and distributors responsible for harm caused by defective products, regardless of whether they exercised care in the product's manufacture and distribution.

107. (A): Strict liability applies regardless of the precautions taken by the defendant. The liability is based on the undertaking of an inherently dangerous activity or the creation of a hazardous condition that leads to harm.

108. (A): Absolute liability is often applied in cases involving inherently dangerous activities such as the handling and disposal of hazardous waste. It ensures that operators cannot escape liability simply by showing they took care, emphasizing the importance of public safety and environmental protection.

109. (A): The principle of absolute liability is particularly relevant in cases involving ultra-hazardous activities. In such cases, the law imposes liability without fault to ensure maximum protection against potentially devastating risks, such as those posed by explosives.

110. (A): Rylands v. Fletcher established a legal principle where a person who brings onto their land and collects and keeps there anything likely to do mischief if it escapes must keep it at their peril. If they fail, they are prima facie answerable for all the damage which is the natural consequence of its escape.

111. (B): Strict liability is often imposed in cases involving inherently dangerous activities such as the use of explosives. The risk posed by such activities is deemed so high that the law holds the actor liable regardless of the level of care exercised.

112. (D): Absolute liability means that a defendant may be held liable without the possibility of presenting defenses related to how reasonable their actions were. The focus is solely on whether the act occurred, not on the precautions or intentions behind it.

113. (D): Strict liability is not applicable to all commercial activities but is reserved for those that involve inherently dangerous activities, such as manufacturing explosives, chemicals, or other hazardous materials where even the utmost care cannot eliminate risk.

114. (A): Absolute liability holds the defendant liable without regard to mitigating factors, defenses, or the level of care taken. This type of liability is especially prevalent in cases involving ultra-hazardous activities or where public safety is of paramount concern.

115. (A): Keeping wild animals is an inherently dangerous activity, and strict liability is imposed on the owners or keepers, regardless of the level of care or security measures implemented, because of the high risk associated with such activities.

116. (A): Rylands v. Fletcher is a foundational English law case that established the principle of strict and absolute liability for inherently dangerous activities. In this case, the court held that the owner of the reservoir was liable for the damage caused by its failure, regardless of negligence.

117. (D): Handling radioactive materials is inherently hazardous and typically subject to absolute liability due to the potential for catastrophic consequences, thus making operators liable regardless of the level of care or safety measures they implement.

118. (B): Strict liability is imposed regardless of fault or negligence. It is based on the nature of the activity and the inherent risks involved, rather than any wrongful conduct on the part of the defendant.

119. (D): Strict liability for harm caused by domestic animals typically applies only if the animal is known to have dangerous propensities unusual for its species. Otherwise, liability usually depends on the owner's knowledge of the particular animal's aggressive behavior.

120. (D): Absolute liability does not require the plaintiff to prove foreseeability of harm. It focuses on the mere fact of harm resulting from the defendant's actions or operations, making defenses related to foreseeability or lack of negligence irrelevant.

121. (A): The principle of strict liability applies particularly to inherently dangerous industrial activities, such as chemical manufacturing. Liability is imposed based on the nature of the activity and its potential risks, irrespective of the level of care exercised.

122. (D): The doctrine of respondeat superior applies to cases where an employer is held strictly liable for the actions of employees, provided those actions occur within the scope of their employment. This legal principle is essential in enforcing responsibility in business and professional settings.

123. (A): Absolute liability in environmental law typically holds parties responsible for any environmental damage they cause, regardless of compliance with existing safety regulations or standards. This approach is particularly relevant in cases where activities have inherently dangerous implications for public health and the environment.

124. (D): Absolute liability in high-risk industries, like nuclear power, serves both to ensure that any damages are automatically addressed through compensation and to mandate that such industries carry sufficient insurance to cover potential claims. This legal approach is designed to protect the public and the environment by ensuring financial accountability for possible catastrophic events, thereby also influencing operational and safety standards within the industry.

125. (B): In many common law jurisdictions, the State can be held vicariously liable for torts committed by its employees during the course of their employment. This principle assumes that the State, like any employer, should be responsible for the acts of its employees if those acts are related to their official duties.

126. (B): The State typically claims immunity from tortious liability when the act involved is part of its sovereign functions, such as law enforcement, military actions, and legislative activities, where the State acts as the representative of sovereign authority.

127. (B): While the State can be held liable for the negligent acts of its employees, there are exceptions, especially when actions are performed under statutory authority or involve discretionary functions, which might not attract liability under the principle of sovereign immunity.

128. (A): Generally, a sovereign state cannot be sued in its own courts without its consent, a principle known as "sovereign immunity." Many states have statutes that waive this immunity to a certain extent to allow for suits in specified situations.

129. (D): The State is generally not liable for the judicial acts of its officers, as judges and other judicial officials are granted immunity when acting within their jurisdiction to ensure that they can perform their functions without fear of personal liability.

130. (B): Sovereign immunity is a legal doctrine that prevents the State from being sued without its consent, embodying the principle that the sovereign or government cannot commit a legal wrong and is immune from civil suit or criminal prosecution.

131. (B): Generally, the State may be held liable for the negligent acts of its employees when these acts occur during the course of routine, non-sovereign functions such as healthcare services provided by state hospitals.

132. (A): To hold the State liable for the tortious acts of its employees, it must be shown that these acts were committed within the scope of employment, linking the wrongful acts to the State's responsibility as an employer.

133. (B): Generally, the State is not held liable for the actions of independent contractors it hires, as these contractors are not considered employees, and their actions do not fall within the scope of state employment.

134. (A): In many jurisdictions, sovereign immunity does not extend to violations of constitutional rights, allowing individuals to seek redress against the State for such violations, particularly in contexts like civil rights abuses.

135. (A): Environmental laws often explicitly hold the State and its agencies liable for violations, including damages caused by illegal activities such as dumping waste, thereby waiving sovereign immunity in these specific contexts.

136. (D): The doctrine of respondeat superior holds an employer (including the State) liable for the actions of its employees performed within the scope of their employment, regardless of whether the actions were expressly authorized or not.

137. (A): Situations with the appropriate legal principle related to State responsibility under the Indian Constitution:

- Government fails to protect citizens during a communal riot: This is a Failure of Constitutional Duty, as the State is obligated to protect citizens' lives and safety under Article 21 (right to life).
- State-owned railway negligently maintains tracks, causing a derailment: This falls under Tortious Liability, as the State is liable for negligence in its operations, similar to a private entity.
- Public official demands a bribe for processing a license: This is an Abuse of Public Office, as the official misuses their authority for personal gain, violating public trust.
- State legislation violates fundamental rights: This is an Unconstitutional Action, as laws infringing on fundamental rights (e.g., under Articles 14, 19, or 21) can be struck down by courts.

Hence, correct match is A-1, B-2, C-3, D-4.

138. (A): The correct sequence begins with determining the nature of the official's act (whether it was within the scope of their duties), followed by establishing that the act was tortious. Next, it is necessary to ascertain whether a statutory waiver of immunity allows for suing the State. Finally, the claim must be filed in accordance with any relevant statutory deadlines.

139. (A): A matches with 1 because the officer's actions, while off-duty, fall outside the scope of employment.

B matches with 4 due to complexities in medical cases where liability could depend on specific factors like consent or expected surgical outcomes.

C matches with 2 as the bus driver's actions during employment directly relate to their job duties.

D matches with 3 because the government as a property owner is directly responsible for ensuring the safety of its premises.

140. (A): The correct sequence starts with confirming the scope of the officer's duties to establish the context of the act. Next, evidence of misconduct is gathered, followed by an analysis of statutory or constitutional breaches. A formal claim must then be filed, typically through processes outlined by governmental claims acts, before moving to litigation if necessary.

141. (B): Sovereign immunity is a legal doctrine that provides the State immunity from being sued without its consent, particularly when performing sovereign functions such as legislative actions, judicial activities, or acts of governance.

142. (A): The State can be held vicariously liable for negligent acts committed by its employees if those acts occur within the scope of their employment, as in the case of a state employee driving a government vehicle for work purposes.

143. (B): Generally, the State is not liable for acts performed by its employees while exercising discretionary functions, such as decision-making or policy formulation, provided these actions are within the bounds of their authority.

144. (C): In cases where sovereign immunity does not apply, claiming against the State for tortious acts involves establishing elements like duty, breach, causation, and damages, similar to any tort case against an individual.

145. (A): The State can be held liable for actions of its employees, such as teachers, when they act outside the scope of accepted educational practices and breach legal or statutory duties, such as prohibitions against physical punishment.

146. (A): State immunity can be waived through legislative statutes that specifically allow for such claims, providing a legal basis for individuals to seek redress for injuries caused by the State or its employees.

147. (B): According to the Consumer Protection Act 1986, a consumer is defined as any person who buys any goods or hires or avails of any services for a consideration which has been paid or promised or partly paid and partly promised, or under any system of deferred payment.

148. (A): The Right to Safety, under the Consumer Protection Act 1986, ensures that consumers are protected against the marketing of goods and services which are hazardous to life and property, part of the rights to be informed about the quality, quantity, potency, purity, standard, and price of goods or services.

149. (A): The Act establishes a three-tier consumer dispute redressal mechanism at the national, state, and district levels, known as National Consumer Disputes Redressal Commission, State Consumer Disputes Redressal Commissions, and District Consumer Disputes Redressal Commissions, respectively.

150. (A): True, Consumer Protection Councils, established at the national, state, and district levels, are advisory bodies designed to promote and protect the rights of the consumers. They advise on policies and programs for consumer welfare.

151. (A): The Act permits recognized consumer associations to file complaints, making it possible for them to represent consumer interests proactively, thus broadening the scope and impact of consumer protection.

152. (A): The Central Consumer Protection Authority (CCPA) is empowered to regulate matters relating to violation of consumer rights, unfair trade practices, and misleading advertisements, and also ensure compliance with the provisions of the Act.

153. (C): The National Consumer Disputes Redressal Commission deals with complaints where the value of the goods or services paid exceeds INR 1 crore, making it the highest level of consumer redressal mechanism under the act.

154. (C): The Consumer Protection Act 1986 does not explicitly include the 'Right to Bargain' as a consumer right. The act provides other rights such as the Right to Safety, Information, Choice, to be Heard, Redress, and Consumer Education, which are designed to protect consumer interests.

155. (A): The act provides for the establishment of consumer councils and other authorities, which play a significant role in settling consumer disputes and advocating consumer rights at various levels from national to district.

156. (A): The act explicitly allows consumers to file complaints against unfair trade practices, which include any deceptive, improper, or unethical methods that may influence transaction decisions.

157. (A): Ensuring the presence of both parties during hearings under the Consumer Protection Act, 1986, promotes a fair and transparent adjudication process, allowing the disputing parties equal opportunity to be heard and to contest evidence.

158. (A): The 2019 amendment to the Consumer Protection Act, 1986, significantly broadened the scope to include e-commerce, emphasizing the protection and enforcement of the rights of online consumers, which reflects the evolving nature of consumer transactions and the need for legal frameworks to keep pace.

159. (B): Consumer Protection Councils, established at the national, state, and district levels, are advisory bodies designed to promote and protect consumer rights. They play a crucial role in advising on consumer protection policies but do not adjudicate disputes or impose penalties.

160. (A): The Consumer Protection Act specifies that a complaint must be filed within two years from the date on which the cause of action has arisen, ensuring timely resolution and relevance of the cases brought before consumer forums.

161. (A): With amendments and updates to the Consumer Protection Act to adapt to modern needs, complaints can now be filed electronically, making the process more accessible and efficient for consumers across the country.

162. (A): The Act allows for the consumer to not only receive compensation for the harm caused but also to potentially recover reasonable expenses and legal costs involved in pursuing the complaint, promoting justice and fairness.

163. (A): Mediation cells are a significant aspect of the consumer dispute resolution mechanism under the Consumer Protection Act, aimed at providing an alternative method to resolve disputes quickly and effectively, reducing the load on the judiciary.

164. (B): The introduction of the Central Consumer Protection Authority (CCPA) marked a significant step in strengthening consumer rights protection in India, focusing on preventing unfair trade practices and ensuring compliance with the provisions of the Act.

165. (B): Under the Consumer Protection Act, product liability extends to all responsible parties in the production and distribution chain and does not require the consumer to have a direct purchase relationship with the manufacturer. This facilitates broader protection for consumers against defective products.

166. (B): The 'right to choose' empowers consumers to have access to a variety of products and services at competitive prices, ensuring they have a range of options from which to select, promoting fair competition and preventing undue restrictions in the market.

167. (A): 'No fault liability' means that compensation for death or permanent disablement due to a motor accident is provided without the need to prove fault or negligence on the part of the driver or owner of the vehicle involved in the accident.

168. (C): The act mandates that all motor vehicle owners must purchase insurance that covers their potential third-party liability concerning bodily injuries or death caused by their vehicles. This is to ensure that victims of road accidents can obtain compensation.

169. (A): Claims Tribunals are established under the Motor Vehicles Act specifically to adjudicate upon claims for compensation in respect of accidents involving the death of, or bodily injury to, persons arising out of the use of motor vehicles, or damages to any property of a third party.

170. (C): Third-party insurance is specifically designed to cover any liability arising from injuries to or the death of third parties, as well as damage to third-party property caused by the insured vehicle. It does not cover personal injuries to the driver or damage to the insured vehicle itself.

171. (A): Under the Motor Vehicles Act, the principle of strict liability ensures that the owner of the vehicle pays compensation in the event of an accident causing death or bodily injury, independent of fault, to facilitate immediate financial support to the victims.

172. (A): The Motor Accident Claims Tribunal specifically addresses compensation claims related to road accidents, streamlining the process and providing a specialized forum that focuses on such disputes, separate from regular civil courts.

173. (A): Under the 'no fault liability' provision of the Motor Vehicles Act, the minimum compensation for the death of a person in a motor vehicle accident is ₹ 50,000. This provision ensures immediate relief to the victim's family irrespective of the fault.

174. (A): The Motor Vehicles Act stipulates a minimum compensation of ₹ 25,000 for grievous hurt caused by a motor vehicle accident under the 'no fault liability' clause, ensuring that victims receive some form of immediate financial support.

175. (A): The Claims Tribunal has the discretion to award compensation amounting to more than what was claimed if it finds that the circumstances of the case and the extent of loss or injury justify a higher compensation. This flexibility helps ensure fair and adequate relief to the victims or their families.

176. (A): The Motor Vehicles Act, 1988 mandates third-party insurance for all types of motor vehicles plying on public roads. This insurance covers the vehicle owner against any legal liability to a third party caused when the insured vehicle is at fault.

177. (A): Under the Motor Vehicles Act, compensation for death is not limited to the loss of income but extends to non-pecuniary damages such as loss of consortium and mental anguish to the deceased's family, ensuring comprehensive compensation.

178. (A): The Motor Accident Claims Tribunal (MACT) is specially set up under the Motor Vehicles Act, 1988 to provide a faster resolution and specific venue for accident-related compensation cases, avoiding the regular civil court delays.

179. (A): No-Fault Liability provides immediate compensation without fault determination, Third-Party Insurance covers damages to others, Claims Tribunals handle disputes arising from motor vehicle accidents, and Permanent Disability Compensation covers long-term impairments from accidents.

180. (A): Initially, the vehicle owner must pay the insurance premium to have an active policy (3). After an accident, a claim is filed (1), followed by an assessment of damages (2), and finally, if approved, compensation is received (4).

181. (B): In cases of third-party injuries, the vehicle owner (Mr. Sharma) must inform his insurance company about the accident. The insurer then manages the compensation process, making it unnecessary for the pedestrian to directly sue Mr. Sharma or negotiate privately.

182. (A): The correct sequence starts with the incident causing damage or injury. The third party should then file a police complaint to ensure there's an official report of the incident (2), followed by submitting a compensation claim to the Claims Tribunal (3). The Tribunal will then assess the claim, possibly hold hearings (4), and finally issue a compensation order (5).

183. (C): Under the Motor Vehicles Act, Mrs. Gupta should file a claim with the Claims Tribunal, which is specifically established to handle such disputes. This tribunal assesses claims related to road accidents and can award compensation for damages and injuries without the need to establish criminal liability.

184. (C): Third-party insurance covers injuries or damages to third parties (i.e., other people, vehicles, or property) but does not cover personal injuries to the insured driver unless additional personal accident cover is taken.

185. (C): The Act provides for ₹ 1,00,000 as compensation for death in hit-and-run cases, where the offending vehicle is untraceable, ensuring that victims or their families receive some relief even when the responsible party cannot be identified.

186. (B): Claims Tribunals are established to adjudicate civil claims for compensation related to motor accidents, not to handle criminal liability cases, which are dealt with by regular criminal courts.

187. (A): The no-fault liability principle ensures that victims receive compensation without the need to establish the negligence or fault of the vehicle owner or driver, allowing for quicker disbursement of claims.

188. (A): Third-party insurance is mandatory to ensure that victims of road accidents receive compensation, even if the vehicle owner is unable or unwilling to pay damages personally.

189. (B): MACT is a specialized tribunal established under the Motor Vehicles Act to handle claims related to compensation for death, injury, and property damage arising from motor vehicle accidents.

190. (A): A (Hit-and-Run Case) matches with 2 as it refers to accidents where the vehicle cannot be traced.

B (No-Fault Liability) matches with 4, as compensation is provided without proving negligence.

C (Third-Party Insurance) matches with 3, which covers liability towards others.

D (Claims Tribunal) matches with 1, a body established to decide compensation claims.

UNIT 6 Commercial Law

ESSENTIAL ELEMENTS OF A VALID CONTRACT

1. Offer and Acceptance

- **Definition:** A proposal or offer is made by one party and accepted by the other.
- **Key Points:**
  - ❑ Offer must be **clear, definite, and communicated.**
  - ❑ Acceptance must be **absolute, unqualified,** and communicated to the offeror.
  - ❑ An offer may be **general (to the public)** or **specific (to a person or group).**

2. Intention to Create Legal Relations

- Agreements must be made with the intention of creating legal obligations.
- **Social or domestic agreements** (e.g., family arrangements) are not enforceable unless intended to create a legal relationship.

3. Lawful Consideration

- **Definition:** Consideration refers to the price paid for a promise.
- **Essentials:**
  - ❑ Must be **real, lawful**, and have value in the eyes of the law.
  - ❑ May move from the romise or any other person.
  - ❑ Past, present, or future considerations are valid.
- **Case Law:** *Chinnaya v. Ramaya* (1876).

4. Capacity of Parties

- Parties must be competent to contract under Section 11 of the Indian Contract Act.
- A person is competent if:
  - ❑ **Of sound mind** (can understand the terms).
  - ❑ **Of the age of majority** (18 years or older).
  - ❑ **Not disqualified by law** (e.g., insolvent or alien enemy).

5. Free Consent

- Consent of the parties must be free and not induced by:
  - ❑ **Coercion** (Section 15): Threat or force.
  - ❑ **Undue Influence** (Section 16): Taking advantage of a dominant position.
  - ❑ **Fraud** (Section 17): Intentional deception.
  - ❑ **Misrepresentation** (Section 18): False statements without intent to deceive.
  - ❑ **Mistake** (Section 20-22): Error of fact or law.

6. Lawful Object

- The object of the agreement must be lawful and not:
  - ❑ Forbidden by law.
  - ❑ Fraudulent.
  - ❑ Injurious to public policy.
  - ❑ Immoral.

7. Agreement Not Expressly Declared Void

- Agreements that are **expressly declared void** under the Act:
  - ❑ Agreements in restraint of marriage (Section 26).
  - ❑ Agreements in restraint of trade (Section 27).
  - ❑ Agreements in restraint of legal proceedings (Section 28).
  - ❑ Wagering agreements (Section 30).

8. Certainty and Possibility of Performance

- Terms of the contract must be **clear** and **certain** (Section 29).
- The contract must be **capable of performance** (Section 56).
  - Example: An agreement to perform an impossible act is void.

9. Writing and Registration (If Required by Law)

- Some contracts must be in writing, e.g.:
  - Lease agreements over one year.
  - Sale of immovable property.
  - Contracts under **Section 25** requiring registration.

10. Legal Formalities

- All prescribed legal formalities (if any) must be followed, such as stamping or registration under applicable laws.

Key Doctrines to Remember

- **Privity of Contract:** Only parties to the contract can sue or be sued.
- **Quasi-Contracts (Sections 68-72):** Obligations resembling contracts (e.g., payment by a person who enjoys non-gratuitous services).
- **Unjust Enrichment:** No one should benefit at another's expense without legal justification.

Essentials of E-Contracts (Electronic Contracts)

E-contracts, governed by the **Indian Contract Act, 1872** and the **Information Technology Act, 2000**, are agreements created and executed in an electronic form.

11. Offer and Acceptance

- Similar to traditional contracts, there must be a **valid offer** and **unqualified acceptance**.
- In e-contracts:
  - Offers are made electronically (via emails, websites, or online platforms).
  - Acceptance can occur through electronic communication like clicking "I Agree" or "Accept" buttons.
  - **Communication of acceptance** is instantaneous, and the **time and place of contract formation** are determined by the provisions of the IT Act.

12. Intention to Create Legal Relations

- Parties must have the intent to create legal obligations.
- Merely visiting a website or engaging in casual communication does not constitute a contract unless there is a clear intent.

13. Lawful Consideration

- There must be valid consideration, which is not forbidden by law.
  - Example: Payment via online platforms (credit/debit cards, net banking) serves as lawful consideration.

14. Capacity of Parties

- Parties entering into e-contracts must be:
  - Of sound mind.
  - Of the age of majority (18 years or older).
  - Not disqualified by law (e.g., bankrupts or alien enemies).
- **Practical Issues:** Ensuring age verification and identity authentication in online contracts.

15. Free Consent

- Consent must be free and not induced by:
  - Coercion, undue influence, fraud, or misrepresentation.
  - Fraudulent practices, such as phishing, can challenge the validity of an e-contract.

16. Lawful Object

- The object of the e-contract must be lawful and not:
  - Prohibited by law.
  - Fraudulent or immoral.
  - Against public policy.

17. Certainty and Possibility of Performance

- The terms and conditions of an e-contract must be clear, definite, and capable of being performed.
- Example: Agreements for delivering specific goods through e-commerce platforms must specify delivery timelines and modes.

18. Compliance with Legal Provisions

- E-contracts must comply with:
  - **Indian Contract Act, 1872** for essential elements.
  - **IT Act, 2000**, which provides legal recognition to electronic records and digital signatures.
- Important Sections of IT Act:
  - **Section 10A:** Validity of contracts formed electronically.

- ❑ **Section 4:** Legal recognition of electronic records.
- ❑ **Section 5:** Legal recognition of electronic signatures.

19. Authentication of E-Contracts

- E-contracts must be authenticated using:
  - ❑ **Electronic or digital signatures**.
  - ❑ Methods ensuring authenticity, integrity, and reliability.
- **Digital Signature Certificates (DSC)** issued under the IT Act ensure security and verification.

20. Mode of Communication

- Modes of communication in e-contracts include:
  - ❑ Email exchanges.
  - ❑ Click-wrap agreements (e.g., "I Agree" checkbox).
  - ❑ Browse-wrap agreements (e.g., terms available on websites).
  - ❑ Shrink-wrap agreements (e.g., pre-installed software).

Writing and Retention

- E-contracts must comply with writing and storage requirements under the IT Act:
  - ❑ **Section 7:** Ensures that electronic records are considered equivalent to paper documents.
  - ❑ **Section 9:** Specifies that e-records must be accessible for future reference.

Jurisdiction and Dispute Resolution

- Determining the jurisdiction in e-contracts is crucial:
  - ❑ Governed by the **Information Technology Act** and applicable laws.
  - ❑ **Place of business or residence** of the parties often determines jurisdiction.
  - ❑ Agreements may include **arbitration clauses** or specify jurisdiction.

Types of E-Contracts

- **Click-Wrap Contracts:** User accepts by clicking a button (e.g., "I Agree").
- **Browse-Wrap Contracts:** Acceptance inferred from the use of a website.
- **Shrink-Wrap Contracts:** Embedded in software or product packaging.
- **Email Contracts:** Offers and acceptances communicated via email.

Advantages of E-Contracts

- Speed and convenience.
- Cost-effectiveness.
- Global reach.
- Reduced paper usage.

Key Issues in E-Contracts

- Identity theft or fraud.
- Enforceability of click-wrap and browse-wrap agreements.
- Data security and privacy concerns.
- Ensuring compliance with cross-border regulations.

BREACH OF CONTRACT

Breach of contract occurs when a party fails to fulfill their obligations under a valid contract, either fully or partially, without a lawful excuse. It is governed by the Indian Contract Act, 1872, and the aggrieved party is entitled to remedies for the breach.

Types of breach of contract

1. Anticipatory Breach:

- Breach occurs before the due date of performance.
- The party declares their intention not to perform their contractual obligations.
- The aggrieved party can:
  - ❑ Treat the contract as repudiated and sue immediately.
  - ❑ Wait until the performance date to take action.
- **Case Law: *Hochster v. De La Tour* (1853).**

2. Actual Breach:

- Breach occurs at the time when the performance is due or during performance.
- Types:
  - ❑ Failure to perform as promised.
  - ❑ Improper or defective performance.
- Example: Non-delivery of goods after payment.

Consequences of Breach of Contract

1. Right to Sue for Damages:

- The aggrieved party can claim compensation for losses caused by the breach (Sections 73-75).
- Types of damages:
  - ❑ **Ordinary Damages:** Direct losses from the breach.

- ❑ **Special Damages:** Indirect losses if they were foreseeable at the time of contract formation.
- ❑ **Nominal Damages:** Awarded when no actual loss is suffered.
- ❑ **Exemplary Damages:** Awarded in exceptional cases (e.g., breach of a promise to marry).

2. Right to Specific Performance (Section 10, Specific Relief Act, 1963):

- Court orders the breaching party to perform their contractual obligations.
- Applicable when:
  - ❑ Damages are not an adequate remedy.
  - ❑ The subject matter is unique (e.g., sale of rare goods).

3. Right to Injunction:

- Court order, restraining a party from doing something prohibited by the contract.

4. Right to Rescind the Contract:

- The aggrieved party can cancel the contract and refuse further performance.

5. Quantum Meruit (As Much as Earned):

- The aggrieved party can claim compensation for the work already done if the contract is terminated prematurely.

Remedies for Breach of Contract

1. Damages:

- Governed under Sections 73-75 of the Indian Contract Act.
- Compensates the aggrieved party for:
  - ❑ Direct losses and damages naturally arising from the breach.
  - ❑ Losses due to special circumstances, if known to both parties at the time of contract formation.

2. Specific Relief:

- Governed under the Specific Relief Act, 1963.
- Includes:
  - ❑ Specific performance.
  - ❑ Rectification.
  - ❑ Rescission.
  - ❑ Injunction.

3. Restitution:

- To restore the aggrieved party to their original position before the contract.

4. Recession:

- The contract is treated as void, releasing both parties from their obligations.

5. Suit for Quantum Meruit:

- Compensation for partial performance or benefits conferred.

Common Causes of Breach

- Non-payment of consideration.
- Delay in performance beyond agreed time.
- Non-performance of a material obligation.
- Defective or improper performance.

FRUSTRATION OF CONTRACT

The **doctrine of frustration** applies when a contract becomes impossible to perform due to unforeseen circumstances, thereby discharging the parties from their contractual obligations. In India, this is governed by **Section 56 of the Indian Contract Act, 1872**.

Definition

Frustration occurs when the performance of a contract becomes **impossible**, **illegal**, or **radically different** from what was originally contemplated due to an unforeseen event beyond the control of the parties.

Legal Provisions

1. Section 56 (Indian Contract Act, 1872):

- An agreement to do an act **impossible in itself** is void.
- A contract to do an act that becomes **impossible or unlawful** after it is made, without the fault of either party, becomes void.

2. Doctrine of Supervening Impossibility:

- The event must render performance:
  - ❑ Impossible or impracticable.
  - ❑ Fundamentally different from what was agreed upon.

Conditions for Frustration

- **Impossibility of Performance**: Performance becomes physically or legally impossible (e.g., destruction of subject matter).
- **Change in Circumstances**: Performance becomes commercially impracticable or radically different due to unforeseen circumstances.

- **No Fault of the Parties**: The event causing frustration must not result from the fault of either party.
- **Unforeseen Events**: The event must be beyond what the parties could reasonably foresee at the time of contracting.

Examples of Frustration

1. **Destruction of Subject Matter**:
   - If the subject matter is destroyed (e.g., a theater burns down), performance becomes impossible.
   - **Case Law:** *Taylor v. Caldwell* (1863) – A music hall was destroyed by fire before a scheduled concert.
2. **Change in Law**:
   - If a new law makes the performance of the contract illegal.
   - **Example:** Export bans imposed after signing an export contract.
3. **Death or Incapacity**:
   - If a contract depends on the personal skill or service of a party, their death or incapacity frustrates the contract.
   - **Case Law:** *Robinson v. Davison* (1871) – A pianist fell ill and could not perform.
4. **Outbreak of War**:
   - War may render a contract impossible or illegal, especially if it involves trading with an enemy.
   - **Case Law:** *Metropolitan Water Board v. Dick Kerr & Co.* (1918) – Government requisition of a contractor's equipment during wartime frustrated the contract.
5. **Non-occurrence of an Event**:
   - If the contract's performance depends on the occurrence of a specific event, and that event does not occur.
   - **Case Law:** *Krell v. Henry* (1903) – A contract for a room to view King Edward VII's coronation procession was frustrated when the event was postponed.

Exceptions to Frustration

- **Self-Induced Frustration**: A party cannot rely on frustration if the impossibility arises due to their own act or negligence.
- **Foreseeable Events**: If the event causing frustration could have been foreseen or anticipated, the doctrine does not apply.
- **Force Majeure Clauses**: If the contract contains a force majeure clause, it will govern the rights and obligations of the parties in case of unforeseen events.
- **Partial Impossibility**: If only part of the contract becomes impossible, frustration may not apply unless it affects the entire basis of the contract.

Effects of Frustration

- **Contract Becomes Void**: Under Section 56, the frustrated contract is void, and parties are discharged from future obligations.
- **Restitution**: Under **Section 65**, if any benefit has been received under the contract, it must be restored.
- **No Damages**: The doctrine discharges both parties from the contract without imposing liability for damages.

Case Laws

- **Satyabrata Ghose v. Mugneeram Bangur & Co. (1954)**: The Supreme Court of India held that frustration occurs when an unforeseen event makes the contract impossible to perform or alters the principal purpose of the agreement.
- **Chand Basha v. Bharat Coking Coal Ltd. (2005)**: Highlighted that frustration does not apply to leases where the lessee's rights continue even if physical possession is temporarily disrupted.
- **NPA Management Group v. Ashok Iron Works (2004)**: Reaffirmed that frustration must involve complete impossibility, not mere inconvenience or hardship.

VOID AND VOIDABLE CONTRACTS

Contracts can be classified as **void** or **voidable** based on their enforceability under the **Indian Contract Act, 1872**.

VOID CONTRACT

A **void contract** is an agreement that is **not enforceable by law** and does not create any legal rights or obligations between the parties.

Features of Void Contracts

- **No Legal Effect**:
  - It is as if the contract never existed.
  - Parties cannot sue for performance or damages.

- **Time Factor**:
  - A contract may be void **ab initio** (from the beginning) or become void later.
- **Causes of Void Contracts**:
  - **Section 2(g)**: Agreements that are not enforceable by law.
  - **Section 20:** Agreements void due to mutual mistake of fact.
  - **Section 23:** Agreements with unlawful consideration or object.
  - **Section 25:** Agreements made without consideration (exceptions apply).
  - Agreements expressly declared void under the Act:
    - Restraint of trade (Section 27).
    - Restraint of marriage (Section 26).
    - Restraint of legal proceedings (Section 28).
    - Wagering agreements (Section 30).
- **Examples**:
  - Contract to commit an illegal act (e.g., smuggling).
  - Agreement between two parties based on a mutual mistake of fact.
- **Important Case Law:**
  - *Sharma v. Gupta*: An agreement with an unlawful object was declared void.

VOIDABLE CONTRACT

A **voidable contract** is an agreement that is **enforceable by law at the option of one of the parties** but not at the option of the other.

Features of Voidable Contracts

- **Option to Rescind**:
  - One party has the right to either enforce or void the contract.
  - The aggrieved party must take action within a reasonable time.
- **Causes of Voidable Contracts**:
  - **Coercion** (Section 15): Use of force to obtain consent.
  - **Undue Influence** (Section 16): Exploiting a dominant position to obtain an unfair advantage.
  - **Fraud** (Section 17): Intentional deception to induce the other party to enter the contract.
  - **Misrepresentation** (Section 18): False statements made without intent to deceive.
  - **Mistake of Law (Section 22):** If one party enters a contract under an error about Indian law.
  - Agreements entered into by a **minor**, when not void ab initio, may also be voidable.
- **Examples**:
  - A contract signed under coercion (e.g., a threat to life).
  - A contract entered into based on fraudulent information.
- **Rights of the Aggrieved Party**:
  - Rescind the contract.
  - Claim damages if applicable.
- Important Case Law:
  - *Undue Influence: Mannoj Kumar Mitra v. Nirmal Krishna Ghose* – A contract was held voidable because of undue influence.

Differences Between Void and Voidable Contracts

Aspect	Void Contract	Voidable Contract
Enforceability	Not enforceable by law.	Enforceable at the option of one party.
Legal Effect	No legal rights or obligations are created.	Rights and obligations depend on the aggrieved party's choice.
Status	Void from the beginning or becomes void later.	Valid until it is rescinded by the aggrieved party.
Cause	Illegal object, unlawful consideration, mutual mistake.	Coercion, undue influence, fraud, or misrepresentation.
Examples	Agreements in restraint of trade, wagering agreements.	Contracts entered under duress or fraud.

STANDARD CONTRACT

Standard form contract- When a large number of contracts have got to be entered into by a person, from a practical point of view and for the sake of convenience, a standard form for the numerous contracts may be used (Documents containing drafted by one party and on the same terms contracts may be made with numerous persons. An insurance policy, shares or a railway ticket are few examples of such standardized as part of the contract only if they are brought to the notice of the acceptor before or at the time of contract.

In standard form contracts, generally the terms of the contract are pre-drafted by one of the parties and the other is supposed to sign on the dotted line, without having any time or opportunity to get the terms changed. In view of the unequal bargaining power of the two parties, the courts and the legislature have evolved certain rules to protect the interest of the weaker party:

- **Reasonable notice:** If the attention of a contract has been drawn to the terms of the contract by a sufficient notice, for example, by printing back", or obtaining his signatures on the document containing terms, or otherwise explaining the terms to him, there arises a binding contract as regards such terms.

  In Henderson v Stevenson (1875) 32 LT 709, held that where an adequate notice is not given the offeree is not bound by the terms. In Special Secy., Govt. of Rajasthan v V.V. Seshaiyar (AIR 1984 A.P.5) held that ;the plaintiff was not bound by the terms printed on the reverse of the ticket. The terms on the ticket were in small print and they were not brought to the notice of the plaintiff either before or at the time of purchase of the ticket.

- **Notice should be contemporaneous with the contract:** If a party to the contract want to have exemption from liability he must give a notice about the exemption while the contract is being entered into and not thereafter [Olley v Marlborough Court, Ltd. (1949) 1 K.B. 532].

- **Terms of contract should be reasonable:** If the terms of the contract are unreasonable and opposed to public white policy, they will not be enforced. Thus, in Central Inland Water Transport Corpn. V Broje Nath (1986 SC 1571), the court struck down clause in a service not agreement whereby the service of a permanent employee could be terminated by giving him a 3 month's notice or 3 month's salary.

- **Fundamental breach of contract:** The main obligation under the contract is not allowed to be negatived by the contract. No exemption clause is allowed any to permit the non-compliance of the basic contractual obligation i.e., obligation which is fundamental or of the contract. Thus, a dry cleaner has to be answerable, even if the contract contains all sorts of exemption clauses, if the cloth is altogether lost (Davies thene Collins (1945) 1 All ER 247].

- **Non-contractual liability:** In case more than one kind of liability arises, exclusion of contractual liability may not negative any other kind of liability e.g. tortious or personal injury [White v John Warwick & Co. (1953) 1 WLR 1285].

- **Strict construction:** A strict construction shall be applied to exemption clause, and any ambiguity is to be resolved in favour of the weaker party [Lee & Sons v Railway Executive (1949) 2 All ER 581].

- **Statutory protection:** The English Unfair Contract Terms Act, 1977 severely limits the right of the contracting parties to exclude or limit their liability through exemption clauses in the agreement. India lacks.

LEADING CASE: INDIAN AIRLINES vs MADHURI CHOWDHURY (AIR 1965 Cal 252)

This case highlights the inadequacy of the Indian Contract Act in providing relief to clauses. The weaker party against the exemption clauses. In this case, the plaintiff's husband was killed in a plane crash. The plaintiff claimed compensation from the defendants i.e. Indian Airlines. The question was regarding the validity of an exemption clause contained in the Air ticket exempting the defendants from liability for negligence, viz. "for death, injury or delay to the passengers or loss, damage, detention, etc. of personal property arising out of the carriage or any other operations of the carrier.

Held that the liability of a common carrier was not not governed by the provisions of Indian Contract Act. The defendants were thus not liable. Holding the exemption clause valid, the Court said: "Any contract which contains conditions enlarging diminishing or excluding a carrier's common law duty of care to his passengers cannot in the absence of a statutory restriction on the imposition of such conditions, be pronounced unreasonable by a court with a view to one party getting more than the contract allows him, but the conditions which wholly unreasonable, are not binding upon a passenger even if steps otherwise reasonable have been taken to give him notice of them. This exemption of liability may be prevented by statute. But in India no Act applies to internal carriage by air. The Warsaw Convention does not apply; nor is there any statute which prevents or limits the scope or content of such an exemption clause."

QUASI CONTRACT

There are many situations in which law as a certain person be required to in whose whom well I as justice requires that conform to an obligation, although he has neither broken any contract nor committed any tort. For example a person in whose home certain goods have been left by mistake is bound to restore them. Such obligations are called as quasi-contractual obligations, because they do not arise out of an agreement (the legal obligations are imposed by law without offer and acceptance). They are manifestly not based upon consent and their description as a quasi-contractual liability serves only to emphasise their remoteness from genuine conception of contract. It may be noted that if an agreement does not create a legal obligation it is not a contract at all.

Chapter V of the Indian Contract Act provides for the "quasi-contracts", however the said term is not used as in view of the clear statutory provisions, the courts in India are not hindered in allowing relief under the different sections by the theoretical considerations concerning quasi-contracts.

In an action for unjust enrichment the following essentials have to be proved:

- The defendant has been 'enriched' by the receipt of a 'benefit'.
- That this enrichment is 'at the expense of the plaintiff.
- That the retention of the enrichment is 'unjust' (Mahabir Kishore v State of M.P. AIR 1990 SC 313).

PAYMENT BY AN INTERESTED PERSON (Sec. 69)

Sec. 69 reads: "A person who is interested in the payment of money, which another is bound by law to pay, and who therefore, pays it, is entitled to be reimbursed by the other."

Illustration: B holds land in Bengal, on a lease granted by A, the zamindar. The revenue payable by A to the Government being in arrears, his land is advertised for sale by Government. Under the revenue law, the consequences of such sale will be the annulment of B's lease. B, to prevent sale and the consequent annulment of his own lease, pays to the Government the sum due from A. A is bound to make good to paid.

The conditions of liability under Sec. 69 are:

- The plaintiff should be interested in making the payment. It is not necessary that he should have a legal proprietary interest in the property in respect of which the payment is made. However, often it is used to determine whether plaintiff was interested. His honest belief that he has an interest to protect is enough. Sec. 69 does not invite such judicial limitation that a person who has not an interest in the property can be interested in a payment in respect of that property.
- The plaintiff himself should not be bound to pay. He should only be interested in making the payment in order to protect his own interest bound to pay interest.
- The defendant should be under legal compulsion (covering obligations of contract or tort) to pay. For example, where a party had agreed to purchase certain mills, he was allowed to recover from the seller the amount of already overdue municipal taxes paid by him in order to save the property from being sold in execution (Govindram Gordhandas v State AIR 1950 PC 99).
- The plaintiff should have made the payment to another person and not to himself. In a case, a zamindar gave his must not land on lease to the Forest Department of Madras land was advertised for sale. The Forest Department made payment of the land revenue. It was held that the payment done by was not made to another person [Secretary of State v Fernandes (1907) 30 Mad 375].

LIABILITY TO PAY FOR NON-GRATUITOUS ACT (SEC. 70)

Three conditions must be satisfied before Sec. 70 can be invoked:

- (1) a person should lawfully do something for another person or deliver something to him;
- (2) in doing the said thing or delivering the said thing he must not intend to act gratuitously; and
- (3) the other person for whom something is done or to whom something is delivered must enjoy the benefit thereof.

Illustrations:

- A, a tradesman, leaves goods at B's house by mistake. B treats goods as his own. He is bound to pay A for them.
- A save B's property from fire. A is not entitled to compensation from B if the circumstances show that he intended to act gratuitously.

Similarly, where a coolie takes the luggage at the railway station without being asked by the passenger or a shoe-shiner starts shining shoes of the passenger without being asked to do so, and if the passenger does not object to that, then he is bound to pay reasonably for the same as the work was not intended to be gratuitous.

In cases falling under Sec. 70, the person doing something for another cannot sue for specific performance, nor ask for damages for – breach, as there is no contract between the parties. All that Sec. 70 provides for is that if the services or goods are accepted a liability to pay arises

Secondly, the person for whom the act is done is not bound to pay unless he had the choice to reject the services. Sec. 70 would not encourage officious interference in the affairs of others.

Thirdly, it is necessary that services should have been rendered without any request. However, reasonable compensation may be recovered for services rendered at request.

Fourthly, services should have been rendered lawfully. Payment for extra work done in connection with a contract without any agreement has been allowed to be recovered under this section.

Lastly, the defendant must have derived a direct benefit from the payment or services. Where the works done by a railway company developed the adjoining lands and consequently the municipality received more taxes, this was held to be not a sufficient benefit to enable the railway company to recover compensation from the municipality. Service rendered to a person incompetent to contract (e.g. minor) at the time cannot be made the basis of an action under this section. Even where the party making payment or rendering services is personally interested in the matter, he can recover proportional contribution from those who have enjoyed the benefits of his services [Damodara Mudaliar v Secy of State, India (1894) 18 Mad 88].

Sec. 70 applies even if there is a non-compliance of constitutional requirement of contracting with the State (viz. Art. 299 of the Constitution). Thus in State of W. B. v B.K. Mondal & Sons (AIR 1962 SC 779), the plaintiff made certain constructions at the request of an officer of State. The State accepted the work but refused to pay pleading that there was no valid contract. The court held in favour of the plaintiff.

FINDER FINDE OF GOODS (Sec. 71)

Sec. 71 reads: "A person, who finds goods belonging to another and takes them into his custody, is subject to the same responsibility as a bailee."

A bailee is bound to take as much care of the goods as a man of ordinary prudence would, under similar circumstances, take of his own goods .To avoid liability for criminal misappropriation of property, the finder must try to find out the real owner of the goods and must not appropriate the property to his own use (Sec. 151, Contract Act).

MISTAKE OR COERCIONS (Sec. 72)

Sec. 72 reads: "A person to whom money has been paid, or anything delivered, by mistake or under coercion, must repay or return it."

Illustrations:

- A and B jointly owe ₹ 100 to C. A alone pays the amount to C, and B, not knowing this fact, pays ₹ 100 over again to C. C is bound to repay the amount to B.
- A railway company refuses to deliver up certain goods to the consignee, except upon the payment of an illegal charge for carriage. The consignee pays the sum charged in order to obtain the goods. He is entitled to recover so much of the charge as was illegally excessive.

Sec. 72 is usually regarded as dealing with the doctrine of 'unjust enrichment'. Lord Mansfield in Moses v Macfertan (1760) 2 Burr 1005, observed that an action lies for money paid by mistake; or upon a consideration which happens to fail or for money got through imposition, extortion or oppression. The defendant in such cases is obliged by ties of natural justice and equity, to refund the money. The view of Lord Mansfield on 'equity' has been accepted by the Supreme Court in Mafatlal Industries Ltd. V Union of India (1997) 5 SCC 536 (discussed below).

In Sales Tax Officer v Kanhaiya Lal Saraf (AIR 1959 SC 135), it has been held that the money paid under mistake is recoverable whether the mistake be of fact or of law. And the term 'mistake' has been used without any limitation under Sec. 72. In this case, a certain amount of sales tax was paid by a firm under the U.P. Sales Tax laws on its forward transactions. Subsequently to the payment the Allahabad High Court ruled the levy of sales tax on such transactions to be ultra vires. The firm sought to recover back the tax money. The Supreme Court allowed it.

It is not that every sum paid under mistake is recoverable. There may be circumstances which disentitle a plaintiff by estoppel or otherwise. The Supreme Court found no ground for any estoppel against the firm and disapproved the following statement of the Nagpur High Court: If the reason for the rule is that a person paying money under mistake is entitled to recover it, because it is against the conscience of the receiver to retain it, then when the receiver has no longer the money with him (e.g. has spent it on his own purposes), different considerations must arise. The Supreme Court said that no such equitable consideration can be imported when the terms of Sec. 72 are clear and unambiguous.

Section 68 of the Indian Contract Act, 1872 (necessities supply)

Text of the Section: "If a person, incapable of entering into a contract, or anyone whom he is legally bound to support, is supplied by another person with necessaries suited to his condition in life, the person who has furnished such supplies is entitled to be reimbursed from the property of such incapable person."

Key Points and Notes

- **Incapable Persons**: Section 68 applies to persons who are not legally capable of contracting, which includes minors, persons of unsound mind, and persons who are disqualified from contracting by any law to which they are subject.
- **Necessaries Defined**: The term "necessaries" is not strictly defined in the Act but generally includes goods or services that are essential for the sustenance and normal living of such a person, considering their particular condition in life and their existing standards of comfort and lifestyle. This could include food, clothing, shelter, health care, education, and legal services deemed necessary.
- **Supplier's Right to Reimbursement**: The supplier of such necessaries is entitled to be reimbursed from the property of the incapable person. It's important to note that the claim is against the property, not against the person directly, as they are deemed incapable of contracting.
- **No Personal Liability**: The incapable person is not personally liable, but their property can be used for reimbursement. This means any claim under this section is to be satisfied only out of the property of the incapable person and does not bring personal liability upon the individual.
- **Legal Support Obligation**: The provision also extends to any person whom the incapable person is legally bound to support, such as a dependent child or spouse, indicating that suppliers can seek reimbursement if they provide necessaries to dependents of an individual who is incapable of contracting.

BAILMENT

Definition of Bailment

- **Definition**:
  - ❑ Section 148 of the Indian Contract Act, 1872 defines Bailment as: *"The delivery of goods by one person to another for some purpose, upon a contract that they shall, when the purpose is accomplished, be returned or otherwise disposed of according to the directions of the person delivering them."*
- **Parties**:
  - ❑ **Bailor**: The person who delivers the goods.
  - ❑ **Bailee**: The person to whom the goods are delivered.
- **Key Features**:
  - ❑ **Delivery of Goods**: Involves transfer of possession, not ownership.
  - ❑ **Purpose**: Goods are delivered for a specific purpose.
  - ❑ **Return of Goods**: Goods must be returned after the purpose is fulfilled.

Essentials of Bailment

- **Delivery of Goods**:
  - ❑ Actual or constructive delivery.
  - ❑ Ownership remains with the bailor.
- **Purpose**: The goods must be delivered for a lawful purpose.
- **Voluntary Agreement**: Both parties must consent to the contract.
- **Return or Disposal of Goods**: Bailee must return the goods or act as per the bailor's instructions.

Duties of a Bailor

- **Duty to Disclose Defects**:
  - ❑ In case of gratuitous bailment, disclose known defects.
  - ❑ In case of bailment for consideration, disclose known and latent defects.
- **Compensation to Bailee**: Bailor must compensate for expenses incurred in keeping the goods.
- **Responsibility for Loss**: Bailor is liable if goods delivered were defective or caused harm to the bailee.

Duties of a Bailee

- **Reasonable Care**:
  - ❑ Take care of goods as an ordinary prudent person would.
  - ❑ Liable for negligence if goods are lost or damaged.
- **Not to Make Unauthorized Use**: Using goods outside the agreed purpose makes the bailee liable for damages.
- **Return the Goods**: Return goods after the purpose is completed or at the bailor's request.
- **Not to Mix Goods**: If bailee mixes goods without consent, they bear the cost of separation.

Rights of a Bailor

- **Demand Return of Goods**: Bailor has the right to demand return when the purpose is fulfilled.
- **Claim Damages**: Can claim damages for unauthorized use or negligence by the bailee.
- **Right to Terminate**: Bailor can terminate the bailment for misuse or breach by bailee.

Rights of a Bailee

- **Right to Compensation**: Bailee has a right to be reimbursed for expenses incurred in maintaining the goods.
- **Right of Lien**: Bailee can retain goods for unpaid expenses or remuneration.
- **Right to Indemnity**: If a third party claims the goods, the bailor must indemnify the bailee.

Types of Bailment

- **Gratuitous Bailment**: No consideration involved; either party can terminate at will.
- **Bailment for Consideration**: Contract involves remuneration or reward.

Termination of Bailment

- **On Completion of Purpose**: Bailment ends when the agreed purpose is fulfilled.
- **By Expiry of Time**: Ends after the agreed time duration.
- **By Act of Parties**: Either party can terminate, provided conditions are met.
- **By Destruction of Goods**: Bailment ends if goods are destroyed or lost.

Finder of Goods as a Bailee

- **Definition**: A person who finds goods belonging to another and takes possession of them.
- **Duties of Finder**:
  - Take reasonable care of the goods.
  - Return the goods to the rightful owner.
- **Rights of Finder**:
  - Right to retain goods until the rightful owner compensates for expenses incurred in preservation.
  - Cannot sell the goods unless:
    - Goods are perishable.
    - Lawful charges exceed two-thirds of the value.

PLEDGE

Essentials of Pledge

A pledge is a **bailment of goods** as security for the payment of a debt or performance of a promise.

Essentials:

- **Delivery of Goods**: Actual or constructive delivery of goods is necessary.
- **Purpose**: The delivery must be for securing a debt or performance of a promise.
- **Ownership**: Ownership remains with the pledger; only possession is transferred.
- **Return of Goods**: The pledgee must return the goods after the debt is paid or the promise is performed.
- **Movable Property**: Only movable property can be pledged.
- **Consent**: There must be a valid agreement between the pledger and pledgee.

Legal Reference:

- Defined under **Section 172** of the **Indian Contract Act, 1872.**

Difference between Bailment and Pledge

Aspect	Bailment	Pledge
Purpose	Goods are delivered for safekeeping or use.	Goods are delivered as security for repayment of debt.
Ownership	Ownership remains with the bailor.	Ownership remains with the pledger.
Consideration	May or may not involve consideration.	Always involves a debt or promise to be secured.
Right to Sell	Bailee cannot sell the goods.	Pledgee can sell goods on default after proper notice.
Law	Sections 148–171 of the Indian Contract Act.	Sections 172–181 of the Indian Contract Act.

Rights and Duties of Pledger and Pledgee

Rights of the Pledger (Borrower):

- **Right to Redeem Goods (Section 177)**: The pledger can reclaim the pledged goods by paying the debt before the pledgee sells them.
- **Right to Demand Sale Proceeds**: If goods are sold, the pledger can claim any surplus amount after the debt is settled.

Duties of the Pledger:

- **Repayment of Debt**: The pledger must pay the debt or fulfill the promise secured by the pledge.

- **Indemnification**: The pledger must indemnify the pledgee for expenses incurred in maintaining the goods.

Rights of the Pledgee (Creditor):

- **Right to Retain Goods (Section 173)**: The pledgee can retain possession of goods until the debt is paid.
- **Right to Sell Goods (Section 176)**: The pledgee can sell the goods after giving reasonable notice if the pledger defaults.
- **Right to Recover Deficiency**: If the sale proceeds are insufficient, the pledgee can sue for the remaining debt.

Duties of the Pledgee:

- **Care of Goods (Section 151)**: The pledgee must take reasonable care of the pledged goods.
- **Return of Goods**: The pledgee must return the goods upon repayment of the debt.

Lien and its Types

Lien: The **right to retain possession** of goods until a debt or obligation is fulfilled.

Types of Lien in Pledge:

- **Particular Lien (Section 173)**:
  - ❑ Right to retain goods for the specific debt for which they were pledged.
  - ❑ Example: A bank retains jewelry pledged against a loan until repayment.

General Lien (Section 174):

- Right to retain goods for any general balance of account.
- Example: Bankers, factors, and warehousemen may have this right if explicitly agreed upon.

Pledge by Non-Owner

Under **Section 178 and 178A** of the Indian Contract Act:

- **Mercantile Agent (Section 178)**:
  - ❑ A mercantile agent, acting within the scope of their authority, can pledge goods even if they do not own them.
  - ❑ Example: A car dealer pledging a vehicle in stock.
- **Possession with Consent**:
  - ❑ If the goods are in possession of the pledger with the owner's consent, the pledge is valid.
  - ❑ Example: Lessee pledging goods in their possession.
- **Finder of Goods (Section 169)**: A finder of goods can pledge goods if expenses are incurred for preservation or finding the owner.
- **Exceptions:** Pledge made by a person who acquired goods through theft or fraud is void.

Enforcement of Rights of the Pledgee

- **Right to Sue**: The pledgee can sue the pledger for the recovery of the debt without selling the pledged goods.
- **Sale of Goods (Section 176)**:
  - ❑ If the pledger defaults, the pledgee can sell the goods after giving reasonable notice.
  - ❑ Example: Auction of pledged shares for a defaulted loan.
- **Right to Retain Proceeds**: The pledgee can retain the sale proceeds to satisfy the debt and return the surplus, if any.

Legal Framework

- **Statutory Provisions**: Governed by **Sections 172–181** of the **Indian Contract Act, 1872.**
- **Banking and Financial Transactions**: Pledge is commonly used in secured loans where movable assets like jewelry or stock are pledged as collateral.
- **Case Laws**:
  - ❑ **Lallan Prasad v. Rahmat Ali (1967)**:
    - ➾ Rights of a pledgee to retain goods until debt is cleared.
- **State Bank of India v. Shyama Devi (1978)**: Sale of pledged goods must be preceded by reasonable notice.
- **International Application**: In cross-border trade, warehouse receipts are often pledged to secure loans.

Breach of Contract in Pledge

Remedies for Breach:

- **For the Pledger**: Claim damages for loss caused by the pledgee's negligence.
- **For the Pledgee**:
  - ❑ Sell goods and recover outstanding debt.
  - ❑ File a lawsuit for the balance amount.

- **Case Laws:**
  - **Bank of Bihar v. Damodar Prasad (1969)**: Pledgee is entitled to retain goods until full payment of the debt.
  - **Suraj Bhan v. Mohd. Ishaq (1925)**: Sale of pledged goods without notice is invalid.

INDEMNITY

Meaning and Definition of Indemnity

- **Definition (Section 124 of the Indian Contract Act, 1872)**:
  - **Indemnity** means a contract by which one party promises to save the other from loss caused:
    - By the conduct of the promisor, or
    - By the conduct of any other person.
  - Example: A contracts to indemnify B if a third party sues B for damages. A is bound to compensate B.
- **Key Features**:
  - **Two Parties**: Indemnifier (promisor) and Indemnity-Holder (promisee).
  - **Promise to Protect Against Loss**: Loss must result from specified events.
  - **Written or Oral Contract**: No specific format required unless statutes prescribe otherwise.

Rights of the Indemnifier and Indemnity-Holder

Rights of Indemnity-Holder:

- **Compensation for Loss (Section 125)**:
  - Right to recover damages caused due to indemnified events.
  - Right to recover all sums paid in settlement of claims.
  - Right to recover all costs incurred due to indemnifier's act or third-party claims.
- **Right to Sue for Anticipated Loss**: Indemnity-holder can seek damages before incurring actual loss if liability is imminent.

Rights of Indemnifier:

- **Right to Subrogation**: Upon indemnification, the indemnifier steps into the shoes of the indemnity-holder and acquires their rights against third parties.
- **Right to Reimbursement**: Indemnifier can seek reimbursement from the indemnity-holder for excess or unjustified claims.

Distinction Between Indemnity and Guarantee

Aspect	Indemnity	Guarantee
Parties	Two parties: Indemnifier and Indemnity-Holder.	Three parties: Creditor, Debtor, and Surety.
Nature of Contract	Promise to save the other party from loss.	Promise to fulfill a third party's obligation in case of default.
Liability	Primary liability rests with indemnifier.	Secondary liability rests with surety.
Scope	Covers loss from indemnified events.	Covers debt, default, or obligation.

Scope of Indemnity Contracts

- **Express Indemnity**: Explicitly mentioned in agreements (e.g., insurance policies, construction contracts).
- **Implied Indemnity**: Arises out of relationships or circumstances (e.g., employer indemnifies employee for work-related acts).
- **Broad Scope**: Applicable in corporate agreements, insurance contracts, and financial dealings.
- **Extent of Coverage**:
  - May include:
    - Direct losses.
    - Consequential losses (if agreed).
    - Third-party claims.

Common Applications of Indemnity

- **Insurance Contracts**: The insurer promises to indemnify the insured against specified risks (e.g., fire, theft).
- **Commercial Contracts**: Indemnity clauses are common in joint ventures, mergers, acquisitions, and agency agreements.
- **Employment Agreements**: Employers often indemnify employees for liabilities arising out of job-related actions.
- **Banking and Finance**: Indemnity used in guarantees and secured loans.

Key Case Laws on Indemnity

- **Gajanan Moreshwar v. Moreshwar Madan (1942)**: The Bombay High Court held that an indemnity-holder can recover damages even before actual payment if liability is certain.
- **Osborne v. Harper (1838)**: Established the principle that indemnity extends only to losses caused by events specified in the contract.

- **United India Insurance Co. Ltd. V. Ajmer Singh Cotton & General Mills (1999)**: Indemnity clauses in insurance contracts must be interpreted strictly as per the terms of the policy.

Interpretation of "Compensatory Liability"

- **Loss Must Be Quantifiable**: Compensation is limited to actual losses suffered due to indemnified events.
- **Exclusion of Remote Damages**: Only foreseeable losses arising directly from indemnified events are covered.

Liability Arising Out of Acts of Third Parties

- **Indemnifier's Responsibility**: Liable for losses caused by third-party claims if specified in the contract.
- **Limits of Indemnity**: Third-party liabilities are enforceable only within the scope of the agreement.

CONTRACT OF GUARANTEE

Definition and Essentials of a Contract of Guarantee

- **Definition**: A **contract of guarantee** is a contract to perform the promise, or discharge the liability, of a third person in case of his default. (Section 126, Indian Contract Act, 1872).
- **Essentials**:
  - **Tripartite Agreement**: Involves three parties – Principal Debtor, Creditor, and Surety.
  - **Consent of All Parties**: Must be mutual and informed.
  - **Primary Liability**: Principal debtor has the primary liability, and surety has a secondary liability.
  - **Lawful Consideration**: The contract must have valid consideration.
  - **Written or Oral**: The guarantee may be expressed in writing or may be oral.
  - **Liability Contingent on Default**: Surety's obligation arises only upon the default of the principal debtor.

Parties to a Guarantee

- **Principal Debtor**:
  - The person who has borrowed money or availed credit.
  - Has the primary obligation to fulfill the promise.
- **Creditor**:
  - The person or entity who gives a loan or credit.
  - Can demand payment from the principal debtor or surety.
- **Surety**:
  - The person who guarantees the performance of the contract or repayment of the debt.
  - Liable only if the principal debtor defaults.

Types of Guarantees

- **Specific Guarantee**:
  - Applies to a specific transaction or debt.
  - Ends once the debt is repaid or the obligation is fulfilled.
- **Continuing Guarantee**:
  - Covers a series of transactions.
  - Remains valid until revoked by the surety or until the specific conditions of the agreement are met.
  - Example: Guarantee for a running account in a bank.

Rights of Surety

- **Against the Principal Debtor**:
  - **Right to Indemnity**: Surety can recover any amount paid on behalf of the debtor.
  - **Subrogation**: Upon payment, surety steps into the shoes of the creditor and can exercise creditor's rights against the debtor.
- **Against the Creditor**:
  - **Right to Securities**: Surety is entitled to the benefit of securities held by the creditor, even if unaware of their existence.
  - **Right to Set-off**: Surety can claim any amounts that the creditor owes to the principal debtor.
- **Against Co-Sureties**:
  - **Right to Contribution**: If there are multiple sureties, they share the liability proportionally.

Liabilities of Surety

- **Primary and Secondary Liability**:
  - The principal debtor has primary liability, while the surety's liability is secondary.

- However, the creditor can directly sue the surety without first proceeding against the principal debtor.

- **Extent of Liability**:
  - Determined by the terms of the contract.
  - Surety's liability cannot exceed what is specified in the contract.

Discharge of Surety from Liability

- **By Revocation**:
  - Surety can revoke a continuing guarantee by giving notice to the creditor.
  - Revocation does not affect prior transactions.
- **By Conduct of Creditor**: Any action by the creditor that prejudices the surety discharges the surety (e.g., loss of security).
- **By Variation of Terms**: Any variation in the terms of the original contract without the surety's consent discharges the surety.
- **By Release of Principal Debtor**: If the principal debtor is discharged by the creditor, the surety is also discharged.
- **By Fraud or Misrepresentation**: If the contract of guarantee was obtained through fraud or misrepresentation, it is voidable at the surety's option.

Difference Between Indemnity and Guarantee

Aspect	Indemnity	Guarantee
Parties	Two parties: Indemnifier and Indemnity-holder.	Three parties: Principal Debtor, Creditor, Surety.
Liability	Only one person (Indemnifier) is liable.	Surety's liability is secondary.
Purpose	To compensate for a loss.	To ensure performance or repayment.
Nature	Contingent upon the happening of an event.	Contingent upon the default of the principal debtor.

Important Case Laws

- **Amrit Lal Goverdhan Lalan v. State Bank of Travancore (1968)**: Emphasized the rights of a surety to securities held by the creditor.
- **Bank of Bihar v. Damodar Prasad (1969)**: Held that the creditor is not bound to exhaust remedies against the principal debtor before suing the surety.
- **State of Maharashtra v. Dr. M.N. Kaul (1967)**: Discussed the discharge of surety when the creditor releases the principal debtor.
- **Birkmyr v. Darnell (1704)**: Early English case laying down the principles of contracts of guarantee.

AGENCY: DEFINITION AND ESSENTIALS

- **Definition:** An agency is a legal relationship where one party (the agent) is authorized to act on behalf of another (the principal) to establish legal relations with third parties.
- Essentials of an Agency Contract:
  - **Principal-Agent Relationship:** Must exist with the agent acting under the principal's authority.
  - **Competency of Principal:** Principal must be competent to contract; the agent need not be competent if acting under valid authority.
  - **Consent:** Both principal and agent must consent to the relationship.
  - **Purpose of Agency:** Must be lawful.
  - **Consideration:** Not mandatory; gratuitous agency is valid.

CREATION OF AGENCY

- **Express Agreement:** Created through written or oral consent.
- **Implied Agreement:** Created by conduct, relationship, or circumstances (e.g., family situations, business conduct).
- **By Estoppel:** When the principal's actions make a third party believe the agent has authority.
- **By Necessity:** Arises in emergencies to protect the principal's interest.
- **By Ratification:**
  - Acts performed by someone without authority can be ratified by the principal.
  - Ratification relates back to the time of the act.

TYPES OF AGENTS AND THEIR AUTHORITY

Types of Agents:

- **General Agent:** Authorized to perform all acts relating to a particular business or employment.
- **Special Agent:** Authorized for a specific purpose or transaction.
- **Sub-Agent:** Appointed by the agent to assist in the principal's work with the principal's consent.
- **Mercantile Agent:** Includes brokers, auctioneers, and factors, who have authority in commercial transactions.

Types of Authority:

- **Actual Authority:**
  - ❑ **Express Authority:** Specifically granted.
  - ❑ **Implied Authority:** Derived from the conduct, customs, or circumstances.
- **Apparent (Ostensible) Authority:** Authority that a third party believes the agent has due to the principal's representations.
- **Authority by Necessity:** For urgent matters when immediate action is required.

RIGHTS AND DUTIES OF PRINCIPAL AND AGENT

Rights of the Principal:

- To obtain true accounts from the agent.
- To claim damages for breach of duty.
- To repudiate transactions done outside authority.

Duties of the Principal:

- To indemnify the agent for lawful acts done in the course of the agency.
- To pay remuneration to the agent unless gratuitous.

Rights of the Agent:

- To be indemnified for lawful acts.
- To claim remuneration and lien over the principal's property until paid.

Duties of the Agent:

- To act within authority.
- To perform duties with due diligence and skill.
- To avoid conflict of interest.
- To remit amounts received on behalf of the principal.

TERMINATION OF AGENCY

Modes of Termination:

- **By Act of Parties:**
  - ❑ Mutual agreement.
  - ❑ Revocation by the principal.
  - ❑ Renunciation by the agent.
- **By Operation of Law:**
  - ❑ Completion of the agency's purpose.
  - ❑ Death or insanity of principal or agent.
  - ❑ Insolvency of the principal.
  - ❑ Destruction of the subject matter.
- **Important Points:**
  - ❑ Revocation must occur before the agent acts on behalf of the principal.
  - ❑ Irrevocable Agency:
    - Cannot be terminated if it is coupled with interest.
    - Agent retains the right to exercise authority for their benefit.

SUB-AGENT VS. SUBSTITUTED AGENT

- **Sub-Agent:**
  - ❑ Appointed by the agent with principal's consent.
  - ❑ Works under the agent's control.
  - ❑ The principal is liable for acts of the sub-agent.
- **Substituted Agent:**
  - ❑ Appointed by the agent.
  - ❑ Works under the principal's control.
  - ❑ Principal is directly liable for acts of the substituted agent.

INTRODUCTION TO THE SALE OF GOODS ACT, 1930

The **Sale of Goods Act, 1930** is a key piece of legislation in India that governs contracts related to the sale and purchase of goods. It provides a legal framework to define, regulate, and enforce the rights and duties of buyers and sellers in a sale transaction. This Act separates the law relating to the sale of goods from the Indian Contract Act, 1872, and establishes specific provisions for contracts of sale.

TYPES OF GOODS UNDER THE SALE OF GOODS ACT, 1930

The **Sale of Goods Act, 1930** classifies goods into different categories based on their nature and the stage of ownership or availability at the time of the contract of sale. Understanding these types of goods is crucial to determining the rights and obligations of the buyer and seller.

Existing Goods

Existing goods are goods that are owned or possessed by the seller at the time of the contract of sale. These are further subdivided into:

- **Specific Goods**
  - ❑ **Definition**: Goods that are identified and agreed upon at the time of the contract of sale.

- ❑ **Example**: A specific car with a unique VIN number, or a particular painting that the buyer and seller agree upon.
- ❑ **Key Feature**: Both parties have explicitly identified the goods to be sold.

- **Ascertained Goods**
  - ❑ **Definition**: Goods that are initially unascertained but later identified and set aside for the purpose of the contract.
  - ❑ **Example**: From a bulk of 100 bags of wheat, the seller and buyer agree to sell and buy 20 specific bags.
  - ❑ **Key Feature**: These are goods that become specific after selection or appropriation.
- **Unascertained Goods**
  - ❑ **Definition**: Goods that are not specifically identified at the time of the contract of sale.
  - ❑ **Example**: Buying 50 bags of rice from a warehouse containing 500 bags.
  - ❑ **Key Feature**: The goods are not separated or distinguished at the time of agreement, and identification occurs later.

Future Goods

- **Definition**: Goods that the seller does not currently own or possess but agrees to manufacture, procure, or acquire in the future.
- **Example**: A contract to sell mangoes from the seller's orchard for the upcoming season.
- **Key Feature**: Future goods do not exist at the time of the contract and depend on future events or production.
- **Legal Provision**: The contract for future goods is an **agreement to sell**, as the goods do not exist at the time of the agreement.

Contingent Goods

- **Definition**: A subtype of future goods, contingent goods are goods whose acquisition by the seller depends on the occurrence or non-occurrence of a specific event.
- **Example**: A seller agrees to sell a batch of fish if they are caught during the next fishing trip.
- **Key Feature**: The performance of the contract is contingent upon a future uncertain event.
- **Legal Provision**: A contract for contingent goods is also treated as an **agreement to sell** until the contingency is fulfilled.

Comparison Between Types of Goods

Type of Goods	Existence at Contract Time	Ownership	Example
Specific Goods	Exist	Identified and agreed upon	A specific car or piece of jewelry
Ascertained Goods	Exist	Identified from a larger quantity	10 bags of rice selected from a stockpile
Unascertained Goods	Exist	Not yet identified or agreed upon	Any 50 liters of milk from a dairy farm
Future Goods	Do not exist	Seller agrees to procure or produce	Mangoes from the next harvest
Contingent Goods	Depend on a future event	Seller's ownership depends on event	Fish from the next fishing trip

CONDITIONS AND WARRANTIES UNDER THE SALE OF GOODS ACT, 1930

The concepts of **conditions** and **warranties** are critical in understanding the contractual obligations in a contract for the sale of goods. They help establish the rights of the buyer and the seller in case of a breach.

Meaning of Conditions and Warranties

Condition

- A **condition** is a **major term** of the contract, the breach of which goes to the root of the contract. If a condition is breached, the aggrieved party has the right to:
  - ❑ Repudiate (cancel) the contract, and
  - ❑ Claim damages.
- **Example**: A buyer orders a car of a specific model, but the seller delivers a different model. The buyer can refuse to accept the car and cancel the contract.

Warranty

- A **warranty** is a **minor term** of the contract. It is not fundamental to the performance of the contract, and its breach does not allow for cancellation. The aggrieved party can only:
  - ❑ Claim damages for the breach.
- **Example**: A seller provides a one-year warranty for free repairs of a car. If the seller refuses to honor this, the buyer can claim damages but cannot reject the car.

Distinction Between Conditions and Warranties

Aspect	Condition	Warranty
Nature	Essential term, fundamental to the contract	Non-essential term, secondary to the contract
Effect of Breach	Right to cancel the contract and claim damages	Right to claim damages only
Example	Delivering goods of the wrong description	Failure to provide a promised free service

Implied Conditions

The **Sale of Goods Act, 1930** specifies certain conditions that are implied in every contract of sale unless the contract states otherwise. These are:

- **Condition as to Title (Section 14(a))**
  - ❑ The seller has the right to sell the goods, and the buyer will enjoy uninterrupted ownership.
  - ❑ **Example**: If the seller does not own the goods or has no right to sell them, the buyer can cancel the contract.
- **Condition as to Description (Section 15)**
  - ❑ Goods must correspond to the description provided in the contract.
  - ❑ **Example**: If a buyer orders "100% cotton shirts" and receives polyester shirts, the condition is breached.
- **Condition as to Quality or Fitness (Section 16(1))**
  - ❑ If the buyer has made the seller aware of the intended purpose for the goods, the goods must be fit for that purpose.
  - ❑ **Example**: If a buyer informs the seller that they need a water pump for irrigation, but the pump is unsuitable, this condition is breached.
- **Condition as to Merchantable Quality (Section 16(2))**
  - ❑ Goods sold must be of merchantable quality, meaning they should be saleable and free from defects.
  - ❑ **Example**: If a buyer purchases packaged milk and it is spoiled, this condition is breached.
- **Condition as to Sample (Section 17)**
  - ❑ When goods are sold by sample, they must match the sample provided.
  - ❑ **Example**: If a sample of high-quality fabric is shown, the bulk of the goods must match that quality.
- **Condition as to Sample and Description (Section 15)**
  - ❑ When goods are sold by both sample and description, they must correspond to both.
- **Condition as to Wholesomeness**
  - ❑ Particularly applicable to food items, goods must be wholesome and fit for consumption.
  - ❑ **Example**: Selling contaminated food violates this condition.

Implied Warranties

Implied warranties are secondary to the contract and exist to safeguard the interests of the buyer:

- Warranty as to Quiet Possession (Section 14(b))
  - ❑ The buyer must enjoy uninterrupted possession of the goods.
  - ❑ **Example**: If a third party claims ownership and disrupts possession, this warranty is breached.
- **Warranty as to Freedom from Encumbrance (Section 14I)**
  - ❑ Goods sold should be free from any undisclosed charges or encumbrances.
  - ❑ **Example**: If the goods are under a lien and the buyer is unaware, this warranty is breached.
- **Warranty as to Quality or Fitness (When Disclosure is Required)**
  - ❑ If goods are purchased for a specific purpose, and the buyer relies on the seller's expertise, it is implied that the goods will be fit for that purpose.
- **Warranty for Repairs or Replacement**
  - ❑ In some contracts, a warranty for after-sales service or replacement of defective goods is implied.

Doctrine of Caveat Emptor (Let the Buyer Beware)

Meaning: The principle of **Caveat Emptor** means that the buyer must take responsibility for checking the quality, fitness, and suitability of the goods before purchase. The seller is not liable for any defects if the buyer does not examine the goods.

Exceptions to Caveat Emptor:

The doctrine is subject to several exceptions under the **Sale of Goods Act, 1930**:

- **When the Seller Knows the Buyer's Purpose (Section 16(1)):** If the buyer informs the seller about the specific purpose for which the goods are needed, and the seller recommends them, the goods must meet that purpose.
- **Sale by Description (Section 15):** When goods are sold based on a description, they must match the description.

- **Sale by Sample (Section 17):** When goods are sold by sample, they must correspond to the sample shown.
- **Merchantable Quality (Section 16(2)):** If goods are purchased from a seller who deals in such goods, they must be of merchantable quality unless the buyer has examined them and found defects.
- **Misrepresentation or Fraud**: If the seller makes a false statement or conceals a material defect, the buyer is protected.
- **Sale of Wholesome Goods**: Particularly for food items, the seller is liable if the goods are not fit for consumption.

Summary Table

Aspect	Condition	Warranty	Caveat Emptor Exception
Nature	Essential to the contract	Secondary to the contract	Protects buyer if seller breaches conditions
Remedy for Breach	Cancel the contract + damages	Claim damages only	Buyer protected under exceptions
Examples	Goods matching description or purpose	Free from encumbrances	Seller misrep-resentation or fraud

TRANSFER OF OWNERSHIP UNDER THE SALE OF GOODS ACT, 1930

The **transfer of ownership** in a contract of sale is a crucial aspect as it determines when the buyer gains the title (ownership rights) to the goods. This also affects other aspects such as the passing of risk, liability, and remedies in case of a breach.

Rules Regarding the Transfer of Property in Goods

The rules governing the transfer of ownership depend on the nature of the goods being sold:

Specific or Ascertained Goods (Section 19–20)

- **Ownership of specific goods is transferred when:**
  - Both parties intend for the ownership to pass, and
  - All conditions agreed upon are fulfilled.
- **If the intention is unclear, the rules of Section 20 apply:** The property in the goods passes when the contract is made, provided the goods are in a deliverable state.

Unascertained Goods (Section 18)

- **Ownership of unascertained goods does not pass until the goods are:**
  - Appropriated (identified and set aside) to the contract.
  - Appropriation can be done by the seller, the buyer, or a third party with mutual consent.

Goods to be Put in a Deliverable State (Section 21)

- If the goods are not in a deliverable state, the seller must do something (e.g., packaging, repairs) to make them deliverable. Ownership passes only when the seller completes this and notifies the buyer.

Sale on Approval or Sale or Return (Section 24)

- **Ownership is transferred when:**
  - The buyer communicates acceptance, or
  - The buyer does not reject the goods within the stipulated time, or
  - The buyer acts in a manner inconsistent with the seller's ownership (e.g., reselling the goods).

Passing of Risk

The **risk of loss or damage to goods** is linked to ownership unless otherwise agreed:

- **General Rule (Section 26):** The risk passes with ownership. The person who owns the goods bears the risk, even if possession is with the other party.
- **Unascertained Goods:** Risk does not pass to the buyer until the goods are ascertained and ownership is transferred.
- **Delay in Delivery:** If delivery is delayed due to the fault of either party, the party at fault bears the risk during the delay.
- **Exceptions:** Parties can contractually agree that risk will pass at a different time (e.g., during shipment).
- **Example:** If goods are sold but remain with the seller, and a fire destroys the goods, the buyer bears the risk if ownership has already passed.

Importance of Delivery

Delivery plays a vital role in the transfer of ownership, as it facilitates the passing of possession and risk:

Types of Delivery:

- **Actual Delivery**: Physical transfer of goods from the seller to the buyer.

- **Symbolic Delivery**: Delivery of a symbol representing the goods, such as handing over a key to a warehouse.
- **Constructive Delivery**: Transfer of control without physical movement of the goods, e.g., transferring ownership papers.

Rules Governing Delivery:

- Delivery must be made according to the contract's terms.
- Goods must be in a deliverable state.

Importance:

- Delivery signifies performance of the seller's obligation.
- It is a precondition for the transfer of risk in most cases.

Reservation of the Right of Disposal (Section 25)

Meaning: The seller may reserve the right to retain ownership of the goods even after they are delivered, typically to secure payment.

Conditions for Reservation:

- Ownership does not pass to the buyer until the seller's conditions are fulfilled (e.g., full payment).

Methods of Reservation:

- **By Contract**: The contract may explicitly state that ownership is retained until payment.
- **Through a Bill of Lading or Transport Document**: If the seller ships goods and retains control over the transport document (e.g., bill of lading), ownership remains with the seller.
- **Example:** A seller agrees to sell goods to a buyer but stipulates that ownership will not transfer until the buyer pays the full amount. If the buyer defaults, the seller can reclaim the goods.

Key Points to Remember

Aspect	Explanation
Transfer of Ownership	Ownership passes when both parties intend it to, as per the type of goods and conditions fulfilled.
Passing of Risk	Risk generally follows ownership unless the contract specifies otherwise.
Importance of Delivery	Delivery symbolizes performance of the seller's obligations and is often linked to risk transfer.
Reservation of Disposal	The seller retains ownership until certain conditions, like payment, are met.

UNPAID SELLER AND ITS RIGHTS UNDER THE SALE OF GOODS ACT, 1930

The concept of the **unpaid seller** is fundamental in the **Sale of Goods Act, 1930**, as it safeguards the seller's interests in situations where the buyer fails to fulfill payment obligations.

Meaning of an Unpaid Seller

- **Definition:** An **unpaid seller** is a seller who:
  - Has not received the full price of the goods sold, or
  - Has received a payment, but the payment has been dishonored (e.g., a bounced cheque).
- **Legal Reference:** Section 45 of the **Sale of Goods Act, 1930** defines the unpaid seller and provides the rights available to them.
  - **Example:** A sells goods worth ₹ 50,000 to B. If B fails to pay or gives a cheque that bounces, A becomes an unpaid seller.

Rights of an Unpaid Seller

The **unpaid seller's rights** are divided into two categories:

- **Rights against thZe goods**: Protecting the seller's interest in the goods sold.
- **Rights against the buyer personally**: Seeking remedies from the buyer directly.

A. Rights Against the Goods

- **Right of Lien (Section 47–49):** The unpaid seller has the right to retain possession of the goods until the buyer pays the full price.
  - **Conditions for Lien**:
    - The seller must be in possession of the goods.
    - The goods must have been sold without a stipulation of credit, or the credit period has expired.
  - **Termination of Lien**:
    - When the goods are delivered to the buyer or their agent.
    - When the seller waives the lien voluntarily.
  - **Example**: If a seller has delivered part of the goods but retains the rest because the buyer has not paid, the seller is exercising their lien.
- **Right of Stoppage in Transit (Section 50–52):** The unpaid seller can stop goods in transit if the

buyer becomes insolvent, even if the goods have been handed over to a carrier.

- **Conditions for Stoppage**:
  - The buyer must be insolvent.
  - The goods must be in transit (not yet delivered to the buyer).
- **How to Stop Transit**: Inform the carrier or bailee not to deliver the goods to the buyer.
- **Termination of Transit**: Transit ends when the buyer or their agent takes delivery.
- **Example**: A seller dispatches goods to the buyer. If the buyer becomes insolvent while the goods are with the courier, the seller can instruct the courier to return the goods.

- **Right of Resale (Section 54):** If the buyer defaults, the seller has the right to resell the goods.
  - **Conditions for Resale**:
    - The seller has exercised their right of lien or stoppage in transit.
    - A reasonable notice of resale is given to the buyer.
  - **Effect of Resale**: If the goods are resold at a lower price, the seller can claim the difference from the original buyer as damages.
  - **Example**: If goods worth ₹ 50,000 are resold for ₹ 40,000, the seller can recover ₹ 10,000 from the buyer.

B. Rights Against the Buyer Personally

If the unpaid seller cannot exercise their rights against the goods, they can seek remedies against the buyer personally:

- **Suit for Price (Section 55):** The seller can sue the buyer for the price of the goods if the buyer refuses or neglects to pay.
- **Suit for Damages (Section 56):** The seller can claim damages for non-acceptance of goods by the buyer.
- **Suit for Interest (Section 61):** If the buyer delays payment, the seller can sue for interest on the unpaid amount.
- **Suit for Repudiation:** If the buyer wrongfully cancels the contract, the seller can sue for damages due to breach of contract.

Summary Table

Rights of Unpaid Seller	Conditions	Example
Rights Against the Goods		
Right of Lien	Seller retains goods if the price is unpaid.	Seller withholds goods when the buyer fails to pay on delivery.
Right of Stoppage in Transit	Goods can be stopped if the buyer is insolvent.	Seller stops goods in transit after learning the buyer has declared bankruptcy.
Right of Resale	Goods can be resold after lien or stoppage if the buyer defaults.	Seller resells goods after notifying the buyer, claiming the price difference as damages.
Rights Against Buyer		
Suit for Price	Seller sues for the price when the buyer refuses to pay.	Buyer fails to pay ₹ 50,000 for delivered goods, so the seller sues.
Suit for Damages	Seller claims damages for non-acceptance or breach of contract.	Buyer refuses to accept goods ordered, causing losses for the seller.
Suit for Interest	Seller sues for interest on the delayed payment.	Buyer delays payment beyond the agreed credit period, and the seller demands interest.

PARTNERSHIP ACT 1932

NATURE OF PARTNERSHIP

Section: Section 4

Definition: "Partnership is the relation between persons who have agreed to share the profits of a business carried on by all or any of them acting for all."

- **Core Concept:** Partnership is a contractual relationship where individuals (partners) collaborate to run a business and share its profits. It's not a status-based entity like a Hindu Undivided Family (HUF) but arises from mutual consent.
- **Essential Elements:**
  - **Agreement:** The foundation of partnership, it can be oral, written (e.g., partnership deed), or implied by conduct (e.g., jointly managing a shop). Without agreement, no partnership exists—e.g., co-owners of property aren't partners unless they agree to a business venture.

- ❑ **Business:** A lawful activity (trade, profession, or occupation) aimed at profit. Mere joint ownership (e.g., inherited land) isn't enough unless actively managed for gain—e.g., A and B renting out property as a business qualifies.
- ❑ **Profit-Sharing:** Partners must agree to share profits, though sharing losses isn't mandatory (can be agreed otherwise). However, profit-sharing alone doesn't prove partnership—e.g., a servant paid 10% profits isn't a partner unless he has agency.
- ❑ **Mutual Agency:** The defining feature—each partner is an agent of the firm and other partners, binding them in business dealings, and a principal, liable for others' acts. E.g., A signs a contract; B and C are bound too.

- **True Test:** Mutual agency is the litmus test, not profit-sharing. In Cox vs. Hickman (1860), a creditor receiving profits as loan repayment wasn't a partner because he lacked agency, showing courts prioritize control over profit distribution.
- **Distinctions:**
  - ❑ **Partnership vs. Co-ownership:** Co-owners lack mutual agency—e.g., A and B owning a house don't bind each other in dealings.
  - ❑ **Partnership vs. Company:** Partnerships have no separate legal entity, unlimited liability, and a maximum of 100 partners (per Companies Act, 2013), unlike companies.
  - ❑ **Partnership vs. HUF:** Partnership is contractual; HUF arises from status (birth).
- **Types (Sections 7, 8):**
  - ❑ Partnership at Will (Section 7): No fixed duration—e.g., A, B, C start a store; any can dissolve it with notice.
  - ❑ Particular Partnership (Section 8): For a specific venture/time—e.g., A and B build a bridge, ends when done.
- **Section 5 Connection:** Reinforces that partnership is a contract, not status—e.g., family ties don't create it without intent.
- **Section 6 Connection:** Courts determine existence by intent, conduct, and agency, not just profit-sharing—e.g., A and B sharing profits but not managing aren't partners.

Relation of Partners to One Another

Sections: 9, 10, 11, 12, 13, 15, 16, 17

- **General Duties (Section 9):**
  - ❑ Partners must act with diligence, good faith, and for the common benefit. E.g., A must keep accurate accounts and not hide profits from B.
  - ❑ Fiduciary duty—e.g., A can't divert firm clients to his personal business without consent.
- **Indemnity for Fraud/Neglect (Section 10):**
  - ❑ A partner must compensate the firm for losses from willful neglect or fraud. E.g., A's fraud in a deal costs ₹ 50,000; he pays it back, protecting B and C.
  - ❑ Neglect example: A ignores tax filings, causing penalties—he's liable.
- **Interest on Capital/Advances (Section 11):**
  - ❑ **Capital:** No interest unless agreed in the deed—e.g., "A gets 5% on ₹ 1 lakh"—and only from profits (Section 13I). No profits, no interest.
  - ❑ **Advances:** Loans beyond capital get 6% p.a., regardless of profits—e.g., A lends ₹ 40,000 extra, earns ₹ 2,400 yearly.
- **Rights of Partners (Section 12):**
  - ❑ **Participation:** All can manage unless restricted—e.g., A and B run a shop, but B can be a sleeping partner per deed.
  - ❑ **Access to Books:** Inspect and copy records—e.g., A checks sales logs for transparency.
  - ❑ **No Remuneration:** No salary unless agreed—e.g., A works full-time, B invests; both share profits equally unless A gets a wage per deed.
- **Mutual Rights and Duties (Section 13):**
  - ❑ Profit-Sharing: Equal unless specified—e.g., A, B, C split 1 : 1 : 1 without a deed; 2 : 1 : 1 if agreed.
  - ❑ Interest on Capital: Only from profits if agreed—e.g., A's ₹ 2 lakh gets 5% if profits allow.
  - ❑ Indemnity: Firm repays partners for business expenses—e.g., A pays ₹ 10,000 to settle a supplier; firm reimburses.
- **Application of Property (Section 15):** Firm property (Section 14) is for business use only—e.g., A contributes a shop; he can't use it personally.
- **Personal Profits (Section 16):**
  - ❑ Partners must account for profits from firm business/name—e.g., A earns ₹ 20,000 using firm goodwill; he pays it to the firm.
  - ❑ Competing business profits must be shared—e.g., A's rival shop using firm resources.
- **Reconstitution (Section 17):** Rights/duties continue post-admission/retirement unless changed—e.g., C joins A and B, profit shifts to 1 : 1 : 1; B retires, A and C keep 1 : 1 unless altered.

- **Practical Example:** A, B, and C run a firm. A works full-time, no salary unless agreed; B contributes ₹ 1 lakh, no interest unless profits and agreed; C's fraud costs ₹ 30,000, he indemnifies. All share profits equally unless specified.

Relation of Partners to Third Parties

Sections: 19, 20, 22, 25, 26, 27

- **Implied Authority (Section 19):**
  - ❑ A partner's acts in the ordinary course of business bind the firm—e.g., A buys goods for a trading firm, B and C are liable.
  - ❑ Scope: Includes buying/selling goods, hiring staff, accepting payments—e.g., A hires a clerk, firm pays.
  - ❑ Exclusions: No authority for arbitration, selling firm property, or admitting liability in a suit without consent—e.g., A can't sell the firm's shop alone.
  - ❑ Depends on business type—e.g., wider in trading firms (buy/sell) than professional firms (consulting).
- **Extension/Restriction of Authority (Section 20):**
  - ❑ Partners can modify authority—e.g., deed says only A signs contracts, or all can sell property.
  - ❑ Example: A's authority restricted to sales; B handles purchases.
- **Mode of Exercising Authority (Section 22):** Acts must be in the firm's name and usual way—e.g., A signs "For XYZ Firm" for supplies, binds all; personal deals don't.
- **Liability for Firm Acts (Section 25):**
  - ❑ Partners are jointly and severally liable—creditors can sue all or one for full debt—e.g., firm owes ₹ 1 lakh, creditor sues A alone, A pays, then seeks from B and C.
  - ❑ Unlimited liability—e.g., personal assets of A, B, C cover firm debts.
- **Liability for Wrongful Acts (Section 26):**
  - ❑ Firm liable for a partner's wrongful acts (e.g., fraud, negligence) in business—e.g., A defrauds a client in a firm deal, all partners pay.
  - ❑ Must be in course of business—e.g., A's personal fraud doesn't bind firm.
- **Liability for Misapplication (Section 27):**
  - ❑ Firm liable if a partner misuses third-party money/property—e.g., A takes ₹ 50,000 from a client and pockets it, firm compensates.
  - ❑ Two cases: (a) Partner receives as firm agent, misapplies; (b) Firm receives, partner misapplies—both bind firm.
- **Practical Example:** A, B, C run a store. A buys stock (Section 19), binds firm; C restricts A's authority (Section 20); B's fraud in a sale (Section 26) makes all liable; firm owes ₹ 2 lakh (Section 25), creditor sues C alone.

Incoming and Outgoing Partners

Sections: 31, 32, 36, 37

- **Incoming Partners (Section 31):**
  - ❑ A new partner can only be admitted with the consent of all existing partners unless the partnership deed specifies otherwise. This ensures mutual trust and agreement among the current partners. For example, if A and B run a firm, they must both agree to admit C; a deed might allow admission by majority vote instead.
  - ❑ Liability: An incoming partner is liable only for debts and obligations arising after their admission, not before, unless they explicitly agree to take on prior liabilities. For instance, if the firm owes ₹ 1 lakh before C joins, C isn't responsible unless the deed states he'll share it. Once admitted, C's liability aligns with other partners for future acts—e.g., a new ₹ 50,000 debt binds A, B, and C equally.
  - ❑ Practical Example: A and B's firm has a ₹ 2 lakh debt. C joins on 1st January 2025 with consent; a debt of ₹ 80,000 incurred on 15th January binds C, but not the earlier ₹ 2 lakh unless agreed.
- **Outgoing Partners (Sections 32, 36, 37):**
  - ❑ **Retirement (Section 32):** A partner can retire in three ways: (a) with the consent of all other partners, (b) as per the terms of the partnership deed (e.g., after 5 years' service), or (c) by giving written notice in a partnership at will. For example, A, B, and C run an at-will firm; A notifies in writing to retire, ending his role.
    - ➾ **Liability:** A retiring partner remains liable for debts incurred before retirement. For acts after retirement, liability ceases only if public notice is given (e.g., in a newspaper or Gazette). Without notice, third parties can hold the retiring partner liable as if still a partner (holding-out principle, Section 45). For instance, A retires without notice;

a creditor sues A for a post-retirement debt of ₹ 60,000—A must pay unless notice was published.

- **Rights to Compete (Section 36):** An outgoing partner (retired or deceased's representative) can start a competing business but cannot use the firm's name or represent themselves as part of it. For example, A retires and opens a rival shop—he can't call it "ABC Firm" (original firm name). The deed may impose a restraint of trade (e.g., no competing within 5 km for 2 years), which is valid if reasonable in scope and duration.
- **Rights to Interest or Profits (Section 37):** If the firm delays settling an outgoing partner's share, they can claim either 6% per annum interest on their capital or a share of profits attributable to their unpaid amount, until settled. For instance, A retires with ₹ 1 lakh capital unsettled; he can claim ₹ 6,000 yearly interest or a portion of profits from B and C's continued use of his funds.
- **Practical Example:** A retires from A, B, C's firm, gives notice, and starts a rival store 10 km away (Section 36 allows). His ₹ 2 lakh share remains unpaid; he opts for 6% interest (₹ 12,000 p.a.) under Section 37 until B and C pay him.

Agreements in Restraint of Trade

Section 36

- **Provision:** An outgoing partner (retired or deceased's representative) may carry on a business competing with the firm and advertise it, but with two key restrictions:
  - They cannot use the firm's name or represent themselves as still part of it.
  - They cannot solicit the firm's existing clients from before their exit.
- **Restraint of Trade:** The partnership deed can include an agreement restraining the outgoing partner from starting a similar business, provided it's reasonable. For example, "A cannot open a shop within 10 km of the firm for 3 years after retirement." Such restraints are exceptions to the general rule under Section 27 of the Indian Contract Act, 1872, which voids agreements in restraint of trade, because they protect the firm's goodwill.
- **Reasonableness:** Courts uphold restraints if they're fair in scope (geographical area), duration, and purpose. For instance:
  - **Valid:** "No competing within 5 km for 2 years"—protects local clientele without overly restricting A's livelihood.
  - **Invalid:** "No trade anywhere in India for 10 years"—too broad, likely struck down.
- **Practical Examples:**
  - A retires from "ABC Traders" and opens "A's Store" 15 km away—legal under Section 36 unless restrained by deed. He can't call it "ABC Traders" or approach ABC's old clients.
  - Deed says "No retail within 8 km for 1 year"—A complies by opening 9 km away; if he violates, B and C can seek an injunction.
- **Connection to Goodwill:** Restraints often tie to protecting the firm's goodwill (Section 55), an asset built by all partners—e.g., A can't exploit it post-exit without consent.

Dissolution of Firm

Sections: 39, 40, 41, 42, 43, 44, 48, 49, 55

- **Dissolution Defined (Section 39):** Dissolution of a firm means the end of all partnerships within it, distinct from a single partnership ending (e.g., one partner retiring). For example, A, B, C's firm dissolves entirely, stopping all business, unlike A retiring while B and C continue.
- **Modes of Dissolution:**
  - **By Agreement (Section 40):** All partners consent to end the firm—e.g., A, B, C agree to close their loss-making store and sign a dissolution deed.
  - **Compulsory Dissolution (Section 41):** Occurs automatically if: (a) all partners (or all but one) become insolvent, or (b) the business becomes unlawful—e.g., a firm trading banned goods must dissolve.
  - **Contingent Dissolution (Section 42):** Triggered by events unless agreed otherwise: (a) expiry of a fixed term (e.g., 5-year partnership ends), (b) completion of a venture (e.g., bridge built), (c) death or insolvency of a partner (e.g., A dies, firm dissolves unless B and C agree to continue).
  - **By Notice (Section 43):** In a partnership at will, any partner can dissolve the firm by written notice—e.g., A notifies B and C, ending their at-will firm on the specified date.
  - **By Court (Section 44):** Court orders dissolution on grounds like: (a) a partner's insanity (e.g., A can't function), (b) permanent incapacity, (c) misconduct (e.g., A's fraud harms the firm), (d) persistent breach (e.g., A falsifies accounts),

I continuous losses (firm unviable), or (f) just and equitable cause (e.g., irreconcilable disputes). For instance, B sues for dissolution due to A's theft.

- **Settlement of Accounts (Section 48): Post-dissolution, accounts are settled:**
  - **Losses:** Paid first from profits, then capital, then partners' personal assets in their profit-sharing ratio—e.g., ₹1 lakh loss wipes out profits, then A's ₹50,000 capital, then B and C contribute.
  - **Assets:** Applied to: (a) pay firm debts (e.g., ₹2 lakh to creditors), (b) repay partner advances (e.g., A's ₹30,000 loan), (c) return capital (e.g., B's ₹1 lakh), (d) surplus shared per profit ratio (e.g., A : B : C = 2 : 1 : 1).
- **Advances vs. Capital (Section 49):** Advances (loans beyond capital) get priority with 6% interest—e.g., A's ₹40,000 advance repaid before his ₹1 lakh capital.
- **Goodwill (Section 55):** After dissolution, surviving partners can use or sell goodwill unless agreed otherwise—e.g., A dies, B and C sell "XYZ Firm" goodwill for ₹3 lakh, sharing proceeds.
- **Practical Example:** A, B, C's at-will firm faces A's misconduct. B seeks court dissolution (Section 44); firm ends, debts of ₹5 lakh paid from ₹6 lakh assets, A's ₹1 lakh advance repaid with interest (Section 49), surplus split 1 : 1 : 1 (Section 48).

Registration of Firm

Sections: 58, 59, 69

- **Procedure (Section 58):** Registration is optional, not mandatory. Partners file an application with the Registrar of Firms, including:
  - Firm name (e.g., "ABC Traders").
  - Principal place of business.
  - Names and addresses of partners.
  - Duration (if any) and joining dates.
  - For example, A, B, C submit a form on 1st March 2025 to register their trading firm in Delhi.
- **Effect of Registration (Section 59):** Registration takes effect when the Registrar enters the details in the Register of Firms—e.g., entry on 10th March 2025 makes "ABC Traders" officially registered, issuing a certificate.
- **Consequences of Non-Registration (Section 69):**
  - **Disabilities:** An unregistered firm or its partners cannot:
    - Sue third parties for debts/contracts—e.g., "ABC Traders" can't sue a debtor for ₹4 lakh.
    - Claim set-off exceeding ₹100 in lawsuits—e.g., can't offset a ₹50,000 claim against a ₹60,000 suit.
  - **Exceptions:** Partners can sue:
    - For dissolution or accounts—e.g., A sues B and C to wind up an unregistered firm.
    - Third parties for criminal acts (e.g., theft).
  - **Third Parties:** Can sue the firm regardless—e.g., a creditor sues "ABC Traders" for ₹3 lakh, registration irrelevant.
  - **Practical Example:** Unregistered "XYZ Firm" (A, B) can't sue a client for ₹2 lakh dues but can dissolve internally. A creditor sues XYZ for ₹1 lakh—suit proceeds.
- **Rationale:** Registration enhances legal enforceability—e.g., registered "ABC Traders" sues a debtor successfully, unregistered firms face hurdles.

LIMITED LIABILITY PARTNERSHIP (LLP)

Introduction to LLPs

A Limited Liability Partnership (LLP) is a hybrid business structure combining features of a partnership firm and a corporate entity. It offers operational flexibility while limiting the liabilities of its partners.

- **Governed by:** The Limited Liability Partnership Act, 2008 (effective April 1, 2009).
- **Objective:** To promote small and medium businesses with a simpler corporate structure.

Key Advantages of LLPs

- Limited liability protection for partners.
- Flexible management without rigid corporate governance norms.
- Separate legal identity, distinct from its partners.

Definition and Characteristics of LLPs

Definition

Under Section 2(1)(n) of the LLP Act, 2008:

- An LLP is a body corporate formed and incorporated under this Act, recognized as a legal entity separate from its partners.

Characteristics of LLPs

- **Separate Legal Entity:**
  - Has its own legal identity, distinct from partners.
  - Can own assets, incur debts, and enter contracts in its own name.
- **Limited Liability:**
  - Liability of each partner is limited to their agreed contribution.
  - Personal assets of partners are protected, except in cases of fraud.
- **Perpetual Succession:** Continues to exist regardless of changes in partnership.
- **Flexibility in Management:** Governed by LLP agreements, offering flexibility compared to rigid company law requirements.
- **Minimum Partners:** Requires at least two designated partners, one of whom must be an Indian resident.
- **No Minimum Capital Requirement:** No prescribed minimum contribution, unlike private companies.
- **Taxation:** Taxed as a partnership, exempt from Dividend Distribution Tax (DDT).
- **Ease of Formation:** Simpler incorporation process than private limited companies.

Comparison between LLP, Partnership Firm, and Private Limited Company

Criteria	LLP	Partnership Firm	Private Limited Company
Legal Entity	Separate legal entity	Not a separate legal entity	Separate legal entity
Liability	Limited to partner's contribution	Unlimited liability	Limited to shareholder's investment
Formation	Registration under LLP Act	Simple, under Partnership Act	Registration under Companies Act
Minimum Members	Two designated partners	Two partners	Two shareholders
Perpetual Succession	Yes	No	Yes
Governance Structure	Flexible via LLP Agreement	Governed by Partnership Act	Governed by MOA and AOA
Taxation	Taxed as a partnership	Taxed as a partnership	Subject to corporate tax
Transferability	Easy transfer of ownership	Restricted	Transfer of shares allowed
Regulatory Compliance	Moderate compliance	Minimal compliance	High compliance (e.g., ROC filing)

Historical Background and Need for LLP Legislation

Historical Context

- Originated in the United States in the 1990s to address liability concerns of professional firms (e.g., law and accounting firms).
- Gained global popularity for limiting partner liabilities.

Need for LLP Legislation in India

- **Encouragement for SMEs:** Offers a flexible, low-compliance structure for small and medium enterprises (SMEs) and service sector businesses.
- **Hybrid Structure:** Combines partnership flexibility with company-like liability protection.
- **Promoting Entrepreneurship:** Supports entrepreneurs with limited liability and simplified compliance.
- **Global Competitiveness:** Aligns with international business structures (e.g., UK, Singapore) to enhance Indian businesses' global standing.
- **Professional Services:** Meets the needs of growing sectors like IT, consulting, and financial services for risk management.
- **Corporate Governance:** Balances governance benefits with operational independence.
- **Ease of Doing Business:** Part of India's reforms to improve its Ease of Doing Business Index ranking.

Legislative Milestones

- Naresh Chandra Committee Report (2003): Recommended introducing LLPs in India.
- J.J. Irani Expert Committee Report (2005): Proposed separate LLP legislation to encourage entrepreneurship.

LIMITED LIABILITY PARTNERSHIP ACT, 2008: AN OVERVIEW

Introduction

- Provides the legal framework for LLPs in India.
- Enacted to introduce a hybrid structure blending partnership and company features.
- Effective Date: April 1, 2009.

Key Features

- **Separate Legal Entity:** Distinct from its partners; can own property, enter contracts, and sue/be sued.
- **Limited Liability:** Partners' liability limited to their contribution, except in fraud cases.
- **Perpetual Succession:** Continues regardless of partnership changes.
- **Flexible Structure:** Combines limited liability with partnership flexibility.

Applicability

- Suitable for small and medium-sized businesses, professionals, and startups.
- Governed by the Ministry of Corporate Affairs (MCA).

Objectives

- Encourage entrepreneurship.
- Provide a simple, cost-effective structure.
- Enhance international competitiveness.

Key Provisions

- **Incorporation (Sections 11-21):** Formed by filing incorporation documents with the Registrar of Companies (RoC).
- **Designated Partners (Sections 7-10):** Requires minimum two designated partners, one resident in India.
- **LLP Agreement (Section 23):** Governs mutual rights and duties of partners.
- **Accounts and Audit (Sections 34-35):** Mandates maintaining books of accounts and filing annual returns.

Amendments

- **LLP (Amendment) Act, 2021:**
  - Decriminalized minor offenses.
  - Introduced relaxed compliance for small LLPs.

Advantages

- Limited liability.
- No minimum capital requirement.
- Lower compliance burden than companies.

Disadvantages

- Not suitable for raising equity capital.
- Certain tax inefficiencies compared to companies.

Registration of LLPs: Legal Requirements and Process

Legal Framework

- Governed by Sections 11-21 of the LLP Act, 2008.
- Registration with the Registrar of Companies (RoC) is mandatory.

Prerequisites

- **Minimum Partners:** At least two partners (no upper limit).
- **Designated Partners:** Minimum two, with one Indian resident.
- **Digital Signature Certificate (DSC):** Required for online filing.
- **Director Identification Number (DIN):** Mandatory for designated partners.

Step-by-Step Process

- Name Reservation
  - File RUN-LLP form for name approval with MCA.
  - Must adhere to LLP Act naming guidelines.
- LLP Incorporation Form
  - File Form FiLLiP with required documents:
    - Proof of registered office address.
    - Identity and address proofs of partners.
    - Consent to act as designated partners.
  - Pay fees based on capital contribution.
- **Certificate of Incorporation:** Issued by RoC with LLP Identification Number (LLPIN).
- **LLP Agreement:** File within 30 days of incorporation using Form 3.

LLP Agreement: Importance, Drafting, and Contents

Definition and Importance

- A written contract defining mutual rights, duties, and operational rules among partners.
- Governed by Section 23 of the LLP Act, 2008.
- Filing with RoC is mandatory within 30 days of incorporation (non-compliance incurs penalties).

Key Features

- **Customizable:** Allows partners to define roles and responsibilities.
- **Legally Binding:** Governs disputes.
- **Supersedes Act Provisions:** Overrides default provisions of the LLP Act where applicable.

Contents of LLP Agreement

- **Basic Details:** Name of LLP, registered office address, details of partners/designated partners.
- **Capital Contribution:** Contribution by each partner (cash, kind, or services); procedure for additional contributions.
- **Profit-Sharing Ratio:** Distribution of profits and losses among partners.
- **Management Structure:** Roles and responsibilities of designated partners; decision-making process.
- **Admission and Exit of Partners:** Process for adding new partners; resignation or expulsion procedures.
- **Meetings and Resolutions:** Frequency, conduct of meetings; voting rights.
- **Dispute Resolution:** Mechanism (e.g., arbitration or mediation).
- **Dissolution and Winding Up:** Terms for dissolution; distribution of remaining assets.

Drafting Considerations

- Seek professional legal assistance.
- Ensure clarity and compliance with the LLP Act.

Importance of Filing

- Ensures transparency and legal validity.
- Non-compliance penalty: ₹ 100 per day (no maximum limit).

Rights and Duties of Partners under the LLP Act, 2008

Statutory Rights of Partners

- **Participation in Management:** Right to participate unless restricted by LLP agreement.
- **Access to Books of Accounts:** Right to inspect and obtain copies at any time.
- **Profit-Sharing:** As per LLP agreement or equally if unspecified.
- **Indemnity:** For acts done in ordinary business or to protect the LLP.

STATUTORY DUTIES OF PARTNERS

- **Act in Good Faith:** In the best interests of LLP and partners.
- **Comply with LLP Agreement:** Adhere to its terms.
- **Avoid Conflict of Interest:** Disclose personal interests in transactions.
- **Act within Authority:** Stay within assigned scope.
- **Contribute to Losses:** As per LLP agreement or equally if unspecified.
- **Duty of Care:** Avoid gross negligence or reckless conduct.

Legal Provisions

- **Section 23:** Defines roles and duties.
- **Breach of Duty:** May lead to legal action.

Role and Responsibilities of Designated Partners

Who Are Designated Partners?

- Minimum two per LLP, with at least one Indian resident (Section 7, LLP Act, 2008).
- Responsible for compliance and legal requirements.

Key Roles

- **Compliance Officer:** Files annual returns, accounts, and solvency statements.
- **Legal Representative:** Represents LLP in legal matters.
- **Signatory for Documents:** Signs e-forms and regulatory submissions.
- **Risk Management:** Monitors financial and operational risks.

Responsibilities

- Ensure legal compliance.
- Maintain statutory records.
- Handle tax compliance (e.g., GST, income tax).
- Represent LLP in official correspondence.
- Accountable for mismanagement penalties.

Liabilities

- Civil Liability: For defaults in filings.
- Criminal Liability: For fraud or gross negligence.
- Personal Liability: For wrongful acts under specific circumstances.

Fiduciary Duties of Partners in an LLP

Definition

- Obligation to act in the best interests of the LLP and partners, maintaining trust.

Key Fiduciary Duties

- **Duty of Loyalty:** Avoid conflicts of interest; no exploitation of LLP opportunities for personal gain.

- **Duty of Good Faith:** Act honestly and with integrity.
- **Duty of Confidentiality:** Protect sensitive LLP information.
- **Duty of Fair Dealing:** Ensure transparency; avoid misrepresentation.
- **Duty to Avoid Self-Dealing:** No transactions benefiting self at LLP's expense.

Consequences of Breach

- Legal action, compensation for losses, or disqualification from partnerships.

Relevant Case Laws

- **Re Gee & Co.:** Emphasized acting in business's best interest.
- **Vasudev Ramchandra Shelat v. Pranlal Jayanand Thakar:** Partners must not exploit opportunities for personal gain.

Legislative Provisions

- **Section 9:** Duties to LLP and partners.
- **Section 30:** Penalties for fraudulent acts.

Extent of Limited Liability in LLPs

Definition

- Partners' personal assets are protected; liability is limited to their capital contribution.

Key Provisions

- **Section 3, LLP Act, 2008:** LLP as a separate legal entity.
- Creditors cannot claim partners' personal assets for LLP debts.

Practical Implications

- Partners not liable for business losses unless agreed otherwise.
- LLP liability confined to the entity.

Exceptions

- **Fraud:** Unlimited personal liability.
- **Personal Guarantees:** Creditors can claim personal assets.
- **Statutory Violations:** Liability for non-compliance.

Judicial Precedents

- United Bank of India v. Satyawati Tondon (2010): No liability unless fraud proven.
- CIT v. M/s Rajendra Goud Chekkala (2020): Reinforced entity-partner distinction.

Benefits

- Reduces personal financial risk.
- Attracts investors and professionals.

Partners' Liability in Case of Fraud or Misrepresentation

General Liability

- Section 26, LLP Act, 2008: Liable for acts within authorized roles.

Fraudulent Acts

- Section 30: Personal liability for fraud or intentional misrepresentation.

Consequences

- Unlimited liability for debts/losses from fraud.
- LLP may also be liable.

Judicial Examples

- Serious Fraud Investigation Office v. Rahul Modi (2019): Fraud removes liability protection.
- State Bank of India v. Kingfisher Airlines Ltd. (2016): Personal guarantees override limited liability.

Doctrine of Piercing the Corporate Veil in LLPs

Concept

- Courts disregard LLP-partner separation to prevent misuse.

When Applied

- Fraud or Illegal Purpose: E.g., tax evasion.
- Evasion of Obligations: Avoiding statutory duties.
- Improper Conduct: Misrepresentation for undue advantage.

Judicial Precedents

- Gilford Motor Co. Ltd. V. Horne (1933): Prevented evasion of agreements.
- Union Bank of India v. Khader International Construction (2001): Fraudulent transactions.

Implications

- Partners lose liability protection; creditors access personal assets.

Modes of Winding Up an LLP

Voluntary Winding Up

- Initiated by partners when LLP is no longer viable.

- Steps:
  - Resolution by three-fourths of partners.
  - Declaration of solvency filed with RoC.
  - Appointment of liquidator.
  - Final report to RoC for dissolution.

Compulsory Winding Up

- Ordered by Tribunal (Section 64, LLP Act).
- Grounds:
  - Non-filing of returns for 5 years.
  - Fewer than two partners for over 6 months.
  - Insolvency or illegal activities.
- Process: Petition to NCLT; liquidator appointed.

Role of National Company Law Tribunal (NCLT) in LLP Dissolution

Key Functions

- Adjudicates winding-up petitions.
- Appoints and supervises liquidators.
- Issues dissolution orders.
- Addresses fraud/misconduct.

Insolvency and Bankruptcy Code (IBC) and LLPs

Relevance

- Applies Corporate Insolvency Resolution Process (CIRP) to LLPs.
- Threshold: Default of ₹ 1 crore or more.

Key Features

- Time-bound (330 days).
- Creditor-driven resolution or liquidation.
- Moratorium on legal actions during process.

Landmark Judicial Pronouncements on LLPs in India

- Re: Global Mutual Funds LLP (2012): Limited liability unless fraud proven.
- MCA v. Goldline LLP (2015): Strict compliance enforced.
- Serco BPO v. Citi Financial (2014): Entity liability distinct from partners.

Amendments to the LLP Act: Key Changes

LLP (Amendment) Act, 2021

- Small LLP: Turnover $\leq$ ₹ 40 lakh, contribution $\leq$ ₹ 25 lakh; reduced compliance.
- Decriminalization: Minor offenses shifted to compliance focus.
- Simplified Incorporation: Single integrated form.

Role of Ministry of Corporate Affairs (MCA) in Regulating LLPs

Responsibilities

- Oversees compliance and incorporation.
- Enforces filings via MCA21 portal.
- Formulates policies for ease of doing business.

NEGOTIABLE INSTRUMENTS ACT, 1881

DEFINITION AND SCOPE OF NEGOTIABLE INSTRUMENTS ACT, 1881

The **Negotiable Instruments Act, 1881** was enacted to define and regulate the law related to negotiable instruments in India. It provides a legal framework for the creation, transfer, and enforcement of negotiable instruments such as promissory notes, bills of exchange, and cheques.

What is a Negotiable Instrument?

A **Negotiable Instrument** is a written document that guarantees the payment of a specific amount of money either on demand or at a future date, with the condition that it is freely transferable from one person to another.

- **Definition (Section 13):** As per Section 13 of the Negotiable Instruments Act, a negotiable instrument means a promissory note, bill of exchange, or cheque payable either to order or to bearer.
- **Explanation:** A negotiable instrument creates a right in the holder to receive the amount mentioned in it and allows them to transfer that right to another person by delivery or endorsement.
- **Common Examples:**
  - **Promissory Note:** A written promise to pay a specified amount to a certain person.
  - **Bill of Exchange:** A written order directing one party to pay a fixed sum to another.
  - **Cheque:** A bill of exchange drawn on a banker and payable on demand.

ESSENTIAL CHARACTERISTICS OF NEGOTIABLE INSTRUMENTS

For an instrument to qualify as a negotiable instrument, it must exhibit the following essential characteristics:

Freely Transferable:

- The most important feature of a negotiable instrument is its transferability.

- Transfer can be done either by **delivery** (for bearer instruments) or by **endorsement and delivery** (for order instruments).

Title Passes Free from Defects:

- The person who acquires a negotiable instrument in good faith and for consideration (known as the **Holder in Due Course**) gets a good title, even if the instrument was defective in the hands of a previous holder.

Written Form:

- A negotiable instrument must always be in written form and signed by the maker, drawer, or endorser.

Unconditional Promise or Order:

- The instrument must contain an **unconditional promise** (in the case of a promissory note) or an **unconditional order** (in the case of a bill of exchange or cheque) to pay a certain amount.

Payable in Money Only:

- The amount mentioned in the negotiable instrument must be payable in **legal currency** and not in kind or goods.

Payable on Demand or at a Future Date:

- The instrument may specify that payment is to be made either **on demand** (e.g., cheques) or at a fixed future date (e.g., bills of exchange or promissory notes).

Certainty of Amount and Parties:

- The amount payable must be certain and determinable.
- The instrument must clearly mention the parties involved (e.g., drawer, drawee, and payee).

Acceptance of Liability:

- In the case of a bill of exchange, the drawee must accept liability to pay the amount mentioned.

Presumption of Consideration:

- It is presumed that every negotiable instrument is drawn or made for valuable consideration unless proven otherwise.

Prompt Payment:

- The negotiable instrument encourages prompt payment and ensures confidence in the commercial system.

Legal Presumptions Under the Act

To ensure smooth functioning and trust in negotiable instruments, the Act provides for certain legal presumptions under Sections 118 and 139:

- **Section 118:** Presumptions regarding:
  - ❑ Consideration
  - ❑ Date of execution
  - ❑ Acceptance of bills of exchange
  - ❑ Endorsement and delivery
  - ❑ Holder being a holder in due course
- **Section 139:** Presumption in favor of the holder that the cheque was issued for discharge of any legally enforceable debt or liability.

Types of Negotiable Instruments

Under the **Negotiable Instruments Act, 1881**, the following are the primary types of negotiable instruments explicitly defined:

- Promissory Note (Section 4)
- Bill of Exchange (Section 5)
- Cheque (Section 6)

Here's a detailed explanation of each type:

Promissory Note (Section 4)

Definition: A promissory note is defined under Section 4 as:

"An instrument in writing (not being a banknote or a currency note), containing an unconditional undertaking, signed by the maker, to pay a certain sum of money to, or to the order of, a certain person, or to the bearer of the instrument."

Key Features:

- **In Writing:** Must be in written form and cannot be oral.
- **Unconditional Undertaking:** The promise to pay must be unconditional.
- **Signed by the Maker:** The instrument must be duly signed by the person making the promise.
- **Definite Amount:** The amount to be paid must be certain.
- **Payable to a Specific Person or Bearer:**
  - ❑ It must mention the person to whom the payment is to be made or to the bearer of the instrument.
- **Not a Currency Note or Banknote:** It cannot be used as legal tender.

Parties Involved:

- **Maker:** The person who makes the promise to pay.
- **Payee:** The person to whom the payment is promised.

Example: "I promise to pay ₹ 10,000 to Mr. X or order on 1st March 2025."

- Signed: Mr. Y

Bill of Exchange (Section 5)

Definition: A bill of exchange is defined under Section 5 as:

"An instrument in writing containing an unconditional order, signed by the maker, directing a certain person to pay a certain sum of money only to, or to the order of, a certain person or to the bearer of the instrument."

Key Features:

- **In Writing:** Must be in written form.
- **Unconditional Order:** The order to pay must not depend on any conditions.
- **Signed by the Drawer:** The person giving the order (drawer) must sign the instrument.
- **Definite Amount:** The amount of money must be clearly specified.
- **Payable to a Certain Person or Bearer:** It must clearly state the payee or the bearer.
- **Tri-Party Instrument:** Involves three parties – the drawer, the drawee, and the payee.

Parties Involved:

- **Drawer:** The person who draws the bill and gives the order to pay.
- **Drawee:** The person who is directed to make the payment.
- **Payee:** The person who is entitled to receive the payment.

Example:

"Pay ₹ 20,000 to Mr. X or order after 60 days from today."

- Signed: Mr. Y (Drawer)

Acceptance:

The drawee must accept the bill of exchange for it to become legally binding.

Cheque (Section 6)

Definition: A cheque is defined under Section 6 as:

"A bill of exchange drawn on a specified banker and not expressed to be payable otherwise than on demand."

Key Features:

- **Drawn on a Bank:** Unlike bills of exchange, cheques are specifically drawn on a banker.
- **Payable on Demand:** A cheque is always payable on demand; no future date can be specified for payment.
- **Unconditional Order:** The order to pay must not be conditional.
- **Specified Amount:** The amount must be clearly mentioned in figures and words.
- **Signed by the Drawer:** The person issuing the cheque (drawer) must sign it.

Parties Involved:

- **Drawer:** The person who writes and issues the cheque.
- **Drawee:** The bank on which the cheque is drawn.
- **Payee:** The person to whom the payment is to be made.

Types of Cheques:

- **Bearer Cheque:** Payable to the person holding the cheque.
- **Order Cheque:** Payable to a specific person or their order.
- **Crossed Cheque:** Contains two parallel lines across the cheque, restricting it to be deposited into a bank account only.
- **Account Payee Cheque:** A cheque that can only be credited to the payee's account.

Example:

"Pay ₹ 5,000 to Mr. X or bearer."

- Signed: Mr. Y (Drawer)
- Bank: ABC Bank

PRESUMPTIONS UNDER THE NEGOTIABLE INSTRUMENTS ACT, 1881

The **Negotiable Instruments Act, 1881**, provides certain legal presumptions to facilitate the smooth functioning of negotiable instruments and ensure confidence in their use. These presumptions reduce the burden of proof on the holder of the instrument.

Relevant Sections:

- **Section 118**: Provides presumptions regarding negotiable instruments.
- **Section 139**: Presumption in favor of the holder of a cheque for the discharge of a debt or liability.

Key Presumptions Under Section 118

- **Presumption of Consideration**
  - It is presumed that every negotiable instrument was made, drawn, accepted, endorsed, or transferred for valuable consideration.
  - The holder is not required to prove that consideration was provided; it is automatically assumed.
  - **Rebuttable Presumption:** The person challenging the validity of the instrument has the burden to prove that it was executed without consideration.

Example:

- If a promissory note is issued, the law assumes it was issued for a valid debt or obligation unless the defendant proves otherwise.

Presumption as to Date

- The date mentioned on a negotiable instrument is presumed to be the actual date of its creation.
- This presumption ensures that the instrument is treated as valid from the date stated on it unless evidence proves otherwise.
- **Importance:** The date is crucial for calculating the due date, maturity, and days of grace (if applicable).

Example:

- A cheque dated "25th January 2025" will be presumed to have been issued on that date unless contrary evidence is provided.

Presumption as to Time of Acceptance

- If a bill of exchange has been accepted, the law presumes that it was accepted within a reasonable time after its issuance and before its maturity.
- This presumption ensures that the instrument's life cycle follows standard business practices.

Key Points:

- The drawee is expected to accept the bill within a reasonable time.
- This presumption can be rebutted with proof of delayed acceptance.

Example:

- If a bill is issued on 1st February 2025, and it matures in 30 days, it is presumed that the drawee accepted it well before the due date.

Presumption as to Transfer and Endorsement

- Every transfer of a negotiable instrument is presumed to have been made properly and legally.
- It is also presumed that every endorsement appearing on the instrument was made in the sequence in which it appears.
- **Rebuttable Presumption:** The person challenging the validity of the transfer or endorsement must prove their claim.

Example:

- If a cheque is endorsed by multiple parties, the law assumes that the endorsements were valid and made in order, even if one of the endorsements is questioned.

HOLDER AND HOLDER IN DUE COURSE

The concepts of **Holder** and **Holder in Due Course** are crucial in understanding the rights and protections offered to parties under the **Negotiable Instruments Act, 1881**.

Definition of Holder (Section 8)

A **Holder** is defined as:

"The person who is entitled in his own name to the possession of a negotiable instrument and to receive or recover the amount due thereon from the parties thereto."

Key Points:

- **A holder must:**
  - Be in **lawful possession** of the negotiable instrument.
  - Have the right to **enforce payment** in their own name.
- **A holder may be:**
  - The original payee or drawer.
  - Any person to whom the instrument has been endorsed or transferred.

Example:

- If a cheque is issued in favor of Mr. X, he becomes the **holder** of the cheque.
- If Mr. X endorses the cheque to Mr. Y, Mr. Y becomes the **holder**.

Rights and Powers of a Holder:

- **Right to Possess the Instrument:** A holder has the legal right to possess the negotiable instrument.

- **Right to Receive Payment:** A holder can demand and receive payment from the drawer, drawee, or acceptor.
- **Right to Sue:** A holder can file a lawsuit in their own name to recover the money due on the instrument.
- **Right to Cross or Endorse:** The holder can cross a cheque or endorse it to another person, transferring ownership.
- **Right Against All Prior Parties:** A holder can hold prior parties (maker, drawer, or endorsers) liable for payment.

Holder in Due Course (Section 9)

A **Holder in Due Course (HDC)** is defined as:

"A person who for consideration becomes the possessor of a negotiable instrument, payable to bearer, or the payee or endorsee thereof, payable to order, before it becomes overdue, and without having sufficient cause to believe that any defect existed in the title of the person from whom he derived his title."

Key Points:

- **Consideration:** The HDC must acquire the instrument for valuable consideration (not as a gift).
- **Before Due Date:** The instrument must be acquired before it is overdue.
- **Good Faith:** The HDC must acquire the instrument in good faith without knowledge of any defect or fraud.
- **Title Free from Defects:** The HDC acquires the instrument free from defects in the previous holder's title.

Example:

- If Mr. A issues a cheque to Mr. B, and Mr. B sells it to Mr. C (for consideration and without knowledge of fraud), Mr. C becomes the **Holder in Due Course**.

Rights of a Holder in Due Course:

- **Better Title:** An HDC gets a better title than the transferor, even if the transferor's title was defective.
- **Right to Enforce Payment:** The HDC can enforce payment from all parties liable on the instrument, irrespective of any disputes between previous parties.
- **No Defenses Against HDC:** Except for specific defenses like forgery, no party can deny liability to an HDC.
- **Right to Sue All Prior Parties:** An HDC can sue all prior parties (drawer, maker, acceptor, or endorsers) in case of dishonor.
- **Presumption of Validity:** Courts presume that an HDC has obtained the instrument for valid consideration and in good faith.

Difference Between Holder and Holder in Due Course

Aspect	Holder	Holder in Due Course (HDC)
Definition	Entitled to possess and enforce payment of the instrument.	Acquires the instrument for consideration, in good faith, and before due date.
Consideration	May or may not have provided consideration.	Must have provided valuable consideration.
Title	Holder gets the same title as the previous holder.	HDC gets a better title, even if the previous title was defective.
Defects in Title	Cannot claim rights if the previous holder's title was defective.	Can claim rights even if the previous holder's title was defective.
Rights	Can sue prior parties and endorse the instrument.	Enjoys additional protections, such as immunity from most defenses.
Good Faith Requirement	Not mandatory.	Must acquire the instrument in good faith.
Defense Against Claims	Liable to genuine defenses raised by parties.	Not affected by most defenses (except forgery or fraud).

COMPANY LAW – INCORPORATION OF A COMPANY, PROSPECTUS, SHARES AND DEBENTURES

DEFINITION OF A COMPANY

A **company** is a legal entity formed by a group of individuals to engage in and operate a business, either commercial or industrial, enterprise.

According to **Section 2(20) of the Companies Act, 2013**, a company means a company incorporated under this Act or under any previous company law.

Features of a Company

- **Separate Legal Entity**:
  - ❑ A company has its own legal identity, separate from its members or shareholders.
  - ❑ It can own property, enter contracts, and sue or be sued in its own name.

- **Limited Liability**: The liability of the members is limited to the amount unpaid on their shares or the amount they have agreed to contribute in the event of liquidation.
- **Perpetual Succession**: A company has a continuous existence, unaffected by changes in membership or the death of its shareholders.
- **Common Seal (optional under Companies Act, 2013):** It acts as the signature of the company for legal purposes.
- **Transferability of Shares**: Shares of a public company are freely transferable unless restricted by its articles.
- **Artificial Legal Person**: A company is created by law and is considered an artificial person with certain legal rights and obligations.
- **Separate Management**: Shareholders own the company, but management is carried out by directors appointed by them.
- **Statutory Compliance**: A company is required to comply with various legal formalities, including regular filings, audits, and meetings.

Characteristics of a Company

- **Incorporation**: A company comes into existence only after being registered under the Companies Act.
- **Corporate Veil**: A company shields its members from personal liability beyond their investment.
- **Capital**: A company raises funds through the issue of shares or debentures.
- **Democratic Setup**: Decisions are made through voting rights at meetings by shareholders and directors.

Types of Companies

Based on Incorporation

- **Statutory Companies**: Created by a special act of Parliament or state legislature (e.g., Reserve Bank of India).
- **Registered Companies**: Incorporated under the Companies Act, 2013.

Based on Liability

- **Limited by Shares**: Members' liability is limited to the unpaid value of their shares.
- **Limited by Guarantee**:Members' liability is limited to a pre-agreed amount they will contribute in case of liquidation.
- **Unlimited Liability Company**: Members' liability is unlimited.

Based on Number of Members

- **Private Company**:
  - ❑ Minimum 2 and maximum 200 members.
  - ❑ Restricts share transferability and cannot invite public to subscribe to its shares.
- **Public Company**:
  - ❑ Minimum 7 members with no upper limit.
  - ❑ Can invite public to subscribe to its shares.
- **One Person Company (OPC)**:
  - ❑ Single individual acts as the sole member and director.
  - ❑ Introduced under the Companies Act, 2013 for small businesses.

Other Types of Companies

- **Holding Company and Subsidiary Company**: Holding company controls the composition of the board or holds more than 50% of the shares in a subsidiary company.
- **Government Company**: At least 51% of shares are held by the central or state government.
- **Foreign Company**: Incorporated outside India but conducts business in India.
- **Section 8 Company**: Formed for charitable purposes such as promoting education, art, or social welfare.
- **Small Company**: Private company with paid-up capital and turnover not exceeding prescribed limits under the Companies Act, 2013.

TYPES OF INCORPORATION

Meaning of Incorporation

Incorporation refers to the legal process of creating a company or a corporate entity that is recognized as a separate legal entity under the law. Once incorporated, a company gains its own identity, separate from its owners, shareholders, or founders, and enjoys certain rights and obligations as defined by the governing law (e.g., Companies Act, 2013 in India).

Incorporation by Registration

Definition: This is the most common method of forming a company. A company is incorporated by filing necessary documents with the Registrar of Companies (RoC) as per the provisions of the **Companies Act, 2013**.

Key Steps:

- **Approval of Name**: File an application to the ROC to reserve the company's name (using forms like SPICe+).
- **Drafting of Documents**: Prepare the **Memorandum of Association (MoA)** and **Articles of Association (AOA)**.
- **Submission of Incorporation Documents**: Submit incorporation forms along with MoA, AOA, and other documents (e.g., identity proof of directors, proof of registered office).
- **Issuance of Certificate of Incorporation (COI)**: Upon approval, the RoC issues a Certificate of Incorporation.

Key Characteristics:

- ❑ Once registered, the company becomes a legal entity separate from its members.
- ❑ Examples: Most private, public, and one-person companies are incorporated through registration.

Incorporation through Statute

Definition: Certain companies are created by specific legislation passed by the Parliament or state legislature. These companies are governed by the provisions of the special statute under which they are created.

Examples:

- **Reserve Bank of India (RBI)**: Incorporated under the Reserve Bank of India Act, 1934.
- **Life Insurance Corporation of India (LIC)**: Incorporated under the LIC Act, 1956.
- **State Bank of India (SBI)**: Incorporated under the SBI Act, 1955.

Key Characteristics:

- These companies are not required to follow the registration process under the Companies Act.
- They are governed by their specific legislation, although certain provisions of the Companies Act may also apply.

Foreign Companies and their Incorporation Process

Definition: A foreign company is one that is incorporated outside India but has a place of business in India, either directly or through an agent, and conducts business in India.

Legal Provisions:

- Governed by **Section 2(42)** and **Sections 379-393** of the **Companies Act, 2013**.
- Foreign companies are also regulated by the rules of the Reserve Bank of India (RBI) and FEMA (Foreign Exchange Management Act).

Process of Registration in India:

- **Submission of Documents**:
  - ❑ **Submit the following documents to the RoC:**
    - ➾ Certified copy of the company's charter documents (e.g., MoA, AOA).
    - ➾ Details of directors, secretary, and authorized representatives in India.
    - ➾ Address of the principal place of business in India.
    - ➾ Financial statements of the company.
- **Approval**: Once approved, the foreign company is registered under the Companies Act, 2013, and can commence operations in India.
- **Compliance Requirements**:
  - ❑ Maintain books of account related to Indian operations.
  - ❑ File annual returns and other required filings with the RoC.

  Examples: Companies like **Google India**, **Microsoft India**, and **Apple India** are foreign companies operating in India.

Comparison of the Three Types of Incorporation

Aspect	Incorporation by Registration	Incorporation through Statute	Foreign Companies
Basis	Filing incorporation documents with RoC	Created through special legislative act	Incorporated abroad, operates in India
Legal Authority	Companies Act, 2013	Specific statute governs the company	Companies Act, FEMA, and RBI rules
Examples	Private companies, public companies	RBI, LIC, SBI	Google India, Microsoft India

PROSPECTUS: MEANING AND IMPORTANCE

Definition of a Prospectus

- A **prospectus** is a legal document issued by a company to invite the public to purchase its securities (shares, debentures, etc.).
- It provides detailed information about the company's business, financials, and the securities being offered, enabling investors to make informed decisions.

- According to **Section 2(70) of the Companies Act, 2013**, a prospectus is any document described or issued as a prospectus, including a red herring prospectus, shelf prospectus, or any notice, circular, advertisement, or other document inviting offers from the public to subscribe to securities.

Key Characteristics of a Prospectus

- **Invitation to the Public**: It is a formal invitation to the public to invest in the company's securities.
- **Legal Document**: It is governed by specific rules and regulations under the Companies Act, 2013.
- **Mandatory for Public Companies**: A prospectus is compulsory for companies offering securities to the public.
- **Disclosure of Information**: It contains details like the company's financial position, future plans, risks involved, and terms of the security issue.

Importance of a Prospectus in Raising Capital

- **Encourages Public Investment**: The prospectus serves as the primary tool to attract potential investors by providing relevant and transparent information about the company and its securities.
- **Builds Investor Confidence**: By disclosing critical details like business plans, financial statements, and potential risks, the prospectus assures investors of the company's credibility.
- **Ensures Compliance**: A prospectus helps ensure compliance with the legal requirements of the Companies Act, safeguarding the interests of both the company and the investors.
- **Acts as a Legal Record**: Since it is a legally binding document, the prospectus holds the company accountable for any misstatements or false information provided.
- **Facilitates Decision-Making**: Investors use the prospectus to evaluate the viability of the investment and assess risks before committing their funds.
- **Transparency and Disclosure**: A prospectus promotes transparency by making it mandatory for the company to disclose all material information regarding its financial health, market potential, and other relevant factors.
- **Compliance with Regulatory Authorities**: Filing and issuing a prospectus is required by law (e.g., under the SEBI regulations in India) to protect the interests of public investors.

Sections and Types of Prospectus under Companies Act, 2013

- **Section 26**: Governs the content and filing requirements of a prospectus.
- **Types of Prospectus**:
  - ❑ **Red Herring Prospectus**: Preliminary document with limited details, issued before the final prospectus.
  - ❑ **Shelf Prospectus**: Allows companies to issue securities multiple times without re-filing.
  - ❑ **Abridged Prospectus**: Shortened version of the main prospectus, containing key highlights.

DEFINITION AND TYPES OF SHARES

Definition of Shares

- A **share** represents a unit of ownership in a company and defines the shareholder's proportion of the company's capital.
- According to **Section 2(84) of the Companies Act, 2013**, a share means a share in the share capital of a company, which can be **equity** or **preference**.

Types of Shares

The **Companies Act, 2013** classifies shares broadly into the following categories:

Equity Shares

Equity shares, also known as ordinary shares, represent the ownership of the company and give shareholders voting rights. They are defined under **Section 43(1)(a)** of the Companies Act, 2013.

- **Features**:
  - ❑ **Voting Rights:** Equity shareholders have voting rights, allowing them to influence key decisions in the company.
  - ❑ **Variable Dividend:** Dividends are paid based on the company's profitability and are not fixed.
  - ❑ **Ownership Rights:** Equity shareholders are considered owners of the company.
  - ❑ **Risk and Return:** High risk and high potential for returns, as they receive residual profits after other obligations are met.
  - ❑ **No Priority in Repayment:** In the event of liquidation, equity shareholders are repaid after creditors and preference shareholders.

Preference Shares

Preference shares are those shares that carry certain preferential rights, such as receiving a fixed dividend before equity shareholders and having priority during the repayment of capital. They are defined under **Section 43(1)(b)** of the Companies Act, 2013.

Types of Preference Shares:

- **Cumulative Preference Shares**: Unpaid dividends accumulate and are paid in the subsequent years.
- **Non-Cumulative Preference Shares**: Unpaid dividends are not carried forward to future years.
- **Convertible Preference Shares**: Can be converted into equity shares after a specified period.
- **Non-Convertible Preference Shares**: Cannot be converted into equity shares.
- **Participating Preference Shares**: Entitled to additional profits after payment of equity dividends.
- **Non-Participating Preference Shares**: Entitled only to fixed dividends.
- **Redeemable Preference Shares**: Redeemed (bought back) by the company after a specific period.
- **Irredeemable Preference Shares**: Cannot be redeemed during the company's lifetime (not permitted in India under the Companies Act, 2013).

Differences Between Equity Shares and Preference Shares

Aspect	Equity Shares	Preference Shares
Definition	Represent ownership in the company.	Have preferential rights over equity shares for dividends and capital repayment.
Dividend	Variable and depends on the company's profitability.	Fixed dividend, paid before equity shareholders.
Voting Rights	Equity shareholders have voting rights in company decisions.	Generally, no voting rights except in special cases.
Risk	Higher risk due to no guaranteed returns.	Lower risk due to fixed dividends and repayment priority.
Priority in Repayment	Paid after creditors and preference shareholders during liquidation.	Paid before equity shareholders but after creditors.
Convertibility	Cannot be converted into preference shares.	May be convertible into equity shares (convertible preference shares).
Ownership	Equity shareholders are the real owners of the company.	Preference shareholders are not considered real owners.
Examples	Common stock issued to the public.	Preferred shares with fixed dividend rate.

DEBENTURES: DEFINITION AND FEATURES

Definition of Debentures

A **debenture** is a debt instrument issued by a company to borrow money from the public. It is a certificate of loan that acknowledges the company's obligation to repay the borrowed amount with a fixed rate of interest at regular intervals.

According to **Section 2(30) of the Companies Act, 2013**, a debenture includes any instrument of a company evidencing a debt, whether it constitutes a charge on the assets of the company or not.

Features of Debentures

- **Loan Instrument**: A debenture is issued by a company to raise long-term funds from the public as debt.
- **Fixed Interest Rate**: Interest on debentures is fixed and is paid periodically, irrespective of the company's profitability.
- **Repayment Obligation**: Debentures have a fixed maturity date, and the principal amount is repaid to the holders at the end of the term.
- **No Voting Rights**: Debenture holders do not have voting rights, as they are creditors, not owners, of the company.
- **Charge on Assets**: Debentures may be secured by a charge on the company's assets or may be unsecured.
- **Tradability**: Debentures can often be traded on stock exchanges, providing liquidity to the holder.
- **Priority Over Equity**: In the event of liquidation, debenture holders have priority over shareholders for repayment.
- **Tax Benefits**: Interest paid on debentures is treated as an expense for the company, reducing its taxable income.

Characteristics of Debentures

- **Creditors, Not Owners**: Debenture holders are creditors of the company, not shareholders.
- **Fixed Income**: They receive interest regularly, which is a fixed charge on the company's income.
- **Types of Security**: Can be secured (backed by assets) or unsecured.
- **Rank in Liquidation**: Debenture holders are repaid before shareholders during liquidation.
- **Convertibility**: Some debentures can be converted into equity shares (convertible debentures).

Types of Debentures

Based on Security

- **Secured Debentures**:
  - ❑ These debentures are backed by a charge on the company's assets, either fixed or floating.
  - ❑ In case of default, debenture holders can claim repayment by selling the secured assets.
- **Unsecured Debentures**: These are not backed by any charge on assets and carry a higher risk.

Based on Convertibility

Convertible Debentures:

- Can be converted into equity shares of the company after a specific period.
- Further classified into:
  - ❑ **Fully Convertible Debentures**: Entire amount is converted into shares.
  - ❑ **Partly Convertible Debentures**: Only a portion is converted into shares.
- **Non-Convertible Debentures**: Cannot be converted into shares; the principal is repaid on maturity.

Based on Redemption

- **Redeemable Debentures**: Redeemed (repaid) after a fixed period.
- **Irredeemable (Perpetual) Debentures**: No fixed maturity date; repaid only during liquidation.

Based on Registration

- **Registered Debentures**: Issued in the name of the holder, and their details are registered in the company's records.
- **Bearer Debentures**: Transferable by delivery without requiring registration, making them like negotiable instruments.

Based on Priority

- **First Debentures**: These debentures have a primary claim on the company's assets.
- **Second Debentures**: These debentures have a subordinate claim, paid after first debenture holders.

DEBENTURE TRUST DEED AND TRUSTEE

Debenture Trust Deed

A **debenture trust deed** is a legal document that outlines the terms and conditions of the debenture issue and creates a charge on the company's assets (if applicable) in favor of debenture holders.

The deed is executed between the company and the **debenture trustee**.

Key Provisions in a Trust Deed:

- Details of the debenture issue (e.g., interest rate, maturity date, redemption terms).
- Rights and obligations of the debenture holders.
- Rights and responsibilities of the debenture trustee.
- Charge on the assets (if any) as security for repayment.
- Remedies in case of default by the company.

Debenture Trustee

- A **debenture trustee** is a third party (typically a financial institution or bank) appointed to protect the interests of debenture holders.
- The appointment of a trustee is mandatory for a public issue of debentures under the **Companies Act, 2013**.

Role and Responsibilities of the Trustee:

- Ensure that the company fulfills its obligations (e.g., timely payment of interest and principal).
- Act as an intermediary between the company and the debenture holders.
- Enforce the security in case of default.
- Represent the debenture holders in any legal or regulatory matters.

COMPANY LAW – DIRECTORS AND MEETINGS

FIRST DIRECTORS AND SUBSEQUENT APPOINTMENTS

First Directors:

- **Private Companies:** The first directors are typically named in the Articles of Association (AOA). If not specified, the subscribers to the Memorandum of Association (MoA) are deemed the first directors.
- **Public Companies:** In public companies, the first directors are usually appointed as per the AOA. If no provision is made in the AOA, the subscribers to the MoA or the shareholders at the general meeting appoint the first directors.

Subsequent Appointments:

- **By Shareholders:** Directors are appointed in the Annual General Meeting (AGM) by ordinary resolution.
- **By the Board of Directors:** The Board can appoint directors to fill casual vacancies or as additional directors, subject to the provisions of the Companies Act.
- **Government Nominees:** In some cases, government bodies can appoint directors for public sector undertakings or companies under regulatory oversight.

Methods of Appointment

- **Appointment by Shareholders:**
  - Regular directors are appointed during the AGM by an ordinary resolution.
  - Special resolution may be required for specific appointments (e.g., exceeding limits on directorships).
- **Appointment by the Board:**
  - **Additional Director:** Can be appointed by the board if authorized by the Articles of Association (Section 161(1)).
  - **Casual Vacancy:** Board fills vacancies arising due to death, resignation, or disqualification of a director (Section 161(4)).
  - **Alternate Director:** Appointed by the board to act in place of an absent director, typically for a period exceeding three months (Section 161(2)).
- **Appointment by Tribunal:** In case of mismanagement or oppression (Section 242), the tribunal may appoint directors to protect the interests of the company or stakeholders.
- **Appointment by Government/Regulators:**
  - Central Government can appoint directors in companies where mismanagement is identified.
  - Nominee directors can be appointed under agreements with financial institutions.

Qualifications of a Director

A director must meet the following eligibility criteria:

- Must be an individual (not a corporate entity).
- Must possess a Director Identification Number (DIN) issued by the Ministry of Corporate Affairs (MCA).
- Should not be disqualified under any provisions of the Companies Act.
- In case of independent directors, must meet the criteria specified under Section 149(6) of the Companies Act (e.g., independence, professional expertise).

Disqualifications Under Company Law

Under Section 164 of the Companies Act, a person is disqualified from being appointed as a director if:

- **Unsound Mind:** Declared by a competent court.
- **Undischarged Insolvent:** Not discharged from insolvency.
- **Conviction of Offense:** Convicted for any offense involving moral turpitude or an offense punishable with imprisonment for at least 6 months (disqualification lasts for 5 years after completion of sentence).
- **Non-Payment of Calls:** Fails to pay any calls in respect of shares of the company held by them and six months have elapsed from the last day fixed for payment.
- **Non-Compliance by Company:**
  - Company has failed to file financial statements or annual returns for 3 consecutive financial years.
  - Company or director has defaulted in repayment of deposits, debentures, or dividends for more than 1 year.
- **Age Criteria:** The 70-year limit and the requirement for a special resolution specifically apply to the appointment of Managing Directors, Whole-Time Directors, or Managers (Section 196(3)). There's no general upper age limit for other types of directors.

Number of Directorships Allowed Under Law

A person can hold directorships in a maximum of **20 companies** at any time.

- **Out of these 20:**
  - Directorships in **public companies** are limited to **10**.
  - This limit includes positions in **private companies** that are subsidiaries or holding companies of public companies.
- **Independent Directors:** Their appointments are governed by Section 149, which specifies limits on their tenure and involvement.
- **Exemptions:** The limit does not include directorships in charitable or non-profit organizations (e.g., Section 8 companies).

TYPES OF DIRECTORS

Here is a detailed breakdown of the different types of directors under company law, along with their roles, responsibilities, and key features, followed by sample multiple-choice questions:

Managing Director

A Managing Director (MD) is a director entrusted with substantial powers of management by the Board of Directors.

Features:

- ❑ The MD has authority over day-to-day business operations.
- ❑ The appointment must comply with Section 196 of the Companies Act, 2013.
- ❑ A company cannot appoint a person as MD if they are already an MD or manager in more than one company unless the company is a subsidiary.

- **Appointment Criteria:**
  - ❑ Must be approved by the board and ratified by shareholders.
  - ❑ Tenure cannot exceed 5 years.

Independent Director

An independent director is a non-executive director who does not have any material or pecuniary relationship with the company, its promoters, or its management.

Key Criteria (Section 149(6)):

- Must possess integrity and relevant expertise.
- Should not be a promoter of the company or its subsidiaries.
- Should not have any financial relationship with the company (e.g., loans, shares, etc.).

Role:

- Ensures the company complies with corporate governance practices.
- Protects the interest of minority shareholders.

Tenure:

- An independent director can hold office for a maximum of 5 years per term, with a possibility of one renewal.

Whole-Time Director

A Whole-Time Director (WTD) is a director who is in full-time employment of the company.

Features:

- They dedicate their time exclusively to the company.
- Often appointed to oversee specific operational functions (e.g., finance, marketing).

Difference from Managing Director:

- A WTD is limited to specific functions, whereas an MD oversees the entire management.

Nominee Director

A Nominee Director is appointed by a specific stakeholder (e.g., government, financial institutions, or creditors) to represent their interests on the board.

Key Features:

- Appointment is typically governed by an agreement, such as a loan agreement or shareholders' agreement.
- They ensure that the stakeholder's interests are protected in decision-making processes.

Examples:

- Nominees from banks to oversee the utilization of loans.

Executive vs. Non-Executive Directors

Executive Directors:

- Actively involved in the day-to-day operations of the company.
- Examples: Managing Director, Whole-Time Director.

Non-Executive Directors:

- Not involved in daily operations but participate in policymaking and strategic decisions.
- Examples: Independent Director, Nominee Director.

Key Role:

- Provides an external perspective on the company's operations.

Woman Director Requirements

- **Mandatory Requirement:** Listed companies and companies with certain thresholds (e.g., paid-up capital of ₹ 100 crores or turnover of ₹ 300 crores) must appoint at least one woman director under Section 149 of the Companies Act, 2013.
- **Purpose:** Promotes gender diversity and inclusion on boards.
- **Eligibility:** The woman director should meet the same qualifications and criteria as other directors.

Comparison Table: Types of Directors

Type	Involvement	Key Role	Appointment
Managing Director	Full-time, executive	Oversees overall management	Board + Shareholder approval
Independent Director	Non-executive	Ensures compliance, governance	Board + Compliance with Section 149(6)
Whole-Time Director	Full-time, executive	Handles specific operational areas	Board approval
Nominee Director	Non-executive	Represents stakeholder interests	Agreement-based appointment
Executive Director	Full-time, executive	Policy and operations	Board approval
Non-Executive Director	Non-executive	Advisory and policymaking	Board approval
Woman Director	Can be executive/non-executive	Enhances gender diversity	Mandatory for specified companies

MEETINGS OF THE BOARD

Here's an in-depth explanation of the key aspects related to board meetings under company law:

Quorum for Board Meetings

Quorum is the minimum number of directors required to be present at a meeting for it to be valid.

Provisions:

- **As per Section 174 of the Companies Act, 2013:**
    - ❑ **Private Companies:** The quorum is **two directors** or as specified in the Articles of Association (AOA).
    - ❑ **Public Companies:**
        - ➾ If the number of directors is up to 8, quorum is **2 directors**.
        - ➾ If the number of directors is between 9 and 15, quorum is **3 directors**.
        - ➾ If the number of directors is more than 15, quorum is **5 directors**.

        (The statutory rule (Section 174(1)) is "one-third of the total strength of the Board, or two directors, whichever is higher.")
- For virtual meetings (video conferencing or other electronic means), directors participating electronically are counted for quorum purposes.

Adjourned Meetings:

- If a meeting is adjourned due to a lack of quorum, it is typically reconvened on the same day and time in the following week, or as specified in the AOA.
- At the reconvened meeting, the directors present form the quorum, irrespective of the number.

Frequency of Board Meetings

Statutory Requirements:

- Section 173 of the Companies Act, 2013 specifies:
    - ❑ The first board meeting must be held **within 30 days** of incorporation.
    - ❑ A minimum of **four board meetings** must be held in a financial year.
    - ❑ The gap between two consecutive board meetings cannot exceed **120 days.**

Exemptions:

- One Person Companies (OPCs), Small Companies, and Dormant Companies need to conduct only **two board meetings** in a financial year.
- The gap between these two meetings must be at least **90 days.**

Notice Requirements

Provisions:

- A notice of at least **7 days** must be sent to every director before a board meeting.
- The notice can be sent in writing, electronically (e.g., email), or as permitted by the AOA.
- The notice must specify:
    - ❑ **Date**
    - ❑ **Time**
    - ❑ **Venue**
    - ❑ **Agenda** of the meeting

Short Notice:

- A meeting can be convened on shorter notice if at least one independent director is present. If not, the decisions taken at the meeting must be ratified by at least one independent director later.

Agenda and Minutes of Board Meetings

Agenda:

- The agenda is the list of items to be discussed during the board meeting.
- It must be included in the notice and should detail:
    - ❑ Routine matters (e.g., approval of accounts, review of performance).
    - ❑ Specific issues requiring board approval (e.g., appointment of directors, capital decisions).
    - ❑ Statutory compliance matters.

Minutes:

- **Definition:** Minutes are a written record of the proceedings of the board meeting.

Key Requirements (Section 118):

- Minutes must be prepared and signed by the chairman within **30 days** of the meeting.
- They must include:
  - ❑ Date, time, and venue of the meeting
  - ❑ Names of directors present
  - ❑ Resolutions passed
  - ❑ Dissenting opinions (if any)
- Minutes must be maintained in a **minutes book**.

Inspection:

- Shareholders cannot inspect board meeting minutes, but they can inspect general meeting minute

CORPORATE SOCIAL RESPONSIBILITY (CSR)

Definitions and Scope of CSR

- **Definition**: Corporate Social Responsibility refers to the practices and policies undertaken by corporations to have a positive impact on the world, including social, economic, and environmental areas.
- **Scope**: CSR initiatives may involve a range of activities such as environmental management, ethical business practices, economic development in the community, and volunteering.

Importance of CSR in Modern Business

- **Brand Image and Reputation**: Effective CSR practices can significantly improve a company's brand and public image, differentiating it in the marketplace and leading to a competitive advantage.
- **Risk Management**: CSR can mitigate risk by fostering a stronger compliance culture and closer ties with stakeholders on social and environmental issues.
- **Attracting and Retaining Employees**: Companies with robust CSR programs often find it easier to attract and retain talent, particularly among younger generations who favor socially conscious employers.

Examples of CSR Practices

- **Patagonia**: The company is known for its environmental and social initiatives, including donating a percentage of its profits to environmental causes and encouraging sustainable practices.
- **Microsoft**: Focuses on digital inclusion, creating opportunities through technology, and maintaining high standards of corporate governance.
- **LEGO**: Invests in sustainable materials for its products and packaging and aims to have a positive impact on the communities where it operates.

CSR Theories and Frameworks

- **Triple Bottom Line**: Proposes that companies should commit to focusing as much on social and environmental concerns as they do on profits ("People, Planet, Profit").
- **Creating Shared Value (CSV)**: Encourages companies to develop profitable business strategies that deliver tangible social benefits.
- **Sustainability Theory**: Focuses on the endurance and ecological aspect of business practices, ensuring that business operations do not harm the environment.

Regulations and Standards for CSR

- **Global Reporting Initiative (GRI)**: Provides a comprehensive set of indicators covering the economic, environmental, and ethical impacts of a company's performance.
- **United Nations Global Compact**: A principle-based framework that encourages businesses to adopt sustainable and socially responsible policies.

Environmental Aspects of CSR

- **Resource Efficiency**: Companies focusing on reducing their resource consumption through recycling, reusing, and reducing materials.
- **Climate Change Mitigation**: Initiatives to reduce greenhouse gas emissions, such as adopting renewable energy technologies and improving energy efficiency.

Social Aspects of CSR

- **Diversity and Inclusion**: Initiatives aimed at enhancing diversity in the workplace through equitable hiring practices and supporting minority groups.
- **Community Development**: CSR often involves programs aimed at improving infrastructure, education, and health services in underserved communities.

Ethical Issues in CSR

- **Corporate Governance**: Strong governance structures that ensure accountability and transparency in how businesses operate.
- **Human Rights**: Ensuring that business practices do not violate human rights, including labor rights, and do not involve exploitative practices.

Impact of CSR on Stakeholders

- **Impact on Suppliers and Consumers**: CSR demands ethical supply chain practices and influences consumer choices and behaviors.
- **Community and Environmental Impact**: Local communities and the environment can benefit from corporate initiatives that focus on sustainable growth and development.

Future Trends in CSR

- **Technology and Innovation for Sustainability**: Companies are increasingly using technology to solve complex sustainability challenges, such as through the use of AI to optimize energy use.
- **Regulatory Pressure**: Increasingly, governments are mandating CSR reporting and sustainable practices, which may shape future trends in CSR.

MULTIPLE CHOICE QUESTIONS

1. Which of the following is NOT an essential element of a valid contract under the Indian Contract Act, 1872?
A. Lawful consideration
B. Offer and acceptance
C. Agreement in writing only
D. Free consent of parties

2. Which of the following is NOT considered a valid mode of communication for an e-contract?
A. Email
B. Verbal telephone conversation
C. Click-wrap agreement
D. Shrink-wrap agreement

3. In an e-contract, the acceptance of an offer can be legally binding through a simple click on the "I Agree" button.
A. True
B. False
C. True, only if the contract is for goods
D. False, as physical signatures are mandatory

4. A contract entered into by a minor is voidable at the option of the minor under Indian law.
A. True
B. False
C. True, only if the minor misrepresented their age
D. False, such contracts are void ab initio (invalid from the beginning)

5. Assertion (A): Consideration is necessary for a valid contract under Indian law.

Reason (R): A contract without consideration is always void, without any exceptions.
A. Both A and R are true, and R is the correct explanation of A
B. Both A and R are true, but R is not the correct explanation of A
C. A is true, R is false
D. A is false, R is true

6. In a contract, an _______ is a proposal made by one party to another, indicating a willingness to enter into an agreement on certain terms.
A. Invitation to offer B. Offer
C. Consideration D. Acceptance

7. In the context of e-contracts, _______ agreements require the user to actively click "I Agree" to be legally bound by the contract terms.
A. Shrink-wrap B. Browse-wrap
C. Click-wrap D. Oral contracts

8. Match the following types of contracts with their definitions:

Contracts	Definitions
A. Void Contract	1. A contract formed electronically through digital communication
B. Voidable Contract	2. A contract that ceases to be enforceable by law
C. E-Contract	3. A contract enforceable by one party but not the other
D. Unilateral Contract	4. A contract where one party makes a promise in exchange for an act

A. A-2, B-3, C-1, D-4
B. A-1, B-4, C-2, D-3
C. A-4, B-1, C-3, D-2
D. A-3, B-2, C-4, D-1

9. Scenario: Rajesh downloads a mobile app and clicks "I Agree" to the terms and conditions without reading them. Later, he disputes a clause related to data sharing, claiming he wasn't aware of it. Is the click-wrap agreement legally binding?
A. Yes, because clicking "I Agree" signifies consent to the contract terms.
B. No, because he did not read the terms.
C. Yes, only if the app had a physical signature requirement.
D. No, unless he verbally confirmed the terms.

10. Which of the following is an essential element of a valid contract under Indian Contract Act, 1872?
A. Written agreement only
B. Mutual consent of parties
C. Government approval
D. Registration with the registrar

11. Which of the following is NOT a type of e-contract?
A. Click-wrap agreement
B. Shrink-wrap agreement
C. Verbal contract over the phone
D. Browse-wrap agreement

12. A contract without consideration is valid if it is made out of natural love and affection between parties standing in a close relationship.
A. True
B. False
C. True, only if it is in writing and registered
D. False, unless witnessed by a public notary

13. In an e-contract, a digital signature has the same legal validity as a handwritten signature.
A. True
B. False
C. True, only for government contracts
D. False, unless notarized

14. **Assertion (A):** An agreement enforceable by law is called a contract.

Reason (R): All agreements, whether legal or illegal, are enforceable under the Indian Contract Act.
A. Both A and R are true, and R is the correct explanation of A
B. Both A and R are true, but R is not the correct explanation of A
C. A is true, R is false
D. A is false, R is true

15. A contract formed through electronic means without any physical meeting of parties is known as a/an ______.
A. Void contract B. E-contract
C. Quasi-contract D. Implied contract

16. For a contract to be valid, the parties must have the ______ to contract, meaning they must be legally competent.
A. Capacity B. Consideration
C. Consent D. Condition

17. Match the following types of consent with their legal consequences in a contract:

Types of Consent	Legal Consequences
A. Coercion	1. Contract is voidable at the option of the aggrieved party
B. Undue Influence	2. Contract is valid and enforceable
C. Fraud	3. Consent obtained by deception
D. Free Consent	4. Consent obtained through physical threats

A. A-4, B-1, C-3, D-2
B. A-3, B-2, C-1, D-4
C. A-1, B-4, C-2, D-3
D. A-2, B-3, C-4, D-1

18. Arrange the following in the correct order for the formation of an e-contract:
1. Offer is made via email or website.
2. Acceptance through electronic means (click, email, etc.)
3. Digital signature or electronic confirmation
4. Consideration is exchanged
5. Contract is enforceable under law

A. 1, 2, 3, 4, 5
B. 2, 1, 4, 3, 5
C. 3, 1, 2, 4, 5
D. 1, 4, 3, 2, 5

19. Scenario: An online shopping website offers products with a detailed "Terms & Conditions" page. Before purchasing, the user must click "I Agree" to proceed. Later, the user claims they were unaware of certain conditions and refuses to comply. Is this contract enforceable?
A. Yes, because clicking "I Agree" signifies acceptance of all terms
B. No, because the user didn't read the terms
C. Yes, only if the website sent a confirmation email
D. No, unless the terms were explained verbally

20. Which of the following is an example of a breach of contract?
A. A delay in performance due to unavoidable natural events
B. Failure to perform contractual obligations without any lawful excuse
C. Performance of contract after mutual consent for extension
D. Termination of the contract due to frustration

21. Which of the following situations will NOT result in the frustration of a contract?
A. Destruction of the subject matter of the contract
B. Death of a party in a personal service contract
C. Change in law making the performance illegal
D. Financial difficulty faced by one party

22. Which of the following agreements is void from the beginning (void ab initio)?
A. A contract with a minor
B. A contract obtained through coercion
C. A contract induced by fraud
D. A contract signed under undue influence

23. A voidable contract becomes void when:
A. Both parties agree to terminate the contract
B. The party entitled to rescind the contract exercises their right
C. The contract is not performed within the stipulated time
D. The contract is illegal

24. Breach of contract always results in the automatic termination of the contract.
A. True
B. False
C. True, if the breach is material
D. False, unless both parties agree

25. A contract is frustrated if performance becomes impossible due to an unforeseen event beyond the control of both parties.
A. True
B. False
C. True, only if there was no force majeure clause
D. False, unless the parties mutually agree

26. Assertion (A): A contract with unlawful consideration is void.

Reason (R): The law does not enforce agreements that involve illegal activities.
A. Both A and R are true, and R is the correct explanation of A
B. Both A and R are true, but R is not the correct explanation of A
C. A is true, R is false
D. A is false, R is true

27. Assertion (A): A contract cannot be frustrated if the event causing frustration was foreseeable.

Reason (R): Frustration applies only to unforeseen and unavoidable events.
A. Both A and R are true, and R is the correct explanation of A
B. Both A and R are true, but R is not the correct explanation of A
C. A is true, R is false
D. A is false, R is true

28. A contract becomes ________ when it is no longer legally enforceable by either party.
A. Void B. Voidable
C. Enforceable D. Executed

29. The legal remedy for a breach of contract is usually the award of ________ to the injured party.
A. Damages B. Punishment
C. Rescission D. Consideration

30. Match the following legal concepts with their definitions:

Legal Concepts	Definitions
A. Breach of Contract	1. A contract that becomes impossible to perform due to unforeseen events
B. Frustration of Contract	2. Failure to perform contractual obligations without lawful excuse
C. Void Contract	3. A contract enforceable by one party but not the other
D. Voidable Contract	4. A contract that is not enforceable from the beginning

A. A-2, B-1, C-4, D-3
B. A-1, B-2, C-3, D-4
C. A-4, B-3, C-2, D-1
D. A-3, B-4, C-1, D-2

31. Arrange the following steps in the correct sequence for claiming damages for breach of contract:
1. Breach of contract occurs
2. Notice of breach to the other party
3. Filing a legal suit
4. Court evaluates the breach
5. Award of damages
A. 1, 2, 3, 4, 5
B. 2, 1, 3, 5, 4
C. 3, 1, 2, 4, 5
D. 1, 4, 3, 2, 5

32. Scenario: A agrees to deliver 500 tons of coal to B. Before delivery, new government regulations ban coal transportation due to environmental concerns. Can A claim frustration of contract?
A. Yes, because the contract has become illegal
B. No, because A could have anticipated the regulation
C. Yes, only if A suffers financial loss
D. No, unless both parties mutually agree to terminate

33. Scenario: X agrees to sell his car to Y. However, before the sale, the car is completely destroyed in an accident. What is the status of the contract?
A. The contract is void due to frustration
B. The contract is voidable at Y's option
C. The contract is still enforceable
D. X must compensate Y for breach of contract

34. Scenario: P enters into a contract with Q by threatening to harm Q's family. Q later wishes to cancel the contract. Is this contract void or voidable?
A. Void from the beginning
B. Voidable at the option of Q
C. Valid and enforceable
D. Illegal contract

35. Which of the following remedies is NOT available for breach of contract under the Indian Contract Act, 1872?
A. Suit for specific performance
B. Suit for injunction
C. Suit for criminal prosecution
D. Suit for damages

36. **Assertion (A):** A contract becomes void if its performance becomes impossible due to an act of God (like an earthquake).

Reason (R): The doctrine of frustration applies when unforeseen events make the performance of a contract impossible.
A. Both A and R are true, and R is the correct explanation of A
B. Both A and R are true, but R is not the correct explanation of A
C. A is true, R is false
D. A is false, R is true

37. A contract entered into under ______ is voidable at the option of the party whose consent was obtained through such means.
A. Coercion B. Free will
C. Legal agreement D. Mutual consent

38. Match the following contract terms with their appropriate legal outcomes:

Contract Terms	Legal Outcomes
A. Breach of Contract	1. Results in a claim for damages
B. Frustration of Contract	2. Automatically terminates due to impossibility
C. Void Agreement	3. Cannot be enforced from the beginning
D. Voidable Agreement	4. Can be canceled by one of the parties

A. A-1, B-2, C-3, D-4
B. A-4, B-3, C-1, D-2
C. A-2, B-1, C-4, D-3
D. A-3, B-1, C-2, D-4

39. Scenario: X agrees to rent out his banquet hall to Y for a wedding scheduled on a particular date. However, before the event, the government imposes a lockdown due to a pandemic, prohibiting public gatherings. What is the status of the contract?
A. The contract is breached by X
B. The contract is frustrated due to supervening impossibility
C. The contract is voidable at Y's option
D. The contract remains valid, and Y must pay compensation

40. Which of the following best describes a standard form of contract?
A. A contract negotiated equally by both parties
B. A pre-drafted contract with fixed terms, offered on a "take it or leave it" basis
C. A contract that requires court approval
D. A verbal agreement between two parties

41. Which of the following is an example of a quasi-contract?
A. A written agreement between two parties
B. A verbal promise to sell goods
C. A situation where someone receives goods by mistake and is legally bound to pay for them
D. A contract that has been registered under law

42. Which of the following is NOT a characteristic of a standard form contract?
A. Non-negotiable terms
B. Equal bargaining power
C. Pre-determined clauses
D. Prepared by one party

43. Which section of the Indian Contract Act deals with quasi-contractual obligations?
A. Section 10
B. Section 31
C. Sections 68 to 72
D. Section 56

44. Standard form contracts are enforceable even if one party did not read the terms before signing.
A. True
B. False
C. True, only if signed before a magistrate
D. False, unless signed in duplicate

45. A quasi-contract is formed through mutual consent of the parties involved.
A. True
B. False
C. True, if consideration is present
D. False, unless supported by a written agreement

46. **Assertion (A):** Standard form contracts are often used by large organizations for efficiency.

Reason (R): These contracts reduce negotiation time as the terms are pre-determined.
A. Both A and R are true, and R is the correct explanation of A
B. Both A and R are true, but R is not the correct explanation of A
C. A is true, R is false
D. A is false, R is true

47. **Assertion (A):** In a quasi-contract, legal obligations arise even without any contract.

Reason (R): Quasi-contracts are created when both parties have expressly agreed to specific terms.
A. Both A and R are true, and R is the correct explanation of A
B. Both A and R are true, but R is not the correct explanation of A
C. A is true, R is false
D. A is false, R is true

48. A contract that is pre-drafted with fixed terms and offered without the possibility of negotiation is known as a ______ contract.
A. Voidable   B. Unilateral
C. Standard Form   D. Bilateral

49. A quasi-contract is based on the principle of ______ enrichment, where one party should not benefit at the expense of another without compensation.
A. Just   B. Mutual
C. Unjust   D. Fair

50. Match the following types of quasi-contracts with their descriptions:

A. Supply of Necessaries	1. A person who finds goods belonging to another must return them
B. Payment by Interested Person	2. Recovery of money accidentally paid to someone
C. Obligation of Finder of Goods	3. Providing essentials to a minor or incapable person with reimbursement rights
D. Money Paid by Mistake	4. A person paying on behalf of another when legally bound

A. A-3, B-4, C-1, D-2
B. A-2, B-3, C-4, D-1
C. A-4, B-1, C-3, D-2
D. A-1, B-2, C-4, D-3

51. Arrange the following steps in the correct sequence for dealing with a quasi-contractual obligation:
1. Unjust enrichment occurs
2. Legal obligation is imposed by law
3. Compensation or restitution is demanded
4. Court enforces the obligation if not voluntarily fulfilled

A. 1, 2, 3, 4   B. 2, 1, 3, 4
C. 4, 3, 2, 1   D. 3, 1, 2, 4

52. Scenario: A mistakenly transfers ₹ 50,000 to B's bank account. B refuses to return the money, claiming there was no contract between them. Can A recover the money?
A. Yes, under quasi-contract for money paid by mistake
B. No, because there was no contract
C. Yes, only if A proves B promised to return it
D. No, unless A files a criminal case

53. Scenario: X's goods are mistakenly delivered to Y. Y uses the goods without informing the delivery company. Is Y liable to pay for the goods?
A. Yes, because of the quasi-contractual obligation
B. No, because Y didn't order the goods
C. Yes, only if Y resells the goods
D. No, unless X files a breach of contract case

54. Scenario: A hotel provides medical assistance to an unconscious guest without any prior agreement. Is the guest legally bound to pay for the services after recovery?

A. Yes, under quasi-contract for supply of necessaries
B. No, because there was no contract
C. Yes, only if the guest signed a consent form
D. No, unless the hotel files a lawsuit

55. Which of the following is a key feature of a standard form contract?
A. Terms are negotiated individually for each party
B. The contract is flexible and open to modification anytime
C. It contains pre-set terms and conditions drafted by one party
D. Requires a government stamp to be valid

56. Assertion (A): In a quasi-contract, the obligation to pay arises even when there is no formal contract between the parties.

Reason (R): Quasi-contracts are based on the principle of preventing unjust enrichment.
A. Both A and R are true, and R is the correct explanation of A
B. Both A and R are true, but R is not the correct explanation of A
C. A is true, R is false
D. A is false, R is true

57. In a quasi-contract, the liability imposed by law is ________ in nature, meaning it is treated like a contract even though no actual contract exists.
A. Criminal B. Tortious
C. Contractual D. Statutory

58. Match the following principles with the type of contracts they apply to:

A. Doctrine of Reasonable Notice	1. Applies to quasi-contracts to prevent benefiting unfairly
B. Unjust Enrichment	2. Obligation to reimburse when essential goods or services are provided
C. Take-it-or-leave-it Contracts	3. Applies to standard form contracts requiring clear notice of terms
D. Obligation to Pay for Necessaries	4. Contracts offered without negotiation

A. A-3, B-1, C-4, D-2
B. A-4, B-2, C-3, D-1
C. A-1, B-4, C-3, D-2
D. A-2, B-3, C-1, D-4

59. Scenario: Mr. A orders 100 chairs from Mr. B, but due to a clerical error, Mr. B delivers 150 chairs. Mr. A uses all 150 chairs without informing Mr. B. Is Mr. A legally bound to pay for the extra 50 chairs?
A. Yes, under quasi-contract, as he has benefited from the extra chairs
B. No, because the contract was for only 100 chairs
C. Yes, only if there was a written agreement for the extra chairs
D. No, unless Mr. B files a breach of contract case

60. Which of the following is an essential element of a contract of bailment?
A. Delivery of goods without consideration
B. Transfer of ownership
C. Delivery of goods for a specific purpose with an obligation to return
D. Sale of goods

61. In a contract of pledge, the person who delivers the goods as security is called:
A. Bailor
B. Pledger (Pawnor)
C. Pledgee (Pawnee)
D. Agent

62. Which of the following is true regarding a contract of indemnity?
A. It involves three parties
B. It is a contract where one party promises to compensate another for loss
C. It requires delivery of goods
D. It is always related to employment contracts

63. Which of the following is NOT a valid duty of an agent under the law of agency?
A. Duty to act in good faith
B. Duty to act according to the principal's instructions
C. Duty to act for personal gain even against the principal's interests
D. Duty to maintain proper accounts

64. A contract of guarantee involves three parties: the principal debtor, the creditor, and the surety.
A. True
B. False
C. True, but only if in writing
D. False, unless notarized

65. In a contract of bailment, the bailor retains ownership of the goods.
A. True
B. False
C. True, only if the contract is registered
D. False, because ownership is transferred to the bailee

66. Assertion (A): In a contract of pledge, the pawnee has the right to sell the pledged goods if the pawnor defaults.

Reason (R): This right arises after giving reasonable notice to the pawnor.

A. Both A and R are true, and R is the correct explanation of A
B. Both A and R are true, but R is not the correct explanation of A
C. A is true, R is false
D. A is false, R is true

67. Assertion (A): In a contract of agency, an agent can delegate their authority to another person.

Reason (R): The principle of "delegatus non potestdelegare" allows agents to freely delegate authority.

A. Both A and R are true, and R is the correct explanation of A
B. Both A and R are true, but R is not the correct explanation of A
C. A is true, R is false
D. A is false, R is true

68. In a contract of guarantee, the person who gives the guarantee is called the ______.

A. Creditor B. Debtor
C. Surety D. Agent

69. A contract of indemnity requires a promise to compensate for a loss that may occur in the ______.

A. Past B. Present
C. Future D. None of the above

70. Match the following terms with their correct definitions:

Terms	Definitions
A. Bailment	1. A contract where goods are delivered as security for a loan
B. Pledge	2. A contract where one party promises to compensate for the loss of another
C. Indemnity	3. Delivery of goods for a specific purpose with an obligation to return
D. Guarantee	4. A contract involving a third party to ensure the performance of an obligation

A. A-3, B-1, C-2, D-4
B. A-4, B-3, C-1, D-2
C. A-1, B-2, C-3, D-4
D. A-2, B-1, C-4, D-3

71. Arrange the following steps for creating a valid contract of guarantee:

1. Existence of a principal debtor
2. A promise by the surety to fulfill obligations if the debtor defaults
3. Acceptance of the guarantee by the creditor
4. Consideration for the guarantee

A. 1, 2, 4, 3
B. 2, 1, 3, 4
C. 1, 4, 2, 3
D. 4, 1, 2, 3

72. Scenario: A lends money to B, and C acts as a surety for the loan. B defaults on the repayment. What is C's liability?

A. C is liable only if A sues B first
B. C is not liable as it was B's responsibility
C. C is liable immediately without A needing to sue B
D. C can refuse payment because he didn't receive the loan

73. Scenario: X gives his gold watch to Y for safe-keeping while he's traveling. Y loses the watch due to his negligence. What is Y's liability?

A. Y is not liable as he was doing a favor
B. Y is liable because he was negligent
C. Y is liable only if X paid him for safekeeping
D. Y can claim ownership since X left it with him

74. Scenario: P agrees to compensate Q for any losses arising from Q's new business venture. What type of contract is this?

A. Bailment B. Pledge
C. Indemnity D. Guarantee

75. In a contract of agency, the principal is bound by the acts of the agent if:

A. The agent acts beyond their authority without informing the principal
B. The agent acts within the scope of their actual or apparent authority
C. The agent makes personal decisions unrelated to the principal's business
D. The agent delegates their authority without permission

76. Assertion (A): In a contract of indemnity, the indemnifier's liability arises only when the indemnified suffers an actual loss.

Reason (R): The indemnifier is not liable for contingent liabilities unless specified in the contract.

A. Both A and R are true, and R is the correct explanation of A

B. Both A and R are true, but R is not the correct explanation of A
C. A is true, R is false
D. A is false, R is true

77. In a contract of pledge, if the pawnor defaults, the pawnee has the right to _______ the pledged goods after giving due notice.
A. Destroy B. Return
C. Sell D. Keep

78. Match the following parties with their roles in specific contracts:

A. Bailor	1. Person who delivers goods as security for a loan
B. Pawnor	2. Person who appoints another to act on their behalf
C. Indemnifier	3. Person who delivers goods to another for safekeeping
D. Principal	4. Person who promises to compensate for a loss

A. A-3, B-1, C-4, D-2
B. A-2, B-3, C-1, D-4
C. A-1, B-4, C-3, D-2
D. A-4, B-1, C-2, D-3

79. Scenario: Rohan appoints Suresh as his agent to buy machinery for his business. Suresh buys machinery from his own company without informing Rohan. Is this transaction valid?
A. Yes, because Suresh acted within his authority
B. No, because Suresh had a conflict of interest
C. Yes, only if Rohan later approves the purchase
D. No, unless Suresh made a profit for Rohan

80. Which of the following is NOT an essential element of a contract of sale under the Sale of Goods Act, 1930?
A. Two parties
B. Transfer of property in goods
C. Goods must be delivered at the time of contract
D. Price consideration

81. Which of the following is an example of specific goods under the Sale of Goods Act, 1930?
A. 50 bags of rice from a warehouse containing 1,000 bags
B. A car with registration number XYZ123
C. Any television from a store
D. 20 kg of sugar from a sack

82. Under the Sale of Goods Act, 1930, the term "goods" does NOT include:
A. Growing crops
B. Stocks and shares
C. Immovable property
D. Things attached to land that can be severed

83. In a contract of sale, when the ownership of goods is transferred immediately from the seller to the buyer, it is known as:
A. Agreement to sell
B. Hire-purchase agreement
C. Sale
D. Contract for service

84. A contract for the sale of future goods is an agreement to sell, not an actual sale.
A. True
B. False
C. True, only if payment is made in advance
D. False, unless the goods are already manufactured

85. The doctrine of 'Caveat Emptor' implies that the seller is responsible for checking the quality of goods before sale.
A. True
B. False
C. True, only in international trade
D. False, unless goods are defective

86. **Assertion (A):** In a contract of sale, the risk of loss of goods usually passes with the ownership.

Reason (R): Ownership and risk are inseparable in all cases.
A. Both A and R are true, and R is the correct explanation of A
B. Both A and R are true, but R is not the correct explanation of A
C. A is true, R is false
D. A is false, R is true

87. **Assertion (A):** In a contract of sale, goods can only be sold if they are physically delivered.

Reason (R): Delivery of goods is mandatory to transfer ownership under the Sale of Goods Act, 1930.
A. Both A and R are true, and R is the correct explanation of A
B. Both A and R are true, but R is not the correct explanation of A
C. A is true, R is false
D. A is false, R is true

88. The principle of _______ means that the buyer must take responsibility for checking the quality and fitness of goods before purchasing.

A. Nemo dat quod non habet
B. Caveat Emptor
C. Pacta Sunt Servanda
D. Res Ipsa Loquitur

89. Goods that are identified and agreed upon at the time of the contract of sale are called ______ goods.

A. Future
B. Unascertained
C. Contingent
D. Specific

90. Match the following types of goods with their correct descriptions:

A. Specific Goods	1. Goods identified and agreed upon at the time of contract
B. Unascertained Goods	2. Goods that will be manufactured or acquired in the future
C. Future Goods	3. Goods not specifically identified at the time of contract
D. Contingent Goods	4. Goods whose acquisition depends on the occurrence of a future uncertain event

A. A-1, B-3, C-2, D-4
B. A-3, B-2, C-4, D-1
C. A-4, B-1, C-3, D-2
D. A-2, B-4, C-1, D-3

91. Arrange the following stages in the correct sequence for a contract of sale:

1. Offer to buy or sell
2. Acceptance of the offer
3. Agreement to sell
4. Transfer of ownership

A. 1, 2, 3, 4
B. 2, 1, 4, 3
C. 3, 4, 1, 2
D. 4, 1, 2, 3

92. Scenario: A agrees to sell 100 bags of wheat to B. Before delivery, the entire stock is destroyed in a fire without A's fault. What is the status of the contract?

A. The contract is still enforceable
B. The contract becomes void due to impossibility of performance
C. B must still pay for the goods
D. A is liable for breach of contract

93. Scenario: X sells a car to Y without owning it. Later, X purchases the car and refuses to deliver it to Y. Is Y entitled to claim the car?

A. Yes, because the sale was valid once X became the owner
B. No, because X was not the owner at the time of sale
C. Yes, only if X had registered the car in Y's name
D. No, unless Y pays additional consideration

94. Scenario: A bought a refrigerator based on B's advice that it was suitable for commercial use. The refrigerator failed to work in A's restaurant. Is B liable?

A. Yes, under the implied condition of fitness for purpose
B. No, because A should have checked before buying
C. Yes, only if there was a written warranty
D. No, unless A paid extra for expert advice

95. Which of the following statements is true regarding the transfer of property in goods under the Sale of Goods Act, 1930?

A. Property in goods passes to the buyer only after delivery
B. Property in goods can never pass without physical possession
C. Property in goods passes when the parties intend it to pass
D. Property in goods always passes at the time of payment

96. Assertion (A): A seller has the right to stop goods in transit if the buyer becomes insolvent.

Reason (R): This right exists even if the property in the goods has already passed to the buyer.

A. Both A and R are true, and R is the correct explanation of A
B. Both A and R are true, but R is not the correct explanation of A
C. A is true, R is false
D. A is false, R is true

97. When goods are delivered to a carrier for transmission to the buyer, it is considered as ______ delivery under the Sale of Goods Act, 1930.

A. Constructive
B. Symbolic
C. Actual
D. Implied

98. Match the following terms with their correct legal implications under the Sale of Goods Act, 1930:

Terms	Legal Implications
A. Unpaid Seller	1. A stipulation essential to the main purpose of the contract
B. Condition	2. A stipulation collateral to the main purpose, breach of which allows for damages
C. Warranty	3. A seller who hasn't received full payment for the goods
D. Agreement to Sell	4. A contract where the transfer of property is to take place at a future date

A. A-3, B-1, C-2, D-4
B. A-1, B-4, C-3, D-2
C. A-4, B-2, C-3, D-1
D. A-2, B-3, C-1, D-4

99. Scenario: A agrees to sell 500 kg of rice to B. The rice was to be delivered after a week. Before delivery, a government ban is imposed on the sale of rice due to a crisis. What is the status of the contract?

A. The contract remains valid, and A must deliver the rice
B. The contract becomes void due to supervening impossibility
C. B can sue A for breach of contract
D. A can deliver substitute goods instead of rice

100. Which of the following is NOT an essential element of a partnership?

A. Agreement between parties
B. Sharing of profits
C. Registration of the firm
D. Mutual agency

101. In a Limited Liability Partnership (LLP), who is liable for the debts of the LLP?

A. All partners equally
B. Only the managing partner
C. The LLP itself, while partners have limited liability
D. The partner who signed the contract

102. Which of the following statements is true about LLPs?

A. LLPs cannot enter into contracts in their own name
B. LLPs require a minimum of three partners
C. LLPs have perpetual succession
D. LLPs do not require registration

103. Which of the following is NOT a characteristic of a partnership firm?

A. Mutual agency
B. Separate legal entity distinct from partners
C. Sharing of profits and losses
D. Based on an agreement

104. A partnership can be formed only through a written agreement.

A. True
B. False
C. True, if the capital exceeds ₹ 1,00,000
D. False, unless registered

105. In an LLP, every partner is considered an agent of the LLP but not of other partners.

A. True
B. False
C. True, unless stated otherwise in the agreement
D. False, except in case of fraud

106. Assertion (A): In a partnership, partners are jointly and severally liable for the firm's debts.

Reason (R): This is because a partnership has a separate legal identity from its partners.

A. Both A and R are true, and R is the correct explanation of A
B. Both A and R are true, but R is not the correct explanation of A
C. A is true, R is false
D. A is false, R is true

107. Assertion (A): LLPs are preferred over traditional partnerships for large businesses.

Reason (R): This is because LLPs provide limited liability protection and perpetual succession.

A. Both A and R are true, and R is the correct explanation of A
B. Both A and R are true, but R is not the correct explanation of A
C. A is true, R is false
D. A is false, R is true

108. In a partnership, the relationship between partners is governed by a ________.

A. Memorandum of Association
B. Deed of Partnership
C. Certificate of Incorporation
D. Articles of Association

109. An LLP must have at least ______ designated partners, one of whom must be a resident of India.

A. 1 B. 2
C. 3 D. 4

110. Arrange the following steps in the correct sequence to register an LLP:

1. Apply for Digital Signature Certificate (DSC)
2. Obtain Director Identification Number (DIN)
3. Reserve the name of the LLP
4. File incorporation documents with the Ministry of Corporate Affairs (MCA)
5. Obtain the Certificate of Incorporation

A. 1, 2, 3, 4, 5 B. 2, 1, 4, 3, 5
C. 3, 2, 1, 4, 5 D. 4, 1, 3, 2, 5

111. Scenario: X and Y are partners in a firm. X borrows money in the firm's name without Y's knowledge for personal use. Is Y liable to repay the loan?

A. Yes, because they are partners
B. No, because the act was outside the scope of the partnership
C. Yes, if X is the managing partner
D. No, unless X had prior written consent from Y

112. Scenario: A, B, and C form an LLP. A commits a fraudulent act without B and C's knowledge. Who is liable?

A. Only A
B. All partners equally
C. The LLP and A
D. Only the LLP

113. Scenario: P and Q are partners. P introduces R as a new partner without Q's consent. Is R a partner in the firm?

A. Yes, because P is already a partner
B. No, because the consent of all existing partners is required
C. Yes, if R agrees to join
D. No, unless R contributes capital

114. Which of the following acts does NOT require the consent of all partners in a partnership firm?

A. Admitting a new partner
B. Change in the nature of the business
C. Transferring the firm's property
D. Day-to-day management decisions

115. Assertion (A): In an LLP, partners are not personally liable for the wrongful acts or omissions of other partners.

Reason (R): LLPs provide limited liability protection to all partners unless the act is fraudulent or wrongful by the concerned partner.

A. Both A and R are true, and R is the correct explanation of A
B. Both A and R are true, but R is not the correct explanation of A
C. A is true, R is false
D. A is false, R is true

116. A person who lends their name to a partnership without being an actual partner, but becomes liable to third parties, is called a ______ partner.

A. Sleeping B. Nominal
C. Active D. Secret

117. Match the following types of partners with their characteristics:

Partners	Characteristics
A. Active Partner	1. Does not take part in daily activities but invests capital
B. Sleeping Partner	2. Actively participates in the management of the firm
C. Nominal Partner	3. Holds out as a partner and becomes liable to third parties
D. Partner by Estoppel	4. Lends name without actual participation

A. A-2, B-1, C-4, D-3
B. A-1, B-2, C-3, D-4
C. A-4, B-3, C-1, D-2
D. A-3, B-4, C-2, D-1

118. Scenario: X, Y, and Z are partners in an LLP. X commits a fraud without the knowledge of Y and Z. A third party suffers a loss due to this fraud. Who is liable?

A. Only X B. X and the LLP
C. All partners equally D. Only the LLP

119. The Indian Partnership Act, 1932 governs:

A. Only registered partnerships
B. Only LLPs
C. Both registered and unregistered partnerships
D. Only partnerships with more than two partners

120. In an LLP, the liability of partners arises in cases of:

A. Ordinary business losses
B. Fraud committed by the partner
C. Acts done with the consent of all partners
D. Administrative errors

121. 18. Match the following CSR-related entities with their roles:

Entities	Roles
A. CSR Committee	1. Recommends CSR policy
B. Board of Directors	2. Approves CSR policy and ensures implementation
C. Implementing Agency	3. Executes CSR activities on behalf of companies
D. Ministry of Corporate Affairs	4. Provides CSR-related regulatory framework

A. A-1, B-2, C-3, D-4
B. A-2, B-1, C-4, D-3
C. A-3, B-4, C-2, D-1
D. A-4, B-3, C-1, D-2

122. Scenario: A, B, and C are partners in a firm. A retires without giving notice to third parties. A third party extends credit to the firm believing A is still a partner. Is A liable?
A. Yes, because A did not give notice of retirement
B. No, because A has retired
C. Yes, only if A still holds shares
D. No, unless A signed the credit agreement

123. Scenario: In an LLP, X, a designated partner, fails to file annual returns. Who is liable?
A. Only X
B. The LLP and X
C. All partners equally
D. Only the LLP

124. Which of the following is NOT a negotiable instrument under the Negotiable Instruments Act, 1881?
A. Promissory Note
B. Bill of Exchange
C. Cheque
D. Fixed Deposit Receipt

125. Which section of the Negotiable Instruments Act, 1881 defines a 'cheque'?
A. Section 4 B. Section 5
C. Section 6 D. Section 9

126. A negotiable instrument can be transferred through:
A. Assignment only
B. Endorsement and delivery
C. Oral agreement
D. Registration with the government

127. Which of the following is true about a promissory note?
A. It is drawn by the creditor
B. It is an unconditional order to pay
C. It requires acceptance by the drawee
D. It is an unconditional promise to pay

128. A cheque is always payable on demand.
A. True
B. False
C. True, if it is crossed
D. False, unless post-dated

129. A bearer cheque can be transferred simply by delivery without endorsement.
A. True
B. False
C. True, if signed by the payee
D. False, unless notarized

130. **Assertion (A):** A dishonoured cheque can result in criminal liability under Section 138 of the Negotiable Instruments Act.

Reason (R): Dishonour of a cheque due to insufficient funds is considered a criminal offense under the Act.

A. Both A and R are true, and R is the correct explanation of A
B. Both A and R are true, but R is not the correct explanation of A
C. A is true, R is false
D. A is false, R is true

131. **Assertion (A):** A negotiable instrument must be in writing.

Reason (R): Verbal promises to pay are legally recognized as negotiable instruments.

A. Both A and R are true, and R is the correct explanation of A
B. Both A and R are true, but R is not the correct explanation of A
C. A is true, R is false
D. A is false, R is true

132. A cheque crossed generally bears two parallel lines with or without the words '______'.
A. Payable to bearer
B. Account payee
C. Not negotiable
D. Payable at sight

133. In a bill of exchange, the person who orders the payment is called the ______.
A. Drawer B. Drawee
C. Payee D. Endorser

134. Match the following types of negotiable instruments with their correct definitions:

A. Promissory Note — 1. An unconditional promise to pay
B. Bill of Exchange — 2. An order to pay a specific amount to a person
C. Cheque — 3. A type of bill of exchange drawn on a banker
D. Endorsement — 4. Signing on the back of an instrument for transfer

A. A-1, B-2, C-3, D-4
B. A-2, B-1, C-4, D-3
C. A-3, B-4, C-2, D-1
D. A-4, B-3, C-1, D-2

135. Arrange the following steps in the correct sequence for legal action under Section 138 for cheque dishonour:

1. Issuance of demand notice to the drawer
2. Presentation of the cheque to the bank
3. Dishonour of cheque
4. Filing a complaint in the court
5. Failure of the drawer to pay within 15 days of notice

A. 2, 3, 1, 5, 4
B. 1, 2, 3, 4, 5
C. 3, 2, 1, 5, 4
D. 4, 1, 3, 2, 5

136. Scenario: A cheque issued by X to Y is dishonoured due to insufficient funds. Y sends a legal notice to X, but X does not respond within 15 days. Can Y file a case?

A. Yes, under Section 138 of the Act
B. No, as cheque dishonour is a civil matter
C. Yes, but only after 30 days
D. No, unless the bank provides written confirmation

137. Scenario: A signs a blank cheque and gives it to B for business expenses. B fills in an amount higher than agreed. Is A liable if the cheque bounces?

A. No, because B misused the cheque
B. Yes, because A authorized B by signing
C. No, unless A filed a police report
D. Yes, only if A explicitly consented to the amount

138. Scenario: Z receives a cheque from Y that is crossed and marked "Account Payee Only." Z wants to endorse it to W. Can Z do this?

A. Yes, because it's a negotiable instrument
B. No, because "Account Payee Only" restricts endorsement
C. Yes, if Y provides written consent
D. No, unless the cheque is uncrossed

139. Which of the following is NOT required for a valid promissory note?

A. Written form
B. Unconditional promise to pay
C. Signature of the drawer
D. Payment in installments

140. The person to whom the amount of a negotiable instrument is payable is called the:

A. Drawer
B. Drawee
C. Payee
D. Endorser

141. Match the following parties with the correct role in a bill of exchange:

A. Drawer — 1. The person who makes the bill
B. Drawee — 2. The person directed to pay
C. Payee — 3. The person receiving payment
D. Endorser — 4. The person transferring the bill

A. A-1, B-2, C-3, D-4
B. A-2, B-1, C-4, D-3
C. A-3, B-4, C-1, D-2
D. A-4, B-3, C-2, D-1

142. Scenario: X issues a cheque to Y. The cheque is post-dated. Y presents it to the bank before the date. What will happen?

A. The bank will honour the cheque
B. The bank will dishonour it as it's presented early
C. The bank will accept it and process later
D. The cheque will be invalid

143. Scenario: A cheque is dishonoured, and the drawer claims there was a 'stop payment' instruction. Is the drawer still liable under Section 138?

A. Yes, stop payment does not absolve liability
B. No, because the drawer stopped payment
C. Yes, only if the drawer was informed by the bank
D. No, unless the cheque was post-dated

144. Which of the following documents is required for the incorporation of a company?

A. Partnership Deed
B. Memorandum of Association (MoA)
C. Letter of Intent
D. Articles of Understanding

145. Which of the following is NOT considered as part of the contents of a prospectus?

A. Name of directors
B. Terms of issue of shares
C. Company's vision and mission statement
D. Risk factors associated with investment

146. Which of the following is true regarding preference shares?
A. Preference shareholders have voting rights in all company matters
B. Preference shareholders receive dividends after equity shareholders
C. Preference shareholders have preferential rights to dividends and repayment of capital
D. Preference shares cannot be redeemed

147. A debenture is best described as:
A. An equity security
B. A form of short-term loan
C. A long-term debt instrument issued by a company
D. A certificate of shareholding

148. A private company can invite the public to subscribe to its shares through a prospectus.
A. True
B. False
C. True, if authorized by the registrar
D. False, unless it converts into a public company

149. Debenture holders are considered owners of the company.
A. True
B. False
C. True, if the debentures are convertible
D. False, unless stated in the Articles of Association

150. **Assertion (A):** A company is a separate legal entity distinct from its members.

Reason (R): Members of a company are liable for the company's debts.
A. Both A and R are true, and R is the correct explanation of A
B. Both A and R are true, but R is not the correct explanation of A
C. A is true, R is false
D. A is false, R is true

151. **Assertion (A):** A company must issue a prospectus before allotting shares to the public.

Reason (R): A prospectus provides information for potential investors to make informed decisions.
A. Both A and R are true, and R is the correct explanation of A
B. Both A and R are true, but R is not the correct explanation of A
C. A is true, R is false
D. A is false, R is true

152. The liability of shareholders in a company limited by shares is limited to the amount ____.
A. Paid on their shares
B. Unpaid on their shares
C. Invested in company's debentures
D. Declared as profit

153. A document issued by a company to invite the public to subscribe to its securities is called a ______.
A. Memorandum of Association
B. Articles of Association
C. Prospectus
D. Certificate of Incorporation

154. Match the following terms with their correct definitions:

A. Equity Shares	1. Ownership interest with voting rights
B. Preference Shares	2. Debt instrument representing a loan
C. Debenture	3. Document inviting public to invest
D. Prospectus	4. Shares with preferential rights for dividends

A. A-1, B-4, C-2, D-3
B. A-2, B-1, C-4, D-3
C. A-3, B-2, C-1, D-4
D. A-4, B-3, C-2, D-1

155. Arrange the following steps in the correct sequence for incorporating a company:
1. Obtain Digital Signature Certificate (DSC)
2. Apply for Director Identification Number (DIN)
3. Reserve company name
4. Draft and file MOA and AOA
5. Obtain Certificate of Incorporation

A. 1, 2, 3, 4, 5 B. 2, 1, 4, 3, 5
C. 3, 2, 1, 4, 5 D. 4, 1, 3, 2, 5

156. Scenario: ABC Ltd. issues shares to the public without filing a prospectus. Which of the following is true?
A. The issue is valid
B. It is a violation of the Companies Act
C. No legal consequences if the shares are sold
D. The issue is valid if shareholders approve

157. Scenario: XYZ Ltd. issues a prospectus with false information. Who is liable?
A. Only the company
B. Only the directors
C. Company, directors, promoters, and all responsible parties
D. Only the underwriters

158. Scenario: Mr. A holds preference shares in ABC Ltd. The company declares dividends but fails to pay Mr. A. Does he have any legal remedy?

A. No, because preference shareholders don't have rights

B. Yes, as he has preferential rights to dividends

C. No, unless he holds equity shares too

D. Yes, but only after equity shareholders are paid

159. Which of the following types of shares cannot be issued by a company limited by shares?

A. Equity Shares

B. Preference Shares

C. Bearer Shares

D. Bonus Shares

160. Which document defines the scope of a company's operations?

A. Articles of Association

B. Memorandum of Association

C. Prospectus

D. Share Certificate

161. Match the following company documents with their purposes:

A. MoA	1. Defines internal rules of the company
B. AOA	2. Invitation to the public to subscribe to securities
C. Prospectus	3. Specifies the objectives and scope of business
D. Share Certificate	4. Proof of ownership of shares

A. A-3, B-1, C-2, D-4

B. A-1, B-2, C-3, D-4

C. A-4, B-3, C-1, D-2

D. A-2, B-3, C-1, D-4

162. Scenario: ABC Ltd. issues secured debentures. What does "secured" mean in this context?

A. Debentures are backed by company profits

B. Debentures are secured against company assets

C. Debentures are insured by the government

D. Debentures have higher interest rates

163. Scenario: DEF Ltd. has unpaid calls on shares. Can these shares be transferred?

A. Yes, without restrictions

B. No, until the calls are paid

C. Yes, but only with board approval

D. Yes, but the unpaid calls remain the liability of the transferor

164. Which of the following is the minimum number of directors required in a public company?

A. 1 B. 2

C. 3 D. 5

165. What is the maximum number of directorships an individual can hold in companies under the Companies Act, 2013?

A. 10 B. 15

C. 20 D. 25

166. Which of the following types of meetings is held annually by a company?

A. Extraordinary General Meeting (EGM)

B. Board Meeting

C. Annual General Meeting (AGM)

D. Statutory Meeting

167. Who among the following can convene a Board Meeting?

A. Any shareholder

B. Company secretary without approval

C. Chairman or any director authorized by the Board

D. Auditor of the company

168. A company must hold its first Board Meeting within 30 days of incorporation.

A. True

B. False

C. True, only if it's a public company

D. False, unless required by the shareholders

169. Independent directors have voting rights in Board Meetings on all matters.

A. True

B. False

C. True, only if nominated by shareholders

D. False, unless the Articles of Association permit

170. **Assertion (A):** The Board of Directors is responsible for the management of the company's affairs.

Reason (R): The shareholders are directly involved in the day-to-day operations of the company.

A. Both A and R are true, and R is the correct explanation of A

B. Both A and R are true, but R is not the correct explanation of A

C. A is true, R is false

D. A is false, R is true

171. Assertion (A): A director can participate in a Board Meeting through video conferencing.

Reason (R): The Companies Act, 2013 permits participation through electronic means to ensure flexibility.

A. Both A and R are true, and R is the correct explanation of A
B. Both A and R are true, but R is not the correct explanation of A
C. A is true, R is false
D. A is false, R is true

172. The quorum for a Board Meeting is ______ of the total strength of directors or two directors, whichever is higher.

A. One-fourth B. One-third
C. Half D. Two-thirds

173. A director who is not involved in the daily operations but attends board meetings and provides strategic advice is known as a ______ director.

A. Managing B. Executive
C. Non-Executive D. Nominee

174. Match the following types of directors with their descriptions:

Directors	Descriptions
A. Managing Director	1. Appointed to protect the interests of financial institutions
B. Independent Director	2. Not involved in daily management, ensures corporate governance
C. Nominee Director	3. Responsible for day-to-day operations
D. Whole-time Director	4. Full-time employee of the company

A. A-3, B-2, C-1, D-4
B. A-1, B-3, C-4, D-2
C. A-4, B-1, C-3, D-2
D. A-2, B-4, C-1, D-3

175. Arrange the following steps in the correct sequence for conducting an Annual General Meeting (AGM):

1. Issue notice to members
2. Prepare agenda and resolutions
3. Hold the meeting
4. Record minutes of the meeting
5. File resolutions with the Registrar of Companies

A. 1, 2, 3, 4, 5
B. 2, 1, 3, 4, 5
C. 1, 3, 2, 4, 5
D. 2, 3, 1, 4, 5

176. Scenario: XYZ Ltd. has 9 directors. For a valid Board Meeting, what is the minimum number of directors required to be present?

A. 2 B. 3
C. 4 D. 5

177. Scenario: ABC Ltd. fails to hold its AGM within the prescribed time. What are the consequences?

A. No consequences if shareholders don't complain
B. The company can delay the AGM indefinitely
C. The company and its officers may face penalties under the Companies Act
D. The AGM can be skipped if the company had losses

178. Scenario: Mr. A, a director of DEF Ltd., has not attended any Board Meeting in the last 12 months. What is the legal implication?

A. No implications as attendance is optional
B. He is automatically disqualified as a director
C. He remains a director until shareholders decide
D. His position is vacated automatically as per the Companies Act

179. Which of the following is NOT a power that can be exercised by the Board of Directors without shareholder approval?

A. Borrowing funds
B. Selling substantial assets of the company
C. Appointing employees
D. Opening bank accounts

180. Who presides over a Board Meeting if the Chairman is absent?

A. The Company Secretary
B. The Senior-most Director present
C. Any shareholder
D. The Managing Director only

181. Match the following company meetings with their characteristics:

A. Board Meeting	1. Mandatory for public companies annually
B. Annual General Meeting (AGM)	2. For urgent business matters outside AGM
C. Extraordinary General Meeting (EGM)	3. Regular meetings of the company's directors
D. Statutory Meeting	4. Held only once in a company's lifetime

A. A-3, B-1, C-2, D-4
B. A-1, B-3, C-4, D-2
C. A-4, B-2, C-1, D-3
D. A-2, B-4, C-3, D-1

182. Scenario: The Board of Directors of PQR Ltd. wants to pass a resolution without holding a physical meeting. Which of the following methods can be used?
A. Only physical meetings are allowed
B. Circulation of the resolution to all directors for approval
C. Shareholders' consent is required
D. Resolution cannot be passed without a meeting

183. Scenario: ABC Ltd. holds a Board Meeting without providing proper notice to all directors. Is the meeting valid?
A. Yes, if decisions were unanimous
B. No, as proper notice is mandatory
C. Yes, if the shareholders approve the decisions
D. Yes, unless someone files a complaint

184. Under the Companies Act, 2013, CSR is applicable to companies having:
A. Net worth of ₹ 100 crores or more
B. Turnover of ₹ 500 crores or more
C. Net profit of ₹ 5 crores or more
D. All of the above

185. What is the minimum percentage of average net profits that companies are required to spend on CSR activities?
A. 1% B. 2%
C. 3% D. 5%

186. Which of the following activities does NOT qualify as CSR under the Companies Act, 2013?
A. Eradicating hunger and poverty
B. Contributions to political parties
C. Promoting education
D. Ensuring environmental sustainability

187. The CSR policy of a company is recommended by:
A. Shareholders in the AGM
B. CSR Committee of the Board
C. Statutory Auditors
D. Ministry of Corporate Affairs

188. CSR spending is mandatory for all companies registered under the Companies Act, 2013.
A. True
B. False
C. True, only for public companies
D. False, unless profits exceed ₹ 1 crore

189. Excess CSR expenditure can be carried forward and set off in subsequent years.
A. True
B. False
C. True, only if approved by the Ministry of Corporate Affairs
D. False, unless the company is a listed entity

190. **Assertion (A):** Companies must form a CSR Committee if CSR provisions are applicable.

Reason (R): The CSR Committee monitors the company's financial performance.
A. Both A and R are true, and R is the correct explanation of A
B. Both A and R are true, but R is not the correct explanation of A
C. A is true, R is false
D. A is false, R is true

191. **Assertion (A):** Companies can undertake CSR activities directly or through registered trusts, societies, or Section 8 companies.

Reason (R): The Companies Act allows flexibility in implementing CSR through third parties.
A. Both A and R are true, and R is the correct explanation of A
B. Both A and R are true, but R is not the correct explanation of A
C. A is true, R is false
D. A is false, R is true

192. CSR activities must be carried out within _______ unless approved otherwise by the Board.
A. India B. South Asia
C. Globally D. Neighboring countries

193. The CSR Committee must have at least _______ directors, including one independent director (if applicable).
A. 1 B. 2
C. 3 D. 4

194. Match the following CSR-related terms with their correct descriptions:

Terms	Descriptions
A. CSR Committee	1. Lists the eligible CSR activities
B. Section 135 of the Companies Act	2. Governs CSR provisions
C. CSR Policy	3. Framework for implementing CSR activities
D. Schedule VII	4. Recommends CSR activities to the Board

A. A-4, B-2, C-3, D-1
B. A-2, B-3, C-4, D-1
C. A-3, B-1, C-2, D-4
D. A-1, B-4, C-2, D-3

195. Arrange the following steps for CSR compliance in the correct sequence:

1. Form CSR Committee
2. Identify CSR projects
3. Allocate budget
4. Implement CSR activities
5. Report CSR in Board's Report

A. 1, 2, 3, 4, 5 B. 2, 1, 3, 4, 5
C. 1, 3, 2, 4, 5 D. 1, 4, 3, 2, 5

196. Scenario: ABC Ltd. has a net profit of ₹ 10 crores. How much should the company spend on CSR as per the Companies Act, 2013?

A. ₹ 10 lakhs B. ₹ 20 lakhs
C. ₹ 50 lakhs D. ₹ 2 crores

197. Scenario: XYZ Ltd. spent ₹ 25 lakhs on CSR in the current year, exceeding the required amount by ₹ 5 lakhs. Can this excess amount be adjusted in the next financial year?

A. Yes, as per the Companies Act
B. No, CSR spending cannot be carried forward
C. Yes, but only after Ministry approval
D. No, unless the company is loss-making

198. Scenario: DEF Ltd. did not spend the required CSR amount and failed to provide any justification in the Board's Report. What are the consequences?

A. No action if it was unintentional
B. Penalty provisions apply under the Companies Act
C. Only a warning from the Ministry
D. CSR obligations are waived automatically

199. Which of the following is NOT included in the calculation of net profit for CSR purposes?

A. Profits from overseas branches
B. Dividends received
C. Income from Indian operations
D. Profits from domestic subsidiaries

200. Which of the following can be considered a valid CSR activity?

A. Sponsorship of sports events for marketing
B. Contribution to a private trust not registered under Section 12A
C. Building sanitation facilities in rural schools
D. Employee welfare activities

ANSWERS

1. **(C):** A contract can be oral, written, or implied unless a specific law requires it to be in writing (like in property transactions). Thus, "in writing only" is not an essential requirement for all contracts.

2. **(B):** E-contracts require digital communication forms like emails, click-wrap, and shrink-wrap agreements. Verbal communication over the phone does not constitute an e-contract unless recorded and backed by digital confirmation.

3. **(A):** Click-wrap agreements, where users click "I Agree" to terms and conditions, are legally binding as long as they meet the essential requirements of a valid contract (offer, acceptance, consideration, etc.).

4. **(D):** Under the Indian Contract Act, a contract with a minor is void ab initio, meaning it is invalid from the outset, not merely voidable.

5. **(C):** While consideration is generally necessary, there are exceptions under Section 25 of the Indian Contract Act, such as agreements made out of natural love and affection, voluntary services, or promises to pay time-barred debts.

6. **(B):** An offer (or proposal) is an essential element of a contract where one party expresses willingness to do or abstain from doing something, intending to obtain the other party's consent.

7. **(C):** Click-wrap agreements are common in e-contracts, where a user clicks "I Agree" to accept the terms and conditions, making it legally enforceable.

8. **(A):** Void Contract (A-2): A contract that becomes unenforceable due to legal reasons.

   Voidable Contract (B-3): A contract enforceable by one party (e.g., in cases of coercion, fraud, etc.).

   E-Contract (C-1): A contract formed digitally through emails, websites, etc.

   Unilateral Contract (D-4): A contract where one party promises something in return for an act by the other.

9. **(A):** In click-wrap agreements, the act of clicking "I Agree" legally binds the user to the contract, even if the terms were not read. The law assumes the user had the opportunity to review them.

10. (B): Free and mutual consent of the parties is an essential element of a valid contract. The contract must reflect the genuine agreement between the parties without coercion, fraud, or undue influence.

11. (C): E-contracts involve electronic/digital means like click-wrap, shrink-wrap, or browse-wrap agreements. A verbal contract over the phone is not considered an e-contract unless supported by electronic confirmation.

12. (C): Under Section 25 of the Indian Contract Act, a contract without consideration can be valid if it is based on natural love and affection, provided it is in writing and registered.

13. (A): The Information Technology Act, 2000 recognizes digital signatures as legally valid and equivalent to handwritten signatures in e-contracts.

14. (C): Only legal agreements are enforceable by law. Illegal agreements are void and unenforceable under the Indian Contract Act.

15. (B): An e-contract is formed electronically through emails, websites, or digital platforms without the physical presence of parties.

16. (A): Capacity to contract refers to the legal ability of parties to enter into a contract, such as being of sound mind, of legal age, and not disqualified by law.

17. (A): Coercion (A-4): Involves physical threats, making the contract voidable.

Undue Influence (B-1): Makes the contract voidable at the aggrieved party's option.

Fraud (C-3): Consent obtained through deception renders the contract voidable.

Free Consent (D-2): Valid and enforceable contract.

18. (A): The proper sequence starts with an offer (1), followed by acceptance (2), then digital confirmation/signature (3), consideration (4), and finally making the contract enforceable by law (5).

19. (A): In a click-wrap agreement, clicking "I Agree" constitutes legal acceptance, even if the user did not read the terms. Courts uphold such contracts as long as the terms were accessible before acceptance.

20. (B): A breach of contract occurs when a party fails to perform their obligations under the contract without any valid legal excuse.

21. (D): Mere financial difficulty does not amount to frustration. Frustration occurs when an unforeseen event renders performance impossible or illegal.

22. (A): A contract with a minor is void ab initio, meaning it is considered invalid from the start.

23. (B): A voidable contract becomes void when the party entitled to rescind it (due to factors like coercion, fraud, etc.) chooses to do so.

24. (B): Not all breaches lead to automatic termination. The non-breaching party can choose to continue with the contract or claim damages, depending on the nature of the breach.

25. (A): Frustration applies when an unforeseen event makes performance impossible, illegal, or radically different from what was agreed.

26. (A): Contracts with unlawful consideration are void because the law does not support agreements that involve illegal activities.

27. (A): The doctrine of frustration applies only to events that are unforeseen and beyond the control of the contracting parties.

28. (A): A void contract is one that is not legally enforceable by either party.

29. (A): The most common legal remedy for breach of contract is the award of damages to compensate the injured party.

30. (A): Breach of Contract: Failure to perform obligations (2)

Frustration of Contract: Performance becomes impossible (1)

Void Contract: Not enforceable from the beginning (4)

Voidable Contract: Enforceable by one party (3)

31. (A): The process starts with the breach of contract (1), followed by notifying the other party (2), then filing a suit (3), court evaluation (4), and finally the award of damages (5).

32. (A): A contract becomes frustrated if its performance becomes illegal due to a change in law, which applies in this scenario.

33. (A): The contract is frustrated because the subject matter (the car) has been destroyed, making performance impossible.

34. (B): Contracts entered into under coercion are voidable at the option of the aggrieved party, in this case, Q.

35. (C): Breach of contract is a civil matter, and the remedies include damages, specific performance, or injunction. Criminal prosecution is not a remedy for breach unless the breach involves a criminal offense like fraud.

36. (A): The doctrine of frustration applies when unforeseen events, like natural disasters (acts of God), make it impossible to perform the contract, rendering it void.

37. (A): A contract entered into through coercion (use of force or threats) is voidable at the option of the party who was coerced.

38. (A): Breach of Contract (A-1): Leads to a claim for damages.

Frustration of Contract (B-2): Automatically terminates the contract.

Void Agreement (C-3): Cannot be enforced from the beginning.

Voidable Agreement (D-4): Can be canceled by one of the parties.

39. (B): The contract is frustrated because an unforeseen government order (due to the pandemic) has made it impossible to perform. This is a classic case of supervening impossibility under the doctrine of frustration.

40. (B): Standard Form of Contract is a pre-drafted contract where the terms are fixed by one party, leaving the other party with little or no ability to negotiate the terms.

41. (C): A quasi-contract arises in situations where no formal contract exists, but the law imposes an obligation to prevent unjust enrichment.

42. (B): In standard form contracts, there is usually unequal bargaining power, with one party setting the terms.

43. (C): Sections 68 to 72 of the Indian Contract Act deal with quasi-contractual obligations, covering cases like supply of necessities, payment by interested persons, etc.

44. (A): Standard form contracts are generally enforceable once signed, even if the signing party did not read the terms, provided there's no element of fraud or misrepresentation.

45. (B): A quasi-contract is not formed through mutual consent but arises by law to prevent unjust enrichment, even though no formal agreement exists.

46. (A): Standard form contracts are used for efficiency because pre-determined terms reduce the need for lengthy negotiations.

47. (C): In quasi-contracts, legal obligations arise without any agreement. They are imposed by law, not through mutual consent.

48. (C): A Standard Form Contract is a pre-drafted contract with non-negotiable terms, often used in mass transactions.

49. (C): The concept of quasi-contracts is based on preventing "unjust enrichment", where one party unfairly benefits without providing compensation.

50. (A): Supply of Necessaries: Essentials provided to a person incapable of contracting (3)

Payment by Interested Person: Paying on behalf of another person (4)

Finder of Goods: Obligation to return found goods (1)

Money Paid by Mistake: Recovering payments made by error (2)

51. (A): The process starts with unjust enrichment (1), followed by the imposition of legal obligation (2), then a demand for restitution (3), and if needed, court enforcement (4).

52. (A): A can recover the money under a quasi-contract as the law imposes an obligation to prevent unjust enrichment when money is paid by mistake.

53. (A): Y is liable under a quasi-contract since he used goods not belonging to him, creating an obligation to pay for the benefit received.

54. (A): The hotel can recover the cost under a quasi-contract because the service provided was a necessity, and the law prevents unjust enrichment even without a formal contract.

55. (C): A standard form contract is drafted by one party with pre-set terms, leaving the other party with little or no opportunity to negotiate, often found in insurance policies, online services, etc.

56. (A): In quasi-contracts, legal obligations arise without a formal agreement to prevent one party from being unjustly enriched at the expense of another.

57. (C): The liability in a quasi-contract is "contractual" in nature because it resembles obligations in a contract, even though no formal contract exists between the parties.

58. (A): Doctrine of Reasonable Notice (A-3): Applies to standard form contracts to ensure parties are aware of key terms.

Unjust Enrichment (B-1): Prevents unfair benefit in quasi-contracts.

Take-it-or-leave-it Contracts (C-4): Standard form contracts offered without negotiation.

Obligation to Pay for Necessaries (D-2): Applies in quasi-contracts for essentials provided.

59. **(A):** Since Mr. A used the extra 50 chairs, he is liable to pay under a quasi-contract because it would be unjust enrichment if he kept the benefit without compensating Mr. B.

60. **(C):** In bailment, goods are delivered for a specific purpose with the condition that they will be returned after the purpose is fulfilled.

61. **(B):** In a pledge, the person who delivers goods as security is called the pawnor (or pledger), and the person receiving the goods is the pawnee (or pledgee).

62. **(B):** A contract of indemnity is an agreement where one party promises to compensate the other for any loss suffered due to the actions of the promisor or a third party.

63. **(C):** An agent must act in the best interest of the principal, and acting for personal gain against the principal's interest is a breach of duty.

64. **(A):** A contract of guarantee involves three parties: the creditor, the principal debtor, and the surety, who guarantees the performance or repayment by the debtor.

65. **(A):** In bailment, only the possession of goods is transferred to the bailee, while the ownership remains with the bailor.

66. **(A):** The pawnee can sell the pledged goods if the pawnor defaults, but reasonable notice must be given before the sale.

67. **(C):** The principle of "delegatus non potestdelegare" means an agent cannot delegate authority unless explicitly permitted or under exceptional circumstances.

68. **(C):** The surety is the person who gives the guarantee to the creditor, promising to fulfill the debtor's obligations if the debtor defaults.

69. **(C):** A contract of indemnity involves a promise to compensate for a loss that may arise in the future due to specific circumstances.

70. **(A):** Bailment: Delivery of goods for a specific purpose (3)

Pledge: Delivery of goods as security (1)

Indemnity: Promise to compensate for loss (2)

Guarantee: Third party ensures performance (4)

71. **(A):** The proper sequence includes the existence of a debtor (1), the surety's promise (2), the consideration (4), and finally the creditor's acceptance (3).

72. **(C):** In a contract of guarantee, the surety (C) is directly liable to the creditor (A) if the principal debtor (B) defaults, without the need to sue B first.

73. **(B):** In bailment, the bailee (Y) must take reasonable care of the goods. If the loss occurs due to negligence, the bailee is liable.

74. **(C):** This is a contract of indemnity, where P promises to compensate Q for any potential losses.

75. **(B):** The principal is bound by the acts of the agent if those acts are performed within the agent's actual or apparent authority, even if the principal is unaware of the specific transactions.

76. **(A):** In a contract of indemnity, the indemnifier's liability arises when the indemnified suffers an actual loss, unless the contract explicitly covers contingent liabilities.

77. **(C):** If the pawnor defaults, the pawnee has the legal right to sell the pledged goods after giving reasonable notice to the pawnor.

78. **(A):** Bailor (A-3): Delivers goods for safekeeping

Pawnor (B-1): Delivers goods as security

Indemnifier (C-4): Promises to compensate for loss

Principal (D-2): Appoints an agent to act on their behalf

79. **(B):** An agent cannot deal on behalf of the principal where there is a conflict of interest, unless the principal has full knowledge and consents. Since Suresh did not disclose his interest, the transaction is invalid.

80. **(C):** Delivery can be immediate, in the future, or as agreed upon. Delivery at the time of contract is not mandatory.

81. **(B):** Specific goods are identified and agreed upon at the time the contract is made, like a car with a specific registration number.

82. **(C):** The term "goods" refers to movable property. Immovable property is not included under this definition.

83. **(C):** A sale involves the immediate transfer of ownership, whereas an agreement to sell refers to a transfer in the future.

84. **(A):** Future goods cannot be sold as ownership does not exist yet. It constitutes an agreement to sell.

85. **(B):** Caveat Emptor means "let the buyer beware," placing the responsibility on the buyer to inspect the quality of goods.

86. (C): While risk generally passes with ownership, they can be separated by agreement or depending on the nature of the contract.

87. (D): Ownership can transfer without physical delivery, through symbolic delivery or constructive delivery.

88. (B): Caveat Emptor translates to "let the buyer beware," implying that the buyer must ensure the goods meet their expectations.

89. (D): Specific goods are those identified and agreed upon at the time the contract is made.

90. (A): Specific Goods (A-1): Already identified goods

Unascertained Goods (B-3): Not specifically identified

Future Goods (C-2): To be manufactured or acquired

Contingent Goods (D-4): Acquisition depends on uncertain events

91. (A): The sequence begins with an offer (1), followed by acceptance (2), forming an agreement to sell (3), and then the transfer of ownership (4).

92. (B): The contract is void under Section 7 of the Sale of Goods Act as the goods have been destroyed without the seller's fault, making performance impossible.

93. (A): This situation falls under the "after-acquired property" rule. Once X becomes the owner, Y can claim the car because the title passes automatically.

94. (A): Under Section 16, there is an implied condition of fitness for purpose if the buyer relies on the seller's skill or judgment.

95. (C): Section 19 of the Act states that property in goods passes when the parties intend it to pass, which can be determined by the terms of the contract, conduct of the parties, and circumstances of the case.

96. (A): Under Section 50, the unpaid seller has the right to stop goods in transit if the buyer becomes insolvent, even if ownership has passed to the buyer.

97. (A): Delivery to a carrier for transmission to the buyer is considered constructive delivery, meaning the buyer gains control through the carrier without physical possession.

98. (A): Unpaid Seller (A-3): A seller who hasn't received full payment

Condition (B-1): Essential stipulation

Warranty (C-2): Collateral stipulation

Agreement to Sell (D-4): Transfer of property in the future

99. (B): Under Section 56 of the Indian Contract Act, the contract becomes void due to supervening impossibility because of the government ban, which makes the performance illegal.

100. (C): Registration of a partnership firm is not mandatory under the Indian Partnership Act, though it is advisable. The essentials are agreement, profit-sharing, and mutual agency.

101. (C): In an LLP, the entity has a separate legal identity, and partners enjoy limited liability unless fraud or wrongful acts are involved.

102. (C): LLPs have perpetual succession, meaning their existence is not affected by changes in partners.

103. (B): A partnership firm does not have a separate legal entity from its partners, unlike an LLP or a company.

104. (B): A partnership can be formed through an oral or written agreement.

105. (A): In an LLP, each partner is an agent of the LLP but not of other partners, which distinguishes it from traditional partnerships.

106. (C): Partners are jointly and severally liable, but a partnership firm does not have a separate legal identity from its partners.

107. (A): LLPs are preferred because they offer limited liability and perpetual succession, making them ideal for large businesses.

108. (B): The Partnership Deed is the document that governs the relationship, rights, and duties of the partners.

109. (B): An LLP must have a minimum of two designated partners, with at least one resident in India.

110. (A): The correct sequence starts with DSC (1) → DIN (2) → Name reservation (3) → Incorporation documents (4) → Certificate of Incorporation (5).

111. (B): Partners are jointly liable only for acts done within the scope of the firm's business. Since this was for personal use, Y is not liable.

112. (C): In case of fraudulent acts, both the LLP and the partner committing the fraud (A) are liable. The liability may extend to personal liability for the fraudulent partner.

113. (B): According to the Indian Partnership Act, adding a new partner requires the consent of all existing partners.

114. (D): Day-to-day management decisions can generally be taken by any partner acting within the scope of the firm's business, while significant decisions like admitting new partners require unanimous consent.

115. (A): In an LLP, partners are generally not personally liable for each other's actions, except in cases of fraud or personal misconduct.

116. (B): A nominal partner lends their name to the firm but does not actively participate in the business. However, they can be held liable to third parties for obligations of the firm.

117. (A): Active Partner (A-2): Involved in daily operations

Sleeping Partner (B-1): Invests capital but not active in management

Nominal Partner (C-4): Lends name without actual involvement

Partner by Estoppel (D-3): Appears as a partner to outsiders, thus liable

118. (B): In case of fraudulent acts, both the LLP and the partner committing the fraud (X) are liable. The innocent partners (Y and Z) are generally not personally liable unless they were complicit.

119. (C): The Act applies to all partnerships, whether registered or unregistered.

120. (B): In cases of fraud, partners can be held personally liable.

121. (A): CSR Committee (A-1): Recommends CSR policy

Board of Directors (B-2): Approves CSR policy and ensures implementation

Implementing Agency (C-3): Executes CSR activities on behalf of companies

Ministry of Corporate Affairs (D-4): Provides CSR-related regulatory framework

122. (A): A retired partner remains liable to third parties unless proper notice of retirement is given.

123. (B): Designated partners are responsible for statutory compliances, and both the LLP and the designated partner can be held liable.

124. (D): A Fixed Deposit Receipt is not a negotiable instrument as it is not transferable like promissory notes, bills of exchange, or cheques.

125. (C): Section 6 defines a cheque as a bill of exchange drawn on a specified banker and payable on demand.

126. (B): Negotiable instruments are typically transferred by endorsement and delivery, especially in the case of order instruments.

127. (D): A promissory note is an unconditional promise made in writing by one person to another to pay a certain sum of money.

128. (A): A cheque is a bill of exchange drawn on a banker and is always payable on demand.

129. (A): A bearer cheque can be transferred by mere delivery without the need for an endorsement.

130. (A): Under Section 138, dishonour of a cheque due to insufficient funds can lead to criminal prosecution.

131. (C): A negotiable instrument must be in writing; verbal promises are not recognized under the Act.

132. (C): A generally crossed cheque has two parallel lines with or without words like "Not Negotiable" or "Account Payee".

133. (A): The drawer is the person who makes the bill and orders the drawee to pay the payee.

134. (A): Promissory Note: Unconditional promise to pay

Bill of Exchange: Order to pay

Cheque: Bill of exchange drawn on a bank

Endorsement: Signing for transfer

135. (A): The correct sequence is: Present the cheque (2) → Dishonour of cheque (3) → Issue demand notice (1) → Wait for 15 days (5) → File complaint (4).

136. (A): Y can file a case under Section 138 after giving 15 days' notice without payment from X.

137. (B): The drawer (A) is liable if the cheque is dishonoured, as signing and handing over a blank cheque implies authorization.

138. (B): A cheque marked "Account Payee Only" can only be deposited in the specified account and cannot be endorsed further.

139. (D): A promissory note must involve an unconditional promise to pay a specific amount, not in installments unless explicitly stated.

140. (C): The payee is the person to whom the money is payable.

141. (A): Drawer (A-1): The person who makes the bill

Drawee (B-2): The person directed to pay

Payee (C-3): The person receiving payment

Endorser (D-4): The person transferring the bill

142. (B): A post-dated cheque cannot be honoured before its due date.

143. (A): Stopping payment does not protect the drawer from liability under Section 138, provided the cheque was issued to discharge a debt or liability.

144. (B): The MOA is a key document required for the incorporation of a company, defining its objectives and scope of operations.

145. (C): The vision and mission are not mandatory disclosures in a prospectus, which focuses on financial and legal information.

146. (C): Preference shareholders have priority in receiving dividends and repayment of capital in case of liquidation.

147. (C): A debenture is a long-term debt instrument used by companies to borrow funds from the public.

148. (B): A private company cannot issue a prospectus as it is prohibited from inviting the public to subscribe to its shares.

149. (B): Debenture holders are creditors, not owners, as they lend money to the company and do not hold ownership rights.

150. (C): A company is a separate legal entity, but members are not personally liable for its debts beyond their shareholding.

151. (A): A prospectus is mandatory for public offerings to provide relevant information to potential investors.

152. (B): Shareholders' liability is limited to the unpaid amount on their shares.

153. (C): A prospectus is an invitation to the public to subscribe to shares or debentures.

154. (A): Equity Shares: Voting rights (1)

Preference Shares: Preferential dividend rights (4)

Debenture: Debt instrument (2)

Prospectus: Invitation document (3)

155. (A): The correct sequence for incorporation starts with DSC, then DIN, name reservation, MOA & AOA filing, and finally, the Certificate of Incorporation.

156. (B): Issuing shares without filing a prospectus is a violation under the Companies Act, 2013.

157. (C): Misstatements in a prospectus lead to liability for all persons involved, including directors, promoters, and the company.

158. (B): Preference shareholders have preferential rights to receive dividends before equity shareholders.

159. (C): Bearer shares are not allowed under Indian company law as they facilitate anonymous ownership, raising security concerns.

160. (B): The MOA defines the scope of operations and objectives of the company.

161. (A): MOA (A-3): Specifies the objectives and scope of business

AOA (B-1): Defines internal rules of the company

Prospectus (C-2): Invitation to the public to subscribe to securities

Share Certificate (D-4): Proof of ownership of shares

162. (B): Secured debentures are backed by specific company assets, which act as security in case of default.

163. (D): Shares with unpaid calls can be transferred, but the liability for unpaid amounts may remain with the transferor, depending on the company's Articles.

164. (C): A public company must have a minimum of 3 directors as per the Companies Act, 2013.

165. (C): A person can be a director in up to 20 companies, with a maximum of 10 public companies.

166. (C): The AGM is held annually to discuss company performance, financial statements, and other statutory matters.

167. (C): A Board Meeting can be convened by the Chairman or any authorized director.

168. (A): As per the Companies Act, 2013, the first Board Meeting must be held within 30 days of incorporation.

169. (A): Independent directors have equal voting rights like other directors in Board Meetings.

170. (C): The Board of Directors manages the company's affairs, while shareholders are not involved in day-to-day operations.

171. (A): The Companies Act, 2013 allows directors to participate via video conferencing to provide flexibility.

172. (B): The quorum for a Board Meeting is one-third of the total strength or two directors, whichever is higher.

173. (C): A Non-Executive Director provides strategic guidance without being involved in daily operations.

174. (A): Managing Director: Day-to-day operations (3)
Independent Director: Governance role (2)
Nominee Director: Protects institutional interests (1)
Whole-time Director: Full-time employee (4)

175. (A): The correct sequence is: issue notice → prepare agenda → hold meeting → record minutes → file resolutions.

176. (C): One-third of 9 = 3, but since the rule is whichever is higher between one-third or two, the quorum is 4 directors.

177. (C): Failure to hold an AGM attracts penalties under the Companies Act for both the company and its officers.

178. (D): Under Section 167(1)(b), a director who fails to attend Board Meetings for 12 consecutive months will have their office vacated automatically.

179. (B): Selling substantial assets requires shareholder approval through a special resolution.

180. (B): If the Chairman is absent, the Board elects one of the directors present to chair the meeting.

181. (A): Board Meeting (A-3): Regular meetings of the company's directors
AGM (B-1): Mandatory for public companies annually
EGM (C-2): For urgent business matters outside AGM
Statutory Meeting (D-4): Held only once in a company's lifetime

182. (B): Resolutions by circulation can be passed if approved by a majority of directors entitled to vote.

183. (B): Proper notice to all directors is mandatory for the validity of a Board Meeting.

184. (D): CSR provisions apply to companies meeting any one of the following criteria: net worth of ₹ 500 crores or more, turnover of ₹ 1,000 crores or more, or net profit of ₹ 5 crores or more in the preceding financial year.

185. (B): Companies meeting CSR applicability criteria must spend at least 2% of their average net profits (calculated over the preceding three financial years) on CSR activities.

186. (B): Contributions to political parties are explicitly excluded from CSR activities under the Act.

187. (B): The CSR Committee, formed by the company's board, is responsible for formulating and recommending the CSR policy.

188. (B): CSR is mandatory only for companies that meet the specified criteria related to net worth, turnover, or net profit.

189. (A): Companies can carry forward excess CSR spending for up to three subsequent financial years, as per the 2021 amendment to CSR rules.

190. (C): While forming a CSR Committee is mandatory for applicable companies, its role is to recommend and monitor CSR activities, not financial performance.

191. (A): Companies can execute CSR activities directly or through eligible entities, providing flexibility in implementation.

192. (A): CSR activities must be undertaken within India to qualify under the Companies Act, 2013.

193. (C): A CSR Committee must consist of at least three directors, with one independent director if the company is required to appoint one.

194. (A): CSR Committee: Recommends CSR activities (4)
Section 135: Governs CSR provisions (2)
CSR Policy: Implementation framework (3)
Schedule VII: Lists eligible CSR activities (1)

195. (A): The correct CSR process is: Form CSR Committee → Identify projects → Allocate budget → Implement → Report.

196. (B): The company must spend 2% of ₹ 10 crores, i.e., ₹ 20 lakhs, on CSR activities.

197. (A): The excess CSR expenditure can be carried forward for up to 3 years, subject to board approval.

198. (B): Non-compliance with CSR provisions leads to penalties under Section 135 of the Companies Act, 2013.

199. (A): Profits from overseas branches are excluded when calculating net profits for CSR.

200. (C): Activities like building sanitation facilities qualify under CSR as per Schedule VII of the Companies Act.

UNIT 7 Family Law

SOURCES OF HINDU LAW

ANCIENT SOURCES OF HINDU LAW

Shruti

- The term "Shruti" translates to "that which has been heard" and is considered the primary and divine revelation in Hindu tradition.
- It includes the Vedas, which are the oldest sacred texts of Hinduism. The Vedas consist of four parts: Rigveda, Yajurveda, Samaveda, and Atharvaveda.
- Shruti is viewed as the absolute authority in matters of law, ethics, and religion.

Smriti

- Smriti means "that which is remembered" and is considered less authoritative than Shruti. It includes texts that are believed to be human interpretations of the divine Shruti.
- Key Smriti texts include Manusmriti (Laws of Manu), Yajnavalkya Smriti, and Narada Smriti, among others. These texts outline detailed rules on various aspects of life, including family law, social norms, and legal principles.

Digests and Commentaries (Nibandhas)

- Digests and commentaries have been written over centuries to explain, interpret, and often expand upon the concepts found in the Smriti and other texts.
- Prominent examples include the Mitakshara by Vijnaneshwara, which is a commentary on the Yajnavalkya Smriti and is foundational for understanding the Mitakshara school of Hindu law.
- These texts are crucial for understanding the evolution and application of Hindu law over time.

Custom

- Custom in Hindu law refers to practices that have been followed for a long time and are considered to have acquired legal force.
- To be recognized as a source of law, a custom must be ancient, certain, and reasonable, and must have been continuously and uniformly followed.
- Custom can override written law, except where the statute is explicitly contrary to the custom.

MODERN SOURCES OF HINDU LAW

Legislation

- Legislation is now the most significant source of Hindu law, consisting of laws enacted by the Parliament and state legislatures.
- Key legislative acts include the Hindu Marriage Act, 1955; the Hindu Succession Act, 1956; the Hindu Minority and Guardianship Act, 1956; and the Hindu Adoption and Maintenance Act, 1956.
- These laws have modernized and codified many aspects of Hindu law, often overriding traditional sources.

Judicial Decisions

- Judicial decisions by the Supreme Court and High Courts play a crucial role in interpreting, defining, and evolving the application of Hindu law.
- Courts interpret both ancient texts and modern statutes to decide cases, thereby contributing to the development of the law.

Equity, Justice, and Good Conscience

- In cases where there is no specific statutory provision or precedent, the principles of equity, justice, and good conscience are applied.
- This source is derived from the British legal system and allows courts to provide fair and just solutions based on general moral and ethical considerations.

SCHOOLS OF HINDU LAW

MITAKSHARA SCHOOL

General Overview

- The Mitakshara school is based on the commentary of the same name written by Vijnaneswara on the Yajnavalkya Smriti. It is one of the most authoritative texts in Hindu law.
- This school is known for its doctrine of joint family and coparcenary. The coparcenary includes only those family members who acquire by birth an interest in the joint or coparcenary property.

Key Principles

- **Joint Family System**: The Mitakshara recognizes the formation of a joint family, which includes all persons lineally descended from a common ancestor and includes their wives and unmarried daughters.
- **Right by Birth**: In the Mitakshara system, the male offspring acquire an interest in the ancestral property right from birth.
- **Survivorship**: Upon the death of a member, the property is distributed by survivorship within the coparceners.

Regional Variations

- **Benares School** - Predominant in North India, it is known for strict adherence to the Mitakshara text, especially in interpretation of joint family property rights.
- **Mithila School** - Found in Bihar and parts of Nepal, it has unique interpretations of the rituals and duties outlined in Mitakshara.
- **Maharashtra School** - Active in Maharashtra and parts of Gujarat and Madhya Pradesh, it sometimes shows a blend of Benares and Dravida characteristics, especially in marital and religious duties.
- **Dravida or Madras School** - Prevalent in South India, this school often exhibits more liberal interpretations, particularly regarding women's rights in property.

DAYABHAGA SCHOOL

Distinct Features

- The Dayabhaga School is a legal doctrine that is based on Jimutavahana's Dayabhaga. It differs significantly from Mitakshara, particularly regarding joint family property and inheritance.
- **No Right by Birth**: Unlike Mitakshara, the Dayabhaga system does not recognize the birth right of sons to claim an interest in ancestral property.
- **Partition**: In Dayabhaga, partition of the property can only be claimed after the death of the father, not merely by birth.
- **Authority of Father**: The father has considerable authority over the disposition of family properties, which is not seen in Mitakshara.

Geographic Prevalence

- This school is primarily followed in West Bengal and parts of Assam. Its distinct practices influence the legal interpretation and application in these regions, affecting how family law is practiced.

DEFINITION AND CONCEPT OF MARRIAGE IN HINDU LAW

- **Definition**: In Hindu law, marriage (vivaha) is considered a sacred and indissoluble union of a man and a woman—both physically, spiritually, and ritually. It is a sacrament, not merely a contract, intended to perpetuate the dharma (religious duty) and praja (progeny).
- **Purpose**: The primary purposes of marriage are dharma, praja (procreation), and rati (pleasure). It is seen as a binding commitment between two families and not just the couple.

Conditions for a Valid Hindu Marriage

Under the Hindu Marriage Act, 1955, several conditions must be met for a marriage to be considered valid:

- **Eligibility Age**: The bridegroom must be 21 years old, and the bride must be 18.
- **Monogamy**: Both parties must be unmarried at the time of the marriage or legally divorced; polygamy is prohibited.
- **Mental Capacity**: Both individuals must be mentally capable of understanding the implications of marriage.

- **Prohibited Relationships**: Parties must not fall within prohibited degrees of relationship unless custom permits.
- **Sapinda Relationship**: Parties should not be sapindas of each other, a relationship extending to five generations on the father's side and three on the mother's side, unless allowed by custom.

Ceremonies and Rituals

- The essential ceremonies include the **Vivaha-samskara**, which can vary by region but generally involves the invocation before the sacred fire (Agni), the saptapadi (seven steps or vows), and the kanyadan (giving away of the daughter).
- The saptapadi is the most crucial rite, legally binding the marriage under the Hindu Marriage Act.

DISSOLUTION OF MARRIAGE

GROUNDS FOR DISSOLUTION

Dissolution of marriage can occur through divorce, annulment, or separation. Each ground has specific legal criteria:

Divorce: A legal termination of a marriage by a court or other competent body. Common grounds for divorce include:

- **Irretrievable breakdown**: Most common ground, indicating that the marriage cannot be saved.
- **Adultery**: One spouse has had voluntary sexual intercourse with a person who is not their spouse.
- **Desertion**: One spouse abandons the other for a continuous period of at least one year.
- **Cruelty**: Physical or mental cruelty that makes living together unsafe or unreasonable.
- **Separation**: Living apart for a statutory period, usually two years with consent or five years without consent.

Annulment: Treats the marriage as if it never legally existed, usually based on grounds existing at the time of marriage:

- **Non-consummation**: Inability or refusal to consummate the marriage.
- **Bigamy**: One spouse was legally married to someone else at the time of marriage.
- **Incapacity**: Mental incapacity or lack of legal age to marry.
- **Fraud or coercion**: Marriage consent was obtained through deceit or under duress.

Legal Separation: Does not legally end the marriage but allows couples to live apart while remaining legally married. Grounds are often similar to those for divorce.

MATRIMONIAL REMEDIES

A. NULLITY OF MARRIAGE

Concept

Nullity of marriage refers to the legal declaration that a marriage is null and void. This is different from a divorce as it asserts that the marriage was never valid.

Grounds for Nullity

- **Void Marriages** (Section 11 of the Hindu Marriage Act, 1955):
  - ❑ Marriage is between prohibited degrees of relationship unless custom permits.
  - ❑ Marriage is between sapindas of each other unless custom permits.
  - ❑ Either party has a living spouse at the time of marriage (bigamy).
- **Voidable Marriages** (Section 12 of the Hindu Marriage Act, 1955):
  - ❑ Marriage not consummated due to impotence of the respondent.
  - ❑ Consent obtained by force or fraud.
  - ❑ Respondent was pregnant by someone other than the petitioner at the time of marriage.
  - ❑ Either party was mentally unfit for marriage and procreation at the time of marriage.

Procedure

A petition must be filed in the family court within the jurisdiction where the marriage took place, where the spouses last lived together, or where the respondent resides.

B. RESTITUTION OF CONJUGAL RIGHTS

Concept

The restitution of conjugal rights is a remedy that can be applied when one spouse withdraws from the society of the other without reasonable cause.

Legal Basis

Section 9 of the Hindu Marriage Act, 1955 enables a spouse to apply to the court for restitution if the other spouse has left without a valid reason.

Procedure

- The aggrieved party must file a petition in the district court, proving the withdrawal from the society was unjustified.
- If the court is satisfied, it may decree restitution, mandating the defaulting spouse to resume cohabitation.

C. JUDICIAL SEPARATION

Concept

Judicial separation allows couples to live apart without dissolving the marriage. It provides a period for reflection and potential reconciliation.

Grounds

The grounds for judicial separation are essentially the same as for divorce, including cruelty, desertion, conversion to another religion, unsound mind, communicable disease, renunciation of the world, and presumption of death.

Procedure

A petition is filed in the court, and if the court deems the grounds valid, it may grant a decree of judicial separation.

D. DIVORCE: GROUNDS AND PROCEDURES

Grounds for Divorce (Section 13 of the Hindu Marriage Act, 1955):

- Adultery.
- Cruelty.
- Desertion for a continuous period of not less than two years.
- Conversion to another religion.
- Unsound mind rendering the spouse unfit for marriage.
- Suffering from a virulent and incurable form of leprosy or communicable disease.
- Renunciation of the world by entering any religious order.
- Not heard of as being alive for a period of seven years or more.

Additional Grounds for Women (Section 13(2)):

- Husband guilty of rape, sodomy, or bestiality.
- Cohabitation not resumed after a decree/order of maintenance.
- Repudiation of marriage (if married before 15 and repudiates the marriage before 18).

CONCEPTUAL OVERVIEW OF LIVE-IN RELATIONSHIPS IN THE INDIAN CONTEXT

DEFINITION AND CONTEXT

A live-in relationship is characterized by two adults cohabiting without being married to each other. This form of partnership allows them to live together in a long-term relationship that resembles a marriage but without the legal recognition of marriage under Indian law. Over the years, live-in relationships have gained visibility and prevalence in India, influenced by shifts in societal attitudes and legal interpretations.

LEGAL PERSPECTIVE

In India, the legal system does not explicitly recognize live-in relationships through any specific statute; however, the judiciary has progressively acknowledged and provided rights under the "right to life" under Article 21 of the Indian Constitution. The Supreme Court of India has recognized live-in relationships as a part of the right to life, and therefore, they are legal. Various court rulings have offered protections similar to those afforded to married couples, particularly regarding alimony and child support. Notably, the Protection of Women from Domestic Violence Act, 2005 provides protection and maintenance rights to women in live-in relationships under some conditions.

Factors Driving Acceptability and Growth

- **Social Modernization**: As Indian society becomes more urbanized and exposed to global cultures, the traditional values that dictate strict marital relationships are evolving. Younger generations are increasingly prioritizing personal freedom, career progression, and financial independence, which align with the flexibility offered by live-in arrangements.
- **Media Influence**: Bollywood and other forms of popular media have played a significant role in normalizing live-in relationships by portraying them as a viable option for modern couples. This has contributed to a shift in societal perceptions, especially among the urban youth.
- **Economic Factors**: Economic independence among the youth, especially women, has empowered more individuals to make personal choices about their relationships outside the traditional bounds of marriage. Live-in relationships can also be economically pragmatic, sharing living costs without the financial burdens often associated with a formal marriage.

- **Legal Support and Protection**: Judicial recognition of live-in relationships provides a semblance of security to couples. Key judgments have acknowledged that women in such relationships should have rights akin to wives, which has helped reduce legal stigmas.
- **Changes in Personal Values**: There is a growing emphasis on partnership based on emotional connections rather than social obligation, leading many to choose live-in relationships as they allow partners to test compatibility before entering into marriage.
- **Education and Liberal Attitudes**: Higher education levels correlate with more liberal attitudes toward cohabitation outside marriage. Educated individuals are more likely to view live-in relationships as acceptable, driven by values of equality, freedom, and personal choice.

Prevalence

The prevalence of live-in relationships in India, while still limited compared to Western countries, has been notably rising in urban areas and among the educated middle and upper classes. The exact numbers are difficult to quantify due to the private nature of such arrangements and social stigma, but the trend is upward, reflecting broader social changes.

LEGAL ASPECTS OF LIVE-IN RELATIONSHIPS IN INDIA

Current Legal Standing:

In India, live-in relationships are not codified but have gained recognition through various Supreme Court rulings. Indian law does not provide a clear legal definition of live-in relationships, and they are not legally sanctified like marriage. However, the judiciary, particularly the Supreme Court, has progressively interpreted the law to provide certain protections to couples in such relationships under the doctrine of 'relationship in the nature of marriage' based on certain conditions.

- **Protection under Domestic Violence Act, 2005:** The Protection of Women from Domestic Violence Act, 2005 is crucial as it recognizes the rights of women to be protected from abuse in live-in relationships. The Act provides a broad definition of a "domestic relationship" that includes women living in a household with persons in consensual, sexual relationships akin to marriage, thus offering them legal protection against physical, emotional, and economic abuse.
- **Precedents Set by Judiciary:** Several landmark judgments have shaped the legal landscape for live-in relationships. For instance, in the cases of *D. Velusamy vs D. Patchaiammal (2010)* and *Indra Sarma vs V.K.V. Sarma (2013)*, the Supreme Court set criteria for live-in relationships to be recognized under the law, which include duration of the relationship, shared household, pooling of resources, sexual relationship, public socialization, intention and conduct of the parties, and children.

Rights and Protections Offered:

- **Status of Children:**
    - **Legitimacy and Inheritance Rights:** Children born out of live-in relationships are considered legitimate for the purposes of inheritance under the Hindu Marriage Act, 1955, provided the parents fulfill certain conditions resembling a marriage-like relationship. Such children have the same rights as those born to legally-wedded parents.

      (The legitimacy of children from such relationships is primarily recognized under Section 16 of the Hindu Marriage Act, 1955, through judicial interpretation for "relationship in the nature of marriage.")
    - **Right to Maintenance:** Under Section 125 of the Criminal Procedure Code, the child born from a live-in relationship has the right to claim maintenance. This provision is crucial for ensuring financial support for children from such unions.
- **Property Rights:** Women in live-in relationships do not automatically have rights to property acquired during the relationship, unlike their married counterparts. Property rights are generally governed by individual contributions unless there is a legal agreement stating otherwise.
- **Protection Against Abuse:** As stated earlier, partners in a live-in relationship can seek protection against abuse under the Domestic Violence Act, 2005, which includes the right to reside in the shared household, protection orders, maintenance, and custody orders for children.
- **Right to Maintenance for Women:** While the law does not explicitly provide for a woman's right to maintenance in a live-in relationship as it does in marriage, courts have on several occasions granted maintenance to women under the provisions of the Domestic Violence Act, interpreting the relationship to be 'in the nature of marriage

CASES

1. Indra Sarma vs. V.K.V. Sarma (2013)

Key Facts:

- Indra Sarma filed a case under the Protection of Women from Domestic Violence Act, 2005, claiming maintenance from her partner, V.K.V. Sarma, with whom she was in a live-in relationship for several years.

Legal Outcome:

- The Supreme Court of India recognized that not all live-in relationships will be treated as relationships in the nature of marriage. Criteria were set to determine such relationships based on duration, shared household, pooling of resources, sexual relationship, public socialization, intention and conduct of the parties, and children.
- This case helped in defining the test of "relationship in the nature of marriage" under the Domestic Violence Act and clarified legal protections available to women in live-in relationships.

2. D. Velusamy vs. D. Patchaiammal (2010)

Key Facts:

- D. Patchaiammal was in a live-in relationship with D. Velusamy, who was already married to another woman.

Legal Outcome:

- The Supreme Court ruled that for a woman in a live-in relationship to be eligible for alimony under the Protection of Women from Domestic Violence Act, 2005, the relationship must resemble a marriage, the couple must hold themselves out to society as being akin to spouses, and must be of legal age to marry or must be qualified to enter into a legal marriage.
- This case provided specific guidelines to recognize 'relationships in the nature of marriage' and discussed the rights of women under the Domestic Violence Act.

RECOGNITION OF FOREIGN DECREES IN INDIA ON MARRIAGE AND DIVORCE

OVERVIEW OF RECOGNITION OF FOREIGN DECREES IN INDIA

Introduction: In the context of globalization, the recognition of foreign decrees by domestic courts is a critical aspect of international law. This process ensures the enforcement of judgments made outside the territorial boundaries of a country. In India, the recognition and enforcement of foreign decrees are governed by specific sections of the Code of Civil Procedure, 1908, along with relevant case law and principles derived from common law.

Basic Principles of International Law Regarding Recognition of Foreign Judgments

- **Comity of Nations**: This principle implies a mutual recognition of legislative, executive, and judicial acts of foreign countries. In practice, it promotes international courtesy and respect, which underpin the recognition of foreign decrees.
- **Natural Justice**: A foreign judgment must be rendered by a judiciary that offers procedures akin to fairness as recognized in Indian law. The judgment must be given after proper notice and in the presence of a fair opportunity to defend, thus ensuring the standards of natural justice are met.
- **Finality of Judgment**: For a foreign decree to be recognized in India, it must be conclusive and final in the country of its origin. It cannot be provisional or interim.
- **Jurisdiction**: The foreign court should have had proper jurisdiction to deal with the case, both according to its own laws and from the perspective of Indian courts. Generally, jurisdiction is considered appropriate if the defendant is a resident of the foreign country or has submitted to its jurisdiction.
- **No Fraud**: The judgment must be obtained without fraud. Any judgment procured on fraudulent grounds is not recognized or enforceable.
- **Public Policy**: The enforcement of the foreign decree must not be contrary to the public policy of India. This includes adherence to fundamental policy concerns and the basic principles of Indian law.

The Role of Indian Courts in Recognizing Foreign Decrees

- **Procedural Framework**: The Code of Civil Procedure, 1908 (Sections 13 and 44A) lays down the procedure and conditions for the recognition of foreign judgments. Section 13 states that a foreign judgment shall be conclusive on any matter thereby directly adjudicated upon between the same parties or between parties under whom they or any of them claim litigating under the same title except in certain cases. Section 44A specifically deals with the execution of decrees from reciprocating territories.

- **Reciprocating and Non-Reciprocating Territories**: India distinguishes between decrees from reciprocating territories (countries notified by the Central Government in the Official Gazette) and non-reciprocating territories. Decrees from reciprocating territories can be enforced directly by filing an execution petition, while decrees from non-reciprocating territories require a lawsuit in an Indian court to establish the decree before enforcement.
- **Judicial Interpretation**: Indian courts frequently engage in the interpretation of what constitutes public policy, jurisdiction, natural justice, and finality. Judicial precedents play a crucial role in shaping the criteria for recognition and enforcement.
- **Limitations**: Certain types of decrees, especially those involving matrimonial or family law from non-secular jurisdictions, may face additional scrutiny to determine compatibility with Indian law and societal norms.
- **Enforcement**: Once a foreign decree passes these criteria, it can be enforced like any domestic judgment. However, the process may involve significant legal complexities, especially when interpreting the substantive and procedural law aspects of the foreign judgment.

LAWS DEALING WITH FOREIGN DECREE IN INDIA

The Code of Civil Procedure, 1908 (CPC) - Sections Dealing with the Enforcement of Foreign Judgments

Section 13: Recognition of Foreign Judgments

A foreign judgment shall be conclusive on any matter thereby directly adjudicated upon between the same parties or between parties under whom they or any of them claim litigating under the same title except:

- Where it has not been pronounced by a court of competent jurisdiction.
- Where it has not been given on the merits of the case.
- Where it appears on the face of the proceedings to be founded on an incorrect view of international law or a refusal to recognize the law of India in cases in which such law is applicable.
- Where the proceedings in which the judgment was obtained are opposed to natural justice.
- Where it has been obtained by fraud.
- Where it sustains a claim founded on a breach of any law in force in India.

Section 44A: Execution of Decrees Passed by Courts in Reciprocating Territory

Allows for the execution of a decree passed by a superior court in any reciprocating territory (countries and territories declared by the Government of India) as if it had been passed by the domestic courts.

Application for execution must be made within three years from the date of the judgment.

The Indian Divorce Act, 1869: Provisions for the Recognition of Foreign Decrees

Recognition of Foreign Divorce Decrees

- Applies predominantly to persons of Christian religion but also includes others where specified.
- A foreign decree of divorce will generally be recognized in India if it is granted by a competent court and follows the judicial or legal procedures of the country in which it was issued.
- Recognition can be denied if the decree contradicts Indian matrimonial law or public policy.

The Special Marriage Act, 1954: Implications for International Marriages

Registration and Recognition of Foreign Marriages

- The Act provides for the solemnization of marriages in accordance with its provisions, irrespective of the religion or nationality of the parties.
- A marriage between an Indian citizen and a foreign national can be solemnized under this Act either in India or abroad.
- Section 17 aligns the legal grounds for divorce under this Act with those under the Hindu Marriage Act, 1955, including cruelty, desertion, conversion to another religion, unsoundness of mind, communicable venereal disease, renouncement of the world, and presumption of death.

Key Implications

- Allows for a civil marriage by registration, providing a legal framework for interfaith and international marriages.
- The Act mandates a notice period of 30 days before the marriage can be solemnized, to allow for objections if any.

Case Studies of Indian Court Decisions on Foreign Decrees

Several Indian court decisions illustrate the application of these criteria:

- **Y. Narasimha Rao and Ors vs. Y. Venkata Lakshmi and Anr (1991)**: The Supreme Court held that foreign matrimonial decrees can only be recognized in India if the decree was issued by a court of competent jurisdiction and according to a law that is in conformity with Indian laws. Additionally, it emphasized that the decree should be granted on grounds that are recognized by Indian matrimonial laws.
- **Neeraja Saraph vs. Jayant V. Saraph (1994)**: The Supreme Court suggested guidelines for protecting the interests of Indian women deserted by their NRI (Non-Resident Indian) husbands, including the necessity of foreign courts to ensure that the summons was duly served.

MAINTENANCE IN HINDU MARRIAGE

Maintenance is a matter of right in case of a Hindu marriage. As soon as the marital tie of the couples comes into being both of the spouses comes under obligation to maintain each other. Even after the divorce a spouse without any means of income can claim maintenance against the other spouse. This concept of maintenance can be studied under two main heads – *viz.* – maintenance *pendente lite* or interim maintenance and permanent alimony.

MAINTENANCE *PENDENTE LITE*

Where in any proceeding under the Hindu Marriage Act, it appears to the Court that either the wife or the husband as the case may be has no independent income sufficient for her or his support and the necessary expenses of the proceeding, it may, on the application of the wife or the husband, order the respondent to pay to the petitioner the expenses of the proceeding, and monthly during the proceeding such sum as having regard the petitioner's own income and the income of the respondent, it may seem to the Court to be reasonable. This provision of law applies to the proceedings under the Hindu Marriage Act, 1955 (Daya v. Sohanlal 78 Punj LR 226). It may be a case of restitution of conjugal rights, judicial separation or nullity of marriage or divorce. Such an application for the purpose of maintenance *Pendente lit* can be filed before the conciliation process as per section 23(2) (Dilipbhai v. State of Maharashtra AIR 1983 Bom 128).

In a significant observation of Supreme Court in *Ramesh Chander* v. *Veera Kaushal* AIR 1978 SC 1807 it was pointed out that maintenance *pendente* lite as per section 24 of the Hindu Marriage Act, 1955 does not check the maintenance under section 125 of the Criminal Procedure Code, 1973 irrespective of the fact, the proceedings under section 24 of the Hindu Marriage Act, 1955 are pending. The magistrate can order higher maintenance even if the interim maintenance has been awarded by the Civil Court. The rational behind it lies in the fact that the order of the Civil Court is not the final determination under Hindu Adoptions and Maintenance Act, 1956, and the maintenance for children is not inclusive in that amount. There are two basic ingredients for the purpose of order of maintenance. Firstly that there should be insufficiency of the income and secondly there should be absence of income. Where the contention of the husband was that the wife could go to her parent's house and live with them it was held that such a contention was not acceptable. Under section 24 of the Hindu Marriage Act, 1955 there is no provision for maintenance for the period subsequent to the disposal of petition (Swarajyawati v. Munnalal (1971)2 An WR 351). Where the order of maintenance was passed without mentioning the facts and grounds for the same it was held to be improper and illegal (Sakuntala v. Amar Nath AIR 1978 P & H 32).

Liability of wife to pay maintenance: In the general cases the interim maintenance *pendente lit* is paid by the husband to the wife but according to wordings of section 24 even the husband can also apply for the interim maintenance. The word that has been used in the section is "respondent" which means the opposite party in the application for maintenance (Rukmani Bai v. Kishanlal AIR 1959 MP 187). The factor that is to be borne in mind while awarding of maintenance under section 24 is that the applicant has not got sufficient means to support himself or herself (Surjit Kaur v. Jirath Singh AIR 1978 P & H 112).

Quantum of Maintenance: As regards the amount of maintenance that needs to be awarded it is to be borne in mind that it should be reasonable amount and only the net or disposable income should be taken into account. The Hon'ble Supreme Court for quantum of maintenance in *Bhagwan Dutta* v. *Kamla Devi* AIR 1985 SC 83, 86 pointed out "what is required by the wife to maintain a standard of living which is neither luxurious nor penurious, but is modestly consistent with the status of the family. The need and requirements of the wife for such moderate living can be fairly determined only if her separate income is also taken into account together with the earnings of the husband and his commitments." In case the income of the husband remains undisclosed the Court is at liberty to rely over the testimony of the wife (Pushpa Rani v. Asanand (1978)80 Punj LR 300).

Time for Application of Interim Maintenance: Regarding the time for application of interim maintenance under section 24 it is to be noted that the section itself does not prescribe any time for filing or presentation of petition for interim maintenance but in general circumstances it is presented when the main petition for relief for matrimonial offence is made. In case the respondent is found to be *ex-parte* in the main petition and notice of interim petition has been served up to the satisfaction of the Court then the Court can make order for the interim relief. However, the respondent cannot be prevented from moving to the Court for canceling or modifying the *ex-parte* order so made. The Court while using its discretion to refuse decree, should be careful and cautious. It should not act capriciously.

PERMANENT ALIMONY AND MAINTENANCE

Any Court exercising jurisdiction under the Hindu Marriage Act, 1955 may at the time of passing any decree or at the time subsequent thereto, on application made to it for the purpose by either the wife or the husband, as the case may be, order that the respondent shall pay to the applicant for her or his maintenance and support such gross sum or such monthly or periodical sum for a term not exceeding the life of the applicant as, having regard to the respondent's own income and other properly, if any, the income and other property of the applicant the conduct of the parties and other circumstances of the case, it may seem to the Court to be just, and any such payment may secured, if necessary, by a charge on the immovable property of the respondent. If the Court is satisfied that there is change in the circumstances of either party at any time after it has made an order as aforesaid, it may, at the instance of either party, vary, modify or rescind any such order in such manner as the Court may deem just. If the Court is satisfied that the party is whose favour an order has been made in the said manner has remarried or, if such party is the wife, that she has not remained chaste, or if such party is the husband, that he has had sexual intercourse with any woman outside wedlock it may at the instance of the other party vary, modify or rescind any such order in such manner as the Court may deem just. Section 25 of the Hindu Marriage Act, 1955 dealing with the permanent alimony corresponds to section 37 of the Special Marriage Act, 1954, section 37 of Divorce Act, 1869 and section 40 of the Parsi Marriage and Divorce Act, 1936. This concept has been imported from the English law where the allowance known as alimony was granted to the wife in case of divorce *mensa et toro*. In case of permanent alimony since the maintenance is awarded by the Court on application made at the time of passing any decree or at any time subsequent thereto therefore if the petition for relief is dismissed the permanent alimony cannot be granted (Chinna Babu v. Parbiti 1967 Orissa 163). The right to permanent alimony is a statutory right in nature and it cannot be abridged or taken away by way of contract between the parties (Hyman v. Hyman 1929 AC 601). However, where an agreement was entered into between the husband and wife to the effect of, husband giving up the right to the custody of child and wife setting aside her right to alimony, it was held that such an agreement is not contrary to the law or public policy (Manjit Singh v. Savita Kiran AIR 1983 P & H 281). It is not for the Court to pass the order of granting permanent alimony as per section 25 *suo moto* rather an application has to be made for this purpose. The wife against whom the decree of divorce has been passed for the reason of adultery is lawfully entitled to claim maintenance from her husband (Gulab v. Kamal AIR 1985 Bom 88).

Maintenance under Hindu Marriage Act vis-à-vis Hindu Adoptions and Maintenance Act: It becomes necessary here to compare section 25 of the Hindu Marriage Act, 1955 relating to the permanent alimony with the corresponding provision of maintenance under the Hindu Adoptions and Maintenance Act, 1956. The object of the provision of permanent alimony to the respondent under Hindu Marriage Act would not have been to confer it the status of a right. It is only after the Hindu Adoptions and Maintenance Act, 1956 came into force that by virtue of section 18 in it, the wife was made entitled to claim maintenance without filing any petition for matrimonial relief. A significant difference between section 25 (1) of the Hindu Marriage Act, 1955 and section 18 of the Hindu Adoptions and Maintenance Act, 1956 is that under the former provision even husband is entitled to get maintenance from wife whereas under the latter provision of law it is only wife who can claim maintenance from the husband (Govind Rao v. Anandi Bai 79 Bom LR 73). The words "at the time of passing any decree" indicate that the permanent alimony can be ordered only if the main petition is decreed but if such petition is dismissed, the maintenance order can not be passed (Purushottam v. Devki, AIR 1973 Raj 3). The order for permanent alimony can be made at the time of passing of decree of main petition or at any time subsequent thereto (Gulab v. Kamal AIR 1985 Bom 88). The maintenance of the son is not inclusive in the allowance of the mother and she is liable to claim it in a separate proceeding (Patel Dharmshi Premji v. Bai Sakar Kanji AIR 1968 Guj 150). Although there is no limitation period within which the application for an order of permanent alimony be made but it should be taken to be a reasonable period rather than an unlimited one (Govindrao v. Anandibai AIR 1976 Bom 433).

STRIDHAN

Definition of Stridhan

- **Stridhan** is a Sanskrit term meaning "woman's property."
- It refers to property that a woman can claim as her own, independent of her marital status.
- Under Hindu law, Stridhan represents wealth gifted to a woman at various stages of her life, either before, during, or after marriage, by her family, in-laws, relatives, or friends.

Nature of Stridhan

- Stridhan is a woman's **absolute property** over which she has complete ownership and control.
- She has the **right to dispose of it** (sell, gift, or will) as she wishes without the consent of her husband or in-laws.
- It includes movable and immovable property acquired by her voluntarily.

Judicial Interpretation

- In **Pratibha Rani v. Suraj Kumar (1985)**, the Supreme Court held that a married woman retains full control over her Stridhan even after marriage, and any misappropriation of the same by her husband or in-laws is punishable under criminal law.

Legal Meaning of Stridhan

Stridhan has been defined under Hindu laws through judicial precedents and customary practices:

- **Textual Basis**: Derived from ancient Hindu texts like Manusmriti and Smritis, it traditionally includes gifts given at marriage, during childbirth, or festivals.
- **Modern Legal Recognition**:
  - ❑ Hindu law, as codified in the **Hindu Succession Act, 1956**, recognizes the concept of Stridhan.
  - ❑ Misappropriation of Stridhan is a criminal offense under **Section 406 of the Indian Penal Code (IPC)**, which deals with criminal breach of trust.
- **Difference from Joint Property**: Stridhan is the personal property of the woman, distinct from the joint family or matrimonial property.

Difference Between Stridhan and Dowry

Aspect	Stridhan	Dowry
Definition	Property voluntarily given to a woman.	Property demanded by the groom or his family as a precondition for marriage.
Ownership	Absolute ownership lies with the woman.	Ownership is often unclear and generally with the husband's family.
Legality	Legal and protected under Hindu law.	Illegal under the Dowry Prohibition Act, 1961.
Purpose	For the woman's financial security and independence.	A societal evil meant to satisfy the demands of the groom's family.
Examples	Jewelry, gifts, and assets given voluntarily.	Cash, goods, and valuables demanded by the groom's side.

Types of Property Included Under Stridhan

Movable Property

- **Gifts Received Before Marriage**:
  - ❑ Property gifted by parents, relatives, or friends.
  - ❑ Includes cash, jewelry, clothes, or other valuables.
- **Gifts Received During Marriage**: Items received at the time of the wedding from the bride's family, groom's family, or others.
- **Gifts Received After Marriage**: Presents given on occasions like festivals, childbirth, anniversaries, or other ceremonies.
- **Self-Acquired Property**: Income earned by the woman through employment, business, or investments.
- **Other Movables**: Property inherited by the woman.

Immovable Property

Land, houses, or other immovable assets voluntarily gifted to the woman at any stage.

Judicial Precedent

- In **Raghunath Das v. Sundar Das (1914)**, it was clarified that property acquired by a woman through her skills or employment also qualifies as Stridhan.

1. Legal Provisions Relating to Stridhan

Stridhan is recognized and protected under various legal frameworks in India, including codified Hindu law, criminal law, and specific statutes. It encompasses property voluntarily given to a woman at any stage of her life.

2. Sections of the Hindu Succession Act, 1956 Relevant to Stridhan

The **Hindu Succession Act, 1956** governs the inheritance and property rights of Hindus, including rights over Stridhan. Key sections related to Stridhan are:

- **Section 14: Property of a Female Hindu to be her Absolute Property**
  - Any property possessed by a female Hindu, including Stridhan, becomes her absolute property.
  - It includes property acquired:
    - Before or after marriage.
    - By inheritance, partition, gift, will, or her own skill or exertion.
  - **Explanation**: Stridhan, regardless of how or when it is acquired, is fully owned by the woman and cannot be taken away by her husband or family.
- **Section 15: General Rules of Succession in the Case of Female Hindus**
  - If a woman dies intestate (without a will), her Stridhan devolves upon her legal heirs in the following order:
    - Sons, daughters, and husband.
    - Heirs of the husband.
    - Parents and their heirs.
- **Section 16: Order of Succession**
  - The order of succession ensures equitable distribution of the deceased woman's property, including Stridhan.

3. Stridhan Under the Hindu Marriage Act, 1955

The **Hindu Marriage Act, 1955** primarily addresses marriage-related matters but also indirectly safeguards Stridhan. Key provisions include:

- **Section 24: Maintenance Pendente Lite and Expenses of Proceedings**
  - A woman is entitled to claim maintenance and litigation expenses during matrimonial disputes. Stridhan cannot be appropriated for such purposes without her consent.
- **Section 25: Permanent Alimony and Maintenance**
  - During or after divorce, Stridhan remains the woman's exclusive property and is not subject to division as part of the matrimonial property.
- **Judicial Precedent**:
  - In **Pratibha Rani v. Suraj Kumar (1985)**, the Supreme Court reaffirmed that Stridhan is a woman's exclusive property, and its misappropriation by the husband or in-laws is punishable under criminal law.

4. Stridhan and its Relationship with the Dowry Prohibition Act, 1961

The **Dowry Prohibition Act, 1961** criminalizes the practice of dowry, which often overlaps with the concept of Stridhan. Key distinctions and relationships are as follows:

- Prohibition of Dowry Demands (Section 3)
  - The Act prohibits giving or taking dowry as a condition of marriage.
  - **Relationship with Stridhan**:
    - Dowry is a coerced transaction, whereas Stridhan is voluntarily given to the woman.
    - Property voluntarily given to a bride as gifts during or after marriage, without demand, qualifies as Stridhan and is not considered dowry.
- **Penalty for Demanding Dowry (Section 4)**
  - Demanding dowry is punishable with imprisonment and fines.
  - However, the Act does not interfere with the woman's right to receive gifts or Stridhan from her family.
- **Judicial Observations**:
  - Courts have clarified that the Act does not apply to gifts freely given without coercion or demand. For example:
    - Gifts given to the bride during her wedding as part of customary practices are Stridhan.
- **Protection of Stridhan**:
  - Misappropriation of Stridhan by the husband or in-laws is addressed under **Section 406 of the IPC (Criminal Breach of Trust)**, which works in tandem with the Dowry Prohibition Act to safeguard women's property.

Landmark Judgments Related to Stridhan

Stridhan, recognized as a woman's absolute property, has been clarified and protected through various landmark judicial pronouncements. The following cases are pivotal for understanding the legal and judicial interpretation of Stridhan:

1. *Pratibha Rani v. Suraj Kumar (1985)*

Facts of the Case

- The petitioner, Pratibha Rani, filed a case against her husband, Suraj Kumar, and in-laws alleging misappropriation of her Stridhan.
- She claimed her Stridhan, which included jewelry, cash, and other valuables, was taken by her husband and not returned despite repeated demands.

Key Legal Issues

- Is Stridhan the absolute property of the woman?
- Can the husband or in-laws be held liable for criminal breach of trust under **Section 406 of the Indian Penal Code (IPC)** for not returning the Stridhan?

Judgment

- The **Supreme Court of India** ruled in favor of Pratibha Rani, holding that:
  - **Stridhan is the woman's exclusive and absolute property**, even after marriage.
  - If the husband or in-laws retain the Stridhan and fail to return it upon demand, it constitutes **criminal breach of trust under Section 406 IPC**.
  - The husband and in-laws do not acquire ownership rights over Stridhan.

Significance of the Judgment

- **Recognition of Women's Property Rights**: It affirmed that Stridhan is the exclusive property of a woman, ensuring her financial independence.
- **Criminal Protection for Misappropriation**: Misappropriation of Stridhan is treated as a criminal offense, providing legal recourse for women against unfair practices.
- **Legal Precedent**: This case became a cornerstone for the interpretation of women's rights over Stridhan in India.

Ownership and Rights Over Stridhan

Stridhan, as recognized under Hindu law and interpreted through judicial pronouncements, is a woman's absolute property, ensuring her financial security and independence. The following aspects explain the ownership and rights over Stridhan in detail:

1. *Ownership of Stridhan*

- **Exclusive Ownership**:
  - A woman is the sole and absolute owner of her Stridhan.
  - She has complete autonomy to use, gift, sell, or bequeath her Stridhan without requiring consent from her husband or family.
- **Nature of Ownership**:
  - Stridhan is distinct from joint family property or matrimonial property.
  - It includes all movable and immovable assets voluntarily gifted to her before, during, or after marriage.

Judicial Precedents:

- **Pratibha Rani v. Suraj Kumar (1985)**: The Supreme Court held that Stridhan is the woman's exclusive property, and any misappropriation amounts to criminal breach of trust.
- **Sushila Devi v. Narayanan (2003)**: Stridhan remains the woman's property even after marriage, and her in-laws or husband cannot claim ownership.

2. *Rights of a Woman Over Her Stridhan During and After Marriage*

During Marriage:

- **Unrestricted Access**:
  - A woman has the right to manage, use, or dispose of her Stridhan at her discretion.
  - Any attempt by her husband or in-laws to restrict her access to Stridhan is unlawful.
- **Legal Remedies Against Misappropriation**:
  - If Stridhan is misappropriated, she can file a criminal case under **Section 406 IPC** for criminal breach of trust.
  - Courts have consistently upheld women's rights over Stridhan.

After Marriage or in Separation:

- **Absolute Right**:
  - Post-separation, the woman retains absolute ownership of her Stridhan.
  - Misuse or withholding of Stridhan by the husband or his family can be challenged legally.
- **Judicial Protection**: **The Protection of Women from Domestic Violence Act, 2005** mandates the return of Stridhan to the woman in cases of matrimonial disputes.

3. *Inheritance Rights of Stridhan*

General Rules of Inheritance:

Under the **Hindu Succession Act, 1956**, a woman's Stridhan is her absolute property and is inheritable. Upon her demise, the inheritance of her Stridhan follows these rules:

- **In Case of Intestate Succession**:
  - ❑ The property devolves upon her heirs as per **Sections 15 and 16 of the Hindu Succession Act**.
  - ❑ The order of succession is as follows:
    - **First Priority**: Sons, daughters, and husband.
    - **Second Priority**: Heirs of the husband.
    - **Third Priority**: Parents and their heirs.
- **In Case of a Will**: If a woman bequeaths her Stridhan through a will, the property is distributed according to her wishes.

4. Protection of Stridhan in Case of Separation or Divorce

Legal Safeguards:

- **Return of Stridhan**:
  - ❑ The husband and his family are legally obligated to return the woman's Stridhan during separation or divorce.
  - ❑ Any refusal to do so constitutes an offense under **Section 406 IPC**.
- **Domestic Violence Act, 2005**:
  - ❑ The Act ensures protection and recovery of Stridhan in cases of domestic abuse or harassment.
  - ❑ Courts can direct the husband or in-laws to return the Stridhan as part of the relief granted.
- **Divorce Proceedings**:
  - ❑ Stridhan remains outside the scope of alimony or maintenance settlements.
  - ❑ It is treated as the woman's separate property and cannot be claimed by the husband.

Judicial Precedents:

- **Neelamma v. Sarojamma (2006)**: The Court ruled that a woman's Stridhan is her personal property, and its return is mandatory in cases of divorce or separation.
- **Sunita v. State of Haryana (2010)**: The husband's failure to return Stridhan was deemed a criminal act under **Section 406 IPC**.

ADOPTION

1. Concept and Definition of Adoption

Adoption is a legal process in which a person (the adoptive parent) assumes the responsibility and rights of a parent for a child (the adopted child) who is not their biological offspring. The legal relationship established through adoption creates permanent parental rights and responsibilities, including rights to inheritance, support, and protection under the law.

Legal Meaning of Adoption:

- **Adoption** is a **permanent** legal relationship between the child and the adoptive parents, as opposed to **guardianship**, which may be temporary.
- The **adopted child** becomes a **legal heir** to the adoptive family, with the same rights as a biological child.
- Adoption is governed by **family law** and is a critical aspect of the legal system in ensuring the welfare of children who cannot be cared for by their biological parents.

Requirements for Adoption:

- **Legal Declaration of Adoption**: A legal process by which a child is formally recognized as a member of the adopting family, often requiring a court decree.
- **Consent of Biological Parents**: If the biological parents are alive, their consent is typically required, especially if they have legal custody of the child.
- **Welfare of the Child**: The best interests of the child must be paramount in any adoption process. Courts consider factors like the emotional, financial, and social welfare of the child.

Purposes of Adoption:

- **To Provide Care**: Adoption helps children who are orphaned, abandoned, or neglected to find permanent, stable homes.
- **To Create Family Bonds**: Adoption allows individuals to form legal familial relationships that might not otherwise exist.
- **To Secure Inheritance Rights**: An adopted child enjoys the same rights to inherit from their adoptive parents as a biological child would.
- **To Promote Child Welfare**: Adoption ensures that children grow up in loving, supportive environments.

2. Laws Governing Adoption in India

Several laws regulate adoption in India, ensuring the protection and welfare of children:

a. The Hindu Adoption and Maintenance Act, 1956 (HAMA):

This law applies to Hindus, Buddhists, Jains, and Sikhs in India. It provides a framework for the adoption process for individuals following these religions.

- **Eligibility for Adoption:**
  - **Hindu male or female**: A male must be at least 21 years old, and a female must be at least 18 years old to adopt a child.
  - **Adoptive parents**: The adoptive parents must be in a position to provide for the child's welfare and should not be an "unfit" parent (e.g., if they are mentally ill, have criminal convictions, etc.).
- **Process of Adoption**:
  - Adoption requires a **formal declaration** made by the adoptive parent(s) to adopt a child.
  - The **adoptive child** must be under 15 years of age.
  - The adoption becomes final with a court decree.
- **Rights and Duties of Adoptive Parents**: Once adoption is completed, the adoptive parents are legally bound to care for the child. The child enjoys full inheritance rights from the adoptive parents.

b. The Juvenile Justice (Care and Protection of Children) Act, 2015 (JJ Act, 2015):

This law deals with children who are in need of care and protection, and it specifically addresses adoption procedures for such children.

- **Key Provisions**:
  - **Central Adoption Resource Authority (CARA)**: A body under the Ministry of Women and Child Development, it governs and monitors the adoption process in India.
  - The **Child Welfare Committees (CWCs)** handle cases of children in need of care and protection, including those eligible for adoption.
  - The **adoption process** under the JJ Act allows for children to be placed for adoption only if all other options (such as reunification with the biological family) have been exhausted.

c. The Adoption Regulation 2017:

This regulation provides detailed procedural aspects for adoption in India under the JJ Act, including:

- **Eligibility Criteria**: It specifies the eligibility of adoptive parents, including their age, financial stability, and willingness to provide a nurturing home environment.
- **Procedure for Adoption**: The detailed process includes the preparation of the child for adoption, matching the child with prospective adoptive parents, and legal formalities.

d. The Guardians and Wards Act, 1890 (Related to Guardianship):

While not directly dealing with adoption, this law addresses **guardianship** of children, and there can be overlaps when adoption is not possible.

3. Conditions for Adoption

The following are the key conditions that must be met for an adoption to be legally valid in India:

a. Eligibility of Adoptive Parents:

- **Age Criteria**:
  - For **Hindus**, an adoptive father must be at least 21 years older than the child, and an adoptive mother must be at least 21 years old.
  - The prospective adoptive parents should be in a position to provide a stable home, financially and emotionally.
- **Married Couples**: In India, adoption is usually allowed for a **married couple**, though single individuals can also adopt, provided they meet other criteria.
- **Single Individuals**: Single men and women can adopt, but there are **restrictions** based on the child's gender (a single male can only adopt a male child, while a single female can adopt both male and female children).

b. Consent of Biological Parents:

- The **biological parents' consent** is crucial for an adoption to proceed, especially if the parents are not legally separated or divorced.
- If the biological parents are unknown, abandoned children may be adopted through the court process after the required waiting period.

c. Age Difference Between Adoptive Parents and Child:

- There must be an appropriate **age difference** between the child and the adoptive parents to ensure the welfare of the child.
- A child should be adopted at an age where they can be given full parental care, usually before the age of 15 (under HAMA), though under the JJ Act, children can be adopted up to the age of 18.

d. Welfare of the Child:

- The welfare of the child is the **primary consideration** for any adoption.
- Courts and adoption agencies evaluate the adoptive parents' suitability, considering factors such as:
  - Financial stability
  - Emotional stability
  - Health and mental fitness
  - A safe and nurturing home environment

e. Process of Adoption:

- **Court Decree**: The adoption becomes legal only when the court issues a decree of adoption, confirming that the adoption complies with all the legal requirements.
- **Post-Adoption Period**: After the adoption, the child's welfare is monitored, and the adoptive parents must meet their responsibilities to the child, including providing maintenance, education, and general welfare.

Rights and Duties of Adoptive Parents

1. Parental Rights of Adoptive Parents

Once the adoption process is completed, adoptive parents acquire full **parental rights** over the child. These rights are equivalent to those of biological parents and carry several legal and social implications:

- **Custody and Control**: Adoptive parents have the right to custody and control over the adopted child, which means they can make decisions regarding the child's upbringing, education, healthcare, and general welfare.
- **Protection and Care**: Adoptive parents have a legal duty to provide the child with **adequate protection**, care, and emotional support.
- **Decision-Making Authority**: They have the authority to make significant decisions concerning the child's education, religion, medical care, and welfare.
- **Parental Authority**: Adoptive parents have the legal right to represent the child in all matters, including legal and educational issues, much like biological parents.

2. Duty to Maintain the Child

Adoptive parents are legally required to **maintain** the adopted child, providing for their **physical, mental, and emotional needs**:

- **Financial Support**: Adoptive parents are obligated to provide the child with food, shelter, clothing, education, medical care, and all other essential needs.
- **Emotional and Psychological Welfare**: Adoptive parents are expected to nurture and provide emotional stability and a loving environment for the child, which is essential for the child's mental well-being.
- **Obligation of Support**: The adoption decree enforces the obligation of the adoptive parents to care for the child until they reach adulthood or are no longer dependent.

3. Legal Status of the Adopted Child

The legal status of the adopted child is very similar to that of a biological child, with some important implications:

- **Legal Recognition**: An adopted child is legally recognized as a **full-fledged member** of the adoptive family. The child has **equal legal status** as a biological child under the law.
- **Inheritance and Succession**: The adopted child inherits the rights of the adoptive parents, including property and succession rights. The child is treated the same as a biological child in matters related to inheritance.
- **Rights to Citizenship**: If the adopted parents are citizens of India, the adopted child acquires the same citizenship rights as any biological child of the parents.

Effects of Adoption

The process of adoption has significant legal and personal effects, especially regarding **inheritance rights, succession, and property rights**. These effects are crucial in understanding the child's place within the adoptive family and their relationship to both the adoptive parents and the biological family.

1. Inheritance Rights of the Adopted Child

- **Equal Rights to Inheritance**: An adopted child has **the same inheritance rights** as a biological child under the Indian legal system. This means the adopted child is entitled to inherit property, both movable and immovable, from the adoptive parents.
- **Property Rights**: Upon adoption, the child becomes a legal heir to the adoptive parents' property. The child has a **right to inherit** the adoptive parents' estate upon their death, as well as any property passed through **wills** or **testamentary dispositions**.
- **Rights to Ancestors' Property**: In certain cases, the adopted child may also inherit from the **ancestors** of the adoptive parents, depending on the terms of the family's **succession laws** and whether the adoption was formalized with the correct legal procedures.

2. Succession Rights of the Adopted Child

The **succession rights** of an adopted child are governed by the personal laws of the adoptive parents, and the effects are as follows:

- **Intestate Succession**: If the adoptive parent dies **intestate** (without a will), the adopted child will inherit the estate along with the biological children, in accordance with the applicable personal law (e.g., Hindu law under the Hindu Succession Act, 1956).
- **Testamentary Succession**: If the adoptive parent leaves a will, the adopted child has the right to be included in the will and can inherit according to the terms specified, similar to a biological child.
- **Right to Ancestor's Property**: An adopted child may also have the right to inherit the property of the **adoptive grandparents** and other relatives, especially under **Hindu law** (Hindu Succession Act, 1956) where an adopted child is treated as a biological child in terms of inheritance.

3. Property Rights of the Adopted Child

- **Right to Property**: The adopted child has the same **right to property** as a biological child. This means the adopted child can claim a share in the adoptive parents' property, which includes immovable assets such as land, house, or any inheritance passed down through the adoptive family.
- **Hindu Law and Adoption**: Under **Hindu law**, once a child is adopted, they become part of the family and are treated as **natural-born children** for property distribution purposes. The adoption severs the child's ties with the biological family in terms of inheritance rights, but it establishes the child's full rights in the adoptive family.
  - For instance, under the **Hindu Adoption and Maintenance Act (HAMA), 1956**, the adopted child can inherit from the adoptive parents' estate.
  - **Stridhan Rights**: An adopted female child can also inherit **stridhan** (property traditionally meant for women) if specified in the family's traditions.

4. Severance of Rights in the Biological Family

- **Termination of Rights with Biological Parents**: Adoption severs the child's legal ties with their biological family concerning inheritance and succession rights.
  - Under the **Hindu Adoption and Maintenance Act, 1956 (HAMA)**, the adopted child no longer has any rights to inherit from their biological parents' property once the adoption is finalized.
  - However, the child may still retain emotional or social ties with their biological family if they choose to maintain such relationships.

5. Adopted Children and Property Division Among Siblings

- **No Discrimination**: Adopted children are not discriminated against in the distribution of property. They have the same rights as biological children in terms of **equal distribution** of the adoptive family's property.
- **Will and Testament**: If a will exists, the adopted child has the right to claim their share according to the will. If no will is present, the child shares in the estate equally with biological siblings.

GUARDIANSHIP

1. Concept and Definition of Guardianship

Guardianship is a legal relationship that arises when an individual or institution is entrusted with the responsibility for the care, welfare, and upbringing of a child who is under the age of majority (usually 18 years). Unlike **adoption**, which creates a permanent legal bond akin to that of a biological parent, guardianship is often temporary and may be subject to change by the courts or the child's biological parents.

Types of Guardianship:

- **Natural Guardianship**:
  - **Natural guardianship** refers to the rights and responsibilities of the **biological parents** or **legal guardians** to provide care and protection for the child.
  - **Under Hindu law**, the father is generally considered the natural guardian of a child, while the **mother** is the natural guardian if the child **is** under the age of 5 years or in the absence of the father.
- **Testamentary Guardianship**:
  - **Testamentary guardianship** is created when the biological parents (particularly the father) name a **guardian** for their child in a **will**. This guardianship takes effect upon the death of the parent.
  - The appointed **testamentary guardian** has the responsibility of the child's upbringing, care, and welfare according to the directions given in the will.
- **Statutory Guardianship**:
  - **Statutory guardianship** refers to the guardianship created by law, particularly when a court appoints a guardian. This occurs under circumstances where the parents are deceased, unable, or unfit to care for the child.
  - The **Guardian and Wards Act, 1890** and the **Hindu Minority and Guardianship Act, 1956** are two of the key legal frameworks that deal with statutory guardianship in India.
- **Legal Framework of Guardianship:**
  - **Guardianship** ensures that a child's **welfare** is safeguarded, and that the child is provided with proper care, education, and emotional development.
  - The key principles of guardianship are based on ensuring the **best interests of the child, protection from harm**, and **support for the child's overall development**.

2. Laws Governing Guardianship in India

Several legal frameworks govern the concept of **guardianship** in India. The most significant ones include:

a. The Guardian and Wards Act, 1890

This law deals with the appointment of guardians and the welfare of minor children. It applies to all children, regardless of their religion, and provides a **judicial process** for appointing a guardian for a child.

- **Objective**: The primary purpose of this law is to ensure the **welfare of the child**. Courts are empowered to appoint guardians based on the child's best interests, whether they are biological parents, relatives, or third-party individuals.
- **Scope of Guardianship**: The guardian appointed under this Act has the **custody** of the child, which includes the responsibility for the child's care, welfare, education, and property management.
- **Court's Role**: The court's **primary concern** is the welfare of the minor, and it has the power to determine the suitability of the person or institution proposed as a guardian. Courts will consider factors such as the **child's welfare, family environment, and the ability of the proposed guardian to provide care**.

b. The Hindu Minority and Guardianship Act, 1956 (HMGA)

This Act governs the guardianship of **Hindu minors** and lays down the rights and duties of parents and guardians.

- **Natural Guardians**: Under **Hindu law**, the **father** is the **natural guardian** of a Hindu minor child. The **mother** becomes the natural guardian in cases where the child is a **minor female** or the father is **unavailable** (e.g., deceased).
- **Father's Rights**: The father has the exclusive right to **appoint a guardian** and has the final say regarding decisions on the child's education, marriage, and other significant matters.
- **Mother's Rights**: The **mother** can act as a guardian in the absence of the father, or for minor daughters, and she has the same legal duties regarding the care and custody of the child.
- **Procedure for Guardianship**: If the parents are **deceased** or unable to act, the courts can appoint a guardian under the **Hindu Minority and Guardianship Act, 1956**.

c. The Juvenile Justice (Care and Protection of Children) Act, 2015

This Act also plays a role in guardianship when the child is found in a state of **abandonment** or **neglect**. It lays out the framework for **adoption, care, and protection** of children who are orphaned or abandoned. The Act emphasizes the **best interests of the child** and ensures that children in need of protection are not left without a guardian or care.

3. Appointment of Guardians:

The **appointment of a guardian** is typically done through the courts under the following conditions:

a. By the Courts (Under the Guardian and Wards Act, 1890)

- **Application to Court**: A petition must be filed in the **District Court** or the **Family Court** for appointing a guardian, either by a parent or any person interested in the welfare of the child.
- **Best Interest of the Child**: The court evaluates the **best interests** of the child, considering factors like the child's emotional, physical, and social needs, and their safety.
- **Custody Orders**: The court can grant either **joint custody** (both parents share custody) or **sole custody** (one parent or other suitable individual is the sole guardian).
- **Consent of Parents**: The court usually requires the **consent** of the biological parents for the appointment of a guardian, although in some cases (e.g., where the parents are unfit or deceased), the court may proceed without their consent.

b. By the Will (Testamentary Guardianship)

- A parent can appoint a guardian for their minor child through a **will**. This guardianship comes into effect upon the **parent's death**.
- **Testamentary guardianship** is subject to the child's welfare being the primary concern. The court may override the appointment if the guardian is deemed unsuitable.

c. Consent Requirements

- Consent of the **biological parents** is often required for appointing a guardian, unless they are unavailable, unwilling, or unfit to act.
- In cases where **both parents are deceased**, the court may appoint a guardian without their consent, but **family members** are usually prioritized.

4. Rights and Duties of Guardians

a. Responsibilities of Guardians Toward the Child

Guardians are entrusted with a range of **duties** toward the child, all centered on ensuring the child's **well-being and development**.

- **Custody**: The guardian is responsible for the **physical custody** of the child, which includes providing for the child's **daily needs** (food, clothing, shelter, etc.).
- **Education and Welfare**: The guardian must ensure that the child receives an **education** and opportunities for development, both physically and intellectually. This includes enrolling the child in school, providing for health care, and guiding their moral and ethical upbringing.
- **Protection**: The guardian must ensure that the child is **protected from harm**, including **physical, emotional, and psychological abuse**.
- **Emotional Support**: The guardian must also provide the child with emotional support, care, and love, crucial for the child's mental and psychological development.
- **Decision-Making**: The guardian has the **legal right and duty** to make decisions regarding the child's **medical treatment**, **education**, and other significant life choices.

b. Duties of Guardians

- **Maintenance**: The guardian has the **legal duty** to maintain the child, which includes providing for all the child's **basic needs**, such as food, shelter, clothing, and medical care.
- **Supervision of Child's Behavior**: The guardian is responsible for supervising the child's **behavior**, ensuring that they grow up to be responsible, law-abiding individuals.
- **Financial Support**: If necessary, the guardian must also manage the child's **financial affairs**, including using the child's funds for their **welfare** (if the child has any property).
- **Protecting the Child's Property**: If the child inherits property, the guardian has a responsibility to **protect** and manage the child's property until they are legally capable of handling it themselves.

ACKNOWLEDGMENT

Acknowledgment : Concept and Legal Significance

Acknowledgment in law refers to the **recognition or acceptance** of a particular fact, debt, or relationship, which is done formally by an individual or a party involved. It is an essential element in various areas of law, including **family law**, **contract law**, and **property law**.

General Concept of Acknowledgment

- **Definition**: Acknowledgment is a formal admission of a fact, such as the existence of a debt, or the recognition of a legal relationship, such as in adoption or guardianship.
- **Importance in Law**: It serves as a vital legal tool to validate certain facts, particularly in confirming responsibilities, rights, or the acknowledgment of legal obligations that are central to forming, changing, or enforcing legal relations.

Acknowledgment in the Context of Adoption

In the context of adoption, **acknowledgment** plays a crucial role in formalizing the legal process, ensuring the rights of the child and the adoptive parents are recognized. It also safeguards the interests of biological parents.

1. Acknowledgment in Adoption Process

- **Definition**: In adoption, acknowledgment refers to the formal acceptance of the **adoptive relationship** by all parties involved, including the **biological parents**, **adoptive parents**, and sometimes the **child** (depending on their age). It is a formal act of recognizing that the child is being legally transferred from biological parents to adoptive parents.
- **Legal Requirements**:
  - ❑ **Consent of Biological Parents**: Acknowledgment by the biological parents, particularly the mother and father, is a mandatory requirement. They must **consent in writing** to the adoption, confirming their acknowledgment that they are relinquishing parental rights over the child. The **Hindu Adoption and Maintenance Act (HAMA), 1956** mandates the **consent of the biological parents** for the adoption to be valid.
  - ❑ **Adoption Deed**: The **adoptive parents** must acknowledge their intent to adopt the child through an **adoption deed**, which is a formal legal document. This deed must clearly state that the child is being adopted voluntarily and with full consent, acknowledging the transfer of rights and responsibilities from the biological parents to the adoptive parents.
- **Role of Acknowledgment in Validating Adoption**:
  - ❑ **Transfer of Rights**: Acknowledgment formalizes the **transfer of parental rights** from the biological parents to the adoptive parents. This step is essential for the adopted child to be granted legal rights, such as **inheritance**, **custody**, and the recognition as a member of the adoptive family.
  - ❑ **Welfare of the Child**: Courts ensure that the adoption process is in the **best interest of the child** and the acknowledgment of both parties (biological and adoptive) serves to validate that the adoption is being carried out under a legal framework that prioritizes the child's welfare.

Acknowledgment in Relation to Paternity and Legitimation

Acknowledgment of paternity is a crucial legal concept, especially in family law, as it directly affects the **legitimacy** of a child and their **inheritance rights**. The legal acknowledgment of paternity can determine whether a child is considered legitimate or illegitimate in the eyes of the law, which has significant consequences for their rights to succession, maintenance, and property inheritance.

1. Legal Acknowledgment of Paternity

- **Definition**: **Acknowledgment of paternity** refers to the formal admission by a man that he is the biological father of a child. This can be done either **voluntarily** (e.g., through a declaration or in writing) or **by implication** (through behavior such as public acknowledgment of the child as his own).
- **Forms of Acknowledgment**:
  - ❑ **Voluntary Admission**: A man may acknowledge his paternity of a child by signing an affidavit, stating that the child is his biological offspring.
  - ❑ **Presumed Paternity**: In certain cases, especially where the father and mother are married, the husband is presumed to be the father of the child, and thus an acknowledgment may be implied from the marriage.
  - ❑ **Court-Ordered Acknowledgment**: In cases of disputed paternity, courts may require a formal acknowledgment, often after genetic testing or other evidence is presented.

2. Effect on Legitimation and Inheritance Rights

- **Legitimacy**: When a man acknowledges paternity, the child's legitimacy is established, meaning the child is treated as a legitimate child in the eyes of the law. This **legitimates** the child, conferring all the legal rights of a legitimate child, including the right to inheritance.

- **Inheritance Rights**:
  - Under **Indian law**, an acknowledged child has the same **rights of inheritance** as a biological child, including the right to inherit property, assets, and wealth from the father.
  - The **Hindu Succession Act, 1956** recognizes the rights of a child to inherit ancestral property if they are legitimate. In cases where the father acknowledges paternity, the child can inherit from both the father and the mother, even if the child was born out of wedlock (though the child must still meet certain legal criteria).
- **Legitimacy under Muslim Law**: Under Muslim personal law, the acknowledgment of paternity by the father establishes the **legitimacy of the child**, especially if the child is born during the marriage or within **270 days** of the dissolution of the marriage. However, an acknowledgment does not automatically grant inheritance rights unless the child is recognized legally as legitimate in the father's will or by customary law.

Legal Consequences of Acknowledgment

The acknowledgment of paternity and family relationships has several important legal consequences, particularly related to **maintenance**, **succession**, and **legitimacy**. These consequences affect both the child and the parent.

1. Maintenance

- **Right to Maintenance**: An acknowledged child has the legal right to receive **maintenance** from the father. This is true whether the child is born within or outside of marriage. Under the **Hindu Adoption and Maintenance Act (HAMA), 1956**, an adopted child has the right to maintenance, but a biological child, whose paternity is acknowledged, is also entitled to **financial support** from the father.
  - The **Maintenance and Welfare of Parents and Senior Citizens Act, 2007**, further strengthens the rights of a child for maintenance, including situations of acknowledged paternity.
- **Maintenance from Biological Father**: If a child is born out of wedlock but the father acknowledges paternity, the child is entitled to financial support. A court can order **maintenance** from the father if he fails to provide support voluntarily, even if the child does not have full inheritance rights.

2. Succession Rights

- **Inheritance of Property**: Acknowledgment of paternity ensures that a child, whether born in or outside of marriage, is **legally recognized** and, therefore, **eligible to inherit property** from the father.
  - In the case of **intestate succession**, where the father dies without a will, an acknowledged child will be entitled to a share in the father's estate, just as a legitimate child would.
  - The **Hindu Succession Act, 1956** grants the **right to inheritance** to legitimate children, and an acknowledged child is treated as legitimate for the purposes of inheritance.
- **Testamentary Succession**: If the father has made a will, the acknowledged child will be entitled to share in the estate as per the terms of the will. The acknowledgment solidifies the child's claim to the inheritance.

3. Legitimacy of the Child

- **Establishing Legitimacy**: Acknowledgment formally establishes the **legitimacy** of the child, which is critical for legal purposes. An acknowledged child is entitled to rights such as inheritance, custody, and the ability to seek maintenance.
  - Under **Indian law**, legitimacy confers upon the child the right to bear the father's surname, inherit his property, and be a part of his family.
  - In **Hindu law**, the **legitimacy of a child** is essential for the **succession** to ancestral property. An acknowledged child is considered a part of the family unit and can share in the family's inheritance rights.

INTESTATE SUCCESSION UNDER HINDU LAW

The succession law of Hindus is governed by the Hindu succession Act, 1956.

The Hindu succession Act has its overriding effect except in cases where it has been expressly provided in this Act. Any text, rule or interpretation of Hindu law or any custom or usage as part of that law in force immediately before the commencement of the Hindu succession Act shall cease to have effect with respect to any matter for which provision is made in this Act. Further, any other law in force immediately before the commencement of this Act shall cease to apply to Hindus insofar as it is inconsistent with any of the provisions contained in this Act.

Prior to the Hindu Succession (Amendment) Act, 2005 the provisions of Hindu Succession Act, 1956 that dealt with the intestate succession among Hindus had no effect on the provisions of any law for the time being in force providing for the prevention of fragmentation of agricultural holdings or for the fixation of ceilings or for the devolution of tenancy rights in respect of such holdings. The state laws as such which dealt with these issues were as such not at all affected and this was discriminatory to the females in the Hindu family because most of the succession laws of the state provided very lower rank to females in the order of succession. In most of the states the law was that if Hindu died intestate leaving behind female heirs only, then in that case the tenancy rights of the agricultural property devolved upon the sons of the brother of the deceased rather than his own daughter. This discrimination has been abrogated by the Hindu Succession (Amendment) Act, 2005 and now the amended Hindu Succession Act would override the discriminatory state laws on agricultural properties. Now, the female heirs can claim equal rights of tenancy even in agricultural properties as that exists to the sons.

INTESTATE SUCCESSION

The Hindu succession Act does not apply to certain properties. Within these properties comes

- Any property succession to which is regulated by the Indian Succession Act, 1925, by reason of the provisions contained in section 21 of the Special Marriage Act, 1954.
- Any estate which descends to a single heir by the terms of any covenant or agreement entered into by the Ruler of any Indian State with the Government of India or by the terms of any enactment passed before the commencement of this Act.
- The Valiamma Thampuran Kovilagam Estate and the Palace Fund administered by the Palace Administration Board by reason of the powers conferred by Proclamation (IX of 1124) dated 29th June, 1949, promulgated by the Maharaja of Cochin.

GENERAL RULES OF SUCCESSION IN THE CASE OF MALES

The property of a male Hindu dying intestate shall devolve in the following manner -

- Firstly, upon the heirs, being the relatives specified in class I (CLASS I – Son; daughter; widow; mother; son of a pre-deceased son; daughter of a pre-deceased son; son of a pre-deceased daughter; daughter of a pre-deceased daughter; widow of a pre-deceased son; son of a pre-deceased son of a pre-deceased son; daughter of a pre-deceased son of a pre-deceased son; widow of a pre-deceased son of a pre-deceased son, son of a pre-deceased daughter of a pre-deceased daughter, daughter of a pre-deceased daughter of a pre-deceased daughter, daughter of a pre-deceased son of a pre-deceased daughter, daughter of a pre-deceased daughter of a pre-deceased son.) of the Schedule;
- Secondly, if there is no heir of class I, then upon the heirs, being the relatives specified in class II (CLASS II— I. Father; II. (1) Son's daughter's son, (2) son's daughter's daughter, (3) brother, (4) sister; III. (1) Daughter's son's son, (2) daughter's son's daughter, (3) daughter's daughter's son, (4) daughter's daughter's daughter; IV. (1) Brother's son, (2) sister's son, (3) brother's daughter, (4) sister's daughter; V. Father's father; father's mother; VI. Father's widow; brother's widow; VII. Father's brother; father's sister; VIII. Mother's father; mother's mother; IX. Mother's brother; mother's sister. *Explanation:* In this Schedule, references to a brother or sister do not include references to a brother or sister by uterine blood.) of the Schedule;
- Thirdly, if there is no heir of any of the two classes, then upon the agnates of the deceased; and
- Lastly, if there is no agnate, then upon the cognates of the deceased.

Interpreting the term "agnate" it is to be noted that one person is said to be an "agnate" of another if the two are related by blood or adoption wholly through males.

Interpreting the term "cognate" it is to be noted that one person is said to be a cognate of another if the two are related by blood or adoption but not wholly through males.

The term "related" means related by legitimate kinship. It is subject to the condition that illegitimate children shall be deemed to be related to their mother and to one another, and their legitimate descendants shall be deemed to be related to them and to one another; and any word expressing relationship or denoting a relative shall be construed accordingly.

It is further to be noted that words imparting the masculine gender shall not be taken to include females.

The Supreme Court in *Yudhister* v. *Ashok Kumar*, AIR 1987 SC 558 held that where the family in question was governed by Mitakshara School of Hindu Law the property devolved on Hindu under S. 8 would not be HUF in his hand vis-a-vis his own sons.

So far as the order of succession among heirs in the Schedule is concerned among the heirs specified in the Schedule, those in class I shall take simultaneously and to the exclusion of all other heirs; those in the first entry in class II shall be preferred to those in the second entry; those in the second entry shall be preferred to those in the third entry; and so on in succession.

DISTRIBUTION OF PROPERTY AMONG HEIRS IN CLASS I OF THE SCHEDULE

The property of an intestate shall be divided among the heirs in class I of the Schedule in accordance with the following rules:

- ***Rule 1:*** The intestate's widow, or if there are more widows than one, all the widows together, shall take one share.
- ***Rule 2:*** The surviving sons and daughters and the mother of the intestate shall each take one share.
- ***Rule 3:*** The heirs in the branch of each pre-deceased son or each pre-deceased daughter of the intestate shall take between them one share.
- ***Rule 4:*** The distribution of the share referred to in Rule 3-
  - among the heirs in the branch of the pre-deceased son shall be so made that his widow (or widows together) and the surviving sons and daughters get equal portions; and the branch of his predeceased sons gets the same portion;
  - among the heirs in the branch of the pre-deceased daughter shall be so made that the surviving sons and daughters get equal portions.

DISTRIBUTION OF PROPERTY AMONG HEIRS IN CLASS II OF THE SCHEDULE

The property of an intestate shall be divided between the heirs specified in any one entry in class II of the Schedule so that they share equally.

ORDER OF SUCCESSION AMONG AGNATES AND COGNATES

The order of succession among agnates or cognates, as the case may be, shall be determined in accordance with the rules of preference laid down hereunder:

- ***Rule 1:*** Of two heirs, the one who has fewer or no degrees of ascent is preferred.
- ***Rule 2:*** Where the number of degrees of ascent is the same or none, that heir is preferred who has fewer or no degrees of descent.
- ***Rule 3:*** Where neither heir is entitled to be preferred to the other under Rule 1 or Rule 2 they take simultaneously.

COMPUTATION OF DEGREES

For the purposes of determining the order of succession among agnates or cognates, relationship shall be reckoned from the intestate to the heir in terms of degrees of ascent or degrees of descent or both, as the case may be. Degrees of ascent and degrees of descent shall be computed inclusive of the intestate. Every generation constitutes a degree either ascending or descending.

PROPERTY OF A FEMALE HINDU TO BE HER ABSOLUTE PROPERTY

Any property possessed by a Female Hindu, whether acquired before or after the commencement of the Hindu succession Act, shall be held by her as full owner thereof and not as a limited owner. Here, "property" includes both movable and immovable property acquired by a female Hindu by inheritance or devise, or at a partition, or in lieu of maintenance or arrears of maintenance, or by gift from any person, whether a relative or not, before, at or after her marriage, or by her own skill or exertion, or by purchase or by prescription, or in any other manner whatsoever, and also any such property held by her as stridhana immediately before the commencement of the Hindu Succession Act.

Nothing as mentioned here shall apply to any property acquired by way of gift or under a will or any other instrument or under a decree or order of a civil court or under an award where the terms of the gift, will or other instrument or the decree, order or award prescribe a restricted estate in such property.

Share devolved upon mother on account of death of her son, would become her streedhana property and husband in absence of any express authority from wife cannot alienate or otherwise dispose of streedhana property of his wife. It can not be said that there is implied authority in favour of husband in respect of separate properties of wife (Smt. Kalipatrapu Atchutamma v. Kommana Sambamurthy, [2003] 6 ILD 110 (AP)).

GENERAL RULES OF SUCCESSION IN THE CASE OF FEMALE HINDUS

The property of a female Hindu dying intestate devolves as per the rules set out in **Section 16** of Hindu Succession Act which has been discussed further:

- firstly, upon the sons and daughters (including the children of any pre-deceased son or daughter) and the husband;
- secondly, upon the heirs of the husband;
- thirdly, upon the mother and father;
- fourthly, upon the heirs of the father; and
- lastly, upon the heirs of the mother.

It is subject to the condition that any property inherited by a female Hindu from her father or mother shall devolve, in the absence of any son or daughter of the deceased (including the children of any pre-deceased son or daughter) not upon the other heirs referred above in the order specified therein, but upon the heirs of the father; and further any property inherited by a female Hindu from her husband or from her father-in-law shall devolve, in the absence of any son or daughter of the deceased (including the children of any pre-deceased son or daughter) not upon the other heirs referred above in the order specified therein, but upon the heirs of the husband.

ORDER OF SUCCESSION AND MANNER OF DISTRIBUTION AMONG HEIRS OF A FEMALE HINDU

The order of succession among the heirs referred above shall be, and the distribution of the intestate's property among those heirs shall take place, according to the following rules, namely:-

- ***Rule 1:*** Among the sons and daughters (including the children of any pre-deceased son or daughter) and the husband, those in one entry shall be preferred to those in any succeeding entry and those including in the same entry shall take simultaneously.
- ***Rule 2:*** If any son or daughter of the intestate had pre-deceased the intestate leaving his or her own children alive at the time of the intestate's death, the children of such son or daughter shall take between them the share which such son or daughter would have taken if living at the intestate's death.
- ***Rule 3:*** The devolution of the property of the intestate on the heirs of husband, heirs of father and heirs of mother shall be in the same order and according to the same rules as would have applied if the property had been the father's or the mother's or the husband's as the case may be, and such person had died intestate in respect thereof immediately after the intestate's death. Similarly, any property inherited by a female Hindu from her father or mother and any property inherited by a female Hindu from her husband or from her father-in-law shall be in the same order and according to the same rules as would have applied if the property had been the father's or the mother's or the husband's as the case may be, and such person had died intestate in respect thereof immediately after the intestate's death.

GENERAL PROVISIONS RELATING TO SUCCESSION

Full blood is always preferred to half blood. Heirs related to an intestate by full blood shall be preferred to heirs related by half blood, if the nature of the relationship is the same in every other respect.

Two persons said to be related to each other by full blood when they are descended from a common ancestor by the same wife, and by half blood when they are descended from a common ancestor but by different wives.

Similarly, two persons are said to be related to each other by uterine blood when they are descended from a common ancestress but by different husbands.

Here, "ancestor" includes the father and "ancestress" the mother.

MODE OF SUCCESSION OF TWO OR MORE HEIRS

If two or more heirs succeed together to the property of an intestate, they shall take the property-

- per capita and not per stripes except in the cases where the Hindu succession Act otherwise expressly provides for it.
- as tenants-in-common and not as joint tenants.

RIGHT OF CHILD IN WOMB

A child who was in the womb at the time of death of an intestate and who is subsequently born alive has the same right to inherit to the intestate as if he or she had been born before the death of the intestate, and the inheritance shall be deemed to vest in such a case with effect from the date of the death of the intestate.

PRESUMPTION IN CASES OF SIMULTANEOUS DEATHS

Where two persons have died in circumstances rendering it uncertain whether either of them, and if so which, survived the other, then for all purposes affecting succession to property, it shall be presumed, until the contrary is proved, that the younger survived the elder.

PREFERENTIAL RIGHT TO ACQUIRE PROPERTY IN CERTAIN CASES

Where, after the commencement of the Hindu Succession Act, interest in any immovable property of an intestate, or in any business carried on by him or her, whether solely or in conjunction with others, devolve upon to two or more heirs specified in class I of the Schedule, and any one of such heirs proposes to transfer his or her interest in the property or business, the other heirs shall have a preferential right to acquire the interest proposed to be transferred.

The consideration for which any interest in the property of the deceased may be transferred as the preferential right to acquire property shall, in the absence of any agreement between the parties, be determined by the court on application being made to it in this behalf, and if any person proposing to acquire the interest is not willing to acquire it for the consideration so determined, such person shall be liable to pay all costs of or incident to the application.

If there are two or more heirs specified in class I of the Schedule proposing to acquire any interest as the preferential right to acquire property, that heir who offers the highest consideration for the transfer shall be preferred.

Here, "court" means the court within the limits of whose jurisdiction the immovable property is situate or the business is carried on, and includes any other court which the State Government may, by notification in the Official Gazette, specify in this behalf.

DAUGHTERS CAN SUE AND CAUSE PARTITION OF DWELLING HOUSES

Prior to the passing of the Hindu Succession (Amendment) Act, 2005, the position was that where a Hindu intestate has left surviving him or her both male and female heirs specified in class I of the Schedule and his or her property includes a dwelling-house wholly occupied by members of his or her family, then subject to anything contained in the Hindu Succession Act, the right of any such female heir to claim partition of the dwelling-house did not arise until the male heirs choose to divide their respective shares therein; but the female heir was entitled to a right of residence therein. But it was subject to the condition that where such female heir was a daughter, she was entitled to a right of residence in the dwelling-house only if she was unmarried or had been deserted by or had separated from her husband or was a widow.

After the passing of the Hindu Succession (Amendment) Act, 2005 this provision of law has been omitted so now the female heir like the male coparceners can sue and cause partition of the dwelling house.

Prior to the passing of the Hindu Succession (Amendment) Act, 2005 the High court of Madras on section 23 of the Hindu Succession Act, 1956 in the case of intestate succession on special provisions respecting dwelling houses held that as per section 23 a female class I heir is disentitled to claim partition of 'dwelling house' when said house is wholly occupied by any one of class I heir and till male heir chooses to effect partition thereof. However, there is no bar on Court under section 23 to declare share of female heir but she can enforce her right for division of share in respect of said property only when contingency contemplated under section 23 is satisfied (Janakiammal v. Pushpa Leelavathi, [2003] 2 ILD 869 (Mad.)). So, earlier the position was that the daughter could go for the suit for declaration of her share in the dwelling house but now she can, being coparcener on equal footings as the son, can cause partition of the dwelling house and receive her share.

INHERITANCE RIGHTS OF REMARRIED WIDOW

Prior to the passing of Hindu Succession (Amendment) Act, 2005 certain widows remarrying were not able to inherit as widows. Any heir who was related to an intestate as the widow of a pre-deceased son, the widow of a pre-deceased son of a pre-deceased son or the widow of a brother was not entitled to succeed to the property of the intestate as such widow, if on the date the succession opens, she had re-married.

But by the passing of the Hindu Succession (Amendment) Act, 2005 this provision of law has also been omitted. The effect of this omission would be that the widows, being class I heirs as per the schedule of the Hindu Succession Act, 1956, would be entitled to inherit the property of her ex-husband irrespective of the fact that she has remarried after his death. This omission of the old section may promote widow re-marriages and their economic position would be highly strengthened.

DISQUALIFICATIONS FOR SUCCESSIONS IN CERTAIN CASES

Some of the persons are disqualified from succession as per law. These are:

Murderer disqualified: A person who commits murder or abets the commission of murder shall be disqualified from inheriting the property of the person murdered, or any other property in furtherance of the succession to which he or she committed or abetted the commission of the murder.

Convert's descendants disqualified: Where, before or after the commencement of Hindu Succession Act, a Hindu has ceased or ceases to be a Hindu by conversion to another religion, children born to him or her after such conversion and their descendants shall be disqualified from inheriting the property of any of their Hindu relatives, unless such children or descendants are Hindus at the time when the succession opens.

Succession when heir disqualified: If any person is disqualified from inheriting any property under the Hindu Succession Act, it shall devolve as if such person had died before the intestate.

Disease, defect, etc. does not to disqualify any person from succession. No person shall be disqualified from succeeding to any property on the ground of any disease, defect or deformity, or save as provided in the Hindu Succession Act, on any other ground whatsoever.

If an intestate has left no heir qualified to succeed to his or her property in accordance with the provisions of the Hindu Succession Act, such property shall devolve on the government; and the government shall take the property subject to all the obligations and liabilities to which an heir would have been subjected.

TESTAMENTARY SUCCESSION

Any Hindu may dispose of by will or other testamentary disposition any property, which is capable of being so disposed of by him or by her, in accordance with the provisions of the Indian Succession Act, 1925, or any other law for the time being in force and applicable to Hindus.

Here, the interest of a male Hindu in a Mitakshara coparcenary property or the interest of a member of a tarwad, tavazhi, illom, kutumba or kavaru in the property of the tarwad, tavazhi, illom, kutumba or kavaru shall, subject to anything contained in the Hindu Succession Act or in any other law for the time being in force, be deemed to be property capable of being disposed of by him or by her.

A Will is liable to be revoked or altered by the maker of it at any time when he is competent to dispose of his property by Will.

PERSON CAPABLE OF MAKING WILLS

Every person of sound mind not being a minor may dispose of his property by will. A married woman may dispose by will of any property which she could alienate by her own act during her life. Persons who are deaf or dumb or blind are not thereby incapacitated for making a will if they are able to know what they do by it. A person who is ordinarily insane may make a will during an interval in which he is of sound mind. No person can make a will while he is in such a state of mind, whether arising from intoxication or from illness or from any other cause, that he does not know what he is doing.

A father, whatever his age may be, may by will appoint a guardian or guardians for his child during minority.

WILL OBTAINED BY FRAUD, COERCION OR IMPORTUNITY

A Will or any part of a will, the making of which has been caused by fraud or coercion, or by such importunity as take away the free agency of the testator, is void.

WORDINGS OF WILL

It is not necessary that any technical words or terms of art be used in a will, but only that the wording be such that the intentions of the testator can be known therefrom. Where any word material to the full expression of the meaning has been omitted, it may be supplied by the context.

If the thing which the testator intended to bequeath can be sufficiently identified from the description of it given in the will, but some parts of the description do not apply, such parts of the description shall be rejected as erroneous, and the bequest shall take effect.

If a will mentions several circumstances as descriptive of the thing which the testator intends to bequeath, and there is any property of his in respect of which all those circumstances exist, the bequest shall be considered as limited to such property, and it shall not be lawful to reject any part of the description as erroneous, because the testator had other property to which such part of the description does not apply. In judging whether a case falls within this provision, any words which would be liable to rejection shall be deemed to have been struck out of the will.

The meaning of any clause in a will is to be collected from the entire instrument, and all its parts are to be construed with reference to each other.

General words may be understood in a restricted sense where it may be collected from the will that the testator meant to use them in a restricted sense, and words may be understood in a wider sense than that which they usually bear, where it may be collected from the other words of the will that the testator meant to use them in such wider sense.

Where a clause is susceptible of two meanings according to one of which it has some effect, and according to the other of which it can have none, the former shall be preferred.

No part of a will shall be rejected as destitute of meaning if it is possible to put a reasonable construction upon it.

If the same words occur in different parts of the same will, they shall be taken to have been used everywhere in the same sense, unless a contrary intention appears.

The intention of the testator shall not be set aside because it cannot take effect to the full extent, but effect is to be given to it as far as possible.

Where two clauses of gifts in a will are irreconcilable, so that they cannot possibly stand together, the last shall prevail.

A will or bequest not expressive of any definite intention is void for uncertainty.

The description contained in a will of property, the subject of gift, shall, unless a contrary intention appears by the will, be deemed to refer to and comprise the property answering that description at the death of the testator.

INHERITANCE

Inheritance is the actual act of receiving property or assets from a deceased person. It is the outcome or result of the succession process. The term "inheritance" is often used interchangeably with "legacy" or "bequest," although these terms can have slightly different connotations:

- **Legacy:** Traditionally refers to a gift of personal property (e.g., money, jewelry, specific items) in a will.
- **Bequest:** Similar to a legacy, often used for gifts of personal property, but can sometimes include real property as well.

Under Hindu Law, inheritance refers to the transfer of property and rights from a deceased person (the "propositus") to their legal heirs. The rules of inheritance are primarily governed by the Hindu Succession Act, 1956, as amended.

Key aspects of Hindu inheritance:

- **Intestate Succession:** This applies when a person dies without a valid will. The property is distributed among the heirs based on their relationship to the deceased and specific classes defined in the Act.
- **Testamentary Succession:** This applies when a person leaves a valid will (testament) specifying how their property should be distributed. The will must be executed according to legal requirements and can be challenged in court if it is found to be invalid.
- **Classes of Heirs:** The Act divides heirs into various classes, with Class I heirs having priority over those in subsequent classes. The order of succession generally follows a descending order of proximity to the deceased.
- **Equal Rights for Daughters:** A significant amendment in 2005 granted daughters equal inheritance rights to sons in both self-acquired and ancestral property.
- **Coparcenary Property:** This refers to joint family property held by male members of a Hindu undivided family (HUF). The rights of coparceners to inherit coparcenary property are governed by specific rules.
- **Exclusion and Disinheritance:** Certain individuals, such as those who have murdered the deceased, may be excluded from inheriting. The deceased may also disinherit specific heirs through a valid will.

FOUNDATIONS OF INHERITANCE IN MUSLIM LAW

- **Divine Origin:** Islamic inheritance law is rooted in the Quran and the Sunnah (teachings and practices of Prophet Muhammad), making it a fundamental aspect of Islamic jurisprudence (fiqh).
- **Justice and Equity:** The system aims to ensure a just and equitable distribution of the deceased's estate among their rightful heirs, upholding the principles of fairness and social responsibility.
- **Family Preservation:** The law prioritizes the protection and support of the deceased's family, particularly women and children, through the inheritance process.

Key Concepts

- **Sharers (Ashabah):** These heirs have fixed shares in the estate, regardless of its size. Key sharers include:
  - **Husband:**
    - If the deceased wife has children (or a child of a son, how low soever): The husband inherits 1/4 (one-fourth) of her estate.
    - If the deceased wife has no children (and no child of a son, how low soever): The husband inherits 1/2 (one-half) of her estate.
  - **Wife:**
    - 1/8 of husband's estate if he has children.
    - 1/4 of husband's estate if he has no children.
  - **Children:** Sons generally inherit twice the share of daughters.
  - **Parents:**
    - **Mother:** Primarily 1/6 or 1/3, depending on the presence of children or multiple siblings.
    - **Father:** Primarily 1/6 (if there are children) plus the residue, or just the residue (if no children).
  - **Grandparents:** Inherit in specific circumstances when parents are not alive.

- **Residuaries (Asabah):** These heirs inherit the remaining estate after the shares of the sharers are distributed. They typically include:
  - Sons
  - Daughters
  - Brothers
  - Sisters
  - Nephews
  - Nieces
  - More distant relatives
- **Wills:** A Muslim can bequeath up to one-third of their estate through a will. However, the will cannot disinherit compulsory heirs (sharers).
- **Exclusion:** Certain individuals, such as those who have killed the deceased, may be excluded from inheritance.
- **Disinheritance:** While generally prohibited for compulsory heirs, there are limited exceptions.
- **Succession to Property:** The rules of succession may differ based on whether the property is ancestral or self-acquired.

MUSLIM LAW

MARRIAGE UNDER MUSLIM LAW OR NIKAH – A PRE-ISLAMIC APPROACH

In the pre-Islamic Arab there was no well defined form or nature of marriage. It was only a sought of sexual union more or less which can be brought into the category of prostitution, adultery or polyandry. Abdur Rahim pointed out at the three major forms of marriage in the pre-Islamic Arab –

- The first among these types of marriage was where the husband used to send his wife to some noble person and have intercourse with him. After the wife got conceived by this person, she used to return back to her husband and give birth to the child. The desire to get the noble offspring was one of the reason for this type of marriage.
- Another class of marriage was where many a persons, less than ten, used to have sexual intercourse with the women. After the women was conceived she used to deliver the child to the father.
- In the third form of marriage, intercourse was done by several persons with a particular class of women who were more or less prostitutes and used to fix a flag at their tents. When such a woman delivered an offspring the paternity of the child was determined by physionomist.

The difference between the ordinary prostitution and the last two discussed forms of marriage was that in ordinary prostitution the paternity cannot be established lawfully or customarily but it was not true in the above mentioned two forms of marriage. Along with these forms of marriage were few other types of marriages prevalent at that time like Muta (temporary) marriages, purchasing the girl for fixed sum from her parents or guardians and marriage with the real sisters as was allowed at that time (one prevalent custom in pre-Islamic Arab was that a person could marry two real sisters at one and the same time.

MARRIAGE – DEFINITION AND NATURE OF

Various Muslim scholars have given the definition of marriage in their own manner and the text related with this religion also provide an outlook of marriage. Few of them are –

- **Hedaya** – "Nikah in its primitive sense, means carnal conjunction. Some have said that it signifies conjunction generally. In the language of the law it implies a particular contract used for the purpose of legalizing generation."
- **Justice Mahmood** – "Marriage among Mohammedans is not a sacrament, but purely a civil contract."
- **Abdur Rahim** – "The Mohammedan jurists regard the institution of marriage as partaking both of the nature of Ibadat or devotional acts and Muamlat or dealings among men."
- **M.U.S. Jung** – "Marriage though essentially a contract is also a devotional act, its objects are the right of enjoyment, procreation of children and the regulation of social life in the interest of the society."
- **Ameer Ali** – "Marriage is an institution ordained for the protection of society, and in order that human beings may guard themselves from foulness and unchastity."

Analyzing these above-mentioned definitions of marriage it becomes necessary here to judge the nature of a Muslim marriage. There exists controversy over the nature of Muslim marriage. Few scholars treat it as purely a civil contract whereas others analyze it something more than a mere civil contract like sacrament. The observation of Mr. Justice Mohammad in *Abdur Kadir* v. *Salima* (1886) All 149 is significant in this regard where he has taken the Muslim marriage as purely a civil contract. The judgment reads as –

"Marriage among Muhammadans is not a sacrament, but purely a civil contract; and though it is solemnized generally with recitation of certain verses from the Koran, yet the Muhammadan law does not positively prescribe any service peculiar to the occasion. That it is a civil contract is manifest from the various ways and circumstances in and under which marriages are contracted or presumed to have been contracted. And though a civil contract, it is not positively prescribed to be reduced to writing, but the validity and operation of the whole are made to depend upon the declaration or proposal of the one, and the acceptance or consent of the other of the contracting parties, or of their natural and legal guardians before competent and sufficient witnesses; as also upon the restrictions imposed, and certain of the conditions required to be abided by according to the peculiarity of the case.

That (the above) is an accurate summary of the Muhammadan law is shown by the best authorities, and Mr. Bailie, at page 4 of his Digest, relying upon the texts of the Kanz, the Kifayah and the Inayah, has well summarized the law; 'Marriage is a contract which has for its design or object the right of enjoyment and the procreation of children. But it was also instituted for the solace of life, and is one of the prime or original necessities of man. It is therefore lawful in extreme old age after hope of offspring has ceased, and even in the last or death illness. The pillars of marriage, as of other contracts, are Ejab-o-Kubool, or declaration or acceptance. The first speech, from whichever side it may proceed, is the declaration, and the other the acceptance.

The Hedaya lays down the same rule as to the constitution of the marriage contract, and Mr. Hamilton has rightly translated the original text: "Marriage is contracted – that is to say, is effected and legally confirmed – by means of declaration and consent, both expressed in the preterite."

For Dower in the same judgment Justice Mohammad pointed out –

"Dower, under the Muhammadan law, is a sum of money or other property promised by the husband to be paid or delivered to the wife in consideration of the marriage... the dower of the Muhammadan law bears a strong resemblance to the *denatio propter nuptias* of the Romans which has subsisted in the English law under the name of marriage settlement. In this sense and in no other can dower under the Muhammadan law be regarded as the consideration for intercourse, and if the authors of the Arabic textbooks of Muhammadan law have compared it to price in the contract of sale, it is simply because marriage is a civil contract under that law, and the sale is the typical contract which Muhammadan jurists are accustomed to refer to in illustrating the incidents of other contracts by analogy."

On the other hand in *Anis Begam* v. *Mohammad Istefa* (1933) 55 All 743 Sir Shah Sulaiman C.J. observed "marriage is not regarded as mere civil contract but a religions sacrament (too)". Great scholar Tahir Mahmood also says that the marriage among Muslim is a "solemn pact" (Mithaq-e-ghalid) which takes the form of a contract (Aqd). Apart from this proceeding to the religious aspect it is said that prophet believed marriage to be equal to Jehad (holy war). Not solemnizing marriage by a fit person is sinful and moreover it is sunna. Traditional aspect of marriage brings out the views "He who marries completes half his religion, it now rest with him to complete the other half by leading a virtuous life in constant fear of God." Moreover "there is no mockery in Islam."

"There are three persons whom the almighty himself has undertaken to help first, he who seeks to buy his freedom; second, he who marries with a view to secure his chastity; and third, he who fights in the cause of God."

"Whoever marries woman in order that he may retain his eyes – God Putteth a blessedness in her for him and in him for her."

So, analyzing these various view it can be said that a Muslim marriage is not merely a civil contract as said by Justice Mahmood rather it also has a sacramental touch in it but that sacramental touch is quite different as it exists in the case of a Hindu marriage. Even Justice Mahmood in his observations relying upon the Baillie's view has accepted that marriage was also instituted for the solace of life.

CONDITIONS OF A VALID MARRIAGE

For a valid Muslim marriage there are few conditions that needs to be fulfilled and they are –

- Offer by one party to the marriage (Ijab)
- Acceptance to that offer by the other party (Qubul)
- Presence of two witnesses if the parties to the marriage are Hanafis. However, in case of Shias no witness is required.
- Adult age or puberty of the parties. The adult age talked of here should not be understood to be the statutory majority age of the parties i.e. 21 years for males and 18 years for females. (Baligh)
- Soundness of mind of the parties. (Rashid)
- The wordings that are used while contracting the marriage should be clear and unambiguous.
- The offer and acceptance to the marriage must be made in the one and same meeting.

As regards the offer and acceptance by the parties, Fyzee points "the offer and acceptance may be made by the parties or by their agents, if both are competent. In case of legal incompetency, like minority or unsoundness of mind, the guardians may validly enter into a contract of marriage on behalf of their wards."

EFFECTS OF A VALID MARRIAGE

The effect of a valid marriages can be illustrated as follows –

- Legitimacy of sexual intercourse and children.
- Entitlement of wife to her dower.
- Power of making reasonable restraint to wife's movement gets vested with the husband.
- Establishment of mutual rights of inheritance.
- Prohibitions with respect to marriage according to rules of affinity comes into operation.
- Observing Iddat becomes compulsory for the wife after the death of the husband or on the dissolution of marriage.
- In case of agreement between the parties entered into at the time of marriage or subsequently; it becomes obligatory on the parties to follow the stipulation in the agreement and the same can be enforced subject to the consistency with the provisions and policy of the law.
- By virtue of marriage the husband does not get any right, title or interest in the property of wife and vice versa.

There are certain conditions that can be validly appended with a marriage contract. Few of them are–

- The guardians of the minor spouses agree that the wife could divorce her husband in case he contracts second marriage without her consent
- That the wife would be entitled to separate maintenance in case the relations between husband and wife becomes stringent.
- That the wife could ask for divorce if the husband forsake Malak-O-Badar community or is expelled from it.
- An agreement to the effect that the wife shall live with her parents and in case of dissension with the husband, he would be liable to pay monthly allowance to her while she lives with her parents. But, where it was agreed that the husband would be living in the house of his in laws; it was found to be bad in law.
- An agreement to the effect that the wife could validly leave her husband house if he is found to be guilty of misbehaviour or cruelty to her or her parents or her relatives.

Besides, there are many other conditions that can be validly imposed at the time of marriage, as it is believed to be a civil contract. On the other hand an agreement for future separation of husband and wife, an agreement whereby the wife was allowed to visit immoral places, an agreement divesting the power of the husband to divorce, an agreement negotiating the mutual right of inheritance or the right of dower and maintenance to the wife are all found to be bad in law. However, there cannot be any exhaustive list of such aforesaid legal or illegal conditions.

CLASSIFICATION OF MARRIAGE

Muslim marriage can be classified under three heads *viz.* – (*i*) Valid (*ii*) Void, and (*iii*) Irregular

- **Valid marriage** – A marriage that conforms all the legal requirements is a valid marriage and no prohibition should be there affecting the parties to marriage in such a case. The prohibitions as said here may be permanent or the temporary. Where the prohibitions are permanent the marriage is void and where it is temporary it comes within the ambit of irregular marriage. A valid marriage conforming all the legal requirements is called "Sahih" or "Correct".
- **Void marriage** – A marriage having no legal results is called a void marriage. So, a marriage contracted in violation of the rules of blood relationship, affinity or fosterage or a marriage with the wife of another person are few examples of void marriages. No mutual rights or obligations emerge out of a *Batil* or void marriage. As such there exist no rights like right to dower or right of inheritance or right to enjoy the company of other party in case of a void marriage. The children born out of a void marriage are not legitimate according to Muslim law.
- **Irregular marriage** – Where the unlawfulness in a marriage is relative in nature rather than an absolute one as in the case of void marriages, the marriage comes within the category of irregular marriage. A marriage in the absence of witnesses, a marriage with a woman observing Iddat, a marriage prohibited due to difference of religion, a marriage with two sisters at the same time and a marriage contracted with the fifth wife are all irregular form of marriage. According to the Shia law all these form of irregular marriage are void

for the reason that there is no difference between the void and irregular marriage in Shia law. There are only two classification of marriage in Shia law *viz.* - valid or void. The children born out of an irregular marriage are legitimate and owe the right of inheritance but this right of inheritance does not exist between the husband and wife. If the marriage is consummated the wife becomes entitled to dower and observance of Iddat for three menstrual courses becomes compulsory for her.

For regularizing the irregular marriage certain impediments are needed to be removed. For example, a marriage solemnized in the absence of witnesses becomes regularized on consummation; similarly a marriage without free consent becomes regular if it is ratified with free consent. More so, marriage with the non-Muslim becomes regular if the party converts to the religion that makes the marriage valid. A marriage with the fifth wife becomes regular if the number of wives reduces to four by way of divorce or death of any of the wife. These are all temporary impediments that can be removed by one way or other but certain irregularities are of permanent nature which cannot be cured. Within this category lies the marriage within the relationship of consanguinity, affinity and fosterage, marriage with the wife of another person that renders the marriage void *ab initio*.

MUTA OR TEMPORARY MARRIAGE

Among the Muslim there is a special form of marriage called Muta or temporary marriage. This kind of marriage is lawful among Shias according to the views of Wilson. It is a contract of marriage for a limited period which may be for a term of year, a month, a day or even a part of a day. After the expiration of the agreed period this type of marriage dissolves by itself and in case no time limit is agreed upon the marriage is presumed to be permanent one. There is no limit to wives in case of Muta marriage as in the case of ordinary marriage where the ceiling of four applies. The children born out of a Muta marriage are legitimate and owe the right of inheritances from the father. This is what distinguishes this marriage from a legalized prostitution. The agreement of Muta becomes void in the absence of specification of the amount of dower. Where there is no express agreement for the purpose of inheritance from the other party or for the purpose of maintenance then in such a case no such right can be claimed by the aggrieved party.

There are two essential conditions of a valid Muta marriage. Firstly – period and secondly – dower or Mahr. As said above the period in case of temporary or Muta marriage can be a year or a mouth or a day or even a part of the day. In case this period remains unfixed the marriage is presumed to be permanent. As the Hyderabad High Court in *Shahzada Qanum* v. *Fakher Jung* AIR 1953 Hyd. 6 observed that where the period has not been fixed either intentionally or unintentionally; in both case permanent Nikah would be the result.

As regards the dower in Muta marriage, it is necessary that such dower should be specified and in the absence of any specification in this regard the marriage becomes void. This right of the wife arises with the consummation of marriage and the whole of the amount can be claimed by her subject to her renouncement of this right before the end of the fixed period.

DIFFERENCE BETWEEN MUTA AND NIKAH

It becomes necessary here to differentiate between the Muta and Nikah. A Muta marriage is temporary in nature whereas Nikah is something permanent. Muta is contracted for the sake of pleasure, on the other side Nikah is a socio-religious union. Muta is lawful among the Shias while Nikah is observed by Shias as well as Sunnis both. Muta is a temporary arrangement and the fixed period is its essential requirement, whereas Nikah is contracted for the lifetime. Fixation of period in case of Nikah gives it the status of Muta. In case of Muta if the dower is unspecified it renders the marriage as void for the reason that it is *quid pro quo* but in case of Nikah, the dower may be implied if not specified. If a Muta marriage remains unconsummated the wife shall be entitled to one half dower only but in case of Nikah she is always entitled to full dower. There is no minimum limit of dower in case of Muta but according to the Hanafi law this minimum limit is ten Dirhams. Muta marriage gets terminated on the expiry of the fixed period but in case of Nikah there is no such automatic termination of marriage. In case of Muta the marriage can be terminated even before the fixed period by paying Hibba-I-muddat i.e. gift for the unexpected period but in Nikah no such question arises. Divorce is not recognized in Muta marriages whereas Nikah can be dissolved by way of divorce. According to Shia law there is no provision for maintenance of wife for the reason that she is not regarded as dependent but Nikah makes the wife entitled to maintenance. Reciprocal right of inheritance between the husband and wife does not exist in case of Muta marriage whereas such right exist in case of Nikah. In case of Muta marriage there is no limit fixed for the number of wives whereas in Nikah the number of wife should not exceed four.

PROHIBITIONS FOR MUSLIM MARRIAGE

While solemnizing a marriage there are certain prohibitions for the Muslims and according to Tyabji there are nine such grounds as mentioned below –

- A Muslim cannot marry within consanguinity i.e. with his own ascendants or descendants or his father's or mother's descendants and with the siblings of any ascendant.
- Affinity is another prohibition for Muslims so it is not lawful for a Muslim to marry ascendants or descendants of his wife and the wife of any ascendant or descendant.
- Another prohibition is with regard to fosterage. It is prohibited under Muslim law to marry within certain limits of fosterage for example a man is not allowed to marry his foster mother or foster sister.
- If there exists some unlawful conjunction then prohibition applies in such a case. Such unlawful conjunction may be because of two things *viz.* – Number or Relationship between the co-wives. As regards numbers a Muslim male may marry any number of wife subject to the maximum limit of four but a Muslim women can be punished under section 494 of the Indian Penal Code if she contracts a second marriage while her first husband is alive. It is significant to note that the Supreme Court recently in *Lily Thomas* v. *Union of India* (2000) 6 SCC 224 has observed that right to plurality of marriage in Islamic law is subject to certain conditions precedent and one such condition is the capacity to do justice between the co-wives. So, it is unjustified to say that a convert is entitled to practice bigamy irrespective of the subsistence of his marriage under the personal law by which he was governed before conversion. On the similar lines, it is prohibited to have two wives at the same time if they are related to each other by consanguinity, affinity or fosterage such that they would not have married each other lawfully if they were belonging to different sexes. So, one inference here can be drawn that marriage with the two sisters at the same time is void as held in *Azizunnisa* v. *Karimunnisa* (1895) 23 Cal 130. However, the Chief Court of Oudh observed such marriage as irregular only.
- The prohibition has also been made with regard to Iddat due to the fact that the object of Iddat lies in determining whether the woman is pregnant or not and in case she is pregnant, to determine the paternity of the child. So, there is prohibition for remarrying or marrying to a widow, a divorcee or a woman who has conceived due to illicit intercourse during the period of Iddat. This period is 4 months and 10 days in case of death of the husband if the wife is not pregnant and if the wife is pregnant then till the delivery of the child. Where the marriage has been consummated and is dissolved by way of divorce the period of Iddat is three menstrual cycles.
- The marriage of the husband with the divorced wife has also been prohibited subject to certain conditions These conditions are that the woman should lawfully marry to second husband and there should be consummation of such marriage. Thereafter this marriage should be dissolved and the Iddat should be observed by the wife.
- Another prohibition has been made with regard to religion. A Muslim man can marry a Muslim woman or a Kitabiya but vice versa is not true i.e. a Muslim woman can marry a Muslim only and exclusively according to Hanafi law. As such it is not lawful to marry an idolatress or a fire worshipper for a Muslim man and a Muslim woman cannot even marry with a Kitabiya. According to Shia law it is not possible to marry a non-Muslim in the form of Nikah but a Muta marriage can be contracted by a Shia male with a Kitabiya including a fire worshipper.
- Supervenient prohibition is another form of restriction imposed in case of marriage. So, a marriage becomes invalid if any party to the marriage becomes a five worshipper, or an idolater or the husband gets baptized.
- Furthermore, if a man has gone to Haj (Pilgrimage) and has entered the sacred abode of Kaba after dressing up in Ahram (Pilgrim's dress), he may not contract a marriage according to Ithna, Ashari and Shafai law. As per the Shia law a deliberate violation of this rule restrains the man and woman from becoming husband and wife for ever.

One ancillary prohibition lies where the parties to the marriage are unequal. So, the marriage should be solemnized with a person of equal status. According to Hanafi law, such status of equality is to be seen with respect to Nasb (family or descent), Islam, profession, freedom (free or slave), honesty, means and potency.

OPTION OF PUBERTY UNDER MUSLIM LAW

Option of puberty is called Khayar-Ul-Bulugh and it is the power to repudiate the marriage on the attainment of puberty by the concerned party if it has been contracted while he or she was minor by his lawful guardian other than the father or paternal grandfather. As per the Shia law if the marriage is contracted in such a manner while the party was minor and it is not ratified on the attainment of puberty then the marriage becomes totally ineffective.

According to Hanafi law if the minor's marriage is contracted by the paternal grandfather the option of puberty does not exist there except in the cases where the marriage was contracted fraudulently or negligently or the dower fixed was improper or there was inequality in the status of minor.

RESTITUTION OF CONJUGAL RIGHT UNDER MUSLIM LAW

In *Munshee Bazloom Raheem* v. *Shumsunnisa Begum* (1867) 11 MIA 551 the restitution of conjugal rights was discussed in detail. Where a party to the marriage has left the company of other spouse without any reasonable cause or has neglected the performance of marital obligation on his or her part the other party can sue him in the Civil Court for the restitution of conjugal rights. But this right is subject to certain condition and defenses. For the wife the defenses may be of various kind like the treatment of the husband is cruel to her or there is neglect of performance of marital obligations by the husband or the marriage is irregular or the husband has been outcaste by his community. In *Itwari* v. *Asghari* AIR 1960 All 684 the Allahabad High Court elucidated the concept of cruelty in the following manner –

"and that the test of cruelty is based on the universal and humanitarian standards, that is to say, conduct of the husband which would cause such bodily or mental pain as to endanger the wife's safety and health..."

Cruelty includes actual violence so as to endanger personal health safety of wife or apprehension of the same, a treatment of lesser degree than actual violence jeopardizing the health or sanctity of wife, throwing ill reputation to wife and false allegations, abusive language, second marriage of the husband causing unbearable conditions to the first wife.

Where the matrimonial obligations have not been performed by the husband the wife can deny his restitution of conjugal right. Payment of dower, proper accommodation separate from the husband's relations and maintenance according to her status of living are all included in the marital obligation of the husband. Where the prompt amount of dower has not been paid a Muslim lady can validly refuse to cohabit in case the marriage is not consummated. There may be conditional restitution in certain cases as held in *Anees Begum* v. *Muhammad Istefa* (1933) 55 All 743 where the wife alleged the husband of keeping mistress in the same house and treating her cruelly. It was observed by Sir Sulaiman, C.J –

"I think that the wife is fully justified in refusing to go and live with her husband so long as there is no undertaking not to keep any mistress in the house; she can go to live with him only if a separate house is given to her. Further, I think that in order to protect her safety it is necessary that she could have the option of keeping one female servant and one male servant, according to her choice, in the house..."

In the landmark judgment of *Mohammad Ahmed Khan* v. *Shah Bano* (1985) 2 SCC 556 it was observed that as per explanation to the second proviso to section 125 (3) of the Code of Criminal Procedure the wife has been conferred with the right to refuse to live with her husband if the husband contracts another marriage for the reason that secular law overrides the personal law.

DOWER OR MAHR

There are various definition of Mahr or dower given by different scholars. Few of them are –

- **Bailie** – The property which is incumbent on a husband either by reason of its being named in the contract of marriage, or by virtue of the contract itself... Dower is not the exchange or consideration given by the man to the woman for entering into the contract; but an effect to the contract imposed by the law on the husband as a token of respect for its subject, the woman.
- **Abdur Rahim (On the basis of Hedaya)** – It is either a sum of money or other form of property to which the wife becomes entitled by marriage... it is an obligation imposed by law on the husband as a mark of respect for the wife... (This definition has been adopted by Mulla also.)
- **Tyabji** – Mahr or dower is a sum that becomes payable by the husband to the wife on marriage, either by agreement between the parties, or by operation of law.

In *Abdul Kadir* v. *Salima* (1886) 8 All 149 Justice Mahmood observed dower as –

"Dower, under the Muhammadan law, is a sum of money or other property promised by the husband to be paid or delivered to the wife in consideration of the marriage, and even where no dower is expressly fixed or mentioned at the marriage ceremony, the law confers the right of dower upon the wife as a necessary effect of marriage. To use the language of the Hedaya, 'the payment of dower is enjoined by the law merely as a token of respect for its object (the woman), wherefore the mention of it is not absolutely essential to the validity of a marriage; and, for the same reason, a marriage is also valid, although a man were to engage in the contract on the special condition that should be no dower".

In the Arabic textbooks many authors of Mohammedan law have compared dower with the price for contract of sale. Controverting this view Sir Shah Sulaiman in *Anees Begum* v. *Mohd. Istefa* ILR 1933 All 743 and in *Wajid Ali Khan* v. *Shaukat Ali Khan* (1912) 15 Oudh cases 127 observed –

"It is quite obvious that the analogy of sale cannot be carried too far. The marriage cannot be regarded as purely a sale of the person by the wife in consideration for the payment of dower."

KINDS OF DOWER

Under Muslim law dower can be classified into two types *viz.* (*i*) specified dower (*ii*) unspecified dower. Further, specified dower has been classified into (*i*) Prompt dower and (*ii*) Deferred dower.

- **Specified dower**: – Where the amount of dower has been settled by the parties at the time of marriage or after the marriage then this type of dower is called specified dower. Where the male is minor it is for his father to fix such amount. In such a case according to Hanafi law the father may not be held personally liable for the dower but according to Shia law the father is personally liable for the amount of dower. The husband becomes bound to pay the amount of dower irrespective of the fact that it is beyond his reach or excessive. However, the excessive amount may be slashed to a reasonable sum in Oudh. As said above specified dower is further classified into prompt and deferred, it is to be conceived in mind that prompt dower is one which is payable on demand by the wife whereas deferred dower is payable on the dissolution of marriage either by way of death of the husband or by divorce. While settling the amount of dower a part of the dower may be prompt and the remaining amount may be deferred. The prompt part of the dower can be demanded and realized by the wife at any time before or after consummation but it is not possible for the wife to demand deferred dower in such a manner. Where the amount of prompt and deferred part of dower remains unsettled then as per the Shia law the whole of the amount of dower is prompt but Sunni law holds that the amount of prompt dower in such a case is to be determined in accordance with the custom, status of parties and the amount of settled dower in the marriage.

  Prompt dower or *Mahr-I-Muajjal* can be understood in its two aspects *viz.* the time factor and the quantum factor. "Prompt" although stands for "immediately on demand" or "at the time of marriage" or "at any time before the consummation of marriage" or "after consummation whenever demand is made for the same" but in practice rarely we find the cases where the dower is paid promptly. Wife can refuse the conjugal rights if prompt dower is not paid on demand. Where the marriage has not been consummated a suit for the restitution of conjugal rights can be successfully resisted by the wife. In case the marriage has been consummated a conditional decree subject to the payment of dower can be passed by the Court. On the death of the husband prompt dower can be charged from the estate of the deceased.

- **Unspecified dower**: Where the dower has not been fixed at the time of marriage or after that, it is settled keeping in view the social status of the family of the wife and her personal qualification and such a form of dower is called unspecified dower. This type of dower is called Mahr-*Ul-Misl* and the age of the wife, beauty, intellect and virtue are few things that are to be borne in mind while deciding it, as Hedaya suggest. A significant thing to note here is that although dower may be unspecified or unsettled yet it is obligatory on the part of the husband to pay the dower for the reason that the wife can claim the implied dower which is also called proper dower or customary dower. The rule of estoppel is not applicable to her. However, as per the *Ithana* Ashari law an adult wife is eligible to waive the requirement of dower.

As regards the subject matter of dower it is to be borne in mind that it can be a sum of money or property and even personal services and other things. Teaching of *Koran* has been recognized as a dower under Muslim personal law. According to Muslim jurists any thing that falls within the ambit of *Mall* has been recognized as Mahr or Dower. As such the profits arising from land or business, debt due to husband, choses-in-action, insurance policies, the sale proceeds of some thing and personal services of husband are all valid dower according to the Muslim Law.

For the amount of dower, in the Hanafi Law the minimum dower is ten dirhams which is equivalent to ` 5-6 after the devaluation whereas under Malikis law it is three dirhams which becomes one Rupee fifty Paise and two rupees after devaluation. Under Shia and Shafis law there is no fixed minimum amount of dower.

There exists no limit to the maximum dower to be fixed under Sunni law but under the Shia law the tendency is not to fix an amount higher than 500 dirham which is equal to ₹ 100 approximately. This is the amount that prophet Mohammed fixed as dower for is beloved daughter Fatima, the wife of Ali.

Where the marriage has been consummated and is dissolved by death then in case of regular marriage whole of the specified dower and if it is unspecified then the proper dower is payable. But, in case of irregular marriage the specified or proper dower whichever is less becomes payable. Where the marriage is not consummated and is dissolved by the act of the party then in case of regular marriage when divorce is given by the husband the half of the specified dower is payable and if it is unspecified then the present of three articles is required. In case it is the wife who has given divorce then no dower is payable. Where the marriage is irregular then also no dower is payable irrespective of the fact that it is the wife or husband who has given divorce.

In the celebrated case of Hamira Bibi v. Zubaida Bibi (1916) 43 IA 294 the Privy Council observed that a widow under the Muslim law has the right to retain possession of the estate of her deceased husband against unpaid dower.

In the same case, it was further held:

> "When a widow is allowed to take possession of her husband's estate in order to satisfy her dower debt with the income thereof, it is either on the basis of some understanding as to the conditions on which she should hold the property, or on no understanding. If there is an agreement, express or implied, that she should not be entitled to claim any sum in excess of her actual dower, she must abide by its terms. But where there is no such understanding, and a claim is made as in the present case, the question arises whether, on equitable considerations, she should not be allowed some reasonable compensation, not only for the labour and responsibility imposed on her for the proper preservation and management of the estate, but also for forbearing to insist on her strict legal right to exact payment of her dower on the death of her husband."

It was observed in this case that a widow couldn't be made liable to account for the profits of the estate without being allowed reasonable compensation; this compensation was allowed in the form of interest upon the dower.

As regards the transferability and heritability of the widow's right of retention, there exists plethora of conflicting judicial opinions over the issue. In the case of *Azizullah* v. *Ahmad* (1885) 7 All. 353 it was held that this right of the widow to retain the property of the husband is a heritable right. Similar opinion was expressed in *Ali Buksh* v. *Allahabad* (1910) 32 All. 551, *Amir Hasan* v. *Mohd. Nazir Hussain* (1932) 54 All. 499, *Mir Vaheed Ali* v. *Rashid Beg* AIR 1951 Bom. 22. However, in *Muzzafar Ali Khan* v. *Parbati* (1907) 29 All. 640, the High Court of Allahabad held that the right is not heritable in these cases.

DOWER *vis-à-vis* MAINTENANCE

Under Muslim law it is the divorce or death which is the farthest point to which payment of dower can be postponed. The payment cannot be deferred beyond it. So the question that arises here is that is it the dower which is to be regarded as an amount payable by husband to the wife on divorce. This question has given rise to a number of controversies. Answering to the question the Supreme Court in *Bai Tahira* v. *Ali Hussain* (1979) 2 SCC 316 held that Mahr or Dower is the amount payable under customary or personal law on divorce as pointed out in section 127(3)(*b*) of the Code of Criminal Procedure. Justice Krishna Iyer stated as "payment of Mahr money as a customary discharge, is within the cognizance of that provision".

Replying to the same question in *Fuzlunbi* v. *K. Khader Vali* (1980) 4 SCC 125 in negative the Supreme Court conveyed an altogether different impression. Justice Krishna Iyer stated as, "Maybe somehow the masculine obsession of jurisprudence linked up this promise or payment as a consolidated equivalent of maintenance after divorce. May be, some legislatures might have taken it in that light, but the law is to be as the law enacted. The language of Section 127(3)(*b*) appears to suggest that payment of the sum and the divorce should be essentially parts of the same transaction so as to make one the consideration for the other. Such customary divorce on payment of a sum of money among the so-called lower castes are not uncommon. At any rate the payment of money contemplated by Section 127(3)(*b*) should be so linked with divorce as to become payable only in the event of the divorce."

Justice Krishna Iyer further remarked that, "The quintessence of Mahr, whether it is prompt or deferred is clearly not a contemplated quantification of a sum of money in lieu of maintenance on divorce. Indeed dower focuses on marital happiness and is an incident of conjugal joy. Divorce is farthest from the thought of the bride and the bridegroom when Mahr is promised. Dower may be prompt, which is payable during marriage and cannot therefore be a recompense for divorce..... Mahr as understood in Muslim law cannot under any circumstances be considered as consideration for divorce or a payment made in lieu of connubial relationship."

In *Mohammed Ahmad Khan* v. *Shah Bano Begum* (1985) 2 SCC 556 the Supreme Court observed that Mahr was not the amount which was payable by the husband to wife on divorce. The Apex Court was of the view that Mahr is the amount which is payable at the time of dissolution of marriage by death or by divorce could not lead to the conclusion that the amount is payable on divorce. Divorce may be believed to be the convenient point of time so as to identify the time at which it is payable. But the expression "on divorce" as used in section 127 leads to meaning that payment is not occasioned by the divorce. The argument that Mahr is the sum payable to the wife as a consideration of marriage is opposite to the contention that it is the amount payable in consideration of divorce. Divorce leads to the dissolution of marriage. As such the amount which is payable as a consideration of the marriage can not be regarded as the amount payable in consideration of divorce. Besides, the dower is regarded as the amount paid by the husband to the wife as a token of respect wholly rebuts the averment that it is the amount payable on divorce. So, the Court was of the view that the amount, which is paid to the wife as a token of respect, cannot be the sum payable "on divorce". The Court stated as:

> "Though *Bai Tahira* is correctly decided, an error has crept into the judgment. There is a statement at p. 321 (SCC, para 11) that 'payment of Mahr-money as a customary discharge, is within the cognizance of that provision'. We have taken the view that Mahr, not being payable on divorce does not fall within the meaning of that provision."

The Court very well had in mind that simply by divorcing dower from divorce would not meet the constitutional objective of economic justice to that one individual namely the destitute divorcee. It's objective lies in removing an obstacle to a maintenance claim for divorcee that would maintain her in fact. The Court also observed that the introduction of the provision contained in section 127(3)(*b*) may have been because of the misconception that dower is the sum payable "on divorce". But it does not lead to the inference that the amount which is payable as a mark of respect for the wife would convert into an amount which is payable on divorce.

To overrule the judgment of *Mohd. Ahmad Khan* v. *Shah Bano Begum* (1985) 2 SCC 556, 572 parliament passed the Muslim Women (Protection of Rights on Divorce) Act, 1986 which is often called the sequel to the Shah Bano decision. Section 3 of the Act hits the ruling of the Shah Bano case and clause 1 (*c*) of this section states as:

"Mahr or other properties of Muslim woman to be given to her at the time of divorce:

(1) Notwithstanding anything contained in any other law for the time being in force, a divorced woman shall be entitled to - (*c*) an amount equal to the sum of Mahr or dower agreed to be paid to her at the time of her marriage or at any time thereafter according to Muslim law."

Muslim Women (Protection of Rights on Divorce) Act, 1986: - About the applicability of this Act it has been held in *Daniel Latifi* v. *Union of India*, (2001) 7 SCC 740 that this Act is not applicable to deserted or separated Muslim women or to a Muslim women whose marriage was solemnized under Special Marriage Act, 1954 or whose marriage was dissolved either under Indian Divorce Act, 1869 or Special Marriage Act, 1954. In the same case it was further held that so as to find out the rights of divorced women the starting point is the Shah Bano case (1985) 2 SCC 556 and not the original text or any other material. Muslim Women (Protection of Rights on Divorce) Act 1986 actually codifies the law as stated in Shah Bano case. Where the interpretation of statute, external aids, history of legislation, statement of objects and reasons are different from the language of the Act, then they would not be of much materiality. The interpretation placed on religious text by an earlier constitutional bench is binding.

Further, the Supreme Court observed that the phrase "Reasonable and fair provision and maintenance" as enshrined under Section 3(1)(*a*) of the Muslim Women (Protection of Rights on Divorce) Act, 1986 is not confined for the Iddat period rather it extends for whole of the life of divorced wife unless she remarries. It is not the nature or duration of such "Provision and Maintenance" over which emphasis has been laid down in the Section rather it is the time "within" which the arrangement for their payment should be finalized and executed. It has further been held that in case the provisions of the Act are construed as less beneficial than the provisions of Chapter IX of the Code of Criminal Procedure and if the husband were held liable to pay maintenance only for the Iddat Period then it would cause irrational discrimination against divorced Muslim women and would render the Act violative of Articles 14, 15 and 21 of the Constitution of India. As per this ruling of the Supreme Court the effect of *Shaik Dada Saheb* v. *Shaik Mastan Bee*, 1995 Cri. LJ 696 (AP), *Nazir Ahmad Ansari* v. *Lateef Bi*, (1996) Cri. LJ 1548 (AP), *Noorunnisha* v. *Maqsood Ahmad*, 1994 Cri. LJ 3129 (MP) seems to be impliedly overruled.

Besides, *Md. Tajuddin* v. *Quamarunnisa Begum*, 1989 Cri. LJ 2285 (AP) seems to be approved by implications.

"A reasonable and fair provision" as referred in Section 3 of the Muslim Women (Protection of Rights on Divorce) Act, 1986 is a right enforceable only against the former husband of the divorced women and it is in addition to what he is obliged to pay as "Maintenance". It should be ascertained with reference to the needs of divorce women, the means of husband and the standard of life enjoyed during the subsistence of marriage. It has been further held that there is no reason why such provision cannot take form of regular payment of alimony. On monetary compensation under Muslim Law it was further held that it is difficult to perceive that the responsibility of providing monetary compensation to the divorced woman would pass on to persons unconnected with the matrimonial life such as heir likely to inherit her property or the Wakf Board. Solutions over the issue needs to be adjudged on considerations other than religion and religious faith or belief or national, sectarian, racial or communal constraints.

DIVORCE UNDER MUSLIM LAW – CONCEPT

The concept of divorce is not new to the Muslim law rather it existed in the Pre-Islamic era also where the husband had unlimited and unrestricted power of divorce. As such the wife could be divorced by the husband even without assigning any reason. They also possessed the power to revoke the divorce and again divorce their wives repeatedly. More so, they could also swear that they would have no intercourse with their wives, though still living with them.

Talaq, *Ila*, *Zihar* and Khula were four types of divorces that existed in Pre-Islamic Arabia. Women after the dissolution of marriage by any of these four modes were free to remarry, but after the passing of the period of Iddat.

With the advent of Islam the prophet gave a systematic look to the concept of divorce. He was not able to eradicate this wide spread evil as a whole so he provided for divorce under certain conditions. Three distinct and separate period were permitted to the divorced parties within which they might endeavour to become reconciled. Where all the attempts of reconciliation proved unsuccessful then in the third period the final separation became effective. Ameer Ali on divorce states as - "The permission (of divorce), therefore in the Koran though it gave a certain countenance to the old custom, has to be read in the light of the law-giver's own enunciations. When it is borne in mind how law and religion are connected in the Islamic system, it will be easy to understand the bearing of his words on the institution of divorce".

IDDAT

Iddat is a significant formality in the dissolution of Muslim marriage. In Hedaya it has been defined as follows:

"The term of probation incumbent upon a women in consequence of the dissolution of marriage after carnal connection". Furthermore, it has been stated that "the most approved definition of Iddat is, the term by the completion of which a new marriage is rendered lawful".

There are different period of Iddat in different circumstances. Where the marriage has been dissolved due to the divorce and it has been consummated duly then in such a case the period of Iddat is three menstruation courses. But if the wife is pregnant then it will be till delivery.

MODES OF DISSOLUTION OF MARRIAGE

There are different modes of dissolution of marriage as stated below:

A. By the death of the husband or wife.

B. By the Act of the parties.

Under this second head i.e. by the act of the parties there is further classification i.e.

- (*i*) By the husband under which lies
  - (*a*) Talak:
    1. Talak-Ul-Sunnat
       - (1.1) Ahsan (Most approved)
       - (1.2) Hasan (Approved)
    2. Talak-Ul-Biddat
       - (2.1) Triple divorce
       - (2.2) One irrevocable divorce (In written form)
  - (*b*) Ila (Vow of continence)
  - (*c*) Zihar (Injurious Comparison)
- (*ii*) By the wife

  Talak-e-Tafwid (delegated divorce)
- (*iii*) By mutual consent
  - (*a*) Khula (redemption)
  - (*b*) Mubarat (mutual freeing)

C. By judicial process, which is further classified as

- (*i*) Lian (Mutual Imprecation)
- (*ii*) Faskh (Judicial annulment)

A. Dissolution of marriage by the death of husband or wife

As it is very clear that with the death of either of the spouse the marital tie comes to an end and as such it is open for the husband to marry immediately after the death of the wife but in case of death of husband the wife has to wait till the expiry of the period of Iddat which is four months and ten days and if the wife is pregnant, till delivery.

B. Dissolution of marriage by the act of the parties:

- **Talak**: The expression "Talak" is an Arabic word that stand for "taking of any tie or restraint" and as such its legality lies in the dissolution of marriage. For the pronouncement of Talak no special form or phrase is prescribed under Hanafi law but as per Ithna and Ashari law the Talak needs to be strictly in Arabic language uttered orally in the presence and hearing of two male witnesses who should be honest and virtuous Muslims. The presence of wife in this case is not essential. In the case of *Ful Chand* v. *Nazab Ali Chaudhari*, ILR (1909) 36 Cal. 185 it was held that the date of effect of wife is on the date when wife came to know about it. In certain cases, for instance, when the wife has to observe Iddat the communication of Talak becomes necessary and the Mahr or Dower becomes payable during Iddat. It is to be borne in mind here that under Sunni law both types of Talak are permissible i.e. oral as well as written but under Shia law, only oral Talak is allowed. Here any word may be used and it may be given at any time. Due to the unrestricted power conferred to the husband with regard to the procedure of Talak, in *Haneefa* v. *Pathummal* 1972 KLT 512 Khalid J. termed the practice as monstrosity.

- ***Talak-Us-Sunnat*** : - It is the form of Talak that has been approved by prophet. It may be in most approved form i.e. Ahsan or Hasan i.e. simply an approved form.

  Ahsan: In Hedaya this form of Talak has been recognized as the most laudable form of divorce. Here the husband by single pronouncement during the period of *Tuhr* (i.e. purity in the sense that the wife is free from her menstrual courses) without having intercourse leaves her for the observance of Iddat. According to the view of Fyzee during the period of Iddat the divorce is revocable and the parties retain the right of inheritance. The period of Iddat in this case is three months or till delivery as the case may be. Where the case is such that the marriage is not yet consummated then Ahsan Talak may be pronounced during the period of menstruation. In the case of *Chand Bibi* v. *Bandesha*, AIR 1960 Bom. 121 it was held that where the husband and wife live separate from each other or the wife has crossed the age of menstruation i.e. (when the wife is old) the condition with respect to *Tuhr* is not applicable. More so, where the divorce is in written form, again, the condition of *Tuhr* is not applicable. This Talak is revocable either by expressed words or impliedly by cohabitation within the Iddat period.

  Hasan: In this form of Talak husband successively pronounces divorce three times during the consecutive periods of purity (*Tuhr*). As such it is believed to be "a divorce upon a divorce" and here the Talak becomes irrevocable only after the pronouncement of third Talak. A condition put forth during the tenure of pronouncement of Talak is that there should be no intercourse during this period. In case the wife is not subject to menstrual courses an interval of thirty days is required between each successive repudiation.

- ***Talak-Ul-Biddat***: - This form of Talak is an escape from the way of pronouncement of Talak as prescribed by prophet i.e. Talak-Us-Sunnat. Here, no attention is paid to the period of purity or to the abstention from intercourse. According to Hedaya the husband in this case repudiates his wife by three divorces in one sentence or he repeats the sentence separately thrice within *Tuhr*. Under Hanafi law this form of divorce is lawful but sinful but under Shia law it is not permissible. For the union of the couples in this type of divorce intermediary marriage is necessary. In *Sara Bhai* v. *Ralia Bai* (1906) ILR 30 Bom. 537 it was held that this form of Talak-Ul-Biddat is good in law but bad in theology and it is the most widely spread form of Talak in India. So it is to be borne in mind that it is on the completion of the period of Iddat that Talak Ahsan becomes irrevocable where as Talak Hasan comes into the force on the very point when third pronouncement is made and Iddat factor has no influence on it. Unapproved form of Talak i.e. Talak-Ul-Biddat is of both types – triple or single and it becomes irrevocable right on pronouncement. Where the marriage has not been consummated Talak becomes irrevocable right on pronouncement. A written form of Talak comes into effect from the movement of its execution, unless it is ambiguous.

With regard to the effect of compulsion, intoxication or jest on the pronouncement of Talak it is to be conceived in mind that Hanafi consider a Talak given by a man under compulsion as valid whereas Imam Shafi, Maliki, Hanbal, and Shia jurists consider it as invalid. As regards the divorce given in the state of intoxication it is to be borne in mind that according to Hanafi law such a divorce is valid but it is not recognized under Shia law. Similarly, unlike Shia law divorce pronounced in jest is valid under Hanafi law.

There is also another category of Talak called contingent and implied Talak. This form of Talak is recognized under Sunni law but Shias do not recognize this Talak. In contingent form of Talak a condition is attached for the Talak to be effected and in implied form of Talak the husband pronounces some other words in substitution to the express words for instance "I have severed all relations with you", or "you are no more my wife" etc.

- **Ila (Vow of Continence)** : Ila is a form of divorce where the husband swears not to have sexual intercourse with his wife and abstains from it for four months. With the completion of the duration of four months in this manner, the divorce is effected. There is difference of opinion with regard to the effect of such abstention between Hanafis on one side and Shafis and Shias on other side. According to Hanafi law such abstention deprives the husband of the benefit of marriage but Shafis and Shias on other hand hold that such a vow is not in itself a divorce rather it only provides the wife a ground to seek judicial divorce. Asharis hold that this form of divorce can be given only after the consummation of marriage. The retraction of Ila is possible by resumption of cohabitation and in case actual cohabitation is not possible due to some reason then there may be verbal retraction as per the Hanafi law. Husband has the power cancel Ila with the accent of the wife even after the expiry of four months.
- **Zihar (Injurious Comparison)**: - Zihar connotes a comparison of the wife by the husband with any female relation that falls within his prohibited degrees. The effect of Zihar is that the sexual intercourse between the husband and wife becomes unlawful till the husband has expiated himself by performing penance. Besides, after the uttering of Zihar, judicial separation or divorce can be claimed by the wife if the husband is in practice of making such comments irresponsibly. Zihar in itself does not lead to the dissolution of marriage. The presence of two witnesses is necessary for testifying Zihar as per the Shia law.

Divorce by the wife (Talak-e-Tafwid or delegated divorce)

The definition of Talak-e-Tafwid or delegated divorce has been given by Baillie in the following words:

> "As a man may in person repudiates his wife, so he may commit the power of repudiating her to herself or to a third party".

As such right has been vested in the husband to delegate the power of divorce to his wife. This doctrine is an exclusive feature of Muslim law and there exists no parallel to it in any other system. Indian High Courts have held these type of agreements (where the wife is authorised by the husband to divorce herself in case the husband marries a second wife without her consent) as valid. There are three forms of Talak-e-Tafwid. These are:

- Ikhtiyar (Choice)
- Amr Biyad (The affairs is in hands)
- Mashiat (At your pleasure)

It is to be conceived in mind here that the terms and circumstances must be clearly made in which the wife (or the guardian of a minor wife) is to exercise the choice and the condition must not be opposed to the public policy. In the case of *Hamidoola* v. *Faizunnissa* (1812) 8 Cal. 327 where the condition was that in case of failure of husband to pay maintenance, the wife was conferred with the right to Talak it was held that this form of Talak was Talak-e-Tafwid or delegated divorce. The option to divorce must be exercised by the wife and mere a happening of a particular condition does not in itself result in effectuation of Talak. The delegation of the power to divorce may be made at the time of nuptial agreement or during the married life and this power so delegated cannot be revoked by the husband. In the case of *Saifuddin* v. *Latifunnissa* (1919) 46 Cal. 141 it was held that this power to divorce may be exercised by the wife to counter the suit for restitution of conjugal rights instituted by the husband and such exercise would result in Talak. A significant thing to note about Talak-e-Tafwid is that in spite of such delegation the husband still retains the right to Talak his wife according to his choice.

Divorce by Mutual Consent

(i) Khula (Redemption)

In this form of divorce the wife relinquishes her claim to dower and seeks a Khula divorce. But it depends over the husband to accept the consideration of dower and to grant the divorce. On the similar lines the husband may also propose a Khula divorce and it is open for the wife whether to accept or refuse it. Where the proposal is accepted by the wife it leads to the inference that the wife has relinquished the right to get dower from the husband. The consideration in case of Khula may be dower, money, property etc. Where the wife fails to tell her consideration agreed upon in a Khula divorce then such a failure does not invalidate the divorce, so as to enable the husband to sue for the restitution of conjugal rights, however it entitles him -

- To sue for any money or property due under the agreement.
- To claim the release of dower.

In the case of *Moonshee Buzul Raheem* v. *Lattefut-oon-Nissa* (1861) 8 MIA 379 it was held that the moment when the husband repudiates the wife the divorce by Khula is at once complete. There is no period for the repudiation of such a divorce. The husband and wife need to be of sound mind and they must have attained puberty at the time of divorce by the way of Khula. Under the Hanafi and Shafai school of Muslim law the guardian of a minor wife can validly enter into Khula on her behalf but the guardian of the minor husband cannot. As per the Shia law in this form of divorce there should not be any compulsion exerted on the mind of the wife but Sunnis hold that Khula obtained even under compulsion is valid. Moreover, a conditional Khula is also recognized under Sunni law but it is not so under the Shia law. Under the Hanafi law an option is left with the wife to revoke Khula. Khula would be deemed to be irrevocable and the option would be void if the husband stipulates such an option. Under the Shia law, for the Khula to be unconditional, both the Khula and the option would be void.

(ii) Mubarat (Mutual Freeing)

When the divorce is effected by the mutual consent of the husband and wife it is called Mubarat (i.e. freeing one another mutually). According to a Pakistani case of *Sayeeda Khanum* v. *Muhammad Sami*, PLD 1952 (WP) Lah. 113 (FB) it has been held that such matter as "incompatibility of temperaments, aversion or dislike cannot form a ground for a wife to seek dissolution of her marriage, at the hands of a *Qazi* or a Court, but they fall to be dealt with under the powers possessed by the husband as well as the wife under Muslim law" which implies the capacity of making a Khula or Mubarat divorce. The nature of this form of divorce is irrevocable as it happens in the case of Khula. Iddat is necessary for the wife in this case and she has the right to maintenance. Any party to the marriage can make the offer in case of Mubarat and no special form has been prescribed for it by Sunnis.

Difference between Khula and Mubarat

Highlighting the difference between Khula and Mubarat it is to be borne in mind that in case of Khula there is redemption of the contract of marriage whereas in case of Mubarat there is mutual release from the marital tie. In case of Khula the offer for divorce comes from the side of wife and it is the husband who accepts it but in case of Mubarat any party may make the offer and the other side accepts it. In Khula consideration passes from wife to husband but in Mubarat there arises no question of consideration. Lastly in Khula, aversion is on the side of the wife while in Mubarat there is a mutual aversion.

Divorce by Judicial Process

(i) Lian (Mutual Imprecation)

Where the husband falsely charges the wife for adultery then in such a case the wife can sue him for divorce. After the suit is filed by the wife, the husband is left with two alternatives. Firstly, the charge leveled against the wife by the husband can be withdrawn by him before the end of trial and in such a case the wife would not get a divorce. Secondly, where the husband uninterruptedly continues to make such charges then he would be required to accuse his wife on oath. After the oath of the husband, the wife would take the oath of innocency. After these "mutual imprecations" the marriage is dissolved by the Court.

There are few conditions for the divorce by way of lian. These are that the parties to the marriage must be sane adult and the charge made by the husband needs to be false. Irrespective of this fact where the husband has merely laid down the charge or the wife has made an application alleging that the husband has falsely charged her of adultery then in such cases divorce would not be result. Besides, for the divorce by the way of lian the marriage needs to be *Sahih* and not *Fasid*. The wife should file a regular suit for the dissolution of marriage. After the dissolution of marriage by the Court the consequences would be irrevocable. The doctrine of lian is in practice in the Indian Courts even today as it was observed in *Nurjahan Bibi* v. *Mohd. Kazim Ali* AIR (1977) Cal. 90 where Bhattacharya, J. stated that the doctrine of lian is not outdated and this is a practice based on tradition. Where the charge of the husband is proved, the wife would loose the ground for the dissolution of marriage. But in case the husband fails to prove the allegations then the wife is entitled to get divorce and at the same time she can also sue the husband for defamation under the Indian Penal Code for bringing the false charge of adultery which tantamount to cruelty against the wife. Here, exception I under section 499 of the Indian Penal Code would not be applicable.

In case of retraction or withdrawal of charge there is conflict of views between different High Courts. The High Court of Allahabad in *Tufail Ahmed* v. *Zamila Khatun* 1962 All. L. J. 971 held that where the husband has withdrawn the charge against the wife before the suit for the dissolution of marriage then such a retraction of charge is sufficient for the dismissal of the suit of wife. The retraction needs to be bonafide and the husband should be punished for the false accusation. The husband can be held liable for slander or defamation. However, in *Ahmed* v. *Fatima* AIR 1931 Bom. 76 it was held that the retraction had no place in the procedure of Indian Courts. On the contrary in *Maomebali* v. *Hazrabai* AIR 1955 Bom. 464 the earlier view of the Bombay High Court was over ruled. In *Shamsunnessa* v. *Mir* AIR 1940 Cal. 95 the High Court of Calcutta allowed retraction or withdrawl of charge at any time before the close of evidence.

(ii) Faskh (Judicial Annulment)

Faskh refers to "annulment" and implies annulment of marriage by the law Court on application of the wife. The root of the law of Faskh rests upon Koran and tradition which says, "if a women be prejudiced by a marriage, let it be broken off". Section 2 of the Dissolution of Muslim Marriages Act, 1939 governs such judicial annulment. A women married under Muslim law shall be entitled to obtain a decree for the dissolution of her marriage on any one or more of the following grounds namely:

- That the whereabouts of the husband have not been known for a period of four years;
- That the husband has neglected or has failed to provide for her maintenance for a period of two years;
- That the husband has been sentenced to imprisonment for a period of seven years or upward;
- That the husband has failed to perform without reasonable cause his marital obligations for a period of three years;
- That the husband was impotent at the time of the marriage and continues to be so;
- That the husband has been insane for a period of two years or is suffering from leprosy or a virulent venereal disease;
- That she, having being given in marriage by her father or other guardian before she attained the age of fifteen years, repudiated the marriage before attaining the age of eighteen years, provided that the marriage has not been consummated;
- That the husband treats her with cruelty, that is to say -
  - ❑ Habitually assaults her or makes her life miserable by cruelty of conduct even if such conduct does not amount to physical ill-treatment, or
  - ❑ Associates with women of ill-repute or leads an infamous life or
  - ❑ Attempts to force her to lead an immoral life, or
  - ❑ Disposes of her property or prevents her from exercising her legal right over it, or
  - ❑ Obstructs her in the observance of her religious profession or practice, or
  - ❑ If he has more wives then one, does not treat her equitably in accordance with the injunctions of the Koran.
- On any other ground which is recognized as valid for the dissolution of marriages under Muslim law:

Provided that -

- ❑ No decree shall be passed on ground (*iii*) until the sentence has become final;
- ❑ A decree passed on ground (*i*) shall not take effect for period of six months form the date of such decree and if the husband appears either in person or through an authorized agent within that period and satisfies the Court that he is prepared to perform his conjugal duties, the Court shall set aside the said decree; and
- ❑ Before passing a decree on ground (*v*) the Court shall, on application by the husband, make an order requiring the husband to satisfy the Court within a period of one year from the date of such order the he has ceased to be impotent and if the husband so satisfies the Court within such period, no decree shall be passed on the said ground.

EFFECTS OF DIVORCE

It becomes necessary here to point out the effects of divorce. One of the effects of divorce is that after the divorce the cohabitation between the couples becomes illegal and the wife becomes entitled for the payment of dower. Moreover, during the period of Iddat, wife becomes entitled to maintenance. The husband and wife get the right of inheritance from each other, if either of them dies during Iddat following a revocable divorce. In case of irrevocable divorce no right of inheritance arises. Remarriage becomes possible between the couples after adhering to the strict procedure. A widow can remarry under Muslim law only after the expiry of the term of Iddat.

For the purpose of remarriage in the cases where the husband has divorced his wife by three pronouncements i.e. irrevocable divorce, there are few conditions that needs to be fulfilled. Among them the first is that after the divorce Iddat should be observed by the wife and after the expiry of the period of Iddat the wife should marry another person and this marriage should be actually consummated. Then the second husband should voluntarily divorce the wife and she needs to observe Iddat accordingly. After observing this Iddat only the remarriage with the first husband is possible. In default of complying with these requirements the remarriage is irregular but not void.

MAINTENANCE BY CRIMINAL COURTS TO DIVORCED MUSLIM WOMEN

Muslim women (Protection of Rights on Divorce) Act, 1986 has made certain special provision for the Muslim women. Section 125 of Code of Criminal Procedure, 1973 can be invoked by the divorced Muslim women only when the divorcee and her former husband on the first date of hearing i.e. on the first date fixed for appearing in the summons declare by affidavit or in writing that they agree to obey and abide Section 125 to 128 of the Code of Criminal Procedure, 1973.

In *Rizwana Begum* v. *Motiullah* 1989 Cri.L.J (No.C) 155 (Ori.) it was held that the magistrate cannot assume jurisdiction unless both the parties give consent in writing to obey the decision in the proceeding under Section 125 of the Code of Criminal Procedure, 1973. Similarly, in *Begum Bibi* v. *Abdul Razak Khan* 1995 Cri.L.J 604 (Ori.) it was observed by the High Court of Orissa that the applicability of Section 125 of the Code of Criminal Procedure over the Muslim divorcee only where both the parties, exercising their option, declare it at the first hearing of the application under Section 3(2) of the Muslim women (Protection of Rights on Divorce) Act 1989. Where no such declaration is made the Muslim divorcee would be entitled to invoke the provisions of Muslim women (Protection of Rights on Divorce) Act, 1986 only. The women who has been divorced by her husband presumably by *Khulanama* would be entitled to claim the following as per Section 3 of the Muslim women (Protection of Rights on Divorce) Act, 1986:

- An amount equal to the Mahr or dower agreed at the time of the marriage or after, according to Mohammedan law.
- Return of Properties given to her during or before or after the marriage by her relatives or friends or the husband or any other relative of her husband or his friends.
- If she has been a menstruating lady to a fair and reasonable provision and maintenance for three lunar months from the date of divorce and
- If she has any child by her former divorcing husband which child resides with her, fair and reasonable provision and maintenance for the child.

In *Shahnaz Bano* v. *Baboo Khan* (1986) 1 DMC 40 it was held that where a Muslim lady has taken divorce by way of Khulanama then she could also ask for maintenance under Section 125 of the Code of Criminal Procedure, 1973. The ratio of this decision was overruled by the Muslim women (Protection of Right on Divorce) Act, 1986. As such in *Mohd. Ismail Shariff* v. *Khairunnissa* (1986) 2 DMC 199 (Mad.) the Madras High Court held that after the passing of the Muslim women (Protection of Rights on Divorce) Act, 1986 the Muslim lady who has taken divorce by Khulanama would not be entitled to maintenance under 125 Cr.P.C. For making an order of maintenance the jurisdiction vests in the magistrate, first class of the place of the residence of the Muslim divorcee and an order can be made by such Magistrate for the payment of dower or properties described above. An order to make reasonable and fair provision and maintenance can also be made by the magistrate but the period of it should not extend beyond iddat. The jurisdiction of the magistrate is limited to make an order and enforcement thereof so as to force the former husband to pay an amount equal to Mahr or dower. The magistrate does not have any jurisdiction to order a fair and reasonable provision after the iddat period. In *Gafur Saha* v. *Sabutan Bibi* (1994) 1 DMC 228 (Ori.) it was held that a Muslim divorcee can claim maintenance for the iddat period and not beyond that.

In a significant decision of *Hamidan* v. *Md. Rafiq* 1994 Cri.L.J 348 (All) the Allahbad High Court was of the view that where the maintenance has been granted to the Muslim divorcee before the Muslim women (Protection of Right on Divorce) Act, 1986, the duration of it cannot be restricted to iddat period and it cannot be extended beyond that period. However, the High Court of Bombay stood on different footings over this issue in *Ali* v. *Sufaira* (1988) 3 Crimes 147 (Bom.) and it was held that a Muslim divorcee in also entitled to a reasonable and fair provision beyond the period of iddat along with the maintenance from her former husband during the period of iddat. The forum for application of maintenance under Section 3 of the Muslim Women (Protection of Rights on Divorce) Act, 1986 is not family court even if established. The appropriate forum is the Judicial Magistrate of first class of the area where the concerned women resides.

Interpreting the term "residence" it was observed in *Avaran Koya* v. *Mariam* (1994) 1 DMC 205 (Ker.) that the said expression does not signify the own residence of the women within the territorial limits of the court rather *animus manendi* or an intention to stay for an indefinite period at a place is sufficient to constitute residence for the aforesaid purpose. A Muslim divorcee has also been empowered under the Act to compel those relatives who would have inherited her on her death so as to pay her an amount equal to Mahr or to make a fair and reasonable provision and maintenance during the iddat period. The divorced Muslim lady has also been empowered to ask for the amount from her parents and where the parents also fail to provide her maintenance due to indigence to turn to the State Board of Wakf.

The Hon'ble Apex Court in *Subanu alias Sairabanu* v. *A.M. Abdul Gafoor* A.I.R. 1987 SC 1103 held that where a Muslim male has contracted second marriage or keeps a mistress, the first wife can proceed under Section 125 of Code of Criminal Procedure, 1973 for getting maintenance. The provisions of the Muslim Women (Protection of Rights on Divorce) Act, 1986 envisages a divorced woman only as such the ratio of the case of *Subanu alias Sairabanu* v. *A.M. Abdul Gafoor* A.I.R. 1987 SC 1103 remains unaffected by this Act. The full bench of the High Court of Andhra Pradesh peeping into the question whether the provisions of Section 125 of the Code of Criminal Procedure, 1973 is applicable to the case of a Muslim divorcee claiming maintenance from her former husband, it was held that the starting clause of Section 3 is a *non-obstante* one and it provides that notwithstanding anything contained in any other law for the time being in force, a divorced woman shall be entitled to the rights which are enumerated therein. Under Section 4 of the said Act if a Muslim divorcee is unable to maintain herself after the period of iddat, the liability to pay maintenance to her is devolved upon the relatives and in case of unavailability of the relatives the liability is shifted on for and during the period of iddat. The obligation to pay maintenance after the iddat period to a Muslim divorcee if she is not able to maintain herself is cast upon the relatives or the Wakf Board under Section 4 of the Act. Section 5 of the Act provides that the husband and wife would be governed by Sections 125 to 128 of the Code of Criminal Procedure, if they exercise their option in the manner stated therein. In case the option is not exercised then it is obvious that they would not be governed by Section 125 to 128 of the Code. When an application is expressly dependent upon the provisions of Section 5 of the Act and on the exercise of the option of the parties concerned it would be too much to say that the claim of maintenance by the Muslim divorcee would still be governed by Section 125 of the code. Moreover, the legislature has clarified its intention under Section 7 of the Act where it has been provided that every application by a divorced women under Section 125 or Section 127 of the code sending before the magistrate on the commencement of the Act of 1986, shall, notwithstanding anything contained in that code and subject to the provisions of Section 5 of the Act of 1986. As such in *Azmath Ali Khan* v. *Qamar Bano* A.I.R. 1990 AP 225 maintenance cannot be claimed by the Muslim divorcee under Section 125 of the Code from her former husband after passing of the Act of 1986.

In a significant observation of *Motiar Rahaman* v. *Sabina Khatun* (1994) 2 DMC 57 (Cal.) it was held that where a Muslim lady obtained order of maintenance before the Act of 1986 then such a lady would not loose the benefit of that order after coming of the Act into force if she is subsequently divorced by her husband. In a celebrated case of *All India Muslim Advocates Forum* v. *Osman Khan Brahamaini* (1990) 2 DMC 541 (AP) (FB) three question were mooted by the Andhra Pradesh High Court which were as follows:

- Whether maintenance under Section 125 Cr.P.C could be claimed by the Muslim divorcee even after the passing of the Act of 1986?
- Whether the maintenance envisaged under Section 3(1)(*a*) of the Act of 1986 is confined only for the period of "iddat" or whether a fair and reasonable provision has also to be made for future within the period of iddat?
- What is the extent of the applicability of Section 125 to 128 the Code of Criminal Procedure, 1973 after enforcement of the Act 1986 and what should be the mode of disposal of the cases pending before the courts under these Sections?

The first question was replied in negative and as to the second question it was said that the obligation of the husband to provide any provision of maintenance after the period of iddat does not exist and the fair reasonable provision and maintenance envisaged under Section 3(1)(*a*) payable by the husband is confined only for the period of iddat. For the third question the full bench was of the view that Sections 125 to 128 of the Code of Criminal Procedure, 1973 are not applicable after the enforcement of the Act of 1986, save in so far as the parties exercise their option under Section 5 of the Act to be governed by the provisions of Section 125 to 128 of the Code. However, it is to be conceived in mind that a Muslim lady cannot be said to be divorced simply due to the suggestion that she has been divorced thrown to her in the witness box. On the similar lines it was held in *P.M. Pareed* v. *C.Aysha* 1988 Cr.L.J 806 that the statement of this nature by the husband in the witness box cannot be said to be communication of Talak to her.

In *Abdul Rehman* v. *Akhtari Begum* (1994) 1 DMC 518 (Mad.) it was observed that where a petition for maintenance was filed by the Muslim lady before her being divorced by Talak for instance on 1985 and subsequent to it the husband by a Talak dissolved the marriage on 13th June, 1986 then in such case the proceedings under Section 125 of Cr.P.C would continue for the reason that the Muslim Women (Protection of Right on Divorce) Act, 1986 envisages a divorcee. In *Basir Khan* v. *Jamila Bee* 1994 Cr.L.J 361 (MP) it was held that the options available under Section 5 of the Act of 1986 is exercisable in a proceeding under Section 3 of the Act of 1986. Where there is no proceeding pending under Section 3 of the Act of 1986, the exercise of options under Section 5 of the Act is out of question.

MAINTENANCE TO MUSLIM CHILDREN OUT OF MARRIAGE DIVORCED

The maintenance of both legitimate and illegitimate children by the parents has been provided under Section 125 of the Code of Criminal Procedure, 1973. Muslim parents are in no way exempted from maintenance of illegitimate minor child/children under Section 125 of the code. It cannot be reasonably held that a Muslim father is not under obligation to maintain his legitimate minor child/children above two years old, when under Section 125 of Cr.P.C an order to maintenance of illegitimate minor child/children can be passed against the Muslim father, after he has divorced his wife through whom the child/children is/are born.

In *Rupsan Begum* v. *Abdus Sattar* (1990) 2 DMC 253 (Gau.) it was held that the right under Section 3(1)(*b*) of the Muslim Women (Protection of Right on Divorce) Act, 1986 is the right of a Muslim divorcee incidental to divorce and it does not stand in conflict with Section 125 of the Code of Criminal Procedure, 1973. More so in *A. Abdul Gafoor Kunju* v. *A.V. Pathumma Beevi* 1989 Cr.L.J 1924 (Ker) it was observed that a Muslim divorcee is not empowered to claim maintenance under Section 125 of the Code of Criminal Procedure, 1973 after the enforcement of the Muslim Women (Protection of Rights on Divorce) Act, 1986 but her minor daughter can claim.

Justice V.A. Mohta in *Shrawan Kumar Ubhale* v. *Sau Durga Sharwan Ubhale* (1990) 1 DMC 299 (Bom) observed "Whether the appeal ends in divorce or not the definition contained in Explanation (*b*) to Section 125 Cr.P.C continues unless parties make adjustments and come to terms regarding the quantum of the right of maintenance". An inference from this observation can also be drawn that where the wife voluntarily relinquishes her right to claim maintenance than such a right cannot be claimed later by her. More so, in *Bai Laxmiben* v. *Bharat Bhai* (1986) 1 DMC 129 it was held that the wife had received amount of maintenance in lump sum it tantamount to surrendering the right to get maintenance under Section 125 of the Code of Criminal Procedure, 1973.

INTER-RELIGIOUS MARRIAGE AND DIVORCE

Special Marriage Act, 1954 is the Act that provides for a special form of marriage in certain cases, for the registration of such and certain other marriages and divorce. It generally deals with the inter-religious and like form of marriage and divorce. This Act is the outcome of the secular nature of our constitution and it takes away the embargo that exists in the society for inter-communal relationship. The law relating to such matrimonial relationship is governed by this Act.

Conditions Relating to Solemnization of Special Marriages

Notwithstanding anything contained in any other law for the time being in force relating to be solemnization of marriages, a marriage between any two persons may be solemnized under the Special Marriage Act, 1954 if at the time of the marriage the following conditions are fulfilled, namely:

- neither party has a spouse living;
- neither party-
  - ❑ is incapable of giving a valid consent to it in consequence of unsoundness of mind; or
  - ❑ though capable of giving a valid consent, has been suffering from mental disorder of such a kind or to such an extent as to be unfit for marriage and the procreation of children; or
  - ❑ has been subject to recurrent attacks of insanity;
- the male has completed the age of twenty-one years and the female the age of eighteen years;
- the parties are not within the degrees of prohibited relationship provided that where a custom governing at least one of the parties permits of a marriage between them, such marriage may be solemnized, notwithstanding that they are within the degrees of prohibited relationship; and

- where the marriage is solemnized in the State of Jammu and Kashmir, both parties are citizens of India domiciled in the territories to which the Special Marriage Act, 1954 extends.

Here, "custom", in relation to a person belonging to any tribe, community, group or family, means any rule which the State Government may, by notification in the Official Gazette, specify in this behalf as applicable to members of that tribe, community, group or family provided that no such notification shall be issued in relation to the members of any tribe, community, group or family, unless the State Government is satisfied:

- that such rule has been continuously and uniformly observed for a long time among those members;
- that such rule is certain and not unreasonable or opposed to public policy; and
- that such rule, if applicable only to a family, has not been discontinued by the family.

POWERS OF MARRIAGE OFFICERS IN RESPECT OF INQUIRIES

For the purpose of any inquiry on the objection made in the marriage, the Marriage Officer shall have all the powers vested in a Civil Court under the Code of Civil Procedure, 1908, when trying a suit in respect of the following matters, namely:

- summoning and enforcing the attendance of witnesses and examining them on oath;
- discovery and inspection;
- compelling the production of documents;
- reception of evidence on affidavits; and
- issuing commissions for the examination of witnesses;

and any proceeding before the Marriage Officer shall be deemed to be a judicial proceeding within the meaning of section 193 of the Indian Penal Code.

Here, for the purpose of enforcing the attendance of any person to give evidence, the local limits of the jurisdiction of the Marriage Officer shall be the local limits of his district.

If it appears to the Marriage Officer that the objection made to an intended marriage is not reasonable and has not been made in good faith he may impose on the person objecting costs by way of compensation not exceeding one thousand rupees and award the whole or any part thereof to the parties to the intended marriage, and any order for costs so made may be executed in the same manner as a decree passed by the District Court within the local limits of whose jurisdiction the Marriage Officer has his office.

REGISTRATION OF MARRIAGES CELEBRATED IN OTHER FORMS

Any marriage celebrated, other than a marriage solemnized under the Special Marriage Act, 1872, or under the Special Marriage Act, 1954 may be registered by a Marriage Officer in the territories to which the Special Marriage Act, 1954 extends if the following conditions are fulfilled, namely: -

- a ceremony of marriage has been performed between the parties and they have been living together as husband and wife ever since;
- neither party has at the time of registration more than one spouse living;
- neither party is an idiot or a lunatic at the time of registration;
- the parties have completed the age of twenty-one years at the time of registration;
- the parties are not within the degree of prohibited relationship provided that in the case of a marriage celebrated before the commencement of the Special Marriage Act, 1954, this condition shall be subject to any law, custom or usage having the force of law governing each of them which permits of a marriage between the two; and
- the parties have been residing within the district of the Marriage Officer for a period of not less than thirty days immediately preceding the date on which the application is made to him for registration of the marriage.

PROCEDURE FOR REGISTRATION

Upon receipt of an application signed by both the parties to the marriage for the registration of their marriage, the Marriage Officer shall give public notice thereof and after allowing a period of thirty days for objections and after hearing any objection received within that period, shall, if satisfied that all the conditions mentioned above are fulfilled, enter a certificate of the marriage in the Marriage Certificate Book in the form specified in the Fifth Schedule, and such certificate shall be signed by the parties to the marriage and by three witnesses.

Any person aggrieved by any order of a Marriage Officer refusing to register a marriage celebrated in other form may, within thirty days from the date of that order, appeal against that order to the District Court within the local limits of whose jurisdiction the Marriage Officer has his office, and the decision of the District Court on such appeal shall be final, and the Marriage Officer to whom the application was made shall act in conformity with such decision.

EFFECT OF REGISTRATION OF MARRIAGE

Where a certificate of marriage has been finally entered in the Marriage Certificate Book, the marriage shall, as from the date of such entry, be deemed to be a marriage solemnized under the Special Marriage Act, 1954.

All children born after the date of the ceremony of marriage (whose names shall also be entered in the Marriage Certificate Book) shall in all respects be deemed to be and always to have been the legitimate children of their parents. It is subject to the proviso that nothing as said here shall be construed as conferring upon any such children any rights in or to the property of any person other than their parents in any case where, but for the passing of the Special Marriage Act, 1954, such children would have been incapable of possessing or acquiring any such rights by reason of their not being the legitimate children of their parents.

LEGITIMACY OF CHILDREN OF VOID AND VOIDABLE MARRIAGES

Even in the case that a marriage is null and void, any child of such marriage who would have been legitimate if the marriage had been valid, shall be legitimate - whether such child is born before or after the commencement of the Marriage Laws (Amendment) Act, 1976; and whether or not a decree of nullity is granted in respect of that marriage and whether or not the marriage is held to be void otherwise than on a petition under the Special Marriage Act, 1954.

Where a decree of nullity is granted in respect of a voidable marriage, any child begotten or conceived before the decree is made, who would have been the legitimate child of the parties to the marriage if at the date of the decree it has been dissolved instead of being annulled, shall be deemed to be their legitimate child notwithstanding the decree of nullity.

Nothing as said above shall be construed as conferring upon any child of a void or voidable marriage, any rights in or to the property of any person, other than the parents, in any case where, but for the passing of the Special Marriage Act, 1954, such child would have been incapable of possessing or acquiring any such rights by reason of his not being the legitimate child of his parents.

BIGAMY

Every person whose marriage is solemnized under the Special Marriage Act, 1954 and who, during the lifetime of his or her wife or husband, contracts any other marriage shall be subject to the penalties provided in section 494 and section 495 of the Indian Penal Code, for the offence of marrying again during the lifetime of a husband or wife, and the marriage so contracted shall be void.

RESTITUTION OF CONJUGAL RIGHTS UNDER SPECIAL MARRIAGE ACT, 1954

When either the husband or the wife has, without reasonable excuse, withdrawn from the society of the other, the aggrieved party may apply by petition to the District Court for restitution of conjugal rights, and the Court, on being satisfied of the truth of the statements made in such petition, and that there is no legal ground why the application should not be granted, may decree restitution of conjugal rights accordingly. Where a question arises whether there has been reasonable excuse for withdrawal from the society, the burden of proving reasonable excuse shall be on the person who has withdrawn from the society.

DIVORCE AND JUDICIAL SEPARATION

A petition for judicial separation or divorce may be presented to the District Court either by the husband or the wife on the ground that the respondent-

- has, after the solemnization of the marriage, had voluntary sexual intercourse with any person other than his or her spouse; or
- has deserted the petitioner for a continuous period of not less than two years immediately preceding the presentation of the petition; or
- is undergoing a sentence of imprisonment for seven years or more for an offence as defined in the Indian Penal Code;
- has since the solemnization of the marriage treated the petitioner with cruelty; or
- has been incurably of unsound mind, or has been suffering continuously or intermittently from mental disorder of such a kind and to such an extent that the petitioner cannot reasonably be expected to live with the respondent. Here, the expression "mental disorder" means mental illness, arrested or incomplete development of mind, psychopathic disorder or any other disorder or disability of mind and includes schizophrenia. The expression "psychopathic disorder" means a persistent disorder or disability of mind (whether or not including sub-normality of intelligence) which results in abnormally aggressive or seriously irresponsible conduct on the part of the respondent, and whether or not it requires or is susceptible to medical treatment; or
- has been suffering from venereal disease in a communicable form; or

- has been suffering from leprosy, the disease not having been contracted from the petitioner; or
- has not been heard of as being alive for a period of seven years or more by those persons who would naturally have heard of the respondent if the respondent had been alive; Here, the expression "desertion" means desertion of the petitioner by the other party to the marriage without reasonable cause and without the consent or against the wish of such party, and includes the willful neglect of the petitioner by the other party to the marriage and its grammatical variations and cognate expressions shall be construed accordingly.
- has failed to comply with a decree for restitution of conjugal rights.

A wife may also present a petition for judicial separation or divorce to the District Court on the ground:

- that her husband has, since the solemnization of the marriage been guilty of rape, sodomy or bestiality;
- that in suit under section 18 of the Hindu Adoptions and Maintenance Act, 1956, or in a proceeding under section 125 of the Code of Criminal Procedure, 1973 (or under the corresponding section 488 of the Code of Criminal Procedure, 1898), a decree or order, as the case may be, has been passed against the husband awarding maintenance to the wife notwithstanding that she was living apart and that since the passing of such decree or order, cohabitation between the parties has not been resumed for one year or upwards; or

The Court, on being satisfied of the truth of the statement made in such petition, and that there is no legal ground why the application should not be granted, may decree judicial separation or divorce accordingly.

Where the Court grants a decree for judicial separation, it shall be no longer obligatory for the petitioner to cohabit with the respondent, but the Court may, on the application by petition of either party and on being satisfied of the truth of the statements made in such petition, rescind the decree if it considers it just and reasonable to do so.

Besides, for the purpose of divorce, either party to a marriage, whether solemnized before or after the commencement of the Special Marriage (Amendment) Act, 1970, may present a petition for divorce to the District Court on the ground:

- that there has been no resumption of cohabitation as between the parties to the marriage for a period of one year or upwards after the passing of a decree for judicial separation in a proceeding to which they were parties; or
- that there has been no restitution of conjugal rights as between the parties to the marriage for a period of one year or upwards after the passing of a decree for restitution of conjugal rights in a proceeding to which they were parties.

DIVORCE BY MUTUAL CONSENT

A petition for divorce may be presented to the District Court by both the parties together on the ground that they have been living separately for a period of one year or more, that they have not been able to live together and they have mutually agreed that the marriage should be dissolved. On the motion of both the parties made not earlier than six months after the date of the presentation of the petition and not later than eighteen months after the said date, if the petition is not withdrawn in the meantime, the District Court shall pass a decree declaring the marriage to be dissolved with effect from the date of the decree.

On a petition for dissolution of marriage by a decree of divorce, the Court may pass instead a decree for judicial separation except in the case where the ground is that the respondent has not been heard of as being alive for a period of seven years or more by those persons who would naturally have heard of the respondent if the respondent had been alive.

There is restriction on petitions for divorce during first three years after marriage except where the case is one of exceptional hardship suffered by the petitioner or of exceptional depravity on the part of the respondent. In such case the District Court shall have regard to the interests of any children of the marriage, and to the question whether there is a reasonable probability of reconciliation between the parties before the expiration of the said one year.

REMARRIAGE OF DIVORCED PERSONS

Where a marriage has been dissolved by a decree of divorce, and either there is no right of appeal against the decree or if there is such a right of appeal, the time for appealing has expired without an appeal having been presented, or an appeal has been presented but has been dismissed, either party to the marriage may marry again.

MAINTENANCE UNDER SPECIAL MARRIAGE ACT, 1954

Alimony Pendente Lit: Where in any proceeding relating to the restitution of conjugal rights and judicial separation or nullity of marriage and divorce it appears to the District Court that the wife has no independent income sufficient for her support and the necessary expenses of the proceeding, it may, on the application of the wife, order the husband to pay to her the expenses of the proceeding, and weekly or monthly during the proceeding such sum as, having regard to the husband's income, it may seem to the Court to be reasonable. It is subject to the proviso that the application for the payment of the expenses of the proceeding and such weekly or monthly sum during the proceeding under the chapters relating to the restitution of conjugal rights and judicial separation and nullity of marriage and divorce, shall, as far as possible, be disposed of within sixty days from the date of service of notice on the husband.

PERMANENT ALIMONY AND MAINTENANCE

At the time of passing any decree or at any time subsequent to the decree, the Court can, on application made to it for the purpose, order that the husband shall secure to the wife for her maintenance and support such gross sum or such monthly or periodical payment of money for a term not exceeding her life, as, having regard to her own property, if any, her husband's property and ability, the conduct of the parties and other circumstances of the case, it may seem to the Court to be just. The Court can create a charge on the husband's property for the purpose. If the District Court is satisfied that there in a change in the circumstances of either party at any time after it has made an order, it may, at the instance of either party, vary, modify or rescind any such order in such manner as it may seem to the Court to be just. More so, if the District Court is satisfied that the wife in whose favour an order has been made has remarried or is not leading a chaste life, it may, at the instance of the husband vary, modify or rescind any such order and in such manner as the Court may deem just.

CUSTODY OF CHILDREN UNDER SPECIAL MARRIAGE ACT, 1954

In any proceeding relating to the restitution of conjugal rights and judicial separation or nullity of marriage and divorce the District Court may, from time to time, pass such interim orders and make such provisions in the decree as it may seem to it to be just and proper with respect to the custody, maintenance and education of minor children, consistently with their wishes wherever possible. After the decree, it can also, upon application by petition for the purpose, make, revoke, suspend or vary, from time to time, all such orders and provisions with respect to the custody, maintenance and education of such children. It is subject to the proviso that the application with respect to the maintenance and education of the minor children, during the proceeding under the chapters relating to the restitution of conjugal rights and judicial separation and nullity of marriage and divorce shall, as far as possible, be disposed of within sixty days from the date of service of notice on the respondent.

MAINTENANCE UNDER SPECIAL MARRIAGE ACT, 1954 : PROCESS

Where in any proceeding under chapter V of this Act dealing with restitution of conjugal rights and judicial separation or chapter VI of this Act dealing with nullity of marriage and divorce it appears to the district court that the wife has no independent income sufficient for her support and the necessary expenses of the proceeding, it may, on the application of the wife, order the husband to pay her the expenses of the proceeding and weekly or monthly during the proceeding such as having regard to the husband's income, it may seem to the court to be reasonable provided that the application for the payment of the expenses of the proceeding and such weekly or monthly sum during the proceeding under chapter V or chapter VI, shall, as far as possible, be disposed of within sixty days from the date of service of notice on the husband.

Any court exercising jurisdiction under chapter V or chapter VI may at the time of passing any decree or at any time subsequent to the decree, or application made to it for the purpose, order that the husband shall secure to the wife for her maintenance and support, if necessary, by a charge on the husband's property, such gross sum or such monthly or periodical payment of money for a term not exceeding her life, as having regard to her own property, if any, her husband's property and ability the conduct of the parties and other circumstances of the case, it may seem to the court to be just. If the district court is satisfied that there is a change in the circumstances of either party at any time after it has made an order, it may, at the instance of either party, vary, modify or rescind any such order in such manner, as it may seem to the court to be just. If the district court is satisfied that the wife in whose favour an order has been made under this section has remarried or is not leading a chaste life, it may, at the instance of the husband vary, modify or rescind any such order and in such manner as the court may deem just.

ALIMONY UNDER CHRISTIAN LAW

The Christian law on alimony is governed by the Divorce Act, 1869. If any suit under the Divorce Act, 1869, whether it be instituted by a husband or a wife and whether or not she has obtained an order of protection the wife may present a petition for expenses of the proceedings and alimony pending the suit. Such petition shall be served on the husband, and the court, on being satisfied of the truth of the statements therein contained, may make such order on the husband for payment to the wife of the expenses of the proceedings and alimony pending the suit as it may deem just provided further that the petition for the expenses of the proceedings and alimony pending the suit, shall, as far as possible, be disposed of within sixty days of service of such petition on the husband.

Where a decree of dissolution of the marriage or a decree of judicial separation is obtained by the wife, the district court may order, that the husband shall to the satisfaction of the court, secure to the wife such gross sum of money, or such annual sum of money for any term not exceeding her own life, as, having regard to her fortune (if any), to the ability of the husband, and to the conduct of the parties, it thinks reasonable and for that purpose may cause a proper instrument to be executed by all necessary parties.

In every such case the court may make an order on the husband for payment to the wife of such monthly or weekly sum for her maintenance and support as the court may think reasonable provided that if the husband afterwards from any cause becomes unable to make such payments, it shall be lawful for the Court to discharge or modify the order, or temporarily to suspend the same as to the whole or any part of the money so ordered to be paid and again to revive the same order wholly or in part as to the court seems fit.

In all cases in which the court makes any decree or order for alimony, it may direct the same to be paid either to the wife herself, or to any trustee on her behalf to be approved by the court, and may impose any terms or restrictions which the court seem expedient, and may from time to time appoint a new trustee, if it appears to the court expedient so to do.

ALIMONY UNDER PARSI LAW

Where in any suit under the Parsi Marriage and Divorce Act, 1936 it appears to the court that either the wife or the husband, as the case may be has no independent income sufficient for her or his support and the necessary expenses of the suit, it may, on the application of the wife or the husband order the defendant to pay to the plaintiff, the expenses of the suit, and such weekly or monthly sum, during the suit, as having regard to the plaintiff's own income and the income of the defendant, it may seem to the court to be reasonable provided that the application for the payment of the expenses of the suit and such weekly or monthly sum during the suit shall, as far as possible, be disposed of within sixty days from the date of service of notice on the wife or the husband, as the case may be.

Any court exercising jurisdiction under the Parsi Marriage and Divorce Act, 1936 may, at the time of passing any decree or at any time subsequent thereto, on an application made to it for the purpose by either the wife or the husband, order that the defendant shall pay to the plaintiff for her or his maintenance and support, such gross sum or such monthly or periodical sum for a term not exceeding the life of the plaintiff as having regard to the defendant's own income and other property, if any, the income and other property of the plaintiff, the conduct of the parties and other circumstances of the case, it may seem to the court to be just and any such payment may be secured, if necessary, by a charge on the movable or immovable property of the defendant. The court if it is satisfied that there is change in the circumstance of either party at any time after it has made an order, it may, at the instance of either party, vary, modify or rescind any such order in such manner as the court may deem just. The court if it is satisfied that the party in whose favour an order has been made under Section 40 of the Parsi Marriage and Divorce Act, 1936 has remarried or if such party is the wife, that she has not remained chaste or if such party is the husband, that he had sexual intercourse with any women outside wedlock, it may, at the instance of the other party, vary, modify or rescind any such order in such manner as the court may deem just.

In *Tehmi Dinyar Mistry* v. *Kaikhushrao Mistry* A.I.R. 1976 Bom. 246 (DB) it was held that it was possible for the court to grant permanent alimony in lump sum and to handover or give a direction for the handing over of the money to the wife.

In all cases in which the court shall make any decree or order for alimony it may direct the same to be paid either to the wife herself or to any trustee on her behalf to be approved by the court or to a guardian appointed by the court, and may impose any terms or restrictions which the court may seem expedient, and may from time to time appoint a new trustee or guardian if for any reason it shall appear to the court expedient so to do.

WILL, GIFT AND WAKF

Wills in Muslim Law

1. Validity and Essentials of a Will

In Muslim law, a will (Wasiyat) is a legal declaration by an individual expressing their intentions regarding the distribution of their property after their demise. To be considered valid, a will must meet certain essential criteria:

- **Legal Capacity of the Testator:** The individual making the will (the testator) must possess sound mental faculties. This implies they understand the nature and consequences of their actions and are not suffering from any mental disorders that could impair their judgment. Additionally, the testator must have attained the age of majority, which varies depending on the specific school of Islamic law.
- **Freedom of Intention:** The will must be executed voluntarily and without any external pressure or coercion. Any undue influence exerted upon the testator can render the will invalid. This includes situations where the testator is coerced, manipulated, or misled into making a particular disposition of their property.
- **Subject Matter Limitations:** A will cannot dispose of the entire estate of the testator. Islamic law imposes a limit, allowing the testator to bequeath only one-third of their estate through a will. The remaining two-thirds are subject to the rules of inheritance (Faraid), which dictate how the property is distributed among the testator's legal heirs.
- **Formalities:** While Islamic law does not mandate strict formalities for the execution of a will, it emphasizes the importance of clear and unambiguous expression of the testator's intentions. A will can be oral or written, but it should be clear and avoid any ambiguity that could lead to disputes among heirs.

2. Revocation of a Will

A will is not an irrevocable document. A testator retains the right to revoke their will at any time during their lifetime. Revocation can occur through various means:

- **Express Revocation:** The most direct method of revocation is through an explicit declaration by the testator. This can be done orally or in writing, with the testator clearly stating their intention to revoke the existing will.
- **Implied Revocation:** Revocation can also be implied through subsequent actions or statements by the testator that contradict the provisions of the original will. For instance, if the testator executes a new will with different provisions, it implicitly revokes the previous will. Similarly, if the testator disposes of the property bequeathed in the will, it can be considered an implied revocation of that specific bequest.
- **Destruction of the Will:** Physically destroying the will, such as tearing it up or burning it, can also constitute a revocation. However, mere possession of the will by someone other than the testator does not automatically imply revocation.

3. Distribution of Property According to a Will

The distribution of property according to a will is subject to certain limitations:

- **Protection of Legal Heirs:** Islamic law recognizes the rights of legal heirs to inherit a portion of the testator's estate. A will cannot completely disinherit legal heirs but can exclude residuaries or distant kindred within the one-third limit, provided bequests to heirs have other heirs' consent post-testator's death.
- **One-Third Limit:** As mentioned earlier, a will cannot dispose of more than one-third of the testator's estate. This limitation ensures that a significant portion of the estate is distributed according to the rules of inheritance, safeguarding the rights of legal heirs.

The order of distribution generally follows these steps:

- **Payment of Debts and Funeral Expenses:** Prior to any other distribution, the testator's debts and funeral expenses are settled from the estate.
- **Fulfillment of Legacies:** If the will contains any specific bequests (legacies) to individuals or charities, these are fulfilled up to the one-third limit.
- **Distribution to Legal Heirs:** The remaining two-thirds of the estate are distributed among the testator's legal heirs according to the rules of inheritance (Faraid). These rules are based on intricate calculations and vary depending on the relationship of each heir to the deceased.

4. Case Laws on Wills in Muslim Law

Numerous case laws have shaped the interpretation and application of Islamic law concerning wills. These cases provide valuable insights into specific legal principles and their practical implications. Some notable examples include:

- **Cases Involving Undue Influence:** Courts have frequently addressed cases where the validity of a will is challenged on the grounds of undue influence exerted upon the testator. These cases often involve situations where a dominant individual or entity coerces the testator into making a particular disposition of their property.

- **Cases Concerning Revocation:** Courts have adjudicated cases involving disputes over the revocation of wills. These cases may involve questions of whether a subsequent act or statement by the testator constitutes an implied revocation or whether the testator had the mental capacity to revoke their will.
- **Cases Involving Ambiguous Language:** Courts have also dealt with cases where the language of the will is ambiguous or unclear. In such situations, courts may interpret the will based on various principles of interpretation, such as considering the testator's intentions and the surrounding circumstances.

GIFTS (HIBA) IN MUSLIM LAW

In Islamic law, a gift (Hiba) is a voluntary and irrevocable transfer of ownership of property from one person (the donor or "wahib") to another (the donee or "mauhub") without any consideration or exchange. It is considered an act of generosity and benevolence, deeply rooted in Islamic values.

Types of Gifts

While the core concept of a gift remains consistent, Islamic jurisprudence recognizes different categories based on the nature of the transfer:

- **Absolute Gift (Hiba-e-Mutlaq):** This is the most common form of gift, characterized by its unconditional nature. The transfer of ownership to the donee is immediate and complete, granting them full rights to possess, use, and dispose of the gifted property as they deem fit. There are no restrictions or conditions attached to the transfer.
- **Conditional Gift (Hiba-e-Mashrut):** Under the dominant Hanafi school, a condition that makes a valid gift contingent or revocable is often void, while the gift itself remains valid and becomes absolute. The property usually does not revert if the condition is not met in such cases.
- **Gift with Consideration (Hiba-bil-Iwaz):** In Indian legal practice, Hiba-bil-Iwaz is essentially treated as a sale where mutual consideration transforms it into an exchange/sale, not primarily a "gift" where intent to bestow generosity is the sole driver and consideration is nominal. The consideration can be substantial, and it doesn't need to be solely an "intent to bestow a gift.

Validity and Essentials of a Gift

For a gift to be considered valid in Islamic law, several essential conditions must be met:

- **Legal Capacity:** Both the donor and the donee must possess legal capacity to enter into the transaction. This generally requires them to be of sound mind, have attained the age of majority, and not be legally prohibited from making such a transfer.
- **Clear Intention:** The donor's intention to make the gift must be clear and unambiguous. This can be expressed through explicit statements, written documents, or even implied through actions.
- **Acceptance by the Donee:** The donee must unequivocally accept the gift. This acceptance can be expressed verbally, in writing, or through actions that demonstrate their acknowledgment and acceptance of the transfer of ownership.
- **Delivery (Qabd):** While not always strictly required in all schools of thought, delivery of the gifted property to the donee is generally considered an essential element for the validity of the gift. This can take various forms, including physical delivery, constructive delivery (such as handing over keys to a property), or symbolic delivery.
- **Absence of Undue Influence or Coercion:** The gift must be made freely and voluntarily, without any pressure, coercion, or undue influence exerted upon the donor. Any evidence of coercion or manipulation can render the gift invalid.

Revocation of a Gift

One of the defining characteristics of a valid gift in Islamic law is its general irrevocability. Once a gift is validly made and accepted, the donor typically cannot unilaterally revoke it. However, there are certain limited circumstances under which revocation may be permissible:

- **Failure to Fulfill Conditions:** In the case of conditional gifts, if the stipulated conditions are not met, the gift may be revoked. This is because the fulfillment of the conditions was a fundamental aspect of the agreement.
- **Gratuitous Revocation:** Some schools of Islamic thought recognize the possibility of revoking a gift based on the donor's subsequent change of mind. However, this is generally subject to significant restrictions and may not be universally accepted.

- **Revocation in Public Interest:** In exceptional circumstances, a gift may be revoked if it is deemed to be contrary to public interest or against the principles of Islamic law. For example, if a gift is made with the intention of harming another individual or undermining public order, it may be considered invalid.

Case Laws on Gifts in Muslim Law

Numerous case laws have arisen in Islamic legal history concerning the validity, interpretation, and revocation of gifts. These cases provide valuable insights into the application of legal principles and the complexities that can arise in real-world situations. Some examples include cases involving disputes over the validity of gifts due to alleged undue influence, challenges to the revocation of gifts, and interpretations of ambiguous language in gift deeds.

WAKF IN MUSLIM LAW

Wakf is a unique and significant institution in Islamic law that involves the permanent dedication of property for religious, charitable, or public welfare purposes. It is considered an act of piety and a means of ensuring the continuous performance of good deeds even after the donor's demise.

Core Concept

The fundamental principle underlying Wakf is the irrevocable transfer of ownership of the property to Allah. The donor, known as the "waqif," relinquishes their ownership rights, effectively transferring them to the divine. Waqif relinquishes all rights, including usufruct, transferring ownership and benefits to Allah for the Wakf's designated purpose.

Types of Wakf

Wakf can be broadly categorized into two main types:

- **Public Wakf (Waqf Khairi):** This type of Wakf is dedicated to the benefit of the general public. The proceeds from the Wakf property are utilized for various public welfare activities, such as:
  - Construction and maintenance of mosques, schools, and hospitals.
  - Providing for the poor and needy.
  - Funding public infrastructure projects, such as roads and bridges.
  - Supporting religious and educational activities.
- **Private Wakf (Waqf Ahli):** This type of Wakf is established for the benefit of specific individuals or families. The beneficiaries may include the donor's descendants, relatives, or other designated individuals. Examples of private Wakf include:
  - Providing for the maintenance of a family mausoleum or grave.
  - Supporting the education and upbringing of specific individuals or groups.
  - Providing for the financial needs of specific individuals or families.

Creation and Administration of a Wakf

The creation of a valid Wakf requires several essential elements:

- **Declaration of Intent:** The donor must clearly and unequivocally express their intention to dedicate the property for Wakf purposes. This can be done through a written deed, an oral declaration, or even implied through actions. The declaration must clearly specify the property being dedicated, the intended beneficiaries, and the purposes for which the property is to be utilized.
- **Subject Matter of the Wakf:** Any type of property can be dedicated as Wakf, including land, buildings, cash, and other valuable assets. However, the property must be legally owned by the donor and must be capable of generating income or providing the intended benefits.
- **Lawful Purpose:** The purpose for which the Wakf is established must be lawful and in accordance with Islamic principles. Purposes that are contrary to Islamic law or public order are not permissible.

Once a Wakf is established, a Mutawalli (trustee) is typically appointed to manage and administer the Wakf property. The Mutawalli is responsible for:

- Collecting and managing the income generated from the Wakf property.
- Disbursing funds for the designated charitable or religious purposes.
- Maintaining and preserving the Wakf property.
- Ensuring that the Wakf property is utilized in accordance with the donor's intentions and the provisions of the Wakf deed.
- Accounting for all income and expenditures related to the Wakf.

Case Laws on Wakf in Muslim Law

Numerous case laws have arisen in Islamic legal history concerning the validity, interpretation, and administration of Wakf. These cases provide valuable insights into the application of legal principles and the complexities that can arise in real-world situations. Some examples include:

- Cases involving disputes over the validity of a Wakf due to ambiguity in the declaration of intent or the designated purpose.
- Cases dealing with the removal of a Mutawalli for mismanagement, breach of trust, or failure to fulfill their duties.
- Cases concerning the diversion of Wakf funds from the intended charitable purposes.
- Cases involving disputes between beneficiaries or between the Mutawalli and beneficiaries regarding the utilization of Wakf funds.

UNIFORM CIVIL CODE

DEFINITION AND PURPOSE OF THE UNIFORM CIVIL CODE (UCC)

What is the Uniform Civil Code? The Uniform Civil Code (UCC) refers to a proposal in India to formulate and implement a single set of laws governing personal matters such as marriage, divorce, adoption, inheritance, and maintenance for all citizens, irrespective of their religion. Currently, such matters are primarily governed by separate personal laws specific to each major religious community in India. The UCC aims to replace these separate personal laws with a common set of rules.

Objectives and Reasons for Proposing a UCC in India:

- **Promotion of National Unity and Integrity:** The UCC seeks to consolidate diverse personal laws under one umbrella, which is seen as a way to promote national unity and reduce divisions based on religious identities.
- **Ensuring Gender Justice:** One of the main driving forces behind the UCC is the aim to provide equal status to all citizens, particularly women, across religions. Many personal laws are perceived as discriminatory towards women. A uniform code is viewed as a means to ensure equal rights in marriage, divorce, inheritance, and family matters, thus empowering women.
- **Modernization of Law:** As society evolves, the need for a set of laws that reflect contemporary values and ethics becomes crucial. The UCC is seen as a step towards modernizing legal frameworks by replacing outdated customs and practices that no longer align with modern views on rights and equality.
- **Legal Simplification:** Having a single, uniform set of laws would simplify the legal system by eliminating the confusion and complexity that arises from the existence of multiple legal systems. This can potentially lead to a more efficient administration of justice.
- **Protection of Vulnerable Groups:** By creating a uniform law, the rights and interests of vulnerable groups, including religious minorities, can be better protected as everyone will be subject to the same laws, thereby ensuring fairness and justice.
- **Encouraging Secularism:** Implementing the UCC is also seen as a step towards reinforcing the secular framework of the nation, where the state does not prioritize one religion over another but instead upholds the same laws for all, irrespective of religious background.
- **Adherence to Constitutional Mandates:** The Indian Constitution in Article 44 of the Directive Principles of State Policy mentions that the state shall endeavor to secure a Uniform Civil Code for the citizens throughout the territory of India. Although directive principles are not enforceable by courts, they are fundamental in the governance of the country, intended to apply principles of justice and equality.
- **International Practices:** Comparing with other secular nations that have uniform civil laws, proponents argue that India too should adopt similar practices to remain competitive and fair in its legal system.

Article 44 of the Indian Constitution and Its Implications

- **Definition:**
  - Article 44 is part of the Directive Principles of State Policy (DPSP) under Part IV of the Indian Constitution.
  - It states, "The State shall endeavour to secure for the citizens a uniform civil code throughout the territory of India."

- **Purpose:** The purpose of Article 44 is to address the disparity in personal laws existing in India based on religious practices. It aims to bring about a uniform legal framework governing personal matters such as marriage, divorce, inheritance, and adoption.
- **Implications:**
  - While Article 44 sets forth an ideal that the State should strive towards, it is not enforceable by any court. However, it serves as a guideline or principle that the government should consider in its legislative agenda.
  - Uniform Civil Code (UCC) intends to promote national unity and integrity by standardizing civil laws, potentially reducing religious conflicts and improving gender justice.

Shah Bano Case (1985)

- **Case Reference:** Mohd. Ahmed Khan v. Shah Bano Begum
- **Summary:** This was a landmark case in which the Supreme Court of India granted alimony to a Muslim woman after her divorce, under Section 125 of the Code of Criminal Procedure, which applies to all Indian citizens regardless of religion.
- **Significance:** The judgment highlighted the conflict between the secular principles enshrined in the Indian Constitution and the personal laws specific to various religious communities. It emphasized the need for a Uniform Civil Code, sparking a nationwide debate. The ruling led to accusations of the court overstepping into personal law territory, followed by the government enacting the Muslim Women (Protection of Rights on Divorce) Act, 1986, which made the judgment effectively redundant in Shah Bano's case but Danial Latifi v. Union of India (2001) upheld broader maintenance rights, preserving the Shah Bano judgment's constitutional significance.

Sarla Mudgal Case (1995)

- **Case Reference:** Sarla Mudgal, President, Kalyani v. Union of India & Ors.
- **Summary:** This case involved Hindu husbands who converted to Islam solely to remarry without divorcing their first wives. The Supreme Court held that a Hindu marriage could only be dissolved under the Hindu Marriage Act, 1955. A conversion to Islam and subsequent marriage by a Hindu spouse does not automatically dissolve the Hindu marriage under the act.
- **Significance:** The judgment brought to the forefront issues of misuse of religious conversions to circumvent legal provisions governing marriage and divorce, highlighting the inconsistency and potential for abuse in personal laws. It reiterated the necessity for a Uniform Civil Code to ensure equality and justice across religions, which could prevent such legal ambiguities and exploitation.

Recent Cases and Their Significance in the UCC Discourse

Jose Paulo Coutinho Case (2019)

- **Case Reference:** Jose Paulo Coutinho v. Maria Luiza Valentina Pereira & Anr.
- **Summary:** The Supreme Court reaffirmed the applicability of the Portuguese Civil Code, 1867, in the state of Goa, where it continues to operate. This code is essentially a uniform civil code by itself, governing all Goans irrespective of their religious affiliation.
- **Significance:** This case is often cited in the UCC debate to illustrate that a uniform civil code is indeed feasible in a diverse and pluralistic society like India. It provides a practical example of a functioning UCC within Indian territory, emphasizing that uniform laws can coexist with religious freedom and cultural diversity.

Shayara Bano Case (2017)

- **Case Reference:** Shayara Bano v. Union of India & Ors.
- **Summary:** The case led to the Supreme Court's landmark judgment declaring the practice of triple talaq (talaq-e-biddat) unconstitutional. Triple talaq is a practice among some Muslims where saying 'divorce' thrice consecutively dissolves a marriage instantaneously.
- **Significance:** The judgment is pivotal in the discourse on UCC as it underscores the role of the judiciary in rectifying practices deemed unconstitutional and discriminatory within personal laws. It highlighted the necessity of reforming personal laws that are inconsistent with the fundamental rights guaranteed under the Indian Constitution, pushing further the agenda for a UCC that would ensure equal rights across different genders and religions.

MULTIPLE CHOICE QUESTIONS

1. Which of the following is NOT a primary source of Hindu Law?
A. Shruti B. Smriti
C. Custom D. Constitution of India

2. Which school of Hindu law is prevalent mainly in Northern India?
A. Mitakshara B. Dayabhaga
C. Smriti D. Mimamsa

3. Which of the following is a source of Muslim Law?
A. Vedas B. Quran
C. Manusmriti D. Upanishads

4. Customs that are valid and recognized under Hindu Law must be:
A. Recent and flexible
B. Continuous, certain, and reasonable
C. Written and codified
D. Approved by a court

5. The Mitakshara School allows for the right of a son to inherit property by birth.
A. True
B. False
C. True, only if the father consents
D. False, unless registered in court

6. Under Dayabhaga Law, inheritance is based on survivorship rather than succession.
A. True
B. False
C. True, if the property is immovable
D. False, unless stated otherwise in a will

7. Assertion (A): Custom is considered a source of both Hindu and Muslim law.

Reason (R): Custom has the power to override statutory laws.
A. Both A and R are true, and R is the correct explanation of A
B. Both A and R are true, but R is not the correct explanation of A
C. A is true, R is false
D. A is false, R is true

8. Assertion (A): The Quran is considered the supreme source of Muslim Law.

Reason (R): All Islamic legal principles are derived exclusively from the Quran.
A. Both A and R are true, and R is the correct explanation of A
B. Both A and R are true, but R is not the correct explanation of A
C. A is true, R is false
D. A is false, R is true

9. The term 'Shruti' refers to that which is ______.
A. Written B. Remembered
C. Heard D. Disputed

10. The Mitakshara School was founded by ______.
A. Vijnaneshwara B. Yajnavalkya
C. Manu D. Kautilya

11. Match the following schools of Hindu Law with their regions of prevalence:

A. Mitakshara	1. Bengal and Assam
B. Dayabhaga	2. Northern India
C. Dravida School	3. Southern India
D. Maharashtra School	4. Western India

A. A-2, B-1, C-3, D-4
B. A-1, B-2, C-4, D-3
C. A-3, B-4, C-1, D-2
D. A-4, B-3, C-2, D-1

12. Arrange the following sources of Hindu Law in chronological order:
1. Shruti
2. Smriti
3. Commentaries and Digests
4. Custom
5. Judicial decisions

A. 1, 2, 3, 4, 5 B. 2, 1, 4, 3, 5
C. 3, 4, 1, 2, 5 D. 5, 4, 3, 2, 1

13. Scenario: A Hindu family follows a local custom where daughters inherit property equally with sons. Can this custom override the Mitakshara inheritance rules?
A. Yes, if the custom is ancient, certain, and reasonable
B. No, Mitakshara rules always prevail
C. Yes, only if registered
D. No, unless approved by the court

14. Scenario: A dispute arises regarding property succession in a Muslim family. The Quran does not directly address the issue. Which source will be referred to next?

A. Indian Penal Code
B. Hadith
C. Hindu Succession Act
D. Indian Evidence Act

15. Scenario: In a joint Hindu family governed by Mitakshara law, the father dies intestate. Who has the right to claim the ancestral property?
A. Only the eldest son
B. All sons equally
C. All coparceners, including daughters after 2005 amendment
D. Only the wife

16. Which of the following is NOT a source of Muslim Law?
A. Quran B. Hadith
C. Ijma D. Upanishads

17. Under Hindu Law, the term 'Smriti' refers to:
A. That which is heard
B. That which is remembered
C. That which is divine
D. That which is written in court

18. Match the following Islamic legal concepts with their meanings:

A. Quran	1. Consensus of scholars
B. Hadith	2. Analogical reasoning
C. Ijma	3. Teachings of Prophet Muhammad
D. Qiyas	4. Holy book of Islam

A. A-4, B-3, C-1, D-2
B. A-1, B-2, C-4, D-3
C. A-2, B-4, C-3, D-1
D. A-3, B-1, C-2, D-4

19. Scenario: A Hindu man claims his right to ancestral property under the Dayabhaga system. Which principle will the court consider?
A. Right by birth
B. Right by survivorship
C. Right through succession
D. Right through custom only

20. Scenario: A custom followed in a community discriminates against women in property rights. Is this custom valid under modern law?
A. Yes, if it's ancient and certain
B. No, as it violates constitutional principles of equality
C. Yes, if approved by community elders
D. No, unless codified in statutory law

21. Under the Hindu Marriage Act, 1955, the minimum age for marriage is:
A. 18 years for both male and female
B. 21 years for male and 18 years for female
C. 18 years for male and 21 years for female
D. 21 years for both male and female

22. Which of the following is NOT a ground for divorce under the Hindu Marriage Act, 1955?
A. Cruelty
B. Conversion to another religion
C. Mutual consent
D. Property disputes

23. In Muslim Law, which form of divorce allows a husband to pronounce divorce three times in one sitting?
A. Talaq-e-Hasan B. Talaq-e-Ahsan
C. Talaq-e-Biddat D. Khula

24. Which of the following is NOT an essential condition for a valid Hindu marriage?
A. Mental capacity
B. Same caste
C. Age criteria
D. Prohibited degrees of relationship

25. A Hindu marriage is considered a sacrament and not a contract.
A. True
B. False
C. True, only if it involves traditional rituals
D. False, unless registered under the Special Marriage Act

26. Under Muslim law, Khula is a form of divorce initiated by the wife.
A. True
B. False
C. True, only with the husband's consent
D. False, unless the wife proves cruelty

27. **Assertion (A):** Adultery is a ground for divorce under the Hindu Marriage Act, 1955.

Reason (R): Adultery is a criminal offense under Indian law.
A. Both A and R are true, and R is the correct explanation of A
B. Both A and R are true, but R is not the correct explanation of A
C. A is true, R is false
D. A is false, R is true

28. **Assertion (A):** A marriage under the Special Marriage Act, 1954 requires registration.

Reason (R): The Special Marriage Act applies only to Hindus.

A. Both A and R are true, and R is the correct explanation of A
B. Both A and R are true, but R is not the correct explanation of A
C. A is true, R is false
D. A is false, R is true

29. Under the Hindu Marriage Act, 1955, marriage within the prohibited degree of relationship is ______.
A. Valid
B. Void
C. Voidable
D. Legal with parental consent

30. The dissolution of marriage by mutual consent requires the couple to live separately for at least ______ before filing for divorce under the Hindu Marriage Act.
A. 6 months B. 1 year
C. 2 years D. 3 years

31. Match the following types of divorce with their characteristics:

Types of divorce	Characteristics
A. Talaq-e-Ahsan	1. Divorce initiated by the wife
B. Talaq-e-Hasan	2. Divorce by mutual consent in Muslim law
C. Khula	3. Divorce pronounced once, followed by abstinence
D. Mubarat	4. Divorce pronounced three times over three lunar cycles

A. A-3, B-4, C-1, D-2
B. A-1, B-3, C-4, D-2
C. A-4, B-1, C-2, D-3
D. A-2, B-1, C-3, D-4

32. Arrange the following steps in the correct sequence for divorce by mutual consent under the Hindu Marriage Act, 1955:
1. Filing a joint petition
2. Mandatory cooling-off period
3. Final hearing
4. Decree of divorce

A. 1, 2, 3, 4 B. 2, 1, 3, 4
C. 1, 3, 2, 4 D. 4, 1, 2, 3

33. Scenario: A Hindu couple has been living separately for three years without reconciliation. They mutually agree to divorce. What is the appropriate legal provision?
A. Divorce under Section 13 of the Hindu Marriage Act
B. Divorce under Section 13B (mutual consent)
C. Nullity of marriage
D. Judicial separation

34. Scenario: In a Muslim marriage, the wife seeks divorce without the husband's consent due to cruelty. What legal provision can she invoke?
A. Talaq B. Khula
C. Mubarat D. Faskh

35. Scenario: A couple married under the Special Marriage Act wants to dissolve their marriage. Which court has jurisdiction?
A. Family Court
B. High Court
C. Supreme Court
D. District Court

36. Under Muslim law, which of the following is a valid ground for divorce for a woman under the Dissolution of Muslim Marriages Act, 1939?
A. Husband's change of religion
B. Husband's inability to bear children
C. Husband's unemployment
D. Husband's failure to provide maintenance for two years

37. Under Hindu law, desertion as a ground for divorce requires a continuous absence for at least:
A. 1 year B. 2 years
C. 3 years D. 5 years

38. Match the following legal provisions with the appropriate personal law statutes in India:

Legal Provisions	Statutes
A. Right to maintenance for a divorced wife	1. Hindu Succession Act
B. Inheritance rights for daughters in ancestral property	2. Muslim Personal Law (Shariat) Application Act
C. Registration of marriage for inter-religious couples	3. Special Marriage Act
D. Divorce by pronouncement of triple talaq (prior to its ban)	4. Section 125 of the Criminal Procedure Code

A. A-4, B-1, C-3, D-2
B. A-2, B-3, C-1, D-4
C. A-3, B-1, C-2, D-4
D. A-1, B-2. C-4, D-3

39. Scenario: A Hindu woman seeks divorce due to her husband's conversion to another religion. Is this a valid ground for divorce?
A. Yes, under Section 13(1)(ii) of the Hindu Marriage Act
B. No, unless the husband consents

C. Yes, only if he converts to Islam
D. No, unless registered under the Special Marriage Act

40. Scenario: A Muslim man pronounces Triple Talaq (Talaq-e-Biddat) in one sitting. Is this valid in India?
A. Yes, as per Sharia law
B. No, it is unconstitutional in India
C. Yes, if pronounced before witnesses
D. No, unless registered in court

41. Which of the following is NOT a recognized theory of divorce?
A. Fault Theory
B. Mutual Consent Theory
C. Irretrievable Breakdown Theory
D. Customary Theory

42. Which section of the Hindu Marriage Act, 1955 deals with divorce by mutual consent?
A. Section 11 B. Section 13
C. Section 13B D. Section 14

43. Under Muslim law, which of the following is NOT a valid form of divorce?
A. Talaq B. Khula
C. Mubarat D. Sati

44. Which theory of divorce is based on the idea that marriage can be dissolved only if one party is at fault?
A. Fault Theory
B. Mutual Consent Theory
C. Irretrievable Breakdown Theory
D. Free Will Theory

45. Irretrievable breakdown of marriage is a ground for divorce under the Hindu Marriage Act, 1955.
A. True
B. False
C. True, only after Supreme Court approval
D. False, unless both parties agree

46. Adultery as a ground for divorce requires proof beyond reasonable doubt.
A. True
B. False
C. True, if both parties agree
D. False, unless filed within a year

47. Assertion (A): Mutual consent is sufficient for granting a divorce under the Hindu Marriage Act.

Reason (R): The court's satisfaction is not required if both parties consent.
A. Both A and R are true, and R is the correct explanation of A
B. Both A and R are true, but R is not the correct explanation of A
C. A is true, R is false
D. A is false, R is true

48. Assertion (A): Desertion is a ground for divorce under the Hindu Marriage Act.

Reason (R): Desertion means physical separation only.
A. Both A and R are true, and R is the correct explanation of A
B. Both A and R are true, but R is not the correct explanation of A
C. A is true, R is false
D. A is false, R is true

49. Under the Hindu Marriage Act, the minimum period of separation required for mutual consent divorce is ______.
A. 6 months B. 1 year
C. 2 years D. 3 years

50. The concept of 'irretrievable breakdown of marriage' was first recognized in ______.
A. United States B. United Kingdom
C. India D. France

51. Match the following theories of divorce with their characteristics:

Theories of Divorce	Characteristics
A. Fault Theory	1. Divorce without proving any fault
B. Mutual Consent Theory	2. Both parties agree to end the marriage
C. Irretrievable Breakdown Theory	3. Requires proof that one party is at fault
D. No-Fault Theory	4. Marriage has broken down beyond repair

A. A-3, B-2, C-4, D-1
B. A-1, B-3, C-4, D-2
C. A-4, B-1, C-2, D-3
D. A-2, B-4, C-1, D-3

52. Arrange the following steps in the correct sequence for divorce by mutual consent under the Hindu Marriage Act:
1. Filing of joint petition
2. Mandatory cooling-off period
3. Final hearing by the court
4. Grant of divorce decree

A. 1, 2, 3, 4 B. 2, 1, 3, 4
C. 1, 3, 2, 4 D. 4, 1, 2, 3

53. Scenario: A husband files for divorce under the Hindu Marriage Act on the ground of cruelty. The wife proves that he also treated her with cruelty. Can the court grant divorce?

A. No, because both parties are at fault
B. Yes, as cruelty by either party is sufficient
C. No, unless the wife consents
D. Yes, if the husband withdraws his allegations

54. Scenario: A Muslim woman seeks divorce due to her husband's failure to provide maintenance for three years. What form of divorce can she seek?

A. Talaq
B. Khula
C. Faskh (judicial divorce)
D. Mubarat

55. Scenario: A couple married under the Special Marriage Act wants to dissolve their marriage. What is the minimum period of separation required before filing for divorce?

A. 1 year   B. 2 years
C. 3 years   D. 6 months

56. Which of the following is NOT a ground for divorce under the Hindu Marriage Act, 1955?

A. Adultery   B. Cruelty
C. Incompatibility   D. Desertion

57. Under the Hindu Marriage Act, the term 'desertion' must continue for at least:

A. 6 months   B. 1 year
C. 2 years   D. 5 years

58. Match the following Muslim family law provisions with the appropriate legal frameworks or sources in India:

Muslim family law provisions	Legal Frameworks/ Sources
A. Divorce initiated by the wife through judicial process	1. Muslim Personal Law (Shariat) Application Act
B. Inheritance share of a daughter in her father's estate	2. Dissolution of Muslim Marriages Act
C. Maintenance for a wife during the iddat period	3. Muslim Women (Protection of Rights on Divorce) Act
D. Marriage contract with stipulated dower (mehr)	4. Quran and Sunnah (as applied under Muslim Personal Law)

A. A-2, B-1, C-3, D-4
B. A-3, B-4, C-1, D-2
C. A-1, B-2, C-3, D-4
D. A-2, B-3, C-4, D-1

59. Scenario: A Hindu husband converts to Islam to marry another woman while his first marriage is still valid. Is this legal?

A. Yes, as conversion permits polygamy
B. No, it amounts to bigamy under Indian law
C. Yes, if both wives consent
D. No, unless approved by the court

60. Scenario: A couple has been living separately for five years, and one party refuses to consent to divorce. Can the court grant divorce?

A. No, unless both parties consent
B. Yes, if it constitutes irretrievable breakdown of marriage
C. No, unless the party proves cruelty
D. Yes, but only after counseling

61. Which section of the Code of Civil Procedure, 1908 deals with the recognition of foreign judgments in India?

A. Section 11   B. Section 13
C. Section 23   D. Section 27

62. A foreign divorce decree will NOT be recognized in India if:

A. It is passed by a competent court
B. It is passed ex-parte without hearing both parties
C. It is based on valid grounds recognized in Indian law
D. It follows the principles of natural justice

63. Which of the following is NOT a ground for refusing recognition of a foreign divorce decree in India?

A. Lack of jurisdiction
B. Contrary to natural justice
C. Based on fraud
D. Recognition would benefit both parties

64. The doctrine that determines if a foreign court had the authority to pass a decree is called:

A. Doctrine of Estoppel
B. Doctrine of Res Judicata
C. Doctrine of Competent Jurisdiction
D. Doctrine of Lis Pendens

65. A foreign divorce decree obtained through fraud is valid in India.

A. True
B. False
C. True, if both parties consented
D. False, unless certified by the Indian Embassy

66. A divorce decree passed by a foreign court will always be automatically recognized in India.

A. True
B. False

C. True, if both parties are Indian citizens
D. False, unless registered in India

67. Assertion (A): A foreign divorce decree based on grounds not recognized by Indian law can be enforced in India.

Reason (R): Indian courts are bound to enforce all foreign judgments under international law.

A. Both A and R are true, and R is the correct explanation of A
B. Both A and R are true, but R is not the correct explanation of A
C. A is true, R is false
D. A is false, R is true

68. Assertion (A): Indian courts may refuse to recognize a foreign divorce decree if it violates public policy.

Reason (R): Public policy includes the basic principles of justice, fairness, and Indian matrimonial laws.

A. Both A and R are true, and R is the correct explanation of A
B. Both A and R are true, but R is not the correct explanation of A
C. A is true, R is false
D. A is false, R is true

69. A foreign decree will not be recognized in India if it is passed without _______ of both parties.

A. Written consent B. Legal representation
C. Proper jurisdiction D. Proper hearing

70. Foreign divorce decrees in India are recognized based on the principle of _______ under Section 13 CPC.

A. Comity of Nations B. Res Judicata
C. Natural Law D. Sovereignty Doctrine

71. Match the following grounds with their relevance to recognition of foreign decrees in India:

Foreign Decrees	Grounds
A. Lack of jurisdiction	1. Decree obtained without hearing both parties
B. Fraud	2. Decree procured through deceitful means
C. Violation of natural justice	3. Decree passed by an incompetent court
D. Contrary to Indian public policy	4. Decree violating basic Indian legal principles

A. A-3, B-2, C-1, D-4
B. A-1, B-4, C-3, D-2
C. A-2, B-3, C-4, D-1
D. A-4, B-1, C-2, D-3

72. Arrange the following steps in the correct sequence to enforce a foreign divorce decree in India:

1. Verification of jurisdiction of the foreign court
2. Check for violation of natural justice
3. Ensure the decree is not obtained by fraud
4. Examine if the decree violates Indian public policy

A. 1, 2, 3, 4
B. 4, 1, 3, 2
C. 2, 1, 4, 3
D. 3, 4, 1, 2

73. Scenario: A divorce decree is passed by a foreign court where the wife was not given notice of the proceedings. Can this decree be recognized in India?

A. Yes, if the court was competent
B. No, as it violates natural justice
C. Yes, if both parties are foreign nationals
D. No, unless the decree is registered in India

74. Scenario: A foreign court granted a divorce based on "irretrievable breakdown of marriage," which is not a ground under the Hindu Marriage Act. Will Indian courts recognize this decree?

A. Yes, if both parties agree
B. No, as the ground is not recognized in Indian law
C. Yes, if the decree is from a recognized country
D. No, unless validated by the Supreme Court

75. Scenario: A foreign divorce decree was obtained through fraudulent documents. Will Indian courts enforce this decree?

A. Yes, if the parties reside abroad
B. No, because it was obtained through fraud
C. Yes, if the fraud was minor
D. No, unless the fraud is proved beyond reasonable doubt

76. Which of the following is NOT a requirement for recognition of foreign divorce decrees in India?

A. Decree passed by a competent court
B. Decree obtained after hearing both parties
C. Decree registered with the Ministry of External Affairs
D. Decree not obtained through fraud

77. Recognition of foreign divorce decrees in India is based on which legal principle?

A. Sovereignty Doctrine
B. Comity of Nations
C. Parliamentary Supremacy
D. Reciprocity of Laws

78. Match the following legal principles with their relevance to foreign decrees:

Principles	Relevance
A. Comity of Nations	1. Promotes international recognition of judgments
B. Natural Justice	2. Ensures fairness and due process
C. Fraud Exception	3. Invalidates judgments obtained deceitfully
D. Public Policy Doctrine	4. Protects national legal norms

A. A-1, B-2, C-3, D-4
B. A-4, B-3, C-2, D-1
C. A-2, B-1, C-4, D-3
D. A-3, B-4, C-1, D-2

79. Scenario: A couple obtains a divorce decree from a foreign court, and both were Indian citizens living abroad. The decree is based on mutual consent. Will it be recognized in India?
A. Yes, as mutual consent is recognized in India
B. No, as Indian citizens must divorce under Indian law
C. Yes, only if approved by an Indian court
D. No, unless the decree is registered in India

80. Scenario: A foreign court granted a divorce without applying Indian matrimonial law, even though both parties were Hindu and Indian citizens. Can the decree be recognized?
A. Yes, if both parties accept it
B. No, as Indian law should have been applied
C. Yes, if the decree is from a recognized country
D. No, unless validated by the Indian High Court

81. Which section of the Hindu Adoption and Maintenance Act, 1956 deals with the right of a wife to claim maintenance?
A. Section 9
B. Section 18
C. Section 14
D. Section 25

82. Under Muslim law, Dower (Mahr) is:
A. A dowry paid by the bride's family
B. A mandatory payment by the husband to the wife
C. A voluntary gift by the husband
D. An optional religious offering

83. Which of the following is considered Stridhan under Hindu law?
A. Property acquired by a woman through inheritance
B. Property gifted to her by her husband at marriage
C. Dowry items given by the in-laws
D. Property received by the husband's family

84. Which of the following is NOT a valid ground for a Hindu wife to claim maintenance under Section 18?
A. Cruelty by the husband
B. Husband's conversion to another religion
C. Husband's unemployment
D. Desertion by the husband

85. A Muslim woman can claim unpaid dower even after divorce.
A. True
B. False
C. True, only if specified in the marriage contract
D. False, unless approved by the husband

86. Stridhan becomes the property of the husband after marriage.
A. True
B. False
C. True, only after ten years of marriage
D. False, unless the wife agrees in writing

87. **Assertion (A):** Maintenance under Section 125 CrPC applies to all religions in India.

Reason (R): Section 125 CrPC is a secular law providing maintenance to wives, children, and parents.
A. Both A and R are true, and R is the correct explanation of A
B. Both A and R are true, but R is not the correct explanation of A
C. A is true, R is false
D. A is false, R is true

88. **Assertion (A):** Dower is a form of consideration for the marriage contract under Muslim law.

Reason (R): Without payment of dower, a Muslim marriage is invalid.
A. Both A and R are true, and R is the correct explanation of A
B. Both A and R are true, but R is not the correct explanation of A
C. A is true, R is false
D. A is false, R is true

89. Stridhan includes property acquired by a woman ______.
A. Before marriage
B. During marriage
C. After marriage
D. All of the above

90. Maintenance under Section 125 CrPC can be claimed by a wife who is ______.
A. Living with her husband
B. Divorced and not remarried
C. Only if married under Hindu law
D. Only if she has children

91. Match the following terms with their correct definitions:

A. Maintenance	1. Property owned exclusively by a woman
B. Dower (Mahr)	2. Financial support provided to a spouse or dependent
C. Stridhan	3. Mandatory payment from husband to wife in Muslim marriage
D. Dowry	4. Property or money illegally demanded in connection with marriage

A. A-2, B-3, C-1, D-4
B. A-1, B-4, C-2, D-3
C. A-3, B-1, C-4, D-2
D. A-4, B-2, C-3, D-1

92. Arrange the following steps for claiming maintenance under Section 125 CrPC:
1. Filing of maintenance application
2. Notice to the opposite party
3. Court hearing and evidence presentation
4. Final order by the court

A. 1, 2, 3, 4 B. 2, 1, 4, 3
C. 3, 1, 2, 4 D. 4, 2, 1, 3

93. Scenario: A Muslim woman is divorced and claims unpaid dower from her ex-husband. Can she legally claim it?
A. No, since the marriage is dissolved
B. Yes, as unpaid dower is a debt owed to her
C. Yes, but only within six months of divorce
D. No, unless she proves financial hardship

94. Scenario: A Hindu woman receives jewelry from her parents at the time of her marriage. After separation, can she claim it as Stridhan?
A. No, as it belongs to her husband's family
B. Yes, as it is her exclusive property
C. No, unless registered in her name
D. Yes, only if gifted in writing

95. Scenario: A woman files for maintenance under Section 125 CrPC, but her husband claims he is unemployed. Will the court deny maintenance?
A. Yes, as he has no income
B. No, as maintenance is the husband's legal obligation
C. Yes, unless the wife is disabled
D. No, unless the wife proves cruelty

96. Which of the following is NOT considered Stridhan?
A. Gifts received by a woman from her parents
B. Property purchased by her husband in his name
C. Gifts received from friends during festivals
D. Jewelry gifted by in-laws at marriage

97. Under Muslim law, Dower (Mahr) is payable:
A. Only at the time of marriage
B. Only after the wife demands it
C. Either immediately (prompt) or deferred as agreed
D. Only upon divorce

98. Match the following types of maintenance with their relevant legal provisions:

A. Maintenance under Hindu Law	1. Section 18 of Hindu Adoption and Maintenance Act
B. Maintenance under Muslim Law	2. Muslim Women (Protection of Rights on Divorce) Act
C. Maintenance under CrPC	3. Section 125 CrPC
D. Maintenance for parents	4. Maintenance and Welfare of Parents and Senior Citizens Act

A. A-1, B-2, C-3, D-4
B. A-2, B-3, C-1, D-4
C. A-3, B-4, C-2, D-1
D. A-4, B-1, C-3, D-2

99. Scenario: A Muslim husband refuses to pay the deferred dower after divorce. What legal remedy does the wife have?
A. She cannot claim after divorce
B. She can file a civil suit to recover the dower
C. She must approach a religious authority
D. She can only claim if remarried

100. Scenario: A woman's in-laws retain her Stridhan after her husband's death. Can she claim it back?
A. No, as it becomes family property
B. Yes, as Stridhan remains her property
C. No, unless her husband left a will
D. Yes, only if she remarries

101. Which of the following laws governs adoption among Hindus in India?
A. Guardians and Wards Act, 1890
B. Hindu Adoption and Maintenance Act, 1956
C. Special Marriage Act, 1954
D. Indian Succession Act, 1925

102. Under Muslim law, adoption is:
A. Recognized as a legal institution
B. Prohibited entirely
C. Recognized only if registered
D. Not legally recognized but acknowledgment can be made

103. Which of the following is NOT a valid condition for adoption under the Hindu Adoption and Maintenance Act, 1956?
A. The adoptive parent must be a Hindu
B. The child must be under 18 years of age
C. A Hindu male cannot adopt without the consent of his wife
D. The child must be from the same caste as the adoptive parent

104. Who is considered the natural guardian of a Hindu minor boy and unmarried girl?
A. Mother B. Father
C. Elder sibling D. Grandparents

105. A Hindu female can adopt a child without the consent of her husband if he is alive.
A. True
B. False
C. True, if the husband is of unsound mind
D. False, unless approved by the court

106. Guardianship automatically ends when the minor attains the age of majority.
A. True
B. False
C. True, unless the guardian is a parent
D. False, unless specified in court orders

107. **Assertion (A):** In Hindu law, adoption creates a legal parent-child relationship.

Reason (R): Adopted children have the same rights as biological children.
A. Both A and R are true, and R is the correct explanation of A
B. Both A and R are true, but R is not the correct explanation of A
C. A is true, R is false
D. A is false, R is true

108. **Assertion (A):** Under Muslim law, acknowledgment of paternity establishes legal rights for the child.

Reason (R): Acknowledgment is necessary because adoption is not legally recognized.
A. Both A and R are true, and R is the correct explanation of A
B. Both A and R are true, but R is not the correct explanation of A
C. A is true, R is false
D. A is false, R is true

109. The minimum age required to adopt a child under Hindu law is ______ years for both men and women.
A. 18 B. 21
C. 25 D. 30

110. A guardian appointed by a court is known as a ______ guardian.
A. Natural B. Testamentary
C. De facto D. Guardian ad litem

111. Match the following types of guardians with their descriptions:

A. Natural Guardian	1. Appointed in a will
B. Testamentary Guardian	2. Guardian by biological relation (parent)
C. Guardian ad Litem	3. Appointed by the court for legal cases
D. De facto Guardian	4. Acts as guardian without legal authority

A. A-2, B-1, C-3, D-4
B. A-1, B-4, C-2, D-3
C. A-3, B-1, C-4, D-2
D. A-4, B-2, C-3, D-1

112. Arrange the following steps in the correct sequence for legal adoption under Hindu law:
1. Consent of the spouse (if applicable)
2. Selection of the child for adoption
3. Execution of an adoption deed
4. Registration of the adoption

A. 2, 1, 3, 4 B. 1, 2, 4, 3
C. 4, 3, 1, 2 D. 3, 1, 2, 4

113. Scenario: A Hindu male wants to adopt a child without his wife's consent, even though she is mentally sound. Is this legally valid?
A. Yes, if the husband is financially capable
B. No, as wife's consent is mandatory
C. Yes, if the child is an orphan
D. No, unless approved by a court

114. Scenario: A Muslim man acknowledges a child as his own, though the child was born before his marriage. Does the child get legal status?
A. Yes, acknowledgment grants legitimacy
B. No, unless the child's mother agrees
C. Yes, only if the acknowledgment is in writing
D. No, as acknowledgment applies only after marriage

115. Scenario: A court appoints a guardian for a minor's property. What type of guardian is this?
A. Natural guardian
B. Testamentary guardian
C. Guardian ad litem
D. Court-appointed guardian

116. Which of the following is NOT a requirement for a valid adoption under Hindu law?

A. The child must be unmarried
B. The adoptive parent must be over 21 years
C. The adoption must be registered in court
D. The adoptive parent must have the capacity to adopt

117. A Hindu widow can adopt a child:

A. Only with court approval
B. With her husband's prior written consent
C. Without anyone's consent
D. Only if she has no children

118. Match the following laws with their relevance to adoption and guardianship:

A. Hindu Adoption and Maintenance Act, 1956	1. Governs adoption for Hindus
B. Guardians and Wards Act, 1890	2. Regulates guardianship for minors
C. Muslim Personal Law	3. Provides acknowledgment of paternity
D. Juvenile Justice (Care and Protection of Children) Act, 2015	4. Governs adoption for all religions

A. A-1, B-2, C-3, D-4
B. A-4, B-3, C-2, D-1
C. A-3, B-1, C-4, D-2
D. A-2, B-4, C-1, D-3

119. Scenario: A man takes care of an orphaned child without legal adoption. What type of guardian is he considered?

A. Natural guardian
B. Testamentary guardian
C. De facto guardian
D. Guardian ad litem

120. Scenario: A father appoints a guardian for his child through a will. What type of guardian is this?

A. Natural guardian
B. Court-appointed guardian
C. De facto guardian
D. Testamentary guardian

121. Which of the following laws governs intestate succession among Hindus in India?

A. Indian Succession Act, 1925
B. Hindu Succession Act, 1956
C. Guardians and Wards Act, 1890
D. Special Marriage Act, 1954

122. In Muslim law, succession is based on:

A. The doctrine of survivorship
B. The rule of primogeniture
C. A combination of inheritance and bequest
D. Joint family property system

123. Which of the following is NOT a Class I heir under the Hindu Succession Act, 1956?

A. Mother B. Son
C. Daughter D. Brother

124. Under the Indian Succession Act, 1925, testamentary succession refers to:

A. Succession based on customary law
B. Succession through a will
C. Succession without a will
D. Succession through joint family property

125. The Hindu Succession (Amendment) Act, 2005 granted equal rights to daughters in coparcenary property.

A. True
B. False
C. True, only for unmarried daughters
D. False, unless specified in the will

126. In Muslim law, a bequest can be made for more than one-third of the estate without the consent of legal heirs.

A. True
B. False
C. True, if registered with the court
D. False, unless the property is immovable

127. **Assertion (A):** In Hindu law, intestate succession applies when a person dies without leaving a will.

Reason (R): The property of the deceased automatically goes to the government in such cases.

A. Both A and R are true, and R is the correct explanation of A
B. Both A and R are true, but R is not the correct explanation of A
C. A is true, R is false
D. A is false, R is true

128. **Assertion (A):** A Muslim woman can inherit property under Islamic law.

Reason (R): Sharia law does not recognize inheritance rights for women.

A. Both A and R are true, and R is the correct explanation of A
B. Both A and R are true, but R is not the correct explanation of A
C. A is true, R is false
D. A is false, R is true

129. Under Hindu law, if a person dies intestate without any Class I heirs, the property will pass to _______.
A. The government
B. Class II heirs
C. Distant relatives
D. The eldest male relative

130. In Muslim law, the residuary heirs are known as _______.
A. Sharers
B. Zawil Arham
C. Asabah
D. Distant kindred

131. Match the following terms with their correct definitions:

A. Intestate Succession	1. Inheritance through a will
B. Testamentary Succession	2. Property inherited without a will
C. Coparcenary	3. Joint ownership in ancestral property
D. Bequest	4. Transfer of property by will after death

A. A-2, B-1, C-3, D-4
B. A-1, B-4, C-2, D-3
C. A-4, B-3, C-1, D-2
D. A-3, B-2, C-4, D-1

132. Arrange the following classes of heirs in the correct order of succession under Hindu law:
1. Class I heirs
2. Class II heirs
3. Agnates
4. Cognates

A. 1, 2, 3, 4
B. 2, 1, 4, 3
C. 1, 3, 2, 4
D. 4, 3, 1, 2

133. Scenario: A Hindu man dies intestate, leaving behind a wife, mother, and brother. Who will inherit the property?
A. Wife only
B. Wife and mother equally
C. Wife, mother, and brother equally
D. Wife and mother only

134. Scenario: A Muslim man dies, leaving a wife, two sons, and one daughter. How will the property be divided?
A. Equally among all
B. Sons get double the share of the daughter
C. Wife gets nothing
D. Daughter inherits more than the sons

135. Scenario: A Christian woman dies intestate, leaving behind her husband and children. How is the property divided?
A. Entire property to the husband
B. Equally among husband and children
C. 1/3 to husband and 2/3 to children
D. Entire property to the children

136. Which of the following is NOT a characteristic of coparcenary property under Hindu law?
A. Inherited from ancestors
B. Joint ownership by male members only
C. Daughters cannot be coparceners after 2005
D. Right to partition

137. Under the Indian Succession Act, the term 'probate' refers to:
A. Transfer of property without a will
B. Legal process of validating a will
C. Sale of ancestral property
D. Division of property among heirs

138. Match the following family law provisions with their governing acts in India:

A. Adoption rights for Hindu couples	1. Hindu Adoptions and Maintenance Act, 1956
B. Divorce by talaq under Muslim law (pre-2019)	2. Muslim Personal Law (Shariat) Application Act, 1937
C. Succession for Christians in intestate cases	3. Indian Succession Act, 1925
D. Maintenance rights for a divorced Muslim wife	4. Muslim Women (Protection of Rights on Divorce) Act, 1986

A. A-1, B-3, C-2, D-4
B. A-1, B-2, C-3, D-4
C. A-2, B-1, C-3, D-4
D. A-3, B-2, C-1, D-4

139. Scenario: A Hindu woman dies intestate without children. Her husband and her father survive. Who inherits the property?
A. Only the husband
B. Husband and father equally
C. Only the father
D. Distant relatives

140. Scenario: A Muslim man dies without making a will, leaving no immediate family. Who inherits the property?
A. The government
B. Distant relatives (Zawil Arham)
C. The local mosque
D. The eldest male in the community

141. Which of the following laws governs wills for Hindus in India?
A. Muslim Personal Law
B. Indian Succession Act, 1925
C. Transfer of Property Act, 1882
D. Hindu Succession Act, 1956

142. A valid gift under the Transfer of Property Act, 1882 must be:
A. Oral only
B. In writing and registered if immovable property
C. Given only to blood relatives
D. Based on mutual consideration

143. In Muslim law, a gift without delivery of possession is:
A. Void
B. Voidable
C. Valid if made in writing
D. Invalid unless registered

144. Which of the following is NOT an essential condition for the creation of a valid wakf?
A. Permanent dedication
B. Specific beneficiary
C. Revocable at the donor's discretion
D. Created for a religious, charitable, or pious purpose

145. A will can be modified or revoked by the testator at any time before death.
A. True
B. False
C. True, only with court approval
D. False, unless it's a registered will

146. In Muslim law, a gift made during the donor's death illness (marz-ul-maut) is void.
A. True
B. False
C. True, unless made to legal heirs
D. False, if made with consent of heirs

147. **Assertion (A):** A will becomes effective immediately upon its execution.

Reason (R): A will is a contract between the testator and the beneficiary.
A. Both A and R are true, and R is the correct explanation of A
B. Both A and R are true, but R is not the correct explanation of A
C. A is true, R is false
D. A is false, R is true

148. **Assertion (A):** A Muslim can create a wakf for private purposes.

Reason (R): Wakf is primarily for religious, pious, or charitable purposes.
A. Both A and R are true, and R is the correct explanation of A
B. Both A and R are true, but R is not the correct explanation of A
C. A is true, R is false
D. A is false, R is true

149. A will must be signed by the testator and attested by at least _______ witnesses.
A. 1 B. 2
C. 3 D. 4

150. In Muslim law, the term 'wakif' refers to the person who _______.
A. Inherits the property
B. Creates the wakf
C. Manages the property
D. Benefits from the wakf

151. Match the following terms with their correct definitions:

A. Will	1. A legal declaration of intent to distribute property after death
B. Gift (Hiba)	2. Voluntary transfer of property without consideration
C. Wakf	3. Permanent dedication of property for religious purposes
D. Probate	4. Legal process of validating a will

A. A-1, B-2, C-3, D-4
B. A-2, B-4, C-1, D-3
C. A-3, B-1, C-4, D-2
D. A-4, B-3, C-2, D-1

152. Arrange the following steps for creating a valid will under Indian law:
1. Writing the will
2. Signing by the testator
3. Attestation by witnesses
4. Optional registration

A. 1, 2, 3, 4 B. 2, 1, 4, 3
C. 4, 3, 1, 2 D. 3, 1, 2, 4

153. Scenario: A person gifts his property to his friend through an oral declaration without any written document. The property is immovable. Is the gift valid under the Transfer of Property Act?
A. Yes, oral gifts are valid
B. No, immovable property gifts require registration
C. Yes, if there were witnesses
D. No, unless the property is agricultural land

154. Scenario: A Muslim man makes a gift (Hiba) to his son without delivering possession. Is the gift valid under Muslim law?

A. Yes, as delivery is not required among family
B. No, delivery of possession is essential
C. Yes, if the gift is made verbally
D. No, unless registered in court

155. Scenario: A person makes a will leaving his entire estate to a charitable trust. After his death, the family challenges the will. What legal process will determine the will's validity?

A. Arbitration B. Probate
C. Mediation D. Succession Certificate

156. Which of the following is NOT an essential element of a valid gift under the Transfer of Property Act, 1882?

A. Acceptance by the donee
B. Consideration
C. Competent donor
D. Transfer of ownership

157. Which of the following is an example of a public wakf?

A. Property dedicated for family maintenance
B. Property dedicated for the construction of a mosque
C. Property gifted to a relative
D. Property held jointly by business partners

158. Match the following types of wakf with their purposes:

A. Wakf-alal-aulad	1. Dedicated for family benefit
B. Public Wakf	2. Established for public religious purposes
C. Private Wakf	3. Used continuously for religious or charitable purposes
D. Wakf by User	4. Beneficiary limited to specific individuals

A. A-1, B-2, C-4, D-3
B. A-2, B-4, C-1, D-3
C. A-3, B-1, C-2, D-4
D. A-4, B-3, C-2, D-1

159. Scenario: A person wishes to donate property for religious purposes and retain the benefits during his lifetime. Which legal mechanism can be used?

A. Gift B. Will
C. Wakf D. Mortgage

160. Scenario: A Hindu man dies leaving a will that is not registered. Can the will be enforced in court?

A. NO, REGISTRATION IS MANDATORY
B. Yes, registration is optional
C. No, unless notarized
D. Yes, only if it was executed in front of a judge

161. Which Article of the Indian Constitution mentions the Uniform Civil Code?

A. Article 25 B. Article 32
C. Article 44 D. Article 21

162. The Uniform Civil Code primarily aims to:

A. Regulate religious practices
B. Ensure uniformity in criminal laws
C. Provide a common set of personal laws
D. Control the judiciary

163. Which of the following states in India has implemented the Uniform Civil Code?

A. Kerala B. Maharashtra
C. Goa D. Gujarat

164. The Uniform Civil Code is part of which part of the Indian Constitution?

A. Part III (Fundamental Rights)
B. Part IV (Directive Principles of State Policy)
C. Part V (Union Government)
D. Part VI (State Governments)

165. The Uniform Civil Code is legally enforceable like Fundamental Rights.

A. True
B. False
C. True, if passed by the Supreme Court
D. False, unless approved by Parliament

166. The Supreme Court of India has supported the implementation of the Uniform Civil Code in several judgments.

A. True
B. False
C. True, only for Hindus
D. False, unless directed by Parliament

167. **Assertion (A):** The Uniform Civil Code promotes gender justice and equality.

Reason (R): Personal laws in India are uniform and do not discriminate based on gender.

A. Both A and R are true, and R is the correct explanation of A
B. Both A and R are true, but R is not the correct explanation of A
C. A is true, R is false
D. A is false, R is true

168. **Assertion (A):** The implementation of the Uniform Civil Code will affect the right to religious freedom under Article 25.

Reason (R): Personal laws are considered part of religious practices.

A. Both A and R are true, and R is the correct explanation of A
B. Both A and R are true, but R is not the correct explanation of A
C. A is true, R is false
D. A is false, R is true

169. The concept of a Uniform Civil Code was borrowed from the legal system of ______.

A. United States B. France
C. Portugal D. United Kingdom

170. The landmark case of ______ highlighted the need for a Uniform Civil Code in the context of maintenance rights for Muslim women.

A. Kesavananda Bharati case
B. Shah Bano case
C. Maneka Gandhi case
D. Vishakha case

171. Match the following cases with their relevance to the Uniform Civil Code:

A. Shah Bano case (1985)	1. Polygamy and conversion issues
B. Sarla Mudgal case (1995)	2. Rights of Christian widows under inheritance laws
C. John Vallamattom case (2003)	3. Maintenance rights for Muslim women
D. Danial Latifi case (2001)	4. Clarification on Muslim Women's Protection Act

A. A-3, B-1, C-2, D-4
B. A-1, B-4, C-3, D-2
C. A-2, B-3, C-4, D-1
D. A-4, B-2, C-1, D-3

172. Arrange the following events in chronological order related to the Uniform Civil Code debate in India:

1. Shah Bano Judgment
2. Constitution of India comes into force
3. Sarla Mudgal Judgment
4. Danial Latifi Judgment

A. 2, 1, 3, 4 B. 1, 2, 3, 4
C. 2, 3, 1, 4 D. 4, 1, 3, 2

173. Scenario: A person converts to another religion to practice polygamy, which is otherwise prohibited in their original religion. Which case dealt with a similar issue?

A. Shah Bano case
B. Sarla Mudgal case
C. Maneka Gandhi case
D. Danial Latifi case

174. Scenario: A Christian woman challenges inheritance laws that discriminate against her. Which case is relevant?

A. Vishakha case
B. John Vallamattom case
C. Shah Bano case
D. Kesavananda Bharati case

175. Scenario: A Muslim woman seeks maintenance after divorce under Section 125 CrPC. The husband claims she's not entitled under Muslim law. Which case applies?

A. Shah Bano case B. Sarla Mudgal case
C. Maneka Gandhi case D. Danial Latifi case

176. Which part of the Indian Constitution contains the Directive Principles of State Policy, including the UCC?

A. Part III B. Part IV
C. Part V D. Part VI

177. The Goa Civil Code is derived from the:

A. British Common Law
B. French Civil Code
C. Portuguese Civil Code
D. Roman Law

178. Match the following Articles with their constitutional provisions:

A. Article 25	1. Right to Equality
B. Article 44	2. Uniform Civil Code
C. Article 14	3. Right to Constitutional Remedies
D. Article 32	4. Freedom of Religion

A. A-4, B-2, C-1, D-3
B. A-1, B-3, C-4, D-2
C. A-3, B-1, C-2, D-4
D. A-2, B-4, C-3, D-1

179. Scenario: A secular country aims to implement a common civil code for all its citizens to ensure equality. Which Indian constitutional principle supports this?

A. Federalism B. Secularism
C. Socialism D. National Integration

180. Scenario: A student claims that the UCC is mandatory because it is part of the Constitution. Is this correct?

A. Yes, because it is enforceable like Fundamental Rights
B. No, because Directive Principles are not enforceable
C. Yes, if the Supreme Court orders its implementation
D. No, unless approved by a religious authority

ANSWERS

1. **(D):** The Constitution of India is a modern legal source but not a primary source of traditional Hindu Law.

2. **(A):** The Mitakshara School is prevalent in Northern India, while the Dayabhaga School dominates in Bengal and Assam.

3. **(B):** The Quran is the primary source of Islamic law.

4. **(B):** For a custom to be valid, it must be ancient, certain, reasonable, and continuous.

5. **(A):** Under the Mitakshara School, a son has a birthright in ancestral property.

6. **(B):** The Dayabhaga School follows the principle of succession, not survivorship.

7. **(C):** Custom is a recognized source, but it cannot override statutory laws unless explicitly provided.

8. **(C):** While the Quran is the supreme source, other sources like Ijma, Qiyas, and Hadith also play key roles.

9. **(C):** Shruti means "that which is heard" and includes sacred texts like the Vedas.

10. **(A):** Vijnaneshwara is the author of the Mitakshara, a key commentary on the Yajnavalkya Smriti.

11. **(A):** Mitakshara: Northern India

    Dayabhaga: Bengal and Assam

    Dravida: Southern India

    Maharashtra: Western India

12. **(A):** The chronological development is: Shruti → Smriti → Commentaries/Digests → Custom → Judicial decisions.

13. **(A):** Custom can override codified law if it is ancient, certain, reasonable, and continuous.

14. **(B):** When the Quran is silent, the next source is the Hadith, followed by Ijma and Qiyas.

15. **(C):** Post the Hindu Succession (Amendment) Act, 2005, daughters are also coparceners with equal rights.

16. **(D):** Upanishads are part of Hindu scriptures, not Islamic sources.

17. **(B):** Smriti means "that which is remembered" and includes texts like Manusmriti.

18. **(A):** Quran (A-4): Holy book of Islam

    Hadith (B-3): Teachings of Prophet Muhammad

    Ijma (C-1): Consensus of scholars

    Qiyas (D-2): Analogical reasoning

19. **(C):** The Dayabhaga School follows the principle of succession, unlike Mitakshara which follows survivorship.

20. **(B):** Customs that violate constitutional rights, such as gender equality, are invalid under modern law.

21. **(B):** As per Section 5(iii) of the Hindu Marriage Act, the minimum age is 21 for males and 18 for females.

22. **(D):** Property disputes are not a ground for divorce. Grounds like cruelty, conversion, and mutual consent are valid.

23. **(C):** Talaq-e-Biddat (Triple Talaq) involves pronouncing talaq three times in one sitting, now declared unconstitutional by the Supreme Court in 2017.

24. **(B):** There is no legal requirement that both parties must belong to the same caste for a valid Hindu marriage.

25. **(A):** Hindu marriage is traditionally viewed as a sacrament rather than a contract.

26. **(A):** Khula is a form of divorce where the wife initiates the dissolution of marriage, often with the husband's consent and compensation.

27. **(C):** Adultery is a ground for divorce but is no longer a criminal offense after the Supreme Court's 2018 judgment decriminalizing it.

28. **(C):** The Special Marriage Act applies to all citizens, regardless of religion, and requires registration for legal validity.

29. **(B):** Marriages within prohibited degrees of relationship are void, unless custom allows otherwise.

30. **(B):** Couples must live separately for at least one year before seeking divorce by mutual consent.

31. **(A):** Talaq-e-Ahsan: Single pronouncement with abstinence

    Talaq-e-Hasan: Pronounced three times over different lunar cycles

    Khula: Wife-initiated divorce

    Mubarat: Mutual consent divorce

32. **(A):** The process involves: filing a joint petition → cooling-off period → final hearing → decree of divorce.

33. **(B):** Section 13B allows divorce by mutual consent after living separately for at least one year.

34. **(D):** Faskh is a form of judicial divorce where the court dissolves the marriage on valid grounds like cruelty.

35. **(D):** Under the Special Marriage Act, 1954, the District Court has jurisdiction for divorce proceedings.

36. **(D):** Failure to provide maintenance for two years is a valid ground for divorce under the Act.

37. **(B):** Desertion must continue for at least 2 years before filing for divorce under Section 13(1)(ib).

38. **(A):** Correct matching:

- **Right to maintenance for a divorced wife:** Covered under Section 125 of the Criminal Procedure Code, which provides maintenance for wives, including divorced wives, across religious communities (e.g., Shah Bano case, 1985, extended it to Muslim women until modified by the Muslim Women (Protection of Rights on Divorce) Act, 1986).
- **Inheritance rights for daughters in ancestral property:** Governed by the Hindu Succession Act (Section 6, amended in 2005), which grants daughters equal coparcenary rights in Hindu joint family property.
- **Registration of marriage for inter-religious couples:** Provided under the Special Marriage Act (3) (Section 5), which allows secular marriage registration for couples of different religions.
- **Divorce by pronouncement of triple talaq (prior to its ban):** Was part of Muslim Personal Law (Shariat) Application Act (2), governing divorce practices like talaq-e-biddat until its criminalization in 2019.

Hence, correct match is A-4, B-1, C-3, D-2.

39. **(A):** Conversion to another religion is a valid ground under Section 13(1)(ii).

40. **(B):** Triple Talaq was declared unconstitutional by the Supreme Court of India in 2017.

41. **(D):** Customary Theory is not a recognized theory of divorce. The major theories include Fault Theory, Mutual Consent Theory, and Irretrievable Breakdown Theory.

42. **(C):** Section 13B of the Hindu Marriage Act provides for divorce by mutual consent.

43. **(D):** Sati is an abolished and illegal practice in India and has nothing to do with divorce.

44. **(A):** The Fault Theory holds that divorce can be granted if one party is at fault for causing the breakdown of the marriage.

45. **(B):** Irretrievable breakdown is not explicitly a ground under the Hindu Marriage Act, but courts, especially the Supreme Court, have granted divorce on this basis under Article 142.

46. **(B):** In civil cases like divorce, the standard of proof is preponderance of probabilities, not beyond reasonable doubt.

47. **(C):** Mutual consent is required, but the court must be satisfied that the consent is free and genuine.

48. **(C):** Desertion includes both physical separation and intention to permanently abandon the relationship.

49. **(B):** The parties must have been living separately for at least one year before filing for mutual consent divorce under Section 13B.

50. **(B):** The United Kingdom first recognized the irretrievable breakdown of marriage as a ground for divorce in the Matrimonial Causes Act, 1969.

51. **(A):** Fault Theory: Requires proving fault (3)

Mutual Consent Theory: Both parties agree (2)

Irretrievable Breakdown Theory: Marriage beyond repair (4)

No-Fault Theory: No need to prove fault (1)

52. **(A):** The process involves filing a joint petition, observing a cooling-off period, conducting the final hearing, and then the grant of divorce decree.

53. **(B):** Under the Hindu Marriage Act, the court can grant divorce even if both parties are at fault.

54. **(C):** Faskh allows a Muslim woman to seek judicial divorce for reasons like failure to provide maintenance.

55. **(A)**

56. **(C):** Incompatibility is not explicitly mentioned as a ground under the Act, though it may be considered under the umbrella of mental cruelty.

57. **(C):** Desertion must continue for at least 2 years before it becomes a valid ground for divorce.

58. (A): Correct match is:

- **Divorce initiated by the wife through judicial process:** Governed by the Dissolution of Muslim Marriages Act (1939, Section 2), which allows a Muslim wife to seek divorce (khula or judicial dissolution) on grounds like cruelty, desertion, or failure to maintain, through a court process.
- **Inheritance share of a daughter in her father's estate:** Regulated by the Muslim Personal Law (Shariat) Application Act (1937), which applies Islamic inheritance rules where a daughter typically receives half the share of a son (e.g., Quran, Surah An-Nisa, 4:11).
- **Maintenance for a wife during the iddat period:** Covered by the Muslim Women (Protection of Rights on Divorce) Act (1986, Section 3), which ensures a divorced Muslim woman receives maintenance during the iddat period (approximately three months post-divorce).
- **Marriage contract with stipulated dower (mehr):** Rooted in the Quran and Sunnah, as applied under Muslim Personal Law in India, where mehr is a mandatory obligation in a nikah contract (Quran, Surah An-Nisa, 4:4).

Hence, correct match is A-2, B-1, C-3, D-4.

59. (B): Such an act amounts to bigamy, punishable under Section 494 IPC, despite conversion.

60. (B): Courts, especially the Supreme Court, have granted divorce on the ground of irretrievable breakdown of marriage, even without mutual consent.

61. (B): Section 13 CPC outlines the conditions under which foreign judgments are recognized in India.

62. (B): Ex-parte decrees without proper opportunity for both parties to be heard may not be recognized in India as it violates natural justice.

63. (D): Recognition is refused based on jurisdiction, fraud, or violation of natural justice, not on whether it benefits the parties.

64. (C): The Doctrine of Competent Jurisdiction ensures the foreign court had proper authority over the matter and parties.

65. (B): Decrees obtained through fraud are not recognized in India under Section 13 CPC.

66. (B): Recognition depends on compliance with conditions under Section 13 CPC, including jurisdiction, natural justice, and public policy.

67. (D): Foreign decrees must be based on grounds recognized by Indian law to be enforceable. Indian courts are not bound to enforce all foreign judgments.

68. (A): Public policy includes justice, fairness, and Indian matrimonial norms, and violations may lead to non-recognition.

69. (D): Lack of a proper hearing violates natural justice, a key ground for non-recognition.

70. (A): The principle of Comity of Nations promotes mutual recognition of judgments between countries, subject to conditions.

71. (A): Lack of jurisdiction: Incompetent court (3)

Fraud: Deceitful means (2)

Violation of natural justice: No fair hearing (1)

Contrary to public policy: Against Indian legal norms (4)

72. (A): Courts first verify jurisdiction, followed by checks for natural justice, fraud, and public policy violations.

73. (B): No notice violates natural justice, a ground for non-recognition under Section 13 CPC.

74. (B): Recognition depends on whether the grounds are recognized under Indian matrimonial laws.

75. (B): Fraudulent decrees are not enforceable under Indian law.

76. (C): Registration with the Ministry of External Affairs is not required for recognition.

77. (B): The principle of Comity of Nations guides mutual recognition of foreign judgments.

78. (A): Comity of Nations (A-1): Promotes international recognition of judgments

Natural Justice (B-2): Ensures fairness and due process

Fraud Exception (C-3): Invalidates judgments obtained deceitfully

Public Policy Doctrine (D-4): Protects national legal norms

79. (A): If the decree is based on mutual consent, which is a valid ground under Indian law, it can be recognized.

80. (B): Indian courts may refuse recognition if the foreign court did not apply Indian matrimonial laws for Indian citizens.

81. (B): Section 18 provides the right of a Hindu wife to claim maintenance from her husband during marriage.

82. (B): Dower (Mahr) is a mandatory obligation upon the husband, payable to the wife as part of the marriage contract.

83. (B): Stridhan includes gifts received by a woman, particularly during marriage, from her husband or family.

84. (C): Unemployment alone is not a ground; however, the wife can claim maintenance even if the husband is unemployed.

85. (A): Unpaid dower (Mahr) is a debt owed by the husband and can be claimed even after divorce.

86. (B): Stridhan remains the exclusive property of the woman, and the husband has no ownership rights over it.

87. (A): Section 125 CrPC is a secular provision applicable to all religions for maintenance.

88. (C): While dower is an obligation, a Muslim marriage is valid even if dower is not paid immediately.

89. (D): Stridhan includes property acquired by a woman before, during, or after marriage through various means like gifts, inheritance, or earnings.

90. (B): A divorced woman who has not remarried can claim maintenance under Section 125 CrPC.

91. (A): Maintenance: Financial support (2)

Dower: Mandatory payment in Muslim marriage (3)

Stridhan: Woman's exclusive property (1)

Dowry: Illegally demanded property in marriage (4)

92. (A): The correct procedure is to file the application, issue notice, conduct hearings, and pass the final order.

93. (B): Unpaid dower (Mahr) is treated as a debt and can be claimed even after divorce.

94. (B): Jewelry gifted to a woman at marriage is her Stridhan and remains her exclusive property.

95. (B): The husband's unemployment is not a valid defense; he must fulfill his legal obligation.

96. (B): Stridhan refers to property owned or gifted to the woman, not property bought by the husband in his name.

97. (C): Mahr can be prompt (payable immediately) or deferred (payable later).

98. (A): Maintenance under Hindu Law (A-1): Section 18 of Hindu Adoption and Maintenance Act

Maintenance under Muslim Law (B-2): Muslim Women (Protection of Rights on Divorce) Act

Maintenance under CrPC (C-3): Section 125 CrPC

Maintenance for parents (D-4): Maintenance and Welfare of Parents and Senior Citizens Act

99. (B): The wife can file a civil suit as unpaid dower is treated as debt.

100. (B): Stridhan remains the woman's exclusive property, and she can recover it from anyone unlawfully possessing it.

101. (B): Adoption among Hindus is governed by the Hindu Adoption and Maintenance Act, 1956.

102. (D): Adoption is not legally recognized under Muslim law; however, acknowledgment of paternity serves a similar purpose.

103. (D): There is no caste restriction for adoption under the Act.

104. (B): Under Hindu law, the father is the natural guardian, and after him, the mother.

105. (C): A Hindu woman can adopt without the husband's consent if he is of unsound mind, renounced the world, or ceased to be Hindu.

106. (A): Guardianship generally terminates when the minor attains majority, i.e., 18 years of age.

107. (A): Adopted children have equal legal rights as biological children under Hindu law.

108. (A): Since adoption is not recognized under Muslim law, acknowledgment of paternity provides legal status to the child.

109. (B): The adoptive parent must be at least 21 years old if adopting a child of the opposite gender.

110. (D): A guardian ad litem is appointed by the court to represent a minor in legal proceedings.

111. (A): Natural Guardian: Parent (2)

Testamentary Guardian: Appointed in a will (1)

Guardian ad Litem: Appointed for court cases (3)

De facto Guardian: Acts without legal authority (4)

112. (A): First, the child is selected, then consent is obtained, followed by the execution and registration of the adoption deed.

113. (B): Consent of the wife is mandatory unless she is of unsound mind or has renounced the world.

114. (A): Acknowledgment of paternity can grant legal status even if the child was born before marriage.

115. (D): The court appoints a guardian specifically to manage the minor's property when necessary.

116. (C): Registration in court is not mandatory; however, it is advisable for legal proof.

117. (C): A Hindu widow can adopt without anyone's consent under the Hindu Adoption and Maintenance Act.

118. (A): Hindu Adoption and Maintenance Act (A-1): Governs adoption for Hindus

Guardians and Wards Act (B-2): Regulates guardianship for minors

Muslim Personal Law (C-3): Provides acknowledgment of paternity

Juvenile Justice Act (D-4): Governs adoption for all religions

119. (C): A de facto guardian is someone who acts as a guardian without legal authority.

120. (D): A testamentary guardian is appointed through a will.

121. (B): Hindu Succession Act, 1956 governs intestate succession among Hindus.

122. (C): Muslim succession is based on both inheritance (faraid rules) and bequest (wasiyat).

123. (D): A brother is a Class II heir, not Class I.

124. (B): Testamentary succession refers to succession through a will.

125. (A): The 2005 amendment granted equal rights to daughters as coparceners in ancestral property.

126. (B): A Muslim can bequeath only one-third of the property without the consent of heirs.

127. (C): In intestate succession, the property is distributed among legal heirs, not automatically to the government.

128. (C): Muslim women have the right to inherit under Islamic law, although their share is often less than that of male heirs.

129. (B): In the absence of Class I heirs, the property goes to Class II heirs.

130. (C): Asabah are the residuary heirs who inherit the remaining estate after sharers receive their fixed portions.

131. (A): Intestate Succession: Without a will (2)

Testamentary Succession: Through a will (1)

Coparcenary: Joint ownership (3)

Bequest: Transfer by will (4)

132. (A): Priority of succession is given to Class I heirs, followed by Class II heirs, agnates, and cognates.

133. (D): Wife and mother are Class I heirs and will inherit equally. Brother, a Class II heir, gets nothing if Class I heirs exist.

134. (B): Under Muslim law, sons receive twice the share of daughters, while the wife gets 1/8 if children exist.

135. (B): Under the Indian Succession Act, 1925, property is equally divided among the husband and children.

136. (C): The 2005 amendment gave daughters equal coparcenary rights.

137. (B): Probate is the legal certification of a will's validity by a competent court.

138. (C): Correct match is:

- **Adoption rights for Hindu couples:** Governed by the Hindu Adoptions and Maintenance Act, 1956 (Section 5), which regulates adoption procedures for Hindus, including eligibility and conditions for adopting a child.
- Divorce by talaq under Muslim law (pre-2019): Regulated by the Muslim Personal Law (Shariat) Application Act, 1937, which applies Islamic principles for divorce, including talaq (e.g., triple talaq) until its criminalization in 2019.
- **Succession for Christians in intestate cases:** Covered by the Indian Succession Act, 1925 (3) (Sections 29–56), which governs intestate and testamentary succession for Christians in India.
- Maintenance rights for a divorced Muslim wife: Provided under the Muslim Women (Protection of Rights on Divorce) Act, 1986 (Section 3), which ensures maintenance during the iddat period and beyond in certain cases.

Hence, correct match is A-1, B-2, C-3, D-4.

139. (B): Both the husband and father, being Class I heirs, will inherit equally.

140. **(B):** In the absence of direct heirs, distant relatives (Zawil Arham) inherit under Muslim law.

141. **(B):** The Indian Succession Act, 1925 governs the creation and execution of wills for Hindus, Christians, Parsis, etc.

142. **(B):** A gift of immovable property must be in writing, signed, and registered as per the Act.

143. **(A):** In Muslim law, a gift (Hiba) requires offer, acceptance, and delivery of possession to be valid.

144. **(C):** A wakf is irrevocable once created.

145. **(A):** A will is revocable and can be modified by the testator any time before their death.

146. **(B):** A gift made during marz-ul-maut is valid but limited to one-third of the estate unless the legal heirs consent.

147. **(D):** A will becomes effective only after the testator's death. It is not a contract but a unilateral declaration.

148. **(D):** A wakf must be for religious, charitable, or pious purposes, though family wakfs (wakf-alal-aulad) are allowed with public benefits.

149. **(B):** A valid will requires the signature of the testator and attestation by at least two witnesses.

150. **(B):** The 'wakif' is the person who creates the wakf by dedicating property for religious or charitable purposes.

151. **(A):** Will: Declaration of intent (1)

Gift (Hiba): Voluntary transfer (2)

Wakf: Dedication for religious purposes (3)

Probate: Legal validation of a will (4)

152. **(A):** The correct process is writing the will, followed by the testator's signature, witness attestation, and optional registration.

153. **(B):** Gifts of immovable property must be in writing, signed, and registered.

154. **(B):** In Muslim law, delivery of possession is mandatory for a valid gift (Hiba).

155. **(B):** Probate is the legal process to validate a will in court.

156. **(B):** A gift is a gratuitous transfer and does not require consideration.

157. **(B):** A public wakf is for religious or charitable purposes, like building a mosque.

158. **(A):** Wakf-alal-aulad (A-1): Dedicated for family benefit

Public Wakf (B-2): Established for public religious purposes

Private Wakf (C-4): Beneficiary limited to specific individuals

Wakf by User (D-3): Used continuously for religious or charitable purposes

159. **(C):** A wakf allows property to be dedicated for religious purposes while the wakif retains some benefits.

160. **(B):** A will does not require registration to be valid; execution and attestation are sufficient.

161. **(C):** Article 44 of the Directive Principles of State Policy (DPSP) directs the State to secure a Uniform Civil Code for all citizens.

162. **(C):** The UCC seeks to create a common set of personal laws governing marriage, divorce, inheritance, adoption, etc., for all citizens, regardless of religion.

163. **(C):** Goa follows a Uniform Civil Code, known as the Goa Family Law, applicable to all communities in the state.

164. **(B):** The UCC is included under Part IV, which contains the Directive Principles of State Policy.

165. **(B):** Directive Principles are non-justiciable, meaning they are not legally enforceable in courts.

166. **(A):** The Supreme Court has supported the UCC in cases like Shah Bano (1985) and Sarla Mudgal (1995).

167. **(C):** The UCC promotes gender justice, but personal laws in India are not uniform and often discriminate based on gender.

168. **(B):** While personal laws may have religious elements, the UCC does not violate religious freedom as it deals with secular matters like marriage and inheritance.

169. **(C):** The Goa Civil Code, which serves as an example of the UCC, is derived from the Portuguese Civil Code.

170. **(B):** The Shah Bano case (1985) was a pivotal judgment where the Supreme Court emphasized the importance of the UCC.

171. **(A):** Shah Bano case: Maintenance for Muslim women (3)

Sarla Mudgal case: Polygamy and conversion (1)

John Vallamattom case: Christian inheritance laws (2)

Danial Latifi case: Muslim Women's Protection Act (4)

172. (A): 1950: Constitution comes into force

1985: Shah Bano Judgment

1995: Sarla Mudgal Judgment

2001: Danial Latifi Judgment

173. (B): The Sarla Mudgal case addressed the issue of conversion to Islam for the purpose of polygamy, emphasizing the need for a UCC.

174. (B): The John Vallamattom case (2003) challenged discriminatory Christian inheritance laws, with the court favoring reforms aligned with the UCC.

175. (A): The Shah Bano case established that Section 125 CrPC applies irrespective of religion, ensuring maintenance rights for Muslim women.

176. (B): The DPSP, including Article 44 (UCC), is part of Part IV of the Constitution.

177. (C): The Goa Civil Code is based on the Portuguese Civil Code, implemented during colonial rule.

178. (A): Article 25 (A-4): Freedom of Religion

Article 44 (B-2): Uniform Civil Code

Article 14 (C-1): Right to Equality

Article 32 (D-3): Right to Constitutional Remedies

179. (B): The UCC aligns with the principle of secularism, ensuring uniform civil laws for all citizens.

180. (B): The UCC is part of the DPSP, which is non-justiciable, meaning it is not enforceable in court but guides state policy.

UNIT 8 Environment and Human Rights Law

ENVIRONMENT AND ENVIRONMENTAL POLLUTION

INTRODUCTION TO THE CONCEPT OF ENVIRONMENT

The environment encompasses all natural systems and elements, including air, water, land, and living organisms. It forms the basic framework in which all living creatures, including humans, interact and sustain themselves. Environmental studies focus on understanding these interactions and the impact of human actions on natural systems. The sustenance and health of the environment are crucial as it provides essential services like climate regulation, oxygen production, and biodiversity, which are indispensable for life on Earth

The Scope of Environmental Pollution

Environmental pollution refers to the introduction of harmful substances or energies into the environment that are detrimental to living organisms and the ecosystem. Types of pollution include:

- **Air Pollution:** Emitted from industrial processes, vehicular emissions, and natural sources like volcanic activity, impacting air quality and contributing to climate change.
- **Water Pollution:** Arises from industrial discharges, agricultural runoff, and wastewater disposal, affecting aquatic life and water usability.
- **Soil Pollution:** Caused by chemical spills, industrial activity, and improper disposal of waste, leading to degraded land quality and affecting food safety.
- **Noise Pollution:** Emanates from industrial and transport activities, affecting human health and wildlife.
- **Thermal Pollution:** Involves the release of heated water or emissions into the environment, affecting aquatic systems.

INTERNATIONAL ENVIRONMENTAL LAW AND UN CONFERENCES

INTRODUCTION TO INTERNATIONAL ENVIRONMENTAL LAW

International environmental law encompasses regulations and agreements designed to protect the global environment. It addresses issues such as climate change, biodiversity loss, and pollution on an international scale. This branch of law relies heavily on treaties, conventions, and protocols agreed upon by multiple countries. These agreements not only set out legal obligations but also establish frameworks for international cooperation.

- **United Nations Framework Convention on Climate Change (UNFCCC)**: Established in 1992, the UNFCCC sets a framework for intergovernmental efforts to tackle the challenge posed by climate change. It recognizes that the climate system is a shared resource whose stability can be affected by industrial and other emissions of carbon dioxide and other greenhouse gases. The Convention enjoys near-universal membership, which underlines the recognition by the world's governments of the need to cooperate and take action against climate change.
- **Kyoto Protocol**: Adopted in December 1997 and entered into force in February 2005, the Kyoto Protocol is a legally binding agreement under which industrialized countries will reduce their collective emissions of greenhouse gases by 5.2% compared to the year 1990. The reductions must be achieved during the commitment period of

2008 to 2012. The Protocol operationalizes the UNFCCC by committing advanced nations to lead the way in cutting emissions.

- **Montreal Protocol**: Agreed on in 1987, the Montreal Protocol on Substances that Deplete the Ozone Layer is designed to reduce the production and consumption of ozone-depleting substances in order to reduce their abundance in the atmosphere, and thereby protect the earth's fragile ozone layer. It has been remarkably successful, with all countries in the world ratifying it to eliminate the production and use of many of the most ozone-depleting chemicals.
- **Convention on Biological Diversity (CBD)**: Opened for signature at the Earth Summit in Rio de Janeiro in 1992 and entering into force in December 1993, the CBD is a key document regarding sustainable development. The Convention has three main goals: the conservation of biological diversity, the sustainable use of its components, and the fair and equitable sharing of benefits arising from genetic resources. Its overall objective is to encourage actions that will lead to a sustainable future.

Impact of International Environmental Conferences on Legal Frameworks

International environmental conferences significantly influence legal frameworks at both the international and national levels. These impacts can be categorized into several key areas:

- **Development of New International Agreements and Protocols:** Major international environmental conferences often result in the drafting, adoption, or amendment of international treaties and agreements. These documents set global standards and obligations for environmental protection, which countries commit to implement through their domestic laws. For instance, the Conference of the Parties (COP) meetings under the UNFCCC have been instrumental in creating binding agreements like the Kyoto Protocol and the Paris Agreement, which compel state parties to undertake emissions reduction and adapt to climate impacts.
- **Harmonization of Environmental Standards:** International conferences facilitate the harmonization of environmental standards across countries. By agreeing on minimum standards, countries ensure that there is a level playing field, reducing the risk of "environmental dumping" where businesses move operations to countries with looser regulations. This harmonization also aids in addressing transboundary environmental issues such as air and water pollution, and wildlife trafficking.
- **Strengthening National Environmental Legislation:** Outcomes from international environmental conferences often require countries to update or introduce new national legislation to meet international obligations. For example, the agreements reached at COP meetings may require countries to establish more stringent national climate policies, enhance renewable energy usage, or protect biodiversity. This can lead to the development of comprehensive environmental protection laws, updated pollution control norms, and enhanced conservation efforts.
- **Enhancement of Enforcement Mechanisms:** International agreements often include mechanisms to monitor and ensure compliance with the commitments made. These mechanisms can influence national legal frameworks by necessitating the creation or enhancement of environmental agencies and enforcement bodies. For instance, the Montreal Protocol includes provisions for monitoring the phase-out of ozone-depleting substances, requiring countries to establish and maintain robust regulatory agencies to ensure compliance.

CONSTITUTIONAL AND LEGAL FRAMEWORK FOR ENVIRONMENTAL PROTECTION IN INDIA

Constitutional Provisions

- **Article 48A and 51A(g)**: Introduced by the 42nd Amendment Act of 1976, Article 48A of the Directive Principles of State Policy requires the State to protect and improve the environment and to safeguard forests and wildlife. Article 51A(g) imposes a duty on every citizen to protect and improve the natural environment, including forests, lakes, rivers, and wildlife, and to have compassion for living creatures.
- **Article 21**: The Supreme Court of India has interpreted Article 21, which guarantees the right to life, to include the right to a clean and healthy environment. This expansive interpretation helps in the enforcement of environmental rights as part of the basic fundamental rights.

Landmark Judicial Decisions

- **M.C. Mehta Cases**: A series of important cases brought by environmental activist M.C. Mehta highlighted the role of the Supreme Court in environmental protection. These cases addressed issues ranging from air pollution in Delhi to the protection of the Taj Mahal from industrial pollution. The court's rulings have often led to significant changes in environmental regulations.
- **Vellore Citizens' Welfare Forum v. Union of India (1996)**: This case recognized the "Precautionary Principle" and the "Polluter Pays Principle" as essential features of sustainable development under Indian law. The court ruled that environmental measures by the state and other authorities must anticipate, prevent, and attack the causes of environmental degradation.

Environmental Legislation

- **The Environment (Protection) Act, 1986**
  - This act was enacted in response to the Bhopal Gas Tragedy and serves as an umbrella law that provides a framework for planning and execution of a nationwide program for environmental protection. The Act empowers the Central Government to:
  - Take all necessary measures to protect the quality of the environment.
  - Set standards for emissions and discharges of pollution in the atmosphere by any person or industry.
  - Regulate the location of industries.
  - Manage hazardous wastes, and protect public health and welfare.
  - The Central Government can also issue direct orders, including closure, prohibition, or regulation of any industry, operation, or process, or stoppage or regulation of the supply of electricity, water, or any other service.
- **The Water (Prevention and Control of Pollution) Act, 1974**
  - This act was the first of its kind to lay down a legal framework for water pollution control activities in India. Key provisions include:
  - Establishment of the Central and State Pollution Control Boards with the power to set wastewater standards for industry and municipalities.
  - Prevention and control of water pollution and maintaining or restoring the wholesomeness of water.
  - Boards can also restrict industrial and other activities that are likely to pollute water bodies.
- **The Air (Prevention and Control of Pollution) Act, 1981**
  - Introduced to combat air pollution, this act provides for the control and prevention of air pollution. It includes:
  - Establishment of Central and State Boards with similar powers as under the Water Act but focused on air pollution.
  - Powers to declare pollution control areas, set emission standards, and regulate appliances that may cause air pollution.
- **The Wildlife Protection Act, 1972**
  - This law provides comprehensive protection to wildlife species and manages the conservation areas where these species live. Its major provisions include:
  - Prohibiting the hunting of endangered species and regulating hunting to other species.
  - Establishment of wildlife sanctuaries, national parks, and closed areas.
  - Regulation and control of trade in parts and products derived from wildlife.
- **The Forest Conservation Act, 1980**
  - Focused specifically on the conservation of forests and to check deforestation, the act includes:
  - Restriction on the de-reservation of forests and use of forest land for non-forest purposes.
  - Mandatory approval of the central government for any diversion of forest land to non-forest uses.
  - Preservation and enhancement of forest cover through strict regulations.
- **The Biological Diversity Act, 2002**
  - This act was implemented to meet India's obligations under the Convention on Biological Diversity. It focuses on:
  - Conservation of biological diversity.
  - Sustainable use of its components.
  - Fair and equitable sharing of benefits arising from the use of genetic resources.
  - Registration of biodiversity-related knowledge with the National Biodiversity Authority.

- **The National Green Tribunal Act, 2010**
  - This act established the National Green Tribunal, a specialized body equipped to handle the expeditious resolution of environmental cases. It provides:
  - Effective and expeditious disposal of cases relating to environmental protection.
  - Enforcement of legal rights related to the environment.
  - Relief and compensation for damages to persons and property.
- **The Hazardous and Other Wastes (Management and Transboundary Movement) Rules, 2016**

  These rules are designed to:
  - Regulate the generation, storage, transportation, reuse, recycling, recovery, and disposal of hazardous waste.
  - Ensure environmentally sound management of hazardous waste.
  - Control the transboundary movement of hazardous waste in and out of India.
- **The Coastal Regulation Zone Notification, 2011**
  - Issued under the Environment Protection Act, it regulates activities along India's coast with the aim of:
  - Protecting and conserving the coastal environment.
  - Promoting sustainable development based on scientific principles taking into account the dangers of natural hazards.
- **The Public Liability Insurance Act, 1991**

  This act provides:
  - Immediate relief to persons affected by accidents while handling hazardous substances.
  - Compulsory insurance policies for handling hazardous substances to provide minimum relief.

ENVIRONMENTAL IMPACT ASSESSMENT (EIA)

Definition and Objective of EIA

- **Definition**: Environmental Impact Assessment (EIA) is a formal process used to anticipate the environmental consequences of a plan, policy, program, or actual projects prior to the decision to move forward with the proposed action.
- **Objective**: The main objectives of EIA are to:
  - Predict environmental impacts at an early stage in project planning and design.
  - Find ways to reduce adverse impacts.
  - Shape projects to suit the local environment.
  - Present the predictions and options to decision-makers and the public.

Principles of EIA

- **Precautionary Principle**: This principle implies that lack of full scientific certainty should not be used as a reason for postponing measures to prevent environmental degradation where there are threats of serious or irreversible damage.
- **Polluter Pays Principle**: This principle asserts that the environmental costs of economic activities, including the cost of preventing potential harm, should be internalized rather than imposed upon society at large.
- **Public Participation Principle**: Ensures that the affected public and their concerns are part of the decision-making process, particularly in approving or rejecting projects based on EIA findings.

Legislative Framework

- **Global Context**: Internationally, EIA processes are influenced by various conventions and declarations, such as the Stockholm Declaration (1972) and the Rio Declaration on Environment and Development (1992), which includes principles to support the integration of environmental considerations into sustainable development.
- **Indian Context**:
  - **The Environment Protection Act (1986)**: This act empowers the government of India to take measures necessary to protect and improve the environment.
  - **EIA Notification (2006)**: This is a procedural document under the Environment Protection Act, 1986, detailing the process to obtain environmental clearances and ensuring that the proposed activities are environmentally sound and sustainable.

EIA Process

- **Screening**: The first step determines if a project requires an EIA and, if so, the level of assessment needed.
- **Scoping**: This step identifies the key issues that are likely to require detailed investigation. This

phase sets the boundaries for the study and focuses the EIA on significant environmental issues.

- **Impact Assessment**: This involves predicting and evaluating the impact of project alternatives including no-action alternatives. It also includes detailed studies to predict the consequences of various alternatives.
- **Mitigation**: In this phase, measures to avoid, minimize, rectify, or reduce adverse environmental impacts are developed.
- **Reporting**: The Environmental Impact Statement (EIS) is prepared, documenting the findings of the study and proposing mitigation strategies. It includes a non-technical summary for the lay public.
- **Review**: The EIS is evaluated by the respective environmental authority and the public for adequacy and the resolution of concerns.
- **Decision-making**: Decisions regarding the approval of the project are taken, incorporating the EIS findings and public opinions.
- **Post-monitoring**: This phase involves checking compliance with required environmental conditions and monitoring the impacts of the development.

Key Case Laws and Judicial Decisions

- **M.C. Mehta vs. Union of India**: A series of rulings focusing on environmental protection by the Supreme Court of India, setting precedents for strict environmental regulation and oversight.
- **T.N. Godavarman Thirumulpad vs. Union of India**: A comprehensive case where the Supreme Court emphasized the importance of forest conservation and expanded the interpretation of what constitutes an 'environmental impact'.

Recent Amendments and Trends

- Recent amendments to the EIA Notification 2020 in India propose changes to streamline the process, which include increasing the validity of the environmental clearances and reducing the need for public consultations for certain project types. This has sparked significant debate concerning the balance between development needs and environmental protection.

Key Changes Proposed in Draft EIA Notification 2020

- **Exemptions from Public Consultation**: Certain projects, such as MSMEs in the dye industry and medium mineral beneficiation units, are exempted from the requirement of an Environmental Impact Assessment (EIA). This includes projects like offshore and onshore oil, gas, and shale exploration, which previously required thorough assessment and public consultation.
- **Reduction in Public Hearing Notice Period**: The period for public consultations has been reduced from 30 days to 20 days. This change has been critiqued for potentially limiting public engagement in the environmental decision-making process, making it more difficult for stakeholders to prepare and participate effectively.
- **Post-facto Clearances**: The draft allows for environmental clearances to be granted even after a project has commenced construction, a move seen by many as a significant dilution of the regulatory regime.
- **Relaxed Compliance Norms**: Under the new draft, the frequency of compliance reports required by project proponents has been reduced from twice a year to just annually. This could potentially delay the identification and mitigation of environmental damages.
- **Expansion and Modernization of Projects**: The draft eases norms for project expansions; projects that involve up to a 25% increase in production capacity may not require a new EIA, and only those with over 50% increase would need to undergo public consultation.

CONTROL OF HAZARDOUS WASTE IN INDIA

Hazardous and Other Wastes (Management and Transboundary Movement) Rules, 2016

These rules are a revision of the earlier 2008 rules and are designed to ensure safe handling, generation, storage, transportation, treatment, disposal, and import-export of hazardous and other wastes. They focus on:

- **Responsibility of the Generator**: Ensure safe disposal, label containers correctly, and provide the authorities with detailed information on waste generated.
- **Manifest System**: A form of tracking the transfer of waste from origin to disposal to ensure traceability and accountability.
- **Import and Export Restrictions**: Regulate import and export of hazardous waste for recycling, recovery, or utilization, not disposal, and align with the Basel Convention's consent requirements for transboundary movement.

Environment (Protection) Act, 1986

This act forms the backbone of environmental regulation in India, under which most environmental rules, including those governing hazardous waste, are framed:

- **Empowers the Government**: To take all necessary measures to protect and improve the quality of the environment and prevent, control, and abate environmental pollution.
- **Sets Standards and Regulations**: The act enables the central government to set standards for emissions and discharges of pollution into the environment, including the handling of hazardous substances.

Role of Central and State Authorities

- **Central Pollution Control Board (CPCB)**: Provides technical assistance and advice to the central government and coordinates activities between the state boards.
- **State Pollution Control Boards (SPCBs)**: Each state's board enforces the rules and regulations within its jurisdiction, including granting consents and approvals for handling hazardous wastes.

Important Legal Cases

- **Bichhri Case (Indian Council for Enviro-Legal Action vs. Union of India, 1996)**: This case dealt with the issue of soil and water contamination due to hazardous chemical waste discharged by several chemical plants in Rajasthan. The Supreme Court emphasized the "polluter pays" principle, holding the polluting industries responsible for environmental restoration.
- **Oleum Gas Leak Case (M.C. Mehta vs. Union of India, 1986)**: This case expanded the scope of Article 21 of the Indian Constitution, establishing the right to a pollution-free environment as integral to the right to life.

International Conventions

- **Basel Convention**: Regulates the transboundary movements of hazardous wastes and their disposal. India's alignment with this convention impacts its policies on the import and export of hazardous wastes.
- **Stockholm Convention**: Aims to eliminate or restrict the production and use of persistent organic pollutants (POPs), influencing India's environmental strategies.

Recent Amendments and Government Initiatives

- **Amendment to Hazardous Waste Rules (2019)**: Introduced changes to include solid plastic waste exclusion from import, prohibition on import of solid plastic waste even in Special Economic Zones (SEZ) and by Export Oriented Units (EOU).
- **E-Waste (Management) Rules, 2016, amended 2018**: Address the production and disposal of electronic waste, which includes hazardous components like heavy metals and flame retardants.

NATIONAL GREEN TRIBUNAL

Establishment and Legislative Background

- The National Green Tribunal (NGT) was established by the National Green Tribunal Act, 2010. It was introduced as a specialized body to handle environmental disputes which could involve multi-disciplinary issues requiring specialized knowledge in the environmental and related sectors. The NGT replaced the National Environment Appellate Authority, 1997, to provide a faster and more effective adjudication of environmental cases.

Structure and Composition

- **Chairperson**: The NGT is headed by a Chairperson who is a retired Judge of the Supreme Court of India or a Chief Justice of a High Court.
- **Judicial Members**: These include judges or retired judges of High Courts.
- **Expert Members**: Individuals with a minimum of 15 years of experience in environmental and related sciences. The tribunal is required to have at least 10 and not more than 20 full-time judicial and expert members.

Jurisdiction and Powers

- **Jurisdiction**: The NGT has jurisdiction over all civil cases with a substantial environmental question, including enforcement of legal rights concerning the environment and giving relief and compensation for damages to persons and property. It handles cases under major laws such as the Environment (Protection) Act, 1986, the Forest (Conservation) Act, 1980, and others.
- **Powers**: Like a civil court, the NGT can summon witnesses, enforce the attendance of witnesses, compel the discovery and production

of documents, receive evidence on affidavits, and issue commissions for the examination of witnesses or documents. It has the power to provide relief, award compensation, and enforce restitution as part of its directives.

Procedural Aspects

- The NGT is not bound by the procedure laid down under the Code of Civil Procedure, 1908, but follows principles of natural justice. This flexibility allows the NGT to handle cases more efficiently and focus on the substantial issues at hand without being bogged down by procedural complexities.

Decision Making and Appeals

- **Decision Making**: Decisions are taken by a majority of the members present. In case of a tie, the Chairperson has the casting vote. Decisions of the NGT are binding and enforceable as decrees of a civil court.
- **Appeals**: Appeals against the NGT's decisions can only be made to the Supreme Court of India within 90 days of the decision.

Challenges and Criticism

- The NGT faces challenges such as limited jurisdiction (it does not cover issues related to wildlife and forest rights), delayed justice despite the mandate for quick resolution, and limited awareness and accessibility, especially in rural areas. The implementation of its orders also poses significant challenges due to bureaucratic inertia and resistance at various levels of governance.

Impact and Landmark Judgments

- The NGT has been instrumental in several landmark judgments, such as the ban on 10-year-old diesel vehicles in Delhi to combat air pollution, and suspension of large-scale industrial projects violating environmental norms. These decisions have significantly contributed to environmental protection and policy changes in India.

CONCEPT AND DEVELOPMENT OF HUMAN RIGHTS

Historical Development of Human Rights

- **Ancient and Philosophical Origins**: Concepts similar to human rights have existed in most early civilizations and religious texts, emphasizing ideas of justice, equality, and dignity.
- **Magna Carta (1215)**: Often regarded as one of the first legal documents to protect human rights, it established the principle that everybody, including the king, was subject to the law.
- **Bill of Rights (1689)**: Enacted in England, strengthening the rights of individuals and Parliament's authority over the monarch.
- **Declaration of the Rights of Man and of the Citizen (1789)**: Adopted during the French Revolution, it articulated fundamental rights and freedoms, emphasizing liberty, property, security, and resistance to oppression.

The 20th Century and the Universal Declaration of Human Rights (UDHR)

- **Post World War II**: The atrocities of World War II led to a renewed focus on human rights protections. This resulted in the formation of the United Nations and the drafting of the Universal Declaration of Human Rights (UDHR) in 1948.
- **UDHR**: A milestone document in the history of human rights, it sets out, for the first time, fundamental human rights to be universally protected. It has been translated into over 500 languages.

International Human Rights Instruments

- **International Covenant on Civil and Political Rights (ICCPR, 1966)**: Enforces civil and political rights, including the right to life, freedom of speech, religion, and voting.
- **International Covenant on Economic, Social, and Cultural Rights (ICESCR, 1966)**: Focuses on socioeconomic rights like the right to health, education, and an adequate standard of living.
- **Convention on the Elimination of All Forms of Discrimination Against Women (CEDAW, 1979)** and **Convention on the Rights of the Child (CRC, 1989)**: Specific treaties to protect the rights of women and children respectively.

Enforcement Mechanisms

- **United Nations Human Rights Council**: Established in 2006, it is an inter-governmental body within the UN system responsible for strengthening the promotion and protection of human rights around the globe.
- **European Court of Human Rights**, **Inter-American Court of Human Rights**, and **African Court on Human and Peoples' Rights**: Regional courts that hear and decide cases on human rights violations.

UNIVERSALISM AND CULTURAL RELATIVISM

UNIVERSALISM

Concept: Universalism posits that certain fundamental human rights are universally applicable to all people, regardless of cultural, geographical, or religious differences. This principle supports the idea that basic rights, like the right to life, liberty, and security, are inherent and not contingent on local customs or beliefs.

Philosophical Roots: The philosophical underpinnings of universalism trace back to natural law theory, which suggests that rights are inherent due to human reason or nature itself, as argued by philosophers such as John Locke and Immanuel Kant.

Implementation in International Law:

- **Universal Declaration of Human Rights (UDHR), 1948:** This key document lays down rights that many agree should be universally protected, including civil, political, economic, social, and cultural rights.
- **International Covenants:** These include the International Covenant on Civil and Political Rights (ICCPR) and the International Covenant on Economic, Social and Cultural Rights (ICESCR), which countries globally have ratified, agreeing to uphold basic human rights.

Challenges: Universalism often faces criticism from those who argue that it imposes Western values on non-Western societies, potentially overriding local traditions and legal practices.

CULTURAL RELATIVISM IN HUMAN RIGHTS

Concept: Cultural relativism holds that human rights and ethical standards are culturally dependent and should be interpreted within the context of individual cultural practices and values. This perspective argues that what is considered a "right" in one society might not necessarily be seen as such in another.

Key Proponents: Cultural relativists like Clifford Geertz and Franz Boas emphasize understanding human behaviors and beliefs through the lens of the respective culture's own context, not through external standards.

Practical Implications in Law: Cultural relativism influences how laws are applied in different contexts, advocating for a more localized approach to rights that respects cultural norms and practices.

- **Example:** Practices such as animal sacrifice might be protected in one culture for religious reasons while being viewed as cruel or illegal in others.

Criticism: Critics argue that cultural relativism can be used to justify human rights abuses, including gender discrimination, corporal punishment, and other practices that would typically be condemned under universal human rights norms.

INTERSECTION AND DIALOGUE

Balancing Perspectives: The tension between universalism and cultural relativism is a central theme in international human rights discussions. Effective dialogue between these perspectives is crucial for developing a nuanced understanding that respects cultural differences while upholding universal human rights principles.

Vienna Declaration, 1993: The Vienna World Conference on Human Rights acknowledged the universality of human rights and noted that while the significance of national and regional particularities and various historical, cultural, and religious backgrounds must be borne in mind, it is the duty of states, regardless of their political, economic, and cultural systems, to promote and protect all human rights and fundamental freedoms.

INTERNATIONAL BILL OF RIGHTS

The International Bill of Rights consists of three core instruments that together outline the fundamental civil, political, economic, social, and cultural rights that are universally guaranteed:

- **Universal Declaration of Human Rights (UDHR)** - 1948
- **International Covenant on Civil and Political Rights (ICCPR)** - 1966
- **International Covenant on Economic, Social and Cultural Rights (ICESCR)** - 1966

Universal Declaration of Human Rights (UDHR)

- **Adoption**: Adopted by the United Nations General Assembly on December 10, 1948.
- **Nature**: Although not a legally binding document, the UDHR is widely regarded as the foundational text of international human rights law. It has inspired more than 60 human rights instruments which together constitute an international standard of human rights.
- **Key Provisions**: It includes rights such as the right to life, liberty, and security of person (Article 3); the right to a fair trial (Article 10); freedom of thought, conscience, and religion (Article 18); and rights to education (Article 26).

International Covenant on Civil and Political Rights (ICCPR)

- **Adoption**: Adopted by the UN General Assembly on December 16, 1966, and came into force on March 23, 1976.
- **Nature**: The ICCPR is a key international treaty that is legally binding to those states that are parties to it. It commits its parties to respect the civil and political rights of individuals, including the right to life, freedom of speech, religion, and voting.
- **Key Provisions**: Articles in the ICCPR cover issues such as the right to life (Article 6), prohibition of torture (Article 7), freedom of expression (Article 19), and rights of minorities (Article 27).
- **Human Rights Committee**: The ICCPR established the Human Rights Committee, which monitors the implementation of the treaty and addresses violations.

International Covenant on Economic, Social and Cultural Rights (ICESCR)

- **Adoption**: Adopted alongside the ICCPR on December 16, 1966, and entered into force on January 3, 1976.
- **Nature**: This Covenant is also legally binding for the states that have ratified it. It emphasizes economic, social, and cultural rights.
- **Key Provisions**: It includes rights to work (Article 6), the right to health (Article 12), the right to education (Article 13), and rights to an adequate standard of living (Article 11).
- **Committee on Economic, Social and Cultural Rights**: This body monitors compliance with the ICESCR and provides guidance through General Comments on thematic issues.

GROUP RIGHTS – WOMEN, CHILDREN, PERSONS WITH DISABILITIES, ELDERLY PERSONS, MINORITIES AND WEAKER SECTIONS

CHILDREN

Major Laws and Initiatives:

- **The Child Labour (Prohibition and Regulation) Amendment Act, 2016**: The Child Labour (Prohibition and Regulation) Amendment Act, 2016, prohibits employment of children below 14 in all occupations and processes, except in non-hazardous family enterprises or as child artists in the entertainment industry (excluding circus) after school hours or during vacations, subject to regulatory conditions.
- **The Protection of Children from Sexual Offences (POCSO) Act, 2012**: Protects children from offenses of sexual assault, sexual harassment, and pornography.
- **Juvenile Justice (Care and Protection of Children) Act, 2015**: Provides a framework for the protection, treatment, and rehabilitation of children in the juvenile justice system.
- **Prohibition of Child Marriage Act, 2006**: Aims to eliminate child marriage by setting the legal age of marriage at 18 for girls and 21 for boys.
- **Government Initiatives:**
  - **National Child Labour Project**: Seeks to eliminate child labor by providing educational and vocational training to children rescued from labor.
  - **Integrated Child Development Services (ICDS)**: Offers health, nutrition, and education services to children under 6 years and their mothers to combat child malnutrition and mortality.

ELDERLY PERSONS

Legal Provisions:

- **The Maintenance and Welfare of Parents and Senior Citizens Act, 2007** - This act provides a legal mechanism for elderly persons to claim maintenance from their children. It also mandates the establishment of old age homes in every district and provides provisions for their medical care and protection.
- **National Policy on Older Persons, 1999** - This policy aims to encourage individuals to make provisions for their own as well as their spouse's old age. It also stresses state support for financial security, health care, shelter, welfare, and other needs of older persons, to improve the quality of their lives.

PERSONS WITH DISABILITIES

Legislative Framework:

- **The Rights of Persons with Disabilities Act, 2016** - Significantly expands the definition of disabilities and stipulates that the appropriate governments and local authorities must ensure that all their public documents are in accessible formats. It also increases the reservation for persons with disabilities in government jobs and higher educational institutions, and provides for the setting up of special courts for the speedy trial of offenses against persons with disabilities.

- **Mental Health Act, 2017** - This act was introduced to meet the requirements of the UN Convention on the Rights of Persons with Disabilities, Mental Healthcare Act, 2017, and clarify that Section 115 presumes a person attempting suicide is under severe stress, effectively reducing punishment under Section 309, IPC, rather than fully decriminalizing suicide.
- **National Trust for Welfare of Persons with Autism, Cerebral Palsy, Mental Retardation, and Multiple Disabilities Act, 1999** - Establishes the National Trust to enable and empower persons with disability to live as independently and as fully as possible within and as close to the community to which they belong.

MINORITIES AND WEAKER SECTIONS

Constitutional Provisions:

- **Articles 29 and 30**: Protect the cultural and educational rights of minorities, allowing them to conserve their language, script, and culture and to establish and administer educational institutions of their choice.
- **Articles 46, 330, 332, 334**: Direct the State to promote the educational and economic interests of the weaker sections, particularly Scheduled Castes and Scheduled Tribes, and to protect them from social injustice and all forms of exploitation. These articles also provide for political representation by reserving seats in the Parliament and State Legislatures.

Specific Laws:

- **Wakf Act, 1995** - Provides for the administration of wakf properties, ensuring that such properties are properly maintained and utilized to help the Muslim community.
- **Commission for Minorities Act, 1992** - Establishes the National Commission for Minorities to evaluate the progress of the development of minorities and monitor the working of safeguards provided in the Constitution and in laws enacted by Parliament.
- **Scheduled Castes and Tribes (Prevention of Atrocities) Amendment Act, 2015** - Strengthens the provisions of the principal Act and adds new offenses to the list of atrocities against Scheduled Castes and Scheduled Tribes.
- **Forest Rights Act, 2006** - Recognizes the rights of forest-dwelling tribal communities over land and other resources which were denied to them over decades as a result of the continuance of colonial forest laws in India.

PROTECTION AND ENFORCEMENT OF HUMAN RIGHTS IN INDIA

NATIONAL HUMAN RIGHTS COMMISSION (NHRC)

Legal Framework and Establishment

- **Background**: The NHRC was established under the Protection of Human Rights Act, 1993. The Act was amended in 2006 and 2019 to include various changes that expanded the NHRC's functions and membership.
- **Purpose**: The commission is tasked with promoting and protecting human rights, which are defined under the Act as rights relating to life, liberty, equality, and dignity of the individual, guaranteed by the Constitution or embodied in the International Covenants.

Composition of the NHRC

- **Members**: The NHRC consists of a Chairperson must be a person who is or has been a Chief Justice of India or a Supreme Court Judge, and two members appointed from among persons having knowledge of, or practical experience in, matters relating to human rights.
- **Term**: The Chairperson and members hold office for a term of three years or until they reach the age of 70, whichever is earlier.

Powers and Functions

- **Investigatory Powers**: The NHRC has the powers of a civil court while trying a suit under the Code of Civil Procedure, 1908. It can summon and enforce the attendance of witnesses and examine them under oath, receive evidence, and requisition records from courts and government offices.
- **Recommendatory Powers**: The NHRC examines the safeguards for human rights under the constitution and other laws, recommends corrective legislative measures, and advises the government on effective implementation of international treaties.

Procedure for Handling Complaints

- **Process**: Individuals can file complaints to the NHRC regarding violations of human rights or negligence in preventing such violation by a public servant. The NHRC can also take suo moto cognizance of serious human rights violations.
- **Follow-up**: Post inquiry, the NHRC may recommend compensation to the victim or prosecution of the offender. However, the recommendations of the NHRC are not binding on the government.

Important Cases and Interventions

- **Cases**: NHRC has been pivotal in several key human rights cases in India, dealing with issues such as custodial deaths, illegal detentions, and enforced disappearances.
- **Impact**: These interventions often lead to remedial actions including compensation to victims and changes in administrative procedures.

Relationship with State Human Rights Commissions

- **Coordination**: The NHRC collaborates with SHRCs to ensure a broader reach and effective monitoring of human rights across India.
- **Guidance**: It provides guidance and advice to SHRCs, can call for reports on specific incidents, and even transfer cases to or from SHRCs.

Recent Developments and Reforms

- **Amendments**: The Protection of Human Rights (Amendment) Act, 2019, introduced changes to the composition and reduced the term of office of chairperson and members to three years.
- **Initiatives**: Recent initiatives include increased focus on human rights education, awareness programs, and special monitoring mechanisms for vulnerable populations.

National Commission for Minorities (NCM)

Establishment and Legal Basis

- **Established**: Under the National Commission for Minorities Act, 1992.
- **Purpose**: To safeguard and improve the socio-economic conditions of minority communities in India.

Composition and Leadership

- **Composition**: The NCM is composed of a Chairperson, a Vice Chairperson, and five members, all of whom must belong to minority communities. Members are appointed by the Central Government and are recognized individuals of eminence, ability, and integrity.
- **Leadership**: The current Chairperson, as mentioned in the sources, is Iqbal Singh Lalpura. The commission also includes various members dedicated to addressing specific minority concerns.

Powers and Functions

- **Civil Court Powers**: The NCM has the powers of a civil court for summoning and enforcing the attendance of any person, examining him/her under oath, and requiring the discovery and production of documents.
- **Functions**:
- **Evaluation and Monitoring**: Assess and monitor the development progress of minorities and the implementation of safeguards provided in the Constitution and various laws.
- **Recommendations**: Propose recommendations to the central and state governments for the effective implementation of minority rights protections.
- **Address Complaints**: Look into specific complaints concerning the deprivation of minority rights and interact with appropriate authorities for redressal.
- **Research and Studies**: Conduct research and studies on issues affecting minorities and suggest measures for improvement.
- **Reporting**: Produce periodic reports on the status of minorities, highlighting any challenges and suggesting ways forward.

Key Constitutional Provisions

- **Article 29**: Protects the rights of minorities to conserve their culture, language, or script.
- **Article 30**: Grants minorities the right to establish and administer educational institutions of their choice, safeguarding their educational rights.

Challenges and Critiques

- **Effectiveness**: One of the significant challenges is the non-binding nature of the NCM's recommendations, which governments are not obliged to follow.
- **Implementation Issues**: There are often gaps in the implementation of the NCM's recommendations by various government bodies.

Significant Contributions and Recent Initiatives

- **Follow-up on Sachar Committee Recommendations**: The NCM has been pivotal in implementing the Sachar Committee's suggestions, particularly concerning the socio-economic development of the Muslim community.
- **Annual Reports and Special Studies**: The commission regularly updates its findings and suggestions through comprehensive reports and targeted studies addressing specific issues.

Recommendations for Enhancements

- **Strengthening Authority**: There are ongoing discussions about enhancing the commission's powers to make its recommendations more impactful and binding on state and central governments.

NATIONAL COMMISSION FOR WOMEN

History and Formation of NCW

- **Establishment**: The National Commission for Women was established in January 1992 under the National Commission for Women Act, 1990.
- **Purpose**: It was set up to review the constitutional and legal safeguards for women, recommend remedial legislative measures, facilitate redressal of grievances, and advise the Government on all policy matters affecting women.

Roles and Functions of NCW

- **Advisory Role**: Advises the Government on policy matters affecting women.
- **Legal Monitoring**: Reviews existing legislation and suggests amendments to meet lacunae in laws related to women.
- **Complaint and Redressal Mechanism**: Processes complaints received regarding violations of women's rights and provides a forum for hearing grievances.
- **Research and Studies**: Undertakes promotional and educational research to suggest ways of ensuring due representation of women in all spheres.

Significant Cases and Interventions

- **Violence against Women**: Played a crucial role in addressing issues like domestic violence, dowry harassment, and acid attacks.
- **Employment and Workplace Safety**: Addressed sexual harassment at the workplace, enforcing compliance with the Sexual Harassment of Women at Workplace (Prevention, Prohibition and Redressal) Act, 2013.
- **Emergency Response and Legal Aid**: Provided legal aid to women in distress and collaborated with NGOs for quick relief.

Programs and Campaigns

- **Awareness Campaigns**: Launched campaigns to raise awareness about legal rights among women, focusing on rural and backward areas.
- **Skill Development and Employment**: Promoted vocational training and skill development programs to enhance women's participation in the workforce.
- **Health and Reproductive Rights**: Advocated for better health facilities for women and supported initiatives aimed at improving maternal health.

Legal Framework and Policies

- **Contribution to Legislation**: Influential in shaping significant legislations such as the Protection of Women from Domestic Violence Act, 2005.
- **Policy Recommendations**: Offers recommendations to ensure that government policies and programs are inclusive of and beneficial to women.

Composition

- **Chairperson**: A woman committed to the cause of women, who is appointed by the Central Government.
- **Member Secretary**: Typically a person who is an expert in the field of management, organizational structure, sociological movement, or an officer who is a member of a civil service of the Union or of an all-India service or holds a civil post under the Union with appropriate experience.
- **Five Members**: Appointed from amongst persons of ability, integrity, and standing who have experience in law or legislation, trade unionism, management of an industry or organization committed to increasing the employment potential of women, women's voluntary organizations (including women activists), administration, economic development, health, education, or social welfare; provided that at least one member each shall be from amongst persons belonging to the Scheduled Castes and Scheduled Tribes respectively.

Appointment and Term

- The Chairperson and members are appointed for a term of three years, which can be renewed.
- They are appointed by the Central Government (Ministry of Women and Child Development) for a term of three years, which can be renewed.
- The commission thus has a varied and comprehensive structure aimed at addressing multiple aspects of women's rights and issues from legal to educational and from health to economic empowerment.

NATIONAL COMMISSION FOR SCHEDULE CASTE

Foundations and Functions of the NCSC

- **Constitutional Basis**: Established under Article 338 of the Indian Constitution, the NCSC is tasked with monitoring all safeguards provided for Scheduled Castes under the Constitution or other laws.
- **Powers and Functions**: The NCSC investigates and monitors matters relating to the safeguards for Scheduled Castes, participates in and advises on the planning process of socio-economic development, and evaluates the progress of their development under the Union and any State.

- **Key Interventions**: Case studies, such as the NCSC's intervention in preventing atrocities against Scheduled Castes or in ensuring implementation of reservation policies in educational institutions and government employment, are crucial to understand the practical role of the commission.

Legislative Framework for Scheduled Castes Welfare

- **Protection of Civil Rights Act, 1955**: This act was an early framework intended to abolish untouchability and prevent atrocities against Scheduled Castes.
- **SC and ST (Prevention of Atrocities) Act, 1989**: Focus on provisions that enhance penalties for crimes against Scheduled Castes, and the establishment of special courts for expedited processing of these cases.
- **Affirmative Action**: Review the reservation policies in education and public sector employment, including recent changes and legal challenges related to these policies.

COMPOSITION

Chairperson

- **Role**: The Chairperson leads the commission and oversees its functions and administration. They represent the commission in official capacities and ensure that it fulfills its mandate.
- **Selection**: Appointed by the President of India.

Vice Chairperson

- **Role**: Assists the Chairperson and may act in their stead if the Chairperson is unavailable.
- **Selection**: Also appointed by the President of India.

Members

- **Number**: The commission typically includes three other members.
- **Role**: These members work collectively to monitor the safeguards provided for Scheduled Castes, investigate complaints, and participate in the planning process of socio-economic development of Scheduled Castes.
- **Selection**: Like the Chairperson and Vice Chairperson, these members are appointed by the President of India.

Terms of Office

- **Duration**: The Chairperson, Vice Chairperson, and other members usually serve for a term specified by the President at the time of their appointment. Often, this term is around three years, but it can vary.
- **Conditions**: Members hold office subject to the pleasure of the President, and their service conditions and salaries are also prescribed by the President.

NATIONAL COMMISSION FOR SCHEDULE TRIBE

Establishment and Function of NCST

- **History and Establishment**: Established through the 89th Amendment of the Constitution of India in 2003, under article 338A of constitution, the NCST was formed by bifurcating the erstwhile National Commission for Scheduled Castes and Tribes to provide more focused attention on issues related to Scheduled Tribes.
- **Key Functions**: The NCST investigates and monitors matters relating to the safeguards provided for the Scheduled Tribes under the Constitution or under any other law. It also advises on the planning process of socio-economic development of the Scheduled Tribes and evaluates the progress of their development under the Union and any State.

Composition of NCST

- **Members**: The Commission consists of a Chairperson, a Vice Chairperson, and three other Members. They are appointed by the President of India.
- **Term of Office**: The members hold office for a term of three years from the date of assumption of charge.

Legislative Framework

- **Relevant Legislations**: Key laws include the Scheduled Castes and Scheduled Tribes (Prevention of Atrocities) Act, 1989, the Forest Rights Act, 2006, and the Panchayats (Extension to Scheduled Areas) Act, 1996.
- **Role in Implementation**: The Commission ensures that these laws are faithfully implemented and the violators are prosecuted to safeguard tribal interests.

Reports and Recommendations

- **Significant Reports**: Annual reports provided to the President of India detail the state of affairs of Scheduled Tribes, highlight particular issues, and suggest measures for improvement.

- **Recommendations**: Typically include enhancement of educational facilities, better healthcare access, and legal support to protect tribal lands and culture.

Role in Policy Making

- **Influence on Policies**: The Commission's recommendations often lead to policy adjustments or new initiatives aimed at improving the welfare and protection of tribal populations.
- **Coordination with Governmental Bodies**: NCST collaborates with central and state governments to ensure that developmental benefits reach the tribal communities effectively.

NATIONAL COMMISSION FOR BACKWARD CASTE

History and Formation of NCBC

- **Establishment**: Formed by the National Commission for Backward Classes Act, 1993, following the recommendations of the Mandal Commission and the directive in the Indra Sawhney case (1992), which addressed the need for an authority to consider the inclusion of various communities within the OBC list and ensure justice and equality in reservations.
- **Constitutional Status**: Received constitutional status with the 102nd Constitutional Amendment in 2018, making it a constitutional body like the National Commission for Scheduled Castes and Scheduled Tribes.

Functions and Powers of NCBC

- **Investigative Powers**: Can investigate and monitor all matters relating to the safeguards provided for backward classes under the Constitution and other laws.
- **Annual Reports**: Required to present annual reports to the President detailing the protection provided to backward classes.
- **Legal Authority**: Empowered to regulate its own procedures and the Government of India is required to consult the Commission on all major policy matters affecting backward classes.

Composition of the National Commission for Backward Classes:

- **Number and Appointment of Members**: The NCBC consists of a Chairperson, a Vice-Chairperson, and three other Members. These members are appointed by the President of India.
- **Qualifications for Membership**: Members are usually eminent persons in public life with deep knowledge and experience in matters relating to backward classes. Typically, the members include people from various fields such as law, public administration, education, or social service, ensuring a well-rounded perspective on issues affecting backward classes.

Term of Office:

- The Chairperson, Vice-Chairperson, and other members hold office for a term of three years from the date they assume office or until they reach the age of 70 years, whichever is earlier.

Roles and Responsibilities:

- The Chairperson has the overall responsibility for the functioning of the Commission and represents the Commission in its dealings with the Government.
- The Vice-Chairperson assists the Chairperson and may act in their capacity during their absence.
- The other Members are responsible for specific areas, like investigation and monitoring, advising on policy and legal matters, and outreach to the community.

Role of NCBC in Reservations

- **Determining Criteria for OBCs**: Responsible for defining and revising the criteria that determine which communities are classified as Other Backward Classes (OBC).
- **Policy Recommendations**: Provides the government with recommendations on setting aside quotas in higher education and government employment.

Significant Judgments and Recommendations

- **Inclusion/Exclusion in OBC Lists**: Has the authority to include or exclude any class from the list of backward classes.
- **Major Judicial Endorsements**: Influential in shaping the legal framework surrounding backward class reservations, as seen in several high-profile court cases affecting reservation policies.

Recent Amendments and Legislative Changes

- **Impact of 102nd Amendment:** Reinforced the NCBC's power by providing it with the constitutional status, previously held by the National Commission (Repealed) which functioned under the Ministry of Social Justice and Empowerment.

MULTIPLE CHOICE QUESTIONS

1. Which of the following is included in the legal definition of the environment under the Environment (Protection) Act, 1986?
A. Air B. Water
C. Land D. All of the above

2. Which of the following is NOT considered an environmental pollutant under the Environment (Protection) Act, 1986?
A. Noise B. Light
C. Water D. Chemical waste

3. Which of the following types of pollution is primarily caused by vehicular emissions?
A. Water pollution B. Soil pollution
C. Air pollution D. Noise pollution

4. The process of accumulation of harmful substances in the environment, leading to adverse effects, is called:
A. Biodegradation B. Pollution
C. Conservation D. Photosynthesis

5. Noise pollution is not considered a part of environmental pollution under Indian law.
A. True
B. False
C. True, only in rural areas
D. False, unless it exceeds 100 decibels

6. The environment only includes natural components like air, water, and land, excluding man-made structures.
A. True
B. False
C. True, unless in urban areas
D. False, unless specified in environmental treaties

7. **Assertion (A):** Deforestation contributes to environmental pollution.
Reason (R): Deforestation reduces the amount of oxygen released into the atmosphere.
A. Both A and R are true, and R is the correct explanation of A
B. Both A and R are true, but R is not the correct explanation of A
C. A is true, R is false
D. A is false, R is true

8. The Environment (Protection) Act, 1986 was enacted after the _______ disaster.
A. Chernobyl B. Fukushima
C. Bhopal Gas D. Three Mile Island

9. The presence of harmful substances in the environment, exceeding permissible limits, is referred to as _______.
A. Biodiversity B. Pollution
C. Sustainability D. Conservation

10. Match the following types of pollution with their major causes:

A. Air Pollution	1. Industrial effluents
B. Water Pollution	2. Vehicle emissions
C. Soil Pollution	3. Use of pesticides
D. Noise Pollution	4. Loudspeakers and traffic

A. A-2, B-1, C-3, D-4
B. A-1, B-4, C-2, D-3
C. A-3, B-2, C-1, D-4
D. A-4, B-3, C-2, D-1

11. Arrange the following events related to environmental awareness in chronological order:
1. Stockholm Conference
2. Earth Summit (Rio)
3. Kyoto Protocol
4. Paris Agreement
A. 1, 2, 3, 4 B. 4, 3, 2, 1
C. 3, 1, 4, 2 D. 2, 1, 3, 4

12. Scenario: A factory discharges untreated chemicals into a nearby river, affecting aquatic life and human health. What type of pollution is this?
A. Air Pollution B. Noise Pollution
C. Water Pollution D. Soil Pollution

13. Scenario: A city experiences severe smog due to heavy traffic and industrial emissions. Which pollutant is likely the cause?
A. Ozone B. Carbon monoxide
C. Nitrogen dioxide D. Both B and C

14. Scenario: An area near an airport suffers from constant loud noise, affecting the residents' health. What type of pollution is this?
A. Soil Pollution B. Air Pollution
C. Water Pollution D. Noise Pollution

15. Which of the following is considered a greenhouse gas contributing to climate change?
A. Oxygen B. Nitrogen
C. Carbon dioxide D. Helium

16. Which Article of the Indian Constitution imposes a duty on the State to protect the environment?

A. Article 14 B. Article 21
C. Article 48A D. Article 32

17. Match the following environmental laws with their year of enactment:

A. Environment (Protection) Act	1. 1986
B. Air (Prevention and Control of Pollution) Act	2. 1981
C. Water (Prevention and Control of Pollution) Act	3. 1974
D. Wildlife Protection Act	4. 1972

A. A-1, B-2, C-3, D-4
B. A-4, B-1, C-2, D-3
C. A-3, B-2, C-4, D-1
D. A-2, B-4, C-1, D-3

18. Scenario: A farmer uses excessive fertilizers, leading to contamination of groundwater. What type of pollution is this?

A. Air Pollution B. Noise Pollution
C. Soil Pollution D. Water Pollution

19. Scenario: A residential area near an industrial zone suffers from chronic respiratory diseases due to air emissions. Which pollutant is most likely responsible?

A. Oxygen B. Sulfur dioxide
C. Helium D. Nitrogen gas

20. Which of the following was the first major international conference on the environment?

A. Rio Earth Summit, 1992
B. Stockholm Conference, 1972
C. Kyoto Protocol, 1997
D. Paris Agreement, 2015

21. The United Nations Framework Convention on Climate Change (UNFCCC) was adopted at:

A. Kyoto Protocol
B. Stockholm Conference
C. Earth Summit, Rio de Janeiro
D. Paris Agreement

22. Which of the following international agreements focuses specifically on the reduction of greenhouse gas emissions?

A. Montreal Protocol
B. Kyoto Protocol
C. Basel Convention
D. Stockholm Convention

23. The Paris Agreement, signed in 2015, aims to:

A. Protect endangered species
B. Limit global warming to below 2°C
C. Control hazardous waste movement
D. Prevent deforestation globally

24. The Rio Declaration on Environment and Development introduced the concept of sustainable development.

A. True
B. False
C. True, but only for developed countries
D. False, it was introduced at the Stockholm Conference

25. The Montreal Protocol deals with the protection of the ozone layer.

A. True
B. False
C. True, but only in the northern hemisphere
D. False, it focuses on climate change mitigation

26. **Assertion (A):** The Kyoto Protocol legally binds developed countries to reduce greenhouse gas emissions.

Reason (R): Developing countries were exempted from binding targets under the Kyoto Protocol.

A. Both A and R are true, and R is the correct explanation of A
B. Both A and R are true, but R is not the correct explanation of A
C. A is true, R is false
D. A is false, R is true

27. **Assertion (A):** The Basel Convention deals with climate change.

Reason (R): The Basel Convention regulates the transboundary movement of hazardous wastes.

A. Both A and R are true, and R is the correct explanation of A
B. Both A and R are true, but R is not the correct explanation of A
C. A is true, R is false
D. A is false, R is true

28. The concept of "common but differentiated responsibilities" was first introduced in the _______.

A. Kyoto Protocol
B. Paris Agreement
C. Rio Declaration
D. Montreal Protocol

29. The Kyoto Protocol was adopted in the year _______.

A. 1987 B. 1992
C. 1997 D. 2001

30. Match the following international environmental agreements with their objectives:

A. Montreal Protocol	1. Reduce greenhouse gas emissions
B. Basel Convention	2. Control hazardous waste movement
C. Paris Agreement	3. Protect the ozone layer
D. Kyoto Protocol	4. Limit global warming below 2°C

A. A-3, B-2, C-4, D-1
B. A-1, B-4, C-3, D-2
C. A-2, B-1, C-3, D-4
D. A-4, B-3, C-2, D-1

31. Arrange the following major environmental conferences in chronological order:
1. Stockholm Conference
2. Earth Summit (Rio)
3. Kyoto Protocol
4. Paris Agreement

A. 1, 2, 3, 4 B. 4, 3, 2, 1
C. 3, 1, 4, 2 D. 2, 1, 3, 4

32. Scenario: A country refuses to reduce its carbon emissions, citing that it is a developing nation with less historical responsibility for climate change. Which principle supports this argument?
A. Polluter Pays Principle
B. Precautionary Principle
C. Common but Differentiated Responsibilities
D. Sustainable Development

33. Scenario: A country signs an international agreement to phase out chlorofluorocarbons (CFCs) to protect the ozone layer. Which agreement is this?
A. Kyoto Protocol
B. Montreal Protocol
C. Paris Agreement
D. Stockholm Convention

34. Scenario: A country faces criticism for exporting hazardous waste to developing nations. Which international agreement addresses this issue?
A. Paris Agreement
B. Basel Convention
C. Rio Declaration
D. Kyoto Protocol

35. Which of the following principles emphasizes that the polluter should bear the cost of environmental damage?
A. Sustainable Development
B. Precautionary Principle
C. Polluter Pays Principle
D. Equity Principle

36. Which of the following is a legally binding agreement under the UNFCCC?
A. Rio Declaration
B. Kyoto Protocol
C. Stockholm Conference
D. Earth Charter

37. Match the following international environmental conferences with their outcomes:

A. Stockholm Conference (1972)	1. UNFCCC adoption
B. Earth Summit (1992)	2. Creation of UNEP
C. Kyoto Protocol (1997)	3. Binding targets for GHG reduction
D. Paris Agreement (2015)	4. Limit temperature rise below 2°C

A. A-2, B-1, C-3, D-4
B. A-4, B-3, C-1, D-2
C. A-1, B-4, C-2, D-3
D. A-3, B-2, C-4, D-1

38. Scenario: A developing country is seeking financial and technical assistance to meet its climate commitments. Which mechanism under the UNFCCC supports this?
A. Clean Development Mechanism (CDM)
B. Polluter Pays Principle
C. Basel Convention
D. Stockholm Declaration

39. Scenario: A country refuses to ratify an international climate agreement, arguing that it affects its economic growth. What is the legal effect of not ratifying the agreement?
A. The country is still legally bound
B. The country has no legal obligations under the agreement
C. The agreement applies automatically after signing
D. The UN can impose penalties directly

40. Which Article of the Indian Constitution imposes a duty on the State to protect and improve the environment?
A. Article 21 B. Article 32
C. Article 48A D. Article 51A(g)

41. Which of the following is a Fundamental Duty related to environmental protection?
A. Duty to vote in elections
B. Duty to develop scientific temper
C. Duty to protect and improve the natural environment
D. Duty to follow traffic rules

42. Which of the following laws was enacted after the Bhopal Gas Tragedy of 1984?

A. Air (Prevention and Control of Pollution) Act, 1981

B. Water (Prevention and Control of Pollution) Act, 1974

C. Environment (Protection) Act, 1986

D. Wildlife Protection Act, 1972

43. Which of the following constitutional provisions ensures the Right to a Clean Environment?

A. Article 19 B. Article 21

C. Article 29 D. Article 14

44. The Right to Pollution-Free Water and Air is considered part of the Right to Life under Article 21.

A. True

B. False

C. True, but only for urban residents

D. False, unless specifically stated in legislation

45. The National Green Tribunal (NGT) was established under the Environment (Protection) Act, 1986.

A. True

B. False

C. True, but only for industrial cases

D. False, it was established under the NGT Act, 2010

46. Assertion (A): The Air (Prevention and Control of Pollution) Act, 1981 aims to control air pollution.

Reason (R): The Act was passed in response to the Stockholm Conference, 1972.

A. Both A and R are true, and R is the correct explanation of A

B. Both A and R are true, but R is not the correct explanation of A

C. A is true, R is false

D. A is false, R is true

47. **Assertion (A):** The Polluter Pays Principle is recognized in Indian environmental law.

Reason (R): The principle states that the polluter must pay for the damage caused to the environment.

A. Both A and R are true, and R is the correct explanation of A

B. Both A and R are true, but R is not the correct explanation of A

C. A is true, R is false

D. A is false, R is true

48. The primary law governing environmental protection in India is the ______.

A. Environment (Protection) Act, 1986

B. Wildlife Protection Act, 1972

C. Forest Conservation Act, 1980

D. Biological Diversity Act, 2002

49. The National Green Tribunal (NGT) was established in the year ______.

A. 2005 B. 2010

C. 2015 D. 2000

50. Match the following constitutional provisions with their relevance to environmental protection:

A. Article 21	1. Right to a Clean Environment
B. Article 48A	2. Duty of the State to protect the environment
C. Article 51A(g)	3. Fundamental Duty of citizens
D. Article 32	4. Right to approach the Supreme Court

A. A-1, B-2, C-3, D-4

B. A-4, B-1, C-2, D-3

C. A-2, B-3, C-4, D-1

D. A-3, B-4, C-1, D-2

51. Scenario: A company is found to be dumping toxic waste into a river, affecting the health of nearby residents. Which principle of environmental law applies?

A. Sustainable Development

B. Polluter Pays Principle

C. Precautionary Principle

D. Doctrine of Public Trust

52. Scenario: A government policy is introduced that allows large-scale deforestation for economic projects. A group of citizens files a petition in the Supreme Court. Which constitutional provision supports their case?

A. Article 14 B. Article 21

C. Article 32 D. Article 51A

53. Which landmark case established the Public Trust Doctrine in Indian environmental law?

A. Vellore Citizens Welfare Forum v. Union of India

B. M.C. Mehta v. Kamal Nath

C. Indian Council for Enviro-Legal Action v. Union of India

D. Subhash Kumar v. State of Bihar

54. Which of the following principles emphasizes that preventive measures should be taken to avoid environmental degradation even in the absence of scientific certainty?

A. Polluter Pays Principle
B. Precautionary Principle
C. Sustainable Development Principle
D. Doctrine of Proportionality

55. The 'Right to Environment' as a part of the 'Right to Life' was first recognized in which landmark case?

A. Maneka Gandhi v. Union of India
B. M.C. Mehta v. Union of India (Oleum Gas Leak Case)
C. Kesavananda Bharati v. State of Kerala
D. Golaknath v. State of Punjab

56. **Assertion (A):** The Forest (Conservation) Act, 1980 aims to prevent deforestation and conserve forest resources.

Reason (R): The Act allows unrestricted use of forest land for industrial purposes.

A. Both A and R are true, and R is the correct explanation of A
B. Both A and R are true, but R is not the correct explanation of A
C. A is true, R is false
D. A is false, R is true

57. The 'Sustainable Development' principle was prominently discussed in the ______ case in India.

A. M.C. Mehta v. Union of India (Ganga Pollution Case)
B. Vellore Citizens Welfare Forum v. Union of India
C. T.N. Godavarman Thirumulpad v. Union of India
D. Indian Council for Enviro-Legal Action v. Union of India

58. Scenario: A public authority allocates a wetland area for commercial construction, affecting biodiversity. Environmental activists challenge this in court. Which legal doctrine can be invoked?

A. Doctrine of Estoppel
B. Public Trust Doctrine
C. Doctrine of Severability
D. Doctrine of Eclipse

59. Match the following environmental principles with their key features:

A. Sustainable Development	1. Prevents degradation of the environment for future generations
B. Polluter Pays Principle	2. Polluter bears the cost of pollution
C. Precautionary Principle	3. Precautionary measures are taken even without full scientific certainty
D. Public Trust Doctrine	4. State acts as a trustee of natural resources

A. A-1, B-2, C-3, D-4
B. A-4, B-3, C-2, D-1
C. A-2, B-1, C-4, D-3
D. A-3, B-4, C-1, D-2

60. The National Green Tribunal (NGT) was established under which Act?

A. Environment (Protection) Act, 1986
B. National Green Tribunal Act, 2010
C. Air (Prevention and Control of Pollution) Act, 1981
D. Water (Prevention and Control of Pollution) Act, 1974

61. The principal bench of the National Green Tribunal is located in:

A. Mumbai B. Chennai
C. Kolkata D. New Delhi

62. Which of the following principles is NOT directly applied by the National Green Tribunal?

A. Polluter Pays Principle
B. Precautionary Principle
C. Sustainable Development Principle
D. Doctrine of Laches

63. The National Green Tribunal has jurisdiction over matters related to:

A. Land disputes
B. Taxation
C. Environmental protection and conservation of natural resources
D. Criminal offenses

64. The National Green Tribunal can impose penalties on industries causing environmental pollution.

A. True
B. False
C. True, but only with Supreme Court approval
D. False, unless directed by the government

65. Only government bodies can approach the National Green Tribunal for environmental matters.
A. True
B. False
C. True, unless it's a public interest case
D. False, unless approved by the Ministry of Environment

66. Assertion (A): The National Green Tribunal can hear cases related to environmental clearances granted for industrial projects.

Reason (R): The NGT has jurisdiction over disputes related to environmental laws listed in Schedule I of the NGT Act, 2010.
A. Both A and R are true, and R is the correct explanation of A
B. Both A and R are true, but R is not the correct explanation of A
C. A is true, R is false
D. A is false, R is true

67. Assertion (A): The National Green Tribunal has both original and appellate jurisdiction.

Reason (R): It only handles appeals against environmental fines imposed by government authorities.
A. Both A and R are true, and R is the correct explanation of A
B. Both A and R are true, but R is not the correct explanation of A
C. A is true, R is false
D. A is false, R is true

68. The National Green Tribunal is required to dispose of cases within _______ months from the date of filing.
A. 3 months B. 6 months
C. 12 months D. 24 months

69. The National Green Tribunal follows the principles of natural justice and operates as a _______ body.
A. Civil Court B. Criminal Court
C. Quasi-judicial D. Legislative

70. Match the following environmental principles with their relevance in NGT cases:

A. Polluter Pays Principle	1. Preventive action for environmental risks
B. Precautionary Principle	2. Economic responsibility for environmental damage
C. Sustainable Development	3. Balancing development with environmental protection
D. Public Trust Doctrine	4. Natural resources held in trust by the State

A. A-2, B-1, C-3, D-4
B. A-4, B-2, C-1, D-3
C. A-3, B-1, C-4, D-2
D. A-1, B-3, C-2, D-4

71. Arrange the following steps in the correct sequence for filing a case with the National Green Tribunal:
1. Filing an application/appeal
2. Admission of the case
3. Hearing and arguments
4. Final judgment and order

A. 1, 2, 3, 4 B. 2, 1, 4, 3
C. 1, 3, 2, 4 D. 4, 1, 2, 3

72. Scenario: A large construction project is approved without proper environmental impact assessment. Local residents want to challenge this approval. Where should they file the case?
A. Supreme Court
B. National Green Tribunal
C. High Court
D. District Court

73. Scenario: An industry is fined for discharging untreated waste into a river. The company wants to appeal the fine. Which forum is appropriate?
A. High Court
B. National Green Tribunal
C. District Magistrate
D. Pollution Control Board

74. Which of the following is NOT a function of the National Green Tribunal?
A. Providing environmental education
B. Hearing environmental disputes
C. Awarding compensation for environmental damage
D. Imposing penalties on polluters

75. The maximum number of judicial and expert members allowed in the NGT is:
A. 10 judicial and 10 expert members
B. 20 judicial and 20 expert members
C. 15 judicial and 15 expert members
D. 25 judicial and 25 expert members

76. Match the following benches of the NGT with their locations:

A. Principal Bench	1. New Delhi
B. Southern Bench	2. Chennai
C. Western Bench	3. Pune
D. Eastern Bench	4. Kolkata

A. A-1, B-2, C-3, D-4
B. A-4, B-3, C-2, D-1
C. A-2, B-1, C-4, D-3
D. A-3, B-4, C-1, D-2

77. Scenario: A local community suffers from groundwater contamination due to industrial activities. They seek compensation. Can the NGT grant compensation?

A. Yes
B. No
C. Yes, only if the case is referred by the High Court
D. No, compensation can only be granted by the Supreme Court

78. Scenario: A mining project in a protected forest area is challenged for violating environmental laws. What doctrine can the NGT apply to protect the forest?

A. Doctrine of Res Judicata
B. Doctrine of Public Trust
C. Doctrine of Estoppel
D. Doctrine of Eclipse

79. Scenario: A delay of 3 years occurs before a community files a petition against industrial pollution. The NGT refuses to hear the case. Why?

A. NGT cannot hear pollution-related cases
B. The case falls under the civil court's jurisdiction
C. The petition was filed beyond the limitation period
D. NGT doesn't have appellate jurisdiction

80. Universalism in human rights suggests that:

A. Rights are specific to each culture
B. Rights are determined by religious norms
C. Human rights apply equally to all people, regardless of culture
D. Rights are subject to change based on societal needs

81. Cultural relativism argues that:

A. Human rights are the same everywhere
B. Moral values are absolute and fixed
C. Moral and cultural practices vary across societies and should be respected
D. International law overrides cultural norms

82. Which of the following documents reflects the principles of universalism?

A. The Magna Carta
B. Universal Declaration of Human Rights (UDHR), 1948
C. Treaty of Versailles
D. Kyoto Protocol

83. Which of the following best illustrates a conflict between universalism and cultural relativism?

A. Freedom of speech in democratic societies
B. Banning of harmful traditional practices like female genital mutilation
C. Adoption of international languages
D. Trade agreements between countries

84. Universalism in human rights allows for cultural exceptions when necessary.

A. True
B. False
C. True, only for economic rights
D. False, unless approved by the UN

85. Cultural relativism supports the idea that no culture's moral code is superior to another's.

A. True
B. False
C. True, but only for ancient cultures
D. False, unless dealing with legal systems

86. **Assertion (A):** Universalism promotes the idea of equal human rights for all.

Reason (R): Universal human rights are based on the belief that all humans share common values.

A. Both A and R are true, and R is the correct explanation of A
B. Both A and R are true, but R is not the correct explanation of A
C. A is true, R is false
D. A is false, R is true

87. **Assertion (A):** Cultural relativism supports the idea of imposing universal moral standards on all societies.

Reason (R): Cultural relativism values diversity and rejects moral absolutism.

A. Both A and R are true, and R is the correct explanation of A
B. Both A and R are true, but R is not the correct explanation of A
C. A is true, R is false
D. A is false, R is true

88. The philosophical foundation of universal human rights is based on the concept of ______.

A. Moral relativism
B. Legal positivism
C. Natural law
D. Cultural diversity

89. Cultural relativism is often criticized for potentially justifying _______ under the guise of cultural practices.

A. Democracy
B. Human rights violations
C. Globalization
D. Environmental conservation

90. Match the following concepts with their correct descriptions:

A. Universalism	1. Rights apply equally to all humans
B. Cultural Relativism	2. Moral codes vary across cultures
C. Natural Rights	3. Rights derived from human nature
D. Legal Positivism	4. Law is valid only if enacted by legitimate authority

A. A-1, B-2, C-3, D-4
B. A-2, B-3, C-1, D-4
C. A-3, B-1, C-4, D-2
D. A-4, B-3, C-2, D-1

91. Arrange the following key events in the evolution of universal human rights in chronological order:

1. Magna Carta (1215)
2. American Declaration of Independence (1776)
3. Universal Declaration of Human Rights (1948)
4. French Declaration of the Rights of Man and Citizen (1789)

A. 1, 2, 4, 3 B. 2, 1, 4, 3
C. 1, 4, 2, 3 D. 4, 3, 1, 2

92. Scenario: A government defends a harmful traditional practice on the grounds that it is part of their cultural heritage. Which perspective does this align with?

A. Universalism
B. Cultural Relativism
C. Natural Law Theory
D. Social Contract Theory

93. Scenario: An international human rights organization criticizes a country for restricting freedom of speech, arguing that it is a universal right. Which concept are they applying?

A. Cultural Relativism
B. Legal Positivism
C. Universalism
D. Ethical Subjectivism

94. Scenario: A court refuses to recognize a foreign law that violates basic human rights, even though it aligns with that country's traditions. What principle is the court following?

A. Cultural Relativism
B. Universalism
C. Moral Relativism
D. Legal Realism

95. Which of the following is a major criticism of universalism?

A. It promotes global equality
B. It ignores cultural diversity
C. It supports cultural autonomy
D. It prevents human rights violations

96. Which philosopher is associated with the development of universal natural rights?

A. Karl Marx
B. John Locke
C. Thomas Hobbes
D. Friedrich Nietzsche

97. Match the following theories with their key proponents:

A. Universalism	1. John Locke
B. Cultural Relativism	2. Franz Boas
C. Natural Rights Theory	3. Immanuel Kant
D. Moral Relativism	4. Ruth Benedict

A. A-3, B-2, C-1, D-4
B. A-1, B-4, C-3, D-2
C. A-2, B-3, C-4, D-1
D. A-4, B-1, C-2, D-3

98. Scenario: A country rejects international pressure to abolish a discriminatory law, claiming it reflects their cultural values. This defense is based on:

A. Universalism
B. Legal Positivism
C. Cultural Relativism
D. Social Contract Theory

99. Scenario: An international court invalidates a law in a country that violates the right to education, citing global human rights norms. This reflects:

A. Moral Relativism
B. Cultural Relativism
C. Universalism
D. Ethical Subjectivism

100. The International Bill of Rights consists of the following documents EXCEPT:

A. Universal Declaration of Human Rights (UDHR)
B. International Covenant on Civil and Political Rights (ICCPR)
C. International Covenant on Economic, Social, and Cultural Rights (ICESCR)
D. Vienna Convention on the Law of Treaties

101. When was the Universal Declaration of Human Rights (UDHR) adopted?
A. 1945 B. 1948
C. 1950 D. 1966

102. Which of the following rights is protected under the International Covenant on Civil and Political Rights (ICCPR)?
A. Right to health
B. Right to education
C. Right to freedom of speech
D. Right to social security

103. Which body monitors the implementation of the International Covenant on Economic, Social, and Cultural Rights (ICESCR)?
A. UN Human Rights Committee
B. International Court of Justice
C. Committee on Economic, Social, and Cultural Rights (CESCR)
D. Security Council

104. The Universal Declaration of Human Rights (UDHR) is legally binding on all UN member states.
A. True
B. False
C. True, only if ratified
D. False, unless incorporated into domestic law

105. The ICCPR has an Optional Protocol that allows individuals to submit complaints about human rights violations.
A. True
B. False
C. True, but only for European countries
D. False, unless authorized by the Security Council

106. Assertion (A): The UDHR applies equally to all individuals, regardless of nationality.

Reason (R): Human rights are universal, inherent, and inalienable.
A. Both A and R are true, and R is the correct explanation of A
B. Both A and R are true, but R is not the correct explanation of A
C. A is true, R is false
D. A is false, R is true

107. Assertion (A): Economic, social, and cultural rights are immediately enforceable under the ICESCR.

Reason (R): The ICESCR requires states to take progressive measures to achieve these rights.
A. Both A and R are true, and R is the correct explanation of A
B. Both A and R are true, but R is not the correct explanation of A
C. A is true, R is false
D. A is false, R is true

108. The ICCPR and ICESCR were both adopted by the United Nations General Assembly in the year ______.
A. 1948 B. 1955
C. 1966 D. 1972

109. The Universal Declaration of Human Rights (UDHR) consists of ______ articles.
A. 20 B. 30
C. 40 D. 50

110. Match the following components of the International Bill of Rights with their focus:

A. UDHR	1. Non-binding declaration of universal rights
B. ICCPR	2. Civil and political rights
C. ICESCR	3. Economic, social, and cultural rights
D. CESCR	4. Monitoring of economic, social, and cultural rights

A. A-1, B-2, C-3, D-4
B. A-4, B-3, C-2, D-1
C. A-2, B-1, C-4, D-3
D. A-3, B-4, C-1, D-2

111. Arrange the following documents in the order of their adoption:
1. Universal Declaration of Human Rights (UDHR)
2. International Covenant on Civil and Political Rights (ICCPR)
3. International Covenant on Economic, Social, and Cultural Rights (ICESCR)
4. First Optional Protocol to the ICCPR

A. 1, 2, 3, 4 B. 1, 3, 2, 4
C. 1, 2, 4, 3 D. 1, 3, 4, 2

112. Scenario: A citizen of a country claims their freedom of speech has been violated by the government. They want to bring the case to an international body. Which document supports their claim?
A. ICESCR B. ICCPR
C. UDHR D. Vienna Declaration

113. Scenario: A country fails to provide basic healthcare to its citizens, citing resource constraints. Under which treaty can this issue be raised?
A. UDHR B. ICCPR
C. ICESCR D. Hague Convention

114. Scenario: An individual wants to file a complaint about a human rights violation directly with the UN. Which protocol allows this under the ICCPR?

A. Second Optional Protocol
B. First Optional Protocol
C. Additional Protocol to ICESCR
D. Geneva Protocol

115. Which of the following rights is NOT explicitly mentioned in the UDHR?

A. Right to education
B. Right to freedom of religion
C. Right to own property
D. Right to bear arms

116. The principle of non-discrimination in the UDHR applies to discrimination based on:

A. Race
B. Gender
C. Religion
D. All of the above

117. Match the following articles of the UDHR with the rights they protect:

A. Article 1	1. Right to freedom of opinion and expression
B. Article 3	2. Right to life, liberty, and security
C. Article 19	3. Right to education
D. Article 26	4. All human beings are born free and equal

A. A-4, B-2, C-1, D-3
B. A-1, B-3, C-4, D-2
C. A-3, B-1, C-4, D-2
D. A-2, B-4, C-3, D-1

118. Scenario: A country ratifies the ICCPR but not the Optional Protocol. What does this imply?

A. The country is not bound by the ICCPR
B. The country can ignore civil and political rights
C. Individuals cannot directly approach the Human Rights Committee
D. The ICCPR is not applicable in the country

119. Scenario: A state claims that economic rights are less important than civil rights. Which document refutes this claim?

A. ICCPR only
B. ICESCR only
C. Both ICCPR and ICESCR
D. Only the UDHR

120. The National Human Rights Commission (NHRC) was established under which Act?

A. Protection of Human Rights Act, 1993
B. Human Rights Act, 1989
C. Social Justice Act, 1995
D. Fundamental Rights Act, 1950

121. Which of the following commissions is responsible for safeguarding the rights of religious and linguistic minorities in India?

A. National Human Rights Commission (NHRC)
B. National Commission for Minorities (NCM)
C. National Commission for Scheduled Tribes (NCST)
D. National Commission for Women (NCW)

122. The National Commission for Women (NCW) was established in which year?

A. 1989 B. 1990
C. 1992 D. 1995

123. Which constitutional article provides for the establishment of the National Commission for Scheduled Castes (NCSC)?

A. Article 338
B. Article 342
C. Article 330
D. Article 368

124. The NHRC has the power to punish individuals for human rights violations.

A. True
B. False
C. True, only for government officials
D. False, unless directed by the Supreme Court

125. The National Commission for Backward Classes (NCBC) has been granted constitutional status through the 102nd Amendment Act, 2018.

A. True
B. False
C. True, only for certain states
D. False, unless passed by Parliament

126. **Assertion (A):** The NHRC can investigate human rights violations committed by private individuals.

Reason (R): The NHRC has jurisdiction over all human rights issues in India.

A. Both A and R are true, and R is the correct explanation of A
B. Both A and R are true, but R is not the correct explanation of A
C. A is true, R is false
D. A is false, R is true

127. **Assertion (A):** The NCW has the power to summon and enforce the attendance of any person for investigation.

Reason (R): The NCW has powers equivalent to a civil court under the Code of Civil Procedure.

A. Both A and R are true, and R is the correct explanation of A
B. Both A and R are true, but R is not the correct explanation of A
C. A is true, R is false
D. A is false, R is true

128. The National Commission for Scheduled Tribes (NCST) was established as a separate body in the year _______.

A. 1999 B. 2003
C. 2005 D. 2010

129. The National Human Rights Commission (NHRC) consists of a Chairperson who is a former _______.

A. Member of Parliament
B. Judge of the Supreme Court
C. Chief Justice of India
D. High Court Judge

130. Match the following commissions with the constitutional or legal provisions under which they were established:

A. NHRC	1. Protection of Human Rights Act, 1993
B. NCM	2. National Commission for Minorities Act, 1992
C. NCW	3. National Commission for Women Act, 1990
D. NCSC	4. Article 338 of the Constitution

A. A-1, B-2, C-3, D-4
B. A-2, B-3, C-1, D-4
C. A-4, B-1, C-2, D-3
D. A-3, B-4, C-1, D-2

131. Arrange the following commissions in the order of their establishment:

1. National Commission for Scheduled Castes (NCSC)
2. National Human Rights Commission (NHRC)
3. National Commission for Women (NCW)
4. National Commission for Minorities (NCM)

A. 1, 3, 4, 2 B. 1, 4, 3, 2
C. 4, 3, 2, 1 D. 3, 1, 4, 2

132. Scenario: A woman faces workplace harassment and is denied proper redressal by her employer. Which commission should she approach?

A. NHRC B. NCW
C. NCSC D. NCM

133. Scenario: A tribal community's land is illegally taken over by a private company with government support. Which commission should investigate this violation?

A. NCST B. NHRC
C. NCBC D. NCM

134. Scenario: A person from a backward class is denied admission to a public educational institution despite qualifying under the reservation quota. Which commission can address this grievance?

A. NCW B. NCM
C. NCBC D. NHRC

135. Which of the following is NOT a function of the NHRC?

A. Inquiring into human rights violations
B. Imposing punishments on offenders
C. Recommending compensation to victims
D. Reviewing laws related to human rights

136. Who appoints the Chairperson of the NHRC?

A. President of India
B. Chief Justice of India
C. Prime Minister
D. Union Public Service Commission

137. Match the following commissions with their key focus areas:

	Focus Areas
A. NHRC	1. Human Rights Violations
B. NCW	2. Women's Rights and Gender Justice
C. NCBC	3. Rights of Backward Classes
D. NCM	4. Protection of Minority Rights

A. A-1, B-2, C-3, D-4
B. A-2, B-4, C-1, D-3
C. A-3, B-1, C-4, D-2
D. A-4, B-3, C-2, D-1

138. Scenario: A Dalit student faces caste-based discrimination at a university. Which commission should handle this case?

A. NCBC B. NCSC
C. NCW D. NHRC

139. Scenario: A linguistic minority group is denied access to government education in their native language. Which commission can be approached?

A. NCM B. NCW
C. NCST D. NCBC

ANSWERS

1. **(D):** The Environment (Protection) Act, 1986 defines the environment to include air, water, land, and the interrelationship between them.
2. **(C):** Water itself is not a pollutant, but contaminated water can cause pollution.
3. **(C):** Vehicular emissions are a major source of air pollution due to the release of harmful gases.
4. **(B):** Pollution refers to the accumulation of harmful substances in the environment, causing adverse effects.
5. **(B):** Noise pollution is recognized as a form of environmental pollution under Indian law.
6. **(B):** The environment includes both natural and man-made components, such as buildings and infrastructure.
7. **(A):** Deforestation reduces oxygen production and increases carbon dioxide, contributing to pollution.
8. **(C):** The Act was enacted following the Bhopal Gas Tragedy in 1984, one of the worst industrial disasters in India.
9. **(B):** Pollution refers to the presence of harmful substances beyond permissible limits, causing environmental harm.
10. **(A):** Air Pollution: Vehicle emissions (2)

    Water Pollution: Industrial effluents (1)

    Soil Pollution: Use of pesticides (3)

    Noise Pollution: Loudspeakers and traffic (4)
11. **(A):** Stockholm Conference (1972)

    Earth Summit (1992)

    Kyoto Protocol (1997)

    Paris Agreement (2015)
12. **(C):** Discharge of chemicals into water bodies causes water pollution, affecting ecosystems and health.
13. **(D):** Smog is primarily caused by carbon monoxide and nitrogen dioxide from vehicle and industrial emissions.
14. **(D):** Noise pollution is caused by loud sounds, like those from airplanes, affecting mental and physical health.
15. **(C):** Carbon dioxide (CO_2) is a major greenhouse gas contributing to global warming.
16. **(C):** Article 48A directs the State to protect and improve the environment.
17. **(A):** Environment (Protection) Act: 1986 (1)

    Air (Prevention and Control of Pollution) Act: 1981 (2)

    Water (Prevention and Control of Pollution) Act: 1974 (3)

    Wildlife Protection Act: 1972 (4)
18. **(D):** The leaching of chemicals from fertilizers causes groundwater contamination, leading to water pollution.
19. **(B):** Sulfur dioxide (SO_2) from industrial emissions is a common cause of respiratory diseases.
20. **(B):** The Stockholm Conference (1972) was the first major international conference focused on environmental issues.
21. **(C):** The UNFCCC was adopted at the Earth Summit in Rio de Janeiro in 1992.
22. **(B):** The Kyoto Protocol (1997) focuses on reducing greenhouse gas emissions to combat climate change.
23. **(B):** The Paris Agreement aims to limit global warming to well below 2°C above pre-industrial levels.
24. **(A):** The Rio Declaration (1992) emphasized the importance of sustainable development globally.
25. **(A):** The Montreal Protocol (1987) aims to protect the ozone layer by phasing out ozone-depleting substances.
26. **(A):** The Kyoto Protocol imposed binding targets on developed countries, while developing nations were exempt under the principle of common but differentiated responsibilities.
27. **(D):** The Basel Convention (1989) focuses on the control of hazardous waste movement, not climate change.
28. **(C):** The concept of "common but differentiated responsibilities" (CBDR) was introduced in the Rio Declaration (1992).

29. (C): The Kyoto Protocol was adopted in 1997 to combat climate change.

30. (A): Montreal Protocol: Protect the ozone layer (3)

Basel Convention: Control hazardous waste movement (2)

Paris Agreement: Limit global warming below 2°C (4)

Kyoto Protocol: Reduce greenhouse gas emissions (1)

31. (A): Stockholm Conference (1972)
Earth Summit (1992)
Kyoto Protocol (1997)
Paris Agreement (2015)

32. (C): This principle acknowledges the different responsibilities of developed and developing countries in addressing environmental issues.

33. (B): The Montreal Protocol (1987) focuses on phasing out substances that deplete the ozone layer, like CFCs.

34. (B): The Basel Convention regulates the transboundary movement of hazardous waste to protect the environment.

35. (C): The Polluter Pays Principle states that those who cause pollution should bear the cost of managing it.

36. (B): The Kyoto Protocol is a legally binding agreement that requires countries to reduce greenhouse gas emissions.

37. (A): Stockholm Conference (1972): Creation of UNEP (2)

Earth Summit (1992): UNFCCC adoption (1)

Kyoto Protocol (1997): Binding targets for GHG reduction (3)

Paris Agreement (2015): Limit temperature rise below 2°C (4)

38. (A): The CDM helps developing countries receive financial and technical support for climate-related projects.

39. (B): A country that does not ratify an international treaty is not legally bound by its provisions.

40. (C): Article 48A directs the State to protect and improve the environment and safeguard forests and wildlife.

41. (C): Article 51A(g) of the Constitution imposes a Fundamental Duty on citizens to protect and improve the environment.

42. (C): The Environment (Protection) Act, 1986 was enacted in response to the Bhopal Gas Tragedy.

43. (B): Article 21 (Right to Life) has been interpreted by the Supreme Court to include the Right to a Clean Environment.

44. (A): The Supreme Court has held that pollution-free water and air are part of the Right to Life under Article 21.

45. (D): The National Green Tribunal (NGT) was established under the NGT Act, 2010, not the Environment (Protection) Act, 1986.

46. (C)

47. (A): The Polluter Pays Principle means that those who cause pollution must bear the cost of managing it.

48. (A): The Environment (Protection) Act, 1986 is the umbrella legislation for environmental protection in India.

49. (B): The NGT was established under the National Green Tribunal Act, 2010.

50. (A): Article 21: Right to a Clean Environment (1)

Article 48A: Duty of the State to protect the environment (2)

Article 51A(g): Fundamental Duty of citizens (3)

Article 32: Right to approach the Supreme Court (4)

51. (B): The Polluter Pays Principle holds the company responsible for the cost of environmental damage.

52. (C): Article 32 allows citizens to approach the Supreme Court for enforcement of Fundamental Rights, including the Right to a Clean Environment.

53. (B): The Supreme Court established the Public Trust Doctrine in the M.C. Mehta v. Kamal Nath case.

54. (B): The Precautionary Principle advocates for preventive actions to avoid environmental harm even if there is no conclusive scientific proof.

55. (B): The Supreme Court recognized the Right to a Clean Environment under Article 21 in the Oleum Gas Leak case.

56. (C): While the Act aims to prevent deforestation, it imposes strict restrictions on the use of forest land for non-forest purposes.

57. (B): The Supreme Court emphasized the principle of Sustainable Development in the Vellore Citizens Welfare Forum case.

58. (B): The Public Trust Doctrine holds that natural resources are meant for public use and the State acts as a trustee to protect them.

59. (A): Sustainable Development: Prevents degradation for future generations (1)

Polluter Pays Principle: Polluter bears the cost (2)

Precautionary Principle: Preventive measures without full certainty (3)

Public Trust Doctrine: State as trustee of resources (4)

60. (B): The NGT was established under the National Green Tribunal Act, 2010 to handle environmental disputes.

61. (D): The principal bench of the NGT is located in New Delhi, with other regional benches across India.

62. (D): The Doctrine of Laches is related to delays in legal claims and is not an environmental principle applied by the NGT.

63. (C): The NGT deals exclusively with environmental protection, conservation of forests, and natural resources.

64. (A): The NGT has the power to impose penalties and award compensation for environmental damage.

65. (B): Any aggrieved person, including individuals, NGOs, and public interest groups, can approach the NGT.

66. (A): The NGT has jurisdiction over matters related to environmental clearances under laws listed in Schedule I of the NGT Act.

67. (C): The NGT has original jurisdiction (for environmental disputes) and appellate jurisdiction (against decisions of authorities), not limited to fines.

68. (B): As per the NGT Act, 2010, cases should be disposed of within 6 months from the date of filing.

69. (C): The NGT is a quasi-judicial body, meaning it has powers similar to a court but functions in an administrative setup.

70. (A): Polluter Pays Principle: Economic responsibility for damage (2)

Precautionary Principle: Preventive action for risks (1)

Sustainable Development: Balancing development and protection (3)

Public Trust Doctrine: Resources held in trust (4)

71. (A): The process involves filing, admission, hearing, and finally the judgment.

72. (B): The NGT has jurisdiction over cases related to environmental clearances and impact assessments.

73. (B): The NGT handles appeals against penalties imposed under environmental laws.

74. (A): While the NGT's decisions may indirectly raise awareness, its primary role is judicial, not educational.

75. (C): The NGT Act, 2010 allows for up to 15 judicial members and 15 expert members.

76. (A): Principal Bench: New Delhi (1)

Southern Bench: Chennai (2)

Western Bench: Pune (3)

Eastern Bench: Kolkata (4)

77. (A): The NGT has the power to grant compensation for environmental damage and its impact on communities.

78. (B): The Doctrine of Public Trust holds that natural resources are to be protected for public use, and the State acts as a trustee.

79. (C): The NGT Act, 2010 provides a limitation period of 6 months, extendable by another 60 days if justified.

80. (C): Universalism holds that human rights are universal and apply to everyone, regardless of culture or context.

81. (C): Cultural relativism emphasizes that values and practices differ between cultures and should be understood in their own context.

82. (B): The UDHR is based on universal principles that apply to all human beings.

83. (B): Cultural relativists may defend such practices as part of cultural identity, while universalists oppose them on human rights grounds.

84. (B): Universalism asserts that human rights are inalienable and non-negotiable, regardless of cultural differences.

85. (A): Cultural relativism promotes moral relativism, suggesting that no single moral framework is universally superior.

86. (A): Universalism is based on the belief in common human values, which justify equal rights for all.

87. (D): Cultural relativism opposes imposing universal standards, valuing diversity and contextual moral frameworks.

88. (C): Natural law theory asserts that rights are inherent and universal, forming the basis of universal human rights.

89. (B): Critics argue that cultural relativism can be used to justify harmful practices that violate basic human rights.

90. (A): Universalism: Rights apply equally to all humans (1)

Cultural Relativism: Moral codes vary across cultures (2)

Natural Rights: Rights derived from human nature (3)

Legal Positivism: Law is valid only if enacted by legitimate authority (4)

91. (A): The historical evolution starts with the Magna Carta, followed by the American Declaration, the French Declaration, and finally the UDHR.

92. (B): Cultural relativism supports the idea that cultural practices should be understood and respected within their own context.

93. (C): Universalism promotes the idea that freedom of speech is a universal right, applicable to all societies.

94. (B): The court is applying universal principles of human rights, prioritizing them over cultural norms.

95. (B): Critics argue that universalism can be ethnocentric, imposing Western values on diverse cultures.

96. (B): John Locke is a key figure in the development of the concept of natural rights, foundational to universal human rights.

97. (A): Universalism: Immanuel Kant (3)

Cultural Relativism: Franz Boas (2)

Natural Rights Theory: John Locke (1)

Moral Relativism: Ruth Benedict (4)

98. (C): The country is using a cultural relativist argument to justify its domestic law despite international criticism.

99. (C): The court's decision reflects universal principles of human rights, emphasizing global standards over local laws.

100. (D): The Vienna Convention deals with treaty law and is not part of the International Bill of Rights.

101. (B): The UDHR was adopted by the United Nations General Assembly on 10 December 1948.

102. (C): The ICCPR focuses on civil and political rights, including freedom of speech.

103. (C): The CESCR is responsible for monitoring compliance with the ICESCR.

104. (B): The UDHR is a declaration, not a legally binding treaty, though it influences international law.

105. (A): The First Optional Protocol to the ICCPR allows individuals to submit complaints to the Human Rights Committee.

106. (A): The UDHR is based on the universality of human rights, applying to all individuals.

107. (D): ICESCR rights are subject to progressive realization, depending on the state's resources.

108. (C): Both the ICCPR and ICESCR were adopted on 16 December 1966.

109. (B): The UDHR contains 30 articles, covering a broad range of civil, political, economic, social, and cultural rights.

110. (A): UDHR: Non-binding declaration of universal rights (1)

ICCPR: Civil and political rights (2)

ICESCR: Economic, social, and cultural rights (3)

CESCR: Monitoring of economic, social, and cultural rights (4)

111. (A): The UDHR (1948) came first, followed by the ICCPR (1966), ICESCR (1966), and the Optional Protocol (1966).

112. (B): The ICCPR protects civil and political rights, including freedom of speech.

113. (C): The ICESCR covers economic, social, and cultural rights, including the right to health.

114. (B): The First Optional Protocol to the ICCPR allows individual complaints to the Human Rights Committee.

115. (D): The UDHR does not mention the right to bear arms.

116. (D): The UDHR prohibits discrimination based on race, gender, religion, and other factors.

117. (A): Article 1: All human beings are born free and equal (4)

Article 3: Right to life, liberty, and security (2)

Article 19: Right to freedom of opinion and expression (1)

Article 26: Right to education (3)

118. (C): Without the Optional Protocol, individuals cannot submit complaints to the Human Rights Committee.

119. (C): Both ICCPR and ICESCR emphasize that civil and economic rights are interdependent and equally important.

120. (A): The NHRC was established under the Protection of Human Rights Act, 1993 to address human rights violations in India.

121. (B): The NCM safeguards the interests of religious and linguistic minorities under the National Commission for Minorities Act, 1992.

122. (C): The NCW was established in 1992 to protect and promote the rights of women in India.

123. (A): Article 338 of the Constitution provides for the National Commission for Scheduled Castes (NCSC).

124. (B): The NHRC is a recommendatory body and does not have punitive powers. It can recommend actions but cannot impose punishments.

125. (A): The NCBC was granted constitutional status by the 102nd Constitutional Amendment Act, 2018 under Article 338B.

126. (A)

127. (A): The NCW has powers equivalent to a civil court for summoning witnesses and collecting evidence.

128. (B): The NCST was created in 2003 after bifurcation from the National Commission for Scheduled Castes and Scheduled Tribes.

129. (C): The Chairperson of the NHRC is a former Chief Justice of India.

130. (A): NHRC: Protection of Human Rights Act, 1993 (1)
NCM: National Commission for Minorities Act, 1992 (2)
NCW: National Commission for Women Act, 1990 (3)
NCSC: Article 338 of the Constitution (4)

131. (B): NCSC: Established under Article 338 (post-1950).
NCM: Established in 1992.
NCW: Established in 1992.
NHRC: Established in 1993.

132. (B): The NCW addresses issues related to women's rights and gender-based discrimination.

133. (A): The NCST protects the rights of Scheduled Tribes, especially concerning land rights and displacement.

134. (C): The NCBC addresses issues related to OBC rights and reservation policies.

135. (B): The NHRC can recommend actions but does not have punitive powers.

136. (A): The President of India appoints the NHRC Chairperson based on the recommendation of a committee.

137. (A): NHRC: Human Rights Violations (1)
NCW: Women's Rights and Gender Justice (2)
NCBC: Rights of Backward Classes (3)
NCM: Protection of Minority Rights (4)

138. (B): The NCSC deals with caste-based discrimination against Scheduled Castes.

139. (A): The NCM protects the rights of religious and linguistic minorities in India.

UNIT 9

Intellectual Property Rights & Information Technology Law

CONCEPT AND MEANING OF INTELLECTUAL PROPERTY (IP)

Intellectual Property (IP) refers to legal rights that are granted to individuals or organizations for their creations, inventions, and innovations. These rights protect the intangible assets that result from human creativity and intellectual effort. IP laws aim to encourage innovation, protect creators' interests, and foster economic growth by granting creators exclusive rights to use and profit from their creations for a certain period.

Types of Intellectual Property

Intellectual property is categorized into various forms, each designed to protect different types of creations:

Copyright

- **Meaning:** Copyright protects the expression of ideas, such as literary works, artistic works, music, films, software, and other original creations.
- **Duration:** Typically lasts for the life of the author plus 60 years.
- **Rights:** It gives the creator the exclusive right to reproduce, distribute, perform, or display the work.

Trademarks

- **Meaning:** A trademark is a sign, design, or expression used to distinguish goods or services of a particular source from those of others.
- **Duration:** Trademark registration lasts for 10 years from the date of registration and can be renewed every 10 years indefinitely, provided the trademark remains in use and renewal fees are paid (Section 25).
- **Rights:** Trademarks protect brand names, logos, slogans, and product packaging, helping consumers identify the source of products and services.

Patents

- **Meaning:** A patent protects new inventions or discoveries, such as a new product, process, or method that provides a unique solution to a technical problem.
- **Duration:** Typically 20 years from the filing date, subject to maintenance fees and specific regulations.
- **Rights:** A patent grants the inventor the exclusive right to make, use, sell, or distribute the invention, and prevents others from doing so without permission.

Trade Secrets

- **Meaning:** Trade secrets encompass confidential business information, processes, or knowledge that gives a company a competitive edge (e.g., formulas, customer lists, or manufacturing methods).
- **Duration:** Indefinite, as long as the trade secret remains confidential.
- **Rights:** Protection lasts as long as the information is kept secret and does not become public knowledge. If the secret is leaked or exposed, protection is lost.

Industrial Designs

- **Meaning:** Industrial design protects the visual appearance or aesthetic features of a product, such as shape, color, or ornamentation.
- **Duration:** Typically lasts 10 to 15 years, depending on the jurisdiction.

- **Rights:** It grants exclusive rights to the creator or designer to use or license the design, preventing unauthorized imitation.

Geographical Indications (GI)

- **Meaning:** GIs identify goods that have a specific geographical origin and possess qualities or a reputation due to that origin (e.g., Darjeeling Tea, Champagne).
- **Duration:** Indefinite, as long as the product continues to meet the criteria for the geographical indication.
- **Rights:** GIs protect regional products from misuse or imitation and can enhance their marketability and value.

Purpose and Importance of Intellectual Property

- **Encourages Innovation:** IP protection incentivizes creativity and innovation by ensuring that creators can profit from their work and ideas.
- **Economic Growth:** IP contributes significantly to the economy by fostering industries such as entertainment, technology, pharmaceuticals, and manufacturing.
- **Consumer Protection:** Trademarks and patents help consumers make informed decisions by ensuring the quality and authenticity of products and services.
- **Cultural Enrichment:** Copyright protection ensures that creators in the arts, music, literature, and media are rewarded for their contributions to cultural development.
- **Global Trade:** IP rights are essential in international trade, as they help businesses protect their inventions, brands, and products across borders.

Enforcement of Intellectual Property Rights

- **National Laws:** IP rights are generally enforced within the legal framework of a specific country. This includes filing claims in national courts for infringement.
- **International Treaties:** Several international agreements, such as the World Intellectual Property Organization (WIPO) treaties, Agreement on Trade-Related Aspects of Intellectual Property Rights (TRIPS), and the Paris Convention, establish global standards for IP protection and enforcement.

THEORIES OF INTELLECTUAL PROPERTY (IP)

Intellectual Property (IP) is a broad field of law that involves the protection of creations, inventions, and other forms of intellectual work. Various theories have been proposed to justify the creation, scope, and limitations of IP rights. These theories aim to provide a philosophical and legal foundation for the protection of intellectual property. Here are some of the major theories of intellectual property:

Natural Rights Theory

- **Overview:** This theory is based on the concept of natural law, which asserts that individuals have inherent rights to the products of their own labor. According to this theory, intellectual property rights arise because creators have a natural right to control and benefit from the fruits of their intellectual labor.
- **Key Proponents:** The natural rights theory was notably advanced by philosopher John Locke. In his "Labor Theory of Property," Locke argued that by mixing one's labor with natural resources, a person creates something that they have the right to own.
- **Principle:** Creators deserve ownership over their intellectual creations because they are extensions of their own personality and labor.
- **Criticism:** Critics argue that intellectual property is not as easily tied to physical labor as physical property is, and therefore the natural rights justification for IP is less convincing in the case of intangible assets like ideas or inventions.

Utilitarian Theory

- **Overview:** The Utilitarian Theory is based on the idea that intellectual property rights are justified because they promote the greater good of society. IP rights are seen as tools to encourage innovation and creativity, which leads to increased economic benefits, social progress, and public welfare.
- **Key Proponents:** This theory is grounded in the works of Jeremy Bentham and John Stuart Mill, who focused on maximizing societal benefits through laws and policies.
- **Principle:** IP rights are granted as a means of encouraging individuals to invest time, money, and effort into creating new ideas, inventions, and artistic works. The exclusivity granted by IP rights is believed to promote innovation, which benefits

society by leading to new products, technologies, and cultural advancements.

- **Criticism:** Some critics argue that the utilitarian justification for IP rights may lead to monopolistic behavior or over-protection, restricting access to knowledge and cultural goods. There is also concern that IP laws may disproportionately benefit large corporations rather than individual creators or society as a whole.

Incentive Theory

- **Overview:** The Incentive Theory focuses on the idea that intellectual property rights are essential to provide creators with financial and moral incentives to innovate and create. The theory suggests that without the promise of exclusive rights, creators would be less motivated to engage in creative activities or invest in research and development.
- **Key Proponents:** This theory has been widely discussed in economic literature and is a foundational justification for IP laws.
- **Principle:** By granting exclusive rights to creators, IP laws provide them with the opportunity to derive economic benefits from their creations, which encourages further innovation and creativity.
- **Criticism:** One of the criticisms of this theory is that it assumes creators are primarily motivated by financial rewards, which may not always be the case. Additionally, excessive IP protection could hinder collaboration and the free flow of ideas, potentially limiting innovation.

Personhood Theory (Personality Theory)

- **Overview:** The Personhood Theory is based on the idea that intellectual property is an extension of an individual's personality and self-expression. IP rights protect creations as a reflection of a creator's identity, creativity, and individuality.
- **Key Proponents:** This theory is rooted in the ideas of Hegel and has been developed further by scholars like Martha Nussbaum and Friedrich Schiller.
- **Principle:** Just as physical property protects an individual's body and physical labor, intellectual property protects the creator's personality and creative spirit. IP is viewed as a natural right that safeguards the creator's moral and personal connection to their work.
- **Criticism:** The concept of personality rights is not universally recognized in IP law, and critics argue that not all intellectual works are deeply personal. Furthermore, the theory's emphasis on personality rights might undermine public access to knowledge and culture.

Social Planning Theory

- **Overview:** The Social Planning Theory focuses on the idea that IP laws should be structured to serve broader societal goals, such as promoting public welfare, ensuring equitable access to knowledge, and fostering social development. This theory posits that IP is a tool of social policy rather than a natural right or economic incentive.
- **Key Proponents:** This theory has been advanced by legal scholars such as Robert Merges and David Lange, who view IP laws as mechanisms for achieving social goals rather than just protecting individual interests.
- **Principle:** IP laws should be crafted and enforced in a way that promotes the public good, balancing the interests of creators, users, and society as a whole. This includes ensuring access to educational and scientific advancements, protecting cultural heritage, and fostering creativity in a collaborative environment.
- **Criticism:** Critics argue that social planning could undermine the primary goal of IP laws, which is to incentivize creators to innovate. There is also concern that excessive regulation could stifle creativity and lead to a lack of fair competition in the marketplace.

Public Goods Theory

- **Overview:** The Public Goods Theory emphasizes the role of intellectual property in the production and dissemination of public goods, such as knowledge and culture. According to this theory, intellectual property is a necessary tool to prevent the free-riding problem associated with public goods, where individuals benefit from creative works without paying for them.
- **Key Proponents:** This theory has roots in economic theory, particularly the work of Arthur Pigou and James Buchanan, who studied the impact of public goods on economic systems.
- **Principle:** Intellectual property protects creators from the free-riding behavior of others who might use their work without contributing to its creation. By granting exclusive rights, IP ensures that creators can capture the benefits of their work, thereby encouraging the continued production of public goods.

- **Criticism:** The public goods theory has been criticized for its emphasis on economic incentives, as some argue that not all creative works are public goods or require IP protection to thrive.

The Fair Use and Public Domain Theory

- **Overview:** The Fair Use and Public Domain Theory emphasizes the balance between IP rights and the public's right to access and use creative works. The theory supports limited protection for IP, arguing that works should eventually enter the public domain and be freely available for use and innovation.
- **Key Proponents:** This theory is often associated with Lawrence Lessig and the Creative Commons movement, which advocates for more flexible licensing of IP.
- **Principle:** IP should not be perpetual, and creators should not hold exclusive rights forever. Instead, works should gradually become part of the public domain, fostering innovation and ensuring that knowledge remains freely accessible.
- **Criticism:** Opponents of this theory argue that the limitations on IP protection could reduce incentives for creators to innovate, as they may not be able to profit from their work in the long term.

INTERNATIONAL CONVENTIONS PERTAINING TO INTELLECTUAL PROPERTY

International conventions play a crucial role in harmonizing intellectual property (IP) laws across different countries, ensuring that creators and innovators are protected worldwide. These conventions promote cooperation between countries, provide a framework for enforcing IP rights across borders, and establish standards for IP protection. Below are some of the key international conventions and treaties relating to intellectual property:

Paris Convention for the Protection of Industrial Property (1883)

- **Overview:** Paris Convention for the Protection of Industrial Property: The Paris Convention (Article 1(2)) protects indications of source and geographical indications.
- **Key Provisions:**
  - ❑ **Provides for the right of priority:** A patent or trademark applicant in one member country can claim priority for applications in other member countries within a specific period (usually 12 months for patents and 6 months for trademarks).
  - ❑ **Establishes national treatment:** Ensures that foreigners are treated the same as domestic applicants for IP protection.
  - ❑ Provides protection for patents, trademarks, and industrial designs.
- **Significance:** It laid the groundwork for global cooperation in IP protection and established fundamental principles like the right of priority and national treatment.

Berne Convention for the Protection of Literary and Artistic Works (1886)

- **Overview:** The Berne Convention provides international protection for the rights of authors of literary and artistic works, such as books, music, and artwork, ensuring that creators have exclusive rights to their creations.
- **Key Provisions:**
  - ❑ Requires member countries to provide protection for the works of authors from other member states without the need for formal registration.
  - ❑ Establishes the principle of "automatic protection" – works are protected as soon as they are created, without the need for formal registration.
  - ❑ Specifies the minimum duration of protection (usually the life of the author plus 50 years).
  - ❑ Provides the right of translation, reproduction, and public performance for creators.
- **Significance:** The Berne Convention is vital for ensuring that authors and creators' rights are respected globally, regardless of where their works are used or reproduced.

Agreement on Trade-Related Aspects of Intellectual Property Rights (TRIPS) (1994)

- **Overview:** The TRIPS Agreement, administered by the World Trade Organization (WTO), sets international standards for IP protection and enforcement. It is a crucial part of global trade law, establishing minimum standards for all forms of IP, including patents, trademarks, copyrights, and trade secrets.

- **Key Provisions:**
  - ❑ Requires all WTO member countries to comply with minimum IP standards (e.g., patents for inventions, copyright for literary and artistic works, etc.).
  - ❑ Addresses enforcement mechanisms, including civil and criminal procedures for IP infringement.
  - ❑ Provides protection for the trade of goods and services using intellectual property, including the protection of undisclosed information (trade secrets).
  - ❑ Allows flexibility in implementing IP laws to accommodate public health needs (e.g., the use of compulsory licensing for pharmaceutical patents).
- **Significance:** The TRIPS Agreement is one of the most comprehensive treaties, impacting global trade and IP protection by setting minimum standards that apply across WTO member states.

World Intellectual Property Organization (WIPO) Copyright Treaty (1996)

- **Overview:** The WIPO Copyright Treaty (WCT) is designed to address the challenges of the digital environment, providing additional protection for creators of works in the digital world.
- **Key Provisions:**
  - ❑ Expands protections to include digital works and online environments.
  - ❑ Establishes a framework for the protection of works distributed over the internet and through digital networks.
  - ❑ Ensures that creators retain rights over the distribution and communication of their works via digital technologies.
- **Significance:** The WCT adapts traditional copyright law to the challenges and opportunities of the digital age, offering creators protection in online and electronic spaces.

WIPO Performances and Phonograms Treaty (1996)

- **Overview:** The WIPO Performances and Phonograms Treaty (WPPT) complements the WCT by providing protection for performers (e.g., musicians, actors) and producers of phonograms (sound recordings) in the digital environment.
- **Key Provisions:**
  - ❑ Extends performers' rights to digital performances and phonograms.
  - ❑ Ensures protection of sound recordings and performers' rights against unauthorized reproduction and distribution.
  - ❑ Provides for equitable remuneration for performers and phonogram producers when their works are used online or in digital media.
- **Significance:** The WPPT addresses the need for performers and producers to receive compensation and protection in the rapidly evolving digital and internet landscape.

Hague Agreement Concerning the International Registration of Industrial Designs (1925)

- **Overview:** The Hague Agreement, administered by WIPO, provides an international system for registering industrial designs. It allows creators to register their designs in multiple countries through a single application.
- **Key Provisions:**
  - ❑ Provides a centralized system for registering industrial designs, which reduces the complexity of international design protection.
  - ❑ Offers a mechanism for obtaining protection for designs in multiple countries simultaneously.
- **Significance:** The Hague Agreement simplifies and streamlines the process for creators seeking global protection for their industrial designs.

Madrid Agreement and Protocol Concerning the International Registration of Marks (1891)

- **Overview:** The Madrid System, administered by WIPO, provides a mechanism for registering trademarks in multiple countries through a single application. It includes the Madrid Agreement (1891) and the Protocol to the Madrid Agreement (1989).
- **Key Provisions:**
  - ❑ Enables trademark owners to file one application and obtain protection in multiple member countries.
  - ❑ Simplifies the process of managing and renewing trademarks internationally.
  - ❑ The Protocol allows for more flexibility and includes provisions for non-member states to join the system.
- **Significance:** The Madrid System helps businesses expand their brand recognition globally by simplifying international trademark registration.

The Patent Cooperation Treaty (PCT) (1970)

- **Overview:** The Patent Cooperation Treaty, administered by WIPO, provides a unified procedure for filing patent applications in multiple countries.
- **Key Provisions:**
  - Allows inventors to file one international patent application that can be recognized in over 150 countries.
  - Provides for a preliminary search and examination to determine the patentability of an invention before entering national phases.
- **Significance:** The PCT simplifies the process for inventors seeking patent protection across multiple jurisdictions, reducing costs and administrative burden.

Convention Relating to the Distribution of Programme-Carrying Signals Transmitted by Satellite (1974)

- **Overview:** This convention aims to protect the rights of broadcasters and satellite operators by regulating the distribution of television signals transmitted via satellite.
- **Key Provisions:**
  - Ensures that unauthorized retransmission of satellite signals is prevented.
  - Offers protection to satellite broadcasters against signal piracy.
- **Significance:** It helps safeguard intellectual property rights in the broadcasting and telecommunications industries, particularly in the satellite era.

COPYRIGHT AND NEIGHBORING RIGHTS: SUBJECT MATTERS, LIMITATIONS AND EXCEPTIONS, INFRINGEMENT AND REMEDIES

Copyright and neighboring rights are essential aspects of intellectual property law, providing creators and performers protection for their works and performances. The concept of copyright primarily focuses on protecting the original works of authorship, while neighboring rights offer protection to performers, producers, and broadcasters. Below is an overview of the key components of copyright and neighboring rights.

Copyright: Subject Matters

Copyright protects the original works of authorship, provided they are fixed in a tangible medium of expression. The subject matter of copyright includes:

- **Literary Works:** Books, articles, plays, poems, and other written content.
- **Dramatic Works:** Plays, scripts, choreographic works, and pantomimes.
- **Musical Works:** Songs, instrumental compositions, and musical arrangements.
- **Artistic Works:** Paintings, drawings, sculptures, architectural works, and other visual art.
- **Cinematographic Works:** Films, videos, and other audiovisual works.
- **Sound Recordings:** Audio recordings of music, spoken word, and other sounds.
- **Architectural Works:** Designs and plans for buildings or other structures.
- **Software and Databases:** Computer programs and collections of data.
- **Broadcasts:** Radio and television broadcasts, including cable and satellite transmissions.

Neighboring Rights (Related Rights)

Neighboring rights, sometimes referred to as "related rights," under the Copyright Act, 1957, neighboring rights include performers' rights (Section 38), producers of phonograms (Section 39), and broadcasters' rights (Section 37), with publication rights typically covered under copyright, not as a separate neighboring right.

- **Performers' Rights:** Protect the rights of actors, musicians, dancers, and other performers in their performances. These rights include the right to control the recording, reproduction, and distribution of their performances.
- **Producers of Sound Recordings (Phonograms):** Grant protection to producers who invest time, effort, and resources in creating sound recordings. This includes the right to control the reproduction and distribution of their recordings.
- **Broadcasters' Rights:** Protect the interests of radio and television broadcasters by granting them exclusive rights to their broadcasts and transmissions.
- **Publication Rights:** Protection for publishers in relation to the first publication of a work.

Limitations and Exceptions to Copyright

Copyright is not absolute, and several limitations and exceptions allow for public access to works and facilitate social, educational, and research purposes. Some key exceptions include:

- **Fair Use / Fair Dealing:** This exception permits limited use of copyrighted works without permission in certain cases such as criticism, comment, news reporting, teaching, research, and parody. However, the extent of the use must not harm the commercial interests of the copyright holder.
- **Libraries and Archives:** Libraries and archival institutions may be permitted to make copies of works for preservation or research purposes under specific conditions.
- **Educational Purposes:** Copyright law allows certain uses of works for educational purposes, such as reproducing material for classroom use or for distance education, within prescribed limits.
- **Public Domain:** Works that have expired or were never eligible for copyright protection enter the public domain and can be freely used by anyone.
- **Temporary Reproduction:** Some temporary copies made in the course of the transmission of works over networks (e.g., web caches or data buffering) are exempt from infringement.
- **Private Use:** Some jurisdictions permit private reproduction for non-commercial purposes, such as making personal copies of music or videos for private use.
- **Quotation and Parody:** Limited use of works for quotation or parody is allowed, especially when it contributes to commentary, criticism, or other forms of public discourse.

Infringement of Copyright

Copyright infringement occurs when someone violates the exclusive rights granted to the copyright holder without proper authorization. Common forms of infringement include:

- **Reproduction Without Permission:** Copying a copyrighted work in any form without permission, including photocopying, printing, or digital reproduction.
- **Public Performance or Display:** Using a work in public (e.g., playing music, screening a movie) without the creator's consent.
- **Distribution:** Selling or distributing copies of a copyrighted work without the author's permission.
- **Adaptation:** Modifying or adapting a copyrighted work, such as creating a derivative work or translating a book into another language, without authorization.
- **Digital Infringement:** This can include illegal downloading or streaming of copyrighted content from the internet, using pirated software, or sharing copyrighted files without consent.

Remedies for Copyright Infringement

When copyright infringement occurs, the copyright holder can seek various legal remedies. These remedies include:

- **Injunctive Relief:** A court order requiring the infringer to stop the infringing activity. Injunctions are often sought to prevent further harm to the copyright holder's rights.
- **Monetary Damages:** The copyright holder may seek monetary compensation for the damages caused by the infringement. This can include:
  - **Actual Damages:** Compensation for the actual loss suffered by the copyright holder due to the infringement, such as lost profits.
  - **Statutory Damages:** Some jurisdictions provide for statutory damages, which are preset damages that the infringer must pay, regardless of the actual harm caused. These damages can serve as a deterrent against infringement.
- **Account of Profits:** The infringer may be required to account for and surrender any profits they made from the infringement, including royalties or earnings from unauthorized sales or performances.
- **Criminal Penalties:** In cases of willful infringement, criminal charges can be brought against the infringer. Criminal penalties may include fines and imprisonment, especially for large-scale piracy or digital infringement.
- **Destruction of Infringing Copies:** The court may order the destruction or forfeiture of all infringing copies of the work.
- **Attorney's Fees and Costs:** The prevailing party in a copyright infringement case may be entitled to recover legal costs and attorney's fees.

Neighboring Rights: Infringement and Remedies

Neighboring rights also have legal protections, and infringement can lead to remedies similar to copyright violations. For example:

- **Performers' Rights Infringement:** If a performer's rights are infringed (e.g., unauthorized recording or broadcasting of a performance), they can seek remedies such as damages or an injunction to prevent further use of their performance.
- **Producers' Rights Infringement:** Unauthorized reproduction or distribution of sound recordings made by a producer is an infringement. Remedies may include damages, royalties, and injunctions.
- **Broadcasters' Rights Infringement:** If a broadcaster's signal is illegally intercepted or rebroadcast without authorization, the broadcaster may seek remedies such as an injunction, damages, and the destruction of illegal copies.

LAW OF PATENT: PATENTABILITY, PROCEDURE FOR GRANT OF PATENT, LIMITATIONS AND EXCEPTIONS, INFRINGEMENT AND REMEDIES

A patent is a form of intellectual property that grants the patent holder exclusive rights over an invention, preventing others from making, using, or selling the invention without permission. The patent system incentivizes innovation by offering creators a limited period of exclusive rights in exchange for public disclosure of the invention. Below is an overview of the key components of patent law.

Patentability

For an invention to be eligible for a patent, it must meet several essential criteria. These criteria ensure that only new, inventive, and useful inventions are granted patents.

- **Novelty:** The invention must be new and not disclosed in prior art. "Prior art" refers to any information that is publicly available before the filing date of the patent application, such as existing patents, publications, or existing knowledge in the field.
- **Inventive Step (Non-Obviousness):** The invention must involve an inventive step, meaning it cannot be obvious to someone skilled in the relevant field of technology based on existing knowledge.
- **Industrial Applicability:** The invention must be capable of being used in some form of industry. This includes manufacturing, agriculture, or any other useful application.
- **Sufficiency of Disclosure:** The patent application must disclose the invention in a way that enables others skilled in the field to replicate it. This ensures transparency and encourages further innovation.
- **Subject Matter:** Certain inventions are not eligible for patent protection, including:
  - **Abstract Ideas:** Theoretical concepts or fundamental scientific principles cannot be patented.
  - **Laws of Nature:** Natural phenomena and discoveries that explain laws of nature cannot be patented.
  - **Scientific Theories and Mathematical Methods:** Theoretical and abstract mathematical models are generally not patentable.
  - **Methods of Medical Treatment:** Under Section 3(i) of the Patents Act, 1970, methods for medicinal, surgical, curative, prophylactic, diagnostic, therapeutic, or other treatment of humans or animals are explicitly excluded from patentability.

Procedure for Grant of Patent

The process of obtaining a patent typically involves several stages, from filing the application to granting the patent. Here is a simplified overview of the typical procedure:

- **Patent Application:** The applicant submits a detailed description of the invention, including the claims (defining the scope of the invention), drawings (if applicable), and an abstract. This can be done through national or regional patent offices.
- **Patent Examination:** After filing, the patent office conducts an examination to ensure the invention meets the patentability requirements (novelty, inventive step, and industrial applicability). The examiner will check for any prior art and assess the claims.
  - **Preliminary Examination:** An initial review of the application is conducted to check for formal requirements.
  - **Substantive Examination:** A detailed review of the invention's patentability, including an examination of prior art and the inventive step.
- **Patent Publication:** After a specified period (usually 18 months), the patent application is published to make it publicly available.
- **Grant of Patent:** If the application meets all the requirements, the patent office grants the patent. The inventor is given exclusive rights for a limited period (usually 20 years from the filing date).
- **Patent Maintenance:** The patent holder must pay maintenance fees to keep the patent in force throughout its term.

Limitations and Exceptions to Patent Protection

Patents are not absolute, and various limitations and exceptions exist to balance the interests of the patent holder and the public.

- **Compulsory Licensing:** In some cases, the government can grant a license to a third party to use a patented invention without the consent of the patent holder. This typically occurs when the patented invention is not being exploited adequately, or there is a public need, such as in the case of essential medicines or national emergencies.
- **Bolar Provision:** In many jurisdictions, the "Bolar Provision" allows generic drug manufacturers to use a patented invention for the purpose of obtaining regulatory approval before the patent expires. This ensures that generics can enter the market as soon as the patent term ends.
- **Exhaustion of Rights (First Sale Doctrine):** Once a patented product is sold or transferred by the patent holder or with their consent, the patent holder cannot control further distribution of the product. This limits the scope of patent rights.
- **Research and Experimental Use:** Patent rights typically do not extend to acts of private, non-commercial research or experimentation. For example, academic institutions may use patented inventions in research without infringing the patent.
- **Use of Patented Inventions by Governments:** Many countries allow the government to use patented inventions without the patent holder's permission in certain circumstances, such as for public health purposes.

Infringement of Patent

Patent infringement occurs when a third party makes, uses, sells, or imports a patented invention without the authorization of the patent holder. Infringement can happen in several ways:

- **Direct Infringement:** When a third party makes, uses, or sells the patented invention exactly as it is described in the claims of the patent.
- **Indirect Infringement:** This occurs when someone contributes to or induces another party to infringe a patent. For example, selling a component that is used in an infringing product.
- **Doctrine of Equivalents:** Even if a product or process does not literally infringe on the patent claims, it may still infringe if it is equivalent to the patented invention in terms of its function, way of operation, and result.

Remedies for Patent Infringement

When a patent is infringed, the patent holder has several legal remedies available:

- **Injunctive Relief:** The patent holder can seek an injunction, which is a court order that prevents the infringer from continuing to use, sell, or manufacture the patented invention. Injunctive relief is a key remedy to prevent further infringement.
- **Monetary Damages:** The patent holder can claim damages for the infringement. These damages may include:
  - **Actual Damages:** Compensation for actual losses suffered by the patent holder due to the infringement, such as lost profits.
  - **Statutory Damages:** In some jurisdictions, statutory damages are available, which are preset amounts that the infringer must pay as a penalty, regardless of actual harm.
  - **Royalties:** The court may award the patent holder royalties based on what the infringer would have paid for a license to use the invention.
- **Account of Profits:** The patent holder may also request an account of the infringer's profits, requiring the infringer to hand over profits made from using the patented invention without authorization.
- **Destruction or Forfeiture:** The court may order the destruction or forfeiture of infringing goods or materials used to infringe the patent.
- **Criminal Penalties:** In cases of willful infringement, criminal penalties, including fines and imprisonment, may be imposed.

Defenses to Patent Infringement

An accused infringer may raise several defenses in a patent infringement lawsuit, including:

- **Invalidity:** The defendant may argue that the patent is invalid because it does not meet the requirements of patentability (e.g., it lacks novelty or inventiveness).
- **Non-Infringement:** The defendant may argue that their product or process does not infringe the patent, either because it does not fall within the scope of the patent claims or due to the doctrine of equivalents.
- **Prior Use Rights:** In some cases, a defendant may assert that they were using the patented invention before the patent application was filed and have prior use rights.

- **Exhaustion of Rights:** The defendant may argue that the patent rights have been exhausted due to the first sale of the patented product.
- **Use for Private, Non-Commercial Purposes:** If the infringing use is non-commercial or for private research purposes, it may fall within an exception.

LAW OF TRADEMARK: REGISTRATION OF TRADEMARKS, KINDS OF TRADEMARKS, INFRINGEMENT AND PASSING OFF, REMEDIES

A trademark is a distinctive sign or symbol used by a business to identify its products or services and distinguish them from those of others. Trademark law provides legal protection to the owner of a trademark and ensures that consumers are not misled by counterfeit or similar marks. Below is an overview of the key components of trademark law.

Registration of Trademarks

Trademark registration is the process by which a business can formally register its trademark with a national or regional authority. The key steps for registration typically include:

- **Trademark Search:** Before applying for registration, it is advisable to conduct a search to ensure that the trademark is not identical or confusingly similar to an existing trademark.
- **Filing the Application:** The applicant files a trademark application with the relevant trademark office. The application should include:
  - ❑ The trademark name or logo (the mark to be protected).
  - ❑ A description of the goods or services for which the mark will be used.
  - ❑ The class or classes under which the trademark is being registered, as trademarks are categorized into classes based on the nature of the goods or services (e.g., Class 25 for clothing, Class 30 for food products).
- **Examination:** After filing, the trademark office examines the application to ensure the mark is distinctive and does not conflict with existing trademarks.
  - ❑ **Absolute Grounds:** The mark must not be descriptive, generic, or offensive.
  - ❑ **Relative Grounds:** The mark must not conflict with existing registered marks.
- **Publication:** Once the trademark passes the examination, it is published in the trademark journal or gazette for a certain period to allow third parties to oppose registration.
- **Opposition and Objection:** If someone objects to the registration of the trademark, they may file an opposition. If no opposition is raised, or the opposition is successfully overcome, the trademark is registered.
- **Grant of Registration:** Upon approval, the trademark office grants the registration, and the trademark owner is given exclusive rights to use the mark in commerce for a specified period (usually 10 years), with the option of renewal.

Kinds of Trademarks

There are several types of trademarks that can be registered, depending on the nature of the mark and its use. Some of the common types include:

- **Word Marks:** A trademark that consists of letters, words, or numbers without any stylization. For example, "Nike" or "Coca-Cola."
- **Logo Marks (Device Marks):** A trademark that consists of a graphic symbol, design, or logo. For example, the "Apple" logo.
- **Combination Marks:** A trademark that combines both word and logo elements. For example, "PepsiCo" with its iconic logo.
- **Shape Marks:** A trademark that protects the unique shape or configuration of a product or packaging. For example, the Coca-Cola bottle's distinct contour shape.
- **Color Marks:** A trademark that is represented by a specific color or combination of colors associated with a brand. For example, Tiffany & Co.'s trademarked blue color.
- **Sound Marks:** A trademark consisting of a specific sound that identifies the goods or services. For example, the "Intel Inside" chime.
- **Scent Marks:** A trademark consisting of a specific scent that distinguishes the product. This is rare and difficult to register.
- **Collective Marks:** A trademark used to distinguish the goods or services of members of a collective organization, such as a trade union or cooperative.
- **Certification Marks:** A mark used to certify that goods or services meet certain standards, such as "ISO certified" or "Made in India."

Infringement and Passing Off

- **Infringement:** Trademark infringement occurs when a person uses a registered trademark without authorization in a way that is likely to cause confusion or deception among consumers regarding the source of goods or services. The key elements of trademark infringement are:
  - ❑ Use of an identical or similar mark.
  - ❑ In relation to identical or similar goods/services.
  - ❑ Likelihood of confusion or association in the mind of the average consumer.
  - ❑ Infringement can be brought before a court or trademark office, and the owner can seek remedies such as injunctions, damages, or destruction of infringing goods.
- **Passing Off:** Passing off is a common law tort that occurs when a person or business misrepresents its goods or services as those of another, thus deceiving consumers. Unlike trademark infringement, passing off does not require the mark to be registered. The key elements of passing off are:
  - ❑ Goodwill: The claimant must demonstrate that its mark or business has acquired goodwill, misrepresentation, and damage.
  - ❑ Misrepresentation: The defendant must have made a misrepresentation that is likely to deceive consumers.
  - ❑ Damage: The claimant must show that the misrepresentation has caused, or is likely to cause, damage to their business or reputation.

Remedies for Trademark Infringement and Passing Off

Trademark holders who successfully prove infringement or passing off are entitled to various remedies:

- **Injunctive Relief:** The most common remedy in trademark cases, which involves a court order that prohibits the infringer from continuing the infringing act. The injunction can be temporary (interim) or permanent.
- **Monetary Damages:** The trademark holder may be awarded financial compensation for the harm caused by the infringement. These damages may include:
  - ❑ **Actual Damages:** Compensation for the actual loss suffered due to the infringement, such as lost profits or lost sales.
  - ❑ **Punitive Damages:** In some cases, the court may award damages that go beyond the actual loss to punish the infringer for willful infringement and deter future misconduct.
  - ❑ **Statutory Damages:** In some jurisdictions, the law allows for statutory damages that can be awarded without requiring proof of actual damages.
- **Account of Profits:** The court may require the infringer to account for the profits they have made from the infringement and to pay them to the trademark holder.
- **Destruction of Infringing Goods:** In cases of infringement, the court may order the destruction or forfeiture of infringing goods, labels, packaging, or materials used to infringe the trademark.
- **Corrective Advertising:** In cases of passing off, the court may require the defendant to issue corrective advertising or statements to inform the public of the truth and to undo the misleading effects of the misrepresentation.
- **Costs and Attorney's Fees:** The prevailing party may be entitled to recover legal costs and attorney's fees, which can serve as a deterrent to infringers and encourage trademark holders to enforce their rights.
- **Criminal Penalties:** In cases of counterfeit goods or intentional and widespread infringement, criminal penalties, including fines and imprisonment, may be imposed on the infringer.

Defenses to Trademark Infringement and Passing Off

The accused infringer may assert several defenses to avoid liability for trademark infringement or passing off:

- **Non-Use of the Mark:** The defendant may argue that they have not used the trademark in a manner that would constitute infringement or passing off.
- **Lack of Likelihood of Confusion:** The defendant may argue that their mark is not likely to cause confusion with the registered trademark, often by demonstrating significant differences between the marks or the goods/services.
- **Fair Use:** The defendant may assert that the use of the mark was fair, such as using the mark for descriptive purposes (e.g., comparative advertising) or for non-commercial purposes.
- **Use of Own Mark:** The defendant may argue that they are using a mark that is similar to the registered mark, but the mark has become widely recognized in its own right and is not likely to cause confusion.

- **Exhaustion of Rights:** In cases involving the resale of goods, the defendant may argue that the trademark holder's rights have been exhausted after the first sale or distribution of the goods.
- **Invalidity of the Registered Mark:** The defendant may challenge the validity of the trademark, asserting that the mark was improperly registered or does not meet the requirements of trademark law.

PROTECTION OF GEOGRAPHICAL INDICATIONS (GIS)

Geographical Indication (GI) refers to a sign used on goods that have a specific geographical origin and possess qualities, reputation, or characteristics inherent to that location. GIs are used to protect products that are closely linked to the place from which they originate, ensuring that consumers can identify the products and their origin. Common examples include Darjeeling Tea, Kanchipuram Sarees, and Roquefort Cheese.

The protection of Geographical Indications is crucial in safeguarding the interests of local producers, preserving cultural heritage, and ensuring fair competition in the market. Here is a detailed overview of the protection of GIs:

Legal Framework for Protection of GIs

International Legal Framework

- **World Trade Organization (WTO):** The protection of Geographical Indications is governed under Trade-Related Aspects of Intellectual Property Rights (TRIPS), which sets out international standards for the protection of GIs. Article 22 of the TRIPS Agreement defines a geographical indication and provides protection against the use of GIs that mislead consumers or unfairly compete with the genuine products.
- **Paris Convention for the Protection of Industrial Property:** The Paris Convention (Article 1(2)) protects indications of source and geographical indications.

National Legal Framework (India Example)

- **The Geographical Indications of Goods (Registration and Protection) Act, 1999:** This is the primary law in India for the registration and protection of Geographical Indications. The Act provides a legal framework for registering GIs, offering them protection against unauthorized use and preventing misleading practices.
  - ❑ **Section 2(e):** Defines Geographical Indication as an indication that identifies goods as originating from a specific geographical location and that quality, reputation, or other characteristics are linked to that origin.
  - ❑ **Registration of GIs:** GIs are registered with the Geographical Indications Registry under the Ministry of Commerce and Industry in India. Once registered, the GI gets protection against misuse and imitation by other producers not originating from the specified geographical region.
  - ❑ **Rights of Registered GIs:** The registered GI holder gains the right to prevent unauthorized use of the GI, ensuring that only goods genuinely originating from the specified region can use the GI.

Criteria for Protection of GIs

For a product to be eligible for GI protection, it must meet certain criteria:

- **Geographical Origin:** The product must originate from a specific geographical area.
- **Link to Quality or Reputation:** There must be a clear link between the product's quality, reputation, or characteristics and its geographical origin.
- **Tradition and Continuity:** The product must be produced using traditional methods that have been practiced for a significant period, reflecting the cultural and historical heritage of the region.
- **Distinctiveness:** The product must have unique characteristics that distinguish it from similar products that come from other regions.

Types of Protection for GIs

Geographical Indications can be protected in various ways, depending on national or regional legal systems:

- **Collective Marks:** GIs can be protected as collective marks, which are owned by a group or association of producers from a specific geographical region. This ensures that only members of the association can use the GI.
- **Certification Marks:** These marks are used to certify that a product has been produced according to certain standards specific to a region, such as "Made in India" or "Organic Certification."
- **Geographical Indication Protection:** Some countries provide direct GI protection, often without requiring the GI to be registered as a collective

or certification mark. This includes products like Champagne or Basmati Rice, which are protected in certain jurisdictions based on their geographical origin and characteristics.

Benefits of GI Protection

- **Economic Benefits:** GI protection can enhance the economic value of a product by preventing unfair competition, ensuring premium pricing, and improving market access both domestically and internationally. It also allows producers to maintain control over the marketing and reputation of their products.
- **Cultural and Heritage Preservation:** GIs often have a deep connection with cultural heritage and traditional knowledge. Protection helps preserve and promote these unique regional practices and craftsmanship.
- **Consumer Protection:** By protecting the authenticity of products and ensuring that only genuine goods from a specific region can carry the GI, consumers are safeguarded from misleading claims and counterfeit goods.
- **Rural Development:** GI protection can boost rural economies by creating niche markets for traditional and artisanal products, leading to better livelihoods for local communities.

Infringement of Geographical Indications

- **Unauthorized Use:** Infringement occurs when a third party uses a geographical indication without authorization, misrepresenting the origin of the goods. This can occur even if the third party does not have any connection with the geographical region in question.
- **False or Misleading Representation:** If a product is marketed under a GI when it does not originate from the specified region, it misleads consumers and infringes upon the registered GI.
- **Deceptive Practices:** Using a name or sign that is identical or confusingly similar to a registered GI, such as the sale of imitation products under a GI or passing off, is considered an infringement.

Remedies for GI Infringement

Trademark-like remedies are available to protect and enforce GIs against infringement:

- **Injunctions:** Courts can issue an injunction to prevent further unauthorized use of a registered GI.
- **Damages:** Infringers may be required to compensate the rightful GI holder for the losses suffered due to the unauthorized use of the GI.
- **Seizure of Goods:** Courts may order the seizure and destruction of goods that infringe upon a registered GI.
- **Criminal Penalties:** In some jurisdictions, willful infringement of a registered GI can lead to criminal sanctions, including fines and imprisonment.

Challenges in Protecting GIs

Despite the legal frameworks in place, there are several challenges to effective protection of GIs:

- **Lack of Awareness:** Producers, consumers, and even some governments may not fully understand the value of GIs and the mechanisms available for their protection.
- **Enforcement Issues:** In some countries, enforcement of GI rights may be weak, and infringers may evade legal action due to inadequate legal infrastructure or resources.
- **Globalization and Counterfeiting:** The global trade of counterfeit goods and imitation products has made it harder to protect GIs internationally. Global brands may face challenges in controlling unauthorized use in foreign markets.
- **Regional Conflicts:** In some cases, GIs may be subject to territorial disputes, where multiple regions or countries lay claim to the same GI.

BIODIVERSITY AND TRADITIONAL KNOWLEDGE

Biodiversity refers to the variety and variability of life on Earth, including the diversity of species, ecosystems, and genetic resources. It is the foundation of ecosystem services such as air and water purification, food production, and disease control. Traditional knowledge refers to the knowledge, practices, and innovations developed over generations by indigenous and local communities. It encompasses cultural, ecological, agricultural, and medicinal knowledge that is closely tied to the community's relationship with the natural environment.

The intersection of biodiversity and traditional knowledge plays a critical role in the conservation of ecosystems and the sustainable use of natural resources. Traditional knowledge has been pivotal in the conservation of biodiversity in many indigenous communities worldwide. Here's an in-depth look at the connection between biodiversity and traditional knowledge.

Relationship Between Biodiversity and Traditional Knowledge

Traditional knowledge is intrinsically linked to biodiversity in several ways:

- **Conservation Practices:** Indigenous and local communities have long practiced sustainable methods of managing natural resources. For example, indigenous groups in the Amazon rainforest employ traditional farming systems, such as agroforestry, which helps maintain the biodiversity of the ecosystem by mimicking natural habitats.
- **Resource Management:** Traditional knowledge includes methods of sustainable harvesting, animal husbandry, crop rotation, and the use of medicinal plants, which help preserve biodiversity by ensuring that ecosystems and species are not over-exploited.
- **Ecosystem Management:** Traditional ecological knowledge (TEK) often incorporates an understanding of the balance between species, the role of predators and prey, and the delicate interactions between different elements of an ecosystem. Such knowledge has contributed to the effective management of resources and the preservation of ecosystem services over millennia.

Role of Traditional Knowledge in Biodiversity Conservation

- **Medicinal Plants:** Many indigenous communities use local plants for medicinal purposes. This traditional knowledge contributes to the discovery of valuable pharmaceuticals and helps protect plant species that have therapeutic properties. For example, the use of Neem *(Azadirachta indica)* in traditional medicine has sparked interest in its ecological benefits and potential for sustainable agriculture.
- **Indigenous Agricultural Systems:** Traditional agricultural systems such as terracing in the Andes or shift cultivation in Southeast Asia help preserve soil fertility, reduce soil erosion, and maintain biodiversity. These systems are designed to be in harmony with the local environment, unlike modern industrial farming techniques that often contribute to biodiversity loss.
- **Cultural and Spiritual Connections:** For many indigenous groups, biodiversity is not only a matter of livelihood but also intertwined with their spiritual beliefs and cultural practices. Sacred groves, ritual use of plants and animals, and conservation practices rooted in religious or cultural beliefs help protect important species and habitats.

Threats to Biodiversity and Traditional Knowledge

While traditional knowledge plays a key role in preserving biodiversity, both are increasingly under threat due to several factors:

- **Globalization and Modernization:** The encroachment of industrialization, urbanization, and agricultural expansion disrupts ecosystems, reduces biodiversity, and leads to the loss of traditional practices. The commercialization of natural resources, such as forests or medicinal plants, often displaces local communities and erodes their traditional knowledge.
- **Climate Change:** Changing climate patterns affect the distribution and survival of species, which in turn impacts the knowledge systems that depend on those species. Traditional knowledge often evolves in response to environmental changes, but the speed and unpredictability of climate change pose challenges to these adaptive systems.
- **Intellectual Property Issues:** There is a growing concern about the misappropriation or biopiracy of traditional knowledge. Companies may patent products derived from indigenous knowledge without compensating the communities that have preserved and developed this knowledge for generations.
- **Loss of Traditional Knowledge:** The younger generation may not be passing on traditional knowledge due to shifts in lifestyle, loss of languages, or formal education systems that do not value indigenous knowledge systems. This is particularly concerning as the loss of knowledge also leads to a loss of sustainable practices that help protect biodiversity.

Legal Protection of Biodiversity and Traditional Knowledge

The protection of biodiversity and traditional knowledge is crucial for both environmental sustainability and the rights of indigenous and local communities. There are several international and national frameworks aimed at safeguarding biodiversity and the rights of communities:

- **Convention on Biological Diversity (CBD):** The CBD, adopted in 1992, is an international treaty that recognizes the importance of biodiversity and calls for the conservation of biodiversity, the sustainable use of biological resources, and the fair and equitable sharing of benefits arising from the use of genetic resources. The Nagoya

Protocol (2010) is an additional protocol to the CBD, focusing on access to genetic resources and the fair sharing of benefits derived from them, including traditional knowledge.

- **The World Intellectual Property Organization (WIPO) and Traditional Knowledge:** WIPO has developed initiatives aimed at recognizing and protecting traditional knowledge, including the establishment of databases of traditional knowledge, intellectual property systems tailored to indigenous peoples, and the protection of traditional cultural expressions.
- **National Legislation:** Many countries have enacted laws to protect traditional knowledge and biodiversity. For example, India's Biological Diversity Act, 2002, includes provisions for the protection of traditional knowledge related to biodiversity, requiring the disclosure of traditional knowledge in patent applications related to biological resources.
- **Community Rights and Bio-piracy:** Legal frameworks such as the Access and Benefit-Sharing (ABS) system aim to prevent bio-piracy, which involves the unauthorized use of indigenous knowledge or genetic resources by commercial entities. These frameworks ensure that communities receive compensation and recognition for their contribution to scientific research and biotechnology.

Sustainable Development and Traditional Knowledge

The concept of sustainable development incorporates the idea of balancing environmental protection, social equity, and economic development. Traditional knowledge offers a wealth of wisdom for sustainable living and can contribute to addressing contemporary environmental challenges, such as:

- **Agroecology:** Traditional agricultural knowledge is a key component of agroecology, which seeks to create more sustainable, resilient farming systems. By incorporating traditional knowledge with modern science, agroecology promotes biodiversity conservation, climate adaptation, and food security.
- **Conservation of Sacred Sites:** Many indigenous communities have long recognized the importance of sacred sites and areas of biodiversity significance, and their protection can contribute to global conservation efforts. These sites are often maintained through traditional practices that balance human use with ecological preservation.
- **Community-Based Conservation:** Local and indigenous communities often engage in community-based conservation initiatives, using traditional ecological knowledge to manage natural resources in a sustainable manner. These initiatives can complement formal protected areas and contribute to the resilience of ecosystems.

INFORMATION TECHNOLOGY LAW : DIGITAL SIGNATURE, ELECTRONIC SIGNATURE, ELECTRONIC GOVERNANCE, ELECTRONIC RECORDS, AND DUTIES OF SUBSCRIBERS

Information Technology Law governs the legal aspects of information technology, focusing on the use of electronic communications, data protection, and cybersecurity. One of the critical areas within IT law is the regulation of electronic transactions and records. The legal recognition and regulation of digital signatures and electronic signatures play a vital role in ensuring the validity and security of electronic documents. Additionally, electronic governance, the management of government services through electronic means, and the legal duties of subscribers in the digital space are also crucial components of IT law.

DIGITAL SIGNATURE AND ELECTRONIC SIGNATURE

Both digital signatures and electronic signatures serve as means of authenticating electronic documents. However, they differ in terms of technology, legal weight, and requirements for security.

Digital Signature

A digital signature is a cryptographic technique used to verify the authenticity and integrity of a message or document in the digital world. It is based on a mathematical algorithm (typically Public Key Infrastructure (PKI)), which uses a pair of keys: a private key and a public key.

- **Legal Recognition:** In India, the Information Technology Act, 2000 (IT Act) recognizes digital signatures as legally valid. According to Section 3 of the IT Act, a digital signature is considered equivalent to a handwritten signature for legal purposes.
- **Creation and Verification:** A digital signature is created using the sender's private key and can be verified by anyone using the corresponding public key, ensuring the authenticity of the document.

- **Use of Certificate Authorities (CAs):** To provide a higher level of security and trust, digital signatures are issued and verified by Certificate Authorities (CAs), which are trusted entities that validate the identity of the individual or organization requesting the digital certificate.

Electronic Signature

An electronic signature is a broader term that refers to any electronic process used to sign a document. It can be a scanned image of a handwritten signature, a click-to-sign option, or a biometric verification system. Unlike digital signatures, electronic signatures do not necessarily involve cryptographic methods.

- **Legal Framework:** Under the IT Act, 2000 (India), electronic signatures include digital signatures (using PKI cryptography) and other reliable methods. Both can be secure if they meet prescribed standards.
- **Use in E-Commerce:** Electronic signatures are commonly used in e-commerce, email communications, and online agreements, where security measures are less stringent than those required for digital signatures.

While both digital and electronic signatures have legal validity, digital signatures offer a higher level of security and are used in more critical and sensitive contexts (e.g., filing government documents, financial transactions).

ELECTRONIC GOVERNANCE (E-GOVERNANCE)

E-Governance refers to the use of information technology (IT) to provide government services to citizens, businesses, and other stakeholders. It involves digital platforms for the delivery of public services and the interaction between government agencies and the public.

Key Aspects of E-Governance:

- **Online Public Services:** The digital delivery of government services, such as e-filing of taxes, online passport applications, electronic voting, and digital licensing.
- **Transparency and Accountability:** E-Governance promotes transparency in government operations and enhances accountability by making data and services publicly accessible through websites and mobile apps.
- **Digital Infrastructure:** E-Governance relies on the development of digital infrastructure, including internet connectivity, data storage, and digital security measures.
- **Legal Framework:** The Information Technology Act, 2000 plays a critical role in facilitating e-governance by providing legal recognition to electronic records, digital signatures, and ensuring the protection of data. The National e-Governance Plan (NeGP) is another initiative in India to implement e-governance in various government departments.

Examples of E-Governance:

- **Income Tax E-Filing:** The ability to file income tax returns online, which has become a common practice in India and many other countries.
- **Digital Identity Systems:** Examples include Aadhaar in India, which provides citizens with a unique digital identity for accessing government services.
- **E-Voting:** Some countries have implemented or are testing electronic voting systems for local and national elections.

ELECTRONIC RECORDS

Electronic records refer to information stored or transmitted in digital form, as opposed to traditional paper records. These records can include emails, online documents, contracts, and transaction logs.

Legal Recognition

- Under the Information Technology Act, 2000 (India), electronic records are legally recognized and can be used in place of paper documents. Section 4 of the IT Act provides that if a law requires information to be in writing or in a printed form, electronic records will be deemed valid if they comply with the provisions of the IT Act.
- **Admissibility of Evidence:** Section 65B of the Indian Evidence Act, 1872, was amended by the IT Act to allow the admissibility of electronic records as evidence in courts. The electronic records must meet certain conditions, such as being authentic and retrieved from a computer system in a reliable manner.

Security and Integrity

- The integrity of electronic records is maintained through techniques such as digital signatures, encryption, and secure storage systems.
- **Data Protection:** The protection of electronic records from unauthorized access, modification, or destruction is vital. The IT Act requires organizations to implement reasonable security practices to ensure the confidentiality and integrity of electronic records.

Duties of Subscribers

Subscribers are individuals or organizations that use electronic signatures or digital signatures for signing documents, executing transactions, or engaging in online agreements. They have certain responsibilities and duties under the Information Technology Act, 2000 and related regulations.

Duties of Subscribers

- **Authenticity and Accuracy:** Subscribers are required to ensure the authenticity and accuracy of the electronic records they sign. If a subscriber uses a digital signature, it must correspond to the person or entity authorized to sign the document.
- **Confidentiality of Private Keys:** A subscriber must protect the private key used to create a digital signature and ensure that it is not compromised. Misuse of the private key can lead to fraudulent activities.
- **Compliance with Legal Requirements:** Subscribers must comply with the legal and regulatory requirements related to electronic signatures and records. This includes keeping records of signed documents and ensuring compliance with e-governance guidelines.
- **Notification of Compromise:** If a subscriber's private key is compromised, they must immediately notify the Certification Authority (CA) to revoke the certificate and prevent unauthorized use.

Liabilities of Subscribers

- **Misuse of Digital Signature:** If a subscriber's digital signature is used fraudulently, they may be held liable for any damages or illegal activities arising from the misuse.
- **Failure to Comply with Security Practices:** Subscribers may face penalties for failing to adhere to security measures that ensure the integrity and confidentiality of electronic records.

CYBER CRIMES, PENALTIES AND ADJUDICATION

Cybercrime refers to criminal activities that involve computers, networks, or electronic devices. These crimes can range from hacking and identity theft to online fraud and the spread of malicious software (malware). The legal framework for addressing cybercrimes is essential to safeguard individuals, organizations, and nations from the harmful effects of digital offenses.

The Information Technology Act, 2000 (IT Act) in India is the primary legislation governing cybercrimes and electronic commerce. It outlines the definition of various cybercrimes, the penalties associated with them, and the adjudication mechanisms for resolving disputes.

Types of Cyber Crimes

The IT Act, 2000 and other relevant laws define various cybercrimes, including:

- **Hacking (Section 66)**
  - **Definition:** Hacking involves unauthorized access to or manipulation of computer systems, networks, or data.
  - **Example:** A person breaking into an online database to steal sensitive information.
- **Identity Theft (Section 66C)**
  - **Definition:** Identity theft occurs when an individual uses someone else's identity for fraudulent purposes, such as accessing their bank account or committing fraud.
  - **Example:** Using someone else's credit card details for online purchases without authorization.
- **Cyberstalking (Section 66A)**
  - **Definition:** Cyberstalking involves the use of the internet, emails, or social media platforms to harass or stalk someone.
  - **Example:** Repeatedly sending threatening emails or messages with the intent to cause distress. Section 66A was struck down in Shreya Singhal v. Union of India (2015).
- **Phishing (Section 66D)**
  - **Definition:** Phishing refers to the fraudulent practice of attempting to obtain sensitive information, such as passwords or bank account details, by impersonating a trustworthy entity via electronic communication.
  - **Example:** Sending fake emails that look like they come from a bank to trick users into revealing their login credentials.
- **Cyber Terrorism (Section 66F)**
  - **Definition:** Cyber terrorism refers to the use of computers or networks to threaten national security or cause harm to individuals or society.
  - **Example:** Hacking into critical infrastructure systems, such as power grids, to cause widespread damage.

- **Data Theft and Privacy Violations (Section 72A)**
  - **Definition:** Data theft occurs when a person intentionally discloses or acquires sensitive personal information without consent.
  - **Example:** Stealing a company's trade secrets or client data for commercial gain.
- **Sending Offensive Messages (Section 66A – Repealed)**
  - **Definition:** Sending offensive or threatening messages via communication services, websites, or applications (the provision was struck down by the Supreme Court in 2015 for being overly broad and violating free speech).

Penalties for Cyber Crimes

The IT Act, 2000 prescribes penalties for various cyber-crimes, and they can range from fines to imprisonment, depending on the severity of the offense.

- **Hacking (Section 66):**
  - Penalty: Imprisonment for up to 3 years, or a fine that may extend to ₹ 5,00,000, or both.
- **Identity Theft (Section 66C)**
  - Penalty: Imprisonment for up to 3 years, or a fine that may extend to ₹ 1,00,000, or both.
- **Cyberstalking (Section 66A - Struck Down)**
  - Penalty: Previously, this provision had a penalty of imprisonment for up to 3 years, but it was struck down by the Supreme Court in 2015 as it was deemed unconstitutional.
- **Phishing (Section 66D)**
  - Penalty: Imprisonment for up to 3 years, or a fine that may extend to ₹ 1,00,000, or both.
- **Cyber Terrorism (Section 66F)**
  - Penalty: Imprisonment for life.
- **Data Theft and Privacy Violations (Section 72A)**
  - Penalty: Imprisonment for up to 3 years, or a fine that may extend to ₹ 5,00,000, or both.
- **Sending Offensive Messages (Section 66A - Repealed)**
  - Penalty: This provision was struck down by the Supreme Court, but prior to that, it imposed imprisonment for up to 3 years, or a fine, or both.
- **Publishing Pornography (Section 67)**
  - Penalty: Imprisonment for up to 5 years and a fine of ₹ 10 lakh for the first offense, and up to 7 years and a fine of ₹ 10 lakh for subsequent offenses.

Adjudication of Cyber Crimes

The adjudication of cybercrimes in India is handled through a specialized legal and institutional framework that includes both adjudicating officers and cyber appellate tribunals.

- **Adjudicating Officers (Section 46 of the IT Act):**
  - The Adjudicating Officer is a person appointed by the government to handle matters related to cybercrimes, violations of the IT Act, and disputes related to contraventions of electronic records and digital signatures.
  - Jurisdiction: The adjudicating officer has the power to impose penalties for offenses under the IT Act, excluding criminal offenses, which are handled by criminal courts.
  - Penalty for Failure to Comply: The adjudicating officer can impose fines for failure to comply with orders regarding the security of data and system management.
- **Cyber Appellate Tribunal (Section 48 of the IT Act):**
  - The Cyber Appellate Tribunal is established to handle appeals against orders passed by adjudicating officers.
  - Appeal Process: Any person who is dissatisfied with the order passed by an adjudicating officer can file an appeal to the Cyber Appellate Tribunal within 45 days of the order.
  - Tribunal's Authority: The tribunal has the authority to confirm, modify, or annul the penalty imposed by the adjudicating officer.
- **Criminal Courts:**
  - Some cybercrimes, such as cyber terrorism or fraudulent activities, are treated as criminal offenses and are prosecuted in regular criminal courts.
  - Specialized Courts: In India, some high courts have established specialized cybercrime cells to handle complex cases involving cybercrimes and digital evidence.
- **Role of Law Enforcement Agencies:**
  - Cyber Crime Cells: Various law enforcement agencies in India, such as the Cyber Crime Cells of the police, have been set up to deal

with cybercrimes, investigate digital evidence, and file charges.

- Centralized Agencies: The Indian Computer Emergency Response Team (CERT-In) plays a role in coordinating responses to cybersecurity incidents and cybercrimes.

Challenges in Cybercrime Adjudication

- **Cross-Jurisdictional Issues:** Cybercrimes often involve multiple countries, which makes enforcement and adjudication complex, as different countries may have different laws and jurisdictions.
- **Technological Advancements:** The rapid evolution of technology and new types of cybercrimes require ongoing updates to laws and regulations, which may lag behind emerging trends in cybercrime.
- **Lack of Awareness:** Both law enforcement agencies and the public may lack sufficient awareness of cybercrimes, which can hinder effective investigation and prosecution.
- **Digital Evidence:** The collection and preservation of digital evidence pose challenges due to the ephemeral nature of data and the complexity of forensic investigations.

MULTIPLE CHOICE QUESTIONS

1. Which of the following best defines Intellectual Property (IP)?
A. Tangible property like land or buildings
B. Property created through mental effort or creativity
C. Government-owned property
D. Natural resources like water and minerals

2. Which of the following is NOT a type of Intellectual Property?
A. Trademark B. Copyright
C. Real estate D. Patent

3. Which international organization administers intellectual property-related treaties globally?
A. United Nations (UN)
B. World Trade Organization (WTO)
C. World Intellectual Property Organization (WIPO)
D. International Monetary Fund (IMF)

4. A patent provides protection for:
A. Artistic expressions
B. Scientific discoveries
C. Inventions with industrial applications
D. Business trademarks

5. Copyright protects the expression of ideas but not the ideas themselves.
A. True
B. False
C. True, only for literary works
D. False, unless the idea is patented

6. Trademarks can only be words or logos, not sounds or colors.
A. True
B. False
C. True, only in the USA
D. False, unless specified by WIPO

7. Assertion (A): Intellectual Property Rights (IPR) encourage innovation and creativity.

Reason (R): IPR provides creators with exclusive rights to benefit from their creations.
A. Both A and R are true, and R is the correct explanation of A
B. Both A and R are true, but R is not the correct explanation of A
C. A is true, R is false
D. A is false, R is true

8. Assertion (A): Copyright protection lasts forever.

Reason (R): Copyright is granted to ensure perpetual benefits to authors.
A. Both A and R are true, and R is the correct explanation of A
B. Both A and R are true, but R is not the correct explanation of A
C. A is true, R is false
D. A is false, R is true

9. The legal protection granted to the creator of original works such as books, music, and films is known as ______.
A. Trademark
B. Patent
C. Copyright
D. Trade secret

10. The agreement that sets minimum standards for IP protection among WTO member countries is known as ________.

A. TRIPS Agreement
B. Berne Convention
C. Paris Agreement
D. Madrid Protocol

11. Match the following types of Intellectual Property with what they protect:

A. Patent	1. Inventions and innovations
B. Trademark	2. Brand names and logos
C. Copyright	3. Original literary, artistic, and musical works
D. Trade Secret	4. Confidential business information

A. A-1, B-2, C-3, D-4
B. A-4, B-3, C-2, D-1
C. A-3, B-1, C-4, D-2
D. A-2, B-4, C-1, D-3

12. Arrange the following international IP treaties in chronological order of their adoption:

1. Paris Convention for the Protection of Industrial Property
2. Berne Convention for the Protection of Literary and Artistic Works
3. TRIPS Agreement
4. Madrid Protocol

A. 1, 2, 4, 3 B. 2, 1, 3, 4
C. 1, 2, 3, 4 D. 4, 1, 2, 3

13. Scenario: A company develops a new technology for faster data processing. To protect its exclusive rights, the company should apply for:

A. Trademark B. Copyright
C. Patent D. Trade secret

14. Scenario: An author writes a novel and wants to ensure that no one can copy or sell it without permission. Which form of IP protection should the author seek?

A. Patent B. Trademark
C. Copyright D. Trade secret

15. Scenario: A soft drink company keeps its formula a secret, giving it a competitive advantage. This is an example of:

A. Trademark
B. Trade secret
C. Patent
D. Copyright

16. Which of the following is NOT a recognized theory of intellectual property?

A. Natural Rights Theory
B. Utilitarian Theory
C. Marxist Theory of IP
D. Personality Theory

17. The Natural Rights Theory of IP is primarily associated with which philosopher?

A. John Locke
B. Immanuel Kant
C. Karl Marx
D. Jeremy Bentham

18. The Utilitarian Theory of IP focuses on:

A. The moral right of creators
B. Maximizing social welfare through incentives
C. Ownership based on personal development
D. The protection of cultural heritage

19. The Personality Theory of IP is associated with which philosopher?

A. Georg Wilhelm Friedrich Hegel
B. Adam Smith
C. Thomas Jefferson
D. David Ricardo

20. Utilitarian Theory of IP suggests that IP rights should be perpetual to maximize innovation.

A. True
B. False
C. True, only for patents
D. False, unless approved by the government

21. According to Natural Rights Theory, individuals have an inherent right to control their creations because of the labor they invested.

A. True
B. False
C. True, only in capitalist economies
D. False, unless registered officially

22. **Assertion (A):** The Utilitarian Theory of IP promotes exclusive rights to creators to benefit them personally.

Reason (R): The main goal of IP under Utilitarian Theory is to ensure creators' economic dominance.

A. Both A and R are true, and R is the correct explanation of A
B. Both A and R are true, but R is not the correct explanation of A
C. A is true, R is false
D. A is false, R is true

23. **Assertion (A):** Personality Theory emphasizes the economic value of intellectual property.

Reason (R): It views intellectual creations as extensions of an individual's personality rather than commodities.

A. Both A and R are true, and R is the correct explanation of A
B. Both A and R are true, but R is not the correct explanation of A
C. A is true, R is false
D. A is false, R is true

24. According to John Locke's theory, property rights arise from mixing one's _______ with natural resources.

A. Capital B. Labor
C. Wealth D. Education

25. The main principle behind the Utilitarian Theory of IP is to create _______ for innovation and creativity.

A. Legal barriers
B. Economic monopolies
C. Incentives
D. Permanent protections

26. Match the following IP theories with their key concepts:

IP theories	Key Concepts
A. Natural Rights Theory	1. Ownership derived from labor
B. Utilitarian Theory	2. Promoting societal welfare through innovation
C. Personality Theory	3. Extension of individual's personality
D. Social Planning Theory	4. Facilitating democratic culture and access

A. A-1, B-2, C-3, D-4
B. A-2, B-1, C-4, D-3
C. A-3, B-4, C-1, D-2
D. A-4, B-3, C-2, D-1

27. Arrange the following philosophers in chronological order based on their contributions to property theories:

1. John Locke
2. Jeremy Bentham
3. Georg Wilhelm Friedrich Hegel
4. Immanuel Kant

A. 1, 4, 2, 3
B. 1, 2, 4, 3
C. 4, 1, 3, 2
D. 1, 3, 4, 2

28. Scenario: A government grants patents to encourage scientific research, believing this will lead to technological progress benefiting society. This policy aligns with which IP theory?

A. Natural Rights Theory
B. Personality Theory
C. Utilitarian Theory
D. Cultural Heritage Theory

29. Scenario: An artist argues that their painting reflects their personal identity and emotions, and thus deserves legal protection. Which theory best supports this claim?

A. Labor Theory
B. Personality Theory
C. Social Planning Theory
D. Economic Incentive Theory

30. Scenario: A company claims ownership over a software it developed, arguing that the employees' efforts justify exclusive rights. Which theory supports this claim?

A. Utilitarian Theory
B. Natural Rights Theory
C. Cultural Theory
D. Moral Rights Theory

31. Which of the following is the oldest international convention for the protection of industrial property?

A. Berne Convention
B. Paris Convention
C. TRIPS Agreement
D. Madrid Protocol

32. The Berne Convention deals with the protection of:

A. Industrial designs
B. Trademarks
C. Literary and artistic works
D. Patents

33. Which international agreement sets minimum standards for IP protection among World Trade Organization (WTO) members?

A. Madrid Protocol
B. TRIPS Agreement
C. Hague Agreement
D. WIPO Copyright Treaty

34. The World Intellectual Property Organization (WIPO) was established in:

A. 1967 B. 1945
C. 1957 D. 1995

35. The TRIPS Agreement applies only to patents and trademarks.

A. True
B. False
C. True, but only for WTO members
D. False, unless specified in national law

36. The Madrid Protocol facilitates the international registration of trademarks.

A. True
B. False
C. True, but only in Europe
D. False, unless approved by WIPO

37. Assertion (A): The Berne Convention requires authors to register their works to receive copyright protection.

Reason (R): Copyright protection under the Berne Convention is automatic without the need for formal registration.

A. Both A and R are true, and R is the correct explanation of A
B. Both A and R are true, but R is not the correct explanation of A
C. A is true, R is false
D. A is false, R is true

38. Assertion (A): The TRIPS Agreement enforces uniform IP laws across all countries.

Reason (R): TRIPS sets minimum standards, but countries can implement stronger IP protections if they choose.

A. Both A and R are true, and R is the correct explanation of A
B. Both A and R are true, but R is not the correct explanation of A
C. A is true, R is false
D. A is false, R is true

39. The _______ administers the Berne Convention for the Protection of Literary and Artistic Works.

A. WTO
B. UN
C. WIPO
D. IMF

40. The _______ allows for the international registration of industrial designs.

A. TRIPS Agreement
B. Hague Agreement
C. Berne Convention
D. Madrid Protocol

41. Match the following international conventions with their focus areas:

A. Paris Convention	1. Protection of industrial property
B. Berne Convention	2. Protection of literary and artistic works
C. Madrid Protocol	3. International registration of trademarks
D. TRIPS Agreement	4. Minimum standards for IP protection in trade

A. A-1, B-2, C-3, D-4
B. A-2, B-3, C-1, D-4
C. A-3, B-1, C-4, D-2
D. A-4, B-1, C-2, D-3

42. Scenario: A company wants to protect its trademark in multiple countries through a single application. Which international agreement should it use?

A. Paris Convention
B. TRIPS Agreement
C. Madrid Protocol
D. Berne Convention

43. Scenario: An author from Country A wants their literary work to be protected automatically in Country B without registering it there. Which convention provides this protection?

A. TRIPS Agreement
B. Paris Convention
C. Berne Convention
D. Madrid Protocol

44. Scenario: A country is a member of the WTO but not of the Berne Convention. Does this country still need to protect copyrights as per Berne standards?

A. No, because it's not a Berne member
B. Yes, because TRIPS incorporates Berne obligations
C. Only if the author registers the work
D. Yes, but only for patents

45. Which legislation governs the registration and protection of trademarks in India?

A. Copyright Act, 1957
B. Patent Act, 1970
C. Trademarks Act, 1999
D. Designs Act, 2000

46. Which of the following can be registered as a trademark?

A. A word
B. A logo
C. A sound
D. All of the above

47. The symbol ® indicates:
A. A trademark that is pending registration
B. A registered trademark
C. A copyright-protected work
D. A patent-protected invention

48. Which of the following is NOT a ground for refusal of trademark registration?
A. Deceptive similarity to an existing trademark
B. Descriptive of the goods or services
C. Unique and distinctive design
D. Generic terms

49. Trademark protection lasts forever as long as the owner continues to use it.
A. True
B. False
C. True, but only for logos
D. False, unless renewed every 10 years

50. The act of 'passing off' applies only to registered trademarks.
A. True
B. False
C. True, unless the mark is famous
D. False, unless approved by the Registrar

51. **Assertion (A):** A generic term can be registered as a trademark.

Reason (R): Generic terms are distinctive and identify the source of goods.
A. Both A and R are true, and R is the correct explanation of A
B. Both A and R are true, but R is not the correct explanation of A
C. A is true, R is false
D. A is false, R is true

52. **Assertion (A):** Trademark infringement occurs only when there is an exact copy of the registered mark.

Reason (R): Minor variations in a trademark do not constitute infringement.
A. Both A and R are true, and R is the correct explanation of A
B. Both A and R are true, but R is not the correct explanation of A
C. A is true, R is false
D. A is false, R is true

53. A _______ trademark identifies the origin of goods and distinguishes them from others.
A. Descriptive B. Generic
C. Distinctive D. Common

54. In India, an application for trademark registration must be filed with the _______.
A. Registrar of Companies
B. Trademark Registry
C. Intellectual Property Appellate Board
D. Ministry of Corporate Affairs

55. Match the types of trademarks with their descriptions:

A. Service Mark	1. Identifies services instead of goods
B. Certification Mark	2. Certifies goods for quality, origin, or other characteristics
C. Collective Mark	3. Indicates membership in an association
D. Trade Dress	4. Refers to the visual appearance or packaging

A. A-1, B-2, C-3, D-4
B. A-2, B-1, C-4, D-3
C. A-4, B-3, C-1, D-2
D. A-3, B-4, C-2, D-1

56. Arrange the following steps in the correct order for trademark registration in India:
1. Filing of trademark application
2. Examination by the Registrar
3. Publication in the Trademark Journal
4. Registration and issuance of certificate

A. 1, 2, 3, 4
B. 2, 1, 4, 3
C. 3, 2, 1, 4
D. 4, 3, 2, 1

57. Scenario: A company uses a logo similar to a well-known brand, causing confusion among consumers. The original brand holds a registered trademark. What legal action can the original brand take?
A. File for copyright infringement
B. File for trademark infringement
C. Apply for patent protection
D. Initiate a passing-off case

58. Scenario: A local business has been using an unregistered logo for years, building strong goodwill. Another company starts using a similar logo. What remedy is available to the original business?
A. Patent infringement claim
B. Trademark infringement claim
C. Passing-off action
D. Copyright infringement claim

59. Scenario: A company registered a trademark but has not used it for five years. A competitor wants to use the same mark. What legal remedy is available to the competitor?

A. Apply for compulsory licensing
B. File for cancellation due to non-use
C. Claim ownership under the Copyright Act
D. Register a new copyright

60. Which of the following legislations governs the protection of Geographical Indications in India?

A. Trademark Act, 1999
B. Geographical Indications of Goods (Registration and Protection) Act, 1999
C. Copyright Act, 1957
D. Patent Act, 1970

61. Which of the following is an example of a Geographical Indication?

A. Nike B. Coca-Cola
C. Darjeeling Tea D. Microsoft

62. Which international agreement provides for the protection of Geographical Indications?

A. Berne Convention B. TRIPS Agreement
C. Madrid Protocol D. Hague Agreement

63. A Geographical Indication is primarily used to identify:

A. The inventor of a product
B. The brand name of a product
C. The origin of goods and their specific qualities
D. The patent holder of a product

64. Geographical Indications can be owned by individuals.

A. True
B. False
C. True, only if registered
D. False, unless granted by the government

65. Geographical Indications can be licensed to third parties for commercial use.

A. True
B. False
C. True, only with government approval
D. False, unless the product is patented

66. **Assertion (A):** Geographical Indications help promote rural development and cultural heritage.

Reason (R): GIs add value to products by associating them with specific regions, traditions, and qualities.

A. Both A and R are true, and R is the correct explanation of A
B. Both A and R are true, but R is not the correct explanation of A
C. A is true, R is false
D. A is false, R is true

67. The term of registration for a Geographical Indication in India is initially valid for ______ years.

A. 5 B. 10
C. 20 D. 25

68. The ______ Agreement under WTO establishes international rules for the protection of Geographical Indications.

A. Berne B. TRIPS
C. Paris D. Madrid

69. Match the following Geographical Indications with their countries of origin:

Geographical Indications	Countries
A. Basmati Rice	1. India
B. Scotch Whisky	2. United Kingdom
C. Parmigiano-Reggiano	3. Italy
D. Pisco	4. Peru

A. A-1, B-2, C-3, D-4
B. A-2, B-1, C-4, D-3
C. A-3, B-4, C-1, D-2
D. A-4, B-3, C-2, D-1

70. Arrange the following international agreements in chronological order based on their adoption related to IP and GIs:

1. Paris Convention
2. Lisbon Agreement
3. TRIPS Agreement
4. Madrid Protocol

A. 1, 2, 4, 3 B. 2, 1, 4, 3
C. 1, 2, 3, 4 D. 4, 1, 2, 3

71. Scenario: A winery in France wants to ensure that only sparkling wine produced in the Champagne region can be labeled as "Champagne." What type of IP protection should it seek?

A. Trademark
B. Copyright
C. Geographical Indication
D. Patent

72. Scenario: An Indian tea company labels its product as "Darjeeling Tea," although the tea is grown in Assam. What legal action can be taken?

A. Trademark infringement
B. Passing-off suit
C. GI infringement action
D. Copyright claim

73. Scenario: A foreign company is using the term "Basmati" for rice grown outside South Asia. Can legal action be taken under international law?
A. Yes, under the Berne Convention
B. No, because GIs are not protected internationally
C. Yes, under the TRIPS Agreement
D. Only if the company is based in India

74. Which of the following international agreements is primarily concerned with the conservation of biodiversity?
A. Kyoto Protocol
B. Convention on Biological Diversity (CBD)
C. Montreal Protocol
D. TRIPS Agreement

75. Which of the following is NOT considered a component of biodiversity?
A. Genetic diversity
B. Species diversity
C. Ecosystem diversity
D. Technological diversity

76. Traditional Knowledge is best described as:
A. Knowledge based on modern scientific research
B. Indigenous knowledge passed through generations
C. Patented scientific innovations
D. Intellectual property owned by corporations

77. In India, which legislation specifically deals with the protection of biodiversity?
A. The Environment Protection Act, 1986
B. The Biological Diversity Act, 2002
C. The Wildlife Protection Act, 1972
D. The Forest Conservation Act, 1980

78. Traditional Knowledge can be protected under the intellectual property system.
A. True
B. False
C. True, only if patented
D. False, unless it is registered

79. The Nagoya Protocol deals with the access to genetic resources and fair benefit-sharing.
A. True
B. False
C. True, only for plant-based resources
D. False, unless it relates to marine biodiversity

80. **Assertion (A):** Traditional Knowledge is often vulnerable to biopiracy.

Reason (R): TK is typically undocumented, making it susceptible to unauthorized exploitation.
A. Both A and R are true, and R is the correct explanation of A
B. Both A and R are true, but R is not the correct explanation of A
C. A is true, R is false
D. A is false, R is true

81. The _______ Protocol under the CBD focuses on access to genetic resources and equitable benefit-sharing.
A. Cartagena B. Nagoya
C. Kyoto D. Montreal

82. The Indian government maintains a ______ to document Traditional Knowledge and prevent biopiracy.
A. Patent Office
B. Traditional Knowledge Digital Library (TKDL)
C. Intellectual Property Board
D. Environmental Registry

83. Match the following biodiversity-related international agreements with their focus areas:

A. Convention on Biological Diversity (CBD)	1. Conservation of biodiversity
B. Nagoya Protocol	2. Access to genetic resources and benefit-sharing
C. Cartagena Protocol	3. Biosafety related to GMOs
D. CITES	4. Trade in endangered species

A. A-1, B-2, C-3, D-4
B. A-2, B-1, C-4, D-3
C. A-3, B-4, C-1, D-2
D. A-4, B-3, C-2, D-1

84. Arrange the following international environmental agreements in chronological order of their adoption:
1. Convention on Biological Diversity (CBD)
2. Nagoya Protocol
3. Cartagena Protocol
4. Kyoto Protocol
A. 1, 4, 3, 2 B. 4, 1, 3, 2
C. 1, 3, 4, 2 D. 4, 3, 1, 2

85. Scenario: A pharmaceutical company develops a new drug using plant extracts traditionally used by an indigenous community. The company patents the drug without compensating the community. What is this practice called?
A. Bioprospecting
B. Biopiracy
C. Biodiversity conservation
D. Genetic engineering

86. Scenario: A community in the Amazon rainforest has unique knowledge of medicinal plants. How can this knowledge be protected under international law?
A. Patent the knowledge
B. Register it under the TRIPS Agreement
C. Protect it under the Convention on Biological Diversity (CBD)
D. Apply for copyright protection

87. Scenario: An Indian traditional remedy is patented in a foreign country without acknowledging its origin. What legal mechanism can India use to challenge this?
A. File a lawsuit under Indian patent law
B. Use the Traditional Knowledge Digital Library (TKDL) to contest the patent
C. Apply for copyright protection
D. Register the remedy as a trademark

88. Which Indian legislation governs digital signatures and electronic records?
A. Indian Evidence Act, 1872
B. Information Technology Act, 2000
C. Companies Act, 2013
D. Contract Act, 1872

89. A digital signature is created using which of the following techniques?
A. Biometric scanning
B. Encryption algorithms
C. Simple passwords
D. OTP verification

90. Which section of the IT Act, 2000 provides legal recognition to electronic records?
A. Section 4 B. Section 10
C. Section 66 D. Section 72

91. Which of the following is NOT a duty of a subscriber under the IT Act, 2000?
A. To generate a public key
B. To exercise reasonable care to retain control of the private key
C. To immediately inform the certifying authority if the private key is compromised
D. To sell their private key to third parties

92. A digital signature and an electronic signature are the same.
A. True
B. False
C. True, but only for government documents
D. False, unless both are issued by the government

93. Electronic records are admissible as evidence in Indian courts under the Indian Evidence Act.
A. True
B. False
C. True, only if notarized
D. False, unless printed

94. **Assertion (A):** Digital signatures ensure data integrity and authenticity.

Reason (R): Digital signatures are created using symmetric encryption.
A. Both A and R are true, and R is the correct explanation of A
B. Both A and R are true, but R is not the correct explanation of A
C. A is true, R is false
D. A is false, R is true

95. **Assertion (A):** Electronic governance allows for faster public service delivery.

Reason (R): E-Governance eliminates the need for any physical documentation.
A. Both A and R are true, and R is the correct explanation of A
B. Both A and R are true, but R is not the correct explanation of A
C. A is true, R is false
D. A is false, R is true

96. A _______ is an electronic record used to establish the identity of the holder of a digital signature certificate.
A. Public key
B. Private key
C. Digital signature certificate
D. Encryption algorithm

97. The IT Act, 2000 provides legal recognition to electronic governance under Section _______.
A. Section 4 B. Section 6
C. Section 10A D. Section 66

98. Match the following types of electronic signatures with their descriptions:

A. Digital Signature	1. Uses encryption and cryptographic keys
B. Biometric Signature	2. Uses fingerprint or iris scans
C. OTP-based Signature	3. Verified through a one-time password
D. Handwritten Signature on a Digital Pad	4. Captured electronically but replicates manual signatures

A. A-1, B-2, C-3, D-4
B. A-2, B-1, C-4, D-3
C. A-3, B-4, C-1, D-2
D. A-4, B-3, C-2, D-1

99. Arrange the following steps for the issuance of a Digital Signature Certificate in the correct order:
1. Submission of application to the certifying authority
2. Verification of identity and credentials
3. Generation of public and private key pair
4. Issuance of the Digital Signature Certificate

A. 1, 2, 3, 4
B. 3, 1, 2, 4
C. 2, 1, 4, 3
D. 1, 3, 2, 4

100. Scenario: A company wants to sign digital contracts with its clients securely. Which technology should they adopt to ensure authenticity and non-repudiation?
A. Scanned handwritten signatures
B. Simple passwords
C. Digital signatures with encryption
D. Watermarked documents

ANSWERS

1. (B): Intellectual Property refers to creations of the mind, such as inventions, artistic works, designs, symbols, and names.

2. (C): Real estate is a form of tangible property, while IP refers to intangible creations.

3. (C): WIPO is a specialized UN agency responsible for promoting and protecting intellectual property worldwide.

4. (C): A patent protects inventions that are novel, involve an inventive step, and have industrial applicability.

5. (A): Copyright protects the expression of ideas in tangible forms, not the ideas themselves.

6. (B): Trademarks can include sounds, colors, shapes, and even smells in some jurisdictions.

7. (A): IPR provides exclusive rights, giving creators the incentive to innovate and create more.

8. (D): Copyright protection lasts for a limited period (usually the author's lifetime + 60 years in many jurisdictions).

9. (C): Copyright protects original works of literature, music, films, art, software, etc.

10. (A): The TRIPS Agreement (Trade-Related Aspects of Intellectual Property Rights) is a WTO agreement that sets minimum IP standards.

11. (A): Patent: Inventions and innovations (1)

Trademark: Brand names and logos (2)

Copyright: Original literary, artistic, and musical works (3)

Trade Secret: Confidential business information (4)

12. (C): Paris Convention: 1883

Berne Convention: 1886

TRIPS Agreement: 1995

Madrid Protocol: 1996

13. (C): Patents protect technological inventions and provide exclusive rights for a specified period.

14. (C): Copyright protects original literary works like novels, ensuring the author's exclusive rights.

15. (B): Trade secrets protect confidential business information like formulas, processes, or strategies.

16. (C): Marxist theory generally opposes private property concepts, including IP. It's not a recognized theory of IP like the others.

17. (A): John Locke's labor theory of property forms the basis of the Natural Rights Theory, linking ownership to the labor invested in creation.

18. (B): The Utilitarian Theory justifies IP rights as a means to encourage innovation and maximize societal benefits.

19. (A): Hegel's Personality Theory suggests that creations are an extension of an individual's personality, deserving protection.

20. (B): Utilitarian Theory supports limited duration for IP rights to balance innovation incentives with public access.

21. (A): The Natural Rights Theory holds that ownership arises from personal labor and effort invested in creation.

22. (C): While exclusive rights are provided, the primary goal is to benefit society through innovation, not personal economic dominance.

23. (D): The Personality Theory focuses on the personal connection to creations, not just their economic value.

24. (B): Locke's theory states that by mixing labor with resources, individuals gain property rights over their creations.

25. (C): The Utilitarian Theory promotes incentives as a way to encourage innovation and benefit society.

26. (A): Natural Rights Theory: Ownership derived from labor (1)

Utilitarian Theory: Promoting societal welfare through innovation (2)

Personality Theory: Extension of individual's personality (3)

Social Planning Theory: Facilitating democratic culture and access (4)

27. (B): John Locke (1632–1704)

Jeremy Bentham (1748–1832)

Immanuel Kant (1724–1804)

Georg Wilhelm Friedrich Hegel (1770–1831)

28. (C): The Utilitarian Theory justifies IP as an incentive to promote societal progress through innovation.

29. (B): The Personality Theory views creations as an extension of the creator's self, deserving protection.

30. (B): The Natural Rights Theory (based on Locke's labor theory) justifies ownership through labor and effort invested.

31. (B): The Paris Convention for the Protection of Industrial Property was signed in 1883, making it the oldest international IP treaty.

32. (C): The Berne Convention (1886) focuses on the protection of literary and artistic works globally.

33. (B): The TRIPS Agreement (1995) establishes minimum IP protection standards for all WTO members.

34. (A): WIPO was established in 1967 as a specialized agency of the United Nations to promote IP protection worldwide.

35. (B): The TRIPS Agreement covers patents, trademarks, copyrights, industrial designs, trade secrets, and geographical indications.

36. (A): The Madrid Protocol allows businesses to register trademarks internationally through a single application.

37. (D): Under the Berne Convention, copyright protection is automatic and does not require registration.

38. (D): TRIPS sets minimum standards for IP protection, but countries can adopt stricter laws if they prefer.

39. (C): The World Intellectual Property Organization (WIPO) administers the Berne Convention.

40. (B): The Hague Agreement facilitates the international registration of industrial designs.

41. (A): A-1, B-2, C-3, D-4

42. (C): The Madrid Protocol allows for the international registration of trademarks through a single application.

43. (C): The Berne Convention provides automatic copyright protection for literary and artistic works in member countries.

44. (B): The TRIPS Agreement incorporates key provisions of the Berne Convention, making them binding on WTO members.

45. (C): The Trademarks Act, 1999 governs registration, protection, and remedies related to trademarks in India.

46. (D): Trademarks can include words, logos, sounds, colors, shapes, etc., as long as they distinguish goods or services.

47. (B): The ® symbol is used for registered trademarks. Unregistered trademarks use the ™ symbol.

48. (C): A unique and distinctive design is generally eligible for registration, while generic or descriptive terms are not.

49. (D): In India, trademark protection lasts for 10 years but can be renewed indefinitely every 10 years.

50. (B): Passing off protects the goodwill of unregistered trademarks. It's a common law remedy.

51. (D): Generic terms cannot be registered as they do not distinguish the source of goods or services.

52. (D): Trademark infringement can occur even with similar marks if they cause consumer confusion.

53. (C): A distinctive trademark helps in identifying the source of goods and differentiating them from competitors.

54. (B): Trademark applications are filed with the Trademark Registry, which operates under the Controller General of Patents, Designs, and Trademarks.

55. (A): A-1, B-2, C-3, D-4

56. (A): The correct process is: Application → Examination → Publication → Registration.

57. (B): Since the trademark is registered, the original brand can sue for infringement.

58. (C): Passing off protects the goodwill of unregistered trademarks.

59. (B): A trademark can be cancelled if it has been unused for five consecutive years.

60. (B): The Geographical Indications of Goods (Registration and Protection) Act, 1999 provides legal protection for GIs in India.

61. (C): Darjeeling Tea is a well-known GI that signifies tea produced in the Darjeeling region of India.

62. (B): The TRIPS Agreement (1995) under the WTO provides the framework for the protection of GIs globally.

63. (C): A GI identifies goods as originating from a specific geographical region, with qualities or characteristics linked to that region.

64. (B): GIs are typically owned by groups, associations, or organizations, not individuals.

65. (A): GIs can be licensed to producers within the designated geographical area, ensuring quality standards are maintained.

66. (A): GIs promote rural development by adding economic value through regional branding and preserving cultural heritage.

67. (B): A GI registration in India is valid for 10 years and can be renewed indefinitely.

68. (B): The TRIPS Agreement (1995) sets minimum standards for the protection of GIs among WTO members.

69. (A): Correct match is:

- **Basmati Rice:** A GI product from India, grown in specific regions like Punjab and Haryana, protected under India's Geographical Indications of Goods Act, 1999, for its unique aroma and grain quality.
- **Scotch Whisky:** A GI spirit from the United Kingdom, produced in Scotland under strict regulations, protected under UK and EU GI laws.
- **Parmigiano-Reggiano:** A GI hard cheese from Italy, originating in regions like Parma and Reggio Emilia, protected under EU's Protected Designation of Origin (PDO) system.
- **Pisco:** A GI grape brandy from Peru, produced in designated coastal regions, protected under Peruvian and international GI regulations.

Hence, correct option is A-1, B-2, C-3, D-4.

70. (C)

71. (C): The protection sought is for origin-based identification, which falls under Geographical Indications.

72. (C): This is a case of GI infringement because Darjeeling Tea is a registered GI for tea grown in the Darjeeling region.

73. (C): The TRIPS Agreement provides for the international protection of GIs, including Basmati.

74. (B): The CBD (1992) focuses on the conservation of biodiversity, sustainable use, and fair benefit-sharing of genetic resources.

75. (D): Biodiversity refers to genetic, species, and ecosystem diversity, not technological diversity.

76. (B): Traditional Knowledge (TK) includes practices, skills, and knowledge developed by indigenous communities over generations.

77. (B): The Biological Diversity Act, 2002 aims to conserve biodiversity, regulate access to genetic resources, and ensure fair benefit-sharing.

78. (A): TK can be protected under IP systems such as patents, copyrights, trademarks, or through sui generis systems.

79. (A): The Nagoya Protocol (2010) under the CBD focuses on Access and Benefit-Sharing (ABS) of genetic resources.

80. (A): TK is often orally transmitted, making it vulnerable to biopiracy due to lack of formal documentation.

81. (B): The Nagoya Protocol (2010) deals with Access and Benefit-Sharing (ABS) related to genetic resources.

82. (B): The TKDL is an initiative to document traditional knowledge and prevent its misappropriation.

83. (A): A-1, B-2, C-3, D-4

84. (A): CBD: 1992, Kyoto Protocol: 1997, Cartagena Protocol: 2000, Nagoya Protocol: 2010

85. (B): Biopiracy refers to the unauthorized commercial use of biological resources or traditional knowledge without fair compensation.

86. (C): The CBD provides a framework for protecting Traditional Knowledge and ensuring benefit-sharing.

87. (B): The TKDL helps prevent biopiracy by providing documented evidence to challenge wrongful patents globally.

88. (B): The Information Technology (IT) Act, 2000 governs digital signatures, electronic records, and cyber laws in India.

89. (B): Digital signatures rely on asymmetric encryption using a private key for signing and a public key for verification.

90. (A): Section 4 of the IT Act, 2000 provides legal recognition to electronic records as valid documents.

91. (D): Subscribers are prohibited from sharing or selling private keys, as this could compromise security.

92. (B): A digital signature is a type of electronic signature that uses encryption, but electronic signatures also include biometrics, OTPs, etc.

93. (A): Electronic records are admissible under Section 65B of the Indian Evidence Act, 1872, after the IT Act amendments.

94. (C): While digital signatures ensure integrity and authenticity, they use asymmetric encryption, not symmetric.

95. (C): While e-governance speeds up service delivery, some processes may still require physical documents.

96. (C): A Digital Signature Certificate (DSC) verifies the identity of the holder and is issued by a certifying authority.

97. (B): Section 6 of the IT Act, 2000 deals with legal recognition of e-governance and electronic records for government functions.

98. (A): A-1, B-2, C-3, D-4

99. (A): The process involves application → verification → key generation → certificate issuance.

100. (C): Digital signatures provide secure authentication and non-repudiation for digital contracts.

UNIT 10 Comparative Public Law and Systems of Governance

FORMS OF GOVERNMENTS : PRESIDENTIAL AND PARLIAMENTARY, UNITARY AND FEDERAL

PRESIDENTIAL AND PARLIAMENTARY SYSTEMS

These systems are based on the relationship between the executive and the legislature.

a. Presidential System:

- **Definition:** In this system, the executive is independent of the legislature and is not accountable to it.
- **Features:**
  - ❑ Separation of Powers: The executive, legislature, and judiciary operate independently.
  - ❑ Fixed Tenure: The President serves for a specific term and cannot be easily removed by the legislature.
  - ❑ Single Executive: The President is both the Head of State and the Head of Government.
  - ❑ Examples: United States, Brazil.

b. Parliamentary System:

- **Definition:** The executive is derived from the legislature and is accountable to it.
- **Features:**
  - ❑ Fusion of Powers: The executive is a part of the legislature.
  - ❑ Collective Responsibility: The Council of Ministers is collectively responsible to the legislature.
  - ❑ Dual Executive: There is a distinction between the Head of State (President/Monarch) and the Head of Government (Prime Minister).
  - ❑ Examples: United Kingdom, India.

Key Differences:

Aspect	Presidential System	Parliamentary System
Executive-Legislature Relationship	Separate	Interdependent
Tenure	Fixed	Variable
Head of Government	President	Prime Minister

UNITARY AND FEDERAL SYSTEMS

These systems are based on the distribution of power between the central and regional governments.

a. Unitary System:

- **Definition:** A system where all powers are concentrated in the central government. Regional governments, if any, function under its control.
- **Features:**
  - ❑ Centralized Authority: The central government has supreme power.
  - ❑ Uniformity: Laws and policies are uniform across the country.
  - ❑ Flexibility: The central government can modify or abolish regional bodies.
  - ❑ Examples: United Kingdom, France.

b. Federal System:

- **Definition:** A system where power is divided between the central and regional governments, each functioning independently within their spheres.

- **Features:**
  - Division of Powers: Powers are constitutionally divided (e.g., Union, State, and Concurrent Lists in India).
  - Supremacy of the Constitution: The constitution is the supreme law governing the relationship between levels of government.
  - Rigid Constitution: Amendments often require the consent of both central and regional governments.
  - Examples: United States, India, Australia.

Key Differences:

Aspect	Unitary System	Federal System
Power Distribution	Centralized	Decentralized
Autonomy of Regions	Limited	Significant
Constitution	Flexible	Rigid

Models of Federalism: USA, Canada, and India

Federalism is a system of governance where powers are divided between a central authority and regional units, both functioning independently within their spheres. The models of federalism in the USA, Canada, and India represent variations based on historical, political, and social contexts.

USA: Dual Federalism

Overview:

- The USA follows the model of "dual federalism," often described as a "layer cake federalism," where the central and state governments function in distinct spheres.

Features:

- Division of Powers: Powers are divided by the Constitution (e.g., enumerated powers for the federal government and reserved powers for states).
- Supremacy Clause: The federal government is supreme within its constitutional sphere (Article VI, Clause 2).
- Independent Judiciary: The U.S. Supreme Court acts as the final arbiter in federal disputes.
- Amendments and Flexibility: Amendments to the Constitution require substantial consensus among states.

Advantages:

- Ensures state autonomy.
- Clear separation of powers.

Examples:

- Defense and foreign affairs are federal responsibilities.
- Education and local law enforcement are state responsibilities.

Canada: Quasi-Federalism

Overview:

- Canada's federalism is often referred to as "quasi-federal" due to the dominant role of the central government in certain areas.

Features:

- Division of Powers: The Constitution Act, 1867 (formerly the British North America Act) divides powers into federal, provincial, and concurrent lists.
- Centralized Federalism: The federal government has significant residual powers and can override provincial laws through the "declaratory power" or "disallowance power."
- Asymmetrical Federalism: Provinces like Quebec have unique powers (e.g., cultural and language preservation).
- Judiciary: The Supreme Court of Canada resolves federal-provincial disputes.

Advantages:

- Allows flexibility to address regional needs.
- Preserves cultural diversity, especially in Quebec.

Examples:

- Federal government controls national defense and trade.
- Provinces handle education, healthcare, and natural resources.

India: Cooperative Federalism

Overview:

- India follows a unique model of "cooperative federalism" with a strong central government but constitutional provisions for state autonomy.

Features:

- Division of Powers: The Constitution of India (Seventh Schedule) provides three lists: Union, State, and Concurrent.
- Strong Centre: In emergencies (Articles 352, 356, 360), the central government can override state powers.

- Single Constitution: Unlike the USA, India has a single constitution applicable to both central and state governments.
- Judiciary: The Supreme Court is the guardian of the Constitution and resolves federal disputes.

Advantages:

- Balances unity with diversity.
- Adaptable to regional differences.

Examples:

- Union List: Defense, foreign affairs, atomic energy.
- State List: Police, agriculture, public health.
- Concurrent List: Education, forests, marriage laws.

Comparison Table: USA, Canada, and India

Aspect	USA	Canada	India
Nature of Federalism	Dual Federalism	Quasi-Federalism	Cooperative Federalism
Division of Powers	Clear and rigid	Central dominance	Strong central bias
Residual Powers	States	Federal Government	Union Government
Asymmetry	No	Yes (e.g., Quebec)	Yes (e.g., J&K, NE states)
Emergency Powers	Limited	Central override	Extensive
Judiciary Role	Strong and independent	Strong and centralized	Supreme authority

RULE OF LAW: FORMAL AND SUBSTANTIVE VERSIONS

The Rule of Law is a foundational principle of governance, emphasizing that all individuals and institutions are subject to and accountable under the law. It ensures the supremacy of law over arbitrary power, equality before the law, and legal certainty. The concept has evolved into two broad interpretations: the formal and the substantive versions.

Formal Rule of Law

The formal version focuses on the procedural aspects of the law rather than its content.

Key Features:

- Emphasis on Procedure: Laws must be enacted, administered, and enforced in a transparent and predictable manner.
- Equality Before the Law: Everyone, including government officials, is subject to the law.
- Predictability: Laws should be clear, publicized, and applied consistently.
- Neutrality of Law: The law itself does not need to adhere to moral or ethical standards; its content is irrelevant as long as procedural principles are followed.

Prominent Theorists:

- A.V. Dicey: Highlighted three elements: supremacy of law, equality before the law, and predominance of legal spirit.
- Joseph Raz: Advocated for formal legality, emphasizing clarity, stability, and prospectivity of laws without delving into their morality.

Substantive Rule of Law

The substantive version integrates the moral and ethical dimensions of law, emphasizing justice, human rights, and fairness.

Key Features:

- Moral Content: Laws must not only be procedurally valid but also uphold fundamental values like justice, liberty, and equality.
- Protection of Rights: Laws should promote and protect human rights and freedoms.
- Accountability: Institutions must ensure that laws serve the welfare of society and reflect democratic principles.
- Focus on Outcomes: Evaluates the impact of laws on individuals and communities, aiming for substantive fairness.

Prominent Theorists:

- Lon Fuller: Advocated for the "inner morality of law," stressing that laws must align with moral principles to be just.
- Ronald Dworkin: Emphasized that the rule of law must embody principles of justice and equality, linking legality with morality.

Criticism:

- Lack of consensus on what constitutes "justice" or "moral values."
- Risk of subjective interpretations, leading to potential judicial overreach.

Comparison: Formal vs. Substantive Rule of Law

Aspect	Formal Rule of Law	Substantive Rule of Law
Focus	Procedures and processes	Content, morality, and justice
Nature	Neutral to morality	Inherently linked to ethics and values
Key Objective	Legal certainty and predictability	Justice and protection of rights
Example	Any law passed through proper process	Laws protecting fundamental rights
Criticism	Permits unjust laws if procedurally correct	Subjective and open to interpretation

SEPARATION OF POWERS IN INDIA, UK, USA, AND FRANCE

The principle of separation of powers, formulated by Montesquieu, proposes that the three branches of government—legislative, executive, and judiciary—should be distinct and independent to prevent abuse of power. The application of this principle varies significantly across different countries.

India: Integrated Separation of Powers

India adopts a system of checks and balances with a functional overlap between branches.

Key Features:

- Legislature: Parliament makes laws and oversees the executive.
- Executive: Headed by the President, the executive includes the Prime Minister and Council of Ministers, responsible to the legislature.
- Judiciary: An independent judiciary led by the Supreme Court ensures constitutional governance and judicial review (Article 50 promotes separation between judiciary and executive).

Functional Overlaps:

- The executive is drawn from the legislature (Council of Ministers).
- The judiciary can legislate through judicial pronouncements (e.g., Vishaka Guidelines).
- The legislature can amend the Constitution, impacting judicial interpretations.

Example of Checks and Balances:

- Judicial review curbs legislative and executive excesses.
- Parliamentary impeachment of judges (Article 124).

United Kingdom: Parliamentary Supremacy

The UK follows a flexible system with no strict separation, leaning towards parliamentary sovereignty.

Key Features:

- Legislature: Parliament (House of Commons and House of Lords) is supreme and enacts laws.
- Executive: The Prime Minister and the Cabinet are members of Parliament and accountable to it.
- Judiciary: Independent but subordinate to Parliament (until the establishment of the Supreme Court in 2009, the House of Lords functioned as the highest judicial authority).

Functional Overlaps:

- The executive is part of the legislature.
- Judicial independence is safeguarded, but Parliament can theoretically override judicial decisions through legislation.

Example of Checks and Balances:

- Parliament controls the executive through no-confidence motions.
- Courts ensure administrative accountability through judicial review.

United States: Strict Separation of Powers

The USA practices a strict separation of powers with a strong system of checks and balances.

Key Features:

- Legislature: Congress (Senate and House of Representatives) makes laws and controls the budget.
- Executive: The President is independent of the legislature, serving as both Head of State and Head of Government.
- Judiciary: The Supreme Court and federal judiciary ensure constitutional compliance and conduct judicial review (established in Marbury v. Madison).

Functional Overlaps:

- The President can veto Congressional bills.
- Congress can impeach the President or judges.
- The judiciary can declare laws or executive actions unconstitutional.

Example of Checks and Balances:

- Presidential appointments require Senate approval.
- Judicial review restrains legislative and executive excesses.

France: Rationalized Parliamentary System

France employs a semi-presidential system with elements of both separation and fusion of powers.

Key Features:

- Legislature: Bicameral Parliament (National Assembly and Senate) legislates and oversees the executive.
- Executive: The President (Head of State) and Prime Minister (Head of Government) share powers. The President has significant authority in foreign affairs and emergencies.
- Judiciary: The judiciary is independent, with a separate Constitutional Council for constitutional review.

Functional Overlaps:

- The President can dissolve the National Assembly (Article 12 of the French Constitution).
- Parliament can remove the executive through a motion of censure.

Example of Checks and Balances:

- The Constitutional Council ensures laws adhere to constitutional principles.
- The judiciary remains independent, safeguarding individual rights.

Comparison Table

Aspect	India	UK	USA	France
Nature	Integrated Separation	Parliamentary Supremacy	Strict Separation	Semi-Presidential
Legislature-Executive Relationship	Interdependent	Fusion	Separate	Interdependent
Judicial Review	Yes	Limited	Yes	Limited
Role of Constitution	Supreme	Unwritten	Supreme	Supreme
Head of State	Ceremonial (President)	Ceremonial (Monarch)	Executive (President)	Executive (President)

INDEPENDENCE OF JUDICIARY, JUDICIAL ACTIVISM, AND ACCOUNTABILITY: INDIA, UK, AND USA

The judiciary is a cornerstone of democracy, ensuring justice, safeguarding constitutional values, and maintaining the balance of power. The concepts of independence, judicial activism, and accountability are essential to understanding the judiciary's role in India, the UK, and the USA.

1. Independence of Judiciary

a. India

- **Constitutional Provisions:**
  - Article 50: Separation of judiciary from the executive.
  - Articles 124–147: Ensure independence by governing appointments, tenure, and removal of judges.
- **Security of Tenure:** Judges can only be removed via impeachment (Articles 124 and 217).
- **Judicial Review:** The judiciary can review executive and legislative actions to ensure constitutional compliance.
- **Challenges:** Allegations of political interference in judicial appointments (e.g., through the collegium system) and delayed judicial reforms.

b. United Kingdom

- **Parliamentary Sovereignty:** The judiciary operates independently but is subordinate to Parliament.
- **Judicial Appointments:** Judges are selected by an independent Judicial Appointments Commission.
- **Security of Tenure:** Judges hold office during good behavior, removable only by Parliament.
- **Reforms:** The Constitutional Reform Act, 2005, established the UK Supreme Court, enhancing judicial independence by separating it from the House of Lords.

c. USA

- **Constitutional Safeguards:** Article III of the U.S. Constitution ensures judicial independence.
- **Appointments:** Judges are nominated by the President and confirmed by the Senate.
- **Lifetime Tenure:** Federal judges serve during "good behavior" to protect them from political pressures.
- **Judicial Review:** Established in Marbury v. Madison, 1803, enabling the judiciary to declare laws unconstitutional.

2. Judicial Activism

a. India

- Definition: Judges actively interpret laws to promote justice and enforce constitutional mandates, often venturing into policymaking.

- **Landmark Cases:**
  - Kesavananda Bharati v. State of Kerala (1973): Basic structure doctrine.
  - Vishaka v. State of Rajasthan (1997): Guidelines on sexual harassment at workplaces.
- **Tools of Activism:** Public Interest Litigation (PIL) has empowered citizens to seek judicial intervention in matters of public concern.
- **Criticism:** Activism sometimes leads to judicial overreach, blurring the lines between the judiciary and legislature.

b. United Kingdom

- **Restraint vs. Activism:** The judiciary traditionally practices restraint due to parliamentary sovereignty but engages in activism in human rights issues (e.g., enforcing the Human Rights Act, 1998).
- **Examples:** The judiciary has challenged executive decisions (e.g., R (Miller) v. Secretary of State for Exiting the European Union).

c. USA

- **Active Role:** The judiciary often interprets the Constitution expansively, reflecting the doctrine of judicial review.
- **Landmark Cases:**
  - Brown v. Board of Education (1954): Declared segregation unconstitutional.
  - Roe v. Wade (1973): Recognized the right to abortion (recently overturned by Dobbs v. Jackson Women's Health Organization, 2022).
- **Judicial Philosophy:** Divided into "judicial activism" and "judicial restraint," reflecting ideological leanings.

3. Judicial Accountability

a. India

- **Mechanisms:**
  - Impeachment: Judges can be removed for misbehavior or incapacity.
  - In-house mechanisms for ethical misconduct.
- **Challenges:** Lack of transparency in the collegium system and limited accountability measures.
- **Recent Reforms:** National Judicial Appointments Commission (NJAC) Act was struck down as unconstitutional, reinforcing the judiciary's control over appointments.

b. United Kingdom

- **Parliamentary Oversight:** Judges are accountable to Parliament in cases of misconduct.
- **Judicial Code of Conduct:** Sets ethical standards for judges.
- **Criticism:** Limited public scrutiny of judicial decisions.

c. USA

- **Impeachment:** Judges can be removed by Congress for "high crimes and misdemeanors."
- **Accountability Tools:**
  - Judicial councils review complaints against judges.
  - Public scrutiny of judicial decisions through dissenting opinions.
- **Challenges:** Lifetime tenure sometimes leads to concerns about accountability and ideological biases.

Comparison Table

Aspect	India	UK	USA
Independence	Constitutional safeguards, collegium system	Parliamentary reforms, Judicial Appointments Commission	Lifetime tenure, Senate confirmation
Judicial Activism	Active (e.g., PILs, basic structure doctrine)	Moderate (human rights focus)	High (expansive interpretation of Constitution)
Accountability	Limited mechanisms, impeachment rare	Parliamentary oversight, Judicial Code of Conduct	Impeachment, judicial councils

SYSTEMS OF CONSTITUTIONAL REVIEW: INDIA, USA, SWITZERLAND, AND FRANCE

Constitutional review refers to the process by which a country's judiciary or other designated bodies ensure that laws, policies, and governmental actions comply with the Constitution. Different countries adopt varying mechanisms for constitutional review based on their legal traditions, political systems, and historical contexts.

1. India: Judicial Review by the Supreme Court and High Courts

System: Decentralized and extensive judicial review.

- **Authority:** The Supreme Court and High Courts are empowered to invalidate laws, executive orders, or actions that contravene the Constitution (Article 13).
- **Scope:**
  - ❑ Both pre-enactment and post-enactment review of legislation.
  - ❑ Judiciary ensures compliance with the basic structure doctrine (Kesavananda Bharati v. State of Kerala, 1973).
- **Mechanism:**
  - ❑ High Courts (under Article 226) and the Supreme Court (under Article 32) exercise writ jurisdiction to safeguard fundamental rights.
  - ❑ Judicial review is integrated into the system, providing a powerful check on legislative and executive actions.

Key Features:

- Constitutionally mandated review (Articles 32, 226, 131, 136).
- Doctrine of Basic Structure limits parliamentary power to amend the Constitution.

Criticism:

- Allegations of judicial overreach in policy matters.
- Delay in judicial proceedings due to the caseload.

2. USA: Judicial Review through the Supreme Court and Federal Courts

System: Decentralized and rigid judicial review.

- **Authority:** Rooted in the landmark case Marbury v. Madison (1803), the Supreme Court has the authority to invalidate laws and executive actions that violate the Constitution.
- **Scope:**
  - ❑ Focuses on post-enactment review of laws.
  - ❑ Ensures compliance with the written Constitution.
- **Mechanism:**
  - ❑ Federal courts review the constitutionality of laws and executive actions through actual cases and controversies.
  - ❑ The Supreme Court acts as the final arbiter of constitutional interpretation.

Key Features:

- Federal structure ensures judicial review at various levels.
- Lifetime tenure for judges promotes independence.

Criticism:

- Accusations of judicial activism based on ideological leanings of the judiciary.
- Limited accessibility due to procedural requirements for standing in court.

3. Switzerland: Popular Referenda and Limited Judicial Review

System: Focus on direct democracy and limited judicial review.

- **Authority:** Federal Tribunal (Supreme Court) has restricted powers of constitutional review.
- **Scope:**
  - ❑ No review of federal legislation for constitutionality due to the principle of popular sovereignty.
  - ❑ Cantonal laws and executive actions are subject to judicial review.
- **Mechanism:**
  - ❑ Constitutional amendments can be initiated through referenda, reducing the role of the judiciary in constitutional interpretation.

Key Features:

- Strong reliance on direct democracy through referenda.
- Laws passed by the people or legislature are presumed constitutional.

Criticism:

- Limited scope for judicial intervention in protecting fundamental rights against federal legislation.
- Public opinion may not always align with constitutional principles.

4. France: Specialized Constitutional Review through the Constitutional Council

System: Centralized and preventive review.

- **Authority:** The Constitutional Council *(Conseil Constitutionnel)* reviews the constitutionality of laws.
- **Scope:**
  - ❑ Pre-enactment review: Conducted before a law is promulgated.
  - ❑ Post-enactment review: Introduced in 2008 (through a Question Prioritaire de Constitutionnalité or QPC), allowing individuals to challenge laws affecting their rights.

- **Mechanism:**
  - Review initiated by political authorities (e.g., President, Prime Minister, parliamentary members) or through QPC.
  - The Council comprises appointed members with limited tenure, ensuring its independence.

Key Features:

- Specialized body separate from the judiciary.
- Strong preventive mechanism to ensure constitutional compliance.

Criticism:

- Limited access for citizens compared to decentralized systems.
- Heavy reliance on political authorities to initiate review.

Comparison Table

Aspect	India	USA	Switzer-land	France
System	Decentralized	Decentral-ized	Limited and indirect	Central-ized
Authority	Supreme Court and High Courts	Supreme Court and Federal Courts	Federal Tribunal	Consti-tutional Council
Scope	Broad (legis-lation, execu-tive actions, amendments)	Broad (legislation, executive actions)	Limited to cantonal laws	Limited (legisla-tion)
Review Timing	Pre- and post-enact-ment	Post-enact-ment	Limited review	Pre-enact-ment and QPC
Key Feature	Basic struc-ture doctrine	Judicial review via case law	Strong direct democracy	Special-ized Council
Criticism	Judicial over-reach	Judicial activism	Limited intervention	Restricted access

AMENDMENT OF THE CONSTITUTION: INDIA, USA, AND SOUTH AFRICA

Amending a constitution reflects the need for adaptability while maintaining its core principles. India, the USA, and South Africa have distinct approaches to constitutional amendments shaped by their legal traditions and governance structures.

1. India

Provision for Amendment:

- Governed by Article 368 of the Constitution.
- The Constitution provides for a flexible and partially rigid amendment process.

Types of Amendments:

- By Simple Majority (outside Article 368): Certain provisions, such as the creation of new states, are amended by a simple majority of Parliament.
- By Special Majority: Most provisions require a two-thirds majority of members present and voting in each House of Parliament, plus a majority of the total membership.
- By Special Majority and Ratification by States: Amendments affecting federal features (e.g., distribution of powers) require ratification by at least half of the state legislatures.

Key Features:

- No time limit for state legislatures to ratify.
- Parliament's power to amend is subject to the Basic Structure Doctrine, established in Kesavananda Bharati v. State of Kerala (1973).
- The judiciary can invalidate amendments that violate the Constitution's basic structure.

Examples:

- **42nd Amendment (1976):** Introduced significant changes, including the term "socialist" in the Preamble.
- **101st Amendment (2016):** Introduced the Goods and Services Tax (GST).

Criticism:

- Alleged misuse of amendment power for political purposes.
- Complexities in achieving consensus for amendments requiring state ratification.

2. United States

Provision for Amendment:

- Article V of the Constitution outlines the amendment process.
- The process is rigid and deliberately complex to ensure stability.

Methods of Amendment:

- Congressional Proposal: Requires a two-thirds majority in both Houses of Congress and ratification by three-fourths (38) of state legislatures.
- Constitutional Convention: Called by two-thirds of state legislatures, with amendments requiring ratification by three-fourths of the states (never used).

Key Features:

- Amendments do not require Presidential assent.
- Amendments must balance federal and state interests, ensuring broad consensus.
- The process is time-bound (e.g., the Equal Rights Amendment failed due to a missed ratification deadline).

Examples:

- 13th Amendment (1865): Abolished slavery.
- 19th Amendment (1920): Granted women the right to vote.

Criticism:

- The process is considered too rigid, leading to a low number of amendments (only 27 in over 230 years).
- Difficulty in addressing contemporary issues like campaign finance reform and gun control.

3. South Africa

Provision for Amendment:

- Governed by Chapter 4, Section 74 of the 1996 Constitution.
- The process is flexible yet provides safeguards for fundamental principles.

Types of Amendments:

- Ordinary Provisions: Require a two-thirds majority in the National Assembly.
- Entrenched Provisions: Require both a two-thirds majority in the National Assembly and support from six of the nine provinces in the National Council of Provinces.
- Foundational Principles (e.g., Bill of Rights): Require a 75% majority in the National Assembly.

Key Features:

- Emphasizes public participation in the amendment process.
- Upholds constitutional values like democracy, human dignity, and equality, which cannot be amended easily.
- The judiciary, especially the Constitutional Court, ensures amendments comply with constitutional principles.

Examples:

- 6th Amendment (2001): Addressed land reform to promote equitable access to land.
- Ongoing debates on amending property rights to allow land expropriation without compensation.

Criticism:

- Challenges in achieving the high thresholds for significant amendments.
- Political debates over land reform and other transformative provisions

Comparison Table

Aspect	India	USA	South Africa
Flexibility	Flexible and partially rigid	Rigid	Flexible yet safeguarded
Authority	Parliament (and states for federal features)	Congress and state legislatures	Parliament and public participation
Judicial Oversight	Yes (Basic Structure Doctrine)	Limited	Yes (Constitutional Court)
Approval Threshold	Varies (simple majority to state ratification)	Two-thirds Congress + 75% states	Two-thirds to 75% majority
Public Participation	Limited	Indirect	Emphasized
Amendment Examples	GST (101st Amendment)	Abolition of slavery (13th)	Land reform debates

OMBUDSMAN: SWEDEN, UK, AND INDIA

An Ombudsman is an independent authority that addresses grievances related to administrative actions and ensures accountability. It acts as a bridge between the public and the administration, promoting transparency and justice.

1. Sweden: The Origin of the Ombudsman

Historical Background:

- Sweden was the first country to introduce the concept of an Ombudsman in 1809 to supervise public administration and protect citizens from maladministration.

Structure and Function:

- Parliamentary Ombudsman: Appointed by Parliament and operates independently.
- **Scope:**
  - ❑ Investigates complaints from citizens regarding public authorities.
  - ❑ Monitors compliance with laws by public officials.
  - ❑ Can initiate investigations *suo motu* (on its own initiative).

- **Powers:**
  - Can recommend disciplinary actions or legal proceedings against public officials.
  - Has the authority to investigate administrative, judicial, and law enforcement agencies.
- **Features:**
  - Focuses on preventing injustice and ensuring accountability.
  - Highly respected and operates with complete autonomy.
- **Strengths:**
  - Comprehensive and independent oversight of public administration.
  - Direct accountability to Parliament ensures transparency.
- **Limitations:**
  - Cannot enforce decisions; can only recommend actions.

2. United Kingdom: Parliamentary and Public Service Ombudsman

Historical Background:

- The UK introduced the Parliamentary Commissioner for Administration (commonly known as the Parliamentary Ombudsman) in 1967, inspired by the Swedish model.

Structure and Function:

- **Parliamentary Ombudsman:**
  - Appointed by the Crown on the recommendation of Parliament.
  - Investigates complaints referred by Members of Parliament (MPs) regarding government departments and agencies.
- Local Government Ombudsman: Handles grievances at the local authority level.
- **Powers:**
  - Can investigate maladministration or failure in service delivery.
  - Issues recommendations for corrective action.
- **Features:**
  - Restricted to complaints referred by MPs (known as the "MP filter").
  - Addresses individual grievances and systemic issues.
- **Strengths:**
  - Provides citizens a mechanism to seek redress for grievances against the government.
  - Reports findings to Parliament, ensuring accountability.
- **Limitations:**
  - Dependence on MPs to refer complaints limits direct access for citizens.
  - Recommendations are advisory and not legally binding.

3. India: Lokpal and Lokayuktas

Historical Background:

- The concept of an Ombudsman was introduced in India with the enactment of the Lokpal and Lokayuktas Act, 2013.

Structure and Function:

- **Lokpal (Central Level):**
  - A multi-member body headed by a Chairperson, with members drawn from judicial and non-judicial backgrounds.
  - Investigates allegations of corruption against public officials, including the Prime Minister, Ministers, and Members of Parliament.
- **Lokayuktas (State Level):**
  - State-level Ombudsman institutions to investigate complaints against state officials.
- **Powers:**
  - Can initiate investigations into allegations of corruption.
  - Authorized to recommend prosecution or disciplinary action.
- **Features:**
  - Lokpal is independent and has the authority to investigate high-level corruption.
  - Investigations are carried out by the Central Bureau of Investigation (CBI) or other designated agencies under Lokpal's supervision.
- **Strengths:**
- Comprehensive anti-corruption mechanism covering both administrative and political corruption.
- Includes provisions for public accountability and whistleblower protection.
- **Limitations:**
  - Delayed implementation and operationalization in many states.
  - Allegations of political interference and inefficiency in Lokayuktas.

Comparison Table

Aspect	Sweden	United Kingdom	India
Introduction	1809 (world's first Ombudsman)	1967 (Parliamentary Ombudsman)	2013 (Lokpal and Lokayuktas Act)
Authority	Parliamentary Ombudsman	Parliamentary Ombudsman	Lokpal (national) and Lokayuktas (state)
Scope	Public administration	Government departments and local authorities	Corruption in public administration and political offices
Independence	Fully independent, reports to Parliament	Reports to Parliament	Independent of executive control
Powers	Investigative and recommendatory	Investigative and recommendatory	Investigative, recommendatory, and prosecutorial
Accessibility	Direct complaints	Complaints via MPs (MP filter)	Direct complaints, including whistleblower reports
Limitations	Recommendations are not enforceable	Limited direct access for citizens	Delays in implementation, political interference

OPEN GOVERNMENT AND RIGHT TO INFORMATION: USA, UK, AND INDIA

Open Government and the Right to Information (RTI) are essential elements in promoting transparency, accountability, and public participation in governance. These principles allow citizens to access government information, ensuring that public authorities act in the public interest and are held accountable for their actions. The concept of Open Government is reinforced through various laws and frameworks across different countries.

1. United States: Freedom of Information Act (FOIA)

Historical Background:

- The Freedom of Information Act (FOIA) was enacted in 1966, establishing the right of citizens to access records held by federal agencies, with certain exceptions.

Key Features:

- **Scope:** FOIA applies to federal executive branch agencies, and individuals can request access to records unless they are classified or protected by specific exemptions (e.g., national security, trade secrets, personal privacy).
- **Process:**
  - ❑ Citizens can request documents from any federal agency, and agencies are required to respond within 20 working days.
  - ❑ FOIA requests must be processed in the order they are received, and agencies must justify the denial of access.
- **Exemptions:** There are nine exemptions under FOIA that allow agencies to withhold certain types of information, such as matters related to national defense, law enforcement, personal privacy, and privileged communications.

Key Features:

- **Transparency:** Ensures transparency in government dealings, fostering public trust in governmental processes.
- **Public Access:** Citizens have the right to request information on a broad range of government activities, including budgets, policies, contracts, and environmental impact assessments.

Strengths:

- Establishes a strong framework for governmental accountability.
- Allows citizens, journalists, and organizations to demand information, contributing to informed public debates.

Criticism:

- Delays in processing requests due to backlogs.
- Broad exemptions can limit access to important information.

2. United Kingdom: Freedom of Information Act (FOIA)

Historical Background:

- The Freedom of Information Act 2000 came into force in 2005, giving the public a general right of access to information held by public authorities.

Key Features:

- **Scope:** The law applies to all public authorities, including government departments, local authorities, NHS bodies, and the police.
- **Process:**
  - ❑ Citizens can make a request for information held by any public authority.
  - ❑ Authorities are required to respond within 20 working days.
- **Exemptions:**
  - ❑ There are several exemptions, including information that would harm national security, law enforcement, or commercial interests.
  - ❑ Public interest tests are applied to balance the need for transparency against the potential harm of disclosure.

Key Features:

- **Public Interest:** The Act requires a balance between the public interest in disclosure and the harm that could result from releasing certain information.
- **Proactive Disclosure:** Public authorities are required to publish certain information regularly, such as annual reports, budget data, and policies.

Strengths:

- Provides wide access to governmental information and data.
- Public interest test allows flexibility in determining whether to release sensitive information.

Criticism:

- Delays and administrative challenges in responding to requests.
- Some key institutions and bodies are not fully covered by the Act.
- Overuse of exemptions, especially on national security grounds, can restrict public access.

3. India: Right to Information Act (RTI)

Historical Background:

- The Right to Information Act (RTI) came into force in 2005, providing a comprehensive framework for citizens to access information from public authorities at the national, state, and local levels. The Act was a significant move towards transparency and accountability in India.

Key Features:

- **Scope:**
  - ❑ Covers all government bodies, including the executive, legislature, judiciary, and public sector enterprises.
  - ❑ Citizens can request information from public authorities related to their work, records, and actions.
- **Process:**
  - ❑ Citizens can submit a request to the Public Information Officer (PIO) of a government body, which must be answered within 30 days.
- **Exemptions:**
  - ❑ Certain types of information, such as national security, personal privacy, and commercial confidentiality, are exempt from disclosure.
  - ❑ Information that could impede an ongoing investigation or prosecution can be withheld.

Key Features:

- Empowerment: Empowers ordinary citizens by providing them a tool to hold public officials accountable.
- Transparency: Provides access to government processes, decisions, and records, thereby ensuring transparency in governance.
- Decentralized Mechanism: Information is provided by the respective public authorities, and if denied, can be appealed to higher authorities or the Central/State Information Commissions.

Strengths:

- The RTI Act has been instrumental in fighting corruption and improving the responsiveness of public authorities.
- The establishment of Information Commissions ensures a process for appeal and grievance redressal.

Criticism:

- Bureaucratic delays and a lack of sufficient capacity to handle a large volume of RTI requests.
- Concerns over the safety of RTI activists and whistleblowers.
- Exemptions have been used to limit access to information on sensitive matters.

Comparison Table

Aspect	USA - FOIA	UK - FOIA	India - RTI
Enacted	1966	2005	2005
Scope	Federal government agencies	Public authorities, including local government, NHS, police	Government bodies at all levels (national, state, local)
Key Features	Public can request information from federal agencies	Public can request information from any public authority	Public can request information from any public authority
Exemptions	National security, law enforcement, privacy, trade secrets	National security, law enforcement, personal privacy, commercial interests	National security, personal privacy, commercial interests
Process	Requests processed within 20 days; exemptions can delay	Requests processed within 20 days; public interest test	Requests processed within 30 days; exemptions can delay
Public Interest Test	Limited; focus on disclosure vs. harm	Yes; balancing public interest against harm	Limited; focus on transparency in governance
Strengths	Promotes transparency, accountability	Facilitates access to government data	Empowers citizens, fights corruption
Criticism	Delays, exemptions limit access	Delays, exemptions, limited coverage	Delays, safety concerns, bureaucratic challenges

MULTIPLE CHOICE QUESTIONS

1. Which of the following is a key feature of a Presidential system of government?
A. Collective responsibility of the cabinet
B. Separation of powers between the executive and legislature
C. Prime Minister as the head of the government
D. Fusion of executive and legislative powers

2. In a parliamentary system of government, the head of the state is usually:
A. Directly elected by the people
B. The leader of the majority party in the legislature
C. Ceremonial with limited powers
D. Both the head of state and government

3. Which of the following countries follows a federal system of government?
A. United Kingdom
B. France
C. United States of America
D. China

4. A unitary system of government is characterized by:
A. Dual citizenship
B. Division of powers between the center and states
C. Centralized authority with limited regional autonomy
D. Sovereignty shared equally between national and sub-national units

5. In a Presidential system, the President cannot be removed before the end of their term.
A. True
B. False
C. True, unless through general elections
D. False, as impeachment is possible

6. A federal government is always more democratic than a unitary government.
A. True
B. False
C. True, only in developed countries
D. False, unless there's a constitutional guarantee

7. Assertion (A): In a parliamentary system, the executive is accountable to the legislature.

Reason (R): The executive and legislature are completely independent in a parliamentary system.
A. Both A and R are true, and R is the correct explanation of A
B. Both A and R are true, but R is not the correct explanation of A
C. A is true, R is false
D. A is false, R is true

8. Assertion (A): In a unitary system, all powers are centralized in the national government.

Reason (R): The constitution of a unitary state divides power equally between the central and regional governments.

A. Both A and R are true, and R is the correct explanation of A
B. Both A and R are true, but R is not the correct explanation of A
C. A is true, R is false
D. A is false, R is true

9. The United Kingdom is an example of a ______ system of government.

A. Federal B. Presidential
C. Unitary D. Confederation

10. The principle of 'separation of powers' is most strongly associated with the ______ system.

A. Parliamentary B. Federal
C. Presidential D. Unitary

11. Match the following countries with their forms of government:

Countries	Forms of Government
A. USA	1. Presidential and Federal
B. India	2. Parliamentary and Federal
C. France	3. Semi-Presidential and Unitary
D. China	4. Unitary and Single-Party

A. A-1, B-2, C-3, D-4
B. A-2, B-1, C-4, D-3
C. A-3, B-4, C-2, D-1
D. A-4, B-3, C-1, D-2

12. Arrange the following forms of government in terms of increasing centralization of power:

1. Federal
2. Unitary
3. Confederation
4. Semi-Federal

A. 3, 4, 1, 2 B. 2, 1, 4, 3
C. 3, 1, 4, 2 D. 1, 2, 3, 4

13. Scenario: In a country, the President is both the head of state and head of government. The President is not a member of the legislature and cannot be removed by a no-confidence motion. What system does this describe?

A. Parliamentary B. Presidential
C. Semi-Presidential D. Federal

14. Scenario: A country has two levels of government, each having its own constitutionally defined powers. The central government cannot unilaterally alter the powers of the states. What system does this describe?

A. Unitary B. Federal
C. Parliamentary D. Presidential

15. Scenario: In a country, the Prime Minister is the leader of the majority party in Parliament and can be removed from office through a vote of no confidence. What type of government is this?

A. Presidential B. Unitary
C. Federal D. Parliamentary

16. Which of the following is a feature of the Indian federal system?

A. Dual citizenship
B. Independent judiciary
C. Equal powers for the center and states
D. No written constitution

17. The 'Westminster model' refers to:

A. A type of federal government
B. A system where the head of government is directly elected
C. A parliamentary system of government
D. A model of judicial independence

18. Match the following features with the appropriate system:

Features	Systems
A. No-confidence motion	1. Parliamentary
B. Fixed term for the executive	2. Presidential
C. Single constitution for the entire country	3. Unitary
D. Dual system of government	4. Federal

A. A-1, B-2, C-3, D-4
B. A-2, B-1, C-4, D-3
C. A-3, B-4, C-1, D-2
D. A-4, B-3, C-2, D-1

19. Scenario: A country allows the central government to dissolve the regional governments at will. What type of system does this indicate?

A. Federal B. Unitary
C. Parliamentary D. Presidential

20. Scenario: A country has both a President and a Prime Minister. The President handles foreign affairs, while the Prime Minister manages domestic policy. This system is known as:

A. Presidential
B. Parliamentary
C. Semi-Presidential
D. Unitary

21. Which of the following countries follows a "dual federalism" model, also known as the "layer cake" federalism?

A. Canada B. India
C. USA D. Australia

22. In India, federalism is described as:
A. Dual federalism
B. Confederal system
C. Cooperative federalism with a unitary bias
D. Loose federation

23. Which of the following features is unique to Canadian federalism?
A. Strong central government with residuary powers to the center
B. Dual citizenship
C. Asymmetrical federalism with special status for Quebec
D. Complete independence of provincial governments

24. Which constitutional amendment in the USA significantly affected the distribution of powers between the federal and state governments?
A. First Amendment
B. Tenth Amendment
C. Fourteenth Amendment
D. Nineteenth Amendment

25. In the Indian model of federalism, the residuary powers lie with the states.
A. True
B. False
C. True, but only in financial matters
D. False, unless amended by Parliament

26. The USA Constitution explicitly mentions the term 'federalism'.
A. True
B. False
C. True, in Article I
D. False, but implied through the Bill of Rights

27. **Assertion (A):** In Canada, provinces have exclusive powers over matters listed in the Constitution Act, 1867.

Reason (R): Canadian federalism provides equal autonomy to all provinces.
A. Both A and R are true, and R is the correct explanation of A
B. Both A and R are true, but R is not the correct explanation of A
C. A is true, R is false
D. A is false, R is true

28. **Assertion (A):** India's federal structure allows for the creation of new states without the consent of the existing state legislature.

Reason (R): The Indian Constitution provides flexibility to the Union to reorganize states for administrative convenience.
A. Both A and R are true, and R is the correct explanation of A
B. Both A and R are true, but R is not the correct explanation of A
C. A is true, R is false
D. A is false, R is true

29. The division of powers between the Union and the States in India is based on the ______.
A. Federal Supremacy Clause
B. Three-list system (Union, State, Concurrent Lists)
C. Tenth Amendment
D. Article 50 of the Constitution

30. In the USA, the powers not delegated to the federal government are reserved to the ______.
A. President
B. Congress
C. States or the people
D. Supreme Court

31. Match the following countries with their key features of federalism:

Countries	Key Features
A. USA	1. Strong dual federalism with clear separation of powers
B. Canada	2. Asymmetrical federalism with special status for Quebec
C. India	3. Quasi-federal with unitary bias

A. A-1, B-2, C-3　　B. A-2, B-1, C-3
C. A-3, B-1, C-2　　D. A-1, B-3, C-2

32. Arrange the following constitutions in the order of their adoption:
1. USA Constitution
2. Indian Constitution
3. Canadian Constitution Act

A. 1, 3, 2　　B. 3, 1, 2
C. 2, 1, 3　　D. 1, 2, 3

33. Scenario: In a country, the federal government cannot interfere in matters exclusively reserved for state legislatures. States have significant autonomy, and residuary powers rest with them. Which country's model does this describe?
A. India　　B. USA
C. Canada　　D. France

34. Scenario: A central government has the power to reorganize state boundaries without the consent of the concerned state legislature. Which federal model does this feature belong to?
A. USA　　B. Canada
C. India　　D. Germany

35. Scenario: In a federal system, one province has powers that other provinces do not possess, such as language autonomy and distinct immigration policies. Which model does this describe?

A. USA
B. India
C. Canada
D. Switzerland

36. Which of the following principles is more prominent in the USA than in India?

A. Strong central government
B. Judicial review
C. Dual citizenship
D. Equal division of residuary powers

37. In Canada, the federal government has the power to disallow provincial legislation through:

A. Veto power of the Prime Minister
B. Disallowance power under the Constitution Act, 1867
C. Judicial review
D. Presidential decree

38. Match the following constitutional provisions with the respective countries:

Constitutional Provisions	Countries
A. Article 44 (Uniform Civil Code)	1. India
B. Section 51 (Division of Powers)	2. Australia
C. Article 9 (Freedom of Religion)	3. Japan
D. Article 21 (Right to Life and Liberty)	4. South Africa

A. A-1, B-3, C-4, D-2
B. A-2, B-1, C-3, D-4
C. A-4, B-3, C-1, D-2
D. A-3, B-2, C-4, D-1

39. Scenario: A country has a Supreme Court that resolves disputes between the federal and state governments, ensuring constitutional supremacy. Which countries follow this model?

A. USA and India
B. Canada and China
C. UK and Canada
D. France and Russia

40. Scenario: A federal government retains residuary powers, and there's a strong central influence over the states, even though the system is called 'federal'. This describes the model of:

A. USA
B. India
C. Canada
D. Switzerland

41. The concept of the 'Rule of Law' was popularized by:

A. John Locke
B. A.V. Dicey
C. Montesquieu
D. Jeremy Bentham

42. Which of the following is a key feature of the 'formal' version of the Rule of Law?

A. Protection of fundamental rights
B. Focus on legal procedures and processes
C. Emphasis on justice and equality
D. Promotion of social welfare

43. The 'substantive' version of the Rule of Law includes:

A. Only the requirement of clear laws
B. Emphasis on moral values and justice
C. Focus on bureaucratic efficiency
D. Strict adherence to technical legal norms

44. Which of the following principles is NOT associated with the Rule of Law?

A. Equality before the law
B. Arbitrary exercise of power
C. Supremacy of the law
D. Accountability of government officials

45. The formal version of the Rule of Law requires that all laws must be morally just.

A. True
B. False
C. True, if approved by the judiciary
D. False, unless specified in the constitution

46. The substantive version of the Rule of Law includes both procedural fairness and the protection of fundamental rights.

A. True
B. False
C. True, but only in democratic countries
D. False, unless supported by international treaties

47. **Assertion (A):** The Rule of Law ensures that no one is above the law.

Reason (R): This principle applies only to common citizens and not government officials.

A. Both A and R are true, and R is the correct explanation of A
B. Both A and R are true, but R is not the correct explanation of A
C. A is true, R is false
D. A is false, R is true

48. The principle of ______ ensures that government powers are exercised according to laws and not arbitrary decisions.
A. Rule of Law
B. Rule of Majority
C. Judicial Activism
D. Parliamentary Sovereignty

49. A.V. Dicey identified three key principles of the Rule of Law: supremacy of law, equality before the law, and ______.
A. Judicial supremacy
B. Protection of minority rights
C. Predominance of legal spirit
D. Separation of powers

50. Match the following characteristics with the correct version of the Rule of Law:

A. Formal Version	1. Focus on procedural fairness and legal certainty
B. Substantive Version	2. Incorporates justice, fairness, and human rights
	3. Concerned only with the structure of legal rules
	4. Emphasizes the moral content of laws

A. A-1, B-2, A-3, B-4
B. A-2, B-3, A-4, B-1
C. A-3, B-4, A-1, B-2
D. A-4, B-1, A-2, B-3

51. Arrange the following key developments in the evolution of the Rule of Law in chronological order:
1. Magna Carta (1215)
2. A.V. Dicey's Theory (1885)
3. Universal Declaration of Human Rights (1948)
4. International Covenant on Civil and Political Rights (1966)

A. 1, 2, 3, 4 B. 2, 1, 4, 3
C. 3, 2, 1, 4 D. 4, 3, 2, 1

52. Scenario: A country has clear and precise laws that are applied consistently. However, the laws discriminate against certain groups. Which version of the Rule of Law is being followed?
A. Substantive B. Formal
C. Both D. Neither

53. Scenario: A court strikes down a law because it violates fundamental human rights, even though it was passed through proper legal procedures. This reflects which version of the Rule of Law?
A. Formal
B. Substantive
C. Legal positivism
D. Parliamentary sovereignty

54. Scenario: In a dictatorship, laws are strictly enforced, and there's no arbitrary power. However, the laws severely restrict freedom of speech. Which version of the Rule of Law applies here?
A. Substantive B. Formal
C. Democratic D. None of these

55. Which of the following is an essential feature of both formal and substantive versions of the Rule of Law?
A. Arbitrary government action
B. Supremacy of law over individuals and government
C. Absolute power of the legislature
D. Dictatorship with legal procedures

56. The substantive version of the Rule of Law aligns closely with the philosophy of:
A. Legal positivism
B. Natural law theory
C. Realism
D. Utilitarianism

57. Match the following thinkers with their contributions to the concept of the Rule of Law:

Thinkers	Contributions
A. A.V. Dicey	1. Formal conception of the Rule of Law
B. Lon L. Fuller	2. Substantive approach focusing on rights and morality
C. Joseph Raz	3. Procedural aspects of law (the 'inner morality of law')
D. Ronald Dworkin	4. Equality before the law and legal supremacy

A. A-4, B-3, C-1, D-2
B. A-3, B-1, C-2, D-4
C. A-1, B-4, C-3, D-2
D. A-2, B-1, C-4, D-3

58. Scenario: A law is passed in a democratic country allowing detention without trial. The judiciary challenges this law for violating the right to personal liberty. Which version of the Rule of Law is the judiciary applying?
A. Formal B. Substantive
C. Legal positivism D. None of these

59. Scenario: A government implements strict legal procedures to ensure compliance with tax laws. However, the tax laws disproportionately affect poor citizens. Which version of the Rule of Law is being followed?

A. Substantive B. Formal
C. Socialist D. Democratic

60. The doctrine of separation of powers was first systematically articulated by:

A. John Locke
B. A.V. Dicey
C. Montesquieu
D. Rousseau

61. Which country follows a strict separation of powers with clear demarcation between the three organs of the state?

A. India
B. United Kingdom
C. United States of America
D. France

62. In India, the separation of powers is:

A. Strict and absolute
B. Flexible with checks and balances
C. Non-existent
D. Only applicable to the judiciary

63. In the UK, which of the following statements is true regarding the separation of powers?

A. The UK has a written constitution enforcing strict separation
B. The Prime Minister cannot be a Member of Parliament
C. There is a fusion of powers between the executive and legislature
D. The judiciary has the power to declare laws unconstitutional

64. The President of the USA is both the head of state and the head of government.

A. True
B. False
C. True, only during emergencies
D. False, unless approved by Congress

65. In India, the judiciary has the power of judicial review, allowing it to strike down unconstitutional laws.

A. True
B. False
C. True, but only with the President's approval
D. False, unless authorized by Parliament

66. **Assertion (A):** The UK strictly follows the doctrine of separation of powers.

Reason (R): The UK has an unwritten constitution, and the legislature and executive are fused.

A. Both A and R are true, and R is the correct explanation of A
B. Both A and R are true, but R is not the correct explanation of A
C. A is true, R is false
D. A is false, R is true

67. **Assertion (A):** In the USA, the doctrine of separation of powers is rigidly applied.

Reason (R): The US Constitution explicitly defines the powers of each organ of the government.

A. Both A and R are true, and R is the correct explanation of A
B. Both A and R are true, but R is not the correct explanation of A
C. A is true, R is false
D. A is false, R is true

68. The French system of government is characterized by a ______ system, blending both presidential and parliamentary features.

A. Parliamentary
B. Presidential
C. Semi-presidential
D. Federal

69. In India, the doctrine of separation of powers is implied through the ______ of the Constitution.

A. Preamble
B. Basic structure doctrine
C. Directive Principles of State Policy
D. Fundamental Duties

70. Match the following countries with their models of separation of powers:

Countries	Models
A. USA	1. Rigid separation with checks and balances
B. UK	2. Fusion of powers between executive and legislature
C. India	3. Flexible separation with overlap of functions
D. France	4. Semi-presidential system

A. A-1, B-2, C-3, D-4
B. A-2, B-1, C-4, D-3
C. A-3, B-4, C-1, D-2
D. A-4, B-3, C-2, D-1

71. Arrange the following key events related to the development of the separation of powers in chronological order:
1. Montesquieu's The Spirit of the Laws
2. US Constitution adopted
3. Indian Constitution adopted
4. French Fifth Republic established

A. 1, 2, 3, 4 B. 2, 1, 4, 3
C. 1, 4, 2, 3 D. 4, 3, 2, 1

72. Scenario: A President in a country cannot dissolve the legislature, and the judiciary has full authority to review laws passed by the legislature. Which country does this system likely represent?
A. India B. UK
C. USA D. France

73. Scenario: A country's Prime Minister is also a member of the legislature, and laws are passed quickly due to executive dominance in the parliament. Which country likely follows this system?
A. USA B. UK
C. France D. India

74. Scenario: In a country, the judiciary has the power to strike down unconstitutional laws, the President exercises real executive powers, and the legislature cannot interfere with the judiciary's functioning. Which model of separation of powers applies?
A. Parliamentary System
B. Semi-Presidential System
C. Federal Presidential System
D. Unitary System

75. Which Article of the Indian Constitution deals with the procedure for amending the Constitution?
A. Article 356 B. Article 368
C. Article 370 D. Article 352

76. In the USA, an amendment to the Constitution can be proposed by:
A. The President alone
B. A simple majority in Congress
C. A two-thirds majority in both Houses of Congress
D. A referendum by the public

77. Which of the following statements is true about constitutional amendments in South Africa?
A. Amendments require approval from the judiciary
B. All amendments require a national referendum
C. Amendments need a two-thirds majority in the National Assembly
D. The Constitution cannot be amended

78. Which of the following amendments in India was struck down for violating the 'basic structure' of the Constitution?
A. 24th Amendment B. 42nd Amendment
C. 44th Amendment D. 86th Amendment

79. In the USA, the President has the power to veto constitutional amendments.
A. True
B. False
C. True, only for amendments related to federal powers
D. False, unless approved by the Supreme Court

80. In South Africa, certain constitutional amendments require the consent of the National Council of Provinces.
A. True
B. False
C. True, only for financial matters
D. False, unless the amendment affects the judiciary

81. **Assertion (A):** The Indian Parliament can amend any part of the Constitution, including Fundamental Rights.

Reason (R): There are no limitations on the amending power of the Parliament in India.
A. Both A and R are true, and R is the correct explanation of A
B. Both A and R are true, but R is not the correct explanation of A
C. A is true, R is false
D. A is false, R is true

82. **Assertion (A):** In the USA, constitutional amendments require ratification by the states.

Reason (R): The federal structure of the USA mandates the involvement of states in the amendment process.
A. Both A and R are true, and R is the correct explanation of A
B. Both A and R are true, but R is not the correct explanation of A
C. A is true, R is false
D. A is false, R is true

83. The 'basic structure doctrine' in India was established in the case of ______.
A. Golaknath v. State of Punjab
B. Kesavananda Bharati v. State of Kerala
C. Minerva Mills v. Union of India
D. S.R. Bommai v. Union of India

84. In the USA, amendments to the Constitution can be ratified by ______ of the state legislatures.
A. One-half B. Two-thirds
C. Three-fourths D. All states

85. Match the following countries with their constitutional amendment procedures:

Countries	Constitutional Amendment Procedures
A. India	1. Requires two-thirds majority in both Houses of Parliament and, in some cases, ratification by states
B. USA	2. Requires proposal by two-thirds of Congress and ratification by three-fourths of states
C. South Africa	3. Requires two-thirds majority in the National Assembly and approval from the National Council of Provinces for certain amendments

A. A-1, B-2, C-3　B. A-2, B-1, C-3
C. A-3, B-1, C-2　D. A-1, B-3, C-2

86. Arrange the following constitutional amendments in chronological order of their adoption:
1. The First Amendment to the Indian Constitution
2. The 13th Amendment to the US Constitution (abolition of slavery)
3. The 17th Amendment to the South African Constitution (expanding jurisdiction of courts)
4. The 44th Amendment to the Indian Constitution

A. 2, 1, 4, 3　B. 1, 2, 3, 4
C. 4, 3, 1, 2　D. 2, 4, 1, 3

87. Scenario: In a country, constitutional amendments can be proposed either by the national legislature or by a constitutional convention. After proposal, amendments require ratification by a specified majority of state legislatures. Which country is this likely to be?

A. India　B. USA
C. South Africa　D. UK

88. Scenario: A Parliament passes a constitutional amendment affecting fundamental rights. The judiciary strikes it down, stating that it violates the 'basic structure' of the Constitution. Which country does this scenario describe?

A. USA　B. South Africa
C. India　D. France

89. Scenario: A constitutional amendment requires a two-thirds majority in the National Assembly and additional approval from the National Council of Provinces if it affects provincial matters. This is characteristic of which country?

A. USA　B. India
C. South Africa　D. Australia

90. Which of the following Acts provides for the Right to Information in India?

A. Freedom of Information Act, 2000
B. Right to Information Act, 2005
C. Open Government Act, 2002
D. Public Disclosure Act, 2001

91. The Freedom of Information Act (FOIA) in the USA was enacted in which year?

A. 1966　B. 1975
C. 1980　D. 1990

92. Which of the following bodies is responsible for overseeing the implementation of the RTI Act in India?

A. Central Information Commission (CIC)
B. Election Commission of India
C. National Human Rights Commission
D. Public Accounts Committee

93. In the UK, which legislation governs the right to access information held by public authorities?

A. Freedom of Information Act, 1966
B. Official Secrets Act, 1989
C. Freedom of Information Act, 2000
D. Public Disclosure Act, 1999

94. The RTI Act in India applies to both government and private organizations.

A. True
B. False
C. True, only for private organizations receiving government funds
D. False, unless authorized by the Central Government

95. The FOIA in the USA allows access to all government records without any exemptions.

A. True
B. False
C. True, but only for non-classified documents
D. False, unless approved by the Attorney General

96. **Assertion (A):** The RTI Act in India promotes transparency and accountability in government functioning.

Reason (R): The RTI Act allows unrestricted access to all classified government documents.

A. Both A and R are true, and R is the correct explanation of A
B. Both A and R are true, but R is not the correct explanation of A
C. A is true, R is false
D. A is false, R is true

97. **Assertion (A):** In the UK, the Freedom of Information Act, 2000 enhances government transparency.

Reason (R): Public authorities are obligated to proactively publish certain categories of information.

A. Both A and R are true, and R is the correct explanation of A
B. Both A and R are true, but R is not the correct explanation of A
C. A is true, R is false
D. A is false, R is true

98. The maximum time limit for providing information under the RTI Act in India is ______.

A. 15 days B. 30 days
C. 45 days D. 60 days

99. In the USA, the agency responsible for enforcing compliance with the FOIA is the ______.

A. Department of Justice
B. Freedom of Information Commission
C. White House
D. Information Rights Tribunal

100. Match the following countries with their respective transparency legislations:

Countries	Transparency Legislations
A. India	1. Right to Information Act, 2005
B. USA	2. Freedom of Information Act, 1966
C. UK	3. Freedom of Information Act, 2000

A. A-1, B-2, C-3 B. A-2, B-3, C-1
C. A-3, B-1, C-2 D. A-1, B-3, C-2

ANSWERS

1. **(B):** In a Presidential system, such as in the USA, there is a clear separation of powers between the executive and legislature.

2. **(C):** In most parliamentary systems (e.g., India, UK), the head of state is ceremonial, while the Prime Minister is the real executive.

3. **(C):** The USA has a federal system with powers divided between the federal government and states.

4. **(C):** In a unitary system (e.g., UK, France), power is centralized, and any regional autonomy is granted by the central government.

5. **(D):** In the Presidential system, the President can be impeached and removed before the end of their term.

6. **(B):** Democracy depends on many factors, not just the federal or unitary nature of the government.

7. **(C):** In a parliamentary system, the executive is accountable to the legislature, but they are not independent; there is a fusion of powers.

8. **(C):** In a unitary system, power is centralized, and any powers given to regional governments are at the discretion of the central government.

9. **(C):** The UK has a unitary system with parliamentary democracy, where power is centralized in the national government.

10. **(C):** The Presidential system, especially in the USA, is based on the separation of powers between the executive, legislature, and judiciary.

11. **(A):** USA: Presidential and Federal (1)
India: Parliamentary and Federal (2)
France: Semi-Presidential and Unitary (3)
China: Unitary and Single-Party (4)

12. **(C):** Confederation (least centralized) → Federal → Semi-Federal → Unitary (most centralized).

13. **(B):** This describes a Presidential system with separation of powers and independent executive authority.

14. **(B):** This is a federal system, where powers are constitutionally divided between the central and state governments.

15. **(D):** This is a parliamentary system, where the Prime Minister is accountable to the legislature.

16. **(B):** The Indian federal system has an independent judiciary to resolve disputes between the center and states.

17. **(C):** The Westminster model refers to the parliamentary system followed in the UK and many Commonwealth countries.

18. **(A):** No-confidence motion: Parliamentary (1)
Fixed term for the executive: Presidential (2)
Single constitution for the entire country: Unitary (3)
Dual system of government: Federal (4)

19. **(B):** In a unitary system, the central government holds the power to create or dissolve regional governments.

20. (C): In a semi-presidential system (e.g., France), executive power is shared between a President and a Prime Minister.

21. (C): The USA follows dual federalism, where the federal and state governments operate independently within their own spheres.

22. (C): India's federalism is often called quasi-federal because of its strong central government with federal features.

23. (C): Canada's federalism is asymmetrical, granting special powers to Quebec due to its distinct language and culture.

24. (B): The Tenth Amendment reserves powers not delegated to the federal government to the states or the people, reinforcing federalism.

25. (B): In India, the residuary powers lie with the Union government, unlike in the USA.

26. (B): The term 'federalism' is not explicitly mentioned in the US Constitution, but the concept is embedded through the structure.

27. (C): While provinces have exclusive powers, not all provinces have equal autonomy, especially Quebec, which has special powers.

28. (A): Under Article 3 of the Indian Constitution, the Union Parliament can reorganize states without state consent.

29. (B): India's federal structure is defined by the Union List, State List, and Concurrent List in the Seventh Schedule.

30. (C): As per the Tenth Amendment, powers not granted to the federal government are reserved for the states or the people.

31. (A): USA: Strong dual federalism with clear separation of powers (1)

Canada: Asymmetrical federalism with special status for Quebec (2)

India: Quasi-federal with unitary bias (3)

32. (A): USA Constitution: 1787

Canadian Constitution Act: 1867

Indian Constitution: 1950

33. (B): The USA's dual federalism ensures state autonomy with residuary powers resting with the states.

34. (C): Under Article 3 of the Indian Constitution, the Parliament can reorganize states without needing the state's consent.

35. (C): Canada's asymmetrical federalism grants Quebec special powers due to its distinct French identity.

36. (C): The USA allows dual citizenship (national and state), while India has single citizenship.

37. (B): The federal government in Canada can disallow provincial laws, though this power is rarely used today.

38. (A): Correct matching is:

- **Article 44 (Uniform Civil Code):** A provision in the India Constitution (Directive Principles, Part IV), which directs the state to endeavor to secure a Uniform Civil Code for all citizens.
- **Section 51 (Division of Powers):** Found in the Australia Constitution, outlining the legislative powers of the Commonwealth Parliament, such as trade, taxation, and defense.
- **Article 9 (Freedom of Religion):** Part of the Japan Constitution (Chapter III), guaranteeing freedom of religion and prohibiting state-sponsored religion.
- **Article 21 (Right to Life and Liberty):** A key provision in the India (1) Constitution (Part III), protecting life and personal liberty, with expansive judicial interpretation (e.g., right to privacy).

39. (A): Both the USA and India have Supreme Courts with powers of judicial review to resolve federal disputes.

40. (B): India's model is often termed "quasi-federal" with residuary powers resting with the Union government, showcasing unitary bias.

41. (B): A.V. Dicey popularized the concept of the Rule of Law in his book "Introduction to the Study of the Law of the Constitution".

42. (B): The formal version of the Rule of Law emphasizes legal certainty, procedural fairness, and adherence to laws, regardless of their content.

43. (B): The substantive version goes beyond procedure, incorporating justice, fairness, and human rights into the legal framework.

44. (B): The Rule of Law opposes arbitrary power; it requires that laws be applied equally and fairly.

45. (B): The formal version focuses on procedural aspects, not the moral content of the law.

46. (A): The substantive version integrates procedural fairness with substantive justice, including fundamental rights.

47. **(C):** The Rule of Law applies to everyone, including government officials, ensuring equality before the law.

48. **(A):** The Rule of Law prevents the arbitrary exercise of power by ensuring legal accountability.

49. **(C):** Dicey's third principle is the predominance of the legal spirit, emphasizing the role of the judiciary in upholding the law.

50. **(A):** Formal Version: Focus on procedural fairness and legal certainty (1)

    Substantive Version: Incorporates justice, fairness, and human rights (2)

    Formal Version: Concerned only with the structure of legal rules (3)

    Substantive Version: Emphasizes the moral content of laws (4)

51. **(A):** The development of the Rule of Law starts with the Magna Carta, followed by Dicey's theory, and later international human rights instruments.

52. **(B):** The formal version emphasizes procedural legality, even if the laws are unjust in substance.

53. **(B):** The substantive version includes the protection of fundamental rights and moral justice.

54. **(B):** This reflects the formal version, where laws are enforced, but moral justice or human rights are not considered.

55. **(B):** Both versions uphold the supremacy of law as a core principle.

56. **(B):** The substantive version aligns with natural law, focusing on justice, morality, and human rights.

57. **(A):** A.V. Dicey: Equality before the law and legal supremacy (4)

    Lon L. Fuller: Procedural aspects of law (the 'inner morality of law') (3)

    Joseph Raz: Formal conception of the Rule of Law (1)

    Ronald Dworkin: Substantive approach focusing on rights and morality (2)

58. **(B):** The judiciary is applying the substantive version, which emphasizes fundamental rights and justice.

59. **(B):** This scenario reflects the formal version, focusing on procedural compliance, regardless of social justice outcomes.

60. **(C):** Montesquieu introduced the doctrine in his work "The Spirit of the Laws", advocating for division of powers into legislative, executive, and judiciary.

61. **(C):** The USA follows a rigid separation of powers, with checks and balances to maintain autonomy between the branches.

62. **(B):** India follows a flexible separation of powers, with some overlapping functions and mutual checks among the organs.

63. **(C):** In the UK, the executive and legislature are fused, as the Prime Minister and cabinet are part of Parliament.

64. **(A):** In the USA, the President is both the head of state and the head of government, reflecting a strict separation of powers.

65. **(A):** The Indian judiciary has the power of judicial review under Articles 13, 32, and 226.

66. **(D):** The UK does not follow strict separation of powers, and the fusion of powers exists between the executive and legislature.

67. **(A):** The US Constitution explicitly outlines the powers of each branch, leading to a rigid application of the doctrine.

68. **(C):** France follows a semi-presidential system, combining features of both parliamentary and presidential systems.

69. **(B):** The separation of powers is part of the basic structure of the Indian Constitution, as held in Kesavananda Bharati v. State of Kerala.

70. **(A):** USA: Rigid separation with checks and balances (1)

    UK: Fusion of powers between executive and legislature (2)

    India: Flexible separation with overlap of functions (3)

    France: Semi-presidential system (4)

71. **(A):** Montesquieu's work: 1748

    US Constitution: 1787

    Indian Constitution: 1950

    French Fifth Republic: 1958

72. **(C):** In the USA, there is a rigid separation of powers, with judicial review and no power for the President to dissolve Congress.

73. **(B):** In the UK, there is a fusion of powers between the executive and legislature, with the Prime Minister being a Member of Parliament.

74. **(C):** This describes the USA's federal presidential system, with strong separation of powers.

75. (B): Article 368 of the Indian Constitution outlines the procedure for constitutional amendments.

76. (C): In the USA, an amendment requires a two-thirds majority in both the House of Representatives and the Senate.

77. (C): In South Africa, most constitutional amendments require a two-thirds majority in the National Assembly.

78. (B): Parts of the 42nd Amendment were struck down in the Minerva Mills case (1980) for violating the basic structure doctrine.

79. (B): In the USA, the President has no role in the constitutional amendment process and cannot veto amendments.

80. (A): Amendments that affect the provinces require approval from the National Council of Provinces.

81. (C): While Parliament can amend any part of the Constitution, it cannot alter the basic structure, as held in the Kesavananda Bharati case (1973).

82. (A): State ratification reflects the federal character of the USA, requiring approval from three-fourths of the states.

83. (B): The basic structure doctrine was laid down in the Kesavananda Bharati case (1973).

84. (C): An amendment requires ratification by three-fourths of the state legislatures in the USA.

85. (A): India: Requires two-thirds majority in both Houses of Parliament and, in some cases, ratification by states (1)

USA: Requires proposal by two-thirds of Congress and ratification by three-fourths of states (2)

South Africa: Requires two-thirds majority in the National Assembly and approval from the National Council of Provinces for certain amendments (3)

86. (A): 13th Amendment (USA): 1865

First Amendment (India): 1951

44th Amendment (India): 1978

17th Amendment (South Africa): 2012

87. (B): In the USA, amendments can be proposed by Congress or a constitutional convention and require ratification by three-fourths of state legislatures.

88. (C): In India, the Supreme Court can strike down amendments that violate the basic structure doctrine.

89. (C): In South Africa, amendments affecting provinces require approval from the National Council of Provinces.

90. (B): The Right to Information Act, 2005 empowers Indian citizens to access information from public authorities, promoting transparency and accountability.

91. (A): The Freedom of Information Act (FOIA) was enacted in the USA in 1966, granting the public the right to access federal government records.

92. (A): The Central Information Commission (CIC) is the apex body for implementing and monitoring the RTI Act in India.

93. (C): The Freedom of Information Act, 2000 governs the right to access public information in the UK.

94. (C): The RTI Act applies to private organizations that are substantially funded by the government.

95. (B): The FOIA has several exemptions, including matters related to national security, law enforcement, and personal privacy.

96. (C): While the RTI Act promotes transparency, it does not allow access to classified documents related to national security, etc.

97. (A): The UK FOIA requires public bodies to proactively publish information, enhancing transparency.

98. (B): Information requested under the RTI Act must be provided within 30 days.

99. (A): The Department of Justice oversees FOIA compliance in the USA.

100. (A): India: Right to Information Act, 2005 (1)

USA: Freedom of Information Act, 1966 (2)

UK: Freedom of Information Act, 2000 (3)